Techniques in Musculoskeletal Rehabilitation

Techniques in Musculoskeletal Rehabilitation

Editors

William E. Prentice, PhD, PT, ATC

Professor, Coordinator of Sports Medicine Specialization
Department of Exercise and Sport Science
Clinical Professor, Division of Physical Therapy
Department of Medical Allied Professions
Associate Professor, Department of Orthopedics
School of Medicine
University of North Carolina at Chapel Hill
Chapel Hill, North Carolina

Michael L. Voight, DPT, OCS, SCS, ATC

Associate Professor
School of Physical Therapy
Belmont University
Nashville, Tennessee

McGraw-Hill
Medical Publishing Division

New York / Chicago / San Francisco / Lisbon
London / Madrid / Mexico City / Milan / New Delhi
San Juan / Seoul / Singapore / Sydney / Toronto

McGraw-Hill

A Division of The McGraw·Hill Companies

TECHNIQUES IN MUSCULOSKELETAL REHABILITATION

34567890   CCW/CCW   098765432

ISBN 0-07-135498-0

This book was set in Adobe Garamond by The PRD Group.
The editors were Stephen Zollo, Catherine Wenz Johnson, and Scott Kurtz.
The production supervisor was Philip Galea.
The cover designer was Janice Bielawa.
The interior design was by Marsha Cohen/Parallelogram Graphics.
The index was prepared by Katherine Pitcoff.

Courier Kendallville was printer and binder.

This book is printed on acid-free paper.

Library of Congress Cataloging-in-Publication Data

Prentice, William E.
  Techniques in musculoskeletal rehabilitation / William E. Prentice, Michael L. Voight.
    p. ; cm.
  Includes bibliographical references and index.
  ISBN 0-07-135498-0
  1. Medical rehabilitation.   I. Voight, Michael L., 1959–   II. Title.
  [DNLM: 1. Physical Therapy—methods.   2. Rehabilitation—methods.   WB 460 P9266t
2001]
  RC930.P74   2001
  615.8′2—dc21   00-055916

CONTENTS

LIST OF CONTRIBUTORS

Turner A. Blackburn, MEd, PT, ATC
Director
Tulane Institute of Sports Medicine
Tulane University
New Orleans, Louisiana

Mike Clark, MS, PT, PES, CSCS
Vice President
National Academy of Sports Medicine
Clark@NASM.ORG

Gray Cook, MSPT, OCS, CSCS
Director of Orthopedic and Sports Physical
    Therapy
Dunn, Cook, and Associates
Creative Director, Sports-Specific Training
Reebok
Danville, Virginia

Craig R. Denegar, PhD, PT, ATC
Associate Professor of Physicial Therapy
Penn State University
State College, Pennsylvania

Phillip B. Donley, MS, PT, ATC
Director, Chester County Orthopaedic and Sports
    Physical Therapy
West Chester, Pennsylavania

Bernie DePalma, MEd, PT, ATC
Head Athletic Trainer
Cornell University
Ithaca, New York

Marc Davis, PT, ATC
Athletic Trainer/Physical Therapist
Division of Sports Medicine
Student Health Service

Robert S. Gailey, PhD, PT
Assistant Professor
University of Miami School of Medicine
Department of Orthopaedics and Rehabilitation
Division of Physical Therapy
Coral Gables, Florida

Lisa Giallonardo, BS, MS
MSPT Program Director
Boston University
Sargent College of Health and Rehabitation
    Science
Boston, Massachusetts

John A. Guido, Jr., MHS, PT, SCS, ATC, CSCS
Lead Physical Therapist
Tulane Institute of Sports Medicine
New Orleans, Louisiana

Kevin M. Guskiewicz, PhD, ATC
Assistant Professor
Department of Physical Education, Exercise, and
    Sport Science
Director, Undergraduate Athletic Training
    Program
University of North Carolina at Chapel Hill
Chapel Hill, North Carolina

John S. Halle, PhD, MPT
Associate Professor
Physical Therapy Program
Belmont University
Nashville, Tennessee

Christopher J. Hirth, MS, PT, ATC
Athletic Trainer/Physical Therapist
Division of Sports Medicine
University of North Carolina at Chapel Hill
Chapel Hill, North Carolina

Dan Hooker, PhD, PT, ScS, ATC
Coordinator of Athletic Training and Physical
    Therapy
Division of Sports Medicine
Student Health Service
University of North Carolina at
    Chapel Hill
Chapel Hill, North Carolina

Patsy Huff, PharmD, FASHP

Director of the Pharmacy, Student Health Service
Professor, School of Pharmacy
University of North Carolina at Chapel Hill
Chapel Hill, North Carolina

Skip Hunter, PT, ATC

Director of Sports Medicine
Clemson Sports Medicine & Rehabilitation
    Center
Clemson, South Carolina

Steven M. Jacoby, ATC

ATC Product Sales Manager for
    Neuromuscular Systems
Biodex Medical Systems
West Sayville, New York

Gina Martin MA, ATC

Head Athletic Trainer
Lake Highland Preparatory School
Orlando, Florida

William E. Prentice, PhD, PT, ATC

Professor, Coordinator of Sports Medicine
    Specialization
Department of Physical Education, Exercise, and
    Sport Science
Clinical Professor, Division of Physical Therapy
Department of Medical Allied Professions
Associate Professor, Department of Orthopaedics
School of Medicine
University of North Carolina at Chapel Hill
Chapel Hill, North Carolina
Director, Sports Medicine Education and
    Fellowship Program
HEALTHSOUTH Rehabilitation
    Corporation
Birmingham, Alabama

Kevin Robinson, MS, PT, OCS

Assistant Professor
Belmont University
Nashville, Tennessee

Sussette Robinson, PT

Sumner Regional Medical Center
Gallatin, Tennessee

Anne Marie Schneider, OTR, CHT

Coordinator, Hand Center
Raleigh Orthopaedic and Rehabilitation
    Specialists
Raleigh, North Carolina

Rob Schneider, MS, PT, ATC

Athletic Trainer/Physical Therapist
Division of Sports Medicine
University of North Carolina at Chapel Hill
Chapel Hill, North Carolina

Brian C. Thompson, BA, CSCS

Belmont University
Nashville, Tennessee

Stephen R. Tippett, MS, PT, SCS, ATC

Assistant Professor
Department of Physical Therapy
Bradley University
Peoria, Illinois

Cissy Voight, PT, GCS

Department of Physical Therapy
Belmont University
Nashville, Tennessee

Michael L. Voight, DPT, PT, SCS, OCS, ATC

Associate Professor
School of Physical Therapy
Belmont University
Nashville, Tennessee

Pete Zulia, PT, ATC

Director, Oxford Physical Therapy
Instructor, Athletic Training Curriculum
Miami University of Ohio
Oxford, Ohio

PREFACE

As the art and science of caring for the injured patient becomes more sophisticated and specialized, the need arises for textbooks that deal with specific aspects of injury management. Rehabilitation is certainly the primary focus for the physical therapist. This first edition of *Techniques in Musculoskeletal Rehabilitation* is for the student physical therapist who is interested in gaining more in-depth exposure to the theory and practical application of rehabilitation techniques used in treating musculoskeletal injuries in a variety of patient populations.

The purpose of this text is to provide the physical therapist with a comprehensive guide to the design, implementation, and supervision of rehabilitation programs for musculoskeletal injuries. It is intended for use in in-depth courses in musculoskeletal rehabilitation that deal with practical application of theory in a clinical setting. The contributing authors have collectively attempted to combine their expertise and knowledge to produce a single text that encompasses all aspects of musculoskeletal rehabilitation.

Organization

The text is essentially divided into five sections. The first section deals with the basic foundations of the rehabilitation process as identified in the *Guide to Physical Therapist Practice*. Chapter 1 begins by discussing the important considerations in designing a rehabilitation program for the patient with a musculoskeletal injury providing a basic overview of the rehabilitative process. Chapter 2 discusses the importance of the evaluation process in first determining the exact nature of an existing injury and then outlines a rehabilitation program based on the findings of that evaluation. It is critical for the physical therapist to understand the importance of the healing process and how it should dictate the course of rehabilitation (Chapter 3). Section 2 discusses the various physiological impairments that may need to be dealt with during the rehabilitative process, including impairment due to pain and its management (Chapter 4); impaired muscle performance and how to regain muscular strength, endurance, and power (Chapter 5); impaired endurance and maintaining aerobic capacity (Chapter 6); impaired mobility and restoring ROM through improving flexibility (Chapter 7); impaired neuromuscular function and reestablishing neuromuscular control (Chapter 8); and impaired postural stability and regaining balance (Chapter 9). Physical therapists have many rehabilitation "tools" with which they can choose to treat a patient with a musculoskeletal injury. How they choose to use these "tools" is often a matter of personal preference.

The third section provides a detailed discussion of how these tools may be best incorporated into a rehabilitation program to achieve the treatment goals. The tools of rehabilitation included in this section are: Isokinetics (Chapter 10), Plyometric Exercise (Chapter 11), Open- Versus Closed-Kinetic Chain Exercise (Chapter 12), Proprioceptive Neuromuscular Facilitation Techniques (Chapter 13), Muscle Energy Techniques (Chapter 14), Joint Mobilization and Traction Techniques (Chapter 15), Core Stabilization Training (Chapter 16), Aquatic Therapy (Chapter 17), Using Therapeutic Modalities (Chapter 18), Using Biofeedback (Chapter 19), Functional Progressions and Functional Testing (Chapter 20), Using Braces, Orthotics, and Prosthetics (Chapter 21), Assistive Gait and Transfer Techniques (Chapter 22), Using Pharmacologic Agents (Chapter 23), Designing Home Exercise Programs and Principles of Patient Self-Management (Chapter 24), and Components of Functional Exercises (Chapter 25).

Section 4 of this text goes into great detail on specific rehabilitation techniques that are used in treating a variety of musculoskeletal injuries. Specific rehabilitation techniques are included for the Shoulder (Chapter 26), the Elbow (Chapter 27), the Hand and Wrist (Chapter 28), the Groin, Hip, and Thigh (Chapter 29), the Knee (Chapter 30), the Lower Leg (Chapter 31), the Ankle and Foot (Chapter 32), and the Spine (Chapter 33). Each chapter begins with a discussion of the pertinent functional anatomy and biomechanics of that region.

The second portion of each chapter involves in-depth discussion of the pathomechanics, injury mechanism, rehabilitation concerns, and rehabilitation progressions for specific injuries. An extensive series of photographs illustrating a wide variety of rehabilitative exercises is presented in each chapter.

The fifth section of the text discusses treatment considerations for some specific patient populations, including the Geriatric Patient (Chapter 34); the Pediatric Patient (Chapter 35); and Amputees (Chapter 36).

Comprehensive Coverage of Research Based Material

As will become readily apparent, this first edition of *Techniques in Musculoskeletal Rehabilitation* offers a comprehensive reference and guide for treating musculoskeletal injuries for the physical therapist overseeing programs of rehabilitation.

Any physical therapist charged with the responsibility of supervising a rehabilitation program knows that the most currently accepted and up-to-date rehabilitation protocols tend to change rapidly. A sincere effort has been made by the contributing authors to present the most recent information on the various aspects of injury rehabilitation currently available from the literature. Additionally, this manuscript has been critically reviewed by selected physical therapists who are well-respected clinicians, educators, and researchers in this field, to further ensure that the material presented is accurate and current.

Pedagogical Aids

The aids provided in this text to assist the student physical therapist in its use include the following:

Objectives.   These are listed at the beginning of each individual chapter to identify the concepts to be presented.

Figures and Tables.   The number of figures and tables included throughout the text has been significantly increased in an effort to provide as much visual and graphic demonstration of specific rehabilitation techniques and exercises as possible.

Summary.   Each chapter has a summary that outlines the major points presented.

References.   A comprehensive list of up-to-date references is presented at the end of each chapter to provide additional information relative to chapter content.

Acknowledgments

The preparation of the manuscripts for this textbook is a long-term, extremely demanding effort. This requires input and cooperation on the part of many different individuals. We would like to personally thank each of the contributing authors. They were asked to contribute to this text because we have tremendous respect for them personally as well as professionally. These individuals have distinguished themselves as educators and clinicians dedicated to the rehabilitation profession. We are exceedingly grateful for their input.

Catherine Wenz-Johnson, our developmental editor at McGraw-Hill, has been persistent and diligent in the completion of this test. She has patiently encouraged us along the way and we certainly appreciate her support.

Finally, we would like to thank our families and friends. To our parents, who started us down the right road by building a foundation of integrity, hard work, and persistance. To our many friends and colleagues who have given us professional direction and taught us how to "seek" answers to questions while at the same time laughing and enjoying life. And most importantly, thank you to our immediate families, who have had to pay the price of our passion for education. Bill would like to thank his family—Tena, Brian, and Zachary—who make an effort such as this worthwhile. Mike would like to give special thanks to his wife Cissy, whose inspiring wisdom and endless support have helped to sustain his passion for being an educator.

Bill Prentice
Mike Voight

Techniques in Musculoskeletal Rehabilitation

P A R T 1

Foundations of the Rehabilitation Process

Introduction to the Rehabilitation Process: "The Guide to Physical Therapist Practice"

Lisa Giallonardo

OBJECTIVES

After completing this chapter, the student therapist should be able to do the following:

- Explain the concepts on which *The Guide to Physical Therapist Practice* was based.
- Explain the four elements of the disablement model as described by Nagi.
- Compare and contrast the disablement model to the medical model of dealing with the effects of disease and injury.
- Identify the components of the examination process as defined by *The Guide.*
- Discuss the decision-making process that is based upon the examination.
- Explain what is meant by the term "intervention" as defined by *The Guide* and demonstrate examples of each.
- Describe the four Preferred Practice Patterns developed in *The Guide.*
- List the impairments that are included in the Musculoskeletal Practice Pattern.

The Guide to Physical Therapist Practice was published in the November 1997 issue of *Physical Therapy* as a document to describe the practice of physical therapy.[1] It was developed by consensus of an expert clinician panel chosen from a variety of practice settings across the United States. The document was edited many times after extensive clinician review before publication.

The Guide was developed in response to a charge from the American Physical Therapy Association's House of Delegates in 1992. Part 1 (Chapters 1 to 3) of *The Guide* was written specifically as a detailed outline of what the practice of physical therapy entailed. The intended audiences include clinicians, educators, administrators, other health care professionals, policymakers, and third-party payers. When CAPTE (Commission for Accreditation of Physical Therapist Education) revised the Guidelines for Accreditation, the language of *The Guide,* Part 1 was adopted.

The Guide is not a cookbook. There are no recommended prices in *The Guide,* nor is there any direct connection to CPT codes. Although some ICD-9 codes are listed and referred to in Part 2, they should not be used to code for billing purposes. *The Guide* does not specify the site of care; rather, it uses the *episode* *of care* concept that crosses all settings related to each episode. *The Guide* also does not address the state-to-state variances in the scope of practice.

THE DISABLEMENT MODEL

The Guide to Physical Therapist Practice is based on the disablement model developed by Saad Nagi in 1965. It was designed to describe the effects of disease and injury at both the person level and society level and their functional consequences. The disablement model is distinctly different from the classic medical model, where the emphasis is on treating the specific diagnosis with pharmacology or surgery. The disablement model emphasizes the functional and health status of individuals, with intervention based on improving these aspects of the patient's condition. The model has four elements to it:

Pathology ⟷ Impairment ⟷
Functional limitation ⟷ Disability

Pathology is the interruption of the normal cellular processes from a biomechanical, physiologic, or anatomic perspective.[1-3]

The body will often go on the defensive to restore the normal state. Examples of this include hemarthrosis, tumor, fracture, connective tissue damage (tear/stretch), diabetes, and rheumatoid arthritis. Intervention at this level is generally handled by physicians and is often pharmacologic and/or surgical in nature.

Impairment is any loss or abnormality of physiologic, psychological, or anatomic structure or function at the level of organs and body systems.[1–3] Physical therapists typically measure the signs and symptoms and try to correct impairments. Examples of physiologic impairments would be muscle weakness, range-of-motion loss, pain, and abnormal joint play. Anatomic impairments would include genu recurvatum, scoliosis, femoral anteversion, and pes planus.

Functional limitation is a deviation from the normal behavior in performing tasks and activities that would be traditional or expected for the individual.[1–3] These are tasks or activities that are not done in the usual efficient or proficient fashion. Problems with transfers, standing, walking, running, and climbing stairs are all examples of functional limitations.

Disability is the incapacity in performing a broad range of tasks and activities that are usually expected in specific social roles.[1–3] Inability to function as a spouse, student, parent, or worker (in the home or outside of the home) constitutes a disability.

The disablement process represents a two-way continuum and is affected by intra-individual and extra-individual risk factors. Intra-individual factors include habits, lifestyle, behavior, psychosocial characteristics, age and sex, educational level and income, weight, and family history. Extra-individual factors are things like the medical care received, the pharmacologic and other therapies available, the physical environment, and any external supports. The relationship between these aspects will vary between individuals and will ultimately determine the impact of the disease or injury. We have all treated patients who suffered from significant impairments but were still extremely functional. We have also treated patients who were disabled by what seemed to be minor limitations. Unfortunately, there are few studies in the literature to show a direct cause-and-effect relationship between impairments and functional limitations/disabilities.

Physical therapists traditionally examine and intervene at the impairment and functional limitation levels. The patient who has weakness in the quadriceps and an inability to climb stairs will be managed with a strengthening program and activities that include stair climbing. This organization is the basis for the preferred practice patterns in Part 2 of *The Guide*.

OVERVIEW OF *THE GUIDE*: PART 1

The purpose of *The Guide to Physical Therapist Practice* is to improve the quality of physical therapy, promote appropriate use of services, enhance customer satisfaction, and reduce unwarranted variations in physical therapy management. Prevention and wellness initiatives are also stressed and will help decrease the need for services.

Chapter 1 is a discussion of who physical therapists are and what they do. There is a description of the various practice settings, including some less traditional ones like corporate or industrial health centers and fitness centers. The terms "patient" and "client" are defined:

- Patient—individuals who receive direct physical therapy intervention.
- Client—individuals/businesses/school systems who are not necessarily ill but benefit from physical therapy consultation or prevention.

The chapter continues with a discussion of the scope of practice for physical therapists. Physical therapists are considered clinicians in the sense of providing direct services to patients as well as interacting with other professionals, providing prevention and wellness services, consulting, engaging in critical inquiry, educating, administrating, and supervising support personnel.

Physical therapy is generally considered an integral part of secondary and tertiary rehabilitative care. Chapter 1 expands on this model with a discussion of the physical therapist's role in primary care and in wellness. This involves "restoring health; alleviating pain; and preventing the onset of impairments, functional limitations, disabilities, or changes in physical function and health status resulting from injury, disease, or other causes."[1]

The clinical decision-making process is explained in the five elements of the patient/client management model: examination, evaluation, diagnosis, prognosis, and intervention. This clinical decision-making model is explored in greater depth in Chapter 2. The physical therapist begins with a thorough *examination*. There are three components to this[1]:

- *History.* A comprehensive investigation of the current and past health from a variety of sources, including the medical record, the patient, and the patient's caregiver. A complete list of data is included in the chapter.
- *Systems review.* A limited examination of the cardiopulmonary, neuromuscular, musculoskeletal, and integumentary systems as a means of screening for other potential health problems. An example of this would be to take a baseline blood pressure and heart rate. Communication ability is also assessed here.
- *Tests and measures.* After gathering and analyzing the above information, specific tests and measures are performed to rule in/out a diagnosis. There is an operational definition for each one followed by a three-part description: general purpose, clinical indications, and specific tests and measures.

There are 24 tests and measures listed alphabetically in *The Guide*. A description of each group includes general purposes, clinical indications, specific tests and measures, and types of data generated. The following is a list of the alphabetically arranged tests and measures:

- Aerobic capacity and endurance
- Anthropometric characteristics
- Arousal, attention, and cognition
- Assistive and adaptive devices
- Circulation and lymphatic drainage
- Community and work integration or reintegration
- Cranial nerve integrity
- Environmental, home, and work barriers
- Ergonomics and body mechanics
- Gait, locomotion, and balance
- Integumentary integrity
- Joint integrity and mobility
- Motor function
- Muscle performance
- Neuromotor development and sensory integration
- Orthotic, protective, and supportive devices
- Pain
- Posture
- Prosthetic requirements
- Range of motion
- Reflex integrity
- Self-care and home management
- Sensory integrity
- Ventilation and respiration

The following are some relevant examples of the tests and measures.

Anthropometric Characteristics

- Clinical indications
  Patient with acute sprained ankle (edema or effusion)
- Tests and measures
  Assessment of edema: palpation/volume/girth measurements
- Data generated
  Girth of lower extremity in inches or centimeters

Assistive and Adaptive Devices

- Clinical indications
  Patient with total knee replacement (impaired gait, locomotion, and balance)
- Tests and measures
  Assessment of safety during use of a cane
- Data generated
  Deviations and malfunctions that can be corrected or alleviated using the cane

Environmental, Home, and Work Barriers

- Clinical indications
  Patient with osteoporosis (impaired muscle performance)
- Tests and measures
  Assessment of current and potential barriers

- Data generated
  Adaptations, additions, or modifications that would enhance safety

Ergonomics and Body Mechanics

- Clinical indications
  Patient with low back injury (pain)
- Tests and measures
  Analysis of preferred postures during performance of tasks and activities
- Data generated
  Body alignment during specific job tasks and activities

Joint Integrity and Mobility

- Clinical indications
  Patient with glenohumeral adhesive capsulitis (impaired ROM)
- Tests and measures
  Assessment of joint hypermobility and hypomobility
- Data generated
  Joint mobility classification and scale

Muscle Performance

- Clinical indications
  Patient with urinary incontinence (impaired bladder function)
- Tests and measures
  Assessment of pelvic floor musculature
- Data generated
  Strength of pelvic floor musculature

Posture

- Clinical indications
  Patient with scoliosis (abnormal body alignment)
- Tests and measures
  Analysis of resting posture in any position
- Data generated
  Alignment and symmetry of body landmarks within segmental planes, while at rest

Prosthetic Requirements

- Clinical indications
  Patient with below the knee amputation (impaired sensory integrity)
- Tests and measures
  Assessment of alignment and fit of the device and inspection of related changes in skin condition
- Data generated
  Skin integrity and edema in the residual limb

The next three steps in the process involve the decision-making. Using the information gathered through the examination, the physical therapist does an *evaluation*. This is the clinical judgement that results from sizing up the situation in its entirety. From there, factors such as loss of function, social considerations, and health status are taken into consideration when developing a *diagnosis* (cluster of signs and symptoms) and *prognosis* (optimal level of improvement and time to get there), which guide management of the patient.[1]

Intervention involves the skilled interaction of the professional in performing the techniques and/or delegating and overseeing the services. The goal is to produce a positive change in the condition. Intervention is constantly being evaluated for effectiveness with an eye for functional outcomes as well as for remediating impairments. Continued care is based on the patient's response and progress toward the determined goals.[1]

There are three components to the intervention: (1) coordination, communication, and documentation; (2) patient/client-related instruction; and (3) direct interventions. Each patient will have some aspect of the first two components and one or more direct interventions. There are nine direct interventions in all, listed by level of importance:

- Therapeutic exercise
- Functional training in self-care and home management
- Functional training in community and work
- Manual therapy techniques
- Prescription, application, and, as appropriate, fabrication of assistive, adaptive, orthotic, protective, supportive, or prosthetic devices and equipment
- Airway clearance techniques
- Wound management
- Electrotherapeutic modalities
- Physical agents and mechanical modalities

Examination findings, the evaluation, diagnosis, and prognosis should support the intervention choice. Factors that might influence the interventions include[1]:

- Chronicity or severity of current condition
- Level of current impairment
- Functional limitation or disability
- Living environment
- Multisite or multisystem involvement
- Physical function and health status
- Potential discharge destinations
- Preexisting conditions or diseases
- Social supports
- Stability of condition

The following are some relevant examples of interventions.

Coordination, Communication, and Documentation

- Clinical indications
  Patient with total knee replacement (discharge destination)

- Anticipated goals
  Care is coordinated with patient, family, caregivers, and other health care professionals
- Specific interventions
  Discharge planning

Patient/Client-Related Instruction

- Clinical indications
  Patient with scoliosis (patient education)
- Anticipated goals
  Intensity of care is decreased
- Specific interventions
  Written and pictorial instruction

Therapeutic Exercise

- Clinical indications
  Patient with below-the-knee amputation (restricted in performing necessary tasks/activities)
- Anticipated goals
  Gait, locomotion, and balance are improved
- Specific interventions
  Gait and balance training with prosthetic device

Functional Training in Self-Care and Home Management

- Clinical indications
  Patient with osteoporosis (restricted in performing self-care and home activities)
- Anticipated goals
  Performance and independence of ADL/IADL increased
- Specific interventions
  Self-care and home management task adaptation

Functional Training in Community and Work

- Clinical indications
  Patient with low back injury (have a known work-related injury and disability)
- Anticipated goals
  Tolerance to positions and activities is increased
- Specific interventions
  Ergonomic stressor reduction training

Manual Therapy Techniques

- Clinical indications
  Patient with glenohumeral adhesive capsulitis (limited ROM)
- Anticipated goals
  Joint integrity and mobility are improved
- Specific interventions
  Joint mobilization and manipulation

Electrotherapeutic Modalities

- Clinical indications
    Patient with urinary incontinence (impaired muscle performance)
- Anticipated goals
    Ability to perform physical tasks is increased
- Specific interventions
    Electrical muscle stimulation and biofeedback

Physical Agents and Mechanical Modalities

- Clinical indications
    Patient with acute sprained ankle (edema or effusion)
- Anticipated goals
    Edema or effusion is decreased
- Specific interventions
    Cryotherapy, pulsed ultrasound

OVERVIEW OF *THE GUIDE:* PART 2

Part 2 of *The Guide* covers preferred practice patterns. There are four sections: musculoskeletal, neuromuscular, cardiopulmonary, and integumentary. The patterns are structured with diagnostic labels based on impairments. The design of each pattern is as follows[1]:

- Description of the patient/client diagnostic group (with includes/excludes list)
- Listing of the likely ICD-9-CM codes
- Description of the history and systems review section of the examination
- List of likely tests and measures (based on clinical indications)
- Prognosis with a range of visits expected for an episode of care
- Anticipated goals for intervention
- List of likely interventions
- Outcomes of care
- Criteria for discharge
- Primary prevention/risk factor reduction strategies

The patterns are followed by a glossary of terms, standards of practice, code of ethics, guide for professional conduct, standards of ethical conduct and guide for conduct of the affiliate member, and guidelines for PT documentation. At the end, there are two handy indexes, one a numerical and the other an alphabetical index to the patterns and ICD-9 codes.[1]

There are four chapters to Part 2, each one distinguished by a specific graphic that relates to the content area. Chapter 4 is the musculoskeletal patterns; Chapter 5 is the neuromuscular patterns; Chapter 6 is the cardiopulmonary patterns; and Chapter 7 is the integumentary patterns.

MUSCULOSKELETAL PRACTICE PATTERNS[1]

The musculoskeletal panel consisted of nine people with a wide range of experience covering all areas of orthopedic practice. The group, though lively and diverse, all shared a similar philosophy toward physical therapy practice. We all were committed to using the patient/client management model as a framework for practice. In describing musculoskeletal practice, we looked for common disorders treated in a variety of settings. From this list, a commonality of intervention was identified. Finally, the patterns, when grouped, would be managed similarly and have comparable outcomes.

The musculoskeletal patterns are either impairment based or pathology based. Primary prevention is a significant component to each pattern, because the progression to pathology, impairment, functional limitation, and disability is not inevitable. There is also a primary prevention pattern. The following is a description of each pattern, the purpose of which is to get a sense of what patients would fall within this category[1]:

1. Primary prevention of skeletal demineralization
    - Includes clients with prolonged nonweight-bearing state, hormonal changes, steroid use, nutritional deficiency, or those in a known high-risk category (e.g., based on sex, ethnicity, age, lifestyle)
    - Excludes patients with acute fractures, neoplasms, osteogenesis imperfecta, Paget's disease
    - Used to design a screening tool and group exercise program or individualized plan
2. Impaired posture
    - Includes patients with primary spinal or appendicular postural dysfunction due to habit, work, pregnancy, or idiopathic
    - Excludes patients with neuromuscular disorders or disease or radicular signs
    - Also patients with recent spinal stabilization surgery are excluded
3. Impaired muscle performance
    - Includes patients with disuse atrophy from systemic disease or prolonged immobilization
    - Also includes patients with pelvic floor muscle dysfunction
    - Excludes patients with amputation, fracture, postmusculoskeletal surgery, specific joint impairments, and neuromuscular disease
4. Impairments due to capsular restriction
    - Follows prolonged immobilization from external support/protective device or from protective muscle guarding
    - Patients will have decreased range of motion and may also have pain
    - Excludes patients with wounds/burns, joint sepsis/hemarthrosis, lack of voluntary movement
5. Impairments due to ligamentous or other connective tissue disorders

- Includes patients with musculotendinous strain and ligamentous sprain
- Patients may have joint hypermobility, muscle guarding/weakness, and/or swelling
- Excludes patients with fractures, neurologic dysfunction, open wounds, or radiculopathy

6. Impairments due to localized inflammation
- Includes patients with bursitis, tendinitis, synovitis, fasciitis, osteoarthritis, epicondylitis
- Patients may have edema, muscle weakness, neurovascular/sensory changes, pain
- Excludes patients with fractures, systemic diseases, open wounds, sepsis, associated surgery, deep vein thrombosis, dislocations

7. Impairments due to spinal disorders
- Includes patients with disk herniation/disease, nerve root compression, stenosis, stable spondylolisthesis
- Patients may have altered sensation, weakness, positive neural tension, deep-tendon reflex changes, surgery
- Excludes patients with failed surgery, fractures, neuromuscular/systemic disease, SCI, tumor

8. Impairments due to fracture
- Includes patients with trauma, hormonal changes, steroid use, nutritional deficiency, or those in a known high-risk category (e.g., based on sex, ethnicity, age, lifestyle)
- Excludes patients with bone neoplasms, osteogenesis imperfecta, and Paget's disease

9. Impairments due to joint arthroplasty
- Patients who have partial or total joint resurfacing of small or large joints
- Includes patients with bone neoplasms, osteoarthritis, rheumatoid arthritis/juvenile rheumatoid arthritis, steroid-induced necrosis, trauma, ankylosing spondylitis
- Excludes patients with failed surgical procedures and unrelated postoperative complications

10. Impairments due to bony or soft-tissue surgical procedures
- Includes patients with arthroplasty, ligamentous/muscle/tendon repair, open-reduction internal-fixation surgeries, bony debridement/graft, external fixators, soft-tissue/fascial/synovial procedures
- Excludes patients with failed surgery, amputation, nonunion, obstetric and gynecologic surgery, vascular/neurologic sequelae, total joint replacements, neoplasms

11. Impairments due to lower-extremity amputation
- Includes patients with uni/bilateral amputation, congenital amputation, residual limb revision
- Patients may have wound needs, prosthetic needs, gait deviations, and other mobility problems
- Excludes patients with ipsilateral hemiparesis

There are areas of musculoskeletal practice not covered by the patterns. For instance, there is no pattern dealing with the management of patients with impairments due to an upper-extremity amputation. *The Guide* is a fluid document and things will be edited as well as added on a regular basis.

THE NEXT STEP: USING *THE GUIDE* IN PRACTICE

There are several ways that the practice patterns can be useful in both the clinical and the education setting.

The first way to incorporate *The Guide* as a whole is to rewrite the initial evaluation form to reflect *Guide* language. "Guidecizing" forms is the quickest way to get clinicians used to using the terminology. From there, *The Guide* can be used for peer review. Group patients according to patterns and then see how closely the examinations and interventions match the ones outlined in the pattern. This is also a helpful way to validate the organization of the patterns. Do the patterns make sense based on what you're seeing in the clinic? Compiling data and keeping the APTA informed is essential in making *The Guide* a true description of our practice.

Another use of *The Guide* and the practice patterns is development of a form to measure outcomes. This is a great way to assess the efficacy of a variety of interventions. The form can also be used to evaluate the relationships between impairments, functional limitations, and disabilities.

Students in the clinic present another opportunity to use the practice patterns. Have the students develop a case study presentation using the patterns. Students can also use the patterns to work through complicated or unfamiliar patient management.

The practice patterns are wonderful tools for teaching in an academic setting. Besides using Part 1 of *The Guide* to describe documentation, Part 2 can be used as a framework for discussion of patient problems. For instance, patients with rotator cuff tendinitis, bicipital tendinitis, and lateral epicondylitis can all be discussed as part of Pattern F: Impairments due to Localized Inflammation. Commonality of examination and interventions can be addressed as well as a discussion of factors that would relate specifically to a particular body segment. Case studies can be presented in class using the practice patterns. And the disablement model is an ideal format for outlining the management of patients.

SUMMARY

- *The Guide to Physical Therapist Practice* was published to describe the practice of physical therapy.
- *The Guide* is not a cookbook of care but rather a document to improve the quality of physical therapy services.
- The guide is broken into two components: Part 1 gives a detailed outline as to what the practice of physical therapy entails. Part 2 describes the four preferred practice

patterns: Musculoskeletal, Neuromuscular, Cardiopulmonary, and Integumentary.
• The preferred practice patterns are structured with diagnostic labels that are based upon impairments.
• Clinicians should use *The Guide.* Use *The Guide* in different ways and gather data using *The Guide.*
• Once you have become familiar with *The Guide,* give APTA feedback on your use of *The Guide.*

REFERENCES

1. The guide to physical therapist practice. *Phys Ther* 77:1163–1650, 1997.
2. Jette A. Physical disablement concepts for physical therapy research and practice. *Phys Ther* 74:375–382, 1994.
3. Pope A, Tarlov A. *Disability in America.* Washington, DC, National Academy Press, 1991.

Clinical Decision Making in Rehabilitation

Lisa Giallonardo

O B J E C T I V E S

After completing this chapter, the student therapist should be able to do the following:

- Understand and discuss the overall process for clinical decision making in rehabilitation.
- Compare and contrast the disablement model with the medical model of patient management.
- Describe the five components of the clinical decision-making model used by *The Guide to Physical Therapist Practice.*
- Describe the sequence of steps in the examination process of clinical decision making.
- Discuss how the evaluation in the clinical decision-making process leads to determination of the diagnosis.
- Define the process of determining the patient prognosis in clinical decision making.
- Describe the three main components to a successful intervention in clinical decision making.
- Define the components of effective documentation in order to ensure the reproducibility and consistency of patient care.

Good clinical decision making is key to effective patient management. Physical therapists play a critical role in assessing neuromusculoskeletal problems. As more patients enter the medical system through the general practitioner, the patient is often referred to physical therapy without a clear diagnosis, especially those patients with musculoskeletal complaints. Physical therapists are educated in both the technical skills to carry out the examination and intervention procedures and the analytical skills to make the appropriate diagnosis and prognosis.

The physical therapy profession continues to move toward more autonomous practice. The majority of "practice acts" in the United States allow for practice without referral by the physical therapist. And the educational level of the physical therapist at the professional level is quickly changing to the Doctorate in Physical Therapy (DPT) degree. The greater the practitioner autonomy, the more critical effective and efficient clinical decision making becomes. The following case is an example of this need.

Your patient is a 35-year-old female runner who comes to you complaining of midback pain for 6 months. The pain disrupts her running in the early morning but not when she runs in the early evening. She tells you she bought a new mattress a month ago, convinced that her old one was "too soft and worn out." No change in symptoms occurred. Ice and heat have not worked either. She called her family physician and asked for a referral to physical therapy. She has not had a physical examination for almost a year and is scheduled for one next month.

Several key issues pertain to this case. The first is that she has had no physician-based medical screening. Second, the symptoms are not consistent with her running, despite the fact that she relates them to this activity. Third, she has tried to manage the pain with simple modalities as well as a change in mattress and nothing has worked. Given these three issues, it is critical that the examination lead to a valid diagnosis.

While asking the patient some historical questions concerning the current condition, she stated that she had not tried anti-inflammatory drugs because they upset her stomach. With further questioning a past medical history revealed stomach ulcers and acid reflux. The patient stated that she had been off her gastric medication for almost a year. Given this information, the questioning then focused on the differential diagnosis of a systemic problem (gastric in nature that will refer pain to the midback) versus a musculoskeletal issue in the thoracic spine and ribcage.

The patient indicated that she ran in the early morning before ingesting any food. In the evening, she would often run a couple hours after a light supper. She also stated that her stress level at work was considerable over the last 6 months and she used running as a way to cope with that. Upon physical examination, the spine range of motion was normal, the ribcage movement was equal and smooth bilaterally, and the muscle strength of the trunk was normal. I was unable to replicate her symptoms, even with having her run for 15 minutes on the treadmill. I sent her back to the physician with my examination findings and my diagnosis, which stated a question of visceral problems (and lack of musculoskeletal ones) that required physician workup. The physician called me after examining the patient and stated that an endoscopy revealed a return of her stomach ulcer. Medication was used to manage the condition, and her symptoms promptly disappeared.

Effective and efficient decision making requires approaching a patient problem in a systematic and orderly fashion. Using the same process over all types of patients facilitates valuable learning so that each case decision allows the clinician to add to the experiential knowledge base. It also helps make the results of the examination reliable (you or someone else can reproduce what you do) and valid (what you do is generalizable and is what you say it is).

Good clinical decision making requires foundation knowledge applied to each patient. The use of anatomic and kinesiologic information is critical to assessing normal and abnormal movement. Understanding both the pathologic and healing processes helps determine the diagnosis, prognosis, and plan of care.

Theory must be combined with evidence from the research literature for effective and efficient use of resources and achieving optimal outcomes. Sacket et al, in *Evidence Based Medicine*, suggest that evidence-based medicine is a combination of the best research evidence available from basic, applied, and clinical research; the clinical expertise of the practitioner, including skills, knowledge, and experience; and the patient's values, including concerns and expectations.[3] It is each and every clinician's responsibility to stay current with the literature, especially as it relates to their patient populations.

DISABLEMENT MODEL

The disablement model is at the core of each clinical decision. As discussed in Chapter 1, the model is a two-way continuum that focuses on the functional outcome of the patient.

Pathology ⟷ Impairment ⟷
Functional limitation ⟷ Disability

The medical model of patient management involves doing a history and physical exam, often in combination with invasive tests and measures. This allows for diagnosis at the cellular or system level (diagnosis of disease) that generally requires management by pharmacologic agents and/or surgery. The outcomes of this management are tissue repair and sometimes cure. Physical therapists rarely use invasive tests and measures and are legally not permitted to do surgery or dispense drugs (except

topically with phonophoresis or iontophoresis). Traditionally, physical therapists do not intervene at this level. However, exceptions to that in the musculoskeletal area include the management of simple strains and sprains; inflammatory processes of the muscle, tendon, bursa, capsule, and fascia; and capsular restriction. The tests and measures needed to diagnose and treat these problems are well within the scope of physical therapy practice.

In 1988, Sahrmann used the term "movement dysfunction" in relationship to diagnosis by the physical therapist.[4] Using the terminology of the disablement model, movement dysfunction can be classified as impairment (e.g., muscle weakness) or functional limitation (e.g., balance dysfunction).[2] The rehabilitation model involves a history and physical exam with *non*invasive tests and measures, which results in a movement diagnosis and intervention geared toward managing the impairments, functional limitations, and disabilities as appropriate. The classification of abnormalities as a diagnosis of impairment, or the classification of restrictions as diagnosis of functional limitation, relates directly to the management of the patient.

PATIENT–CLIENT MANAGEMENT MODEL

The patient–client management model described in Chapter 1 is the clinical decision-making model used in *The Guide to Physical Therapist Practice*.[1] The model has five components: examination, evaluation, diagnosis, prognosis, and intervention. The end result of this model is effective outcomes.

Examination is the first step of the process. It has three parts: the history, systems review, and tests and measures. The examination should be thorough and use all sources, including the patient, family, medical record, and other health care professionals. The history is an account of past and current health status. It is used to identify health risk factors, health needs, and coexisting health problems. An initial diagnosis is also determined based on the information gleaned from the history. The systems review and tests and measures are then used to rule in or out the initial diagnosis. Table 2-1 is the complete list of history categories from *Guide to Physical Therapist Practice*.[1]

A systems review is a very brief, limited exam designed to give you information concerning the general health of the patient; it helps in formulating a diagnosis and prognosis. This is a general screening that should be done as part of every patient's routine exam. It increases the emphasis on managing the whole person. For an autonomous practitioner, this is the key to good patient care. There are five categories: musculoskeletal, neuromuscular, cardiopulmonary, integumentary, and communication. Table 2-2 outlines the specific tests under each category.

At this point in the examination process, the clinician generally has a good idea of what is wrong with the patient. The last section of the exam is used to confirm or deny this diagnosis and redirect the thought process as necessary. There are 24 tests and measures listed alphabetically in *Guide to Physical Therapist Practice* (Table 2-3).[1] These are not all done at once, nor are

---

TABLE 2-1

Data Generated from a Patient History

- General demographics
- Social history and social habits
- Occupation/employment
- Growth and development
- Living environment
- History of current condition
- Functional status and activity level
- Medications
- Other tests and measures
- Past history of current condition
- Past medical/surgical history
- Family history
- Health status

---

they appropriate for every patient. The appropriate test and measure is chosen based on the results of the history and systems review. For example, the patient is a 21-year-old male college student who comes into the clinic with the complaint of a painful ankle. If he indicates a particular traumatic incident during the history, you would assume he has a sprained ankle and do anthropometric measurements to assess swelling, joint integrity tests to assess ligamentous integrity, range-of-motion measurement, and gait assessment. If the results of these tests and measures are positive, then a sprained ankle is a reasonable diagnosis. However, if the patient has had no trauma and cannot indicate any activity that would have triggered pain that caused him to seek medical attention, then other diagnoses must be considered. For instance, a history of multiple joint pain and inflammation, and/or a history of recent urinary tract infections and conjunctivitis, may indicate a systemic condition such as Reiter's syndrome or other rheumatoid diseases. In that case, anthropometric measures, integumentary integrity, joint integrity, range of motion, and gait will all be important to consider before referring back to a physician. A history of an old ankle injury may point toward structural or postural issues that must be carefully examined.

TABLE 2-2

The Systems Review

- Musculoskeletal: Gross range of motion, functional strength, and symmetry
- Neuromuscular: General movement patterns
- Cardiopulmonary: Heart rate, blood pressure, respiratory rate, edema
- Integumentary: Skin integrity, color, scar, temp, height, weight
- Communication/learning ability: Ability to make needs known, consciousness, orientation, expected emotional/behavioral responses, learning preferences

---

TABLE 2-3

Tests and Measures

- Aerobic capacity and endurance
- Anthropometric characteristics
- Arousal, attention, and cognition
- Assistive and adaptive devices
- Circulation and lymphatic drainage
- Community and work integration/reintegration
- Cranial nerve integrity
- Environmental, home, work barriers
- Ergonomics and body mechanics
- Gait, locomotion, and balance
- Integumentary integrity
- Joint integrity and mobility
- Motor function (motor control and learning)
- Muscle performance (strength/power/endurance)
- Neuromotor development/sensory integration
- Orthotic, protective, and supportive devices
- Pain
- Posture
- Prosthetic requirements
- Range of motion (including muscle length)
- Reflex integrity
- Self-care and home management (ADL/IADL)
- Sensory integrity (including proprioception and kinesthesia)
- Ventilation and respiration

The critical thinking and decision making that follows the examination process is known as the evaluation. It is the most important part of the process, because it leads directly to determination of the diagnosis. Using all the data—including clinical findings, loss of function, social considerations, chronicity of the problem, and patient's overall health status—the clinician formulates an impression. In the case of the 21-year-old college student, the history of an injury followed by the positive ankle swelling, positive anterior drawer test, decreased range of motion, and antalgic gait all led me to believe that this young man sprained his anterior talofibular ligament.

A diagnosis is a label based on a cluster of signs and symptoms after the collection, organization, and interpretation of information reached through the evaluation process. For the physical therapist, these are generally movement-related impairments or functional limitations. Sometimes, as in the case of the patient with the ankle sprain, the diagnosis is at the pathology level.

Diagnosis by the physical therapist is the key to good intervention planning. The medical diagnosis is often not useful. For instance, your patient is a 32-year-old female with a referral that states "chondromalacia patella—evaluate and treat." As physical therapists, we are not going to treat the actual softening of the cartilage, the pathology of chondromalacia patella. Surgery is generally required to accomplish that. Therefore, that leaves us to explore the multiple possible movement dysfunctions that may be ultimately causing the chondromalacia patella. Only once we discover the key impairment(s) will we know how to organize our treatment approach. Not all patients with chondromalacia patella are treated the same. If the key impairment is muscle weakness of the quadriceps, then the program emphasizes muscle performance. If the patella is not tracking properly because of structural issues, then patella taping may be in order. The mechanics at the foot should be explored, because excessive subtalar and midtarsal joint pronation during gait can increase the torsional forces on the patella femoral joint, causing pain. Treatment in that case would be proper footwear and even orthoses. All of these patients may have an appropriate medical diagnosis of chondromalacia patella, but all require a more specific movement diagnosis for determining the plan of care.

Prognosis—the predicted optimal level of functional improvement within a time frame—will also help determine intervention strategies. Predicting the level of improvement guides the intensity, duration, and style of intervention. The combination of diagnosis and prognosis is used to justify physical therapy management. The prognosis for the patient with an ankle sprain will depend on such things as the degree of sprain and the number of previous ankle sprains.

Intervention is the purposeful and skilled interaction between either the physical therapist or ancillary staff and the patient, based heavily on the patient's functional needs. Decisions are contingent upon the timely monitoring of the patient's response and progression toward mutually agreed-upon goals. There are a number of issues that guide the type, duration, and intensity of treatment. Table 2-4 outlines key questions that assist in these decisions. If your patient has a chronic case of subacromial bursitis, it will probably take longer to treat than if the patient was in the acute stage, although the latter stage would not tolerate aggressive treatment. The patient's activity level should always play a major role in the types of exercises as well as the intensity of treatment. If your patient with chronic subacromial bursitis wants to return to golfing weekly, then exercises mimicking the golf swing and even using the golf clubs are a critical component of the plan of care.

T A B L E   2 - 4
Key Questions for Interventions

- What is the stage of healing: acute, subacute, or chronic?
- How long do you have to treat the patient?
- What does patient do for activities?
- How compliant is the patient?
- How much *skilled* physical therapy is needed?
- What needs to be taught to prevent recurrence?
- Are there any referrals needed?
- What has worked for other patients with similar problems?
- Are there any precautions?
- What is your skill level?

T A B L E   2 - 5
Direct Interventions

- Therapeutic exercise (inc. aerobic conditioning)
- Functional training in self-care and home management (ADL)
- Functional training in community and work integration/reintegration (IADL)
- Manual therapy
- Prescription, application, and fabrication of devices and equipment
- Airway clearance techniques
- Wound management
- Electrotherapeutic modalities
- Physical agents and mechanical modalities

There are three main components to intervention: (1) coordination, communication, and documentation; (2) patient/client-related instruction; and (3) direct interventions. The first two components are done by all physical therapists on all patients. There are nine direct interventions, listed in order of importance in Table 2-5.

Notice patient's reactions, both generally and locally while treating the patient. Watch the patient's face; there's no need to inflict unnecessary pain. Also watch for tissue reaction like swelling and redness because you may be causing too much of a reaction. Too little a reaction is just as problematic. A patient who has a chronic adhesive capsulitis should be showing some gradual improvement with grade-4 joint mobilization. If there is no change during or after treatment, then the therapist must consider whether the technique is appropriate and if it's being performed correctly, as well as whether the original diagnosis is correct or something else is causing the limited range of motion.

The reexamination is performing selected tests and measures to evaluate the patient's progress. It is also used to modify or redirect intervention and may require a change in diagnosis and/or prognosis. The patient with adhesive capsulitis should have the range of motion, joint mobility, and functional capacity reexamined regularly.

Outcomes relate to the following: functional limitation/disability, patient/client satisfaction, and secondary prevention. Remediation of impairments is important, but the overriding purpose of physical therapy management is function. If the patient recovering from adhesive capsulitis cannot return to playing golf, despite an increase in range of motion and joint play, then the outcome (even with an improvement in impairments) may not be considered positive.

DOCUMENTATION

Good documentation is a critical component to the decision-making process. It allows you to manage the patient's case and communicate with other health care professionals while keeping your thoughts organized. Effective note writing also improves the reproducibility and consistency of care, allowing for quality assurance in the clinical setting and providing data for needed clinical research. Of course, third-party payers demand complete notes for service justification; billing equals documentation.

SOAP notes are a common form of progress notes that are used by all disciplines in many facilities. There are four aspects of the SOAP note: *s*ubjective, *o*bjective, *a*ssessment, and *p*lan.

Subjective

The subjective portion of the note provides the reader with information about the patient, including history of present illness, pain behavior, past and current medical history, medications, prior and current function and lifestyle, home life, the patient's goals, and the communication section of the systems review.

Objective

The objective section is where the results of the tests and measures are recorded, including the systems review, observation, and any of the 24 tests and measures, such as range of motion, muscle performance, and aerobic capacity. Any treatment that is performed during the session should be documented in the objective section as well.

Assessment

The assessment statement includes the problem list, short-term goals (anticipated goals), long-term goals (functional outcomes), diagnosis, and prognosis. It should include an evaluative statement that logically flows from the diagnosis, the factors affecting the diagnosis, and the prognosis (Fig. 2-1).

Plan

The plan section includes coordination and communication of services and referrals that are needed, patient education, direct

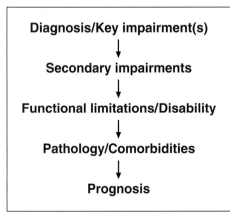

FIGURE 2 - 1
Evaluative statement for assessment.

interventions, outcomes (functional limitations and disabilities, patient satisfaction, and secondary prevention). Discharge planning is also included in this section.

The SOAP note terminology is easily coordinated with the terminology from *Guide to Physical Therapist Practice*. It is really just semantics, with assessment the same as evaluation and plan the same as intervention; short-term goals are the same as anticipated goals and long-term goals are the same as outcomes.

SUMMARY

- As physical therapists strive to become autonomous practitioners, it is essential that clinical reasoning skills be enhanced. Effective decision making requires approaching the problem in a systematic and orderly fashion.
- The patient management model is the clinical decision-making model used in *The Guide to Physical Therapist Practice*. The model has five components: examination, evaluation, diagnosis, prognosis, and intervention.
- The first step in the clinical decision-making process is performing a thorough examination. The examination has three steps: the history, system review, and tests and measures.
- The next step in the clinical decision-making process, the evaluation, is the most important step because it leads directly to determination of the diagnosis.
- A diagnosis is a label based on a cluster of signs and symptoms after the collection of all the relevant data.
- Intervention is the purposeful and skilled interaction based upon the patient's functional needs. There are three main components to intervention: coordination, communication and documentation; patient/client-related instruction; and direct interventions.
- A consistent pattern of decision making requires foundation knowledge applied to each patient. The use of anatomic and kinesiologic information is critical to assessing normal and abnormal movement. Understanding both the pathologic and healing process will help to determine the diagnosis, prognosis, and plan of care.
- Successful decision making requires good documentation in order to communicate with other health care professionals and improve the reproducibility and consistency of care.

REFERENCES

1. The guide to physical therapist practice. *Phys Ther* 77: 1163–1650, 1997.
2. Jette AM. Physical disablement concepts for physical therapy research and practice. *Phys Ther* 74:380–386, 1994.
3. Sacket D et al. *Evidence Based Medicine*, 2nd ed. London, Churchill Livingstone, 2000.
4. Sahrmann SA. Diagnosis by the physical therapist. *Phys Ther* 68:1703–1706, 1988.

Understanding and Managing the Healing Process Through Rehabilitation

William E. Prentice

O B J E C T I V E S

After completing this chapter, the student therapist should be able to do the following:

- Describe the pathophysiology of the healing process.
- Identify those factors that can impede the healing process.
- Identify the four types of tissue in the human body.
- Discuss the etiology and pathophysiology of various musculoskeletal injuries associated with various types of tissue.
- Discuss the healing process relative to specific musculoskeletal structures.
- Explain the importance of initial first aid and management of these injuries and their impact on the rehabilitation process.

Injury rehabilitation requires sound knowledge and understanding of the etiology and pathology involved in various musculoskeletal injuries that may occur.[6,38,63] When injury occurs, the therapist is charged with designing, implementing, and supervising the rehabilitation program. Rehabilitation protocols and progressions must be based primarily on the physiologic responses of the tissues to injury and on an understanding of how various tissues heal.[34,35] Thus the therapist must understand the healing process to effectively supervise the rehabilitative process. This chapter discusses the healing process relative to the various musculoskeletal injuries that may be encountered by a therapist.

UNDERSTANDING THE HEALING PROCESS

Rehabilitation programs must be based on the framework of the healing process (Fig. 3-1). The therapist must have a sound understanding of that process in terms of the sequence of the various phases of healing that take place. The physiologic responses of the tissues to trauma follow a predictible sequence and time course of events.[35] Decisions on how and when to alter and progress a rehabilitation program should be primarily based on recognition of signs and symptoms, as well as some

awareness of the time frames associated with the various phases of healing.[2,47]

The healing process consists of the inflammatory response phase, the fibroblastic-repair phase, and the maturation-remodeling phase. It must be stressed that although the phases of healing are presented as three separate entities, the healing process is a continuum. Phases of the healing process overlap one another and have no definitive beginning or end points.[21]

The Primary Injury

Primary injuries are almost always described as being either chronic or acute in nature and are a result of **macrotraumatic** or **microtraumatic** forces. Injuries classified as macrotraumatic injuries occur as a result of acute trauma and produce immediate pain and disability. Macrotraumatic injuries include fractures, dislocations, subluxations, sprains, strains, and contusions. Microtraumatic injuries are most often called overuse injuries and result from repetitive overloading or incorrect mechanics associated with continuous training.[49] Microtraumatic injuries include tendinitis, tenosynovitis, bursitis, and so forth. A **secondary injury** is essentially the inflammatory or hypoxic response that occurs with the primary injury.

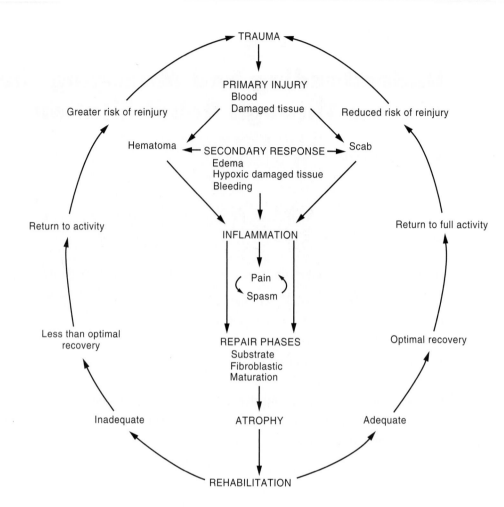

FIGURE 3-1

A cycle of sport-related injury. (Reproduced, with permission, from Booher JM, Thibodeau GA. *Athletic Injury Assessment,* 2nd ed. St. Louis, MO, Mosby, 1994.)

Inflammatory Response Phase

Once a tissue is injured, the process of healing begins immediately (Fig. 3-2).[1,7] The destruction of tissue produces direct injury to the cells of the various soft tissues.[27] Cellular injury results in altered metabolism and the liberation of materials that initiate the inflammatory response. It is characterized symptomatically by redness, swelling, tenderness, and increased temperature.[11,42] *This initial inflammatory response is critical to the entire healing process. If this response does not accomplish what it is supposed to or if it does not subside, normal healing cannot take place.*

Inflammation is a process through which **leukocytes** and other **phagocytic cells** and exudate are delivered to the injured tissue. This cellular reaction is generally protective, tending to localize or dispose of injury by-products (for example, blood and damaged cells) through phagocytosis, thus setting the stage for repair. Local vascular effects, disturbances of fluid exchange, and migration of leukocytes from the blood to the tissues occur.

VASCULAR REACTION

The vascular reaction involves vascular spasm, formation of a platelet plug, blood coagulation, and growth of fibrous tissue.[61]

The immediate response to tissue damage is a vasoconstriction of the vascular walls that lasts for approximately 5 to 10 minutes. This spasm presses the opposing endothelial linings together to produce a local anemia that is rapidly replaced by hyperemia of the area due to dilation. This increase in blood flow is transitory and gives way to slowing of the flow in the dilated vessels, which then progresses to stagnation and stasis. The initial effusion of blood and plasma lasts for 24 to 36 hours.

CHEMICAL MEDIATORS

Three chemical mediators, **histamine, leukotaxin,** and **necrosin,** are important in limiting the amount of exudate and swelling after injury. Histamine released from the injured mast cells causes vasodilation and increased cell permeability. This is due to swelling of endothelial cells and then separation between the cells. Leukotaxin is responsible for **margination,** in which leukocytes line up along the cell walls. It also increases cell permeability locally, thus affecting passage of the fluid and white blood cells through cell walls via diapedesis to form exudate. Therefore, vasodilation and active hyperemia are important in exudate (plasma) formation and supplying leukocytes to the injured area. Necrosin is responsible for phagocytic activity.

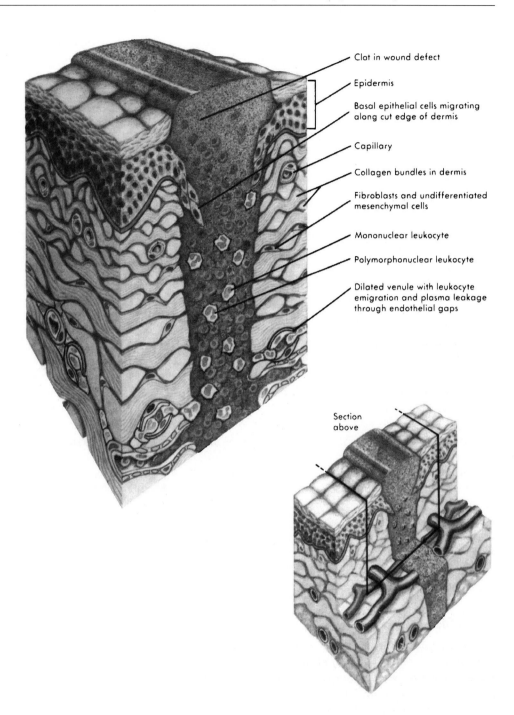

Clot in wound defect

Epidermis

Basal epithelial cells migrating along cut edge of dermis

Capillary

Collagen bundles in dermis

Fibroblasts and undifferentiated mesenchymal cells

Mononuclear leukocyte

Polymorphonuclear leukocyte

Dilated venule with leukocyte emigration and plasma leakage through endothelial gaps

Section above

FIGURE 3-2

The healing process: Inflammatory response phase.

The amount of swelling that occurs is directly related to the extent of vessel damage.

FORMATION OF A CLOT

Platelets do not normally adhere to the vascular wall; however, injury to a vessel disrupts the endothelium and exposes the collagen fibers. Platelets adhere to the collagen fibers to create a sticky matrix on the vascular wall, to which additional platelets and leukocytes adhere and eventually form a plug. These plugs obstruct local lymphatic fluid drainage and localize the injury response.

The initial event that precipitates clot formation is the conversion of **fibrinogen** to **fibrin.** This transformation occurs because of a cascading effect beginning with the release of a protein molecule called **thromboplastin** from the damaged cell. Thromboplastin causes **prothrombin** to be changed into **thrombin,** which in turn causes the conversion of fibrinogen into a very sticky fibrin clot that shuts off blood supply to the injured area. Clot formation begins around 12 hours after injury and is completed within 48 hours.

As a result of a combination of these factors, the injured area becomes walled off during the inflammatory stage of healing.

The leukocytes phagocytize most of the foreign debris toward the end of the inflammatory phase, setting the stage for the fibroblastic phase. This initial inflammatory response lasts for approximately 2 to 4 days after initial injury.

CHRONIC INFLAMMATION

A distinction must be made between the acute inflammatory response, as just described, and chronic inflammation. **Chronic inflammation** occurs when the acute inflammatory response does not eliminate the injuring agent and restore tissue to its normal physiologic state. Chronic inflammation involves the replacement of leukocytes with **macrophages, lymphocytes, and plasma cells.** These cells accumulate in a highly vascularized and innervated loose connective tissue matrix in the area of injury.[41]

The specific mechanisms that convert an acute inflammatory response to a chronic inflammatory response are, to date, unknown; however, they seem to be associated with situations that involve overuse or overload, with cumulative microtrauma to a particular structure.[20,41] Similarly, there is no specific time frame in which the classification of acute is changed to chronic inflammation. It does appear that chronic inflammation is resistant to both physical and pharmacologic treatments.[35]

USE OF ANTI-INFLAMMATORY MEDICATIONS

It is a common practice for a physician to prescribe nonsteroidal anti-inflammatory drugs (NSAIDs) for patients who have sustained an injury. These medications are certainly effective in minimizing pain and swelling associated with inflammation and may enhance return to full activity. However, there are some concerns that use of NSAIDs acutely following injury may actually interfere with inflammation and delay the healing process. The use of NSAIDs will be further discussed in Chapter 23.

Fibroblastic-Repair Phase

During the fibroblastic phase of healing, proliferative and regenerative activity leading to scar formation and repair of the injured tissue follows the vascular and exudative phenomena of inflammation (Fig. 3-3).[32] The period of scar formation, referred to as **fibroplasia,** begins within the first few hours after injury and may last for as long as 4 to 6 weeks. During this period, many of the signs and symptoms associated with the inflammatory response subside. The patient may still indicate some tenderness to touch and will usually complain of pain when particular movements stress the injured structure. As scar formation progresses, complaints of tenderness or pain gradually disappear.[59]

During this phase, growth of endothelial capillary buds into the wound is stimulated by a lack of oxygen, after which the wound is capable of healing aerobically.[15] Along with increased oxygen delivery comes an increase in blood flow, which delivers nutrients essential for tissue regeneration in the area.[12]

The formation of a delicate connective tissue, called **granulation tissue,** occurs with the breakdown of the fibrin clot. Granulation tissue consists of **fibroblasts,** collagen, and capillaries. It appears as a reddish granular mass of connective tissue that fills in the gaps during the healing process.

As the capillaries continue to grow into the area, fibroblasts accumulate at the wound site, arranging themselves parallel to the capillaries. Fibroblastic cells begin to synthesize an **extracellular matrix** that contains protein fibers of **collagen** and **elastin,** a **ground substance** that consists of nonfibrous proteins called **proteoglycans, glycosaminoglycans,** and fluid. On about day 6 or 7, fibroblasts also begin producing collagen fibers that are deposited in a random fashion throughout the forming scar. As the collagen continues to proliferate, the tensile strength of the wound rapidly increases in proportion to the rate of collagen synthesis. As the tensile strength increases, the number of fibroblasts diminishes to signal the beginning of the maturation phase.

This normal sequence of events in the repair phase leads to the formation of minimal scar tissue. Occasionally, a persistent inflammatory response and continued release of inflammatory products can promote extended fibroplasia and excessive fibrogenesis that can lead to irreversible tissue damage.[69] Fibrosis can occur in synovial structures, as with adhesive capsulitis in the shoulder; in extraarticular tissues, including tendons and ligaments; in bursa; or in muscle.

Maturation-Remodeling Phase

The maturation-remodeling phase of healing is a long-term process (Fig. 3-4). This phase features a realignment or remodeling of the collagen fibers that make up scar tissue according to the tensile forces to which that scar is subjected. Ongoing breakdown and synthesis of collagen occur with a steady increase in the tensile strength of the scar matrix. With increased stress and strain, the collagen fibers realign in a position of maximum efficiency parallel to the lines of tension. The tissue gradually assumes normal appearance and function, although a scar is rarely as strong as the normal injured tissue. Usually by the end of approximately 3 weeks, a firm, strong, contracted, nonvascular scar exists. The maturation phase of healing may require several years to be totally complete.

THE ROLE OF PROGRESSIVE CONTROLLED MOBILITY DURING THE HEALING PROCESS

Wolff's law states that bone and soft tissue will respond to the physical demands placed on them, causing them to remodel or realign along lines of tensile force.[72] Therefore, it is critical that injured structures be exposed to progressively increasing loads throughout the rehabilitative process.[55]

Controlled mobilization is superior to immobilization for scar formation, revascularization, muscle regeneration, and reorientation of muscle fibers and tensile properties in animal models.[74] A brief period of immobilization of the injured

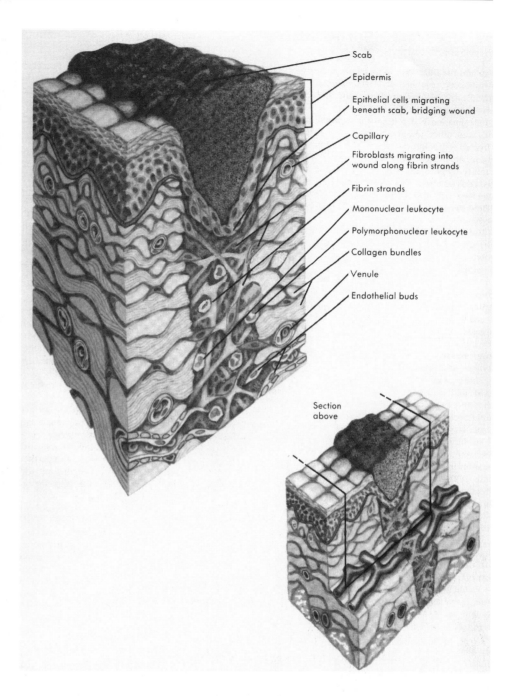

Scab
Epidermis
Epithelial cells migrating beneath scab, bridging wound
Capillary
Fibroblasts migrating into wound along fibrin strands
Fibrin strands
Mononuclear leukocyte
Polymorphonuclear leukocyte
Collagen bundles
Venule
Endothelial buds

Section above

FIGURE 3-3

The healing process: Fibroblastic-repair phase.

tissue during the inflammatory response phase is recommended and will likely facilitate the process of healing by controlling inflammation, thus reducing clinical symptoms. As healing progresses to the repair phase, controlled activity directed toward return to normal flexibility and strength should be combined with protective support or bracing.[37] Generally, clinical signs and symptoms disappear at the end of this phase.

As the remodeling phase begins, aggressive active range-of-motion and strengthening exercises should be incorporated to facilitate tissue remodeling and realignment. To a great extent, pain will dictate rate of progression. With initial injury, pain is intense and tends to decrease and eventually subside altogether as healing progresses. Any exacerbation of pain, swelling, or other clinical symptoms during or after a particular exercise or activity indicates that the load is too great for the level of tissue repair or remodeling. The therapist must be aware of the time required for the healing process and realize that being overly aggressive can interfere with that process.

Factors that Impede Healing

EXTENT OF INJURY The nature or amount of the inflammatory response is determined by the extent of the tissue injury. **Microtears** of soft tissue involve only minor damage and are most often associated with overuse. **Macrotears** involve significantly

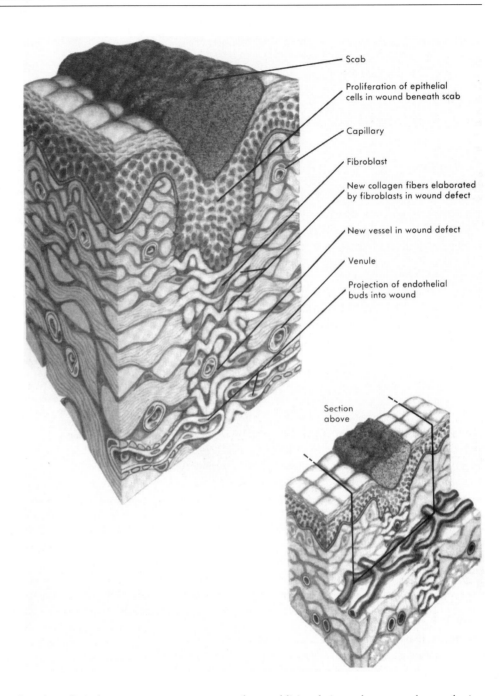

- Scab
- Proliferation of epithelial cells in wound beneath scab
- Capillary
- Fibroblast
- New collagen fibers elaborated by fibroblasts in wound defect
- New vessel in wound defect
- Venule
- Projection of endothelial buds into wound

Section above

F I G U R E   3 - 4

The healing process:
Maturation-remodeling
phase.

greater destruction of soft tissue and result in clinical symptoms and functional alterations. Macrotears are generally caused by acute trauma.[37]

EDEMA   The increased pressure caused by swelling retards the healing process, causes separation of tissues, inhibits neuromuscular control, produces reflexive neurologic changes, and impedes nutrition in the injured part. Edema is best controlled and managed during the initial first-aid management period as described previously.[10]

HEMORRHAGE   Bleeding occurs with even the smallest amount of damage to the capillaries. Bleeding produces the same negative effects on healing as does the accumulation of edema, and its presence produces additional tissue damage and exacerbation of the injury.[54]

POOR VASCULAR SUPPLY   Injuries to tissues with a poor vascular supply heal poorly and at a slow rate. This response is likely related to a failure in the initial delivery of phagocytic cells and fibroblasts necessary for scar formation.[54]

SEPARATION OF TISSUE   Mechanical separation of tissue can significantly impact the course of healing. A wound that has smooth edges that are in good apposition will tend to heal by primary intention with minimal scarring. Conversely, a wound that has jagged, separated edges must heal by secondary intention, with granulation tissue filling the defect and excessive scarring.[60]

MUSCLE SPASM   Muscle spasm causes traction on the torn tissue, separates the two ends, and prevents approximation. Local and generalized ischemia can result from spasm.

ATROPHY   Wasting away of muscle tissue begins immediately with injury. Strengthening and early mobilization of the injured structure retard atrophy.

CORTICOSTEROIDS   Use of corticosteroids in the treatment of inflammation is controversial. Steroid use in the early stages of healing has been demonstrated to inhibit fibroplasia, capillary proliferation, collagen synthesis, and increases in tensile strength of the healing scar. Their use in the later stages of healing and with chronic inflammation is debatable.

KELOIDS AND HYPERTROPHIC SCARS   Keloids occur when the rate of collagen production exceeds the rate of collagen breakdown during the maturation phase of healing. This process leads to hypertrophy of scar tissue, particularly around the periphery of the wound.

INFECTION   The presence of bacteria in the wound can delay healing, causes excessive granulation tissue, and frequently causes large, deformed scars.[29]

HUMIDITY, CLIMATE, AND OXYGEN TENSION   Humidity significantly influences the process of epithelialization. Occlusive dressings stimulate the epithelium to migrate twice as fast without crust or scab formation. The formation of a scab occurs with dehydration of the wound and traps wound drainage, which promotes infection. Keeping the wound moist provides an advantage for the necrotic debris to go to the surface and be shed.

Oxygen tension relates to the neovascularization of the wound, which translates into optimal saturation and maximal tensile strength development. Circulation to the wound can be affected by ischemia, venous stasis, hematomas, and vessel trauma.

HEALTH, AGE, AND NUTRITION   The elastic qualities of the skin decrease with aging. Degenerative diseases, such as diabetes and arteriosclerosis, also become a concern of the older patient and may affect wound healing. Nutrition is important for wound healing. In particular, vitamins C (collagen synthesis and immune system), K (clotting), and A (immune system); zinc for the enzyme systems; and amino acids play critical roles in the healing process.

PATHOPHYSIOLOGY OF INJURY TO VARIOUS BODY TISSUES

Classification of Body Tissues

There are four types of fundamental tissues in the human body: epithelial, connective, muscular, and nervous[66] (Table 3-1). According to Guyton, all tissues of the body can be defined as soft

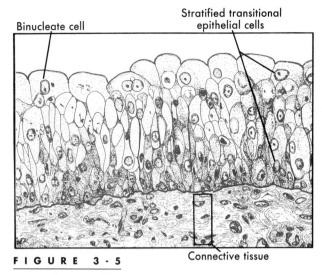

FIGURE   3 - 5

Epithelial cells exist in several layers.

tissue except bone.[30] Cailliet, however, more technically defines **soft tissue** as the matrix of the human body comprised of cellular elements within a ground substance. Furthermore, Cailliet believes that soft tissue is the most common site of functional impairment of the musculoskeletal system.[9] Therefore, most musculoskeletal injuries occur to the soft tissues.

EPITHELIAL TISSUE

The first fundamental tissue is epithelial tissue (Fig. 3-5). This specific tissue covers all internal and external body surfaces and, therefore, encompasses structures such as the skin, the outer layer of the internal organs, and the inner lining of the blood vessels and glands. A basic purpose of epithelial tissue, as presented by Fahey, is to protect and form structure for other tissues and organs.[19] In addition, this tissue functions in absorption (for example, in the digestive tract) and secretion (as in glands). A principal physiologic characteristic of epithelial tissue is that it contains no blood supply per se, so it must depend on the process of diffusion for nutrition, oxygenation, and elimination of waste products. Most injuries to this type of tissue are traumatic, including abrasions, lacerations, punctures, and avulsions. Other injuries to this tissue may include infection, inflammation, or disease.

CONNECTIVE TISSUE

The functions of connective tissue in the body are to support, provide a framework, fill space, store fat, help repair tissues, produce blood cells, and protect against infection. It consists of various types of cells separated from one another by some type of extracellular matrix. This matrix consists of fibers and ground substance and may be solid, semisolid, or fluid. The primary types of connective tissue cells are **macrophages,** which function as phagocytes to clean up debris; **mast cells,** which release chemicals (histamine and heparin) associated with inflammation; and the **fibroblasts,** which are the principal cells of the connective tissue.

TABLE 3-1

Tissues

TISSUE	LOCATION	FUNCTION
EPITHELIAL		
Simple squamous	Alveoli of lungs	Absorption by diffusion of respiratory gases between alveolar air and blood
	Lining of blood and lymphatic vessels	Absorption by diffusion, filtration, and osmosis
Stratified squamous	Surface of lining of mouth and esophagus	Protection
	Surface of skin (epidermis)	
Simple columnar	Surface layer of lining of stomach, intestines, and parts of respiratory tract	Protection; secretion; absorption
Stratified transitional	Urinary bladder	Protection
CONNECTIVE (MOST WIDELY DISTRIBUTED OF ALL TISSUES)		
Areolar	Between other tissues and organs	Connection
Adipose (fat)	Under skin	Protection
	Padding at various points	Insulation; support; reserve food
Dense fibrous	Tendons: ligaments	Flexible but strong connection
Bone	Skeleton	Support; protection
Cartilage	Part of nasal septum; covering articular surfaces of bones; larynx; rings in trachea and bronchi	Firm but flexible support
	Disks between vertebrae	
	External ear	
Blood	Blood vessels	Transportation
MUSCLE		
Skeletal (striated voluntary)	Muscles that attach to bones	Movement of bones
	Eyeball muscles	Eye movements
	Upper third of esophagus	First part of swallowing
Cardiac (striated involuntary)	Wall of heart	Contraction of heart
Visceral (nonstriated involuntary or smooth)	In walls of tubular viscera of digestive, respiratory, and genitourinary tracts	Movement of substances along respective tracts
	In walls of blood vessels and large lymphatic vessels	Changing of diameter of blood vessels
	In ducts of glands	Movement of substances along ducts
	Intrinsic eye muscles (iris and ciliary body)	Changing of diameter of pupils and shape of lens
	Arrector muscles of hairs	Erection of hairs (gooseflesh)
NERVOUS		
	Brain, spinal cord, nerves	Irritability; conduction

Collagen

Fibroblasts produce collagen and elastin found in varying proportions in different connective tissues. **Collagen** is a major structural protein that forms strong, flexible, inelastic structures that hold connective tissue together. Collagen enables a tissue to resist mechanical forces and deformation. **Elastin,** however, produces highly elastic tissues that assist in recovery from deformation. Collagen fibrils are the load-bearing elements of connective tissue. They are arranged to accommodate tensile stress but are not as capable of resisting shear or compressive stress.

Consequently, the direction of orientation of collagen fibers is along lines of tensile stress.

Collagen has several mechanical and physical properties that allow it to respond to loading and deformation, permitting it to withstand high tensile stress. The mechanical properties of collagen include *elasticity,* which is the capability to recover normal length after elongation; *viscoelasticity,* which allows for slow return to normal length and shape after deformation; and *plasticity,* which allows for permanent change or deformation. The physical properties include *force-relaxation,* which indicates the decrease in the amount of force needed to maintain a tissue at a set amount of displacement or deformation over time; the *creep response,* which is the ability of a tissue to deform over time while a constant load is imposed; and *hysteresis,* which is the amount of relaxation a tissue has undergone during deformation and displacement. If the mechanical and physical limitations of connective tissue are exceeded, injury results.

Types of Connective Tissue

There are several different types of connective tissue.[5,33,62] **Fibrous connective tissue** is composed of strong collagenous fibers that bind tissues together. There are two types of fibrous connective tissue. **Dense connective tissue** is composed primarily of collagen and is found in tendons, fascia, aponeurosis, ligaments, and joint capsule. **Tendons** connect muscles to bone. An **aponeurosis** is a thin, sheetlike tendon. A **fascia** is a thin membrane of connective tissue that surrounds individual muscles and tendons or muscle groups. **Ligaments** connect bone to bone. All synovial joints are surrounded by a **joint capsule,** which is a type of connective tissue similar to a ligament. The orientations of collagen fibers in ligaments and joint capsules are less parallel than in tendons. **Loose connective tissue** forms many types of thin membranes found beneath the skin, between muscles, and between organs. **Adipose tissue** is a specialized form of loose connective tissue that stores fat, insulates, and acts as a shock absorber. The blood supply to fibrous connective tissue is relatively poor, so healing and repair are slow processes.

Cartilage is a type of rigid connective tissue that provides support and acts as a framework in many structures. It is composed of chondrocyte cells contained in small chambers called lacunae and surrounded completely by an intracellular matrix. The matrix consists of varying ratios of collagen and elastin and a ground substance made of proteoglycans and glycosaminoglycans, which are nonfibrous protein molecules. These proteoglycans act as sponges and trap large quantities of water, which allows cartilage to spring back after being compressed. Cartilage has a poor blood supply, thus healing after injury is very slow. There are three types of cartilage. **Hyaline cartilage** is found on the articulating surfaces of bone and in the soft part of the nose. It contains large quantities of collagen and proteoglycan. **Fibrocartilage** forms the intervertebral disks and menisci located in several joint spaces. It has greater amounts of collagen than proteoglycan and is capable of withstanding a great deal of pressure. **Elastic cartilage** is found in the auricle of the ear and the larynx. It is more flexible than the other

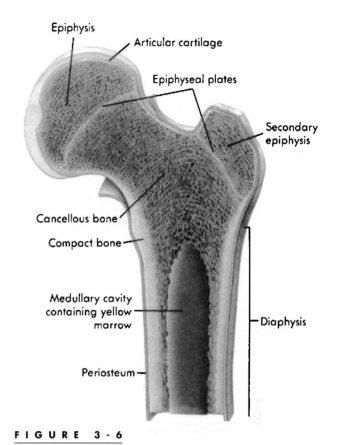

FIGURE 3-6

Structure of bone shown in cross-section.

types of cartilage and consists of collagen, proteoglycan, and elastin.

Reticular connective tissue is also composed primarily of collagen. It provides the support structure of the walls of various internal organs including the liver and kidneys.

Elastic connective tissue is composed primarily of elastic fibers. It is found primarily in the walls of blood vessels, airways, and hollow internal organs.

Bone is a type of connective tissue consisting of both living cells and minerals deposited in a matrix (Fig. 3-6). Each bone consists of three major components. The **epiphysis** is an expanded portion at each end of the bone that articulates with another bone. Each articulating surface is covered by an articular or **hyaline** cartilage. The **diaphysis** is the shaft of the bone. The **epiphyseal,** or **growth plate,** is the major site of bone growth and elongation. Once bone growth ceases, the plate ossifies and forms the epiphyseal line. With the exception of the articulating surfaces, the bone is completely enclosed by the **periosteum,** a tough, highly vascularized and innervated fibrous tissue.[43]

The two types of bone material are **cancellous,** or spongy, bone and **cortical,** or compact, bone. Cancellous bone contains a series of air spaces referred to as **trabeculae,** whereas cortical bone is relatively solid. Cortical bone in the diaphysis forms a hollow **medullary canal** in long bone, which is lined with **endosteum** and filled with bone **marrow.** Bone has a rich blood supply that certainly facilitates the healing process after injury. Bone has the functions of support, movement, and protection. Furthermore, bone stores and releases calcium into the bloodstream and manufactures red blood cells.

One additional type of connective tissue in the body is **blood.** Blood is composed of various cells suspended in a fluid intracellular matrix referred to as plasma. Plasma contains red blood cells, white blood cells, and platelets. Although this component does not function in structure, it is essential for the nutrition, cleansing, and physiology of the body.

With connective tissue playing such a major role throughout the human body, it is not surprising that many musculoskeletal injuries involve structures composed of connective tissue. Although tendons are classified as connective tissue, injuries to tendons and tendon healing will be incorporated into the discussion of the musculotendinous unit.

LIGAMENT SPRAINS

A sprain involves damage to a ligament that provides support to a joint. A ligament is a tough, relatively inelastic band of tissue that connects one bone to another. A ligament's primary function is threefold; to provide stability to a joint, to provide control of the position of one articulating bone to another during normal joint motion, and to provide proprioceptive input or a sense of joint position through the function of free nerve endings or mechanoreceptors located within the ligament.

Before discussing injuries to ligaments, a review of joint structure is in order[53] (Fig. 3-7). All **synovial joints** are composed of two or more bones that articulate with one another to allow motion in one or more places. The articulating surfaces

of the bone are lined with a very thin, smooth, cartilaginous covering called a hyaline cartilage. All joints are entirely surrounded by a thick, ligamentous **joint capsule.** The inner surface of this joint capsule is lined by a very thin **synovial membrane** that is highly vascularized and innervated. The synovial membrane produces **synovial fluid,** the functions of which include lubrication, shock absorption, and nutrition of the joint.

Some joints contain a thick fibrocartilage called a **meniscus.** The knee joint, for example, contains two wedge-shaped menisci that deepen the articulation and provide shock absorption in that joint. Finally, the main structural support and joint stability is provided by the ligaments, which may be either thickened portions of a joint capsule or totally separate bands. Ligaments are composed of dense connective tissue arranged in parallel bundles of collagen composed of rows of fibroblasts. Although bundles are arranged in parallel, not all collagen fibers are arranged in parallel.

Ligaments and tendons are very similar in structure; however, ligaments are usually more flattened than tendons, and collagen fibers in ligaments are more compact. The anatomic positioning of the ligaments determines in part what motions a joint can make.

If stress is applied to a joint that forces motion beyond its normal limits or planes of movement, injury to the ligament is likely[23] (Fig. 3-8). The severity of damage to the ligament is classified in many different ways; however, the most commonly used system involves three grades (degrees) of ligamentous sprain.

GRADE 1 SPRAIN   There is some stretching or perhaps tearing of the ligamentous fibers with little or no joint instability. Mild pain, little swelling, and joint stiffness may be apparent.

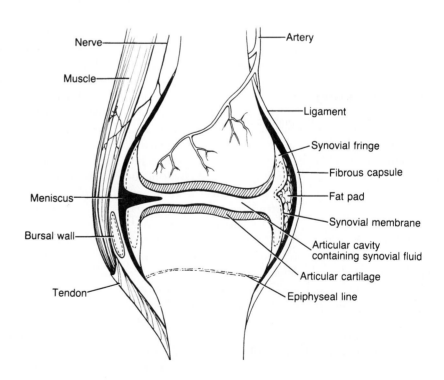

F I G U R E   3 - 7

Structure of a synovial joint.

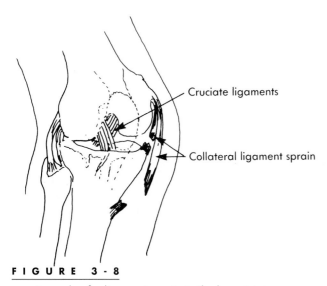

Cruciate ligaments

Collateral ligament sprain

FIGURE 3-8

Example of a ligament sprain in the knee joint.

GRADE 2 SPRAIN   There is some tearing and separation of the ligamentous fibers and moderate instability of the joint. Moderate-to-severe pain, swelling, and joint stiffness should be expected.

GRADE 3 SPRAIN   There is total rupture of the ligament, manifested primarily by gross instability of the joint. Severe pain may be present initially, followed by little or no pain due to total disruption of nerve fibers. Swelling may be profuse, and the joint tends to become very stiff some hours after the injury. A third-degree sprain with marked instability usually requires some form of immobilization lasting several weeks. Frequently the force producing the ligament injury is so great that other ligaments or structures surrounding the joint may also be injured. With cases in which there is injury to multiple joint structures, surgical repair or reconstruction may be necessary to correct an instability.

Ligament Healing

The healing process in the sprained ligament follows the same course of repair as with other vascular tissues. Immediately after injury, and for approximately 72 hours, there is a loss of blood from damaged vessels and attraction of inflammatory cells into the injured area. If a ligament is sprained outside of a joint capsule (extraarticular ligament), bleeding occurs in a subcutaneous space. If an intraarticular ligament is injured, bleeding occurs inside of the joint capsule until either clotting occurs or the pressure becomes so great that bleeding ceases.

During the next 6 weeks, vascular proliferation with new capillary growth begins to occur along with fibroblastic activity, resulting in the formation of a fibrin clot. It is essential that the torn ends of the ligament are reconnected by bridging of this clot. Synthesis of collagen and ground substance of proteoglycan as constituents of an intracellular matrix contributes to the proliferation of the scar that bridges between the torn ends of

the ligament. Initially, this scar is soft and viscous but eventually becomes more elastic. Collagen fibers are arranged in a random woven pattern with little organization. Gradually, there is a decrease in fibroblastic activity, a decrease in vascularity, and an increase to a maximum in collagen density of the scar.[3] Failure to produce enough scar and failure to reconnect the ligament to the appropriate location on a bone are the two reasons why ligaments are likely to fail.

Over the next several months the scar continues to mature with the realignment of collagen occurring in response to progressive stresses and strains. The maturation of the scar may require as long as 12 months to complete.[3] The exact length of time required for maturation depends on mechanical factors such as apposition of torn ends and length of immobilization.

FACTORS AFFECTING LIGAMENT HEALING

Surgically repaired extraarticular ligaments have healed with decreased scar formation and are generally stronger than unrepaired ligaments initially, although this strength advantage may not be maintained as time progresses. Nonrepaired ligaments heal by fibrous scarring effectively lengthening the ligament and producing some degree of joint instability. With intraarticular ligament tears, the presence of synovial fluid dilutes the hematoma, thus preventing formation of a fibrin clot and spontaneous healing.[33]

Several studies have shown that actively exercised ligaments are stronger than those that are immobilized. Ligaments that are immobilized for periods of several weeks after injury tend to decrease in tensile strength and also exhibit weakening of the insertion of the ligament to bone.[44] Thus, it is important to minimize periods of immobilization and progressively stress the injured ligaments while exercising caution relative to biomechanical considerations for specific ligaments.[3,52]

It is not likely that the inherent stability of the joint provided by the ligament before injury will be regained. To restore stability to the joint, the other structures that surround that joint, primarily muscles and their tendons, must be strengthened. The increased muscle tension provided by strength training can improve stability of the injured joint.[64,65]

FRACTURES OF BONE

Fractures can be generally classified as being either **open** or **closed.** A closed fracture involves little or no displacement of bones and little or no soft tissue disruption. An open fracture involves enough displacement of the fractured ends that the bone actually disrupts the cutaneous layers and breaks through the skin. Both fractures can be relatively serious if not managed properly, but an increased possibility of infection exists in an open fracture.[71] Fractures may also be considered complete, in which the bone is broken into at least two fragments, or incomplete, where the fracture does not extend completely across the bone.

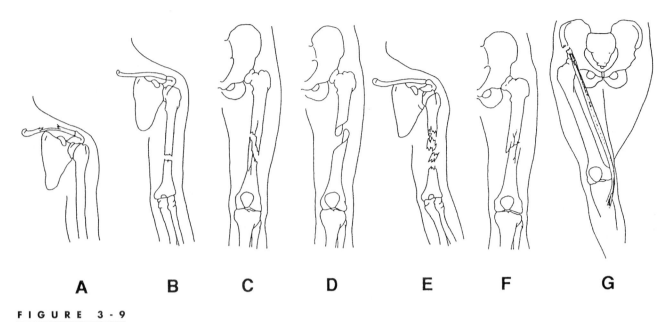

FIGURE 3-9

Fractures of bone. **A,** Greenstick; **B,** transverse; **C,** oblique; **D,** spiral; **E,** comminuted; **F,** impacted; and **G,** avulsion.

The varieties of fractures that can occur include greenstick, transverse, oblique, spiral, comminuted, impacted, avulsive, and stress. A **greenstick** fracture (Fig. 3-9A) occurs most often in children whose bones are still growing and have not yet had a chance to calcify and harden. It is called a greenstick fracture because of the resemblance to the splintering that occurs to a tree twig that is bent to the point of breaking. Because the twig is green, it splinters but can be bent without causing an actual break.

A **transverse** fracture (Fig. 3-9B) involves a crack perpendicular to the longitudinal axis of the bone that goes all the way through the bone. Displacement may occur; however, because of the shape of the fractured ends, the soft tissue (for example, muscles, tendons, and fat) that surrounds it sustains relatively little damage. A **linear** fracture runs parallel to the long axis of a bone and is similar in severity to a transverse fracture.

An **oblique** fracture (Fig. 3-9C) results in a diagonal crack across the bone and two very jagged, pointed ends that, if displaced, can potentially cause a good bit of soft tissue damage. Oblique and spiral fractures are the two types most likely to result in compound fractures.

A **spiral** fracture (Fig. 3-9D) is similar to an oblique fracture in that the angle of the fracture is diagonal across the bone. In addition, an element of twisting or rotation causes the fracture to spiral along the longitudinal axis of the bone. Spiral fractures used to be fairly common in ski injuries occurring just above the top of the boot when the bindings on the ski failed to release when the foot was rotated. These injuries are now less common due to improvements in equipment design.

A **comminuted** fracture (Fig. 3-9E) is a serious problem that may require an extremely long time for rehabilitation. In the comminuted fracture, multiple fragments of bone must be surgically repaired and fixed with screws and wires. If a fracture of this type occurs to a weight-bearing bone, as in the leg, a permanent discrepancy in leg length may develop.

In an **impacted** fracture (Fig. 3-9F), one end of the fractured bone is driven up into the other end. As with the comminuted fracture, correcting discrepancies in the length of the extremity may require long periods of intensive rehabilitation.

An **avulsion** fracture occurs when a fragment of bone is pulled away at the bony attachment of a muscle, tendon, or ligament. Avulsion fractures are common in the fingers and some of the smaller bones but can also occur in larger bones with tendinous or ligamentous attachments that are subjected to a large amount of force (Fig. 3-9G).

Perhaps the most common fracture resulting from physical activity is the **stress fracture.** Unlike the other types of fractures that have been discussed, the stress fracture results from overuse or fatigue rather than acute trauma.[40,50] Common sites for stress fractures include the weight-bearing bones of the leg and foot. In either case, repetitive forces transmitted through the bones produce irritations and microfractures at a specific area in the bone. The pain usually begins as a dull ache that becomes progressively more painful day after day. Initially, pain is most severe during activity. When a stress fracture actually develops, however, pain tends to become worse after the activity is stopped.

The biggest problem with a stress fracture is that often it does not show up on an x-ray film until the osteoblasts begin laying down subperiosteal callus or bone, at which point, a small white line, or a callus, appears. A bone scan, however, can reveal a potential stress fracture in as little as 2 days after onset of symptoms. If a stress fracture is suspected, the patient should stop any activity that produces added stress or fatigue to the area for a minimum of 14 days. Stress fractures do not usually require casting but can become normal fractures that must be immobilized if handled incorrectly. If a stress fracture occurs, it should be managed and rehabilitated by a qualified orthopedist and therapist.

Bone Healing

Healing of injured bone tissue is similar to soft tissue healing in that all phases of the healing process may be identified, although bone regeneration capabilities are somewhat limited. However, the functional elements of healing differ significantly from those of soft tissue. Tensile strength of the scar is the single most critical factor in soft tissue healing, whereas bone has to contend with a number of additional forces including torsion, bending, and compression.[22] Trauma to bone can vary from contusions of the periosteum to closed, nondisplaced fractures to severely displaced open fractures that also involve significant soft tissue damage. When a fracture occurs, blood vessels in the bone and the periosteum are damaged, resulting in bleeding and subsequent clot formation. Hemorrhaging from the marrow is contained by the periosteum and the surrounding soft tissue in the region of the fracture. In about 1 week, fibroblasts have begun laying down a fibrous collagen network. The fibrin strands within the clot serve as the framework for proliferating vessels. **Chondroblast** cells begin producing fibrocartilage, creating a **callus** between the broken bones. At first, the callus is soft and firm because it is composed primarily of collagenous fibrin. The callus becomes firm and more rubbery as cartilage begins to predominate. Bone-producing cells called **osteoblasts** begin to proliferate and enter the callus, forming cancellous bone trabeculae, which eventually replace the cartilage. Finally the callus crystalizes into bone, at which point remodeling of the bone begins. The callus can be divided into two portions, the external callus located around the periosteum on the outside of the fracture and the internal callus found between the bone fragments. The size of the callus is proportional both to the damage and to the amount of irritation to the fracture site during the healing process. Also during this time, **osteoclasts** begin to appear in the area to resorb bone fragments and clean up debris.[33,62]

The remodeling process is similar to the growth process of bone in that the fibrous cartilage is gradually replaced by fibrous bone and then by more structurally efficient lamellar bone. Remodeling involves an ongoing process during which osteoblasts lay down new bone and osteoclasts remove and break down bone according to the forces placed upon the healing bone.[71] Wolff's law maintains that a bone will adapt to mechanical stresses and strains by changing size, shape, and structure. Therefore, once the cast is removed, the bone must be subjected to normal stresses and strains so that tensile strength may be regained before the healing process is complete.[28,67]

The time required for bone healing is variable and based on a number of factors such as severity of the fracture, site of the fracture, extensiveness of the trauma, and age of the patient. Normal periods of immobilization range from as short as 3 weeks for the small bones in the hands and feet to as long as 8 weeks for the long bones of the upper and lower extremities. In some instances, for example, the four small toes, immobilization may not be required for healing. The healing process is certainly not complete when the splint or cast is removed. Osteoblastic and osteoclastic activity may continue for 2 to 3 years after severe fractures.

CARTILAGE DAMAGE

Osteoarthrosis is a degenerative condition of bone and cartilage in and about the joint. **Arthritis** should be defined as primarily an inflammatory condition with possible secondary destruction. **Arthrosis** is primarily a degenerative process with destruction of cartilage, remodeling of bone, and possible secondary inflammatory components.

Cartilage fibrillates, that is, releases fibers or groups of fibers and ground substance into the joint. Peripheral cartilage that is not exposed to weight-bearing or compression-decompression mechanisms is particularly likely to fibrillate. Fibrillation is typically found in the degenerative process associated with poor nutrition or disuse. This process can then extend even to weight-bearing areas with progressive destruction of cartilage proportional to stresses applied on it. When forces are increased, thus increasing stress, osteochondral or subchondral fractures can occur. Concentration of stress on small areas may produce pressures that overwhelm the tissue's capabilities. Typically, lower limb joints have to handle greater stresses, but their surface area is usually larger than the surface area of upper limbs. The articular cartilage is protected to some extent by the synovial fluid, which acts as a lubricant. It is also protected by the subchondral bone, which responds to stresses in an elastic fashion. It is more compliant than compact bone, and microfractures can be a means of force absorption. Trabeculae can fracture or be displaced due to pressures applied on the subchondral bone. In compact bone, fracture can be a means of defense to dissipate force. In the joint, forces can be absorbed by joint movement and eccentric contraction of muscles.

In the majority of joints where the surfaces are not congruent, the applied forces tend to concentrate in certain areas, which increases joint degeneration. **Osteophytosis** occurs as a bone attempts to increase its surface area to decrease contact forces. Typically, people describe this growth as "bone spurs." **Chondromalacia** is the nonprogressive transformation of cartilage with irregular surfaces and areas of softening. It occurs in nonweight-bearing areas at first and can progress to areas of excessive stress.

In patients, certain joints may be more susceptible to a response resembling osteoarthrosis.[57] The proportion of body weight resting on the joint, the pull of musculotendinous unit, and any significant external force applied to the joint are predisposing factors. Altered joint mechanics caused by laxity or previous trauma are also factors that come into play. The intensity of forces may be great, as in the hip, where the previously mentioned factors can produce pressures or forces that can be four times that of body weight and up to ten times that of body weight on the knee.

Typically, muscle forces generate more stress than body weight itself. Particular injuries are conducive to osteoarthritic changes such as subluxation and dislocation of the patella, osteochondritis dissecans, recurrent synovial effusion, and hemarthrosis. Also, ligamentous injuries may bring about a disruption of proprioceptive mechanisms, loss of adequate joint alignment, and meniscal damage in the knees with removal of the injured meniscus.[31] Other factors that have an impact are loss of full range of motion, poor muscular power and strength, and altered biomechanics on the joint. Spurring and spiking of bone are not synonymous with osteoarthrosis if the joint space is maintained and the cartilage lining is intact. It may simply be an adaptation to the increased stress of physical activity.

Cartilage Healing

Cartilage has a relatively limited healing capacity. When chondrocytes are destroyed and the matrix is disrupted, the course of healing is variable, depending on whether damage is to cartilage alone or also to subchondral bone. Injuries to articular cartilage alone fail to elicit clot formation or a cellular response. For the most part, the chondrocytes adjacent to the injury are the only cells that show any signs of proliferation and synthesis of matrix. Thus, the defect fails to heal, although the extent of the damage tends to remain the same.[25,48]

If subchondral bone is also affected, inflammatory cells enter the damaged area and formulate granulation tissue. In this case, the healing process proceeds normally with differentiation of granulation tissue cells into chondrocytes occurring in about 2 weeks. At approximately 2 months, normal collagen has been formed.

INJURIES TO MUSCULOTENDINOUS STRUCTURES

Muscle is often considered to be a type of connective tissue, but here it is treated as the third of the fundamental tissues. The three types of muscles are smooth (involuntary), cardiac, and skeletal (voluntary). **Smooth muscle** is found within the viscera, where it forms the walls of the internal organs, and within many hollow chambers. **Cardiac muscle** is found only in the heart and is responsible for its contraction. A significant characteristic of the cardiac muscle is that it contracts as a single fiber, unlike smooth and skeletal muscles, which contract as separate units. This characteristic forces the heart to work as a single unit continuously; therefore if one portion of the muscle should die (as in myocardial infarction), contraction of the heart does not cease.

Skeletal muscle is the striated muscle within the body responsible for the movement of bony levers (Fig. 3-10). Skeletal muscle consists of two portions: (1) the muscle belly and (2) its tendons, which are collectively referred to as a **musculotendinous unit.** The muscle belly is composed of sep-

arate, parallel elastic fibers called **myofibrils.** Myofibrils are composed of thousands of small **sarcomeres,** which are the functional units of the muscle. Sarcomeres contain the contractile elements of the muscle, as well as a substantial amount of connective tissue that holds the fibers together. **Myofilaments** are small contractile elements of protein within the sarcomere. There are two distinct types of myofilaments: thin **actin** myofilaments and thicker **myosin** myofilaments. Fingerlike projections, or **crossbridges,** connect the actin and myosin myofilaments. When a muscle is stimulated to contract, the crossbridges pull the myofilaments closer together, thus shortening the muscle and producing movement at the joint that the muscle crosses.[20]

The **muscle tendon** attaches muscle directly to bone. The muscle tendon is composed primarily of collagen fibers and a matrix of proteoglycan, which is produced by the **tenocyte** cell. The collagen fibers are grouped together into **primary bundles.** Groups of primary bundles join together to form hexagonal shaped **secondary bundles.** Secondary bundles are held together by intertwined loose connective tissue containing elastin called the **endotenon.** The entire tendon is surrounded by a connective tissue layer called the **epitenon.** The outermost layer of the tendon is the **paratenon,** which is a double-layer connective tissue sheath lined on the inside with synovial membrane (Fig. 3-11).

All skeletal muscles exhibit four characteristics: (1) elasticity, the ability to change in length or stretch; (2) extensibility, the ability to shorten and return to normal length; (3) excitability, the ability to respond to stimulation from the nervous system; and (4) contractility, the ability to shorten and contract in response to some neural command.[74]

Skeletal muscles show considerable variation in size and shape. Large muscles generally produce gross motor movements at large joints, such as knee flexion produced by contraction of the large, bulky hamstring muscles. Smaller skeletal muscles, such as the long flexors of the fingers, produce fine motor movements. Muscles producing movements that are powerful in nature are usually thicker and longer, whereas those producing finer movements requiring coordination are thin and relatively shorter. Other muscles may be flat, round, or fanshaped.[33,62]

Muscles may be connected to bone by a single tendon or by two or three separate tendons at either end. Those muscles that have two separate muscle and tendon attachments are called *biceps,* and those muscles with three separate muscle and tendon attachments are called *triceps.*

Muscles contract in response to stimulation by the central nervous system. An electrical impulse transmitted from the central nervous system through a single motor nerve to a group of muscle fibers causes a depolarization of those fibers. The motor nerve and the group of muscle fibers that it innervates are referred to collectively as a **motor unit.** An impulse coming from the central nervous system and traveling to a group of fibers through a particular motor nerve causes all the muscle fibers in that motor unit to depolarize and contract. This is

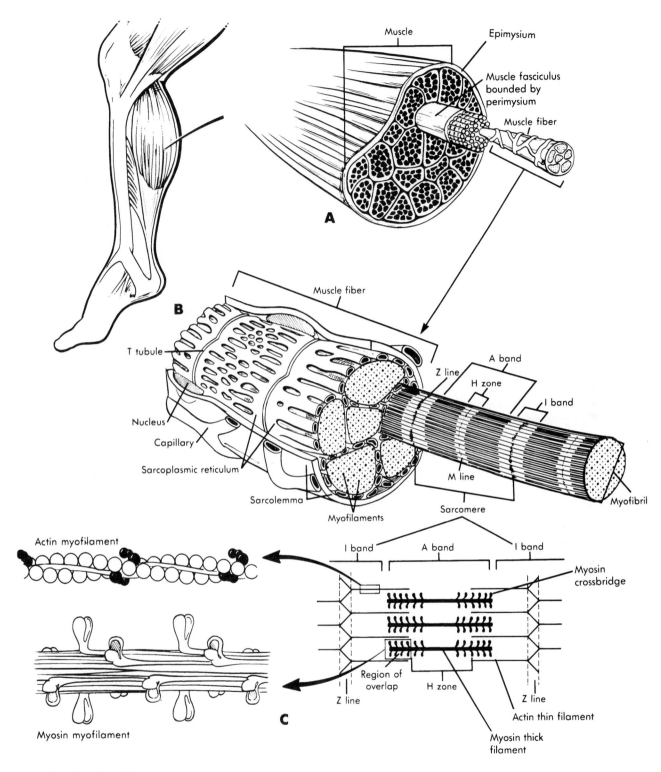

FIGURE 3 - 1 0

Parts of a muscle. **A,** Muscle is composed of muscle fasciculi, which can be seen by the unaided eye as striations in the muscle. The fasciculi are composed of bundles of individual muscle fibers (muscle cells). **B,** Each muscle fiber contains myofibrils in which the banding patterns of the sarcomeres are seen. **C,** The myofibrils are composed of actin myofilament and myosin myofilaments, which are formed from thousands of individual actin and myosin molecules.

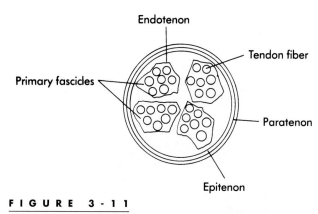

FIGURE   3 - 1 1

Structure of a tendon.

referred to as the **all-or-none** response and applies to all skeletal muscles in the body.[33]

Muscle Strains

If a musculotendinous unit is overstretched or forced to contract against too much resistance, exceeding the extensibility limits or the tensile capabilities of the weakest component within the unit, damage may occur to the muscle fibers, at the musculo-tendinous juncture, in the tendon, or at the tendinous attachment to the bone.[26,36] Any of these injuries can be referred to as a **strain** (Fig. 3-12). Muscles strains, like ligament sprains, are subject to various classification systems. The following is a simple system of classification of muscle strains.

GRADE 1 STRAIN   Some muscle or tendon fibers have been stretch-ed or actually torn. Active motion produces some tenderness and pain. Movement is painful, but full range of motion is usually possible.

GRADE 2 STRAIN   Some muscle or tendon fibers have been torn, and active contraction of the muscle is extremely painful. Usu-ally, a palpable depression or divot exists somewhere in the muscle belly at the spot where the muscle fibers have been torn. Some swelling can occur because of capillary bleeding.

GRADE 3 STRAIN   There is a complete rupture of muscle fibers in the muscle belly, in the area where the muscle becomes tendon, or at the tendinous attachment to the bone. The patient has sig-nificant impairment to or perhaps total loss of movement. Pain is intense initially but diminishes quickly because of complete separation of the nerve fibers. Musculotendinous ruptures are most common in the biceps tendon of the upper arm or in the Achilles heelcord in the back of the calf. When either of these tendons rupture, the muscle tends to bunch toward its prox-imal attachment. With the exception of an Achilles rupture, which is frequently surgically repaired, the majority of third-degree strains are treated conservatively with some period of immobilization.

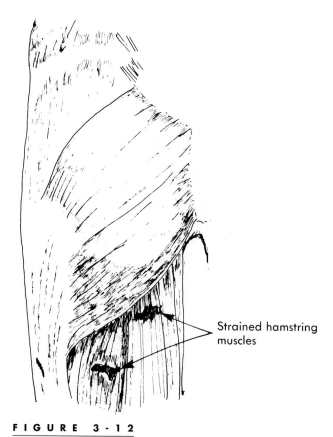

Strained hamstring muscles

FIGURE   3 - 1 2

A muscle strain results in tearing or separation of fibers.

Muscle Healing

Injuries to muscle tissue involve similar processes of healing and repair as discussed with other tissues. Initially, there will be hemorrhage and edema followed almost immediately by phago-cytosis to clear debris. Within a few days, there is a proliferation of ground substance and fibroblasts begin producing a gel-type matrix that surrounds the connective tissue, leading to fibrosis and scarring. At the same time, myoblastic cells form in the area of injury, which will eventually lead to regeneration of new myofibrils. Regeneration of both connective tissue and muscle tissue has begun.[73]

Collagen fibers undergo maturation and orient themselves along lines of tensile force according to Wolff's law. Active con-traction of the muscle is critical in regaining normal tensile strength.[4,45]

Regardless of the severity of the strain, the time required for rehabilitation is fairly lengthy. In many instances, rehabilitation time for a muscle strain is longer than for a ligament sprain. These incapacitating muscle strains occur most frequently in the large, force-producing hamstring and quadriceps muscles of the lower extremity. The treatment of hamstring strains requires a healing period of at least 6 to 8 weeks and a considerable amount of patience. Trying to return to activity too soon frequently causes reinjury to the area of the musculotendinous unit that has been strained, and the healing process must begin again.

Tendinitis

Of all the overuse problems associated with physical activity, tendinitis is among the most common. **Tendinitis** is a catch-all term that can describe many different pathologic conditions of a tendon. It essentially describes any inflammatory response within the tendon without inflammation of the paratenon. The term **paratenonitis** describes inflammation of the outer layer of the tendon only and usually occurs when the tendon rubs over a bony prominence. **Tendinosis** describes a tendon that has significant degenerative changes with no clinical or histologic signs of an inflammatory response.[16]

In cases of what is most often called **chronic tendinitis,** there is evidence of significant tendon degeneration, loss of normal collagen structure, and loss of cellularity in the area, but absolutely no inflammatory cellular response in the tendon. The inflammatory process is an essential part of healing. Inflammation is supposed to be a brief process with an end point after its function in the healing process has been fulfilled. The point or the cause in the pathologic process where the acute inflammatory cellular response terminates and the chronic degeneration begins is difficult to determine. As mentioned previously, with chronic tendinitis the cellular response involves a replacement of leukocytes with macrophages and plasma cells.

During muscle activity a tendon must move or slide on other structures around it whenever the muscle contracts. If a particular movement is performed repeatedly, the tendon becomes irritated and inflamed. This inflammation is manifested by pain on movement, swelling, possibly some warmth, and usually crepitus. Crepitus is a crackling sound similar to the sound produced by rolling hair between the fingers by the ear. Crepitus is usually caused by the adherance of the paratenon to the surrounding structures while it slides back and forth. This adhesion is caused primarily by the chemical products of inflammation that accumulate on the irritated tendon.[16]

The key to treating tendinitis is rest. If the repetitive motion causing irritation to the tendon is eliminated, chances are the inflammatory process will allow the tendon to heal. Unfortunately, a patient who is seriously involved with some physical activity may have difficulty in resting for 2 weeks or more while the tendinitis subsides. Anti-inflammatory medications and therapeutic modalities are also helpful in reducing the inflammatory response. An alternative activity, such as bicycling or swimming, is necessary to maintain fitness levels to a certain degree while allowing the tendon a chance to heal.

Tendinitis most commonly occurs in the Achilles tendon in the back of the lower leg in runners or in the rotator cuff tendons of the shoulder joint in swimmers or throwers, although it can certainly flare up in any tendon in which overuse and repetitive movements occur.

Tenosynovitis

Tenosynovitis is very similar to tendinitis in that the muscle tendons are involved in inflammation. However, many tendons are subject to an increased amount of friction due to the tightness of the space through which they must move. In these areas of high friction, tendons are usually surrounded by synovial sheaths that reduce friction on movement. If the tendon sliding through a synovial sheath is subjected to overuse, inflammation is likely to occur. The inflammatory process produces by-products that are "sticky" and tend to cause the sliding tendon to adhere to the synovial sheath surrounding it.

Symptomatically, tenosynovitis is very similar to tendinitis, with pain on movement, tenderness, swelling, and crepitus. Movement may be more limited with tenosynovitis because the space provided for the tendon and its synovial covering is more limited. Tenosynovitis occurs most commonly in the long flexor tendons of the fingers as they cross over the wrist joint and in the biceps tendon around the shoulder joint. Treatment for tenosynovitis is the same as for tendinitis. Because both conditions involve inflammation, mild anti-inflammatory drugs, such as aspirin, may be helpful in chronic cases.

Tendon Healing

Unlike most soft tissue healing, tendon injuries pose a particular problem in rehabilitation.[34] The injured tendon requires dense fibrous union of the separated ends and both extensibility and flexibility at the site of attachment. Thus an abundance of collagen is required to achieve good tensile strength. Unfortunately, collagen synthesis can become excessive, resulting in fibrosis, in which adhesions form in surrounding tissues and interfere with the gliding that is essential for smooth motion. Fortunately, over a period of time the scar tissue of the surrounding tissues becomes elongated in its structure because of a breakdown in the cross-links between fibrin units and allows the necessary gliding motion. A tendon injury that occurs where the tendon is surrounded by a synovial sheath can be potentially devastating.

A typical time frame for tendon healing would be that during the second week the healing tendon adheres to the surrounding tissue to form a single mass. During the third week, the tendon separates to varying degrees from the surrounding tissues; however, the tensile strength is not sufficient to permit a strong pull on the tendon for at least 4 to 5 weeks, the danger being that a strong contraction can pull the tendon ends apart.

INJURY TO NERVE TISSUE

The final fundamental tissue is nerve tissue (Fig. 3-13). This tissue provides sensitivity and communication from the central nervous system (brain and spinal cord) to the muscles, sensory organs, various systems, and the periphery. The basic nerve cell is the neuron. The neuron cell body contains a large **nucleus** and branched extensions called **dendrites,** which respond to neurotransmitter substances released from other nerve cells. From each nerve cell arises a single **axon,** which conducts the nerve impulses. Large axons found in peripheral nerves are

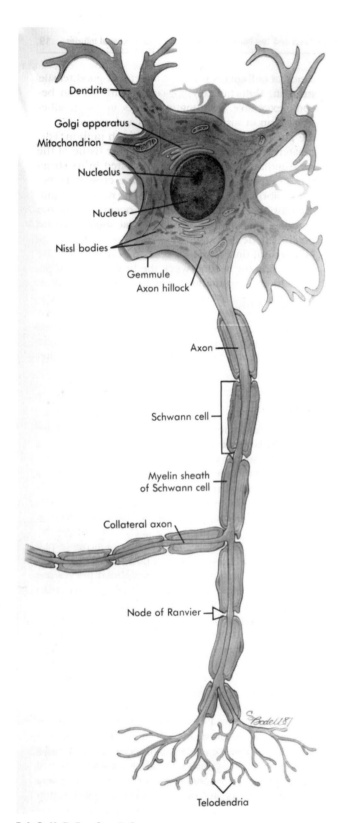

FIGURE   3-13

Structural features of a nerve cell.

enclosed in sheaths composed of **Schwann cells,** which are tightly wound around the axon. A nerve is a bundle of nerve cells held together by some connective tissue, usually a lipid-protein layer called the **myelin sheath** on the outside of the axon. Neurology is an extremely complex science, and only a brief presentation of its relevance to sports-related injuries is covered here.[7]

Nerve injuries often involve either contusions or inflammations. More serious injuries involve the crushing of a nerve or complete division (severing). This type of injury can produce a life-long physical disability, such as paraplegia or quadriplegia, and should therefore not be overlooked in any circumstance.

Of critical concern to the therapist is the importance of the nervous system in proprioception and neuromuscular control of movement as an integral part of a rehabilitation program. This is discussed in detail in Chapter 8.

Nerve Healing

Specialized tissue, such as nerve cells, cannot regenerate once the nerve cell dies. In an injured peripheral nerve, however, the nerve fiber can regenerate significantly if the injury does not affect the cell body. The proximity of the axonal injury to the cell body can significantly affect the time required for healing. The closer an injury is to the cell body, the more difficult the regenerative process. In the case of a severed nerve, surgical intervention can markedly enhance regeneration.

For regeneration to occur, an optimal environment for healing must exist. When a nerve is cut, several degenerative changes occur that interfere with the neural pathways. Within the first 3 to 5 days, the portion of the axon distal to the cut begins to degenerate and breaks into irregular segments. There is also a concomitant increase in metabolism and protein production by the nerve cell body to facilitate the regenerative process. The neuron in the cell body contains the genetic material and produces chemicals necessary for maintenance of the axon. These substances cannot be transmitted to the distal part of the axon, and eventually there will be complete degeneration.

In addition, the myelin portion of the Schwann cells around the degenerating axon also degenerates, and the myelin is phagocytized. The Schwann cells divide, forming a column of cells in place of the axon. If the cut ends of the axon contact this column of Schwann cells, the chances are good that an axon may eventually reinnervate distal structures. If the proximal end of the axon does not make contact with the column of Schwann cells, reinnervation will not occur.

The axon proximal to the cut has minimal degeneration initially and then begins the regenerative process with growth from the proximal axon. Bulbous enlargements and several axon sprouts form at the end of the proximal axon. Within about 2 weeks, these sprouts grow across the scar that has developed in the area of the cut and enter the column of Schwann cells. Only one of these sprouts will form the new axon and the others will degenerate. Once the axon grows through the Schwann cell columns, remaining Schwann cells proliferate along the length of the degenerating fiber and form new myelin around the growing axon, which will eventually reinnervate distal structures.

Regeneration is slow, at a rate of only 3 to 4 millimeters per day. Axon regeneration can be obstructed by scar formation due to excessive fibroplasia. Damaged nerves within the central nervous system regenerate very poorly compared to nerves in the peripheral nervous system. Central nervous system axons lack connective tissue sheaths, and the myelin-producing Schwann cells fail to proliferate.[33,62]

ADDITIONAL MUSCULOSKELETAL INJURIES

Dislocations and Subluxations

A dislocation occurs when at least one bone in an articulation is forced out of its normal and proper alignment and stays out until it is either manually or surgically put back into place or reduced.[51] Dislocations most commonly occur in the shoulder joint, elbow, and fingers, but they can occur wherever two bones articulate.

A subluxation is like a dislocation except that in this situation a bone pops out of its normal articulation but then goes right back into place. Subluxations most commonly occur in the shoulder joint, as well as in the knee cap in females.

Dislocations should never be reduced immediately, regardless of where they occur. The therapist should take the patient to an x-ray facility and rule out fractures or other problems before reduction. Inappropriate techniques of reduction may only exacerbate the problem. Return to activity after dislocation or subluxation is largely dependent on the degree of soft tissue damage.

Bursitis

In many areas, particularly around joints, friction occurs between tendons and bones, skin and bone, or two muscles. Without some mechanism of protection in these high-friction areas, chronic irritation would be likely.

Bursae are essentially pieces of synovial membrane that contain small amounts of synovial fluid. This presence of synovium permits motion of surrounding structures without friction. If excessive movement or perhaps some acute trauma occurs around these bursae, they become irritated and inflamed and begin producing large amounts of synovial fluid. The longer the irritation continues or the more severe the acute trauma, the more fluid is produced. As the fluid continues to accumulate in a limited space, pressure tends to increase and causes irritation of the pain receptors in the area.

Bursitis can be extremely painful and can severely restrict movement, especially if it occurs around a joint. Synovial fluid continues to be produced until the movement or trauma producing the irritation is eliminated.

A bursa that occasionally completely surrounds a tendon to allow more freedom of movement in a tight area is referred to as a **synovial sheath.** Irritation of this synovial sheath may restrict tendon motion.

All joints have many bursae surrounding them. Perhaps the three bursae most commonly irritated as a result of various types of physical activity are the subacromial bursa in the shoulder joint, the olecranon bursa on the tip of the elbow, and the prepatellar bursa on the front surface of the patella. All three of these bursae have produced large amounts of synovial fluid, affecting motion at their respective joints.

Muscle Soreness

Overexertion in strenuous muscular exercise often results in muscular pain. At one time or another most everyone has experienced **muscle soreness,** usually resulting from some physical activity to which we are unaccustomed.

There are two types of muscle soreness. The first type of muscle pain is acute and accompanies fatigue. It is transient and occurs during and immediately after exercise. The second type of soreness involves delayed muscle pain that appears approximately 12 hours after injury. It becomes most intense after 24 to 48 hours and then gradually subsides so that the muscle becomes symptom free after 3 or 4 days. This second type of pain may best be described as a syndrome of delayed muscle pain, leading to increased muscle tension, edema formation, increased stiffness, and resistance to stretching.[46]

The cause of **delayed-onset muscle soreness (DOMS)** is debated. Initially, it was hypothesized that soreness was due to an excessive buildup of lactic acid in exercised muscles; however, recent evidence has essentially ruled out this theory.[18]

It has also been hypothesized that DOMS is caused by the tonic, localized spasm of motor units, varying in number with the severity of pain. This theory maintains that exercise causes varying degrees of ischemia in the working muscles. This ischemia causes pain, which results in reflex tonic muscle contraction that increases and prolongs the ischemia. Consequently, a cycle of increasing severity is begun.[17] As with the lactic acid theory, the spasm theory has also been discounted.

Currently, there are two schools of thought relative to the cause of DOMS. DOMS seems to occur from very small tears in the muscle tissue, which seem to be more likely with eccentric or isometric contractions.[18] It is generally believed that the initial damage caused by eccentric exercise is mechanical damage to either the muscular or connective tissue. Edema accumulation and delays in the rate of glycogen repletion are secondary reactions to mechanical damage.[56]

DOMS may be caused by structural damage to the elastic components of connective tissue at the musculotendinous junction. This damage results in the presence of hydroxyproline, a protein by-product of collagen breakdown, in blood and urine.[13] It has also been documented that structural damage to the muscle fibers results in an increase in blood serum levels of various protein and enzymes, including creatine kinase. This increase indicates that there is likely some damage to the muscle fiber as a result of strenuous exercise.[18]

Muscle soreness can best be prevented by beginning at a moderate level of activity and gradually progressing the intensity of the exercise over time. Treatment of muscle soreness usually also involves some type of stretching activity. As for other conditions discussed in this chapter, ice is important as a treatment for muscle soreness, particularly within the first 48 to 72 hours.

Contusions

A **contusion** is synonymous with the term *bruise*. The mechanism that produces it is a blow from some external object that causes soft tissues (for example, skin, fat, muscle, ligaments, or joint capsule) to be compressed against the hard bone underneath. If the blow is hard enough, capillaries rupture and allow bleeding into the tissues. The bleeding, if superficial enough, causes a bluish-purple discoloration to the skin that persists for several days. The contusion can be very sore to the touch. If damage has occurred to muscle, pain can be elicited on active movement. In most cases, the pain ceases within a few days and discoloration disappears in 2 to 3 weeks.

The major problem with contusions occurs where an area is subjected to repeated blows. If the same area, or more specifically a muscle, is bruised over and over again, small calcium deposits may begin to accumulate in the injured area. These pieces of calcium may be found between several fibers in the muscle belly, or calcium may form a spur that projects from the underlying bone. These calcium formations, which can significantly impair movement, are referred to as **myositis ossificans.** In some cases, myositis ossificans can develop from a single trauma.

The key to preventing myositis ossificans from occurring from repeated contusion is protection of the injured area by padding. If the area is properly protected after the first contusion, myositis ossificans may never develop. Protection, along with rest, may frequently allow the calcium to be reabsorbed and eliminate any need for surgical intervention.

The two areas that seem to be the most vulnerable to repeated contusions during physical activity are the quadriceps muscle group on the front of the thigh and the biceps muscle on the front of the upper arm. The formation of myositis ossificans in either of these or any other areas may be detected on x-ray films.

MANAGING THE HEALING PROCESS THROUGH REHABILITATION

Rehabilitation exercise progressions can generally be subdivided into three phases based primarily on the three stages of the healing process: Phase 1, the acute phase; Phase 2, the repair phase; and Phase 3, the remodeling phase. Depending on the type and extent of injury and the individual response to healing, phases will usually overlap. Each phase must include carefully considered goals and criteria for progressing from one phase to another.

Presurgical Exercise Phase

This phase would only apply to those patients who sustain injuries that require surgery. If surgery can be postponed, exercise may be used as a means to improve its outcome. By allowing the initial inflammatory response phase to resolve, by maintaining or, in some cases, increasing muscle strength and flexibility, levels of cardiorespiratory fitness, and improving neuromuscular control, the patient may be better prepared to continue the exercise rehabilitative program after surgery.

Phase 1: The Acute Injury Phase

Phase 1 begins immediately when injury occurs and may last as long as day 4 following injury. During this phase, the inflammatory stage of the healing process is attempting to "clean up the mess" by creating an environment that is conducive to the fibroblastic stage. Initial first aid and management techniques are perhaps the most critical part of any rehabilitation program. The manner in which the injury is managed initially unquestionably has a significant impact on the course of the rehabilitative process.[58]

Regardless of the type of injury, the one problem they all have in common is swelling. Swelling can be caused by any number of factors, including bleeding, production of synovial fluid, an accumulation of inflammatory by-products, edema, or a combination of several factors. No matter which mechanism is involved, swelling produces an increased pressure in the injured area, and increased pressure causes pain.[17] Swelling can also cause neuromuscular inhibition, which results in weak muscle contraction. Swelling is most likely during the first 72 hours after an injury.

Once swelling has occurred, the healing process is significantly retarded. The injured area cannot return to normal until all the swelling is gone. Therefore, everything that is done in first aid management of any of these conditions should be directed toward controlling the swelling. If the swelling can be controlled initially in the acute stage of injury, the time required for rehabilitation is likely to be significantly reduced.

To control and significantly limit the amount of swelling, the PRICE principle—protection, restricted activity, ice, compression, and elevation—should be applied. Each factor plays a critical role in limiting swelling, and all of these elements should be used simultaneously (Fig. 3-14).

PROTECTION

The injured area should be protected from additional injury by applying appropriate splints, braces, pads, or other immobilization devices. If the injury involves the lower extremity, it is recommended that the athlete go nonweight-bearing on crutches at least until the acute inflammatory response has subsided.

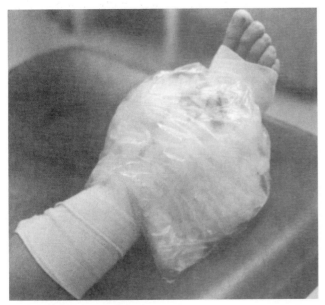

FIGURE 3-14

Musculoskeletal injuries should be treated initially with protection, restricted activity, ice, compression, and elevation.

RESTRICTED ACTIVITY (REST)

The period of restricted activity following any type of injury is absolutely critical in any treatment program. Once an anatomic structure is injured, it immediately begins the healing process. In an injured structure that is not rested and is subjected to unnecessary external stress and strains, the healing process never really gets a chance to begin. Consequently, the injury does not get well, and the time required for rehabilitation is markedly increased. This is not to minimize the importance of early mobility. Controlled mobility has been shown to be superior to immobilization for scar formation, revascularization, muscle regeneration, and reorientation of muscle fibers and tensile properties.[74] The amount of time necessary for resting varies with the severity of the injury, but most minor injuries should rest for approximately 24 to 48 hours before an active rehabilitation program is begun.

ICE

The use of cold is the initial treatment of choice for virtually all conditions involving injuries to the musculoskeletal system.[58] It is most commonly used immediately after injury to decrease pain and promote local vasoconstriction, thus controlling hemorrhage and edema. Cold applied to an acute injury will lower metabolism in the injured area and the tissue demands for oxygen, therefore reducing hypoxia.[39] This benefit extends to uninjured tissue, preventing injury-related tissue death from spreading to adjacent normal cellular structures. It is also used in the acute phase of inflammatory conditions, such as bursitis, tenosynovitis, and tendinitis, in which heat can cause additional pain and swelling.[39] Cold is also used to reduce the reflex muscle

guarding and spastic conditions that accompany pain. Its analgesic effect is probably one of its greatest benefits. One explanation of the analgesic effect is that cold decreases the velocity of nerve conduction, although it does not entirely eliminate it. Cold may also bombard cutaneous sensory nerve receptor areas with so many cold impulses that pain impulses are lost. With ice treatments, the athlete reports an uncomfortable sensation of cold, followed by burning, an aching sensation, and finally complete numbness.[58]

Because of the low thermal conductivity of underlying subcutaneous fat tissues, applications of cold for short periods are ineffective in cooling deeper tissues. For this reason, longer treatments of 20 to 30 minutes are recommended. Cold treatments are generally believed to be more effective in reaching deeper tissues than most forms of heat. Cold applied to the skin is capable of significantly lowering the temperature of tissues at a considerable depth. The extent of this lowered tissue temperature depends on the type of cold applied to the skin, the duration of its application, the thickness of the subcutaneous fat, and the region of the body to which it is applied. Ice should be applied to the injured area until the signs and symptoms of inflammation have disappeared and there is little or no chance that swelling will be increased by using some form of heat. Ice should be used for at least 72 hours after an acute injury.[58]

COMPRESSION

Compression is likely the single most important technique for controlling initial swelling. The purpose of compression is to mechanically reduce the amount of space available for swelling by applying pressure around an injured area. The best way of applying pressure is to use an elastic wrap, such as an Ace bandage, to apply firm but even pressure around the injury.

Because of the pressure buildup in the tissues, having a compression wrap in place for a long time may become painful; however, the wrap must be kept in place despite significant pain because it is so important in the control of swelling. The compression wrap should be left in place continuously for at least 72 hours after an acute injury. In many overuse problems (such as tendinitis, tenosynovitis, and particularly, bursitis) that involve ongoing inflammation, the compression wrap should be worn until the swelling is almost entirely gone.

ELEVATION

The final factor that assists in controlling swelling is elevation. The injured part, particularly an extremity, should be elevated to eliminate the effects of gravity on blood pooling in the extremities. Elevation assists venous and lymphatic drainage of blood and other fluids from the injured area back to the central circulatory system. The greater the degree of elevation, the more effective the reduction in swelling. For example, in an ankle sprain, the leg should be placed in such a position that the ankle is virtually straight up in the air. The injured part should be elevated as much as possible during the first 72 hours.

The appropriate technique for initial management of the acute injuries discussed in this chapter, regardless of where they occur, would be the following.

1. Apply a compression wrap directly over the injury. Wrapping should be from distal to proximal. Tension should be firm and consistent. Wetting the elastic wrap to facilitate the passage of cold from ice packs may be helpful.
2. Surround the injured area entirely with ice bags, and secure them in place. Ice bags should be left on for 45 minutes initially and then 1 hour off and 30 minutes on as much as possible over the next 24 hours. During the following 48-hour period, ice should be applied as often as possible.
3. The injured part should be elevated as much as possible during the initial 72-hour period after injury. Keeping the injured part elevated while sleeping is particularly important.
4. Allow the injured part to rest for approximately 24 hours after the injury.

By day 3 or 4, swelling begins to subside and eventually stops altogether. The injured area may feel warm to the touch, and some discoloration is usually apparent. The injury is still painful to the touch, and some pain is elicited on movement of the injured part.[70] At this point the patient should have already begun active mobility exercises working through a pain-free range of motion. If the injury involves the lower extremity, the patient should be encouraged to progressively bear more weight.

A physician may choose to have the patient take non-steroidal anti-inflammatory drugs (NSAIDs) to help control swelling and inflammation. It is usually helpful to continue this medication throughout the rehabilitative process.

Phase 2: The Repair Phase

Once the inflammatory response has subsided, the repair phase begins. During this stage of the healing process, fibroblastic cells are laying down a matrix of collagen fibers and forming scar tissue. This stage may begin as early as 2 days after the injury and may last for several weeks. At this point, swelling has stopped completely. The injury is still tender to the touch but is not as painful as during the last stage. Pain is also less on active and passive motion.[58]

As soon as inflammation is controlled, the therapist should immediately begin to incorporate activities into the rehabilitation program that can maintain levels of cardiorespiratory fitness, restore full range of motion, restore or increase strength, and re-establish neuromuscular control as discussed in the subsequent chapters.

As in the acute phase, modalities should be used to control pain and swelling. Cryotherapy should still be used during the early portion of this phase to reduce the likelihood of swelling. Electrical stimulating currents can help with controlling pain and improving strength and range of motion.[58]

Phase 3: The Remodeling Phase

The remodeling phase is the longest of the three phases and may last for several years, depending on the severity of the injury. The ultimate goal during this maturation stage of the healing process is return to activity. The injury is no longer painful to the touch, although some progressively decreasing pain may still be felt on motion. The collagen fibers must be realigned according to tensile stresses and strains placed upon them during functional sport-specific exercises.

The focus during this phase should be on regaining activity-specific skills. Dynamic functional activities should be incorporated into the rehabilitation program. Strengthening exercises should progressively place stresses and strains on the injured structures that are normally encountered during that sport. Functional testing should be done to determine specific skill weaknesses that need to be addressed.

At this point some type of heating modality is beneficial to the healing process. The deep-heating modalities, ultrasound, or the diathermies should be used to increase circulation to the deeper tissues. Massage and gentle mobilization may also be used to reduce guarding, increase circulation, and reduce pain. Increased blood flow delivers the essential nutrients to the injured area to promote healing, and increased lymphatic flow assists in breakdown and removal of waste products.[58]

REHABILITATIVE PHILOSOPHY

The rehabilitation philosophy relative to inflammation and healing after injury is to assist the natural processes of the body while doing no harm.[41] The course of rehabilitation chosen by the therapist must focus on their knowledge of the healing process and its therapeutic modifiers to guide, direct, and stimulate the structural function and integrity of the injured part. The primary goal should be to have a positive influence on the inflammation and repair process to expedite recovery of function in terms of range of motion, muscular strength and endurance, neuromuscular control, and cardiorespiratory endurance.[22] The therapist must try to minimize the early effects of excessive inflammatory processes including pain modulation, edema control, and reduction of associated muscle spasm, which can produce loss of joint motion and contracture. Finally, the therapist should concentrate on preventing the recurrence of injury by influencing the structural ability of the injured tissue to resist future overloads by incorporating various therapeutic exercises.[41] The subsequent chapters of this book can serve as a guide for the therapist in using the many different rehabilitation tools available.

SUMMARY

• The three phases of the healing process are the inflammatory response phase, the fibroblastic-repair phase, and maturation-remodeling phase, which occur in sequence but overlap one another in a continuum.

- Factors that may impede the healing process include edema, hemorrhage, lack of vascular supply, separation of tissue, muscle spasm, atrophy, corticosteroids, hypertrophic scars, infection, climate and humidity, age, health, and nutrition.
- The four fundamental types of tissue in the human body are epithelial, connective, muscle, and nerve.
- Ligament sprains involve stretching or tearing the fibers that provide stability at the joint.
- Fractures can be classified as either greenstick, transverse, oblique, spiral, comminuted, impacted, avulsive, or stress.
- Osteoarthritis involves degeneration of the articular cartilage or subchondral bone.
- Muscle strains involve a stretching or tearing of muscle fibers and their tendons and cause impairment to active movement.
- Tendinitis, an inflammation of a muscle tendon that causes pain on movement, usually occurs because of overuse.
- Tenosynovitis is an inflammation of the synovial sheath through which a tendon must slide during motion.
- Dislocations and subluxations involve disruption of the joint capsule and ligamentous structures surrounding the joint.
- Bursitis is an inflammation of the synovial membranes located in areas where friction occurs between various anatomic structures.
- Muscle soreness may be caused by spasm, connective tissue damage, muscle tissue damage, or some combination of each of these factors.
- Repeated contusions can lead to the development of myositis ossificans.
- All injuries should be initially managed with protection, rest, ice, compression, and elevation to control swelling and thus reduce the time required for rehabilitation.

REFERENCES

1. The healing process. *Nursing Times.* 90:95, 1994.
2. Arnheim D, Prentice W. *Principles of Athletic Training,* 10th ed. New York, McGraw-Hill, 2000.
3. Arnoczky SP. Physiologic principles of ligament injuries and healing. In: Scott WN, ed. *Ligament and Extensor Mechanism Injuries of the Knee.* St. Louis, Mosby, 1991, 67–82.
4. Bandy W, Dunleavy K. Adaptability of skeletal muscle: Response to increased and decreased use. In: Zachazewski J, Magee D, Quillen W, eds. *Athletic Injuries and Rehabilitation.* Philadelphia, Saunders, 1996.
5. Beck EW. *Mosby's Atlas of Functional Human Anatomy.* St. Louis, Mosby, 1982.
6. Booher JM, Thibodeau GA. *Athletic Injury Assessment,* 2nd ed. St. Louis, Mosby, 1994.
7. Bryant MW. Wound healing. *CIBA Clinical Symposia* 29.2–36, 1977.
8. Butler U. Nerve structure, function, and physiology. In: Zachazewski J, Magee D, Quillen W, eds. *Athletic Injuries and Rehabilitation.* Philadelphia, Saunders, 1996, 170–188.
9. Cailliet R. *Soft Tissue Pain and Disability,* 2nd ed. Philadelphia, Davis, 1988.
10. Carley PJ, Wainapel SF. Electrotherapy for acceleration of sound healing: Low intensity direct current. *Arch Phys Med Rehabil* 66:443–446, 1985.
11. Carrico TJ, Mehrhof AI, Cohen IK. Biology and wound healing. *Surg Clin North Am* 64:721–734, 1984.
12. Cheng N. The effects of electrocurrents on ATP generation, protein synthesis and membrane transport. *J Orth Res* 171:264–272, 1982.
13. Clancy W. Tendon trauma and overuse injuries. In: Leadbetter W, Buckwalter J, Gordon S, ed. *Sports-Induced Inflammation.* Park Ridge, IL, American Academy of Orthopaedic Surgeons, 1990.
14. Clarkson PM, Tremblay I. Exercise-induced muscle damage, repair and adaptation in humans. *J Appl Physiol* 65:1–6, 1988.
15. Cox D. Growth factors in wound healing. *J Wound Care* 2:339–342, 1993.
16. Curwin S. Tendon injuries: pathophysiology and treatment. In: Zachazewski J, Magee D, Quillen W, eds. *Athletic Injuries and Rehabilitation.* Philadelphia, Saunders, 1996, 27–50.
17. deVries HA. Quantitative EMG investigation of spasm theory of muscle pain. *Am J Phys Med* 45:119–134, 1996.
18. Evans WJ. Exercise induced skeletal muscle damage. *Phys Sports Med* 15:189–200, 1987.
19. Fahey TD. *Athletic Training: Principles and Practice.* Palo Alto, CA, Mayfield Publishing, 1986.
20. Fantone J. Basic concepts in inflammation. In: Leadbetter W, Buckwalter J, Gordon S, ed. *Sports-Induced Inflammation.* Park Ridge, IL, American Academy of Orthopaedic Surgeons, 1990, 25–54.
21. Fernandez A, Finlew JM. Wound healing: Helping a natural process. *Postgrad Med J* 74:311–318, 1983.
22. Flynn M, Rovee D. Influencing repair and recovery. *Am J Nurs* 82:1550–1558, 1982.
23. Frank C. Ligament injuries: Pathophysiology and healing. In: Zachazewski J, Magee D, Quillen W, eds. *Athletic Injuries and Rehabilitation.* Philadelphia, Saunders, 1996, 9–25.
24. Frankel VH, Nordin M. *Basic Biomechanics of the Skeletal System.* Philadelphia, Lea & Febiger, 1980.
25. Gelberman R, Goldberg V, An K-N, et al. Soft tissue healing. In: Woo SL-Y, Buckwalter J, eds. *Injury and Repair of Musculoskeletal Soft Tissues.* Park Ridge, IL, American Academy of Orthopaedic Surgeons, 1988, 103–117.
26. Glick JM. Muscle strains: Prevention and treatment. *Phys Sports Med* 8:73–77, 1980.

27. Goldenberg M. Wound care management: Proper protocol differs from athletic trainers' perceptions. *J Ath Train* 31:12–16, 1996.

28. Gradisar IA. Fracture stabilization and healing. In: Gould JA, Davies GJ, eds. *Orthopaedic and Sports Physical Medicine*. St. Louis, Mosby, 1985, 118–134.

29. Gross A, Cutright D, Bhaskar S, et al. Effectiveness of pulsating water jet lavage in treatment of contaminated crush wounds. *Am J Surg* 124:373–375, 1972.

30. Guyton AC. *Textbook of Medical Physiology*. Philadelphia, Saunders, 1986.

31. Henning CE. Semilunar cartilage of the knee: Function and pathology. In: Pandolf KB, ed. *Exercise and Sport Science Review*. New York, Macmillan 1988.

32. Hettinga DL. Inflammatory response of synovial joint structures. In: Gould JA, Davies GJ, eds. *Orthopaedic and Sports Physical Therapy*. St. Louis, Mosby, 1985, 87–117.

33. Hole J. *Human Anatomy and Physiology*. Dubuque, Brown, 1984.

34. Houglum P. Soft tissue healing and its impact on rehabilitation. *J Sport Rehabil* 1:19–39, 1992.

35. Hubbel S, Buschbacher R. Tissue injury and healing: Using medications, modalities, and exercise to maximize recovery. In: Bushbacher R, Branddom R, eds. *Sports Medicine and Rehabilitation: A Sport Specific Approach*. Philadelphia, Hanley & Belfus, 1994.

36. Keene JS. Ligament and muscle tendon unit injuries. In: Gould JA, Davies GJ, eds. *Orthopaedic and Sports Physical Therapy*. St. Louis, Mosby, 1985, 135–167.

37. Kibler WB. Concepts in exercise rehabilitation of athletic injury. In: Leadbetter W, Buckwalter J, Gordon S, eds. *Sports-Induced Inflammation*, Park Ridge, IL, American Academy of Orthopaedic Surgeons, 1990.

38. Kissane JM. *Anderson's Pathology*, 8th ed. St. Louis, Mosby, 1985.

39. Knight KL. *Cryotherapy in Sport Injury Management*. Champaign, IL, Human Kinetics, 1995.

40. Lane NE, Bloch D, Wood P, et al. Aging, long-distance running, and the development of musculoskeletal disability. *Am J Med* 82:772–780, 1987.

41. Leadbetter W. Introduction to sports-induced soft-tissue inflammation. In: Leadbetter W, Buckwalter J, Gordon S, eds. *Sports-Induced Inflammation*. Park Ridge, IL, American Academy of Orthopaedic Surgeons, 1990, 3–24.

42. Leadbetter W, Buckwalter J, Gordon S. *Sports-Induced Inflammation*. Park Ridge, IL, American Academy of Orthopaedic Surgeons, 1990.

43. Loitz-Ramage B, Zernicke R. Bone biology and mechanics. In: Zachazewski J, Magee D, Quillen W, eds. *Athletic Injuries and Rehabilitation*. Philadelphia, Saunders, 1996, 99–118.

44. MacMaster JH. *The ABC's of Sports Medicine*. Melbourne, FL, Kreiger Publishing, 1982.

45. Malone T, Garrett W, Zachewski J. Muscle: Deformation, injury and repair. In: Zachazewski J, Magee D, Quillen W, eds. *Athletic Injuries and Rehabilitation*. Philadelphia, Saunders, 1996, 71–91.

46. Malone T, McPhoil T, eds. *Orthopaedic and Sports Physical Therapy*. St. Louis, Mosby, 1996.

47. Marchesi VT. Inflammation and healing. In: Kissane JM, ed. *Anderson's Pathology*, 8th ed. St. Louis, Mosby, 1985.

48. Martinez-Hernandez A, Amenta P. Basic concepts in wound healing. In: Leadbetter W, Buckwalter J, Gordon S, eds. *Sports-Induced Inflammation*. Park Ridge, IL, American Academy of Orthopaedic Surgeons, 1990, 55–102.

49. Matheson G, MacIntyre J, Taunton J. Musculoskeletal injuries associated with physical activity in older adults. *Med Sci Sport Exerc* 21:379–385, 1989.

50. Messier SP, Pittala KA. Etiologic factors associated with selected running injuries. *Med Sci Sports Exerc* 20:501–505, 1988.

51. Muckle DS. *Outline of Fractures and Dislocations*. Bristol, England, Wright Publishing, 1985.

52. Musacchia XJ. Disuse atrophy of skeletal muscle: Animal models. In: Padolf KB, ed. *Exercise and Sport Sciences Review*. New York, Macmillan, 1988.

53. Norkin C, Levangie P. Joint structure and function: A comprehensive analysis. Philadelphia, Davis, 1983.

54. Norris S, Provo B, Stotts N. Physiology of wound healing and risk factors that impede the healing process. *AACN Clin Issue Crit Care Nurs* 1:545–552, 1990.

55. Noyes FR. Functional properties of knee ligaments and alterations induced by immobilization. *Clin Orthop* 123:210–242, 1977.

56. O'Reilly K, Warhol M, Fielding R, et al. Eccentric exercise induced muscle damage impairs muscle glycogen depletion. *J Appl Physiol* 63:252–256, 1987.

57. Panush RS, Brown DG. Exercise and arthritis. *Sports Med* 4:54–64, 1987.

58. Prentice WE, ed. *Therapeutic Modalities in Sports Medicine*. St. Louis, McGraw-Hill, 1999.

59. Riley WB. Wound healing. *Am Fam Physician* 24:5, 1981.

60. Robbins SL, Cotran RS, Kumar V. *Pathologic Basis of Disease*, 3rd ed. Philadelphia, Saunders, 1984.

61. Rywlin AM. Hemopoietic system. In: Kissane JM, ed. *Anderson's Pathology*, 8th ed. St. Louis, Mosby, 1985.

62. Seeley R, Stephens T, Tate P. *Anatomy and Physiology*. St. Louis, Mosby, 1995.

63. Seller RH. *Differential Diagnosis of Common Complaints*. Philadelphia, Saunders, 1986.

64. Stanish WD, Gunnlaugson B. Electrical energy and soft tissue injury healing. *Sportcare and Fitness* 9:12, 1988.

65. Stanish WD, Rubinovich M, Kozey J, et al. The use of electricity in ligament and tendon repair. *Phys Sports Med* 13:8, 1985.

66. Stewart J. *Clinical Anatomy and Physiology*. Miami, Medmaster, 1986.

67. Stone MH. Implications for connective tissue and bone

alterations resulting from rest and exercise training. *Med Sci Sports Exerc* 20:S162–168, 1988.

68. Walker J. Cartilage of human joints and related structurs. In: Zachazewski J, Magee D, Quillen W, eds. *Athletic Injuries and Rehabilitation.* Philadelphia, Saunders, 1996, 120–151.

69. Wahl S, Renstrom P. Fibrosis in soft-tissue injuries. In: Leadbetter W, Buckwalter J, Gordon S, eds. *Sports-Induced Inflammation.* Park Ridge, IL, American Academy of Orthopaedic Surgeons, 1990, 637–653.

70. Wells PE, Frampton V, Bowsher D. *Pain Management in Physical Therapy.* Norwalk, CT, Appleton & Lange, 1988.

71. Whiteside JA, Fleagle SB, Kalenak A. Fractures and refractures in intercollegiate patients: An eleven year experience. *Am J Sports Med* 9:369–377, 1981.

72. Woo SL-Y, Buckwalter J, eds. *Injury and Repair of Musculoskeletal Soft Tissues.* Park Ridge, IL, American Academy of Orthopaedic Surgeons, 1988.

73. Woodman R, Pare L. Evaluation and treatment of soft tissue lesions of the ankle and foot using the Cyriax approach. *Phys Ther* 62:1144–1147, 1982.

74. Zachezewski J. Flexibility for sports. In: Sanders B, ed. *Sports Physical Therapy.* Norwalk, CT, Appleton & Lange, 1990, 201–238.

PART 2

Treating Physiologic Impairments During Rehabilitation

Impairment Due to Pain: Managing Pain During the Rehabilitation Process

Craig R. Denegar and Phillip B. Donley

O B J E C T I V E S

After completing this chapter, the student therapist should be able to do the following:

- Define pain, its types, and its positive and negative effects.
- Discuss the various techniques for assessing pain.
- Describe the characteristics of sensory receptors.
- Describe how the nervous system relays information about painful stimuli.
- Describe an appropriate neurophysiologic mechanism for pain control for the therapeutic modalities used by therapists.
- Describe how pain perception can be modified by cognitive factors.

UNDERSTANDING PAIN

The International Association for the Study of Pain defines **pain** as "an unpleasant sensory and emotional experience associated with actual or potential tissue damage, or described in terms of such damage."[22] Pain is a subjective sensation with more than one dimension and an abundance of descriptors of its qualities and characteristics. Despite its universality, pain is composed of a variety of human discomforts, rather than being a single entity.[21] The perception of pain can be subjectively modified by past experiences and expectations. Much of what we do to treat patients' pain is to change their perceptions of pain.[4]

Pain does have a purpose. It warns us that there is something wrong and can provoke a withdrawal response to avoid further injury. It also results in muscle spasm and guarding or protection of the injured part. Pain, however, can persist after it is no longer useful. It can become a means of enhancing disability and inhibiting efforts to rehabilitate the patient. Prolonged spasm, which leads to circulatory deficiency, muscle atrophy, disuse habits, and conscious or unconscious guarding, can lead to a severe loss of function.[17] Chronic pain can become a disease state in itself. Often lacking an identifiable cause, chronic pain can totally disable a patient. Research in recent years has led to a better understanding of pain and pain relief. This research also has raised new questions, while leaving many unanswered.

The control of pain is an essential aspect of caring for the injured patient. The therapist has several therapeutic approaches to pain modulation from which to choose.[31] We now have a better understanding of the psychology of pain; however, newer approaches to pain management challenge our understanding of injury and pain. The evolution of the treatment of pain is, however, incomplete. This chapter presents an overview of some theories of pain control that are intended to provide a stimulus for the therapist to develop his or her own rationale for using various techniques of pain modulation in the plan of care for patients they treat. Ideally, it also will interest some in research to establish the physiologic and psychological soundness of the use of a variety of techniques for pain relief and to expand our understanding of pain. Some understanding of what pain is, how it affects us, and how it is perceived is essential for the therapist.

TYPES OF PAIN

Traditionally, pain has been categorized as either **acute** or **chronic**. Acute pain is experienced when tissue damage is impending and after injury has occurred. Pain lasting for more than 6 months is generally classified as chronic.[5] More recently the term **persistent pain** has been used to differentiate chronic pain that defies intervention from conditions where continuing (persistent) pain is a symptom of a treatable condition.[12,24]

There is more research devoted to chronic pain and its treatment, but acute and persistent pain confront the therapist most often.

Referred pain, which also can be either acute or chronic, is pain that is perceived to be in an area that seems to have little relation to the existing pathology. For example, injury to the spleen often results in pain in the left shoulder. This pattern, known as **Kehr's sign,** is useful for identifying this serious injury and arranging prompt emergency care. Referred pain can outlast the causative events because of altered reflex patterns, continuing mechanical stress on muscles, learned habits of guarding, or the development of hypersensitive areas, called **trigger points.** Irritation of nerves and nerve roots can cause **radiating pain.** Pressure on the lumbar nerve roots associated with a herniated disk or a contusion of the sciatic nerve can result in pain radiating down the lower extremity to the foot.

Deep somatic pain is a type that seems to be **sclerotomic** (associated with a sclerotome, a segment of bone innervated by a spinal segment). There is often a discrepancy between the site of the disorder and the site of the pain.

PAIN ASSESSMENT

Pain is a complex phenomenon that is difficult to evaluate and quantify because it is subjective and is influenced by attitudes and beliefs of the therapist and the patient. Quantification is hindered by the fact that pain is a very difficult concept to put into words.[1]

Obtaining an accurate and standardized assessment of pain is problematic. Several tools have been developed. These pain profiles identify the type of pain, quantify the intensity of pain, evaluate the effect of the pain experience on the patient's level of function, and/or assess the psychosocial impact of pain.

The pain profiles are useful. They compel the patient to verbalize the pain and thereby provide an outlet for the patient and provide the therapist a better understanding of the pain experience. They assess the psychosocial response to pain and injury. The pain profile can assist with the evaluation process by improving communication and directing the therapist toward appropriate diagnostic tests. These assessments also assist the therapist in identifying which therapeutic techniques may be effective and when they should be applied. Finally, these profiles provide a standard measure to monitor treatment progress.[12]

Pain Assessment Scales

The following profiles are used in the evaluation of acute and chronic pain associated with illnesses and injuries. Visual analogue scales are quick and simple tests completed by the patient (Fig. 4-1). These scales consist of a line, usually 10 cm in length, the extremes of which are taken to represent the limits of the pain

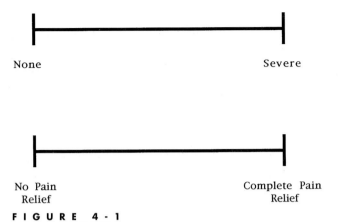

FIGURE   4 - 1

Visual analogue scales. (Reproduced, with permission, from Prentice WE. *Therapeutic Modalities for Allied Health Professionals.* New York, McGraw-Hill, 1998.)

experience. One end is defined as "NO PAIN" and the other as "SEVERE PAIN." The patient is asked to mark the line at a point corresponding to the severity of the pain. The distance between "NO PAIN" and the mark represents pain severity. A similar scale can be used to assess treatment effectiveness by placing "NO PAIN RELIEF" at one end of the scale and "COMPLETE PAIN RELIEF" at the other. These scales can be completed daily or more often as pre- and posttreatment assessments.[15]

Pain charts can be used to establish spatial properties of pain. These two-dimensional graphic portrayals are completed by the patient to assess the location of pain and a number of subjective components. Simple line drawings of the body in several postural positions are presented to the patient (Fig. 4-2). The patient draws or colors the pictures in areas which correspond to their pain experience. Different colors are used for different sensations. For example, blue for aching pain, yellow for numbness or tingling, red for burning pain, and green for cramping pain. Descriptions can be added to the form to enhance the communication value. The form could be completed daily.[18]

The McGill Pain Questionnaire (MPQ) is a tool with 78 words that describe pain (Fig. 4-3). These words are grouped into 20 sets, which are divided into 4 categories representing dimensions of the pain experience. Completion of the MPQ can take 20 minutes and is often frustrating for patients that do not speak English well. It is commonly administered to patients with low back pain. When administered every 2 to 4 weeks, it demonstrated changes in status very clearly.[21]

The Activity Pattern Indicators Pain Profile measures patient activity. It is a 64-question, self-report tool that can be used to assess functional impairment associated with pain. The instrument measures the frequency of certain behaviors such as housework, recreation, and social activities.[13]

The most common acute pain profile used in outpatient clinics today is a numeric pain scale. The patient is asked to rate their pain on a scale from 1 to 10, with 10 representing the worst pain they have experienced or could imagine. The question is

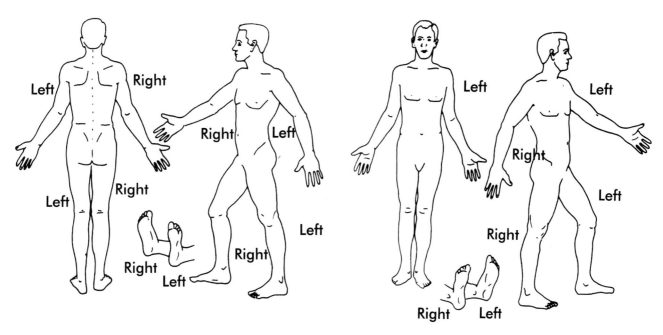

FIGURE 4-2

The pain chart. Use the following instructions: Please use all of the figures to show me exactly where all your pains are, and where they radiate to. Shade or draw with *blue marker*. Only the patient is to fill out this sheet. Please be as precise and detailed as possible. Use *yellow marker* for numbness and tingling. Use *red marker* for burning or hot areas, and *green marker* for cramping. Please remember: blue = pain; yellow = numbness and tingling; red = burning or hot areas; green = cramping. (Reproduced, with permission, from Melzack R. *Pain Measurement and Assessment.* New York, Raven Press, 1983.)

asked before and after treatment. When treatments provide pain relief, patients are asked about the extent and duration of the relief. In addition, the patient may be asked to estimate the portion of the day that they experience pain and about specific activities that increase or decrease their pain. When pain affects sleep, the patient may be asked to estimate the amount of sleep they got in the previous 24 hours. In addition, the amount of medication required for pain can be noted. This information helps the therapist assess changes in pain, select appropriate treatments, and communicate more clearly with the patient about the course of recovery from injury or surgery.

All of these scales help the patient to communicate the severity and duration of his or her pain and appreciate changes that occur. Often in a long recovery, patients lose sight of how much progress has been made in terms of the pain experience and return to functional activities. A review of these pain scales often can serve to reassure the patient, foster a brighter, more positive outlook, and reinforce the commitment to the plan of treatment.

The efficacy of many of the treatments used by therapists has not been fully substantiated. These scales are one source of data that can help therapists identify the most effective approaches to managing common injuries. These assessment tools can also be useful when reviewing a patient's progress with physicians and third party payors.

TISSUE SENSITIVITY

The structures most sensitive to damaging (noxious) stimuli are, first, the periosteum and joint capsule; second, subchondral bone, tendons, and ligament; third, muscle and cortical bone; and finally, the synovium and articular cartilage. A variety of "silent" fractures produce little or no pain. Different anatomic tissues exhibit varying degrees of sensitivity to pain. Avulsion fractures tend to be quite painful because they tear away the periosteum. Musculoskeletal pain is usually spread over a large area unless it is close to the surface. For example, a hamstring strain usually results in pain over the posterior thigh, whereas an acromioclavicular sprain usually localizes over the joint.

GOALS IN MANAGING PAIN

Regardless of the cause of pain, its reduction is an essential part of treatment. Pain signals the patient to seek assistance and often

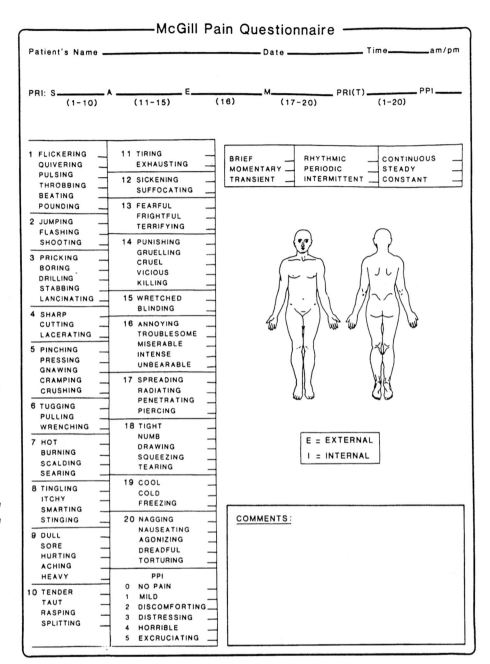

FIGURE 4-3

McGill Pain Questionnaire. The descriptors fall into four major groups: sensory, 1 to 10; affective, 11 to 15; evaluative, 16; and miscellaneous, 17 to 20. The rank value for each descriptor is based on its position in the word set. The sum of the rank values is the pain rating index (PRI). The present pain intensity (PPI) is based on a scale of 0 to 5. (Reproduced, with permission, from Melzack R. *Pain Measurement and Assessment.* New York, Raven Press, 1983.)

is useful in establishing a diagnosis. Once the injury or illness is diagnosed, pain serves little purpose. Medical or surgical treatment or immobilization is necessary to treat some conditions, but physical therapy and an early return to activity are appropriate following many injuries. The therapist's objectives are to encourage the body to heal through exercise designed to progressively increase functional capacity and to return the patient to work, recreational, and other activities as swiftly and safely as possible. Pain will inhibit therapeutic exercise. The challenge for the therapist is to control acute pain and protect the patient from further injury, while encouraging progressive exercise in a supervised environment.

PAIN PERCEPTION AND NEURAL TRANSMISSION

Sensory Receptors

There are several types of sensory receptors in the body, and the therapist should be aware of their existence and the types of stimuli that activate them (Table 4-1). Activation of some of these sense organs with therapeutic agents will decrease the patient's perception of pain. Six different types of receptor nerve endings are commonly described:

Some Characteristics of Selected Sensory Receptors

TYPE OF SENSORY RECEPTORS	STIMULUS		RECEPTOR	
	GENERAL TERM	SPECIFIC NATURE	TERM	LOCATION
Mechanoreceptors	Pressure	Movement of hair in a hair follicle	Afferent nerve fiber	Base of hair follicles
		Light pressure	Meissner's corpuscle	Skin
		Deep pressure	Pacinian corpuscle	Skin
		Touch	Merkel's touch corpuscle	Skin
Nociceptors	Pain	Distension (stretch)	Free nerve endings	Wall of gastrointestinal tract, pharynx, skin
Proprioceptors	Tension	Distension	Corpuscles of Ruffini	Skin and capsules in joints and ligaments
		Length changes	Muscle spindles	Skeletal muscle
		Tension changes	Golgi tendon organs	Between muscles and tendons
Thermoreceptors	Temperature change	Cold	Krause's end bulbs	Skin
		Heat	Corpuscles of Ruffini	Skin and capsules in joints and ligaments

SOURCE: Previte JJ. *Human Physiology.* New York, McGraw-Hill, 1983.

1. Meissner's corpuscles are activated by light touch.
2. Pacinian corpuscles respond to deep pressure.
3. Merkel's corpuscles respond to deep pressure, but more slowly than pacinian corpuscles, and also are activated by hair follicle deflection.
4. Ruffini's corpuscles in the skin are sensitive to touch, tension, and possibly heat; those in the joint capsules and ligaments are sensitive to change in position.
5. Krause's end bulbs are thermoreceptors that react to a decrease in temperature and touch.[26]
6. Pain receptors, called **nociceptors** or **free nerve endings,** are sensitive to extreme mechanical, thermal, or chemical energy.[3] They respond to noxious stimuli, in other words, to impending or actual tissue damage (for example, cuts, burns, sprains, and so on). The term *nociceptive* is from the Latin *nocere,* to damage, and is used to imply pain information. These organs respond to superficial forms of heat and cold, analgesic balms, and massage.

Proprioceptors found in muscles, joint capsules, ligaments, and tendons provide information regarding joint position and muscle tone. The muscle spindles react to changes in length and tension when the muscle is stretched or contracted. The Golgi tendon organs also react to changes in length and tension within the muscle. See Table 4-1 for a more complete listing.

Some sensory receptors respond to phasic activity and produce an impulse when the stimulus is increasing or decreasing, but not during a sustained stimulus. They adapt to a constant stimulus. Meissner's corpuscles and pacinian corpuscles are examples of such receptors.

Tonic receptors produce impulses as long as the stimulus is present. Examples of tonic receptors are muscle spindles, free nerve endings, and Krause's end bulbs. The initial impulse is at a higher frequency than later impulses that occur during sustained stimulation.

Adaptation is the decline in generator potential and the reduction of frequency that occurs with a prolonged stimulus or with frequently repeated stimuli. If some physical agents are used too often or for too long, the receptors can adapt to or accommodate the stimulus and reduce their impulses. The accommodation phenomenon can be observed with the use of superficial hot and cold agents, such as ice packs and hydrocollator packs.

As a stimulus becomes stronger, the number or receptors excited increases, and the frequency of the impulses increases. This provides more electrical activity at the spinal cord level, which may facilitate the effects of some physical agents.

NEURAL TRANSMISSION

Afferent nerve fibers transmit impulses from the sensory receptors toward the brain; whereas **efferent** fibers, such as motor neurons, transmit impulses from the brain toward the periphery. First-order, or primary, afferents transmit the impulses from the sensory receptor to the dorsal horn of the spinal cord (Fig. 4-4). There are four different types of first-order

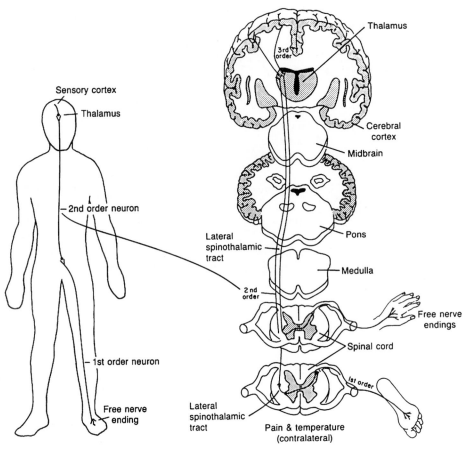

FIGURE 4-4

The lateral spinothalamic tract carries impulses of pain and temperature from the sensory receptors to the cortex. (Reproduced, with permission, from Prentice WE. *Therapeutic Modalities for Allied Health Professionals.* New York, McGraw-Hill, 1998.)

neurons (Table 4-2). Note that A-alpha and A-beta fibers are characterized as being large diameter afferents and A-delta and C fibers as small diameter afferents.

Second-order afferent fibers carry sensory messages from the dorsal horn to the brain. Second-order afferent fibers are categorized as wide dynamic range or nociceptive specific. The wide dynamic range second-order afferents receive input from A-beta, A-delta, and C fibers. These second-order afferents serve relatively large, overlapping receptor fields. The nociceptive specific second-order afferents respond exclusively to noxious stimulation. They receive input only from A-delta and C fibers. These afferents serve smaller receptor fields that do not overlap. All of these neurons synapse with third-order neurons that carry information to various brain centers where the input in integrated, interpreted, and acted upon.

Facilitators and Inhibitors of Synaptic Transmission

For information to pass between neurons, a transmitter substance must be released from one neuron terminal (presynaptic membrane), enter the synaptic cleft, and attach to a receptor site on the next neuron (postsynaptic membrane). In the past, all the activity within the synapse was attributed to neurotransmitters, such as acetylcholine. The neurotransmitters, when released in sufficient quantities, are known to cause depolarization of the postsynaptic neuron. In the absence of the neurotransmitter, no depolarization occurs.

It is now apparent that several compounds that are not true neurotransmitters can facilitate or inhibit synaptic activity. These compounds are classified as biogenic amine transmitters or neuroactive peptides. Serotonin and norepinephrine are examples of biogenic amine transmitters. About two dozen neuroactive peptides have been identified, including **substance P, glutamate, enkephalins,** and **β-endorphin.**[3]

Serotonin and enkephalins are active in descending (efferent) pathways, which block the pain message.[7] Enkephalin is an endogenous (made by the body) opioid that inhibits the depolarization of second-order nociceptive nerve fibers. It is released from interneurons, enkephalin neurons with short axons. The enkephalins are stored in nerve-ending vesicles found in the substantia gelatinosa and several areas of the brain. When

TABLE 4-2

Classification of Afferent Neurons

SIZE	TYPE	GROUP	SUBGROUP	DIAMETER (MICROMETERS)	CONDUCTION VELOCITY (m/sec)	RECEPTOR	STIMULUS
Large	A α	I	1a	12–20 (22)	70–120	Proprioceptive mechanoreceptor	Muscle velocity and length change, muscle shortening of rapid speed
	A α	I	1b				
	A α	II	Muscle	6–12	36–72	Proprioceptive mechanoreceptor	Muscle length information from touch and pacinian corpuscles
	A β	II	Skin			Cutaneous receptors	Touch, vibration, hair receptors
	A δ	III	Muscle	1–5 (6)	6(12)–36(80)	75% mechanoreceptors and thermoreceptors	Temperature change
Small	A δ	III	Skin			25% nociceptors, mechanoreceptors, and thermoreceptors (hot and cold)	Noxious, mechanical, and temperature (>45°C, <10°C)
	C	IV	Muscle	0.3–1.0	0.4–1.0	50% mechanoreceptors and thermoreceptors	Touch and temperature
	C	IV	Skin			50% nociceptors, 20% mechanoreceptors, and 30% thermoreceptors (hot and cold)	Noxious, mechanical, and temperature (>45°C, <10°C)

released, enkephalin may bind to presynaptic or postsynaptic membranes.[3]

Norepinephrine is a biogenic amine transmitter that is released by the depolarization of some neurons and that binds to the postsynaptic membranes. Norepinephrine is found in several areas of the nervous system including a tract that descends from the pons that inhibits synaptic transmission between first-order and second-order nociceptive fibers, thus decreasing pain sensation.[16]

Other endogenous opioids may be active analgesic agents. These neuroactive peptides are released into the central nervous system and have an action similar to that of morphine, an opiate analgesic. There are specific receptors located at strategic sites, called binding sites, to receive these compounds. β-Endorphin, a 31-amino acid peptide, and **dynorphin** have potent analgesic effects. These are released within the central nervous system by mechanisms that are not fully understood at this time.

NOCICEPTION

A nociceptive neuron is one that transmits pain signals. Its cell body is in the dorsal root ganglion near the spinal cord. Approximately 25 percent of the myelinated A-delta and 50 percent of the unmyelinated C fibers contact nociceptors and are considered nociceptive, afferent neurons (Table 4-2). Once a nociceptor is stimulated, it releases a neuropeptide (substance P) that initiates the electrical impulses along the afferent fiber toward the spinal cord. Substance P also serves as a transmitter substance between the first-order afferent fiber and a second-order afferent fiber (Fig. 4-4) at the dorsal horn of the spinal column.

The A-delta and C fibers, which transmit sensations of pain and temperature, have different diameters (A-delta are larger) and different conduction velocities (A-delta are faster). The C fibers also are connected to more of the nociceptive specific second-order afferents. These differences result in two qualitatively different types of pain, termed fast and slow.[3] Fast pain is brief, well-localized, and well-matched to the stimulus—for example, the initial pain of an unexpected pinprick. Slow pain is an aching, throbbing, or burning sensation that is poorly localized and less specifically related to the stimulus. There is a delay in the perception of slow pain following injury, but the pain will continue long after the noxious stimulus is removed. Fast pain is transmitted over the larger, faster-conducting A-delta afferent neurons and originates from receptors located in the skin. Slow pain is transmitted by the C afferent neurons and originates from both superficial tissue (skin) and deeper tissue (ligaments and muscle).[3]

The various types of afferent fibers follow different courses as they ascend toward the brain. Some A-delta and most

C afferent neurons enter the spinal cord through the dorso-lateral tract of Lissauer and synapse in marginal zone (lamina 1) or the substantia gelatinosa (lamina 2) with a second-order neuron.[16] Most nociceptive second-order neurons ascend to higher centers along one of three tracts, (1) lateral spinothalamic tract, (2) spinoreticular tract, and (3) spinoencephalic tract, with the remainder ascending along the spinocervical tract or as projections to the cuneate and gracile nuclei of the medulla.[16] Approximately 90 percent of the wide dynamic range second-order afferents terminate in the thalamus.[16] Third-order neurons project to the sensory cortex and numerous other centers in the central nervous system. These projections allow us to perceive pain. They also permit the integration of past experiences and emotions, which form our response to the pain experience. These connections are also believed to be parts of complex circuits that the therapist may stimulate to manage pain. Most analgesic physical agents are believed to slow or block the impulses ascending along the A-delta and C afferent neuron pathways through direct input into the dorsal horn or through descending mechanisms. These pathways are discussed in more detail in the following section.

NEUROPHYSIOLOGIC EXPLANATIONS OF PAIN CONTROL

The neurophysiologic mechanisms of pain control through stimulation of cutaneous receptors have not been fully explained. Much of what is known and current theory are the result of work involving electroacupuncture and transcutaneous electrical nerve stimulation. The concepts of the analgesic response to cutaneous receptor stimulation presented here were first proposed by Melzack and Wall[20] and Castel.[7] These models essentially present three analgesic mechanisms.

1. Stimulation from ascending A-beta afferents results in the blocking of impulses (pain messages) carried along A-delta and C afferent fibers.
2. Stimulation of descending pathways in the dorsolateral tract of the spinal cord by A-delta and C fiber afferent input results in a blocking of the impulses carried along the A-delta and C afferent fibers.
3. The stimulation of A-delta and C afferent fibers causes the release of endogenous opioids (β-endorphin) resulting in a prolonged activation of descending analgesic pathways.

These theories or models are not necessarily mutually exclusive. Recent evidence suggests that pain relief may result from combinations of dorsal horn and central nervous system activity.[2,9]

A decrease in input along nociceptive afferents also results in pain relief. Cooling afferent fibers decreases the rate at which they conduct impulses. Thus, a 20 minute application of cold is effective in relieving pain because of the decrease in activity, rather than an increase in activity along afferent pathways.

Blocking the Pain Impulses with Ascending A-beta Input

Pain modulation due to sensory stimulation and the resultant increase in the impulses in the large diameter (A-beta) afferent fibers was proposed by the gate control theory of pain[20] (Fig. 4-5). Impulses ascending on these fibers stimulate the substantia gelatinosa as they enter the dorsal horn of the spinal cord. Stimulation of the substantia gelatinosa inhibits synaptic transmission in the large and small (A-delta and C) fiber afferent pathways. The "pain message" carried along the smaller diameter fibers is not transmitted to the second-order neurons

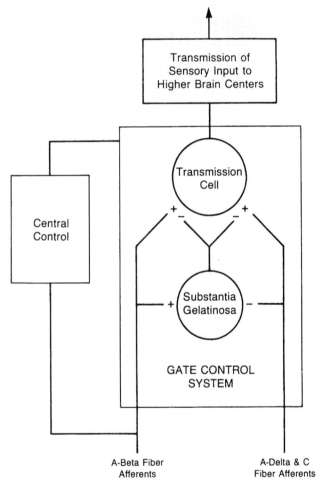

F I G U R E   4 - 5

The gate control system. Increases A-beta input and stimulates the substantia gelatinosa which inhibits the flow of afferent input to sensory centers. (Reproduced, with permission, from Prentice WE. *Therapeutic Modalities for Allied Health Professionals.* New York, McGraw-Hill, 1998.)

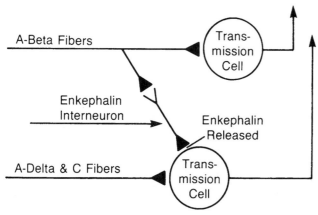

F I G U R E   4 - 6

Presynaptic inhibition of dorsal horn synapse transmission due to A-beta fiber stimulation at enkephalin interneurons. (Reproduced, with permission, from Prentice WE. *Therapeutic Modalities for Allied Health Professionals.* New York, McGraw-Hill, 1998.)

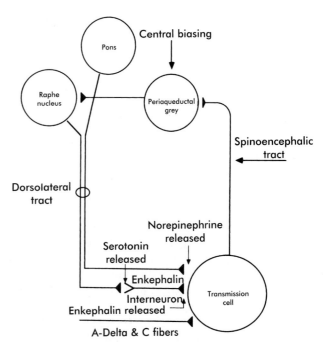

F I G U R E   4 - 7

Stimulation of the periaqueductal grey region of the midbrain and the raphe nucleus in the pons and medulla by ascending neural input, especially from A-delta and C fiber afferents, and possibly central biasing, activates the descending mechanism. (Reproduced, with permission, from Prentice WE. *Therapeutic Modalities for Allied Health Professionals.* New York, McGraw-Hill, 1998.)

and never reaches sensory centers. The balance between the input from the small- and large-diameter afferents determines how much of the pain message is blocked or gated.

The concept of sensory stimulation for pain relief, as proposed by the gate control theory, has empirical support. Rubbing a contusion, applying moist heat, or massaging sore muscles decreases the perception of pain. The analgesic response to these treatments is attributed to the increased stimulation of large-diameter afferent fibers.

The gate control theory also proposes that A-delta and C fiber impulses inhibit the substantia gelatinosa, facilitating the perception of pain. The sensation of pain does not diminish rapidly because free nerve endings do not accommodate and the afferent impulses from them "open the gate" to further pain message transmission.

The discovery and isolation of endogenous opioids in the 1970s led to new theories of pain relief. Castel[7] introduced an endogenous opioid analogue to the gate control theory (Fig. 4-6). This theory proposes increased neural activity in A-alpha and A-beta primary afferent pathways, which triggers a release of enkephalin from enkephalin interneurons found in the dorsal horn. These neuroactive amines inhibit synaptic transmission in the A-delta and C fiber afferent pathways. The end result, as in the gate control theory, is that the pain message is blocked before it reaches sensory levels.

Descending Pain Control Mechanisms

The gate control theory[20] proposed a second analgesic mechanism that involves descending efferent fibers. The central control, originating in higher centers of the central nervous system, could affect the dorsal horn gating process. Impulses from the thalamus and brain stem (central biasing) are carried into the

dorsal horn on efferent fibers in the dorsal or dorsal lateral paths (or tracts). Impulses from the higher centers act to close the gate and block transmission of the pain message at the dorsal horn synapse. Through this system, it was theorized, previous experiences, emotional influences, sensory perception, and other factors could influence the transmission of the pain message and the perception of pain.

Castel[7] offers an endogenous opioid model of descending influence over dorsal horn synapse activity (Fig. 4-7). Stimulation of the **periaqueductal grey** region of the midbrain and the **raphe nucleus** in the pons and medulla by ascending neural input, especially from A-delta and C fiber afferents, and possibly central biasing, activates the descending mechanism. The periaqueductal grey stimulates the raphe nucleus. The raphe nucleus in turn sends impulses along serontonergic efferent fibers in the dorsal lateral tract, which synapse with enkephalin interneurons. The interneurons release enkephalin into the dorsal horn, inhibiting the synaptic transmission of impulses to the second-order afferent neurons.

More recently, a second descending, norandrenergic pathway projecting from the pons to the dorsal horn has been identified.[16] The significance of these parallel pathways is not fully understood. It is also not known if these norandrenergic fibers directly inhibit dorsal horn synapses or stimulate the enkephalin interneurons.

This model provides a physiologic explanation for the analgesic response to brief, intense stimulation. The analgesia following accupressure and the use of some transcutaneous electrical nerve simulators (TENS), such as point simulators, is attributed to this descending pain control mechanism.

β-Endorphin and Dynorphin

There is evidence that stimulation of the small-diameter afferents (A-delta and C) can stimulate the release of other endogenous opioids.[8,10,19,23–25,27–30] **β-Endorphin** (BEP) and **dynorphin** are neuroactive peptides, with potent analgesic affects. The term endorphin refers to an opiate-like substance produced by the body. The mechanisms regulating the release of BEP and dynorphin have not been fully elucidated. It is apparent, however, that these large endogenous substances play a role in the analgesic response to some forms of stimuli used in the treatment of patients in pain.

One of the main sources of BEP is the anterior pituitary. Here, it shares the prohormone **propiomelanocortin** (POMC) with adrenocorticotropin (ACTH). Prolonged (20 to 40 minutes) small-diameter afferent fiber stimulation has been thought to trigger the release of BEP from the anterior pituitary gland. Electroacupuncture, and possibly TENS with long phase durations and low pulse rates (1 to 5 pulses/second), will cause small diameter afferent fiber depolarization necessary for BEP release. The anterior pituitary gland, however, may not be a source of BEP in low pulse rate, long pulse width TENS-induced analgesia.[11] These results and the recognition that BEP does not readily cross the blood–brain barrier[3] suggesting that if BEP or other endogenous opioids are active analgesic agents within the central nervous system, they are released from areas within the brain.

The neurons in the hypothalamus that send projections to the PAG and noradrenergic nuclei in the brain stem contain BEP. It is possible that BEP released from these neurons by stimulation of the hypothalamus is responsible for the analgesic response to the treatments (Fig. 4-8).[6]

Dynorphin, a more recently isolated endogenous opioid, is found in the PAG, rostroventral medulla, and the dorsal horn.[16] It has been demonstrated that dynorphin is released during electroacupuncture.[14] Dynorphin may be responsible for suppressing the response to noxious mechanical stimulation.[16]

Summary of Pain Control Mechanisms

The body's pain control mechanisms are probably not mutually exclusive. Rather, analgesia is the result of overlapping processes. It is also important to realize that the theories presented are only models. They are useful in conceptualizing the perception of pain and pain relief. These models will help the therapist understand the effects of therapeutic modalities and form a

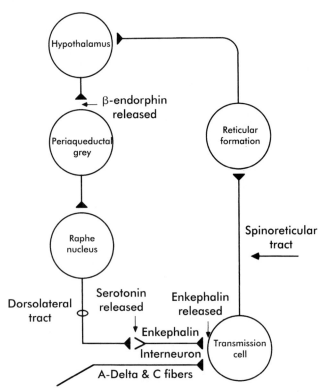

F I G U R E   4 - 8

The neurons in the hypothalamus that send projections to the periaqueductal grey and noradrenergic nuclei in the brain stem contain β-endorphin. It is possible that β-endorphin released from these neurons by stimulation of the hypothalamus is responsible for the analgesic response to the treatments. (Reproduced, with permission, from Prentice WE. *Therapeutic Modalities for Allied Health Professionals.* New York, McGraw-Hill, 1998.)

sound rationale for modality application. As more research is conducted and as the mysteries of pain and neurophysiology are solved, new models will emerge. The therapist should adapt these models to fit new developments.

COGNITIVE INFLUENCES

Pain perception and the response to a painful experience can be influenced by a variety of cognitive processes, including anxiety, attention, depression, past pain experiences, and cultural influences. These individual aspects of pain expression are mediated by higher centers in the cortex in ways that are not clearly understood. They can influence both the sensory discriminative and motivational affective dimensions of pain.

Many mental processes modulate the perception of pain through descending systems. Behavior modification, the excitement of the moment, happiness, positive feelings, focusing (directed attention toward specific stimuli), hypnosis, and suggestion may modulate pain perception. Past experiences, cultural background, personality, motivation to play, aggression, anger, and fear are all factors that could facilitate or inhibit pain perception. Strong central inhibition may mask severe injury for a period of time. At such times, evaluation of the injury is quite difficult. Patients with chronic pain can become very depressed and experience a loss of fitness. They tend to be less active and may have altered appetites and sleep habits. They have a decreased will to work and exercise and often develop a reduced sex drive. They may turn to self-abusive patterns of behavior. Tricyclic drugs are often used to inhibit serotonin depletion for the patient with chronic pain.

Just as pain may be inhibited by central modulation, it may also arise from central origins. Phobias, fear, depression, anger, grief, and hostility are all capable of producing pain in the absence of local pathologic processes. In addition, pain memory, which is associated with old injuries, can result in pain perception and pain response that are out of proportion to a new, often minor, injury. Substance abuse can also alter and confound the perception of pain. Substance abuse may cause the chronic pain patient to become more depressed or may lead to depression and psychosomatic pain.

PAIN MANAGEMENT

How should the therapist approach pain? First, the source of the pain must be identified. Unidentified pain may hide a serious disorder, and treatment of such pain may delay the appropriate treatment of the disorder. Once a diagnosis has been made, several different approaches can provide pain relief. Pain control strategies may include the following.

1. Encourage central biasing through cognitive processes, such as motivation, tension diversion, focusing, relaxation techniques, positive thinking, thought stopping, and self-control.
2. Minimize the tissue damage through the application of proper first aid and immobilization.
3. Maintain a line of communication with the patient. Let the patient know what to expect following an injury. Pain, swelling, dysfunction, and atrophy will occur following injury. The patient's anxiety over these events will increase his or her perception of pain. Often, a patient who has been told what to expect by someone he or she trusts will be less anxious and suffer less pain.
4. Recognize that all pain, even psychosomatic pain, is very real to the patient.
5. Encourage supervised exercise to encourage blood flow, promote nutrition, increase metabolic activity, and reduce stiffness and guarding, if the activity will not cause further harm to the patient.

The physician may choose to prescribe oral or injectable medications in the treatment of the patient. The most commonly used medications are classified as analgesics, anti-inflammatory agents, or both. The therapist should become familiar with these drugs and note if the patient is taking any medications. It is also important to work with the referring physician to assure that the patient takes the medications appropriately (see Chapter 23).

When using physical agents, the therapist should match the physical agent to each patient's situation. Casts and braces may prevent the application of ice or moist heat; however, TENS electrodes often can be positioned under a cast or brace for pain relief. Following acute injuries, ice may be the therapeutic agent of choice because of the effect of cold on the inflammatory process. There is not one "best" physical agent for pain control. The therapist must select the physical agent that is most appropriate for each patient based on the knowledge of the modalities and professional judgment. In no situation should the therapist apply a physical agent without first developing a clear rationale for the treatment (see Chapter 18).

In general, physical agents can be used to:

1. Stimulate large-diameter afferent fibers. This can be done with TENS, massage, and analgesic balms.
2. Decrease pain fiber transmission velocity with cold or ultrasound.
3. Stimulate small-diameter afferent fibers and descending pain control mechanisms with accupressure, deep massage, or TENS over acupuncture points or trigger points.
4. Stimulate a release of BEP or other endogenous opioids through prolonged small-diameter fiber stimulation with TENS.

The goal of most treatment programs is to encourage early pain-free exercise. The physical agents used to control pain do little to promote tissue healing. They should be used to relieve acute pain following injury or surgery or to control pain and other symptoms, such as swelling, to promote progressive exercise. The therapist should not lose sight of the effects of the physical agents or the importance of progressive exercise in restoring the patient's functional ability.

Reducing the perception of pain is as much an art as a science. The therapist's approach to the patient has a great impact on the success of the treatment. The patient will not be convinced of the efficacy and importance of the treatment unless the therapist appears confident about it. The therapist must make the patient a participant rather than a passive spectator in the treatment and rehabilitation process. The therapist is encouraged to keep abreast of the neurophysiology of pain and the physiology of tissue healing to maintain a current scientific basis for selecting treatment approaches and managing the pain experienced by patients.

SUMMARY

- Pain is a response to a noxious stimulus that is subjectively modified by past experiences and expectations.

- Pain is classified as either acute or chronic and can exhibit many different patterns.
- Early reduction of pain in a treatment program will facilitate therapeutic exercise.
- Stimulation of sensory receptors via the therapeutic modalities can modify the patient's perception of pain.
- Four mechanisms of pain control may include:
  - ➤ Decreased transmission of input along nociceptive pathways.
  - ➤ Dorsal horn modulation due to the input from large-diameter afferents through a gate control system, the release of enkephalins, or both.
  - ➤ Descending efferent fiber activation due to the effects of small fiber afferent input on higher centers including the thalamus, raphe nucleus, and periaqueductal grey region.
  - ➤ The central release of endogenous opioids, including β-endorphin, through prolonged small-diameter afferent stimulation.
- Pain perception may be influenced by a variety of cognitive processes mediated by the higher brain centers.
- The selection of a physical agent for controlling pain should be based on current knowledge of neurophysiology and the psychology of pain.
- The application of physical agents for the control of pain should not occur until the diagnosis of the injury has been established.

REFERENCES

1. Addison R. Chronic pain syndrome, *Am J Med* 77:54, 1985.
2. Anderson S, Ericson T, Holmgren E. Electroacupuncture affects pain threshold measured with electrical stimulation of teeth. *Brain* 63:393–396, 1973.
3. Berne R, Levy M. *Physiology.* St. Louis, Mosby, 1988.
4. Bishop B. Pain: Its physiology and rationale for management. *Phys Ther* 60:13–37, 1980.
5. Bonica J. *The Management of Pain.* Philadelphia, Lea & Febiger, 1990.
6. Bowsher D. Central pain mechanisms. In: Wells P, Frampton V, Bowsher D, eds. *Pain Management in Physical Therapy.* Norwalk, CT, Appleton & Lange, 1988.
7. Castel J. *Pain Management: Acupuncture and Transcutaneous Electrical Nerve Stimulation Techniques.* Lake Bluff, IL, Pain Control Services, 1979.
8. Chapman C, Benedetti C. Analgesia following electrical stimulation: Partial reversal by a narcotic antagonist. *Life Sci* 26:44–48, 1979.
9. Cheng R. Pomeranz B. Electroacupuncture analgesia could be mediated by at least two pain relieving mechanisms: Endorphin and non-endorphin systems. *Life Sci* 25:1957–1962, 1979.
10. Clement-Jones V, McLaughlin L, Tomlin S. Increased beta-endorphin but not metenkephalin levels in human cerebrospinal fluid after electroacupuncture for recurrent pain. *Lancet* 2:946–948, 1980.
11. Denegar G. Perrin D, Rogol A. Influence of transcutaneous electrical nerve stimulation on pain, range of motion and serum cortisol concentration in females with induced delayed onset muscle soreness. *J Orthop Sports Phys Ther* 11:101–103, 1989.
12. Dickerman J. The use of pain profiles in clinical practice. *Fam Pract Recert* 14:35–44, 1992.
13. Gatchel R. Million behavioral health inventory: Its utility in predicting physical functioning patients with low back pain. *Arch Phys Med Rehabil* 67:878, 1986.
14. Ho W, Wen H. Opioid-like activity in the cerebrospinal fluid of pain patients treated by electroacupuncture. *Neuropharmacology* 28:961–966, 1989.
15. Huskisson E. Visual analogue scales. Pain measurement and assessment. In: Melzack R, ed. *Pain Measurement and Assessment.* New York, Raven Press, 1983, p. 103.
16. Jessell T, Kelly D. Pain and analgesia. In: Kandel E, Schwartz J, Jessell T eds. *Principles of Neural Science.* Norwalk, CT, Appleton & Lange, 1991, pp. 96–98.
17. Kuland DN. The injured athletes' pain. *Curr Concepts Pain* 1:3–10, 1983.
18. Margoles M. The pain chart: Spatial properties of pain. Pain measurement and assessment. In: Melzack R, ed. *Pain Measurement and Assessment.* New York, Raven Press, 1983, p. 52.
19. Mayer, D. Price D, Rafii A. Antagonism of acupuncture analgesia in man by the narcotic antagonist naloxone. *Brain Res* 121:368–372, 1977.
20. Melzack R, Wall P. Pain mechanisms: A new theory. *Science* 150:971–979, 1965.
21. Melzack R. Concepts of pain measurement. In: Melzack R, ed. *Pain Measurement and Assessment.* New York, Raven Press, 1983.
22. Merskey H, Albe Fessard D, Bonica J. Pain terms: A list with definitions and notes on usage. *Pain* 6:249–252, 1979.
23. Pomeranz B, Paley D. Brain opiates at work in acupuncture. *New Scientist* 73:12–13, 1975.
24. Pomeranz B, Chiu D. Naloxone blockade of acupuncture analgesia: Enkephalin implicated. *Life Sci* 19:1757–1762, 1976.
25. Pomeranz B, Paley D. Electro-acupuncture hypoanalgesia is mediated by afferent impulses: An electrophysiological study in mice. *Exp Neurol* 66:398–402, 1979.
26. Previte J. *Human Physiology.* New York, McGraw-Hill, 1983.
27. Salar G, Job I, Mingringo S. Effects of transcutaneous electrotherapy on CSF beta-endorphin content in patients without pain problems. *Pain* 10:169–172, 1981.

28. Sjolund B, Eriksson M. Electroacupuncture and endoge-
    nous morphines. *Lancet* 2:1085, 1976.

29. Sjoland B, Eriksson M. Increased cerebrospinal fluid lev-
    els of endorphins after electro-acupuncture. *Acta Physiol
    Scand* 100:382–384, 1977.

30. Wen H, Ho W, Ling N. The influence of electroacupunc-
    ture on naloxone: Induces morphine withdrawal: Eleva-
    tion of immunoassayable beta-endorphin activity in the
    brain but not in the blood. *Am J Clin Med* 7:237–240,
    1979.

31. Willis W, Grossman R. *Medical Neurobiology,* 3rd ed.
    St.Louis, Mosby, 1981.

32. Wolf S. Neurophysiologic mechanisms in pain modula-
    tion: Relevance to TENS. In: Manheimer J, Lampe G,
    eds. *Clinical Applications of TENS.* Philadelphia, Davis,
    1984, pp. 119–126.

C H A P T E R 5

Impaired Muscle Performance: Regaining Muscular Strength and Endurance

William E. Prentice

O B J E C T I V E S

After completing this chapter, the student therapist should be able to do the following:

- Define muscular strength, endurance, and power and discuss their importance in a program of rehabilitation following injury.
- Discuss the anatomy and physiology of skeletal muscle.
- Discuss the physiology of strength development and factors that determine strength.
- Describe specific methods for improving muscular strength.
- Differentiate between muscle strength and muscle endurance.
- Discuss differences between males and females in terms of strength development.

Following all musculoskeletal injuries, there will be some degree of impairment in muscular strength and endurance. For the therapist supervising a rehabilitation program, regaining, and in many instances improving, levels of strength and endurance is critical for discharging and returning the patient to a functional level following injury.

By definition, **muscular strength** is the ability of a muscle to generate force against some resistance. Maintenance of at least a normal level of strength in a given muscle or muscle group is important for normal healthy living. Muscle weakness or imbalance can result in abnormal movement or gait and can impair normal functional movement. Resistance training plays a critical role in injury rehabilitation.

Muscular strength is closely associated with muscular endurance. **Muscular endurance** is the ability to perform repetitive muscular contractions against some resistance for an extended period of time. As we will see later, as muscular strength increases, there tends to be a corresponding increase in endurance. For the average person in the population, developing muscular endurance is likely more important than developing muscular strength because muscular endurance is probably more critical in carrying out the everyday activities of living. This statement becomes increasingly true with age.

TYPES OF SKELETAL MUSCLE CONTRACTION

Skeletal muscle is capable of three different types of contraction: (1) an **isometric contraction,** (2) a **concentric contraction,** and (3) an **eccentric contraction.** An isometric contraction occurs when the muscle contracts to produce tension, but there is no change in muscle length. Considerable force can be generated against some immovable resistance even though no movement occurs. In a concentric contraction, the muscle shortens in length while tension increases to overcome or move some resistance. In an eccentric contraction, the resistance is greater than the muscular force being produced, and the muscle lengthens while producing tension. Concentric and eccentric contractions are considered dynamic movements.[46]

Recently, an **econcentric** contraction, which combines both a controlled concentric and a concurrent eccentric contraction of the same muscle over two separate joints, has been introduced.[15,26] An econcentric contraction is possible only in those muscles which cross at least two joints. An example of an econcentric contraction would be a prone, open-kinetic chain hamstring curl. The hamstrings contract concentrically to flex the knee, while the hip tends to flex eccentrically, lengthening the hamstring. Rehabilitation exercises have traditionally concentrated on strengthening of isolated single joint motions despite the fact that the same muscle is functioning at a second joint simultaneously. Therefore, it has been recommended that exercises be included in the strengthening program that strengthen the muscle in the manner in which it contracts functionally.

Slow-Twitch Versus Fast-Twitch Fibers

All fibers in a particular motor unit are either **slow-twitch fibers** or **fast-twitch fibers,** each of which has distinctive metabolic and contractile capabilities.

SLOW-TWITCH FIBERS

Slow-twitch fibers are also referred to as *type I,* or *slow-oxidative (SO),* fibers. They are more resistant to fatigue than are fast-twitch fibers; however, the time required to generate force is much greater in slow-twitch fibers.[25] Because they are relatively fatigue resistant, slow-twitch fibers are associated primarily with long-duration, aerobic-type activities.

FAST-TWITCH FIBERS

Fast-twitch fibers are capable of producing quick, forceful contractions but have a tendency to fatigue more rapidly than do slow-twitch fibers. Fast-twitch fibers are useful in short-term, high-intensity activities, which mainly involve the anaerobic system. Fast-twitch fibers are capable of producing powerful contractions, whereas slow-twitch fibers produce a long-endurance force.[12] There are two subdivisions of fast-twitch fibers. Although both types of fast-twitch fibers are capable of rapid contraction, *type IIa fibers,* or *fast-oxidative glycolytic (FOG),* are moderately resistant to fatigue. *Type IIb fibers,* or *fast-glycolytic (FG) fibers,* fatigue rapidly and are considered the "true" fast-twitch fibers. Recently, a third group of fast-twitch fibers, *type IIx,* has been identified in animal models. Type IIx fibers are fatigue resistant and are thought to be less than type IIb but greater than type IIa fibers in terms of their maximum power capacity.[36]

RATIO IN MUSCLE

Within a particular muscle are both types of fibers, and the ratio in an individual muscle varies with each person.[28] Those muscles with a primary function to maintain posture against gravity require more endurance and have a higher percentage of slow-twitch fibers. Muscles that produce powerful, rapid, explosive-strength movements tend to have a much greater percentage of fast-twitch fibers. The question of whether fiber types can change as a result of training has, to date, not been conclusively resolved.[9] Both types of fibers, however, can improve their metabolic capabilities through specific strength and endurance training.[6]

FACTORS THAT DETERMINE LEVELS OF MUSCULAR STRENGTH AND ENDURANCE

Size of the Muscle

Muscular strength is proportional to the cross-sectional diameter of the muscle fibers. The greater the cross-sectional diameter or the bigger a particular muscle, the stronger it is, and thus the more force it is capable of generating. The size of a muscle tends to increase in cross-sectional diameter with resistance training. This increase in muscle size is referred to as **hypertrophy.**[33] Conversely a decrease in the size of a muscle is referred to as **atrophy.**

Number of Muscle Fibers

Strength is a function of the number and diameter of muscle fibers composing a given muscle. The number of fibers is an inherited characteristic, thus a person with a large number of muscle fibers to begin with has the potential to hypertrophy to a much greater degree than does someone with relatively few fibers.[31]

Neuromuscular Efficiency

Strength is also directly related to the efficiency of the neuromuscular system and the function of the motor unit in producing muscular force.[37] As will be indicated later in this chapter, initial increases in strength during the first 8 to 10 weeks of a resistance training program can be attributed primarily to increased neuromuscular efficiency.[49] Resistance training will increase neuromuscular efficiency in three ways: (1) there is an increase in the number of motor units being recruited; (2) there is an increase in the firing rate of each motor unit; and (3) there is increased synchronization of motor unit firing.[6]

Biomechanical Considerations

Strength in a given muscle is determined not only by the physical properties of the muscle but also by biomechanical factors that dictate how much force can be generated through a system of levers to an external object.[27,31,51]

POSITION OF TENDON ATTACHMENT

If we think of the elbow joint as one of these lever systems, we would have the biceps muscle producing flexion of this joint (Fig. 5-1). The position of attachment of the biceps muscle on the forearm will largely determine how much force this muscle is capable of generating. If there are two patients A and B, and A has a biceps attachment that is closer to the fulcrum (the elbow joint) than B, then A must produce a greater effort with the biceps muscle to hold the weight at a right angle because the length of the effort arm will be greater than with B.

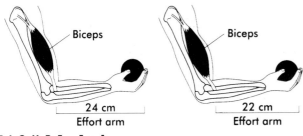

FIGURE 5-1

Muscle attachments. The position of attachment of the muscle tendon on the lever arm can affect the ability of that muscle to generate force. **B** should be able to generate greater force than **A** because the tendon attachment on the lever arm is closer to the resistance.

LENGTH–TENSION RELATIONSHIP

The length of a muscle determines the tension that can be generated. By varying the length of a muscle, different tensions can be produced.[27] This length–tension relationship is illustrated in Figure 5-2. At position B in the curve, the interaction of the crossbridges between the actin and myosin myofilaments within the sarcomere is at maximum. Setting a muscle at this particular length will produce the greatest amount of tension. At position A, the muscle is shortened, and at position C, the muscle is lengthened. In either case, the interaction between the actin and myosin myofilaments through the crossbridges is greatly reduced and the muscle is not capable of generating significant tension.

Age

The ability to generate muscular force is also related to age.[2] Both men and women seem to be able to increase strength throughout puberty and adolescence, reaching a peak around

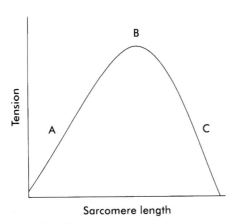

FIGURE 5-2

The length–tension relation of the muscle. Greatest tension is developed at point *B* with less tension developed at points *A* and *C*.

20 to 25 years of age, at which time this ability begins to level off and, in some cases, decline. After about age 25, a person generally loses an average of 1 percent of his or her maximal remaining strength each year. Thus at age 65 years, a person would have only about 60 percent of the strength he or she had at age 25.[36] This loss in muscle strength is definitely related to individual levels of physical activity. Those people who are more active or, perhaps, those who continue to strength train considerably decrease this tendency toward declining muscle strength. In addition to retarding this decrease in muscular strength, exercise may also have an effect in slowing the decrease in cardiorespiratory endurance and flexibility, as well as slowing increases in body fat. Thus strength maintenance is important for all patients regardless of age for achieving total wellness and good health and in rehabilitation after injury.[50]

Overtraining

Overtraining can have a negative effect on the development of muscular strength. Overtraining is an imbalance between exercise and recovery in which the training program exceeds the body's physiologic and psychological limits. Overtraining can result in psychological breakdown (staleness) or physiologic breakdown, which can involve musculoskeletal injury, fatigue, or sickness. Engaging in proper and efficient resistance training, eating a proper diet, and getting appropriate rest can all minimize the potential negative effects of overtraining.

PHYSIOLOGY OF STRENGTH DEVELOPMENT

Muscle Hypertrophy

There is no question that resistance training to improve muscular strength results in an increased size, or hypertrophy, of a muscle. What causes a muscle to become hypertrophied? A number of theories have been proposed to explain this increase in muscle size.[18]

Some evidence exists that there is an *increase in the number of muscle fibers (hyperplasia)* due to fibers splitting in response to training.[24] However, this research has been conducted in animals and should not be generalized to humans. It is generally accepted that the number of fibers is genetically determined and does not seem to increase with training.

Secondly, it has been hypothesized that because the muscle is working harder in resistance training, more blood is required to supply that muscle with oxygen and other nutrients. Thus it is thought that *the number of capillaries is increased.* This hypothesis is only partially correct; *no new* capillaries are formed during resistance training; however, a number of dormant capillaries may well become filled with blood to meet this increased demand for blood supply.[36]

FIGURE   5-3

Muscle contraction.
Muscles contract when
an electrical impulse
from the central nervous
system causes the
myofilaments in a muscle
fiber to move closer
together.

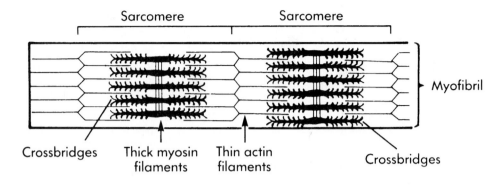

A third theory to explain this increase in muscle size seems the most credible. Muscle fibers are composed primarily of small protein filaments, called myofilaments, which are contractile elements in muscle. **Myofilaments** are small contractile elements of protein within the sarcomere. There are two distinct types of myofilaments: thin **actin** myofilaments and thicker **myosin** myofilaments. Fingerlike projections or **crossbridges** connect the actin and myosin myofilaments. When a muscle is stimulated to contract, the crossbridges pull the myofilaments closer together, shortening the muscle, and producing movement at the joint that the muscle crosses (Fig. 5-3).[4]

These *myofilaments increase in size and number* as a result of resistance training, causing the individual muscle fibers to increase in cross-sectional diameter.[48] This increase is particularly true in men, although women will also see some increase in muscle size.[20] More research is needed to further clarify and determine the specific reasons for muscle hypertrophy.

REVERSIBILITY

If resistance training is discontinued or interrupted, the muscle will atrophy, decreasing in both strength and mass. Adaptations in skeletal muscle that occur in response to resistance training may begin to reverse in as little as 48 hours. It does appear that consistent exercise of a muscle is essential to prevent reversal of the hypertrophy that occurs due to strength training.

Other Physiologic Adaptations to Resistance Exercise

In addition to muscle hypertrophy, there are a number of other physiologic adaptations to resistance training. The strength of noncontractile structures, including tendons and ligaments, is increased. The mineral content of bone is increased, thus making the bone stronger and more resistant to fracture. Maximal oxygen uptake is improved when resistance training is of sufficient intensity to elicit heart rates at or above training levels. However, it must be emphasized that these increases are minimal and if increased maximal oxygen uptake is the goal, aerobic exercise rather than resistance training is recommended. There is also an increase in several enzymes important in aerobic and anaerobic metabolism.[1,21,22] All of these adaptations contribute to strength and endurance.

TECHNIQUES OF RESISTANCE TRAINING

There are a number of different techniques of resistance training for strength improvement including isometric exercise, progressive resistive exercise, isokinetic training, circuit training, and plyometric exercise.

The Overload Principle

Regardless of which of these techniques is used, one basic principle of reconditioning is extremely important. For a muscle to improve in strength, it must be forced to work at a higher level than that to which it is accustomed.[45] In other words, the muscle must be overloaded. Without overload, the muscle will be able to maintain strength as long as training is continued against a resistance to which the muscle is accustomed. No additional strength gains will be realized. This maintenance of existing levels of muscular strength may be more important in resistance programs that emphasize muscular endurance rather than strength gains. Many individuals can benefit more in terms of overall health by concentrating on improving muscular endurance. To most effectively build muscular strength, however, resistance training requires a consistent, increasing effort against progressively increasing resistance.[31,46]

Resistive exercise is based primarily on the principles of overload and progression. If these principles are applied, all of the following resistance training techniques will produce improvement of muscular strength over time.

In a rehabilitation setting, progressive overload is limited to some degree by the healing process. Because the therapist often takes an aggressive approach to rehabilitation, the rate of progression is perhaps best determined by the injured patient's response to a specific exercise. Exacerbation of pain or increased swelling should signal the therapist that the rate of progression is too aggressive.

Isometric Exercise

An **isometric exercise** involves a muscle contraction in which the length of the muscle remains constant while tension develops toward a maximal force against an immovable resistance[5]

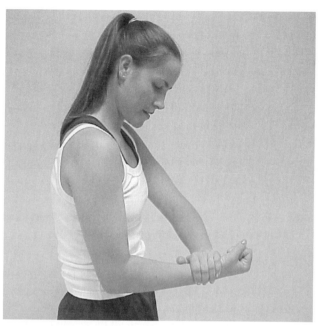

FIGURE 5-4

Isometric exercises. Isometric exercises involve contraction against some immovable resistance.

(Fig. 5-4). Isometric exercises are capable of increasing muscular strength[44]; however, strength gains are relatively specific, with as much as a 20 percent overflow to the joint angle at which training is performed. At other angles, the strength curve drops off dramatically because of a lack of motor activity at that angle. Thus strength is increased at the specific angle of exertion, but there is no corresponding increase in strength at other positions in the range of motion.

Another major disadvantage of isometric exercises is that they tend to produce a spike in systolic blood pressure that can result in potentially life-threatening cardiovascular accidents.[25] This sharp increase in systolic blood pressure results from a Valsalva maneuver, which increases intrathoracic pressure. To avoid or minimize this effect, it is recommended that breathing be done during the maximal contraction to prevent this increase in pressure.

The use of isometric exercises in injury rehabilitation or reconditioning is widely practiced. There are a number of conditions or ailments resulting from trauma or overuse that must be treated with strengthening exercises. Unfortunately, these problems may be exacerbated with full range-of-motion resistance exercises. It may be more desirable to make use of positional or functional isometric exercises, which involve the application of isometric force at multiple angles throughout the range of motion. Functional isometrics should be used until the healing process has progressed to the point that full-range activities can be performed.

During rehabilitation, it is often recommended that a muscle be contracted isometrically for 10 seconds at a time at a frequency of 10 or more contractions per hour. Isometric

exercises may also offer significant benefit in a strengthening program.[52]

There are certain instances in which an isometric contraction can greatly enhance a particular movement. For example, one of the exercises in power weight lifting is a squat. A squat is an exercise in which the weight is supported on the shoulder in a standing position. The knees are then flexed, and the weight is lowered to a three-quarter squat position, from which the lifter must stand completely straight once again.

It is not uncommon for there to be one particular angle in the range of motion at which smooth movement is difficult because of insufficient strength. This joint angle is referred to as a sticking point. A power lifter will typically use an isometric contraction against some immovable resistance to increase strength at this sticking point. If strength can be improved at this joint angle, then a smooth, coordinated power lift can be performed through a full range of movement.

Progressive Resistive Exercise

A second technique of resistance training is perhaps the most commonly used and most popular technique among therapists for improving muscular strength in a rehabilitation program. **Progressive resistive exercise** training uses exercises that strengthen muscles through a contraction that overcomes some fixed resistance such as with dumbells, barbells, various exercise machines, or resistive elastic tubing. Progressive resistive exercise uses isotonic, or *isodynamic,* contractions in which force is generated while the muscle is changing in length.

CONCENTRIC VERSUS ECCENTRIC CONTRACTIONS

Isotonic contractions can be concentric or eccentric. In performing a bicep curl, to lift the weight from the starting position the biceps muscle must contract and shorten in length. This shortening contraction is referred to as a **concentric** or **positive** contraction. If the biceps muscle does not remain contracted when the weight is being lowered, gravity would cause this weight to simply fall back to the starting position. To control the weight as it is being lowered, the biceps muscle must continue to contract while gradually lengthening at the same time. A contraction in which the muscle is lengthening while still applying force is called an **eccentric** or **negative** contraction.

It is possible to generate greater amounts of force against resistance with an eccentric contraction than with a concentric contraction because eccentric contractions require a much lower level of motor unit activity to achieve a certain force than do concentric contractions. Because fewer motor units are firing to produce a specific force, additional motor units may be recruited to generate increased force. In addition, oxygen use is much lower during eccentric exercise than in concentric exercise. Eccentric contractions are less resistant to fatigue than are concentric contractions. The mechanical efficiency of eccentric exercise can be several times higher than that of concentric exercise.[46]

Traditionally, progressive resistive exercise has concentrated primarily on the concentric component without paying much

FIGURE 5-5

Isotonic equipment.
A, Most exercise
machines are isotonic.
B, Resistance may be
easily changed by
changing the key in the
stack of weights.

A

B

attention to the importance of the eccentric component.[46] The use of eccentric contractions has received considerable emphasis in recent years. Eccentric contractions are critical for deceleration of limb motion, especially during high-velocity dynamic activities. For example, a baseball pitcher relies on an eccentric contraction of the external rotators of the glenohumeral joint to decelerate the humerus, which may be internally rotating at speeds as high as 8000 degrees/second. Certainly, strength deficits or an inability of a muscle to tolerate these eccentric forces can predispose an injury. Thus in a rehabilitation program the therapist should incorporate eccentric strengthening exercises. Eccentric contractions are possible with all free weights, with the majority of isotonic exercise machines, and with most isokinetic devices. Eccentric contractions are used with plyometric exercise discussed in Chapter 11 and may also be incorporated with functional proprioceptive neuromuscular facilitation (PNF) strengthening patterns discussed in Chapter 13.

In progressive resistive exercise, it is essential to incorporate both concentric and eccentric contractions.[29] Research has clearly demonstrated that the muscle should be overloaded and fatigued both concentrically and eccentrically for the greatest strength improvement to occur.[2,18,36] When training specifically for the development of muscular strength, the concentric portion of the exercise should require 1 to 2 seconds, while the eccentric portion of the lift should require 2 to 4 seconds. The ratio of the concentric component to the eccentric component should be approximately 1 to 2. Physiologically, the muscle will fatigue much more rapidly concentrically than eccentrically.[35]

FREE WEIGHTS VERSUS EXERCISE MACHINES

There are various types of exercise equipment that can be used with progressive resistive exercise including free weights (barbells and dumbbells) or exercise machines such as Cybex, Universal, Nautilus, Eagle, Body Master, Keiser, Paramount, Continental, Pyramid, Sprint, Hydrafitness, Dynatrac, Future, and Bull. Dumbbells and barbells require the use of iron plates of varying weights that can be easily changed by adding or subtracting equal amounts of weight to both sides of the bar. The exercise machines commonly have stacks of weights that are lifted through a series of levers or pulleys. The stack of weights slides up and down on a pair of bars that restrict the movement

to only one plane. Weight can be increased or decreased simply by changing the position of a weight key (Fig. 5-5).

There are advantages and disadvantages to free weights and machines. The exercise machines are relatively safe to use in comparison with free weights. For example, a bench press with free weights requires a partner to help lift the weight back onto the support racks if the lifter does not have enough strength to complete the lift; otherwise the weight may be dropped on the chest. With the machines, the weight may be easily and safely dropped without fear of injury.

It is also a simple process to increase or decrease the weight by moving a single weight key with the exercise machines, although changes can generally be made only in increments of 10 or 15 pounds. With free weights, iron plates must be added or removed from each side of the barbell.

Patients who have strength trained using free weights and exercise machines realize the difference in the amount of weight that can be lifted. Unlike the machines, free weights have no restricted motion and can thus move in many different directions, depending on the forces applied. With free weights, an element of muscular control on the part of the lifter to prevent the weight from moving in any other direction other than vertical will usually decrease the amount of weight that can be lifted.[54]

SURGICAL TUBING OR THERABAND™

Surgical tubing or Theraband, as a means of providing resistance, has been widely used in rehabilitation (Fig. 5-6). The advantage of exercising with surgical tubing or Theraband is that the direction of movement is less restricted than with free weights or exercise machines. Exercise can be done against resistance in more functional movement planes. The use of surgical tubing exercise in plyometrics and PNF strengthening techniques will be discussed in Chapters 11 and 13. Surgical tubing may be used to provide resistance with the majority of the strengthening exercises shown in Chapters 25 through 31. Regardless of which type of equipment is used, the same principles of progressive resistive exercise may be applied.

VARIABLE RESISTANCE

One problem often mentioned in relation to progressive resistive exercise reconditioning is that the amount of force necessary to

FIGURE 5-6

Strengthening exercises. Strengthening exercises using surgical tubing are widely used in sports injury rehabilitation.

move a weight through a range of motion changes according to the angle of pull of the contracting muscle. It is greatest when the angle of pull is approximately 90 degrees. In addition, once the inertia of the weight has been overcome and momentum has been established, the force required to move the resistance varies according to the force that muscle can produce through the range of motion. Thus it has been argued that a disadvantage of any type of isotonic exercise is that force required to move the resistance is constantly changing throughout the range of movement. This change in resistance at different points in the range of motion has been labeled **accommodating resistance** or **variable resistance.**

A number of exercise machine manufacturers have attempted to alleviate this problem of changing force capabilities by using a cam in the machine pulley system (Fig. 5-7). The cam is individually designed for each piece of equipment so that the resistance is variable throughout the movement. It attempts to alter resistance so that the muscle can handle a greater load, but at the points where the joint angle or muscle length is mechanically disadvantageous, it reduces the resistance to muscle movement. Whether this design does what it claims is debatable.

PROGRESSIVE RESISTIVE EXERCISE TERMINOLOGY

Perhaps the single most confusing aspect of progressive resistive exercise is the terminology used to describe specific programs.[28] The following list of terms with their operational definitions may help clarify the confusion.

Repetitions = Number of times a specific movement is repeated.
Repetition maximum (RM) = Maximum number of repetitions at a given weight.
Set = A particular number of repetitions.
Intensity = The amount of weight or resistance lifted.
Recovery period = The rest interval between sets.
Frequency = The number of times an exercise is done in a week's period.

FIGURE 5-7

Exercise machines.
A, Bench press machine.
B, The cam is designed to equalize resistance throughout the full range of motion.

A

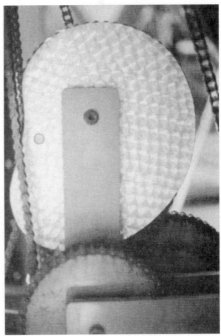

B

T A B L E   5 - 1

T A B L E   5 - 1

DeLorme's Program

SET	AMOUNT OF WEIGHT	REPETITIONS
1	50% of 10 RM	10
2	75% of 10 RM	10
3	100% of 10 RM	10

RM, repetition maximum.

T A B L E   5 - 2

The Oxford Technique

SET	AMOUNT OF WEIGHT	REPETITIONS
1	50% of 10 RM	10
2	75% of 10 RM	10
3	100% of 10 RM	10

RM, repetition maximum.

T A B L E   5 - 3

MacQueen's Technique

SETS	AMOUNT OF WEIGHT	REPETITIONS
3 (Beginning/ intermediate)	100% of 10 RM	10
4–5 (Advanced)	100% of 2–3 RM	2–3

RM, repetition maximum.

T A B L E   5 - 4

Sanders' Program

SETS	AMOUNT OF WEIGHT	REPETITIONS
Total of 4 sets		
(3 times per week)	100% of 5 RM	5
Day 1 4 sets	100% of 5 RM	5
Day 2 4 sets	100% of 3 RM	5
Day 3 1 set	100% of 5 RM	5
2 sets	100% of 3 RM	5
2 sets	100% of 2 RM	5

RM, repetition maximum.

T A B L E   5 - 5

Knight's DAPRE Program

SET	AMOUNT OF WEIGHT	REPETITIONS
1	50% of RM	10
2	75% of RM	6
3	100% of RM	Maximum
4	Adjusted working weight[a]	Maximum

RM, repetition maximum.
[a] See Table 5-6.

RECOMMENDED TECHNIQUES OF RESISTANCE TRAINING

Specific recommendations for techniques of improving muscular strength are controversial among therapists. A considerable amount of research has been done in the area of resistance training relative to (1) the amount of weight to be used, (2) the number of repetitions, (3) the number of sets, and (4) the frequency of training.

A variety of specific programs have been proposed that recommend the optimal amount of weight, number of sets, number of repetitions, and frequency for producing maximal gains in levels of muscular strength. Regardless of the techniques used, however, the healing process must dictate the specifics of any strength-training program. Certainly to improve strength the muscle must be progressively overloaded. The amount of weight used and the number of repetitions must be sufficient to make the muscle work at higher intensity than it is used to working. This factor is the most critical in any resistance training program. The resistance training program must also be designed to ultimately meet the specific competitive needs of the patient.

One of the first widely accepted strength-development programs to be used in a rehabilitation program was developed by DeLorme and was based on a repetition maximum of 10 (10 RM).[14] The amount of weight used is what can be lifted exactly 10 times (Table 5-1).

Zinovieff proposed the Oxford technique, which, like DeLorme's program, was designed to be used in beginning, intermediate, and advanced levels of rehabilitation.[56] The only difference is that the percent of maximum was reversed in the three sets (Table 5-2). MacQueen's technique[39] differentiates between beginning to intermediate and advanced levels as is shown in Table 5-3.

Sanders' program (Table 5-4) was designed to be used in the advanced stages of rehabilitation and was based on a formula that used a percentage of body weight to determine starting weights.[46] The percentages that follow represent median starting points for different exercises.

Barbell squat—45 percent of body weight
Barbell bench press—30 percent of body weight
Leg extension—20 percent of body weight
Universal bench press—30 percent of body weight

TABLE 5-6

DAPRE Adjusted Working Weight

NUMBER OF REPETITIONS PERFORMED DURING THIRD SET	ADJUSTED WORKING WEIGHT DURING FOURTH SET	NEXT EXERCISE SESSION
0–2	– 5–10 lb	– 5–10 lb
3–4	– 0–5 lb	Same weight
5–6	Same weight	+5–10 lb
7–10	+5–10 lb	+5–15 lb
11	+10–15 lb	+10–20 lb

Universal leg extension—20 percent of body weight
Universal leg curl—10 percent to 15 percent of body weight
Universal leg press—50 percent of body weight
Upright rowing—20 percent of body weight

Knight applied the concept of progressive resistive exercise in rehabilitation. The DAPRE (daily adjusted progressive resistive exercise) program (Tables 5-5 and 5-6) allows for individual differences in the rates at which patients progress in their rehabilitation programs.[30]

Berger has proposed a technique that is adjustable within individual limitations (Table 5-7). For any given exercise, the amount of weight selected should be sufficient to allow 6 to 8 RM in each of the three sets with a recovery period of 60 to 90 seconds between sets. Initial selection of a starting weight may require some trial and error to achieve this 6 to 8 RM range. If at least three sets of 6 RM cannot be completed, the weight is too heavy and should be reduced. If it is possible to do more than three sets of 8 RM, the weight is too light and should be increased.[7] Progression to heavier weights is determined by the ability to perform at least 8 RM in each of three sets. When progressing weight, an increase of about 10 percent of the current weight being lifted should still allow at least 6 RM in each of three sets.[8]

For rehabilitation purposes, strengthening exercises should be performed on a daily basis initially, with the amount of weight, number of sets, and number of repetitions governed by the injured patient's response to the exercise. As the healing process progresses and pain or swelling is no longer an issue, a particular muscle or muscle group should be exercised consistently every other day. At that point, the frequency of

TABLE 5-7

Berger's Adjustment Technique

SETS	AMOUNT OF WEIGHT	REPETITIONS
3	100% of 10 RM	6–8

RM, repetition maximum.

weight training should be at least three times per week but no more than four times per week. It is common for serious weight lifters to lift every day; however, they exercise different muscle groups on successive days. For example, Monday, Wednesday, and Friday may be used for upper body muscles, whereas Tuesday, Thursday, and Saturday are used for lower body muscles.

It has been suggested that if training is done properly, using both concentric and eccentric contractions, resistance training is necessary only twice each week, although this schedule has not been sufficiently documented.

Isokinetic Exercise

An **isokinetic exercise** involves a muscle contraction in which the length of the muscle is changing while the contraction is performed at a constant velocity. In theory, maximal resistance is provided throughout the range of motion by the machine. The resistance provided by the machine will move only at some preset speed, regardless of the torque applied to it by the individual. The key to isokinetic exercise is not the resistance but the speed at which resistance can be moved.

Several isokinetic devices are available commercially; Cybex, Biodex, and KinCom are among the more common isokinetic devices (Fig. 5-8). In general, they rely on computer-controlled hydraulic, pneumatic, and mechanical pressure systems to produce this constant velocity of motion. The majority of isokinetic devices are capable of resisting concentric and eccentric contractions at a fixed speed to exercise a muscle.

ISOKINETICS AS A CONDITIONING TOOL

Isokinetic devices are designed so that regardless of the amount of force applied against a resistance, it can only be moved at a certain speed. That speed will be the same whether maximal force or only half the maximal force is applied. Consequently, when training isokinetically, it is absolutely necessary to exert as much force against the resistance as possible (maximal effort) for maximal strength gains to occur. Maximal effort is one of the major problems with an isokinetic strength-training program.

Anyone who has been involved in a resistance training program knows that on some days it is difficult to find the motivation to work out. Because isokinetic training requires a maximal effort, it is very easy to "cheat" and not go through the workout at a high level of intensity. In a progressive resistive exercise program, the patient knows how much weight has to be lifted with how many repetitions. Thus isokinetic training is often more effective if a partner system is used primarily as a means of motivation toward a maximal effort. When isokinetic training is done properly with a maximal effort, it is theoretically possible that maximal strength gains are best achieved through the isokinetic training method in which the velocity and force of the resistance are equal throughout the range of motion. There is, however, no conclusive research to support this theory.

Whether this changing force capability is a deterrent to improving the ability to generate force against some resistance

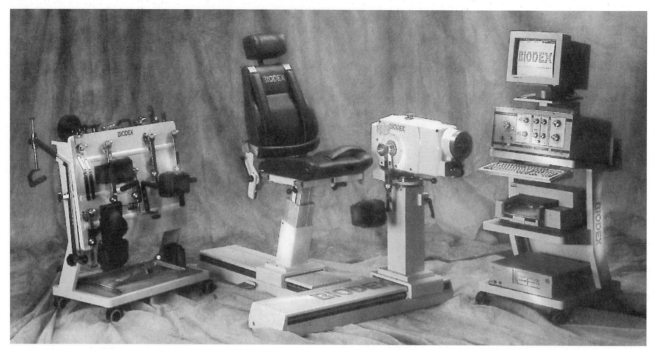

F I G U R E   5 - 8

Isokinetic exercise. The KinCom is an isokinetic device that provides resistance at a constant velocity.

is debatable. In real life it does not matter whether the resistance is changing; what is important is that an individual develops enough strength to move objects from one place to another. The amount of strength necessary for patients is largely dependent on their level of competition.

Another major disadvantage of using isokinetic devices as a conditioning tool is their cost. With initial purchase costs ranging between $40,000 and $75,000 and the necessity of regular maintenance and software upgrades, the use of an isokinetic device for general conditioning or resistance training is for the most part unrealistic. Thus isokinetic exercises are primarily used as a diagnostic and rehabilitative tool.

ISOKINETICS IN REHABILITATION

Isokinetic strength testing gained a great deal of popularity throughout the 1980s in rehabilitation settings, primarily because it provided an objective means of quantifying existing levels of muscular strength and became useful as a diagnostic tool.[40]

Because the capability exists for training at specific speeds, comparisons have been made regarding the relative advantages of training at fast or slow speeds in a rehabilitation program. The research literature seems to indicate that strength increases from slow-speed training are relatively specific to the velocity used in training. Conversely, training at faster speeds seems to produce a more generalized increase in torque values at all velocities. Minimal hypertrophy was observed only while training at fast speeds, affecting only type II or fast-twitch fibers.[13,43] An increase in neuromuscular efficiency caused by more effective

motor unit firing patterns has been demonstrated with slow-speed training.[36]

During the early 1990s, the value of isokinetic devices for quantifying torque values at functional speeds was questioned. This issue, in addition to the theory and use of isokinetic exercise in a rehabilitation setting, will be discussed in detail in Chapter 10.

Circuit Training as a Rehabilitation Technique

Circuit training is a technique that may be useful to the therapist to maintain or perhaps improve levels of muscular strength or endurance in other parts of the body while the patient allows for healing and reconditioning of an injured body part. Circuit training uses a series of exercise stations that consist of various combinations of weight training, flexibility, calisthenics, and brief aerobic exercises. Circuits can be designed to accomplish many different training goals. With circuit training, the patient moves rapidly from one station to the next, performing whatever exercise is to be done at that station within a specified time period. A typical circuit would consist of 8 to 12 stations, and the entire circuit would be repeated three times.

Circuit training is most definitely an effective technique for improving strength and flexibility. Certainly if the pace or time interval between stations is rapid and if work load is maintained at a high level of intensity with heart rates at or above target training levels, the cardiorespiratory system may benefit from this circuit. However, there is little research evidence that shows that circuit training is very effective in improving cardiorespiratory endurance. It should be and is most often used as a technique for developing and improving muscular strength and endurance.[23]

Plyometric Exercise

Plyometric exercise is a technique that is being increasingly incorporated into later stages of the rehabilitation program by the therapist. Plyometric training includes specific exercises that encompass a rapid stretch of a muscle eccentrically, followed immediately by a rapid concentric contraction of that muscle to facilitate and develop a forceful explosive movement over a short period of time.[16] The greater the stretch put on the muscle from its resting length immediately before the concentric contraction, the greater the resistance the muscle can overcome. Plyometrics emphasize the speed of the eccentric phase. The rate of stretch is more critical than the magnitude of the stretch. An advantage to using plyometric exercises is that they can help to develop eccentric control in dynamic movements.[34]

Plyometric exercises involve hops, bounds, and depth jumping for the lower extremity and the use of medicine balls and other types of weighted equipment for the upper extremity.[10,11] Depth jumping is an example of a plyometric exercise in which an individual jumps to the ground from a specified height and then quickly jumps again as soon as ground contact is made.[3]

Plyometrics tend to place a great deal of stress on the musculoskeletal system. The learning and perfection of specific jumping skills and other plyometric exercises must be technically correct and specific to one's age, activity, physical, and skill development. Plyometric exercise will be discussed in detail in Chapter 11.

OPEN- VERSUS CLOSED-KINETIC CHAIN EXERCISES

The concept of the kinetic chain deals with the anatomic functional relationships that exist in the upper and lower extremities. In a weight-bearing position, the lower extremity kinetic chain involves the transmission of forces between the foot, ankle, lower leg, knee, thigh, and hip. In the upper extremity, when the hand is in contact with a weight-bearing surface, forces are transmitted to the wrist, forearm, elbow, upper arm, and shoulder girdle.

An **open-kinetic chain** exists when the foot or hand is not in contact with the ground or some other surface. In a **closed-kinetic chain,** the foot or hand is weight bearing. Movements of the more proximal anatomic segments are affected by these open- versus closed-kinetic chain positions. For example, the rotational components of the ankle, knee, and hip reverse direction when changing from an open- to closed-kinetic chain activity. In a closed-kinetic chain, the forces begin at the ground and work their way up through each joint. Also, in a closed-kinetic chain, forces must be absorbed by various tissues and anatomic structures rather than simply dissipating as would occur in an open chain.

In rehabilitation, the use of closed-chain strengthening techniques has become a treatment of choice for many therapists. Because most functional activities involve some aspect of weight bearing with the foot in contact with the ground or the hand in a weight-bearing position, closed-kinetic chain strengthening activities are more functional than are open-chain activities. Therefore, rehabilitative exercises should be incorporated that emphasize strengthening of the entire kinetic chain rather than an isolated body segment. Chapter 12 will discuss closed-kinetic chain activities in detail.

TRAINING FOR MUSCULAR STRENGTH VERSUS MUSCULAR ENDURANCE

Muscular endurance was defined as the ability to perform repeated muscle contractions against resistance for an extended period of time. Most resistance training experts believe that muscular strength and muscular endurance are closely related.[17,41,47] As one improves, there is a tendency for the other to improve also.

It is generally accepted that when resistance training for strength, heavier weights with a lower number of repetitions should be used.[53] Conversely, endurance training uses relatively lighter weights with a greater number of repetitions.

It has been suggested that endurance training should consist of three sets of 10 to 15 repetitions[8] using the same criteria for weight selection progression and frequency as recommended for progressive resistive exercise. Thus suggested training regimens for muscular strength and endurance are similar in terms of sets and numbers of repetitions.[55] People who possess great levels of strength tend to also exhibit greater muscular endurance when asked to perform repeated contractions against submaximal resistance.[39]

RESISTANCE TRAINING DIFFERENCES BETWEEN MALES AND FEMALES

The approach to strength training is no different for female than for male patients; however, some obvious physiologic differences exist between genders. The average woman will not build significant muscle bulk through resistance training. Significant muscle hypertrophy is dependent on the presence of a steroidal hormone known as **testosterone.** Testosterone is considered a male hormone, although all females possess some level of testosterone in their systems. Women with higher testosterone levels tend to have more masculine characteristics, such as increased facial and body hair, a deeper voice, and the potential to develop a little more muscle bulk.[19,41] For the average female patient, developing large, bulky muscles through strength training is unlikely, although muscle tone may be improved. Muscle tone basically refers to the firmness of tension of the muscle during a resting state.

The initial stages of a resistance training program are likely to produce dramatic increases in levels of strength very rapidly. For a muscle to contract, an impulse must be transmitted from the nervous system to the muscle. Each muscle fiber is innervated by a specific motor unit. By overloading a particular muscle, as in weight training, the muscle is forced to work more efficiently. Efficiency is achieved by getting more motor units to fire, thus causing more muscle fibers to contract, which results in a stronger contraction of the muscle. Consequently, both women and men often see extremely rapid gains in strength when a weight-training program is first begun. In the female, these initial strength gains, which can be attributed to improved neuromuscular efficiency, tend to plateau, and minimal improvement in muscular strength is realized during a continuing resistance training program. These initial neuromuscular strength gains are also seen in men, although their strength continues to increase with appropriate training. Again, women who possess higher testosterone levels have the potential to increase their strength further because of the development of greater muscle bulk.

Differences in strength levels between males and females are best illustrated when strength is expressed in relation to body weight minus fat. The reduced **strength–body weight ratio** in women is the result of their percentage of body fat. The strength–body weight ratio may be significantly improved through resistance training by decreasing the body fat percentage while increasing lean weight.[36]

The absolute strength differences are considerably reduced when body size and composition are considered. Leg strength may actually be stronger in the female than in the male, although upper extremity strength is much greater in the male.[36]

RESISTANCE TRAINING IN THE YOUNG PATIENT

The principles of resistance training discussed previously may be applied to the young patient. There are certainly a number of sociological questions regarding the advantages and disadvantages of younger, in particular prepubescent, patients engaging in rigorous strength training programs. From a physiologic perspective, experts have debated the value of strength training in young patients for years. Recently, a number of studies have indicated that if properly supervised, young patients can improve strength, power, endurance, balance and proprioception; develop a positive body image; improve sport performance; and prevent injuries.[32] A prepubescent child can experience gains in levels of muscle strength without muscle hypertrophy.[42]

A therapist supervising a rehabilitation program for an injured young patient should certainly incorporate resistive exercise into the program. Close supervision, proper instruction, and appropriate modification of progression and intensity based on the extent of physical maturation of the individual is critical to the effectiveness of the resistive exercises.[32]

SPECIFIC RESISTIVE EXERCISES USED IN REHABILITATION

Because muscle contractions result in joint movement, the goal of resistance training in a rehabilitation program should be to regain and, perhaps, increase the strength of either a specific muscle that has been injured or to increase the efficiency of movement about a given joint.[36]

The exercises included throughout Chapters 25 through 32 show exercises for all motions about a particular joint rather than for each specific muscle. These exercises are demonstrated using free weights (dumbbells or bar weights) and some exercise machines. Other strengthening techniques widely used for injury rehabilitation involving isokinetic exercise, plyometrics, closed-kinetic chain exercises, and PNF strengthening techniques, will be discussed in greater detail in subsequent chapters.

SUMMARY

- Muscular strength can be defined as the maximal force that can be generated against resistance by a muscle during a single maximal contraction.
- Muscular endurance is the ability to perform repeated isotonic or isokinetic muscle contractions or to sustain an isometric contraction without undue fatigue.
- Muscular endurance tends to improve with muscular strength, thus training techniques for these two components are similar.
- Muscular strength and endurance are essential components of any rehabilitation program.
- The ability to generate force is dependent on the physical properties of the muscle, neuromuscular efficiency, as well as the mechanical factors that dictate how much force can be generated through the lever system to an external object.
- Hypertrophy of a muscle is caused by increases in the size and perhaps the number of actin and myosin protein myofilaments, which result in an increased cross-sectional diameter of the muscle.
- The key to improving strength through resistance training is using the principle of overload within the constraints of the healing process.
- Five resistance training techniques that can improve muscular strength are isometric exercise, progressive resistive exercise, isokinetic training, circuit training, and plyometric training.
- Improvements in strength with isometric exercise occur at specific joint angles.
- Progressive resistive exercise is the most common strengthening technique used by the therapist for rehabilitation after injury.

- Circuit training involves a series of exercise stations consisting of resistance training, flexibility, and calisthenic exercises that can be designed to maintain fitness while reconditioning an injured body part.
- Isokinetic training provides resistance to a muscle at a fixed speed.
- Plyometric exercise uses a quick eccentric stretch to facilitate a concentric contraction.
- Closed-kinetic chain exercises may provide a more functional technique for strengthening of injured muscles and joints in the athletic population.
- Women can significantly increase strength levels but generally will not build muscle bulk as a result of strength training because of a relative lack of the hormone testosterone.

REFERENCES

1. Alway SE, MacDougall D, Sale G, et al. Functional and structural adaptations in skeletal muscle of trained athletes. *J Appl Physiol* 64:1114, 1988.
2. Astrand PO, Rodahl K. *Textbook of Work Physiology.* New York, McGraw-Hill, 1986.
3. Arnheim D, Prentice WE. *Principles of Athletic Training.* New York, McGraw-Hill, 2000.
4. Baechle T, Groves B. *Weight Training: Steps To Success.* Champaign, IL, Leisure Press, 1992.
5. Baker D, Wilson G, Carlyon B. Generality vs. specificity: A comparison of dynamic and isometric measures of strength and speed-strength. *Eur J Appl Physiol* 68:350–355, 1994.
6. Bandy W, Lovelace-Chandler V, Bandy B, et al. Adaptation of skeletal muscle to resistance training, *J Orthop Sports Phys Ther* 12:248–255, 1990.
7. Berger R. *Conditioning for Men.* Boston, Allyn & Bacon, 1973.
8. Berger R. Effect of varied weight training programs on strength. *Res Q Exerc Sport* 33:168, 1962.
9. Booth F, Thomason D. Molecular and cellular adaptation of muscle in response to exercise; perspectives of various models. *Physiol Rev* 71:541–585, 1991.
10. Chu D. *Jumping into Plyometrics.* Champaign, IL, Human Kinetics, 1992.
11. Chu D: *Plyometric Exercise with the Medicine Ball.* Livermore, CA, Bittersweet, 1989.
12. Costill D, Daniels J, Evan W, et al. Skeletal muscle enzymes and fiber compositions in male and female track athletes. *J Appl Physiol* 40:149, 1976.
13. Coyle E, Feiring D, Rotkis T, et al. Specificity of power improvements through slow and fast speed isokinetic training. *J Appl Physiol* 51:1437, 1981.
14. DeLorme T, Wilkins A. *Progressive Resistance Exercise.* New York, Appleton-Century-Crofts, 1951.
15. Deudsinger RH. Biomechanics in clinical practice. *Phys Ther* 64:1860–1868, 1984.
16. Duda M. Plyometrics: A legitimate form of power training. *Phys Sports Med* 16:213, 1988.
17. Dudley GA, Fleck SJ. Strength and endurance training: Are they mutually exclusive? *Sports Med* 4:79, 1987.
18. Etheridge G, Thomas T. Physiological and biomedical changes of human skeletal muscle induced by different strength training programs. *Med Sci Sports Exerc* 14:141, 1982.
19. Fahey T. *Basic Weight Training for Men and Women.* Mountain View, CA, Mayfield, 1994.
20. Faulkner J, Green H, White T. Response and adaptation of skeletal muscle to change in physical activity. In: Bouchard C, Shepard R, Stephens J, eds. *Physical Activity, Fitness, and Health.* Champaign, IL, Human Kinetics, 1994.
21. Fleck SJ, Kramer WJ. Resistance training: Physiological responses and adaptations. *Physician Sports Med* 16:108, 1988.
22. Gettman L, Ward P, Hagan R. A comparison of combined running and weight training with circuit weight training. *Med Sci Sports Exerc* 14:229, 1982.
23. Gettman L. Circuit weight training: A critical review of its physiological benefits. *Phys Sports Med* 9:44, 1981.
24. Gonyea W. Role of exercise in inducing increases in skeletal muscle fiber number. *J Appl Physiol* 48:421, 1980.
25. Graves JE, Pollack M, Jones A, et al. Specificity of limited range of motion variable resistance training. *Med Sci Sports Exerc* 21:84, 1989.
26. Gray GW. Ecocentrics—a theoretical model for muscle function. JOSPT, submitted for publication.
27. Harmen E. The biomechanics of resistance training. In: Baechle T, ed. *Essentials of Strength Training and Conditioning.* Champaign, IL, Human Kinetics, 1994.
28. Hickson R, Hidaka C, Foster C. Skeletal muscle fiber type, resistance training and strength-related performance. *Med Sci Sports Exer* 26:593–598, 1994.
29. Hortobagyi T, Katch FI. Role of concentric force in limiting improvement in muscular strength. *J Appl Physiol* 68:650, 1990.
30. Knight K. Knee rehabilitation by the DAPRE technique. *Am J Sports Med Phys Fitness* 7:336, 1979.
31. Komi P. *Strength and Power in Sport.* London, Blackwell Scientific Publications, 1992.
32. Kraemer WJ, Fleck SJ. *Strength Training for Young Athletes.* Champaign, IL, Human Kinetics, 1993.
33. Kraemer WJ. General adaptations to resistance and endurance training programs. In: Baechle T, ed. *Essentials of Strength Training and Conditioning.* Champaign, IL, Human Kinetics, 1994.
34. Kramer J, Morrow A, Leger A. Changes in rowing ergometer, weight lifting, vertical jump and isokinetic performance in response to standard and standard plus plyometric training programs. *Int J Sports Med* 14:440–454, 1993.
35. Mastropaolo J. A test of maximum power theory for strength. *Eur J Appl Physiol* 65:415–420, 1992.

36. McArdle W, Katch F, Katch V. *Exercise Physiology, Energy, Nutrition, and Human Performance.* Philadelphia, Lea & Febiger, 1994.

37. McComas A. Human neuromuscular adaptations that accompany changes in activity. *Med Sci Spor Exer* 26:1498–1509, 1994.

38. McGlynn GH. A reevaluation of isometric training. *J Sports Med Phys Fitness* 12:258, 1972.

39. MacQueen I. Recent advance in the techniques of progressive resistance. *Br Med J* 11:11993, 1954.

40. Nicholas JJ. Isokinetic testing in young nonathletic able-bodied subjects. *Arch Phys Med Rehabil* 70:210, 1989.

41. Nygard CH, Luophaarui T, Suurnakki T, et al. Muscle strength and muscle endurance of middle-aged women and men associated to type, duration and intensity of muscular load at work. *Int Arch Occup Environ Health* 60:291, 1988.

42. Ozmun J, Mikesky A, Surburg P. Neuromuscular adaptations following prepubescent strength training. *Med Sci Sport Exer* 26:514, 1994.

43. Pipes T, Wilmore J. Isokinetic vs. isotonic strength training in adult men. *Med Sci Sports Exerc* 7:262, 1975.

44. Rehfeldt H, Caffiber G, Kramer H, et al. Force, endurance time, and cardiovascular responses in voluntary isometric contractions of different muscle groups. *Biomed Biochim Acta* 48:S509, 1989.

45. Sale D, MacDougall D. Specificity in strength training: A review for the coach and athlete. *Can J Appl Sports Sci* 6:87, 1981.

46. Sanders M. Weight training and conditioning. In: Sanders B, ed. *Sports Physical Therapy.* Norwalk, CT, Appleton & Lange, 1990, 239–250.

47. Smith TK. Developing local and general muscular endurance. *Athletic J* 62:42, 1981.

48. Soest A, Bobbert M. The role of muscle properties in control of explosive movements. *Biol Cybern* 69:195–204, 1993.

49. Staron RS, Karapondo DL, Kreamer WJ. Skeletal muscle adaptations during early phase of heavy resistance training in men and women. *J App Physiol* 76:1247–1255, 1994.

50. Stone M, Fleck S, Triplett N. Health and performance related potential of resistance training. *Sports Med* 11:210–231, 1991.

51. Strauss RH, ed. *Sportsmedicine.* Philadelphia, Saunders, 1991.

52. Ulmer H, Knierman W, Warlow T, et al. Interindividual variability of isometric endurance with regard to the endurance performance limit for static work. *Biomed Biochim Acta* 48:S504, 1989.

53. Van Etten L, Verstappen F, Westerterp K. Effect of body building on weight training induced adaptations in body composition and muscular strength. *Med Sci Sport Exer* 26:515–521, 1994.

54. Weltman A, Stamford B. Strength training: Free weights vs. machines. *Phys Sports Med* 10:197, 1982.

55. Yates JW. Recovery of dynamic muscular endurance. *Eur Appl Physiol* 56:662, 1987.

56. Zinovieff A. Heavy resistance exercise, the Oxford technique. *Br J Physiol Med* 14:129, 1951.

CHAPTER 6

Impaired Endurance: Maintaining Aerobic Capacity and Endurance

William E. Prentice

OBJECTIVES

After completing this chapter, the student therapist should be able to do the following:

- Explain the relationships between heart rate, stroke volume, cardiac output, and rate of oxygen use.
- Describe the function of the heart, blood vessels, and lungs in oxygen transport.
- Describe the oxygen transport system and the concept of maximal rate of oxygen use.
- Describe the principles of continuous and interval training and the potential of each technique for improving aerobic activity.
- Describe the difference between aerobic and anaerobic activity.

Although strength and flexibility are commonly regarded as essential components in any injury rehabilitation program, often relatively little consideration is given toward maintaining aerobic capacity and cardiorespiratory endurance. When musculoskeletal injury occurs, the patient is forced to decrease physical activity and levels of cardiorespiratory endurance may decrease rapidly. Thus the therapist must design or substitute alternative activities that allow the individual to maintain existing levels of aerobic capacity during the rehabilitation period.

By definition, **cardiorespiratory endurance** is the ability to perform whole-body activities for extended periods of time without undue fatigue.[10,15] The cardiorespiratory system provides a means by which oxygen is supplied to the various tissues of the body. Without oxygen the cells within the human body cannot possibly function, and ultimately death will occur. Thus the cardiorespiratory system is the basic life-support system of the body.[10]

TRAINING EFFECTS ON THE CARDIORESPIRATORY SYSTEM

Basically, transport of oxygen throughout the body involves the coordinated function of four components: (1) heart, (2) blood vessels, (3) blood, and (4) lungs. The improvement of cardiorespiratory endurance through training occurs because of increased capability of each of these four elements in providing necessary oxygen to the working tissues.[42] A basic discussion of the training effects and response to exercise that occur in the heart, blood vessels, blood, and lungs should make it easier to understand why the training techniques to be discussed later are effective in improving cardiorespiratory endurance.

Adaptation of the Heart to Exercise

The heart is the main pumping mechanism and circulates oxygenated blood throughout the body to the working tissues. The heart receives deoxygenated blood from the venous system and then pumps the blood through the pulmonary vessels to the lungs, where carbon dioxide is exchanged for oxygen. The oxygenated blood then returns to the heart, from which it exits through the aorta to the arterial system and is circulated throughout the body, supplying oxygen to the tissues.

HEART RATE

As the body begins to exercise, the muscles use the oxygen at a much higher rate, and the heart must pump more oxygenated blood to meet this increased demand. The heart is capable of adapting to this increased demand through several mechanisms. **Heart rate** shows a gradual adaptation to an increased workload by increasing proportionally to the intensity of the exercise, and will plateau at a given level after about 2 to 3 minutes (Fig. 6-1).

Monitoring heart rate is an indirect method of estimating oxygen consumption.[15] In general, heart rate and oxygen consumption have a linear relationship, although at very low intensities as well as at high intensities this linear relationship breaks

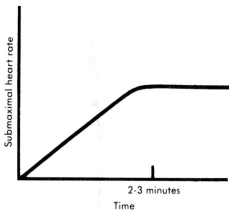

F I G U R E   6 - 1

Plateau heart rate. For the heart rate to plateau at a given level, 2 to 3 minutes are required.

down (Fig. 6-2). During higher-intensity activities, maximal heart rate may be achieved before maximum oxygen consumption, which will continue to rise.[31] The greater the intensity of the exercise, the higher the heart rate. Because of these existing relationships, it should become apparent that the rate of oxygen consumption can be estimated by taking the heart rate.[12]

STROKE VOLUME

A second mechanism by which the heart is able to adapt to increased demands during exercise is to increase the **stroke volume,** the volume of blood being pumped out with each beat. The heart pumps out approximately 70 mL of blood per beat. Stroke volume can continue to increase only to the point at which there is simply not enough time between beats for the heart to fill up. This occurs at about 40 to 50 percent of maximal aerobic capacity, or at a heart rate of 110 to 120 beats per minute; above this level, increases in the volume of blood being pumped out per unit of time must be caused entirely by increases in heart rate (Fig. 6-3).[11]

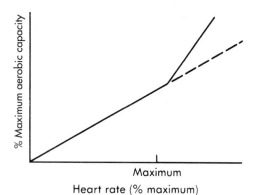

F I G U R E   6 - 2

Maximum heart rate. Maximum heart rate is achieved at about the same time as maximal aerobic capacity.

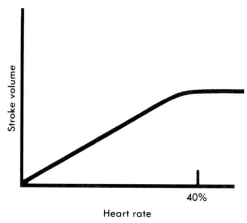

F I G U R E   6 - 3

Stroke volume plateaus. Stroke volume plateaus at about 40 percent of maximal heart rate.

CARDIAC OUTPUT

Stroke volume and heart rate collectively determine the volume of blood being pumped through the heart in a given unit of time. Approximately 5 L of blood are pumped through the heart during each minute at rest. This is referred to as the **cardiac output,** which indicates how much blood the heart is capable of pumping in exactly 1 minute. Thus cardiac output is the primary determinant of the maximal rate of oxygen consumption possible (Fig. 6-4). During exercise, cardiac output increases to approximately four times that experienced during rest (to about 20 L) in the normal individual and may increase as much as six times in the elite endurance athlete (to about 30 L).

$$\text{Cardiac output} = \text{Stroke volume} \times \text{Heart rate}$$

A training effect that occurs with regard to cardiac output of the heart is that the stroke volume increases while the exercise heart rate is reduced at a given standard exercise load. The heart becomes more efficient because it is capable of pumping more

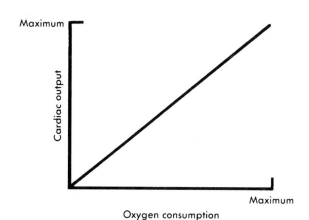

F I G U R E   6 - 4

Cardiac output limits maximal aerobic capacity.

blood with each stroke. Because the heart is a muscle, it will hypertrophy, or increase in size and strength, to some extent, but this is in no way a negative effect of training.

Training Effect

Increased stroke volume $\times$ Decreased heart rate $=$ Cardiac output

During exercise, females tend to have a 5 to 10 percent higher cardiac output than males do at all intensities. This is likely due to a lower concentration of hemoglobin in the female, which is compensated for during exercise by an increased cardiac output.[45]

ADAPTATION IN BLOOD FLOW

The amount of blood flowing to the various organs increases during exercise. However, there is a change in overall distribution of cardiac output; the percentage of total cardiac output to the nonessential organs is decreased, whereas it is increased to active skeletal muscle. Volume of blood flow to the heart muscle or myocardium increases substantially during exercise, even though the percentage of total cardiac output supplying the heart muscle remains unchanged. In skeletal muscle, there is increased formation of blood vessels or capillaries, although it is not clear whether new ones form or dormant ones simply open up and fill with blood.[38]

The total peripheral resistance is the sum of all forces that resist blood flow within the vascular system. Total peripheral resistance decreases during exercise primarily because of vessel vasodilation in the active skeletal muscles.

BLOOD PRESSURE

Blood pressure in the arterial system is determined by the cardiac output in relation to total peripheral resistance to blood flow. Blood pressure is created by contraction of the heart muscle. Contraction of the ventricles of the heart creates systolic pressure, and relaxation of the heart creates diastolic pressure. During exercise, there is a decrease in total peripheral resistance and an increase in cardiac output. Systolic pressure increases in proportion to oxygen consumption and cardiac output while diastolic pressure shows little or no increase.[5] Blood pressure falls below preexercise levels after exercise and may stay low for several hours. There is general agreement that engaging in consistent aerobic exercise will produce modest reductions in both systolic and diastolic blood pressure at rest as well as during submaximal exercise.[14]

ADAPTATIONS IN THE BLOOD

Oxygen is transported throughout the system bound to **hemoglobin.** Found in red blood cells, hemoglobin is an iron-containing protein that has the capability of easily accepting or giving up molecules of oxygen as needed. Training for improvement of cardiorespiratory endurance produces an increase in total blood volume, with a corresponding increase in the

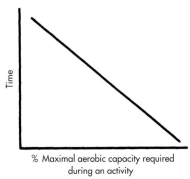

FIGURE 6-5

Maximal aerobic capacity required during activity. The greater the percentage of maximal aerobic capacity required during an activity, the less time that activity can be performed.

amount of hemoglobin. The concentration of hemoglobin in circulating blood does not change with training; it may actually decrease slightly.

ADAPTATION OF THE LUNGS

As a result of training, pulmonary function is improved in the trained individual relative to the untrained individual. The volume of air that can be inspired in a single maximal ventilation is increased. The diffusing capacity of the lungs is also increased, facilitating the exchange of oxygen and carbon dioxide. Pulmonary resistance to air flow is also decreased.[29] Figure 6-5 summarizes the effects of training on the cardiorespiratory system.

MAXIMAL AEROBIC CAPACITY

The maximal amount of oxygen that can be used during exercise is referred to as **maximal aerobic capacity** (exercise physiologists refer to this as $\dot{V}O_2$ max). It is considered to be the best indicator of the level of cardiorespiratory endurance. Maximal aerobic capacity is most often presented in terms of the volume of oxygen used relative to body weight per unit of time ($mL \times kg^{-1} \times min^{-1}$).[3] A normal maximal aerobic capacity for most collegiate men and women would fall in the range of 35 to 50 $mL \times kg^{-1} \times min^{-1}$.[31]

Rate of Oxygen Consumption

The performance of any activity requires a certain rate of oxygen consumption, which is about the same for all persons, depending on their present level of fitness. Generally the greater the rate or intensity of the performance of an activity, the greater will be the oxygen consumption. Each person has his or her own maximal rate of oxygen consumption. That person's ability to perform an activity is closely related to the amount of oxygen required by that activity. This ability is limited by the maximal amount of oxygen the person is capable of delivering into the lungs. Fatigue occurs when insufficient oxygen is supplied to muscles. It should be apparent that the greater percentage of maximal aerobic capacity required during an activity, the less time the activity may be performed (see Fig. 6-5).

Three factors determine the maximal rate at which oxygen can be used: (1) external respiration, involving the ventilatory process, or pulmonary function; (2) gas transport, which is accomplished by the cardiovascular system (that is, the heart, blood vessels, and blood); and (3) internal respiration, which involves the use of oxygen by the cells to produce energy. Of these three factors the most limiting is generally the ability to transport oxygen through the system; thus the cardiovascular system limits the overall rate of oxygen consumption. A high maximal aerobic capacity within a person's range indicates that all three systems are working well.

Maximal Aerobic Capacity: An Inherited Characteristic

The maximal rate at which oxygen can be used is a genetically determined characteristic; we inherit a certain range of maximal aerobic capacity, and the more active we are, the higher the existing maximal aerobic capacity will be within that range.[37,44] Therefore a training program is capable of increasing maximal aerobic capacity to its highest limit within our range.[44]

FAST-TWITCH VERSUS SLOW-TWITCH MUSCLE FIBERS

The range of maximal aerobic capacity that is inherited is in a large part determined by the metabolic and functional properties of skeletal muscle fibers. As discussed in detail in Chapter 5, there are two distinct types of muscle fibers: **slow-twitch** or **fast-twitch** fibers, each of which has distinctive metabolic as well as contractile capabilities. Because they are relatively fatigue resistant, slow-twitch fibers are associated primarily with long-duration, aerobic-type activities. Fast-twitch fibers are useful in short-term, high-intensity activities, which mainly involve the anaerobic system. In general if a patient has a high ratio of slow-twitch to fast-twitch muscle fibers, he or she will be able to use oxygen more efficiently and thus will have a higher maximal aerobic capacity.

Cardiorespiratory Endurance and Work Ability

Cardiorespiratory endurance plays a critical role in our ability to carry out normal daily activities.[35] Fatigue is closely related to the percentage of maximal aerobic capacity that a particular workload demands.[43] For example, Figure 6-6 presents two people, A and B. A has maximal aerobic capacity of 50 mL/kg per minute, whereas B has a maximal aerobic capacity of only 40 mL/kg per minute. If both A and B are exercising at the same intensity, then A will be working at a much lower percentage of maximal aerobic capacity than B. Consequently,

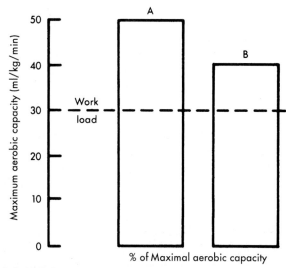

F I G U R E   6 - 6

Patient A should be able to work longer than patient B as a result of a lower percentage use of maximal aerobic capacity.

A should be able to sustain his or her activity over a much longer period of time. Everyday activities may be adversely affected if the ability to use oxygen efficiently is impaired. Thus improvement of cardiorespiratory endurance should be an essential component of any conditioning program and must be included as part of the rehabilitation program for the injured patient.[8]

Regardless of the training technique used for the improvement of cardiorespiratory endurance, one principal goal remains the same: **to increase the ability of the cardiorespiratory system to supply a sufficient amount of oxygen to working muscles.** Without oxygen, the body is incapable of producing energy for an extended period of time.

PRODUCING ENERGY FOR EXERCISE

All living systems need to perform a variety of activities such as growing, generating energy, repairing damaged tissues, and eliminating wastes. All of these activities are referred to as metabolic or cellular **metabolism.**

Muscles are metabolically active and must generate energy to move. Energy is produced from the breakdown of certain nutrients from foodstuffs. This energy is stored in a compound called *adenosine triphosphate (ATP)*, which is the ultimate usable form of energy for muscular activity. ATP is produced in the muscle tissue from blood glucose or glycogen. Fats and proteins can also be metabolized to generate ATP. Glucose not needed immediately is stored as glycogen in the resting muscle and liver. Stored glycogen in the liver can later be converted back to glucose and transferred to the blood to meet the body's energy needs.[6]

If the duration or intensity of the exercise increases, the body relies more heavily on fats stored in adipose tissue to meet its energy needs. The longer the duration of an activity, the greater the amount of fat used, especially during the later stages of endurance events. During rest and submaximal exertion, both fat and carbohydrates are used to provide energy in approximately a 60 to 40 percent ratio. Carbohydrate must be available to use fat. If glycogen is totally depleted, fat cannot be completely metabolized. Regardless of the nutrient source that produces ATP, it is always available in the cell as an immediate energy source. When all available sources of ATP are used, more must be regenerated for muscular contraction to continue.[7,24]

Various sports activities involve specific demands for energy. For example, sprinting and jumping are high-energy-output activities, requiring a relatively large production of energy for a short time. Long-distance running and swimming, on the other hand, are mostly low-energy-output activities per unit of time, requiring energy production for a prolonged time. Other physical activities demand a blend of both high- and low-energy output. These various energy demands can be met by the different processes in which energy can be supplied to the skeletal muscles.[16]

Anaerobic Versus Aerobic Metabolism

Two major energy-generating systems function in muscle tissue: anaerobic and aerobic metabolism. Each of these systems produces ATP.[19] During sudden outbursts of activity in intensive, short-term exercise, ATP can be rapidly metabolized to meet energy needs. After a few seconds of intensive exercise, however, the small stores of ATP are used up. The body then turns to stored glycogen as an energy source. Glycogen can be broken down to supply glucose, which is then metabolized within the muscle cells to generate ATP for muscle contractions.[31]

Glucose can be metabolized to generate small amounts of ATP energy without the need for oxygen. This energy system is referred to as **anaerobic metabolism** (occurring in the absence of oxygen). As exercise continues, the body has to rely on a more complex form of carbohydrate and fat metabolism to generate ATP. This second energy system requires oxygen and is therefore referred to as **aerobic metabolism** (occurring in the presence of oxygen). The aerobic system of producing energy generates considerably more ATP than the anaerobic one.

In most activities, both aerobic and anaerobic systems function simultaneously. The degree to which the two major energy systems are involved is determined by the intensity and duration of the activity.[41] If the intensity of the activity is such that sufficient oxygen can be supplied to meet the demands of working tissues, the activity is considered to be **aerobic**. Conversely, if the activity is of high enough intensity or the duration is such that there is insufficient oxygen available to meet energy demands, the activity becomes **anaerobic**.[45]

EXCESS POSTEXERCISE OXYGEN CONSUMPTION (OXYGEN DEFICIT)

As the intensity of the exercise increases and insufficient amounts of oxygen are available to the tissues, an oxygen deficit is incurred. Oxygen deficit occurs in the beginning of exercise (within the first 2 to 3 minutes) when the oxygen demand is greater than the oxygen supplied. It was been hypothesized that this oxygen debt was caused by lactic acid produced during anaerobic activity and that this debt must be "paid back" during the postexercise period. However, there is presently a different rationale for this oxygen deficit, which is currently referred to as "excess postexercise oxygen consumption." It is theoretically caused by disturbances in mitochondrial function from an increase in temperature.[31]

TECHNIQUES FOR MAINTAINING CARDIORESPIRATORY ENDURANCE

There are several different training techniques that may be incorporated into a rehabilitation program through which cardiorespiratory endurance can be maintained. Certainly, a primary consideration for the therapist would be whether the injury involves the upper or lower extremity. With injuries that involve the upper extremity, weight-bearing activities can be used, such as walking, running, stair climbing, and modified aerobics. However, if the injury is to the lower extremity, alternative nonweight-bearing activities, such as swimming or stationary cycling, may be necessary. The goal of the therapist is to try to maintain a cardiorespiratory endurance throughout the rehabilitation process.

The principles of the training techniques discussed below can be applied with running, cycling, swimming, stair climbing, or any other activity designed to maintain levels of cardiorespiratory fitness.

Continuous Training

Continuous training involves the following considerations:

- The **F**requency of the activity.
- The **I**ntensity of the activity.
- The **T**ype of activity.
- The **T**ime (duration) of the activity.

FREQUENCY OF TRAINING

To see at least minimal improvement in cardiorespiratory endurance, it is necessary for the average person to engage in no less than three sessions per week. A competitive athlete should be prepared to train as often as six times per week. Everyone should take off at least one day per week to give damaged tissues a chance to repair themselves.

INTENSITY OF TRAINING

The intensity of exercise is also a critical factor, though recommendations regarding training intensities vary.[22] This statement is particularly true in the early stages of training, when the body is forced to make a lot of adjustments to increased workload demands. Because heart rate is linearly related to the intensity of the exercise and to the rate of oxygen consumption, it becomes a relatively simple process to identify a specific workload (pace) that will make the heart rate plateau at the desired level.[40] By monitoring heart rate, we know whether the pace is too fast or too slow to get the heart rate into a target range.[27]

Monitoring Heart Rate

There are several points at which heart rate is easily measured. The most reliable is the radial artery. The carotid artery is simple to find, especially during exercise. However, there are pressure receptors located in the carotid artery that if subjected to hard pressure from the two fingers will slow down the heart rate, giving a false indication of exactly what the heart rate is. Thus the pulse at the radial artery proves the most accurate measure of heart rate. Regardless of where the heart rate is taken, it should be monitored within 15 seconds after stopping exercise. Another factor must be considered when measuring heart rate during exercise. The patient is trying to elevate heart rate to a specific target rate and maintain it at that level during the entire workout.[20] Heart rate can be increased or decreased by speeding up or slowing down the pace. It has already been indicated that heart rate increases proportionately with the intensity of the workload and will plateau after 2 to 3 minutes of activity. Thus the patient should be actively engaged in the workout for 2 to 3 minutes before measuring pulse.[47]

There are several formulas that will easily allow the therapist to identify a target training heart rate.[39] Exact determination of maximal heart rate involves exercising a patient at a maximal level and monitoring the heart rate using an electrocardiogram. This process is difficult outside of a laboratory. However, an approximate estimate of maximal heart rate (MHR) for both males and females in the population is thought to be about 220 beats per minute.[36] MHR is related to age. With aging, MHR decreases.[28] Thus a relatively simple estimate of MHR would be MHR = 220 – age. For a 40-year-old patient, MHR would be about 180 beats per minute (220 − 40 = 180). If you are interested in working at 70 percent of your maximal heart rate, the target heart rate can be calculated by multiplying 0.7 × (220 − age). Again using a 40-year-old as an example, a target heart rate would be 126 beats per minute (0.7 × [220 − 40] = 126).

Another commonly used formula that takes into account your current level of fitness is the Karvonen equation[23,25]:

$$\text{Target training HR} = \text{Resting HR} + (0.6\,[\text{Maximum HR} - \text{Resting HR}])$$

Resting heart rate generally falls between 60 and 80 beats per minute. A 40-year-old patient with a resting pulse of 70 beats per minute, according to the Karvonen equation, would have a target training heart rate of 136 beats per minute (70 + 0.6 [180 − 70] = 136).

Regardless of the formula used, to see minimal improvement in cardiorespiratory endurance, the patient must train with the heart rate elevated to at least 60 percent of its maximal rate.[1,21,26] Exercising at a 70 percent level is considered moderate, because activity can be continued for a long period of time with little discomfort and still produce a training effect.[32] In a trained individual it is not difficult to sustain a heart rate at the 85 percent level.[13]

Rating of Perceived Exertion

Rating of perceived exertion (RPE) can be used in addition to monitoring heart rate to indicate exercise intensity.[4] During exercise, individuals are asked to rate subjectively on a numerical scale from 6 to 20 exactly how they feel relative to their level of exertion (Table 6-1). More intense exercise that requires a higher level of oxygen consumption and energy expenditure is directly related to higher subjective ratings of perceived exertion. Over a period of time, patients can be taught to exercise at a specific RPE that relates directly to more objective measures of exercise intensity.[18,33]

TYPE OF EXERCISE

The type of activity used in continuous training must be aerobic. Aerobic activities are activities that generally involve repetitive, whole-body, large-muscle movements that are rhythmical in nature and that use large amounts of oxygen, elevate the

T A B L E   6 - 1

Rating of Perceived Exertion

SCALE	VERBAL RATING
6	
7	Very, very light
8	
9	Very light
10	
11	Fairly light
12	
13	Somewhat hard
14	
15	Hard
16	
17	Very hard
18	
19	Very, very hard
20	

SOURCE: Borg GA. Psychophysical basis of perceived exertion. *Med Sci Sports Exerc* 14:377, 1982.

heart rate, and maintain it at that level for an extended period of time. Examples of aerobic activities are walking, running, jogging, cycling, swimming, rope skipping, stepping, aerobic dance exercise, roller blading, and cross-country skiing.

The advantage of these aerobic activities as opposed to more intermittent activities—such as racquetball, squash, basketball, or tennis—is that aerobic activities are easy to regulate in intensity by either speeding up or slowing down the pace.[30] Because we already know that a given intensity of the workload elicits a given heart rate, these aerobic activities allow us to maintain heart rate at a specified or target level. Intermittent activities involve variable speeds and intensities that cause the heart rate to fluctuate considerably. Although these intermittent activities will improve cardiorespiratory endurance, they are much more difficult to monitor in terms of intensity. It is important to point out that any type of activity, from gardening to aerobic exercise, can improve fitness.[34]

TIME (DURATION)

For minimal improvement to occur, the patient must participate in at least 20 minutes of continuous activity with the heart rate elevated to its working level. The American College of Sports Medicine (ACSM) recommends 20 to 60 minutes of workout/activity with the heart rate elevated to training levels.[3] Generally, the greater the duration of the workout, the greater the improvement in cardiorespiratory endurance.

Interval Training

Unlike continuous training, **interval training** involves activities that are more intermittent. Interval training consists of alternating periods of relatively intense work and active recovery. It allows for performance of much more work at a more intense workload over a longer period of time than if working continuously. We have stated that it is most desirable in continuous training to work at an intensity of about 60 to 80 percent of maximal heart rate. Obviously, sustaining activity at a relatively high intensity over a 20-minute period would be extremely difficult. The advantage of interval training is that it allows work at this 80 percent or higher level for a short period of time followed by an active period of recovery during which you may be working at only 30 to 45 percent of maximal heart rate. Thus the intensity of the workout and its duration can be greater than with continuous training.

There are several important considerations in interval training. The training period is the amount of time that continuous activity is actually being performed, and the recovery period is the time between training periods. A set is a group of combined training and recovery periods, and a repetition is the number of training/recovery periods per set. Training time or distance refers to the rate or distance of the training period. The training/recovery ratio indicates a time ratio for training versus recovery.

An example of interval training would be a patient exercising on a stationary bike. An interval workout would involve ten repetitions of pedaling at a maximum speed for 20 seconds followed by pedaling at 40 percent of maximum speed for 90 seconds. During this interval training session, heart rate would probably increase to 85 to 95 percent of maximal level while pedaling at maximum speed, and should probably fall to the 35 to 45 percent level during the recovery period.

Older adults should exercise some caution when using interval training as a method for improving cardiorespiratory endurance. The intensity levels attained during the active periods may be too high for the older adult.

COMBINING CONTINUOUS AND INTERVAL TRAINING

As indicated previously, most physical activities involve some combination of aerobic and anaerobic metabolism.[46] Continuous training is generally done at an intensity level that primarily uses the aerobic system. In interval training, the intensity is sufficient to necessitate a greater percentage of anaerobic metabolism.[17] Therefore for the physically active patient, the therapist should incorporate both training techniques into a rehabilitation program to maximize cardiorespiratory fitness.

SUMMARY

- The therapist should routinely incorporate activities that will help maintain levels of cardiorespiratory endurance into the rehabilitation program.
- Cardiorespiratory endurance involves the coordinated function of the heart, lungs, blood, and blood vessels to supply sufficient amounts of oxygen to the working tissues.
- The best indicator of how efficiently the cardiorespiratory system functions is the maximal rate at which oxygen can be used by the tissues.
- Heart rate is directly related to the rate of oxygen consumption. It is therefore possible to predict the intensity of the work in terms of a rate of oxygen use by monitoring heart rate.
- Aerobic exercise involves an activity in which the level of intensity and duration is low enough to provide a sufficient amount of oxygen to supply the demands of the working tissues.
- In anaerobic exercise, the intensity of the activity is so high that oxygen is being used more quickly than it can be supplied; thus an oxygen debt is incurred that must be repaid before working tissue can return to its normal resting state.
- Continuous or sustained training for maintenance of cardiorespiratory endurance involves selecting an activity that is aerobic in nature and training at least three times per week for a time period of no less than 20 minutes with the heart rate elevated to at least 60 percent of maximal rate.
- Interval training involves alternating periods of relatively intense work followed by active recovery periods. Interval training allows performance of more work at a relatively higher workload than continuous training.

REFERENCES

1. American College of Sports Medicine. *Guidelines for Exercise Testing and Prescription*. Philadelphia, Lea & Febiger, 1995.

2. Åstrand PO, Rodahl K. *Textbook of Work Physiology*. New York, McGraw-Hill, 1986.

3. Åstrand PO. Åstrand-rhyming nomogram for calculation of aerobic capacity from pulse rate during submaximal work. *J Appl Physiol* 7:218, 1954.

4. Borg GA. Psychophysical basis of perceived exertion. *Med Sci Sports Exerc* 14:377, 1982.

5. Brooks G, Fahey T, White T. *Exercise Physiology: Human Bioenergetics and Its Applications*. Mountain View, CA, Mayfield, 1996.

6. Brooks G, Mercier J. The balance of carbohydrate and lipid utilization during exercise: The crossover concept. *J App Physiol* 76:2253–2261, 1994.

7. Cerretelli P. Energy sources for muscle contraction. *Sports Med* 13:S106–S110, 1992.

8. Chillag SA. Endurance patients: Physiologic changes and nonorthopedic problems. *South Med J* 79:1264, 1986. Review.

9. Convertino VA. Aerobic fitness, endurance training, and orthostatic intolerance. *Exerc Sport Sci Rev* 15:223, 1987. Review.

10. Cooper KH. *The Aerobics Program for Total Well-Being*. New York, Bantam Books, 1982.

11. Cox M. Exercise training programs and cardiorespiratory adaptation. *Clin Sports Med* 10:19–32, 1991.

12. deVries H. *Physiology of Exercise for Physical Education and Athletics*. Dubuque, IA, William C. Brown, 1986.

13. Dicarlo L, Sparling P, Millard-Stafford M. Peak heart rates during maximal running and swimming: Implications for exercise prescription. *Int J Sports Ed* 12:309–312, 1991.

14. Durstein L, Pate R, Branch D. Cardiorespiratory responses to acute exercise. In: American College of Sports Medicine. *Resource Manual for Guidelines for Exercise Testing and Prescription*. Philadelphia, Lea & Febiger, 1993.

15. Fahey T, ed. *Encyclopedia of Sports Medicine and Exercise Physiology*. New York, Garland, 1995.

16. Fox E, Bowers R, Foss M. *The Physiological Basis of Physical Education and Athletics*. Philadelphia, Saunders, 1981.

17. Gaesser GA, Wilson LA. Effects of continuous and interval training on the parameters of the power–endurance time relationship for high-intensity exercise. *Int J Sports Med* 9:417, 1988.

18. Glass S, Whaley M, Wegner M. A comparison between ratings of percieved exertion among standard protocols and steady state running. *Int J Sports Ed* 12:77–82, 1991.

19. Green J, Patla A. Maximal aerobic power: Neuromuscular

and metabolic considerations. *Med Sci Sport Exerc* 24:38–46, 1992.

20. Greer N, Katch F. Validity of palpation recovery pulse rate to estimate exercise heart rate following four intensities of bench step exercise. *Res Q Exerc Sport* 53:340, 1982.

21. Hage P. Exercise guidelines: Which to believe? *Phys Sports Med* 10:23, 1982.

22. Hawley J, Myburgh K, Noakes T. Maximal oxygen consumption: A contemporary perspective. In: Fahey T, ed. *Encyclopedia of Sports Medicine and Exercise Physiology*. New York, Garland, 1995.

23. Hickson RC, Foster C, Pollac M, et al. Reduced training intensities and loss of aerobic power, endurance, and cardiac growth. *J Appl Physiol* 58:492, 1985.

24. Honig C, Connett R, Gayeski T. O_2 transport and its interaction with metabolism. *Med Sci Sports Exerc* 24:47–53, 1992.

25. Karvonen MJ, Kentala E, Mustala O. The effects of training on heart rate: A longitudinal study. *Ann Med Exp Biol* 35:305, 1957.

26. Koyanagi A, Yamamoto K, Nishijima K. Recommendation for an exercise perscription to prevent coronary heart disease. *Ed Syst* 17:213–217, 1993.

27. Levine G, Balady G. The benefits and risks of exercise testing: The exercise prescription. *Adv Intern Ed* 38:57–79, 1993.

28. Londeree B, Moeschberger M. Effect of age and other factors on maximal heart rate. *Res Q Exerc Sport* 53:297, 1982.

29. MacDougall D, Sale D. Continuous vs. interval training: A review for the patient and coach. *Can J Appl Sport Sci* 6:93, 1981.

30. Marcinik EJ, Hogden K, Mittleman K, et al. Aerobic/calisthenic and aerobic/circuit weight training programs for Navy men: A comparative study. *Med Sci Sports Exerc* 17:482, 1985.

31. McArdle W, Katch F, Katch V. *Exercise Physiology, Energy, Nutrition, and Human Performance*. Philadelphia, Lea & Febiger, 1994.

32. Mead W, Hartwig R. Fitness evaluation and exercise prescription. *Fam Pract* 13:1039, 1981.

33. Monahan T. Perceived exertion: An old exercise tool finds new applications. *Phys Sports Med* 16:174, 1988.

34. Pate R, Pratt M, Blair S. Physical activity and public health: A recommendation from the CDC and ACSM. *JAMA* 273:402–407, 1995.

35. Powers S. Fundamentals of exercise metabolism. In: American College of Sports Medicine. *Resource Manual for Guidelines for Exercise Testing and Prescription*. Philadelphia, Lea & Febiger, 1993.

36. Rowland TW, Green GM. Anaerobic threshold and the determination of training target heart rates in premenarcheal girls. *Pediatr Cardiol* 10:75, 1989.

37. Saltin B, Strange S. Maximal oxygen uptake: Old and new arguments for a cardiovascular limitation. *Med Sci Sports Exerc* 24:30–37, 1992.

38. Smith M, Mitchell J. Cardiorespiratory adaptations to exercise training. In: American College of Sports Medicine. *Resource Manual for Guidelines for Exercise Testing and Prescription.* Philadelphia, Lea & Febiger, 1993.

39. Stachenfeld N, Eskenazi M, Gleim G. Predictive accuracy of criteria used to assess maximal oxygen consumption. *Am Heart J* 123:922–925, 1992.

40. Swain D, Abernathy K, Smith C. Target heart rates for the development of cardiorespiratory fitness. *Med Sci Sports Exerc* 26:112–116, 1994.

41. Vago P, Mercier M, Ramonatxo M, et al. Is ventilatory anaerobic threshold a good index of endurance capacity? *Int J Sports Med* 8:190, 1987.

42. Wagner P. Central and peripheral aspects of oxygen transport and adaptations with exercise. *Sports Med* 11:133–142, 1991.

43. Weltman A, Weltman J, Ruh R, et al. Percentage of maximal heart rate reserve, and $\dot{V}O_2$ peak for determining endurance training intensity in sedentary women. *Int J Sports Med* 10:212, 1989. Review.

44. Weymans M, Reybrouck T. Habitual level of physical activity and cardiorespiratory endurance capacity in children. *Eur J Appl Physiol* 58:803, 1989.

45. Williford H, Scharff-Olson M, Blessing D. Exercise prescription for women: Special considerations. *Sports Ed* 15:299–311, 1993.

46. Wilmore J, Costill D. *Physiology of Sport and Exercise.* Champaign, IL, Human Kinetics, 1994.

47. Zhang Y, Johnson M, Chow N. Effect of exercise testing protocol on parameters of aerobic function. *Med Sci Sports Exerc* 23:625–630, 1991.

CHAPTER 7

Impaired Mobility: Restoring Range of Motion and Improving Flexibility

William E. Prentice

OBJECTIVES

After completing this chapter, the student therapist should be able to do the following:

- Define flexibility and describe its importance in injury rehabilitation.
- Identify factors that limit flexibility.
- Differentiate between active and passive range of motion.
- Explain the difference between ballistic, static, and PNF stretching.
- Discuss the neurophysiologic principles of stretching.
- Describe stretching exercises that may be used to improve flexibility at specific joints throughout the body.

When injury occurs, there is almost always some associated loss of the ability to move normally. Loss of motion may be due to pain, swelling, muscle guarding, or spasm; inactivity resulting in shortening of connective tissue and muscle; loss of neuromuscular control; or some combination of these factors. Restoring normal range of motion following injury is one of the primary goals in any rehabilitation program.[66] Thus the therapist must routinely include stretching exercises designed to restore normal range of motion to regain normal function.

Flexibility has been defined as the ability to move a joint or series of joints through a full, nonrestricted, pain-free range of motion.[1,2,18,27,31,48,59] Flexibility is dependent on a combination of (1) joint range of motion, which may be limited by the shape of the articulating surfaces and by capsular and ligamentous structures surrounding that joint; and (2) muscle flexibility, or the ability of the musculotendinous unit to lengthen.[67] In this chapter we will concentrate primarily on rehabilitative stretching techniques used to increase the length of the musculotendinous unit. Loss of the ability to control movement due to impairment in neuromuscular control will be discussed in Chapter 8. Joint mobilization and traction techniques used to address tightness in the joint capsule and surrounding ligaments will be discussed in Chapter 15.

IMPORTANCE OF FLEXIBILITY TO THE PATIENT

For the therapist, the restoration of, or improvement in, normal preinjury range of motion is an important goal of any rehabilitation program.[57,65] Most activities of daily living require relatively "normal" amounts of flexibility. However, some sport-related activities, such as gymnastics, ballet, diving, or karate, require increased flexibility for superior performance (Fig. 7-1). A patient who has a restricted range of motion will probably realize a decrease in performance capabilities.[10] Lack of flexibility may also result in uncoordinated or awkward movement patterns.

Most therapists would agree that good flexibility is essential for normal movement. Likewise, they also believe that maintaining good flexibility is important in prevention of injury to the musculotendinous unit. They will generally insist that stretching exercises be included as part of the warm-up before engaging in strenuous activity,[16,42,52] although little or no research evidence is available to support this practice.

Flexibility can be discussed in relation to movement involving only one joint, such as the knees, or movement involving a whole series of joints, such as the spinal vertebral joints, which

FIGURE   7 - 1

Some sport activities require superior levels of flexibility.

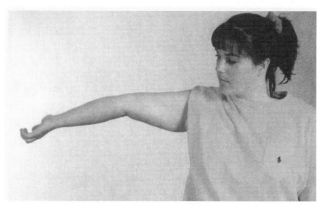

FIGURE   7 - 2

Excessive joint motion, such as the hyperextended elbow, can predispose a joint to injury.

must all move together to allow smooth bending or rotation of the trunk. Flexibility is specific to a given joint or movement. A person may have good range of motion in the ankles, knees, hips, back, and one shoulder joint. If the other shoulder joint lacks normal movement, however, then a problem exists that needs to be corrected before the person can function normally.[9]

ANATOMIC FACTORS THAT LIMIT FLEXIBILITY

A number of anatomic factors may limit the ability of a joint to move through a full, unrestricted range of motion. **Muscles and their tendons,** along with their surrounding fascial sheaths, are most often responsible for limiting range of motion. When performing stretching exercises to improve flexibility about a particular joint, you are attempting to take advantage of the highly elastic properties of a muscle. Over time it is possible to increase the elasticity, or the length that a given muscle can be stretched. Persons who have a good deal of movement at a particular joint tend to have highly elastic and flexible muscles.

Connective tissue surrounding the joint, such as ligaments on the joint capsule, may be subject to **contractures.** Ligaments and joint capsules have some elasticity; however, if a joint is immobilized for a period of time, these structures tend to lose some elasticity and actually shorten. This condition is most commonly seen after surgical repair of an unstable joint, but it can also result from long periods of inactivity.

It is also possible for a person to have relatively slack ligaments and joint capsules. These people are generally referred to as being loose-jointed. Examples of this trait would be an elbow or knee that hyperextends beyond 180 degrees (Fig. 7-2). Frequently there is instability associated with loose-jointedness that may present as great a problem in movement as ligamentous or capsular contractures.

Bony structure may restrict the endpoint in the range. An elbow that has been fractured through the joint may lay down excess calcium in the joint space, causing the joint to lose its ability to fully extend. However, in many instances we rely on bony prominences to stop movements at normal endpoints in the range.

Fat may also limit the ability to move through a full range of motion. A person who has a large amount of fat on the abdomen may have severely restricted trunk flexion when asked to bend forward and touch the toes. The fat may act as a wedge between two lever arms, restricting movement wherever it is found.

Skin might also be responsible for limiting movement. For example, a person who has had some type of injury or surgery involving a tearing incision or laceration of the skin, particularly over a joint, will have inelastic scar tissue formed at that site. This scar tissue is incapable of stretching with joint movement.

Over time, skin contractures caused by scarring of ligaments, joint capsules, and musculotendinous units are each capable of improving elasticity to varying degrees through stretching. With the exception of bone structure, age, and gender, all the other factors that limit flexibility may be altered to increase range of joint motion.

ACTIVE AND PASSIVE RANGE OF MOTION

Active range of motion, also called *dynamic flexibility,* refers to the degree to which a joint can be moved by a muscle contraction, usually through the midrange of movement. Dynamic flexibility is not necessarily a good indicator of the stiffness or looseness of a joint because it applies to the ability to move a joint efficiently, with little resistance to motion.[25]

Passive range of motion, sometimes called *static flexibility,* refers to the degree to which a joint may be passively moved to the endpoints in the range of motion. No muscle contraction is involved to move a joint through a passive range.

When a muscle actively contracts, it produces a joint movement through a specific range of motion.[48,56] However, if passive pressure is applied to an extremity, it is capable of moving farther in the range of motion.

Passive range of motion is important for injury prevention. If a muscle is forced to stretch beyond its normal active limits and there is not enough elasticity to compensate for this additional stretch, it is likely that the musculotendinous unit will be injured.

Assessment of Active and Passive Range of Motion

Accurate measurement of active and passive range of joint motion is difficult.[28] Various devices have been designed to accommodate variations in the size of the joints, as well as the complexity of movements in articulations that involve more than one joint.[30] Of these devices, the simplest and most widely used is the **goniometer** (Fig. 7-3).

A goniometer is a large protractor with measurements in degrees. By aligning the individual arms of the goniometer parallel to the longitudinal axis of the two segments involved in motion about a specific joint, it is possible to obtain reasonably

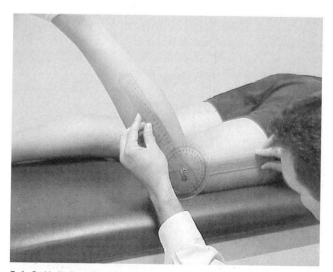

FIGURE 7 - 3

Goniometric measurement. Measurement of active knee joint flexion using a goniometer.

TABLE 7 - 1

Active Ranges of Joint Motions

JOINT	ACTION	DEGREES OF MOTION
Shoulder	Flexion	0–180
	Extension	0–50
	Abduction	0–180
	Medial rotation	0–90
	Lateral rotation	0–90
Elbow	Flexion	0–160
Forearm	Pronation	0–90
	Supination	0–90
Wrist	Flexion	0–90
	Extension	0–70
	Abduction	0–25
	Adduction	0–65
Hip	Flexion	0–125
	Extension	0–15
	Abduction	0–45
	Adduction	0–15
	Medial rotation	0–45
	Lateral rotation	0–45
Knee	Flexion	0–140
Ankle	Plantarflexion	0–45
	Dorsiflexion	0–20
Foot	Inversion	0–30
	Eversion	0–10

accurate measurement of range of movement. To enhance reliability, standardization of measurement techniques and methods of recording active and passive ranges of motion are critical in individual clinics where successive measurements may be taken by different therapists to assess progress. Table 7-1 provides a list of what would be considered normal active ranges for movements at various joints.

The goniometer has an important place in a rehabilitation setting, where it is essential to assess improvement in joint flexibility to modify injury rehabilitation programs.

STRETCHING TECHNIQUES

Flexibility has been defined as the range of motion possible about a single joint or through a series of articulations. The maintenance of a full, nonrestricted range of motion has long been recognized as an essential component of a rehabilitation program.[11–13] Flexibility is important not only for normal movement but also for the prevention of injury.[2,7,8,43,60] The goal of any effective flexibility program should be to improve the range of motion at a given articulation by altering the extensibility of the musculotendinous units that produce movement at that joint. It is well documented that exercises that stretch these musculotendinous units over time will increase the range of movement possible about a given joint.[23,45]

Stretching techniques for improving flexibility have evolved over the years.[33] The oldest technique for stretching is called **ballistic stretching,** which makes use of repetitive bouncing motions. A second technique, known as **static stretching,** involves stretching a muscle to the point of discomfort and then holding it at that point for an extended time. This technique has been used for many years. More recently, another group of stretching techniques known collectively as **proprioceptive neuromuscular facilitation (PNF)** techniques, involving alternating contractions and stretches, has also been recommended.[34,62] Researchers have had considerable discussion about which of these techniques is most effective for improving range of motion, although no clearcut consensus currently exists.[23,37,45,49,63]

Agonist Versus Antagonist Muscles

Before discussing the three different stretching techniques, it is essential to define the terms **agonist** and **antagonist muscles.** Most joints in the body are capable of more than one movement. The knee joint, for example, is capable of flexion, extension, and rotation. Contraction of the quadriceps group of muscles on the front of the thigh causes knee extension, whereas contraction of the hamstring muscles on the back of the thigh produces knee flexion.

To achieve knee extension, the quadriceps group contracts while the hamstring muscles relax and stretch. Muscles that work in concert with one another in this manner are called **synergistic** muscle groups.[5] The muscle that contracts to produce a movement, in this case the quadriceps, is referred to as the **agonist** muscle. Conversely, the muscle being stretched in response to contraction of the agonist muscle is called the **antagonist** muscle.[21] In this example of knee extension, the antagonist muscle would be the hamstring group. Some degree of balance in strength must exist between agonist and antagonist muscle groups. This balance is necessary for normal, smooth, coordinated movement, as well as for reducing the likelihood of muscle strain caused by muscular imbalance. Comprehension of this synergistic muscle action is essential to understanding the three techniques of stretching.

Ballistic Stretching

If you were to walk out to a jogging track on any spring or fall afternoon and watch people who are warming up with stretching exercises before they run, you would probably see them use bouncing movements to stretch a particular muscle. This bouncing technique is more appropriately known as ballistic stretching, in which repetitive contractions of the agonist muscle are used to produce quick stretches of the antagonist muscle.

Over the years, many fitness experts have questioned the safety of the ballistic stretching technique.[3,32] Their concerns have been primarily based on the idea that ballistic stretching creates somewhat uncontrolled forces within the muscle that may exceed the extensibility limits of the muscle fiber, thus producing small microtears within the musculotendinous

unit.[19,20,22,41,67] Certainly this may be true in sedentary individuals, or perhaps in patients who have sustained muscle injuries.

Most sports activities are dynamic and require ballistic-type movements. The antagonist hamstrings are contracting eccentrically to decelerate the lower leg. Ballistic stretching of the hamstring muscle before engaging in this type of activity should allow the muscle to gradually adapt to the imposed demands and reduce the likelihood of injury. Because ballistic stretching is more functional, it should be integrated into a reconditioning program for a physically active patient during the later stages of healing when appropriate.

Static Stretching

The static stretching technique is another extremely effective and widely used technique of stretching.[26] This technique involves passively stretching a given antagonist muscle by placing it in a maximal position of stretch and holding it there for an extended time. Recommendations for the optimal time for holding this stretched position vary, ranging from as short as 3 seconds to as long as 60 seconds.[25] Several studies have indicated that holding a stretch for 15 to 30 seconds is the most effective for increasing muscle flexibility.[4,35,38] Stretches lasting for longer than 30 seconds seem to be uncomfortable for the patient. A static stretch of each muscle should be repeated 3 or 4 times. A static stretch may be accomplished by using a contraction of the agonist muscle to place the antagonist muscle in a position of stretch. A passive static stretch requires the use of body weight, assistance from the therapist or partner, or use of a T-bar, primarily for stretching the upper extremity.

Much research has been done comparing ballistic and static stretching techniques for the improvement of flexibility. Static and ballistic stretching appear to be equally effective in increasing flexibility, and there is no significant difference between the two.[20,51] However, much of the literature states that with static stretching there is less danger of exceeding the extensibility limits of the involved joints because the stretch is more controlled. Most of the literature indicates that ballistic stretching is apt to cause muscular soreness, especially in sedentary individuals, whereas static stretching generally does not cause soreness and is commonly used in injury rehabilitation of sore or strained muscles.[19,64] Static stretching is likely a much safer stretching technique, especially for sedentary or untrained individuals. However, because many physical activities involve dynamic movement, stretching in a warm-up should begin with static stretching followed by ballistic stretching, which more closely resembles the dynamic activity.

A progressive velocity flexibility program (PVFP) has been proposed which takes the patient through a series of stretching exercises where the velocity of the stretch and the range of lengthening are progressively controlled.[67] The stretching exercises progress from slow static stretching; to slow, short, end-range stretching; to slow, full-range stretching; to fast, short, end-range stretching; to fast, full-range stretching. This program allows the patient to control both the range and the speed with no assistance from a therapist.

Proprioceptive Neuromuscular Facilitation Stretching Techniques

Proprioceptive neuromuscular facilitation (PNF) techniques were first used by physical therapists for treating patients who had various neuromuscular disorders.[34] More recently, PNF stretching exercises have increasingly been used as a stretching technique for improving flexibility.[17,39,44,47]

There are three different PNF techniques currently being used for stretching, including slow-reversal-hold-relax, contract-relax, and hold-relax techniques.[58] All three techniques involve some combination of alternating isometric or isotonic contractions and relaxation of both agonist and antagonist muscles (a 10-second pushing phase followed by a 10-second relaxing phase).

Contract-relax (CR) is a stretching technique that moves the body part passively into the agonist pattern. The patient is instructed to push by contracting the antagonist (muscle that will be stretched) isotonically against the resistance of the therapist. The patient then relaxes the antagonist while the therapist moves the part passively through as much range as possible to the point where limitation is again felt. This contract-relax technique is beneficial when range of motion is limited by muscle tightness.

Hold-relax (HR) is very similar to the contract-relax technique. It begins with an isometric contraction of the antagonist (muscle that will be stretched) against resistance, followed by a concentric contraction of the agonist muscle combined with light pressure from the therapist to produce maximal stretch of the antagonist. This technique is appropriate for producing muscle tension on one side of a joint and may be used with either the agonist or antagonist.

Slow reversal-hold-relax (SRHR), also occasionally referred to as the *contract-relax-agonist-contraction (CRAC)* technique, begins with an isotonic contraction of the agonist, which often limits range of motion in the agonist pattern, followed by an isometric contraction of the antagonist (muscle that will be stretched) during the push phase. During the relax phase, the antagonists are relaxed while the agonists are contracting, causing movement in the direction of the agonist pattern and thus stretching the antagonist. The technique, like the contract-relax and hold-relax, is useful for increasing range of motion when the primary limiting factor is the antagonistic muscle group.

PNF stretching techniques can be used to stretch any muscle in the body.[14,15,39,41,46,47,49,58,63] PNF stretching techniques are perhaps best performed with a partner, although they may also be done using a wall as resistance.

NEUROPHYSIOLOGIC BASIS OF STRETCHING

All three stretching techniques are based on a neurophysiologic phenomenon involving the **stretch reflex** (see Fig. 13-1).[44] Every muscle in the body contains various types of mechanoreceptors that when stimulated inform the central nervous system

of what is happening with that muscle. Two of these mechanoreceptors are important in the stretch reflex: the **muscle spindle** and the **Golgi tendon organ.** Both types of receptors are sensitive to changes in muscle length. The Golgi tendon organs are also affected by changes in muscle tension.

When a muscle is stretched, both the muscle spindles and Golgi tendon organs immediately begin sending a volley of sensory impulses to the spinal cord. Initially impulses coming from the muscle spindles inform the central nervous system that the muscle is being stretched. Impulses return to the muscle from the spinal cord, which causes the muscle to reflexively contract, thus resisting the stretch.[44] The Golgi tendon organs respond to the change in length and the increase in tension by firing off sensory impulses of their own to the spinal cord. If the stretch of the muscle continues for an extended period of time (at least 6 seconds), impulses from the Golgi tendon organ begin to override muscle spindle impulses. The impulses from the Golgi tendon organs, unlike the signals from the muscle spindle, cause a reflex relaxation of the antagonist muscle. This reflex relaxation serves as a protective mechanism that will allow the muscle to stretch through relaxation before the extensibility limits are exceeded, causing damage to the muscle fibers.[61]

With the jerking, bouncing motion of ballistic stretching, the muscle spindles are being repetitively stretched; thus there is continuous resistance by the muscle to further stretch. The ballistic stretch is not continued long enough to allow the Golgi tendon organs to have a relaxing effect.

The static stretch involves a continuous sustained stretch lasting anywhere from 6 to 60 seconds, which is sufficient time for the Golgi tendon organs to begin responding to the increase in tension. The impulses from the Golgi tendon organs can override the impulses coming from the muscle spindles, allowing the muscle to reflexively relax after the initial reflex resistance to the change in length. Thus lengthening the muscle and allowing it to remain in a stretched position for an extended period of time is unlikely to produce any injury to the muscle.

The effectiveness of the PNF techniques may be attributed in part to these same neurophysiologic principles. The slow-reversal-hold technique discussed previously takes advantage of two additional neurophysiologic phenomena.[47]

The maximal isometric contraction of the muscle that will be stretched during the 10-second "push" phase again causes an increase in tension that stimulates the Golgi tendon organs to affect a reflex relaxation of the antagonist even before the muscle is placed in a position of stretch. This relaxation of the antagonist muscle during contractions is referred to as **autogenic inhibition.**

During the relaxing phase the antagonist is relaxed and passively stretched while there is a maximal isotonic contraction of the agonist muscle pulling the extremity further into the agonist pattern. In any synergistic muscle group, a contraction of the agonist causes a reflex relaxation in the antagonist muscle, allowing it to stretch and protecting it from injury. This phenomenon is referred to as **reciprocal inhibition** (see Fig. 13-2).[53]

Thus with the PNF techniques, the additive effects of autogenic and reciprocal inhibition should theoretically allow the muscle to be stretched to a greater degree than is possible with static or ballistic stretching.[44]

EFFECT OF STRETCHING ON THE PHYSICAL AND MECHANICAL PROPERTIES OF MUSCLE

The neurophysiologic mechanisms of both autogenic and reciprocal inhibition result in reflex relaxation with subsequent lengthening of a muscle. Thus the mechanical properties of that muscle that physically allow lengthening to occur are dictated via neural input.

Both muscle and tendon are composed largely of noncontractile collagen and elastin fibers. (The physical and mechanical properties of collagen and elastin were discussed in Chapter 3.) Collagen enables a tissue to resist mechanical forces and deformation. Elastin composes highly elastic tissues that assist in recovery from deformation.

Unlike tendon, muscle also has active contractile components, which are the actin and myosin myofilaments. Collectively, the contractile and noncontractile elements determine the muscle's capability of deforming and recovering from deformation.[67]

Both the contractile and noncontractile components appear to resist deformation when a muscle is stretched or lengthened. The percentage of their individual contribution to resisting deformation depends on the degree to which the muscle is stretched or deformed and on the velocity of deformation. The noncontractile elements are primarily resistant to the degree of lengthening, while the contractile elements limit high-velocity deformation. The greater the stretch, the more the noncontractile components contribute.

Lengthening of a muscle via stretching, which is maintained for a period long enough to allow for autogenic inhibition to reflexively relax the muscle, allows for viscoelastic and plastic changes to occur in the collagen and elastin fibers. The viscoelastic changes, which allow slow deformation with imperfect recovery, are not permanent. However, plastic changes—although difficult to achieve—result in residual or permanent change in length due to deformation created by long periods of stretching.

The greater the velocity of deformation, the greater the chance for exceeding that tissue's capability to undergo viscoelastic and plastic changes.[67]

PRACTICAL APPLICATION

Although all three stretching techniques have been demonstrated to effectively improve flexibility, there is still considerable debate as to which technique produces the greatest increases in range of movement. The ballistic technique is recommended for any patient involved in dynamic activity, despite its potential

for causing muscle soreness in the sedentary or untrained individual. In highly trained individuals, it is unlikely that ballistic stretching will result in muscle soreness.

Static stretching is perhaps the most widely used technique. It is a simple technique and does not require a partner. A fully nonrestricted range of motion can be attained through static stretching over time. PNF stretching techniques are capable of producing dramatic increases in range of motion during one stretching session. Studies comparing static and PNF stretching suggest that PNF stretching is capable of producing greater improvement in flexibility over an extended training period.[24,46] The major disadvantage of PNF stretching is that a partner is usually required to assist with the stretch, although stretching with a partner may have some motivational advantages.

The length of time that increases in muscle flexiblity can be sustained once stretching stops is debatable.[63,68] One study indicated that a significant loss of flexibility was evident after only 2 weeks.[68] It was recommended that flexibilty can be maintained by engaging in stretching activities at least once a week. However, to see improvement in flexibility, stretching must be done 3 to 5 times per week.[63]

Importance of Warm-Up Prior to Stretching

To most effectively stretch a muscle during a program of rehabilitation, intramuscular temperature should be increased prior to stretching.[42] Increasing the temperature has a positive effect on the ability of the collagen and elastin components within the musculotendinous unit to deform. Also the capability of the Golgi tendon organs to reflexively relax the muscle through autogenic inhibition is enhanced when the muscle is heated. It appears that the optimal temperature of muscle to achieve these beneficial effects is 39°C or 103°F. This increase in intramuscular temperature may be achieved either through low-intensity warm-up type exercise or through the use of various therapeutic modalities.[52] It is recommended that exercise be used as the primary means for increasing intramuscular temperature.

The use of cold prior to stretching has also been recommended. Cold appears to be most useful when there is some muscle guarding associated with delayed-onset muscle soreness.[46]

RELATIONSHIP OF STRENGTH AND FLEXIBILITY

We often hear about the negative effects that strength training has on flexibility. For example, someone who develops large bulk through strength training is often referred to as "muscle bound," with negative connotations in terms of the ability of that person to move. We tend to think of people who have highly developed muscles as having lost much of their ability to move freely through a full range of motion.[36]

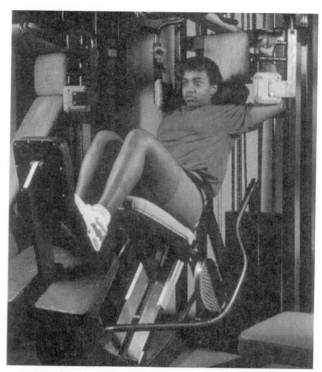

FIGURE 7-4

Strength training can improve flexibility. Strength training through a full range of motion will not impair flexibility.

Occasionally a person develops so much bulk that the physical size of the muscle prevents a normal range of motion. Strength training that is not properly done can impair movement; however, there is no reason to believe that weight training, if done properly through a full range of motion, will impair flexibility. Therefore, during a rehabilitation program the patient must be encouraged to strength train through a full, pain-free range of motion, progressing as rapidly as pain decreases will allow. Proper strength training probably improves dynamic flexibility and, if combined with a rigorous stretching program, can greatly enhance powerful and coordinated movements that are essential for success in many athletic activities. In all cases a heavy weight training program should be accompanied by a strong flexibility program (Fig. 7-4).

GUIDELINES AND PRECAUTIONS FOR STRETCHING

The following guidelines and precautions should be incorporated into a sound stretching program[6,43,54,55]:

- Warm up using a slow jog or a stationary exercise bike before stretching vigorously.
- To increase flexibility, the muscle must be overloaded or stretched beyond its normal range but not to the point of pain.

- Stretch only to the point where you feel tightness or resistance to stretch or perhaps some discomfort. Stretching should not be painful.[6]
- Increases in range of motion will be specific to whatever muscle or joint is being stretched.
- Exercise caution when stretching muscles that surround painful joints. Pain is an indication that something is wrong, and should not be ignored.
- Avoid overstretching the ligaments and capsules that surround joints.
- Stretching from a seated rather than a standing position takes stress off the low back and decreases the chances of back injury.
- Be sure to continue normal breathing during a stretch. Do not hold your breath.
- Static and PNF techniques are most often recommended for individuals who want to improve their range of motion.
- Ballistic stretching should be done only by those who are already flexible or accustomed to stretching and done only after static stretching.
- Stretching should be done at least 3 times per week to see minimal improvement. It is recommended to stretch between 5 and 6 times per week to see maximum results.

SPECIFIC STRETCHING EXERCISES

Chapters 25 through 32 will include examples of various stretching exercises that may be used to improve flexibility at specific joints or in specific muscle groups throughout the body. The exercises described may be done statically or with slight modification; they may also be done with a partner using a PNF technique. There are many possible variations to each of these exercises.[29] The exercises selected are those that seem to be the most effective for stretching of various muscle groups.

SUMMARY

- Flexibility is the ability to move a joint or a series of joints smoothly through a full range of motion.
- Flexibility is specific to a given joint, and the term *good flexibility* implies that there are no joint abnormalities restricting movement.
- Flexibility may be limited by muscles and tendons, joint capsules or ligaments, fat, bone structure, or skin.
- Passive range of motion refers to the degree to which a joint may be passively moved to the endpoints in the range of motion, whereas active range of motion refers to movement through the midrange of motion resulting from active contraction.
- Measurement of joint flexibility is accomplished through the use of a goniometer.

- An agonist muscle is one that contracts to produce joint motion; the antagonist muscle is stretched with contraction of the agonist.
- Ballistic, static, and proprioceptive neuromuscular facilitation (PNF) techniques have all been used as stretching techniques for improving flexibility.
- Each of these stretching techniques is based on the neurophysiologic phenomena involving the muscle spindles and Golgi tendon organs. PNF techniques appear to be the most effective in producing increases in flexibility.
- Stretching should be included as part of the warm-up period to prepare the muscles for what they are going to be asked to do and to prevent injury, as well as in the cool-down period to help reduce injury. Stretching after an activity may prevent muscle soreness and will help increase flexibility by stretching a loose, warmed up muscle.
- Strength training, if done correctly through a full range of motion, will likely improve flexibility.

REFERENCES

1. Alter MJ. *The Science of Stretching*. Champaign, IL, Human Kinetics, 1988.
2. Arnheim DD, Prentice WE. *Principles of Athletic Training*. Madison, Brow & Benchmark, 1997.
3. Astrand PO, Rodahl K. *Textbook of Work Physiology*. New York, McGraw-Hill, 1986.
4. Bandy WD, Irion JM. The effect of time of static stretch on the flexibility of the hamstring muscles. *Phys Ther* 74:845–852, 1994.
5. Basmajian J. *Therapeutic Exercise*, 4th ed. Baltimore, Williams & Wilkins, 1984.
6. Bealieu JE. Developing a stretching program. *Phys Sports Med* 9:59, 1981.
7. Bealieu JE. *Stretching for All Sports*. Pasadena, CA, Athletic Press, 1980.
8. Blanke D. Flexibility. In: Mellion M. *Sports Medicine Secrets*. Philadelphia, Hanley & Belfus, 1994.
9. Chapman EA, deVries HA, Swezey R. Joint stiffness: Effect of exercise on young and old men. *J Gerontol* 27:218, 1972.
10. Condon SA, Hutton RS. Soleus muscle EMG activity and ankle dorsiflexion range of motion from stretching procedures. *Phys Ther* 67:24–30, 1987.
11. Corbin C, Fox K. Flexibility: The forgotten part of fitness. *J Phys Educ* 16:191, 1985.
12. Corbin C, Noble L. Flexibility: A major component of physical fitness. In: Cundiff DE, ed. *Implementation of Health Fitness Exercise Programs*. Reston, VA, American Alliance for Health, Physical Education, Recreation, and Dance, 1985.
13. Corbin C, Noble L. Flexibility. *J Phys Educ Rec Dance* 51:23, 1980.
14. Cornelius WL. *PNF and Oher Flexibility Techniques*. Arlington, VA, Computer Microfilm International (microfiche; 20 fr), 1986.
15. Cornelius WL. Two effective flexibility methods. *Athlet Train* 16:23, 1981.
16. Cornelius WL, Hagemann RW Jr, Jackson AW. A study on placement of stretching within a workout. *J Sports Med Phys Fitness* 28:234, 1988.
17. Cornelius WL, Jackson AW. The effects of cryotherapy and PNF on hip extensor flexibility. *J Athlet Train* 19:183–184, 1984.
18. Couch J. *Runners World Yoga Book*. Mountain View, CA, World Publications, 1982.
19. deVries HA. *Physiology of Exercise for Physical Education and Athletics*. Dubuque, IA, Brown, 1986.
20. deVries HA. Evaluation of static stretching procedures for improvement of flexibility. *Res Q Exerc Sport* 3:222–229, 1962.
21. Entyre BR, Abraham LD. Antagonist muscle activity during stretching: A paradox reassessed. *Med Sci Sports Exerc* 20:285–289, 1988.
22. Entyre BR, Abraham LD. Ache-reflex changes during static stretching and two variations of proprioceptive neuromuscular facilitation techniques. *Electroencephalogr Clin Neurophysiol* 63:174–179, 1986.
23. Entyre BR, Lee EJ. Chronic and acute flexibility of men and women using three different stretching techniques. *Res Q Exerc Sport* 59:222–228, 1988.
24. Godges JJ, MacRae H, Longdon C, et al. The effects of two stretching procedures on hip range of motion and joint economy. *J Orthop Sports Phys Ther* 11:350–357, 1989.
25. Herling J. It's time to add strength training to our fitness programs. *J Phys Educ Program* 79:17, 1981.
26. Hubley CL, Kozey JW, Stanish WD. The effects of static stretching exercises and stationary cycling on range of motion at the hip joint. *J Orthop Sports Phys Ther* 6:104–109, 1984.
27. Humphrey LD. Flexibility. *J Phys Educ Rec Dance* 52:41, 1981.
28. Hutinger P. How flexible are you? *Aquatic World Magazine*, Jan 1974.
29. Ishii DK. Flexibility strexercises for co-ed groups. *Scholastic Coach* 45:31, 1976.
30. Jackson AW, Baker AA. The relationship of the sit-and-reach test to criterion measures of hamstring and back flexibility in young females. *Res Q Exerc Sport* 57:183, 1986.
31. Jensen C, Fisher G. *Scientific Basis of Athletic Conditioning*. Philadelphia, Lea & Febiger, 1979.
32. Johnson P. *Sport, Exercise and You*. New York, Holt, Rinehart, & Winston, 1975.
33. Knortz K, Ringel C. Flexibility techniques. *Nat Strength Conditioning Assoc J* 7:50, 1985.
34. Knott M, Voss P. *Proprioceptive Neuromuscular Facilitation*, 3rd ed. New York, Harper & Row, 1985.

35. Lentell G, Hetherington T, Eagan J, et al. The use of thermal agents to influence the effectiveness of a low-load prolonged stretch. *J Orthop Sports Phys Ther* 5:200–207, 1992.

36. Liemohn W. Flexibility and muscular strength. *J Phys Educ Rec Dance* 59:37, 1988.

37. Louden KL, Bolier CE, Allison KA, et al. Effects of two stretching methods on the flexibility and retention of flexibility at the ankle joint in runners. *Phys Ther* 65:698, 1985.

38. Madding SW, Wong JG, Hallum A. Effects of duration of passive stretching on hip abduction range of motion. *J Orthop Sports Phys Ther* 8:409–416, 1987.

39. Markos PD. Ipsilateral and contralateral effects of proprioceptive neuromuscular facilitation techniques on hip motion and electromyographic activity. *Phys Ther* 59:1366–1373, 1979.

40. McAtee R. *Facilitated Stretching*. Champaign, IL, Human Kinetics, 1993.

41. Moore M, Hutton R. Electromyographic investigation of muscle stretching techniques. *Med Sci Sports Exerc* 12:322–329, 1980.

42. Murphy P. Warming up before stretching advised. *Phys Sports Med* 14:45, 1986.

43. Norris C. *Flexibility Principles and Practices*. London, A&C Black, 1994.

44. Prentice WE. A review of PNF techniques—implications for athletic rehabilitation and performance. *Forum Med* 4(1):1–13, 1989.

45. Prentice WE. A comparison of static stretching and PNF stretching for improving hip joint flexibility. *J Athlet Train* 18:56–59, 1983.

46. Prentice WE. An electromyographic analysis of heat or cold and stretching for inducing muscular relaxation. *J Orthop Sports Phys Ther* 3:133–140, 1982.

47. Prentice WE, Kooima E. The use of PNF techniques in rehabilitation of sport-related injury. *Athlet Train* 21:26–31, 1986.

48. Rasch P. *Kinesiology and Applied Anatomy*. Philadelphia, Lea & Febiger, 1989.

49. Sady SP, Wortman M, Blanke D. Flexibility training: Ballistic, static, or proprioceptive neuromuscular facilitation? *Arch Phys Med Rehab* 63:261–263, 1982.

50. Sapega AA, Quedenfeld T, Moyer R, et al. Biophysical factors in range-of-motion exercise. *Phys Sports Med* 9:57, 1981.

51. Schultz P. Flexibility: Day of the static stretch. *Phys Sports Med* 8:73–77, 1979.

52. Shellock F, Prentice WE. Warm-up and stretching for improved physical performance and prevention of sport-related injury. *Sports Med* 2:267–278, 1985.

53. Shindo M, Harayama H, Kondo K, et al. Changes in reciprocal Ia inhibition during voluntary contraction in man. *Exp Brain Res* 53:400–408, 1984.

54. St. George F. *The Stretching Handbook: Ten Steps to Muscle Fitness*. Rosevill, IL, Simon & Schuster, 1994.

55. Stamford B. A stretching primer. *Phys Sports Med* 22:85–86, 1994.

56. *Staying Flexible: The Full Range of Motion*. Alexandria, VA, Time Life Books, 1987.

57. Surburg P. Flexibility training program design. In: Miller P, ed. *Fitness Programming and Physical Disability*. Champaign, IL, Human Kinetics, 1995.

58. Tanigawa MC. Comparison of the hold relax procedure and passive mobilization on increasing muscle length. *Phys Ther* 52:725, 1972.

59. Tobias M, Sullivan JP. *Complete Stretching*. New York, Knopf, 1992.

60. van Mechelen P. Prevention of running injuries by warm-up, cool-down, and stretching. *Am J Sports Med* 21:711–719, 1993.

61. Verrill D, Pate R. Relationship between duration of static stretch in the sit and reach position and biceps femoris electromyographic activity. *Med Sci Sports Exerc* 14:124, 1982.

62. Voss DE, Ionta MK, Myers GJ. *Proprioceptive Neuromuscular Facilitation: Patterns and Techniques*, 3rd ed. Philadelphia, Lippincott, 1985.

63. Wallin D, Ekblom B, Grahn R. Improvement of muscle flexibility, a comparison between two techniques. *Am J Sports Med* 13:263–268, 1985.

64. Wessel J, Wan A. Effect of stretching on intensity of delayed-onset muscle soreness. *J Sports Med* 2:83–87, 1994.

65. Wiktorsson-Moeller M, Oberg B, Ekstrand J. Effects of warming-up, massage, and stretching on range of motion and muscle strength in the lower extremity. *Am J Sports Med* 11:249–252, 1983.

66. Worrell T, Smith T, Winegardner J. Effect of hamstring stretching on hamstring muscle performance. *J Orthop Sports Phys Ther* 20:154–159, 1994.

67. Zachewski J. Flexibility for sports. In: Sanders B, ed. *Sports Physical Therapy*. Norwalk, CT, Appleton & Lange, 1990.

68. Zebas CJ, Rivera ML. Retention of flexibility in selected joints after cessation of a stretching exercise program. In: Dotson CO, Humphrey JH, eds. *Exercise Physiology: Current Selected Research Topics*. New York, AMS Press, 1985.

CHAPTER 8

Impaired Neuromuscular Control: Reactive Neuromuscular Training

Michael L. Voight and Gray Cook

OBJECTIVES

After completing this chapter, the student therapist should be able to do the following:

- Explain why neuromuscular control is important in the rehabilitation process.
- Define and discuss the importance of proprioception in the neuromuscular control process.
- Define and discuss the different levels of CNS motor control and the neural pathways responsible for the transmission of afferent and efferent information at each level.
- Define and discuss the two motor mechanisms involved with interpreting afferent information and coordinating an efferent response.
- Develop a rehabilitation program that uses various techniques of neuromuscular control exercises.

WHAT IS NEUROMUSCULAR CONTROL AND WHY IS IT IMPORTANT?

The basic goal in rehabilitation is to enhance one's ability to function within the environment and to perform the specific activities of daily living (ADL). The entire rehabilitation process should be focused on improving the functional status of the patient. The concept of functional training is not new. In fact, functional training has been around for many years. It is widely accepted that in order to get better at a specific activity, or to get stronger for an activity, one must practice that specific activity. Therefore, the functional progression for return to ADL can be defined as breaking the specific activities down into a hierarchy and then performing them in a sequence that allows for the acquisition or reacquisition of that skill.

From a historical perspective, the rehabilitation process following injury has focused upon the restoration of muscular strength, endurance, and joint flexibility without any consideration of the role of the neuromuscular mechanism. This is a common error in the rehabilitation process. We cannot assume that clinical programs alone using traditional methods will lead to a safe return to function. Limiting the rehabilitation program to these traditional programs alone often results in an incomplete restoration of ability and quite possibly leads to an increased risk of reinjury.

The overall objective of the functional exercise program is to return the patient to the preinjury level as quickly and as safely as possible. Specific training activities should be designed to restore both dynamic stability about the joint and specific ADL skills. In order to accomplish this objective, a basic tenet of exercise physiology is employed. The SAID principle (Specific Adaptions to Imposed Demands) states that the body will adapt to the stress and strain placed upon it.[130] Patients cannot succeed in ADL if they have not been prepared to meet all of the demands of their specific activity.[130] Reactive Neuromuscular Training (RNT) is not intended to replace traditional rehabilitation but rather to help bridge the gap left from traditional rehabilitation in a complementary fashion via proprioceptive and balance training in order to promote a more functional return to activity.[130] The main objective of the RNT program is to facilitate the unconscious process of interpreting and integrating the peripheral sensations received by the CNS into appropriate motor responses.

TERMINOLOGY: WHAT DO WE REALLY NEED TO KNOW?

Success in skilled performance depends upon how effectively the individual detects, perceives, and uses relevant sensory information. Knowing exactly where our limbs are in space and how much muscular effort is required to perform a particular action is critical for the successful performance in all activities requiring intricate coordination of the various body parts. Fortunately, information about the position and movement of various body parts is available from the peripheral receptors located in and around the articular structures.

About the normal healthy joint, both static and dynamic stabilizers serve to provide support. The role of the capsuloligamentous tissues in the dynamic restraint of the joint has been well established in the literature.[2,3,19,33,45–50,110] Although the primary role of these structures is mechanical in nature by providing structural support and stabilization to the joint, the capsuloligamentous tissues also play an important sensory role by detecting joint position and motion.[33,34,105] Sensory afferent feedback from the receptors in the capsuloligamentous structures projects directly to the reflex and cortical pathways, thereby mediating reactive muscle activity for dynamic restraint.[2,3,33,34,67] The efferent motor response that ensues from the sensory information is called neuromuscular control. Sensory information is sent to the CNS to be processed, and appropriate motor activities are executed.

PHYSIOLOGY OF PROPRIOCEPTION

Although there has been no definitive definition of proprioception, Beard et al described proprioception as consisting of three similar components: (1) a static awareness of joint position, (2) kinesthetic awareness, and (3) a closed-loop efferent reflex response required for the regulation of muscle tone and activity.[7] From a physiologic perspective, proprioception is a specialized variation of the sensory modality of touch. Specifically defined, proprioception is the cumulative neural input to the central nervous system from mechanoreceptors in the joint capsules, ligaments, muscles, tendons, and skin.

A rehabilitation program that addresses the need for restoring normal joint stability and proprioception cannot be constructed until one has a total appreciation of both the mechanical and sensory functions of the articular structures.[12] Knowledge of the basic physiology of how these muscular and joint mechanoreceptors work together in the production of smooth controlled coordinated motion is critical in developing a rehabilitation-training program. This is because the role of the joint musculature extends beyond absolute strength and the capacity to resist fatigue. Simply restoring mechanical restraints or strengthening the associated muscles neglects the smooth coordinated neuromuscular controlling mechanisms required for joint stability.[12] The complexity of joint motion necessitates synergy and synchrony of muscle firing patterns, thereby permitting proper joint stabilization, especially during sudden changes in joint position, which is common in functional activities. Understanding these relationships and functional implications will allow the clinician greater variability and success in returning patients safely back to their playing environment.

Sherrington first described the term proprioception in the early 1900s when he noted the presence of receptors in the joint capsular structures that were primarily reflexive in nature.[105] Since that time, mechanoreceptors have been morphohistologically identified about the articular structures in both animal and human models. Mechanoreceptors are specialized end organs that function as biological transducers that can convert the mechanical energy of physical deformation (elongation, compression, and pressure) into action nerve potentials yielding proprioceptive information.[45] Although receptor discharge varies according to the intensity of the distortion, mechanoreceptors can also be based upon their discharge rates. Quickly adapting receptors cease discharging shortly after the onset of a stimulus, while slowly adapting receptors continue to discharge while the stimulus is present.[21,33,45] About the healthy joint, quickly adapting receptors are responsible for providing conscious and unconscious kinesthetic sensations in response to joint movement or acceleration, while slowly adapting mechanoreceptors provide continuous feedback and thus proprioceptive information relative to joint position.[21,45,71]

Once stimulated, mechanoreceptors are able to adapt. With constant stimulation, the frequency of the neural impulses decreases. The functional implication is that mechanoreceptors detect change and rates of change, as opposed to steady-state conditions.[104] This input is then analyzed in the CNS for joint position and movement.[139] The status of the articular structures is sent to the CNS so that information regarding static versus dynamic conditions, equilibrium versus disequilibrium, or biomechanical stress and strain relations can be evaluated.[129,130] Once processed and evaluated, this proprioceptive information becomes capable of influencing muscle tone, motor execution programs, and cognitive somatic perceptions or kinesthetic awareness.[92] Proprioceptive information also protects the joint from damage caused by movement exceeding the normal physiologic range of motion and helps to determine the appropriate balance of synergistic and antagonistic forces. All of this information helps to generate a somatosensory image within the CNS. Therefore, the soft tissues surrounding a joint serve a double purpose: they provide biomechanical support to the bony partners making up the joint, keeping them in relative anatomic alignment, and through an extensive afferent neurologic network, they provide valuable proprioceptive information.

Before the 1970s, articular receptors in the joint capsule were held primarily responsible for joint proprioception.[104] Since then there has been considerable debate as to whether muscular and articular mechanoreceptors interact. As originally described, the articular mechanoreceptors were located primarily on the parts of the joint capsule that are stretched the most when the joint is moved. This led investigators to believe that these receptors were primarily responsible for perception of joint motion. Skoglund found individual receptors that were active at very specific locations in the range of limb movement (e.g., from 150 to 180 degrees of joint angle for a particular cell).[113] Another cell would fire at a different set of joint angles. By integrating the information, the central nervous system could "know" where the limb was in space by detecting which receptors were active. The problem with this theory is that several studies have shown that the majority of the capsular receptors only respond at the extremes of the range of motion or during other situations when a strong stimulus is imparted onto the structures such as distraction or compression.[21,43,48,49] Furthermore, other studies have found that the nature of the firing pattern is dependent on whether the movement is active or passive.[14] In addition, the mechanoreceptor firing is dependent on the direction of motion from the joint.[115] The fact that the firing pattern of the joint receptors is dependent on factors other than simple position sense has seriously challenged the thought that the articular mechanoreceptors alone are the means by which the system determines joint position.

A more contemporary viewpoint is that muscle receptors play a more important role in signaling joint position.[25,42] There are two main types of muscle receptors that provide complementary information about the state of the muscles. The muscle spindle is located within the muscle fibers and is most active when the muscle is stretched. The Golgi tendon organ is located in the junction between the muscle and the tendon and is most active when the muscle contracts.

The Muscle Spindle

The muscle spindle consists of three main components: small muscle fibers called intrafusial fibers that are innervated by the gamma efferent motor neurons, and types Ia and II afferent neurons (Fig. 8-1). The intrafusial fibers are made up of two types, bag and chain fibers, the polar ends of which provide a tension on the central region of the spindle, called the equatorial region. The sensory receptors located here are sensitive to the length of the equatorial region when the spindle is stretched. The major neurologic connection to this sensory region is the Ia afferent fiber, whose output is related to the length of the equatorial region (position information) as well as to the rate of change in length of this region (velocity information). The spindle connects to the alpha motor neurons for the same muscle, providing excitation to the muscle when it is stretched.

There has been a great deal of controversy about what the spindle actually signals to the CNS.[36] A major conceptual problem in the past was that the output of the Ia afferent that presumably signals stretch or velocity is related to two separate factors.[102] First, Ia output is increased by the elongation of the overall muscle via elongation of the spindle as a whole. However, the Ia output is also related to the stretch placed on the equatorial region by the intrafusial fibers by the gamma motor neurons. Therefore, the CNS would have difficulty in interpreting changes in the Ia output as being due to changes in the overall muscle length with a constant gamma motor neuron activity, changes in gamma motor neuron activity with a constant muscle length, or perhaps changes in both.[102] Another problem was presented by Gelfan and Carter, who suggested that there was no strong evidence that the Ia afferent fibers actually sent their information to the primary sensory cortex.[39] Because of these factors, it was widely held that the muscle spindle was not important for the conscious perception of movement or position.

Goodwin et al were the first to refute this viewpoint.[43] They found as much as 40 degrees of misalignment of arm that had vibration applied to the biceps tendon.[43] The vibration of the tendon produces a small, rapid, alternating stretch and release of the tendon, which affects the muscle spindle and distorts the output of the Ia afferents from the spindles located in the vibrated muscle. The interpretation was that the vibration distorted the Ia information coming from the same muscle, which led to a misperception of the limb's position. Others have found the same results when applying vibration to a muscle tendon.[97,108,109] This information supports the idea that the muscle spindle is important in providing information to the CNS about limb position and velocity of movement.

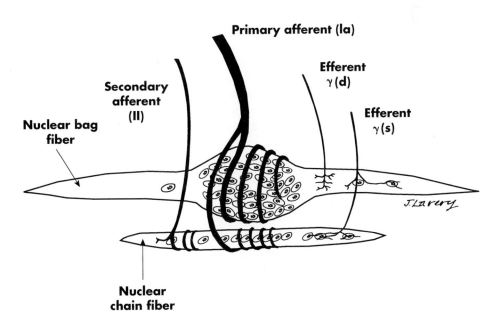

FIGURE 8-1

The anatomy of muscle receptors: Muscle spindle and Golgi tendon organ. (Reproduced, with permission, from Shumway-Cook A, Woollacott M. Physiology of motor control. In: Shumway-Cook A, Woollacott M, eds. *Motor Control: Theory and Practical Applications.* Baltimore, Williams & Wilkins, 1995, p. 53.)

Primary afferent (Ia)

Secondary afferent (II)

Efferent γ(d)

Efferent γ(s)

Nuclear bag fiber

Nuclear chain fiber

The Golgi Tendon Organ

The Golgi tendon organs are tiny receptors located in the junction where the muscle "blends into" the tendon. They are ideally located to provide information about the tension within the muscles because they lie in series with the muscle force-producing contractile elements. The Golgi tendon organ has been shown to produce an inhibition of the muscle in which it is located when a stretch to the active muscle is produced. The fact that a stretch force near the physiologic limit of the muscle was required to induce the tendon organ to fire led to the speculation that this receptor was primarily a protective receptor that would prevent the muscle from contracting so forcibly that it would rupture the tendon. Houk and Henneman[62] and Stuart et al[119] have provided a more precise understanding of the sensitivity of the Golgi tendon organs. Anatomic evidence reveals that each organ is connected to only a small group (3 to 25) of muscle fibers, not to the entire muscle as had been previously suspected. Therefore, the Golgi tendon organ appears to be in a good position to sense the tensions produced in a limited number of individual motor units, not in the whole muscle. Houk and Henneman determined that the tendon organs could respond to forces of less than 0.1 G.[62] Therefore, the Golgi tendon organs are very sensitive detectors for active tension in localized portions of a muscle, in addition to having a protective function.

It is most likely that the muscle and joint receptors work complementary to one another in this complex afferent system, with each modifying the function of the other.[15,46] An important concept is that any one of the receptors in isolation from the others is generally ineffective in signaling information about the movements of the body. The reason for this is that the various receptors are often sensitive to a variety of aspects of body motion at the same time. For example, the Golgi tendon organs probably cannot signal information about movement, because they cannot differentiate between the forces produced in a static contraction and the same forces produced when the limb is moving.[102] Although the spindle is sensitive to muscle length, it is also sensitive to the rate of change in length (velocity) and to the activity in the intrafusal fibers that are known to be active during contractions. Therefore, the spindle confounds information about the position of the limb and the level of contraction of the muscle. The joint receptors are sensitive to joint position, but their output can be affected by the tensions applied and by the direction of movement.

Because both the articular and muscle receptors have well-described cortical connections to substantiate a central role in proprioception, some have suggested that the central nervous system combines and integrates the information in some way to resolve the ambiguity in the signals produced by any one of the receptors.[102,138] Producing an ensemble of information by combining the various separate sources could enable the generation of less ambiguous information about movement.[36] Therefore, the sensory mechanoreceptors may represent a continuum rather than separate distinct classes of receptor.[105] This concept is further illustrated by research that demonstrated a relationship between the muscle spindle sensory afferent and joint mechanoreceptors.[18] McCloskey has also demonstrated a relationship between the cutaneous afferent and joint mechanoreceptors.[78] These studies suggest a complex role for the joint mechanoreceptors in smooth, coordinated, and controlled movement.

Neural Pathways

Information generated and encoded by the mechanoreceptors in the muscle tendon units is projected upwards via specialized pathways toward the cortex, where it is further analyzed and integrated with other sensory inputs.[99] Proprioceptive information is relayed to the cerebral cortex via one of two major ascending systems, the dorsal column and the spinothalamic tract. Both of these pathways involve three orders of neurons and three synapses in transmitting sensory input from the periphery to the cortex. The primary afferent, which is connected to the peripheral receptor, synapses with a second neuron in the spinal cord or lower brain, depending upon the type of sensation. Before reaching the cerebral cortex, all sensory information passes through an important group of nuclei located in the area of the brain called the *diencephalon*. It is within this group of more than 30 nuclei, collectively called the *thalamus,* that neurophysiologists consider the initial stages of sensory integration and perceptual awareness to begin. Therefore, the second neuron then conveys the information to the thalamus where it synapses with the third and final neuron in the area of the thalamus called the *ventroposterolateral (VPL)* area. The thalamus achieves these functions by "gating out" irrelevant sensory inputs and directing those that are relevant to an impending or ongoing action toward primary sensory areas within the cortex. The sensory pathways finally terminate in the primary sensory areas located in different regions of the cortex. It is at this point that we become consciously aware of the sensations.

The final perception of what is occurring in the environment around us is achieved after all of these sensations are integrated and then interpreted by the association areas that lie adjacent to the various primary sensory areas associated with the different types of sensory input. With the assistance of memory, objects seen or felt can be interpreted in a meaningful way. The dorsal column plays an important role in motor control because of its speed in transmission. In order for proprioception to play a protective role through reflex muscle splinting, the information must be transmitted and processed rapidly. The heavily myelinated and wide-diameter axons within this system transmit at speeds of 80 to 100 meters per second. This characteristic facilitates rapid sampling of the environment, which enhances the accuracy of motor actions about to be executed and of those already in progress. By comparison, nociceptor transmission occurs at a rate of about 1 meter per second. Thus proprioceptive information may play a more significant role than pain in the prevention of injuries.

In contrast to the transmission properties associated with the dorsal column system, neurons that make up the spinothalamic tract are small in diameter (some of which are unmyelinated) and conduct slowly (1 to 40 meters per second). The four spinocerebellar tracts also convey important proprioceptive information from the neuromuscular receptors to the cerebellum. Unlike the dorsal column, these pathways do not synapse in either the thalamus or cerebral cortex. As a result, the proprioceptive information conveyed by the spinocerebellar tracts does not lead to conscious perceptions of limb position. The afferent sources are believed to contribute to kinesthesia.

ASSESSMENT OF JOINT PROPRIOCEPTION

Assessment of proprioception is valuable for identifying proprioceptive deficits. If deficiencies in proprioception can be clinically diagnosed in a reliable manner, a clinician would know when and if a problem exists and when the problem has been corrected.[130] There are several ways to measure or assess proprioception about a joint. From an anatomic perspective, histologic studies can be conducted to identify mechanoreceptors within the specific joint structures. Neurophysiologic testing can assess sensory thresholds and nerve conduction velocities. From a clinical perspective, proprioception can be assessed by measuring the components that make up the proprioceptive mechanism: kinesthesia (perception of motion) and joint position sensibility (perception of joint position).

Measuring either the angle or time threshold to detection of passive motion can assess kinesthetic sensibility. With the subject seated, the patient's limb is mechanically rotated at a slow constant angular velocity (2 degrees/sec). With passive motion,

the capsuloligamentous structures come under tension and deform the mechanoreceptors located within. The mechanoreceptor deformation is converted into an electrical impulse, which is then processed within the CNS. Patients are instructed to stop the lever arm movement as soon as they perceive motion. Depending on which measurement is used, either the time to detection or degrees of angular displacement is recorded.

Joint position sense is assessed through the reproduction of both active and passive joint repositioning. The examiner places the limb at a preset target angle and holds it there for a minimum of 10 seconds to allow the patient to mentally process the target angle. Following this, the limb is returned to the starting position. The patient is asked to either actively reproduce or stop the device when passive repositioning of the angle has been achieved (Fig. 8-2). The examiner measures the ability of an individual to accurately reproduce the preset target angle position. The angular displacement is recorded as the error in degrees from the preset target angle. Active angle reproduction measures the ability of both the muscle and capsular receptors while passive repositioning primarily measures the capsular receptors. With both tests of proprioception, the patient is blindfolded during testing to eliminate all visual cueing. In patients with unilateral involvement, the contralateral uninjured limb can serve as an external control for comparison.

The main limitation to current proprioceptive testing is that either time/angle threshold to detection of passive motion does not provide an assessment of the unconscious reflex arc believed to provide dynamic joint stability. The assessment of reflex capabilities is usually performed by measuring the latency of muscular activation to involuntary perturbation through EMG interpretation of firing patterns of those muscles crossing the respective joint (Fig. 8-3).[132] The ability to quantify the sequence

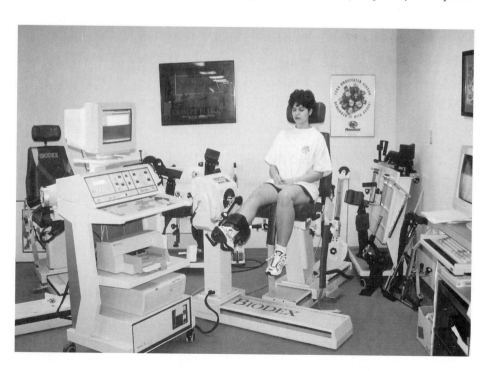

FIGURE 8-2

Open-chain proprioceptive testing using the Biodex dynamometer.

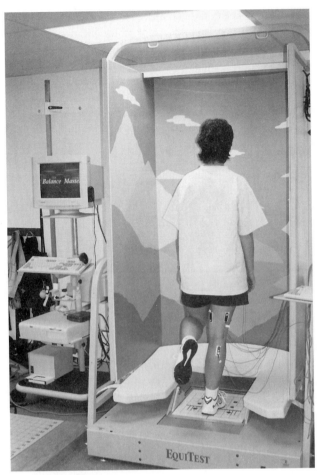

FIGURE 8 - 3

EMG assessment of reflex muscle firing as a result of
perturbation on the Neurocom EquiTest.

of muscle firing can provide a valuable tool for the assessment
of asynchronous neuromuscular activation patterns following
injury.[74,140] A delay or lag in the firing time of the dynamic stabilizers about the joint can result in recurrent joint subluxation
and joint deterioration.

PROPRIOCEPTION AND MOTOR CONTROL

The efferent response that is produced as the result of the proprioceptive afferent input is termed *neuromuscular control*. In
general, there are two motor control mechanisms involved in
the interpretation of afferent information and coordinating an
efferent response. One of the ways in which motor control is
achieved relies heavily on the concept that sensory feedback information is used to regulate our movements. This is a more
traditional viewpoint of motor control. The closed-loop system
of motor control emphasizes the essential role of the reactive
or sensory feedback in the planning, execution, and modification of action. The closed-loop systems involve the processing of

feedback against a reference of correctness, the determination of
error, and a subsequent correction.[102] The feedback mechanism
of motor control relies on the numerous reflex pathways in an
attempt to continuously adjust ongoing muscle activation.[29,102]
The receptors for the feedback supplied to closed-loop systems
are the eyes, vestibular apparatus, joint receptors, and muscle
receptors. One important point to note about the closed-loop
system of feedback motor control is that this loop requires a
great deal of time in order for a stimulus to be processed and
yield a response. Rapid actions do not provide sufficient time for
the system to (1) generate an error, (2) detect the error, (3) determine the correction, (4) initiate the correction, and (5) correct
the movement before a rapid movement is completed.[102] The
best example of this concept is demonstrated by the left jab of
former boxing champion Muhammad Ali. The movement itself
was approximately 40 msec, yet visually detecting an aiming error and correcting it during the same movement should require
approximately 200 msec.[102] The movement is finished before
any correction can begin. Therefore, closed-loop feedback control models seem to have their greatest strength in explaining
movements that are very slow in time or that have very high
movement accuracy requirements.[102]

In contrast, a more contemporary theory emphasizes the
open-loop system, which focuses upon the a priori generation
of action plans in anticipation of movement produced by a central executor somewhere in the cerebral cortex.[102] The ability
to prepare the muscles prior to movement is called pretuning
or feed-forward motor control. The spring-like qualities of a
muscle can be exploited (through preactivation) by the CNS
in anticipation of movements and joint loads. This concept
has been termed feed-forward motor control, in which prior
sensory feedback (experience) concerning a task is fed forward
to preprogram muscle activation patterns.[62] Vision serves an
important feed-forward function by preparing the motor system in advance of the actual movement. Preactivated muscles
can provide quick compensation for external loads and are critical for dynamic joint stability. Researchers have shown that
corrections for rapid changes in body position can occur far
more rapidly (30 to 80 msec) than the closed-loop latencies
of 200 msec that have previously been reported.[27,63,69] Therefore, the motor control system operates with a feed-forward
mode in order to send some signals "ahead of" the movement
that (1) readies the system for the upcoming motor command
and/or (2) readies the system for the receipt of some particular
kind of feedback information.

Anticipatory muscle activity contributes to the dynamic
restraint system in several capacities. By increasing muscle activation levels in anticipation of an external load, the stiffness
properties of the entire muscular unit can be increased.[84] Stiffness is one of the measures used to describe the characteristics
of elastic materials. It is defined in terms of the amount of tension increase required to increase the length of the object by a
certain amount. From a mechanical perspective, muscle stiffness can be defined as the ratio of the change of force to the

change in length. If a spring is very stiff, a great deal of tension is needed to increase its length by a given amount; for a less stiff spring, much less tension is required. When a muscle is stretched, the change in tension is instantaneous, just as the change in length of a spring. An increase in tension would off-set the perturbation or deforming force and bring the system back to its original position. Research has demonstrated that the muscle spindle is responsible for the maintenance of the muscle stiffness when the muscle is stretched, so that it can still act as a spring in the control of an unexpected perturbation.[60,63,86] Therefore, stiff muscles can resist stretching episodes more effectively, have greater tone, and provide a more effective dynamic restraint to joint displacement. Increased muscle stiffness can improve the stretch sensitivity of the muscle spindle system while at the same time reduce the electromechanical delay required to develop muscle tension.[28,60,80,84] Heightening the stretch sensitivity can improve the reactive capabilities of the muscle by providing additional sensory feedback.[28]

CNS MOTOR CONTROL INTEGRATION

It has already been established that the CNS input provided by the peripheral mechanoreceptors as well as the visual and vestibular receptors is integrated by the CNS to generate a motor response. In addition to the many conscious modifications that can be made while movement is in progress, certain neural connections within the CNS contribute to the modification of movements in progress by providing sensory information at a subconscious level. The influence of some of these reflexive loops is limited to local control of muscle force, but others are capable of influencing force levels in muscle groups quite distant from those originally stimulated. These longer reflex loops are therefore capable of modifying movements to a much larger extent than the shorter reflex loops that are confined to single segments within the spinal cord.

In general, the CNS response falls under three categories or levels of motor control: spinal reflexes, brainstem processing, and cognitive cerebral cortex program planning. The goal of the rehabilitation process is to retrain the altered afferent pathways in order to enhance the neuromuscular control system. In order to accomplish this goal, the objective of the rehabilitation program should be to hyperstimulate the joint and muscle receptors in order to encourage maximal afferent discharge to the respective CNS levels.[12,71,122,126,127]

First Level of Integration: The M1 Reflex

When faced with an unexpected load, the first reflexive muscle response is a burst of EMG activity that occurs after between 30 and 50 msec. The afferent fibers of the mechanoreceptors synapse with the spinal interneurons and produce a reflexive facilitation or inhibition of the motor neurons.[122,126,131] The

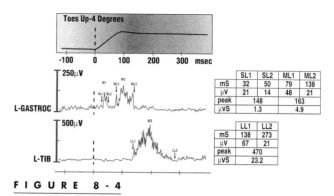

FIGURE 8-4

CNS levels of integration: Short- and long-loop postural reflexes. The components of the evoked postural assessed: (M1) myotatic reflex, (M2) segmental (polysynaptic) response, and (M3) long-loop response involving the brainstem, cortex, and ascending and descending spinal pathways. (Modified, with permission, from NeuroCom International, Clackamas, OR.)

monosynaptic stretch reflex or M1 reflex is one of the most rapid reflexes underlying limb control (Fig. 8-4). The latency or time of this response is very short because it involves only one synapse and the information has a relatively short distance to travel. Unfortunately, the muscle response is brief, which does not result in much added contraction of the muscle. The M1 short reflex loop is most often called into play when minute adjustments in muscle length are needed. The stimulus of small muscular stretches occurs during postural sways or when our limbs are subjected to unanticipated loads. Therefore, this mechanism is responsible for regulating motor control of the antagonistic and synergistic patterns of muscle contraction.[99] These adjustments are necessary when misalignment exists between intended muscle length and actual muscle length. This misalignment is most likely to occur in situations where unexpected forces are applied to the limb or the muscle begins to fatigue. In the situation of involuntary and undesirable lengthening of muscles about a joint during conditions of abnormal stress, the short M1 loop must provide for reflex muscle splinting in order to prevent injury from occurring. The M1 reflex occurs at an unconscious level and is not affected by outside factors. These responses can occur simultaneously to control limb position and posture. Because they can occur at the same time, are in parallel, are subconscious, and are without cortical interference, they do not require attention and are thus automatic.

There are two important short reflex loops acting in the body: the stretch reflex and the gamma reflex loop. The stretch reflex (Fig. 8-5) is triggered when the length of an extrafusal muscle fiber is altered, causing the sensory endings within the muscle spindle to be mechanically deformed. Once deformed, these sensory endings fire, sending nerve impulses into the spinal cord via an afferent sensory neuron located just outside the spinal cord. The information from the Ia afferent is sent essentially to two places: to the alpha motor neurons in the same

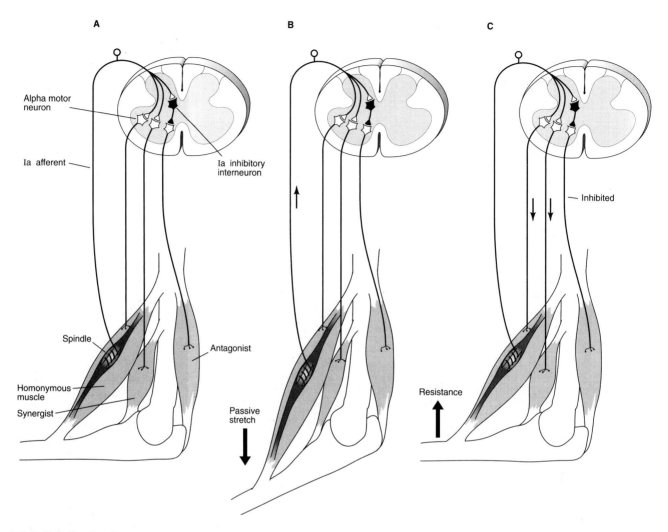

A   **B**   **C**

Alpha motor
neuron

Ia afferent

Ia inhibitory
interneuron

Spindle

Antagonist

Homonymous
muscle

Synergist

Resistance

Passive
stretch

Inhibited

F I G U R E   8 - 5

Excitation of the muscle spindle is responsible for the stretch reflex. **A,** Ia afferent fibers making monosynaptic excitatory connections to alpha motor neurons innervating the same muscle from which they arise and motor neurons innervating synergist muscles. They also inhibit motor neurons to antagonist muscles through an inhibitory interneuron. **B,** When a muscle is stretched, the Ia afferents increase their firing rate. **C,** This leads to contraction of the same muscle and its synergists and relaxation of the antagonist. The reflex therefore tends to counteract the stretch, enhancing the spring-like properties of the muscle. (Reproduced, with permission, from Gordon J, Ghez C. Muscle receptors and stretch reflexes. In: Kandel E. et al (eds). *Principles of Neural Science,* 3rd ed. East Norwalk, CT, Appleton & Lange, 1991, p. 576.)

muscle and also upward to the various sensory regions in the cerebral cortex. As soon as these impulses reach the spinal cord, they are transferred to alpha motor neurons that innervate the very same muscle that houses the activated muscle spindles. The loop time, or the time from the initial stretch until the extrafusial fibers are increased in their innervation, is about 30 to 40 msec in humans.[102] Stimulation of the muscle spindle ceases when the muscle contracts, because the spindle fibers, which lie parallel to the extrafusial fibers, return to their original length. It is through the operation of this reflex that we are able to con-

tinuously alter muscle tone and/or make subtle adjustments in muscle length during movement. These latter adjustments may be in response to external factors producing unexpected loads or forces on the moving limbs.

For example, consider what happens when an additional load is applied to an already loaded limb being held in a given position in space.[27] The muscles of the limb are set at a given length, and alpha motor neurons are firing in order to maintain the desired limb position in spite of the load and gravity. Now an additional load is added to the end of the limb, causing the muscles to lengthen as the limb drops. This stretching of the extrafusial muscle fibers results in almost simultaneous stretching of the muscle spindle, which then fires and sends signals to the spinal cord and alpha motor neurons that serve the same muscle. The firing rate of these alpha motor neurons is subsequently increased, causing the muscles in the dropping limb to be further contracted, and the limb is restored to its previous position. Visual information to the stimulus of loading would also lead to increased contraction in the falling limb, but initiating the corrective response consciously would involve considerably longer delays because of additional processing at the cortical level.[27] The short-loop M1 stretch reflex response times are possible within 30 to 50 msec.[58] Visual-based corrections involved corrective delays on the order of 150 to 200 msec.[58] Given that the rapid correction is required for injury prevention, it is important that these short-loop reflex pathways are available for use.

Muscle spindles also play an important role in the ongoing control and modification of movement by virtue of their involvement in a spinal reflex loop known as the gamma reflex loop. The afferent information from the muscle spindle synapses with both the alpha and gamma motor neurons. The alpha motor neuron sends the information it receives to the muscles involved in the movements. The gamma motor neuron sends the same information back to the muscle spindle, which can be stimulated to begin firing at its polar ends. The independent innervation of the muscle spindle by the gamma motor neuron is thought to be important during muscle contractions when the intrafusial fibers of the spindle would normally be slack. Gamma activation of the spindle results in stretching of the intrafusial even though the extrafusial fibers are contracting. In essence, the gamma system takes up the slack in the spindle caused by muscle contraction, thereby making corrections in minute changes in length of the muscle more quickly.

In the short-loop system of spinal control, the activity of the Ia afferent fibers is determined by two things: (1) the length and the rate of the stretch of the extrafusial muscle fibers; and (2) the amount of tension in the intrafusial fibers, which is determined by the firing of the gamma efferent fibers. Both alpha and gamma motor neurons can be controlled by higher motor centers, and they are thought to be "coordinated" in their action by a process termed *alpha-gamma coactivation*.[44,98] Therefore, the output to the main body of the muscle is determined by (1) the level of innervation provided directly from higher centers and (2) the amount of added innervation provided indirectly from the Ia afferent.[102] This helps to explain how an individual can respond quickly to an unexpected event without conscious involvement of the CNS. When an unexpected event or perturbation causes a muscle to stretch, the spindle's sensory receptors are stimulated. The resulting Ia afferent firing causes a stretch reflex that will increase the activity in the main muscle, all within 40 msec. All of this activity occurs at the same level of the spinal cord as did the innervation of the muscle in the first place. Therefore, no high centers were involved in this 40-msec loop.

At this level of motor control, activities to encourage short-loop reflex joint stabilization should dominate.[12,71,110,126]

These activities are characterized by sudden alterations in joint position that require reflex muscle stabilization. With sudden alterations or perturbations, both the articular and muscular mechanoreceptors will be stimulated for the production of reflex stabilization. Rhythmic stabilization exercises encourage monosynaptic co-contraction of the musculature, thereby producing a dynamic neuromuscular stabilization.[114] These exercises serve to build a foundation for dynamic stability.

Second Level of Integration: The M2 Reflex

For larger adjustments in limb and overall body position, it is necessary to involve the longer reflex loops that extend beyond single segments within the spinal cord. When the muscle spindle is stretched and the Ia afferent fibers are activated, the information is relayed to the spinal cord, where it synapses with the alpha motor neuron. Additionally, information is sent to higher levels of control, where the Ia information is integrated with other information in the sensory and motor centers in the cerebral cortex to produce a more complete response to the imposed stretch. Approximately 50 to 80 msec after an unexpected stimulus, there is a second burst of EMG activity (see Fig. 8-4). Because the pathways involved in these neural circuits travel to the more distant subcortical and cortical levels of the CNS to connect with structures such as the motor cortex and cerebellum within the larger projection system, the reflex requires more time or has a longer latency. Therefore, the 80-msec loop time for this activity corresponds not only to the additional distance that the impulses have to travel but also to the multiple synapses that must take place to close the circuit. Both the M1 and M2 responses are responsible for the reflex response that occurs when a tendon is tapped. An example of this occurs when the patellar tendon is tapped with a reflex hammer. The quadricep muscle is stretched, initiating a reflex response that contracts the quadriceps and produces an involuntary extension of the lower leg.

Even though there is a time lapse for the longer-loop reflexes to take place, there are two important advantages for these reflexes. First, the EMG activity from the long-loop reflex is far stronger than that involved in the monosynaptic stretch reflex. The early short-loop monosynaptic reflex system does not result in much actual increase in force. The long-loop reflex can, however, produce enough force necessary to move the limb/joint back into a more neutral position. Second, because the long-loop reflexes are organized in a higher center, they are more flexible than the monosynaptic reflex. By allowing for the involvement of a few other sources of sensory information during the response, an individual can voluntary adjust the size or amplitude of the M2 response for a given input to generate a powerful response when the goal is to hold the joint as firmly as possible, or to produce no response if the goal is to release under the increasing load. The ability to regulate this response allows an individual to prepare the limb to conform to different environmental demands.

Therefore, the second level of motor control interaction is at the level of the brainstem.[11,122,130] At this level, afferent mechanoreceptors interact with the vestibular system and visual input from the eyes to control or facilitate postural stability and equilibrium of the body.[12,71,122,127,130] Afferent mechanoreceptor input also works in concert with the muscle spindle complex by inhibiting antagonistic muscle activity under conditions of rapid lengthening and periarticular distortion, both of which accompany postural disruption.[92,126] In conditions of disequilibrium where simultaneous neural input exists, a neural pattern is generated that affects the muscular stabilizers, thereby returning equilibrium to the body's center of gravity.[122] Therefore, balance is influenced by the same peripheral afferent mechanism that mediates joint proprioception and is at least partially dependent upon the individual's inherent ability to integrate joint position sense with neuromuscular control.[120]

INTEGRATION OF BALANCE TRAINING: THE SECOND LEVEL OF MOTOR CONTROL

Both proprioception and balance training have been advocated to restore motor control to the lower extremity. In the clinic, the term "balance" is often used without a clear definition. It is important to remember that proprioception and balance are not the same. Proprioception is a precursor of good balance and adequate function. Balance is the process by which we control the body's center of mass with respect to the base of support, whether it is stationary or moving.

Berg has attempted to define balance in three ways: the ability to maintain a position, the ability to voluntarily move, and the ability to react to a perturbation.[9] All three of these components of balance are important in the maintenance of upright posture. Static balance refers to an individual's ability to maintain a stable antigravity position while at rest by maintaining the center of mass within the available base of support. Dynamic balance involves automatic postural responses to the disruption of the center of mass position. Reactive postural responses are activated to recapture stability when an unexpected force displaces the center of mass.[85]

Postural sway is a commonly used indicator of the integrity of the postural control system. Horak defined postural control as the ability to maintain equilibrium and orientation in the presence of gravity.[57] Researchers measure postural sway as either the maximum or the total excursion of center of pressure while standing on a forceplate. Little change is noted in healthy adults in quiet standing, but the frequency, amplitude, and total area of sway increase with advancing age or when vision or proprioceptive inputs are altered.[32,59,89,91]

In order to maintain balance, the body must make continual adjustments. Most of what is currently known about postural control is based upon stereotypical postural strategies activated in response to anteroposterior perturbation.[57,58,85] Horak and Nashner described several different strategies used to maintain balance.[58] These strategies include the ankle, hip, and stepping strategies. These strategies adjust the body's center of gravity so that the body is maintained within the base of support to prevent the loss of balance or falling. There are several factors that determine which strategy would be the most effective

response to postural challenge: speed and intensity of the displacing forces, characteristics of the support surface, and magnitude of the displacement of the center of mass. The automatic postural responses can be categorized as a class of functionally organized long-loop responses that produce muscle activation that brings the body's center of mass into a state of equilibrium.[85] Each of the strategies has reflex, automatic, and volitional components that interact to match the response to the challenge.

Small disturbances in the center of gravity can be compensated by motion at the ankle. The ankle strategy repositions the center of mass after small displacements due to slow-speed perturbations, which usually occur on a large, firm, supporting surface. The oscillations around the ankle joint with normal postural sway are an example of the ankle strategy. Anterior sway of the body is counteracted by gastrocnemius activity, which pulls the body posterior. Conversely, posterior sway of the body is counteracted by contraction of the anterior tibial muscles. If the disturbance in the center of gravity is too great to be counteracted by motion at the ankle, the patient will use a hip or stepping strategy to maintain the center of gravity within the base of support. The hip strategy uses rapid compensatory hip flexion or extension to redistribute the body weight within the available base of support when the center of mass is near the edge of the sway envelope. The hip strategy is usually in response to a moderate or large postural disturbance, especially on an uneven, narrow, or moving surface. The hip strategy is often employed while standing on a bus that is rapidly accelerating. When sudden, large-amplitude forces displace the center of mass beyond the limits of control, a step is used to enlarge the base of support and redefine a new sway envelope. New postural control can then be reestablished. An example of the stepping strategy is the uncoordinated step that often follows a stumble on an unexpected or uneven sidewalk.

The maintenance of balance requires the integration of sensory information from a number of different systems: vision, vestibular, and proprioception. For most healthy adults, the preferred sense for postural control comes from proprioceptive information. Therefore, if proprioception is altered or diminished, balance will also be altered. The functional assessment of the combined peripheral, visual, and vestibular contributions to neuromuscular control can be measured with computerized balance measures of postural stability. The sensory organization test protocol is used to evaluate the relative contribution of vision, vestibular, and proprioceptive input to the control of postural stability when conflicting sensory input occurs.[85] Postural sway is assessed (NeuroCom Smart System) under six increasingly challenging conditions (Fig. 8-6). Baseline sway is recorded in quiet standing with the eyes open. The reliance on vision is evaluated by asking the patient to close the eyes. A significant increase in sway or loss of balance suggests an overreliance on visual input.[85,107,143] Sensory integration is evaluated when the visual surround moves in concert with sway (sway-referenced vision), creating inaccurate visual input. The patient is then retested on a support surface that moves with sway (sway-referenced support), thereby reducing the quality

Sensory Organization Test (SOT)

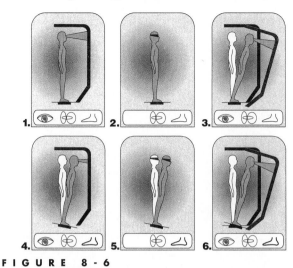

FIGURE 8-6

The sensory organization conditions integrating vestibular, visual, and somatosensory contributions to balance. (Reproduced, with permission, from NeuroCom International, Clackamas, OR.)

and availability of proprioceptive input for sensory integration. With the eyes open, vision and vestibular input contribute to the postural responses. With the eyes closed, vestibular input is the primary source of information, because proprioceptive input is altered. The most challenging condition includes sway-referenced vision and sway-referenced support surface.[57,85,107]

Balance activities, both with and without visual input, will enhance motor function at the brainstem level.[11,122] It is important that these activities remain specific to the types of activities or skills that will be required of the athlete upon return to sport.[96] Static balance activities should be used as a precursor to more dynamic skill activity.[96] Static balance skills can be initiated once the individual is able to bear weight on the lower extremity. The general progression of static balance activities is to progress from bilateral to unilateral and from eyes open to eyes closed.[71,96,122,133,134] With balance training, it is important to remember that sensory systems respond to environmental manipulation. To stimulate or facilitate the proprioceptive system, vision must disadvantaged. This can be accomplished in several ways: remove vision with either the eyes closed or blindfolded, destabilize vision by demanding hand and eye movements (ball toss) or moving the visual surround, or confuse vision with unstable visual cues that disagree with the proprioceptive and vestibular inputs (sway referencing).

In order to stimulate vision, proprioception must be either destabilized or confused. The logical progression to destabilize proprioception is to progress the balance training from a stable surface to an unstable surface such as a mini-tramp, balance board, or dynamic stabilization trainer.[71,122,130] As joint position changes, dynamic stabilization must occur for the patient to control the unstable surface (Fig. 8-7). Vision can be confused

during balance training by having the patient stand on a compliant surface such as a foam mat or using a sway-referenced moving forceplate.

Disadvantaging both vision and proprioceptive information can stimulate the vestibular system. This can be accomplished by several different methods. Absent vision with an unstable or compliant surface is achieved with eyes-closed training on an unstable surface. Demanding hand and eye movements while on a floor mat or foam pad will destabilize both vision and proprioception. A moving surround with a moving forceplate will confuse both vision and proprioceptive input.

The patients should initially perform the static balance activities while concentrating on the specific task (position sense and neuromuscular control) to facilitate and maximize sensory output. As the task becomes easier, activities to distract the athlete's concentration (catching a ball or performing mental exercises) should be incorporated into the training program. This will help to facilitate the conversion of conscious to unconscious motor programming.[122,130] Balance training exercises should induce joint perturbations in order to facilitate reflex muscle activation.

There have been several studies to assess the effect of lower-quarter injury on standing balance. Usually the balance characteristics of the injured extremity are compared to those of the uninjured extremity. Mizuta et al measured postural sway in two groups: a functionally stable group and a functionally unstable group, both of which had unilateral ACL-deficient knees.[83] An additional group of individuals was also studied to serve as a control group. When compared to the control group, impairment in standing balance was found in the functionally unstable group but not in the functionally stable group. These results suggest that stabiliometry was a useful tool in the assessment of functional knee stability. Both Friden et al and Gauffin et al demonstrated impaired standing balance during unilateral stance in individuals with chronic ACL-deficient knees.[35,38] Following injury to the lower quarter, impaired standing balance may be due to the loss of muscular coordination, which could have resulted from the loss of normal proprioceptive feedback.[4,67]

Third Level of Integration: The Voluntary Reaction—Time Response (M3)

The final response that occurs when an unexpected load is applied to the limb is the voluntary long-loop reaction or M3 response (see Fig. 8-4). Seen as the third burst of EMG activity, it is a powerful and sustained response that brings the limb back into the desired position. The latency of the M3 response is about 120 to 180 msec, depending upon the task and the circumstances. Information is processed at the cerebral cortex, where the mechanoreceptors interact and influence cognitive awareness of body position and movement in which motor commands are initiated for voluntary movements.[12,92,99,122] It is in this region of the primary sensory cortex that there is a high degree of spatial orientation.

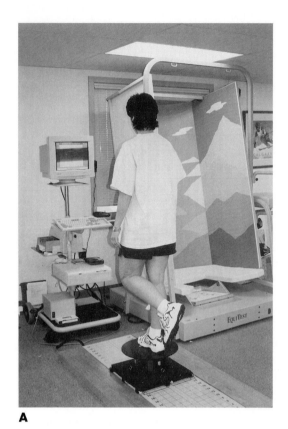
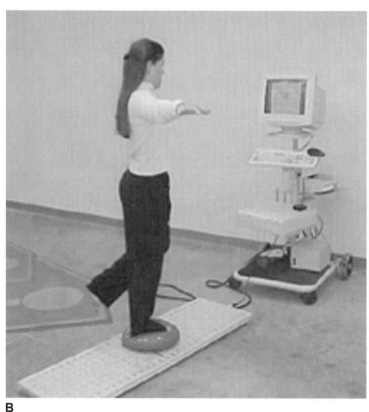

A

B

F I G U R E   8 - 7

Unstable surface training on the Neurocom BalanceMaster. **A,** Dynamic Stabilization Trainer. **B,** Dynadisc.

The M3 response is very flexible and can be modified by a host of factors such as verbal instructions or anticipation of the incoming sensory information. The delay in the M3 response makes it sensitive to a number of stimulus-alternatives. Therefore, the individual's ability to respond will require some conscious attention. Training at this level of the cerebral cortex stimulates the conversion of conscious programming to unconscious programming. These responses have often been referred to as triggered reactions. Triggered reactions are prestructured, coordinated reactions in the same or closely related musculature that are "triggered" into action by the mechanoreceptors. The triggered reaction may bypass the information-processing centers because the reaction is stereotyped, predictable, and well practiced. These reactions have latencies from 80 to 180 msec and are far more variable than the latencies of the faster reflexes.[102] The triggered reactions can be learned and can become a more or less automatic response. The individual does not have to spend time processing a response reaction and programming; the reaction is just "triggered off" almost as if it were automatic.[101] Therefore, with training the speed of the M3 response could be increased in order to produce a more automatic reflex response.

The appreciation of joint position at the highest or cognitive level needs to be included in the RNT program. These types of activities are initiated on the cognitive level and include programming motor commands for voluntary movement. The repetitions of these movements will maximally stimulate the conversion of conscious programming to unconscious programming.[12,71,122,126,127,130] The term for this type of training is the *forced-use paradigm.* By making a task significantly more difficult or asking for multiple tasks, we bombard the CNS with input. The CNS attempts to sort and process this overload information by opening additional neural pathways. When the individual goes back to a basic task of ADL, the task becomes easier. This information can then be stored as a central command and ultimately performed without continuous reference to the conscious as a "triggered response."[12,71,122,126,127] As with all training, the single greatest obstacle to motor learning is the conscious mind. We must get the conscious mind out of the act!

COORDINATING THE MUSCLE RESPONSE WITH UNEXPECTED LOADS

The relative roles of these three muscle responses depend upon the duration of the movement. As previously discussed, the quickest action occurring in the body has a movement time of about 40 msec. When this type or action occurs, the M2 response is incapable of completing or modifying the activity once it is initiated. Even the M1 response has only enough time to begin influencing the muscles near the end of the movement. As the movement time increases, there is a greater potential for the M1 and M2 responses to contribute to the intended action. Movements that take a longer time to be completed (>100 msec) will allow both the M1 and M2 responses sufficient time to contribute to all levels of the action. Only when the duration of the movement is 300 msec or longer is there potential for the M3 long-loop response to be involved in amending the movement. Therefore, for movements that take longer than 300 msec for individuals to complete, closed-loop control is possible at several levels of integration at the same time.

Why Is Response Time Important?

When an unexpected load is placed upon a joint, ligamentous damage occurs after between 70 and 90 msec unless an appropriate response ensues.[7,94,140] Therefore, reactive muscle activity must occur with sufficient magnitude in the 40- to 80-msec time frame after loading begins in order to protect the capsuloligamentous structures. The closed-loop system of CNS integration may not be fast enough to produce a response in order to increase muscle stiffness. Simply, there is no time for the system to process the information and process the feedback about the condition. Failure of the dynamic restraint system to control these abnormal forces will expose the static structures to excessive forces. In this case, the open-loop system of anticipation becomes more important in producing the desired response. Preparatory muscle activity in anticipation of joint loading can influence the reactive muscle activation patterns. Anticipatory activation increases the sensitivity of the muscle spindles, thereby allowing the unexpected perturbations to be detected more quickly.[29]

Very quick movements are completed before feedback can be used to produce an action to alter the course of movement. Therefore, if the movement is fast enough, a mechanism like a motor program would have to be used to control the entire action, with the movement being carried out without any feedback. Fortunately, the open-loop control system allows the motor control system to organize an entire action ahead of time. In order for this to occur, previous knowledge of the following needs to be preprogrammed into the primary sensory cortex:

- The particular muscles that are needed to produce an action.
- The order in which these muscles need to be activated.
- The relative forces of the various muscle contractions.
- The relative timing and sequencing of these actions.
- The duration of the respective contractions.

In the open-loop system, movement is organized in advance by a program that sets up some kind of neural mechanism or network that is preprogrammed. A classic example of this occurs in the body as postural adjustments are made before

the intended movement. When an individual raises the arm up into forward flexion, the first muscle groups to fire are not even in the shoulder girdle region. The first muscles to contract are those in the lower back and legs (approximately 80 msec before noticeable activity in the shoulder).[8] Since the shoulder muscles are linked to the rest of the body, their contraction affects posture. If no preparatory compensations in posture were made, raising the arm would shift the center of gravity forward, causing a slight loss of balance. The feed-forward motor control system takes care of this potential problem by preprogramming the appropriate postural modification first, rather than requiring the body to make adjustments after the arm begins to move.

Lee has demonstrated that these preparatory postural adjustments are not independent of the arm movement, but rather a part of the total motor pattern.[70] When the arm movements are organized, the motor instructions are preprogrammed to adjust posture first and then move the arm. Therefore, arm movement and postural control are not separate events but rather different parts of an integrated action that raises the arm while maintaining balance. Lee showed that these EMG preparatory postural adjustments disappear when the individual leans against some type of support prior to raising the arm. The motor control system recognizes that advance preparation of postural control is not needed when the body is supported against the wall.

It is important to remember that most motor tasks are a complex blend of both open- and closed-loop operations. Therefore, both types of control are often at work simultaneously. Both feed-forward and feedback neuromuscular control can enhance dynamic stability if the sensory and motor pathways are frequently stimulated.[71] Each time a signal passes through a sequence of synapses, the synapses become more capable of transmitting the same signal.[50,56] When these pathways are "facilitated" regularly, memory of that signal is created and can be recalled to program future movements.[50,102]

REESTABLISHING PROPRIOCEPTION AND NEUROMUSCULAR CONTROL

Although the concept and value of proprioceptive mechanoreceptors have been documented in the literature, treatment techniques directed at improving their function generally have not been incorporated into the overall rehabilitation program. The neurosensory function of the capsuloligamentous structures has taken a backseat to the mechanical structural role. This is mainly due to the lack of information about how mechanoreceptors contribute to the specific functional activities and how they can be specifically activated.[37,42] Following injury to the capsuloligamentous structures, it is thought that a partial deafferentation of the joint occurs as the mechanoreceptors become disrupted. This partial deafferentation, which is secondary to injury, may be related to either direct or indirect injury. Direct trauma effects would include disruption of the joint capsule or ligaments, whereas posttraumatic joint effusion or hemarthrosis[67] can illustrate indirect effects.

Whether a direct or indirect cause, the resultant partial deafferentation alters the afferent information into the CNS and therefore the resulting reflex pathways to the dynamic stabilizing structures. These pathways are required by both the feed-forward and feedback motor control systems to dynamically stabilize the joint. A disruption in the proprioceptive pathway will result in an alteration of position and kinesthesia.[4,111] Barrack et al showed an increase in the threshold to detect passive motion in a majority of patients with ACL rupture and functional instability.[4] Corrigan et al, who also found diminished proprioception after ACL rupture, confirmed this finding.[24] Diminished proprioceptive sensitivity has also been shown to cause giving way or episodes of instability in the ACL-deficient knee.[13] Therefore, injury to the capsuloligamentous structures not only reduces the joint's mechanical stability but also diminishes the capability of the dynamic neuromuscular restraint system. Therefore, any aberration in joint motion and position sense will impact both the feed-forward and feedback neuromuscular control systems. Without adequate anticipatory muscle activity, the static structures may be exposed to insult unless the reactive muscle activity can be initiated to contribute to dynamic restraint.

Deficits in the neuromuscular reflex pathways may have a detrimental effect on the motor control system as a protective mechanism. Diminished sensory feedback can alter the reflex stabilization pathways, thereby causing a latent motor response when faced with unexpected forces or trauma. Beard et al demonstrated disruption of the protective reflex arc in subjects with ACL deficiency.[7] A significant deficit in reflex activation of the hamstring muscles after a 100-Newton anterior shear force in a single-legged closed-chain position was identified, as compared to the contralateral uninjured limb.[7] Beard demonstrated that the latency was directly related to the degree of knee instability, the greater the instability, the greater the latency. Other researchers found similar alterations in the muscle-firing patterns in the ACL-deficient patient.[65,116,140] Solomonow et al found that a direct stress applied to the ACL resulted in reflex hamstring activity, thereby contributing to the maintenance of joint stability.[116] Although this response was also present in ACL-deficient knees, the reflex was significantly slower.

Although it has been demonstrated that a proprioceptive deficit occurs following knee injury, both kinesthetic awareness and reposition sense can be at least partially restored with surgery and rehabilitation. A number of studies have examined proprioception following ACL reconstruction. Barrett measured proprioception after autogenous graft repair and found that the proprioception was better than that of the average ACL-deficient patient but still significantly worse than the proprioception in the normal knee.[5] Barrett further noted that the patients' satisfaction was more closely correlated with their proprioception than with their clinical score.[5] Harter et al could not demonstrate a significant difference in the reproduction of passive positioning between the operative and nonoperative knee

at an average of 3 years after ACL reconstruction.[53] Kinesthesia has been reported to be restored after surgery as detected by the threshold to the detection of passive motion in the midrange of motion.[4] A longer threshold to the detection of passive motion was observed in the ACL-reconstructed knee compared with the contralateral uninvolved knee when tested at the end range of motion.[4] Lephart et al found similar results in patients after either arthroscopically assisted patellar-tendon autograft or allograft ACL reconstruction.[74] The importance of incorporating a proprioceptive element in any comprehensive rehabilitation program is justified based upon the results of these studies.

The effects of how surgical and nonsurgical interventions may facilitate the restoration of the neurosensory roles is unclear; however, it has been shown that ligamentous retensioning coupled with rehabilitation can restore proprioceptive sensitivity.[72] Since afferent input is altered after joint injury, proprioceptive rehabilitation must focus on restoring proprioceptive sensitivity to retrain these altered afferent pathways and enhance the sensation of joint movement. Restoration may be facilitated by (1) enhancing mechanoreceptor sensitivity, (2) increasing the number of mechanoreceptors stimulated, and (3) enhancing the compensatory sensation from the secondary receptor sites. Research should be directed toward developing new techniques to improve proprioceptive sensitivity.

Methods to improve proprioception after injury or surgery could improve function and decrease the risk for reinjury. Ihara and Nakayama demonstrated a reduction in the neuromuscular lag time with dynamic joint control following a 3-week training period on an unstable board.[65] The maintenance of equilibrium and improvement in reaction to sudden perturbations on the unstable board served to improve the neuromuscular coordination. This phenomenon was first reported by Freeman and Wyke in 1967 when they found that proprioceptive deficits could be reduced with training on an unstable surface.[33] They found that proprioceptive training through stabiliometry, or training on an unstable surface, significantly reduced the episodes of giving way following ankle sprains. Tropp et al confirmed the work of Freeman by demonstrating that the results of stabiliometry could be improved with coordination training on an unstable board.[124] Hocherman et al also showed an improvement in the movement amplitude of an unstable board and the weight distribution on the feet found in hemiplegic patients who received training on an unstable board.[55]

Barrett[5] has demonstrated the relationship between proprioception and function. Barrett's study suggests that limb function relies more on proprioceptive input than on strength during activity. Borsa et al also found a high correlation between diminished kinesthesia with the single-leg hop test.[12] The single-leg hop test was chosen for its integrative measure of neuromuscular control, because a high degree of proprioceptive sensibility and functional ability is required to successfully propel the body forward and land safely on the limb. Giove et al reported a higher success rate in returning athletes to competitive sports through adequate hamstring rehabilitation.[40] Tibone et al and Ihara and

Nakayama found that simple hamstring strengthening alone was not adequate; it was necessary to obtain voluntary or reflex-level control on knee instability in order to return to functional activities.[65,121] Walla et al found that 95 percent of patients were able to successfully avoid surgery after ACL injury when they were able to achieve "reflex-level" hamstring control.[136] Ihara and Nakayama found that the reflex arc between stressing the ACL and hamstring contraction could be shortened with training.[65] With the use of unstable boards, the researchers were able to successfully decrease the reaction time. Since afferent input is altered after joint injury, proprioceptive sensitivity to retrain these altered afferent pathways is critical to shorten the time lag of muscular reaction in order to counteract the excessive strain on the passive structures and guard against injury.

What About Muscle Fatigue?

It has been well established in the literature that muscle fatigue can play a major role in destabilizing a joint.[100,111,117,129] With fatigue, an increase in knee joint laxity has been noted in both males and females.[100,117,118] More importantly, the body's ability to receive and accurately process proprioceptive information is affected by muscular fatigue. There is evidence that exercise to the point of clinical fatigue does have an effect on proprioception.[111,129] Research has demonstrated that the ability to learn or make improvement in joint position sense is severely impaired with muscle fatigue.[75,100] Likewise, muscle fatigue has been shown to alter both kinesthesia and joint position sense.[2,111,129] Skinner et al showed that the reproduction of passive positioning was significantly diminished following a fatigue protocol.[111] Voight et al also demonstrated a significant proprioceptive deficit following a fatigue protocol.[129] This suggests that patients who are fatigued may have a change in their proprioceptive abilities and be more prone to injury. Following a lower-quarter isokinetic fatigue protocol, postural sway as measured with EMG and forceplates is also increased following muscular fatigue.[66,129] This suggests that muscular fatigue results in a possible motor control deficit. In addition to disruption balance or postural sway, Nyland et al also demonstrated on EMG that muscular fatigue affects muscle activity by extending the latency of the muscle firing.[87]

Modifying Afferent/Efferent Characteristics: How Do We Do It?

The mechanoreceptors in and around the respective joints offer information about the change of position, motion, and loading of the joint to the central nervous system, which in turn stimulates the muscles around the joint to function.[65] If a time lag exists in the neuromuscular reaction, injury may occur. The shorter the time lag, the less stress to the ligaments and other soft-tissue structures about the joint. Therefore, the foundation of neuromuscular control is to facilitate the integration of peripheral sensations relative to joint position and then process this information into an effective efferent motor response. The main objective of the rehabilitation program for neuromuscular control is to develop or reestablish the afferent and efferent characteristics about the joint that are essential for dynamic restraint.[71]

There are several different afferent and efferent characteristics that contribute to the efficient regulation of motor control. As discussed previously, these characteristics include the sensitivity of the mechanoreceptors and facilitation of the afferent neural pathways, enhancing muscle stiffness, and the production of reflex muscle activation. The specific rehabilitation techniques must also take into consideration the levels of CNS integration. For the rehabilitation program to be complete, each of the three levels must be addressed in order to produce dynamic stability. The plasticity of the neuromuscular system permits rapid adaptations during the rehabilitation program that enhance preparatory and reactive activity.[7,56,65,71,74,141] Specific rehabilitation techniques that produce adaptations that enhance the efficiency of these neuromuscular techniques include balance training, biofeedback training, reflex facilitation through reactive training, and eccentric and high-repetition/low-load exercises.[71]

OBJECTIVES OF NEUROMUSCULAR CONTROL: REACTIVE NEUROMUSCULAR TRAINING

Reactive Neuromuscular Training (RNT) activities are designed both to restore functional stability about the joint and to enhance motor control skills. The Reactive Neuromuscular Training program centers around the stimulation of both the peripheral and central reflex pathways to the skeletal muscles. The first objective that should be addressed in the RNT program is the restoration of dynamic stability. Reliable kinesthetic and proprioceptive information provides the foundation on which dynamic stability and motor control are based. It has already been established that altered afferent information into the CNS can alter the feed-forward and feedback motor control systems. Therefore, the first objective of the Reactive Neuromuscular Training program is to restore the neurosensory properties of the damaged structures while at the same time enhancing the sensitivity of the secondary peripheral afferents.[74] The restoration of dynamic stability allows for the control of abnormal joint translation during functional activities. In order for this to occur, the reestablishment of dynamic stability is dependent upon the CNS receiving appropriate information from the peripheral receptors. If the information into the system is altered or inappropriate for the stimulus, a bad motor response will ensue.

To facilitate appropriate kinesthetic and proprioceptive information to the CNS, joint reposition exercises should be used to provide a maximal stimulation of the peripheral mechanoreceptors. The use of closed kinetic chain activities creates axial loads that maximally stimulate the articular mechanoreceptors via the increase in compressive forces.[22,45] The use of closed-chain exercises not only enhances joint congruency and neurosensory feedback but also minimizes the shearing stresses about the joint.[128] At the same time, the muscle receptors are facilitated by both the change in length and tension.[22,45] The objective is to induce unanticipated perturbations, thereby stimulating reflex stabilization. The persistent use of these pathways will decease the response time when faced with an unanticipated joint load.[88] In addition to weight-bearing exercises, joint repositioning exercises can be used to enhance the conscious appreciation of proprioception. Rhythmic stabilization exercises can be included early in the RNT program to enhance neuromuscular coordination in response to unexpected joint translation. The intensity of the exercises can be manipulated by increasing either the weight loaded across the joint or the size of the perturbation. The addition of a compressive sleeve, wrap, or taping about the joint can also provide additional proprioceptive information by stimulating the cutaneous mechanoreceptors.[5,71,76,90] Following the restoration of ROM and strength, dynamic stability can be enhanced with reflex stabilization and basic motor learning exercises.

The second objective of the Reactive Neuromuscular Training program is to encourage preparatory agonist–antagonist co-contraction. Efficient coactivation of the musculature restores the normal force couples that are necessary to balance joint forces and increase joint congruency, thereby reducing the loads imparted onto the static structures.[71] The cornerstone of rehabilitation during this phase is postural stability training. Environmental conditions are manipulated to produce a sensory response. Specifically, the three variables of balance that are manipulated include bilateral to unilateral stance, eyes open to eyes closed, and stable to unstable surfaces. The use of unstable surfaces allows the clinician to use positions of compromise in order to produce maximal afferent input into the spinal cord, thereby producing a reflex response. Dynamic coactivation of the muscles about the joint to produce a stabilizing force requires both the feed-forward and feedback motor control systems. In order to facilitate these pathways, the joint must be placed into positions of compromise in order for the patient to develop reactive stabilizing strategies. Although it was once believed that the speed of the stretch reflexes could not be directly enhanced, efforts to do so have been successful in human and animal studies. This has significant implications for reestablishing the reactive capability of the dynamic restraint system. Reducing the electromechanical delay between joint loading and the protective muscle activation can increase dynamic stability. In the controlled clinical environment, positions of vulnerability can be used safely.

Proprioceptive training for functionally unstable joints has been documented in the literature following injury.[65,106,123,125] Tropp et al[124] and Wester et al[137] reported that ankle disk training significantly reduced the incidence of ankle sprain. Concerning the mechanism of effects, Tropp et al suggested that unstable surface training reduced the proprioceptive deficit.[124] Sheth et al demonstrated changes with healthy adults in the patterns of contractions on the inversion and eversion musculature before and after training on an unstable surface.[106] They concluded that the changes would be supported by the concept of reciprocal Ia inhibition via the mechanoreceptors in the muscles. Konradsen and Ravin also suggested that the afferent input from the calf musculature was responsible for dynamic protection against sudden ankle inversion stress.[68] Pinstaar et al reported that postural sway was restored after 8 weeks of ankle disk training when carried out 3 to 5 times a week.[93] Tropp and Odenrick also showed that postural control improved after 6 weeks of training when performed 15 minutes per day.[125] Bernier and Perrin, whose program consisted of balance exercises progressing from simple to complex sessions (3 times a week for 10 minutes), also found that postural sway was improved after 6 weeks of training.[10] Although there were some differences in each of these training programs, the postural control improved after 6 to 8 weeks of proprioceptive training for participants with functional instability of the ankle.

Once dynamic stability has been achieved, the focus of the RNT program is to restore ADL and sport-specific skills. Exercise and training drills should be incorporated into the program that will refine the physiologic parameters that are required for the return to preinjury levels of function. Emphasis in the RNT program must be placed upon a progression from simple to complex neuromotor patterns that are specific to the demands placed upon the patient during function. The training program should begin with simple activities, such as walking/running, and then progress to highly complex motor skills requiring refined neuromuscular mechanisms including proprioceptive and kinesthetic awareness that provide reflex joint stabilization.

EXERCISE PROGRAM/PROGRESSION

Dynamic reactive neuromuscular control activities should be initiated into the overall rehabilitation program once adequate healing has occurred. The progression to these activities is predicated on the athlete satisfactorily completing the activities that are considered prerequisites for the activity being considered. Keeping this in mind, the progression of activities must be goal oriented and specific to the tasks that will be expected of the athlete.

The general progression for activities to develop dynamic reactive neuromuscular control is from slow-speed to fast-speed activities, from low-force to high-force activities, and from controlled to uncontrolled activities. Initially these exercises should evoke a balance reaction or weight shift in the lower extremities and ultimately progress to a movement pattern. These reactions can be as simple as a static control with little or no visible movement or as complex as a dynamic plyometric response requiring explosive acceleration, deceleration, or change in direction. The exercises will allow the clinician to challenge the patient using visual and/or proprioceptive input via tubing and other devices (medicine balls, foam rolls, visual obstacles). Although these exercises will improve physiologic parameters, they are specifically designed to facilitate neuromuscular reactions. Therefore, the clinician must be concerned with the kinesthetic input and quality of the movement patterns rather than the particular number of sets and repetitions. Once fatigue occurs, motor control becomes poor and all training effects are lost. Therefore, during the exercise progression, all aspects of normal should be observed. These should include isometric, concentric, and eccentric muscle control; articular loading and unloading; balance control during weight shifting and direction changes; controlled acceleration and deceleration; and demonstration of both conscious and unconscious control.

Phase I: Static Stabilization (Closed-Chain Loading/Unloading)

Phase I involves minimal joint motion and should always follow a complete open-chain exercise program that restores near-full active range of motion. The patient should stand bearing full weight with equal distribution on the affected and unaffected lower extremity. The feet should be positioned approximately shoulder width apart. Greater emphasis can be placed on the affected lower extremity by having the patient put the unaffected lower extremity on a 6- to 8-inch stool or step bench. This flexes the hip and knee and forces a greater weight shift to the affected side yet still allows the unaffected extremity to assist with balance reactions (Fig. 8-8). The weight-bearing status then progresses to having the unaffected extremity suspended in front or behind the body, forcing a single-leg stance on the affected side (Fig. 8-9). The patient is then asked to continue the single-leg stance while shifting weight to the forefoot and toes by lifting the heel and plantarflexing the ankle. This places the complete responsibility of weight-bearing and balance reactions on the affected lower extremity. This position will also require slight flexion of the hip and knee. Support devices are often helpful and can minimize confusion. When the patient is first asked to progress weight bearing to the forefoot and toes, a heel lift device can be used. A support device can also be used to place the ankle in dorsiflexion, inversion, or eversion to increase kinesthetic input or decrease biomechanical stresses on the hip, knee, and ankle.

At each progression, the clinician may ask that the patient train with eyes closed to decrease the visual input and increase kinesthetic awareness. The clinician may also use an unstable surface with training in this phase to increase the demands on the mechanoreceptor system. The unstable surface will facilitate the reflex pathways mediated by the peripheral efferent receptors. Single or multidirectional rocker devices will assist the progression to the next phase (Fig. 8-10).

The physiologic rationale for this phase of reactive neuromuscular training is the use of static compression of the articular structures to produce maximal output of the mechanoreceptors, thereby facilitating isometric contractions of the musculature and providing a dynamic reflex stabilization. The self-generated oscillations will help increase the interplay between visual, mechanoreceptor, and equilibrium reaction. Changes in the isometric muscle tension will assist in the sensitization of the muscle spindle (gamma bias).

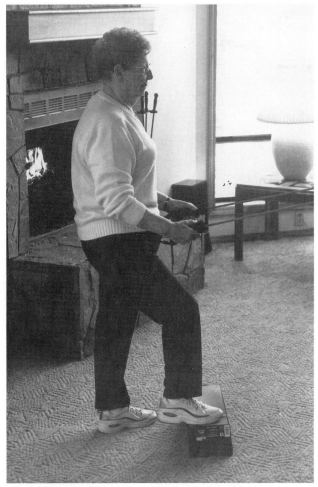

FIGURE 8-8

Static stabilization weight shifting technique to enhance transfer onto the left leg.

The exercise tubing technique used in this phase is called Oscillating Technique for Isometric Stabilization (OTIS). The technique can be used to stimulate muscle spindle and mechanoreceptor activity. The exercises involve continuously loaded short-arc movements of one body part, which in turn causes an isometric stabilization reaction of the involved body part. This is accomplished by pulling two pieces of tubing toward the body and returning the tubing to a start position in a smooth rhythmical fashion with increasing speeds. Resistance builds as the tubing is stretched. This forces a transfer of weight in the direction of the tubing. Because the involved body part is only required to react or respond to a simple stimulus, the oscillating stimulus will produce an isometric contraction in the lower extremity that must produce a stabilizing force in the direction opposite the tubing pull. The purpose of this technique is to quickly involve the proprioceptive system with minimal verbal and visual cueing. Ognibene et al demonstrated a significant improvement in both single-leg postural stability and reaction time with a 4-week training program using OTIS techniques.[88]

A

B

FIGURE 8-9

Static stabilization: Uniplanar anterior weight shift. **A,** Home health setting. **B,** Clinical setting.

A

B

FIGURE 8-10

Static stabilization: Single-leg stance/unstable surface. **A,** Using pillows in the home health setting. **B,** Using a Dynadisc in the clinical setting.

Change in direction—according to anterior, posterior, medial, and lateral weight shifting—will create specific planar demands. Each technique is given a name, which is related to the weight shift produced by the applied tension. The body will then react with an equal and opposite stabilization response. Therefore, the exercise is named for the cause and not the effect.

The goal during this phase is static stabilization. Numerous successful repetitions demonstrating stability are required to achieve motor learning and control.

UNIPLANAR EXERCISE

ANTERIOR WEIGHT SHIFT (AWS) The patient faces the tubing and pulls the tubing toward the body using a smooth, comfortable motion. This causes forward weight shift that is stabilized with an isometric counterforce consisting of hip extension, knee extension, and ankle plantarflexion. There should be little or no movement noted in the lower extremity. If movement is noted, resistance should be decreased to achieve the desired stability (see Fig. 8-9).

LATERAL WEIGHT SHIFT (LWS) The patient stands with the affected side facing the tubing. The tubing is pulled by one hand in front of the body and the other hand behind the body to equalize the force and minimize the rotation. This causes a lateral weight shift, which is stabilized with an isometric counterforce consisting of hip abduction, knee co-contraction, and ankle eversion.

MEDIAL WEIGHT SHIFT (MWS) The patient stands with the unaffected side facing the tubing. The tubing is pulled in the same fashion as above. This causes a medial weight shift, which is stabilized with an isometric counterforce consisting of hip adduction, knee co-contraction, and ankle inversion.

POSTERIOR WEIGHT SHIFT (PWS) The patient stands with his or her back to the tubing in the frontal plane. The tubing is pulled to the body from behind causing a posterior weight shift, which is stabilized by an isometric counterforce consisting of hip flexion, knee flexion, and ankle dorsiflexion.

MULTIPLANAR EXERCISE

The basic exercise program can be progressed to multiplanar activity by combining the PNF chop and lift patterns of the upper extremities. The chop patterns from the affected and unaffected side will cause a multiplanar stress requiring isometric stabilization. The patient will now be forced to automatically integrate the isometric responses that were developed in the previous uniplanar exercises. The force will be representative of the PNF diagonals of the lower extremities (Fig. 8-11). The lift patterns from the affected to the unaffected side will add multiplanar stress in the opposite direction (Fig. 8-12). Changing the resistance, speed of movement, or spatial orientation relative to the resistance can make modifications to the multiplanar exercise. If resistance is increased, the movement speed should be decreased to allow for a strong stabilizing counterforce. If the speed of

movement is increased, then resistance should be decreased to allow for a quick counterforce response. By altering the angle of the body in relation to the resistance, the quality of the movement is changed. A greater emphasis can be placed on one component while reducing the emphasis on another component.

TECHNIQUE MODIFICATION

These techniques can also be used with medicine ball exercises. The posture and position are nearly the same, but the medicine ball does not allow for the oscillations provided by the tubing. The medicine ball provides impulse activity and a more complex gradient of loading and unloading (Fig. 8-13). This is referred to as Impulse Technique for Isometric Stabilization (ITIS). As described, the patient is positioned to achieve the desired stress. The medicine ball is then used with a rebounding device or thrown by the clinician. Progression to ball toss while stabilizing on an unstable surface will disrupt concentration, thereby facilitating the conversion to unconscious reflex adaptation.

The elastic tubing and medicine ball techniques are similar in position but differ somewhat in physiologic demands. Therefore, they should be used to complement each other and not replace or substitute the other at random. When performing an ITIS activity with a medicine ball, the force exerted by the exercise device names the weight shift. The tubing will exert a pull and the ball will exert a push; therefore, they will be performed from the opposite sides to achieve the same weight shift.

Phase II: Transitional Stabilization (Conscious Controlled Motion Without Impact)

Phase II replaces isometric activity with controlled concentric and eccentric activity progressing through a full range of functional motion. The forces of gravity are coupled with tubing to simulate stress in both the vertical and horizontal planes. In phase I, gravitational forces statically load the neuromuscular system. Varying degrees of imposed lateral stress via the tubing are used to stimulate isometric stabilization. Phase II requires that the movement occur in the presence of varying degrees of imposed lateral stress. The movement stimulates the mechanoreceptors in two ways: (1) articular movement causes capsular stretch in a given direction at a given speed, and (2) the changes in the body position cause loading and unloading of the articular structures and pressure changes in the intracapsular fluid. The exercises in this phase use simple movements such as the squat and lunge. The addition of tubing adds a horizontal stress. Other simple movements such as walking, sidestepping, and the lateral slide board can also be emphasized to stimulate a more efficient and controlled movement.

The physiologic rationales for activities in this phase are the stimulation of dynamic postural responses and facilitation of concentric and eccentric contractions via the compression and translation of the articular structures. This is turn helps to increase muscle stiffness, which has a significant role in producing dynamic stabilization about the joint by resisting and absorbing joint loads.[80,81] Research has established that eccentric loading

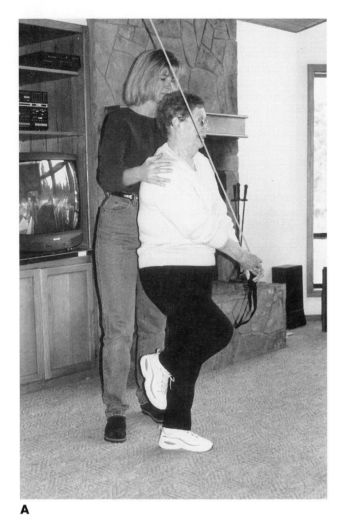

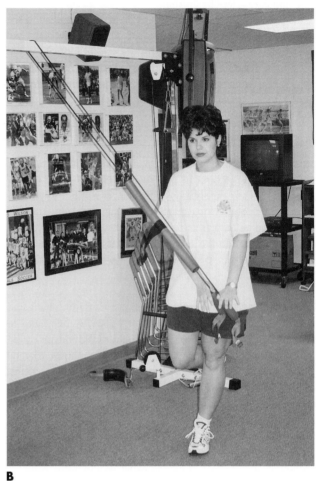

A   **B**

FIGURE 8-11

Static stabilization: Multiplanar PNF chop technique to provide rotational stress.
A, Home health setting. **B,** Clinical setting.

increases both muscle stiffness and tone.[16,95] Chronic overloading of the musculotendinous unit via eccentric contractions will result in not only connective tissue proliferation but also a desensitization of the GTO and increased muscle spindle activity.[64]

The self-generated movements require dynamic control in the midrange and static control at the end range of motion. Because a change in direction is required at the end ranges of motion, the interplay between visual, mechanoreceptor, and equilibrium reactions continues to increase. The "gamma bias" now responds to changes in both length and tension of the involved musculature.

Assisted techniques can also be used in this phase to progress patients who may find phase II exercise fatiguing or difficult. Assisted exercise is used to reduce the effect of gravity on the body or an extremity to allow for an increase in the quality or quantity of a desired movement. The assisted technique will offset the weight of the body or extremity by a percentage of the total weight. This will allow improved range of motion, a

reduction in substitution, minimal eccentric stress, and a reduction in fatigue. The closed-chain tubing program can also benefit from assisted techniques, which allow for a reduction in vertical forces by decreasing relative body weight on one or both lower extremities.

The need for assisted exercise is only transitional in nature. The goal is to progress from unweighted to weight with overloading. The tubing, if used effectively, can also provide an overloading effect by causing exaggerated weight shifting. This overloading will be referred to as resisted techniques (RT) for all closed-chain applications. The two basic exercises used are the squat and the lunge.

SQUAT

The squat is used first because it employs symmetrical movement of the lower extremities. This allows the affected lower extremity to benefit from the visual and proprioceptive feedback from the unaffected lower extremity. The clinician should

A   **B**

FIGURE 8-12

Static stabilization: Multiplanar PNF lift technique to provide rotation stress. **A,** Home health setting. **B,** Clinical setting.

observe the patient's posture and look for weight shifting, which almost always occurs away from the affected limb. Each joint can be compared to its unaffected counterpart. In performing the squat, a weight shift may be provided in one of four different directions. The tubing is used to assist, resist, and modify movement patterns. The posterior weight shift works to identify closed-chain ankle dorsiflexion. A chair or bench can be used as a range-of-motion block (range-limiting device) when necessary. This minimizes fear and increases safety. The anterior weight shift provides an anterior pull that helps facilitate the hip flexion mobility during the descent. Medial and lateral changes may be provided with resistance in order to promote weight bearing on the involved side or decrease weight bearing on the involved side as progression is made (Fig. 8-14). The varying weight shifts may be used to intentionally increase the load or resistance on a particular side for means of strengthening or to facilitate a neuromuscular response on the opposite side. For example, an individual who is reluctant to weight bear on the

involved side may be helped in doing so by causing increased weight shift to the uninvolved side. This will create the need to shift weight to the involved side, thus encouraging a joint response to the required stimulus.

ASSISTED TECHNIQUE (AT)   The patient faces the tubing, which is placed at a descending angle and is attached to a belt. The belt is placed under the buttocks to simulate a swing. The bench is used to allow a proper stopping point. The elastic tension of the tubing is at its greatest when the patient is in the seated position and decreases as the mechanical advantage increases. Therefore, the tension curve of the tubing complements the needs of the patient. The next four exercises follow the assisted squat in difficulty. The tubing is now used to cause weight shifting and demands a small amount of dynamic stability.

ANTERIOR WEIGHT SHIFT (AWS)   The patient faces the tubing, which comes from a level halfway between the hips and the knees and

FIGURE 8-13

Static stabilization: ITIS technique in unilateral stance using a plyoball and plyoback for an impulse stimulus.

attaches to a belt. The belt is worn around the waist and causes an anterior weight shift. During the squat movement, the ankles plantarflex as the knees extend.

POSTERIOR WEIGHT SHIFT (PWS)   The patient faces away from the tubing at the same level as above and attaches to a belt. The belt is worn around the waist and causes a posterior weight shift. This places a greater emphasis on the hip extensors and less emphasis on the knee extensors and plantar flexors.

MEDIAL WEIGHT SHIFT (MWS)   The patient stands with the unaffected side toward the tubing at the same level as above. The belt is around the waist and causes a medial weight shift. This places less stress on the affected lower extremity and allows the patient to lean onto the affected lower extremity without incurring excessive stress or loading.

LATERAL WEIGHT SHIFT (LWS)   The patient stands with the affected side toward the tubing that is at the same level as above. The belt is worn around the waist, which causes a weight shift onto the affected lower extremity. This exercise will place a greater stress on the affected lower extremity, thereby demanding increased balance and control. The exercise simulates a single-leg squat but adds balance and safety by allowing the unaffected extremity to remain on the ground.

LUNGE

The lunge is more specific in that it simulates sports and normal activity. The exercise decreases the base while at the same time producing the need for independent disassociation. The range of motion can be stressed to a slightly higher degree. If the patient is asked to alternate the lunge from the right to the left leg, the clinician can easily compare the quality of the movement between the limbs. When performing the lunge, the patient may often use exaggerated extension movements of the lumbar region to assist weak or uncoordinated hip extension. This substitution is not produced during the squat exercise. Therefore, the lunge must be used not only as an exercise but also as a part of the functional assessment. The substitution must be addressed by asking the patient to maintain a vertical torso (note that the assisted technique will assist the clinician in minimizing this substitution).

ASSISTED TECHNIQUE (AT)—FORWARD LUNGE   The patient faces away from the tubing, which descends at a sharp angle (about 60 degrees). This angle parallels the patient's center of gravity, which moves forward and down (Fig. 8-15). This places a stretch on the tubing and assists the patient up from the low point of the lunge position. The ability to perform a lunge with correct technique is often negated due to the inability to support one's body weight. The assisted lunge corrects this by modifying the load required of the patient, thus improving the quality of the movement. The assistance also minimizes eccentric demands for deceleration when lowering and provides balance assistance by helping the patient focus on the center of gravity (anatomically located within the hip and pelvic region). The patient is asked to first alternate the activity to provide kinesthetic feedback. The clinician can then use variations of full and partial motion to stimulate the appropriate control before moving on to the next exercise.

FIGURE 8-14

Transitional stabilization: Resisted squat with a lateral weight shift in the home health setting.

RESISTED TECHNIQUE (RT)—FORWARD LUNGE The patient faces the tubing, which is at an ascending angle from the floor to the level of the waist (Fig. 8-16). The tubing will now increase the eccentric loading on the quadriceps with the deceleration on the downward movement. For the upward movement, the patient is asked to focus on hip extension and not knee extension. The patient must learn to initiate movement from the hip and not from lumbar hyperextension or excessive knee extension. Initiation of hip extension should automatically stimulate isometric lumbar stabilization along with the appropriate amounts of knee extension and ankle plantarflexion. A foam block is often used to protect the rear knee from flexing beyond 90 degrees and touching the floor. The block can also be made larger to limit range of motion at any point in the lunge.

RESISTED TECHNIQUE (RT)—LATERAL (LWS) AND MEDIAL WEIGHT SHIFT (MWS)
Forward lunges can be performed to stimulate static lateral and medial stabilization during dynamic flexion and extension movements of the lower extremities. The LWS lunge is performed by positioning the patient with the affected lower ex-

tremity toward the direction of resistance. The tubing is placed at a level halfway between the waist and the ankle. The patient is then asked to perform a lunge with minimal lateral movement. This movement stimulates static lateral stabilization of the hip, knee, ankle, and foot during dynamic flexion (unloading) and extension (loading). The MWS lunge is performed by positioning the patient with the affected extremity opposite to the resistance. The tubing is attached as described in the LWS. The movement stimulates static medial stabilization of the affected lower extremity in the presence of dynamic flexion and extension.

The lunge techniques teach weight shifting onto the affected lower extremity during lateral body movements. The assisted technique (AT) lateral lunge will compliment the AT forward lunge, because it also reduces relative body weight while allowing closed-chain function. The prime mover is the unaffected lower extremity that moves the center of gravity over the affected lower extremity for the sole purpose of visual and proprioceptive input prior to excessive loading. The resisted technique (RT) lateral lunge will compliment the RT forward lunge, because it also provides an overloading effect on the affected lower extremity. In this exercise, the affected lower extremity is the prime mover, as well as the primary weight-bearing extremity. The affected lower extremity must not only produce the weight shift but also react, respond, and repeat the movement. Sets, repetitions, and resistance for all of the exercises described are selected by the clinician to produce the appropriate reaction without pain or fatigue.

TECHNIQUE MODIFICATION

As in phase I, the medicine ball can be used to add variety and increase stimulation. However, it is used to stimulate control in the beginning, middle, and end ranges of the squat and lunges. The tubing can also be used to create ITIS and OTIS applications to reinforce stability throughout the range of motion.

FUNCTIONAL TESTING

Functional testing provides objective criteria and can help the clinician to justify a progression to phase III or an indication that the patient should continue working in phase II. A single-leg body weight squat or lunge can be performed. The quality and quantity of the repetitions are compared to the unaffected lower extremity and a deficit can be calculated. An isotonic leg press machine can also be used in this manner by setting the weight at the patient's body weight and comparing the repetitions. Open-chain isotonic and isokinetic testing can also be helpful in identifying problem areas when specificity is needed. Regardless of the mode of testing, it is recommended that the affected lower extremity display 70 to 80 percent of the capacity demonstrated by the unaffected lower extremity, or no more than a 20 to 30 percent strength deficit. When the patient has met these criteria, he or she can move safely into phase III.

A

B

FIGURE 8-15

Transitional stabilization: Assisted lunge technique. **A,** Home health setting. **B,** Clinical setting.

Phase III: Dynamic Stabilization (Unconscious Control/Loading)

Phase III introduces impact and ballistic exercise to the patient. This movement will produce a stretch-shortening cycle that has been described in plyometric exercises. Plyometric function is not a result of the magnitude of the prestretch, but rather relies on the rate of stretch to produce a more forceful contraction. This is done in two ways.

1. The stretch reflex is a neuromuscular response to tension produced in the muscle passively. The muscle responds with an immediate contraction to reorient itself to the new position, protect it, and maintain posture. If a voluntary

FIGURE 8-16

Transitional stabilization: Resisted forward lunge to facilitate deceleration stress.

contraction is added in conjunction with this reflex, a more forceful contraction can be produced.

2. The elastic properties of the tendon allow it to temporarily store energy and release it. When a quick prestretch is followed by a voluntary contraction, the tendon will add to the strength of the contraction by providing force in the direction opposite the prestretch.

Dynamic training at this level can increase the descending cortical drive to the large motor nerves of the skeletal muscles as well as the small efferent nerves to the muscle spindle.[79] If both the muscle tension and efferent output to the muscle spindles are increased, the stretch sensitivity of the muscle spindle will also be increased, thereby reducing the reflex latency.[64] Both feed-forward and feedback loops are used concurrently to superimpose stretch reflexes on preprogrammed motor activity.

As has been previously discussed, there have been previous studies that have been directed toward reducing muscle reaction times.[7,65,141] Ihara and Nakayama significantly reduced the latency of muscle reaction times with a 3-week training period of unanticipated perturbations via the use of unstable wobble boards.[65] Both Beard et al and Wojtys et al found similar results when comparing agility training with traditional strength training.[7,141] Reducing the muscle reaction time in order to produce a protective response following an abnormal joint load will enhance dynamic stability about the joint.

Before the patient is asked to learn any new techniques, he or she is instructed to demonstrate unconscious control by performing various phase II activities while throwing and catching the medicine ball. The squat and lunge exercises are performed with various applications of tubing at the waist level. This activity removes the attention from the lower extremity exercise, thereby stimulating unconscious control. The forces added by throwing and catching the medicine ball stimulate balance reactions needed for the progression to plyometric activities. Simple rope jumping is another transitional exercise that can be used to provide early plyometric information. The double-leg rope jumping is done first. The patient is then asked to perform alternating leg jumping. Rope jumping is effective in building confidence and restoring a plyometric rhythm to movement. Four-way resisted stationary running is an exercise technique used to orient the patient to light plyometric activity.

RESISTED WALKING

Resisted walking uses the same primary components as in gait training. The applied resistance of the tubing, however, allows for a reactive response unavailable in nonresisted activities. For example, a patient may present with a slight Trendelenburg gait associated with a weak gluteus medius. By initiating a program that would incorporate a progression such as that used with the squat, the patient should be able to progress to resisted walking. The addition of resistance permits for increased loading and also brings about the need for improved balance and weight shift.

RESISTED HOPPING

Bilateral hopping should be introduced following adequate training with the jump rope, then followed by increased unilateral training. The use of resistance in the hopping technique is to promote increased resistance in one of four directions. This increased resistance is used to simulate those forces normally seen on the field or court in the return to activity. Introduction of the program should begin with bilateral training and then progress to a unilateral format, which may be accommodated with box drills or diagonal training. At higher levels, implementing cones, hurdles, and/or foam rolls may be used in order to increase the plyometric demands during the hopping drills.

RESISTED RUNNING

Resisted running simply involves jogging or running in place with tubing attached to a belt around the waist. The clinician can analyze the jogging or running activity because it is a stationary drill. The tubing resistance is applied in four different directions, providing simulation of the different forces that the patient will experience as he or she returns to full activity.

1. The **posterior weight shift (PWS)** run causes a balance reaction that results in an anterior weight shift (opposite direction) and simulates the acceleration phase of jogging or running (Fig. 8-17). The patient faces opposite the direction of the tubing resistance and should be encouraged to stay on the toes (for all running exercises). The initial light stepping activity can be progressed to jogging and then running. The most advanced form of the PWS run involves the exaggeration of the hip flexion called "high knees." Exaggeration of hip flexion helps to stimulate a plyometric action in the hip extensors, thus facilitating acceleration. This form of exercise lends itself to slow, controlled endurance conditioning (greater than 3 minutes), or interval training, which depends greatly on the intensity of the resistance, cadence, and rest periods. The interval-training program is most effective and shows the greatest short-term gains. Intervals can be 10 seconds to 1 minute; however, the most common drills are 15 to 30 seconds in length. The patient is usually allowed a 1- to 2-minute rest and is required to perform 3 to 5 sets. To make sure that the patient is delivering maximum intensity, the clinician should count the number of foot touches (repetitions) that occur during the interval. The clinician needs to only count the touches of the affected lower extremity. The patient is then asked to equal or exceed the amount of foot touches on the next interval (set). This is also extremely effective as a functional test for acceleration. The interval time/repetitions can be recorded and compared to future tests. The clinician should note that the PWS places particular emphasis on the hip flexors and extensors, as well as the plantar flexors of the ankle.

2. The **medial weight shift (MWS)** run follows the same progression as the PWS run (from light jogging to high knees) with the resistance now applied medial to the affected lower

A

B

FIGURE 8-17

Dynamic stabilization—stationary run. **A,** Posterior weight shifting in the home health setting. **B,** Anterior weight shifting in the clinical setting.

extremity (which causes an automatic weight shift lateral). Endurance training, interval training, and testing should also be performed for this technique. This technique simulates the forces that the patient will experience when cutting or turning quickly away from the affected side. This drill is the same as in phase I MWS. Although the phase I MWS is static, the same muscles are responsible for dynamic stability. This exercise represents the forces that the patient will encounter when sprinting into a turn on the affected side.

3. The **lateral weight shift (LWS)** run should follow the same progression as above except that the resistance is now lateral to the affected lower extremity (which causes an automatic medial weight shift). This technique simulates the forces that the patient will experience when cutting or turning quickly toward the affected side. When performing the MWS and LWS runs, high knees should be used when working on acceleration. Instructing the patient to perform exaggerated knee flexion or "butt kicks" can emphasize deceleration. The exaggeration of knee flexion places greater plyometric stress on the knee, which has a large amount of eccentric responsibility during deceleration. This exercise represents the forces that the patient will encounter when sprinting into a turn on the unaffected side.

4. The **anterior weight shift (AWS)** run is probably the most difficult technique to perform correctly and is therefore taught last. The tubing that is set to pull the patient forward stimulates a posterior weight shift. This technique simulates deceleration and eccentric loading of the knee

extensors. The patient should start with light jogging on the toes and progress to "butt kicks." This is a plyometric exercise that incorporates exaggerated knee flexion and extension. This exercise will then serve to assist the patient in developing eccentric/concentric reactions that are required in function. The clinician should note that injuries occur more frequently during deceleration and direction changes than on acceleration or straightforward running. Therefore, AWS training is extremely important to the athlete returning to the court or field.

RESISTED BOUNDING

The bounding exercise is a progression taken from both the hopping and running exercise to increase demands placed on the horizontal component. Therefore, bounding is an exercise technique that will place greater emphasis on the lateral movements. The progression of the bounding exercises will follow the same weight shifting sequence as the previous running exercise. Side-to-side bounding in a lateral resisted exercise promotes symmetrical balance and endurance required for progression to higher-level strength and power applications. Distraction activities may also be included in the bounding and/or running exercises in order to promote increased upper extremity demands and to detract from visual and/or verbal reference needed on the lower extremity.

It is suggested that the patient be taught how to perform the bounding exercise without the tubing first. A foam roll, cone, or other obstacle can be used to simulate jump height and/or distance. The tubing can then be added to provide the secondary forces to cause anterior, lateral, medial, or posterior weight shifting. Bounding should be taught as a jump from one foot to another. A single lateral bound can be used as a supplementary functional test. Measurements can be taken for a left and right lateral bound. Bounding is only considered valid if the patient can maintain his or her balance when landing. To standardize the bounding exercise, the body height is used for the bound stride and markers can be placed for the left and right foot landings.

1. The **anterior weight shift (AWS)** lateral combines lateral motion with an automatic posterior weight shift or deceleration reaction. It is slightly more demanding than the stationary running exercises because the body weight is driven a greater distance.

2. The **lateral weight shift (LWS)** bound causes an excessive lateral plyometric force and will help to develop lateral acceleration and deceleration in the affected lower extremity. This is the most strenuous of the lateral bounding activities because it actually accelerates the body weight onto the affected lower extremity. This is, however, necessary so that the clinician can observe the ability of the affected limb to perform a quick direction change and controlled acceleration/deceleration.

3. The **medial weight shift (MWS)** bound is used as an assisted plyometric exercise. The patient works with the total body weight but impact is greatly lowered by reducing both acceleration and deceleration forces. This exercise is an excellent transitional exercise at the end of phase II as well as at the beginning of phase III. It also serves as a warm-up drill providing submaximal stimulation of the proprioceptive system prior to a phase III exercise session.

4. The **posterior weight shift (PWS)** bound facilitates an anterior lateral push-off of each leg and will stimulate an anterior weight shift. This exercise will assist in teaching acceleration and lateral cutting movements.

MULTIDIRECTIONAL DRILLS

Multidirectional drills include jumping (two-foot takeoff followed by a two-foot landing), hopping (one-foot takeoff followed by a landing on the same foot), and bounding (one-foot takeoff followed by an opposite-foot landing). A series of floor markers can be placed in various patterns to simulate functional movements. A weight shift can be produced in any direction by the orientation of the tubing. Obstacles can also be used to make the exercise more complicated.

The jumping exercise can be developed to simulate downhill skiing, while the hopping exercise can be designed to stress single-leg pushoff for vertical jumping sports such as basketball and volleyball.

SUMMARY

- There has been increased attention to the development of balance and proprioception in the rehabilitation and reconditioning of athletes following injury. It is believed that injury results in altered somatosensory input that influences neuromuscular control.

- If static and dynamic balance and neuromuscular control are not reestablished following injury, then the patient will be susceptible to recurrent injury and his or her performance may decline.

- The following rules should be employed when designing the Reactive Neuromuscular Training program:

  ➤ Make sure that the exercise program is specific to the patient's needs. The most important thing to consider during the rehabilitation of patients is that they should be performing functional activities that simulate their ADL requirements. This rule applies to not only the specific joints involved but also the speed and amplitude of movement required in ADL.

  ➤ Practice does appear to be task specific in both athletes and people who have motor control deficits.[73] As retraining of balance continues, it is best to practice complex skills in their entirety rather than in isolation because the skills will transfer more effectively.[1]

  ➤ Make sure to include a significant amount of "controlled chaos" in the program. Unexpected activities with the ADL are by nature unstable. The more the patient rehearses in this type of environment, the better he or she will react under unrehearsed conditions.

  ➤ Progress from straight plane to multiplane movement patterns. In ADL, movement does not occur along a single joint or plane of movement. Therefore, exercise for the kinetic chain must involve all three planes simultaneously.

  ➤ Begin your loading from the inside out. Load the system first with body weight and then progress to external resistance. The core of the body must be developed before the extremities.

  ➤ Have causative cures as a part of the rehabilitation process. The cause of the injury must eventually become a part of the cure. If rotation and deceleration were the cause of the injury, then use this as a part of the rehab program in preparation for return to activity.

  ➤ Be progressive in nature. Remember to progress from simple to complex. The function progression breaks an activity down into its component parts and then performs them in a sequence that allows for the acquisition or reacquisition of the activity. Basic conditioning and skill acquisition must be acquired before advanced conditioning and skill acquisition.

  ➤ Always ask: Does the program make sense? If it doesn't make sense, chances are that it is not functional and therefore not optimally effective.

  ➤ Make the rehabilitation program fun. The first three letters of functional are FUN. If it is not fun, then compliance will suffer and so will the results.

  ➤ An organized progression is the key to success. Failing to plan is planning to fail.

REFERENCES

1. Barnett M, Ross D, Schmidt R, Todd B. Motor skills learning and the specificity of training principle. *Res Q Exerc Sport* 44:440–447, 1973.

2. Barrack RL, Lund PJ, Skinner HB. Knee joint proprioception revisited. *J Sport Rehabil* 3:18–42, 1994.

3. Barrack RL, Skinner HB. The sensory function of knee ligaments. In: Daniel D, ed. *Knee Ligaments: Structure, Function, Injury, and Repair.* New York, Raven Press, 1990.

4. Barrack RL, Skinner HB, Buckley SL. Proprioception in the anterior cruciate deficient knee. *Am J Sports Med.* 17:1–6, 1989.

5. Barrett DS. Proprioception and function after anterior cruciate reconstruction. *JBJS* 73B:833–837, 1991.

6. Basmajian JV, ed. *Biofeedback: Principles and Practice for Clinicians.* Baltimore, Williams and Wilkins, 1979.

7. Beard DJ, Dodd CF, Trundle HR, et al. Proprioception after rupture of the ACL: An objective indication of the need for surgery? *JBJS* 75B:311, 1993.

8. Belen'kii VY, Gurfinkle VS, Pal'tsev YI. Elements of control of voluntary movements. *Biofizika* 12:135–141, 1967.

9. Berg K. Balance and its measure in the elderly: A review. *Physiolother Can* 41:240–246, 1989.

10. Bernier JN, Perrin DH. Effect of coordination training on proprioception of the functionally unstable ankle. *J Orthop Sports Phys Ther* 27:264–275, 1998.

11. Blackburn TA, Voight ML. Single leg stance: Development of a reliable testing procedure. In: *Proceedings of the 12th International Congress of the World Confederation for Physical Therapy,* Alexandria, VA: APTA, 1995.

12. Borsa PA, Lephart SM, Kocher MS, Lephart SP. Functional assessment and rehabilitation of shoulder proprioception for glenohumeral instability. *J Sports Rehabil* 3:84–104, 1994.

13. Borsa PA, Lephart SM, Irrgang JJ, Safran MR, Fu F. The effects of joint position and direction of joint motion on proprioceptive sensibility in anterior cruciate ligament deficient athletes. *Am J Sports Med* 25:336–340, 1997.

14. Boyd IA, Roberts TDM. Proprioceptive discharges from stretch-receptors in the knee joint of the cat. *J Physiol* 122:38–59, 1953.

15. Braxendale RA, Ferrel WR, Wood L. Responses of quadriceps motor units to mechanical stimulation of knee joint receptors in decerebrate cat. *Brain Res* 453:150–156, 1988.

16. Bulbulian R, Bowles DK. The effect of downhill running on motorneuron pool excitability. *J Applied Physiol* 73(3):968–973, 1992.

17. Burgess PR. Signal of kinesthetic information by peripheral sensory receptors. *Annu Rev Neurosci* 5:171, 1982.

18. Cafarelli E, Bigland B. Sensation of static force in muscles of different length. *Exp Neurol* 65:511–525, 1979.

19. Ciccotti MR, Kerlan R, Perry J, Pink M. An electromyographic analysis of the knee during functional activities: I. The normal profile. *Am J Sports Med* 22:645–650, 1994.

20. Ciccotti MR, Kerlan R, Perry J, Pink M. An electromyographic analysis of the knee during functional activities: II. The anterior cruciate ligament—Deficient knee and reconstructed profiles. *Am J Sports Med* 22:651–658, 1994.

21. Clark FJ, Burgess PR. Slowly adapting receptors in cat knee joint: Can they signal joint angle? *J Neurophysiol* 38:1448–1463, 1975.

22. Clark FJ, Burgess RC, Chapin JW, Lipscomb WT. Role of intramuscular receptors in the awareness of limb position. *J Neurophysiol* 54:1529–1540, 1985.

23. Cohen H, Keshner E. Current concepts of the vestibular system reviewed: Visual/vestibular interaction and spatial orientation. *Am J Occup Ther* 43:331–338, 1989.

24. Corrigan JP, Cashman WF, Brady MP. Proprioception in the cruciate deficient knee. *JBJS.* 74B:247–250, 1992.

25. Cross MJ, McCloskey DI. Position sense following surgical removal of joints in man. *Brain Res* 55:443–445, 1973.

26. Crutchfield A, Barnes M. *Motor Control and Motor Learning in Rehabilitation.* Atlanta, GA, Stokesville, 1993.

27. Dewhurst DJ. Neuromuscular control system. *IEEE Trans Biomed Eng* 14:167–171, 1965.

28. Dietz VJ, Schmidtbleicher D. Interaction between preactivity and stretch reflex in human triceps bracii during landing from forward falls. *J Physiol* 311:113–125, 1981.

29. Dunn TG, Gillig SE, Ponser ES, Weil N. The learning process in biofeedback: Is it feed-forward or feedback? *Biofeedback Self Regul* 11:143–155, 1986.

30. Ekdhl C, Jarnlo G, Anderson S. Standing balance in healthy subjects. *Scand J Rehabil Med* 21:187–195, 1989.

31. Eklund J. Position sense and state of contraction: The effects of vibration. *J Neurol Neurosurg Psychiatry* 35:606, 1972.

32. Era P, Heikkinen E. Postural sway during standing and unexpected disturbances of balance in random samples of men of different ages. *J Gerontol* 40:287–295, 1985.

33. Freeman MAR, Wyke B. Articular reflexes of the ankle joint. An electromyographic study of normal and abnormal influences of ankle-joint mechanoreceptors upon reflex activity in leg muscles. *Br J Surg* 54:990–1001, 1967.

34. Freeman MAR, Wyke B. Articular contributions to limb reflexes. *Br J Surg* 53:61–69, 1966.

35. Friden T, Zatterstrom R, Lindstand A, Moritz U. Disability in anterior cruciate ligament insufficiency: An analysis of 19 untreated patients. *Acta Orthop Scand* 61:131–135, 1990.

36. Gandevia SC, Burke D. Does the nervous system depend

on kinesthetic information to control natural limb movements? *Behav Brain Sci* 15:614–632, 1992.

37. Gandevia SC, McCloskey DI. Joint sense, muscle sense and their contribution as position sense, measured at the distal interphalangeal joint of the middle finger. *J Physiol* 260:387–407, 1976.

38. Gauffin H, Pettersson G, Tegner Y, Tropp H. Function testing in patients with old rupture of the anterior cruciate ligament. *Int J Sports Med* 11:73–77, 1990.

39. Gelfan S, Carter S. Muscle sense in man. *Exp Neurol* 18:469–473, 1967.

40. Giove TP, Miller SJ, Kent BE, Sanford TL, Garrick JG. Non-operative treatment of the torn anterior cruciate ligament. *JBJS* 65A:184–192, 1983.

41. Glaros AG, Hanson K. EMG biofeedback and discriminative muscle control. *Biofeedback Self Regul* 15:135–143, 1990.

42. Glenncross D, Thornton E. Position sense following joint injury. *Am J Sports Med* 21:23–27, 1981.

43. Goodwin GM, McCloskey DI, Matthews PC. The contribution of muscle afferents to kinesthesia shown by vibration induced illusions of movement and by effects of paralyzing joint afferents. *Brain* 95:705–748, 1972.

44. Granit R. *The Basis of Motor Control.* New York, Academic Press, 1970.

45. Grigg P. Peripheral neural mechanisms in proprioception. *J Sport Rehabil* 3:1–17, 1994.

46. Grigg P. Response of joint afferent neurons in cat medial articular nerve to active and passive movements of the knee. *Brain Res* 118:482–485, 1976.

47. Grigg P, Finerman GA, Riley LH. Joint position sense after total hip replacement. *JBJS* 55A:1016–1025, 1973.

48. Grigg P, Hoffman AH. Ruffini mechanoreceptors in isolated joint capsule. Reflexes correlated with strain energy density. *Somatosens Mot Res* 2:149–162, 1984.

49. Grigg P, Hoffman AH. Properties of Ruffini afferents revealed by stress analysis of isolated sections of cats knee capsule. *J Neurophysiol* 47:41–54, 1982.

50. Guyton AC. *Textbook of Medical Physiology,* 6th ed. Philadelphia, Saunders, 1991.

51. Haddad B. Protection of afferent fibers from the knee joint to the cerebellum of the cat. *Am J Physiol* 172:511–514, 1953.

52. Hagood SM, Solomonow R, Baratta BH, et al. The effect of joint velocity on the contribution of the antagonist musculature to knee stiffness and laxity. *Am J Sports Med* 18:182–187, 1990.

53. Harter RA, Osternig LR, Singer SL, Larsen RL, Jones DC. Long-term evaluation of knee stability and function following surgical reconstruction for anterior cruciate ligament insufficiency. *Am J Sports Med* 16:434–442, 1988.

54. Hellenbrant FA. Motor learning reconsidered: A study of change. In: *Neurophysiologic Approaches to Therapeutic Exercise.* Philadelphia, Davis, 1978.

55. Hocherman S, Dickstein R, Pillar T. Platform training and postural stability in hemiplegia. *Arch Phys Med Rehabil* 65:588–592, 1984.

56. Hodgson JA, Roy RR, DeLeon R, et al. Can the mammalian lumbar spinal cord learn a motor task? *Med Sci Sports* 26:1491–1497, 1994.

57. Horak FB. Clinical measurement of postural control in adults. *Phys Ther* 67:1881–1885, 1989.

58. Horak FB, Nashner LM. Central programming of postural movements. Adaption to altered support surface configurations. *J Neurophysiol* 55:1369–1381, 1986.

59. Horak FB, Shupert CL, Mirka A. Components of postural dyscontrol in the elderly. *Neurobiol Aging* 10:727–738, 1989.

60. Houk JC. Regulation of stiffness by skeletomotor reflexes. *Ann Rev Phys* 41:99–114, 1979.

61. Houk JC, Crago PE, Rymer WZ. Function of the dynamic response in stiffness regulation: A predictive mechanism provided by non-linear feedback. In: Taylor A, Prochazka A, eds. *Muscle Receptors and Feedback.* London, Macmillan, 1981.

62. Houk JC, Henneman E. Responses of Golgi tendon organs to active contractions of the soleus muscle in the cat. *J Neurophysiol* 30:466–481, 1967.

63. Houk JC, Rymer WZ. Neural controls of muscle length and tension. In: Brooks VB, ed. *Handbook of Physiology: Section 1: The Nervous System. Vol 2. Motor Control.* Bethesda, American Physiological Society, 1981.

64. Hutton RS, Atwater SW. Acute and chronic adaptations of muscle proprioceptors in response to increased use. *Sports Med* 14:406–421, 1992.

65. Ihara H, Nakayama A. Dynamic joint control training for knee ligament injuries. *Am J Sports Med* 14:309–315, 1986.

66. Johnson RB, Howard ME, Cawley PW, Losse GM. Effect of lower extremity muscular fatigue on motor control performance. *Med Sci Sports* 30:1703–1707, 1998.

67. Kennedy JC, Alexander IJ, Hayes KC. Nerve supply to the human knee and its functional importance. *Am J Sports Med* 10:329–335, 1982.

68. Konradsen L, Ravin JB. Prolonged peroneal reaction time in ankle instability. *Int J Sports Med* 12:290–292, 1991.

69. Lee RG, Murphy JT, Tatton WG. Long latency myotatic reflexes in man: Mechanisms, functional significance, and changes in patients with Parkinson's disease or hemiplegia. In: Desmedt J, ed. *Advances in Neurology.* Basel, Karger, 1983.

70. Lee WA. Anticipatory control of postural and task muscles during rapid arm flexion. *J Mot Behav* 12:185–196, 1980.

71. Lephart SM. Reestablishing proprioception, kinesthesia, joint position sense and neuromuscular control in rehab. In: Prentice WE, ed. *Rehabilitation Techniques in Sports Medicine,* 2nd ed. St. Louis, Mosby, 1994.

72. Lephart SM, Henry TJ. Functional rehabilitation for the upper and lower extremity. *Orthop Clin North Am* 26:579–592, 1995.

73. Lephart SM, Kocher MS, Fu FH, et al. Proprioception following ACL reconstruction. *J Sport Rehabil* 1:188–196, 1992.

74. Lephart SM, Pincivero DM, Giraldo JL, Fu F. The role of proprioception in the management and rehabilitation of athletic injuries. *Am J Sports Med* 25:130–137, 1997.

75. Marks R, Quinney HA. Effect of fatiguing maximal isokinetic quadriceps contractions on the ability to estimate knee position. *Percept Mot Skills* 77:1195–1202, 1993.

76. Matsusaka N, Yokoyama S, Tsurusaki T, et al. Effect of ankle disk training combined with tactile stimulation to the leg and foot in functional instability of the ankle. Submitted to *Am J Sport Med,* 2001.

77. Matthews PC. Where does Sherrington's "muscular sense" originate? Muscle, joints, corollary discharges? *Annu Rev Neurosci* 5:189, 1982.

78. McCloskey DI. Kinesthetic sensitivity. *Physiol Rev* 58:763–820, 1978.

79. McComas AJ. Human neuromuscular adaptations that accompany changes in activity. *Med Sci Sports* 26:1498–1509, 1994.

80. McNair PJ, Marshall RN. Landing characteristics in subjects with normal and anterior cruciate ligament deficient knee joints. *Arch Phys Med* 75:584–589, 1994.

81. McNair PJ, Wood GA, Marshall RN. Stiffness of the hamstring muscles and its relationship to function in anterior cruciate deficient individuals. *Clin Biomechanics* 7:131–173, 1992.

82. Melville-Jones GM, Watt GD. Observations of the control stepping and hopping in man. *J Physiol* 219:709–727, 1971.

83. Mizuta H, Shiraishi M, Kubota K, Kai K, Takagi K. A stabiliometric technique for the evaluation of functional instability in the anterior cruciate ligament-deficient knee. *Clin J Sports Med* 2:235–239, 1992.

84. Morgan DL. Separation of active and passive components of short-range stiffness of muscle. *Am J Physiol* 32:45–49, 1977.

85. Nashner LM. Sensory, neuromuscular, and biomechanical contributions to human balance. In: Duncan PW, ed. *Balance: Proceedings of the APTA Forum.* Alexandria, VA, APTA, 1986, p. 550.

86. Nichols TR, Houk JC. Improvement of linearity and regulation of stiffness that results from actions of stretch reflex. *J Neurophysiol* 39:119–142, 1976.

87. Nyland JA, Shapiro R, Stine RL, et al. Relationship of fatigued run and rapid stop to ground reaction forces, lower extremity kinematics, and muscle activation. *J Orthop Sports Phys Ther* 20:132–137, 1994.

88. Ognibene J, McMahan K, Harris M, Dutton S, Voight M: Effects of unilateral proprioceptive perturbation training on postural sway and joint reaction times of healthy subjects. In: *Proceedings of National Athletic Training Association Annual Meeting.* Champaign, IL, Human Kinetics, 2000.

89. Palta AE, Winter DA, Frank JS. Identification of age-related changes in the balance control system. In: Duncan PW, ed. *Balance: Proceedings of the APTA Forum.* Alexandria, VA, APTA, 1986.

90. Perlau RC, Frank C, Fick G. The effects of elastic bandages on human knee proprioception in the uninjured population. *Am J Sports Med* 23:251–255, 1995.

91. Peterka RJ, Black OF. Age related changes in human postural control: Sensory organization tests. *J Vestib Res* 1:73–85, 1990.

92. Phillips CG, Powell TS, Wiesendanger M. Protection from low threshold muscle afferents of hand and forearm area 3A of Babson's cortex. *J Physiol* 217:419–446, 1971.

93. Pinstaar A, Brynhildsen J, Tropp H. Postural corrections after standardized perturbations of single limb stance: Effect of training and orthotic devices in patients with ankle instability. *Br J Sports Med* 30:151–155, 1996.

94. Pope MH, Johnson DW, Brown DW, Tighe C. The role of the musculature in injuries to the medial collateral ligament. *JBJS* 61A:398–402, 1972.

95. Pousson M, Hoecke JV, Goubel F. Changes in elastic characteristics of human muscle and induced by eccentric exercise. *J Biomechanics* 23:343–348, 1990.

96. Rine RM, Voight ML, Laporta L, Mancini R. A paradigm to evaluate ankle instability using postural sway measures. *Phys Ther* 74:S72, 1994.

97. Rogers DK, Bendrups AP, Lewis MM. Disturbed proprioception following a period of muscle vibration in humans. *Neurosci Lett* 57:147–152, 1985.

98. Rothwell J. *Control of Human Voluntary Movement,* 2nd ed. London, Chapman & Hall, 1994.

99. Rowinski, MJ. Afferent neurobiology of the joint. In: The role of eccentric exercise. In: *ProClinics.* Shirley, NY, Biodex, 1988.

100. Sakai H, Tanaka S, Kurosawa H, Masujima A. The effect of exercise on anterior knee laxity in female basketball players. *Int J Sports Med* 13:552–554, 1992.

101. Schmidt RA. The acquisition of skill: Some modifications to the perception-action relationship through practice. In: Heuer H, Sanders AF, eds. *Perspectives on Perception and Action.* Hillsdale, NJ, Erlbaum, 1987.

102. Schmidt RA. *Motor Control and Learning.* Champaign, IL, Human Kinetics, 1988.

103. Schulmann D, Godfrey B, Fisher A. Effect of eye movements on dynamic equilibrium. *Phys Ther* 67:1054–1057, 1987.

104. Schulte MJ, Happel LT. Joint innervation in injury. *Clin Sports Med* 9:511–517, 1990.

105. Sherrington CS. *The Interactive Action of the Nervous System.* New Haven, Yale University Press, 1911.

106. Sheth P, Yu B, Laskowski ER, et al. Ankle disk training influences reaction times of selected muscles in a simulated ankle sprain. *Am J Sports Med* 25:538–543, 1997.

107. Shumway-Cook A, Horak FB. Assessing the influence of sensory interaction on balance. *Phys Ther* 66:1548–1550, 1986.

108. Sittig AC, Denier van der Gon JJ, Gielen CM. Different control mechanisms for slow and fast human arm movements. *Neurosci Lett* 22:S128, 1985.

109. Sittig AC, Denier van der Gon JJ, Gielen CM. Separate control of arm position and velocity demonstrated by vibration of muscle tendon in man. *Exp Brain Res* 60:445–453, 1985.

110. Skinner HB, Barrack RL, Cook SD, Haddad RJ. Joint position sense in total knee arthroplasty. *J Orthop Res* 1:276–283, 1984.

111. Skinner HB, Wyatt MP, Hodgdon JA, Conrad DW, Barrack RI. Effect of fatigue on joint position sense of the knee. *J Orthop Res* 4:112–118, 1986.

112. Skoglund CT. Joint receptors and kinesthesia. In: Iggo A, ed. *Handbook of Sensory Physiology.* Berlin, Springer-Verlag, 1973.

113. Skoglund S. Anatomical and physiological studies of the knee joint innervation in the cat. *Acta Physiol Scand Suppl* 36, 1956.

114. Small C, Waters CL, Voight ML. Comparison of two methods for measuring hamstring reaction time using the Kin-Com Isokinetic Dynamometer. *J Orthop Sports Phys Ther* 19, 1994.

115. Smith JL. Sensorimotor integration during motor programming. In: Stelmach GE, ed. *Information Processing in Motor Control and Learning.* New York, Academic Press, 1978.

116. Solomonow M, Baratta R, Zhou BH, et al. The synergistic action of the anterior cruciate ligament and thigh muscles in maintaining joint stability. *Am J Sports Med* 15:207–213, 1987.

117. Steiner ME, Brown C, Zarins B, et al. Measurements of anterior–posterior displacement of the knee: A comparison of results with instrumented devices and with clinical examination. *JBJS* 72A:1307–1315, 1990.

118. Stoller DW, Markoff KL, Zager SA, Shoemaker SC. The effect of exercise, ice, and ultrasonography on torsional laxity of the knee. *Clin Orthop* 174:172–180, 1983.

119. Stuart DG, Mosher CG, Gerlack RL, Reinking RM. Mechanical arrangement and transducing properties of Golgi tendon organs. *Exp Brain Res* 14:274–292, 1972.

120. Swanik CB, Lephart SM, Giannantonio FP, Fu F. Reestablishing proprioception and neuromuscular control in the ACL-injured athlete. *J Sport Rehab* 6:183–206, 1997.

121. Tibone JE, Antich TJ, Funton GS, Moynes DR, Perry J. Functional analysis of anterior cruciate ligament instability. *Am J Sports Med* 14:276–284, 1986.

122. Tippett S, Voight ML. *Functional Progressions for Sports Rehabilitation.* Champaign, IL. Human Kinetics, 1995.

123. Tropp H, Askling C, Gillquist J. Prevention of ankle sprains. *Am J Sports Med* 13:259–262, 1985.

124. Tropp H, Ekstrand J, Gillquist J. Factors affecting stabiliometry recordings of single leg stance. *Am J Sports Med* 12:185–188, 1984.

125. Tropp H, Odenrick P. Postural control in single limb stance. *J Orthop Res* 6:833–839, 1988.

126. Voight ML. Proprioceptive concerns in rehabilitation. In: *Proceedings of the XXVth FIMS World Congress of SportsMedicine.* Athens, Greece, International Sports Medicine Federation, 1994.

127. Voight ML. Functional Exercise Training. Presented at the 1990 National Athletic Training Association Annual Conference, Indianapolis, IN.

128. Voight ML, Bell S, Rhodes D. Instrumented testing of tibial translation during a positive Lachman's test and selected closed-chain activities in anterior cruciate deficient knees. *J Orthop Sports Phys Ther* 15:49, 1992.

129. Voight ML, Blackburn TA, Hardin JA. Effects of muscle fatigue on shoulder proprioception. *J Orthop Sports Phys Ther* 21:348–352, 1996.

130. Voight ML, Cook G, Blackburn TA. Functional lower quarter exercises through reactive neuromuscular training. In: Bandy WD, ed. *Current Trends for the Rehabilitation of the Athlete.* Lacrosse, WI, Sports Physical Therapy Section Home Study Course, 1997.

131. Voight ML, Draovitch P. Plyometric training. In: Albert, M (ed.). *Muscle Training in Sports and Orthopaedics.* New York, Churchill Livingstone, 1991.

132. Voight ML, Nashner LM, Blackburn TA. Neuromuscular function changes with ACL functional brace use: A measure of reflex latencies and lower quarter EMG responses. Abstract: Conference Proceedings, American Orthopedic Society for Sports Medicine, 1998.

133. Voight ML, Rine RM, Apfel P, et al. The effects of leg dominance and AFO on static and dynamic balance abilities. *Phys Ther* 73:S51, 1993.

134. Voight ML, Rine RM, Briese K, Powell C. Comparison of sway in double versus single leg stance in unimpaired adults. *Phys Ther* 73(6):S51, 1993.

135. Voss DE, Ionta MK, Myers BJ. *Proprioceptive Neuromuscular Facilitation: Patterns and Techniques.* Philadelphia, Harper & Row, 1985.

136. Walla DJ, Albright JP, McAuley E, Martin V, Eldridge V, El-khoury G. Hamstring control and the unstable anterior cruciate ligament-deficient knee. *Am J Sports Med* 13:34–39, 1985.

137. Wester JU, Jespersen SM, Nielsen KD, et al. Wobble board training after partial sprains of the lateral ligaments of the ankle: A prospective randomized study. *J Orthop Sports Phys Ther* 23:332–336, 1996.

138. Wetzel MC, Stuart DC. Ensemble characteristics of cat locomotion and its neural control. *Prog Neurobiol* 7: 1–98, 1976.

139. Willis WD, Grossman RG. *Medical Neurobiology,* 3rd ed. St Louis, CV Mosby, 1981.

140. Wojtys E, Huston L. Neuromuscular performance in normal and anterior cruciate ligament–deficient lower extremities. *Am J Sports Med* 22:89–104, 1994.

141. Wojtys E, Huston L, Taylor PD, Bastian SD. Neuromuscular adaptations in isokinetic, isotonic, and agility training programs. *Am J Sports Med* 24(2):187–192, 1996.

142. Woollacott MH. Postural control mechanisms in the young and the old. In: Duncan PW, ed. *Balance: Proceedings of the APTA Forum.* Alexandria, VA, APTA, 1990.

143. Wollacott MH, Shumway-Cook A, Nashner LM. Aging and postural control: Changes in sensory organs and muscular coordination. *Int J Aging Hum Dev* 23:97–114, 1986.

CHAPTER 9

Impaired Postural Stability: Regaining Balance

Kevin M. Guskiewicz

OBJECTIVES

After completing this chapter, the student therapist should be able to do the following:

- Define and explain the role of the three sensory modalitites responsible for maintaining balance.
- Explain how movement strategies along a closed-kinetic chain help to maintain the COG in a safe and stable area.
- Differentiate between subjective and objective balance assessment.
- Differentiate between static and dynamic balance assessment.
- Explain the effect that injury to the ankle, knee, and head has on balance and postural equilibrium.
- Discuss the goals of each phase of balance training and how to progress the patient through each phase.
- Discuss the difference between static, semidynamic, and dynamic balance training exercises.

WHY BALANCE IS IMPORTANT IN THE REHABILITATION PROCESS

Although maintaining balance while standing may appear to be a rather simple motor skill, this feat cannot be taken for granted in a patient with musculoskeletal dysfunction. Muscular weakness, proprioceptive deficits, and range of motion (ROM) deficits can challenge a patient's ability to maintain his or her center of gravity (COG) within the body's base of support, or in other words, cause them to lose balance. Balance is the single most important element dictating movement strategies within the closed-kinetic chain. Acquisition of effective strategies for maintaining balance is, therefore, essential normal activities of daily living. Although balance is often thought of as a static process, it is actually a highly integrative dynamic process involving multiple neurologic pathways. Although balance is the more commonly used term, **postural equilibrium** is a broader term that involves the alignment of joint segments in an effort to maintain the COG within an optimal range of the maximum limits of stability (LOS), which will be discussed later.

Despite being classified at the end of the continuum of goals associated with therapeutic exercise,[45] maintenance of balance

is a vital component in the rehabilitation of joint injuries and should not be overlooked. Traditionally, musculoskeletal rehabilitation has placed the emphasis on isolated joint mechanics such as improving ROM and flexibility and increasing muscle strength and endurance, rather than on afferent information obtained by the joint(s) to be processed by the postural control system. More recently, however, research in the area of proprioception and kinesthesia has emphasized the need to train the joint's neural system (see Chapter 8).[46–50] Joint position sense, proprioception, and kinesthesia are vital to all activities requiring balance. Current rehabilitation protocols are focusing more on closed-kinetic chain exercises, and **balance training** is receiving more attention in the clinical setting. This chapter focuses on the postural control system, various balance training techniques, and technologic advancements that are enabling clinicians to assess and treat balance deficits in patients with musculoskeletal injuries.

POSTURAL CONTROL SYSTEM

The therapist must first have an understanding of the postural control system and its various components. The postural control system uses complex processes involving both sensory and

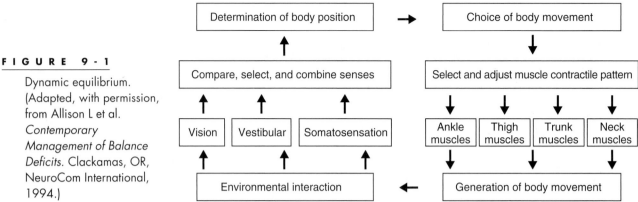

F I G U R E   9 - 1

Dynamic equilibrium. (Adapted, with permission, from Allison L et al. *Contemporary Management of Balance Deficits.* Clackamas, OR, NeuroCom International, 1994.)

motor components. Maintenance of postural equilibrium includes sensory detection of body motions, integration of sensorimotor information within the central nervous system (CNS), and execution of appropriate musculoskeletal responses. Most daily activities, such as walking, climbing stairs, or reaching overhead, require static foot placement with controlled balance shifts, especially if a favorable outcome is to be attained. So, balance should be considered both a dynamic and static process. The successful accomplishment of static and dynamic balance is based on the interaction between body and environment.[44] The complexity of this dynamic process can be seen in Figure 9-1. From a clinical perspective, separating the sensory and motor processes of balance means that a person can have impaired balance for one or a combination of two reasons: (1) the position of the COG relative to the base of support is

not accurately sensed; and (2) the automatic movements required to bring the COG to a balanced position are not timely or effectively coordinated.[55,56]

The position of the body in relation to gravity and its surroundings is sensed by combining visual, vestibular, and somatosensory inputs. Balance movements also involve motions of the ankle, knee, and hip joints, which are controlled by the coordinated actions along the kinetic chain (Fig. 9-2).

CONTROL OF BALANCE

The human body is a very tall structure balanced on a relatively small base, and its COG is quite high, being just above the pelvis.[77] Many factors enter into the task of controlling balance

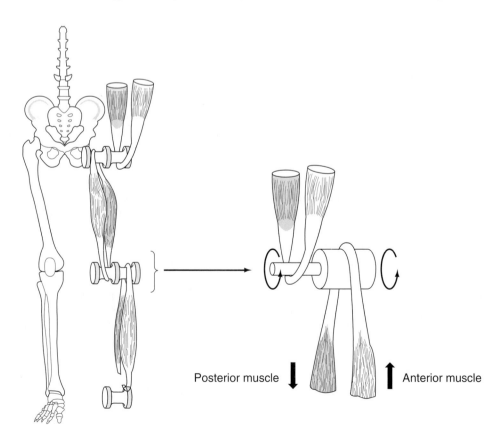

F I G U R E   9 - 2

Paired relationships between major postural musculature that executes coordinated actions along the kinetic chain to control the center of gravity.

Posterior muscle   Anterior muscle

within the base of support. Balance control involves a complex network of neural connections and centers that are related by peripheral and central feedback mechanisms.[34]

The postural control system operates as a feedback control circuit between the brain and the musculoskeletal system. The sources of afferent information supplied to the postural control system collectively come from visual, vestibular, and somatosensory inputs. The central nervous system (CNS) involvement in maintaining upright posture can be divided into two components. The first component, **sensory organization,** involves those processes that determine the timing, direction, and amplitude of corrective postural actions based on information obtained from the vestibular, visual, and somatosensory (proprioceptive) inputs.[59] Despite the availability of multiple sensory inputs, the central nervous system generally relies on only one sense at a time for orientation information. For healthy adults, the preferred sense for balance control comes from somatosensory information (i.e., feet in contact with the support surface and detection of joint movement).[37,59] In considering musculoskeletal injuries, the somatosensory system is of most importance and is the focus of this chapter.

The second component, "muscle coordination," describes processes that determine the temporal sequencing and distribution of contractile activity among the muscles of the legs and trunk, which generate supportive reactions for maintaining balance. Research suggests that balance deficiencies in people with neurologic problems can result from inappropriate interaction among the three sensory inputs that provide orientation information to the postural control system. A patient can be inappropriately dependent on one sense for situations presenting intersensory conflict.[59,69]

From a clinical perspective, stabilization of upright posture requires the integration of afferent information from the three senses, which work in combination and are all critical to the execution of coordinated postural corrections. Impairment of one component is usually compensated for by the remaining two. Often, one of the systems provides faulty or inadequate information, for example, different surfaces and/or changes in visual acuity and/or peripheral vision. In this case, it is crucial that one of the other senses provides accurate and adequate information so that balance can be maintained. When somatosensory conflict is present, such as a moving platform or a compliant foam surface, balance is significantly decreased with the eyes closed as compared to eyes open.

Somatosensory inputs provide information concerning the orientation of body parts to one another and to the support surface.[21,55] **Vision** measures the orientation of the eyes and head in relation to surrounding objects and plays an important role in the maintenance of balance. On a stable surface, closing the eyes should cause only minimal increases in postural sway in healthy subjects. However, if somatosensory input is disrupted due to ligamentous injury, closing the eyes will increase sway significantly.[12,16,37,38,55] The **vestibular** apparatus supplies information that measures gravitational, linear, and angular accelerations of the head in relation to inertial space. It does not, however, provide orientation information in relation to external objects and, therefore, plays only a minor role in the maintenance of balance when the visual and somatosensory systems are providing accurate information.[55,56]

SOMATOSENSATION AS IT RELATES TO BALANCE

The terms *somatosensation, proprioception, kinesthesia,* and *balance* are often used to describe similar phenomena. Somatosensation is a more global term used to describe the proprioceptive mechanisms related to postural control and can accurately be used synonomously. Somatosensation is best defined as a specialized variation of the sensory modality of touch that encompasses the sensation of joint movement (kinesthesia) and joint position (joint position sense).[46,50] As discussed previously, balance refers to the ability to maintain the body's COG within the base of support provided by the feet. Somatosensation and balance work closely, as the postural control system utilizes sensory information related to movement and posture from peripheral sensory receptors (e.g., muscle spindles, Golgi tendon organs (GTO), joint afferents, cutaneous receptors). So the question remains, how does proprioception influence postural equilibrium and balance?

Somatosensory input is received from mechanoreceptors; however, it is unclear as to whether the tactile senses, spindles, or GTOs are more responsible for controlling balance. Nashner[60] concluded, after using electromyography (EMG) responses following platform perturbations, that other pathways had to be involved in the responses they recorded because the latencies were longer than those normally associated with a classic myotatic reflex. The stretch-related reflex is the earliest mechanism for increasing the activation level of muscles about a joint following an externally imposed rotation of the joint. Rotation of the ankles is the most probable stimulus of the myotatic reflex that occurs in many persons. It appears to be the first useful phase of activity in the leg muscles after a change in erect posture.[60] The myotatic reflex can be seen when perturbations of gait or posture automatically evoke functionally directed responses in the leg muscles to compensate for imbalance or increased postural sway.[14,60] Muscle spindles sense a stretching of the agonist, thus sending information along its afferent fibers to the spinal cord. There, the information is transferred to alpha and gamma motor neurons that carry information back to the muscle fibers and muscle spindle, respectively, and contract the muscle to prevent or control additional postural sway.[14]

Postural sway was assessed on a platform moving into a "toes-up" and "toes down" position, and a stretch reflex was found in the triceps surae after a sudden ramp displacement into the "toes up" position.[13] A medium latency response (103 to 118 msec) was observed in the stretched muscle, followed by a delayed response of the antagonistic anterior tibialis muscle (108 to 124 msec). The investigators also blocked afferent proprioceptive information in an attempt to study the role of proprioceptive information from the legs for the maintenance of upright posture. These results suggested that proprioceptive information from pressure and/or joint receptors of the foot (ischemia applied at ankle) plays an important role in postural stabilization during low frequencies of movement, but is of minor importance for the compensation of rapid displacements. The experiment also included a "visual" component, as subjects were tested with eyes closed, followed by eyes open. Results suggested that when subjects were tested with eyes open, visual information compensated for the loss of proprioceptive input.

Another study[14] used compensatory EMG responses during impulsive disturbance of the limbs during stance on a treadmill to describe the myotatic reflex. Results revealed that during backward movement of the treadmill, ankle dorsiflexion caused the COG to be shifted anteriorly, thus evoking a stretch reflex in the gastrocnemius muscle, followed by weak anterior tibialis activation. In another trial, the movement was reversed (plantarflexion), thus shifting the COG posteriorly and evoking a stretch reflex of the anterior tibialis muscle. Both of these studies suggest that stretch reflex responses help to control the body's COG and that the vestibular system is unlikely to be directly involved in the generation of the necessary responses.

Elimination of all sensory information from the feet and ankles revealed that proprioceptors in the leg muscles (gastrocnemius and tibialis anterior) were capable of providing sufficient sensory information for stable standing.[20] Researchers speculated that group I or group II muscle spindle afferents and group Ib afferents from GTOs were the probable sources of this proprioceptive information. The study demonstrated that normal subjects stand in a stable manner when receptors in the leg muscles are the only source of information about postural sway.

Other studies[5,38] have examined the role of somatosensory information by altering or limiting somatosensory input through the use of platform sway referencing or foam platforms. These studies reported that subjects still responded with well-coordinated movements, but the movements were often either ineffective or inefficient for the environmental context in which they were used.

BALANCE AS IT RELATES TO THE CLOSED-KINETIC CHAIN

Balance is the process of maintaining the center of gravity (COG) within the body's base of support. The human body has its center of gravity quite high, just above the pelvis.[77] Many factors enter into the task of controlling balance within this designated area. One component often overlooked is the role balance plays within the **kinetic chain.** Ongoing debates as to how the kinetic chain should be defined and whether open- or closed-kinetic chain exercises are best has caused many therapists to lose sight of what is most important. An understanding of the postural control system as well as the theory of the kinetic (segmental) chain about the lower extremity

helps conceptualize the role of the chain in maintaining balance. Within the kinetic chain, each moving segment transmits forces to every other segment along the chain, and its motions are influenced by forces transmitted from other segments (see Chapter 12).[10] The act of maintaining equilibrium or balance is associated with the closed-kinetic chain, as the distal segment (foot) is fixed beneath the base of support.

The coordination of automatic postural movements during the act of balancing is not determined solely by the muscles acting directly about the joint. Leg and trunk muscles exert indirect forces on neighboring joints through the inertial interaction forces among body segments.[57,58] A combination of one or more strategies (ankle, knee, hip) are used to coordinate movement of the COG back to a stable or balanced position when a person's balance is disrupted by an external perturbation. Injury to any one of the joints or corresponding muscles along the kinetic chain can result in a loss of appropriate feedback for maintaining balance.

BALANCE DISRUPTION

Let us say, for example, that a patient accidently steps in a hole causing him or her to land in an unexpected position, therefore compromising his or her normal balance. In order to prevent a fall from occurring, the body must correct itself by returning the COG to a position within a more safe LOS. Afferent mechanoreceptor input from the hip, knee, and ankle joints are responsible for initiating automatic postural responses through the use of one of three possible movement strategies.

Selection of Movement Strategies

Three principal joint systems (ankles, knees, and hips) are located between the base of support and the COG. This allows for a wide variety of postures, which can be assumed while the COG is still positioned above the base of support. As described by Nashner,[55] motions about a given joint are controlled by the combined actions of at least one pair of muscles working in opposition. When forces exerted by pairs of opposing muscle about a joint (e.g., anterior tibialis and gastrocnemius/soleus) are combined, the effect is to resist rotation of the joint relative to a resting position. The degree to which the joint resists rotation is called joint stiffness. The resting position and the stiffness of the joint are each altered independently by changing the activation levels of one or both muscle groups.[39,55] Joint resting position and joint stiffness are by themselves an inadequate basis for controlling postural movements, and it is theorized that the myotatic stretch reflex is the earliest mechanism for increasing the activation level of the muscles of a joint following an externally imposed rotation of the joint.[55]

When a person's balance is disrupted by an external perturbation, movement strategies involving joints of the lower extremity coordinate movement of the COG back to a balanced

TABLE 9-1

Function Anatomy of Muscles Involved in Balance Movements

| JOINT | EXTENSION | | FLEXION | |
	ANATOMIC	FUNCTION	ANATOMIC	FUNCTION
Hip	Paraspinals Hamstrings	Paraspinals Hamstrings Tibialis	Abdominal Quadriceps	Abdominals Quadriceps Gastrocnemius
Knee	Quadriceps	Paraspinals Quadriceps Gastrocnemius	Hamstrings Gastrocnemius	Abdominals Hamstrings Tibialis
Ankle	Gastrocnemius	Abdominals Quadriceps Gastrocnemius	Tibialis	Paraspinals Hamstrings Tibialis

SOURCE: Nashner LM. Physiology of Balance. In: *Handbook of Balance Function and Testing*, edited by G. Jacobson, C. Newman, and J. Kartush, pp. 261–279. St. Louis, Mosby Yearbook, 1993.

position. Three strategies (ankle, hip, stepping) have been identified along a continuum.[37] In general, the relative effectiveness of ankle, hip, and stepping strategies in repositioning the COG over the base of support depends on the configuration of the base of support, the COG alignment in relation to the LOS, and the speed of the postural movement.[37,38]

The **ankle strategy** shifts the COG while maintaining the placement of the feet by rotating the body as a rigid mass about the ankle joints. This is achieved by contracting either the gastrocnemius or anterior tibialis muscles to generate torque about the ankle joints. Anterior sway of the body is counteracted by gastrocnemius activity, which pulls the body posteriorly. Conversely, posterior sway of the body is counteracted by contraction of the tibialis anterior. Thus, the importance of these muscles should not be underestimated when designing a rehabilitation program. The ankle strategy is most effective in executing relatively slow COG movements when the base of support is firm and the COG is well within the LOS perimeter. The ankle strategy is also believed to be effective in maintaining a static posture with the COG offset from the center. The thigh and lower trunk muscles contract and resist the destabilization of these proximal joints due to the indirect effects of the ankle muscles on the proximal joints (Table 9-1). Under normal sensory conditions, activation of ankle musculature is almost exclusively selected to maintain equilibrium. However, there are subtle differences associated with loss of somatosensation and with vestibular dysfunction in terms of postural control strategies. Persons with somatosensory loss appear to rely on their hip musculature to retain their COG while experiencing forward or backward perturbation or with different support surface lengths.[21]

If the ankle strategy is not capable of controlling excessive sway, the **hip strategy** is available to help control motion of the COG through the initiation of large and rapid motions at the hip joints with antiphase rotation of the ankles. It is most effective when the COG is located near the LOS perimeter and when the LOS boundaries are contracted by a narrowed base of support. Finally, when the COG is displaced beyond the LOS, a step or stumble (**stepping strategy**) is the only strategy that can be used to prevent a fall.[55,57]

It is proposed that LOS and COG alignment are altered in individuals exhibiting a musculoskeletal abnormality such as an ankle or knee sprain. For example, weakness of ligaments following acute or chronic sprain about these joints is likely to reduce range of motion, therefore, shrinking LOS and placing the person at greater risk for a fall with a relatively smaller sway envelope.[57] Pintsaar et al[67] revealed that impaired function was related to a change from ankle synergy toward hip synergy for postural adjustments among patients with functional ankle instability. This finding, which was consistent with previous results reported by Tropp et al,[74] suggests that sensory proprioceptive function for the injured patients was affected.

ASSESSMENT OF BALANCE

Several methods of balance assessment have been proposed for clinical use. Many of the techniques have been criticized for offering only subjective information, or a "qualitative" measurement of balance, rather than an objective, or "quantitative," measure.

Subjective (Clinical) Assessment

Prior to the mid-1980s, there were very few methods for systematic and controlled assessment of balance. The assessment of static balance in patients has traditionally been performed

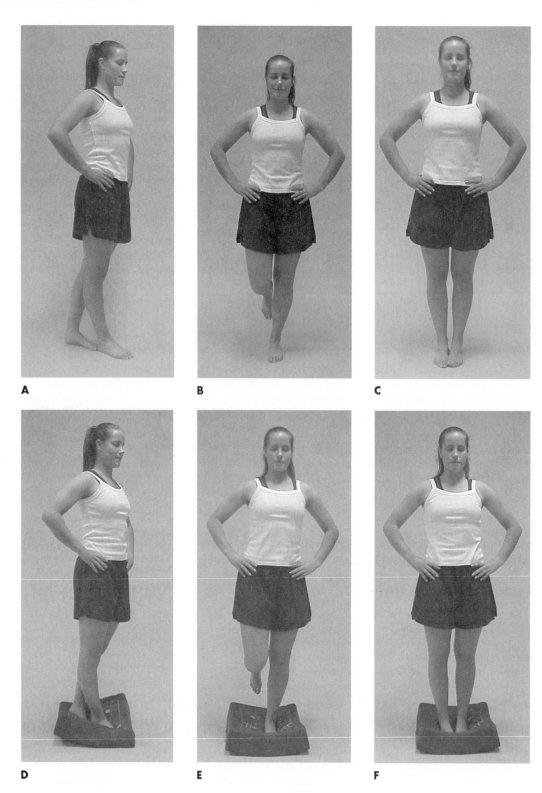

A   **B**   **C**

D   **E**   **F**

F I G U R E   9 - 3

Stance positions for BESS. **A,** Tandem; hard surface. **B,** Single-leg; hard surface. **C,** Double-leg; hard surface. **D,** Tandem; foam. **E,** Single-leg; foam. **F,** Double-leg; foam.

through the use of the standard Romberg test. This test is performed standing with feet together, arms at the side, and eyes closed. Normally, a person can stand motionless in this position, but the tendency to sway or fall to one side is considered a positive Romberg's sign indicating a loss of proprioception.[8] The standard Romberg test has, however, been criticized for its lack of sensitivity and objectivity. It is considered to be a rather qualitative assessment of static balance because a considerable amount of stress is required to make the subject sway enough for an observer to characterize the sway.[42]

The use of a quantifiable clinical test battery called the *Balance Error Scoring System (BESS)* is recommended over the standard Romberg test. Three different stances (double, single, and tandem) are completed twice, once while on a firm surface and once while on a 10-cm thick piece of medium-density foam (45 cm^2 by 13 cm thick, density 60 kg/m^3, load deflection 80 to 90 for a total of six trials (Fig. 9-3A–F). Athletes are asked to assume the required stance by placing their hands on the iliac crests, and upon eye closure the 20-second test begins. During the single-leg stances, subjects are asked to maintain the contralateral limb in 20 to 30 degrees of hip flexion and 40 to 50 degrees of knee flexion. Additionally, the athlete is asked to stand quietly and as motionless as possible in the stance position, keeping the hands on the iliac crests and eyes closed. The single-limb stance tests are performed on the nondominant foot. This same foot is placed toward the rear on the tandem stances. Subjects are told that upon losing their balance, they are to make any necessary adjustments and return to the testing position as quickly as possible. Performance is scored by adding one error point for each error committed (Table 9-2). Trials are considered to be incomplete if the athlete is unable to sustain the stance position for longer than 5 seconds during the entire 20-second testing period. These trials are assigned a standard maximum error score of 10. Balance test results during injury recovery are best utilized when compared to baseline measurements, and clinicians working with athletes or patients on a regular

basis should attempt to obtain baseline measurements when possible.

Dynamic balance assessment can also be performed through functional reach tests, timed agility tests such as the figure-eight test,[15,19,63,79] carioca or hop test,[40] BESS test for dynamic balance,[75] timed "T-band kicks," and timed balance beam walking with the eyes open or closed. The objective in most of these tests is to decrease the size of the base of support in an attempt to determine a patient's ability to control upright posture while moving. Many of these tests have been criticized for failing to quantify balance adequately, as they merely report the time that a particular posture is maintained, angular displacement, or the distance covered after walking.[6,21,46,55,63] At any rate, they can often provide the clinician with valuable information about a patient's function.

Objective (Instrumental) Assessment

More recently, advancements in technology have provided the medical community with commercially available balance systems (Table 9-3) for quantitatively assessing and training static and dynamic balance. These systems provide an easy, practical, and cost-effective method of quantitatively assessing and training functional balance through analysis of postural stability. Thus, the potential exists to assess injured patients and (1) identify possible abnormalities that might be associated with injury; (2) isolate various systems that are affected; (3) develop recovery curves based on quantitative measures for determining readiness to return to activity; and (4) train the injured patient.

Most manufacturers use computer-interfaced forceplate technology consisting of a flat, rigid surface supported on three or more points by independent force-measuring devices. As the patient stands on the forceplate surface, the position of the center of vertical forces exerted on the forceplate over time is calculated (Fig. 9-4). The center of vertical force movements provides an indirect measure of postural sway activity.[56] The Kistler forceplate was used for much of the early work in the area of postural stability and balance.[6,17,27,52,54] Manufacturers

---

TABLE 9-2

Balance Error Scoring System (BESS)

ERRORS
Hands lifted off iliac crests Opening eyes Step, stumble, or fall Moving hip into more than 30 degrees   of flexion or abduction Lifting forefoot or heel Remaining out of testing position for more than 5 sec

The BESS score is calculated by adding one error point for each erorr or any combination of errors occurring during one movement.

TABLE 9-3

High-Technology Balance Assessment Systems

STATIC SYSTEMS	DYNAMIC SYSTEMS
Chattecx Balance System	Biodex Stability System
	Chattecx Balance System
EquiTest	EquiTest
Forceplate System	EquiTest with EMG
(Kistler, Bertec)	Forceplate
Pro Balance Master	Kinesthetic Ability Trainer (KAT)
Smart Balance Master	Pro Balance Master
	Smart Balance Master

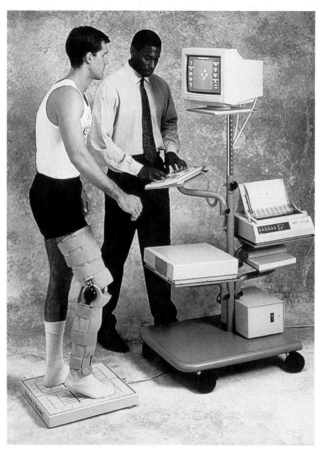

FIGURE   9 - 4

Athlete training on the Balance Master.

FIGURE   9 - 5

EquiTest.

such as Chattecx Corporation (Hixson, TN) and NeuroCom International, Inc. (Clackamas, OR) have developed more sophisticated systems with expanded diagnostic and training capabilities.

Force platforms ideally evaluate three aspects of postural control: steadiness, symmetry, and dynamic stability. **Steadiness** is the ability to keep the body as motionless as possible. This is a measure of postural sway. **Symmetry** is the ability to distribute weight evenly between the two feet in an upright stance. This is a measure of center of pressure (COP), center of balance (COB), or center of force (COF), depending on which testing system is used. **Dynamic stability** is the ability to transfer the vertical projection of the COG around a stationary supporting base.[27] This is often referred to as a measure of a person's perception of his or her "safe" limits of stability, as the goal is to lean or reach as far as possible without losing the balance. **Dynamic balance assessment** is somewhat different, in that postural responses are measured in response to external perturbations from a moving platform in one of four directions: tilting toes up, tilting toes down, shifting medial–lateral (M–L), and shifting anterior–posterior (A–P). Platform perturbation on some systems is unpredictable and determined by the positioning and sway movement of the participant. In such cases, a person's reaction response can be determined

(Fig. 9-5). Other systems have a more predictable sinusoidal waveform, which remains constant regardless of patient positioning (Fig. 9-6).

Many of these force platform systems measure the vertical ground reaction force and provide a means of computing the COP. The COP represents the center of the distribution of the total force applied to the supporting surface. The COP is calculated from horizontal moment and vertical force data generated by triaxial force platforms. Center of balance, in the case of the Chattecx Balance System, is the point between the feet where the ball and heel of each foot has 25 percent of the body weight. This point is referred to as the relative weight positioning over the four load cells as measured only by vertical forces. The center of vertical force, on NeuroCom's Equitest, is the center of the vertical force exerted by the feet against the support surface. In any case (COP, COB, or COF), the total force applied to the force platform fluctuates because it includes both body weight and the inertial effects of the slightest movement of the body, which occur even when a person attempts to stand motionless. The movement of these force-based reference points are theorized to vary according to the movement of the body COG and the distribution of muscle forces required to control posture. Ideally, healthy patients should maintain their COP very near the A–P and M–L midlines.

Once the COP, COB, or COF is calculated, several other balance parameters can be attained. Deviation from this point in any direction represents a person's postural sway. Postural sway can be measured in various ways, depending on which

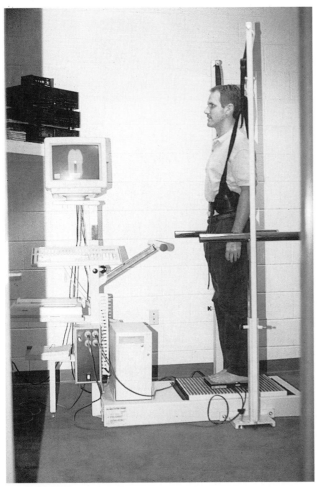

F I G U R E   9 - 6
Chattecx Balance System.

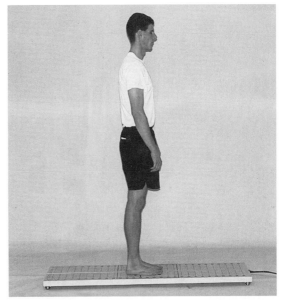

F I G U R E   9 - 7
Balance Master with accessory 5-ft forceplate.

system is being used. Mean displacement, length of sway path, length of sway area, amplitude, frequency, and direction with respect to the COP can be calculated on most systems. An equilibrium score, comparing the angular difference between the calculated maximum anterior to posterior COG displacements to a theoretic maximum displacement, is unique to the NeuroCom International Equitest. Sway index (SI), representing the degree of scatter of data about the COB, is unique to the Chattecx Balance System.

Forceplate technology allows for quantitative analysis and understanding of a participant's postural instability. These systems are fully integrated with hardware and software systems for quick and quantitative assessment and rehabilitation in balance disorders. Most manufacturers allow for both static and dynamic balance assessment in either double- or single-leg stances, with eyes open or eyes closed. The NeuroCom Equitest System is equipped with a moving visual surround (wall) that allows for the most sophisticated technology available for isolating and assessing sensory modality interaction.

Long forceplates have been developed by some manufacturers in an attempt to combat criticism that balance assess-

ment is not functional. This newer variation on some systems (Fig. 9-7) adds a vast array of dynamic balance exercises for training, such as walking, step-up and over, side and crossover steps, hopping, leaping, and lunging. These important return-to-sport activities can be practiced and perfected through the use of visual feedback from the computer.

Biodex Medical Systems (Shirley, NY) and Breg, Inc. (Vista, CA) both manufacture a dynamic multiaxial tilting platform that offers computer-generated data similar to that of a forceplate system. The Biodex Stability System (Fig. 9-8) uses a dynamic multiaxial platform that allows up to 20 degrees of deflection in any direction. It is theorized that this degree of deflection is sufficient to stress joint mechanoreceptors, which provide proprioceptive feedback (at end ranges of motion) necessary for balance control. Clinicians can assess deficits in dynamic muscular control of posture relative to joint pathology. The patient's ability to control the platform's angle of tilt is quantified as a variance from center, as well as degrees of deflection over time, at various stability levels. A large variance is indicative of poor muscle response. The Kinesthetic Ability Trainer, or KAT (Fig. 9-9), is similar to the Biodex Stability System in that it utilizes a multiaxial unstable platform. Exercises performed on these multiaxial unstable systems are similar to those of the Biomechanical Ankle Platform System (BAPS board) and are especially effective for regaining proprioception and balance following injury to the ankle joint.

The FASTEX System (Cybex Division of Lumex, Inc. Ronkonkoma, NY) is another device available for assessing and training functional balance. The FASTEX consists of 8 deformable force platforms that include piezoelectric sensors. The sensor encircles each platform, which allows it to capture the entire shock wave from each impact (Fig. 9-10). On impact,

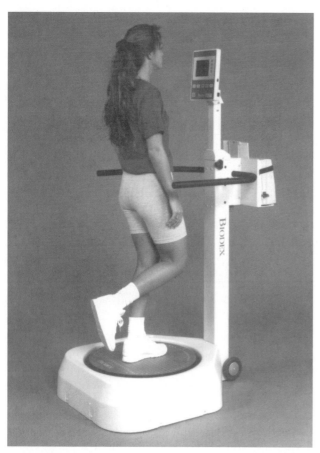

F I G U R E   9 - 8

Biodex Stability System.

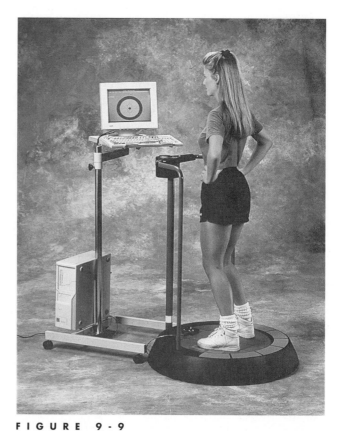

F I G U R E   9 - 9

Kinesthetic Awareness Trainer (KAT).

a measurable electric impulse is produced and translated into one of several quantitative variables. Although this system is not a forceplate capable of measuring COG alignment or postural sway, it can assess reaction time, mobility, and time to stability.[75]

INJURY AND BALANCE

It has long been theorized that failure of stretched or damaged ligaments to provide adequate neural feedback in an injured extremity may contribute to decreased proprioceptive mechanisms necessary for maintenance of proper balance. Research has revealed these impairments in individuals with ankle injury[23,31,73] and anterior cruciate ligament (ACL) injury.[4,65] A lack of proprioceptive feedback resulting from such injuries may allow excessive or inappropriate loading of a joint. Furthermore, although the presence of a capsular lesion may interfere with the transmission of afferent impulses from the joint, a more important effect may be alteration of the afferent neural code that is conveyed to the CNS.[80] Decreased reflex excitation of motor neurons may result from either or both of the following events: (1) a decrease in proprioceptive input to the CNS; and (2) an increase in the activation of inhibitory interneurons within the

spinal cord. All of these factors may lead to progressive degeneration of the joint and continued deficits in joint dynamics, balance, and coordination.[32]

Ankle Injuries

Joint proprioceptors are believed to be damaged during injury to the lateral ligaments of the ankle because joint receptor fibers possess less tensile strength than the ligament fibers. Damage to the joint receptors is believed to cause joint deafferentation, therefore diminishing the supply of messages from the injured joint up the afferent pathway disrupting proprioceptive function. Freeman et al[24] were the first to report a decrease in the frequency of functional instability following ankle sprains when coordination exercises were performed as part of rehabilitation. The term *articular deafferentation* was introduced to designate the mechanism that they believed to be the cause of functional instability of the ankle. This finding led to the inclusion of balance training in ankle rehabilitation programs.

Since 1965, Freeman[23] has theorized that if ankle injuries cause partial deafferentation and functional instability, a person's postural sway would be altered due to a proprioception deficit. Whereas some studies[72,73] have not supported Freeman's theory, other more recent studies using high-technology equipment (forceplate, kinesthesiometer, etc.) have revealed balance deficits in ankles following acute sprains[25,31,66] and/or in ankles with chronic instabilities.[9,22,26,67]

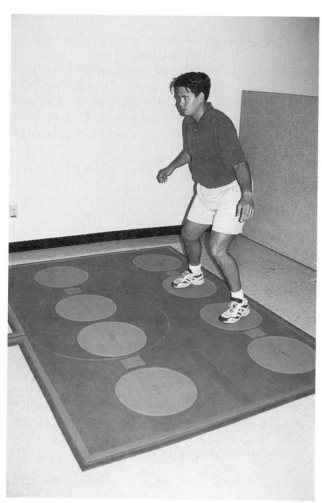

FIGURE 9-10

FASTEX.

Differences were identified between injured and uninjured ankles in 14 ankle-injured participants using a computerized strain gauge forceplate.[25] Four postural sway parameters (standard deviation of the mean center of pressure dispersion, mean sway amplitude, average speed, and number of sway amplitudes exceeding 5 and 10 mm) taken in the frontal plane from a single-leg stance position were reported to discriminate between injured and uninjured ankles. The authors reported that the application of an ankle brace eliminated the differences between injury status when tested on each parameter, therefore improving balance performance. More importantly, this study suggests that the stabiliometry technique of selectively analyzing postural sway movements in the frontal plane, where the diameter of the supporting area is smallest, leads to higher sensitivity. Because difficulties of maintaining balance after a ligament lesion involves the subtalar axis, it is proposed that increased sway movements of the different body segments would be found primarily in the frontal plane. The authors speculated that this could explain nonsignificant findings of earlier stabiliometry studies[72,73] involving injured ankles.

Orthotic intervention and postural sway were studied in 13 participants with acute inversion ankle sprains and 12 uninjured

participants under two treatment conditions (orthotic, nonorthotic) and four platform movements (stable, inversion and eversion, plantarflexion and dorsiflexion, and medial–lateral perturbations).[31] Results revealed that ankle-injured participants swayed more than uninjured participants when assessed in a single-leg test on the Chattecx Balance System. The analysis also revealed that custom-fit orthotics may restrict undesirable motion at the foot and ankle, enhance joint mechanoreceptors to detect perturbations, and provide structural support for detecting and controlling postural sway in ankle-injured participants. A similar study[66] reported improvements in static balance for injured participants while wearing custom-made orthotics.

Studies involving participants with chronic ankle instabilities[9,22,26,67] indicate that individuals with a history of inversion ankle sprain are less stable in single-limb stance on the involved leg as compared to the uninvolved leg and/or uninjured participants. Significant differences between injured and uninjured participants for sway amplitude, but not sway frequency, using a standard forceplate were revealed.[9] The effect of stance perturbation on frontal plane postural control in three groups of participants: (1) control (no previous ankle injury); (2) functional ankle instability and 8-week training program; and (3) mechanical instability without functional instability (without shoe, with shoe, with brace and shoe) was studied.[67] Results revealed a relative change from ankle to hip synergy at medially directed translations of the support surface on the NeuroCom Equitest. The impairment was restored after 8 weeks of ankle disk training. The effect of a shoe and brace did not exceed the effect of the shoe alone. Impaired ankle function was shown to be related to coordination, as participants changed from ankle toward hip strategies for postural adjustments.

Similarly, researchers[36] reported that lateral ankle joint anesthesia does not alter postural sway or passive joint position sense, but affects the center of balance position (similar to center of pressure) during both static and dynamic testing. This suggests the presence of an adaptive mechanism to compensate for the loss of afferent stimuli from the region of the lateral ankle ligaments.[36] Participants tended to shift the center of balance medially during dynamic balance testing and slightly laterally during static balance testing. The authors speculated that center of balance shifting may provide additional proprioceptive input from cutaneous receptors in the sole of the foot and/or stretch receptors in the peroneal muscle tendon unit, which, therefore, prevents increased postural sway.

Increased postural sway frequency and latencies are parameters thought to be indicative of impaired ankle joint proprioception.[13,68] Cornwall and Murrell[9] and Pintsaar et al,[67] however, found no differences between chronically injured and control participants on these measures. This raises the question as to whether postural sway was, in fact, caused by a proprioceptive deficit. Increased postural sway amplitudes in the absence of sway frequencies might suggest that chronically injured patients recover ankle joint proprioception over time. Thus, more research is warranted for investigating loss of joint proprioception and postural sway frequency.[9]

In summary, results of studies involving both chronic and acute ankle sprains suggest that increased postural sway and/or balance instability may not be due to a single factor but to disruption of both neurologic and biomechanical factors at the ankle joint. Loss of balance may result from abnormal or altered biomechanical alignment of the body, thus affecting the transmission of somatosensory information from the ankle joint. It is possible that observed postural sway amplitudes following injury is a result of joint instability along the kinetic chain, rather than deafferentation. Thus, the orthotic intervention[31,61,62] may have provided more optimal joint alignment.

Knee Injuries

Ligamentous injury to the knee has proven to affect the ability of participants to accurately detect position.[2–4,46,49,50] The general consensus among numerous investigators performing proprioceptive testing is that a clinical proprioception deficit occurs in most patients after an ACL rupture who have functional instability and that this deficit seems to persist to some degree after an ACL reconstruction.[2] Because of the relationships between proprioception (somatosensation) and balance, it has been suggested that the patient's ability to balance on the ACL-injured leg may also be decreased.[4,65,79]

Studies have evaluated the effects of ACL ruptures on standing balance using forceplate technology, and some studies have revealed balance deficits[25,53]; others have not.[18,35] Thus, there appears to be conflicting results from these studies depending on which parameters are measured. Mizuta et al[53] found significant differences in postural sway when measuring center of pressure and sway distance area between 11 functionally stable and 15 functionally unstable participants who had unilateral ACL-deficient knees. Faculjak et al,[18] however, found no differences in postural stability between 8 ACL-deficient participants and 10 normal participants when measuring average latency and response strength on an EquiTest System.

Several potential reasons for this discrepancy exist. It has been suggested[1] that there may be a link between static balance and isometric strength of the musculature at the ankle and knee. Isometric muscle strength could, therefore, compensate for any somatosensory deficit present in the involved knee during a closed-chain static balance test. Second, many studies fail to discriminate between "functionally unstable" ACL-deficient knees and those that involved knees that were not functionally unstable. This presents a design flaw, especially considering that functionally stable knees would most likely provide adequate balance despite ligamentous pathology. Another suggested reason for not seeing differences between injured knees and uninjured knees on static balance measures could be explained by the role that joint mechanoreceptors play. Neurophysiologic studies[28,29,43,46] have revealed that joint mechanoreceptors provide enhanced kinesthetic awareness in the near-terminal range of motion or extremes of motion. Therefore, it could be speculated that if the maximum LOS are never reached during a static balance test, damaged mechanoreceptors (muscle or joint) may not even become a factor. Dynamic balance tests or functional hop tests that involve dynamic balance could challenge the postural control system (ankle strategies are taken over by hip and/or stepping strategies) requiring more mechanoreceptor input. These tests would most likely discriminate between functionally unstable ACL-deficient knees and normal knees. Most recently, the shoulder joint and its surrounding musculature has been found to respond favorably to closed-kinetic chain training. More research in this area should substantiate these findings.[76]

Head Injury

Neurologic status following mild head injury has been assessed using balance as a criterion variable. Romberg's test of sensory modality function has been used to test "balance." This is an easy and effective objective test; however, the literature suggests there is more to posture control than just balance and sensory modality,[59–61,64,69] especially when assessing people with head injury.[30,33] The postural control system, which is responsible for linking brain to body communication, is often affected as a result of mild head injury. Recent studies have identified postural stability deficits in patients up to 3 days postinjury using commercially available balance systems.[30,33] It appears that this deficit is related to a sensory interaction problem, whereby the injured patient fails to use the visual system effectively. This research suggests that objective balance assessment can be used for establishing recovery curves when treating concussed patients. Rehabilitation of concussed patients using balance techniques has yet to be studied.

BALANCE TRAINING

Developing a rehabilitation program that includes exercises for improving balance and postural equilibrium is vital for correcting impairment following lower extremity injury. Regardless of whether the patient has sustained a quadriceps strain or an ankle sprain, the injury has caused a disruption at some point between the body's COG and base of support. This is likely to have caused compensatory weight shifts and gait changes along the kinetic chain, which have resulted in balance deficits. These deficits may be detected through the use of functional assessment tests and/or computerized instrumentation previously discussed for assessing balance. Having the advanced technology available to quantify balance deficits is an amenity, but not a necessity. Imagination and creativity are often the best tools available to clinicians with limited resources who are trying to design balance training protocols.

Because so many activities involve closed-chain lower extremity function, functional rehabilitation should be performed in the closed-kinetic chain. However, ROM, movement speed, and additional resistance may be more easily controlled in the open chain initially. Therefore, adequate, safe function in an open chain may be the first step in the rehabilitation process, but should not be the focus of the rehabilitation plan. The clinician should attempt to progress the patient to functional closed-chain exercises quickly and safely. Depending on severity of injury, this could be as early as 1 day postinjury.

As previously mentioned, there is a close relationship between somtosensation, kinesthesia, and balance. Therefore, many of the exercises proposed for kinesthetic training are indirectly enhancing balance. Several methods of regaining balance have been proposed in the literature and are included in the most current rehabilitation protocols for ankle[41,71,81] and knee injury.[11,40,51,70,80]

A variety of activities can be used to improve balance, but the therapist should consider five general rules before beginning.

- The exercises must be safe yet challenging.
- Stress multiple planes of motion.
- Incorporate a multisensory approach.
- Begin with static, bilateral, and stable surfaces and progress to dynamic, unilateral, and unstable surfaces.
- Progress to sport-specific exercises.

There are several ways in which the clinician can meet these goals. Balance exercises should be performed in an open area, where the patient will not be injured in the event of a fall. It is best to perform exercises with an assistive device within an arm's reach (i.e., chair, railing, table, wall), especially during the initial phase of rehabilitation. When considering exercise duration for balance exercises, the therapist can use either sets and repetitions or a time-based protocol. The patient can perform 2 to 3 sets of 15 repetitions and progress to 30 repetitions as tolerated, or perform 10 of the exercises for a 15-second period and progress to 30-second periods later in the program.

Phase I

The progression of activities during this phase should include nonballistic types of drills. Training for static balance can be initiated once the patient is able to bear weight on the extremity. The patient should first be asked to perform a bilateral 20-second Romberg test (Fig. 9-11), followed by a unilateral test (Fig. 9-12) on both the involved and uninvolved extremities. The therapist should make comparisons from these tests to determine the patient's ability to balance bilaterally and unilaterally. It should be noted that even though this is termed *static balance,* the patient does not remain perfectly motionless. To maintain static balance, the patient must make many small corrections at the ankle, hip, trunk, arms, or head, as previously discussed (see "Selection of Muscle Strategies"). If the patient is having difficulties performing these activities, he or she should not be progressed. Repetitions of modified Romberg tests can be performed by first using the arms as a counterbalance, then attempting the activity without using the arms. Static balance activities should be used as a precurser to more dynamic activities. The general progression of these exercises should be from bilateral to unilateral, with eyes open to eyes closed. The exercises should attempt to eliminate or alter the various sensory information (visual, vestibular, and somatosensory) to challenge the other systems. In most musculoskeletal rehabilitation situations, this will involve eye closure and changes in the support surface

FIGURE   9-11

Bilateral Romberg with the eyes closed.

so the somatosensory system can be overloaded or stressed. This theory is synonymous with the overload principle in therapeutic exercise. Research suggests that balance activities, both with and without visual input, will enhance motor function at the brainstem level.[7,71] However, as the patient becomes more efficient at performing activities involving static balance, eye closure is recommended so that only the somatosensory system is left to control balance.

As improvement occurs on a firm surface, static balance drills should progress to an unstable surface such as foam (Fig. 9-13), mini-tramp (Fig. 9-14), BAPS board (Fig. 9-15), or rocker board (Fig. 9-16). Additionally, the therapist can introduce light shoulder, back, or chest taps in an attempt to challenge the patient's ability to maintain balance (Fig. 9-17). Finally, the use of multiaxial devices such as the Biodex Stability System or Kinesthetic Ability Trainer on a relatively easy level can be initiated during the later part of phase I. These exercises increase awareness of the location of the COG under a challenged condition, thereby helping to increase ankle strength in the closed-kinetic chain. Such training may also increase sensitivity of the muscle spindle and increase proprioceptive input to the spinal cord, which may provide compensation for altered joint afference.[46]

Although static balance exercises are likely not very functional for most dynamic activities, they are the first step toward

FIGURE 9-12

Unilateral Romberg with the eyes closed.

FIGURE 9-14

Unilateral stance on mini-tramp.

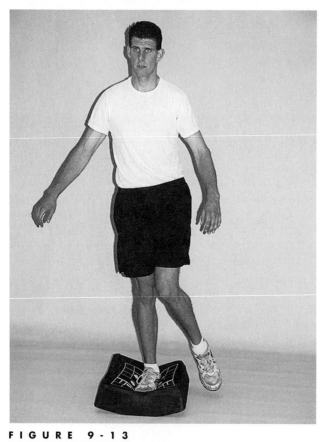

FIGURE 9-13

Unilateral stance on medium-density foam.

FIGURE 9-15

Unilateral stance on BAPS board.

FIGURE 9-16

Unilateral stance on rocker board.

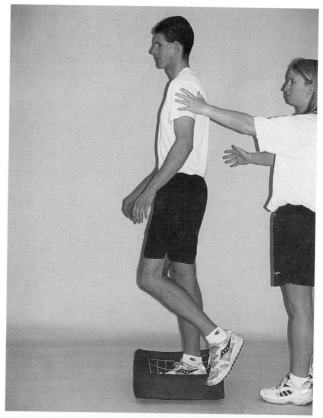

FIGURE 9-17

Clinician causing perturbations using shoulder taps.

regaining proprioceptive awareness, reflex stabilization, and postural orientation. The patient should attempt to assume a functional stance while performing static balance drills. Training in different positions places a variety of demands on the musculotendinous structures about the ankle, knee, and hip joints. For example, an injured gymnast should practice static balance with the hip in neutral and external rotation, as well as during a tandem stance (Fig. 9-18) to mimic performance on a balance beam.

Phase II

This phase should be considered the transition phase from static to more dynamic balance activities. Dynamic balance will be especially important for patients who perform activities such as running, jumping, and cutting, which encompasses about 95 percent of all patients. Such activities require the patient to repetitively lose and gain balance to perform a sport without falling or becoming injured.[41] Dynamic balance activities should only be incorporated into the rehabilitation program once sufficient healing has occurred and the patient has adequate ROM, muscle strength, and endurance. This could be as early as a few days postinjury, in the case of a grade I ankle sprain, or as late as 6 weeks postsurgery in the case of an anterior cruciate reconstruction. Before the therapist progresses the patient to more challenging dynamic balance drills, several semidynamic (intermediate) exercises should be introduced.

These semidynamic balance drills involve displacement or perturbation of the COG away from the base of support. The

patient is challenged to return and/or steady the COG above the base of support throughout several repetitions of the exercise. Some of these exercises involve a bilateral stance, some involve a unilateral stance, and others involve transferring of weight from one extremity to the other.

The bilateral stance balance drills include the minisquat, which is performed with the feet shoulder-width apart and the COG centered over a stable base of support. The trunk should be positioned upright over the legs as the patient slowly flexes the hips and knees into a partial squat with approximately 45 to 60 degrees of knee flexion (Fig. 9-19). The patient then returns to the starting position and repeats the task several times. Once ROM, strength, and stability have improved, the patient can progress to a full squat, which approaches 90 degrees of knee flexion. These should be performed in front of a mirror so the patient can observe the amount of stability on return to the extended position. A large PhysioBall can also be used to perform sit-to-stand activities (Fig. 9-20). These exercises are important in the rehabilitation of knee and hip injuries, as they help improve weight transfer, COG sway velocity, and left and right weight symmetry.

The lunge is a more specific bilateral drill. This exercise decreases the base of support and increases the stress to one extremity at a given moment. ROM can be stressed to a higher degree than with the squatting exercises. When lunges are used to improve balance, it is important that the patient perform

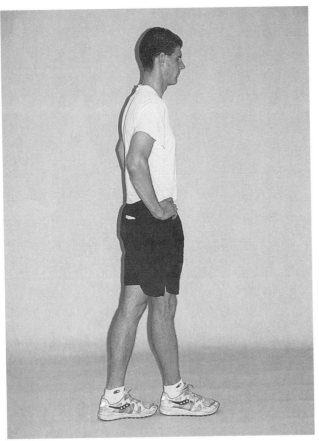

F I G U R E   9 - 1 8

Tandem stance.

F I G U R E   9 - 1 9

Minisquat.

the drill slowly so that the COG can be steadied over each support leg. When performing the forward lunge, the patient may use exaggerated extension movements of the lumbar region to assist weak or uncoordinated hip extension (Fig. 9-21). This substitution is not produced during the squatting exercises.[77] Normal lunge distances should approach, but not reach, the patient's total height.

FORWARD LUNGE

The patient's hands should be placed on the hips, while the involved leg is placed forward and the uninvolved backward. The progression for lunges should be from standard short lunges without tubing, to assisted lunges and resisted lunges using tubing. During the **assisted forward lunge,** the patient faces away from the tubing, which descends at a sharp angle (approximately 60 degrees) and wraps around the waist. The tubing angle parallels the patient's COG, which moves forward and down (Fig. 9-22), thereby assisting the patient up from the lowest point. The assistance also minimizes eccentric demands for deceleration when lowering and improves balance by helping the patient focus on the COG.[78]

During the **resisted forward lunge,** the uninvolved leg remains forward. The patient faces the tubing, which is now ascending from the floor to the level of the waist. The patient

should be positioned far enough from the tubing so that tension is created when kneeling on the uninvolved (back) leg (Fig. 9-23). During the upward movement, the focus should be hip extension and not knee extension. The patient should initiate movement from the hip and not from lumbar hyperextension

F I G U R E   9 - 2 0

Sit-to-stand using PhysioBall.

FIGURE 9-21
Forward lunge.

FIGURE 9-23
Resisted forward lunge with block.

or excessive knee extension.[71,78] During the downward movement, the tubing will increase the eccentric loading on the quadriceps.

LATERAL LUNGE

The **assisted lateral lunge** positions the involved leg opposite the side of the tubing (Fig. 9-24). The tubing reduces relative body weight while allowing closed-kinetic chain function in

FIGURE 9-22
Assisted forward lunge.

FIGURE 9-24
Assisted lateral lunge.

F I G U R E   9 - 2 5
Resisted lateral lunge.

F I G U R E   9 - 2 6
Forward step-up.

F I G U R E   9 - 2 7
Lateral step-up.

a lateral direction. The uninvolved extremity initiates movement of the COG over the involved extremity, followed by an assisted push-off from the involved extremity toward the uninvolved side. The **resisted lateral lunge** positions the involved leg on the same side as the tubing (Fig. 9-25). During this drill, the involved leg initiates the movement and acts as the primary weight-bearing extremity. Similar to the forward resisted lunge, it provides overloading on the involved extremity.[71,78]

The therapist has a variety of options for unilateral semi-dynamic balance exercises. A unilateral minisquat is a good starting point. These can be performed while holding onto a chair or support rail with the uninvolved knee flexed to 45 degrees. The patient should emphasize controlled hip and knee flexion, followed by a smooth return to the starting position on the involved extremity. Once this skill is mastered, the patient can progress to a step-up. Step-ups can be performed either in the sagittal plane (forward step-up) or in the transverse plane (lateral step-up). These drills should begin with the heel of the uninvolved extremity on the floor. Using a 3 count, the patient should shift the weight toward the involved side and use the involved extremity to slowly raise the body onto the step.[71] The involved knee should not be "locked" into full extension. Instead, the knee should be positioned in approximately 5 degrees of flexion, while balancing on the step for 3 seconds. Following

FIGURE 9-28

Step-up and over while ascending and descending on the involved extremity.

FIGURE 9-29

Step-up and over while ascending on the involved extremity and descending on the uninvolved extremity.

FIGURE 9-30

Rocker board used in conjunction with foam padding.

FIGURE 9-32

Thera Band kicks.

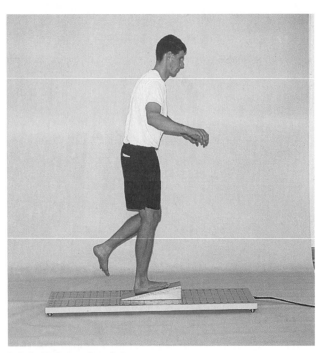

FIGURE 9-31

Unilateral stance on slant board.

FIGURE 9-33

Bilateral hop side to side.

F I G U R E   9 - 3 4

Diagonal hop.

F I G U R E   9 - 3 5

Lateral jumps over box.

the 3 count, the body weight should be shifted toward the uninvolved side and lowered to the heel of the uninvolved side (Figs. 9-26 and 9-27). **Step-up and over** activities are similar to step-ups, but involve more dynamic transfer of the COG. These can be performed by either having the patient both ascend and descend using the involved extremity (Fig. 9-28) or ascend with the involved extremity and descend with the uninvolved extremity forcing the involved leg to support the body on the descend (Fig. 9-29).

The therapist can also introduce the patient to more challenging static tests during this phase. For example, the foam padding can be used in conjunction with the rocker board (Fig. 9-30). A slant board can be used to stretch the heel cord while attempting to balance (Fig. 9-31). Finally, the very popular Thera Band kicks (T-Band kicks or steamboats) are excellent for improving balance. Thera Band kicks are performed with an elastic material (attached to the ankle of the uninvolved leg) serving as a resistance against a relatively fast kicking motion. The patient balance on the involved extremity is challenged by perturbations caused by the kicking motion of the uninvolved leg (Fig. 9-32). Four sets of these exercises should be performed, one for each of four possible kicking motions: hip flexion, hip extension, hip abduction, and hip adduction.

T-Band kicks can also be performed on foam or a mini-tramp if additional somatosensory challenges are desired.[70]

Phase III

Once the patient can successfully complete the semidynamic exercises presented in phase II, he or she should be ready to perform more dynamic and functional types of exercises. The general progression for activities to develop dynamic balance and control is from slow-speed to fast-speed activities, from low-force to high-force activities, and from controlled to uncontrolled activities.[41] As previously mentioned, the therapist often needs to use his or her imagination to develop the best protocol for a patient.

Bilateral jumping drills are a good place to begin once the patient has reached phase III. These can be performed either front to back or side to side. The patient should concentrate on landing on each side of the line as quickly as possible (Fig. 9-33).[70,71] As the patient progresses through these exercises, eye closure can be used to further challenge somatosensation. After mastering these straight-plane jumping patterns, the patient can begin diagonal jumping patterns through the use of a cross on the floor formed by two pieces of tape (Fig. 9-34). The intersecting lines create four quadrants that can be numbered

F I G U R E   9 - 3 6

Lateral bounding.

F I G U R E   9 - 3 7

Control dynamic balance while throwing and catching a ball.

and used to perform different jumping sequences, such as 1, 3, 2, 4 for the first set and 1, 4, 2, 3 for the second set.[70,71] A larger grid can be designed to allow for longer sequences and longer jumps, both of which require additional strength, endurance, and balance control.

Bilateral dynamic balance exercises should progress to unilateral dynamic balance exercises as quickly as possible during phase III. At this stage of the rehabilitation, pain and fatigue should not be as much of a factor. All jumping drills performed bilaterally should now be performed unilaterally, by practicing first on the uninvolved extremity. If additional challenges are needed, a vertical component can be added by having the patient jump over an object such as a box or some other suitable object (Fig. 9-35).

Resistance can be added to dynamic unilateral training exercises through the use of tubing. The patient can perform stationary running against the tube's resistance, followed by lateral and diagonal bounding exercises. Bounding, which involves jumping from one foot to another, places greater emphasis on lateral movements. It is recommended that the patient first learn the bounding exercise without tubing, and then attempt the exercise with tubing. A foam roll, towel, or other obstacle can be used to increase jump height and/or distance (Fig. 9-36).[78] The final step in trying to improve dynamic balance should involve throwing and catching a ball. At this stage of the rehabilitation

program, the patient should be able to safely concentrate on the functional activity (catching and throwing) while subconsciously controlling dynamic balance (Fig. 9-37).

CLINICAL VALUE OF HIGH-TECHNOLOGY TRAINING AND ASSESSMENT

The benefit of using the commercially available balance systems is that not only can deficits be detected, but progress can be charted quantitatively through the computer-generated results. For example, NeuroCom's NEW Balance Master 6.0 is capable of assessing a patient's ability to perform coordinated movements essential for sport performance. The system, equipped with a 5-ft long force platform, is capable of identifying specific components underlying performance of several functional tasks. Exercises are also available on the system that help to improve the deficits.[62]

Results of a step-up and over test are presented in Fig. 9-38. The components analyzed in this particular task are: (1) **lift-up index**—quantifies the maximum lifting (concentric) force exerted by the leading leg and is expressed as a percentage of the person's weight; (2) **movement time**—quantifies the number

Name:	Doe, John J	Diagnosis:	ACL Tear L Knee	File:	HBM1.QBM
ID:	ATID00001	Operator ID:	Jodi Bower	Date:	03/06/97
DOB:	11/22/55	Referred by:	Dr. Tom Merkle	Time:	6:35:06 PM
Height:	5'11"	Comments:	DOI: 7/4/96; DOS: 7/6/96		

STEP UP/OVER TEXT (8 inch curb)

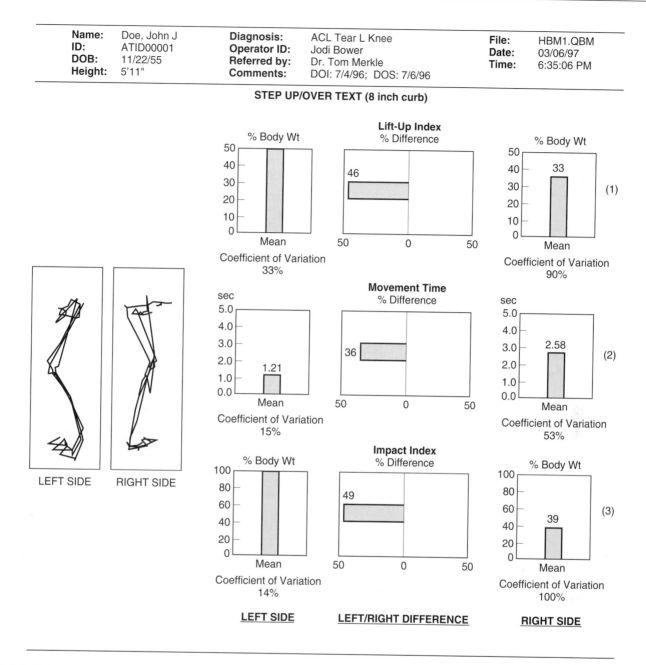

LEFT SIDE   **LEFT/RIGHT DIFFERENCE**   **RIGHT SIDE**

F I G U R E   9 - 3 8

Results from a step-up and over protocol on the NEW Balance Master 6.0.

of seconds required to complete the task, beginning with initial weight shift to the nonstepping leg and ending with impact of the lagging leg onto the surface; and (3) **impact index**—quantifies the maximum vertical impact force (percent of body weight) as the lagging leg lands on the surface.[62]

Early research on the clinical applicability of these measures has revealed interesting results. Preliminary observations from two studies in progress suggest that deficits in impact control are a common feature of patients with ACL injuries, even when strength and range of motion of the involved knee are within normal limits. Several other performance assessments are

available on this system, including *sit to stand, walk test, step and quick turn, forward lunge, weight bearing/squat, and rhythmic weight shift*.

SUMMARY

- There is a very close relationship between proprioception, kinesthesia, and balance.
- The most common form of proprioception training involves unilateral balance drills on challenging surfaces.
- Exercises performed on foam or multiaxial devices are a good

precursor for more dynamic balance exercises such as lunges, lateral bounding, or unilateral hopping drills.

- The goal of any rehabilitation program should be to move safely through a progression of balance exercises (phase I through phase III).
- The use of commercially manufactured balance systems adds a nice feature to balance training and assessment because the therapist can quantify progress.
- With a little creativity, the therapist can design low-cost, yet very effective, exercises for regaining balance.

REFERENCES

1. Balogun JA, Adesinasi CO, Marzouk DK. The effects of a wobble board exercise training program on static balance performance and strength of lower extremity muscle. *Physiotherapy Can* 44:23–30, 1992.
2. Barrack RL, Lund P, Skinner H. Knee joint proprioception revisited. *J Sport Rehabil* 3:18–42, 1994.
3. Barrack RL, Skinner HB, Buckley SL. Proprioception in the anterior cruciate deficient knee. *Am J Sports Med* 17:1–6, 1989.
4. Barrett D. Proprioception and function after anterior cruciate reconstruction. *J Bone Joint Surg* (Br) 73:833–837, 1991.
5. Black F, Wall C, Nashner L. Effect of visual and support surface orientations upon postural control in vestibular deficient subjects. *Acta Otolaryngol* 95:199–210, 1983.
6. Black O, Wall C, Rockette H, Kitch R. Normal subject postural sway during the Romberg test. *Am J Otolaryngol* 3:309–318, 1982.
7. Blackburn T, Voight M. Single leg stance: Development of a reliable testing procedure. In: *Proceedings of the 12th International Congress of the World Confederation for Physical Therapy*, 1995.
8. Booher J, Thibodeau G. *Athletic Injury Assessment*. St. Louis, MO, Mosby College Publishing, 1994, p. 285.
9. Cornwall M, Murrell P. Postural sway following inversion sprain of the ankle. *J Am Podiatr Med Assoc* 81:243–247, 1991.
10. Davies G. The need for critical thinking in rehabilitation. *J Sport Rehabil* 4:1–22, 1995.
11. DeCarlo M, Klootwyk T, Shelbourne K. ACL surgery and accelerated rehabilitation: Revisited. *J Sport Rehabil* 6:144–156, 1997.
12. Diener H, Dichgans J, Guschlbauer B, et al. Role of visual and static vestibular influences on dynamic posture control. *Hum Neurobiol* 5:105–113, 1986.
13. Diener H, Dichgans J, Guschlbauer B, Mau H. The significance of proprioception on postural stabilization as assessed by ischemia. *Brain Res* 296:103–109, 1984.
14. Dietz V, Horstmann G, Berger W. Significance of proprioceptive mechanisms in the regulation of stance. *Prog Brain Res* 80:419–423, 1989.
15. Donahoe B, Turner D, Worrell T. The use of functional reach as a measurement of balance in healthy boys and girls ages 5–15. *Phys Ther* 73:S71, 1993.
16. Dornan J, Fernie G, Holliday P. Visual input: It's importance in the control of postural sway. *Arch Phys Med Rehabil* 59:586–591, 1978.
17. Ekdahl C, Jarnlo G, Anderson S. Standing balance in healthy subjects: Evaluation of a quantitative test battery on a force platform. *Scand J Rehabil Med* 21:187–195, 1989.
18. Faculjak P, Firoozbakshsh K, Wausher D, McGuire M. Balance characteristics of normal and anterior cruciate ligament deficient knees. *Phys Ther* 73:S22, 1993.
19. Fisher A, Wietlisbach S, Wilberger J. Adult performance on three tests of equilibrium. *Am J Occup Ther* 42:30–35, 1988.
20. Fitzpatrick R, Rogers DK, McCloskey DI. Stable human standing with lower-limb muscle afferents providing the only sensory input. *J Physiol* 480:395–403, 1994.
21. Flores A. Objective measures of standing balance. *Neurol Rep Am Phys Ther Assoc* 16:17–21, 1992.
22. Forkin DM, Koczur C, Battle R, Newton RA. Evaluation of kinestic deficits indicative of balance control in gymnasts with unilateral chronic ankle sprains. *J Orthop Sports Phys Ther* 23:245–250, 1996.
23. Freeman M. Instability of the foot after injuries to the lateral ligament of the ankle. *J Bone Joint Surg* 47B:678–685, 1965.
24. Freeman M, Dean M, Hanham I. The etiology and prevention of functional instability of the foot. *J Bone Joint Surg* 47B:669–677, 1965.
25. Friden T, Zatterstrom R, Lindstrand A, Moritz U. A stabilometric technique for evaluation of lower limb instabilities. *Am J Sports Med* 17:118–122, 1989.
26. Garn SN, Newton RA. Kinesthetic awareness in subjects with multiple ankle sprains. *Phys Ther* 68:1667–1671, 1988.
27. Goldie P, Bach T, Evans O. Force platform measures for evaluating postural control: Reliability and validity. *Arch Phys Med Rehabil* 70:510–517, 1989.
28. Grigg P. Mechanical factors influencing response of joint afferent neurons from cat knee. *J Neurophysiol* 38:1473–1484, 1975.
29. Grigg P. Response of joint afferent neurons in cat medial articular nerve to active and passive movements of the knee. *Brain Res* 118:482–485, 1976.
30. Guskiewicz KM, Perrin DH, Gansneder B. Effect of mild head injury on postural stability. *J Athlet Train* 31:300–306, 1996.
31. Guskiewicz KM, Perrin DH. Effect of orthotics on postural sway following inversion ankle sprain. *J Orthop Sports Phys Ther* 23:326–331, 1996.
32. Guskiewicz KM, Perrin DH. Research and clinical applications of assessing balance. *J Sport Rehabil* 5:45–63, 1996.

33. Guskiewicz KM, Riemann BL, Perrin DH, Nashner LM. Alternative approaches to the assessment of mild head injury in athletes. *Med Sci Sport Exer* 29:S213–S221, 1997.

34. Guyton A. *Textbook of Medical Physiology,* 8th ed. Philadelphia, Saunders, 1991.

35. Harrison E, Duenkel N, Dunlop R, Russell G. Evaluation of single-leg standing following anterior cruciate ligament surgery and rehabilitation. *Phys Ther* 74:245–252, 1994.

36. Hertel JN, Guskiewicz KM, Kahler DM, Perrin DH. Effect of lateral ankle joint anesthesia on center of balance, postural sway and joint position sense. *J Sport Rehabil* 5:111–119, 1996.

37. Horak FB, Nashner LM, Diener HC. Postural strategies associated with somatosensory and vestibular loss. *Exp Brain Res* 82:167–177, 1990.

38. Horak F, Nashner L. Central programming of postural movements: Adaptation to altered support surface configurations. *J Neurophysiol* 55:1369–1381, 1986.

39. Houk J. Regulation of stiffness by skeleto-motor reflexes. *Ann Rev Physiol* 41:99–114, 1979.

40. Irrgang J, Harner C. Recent advances in ACL rehabilitation: Clinical factors. *J Sport Rehab* 6:111–124, 1997.

41. Irrgang J, Whitney S, Cox E. Balance and proprioceptive training for rehabilitation of the lower extremity. *J Sport Rehab* 3:68–83, 1994.

42. Jansen E, Larsen R, Mogens B. Quantitative Romberg's test: Measurement and computer calculations of postural stability. *Acta Neurol Scand* 66:93–99, 1982.

43. Johansson H, Alexander IJ, Hayes KC. Nerve supply of the human knee and its functional importance. *Am J Sports Med* 10:329–335, 1982.

44. Kauffman TL, Nashner LM, Allison LK. Balance is a critical pararmeter in orthopedic rehabilitation. *Orthop Phys Ther Clin North Am* 6:43–78, 1997.

45. Kisner C, Colby LA. *Therapeutic Exercise: Foundations and Techniques,* 3rd ed. Philadelphia, Davis, 1996.

46. Lephart SM. Re-establishing proprioception, kinesthesia, joint position sense, and neuromuscular control in rehabilitation. In: Prentice WE, ed. *Rehabilitation Techniques in Sports,* 2nd ed. St. Louis, MO, Times Mirror/Mosby College, 1993, pp. 118–137.

47. Lephart SM, Henry TJ. Functional rehabilitation for the upper and lower extremity. *Orthop Clin North Am* 26:579–592, 1995.

48. Lephart SM, Kocher MS. The role of exercise in the prevention of shoulder disorders. In: Matsen FA, Fu FH, Hawkins RJ, eds. *The Shoulder: A Balance of Mobility and Stability.* Rosemont, IL, American Academy of Orthopaedic Surgeons, 1993, pp. 597–620.

49. Lephart SM, Kocher MS, Fu FH, et al. Proprioception following ACL reconstruction. *J Sport Rehabil* 1:186–196, 1992.

50. Lephart SM, Pincivero D, Giraldo J, Fu F. The role of proprioception in the management and rehabilitation of athletic injuries. *Am J Sports Med* 25:130–137, 1997.

51. Mangine R, Kremchek T. Evaluation-based protocol of the anterior cruciate ligament. *J Sport Rehab* 6:157–181, 1997.

52. Mauritz K, Dichgans J, Hufschmidt A. Quantitative analysis of stance in late cortical cerebellar atrophy of the anterior lobe and other forms of cerebellar ataxia. *Brain* 102, 461–482, 1979.

53. Mizuta H, Shiraishi M, Kubota K, Kai K, Takagi K. A stabilometric technique for evaluation of functional instability in the anterior cruciate ligament deficient knee. *Clin J Sports Med* 2:235–239, 1992.

54. Murray M, Seireg A, Sepic S. Normal postural stability: Qualitative assessment. *J Bone Joint Surg* 57A:510–516, 1975.

55. Nashner L. Practical biomechanics and physiology of balance. In: Jacobson G, Newman C, Kartush J, eds. *Handbook of Balance Function and Testing.* St. Louis, MO, Mosby Year Book, 1993, pp. 261–279.

56. Nashner L. Computerized dynamic posturography. In: Jacobson G, Newman C, Kartush J, eds. *Handbook of Balance Function and Testing.* St. Louis, MO, Mosby Year Book, 1993, pp. 280–307.

57. Nashner L. Sensory, neuromuscular and biomechanical contributions to human balance. In: *Balance: Proceedings of the APTA Forum,* June 13–15, Duncan P, ed. 1989, pp. 5–12.

58. Nashner L. A functional approach to understanding spasticity. In: Struppler A, Weindl A, eds. *Electromyography and Evoked Potentials.* Berlin, Springer-Verlag, 1985, pp. 22–29.

59. Nashner L. Adaptation of human movement to altered environments. *Trend Neurosci* 5:358–361, 1982.

60. Nashner L. Adapting reflexes controlling the human posture. *Exp Brain Res* 26:59–72, 1976.

61. Nashner L, Black F, Wall C III. Adaptation to altered support and visual conditions during stance: Patients with vestibular deficits. *J Neurosci* 2:536–544, 1982.

62. NeuroCom International, Inc. *The Objective Quantification of Daily Life Tasks: The NEW Balance Master 6.0 (manual).* Clackamas, OR, 1997.

63. Newton R. Review of tests of standing balance abilities. *Brain Inj* 3:335–343, 1992.

64. Norre M. Sensory interaction testing in platform posturography. *J Laryngol Otol* 107:496–501, 1993.

65. Noyes F, Barber S, Mangine R. Abnormal lower limb symmetry determined by function hop test after anterior cruciate ligament rupture. *Am J Sports Med* 19:516–518, 1991.

66. Orteza L, Vogelbach W, Denegar C. The effect of molded and unmolded orthotics on balance and pain while jogging following inversion ankle sprain. *J Athlet Train* 27:80–84, 1992.

67. Pintsaar A, Brynhildsen J, Tropp H. Postural corrections after standardised perturbations of single limb stance:

Effect of training and orthotic devices in patients with ankle instability. *Br J Sports Med* 30:151–155, 1996.

68. Shambers GM. Influence of the fusimotor system on stance and volitional movement in normal man. *Am J Phys Med* 48:225–227, 1969.

69. Shumway-Cook A, Horak F. Assessing the influence of sensory interaction on balance. *Phys Ther.* 66:1548–1550, 1986.

70. Swanik CB, Lephart SM, Giannantonio FP, Fu FH. Re-establishing proprioception and neuromuscular control in the ACL-injured athlete. *J Sport Rehab* 6:182–206, 1997.

71. Tippett S, Voight M. *Functional Progression for Sports Rehabilitation.* Champaign, IL, Human Kinetics, 1995.

72. Tropp H, Ekstrand J, Gillquist J. Factors affecting stabilometry recordings of single limb stance. *Am J Sports Med* 12:185–188, 1984.

73. Tropp H, Ekstrand J, Gillquist J. Stabilometry in functional instability of the ankle and its value in predicting injury. *Med Sci Sport Exer* 16:64–66, 1984.

74. Tropp H, Odenrick P. Postural control in single limb stance. *J Orthop Res* 6:833–839, 1988.

75. Trulock SC. A comparison of static, dynamic and functional methods of objective balance assessment. Masters thesis, The University of North Carolina, Chapel Hill, NC, 1996.

76. Ubinger ME, Prentice WE, Guskiewicz K. Effect of closed kinetic chain training on neuromuscular control in the upper extremity using the functional activity system for testing and exercise (FASTEX). *J Sport Rehab* 8:187–194, 1999.

77. Vander A, Sherman J, Luciano D. *Human Physiology: The Mechanisms of Body Function,* 5th ed. New York, McGraw-Hill, 1990.

78. Voight M, Cook G. Clinical application of closed kinetic chain exercise. *J Sport Rehab* 5:25–44, 1996.

79. Wilk K, Zheng N, Fleisig G, Andrews J, Clancy W. Kinetic chain exercise: Implications for the anterior cruciate ligament patient. *J Sport Rehab* 6:125–143, 1997.

80. Wilkerson G, Nitz J. Dynamic ankle stability: Mechanical and neuromuscular interrelationships. *J Sport Rehab* 3:43–57, 1994.

Isokinetics in Rehabilitation

Steven M. Jacoby

OBJECTIVES

After completing this chapter, the student therapist should be able to do the following:

- Describe the concept of isokinetic resistance.
- Identify the advantages and disadvantages of isokinetic exercise.
- Understand the testing parameters associated with isokinetic testing.
- Understand how to interpret the data.
- Understand how the Multi-Joint Systems are incorporated into the rehabilitation process.
- Have general knowledge of treatment considerations with an ACL-reconstructed, lateral ankle sprain, and shoulder instability patient.
- Understand new advancements in isokinetic data presentation.

Though "constant angular devises" have been used to determine muscle function for over 70 years,[44] Hislop and Perrin first described the concept of isokinetics in 1967.[17] The isokinetic concept is based on the principle that the angular velocity of a moving limb can be constantly maintained by changing the force generated by a device to resist the intended movement. Therefore, as the limb accelerates from a resting position to the preset angular velocity, the isokinetic device produces a counterforce equal to the isokinetic speed to maintain this preset speed.

Deceleration begins once the muscle's length–tension relationship is reached. The ability of a muscle to generate torque (rotational force) about a joint is a function of a number of physiologic and cross-sectional areas including muscle moment arm, motor unit recruitment, and firing frequency.[43] During normal activity, the body must handle the constant acceleration and deceleration forces that occur naturally throughout activities of daily living. Currently, clinicians and researchers have the opportunity to evaluate how fast a muscle can accelerate to a preset angular velocity as well as decelerate from this velocity.

DEFINITION OF TERMS

A common method used in clinical practice to determine muscle strength is the manual muscle test (MMT).[20] Although the MMT is commonly used clinically, it has been scrutinized because of the inherent limitations.[25] These limitations include inconsistency in grading and method,[9] the subjectivity reported,[23] and the fact that the MMT is a static test, not a dynamic one. Because of these limitations, the MMT should not be used when determining precise isolated physical impairments or readiness to progress to the next phase in the rehabilitation process.

Although commonly referred to as isokinetic dynamometers (Fig. 10-1), Multi-Joint systems (MJS) are truly multimode dynamometers capable of evaluating isokinetic, isometric, isotonic, and reactive-eccentric methods, and, when needed, can even be used to estimate spasticity in hemiparetic stroke patients.[8] During its initial introduction, isokinetics was highly regarded as a testing medium. Today, technologic advances allow clinicians to advance patients from the acute phases of rehabilitation to the more functional movement patterns faster and safer than ever. To take advantage of the MJS, we first must understand the terminology used.

Isometrics

Popularized as an effective method of muscle strengthening, isometrics has been used throughout the rehabilitation process for decades. Isometric by definition means "same length." Thus, as the muscle contracts, there is no associated lengthening or shortening. Clinically, isometrics are commonly used during the early phases of rehabilitation when motion is limited

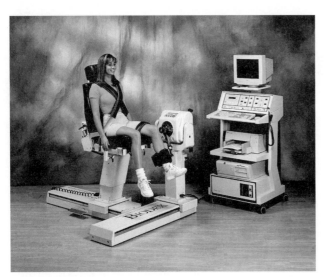

FIGURE 10-1

Biodex System 3 Multi-Joint System (MJS).

or painful arcs are noted (such as patellofemoral dysfunction). When initiating isometrics, an important parameter to keep in mind is that of the physiologic overflow. Atha noted that because a 20-degree physiologic overflow exists with isometric training, patients could rehabilitate within pain-free ranges and still improve strength in the affected ranges.[2] Isometrics can be relatively inexpensive, but without proper supervision patients can overload the healing structure beyond its capabilities. The goal of any rehabilitation program is to strengthen the muscles that surround the joint without overstressing the healing structures. Multi-Joint Systems provide the feedback necessary to safely load the muscle at various points.

Isotonics

In isotonic exercise, the mass remains a constant while the rate of contraction changes. For example, if a person holds a 5-pound weight and performs a knee extension exercise, the weight will not change throughout the range of motion, but the speed of movement is variable. A major drawback to isotonic exercise is that the muscle is maximally loaded at its weakest point in the range of motion. If a weight is placed on the foot and the knee is extended from a flexed position, only the extended position is maximally loaded (the muscle is in a shortened position) while the rest of the range of motion is "underloaded." Safety is another issue that must be considered when incorporating isotonics into the treatment program. Because the muscle is maximally loaded at its weakest point in the range of motion, and if pain is noted and muscle force is eliminated, the limb will return to the starting point. To safely incorporate isotonics into the treatment program, the clinician can use the MJS in the isotonic mode. Multi-Joint Systems offer a concentric/concentric isotonic contraction, which can be configured to ensure safe muscular contractions.

Isokinetics

Following the acceptance of isokinetics, clinicians initially emphasized isolated joint testing and rehabilitation. In recent years, an integrated approach to rehabilitation has become the method of choice.[10A]

Integrated physical medicine blends the value of isolated joint testing where an impairment is identified, isolated joint training where the impairment is treated, and functional movement training. The advantage to this approach is that functional activities are not initiated prior to the elimination of the impairment. This sequential method supports proper kinematics, is safer, and leads to better, faster outcomes. Isokinetics is simply defined as "constant velocity." The clinician presets the velocity, not the force, which is applied by the patient. The clinical significance of this mode is that if a patient feels any pain, or when fatigue sets in, the patient will be able to continue the dynamic contraction throughout a full range of motion, but torque production will decrease. Because both isokinetic and isotonic exercise are dynamic, the patient can perform exercises both concentrically (muscle shortens as it contracts) and eccentrically (muscle lengthens as it contracts). Much of the isokinetic research has been completed using concentric contractions, but new research evaluating total neuromuscular performance is approaching. It has been noted that rehabilitation programs incorporating isokinetic exercise are more efficient and effective than programs that do not include isokinetic activity.[29]

TESTING PARAMETERS: WHAT TO LOOK FOR

The data that are collected during isokinetic testing are commonly used to make important decisions on a patient's rehabilitation program. Most commonly, a patient's data are compared bilaterally because this gives a useful comparison of the involved to noninvolved side. Research has shown this to be a reliable method to analyze data because limb dominance has little to no effect. In addition to the bilateral comparison, a patient's data can be compared to a normative or "goal" database. When performing an isokinetic evaluation, Wilk and Arrigo noted 15 parameters for standardized testing (Table 10-1).[39]

PLANES OF MOTION   When testing shoulder musculature, the clinician must decide which pattern(s) to test. It is important to keep in mind the specific motions and actions the patient will be performing throughout daily function. If the patient is an overhead athlete, then testing of the shoulder internal and external rotators should be performed in 90 degrees of shoulder abduction and 90 degrees of elbow flexion (90°/90° position) (Fig. 10-2). This approximates the normal length–tension relationships of the overhead athlete.

Guidelines for Standardized Isokinetic Testing

1.	Planes of motion to evaluate
2.	Testing position/stabilization
3.	Axis of joint motion
4.	Client education
5.	Active warm-up
6.	Gravity compensation
7.	Rest intervals
8.	Test collateral extremity first
9.	Standardize verbal feedback
10.	Standardize visual feedback
11.	Testing velocities utilized
12.	Test repetitions
13.	System calibration/verification
14.	System level/stabilized
15.	Use semihard end stop

POSITION AND STABILIZATION   It is extremely important to eliminate excessive movements above and below the joint being evaluated. Adequate stabilization is a must for accurate data collection.

ALIGN THE AXIS OF ROTATION OF THE PATIENT WITH THAT OF THE DYNAMOMETER   Wilk noted that this was important for accurate torque measurements.[35]

CLIENT EDUCATION   Prior to testing, the patient must understand exactly what is expected of him or her and what to expect from the test. How it "feels," what to do, and when to do it are questions that should be answered prior to testing. Investigators[21] have noted significant changes in results from the first testing session to all others.

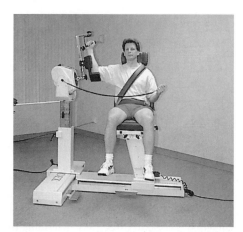

F I G U R E   1 0 - 2

Planes of motion. Testing of the shoulder internal/external rotators on an overhead athlete should be performed at a 90°/90° position.

ACTIVE WARM-UP   The active warm-up should serve two very important purposes. First, it serves to increase core temperature and prepare the muscles for strenuous activity, and, second, it familiarizes the patient with the testing velocities being used.

GRAVITY COMPENSATION   When the knee goes from a flexed position to an extended position, gravity works against this motion. The exact opposite occurs when the patient begins to flex the knee from full extension (i.e., gravity assists). To eliminate the effects of gravity, it is suggested that limb weight be taken and automatically factored into the data.

REST INTERVALS   For the purpose of this chapter, rest intervals deal with the time between each test speed. Touey et al[31] noted that 120 seconds was the optimal rest period, whereas Ariki et al[1] noted that the optimal rest period was 90 seconds. In either case, it is important to keep in mind the total amount of time available for testing. If two to three positions are going to be evaluated, 90 to 120 seconds between test speeds greatly increases the time needed to complete the test.

TESTING THE UNINVOLVED EXTREMITY FIRST   This is an important step in the familiarization process and greatly reduces potential apprehension.

STANDARDIZATION OF VERBAL COMMANDS   According to Wilk,[35] verbal commands need to be consistent, encouraging, and moderate in intensity.

USE (OR NONUSE) OF VISUAL INPUT   It has been noted by researchers that knowledge of results does not affect mean peak torque.[18] Others, however, have noted an increase in performance during isokinetic testing when knowledge of results was present.[12,14] For this reason, it is important to choose one and remain consistent throughout the testing protocol.

TESTING VELOCITIES   The joint under evaluation will determine exactly what test speeds are suggested (Table 10-2). Much of the current research dealing with shoulders and knees looks to higher velocity testing (180° to 300°/second)[41] to accommodate for the high angular velocities faced with normal activity. Smaller joints, wrist, ankle, and forearm are generally tested at slower velocities.

NUMBER OF TEST REPETITIONS   Davies[10] reported that 10 isokinetic repetitions produced optimal training effects for both peak torque to body weight and average power testing parameters. The important aspect to keep in mind is to ensure consistency of test repetitions.

SYSTEM CALIBRATION AND VERIFICATION   According to manufacturer specifications, the isokinetic systems should be calibrated and verified every 30 days,[5] but if the testing is going to be used for legal purposes, the system should be calibrated and verified just prior to testing. Today's calibration/verification procedures are quite simple and take only a moment to complete.

T A B L E   1 0 - 2

Suggested Test Speeds

JOINT	PATTERN	ORTHOPEDIC PATIENT	ATHLETE
Knee	Extension/Flexion	(60), 180, 300	180, 300, 450
Knee	Tibial External/Internal Rotation	(60), 60, 120	120, 180, 240
Shoulder	Abduction/Adduction	(60), 180, 300	180, 300, 450
Shoulder	Flexion/Extension	(60), 180, 300	180, 300, 450
Shoulder	External/Internal Rotation	(60), 180, 300	180, 300, 450
Shoulder	D1, D2	(60), 180, 300	180, 300, 450
Shoulder	Horizontal Abduction/Adduction	(60), 180, 300	180, 300, 450
Elbow	Flexion/Extension	(60), 180, 300	180, 300
Wrist	Extension/Flexion	60, 120	120, 180
Wrist	Radial/Ulnar Deviation	60, 120	120, 180
Forearm	Supination/Pronation	60, 120	120, 180, 240
Ankle	Plantarflexion/Dorsiflexion	60, 120	(60), 120, 180
Ankle	Eversion/Inversion	60, 120	(60), 120, 180
Hip	Flexion/Extension	(120), 180, 300	180, 300, 450
Hip	Abduction/Adduction	(120), 180, 300	180, 300, 450
Hip	Internal/External Rotation	60, 120	120, 180

Test speeds in parentheses may be approximate, depending on pathology.

LEVEL INSTALLATION   When the system is installed, the technician should ensure that the system is level.

USE OF A SEMIHARD END STOP   Once a range of motion is selected, end stops will be created. As the patient moves through the range of motion toward the end stop, the machine will begin to decelerate the limb. This deceleration is caused by the machine's cushion value. A cushion value can be adjusted from hard to soft or numerically, one to nine. A hard cushion yields minimal machine-induced deceleration, whereas a soft cushion yields a greater machine deceleration. If a large joint is tested (shoulder elevators or back), a softer cushion is recommended. For smaller joints, a harder cushion is recommended. If a harder cushion is selected, it is vital to ensure that "artifact spiking" does not occur

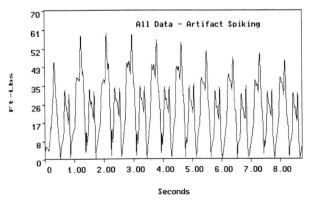

F I G U R E   1 0 - 3

Artifact spiking caused by dynamometer's hard endstop.

(see Fig. 10-3). This occurs when a patient rapidly decelerates into the end range of motion, causing a spike and potentially misrepresenting a peak torque. It is important to understand this concept when choosing a cushion for testing.

The most important concept to remember when testing patients or research participants is to maintain consistency. If the therapist is working in a setting where more than one person will be testing patients, time should be taken to discuss the previously described parameters and determine exactly how testing will occur.

RELIABILITY OF ISOKINETIC DYNAMOMETERS

There are several published studies that illustrate the reliability of isokinetic dynamometers.[3,11,13] Factors affecting the reliability of test results have been previously discussed in this chapter. Only by eliminating inconsistent variables can the clinician be assured that the test results are reliable. The important questions that need to be answered are when is a test "nonreliable" and should the patient retest.

A common parameter noted on all reports is the coefficient of variance (CV). The CV is the ratio between the standard deviation and the mean value for a statistical population expressed as a percentage. It is used to objectively determine the reproducibility of test data. A patient with a high CV (25 percent or greater) is not producing a consistent effort. This is not to say that he or she is not trying, it only represents a patient's level of consistency. Pain, lack of understanding, and apprehension all

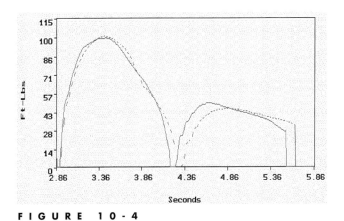

FIGURE 10-4

"Bell-shaped" torque curve.

lead to excessive CVs. It is important to evaluate the CV just after the completion of each test speed. If excessive CVs are noticed at a specific speed, a retest can occur after a brief rest period. This saves the evaluator a great deal of time in the long run.

TORQUE CURVE ANALYSIS

Because isokinetic testing evaluates a specific muscle group, the therapist can easily determine the effect this muscle has on the surrounding joint structure. A normal torque curve at slower velocities is said to be "bell shaped" (Fig. 10-4). This is due to the normal human leverage system and length–tension relationships. When pain is present, this "normal" curve changes in its appearance. For example, if a patient is suffering from a deterioration of the articular surface on the underside of the patella (chondromalacia patella), he or she tends to feel pain throughout the middle of knee range of motion. This pain causes an insufficient quadriceps contraction that leads to a poorly shaped curve (Fig. 10-5). When performing a bilateral comparison, curve analysis can assist with a graphical representation of the

involved and uninvolved sides. This can be especially helpful when explaining the results of a test to a patient (Fig. 10-6).

An important parameter in torque curve analysis is the ability for the MJS to store all the collected data. Once the test or training is complete, torque curve analysis can begin. It is important to be able to view all curves from a particular test set. Without the storage of the data points, this would be impossible. There is little published on the ability to diagnose an injury through curve analysis; however, clinicians should combine the curve analysis with their clinical findings to assist with the diagnosis. It should be noted, however, that Timm noted a distinct isokinetic torque curve for the impingement syndrome compared with the noninvolved shoulder.[30]

DATA INTERPRETATION

Understanding the data as presented on the isokinetic report is probably one of the most overlooked aspects in the education process. The purpose of the isokinetic test is threefold: first, *find the problem.* Is there an isolated physical impairment that is causing a functional deficit? Does this manifest itself during a concentric or eccentric contraction type? Where in the range of motion is the problem—in the beginning, middle, or end range of motion?

Next, *is the rehabilitation program effective in decreasing this isolated physical impairment?* Clinicians should be able to determine if the treatment program is having a positive or negative effect on patients' progress. Throughout the rehabilitation process, clinicians should be measuring progress objectively to determine if the treatment is effective.

Finally, *has the patient been rehabilitated?* This question goes beyond the realm of isokinetic evaluations only. Although the isokinetic test provides valuable information about the isolated muscle function about a joint, it is just one piece of the total process. To return to function, the patient must also have adequate joint stability. Lower extremity joint stability is

FIGURE 10-5

Poor quadriceps contraction.

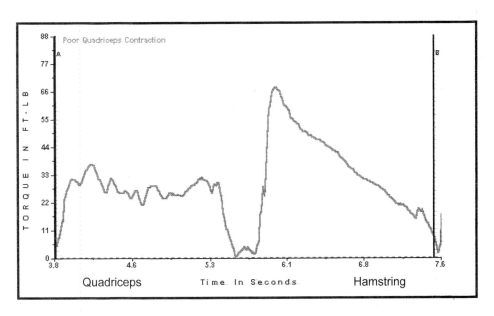

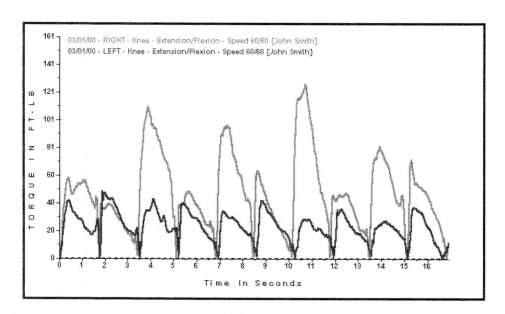

FIGURE   10-6

Bilateral overlay.

comprised of three areas: muscle performance, postural balance, and structural integrity (Fig. 10-7). A deficit in any one of these parameters will lead to inadequate joint stability and, thus, a decrease in function.

These questions should begin with the patient's first visit and last until the end of the treatment regimen. The data printed on the reports should be utilized to answer these questions and may include the following (see next page):

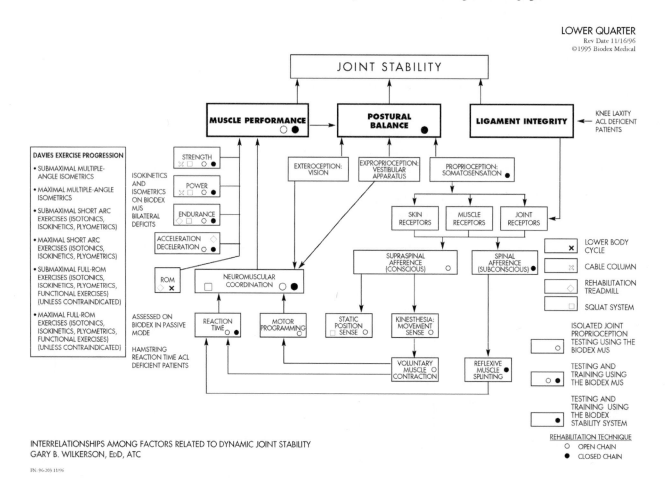

FIGURE   10-7

Lower extremity joint stability flowchart.

PEAK TORQUE   The highest value of torque developed throughout the range of motion.

AVERAGE PEAK TORQUE   Instead of using just one repetition for measuring peak torque, all the repetitions' peak torque are averaged together.

TIME TO PEAK TORQUE   A measure of time from the start of the muscular contraction to the point of highest torque development. An indicator of the functional ability to produce torque.

ANGLE OF PEAK TORQUE   Point in the range of motion where peak torque is achieved. A task-specific test of functional ability of a joint. Peak torque usually occurs in a similar point in the range of motion for like speeds and movement patterns.

- **Torque at various angles (30 degrees of knee flexion)**: Displays the torque produced for each direction at the preselected position.
- **Torque in a certain amount of time (0.20 seconds)**: Displays the time rate torque development, that is, how quickly the patient can achieve a certain level of torque.

PEAK TORQUE TO BODY WEIGHT   A ratio displayed as a percentage of the maximum torque production to the patient's body weight.

MAXIMUM REPETITION WORK   The maximum work (force × distance) produced in a single repetition. This could be a better representation of functional ability (over peak torque) because the muscle must maintain force throughout the range of motion as opposed to force at one instant.

WORK TO BODY WEIGHT   A ratio displayed as a percentage of the maximum repitition work to the patient's body weight.

TOTAL WORK   The sum work for every repetition performed in the bout.

WORK FIRST THIRD, WORK LAST THIRD   This is the total work of the first third divided by work in the last third of the test bout.

AVERAGE POWER   The total work divided by the time it takes to perform the work. Power is used to measure muscular efficiency.

MAXIMUM GRAVITY EFFECT ON TORQUE   Limb weight is measured, then added to torque values when working against gravity and subtracted from torque values when working with gravity.

ACCELERATION TIME   The time it takes the limb to accelerate from a resting position to achieve the preset isokinetic velocity. This should not be controlled by the computer, but controlled by the patient. The harder and faster the patient contracts, the quicker he or she should achieve isokinetic speed.

DECELERATION TIME   This is the time it takes to go from isokinetic speed back down to zero degrees per second.

AGONIST–ANTAGONIST RATIO   A ratio between the agonist and antagonist muscle group tested. An important parameter in determining excessive muscular imbalance.

BILATERAL AND UNILATERAL COMPARISONS   Once the test is complete, the clinician must compare the test result to one of two parameters: the noninvolved (injured) extremity or a normative (goal) database. In the case of extremity testing, having a noninvolved side to compare to makes the determination of impairment quite easy. Several investigators noted no significant difference between the dominant and nondominant throwing arm in internal and external rotator muscle strength (peak torque).[24,37] Wilk et al noted that there was no significant difference between the dominant and nondominant throwing arm in abductor muscle strength, but there was a significant difference in adductor strength.[38] Capranica et al reported no significant difference in force and power values between the dominant and nondominant lower limb.[8] From a shoulder proprioception standpoint, Voight et al determined that there was no relationship between arm dominance and shoulder proprioception.[32] Thus, it is important to understand that limb dominance does not play a significant role when using bilateral comparisons.

Another parameter to consider is the detraining effect. Once an injury occurs, both the involved and noninvolved extremities begin to lose their strength characteristics. During the rehabilitation process, focus is usually placed on the injured or surgically repaired extremity only. Exercises to regain strength, power, and endurance are unilaterally focused on the involved extremity. During this time, the noninvolved extremity will lose strength as well. This loss of strength to the noninvolved leg makes it difficult to compare bilaterally late in the rehabilitation process. As the involved extremity gains strength, the noninvolved extremity loses strength. It should be noted that some investigators have noted a crossover effect of training. Weir et al noted that when participants were trained unilaterally (three sets of six concentric repetitions), their isometric strength increased at all test angles bilaterally.[34]

Because confusion exists, the use of preseason, preemployment, or preparticipation isokinetic strength tests can serve as an important baseline used for comparison later in the rehabilitation process. Most notably a patient, athlete, or employee would be tested prior to activity or employment. These numbers can be used to determine when the individual has regained normal (preinjury) neuromuscular control. Objective test data can also be useful when progressing patients through the various phases of rehabilitation.

Another important consideration is the use of normative or goal data. In certain instances, bilateral comparisons are impossible. For example, consider a patient with bilateral injuries or a test of the lumbar spine. In these cases, there is no side-to-side comparison available. To determine if the patient has returned to normal strength levels, it is important to be able to compare to a goal database. The use of normative data is quite popular, but there are many important parameters that need to be noted prior to its use. Is the patient population similar to the one being tested? Are the normative values from athletes, industrial workers, pediatric or geriatric groups, or a sedentary population? Are the data age and gender specific? How were the data collected? Did the participants receive visual feedback? Were there verbal commands? What type of warm-up was used? All of these parameters must be established prior to the inclusion of any normative values.

Because normative values are difficult to use, it is the author's opinion that a "goal" database be used only for comparison. These data will provide the clinician with a general overview of performance. We are not using this information to note normality, it is simply used to note when a patient has achieved adequate muscle performance. It should be restated that strength alone is not adequate in determining if a patient is ready to return to activity. For the lower extremity, postural balance and structural integrity should be quantified as well.

TRAINING PARAMETERS AND MODES OF OPERATION

Multi-Joint or isokinetic systems are capable of much more than isokinetic testing and training. Isometric, isotonic, reactive eccentric, and passive modes of operation all combine to advance patients from injury or surgery to function as quickly and safely as possible. The goal of any rehabilitation program is to progress patients from postinjury or surgery to the more functional phases of rehabilitation as quickly and safely as possible. Only by combining the various modes of operation can the clinician take the fullest advantage of the Multi-Joint System.

Isometrics, which is commonly used early in the rehabilitation process, provides angle-specific contractions, with varying torque outputs. To gain the full benefits of the **isometric mode**, the clinician will be able to select the specific angles of contraction, time of contraction, and time of relaxation. The clinician can also choose which muscle groups (agonist only, antagonist only, or both the agonist and antagonist) to work. Testing can be completed quite simply and is an effective outcome measure.

As discussed previously in this chapter, the MJS allows for a safe progressive isotonic contraction, first beginning with concentric/concentric contractions and progressing to concentric/eccentric or eccentric/concentric contractions. In the **isotonic mode**, the muscle must overcome the torque selected prior to the limb moving in either direction. Because both the agonist and antagonist muscle groups contract concentrically, two different torques can be selected. Thus, the agonist torque can be set to a low weight (5 ft/lb) while the antagonist weight higher (100 ft/lb) and vise versa.

As the patient progresses, an isotonic eccentric contraction can be introduced into the rehabilitation program. The clinician has the ability to adjust the concentric and eccentric torque levels as needed as well as the speed of the eccentric contraction. This greatly enhances the clinician's ability to control

the movement and maintain a safe rehabilitation environment. Thus, a patient could be asked to lift 10 ft/lb concentrically and lower 30 ft/lb eccentrically at 60 degrees/second. This would be very similar to using two weight stacks on a single piece of exercise equipment.

Another mode of operation is the **reactive eccentric** mode. The reactive eccentric mode allows for an eccentric/eccentric contraction only. To accomplish an eccentric contraction, the clinician sets both the maximum amount of torque the patient can apply and the minimum amount of torque needed to begin the movement. Thus, a window is created for a patient to stay within. If torque levels go too high, the lever arm stops moving. If the torque levels go too low, the lever arm again stops moving. Therefore, for the patient to keep the limb moving the entire time, torque levels must stay between the two limits. This is an excellent way to enhance motor control early in the rehabilitation process.

Aside from the isokinetic mode, the **passive** mode is used most often on the MJS. The passive mode is very similar to that of a continual passive motion (CPM) device in which the clinician sets a range of motion that the limb will move through without any effort from the patient. This is extremely important in the early phases of the rehabilitation process when the focus is on reducing edema and increasing range of motion. Noyes et al demonstrated the negative effect of prolonged immobilization on joint surfaces.[26] If a patient is noted to have motion complications, the passive mode can be an excellent tool to restore full range to the joint. The passive mode can also assist with active muscle contractions as well. The clinician can instruct the patient to "kick up" or "pull back" as needed. Thus, concentric, eccentric, and isometric contractions can be accomplished in this one mode. The clinician has the ability to adjust the passive speed, eccentric torque limits, pauses at the end ranges of motion, and range of motion as needed. Therefore, it is important to understand that an MJS is capable of much more than just isokinetic testing. Clinicians should have the ability to adjust the necessary parameters anytime during the rehabilitation process.

CLINICAL CONSIDERATIONS

Prior to the discussion of pathologic conditions, it is important to understand the relation of angular velocity to torque outputs. When initiating a treatment regimen, it is important to note the effects of slow angular velocities on the joint as compared to higher velocities (Table 10-3). Because it is important to understand how MJS can be used to treat various pathologies, the following examples give an illustration of exactly where the MJS fits into the rehabilitation process.

Anterior Cruciate Ligament Reconstruction

For the anterior cruciate ligament (ACL)-reconstructed patient (patella tendon graft), begin in the passive mode to regain

TABLE 10-3

Angular Velocity and Torque Outputs

VELOCITY	CONCENTRIC	ECCENTRIC
Slow (30–120 degrees/second)	High	Low
Moderate (120–270 degrees/second)	Moderate	Moderate
Fast (300 degrees/second and above)	Low	High

range of motion. After selecting a safe range to work within, the clinician can incorporate additional modalities (cold, heat, electrotherapy) to assist with the rehabilitation process. While in the passive mode, patients can be instructed to "pull back" or use their hamstrings to begin the strengthening process.

Because the tibia moves posterior in relation to the femur from 90 degrees to 70 degrees of knee flexion, it would be safe to begin submaximal quadriceps contractions. Bouchard et al noted that maximal isometrics at 70 degrees of knee flexion caused patella fractures in three subjects that were approximately 7, 11, and 12 weeks post–ACL reconstruction.[7] Submaximal quadriceps contractions could begin in the passive mode, but the clinician cannot prevent the patient from excessive concentric force production.

The reactive eccentric mode might provide a safer progression. First, the range of motion should be set to protect excessive anterior tibial translation. Wilk et al noted that during open-chain knee extension, there was an anterior shear force from 38 degrees to 0 degrees (peaking at 14 degrees) and a posterior shear force from 40 degrees to 101 degrees of knee flexion.[40]

Next, the torque limit for the quadriceps should be set at 20 ft/lb. Yack et al noted that a 20-lb Lachman evaluation produces less anterior tibial displacement than an open-chain knee extension at 18 degrees of knee flexion.[45] The torque limit for the hamstrings can be set to a greater limit. The patient should be instructed to "pull back" to get the limb to move upward and "kick up" to get the limb to move back into the flexed position. Thus, an eccentric/eccentric contraction sequence occurs. The patient needs to understand that the attachment should always be moving. If the patient applied too much or too little torque, the attachment will stop moving, and this is not the appropriate response.

When the patient is ready to progress to active concentric quadriceps contractions, a few parameters must be kept in mind. If graft strength is in question, set the extension stop below 30 degrees of knee flexion. Next, higher speeds (180 degrees/second to 300 degrees/second) should be used early in the rehabilitation process. Finally, raise the tibial pad proximally. All three reduce the stress placed on the healing graft.[36]

Beynnon and Johnson noted that biomechanical studies of healing ACL grafts performed in animals have shown that the graft requires a long time to revascularize and heal and that the biomechanical behavior of the graft never returns to normal.[4] During this phase, the patient can progress to the use of the isotonic mode. Begin with concentric/concentric movements (less than 20 ft/lb on the quadriceps) and progress to concentric/eccentric movements. When determining the readiness to return to activity, ensure adequate muscular strength, power, endurance, acceleration, and deceleration as well as postural balance and structural integrity.

Lateral Ankle Sprain

As with any acute injury, the range of motion needs to be restored. The passive mode can be utilized early in the rehabilitation process. Begin with plantar and dorsiflexion and progress to inversion and eversion. The Biodex closed-chain (Fig. 10-8) attachment can be a useful tool in this early stage as well. The patient can place the foot in the closed-chain attachment and begin actively loading the joint prior to full weight bearing.

The isometric mode can be used to prevent disuse atrophy. Place the ankle in the neutral position and have the patient perform submaximal contractions without the fear of excessive motion. Next, progress to dynamic strengthening of the plantar and dorsiflexors. Begin with slower speed (30 degrees/second to 60 degrees/second) and progress to faster (120 degrees/second to 180 degrees/second) speeds.

When exercising the plantar and dorsiflexors, remember that the dorsiflexors will fatigue much quicker than the plantar flexors. A simple method to allow for similar fatigue responses is to set the plantar flexor speed slow (60 degrees/second) and the dorsiflexor speed faster (120 degrees/second). Next, progress to concentric/eccentric muscle strengthening. Wilkerson et al noted that a lateral ankle ligament injury might be associated with an invertor muscle performance deficiency.[42] Again, remember to ensure adequate dynamic functional stability prior to returning to activity.

Shoulder Instability/Impingement

Glenohumeral stability is maintained statically by the capsulolabral complex and dynamically by the rotator cuff

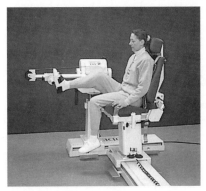

FIGURE 10-8

The Biodex closed-chain attachment.

musculature.[33] These rotator cuff muscles must function synergistically to allow for normal shoulder arthrokinematics. When imbalance or injury occurs, shoulder function diminishes.

An important aspect to consider when testing or training using the isokinetic mode is the position in which the patient is placed. During the initial phases of rehabilitation, the 90-degree abduction 90-degree elbow flexed (90°/90°) position should be limited. This is the same position Hoppenfeld describes for the apprehension test and could cause episodes of instability.[19] On the other hand, Rathburn noted that a position placing the humerus against the body could cause a "wringing out" of the supraspinatus tendinous insertion[27] and thus eliminates this position as well. The recommended starting position places the humerus in 20 degrees to 30 degrees forward flexion and abduction (scapular plane), therefore decreasing the chance of instability and impingement.[22]

According to Wilk et al,[39] when testing throwers, the 90°/90° position closely approximates that of normal throwing motion while ensuring muscle isolation. This position also optimizes the length–tension relationship of the internal and external rotation as they perform the throwing sequence. Based on this information, it is important that clinicians not overlook the various testing positions. Both the scapular plane and 90°/90° positions have benefits and drawbacks when testing. It is the clinician's responsibility to determine when it is safe to progress from the scapular plane to the 90°/90° position. Traditionally, when an isokinetic test is performed, "end stops" are placed at 90-degree external rotation and 0 degrees of internal rotation. Thus, as the patient reaches the end stop the MJS plays a role in the deceleration of the humerus. During normal function when the arm is externally rotating, the internal rotators coactivate to decelerate the humerus. Therefore, the clinician might want to extend the end limit for external rotation beyond 90 degrees to approximately 130 degrees of external rotation and evaluate the patient's ability to decelerate the humerus. The same could be true for the evaluation of the external rotators. This time, have the patient working in a D2 position (Fig. 10-9) seated. Now have the patient concentrically D2 extend toward the body. As the arm passes the horizontal position, the external rotators must contract eccentrically to decelerate the arm. Progress to standing D2 and incorporate a total body movement (Fig. 10-10).

PROPRIOCEPTION

One area of great concern to clinicians is that of proprioception. Proprioception is defined as the cumulative neural input to the central nervous system from specialized nerve endings called mechanoreceptors.[32] When the topic of proprioceptive training comes up, most clinicians think of weight-bearing exercises. This has been an established treatment practice for both the upper and lower extremities. Current research is focusing

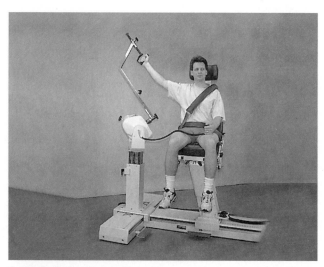

FIGURE   10-9

Coactivation of the external rotators in a seated D2 position.

on a new area of proprioception in the nonweight-bearing position.[6,16] The three types of proprioceptive tests noted in the literature are passive repositioning, active repositioning, and threshold to detect passive motion.[6,16] Each of these tests can be completed on the MJS. In fact, some systems are even

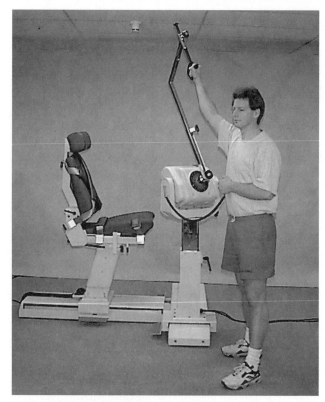

FIGURE   10-10

Coactivation of the external rotators in a standing D2 position, incorporating total body movement.

capable of reporting these findings (Fig. 10-11). To complete the passive and active repositioning tests, simply place the patient in the chair and fix the attachment to the limb. Next, blindfold the patient to remove visual feedback. Place the limb at the "target" angle (this is the angle the patient will replicate, 15 degrees of knee flexion or 75 degrees of shoulder external rotation, for example).Return the patient to the starting angle (90 degrees of knee flexion or neutral shoulder rotation). The MJS should be set to the appropriate mode [isokinetic for active repositioning and passive mode (2 degrees/second) for passive repositioning], and testing is now ready to begin. The patient should move (or be moved) toward the target angle and disengage the system when he or she perceives that he or she is there. A record of the exact position (and difference from the target angle) is noted. An average of three test trials is often used in testing. The threshold to detect passive motion works in a similar manner. First, place the patient at the target angle (45 degrees of knee flexion or 45 degrees of shoulder rotation). Place the MJS in the passive mode at 2 degrees/second. Explain to the patient that he or she should disengage the system as soon as any motion is sensed. The MJS will record the exact degrees of movement from the target angle. Although proprioceptive testing is becoming more mainstream, there are limited treatment options available and further research is needed. Lephart

Name	: Smith, J.	Clinician	: AB	Joint	: Knee
ID	: 11999933	Referral	:	Pattern	: Extension/Flexion
Age	: 30	Cal. Verification	: SEP 01, 1999 08:00:00	Treatment	:
Sex	: M	Test Date	: FEB 23, 2000	Involved Side	:
Height (in):	55	Settings	:	Contraction	: N/A
Weight (lbs):	200	Data Reported	: All Data	Mode	:

JOINT POSITION SENSE TEST

Test Direction ___Extension___

Active Positioning (patient moves limb)

Target Position :   15.0   15.0

		Uninvolved	Involved	Difference
Degrees from Target :	Rep 1 :	2.0	31.0	-29.0
	Rep 2 :	4.0	24.0	-20.0
	Rep 3 :	6.0	31.0	-25.0
	Average :	4.0	28.7	-24.7

Passive Positioning (BIODEX moves limb)

Target Position :   15.0   15.0

		Uninvolved	Involved	Difference
Degrees from Target :	Rep 1 :	9.0	25.0	-16.0
	Rep 2 :	2.0	14.0	-12.0
	Rep 3 :	2.0	15.0	-13.0
	Average :	4.3	18.0	-13.7

Kinesthesia Test: Degrees to Detect Motion

Target Position :   45.0   45.0

		Uninvolved	Involved	Difference
Degrees from Target :	Rep 1 :	10.0	8.0	2.0
	Rep 2 :	13.0	11.0	2.0
	Rep 3 :	8.0	12.0	-4.0
	Average :	10.3	10.3	0

FIGURE 10-11

Biodex proprioception report.

did note three things concerning proprioceptive testing: arm dominance is not a factor in the proprioceptive mechanism; functional instability produced diminished sense of proprioception, especially in the functional position of abduction and external rotation; and finally, surgery combined with rehabilitation may restore some, if not all, of the proprioceptive sensibility and may ultimately improve function and prevent the recurrence of symptoms.[6]

ADVANCED TECHNOLOGIES

During the last 3 years, a new form of isokinetic evaluation has become commercially available. This new report is designed to reduce the emphasis on "numbers" from an isokinetic evaluation. Isomap is a graphical representation and qualitative analysis of muscle performance (Fig. 10-12). Isomap uses the same isokinetic information necessary to generate a three-speed bilateral report. Instead of the numeric report, a graphical report of neuromuscular performance is generated. The goal of an Isomap evaluation is to identify where in the range of motion, which angular velocities, and which muscle groups or contraction types are most effected. By determining this, clinicians can create treatment protocols designed to eliminate the isolated physical impairments.

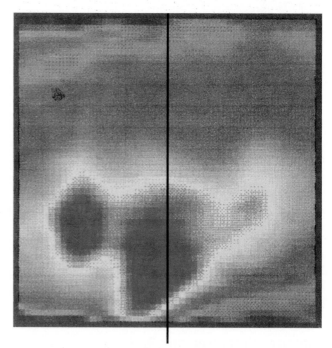

FIGURE 10-12

Isomap is a graphical, rather than numeric, representation and qualitative analysis of muscle performance.

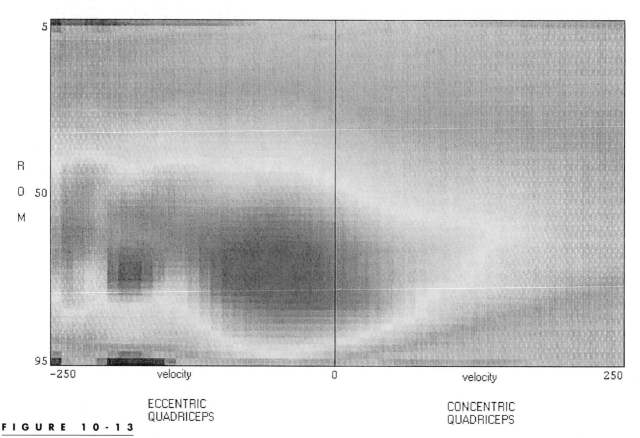

ECCENTRIC
QUADRICEPS

CONCENTRIC
QUADRICEPS

FIGURE 10-13

Isomaps are broken into three different axes—*x*-axis (contraction type/muscle group and speeds), *y*-axis (range of motion), and *z*-axis (torque values).

To understand the Isomap image, one must first break down the map into three different axes: The x-axis, the y-axis, and the z-axis. On the map (Fig. 10-13), the x-axis represents the angular velocities selected. The centerline represents no angular velocity. By moving further to the right, the concentric angular velocity increases. To the far left, the eccentric velocity increases. The y-axis represents the range of motion covered during the test. The top of the map indicates full extension, and the bottom of the map indicates full flexion. The z-axis represents torque output. The greater the torque output, the redder the map gets. Red represents areas of great strength, and blue represents areas of weaker strength. On the "deficit map" the area in red indicates where in the range of motion, at what speeds, and which contraction type the greatest difference occurred between the involved and uninvolved sides. Hence, clinicians now have the opportunity to identify the neuromuscular performance associated with isolated muscle testing. Hiemstra et al noted that during an Isomap evaluation (five speeds concentric and five speed eccentric) a combined ACL group (n = 8 patella tendon) (n = 16 hamstring) revealed a global 25.5 percent extensor strength deficit, with eccentric regional (angle and velocity matched) deficits up to 50 percent of control (n = 30).[15] Now that Isomap evaluations are commercially available, clinicians and researchers alike can benefit from these technologic advances.

SUMMARY

- Isokinetic exercise is movement that occurs at a constant angular velocity with accommodating resistance.
- It is important to be consistent with testing parameters to ensure reliable and valid data.
- Various parameters are defined on the output report. It is best to consider peak torque, total work, and average power when creating a treatment plan.
- Multijoint systems have several modes of operation (isometric, isotonic, reactive eccentric, passive, and isokinetic modes) that can be used throughout the rehabilitation process.
- Slow isokinetic velocities increase compressive and translational forces versus faster isokinetic velocities.
- When treating the anterior cruciate ligament–reconstructed patient, remember there is a posterior shear force from 40 degrees to 101 degrees and anterior shear force from 38 degrees to 0 degrees (peaking at 14 degrees).
- Prior to return to normal functional activities, ensure that adequate muscle strength, postural stability, and structural integrity have been established.

REFERENCES

1. Ariki PK, Davies GJ, Siewert MW, et al. Optimum rest interval between isokinetic velocity spectrum rehabilitation speeds. *Phys Ther* 65:735, 1985.
2. Atha J. Strengthening muscle. *Exerc Sport Sci* 9:1–73, 1981.
3. Bemdem MG, Johnson DA. Reliability of the Biodex B-2000. Isokinetic dynamometer and the evaluation of a sport-specific determination for the angle of peak torque during knee extension. *Isokin Exerc Sci* 3:164–168, 1993.
4. Beynnon BD, Johnson RJ. Anterior cruciate ligament injury rehabilitation in athletes. Biomechanical considerations. *Sports Med* 22:54–64, 1996.
5. *Biodex Advantage Software Manual.* 1994.
6. Borsa PA, Lephart SM, Kocher MS, et al. Functional assessment and rehabilitation of shoulder proprioception for glenohumeral instability. *J Sport Rehabil* 6:327–334, 1997.
7. Bouchard CS, Theriault G, Gauthier JM, et al. Fracture of the patella during rehabilitation of the knee extensor muscles following reconstruction of the anterior cruciate ligament: A brief report. *Clin J Sports Med* 3:126–130, 1993.
8. Capranica L, Cama G, Fanton F, et al. Force and power of preferred and non-preferred leg in young soccer players. *J Sports Med Phys Fitness* 32:358–363, 1992.
9. Daniels L, Worthington C. *Muscle Testing: Techniques of Manual Examination*, 5th ed. Philadelphia, Saunders, 1986.
10. Davies G. *A Compendium of Isokinetic in Clinical Usage*, 3rd ed. Onolaska, WI, S & S Publishers, 1987.
10A. Davies GJ. The need for critical thinking in rehabilitation. *J Sport Rehabil* 4:1–22, 1995.
11. Feiring DC, Ellenbecher TS, Derscheid GL. Test-reliability of the Biodex isokinetic dynamometer. *J Orthop Sports Phys Ther* 23:348–352, 1996.
12. Figoni FI, Morris AF. Effects of knowledge of results on reciprocal isokinetic strength and fatigue. *J Orthop Sports Phys Ther* 6:104–106, 1984.
13. Grabiner MD, Jexiorowski JJ, Divekar AD. Isokinetic measurements of trunk extension and flexion performance collected with the Biodex clinical data station. *J Orthop Sports Phys Ther* 11:590–598, 1990.
14. Hald RD, Bottken EJ. Effects of visual input on maximal and submaximal isokinetic test measurements of normal quadriceps and hamstring. *J Orthop Sports Phys Ther* 9:86, 1987.
15. Hiemstra LA, Webber S, MacDonald PT, et al. Graft site dependent knee strength deficits after patellar tendon and hamstring tendon ACL reconstuction. *Med Sci Sports Exerc* 32(8):1472–1479, 2000.
16. Higgins MJ, Perrin DH. Comparison of weight-bearing and non-weight-bearing conditions on knee joint reposition sense. *J Sport Rehabil* 6:327–334, 1997.
17. Hislop H, Perrin J. The isokinetic concept of exercise. *Phys Ther* 47:114–117, 1967.
18. Hobbel SL, Rose DJ. The relative effectiveness of three forms of visual knowledge of results on peak torque output. *J Orthop Sports Phys Ther* 18(5):601–608, 1993.
19. Hoppenfield S. *Physical Examination of the Spine and*

Extremities. Norwalk, CT, Appleton-Century-Crofts, 1976, p. 34.

20. Kendall FD, McCreary EK. *Muscle Testing and Function*, 3rd ed. Baltimore, Williams & Wilkins, 1983.

21. Mawdsley RH, Knapik J. Comparison of isokinetic measurements with test repetitions. *Phys Ther* 62:169–172, 1882.

22. Neer CS II. Anterior acromioplasty for the chronic impingement syndrome in the shoulder. A preliminary report. *JBJS* 54A:41–50, 1972.

23. Nelson SG, Duncan PW. Correction of isokinetic and isometric torque readings for the effect of gravity. *Phys Ther* 63:674–676, 1983.

24. Newsham KR, Keith CS, Saunders JE, et al. Isokinetic profile of baseball pitchers' internal/external rotation 180, 300, 450°/second. *Med Sci Sports Exerc* 30:1489–1495, 1998.

25. Nicholas J, Sapega A, Kraus H, et al. Factors influencing manual muscle tests in physical therapy. *J Bone Joint Surg* 60:186, 1978.

26. Noyes FR, Mangine RE, Barber S. Early knee motion after open and arthroscopic anterior cruciate ligament reconstruction. *Am J Sport Med* 15:149–160, 1987.

27. Rathburn JB, McNab I. The microvascular pattern of the rotator cuff. *JBJS* 52B:540–553, 1970.

28. Schmit BD, Dewald J, Zev Rymer W. Variability of the Stretch Reflex During Quantification of Spasticity Using Constant Velocity Ramp Stretches. *Med Rehabil* 81(3):269–278, 2000.

29. Timm KE. Postsurgical knee rehabilitation: A five year study of four methods and 5,381 patients. *Am J Sports Med* 16:463–468, 1988.

30. Timm KE. The isokinetic torque curve of shoulder instability in high school baseball pitchers. *J Orthop Sports Phys Ther* 11:590–598, 1990.

31. Touey PA, Sforzo GA, McManis BG. Effect of manipulating rest periods on isokinetic muscle performance. *Med Sci Sports Exerc* 26:S170, 1994.

32. Voight ML, Hardin JA, Blackburn TA, et al. The effects of muscle fatigue on and the relationship of arm dominance to shoulder proprioception. *J Orthop Sports Phys Ther* 23:348–352, 1996.

33. Warner JJ, Micheli LS, Arslanian LE, et al. Patterns of flexibility, laxity, and strength in normal shoulder and shoulder with instability and impingement. *Am J Sports Med* 18:366–374, 1990.

34. Weir JP, Housh DJ, Housh TL, et al. The effect of unilateral concentric weight training and detraining on joint angle specificity, cross-training, and bilateral deficits. *J Orthop Sports Phys Ther* 25:264–270, 1997.

35. Wilk KE. *Dynamic Muscle Strength Testing: Instrumented and Non-Instrumented Systems.* New York, Churchill-Livingstone, 1990, pp. 123–150.

36. Wilk KE, Andrews JR. The effects of pad placement and angular velocity on tibial pad placement during isokinetic exercise. *J Orthop Sports Phys Ther* 17:24–30, 1993.

37. Wilk KE, Andrews JR, Arrigo CA. The abductor and adductor strength characteristics of professional baseball pitchers. *Am J Sports Med* 23:307–311, 1995.

38. Wilk KE, Andrews JR, Arrigo CA, et al. The strength characteristics of internal and external rotator muscles in professional baseball pitchers. *Am J Sports Med* 21:61–66, 1993.

39. Wilk KE, Arrigo CA. Standardized isokinetic testing protocol for the throwing shoulder: The throwers' series. *Isokin Exerc Sci* 1:63–71, 1991.

40. Wilk KE, Escamilla RF, Fleisig GS, et al. A comparison of tibiofemoral joint forces and electromyographic activity during open and closed kinetic chain exercises. *Am J Sports Med* 24:518–527, 1996.

41. Wilk KE, Romaniello WT, Soscia SM, et al. The relationship between subjective knee scores, isokinetic testing, and functional testing in the ACL-reconstructed knee. *J Orthop Sports Phys Ther* 20:60–73, 1994.

42. Wilkerson GB, Pinerola JJ, Caturano RW. Invertor vs. evertor peak torque and power deficiencies associated with lateral ankle injury. *J Orthop Sports Phys Ther* 26:79–87, 1997.

43. Wrigley T, Grant M. Isokinetic dynamometry, in *Sports Physiology: Applied Science and Practice.* Edinburgh, Churchill Livingstone, 1995, pp. 259–287.

44. Wyman J. Studies on the relation of work and heat in tortoise muscle. *J Physiol* 61:337–352, 1926.

45. Yack JH, Colline CE, Whieldon TJ. Comparison of closed and open kinetic chain exercise in the anterior cruciate ligament-deficient knee. *Am J Sports Med* 21:49–54, 1993.

Plyometric Exercise in Rehabilitation

Michael Voight and Steve Tippett

O B J E C T I V E S

After completing this chapter, the student therapist should be able to do the following:

- Describe the mechanical, neurophysiologic, and neuromuscular control mechanisms involved in plyometric training.
- Discuss how biomechanical evaluation, stability, dynamic movement, and flexibility should be assessed before beginning a plyometric program.
- Explain how a plyometric program can be modified by changing intensity, volume, frequency, and recovery.
- Discuss how plyometrics can be integrated into a rehabilitation program.

WHAT IS PLYOMETRIC EXERCISE?

In sports training and rehabilitation of athletic injuries, the concept of specificity has emerged as an important parameter in determining the proper choice and sequence of exercise in a training program. The jumping movement is inherent in numerous sport activities such as basketball, volleyball, gymnastics, and aerobic dancing. Even running is a repeated series of jump-landing cycles. Therefore jump training should be used in the design and implementation of the overall training program.

Peak performance in sport requires technical skill and power. Skill in most activities combines natural athletic ability and learned specialized proficiency in an activity. Success in most activities is dependent upon the speed at which muscular force or power can be generated. Strength and conditioning programs throughout the years have attempted to augment the force production system to maximize the power generated. Because power combines strength and speed, it can be increased by increasing the amount of work or force that is produced by the muscles or by decreasing the amount of time required to produce the force. Although weight training can produce increased gains in strength, the speed of movement is limited. The amount of time required to produce muscular force is an important variable for increasing the power output. A form of training that attempts to combine speed of movement with strength is plyometrics.

The term **plyometric training** is relatively new, but the concept of plyometric training is not. The roots of plyometric training can be traced to Eastern Europe, where it was known simply as jump training. The term *plyometrics* was coined by an American track and field coach, Fred Wilt.[35] The development of the term is confusing. *Plyo-* comes from the Greek word *plythein*, which means "to increase." *Plio* is the Greek word for "more," and *metric* literally means "to measure." Practically, plyometrics is defined as a quick, powerful movement involving prestretching the muscle and activating the stretch–shortening cycle to produce a subsequently stronger concentric contraction. It takes advantage of the length–shortening cycle to increase muscular power.

In the late 1960s and early 1970s when Eastern European countries began to dominate sports requiring power, their training methods became the focus of attention. After the 1972 Olympics, articles began to appear in coaching magazines outlining a strange new system of jumps and bounds that had been used by the Soviets to increase speed. Valery Borzov, the 100-meter gold medalist, credited plyometric exercise for his success. As it turns out, the Eastern European countries were not the originators of plyometrics, just the organizers. This system of hops and jumps has been used by American coaches for years as a method of conditioning. Both rope jumping and bench hops have been used to improve quickness and reaction times. The organization of this training method has been credited to the legendary Soviet jump coach Yuri Verkhoshanski, who during the late 1960s began to tie this method of miscellaneous hops and jumps into an organized training plan.[30]

The main purpose of plyometric training is to heighten the excitability of the nervous system for improved reactive ability of the neuromuscular system.[32] Therefore, any type of exercise that uses the myotatic stretch reflex to produce a more powerful response of the contracting muscle is plyometric in nature. All movement patterns in athletes and in activities of daily living (ADL) involve repeated stretch–shortening cycles. Picture a jumping athlete preparing to transfer forward energy to upward energy. As the final step is taken before jumping, the loaded leg must stop the forward momentum and change it into an upward direction. As this happens, the muscle undergoes a lengthening eccentric contraction to decelerate the movement and prestretch the muscle. This prestretch energy is then immediately released in an equal and opposite reaction, thereby producing kinetic energy. The neuromuscular system must react quickly to produce the concentric shortening contraction to prevent falling and produce the upward change in direction. Most elite athletes will naturally exhibit with great ease this ability to use stored kinetic energy Less gifted athletes can train this ability and enhance their production of power. Consequently, specific functional exercise to emphasize this rapid change of direction must be used to prepare patients and athletes for return to activity. Because plyometric exercises train specific movements in a biomechanically accurate manner, the muscles, tendons, and ligaments are all strengthened in a functional manner.

Most of the literature to date on plyometric training has been focused on the lower quarter. Because all movements in athletics involve a repeated series of stretch–shortening cycles, adaptation of the plyometric principles can be used to enhance the specificity of training in other sports or activities that require a maximum amount of muscular force in a minimal amount of time. Whether the athlete is jumping or throwing, the musculature around the involved joints must first stretch and then contract to produce the explosive movement. Because of the muscular demands during the overhead throw, plyometrics have been advocated as a form of conditioning for the overhead throwing athlete.[31,34] Although the principles are similar, different forms of plyometric exercises should be applied to the upper extremity to train the stretch–shortening cycle. Additionally, the intensity of the upper extremity plyometric program is usually less than that of the lower extremity, due to the smaller muscle mass and type of muscle function of the upper extremity compared to the lower extremity.

BIOMECHANICAL AND PHYSIOLOGIC PRINCIPLES OF PLYOMETRIC TRAINING

The goal of plyometric training is to decrease the amount of time required between the yielding eccentric muscle contraction and the initiation of the overcoming concentric contraction. Normal physiologic movement rarely begins from a static starting

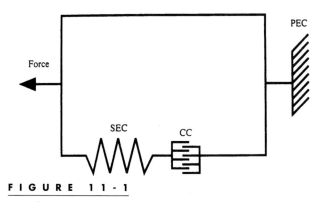

FIGURE 11-1

Three-component model.

position but rather is preceded by an eccentric prestretch that loads the muscle and prepares it for the ensuing concentric contraction. The coupling of the eccentric–concentric muscle contraction is known as the stretch–shortening cycle. The physiology of this stretch–shortening cycle can be broken down into two components: proprioceptive reflexes and the elastic properties of muscle fibers. These components work together to produce a response, but they will be discussed separately for the purpose of understanding.

Mechanical Characteristics

The mechanical characteristics of a muscle can best be represented by a three-component model (Fig. 11-1). A contractile component (CC), series elastic component (SEC), and parallel elastic component (PEC) all interact to produce a force output. Although the CC is usually the focal point of motor control, the SEC and PEC also play an important role in providing stability and integrity to the individual fibers when a muscle is lengthened. During this lengthening process, energy is stored within the musculature in the form of kinetic energy.

When a muscle contracts in a concentric fashion, most of the force that is produced comes from the muscle fiber filaments sliding past one another. Force is registered externally by being transferred through the SEC. When eccentric contraction occurs, the muscle lengthens like a spring. With this lengthening, the SEC is also stretched and allowed to contribute to the overall force production. Therefore the total force production is the sum of the force produced by the CC and the stretching of the SEC. An analogy would be the stretching of a rubber band. When a stretch is applied, potential energy is stored and applied as it returns to its original length when the stretch is released.

Significant increases in concentric muscle force production have been documented when immediately preceded by an eccentric contraction.[2,5,9] This increase might be partly due to the storage of elastic energy, because the muscles are able to use the force produced by the SEC. When the muscle contracts in a concentric manner, the elastic energy that is stored in the SEC can be recovered and used to augment the shortening contraction. The ability to use this stored elastic energy is affected by three variables: time, magnitude of stretch, and velocity of stretch.[17] The concentric contraction can be magnified only if the preceding eccentric contraction is of short range and performed quickly without delay.[2,5,9] Bosco and Komi proved this concept experimentally when they compared damped versus undamped jumps.[5] Undamped jumps produced minimal knee flexion upon landing and were followed by an immediate rebound jump. With damped jumps, the knee flexion angle increased significantly. The power output was much higher with the undamped jumps. The increased knee flexion seen in the damped jumps decreased elastic behavior of the muscle, and the potential elastic energy stored in the SEC was lost as heat. Similar investigations produced greater vertical jump height when the movement was preceded by a countermovement as opposed to a static jump.[2,4,6,22]

The type of muscle fiber involved in the contraction can also affect storage of elastic energy. Bosco et al noted a difference in the recoil of elastic energy in slow-twitch versus fast-twitch muscle fibers.[7] This study indicates that fast-twitch muscle fibers respond to a high-speed, small-amplitude prestretch. The amount of elastic energy used was proportional to the amount stored. When a long, slow stretch is applied to muscle, slow- and fast-twitch fibers exhibit a similar amount of stored elastic energy; however, this stored energy is used to a greater extent with the slow-twitch fibers. This trend would suggest that slow-twitch muscle fibers might be able to use elastic energy more efficiently in ballistic movement characterized by long and slow prestretching in the stretch–shortening cycle.

Neurophysiologic Mechanisms

The proprioceptive stretch reflex is the other mechanism by which force can be produced during the stretch–shortening cycle. Mechanoreceptors located within the muscle provide information about the degree of muscular stretch. This information is transmitted to the central nervous system and becomes capable of influencing muscle tone, motor execution programs, and kinesthetic awareness. The mechanoreceptors that are primarily responsible for the stretch reflex are the Golgi tendon organs and muscle spindles.[24] The muscle spindle is a complex stretch receptor that is located in parallel within the muscle fibers. Sensory information regarding the length of the muscle spindle and the rate of the applied stretch is transmitted to the central nervous system. If the length of the surrounding muscle fibers is less than that of the spindle, the frequency of the nerve impulses from the spindle is reduced. When the muscle spindle becomes stretched, an afferent sensory response is produced and transmitted to the central nervous system. Neurologic impulses are in turn sent back to the muscle, causing a motor response. As the muscle contracts, the stretch on the muscle spindle is relieved, thereby removing the original stimulus. The strength of the muscle spindle response is determined by the rate of stretch.[24] The more rapidly the load is applied to the muscle, the greater the firing frequency of the spindle and resultant reflexive muscle contraction.

The Golgi tendon organ lies within the muscle tendon near the point of attachment of the muscle fiber to the tendon. Unlike the facilitory action of the muscle spindle, the Golgi tendon organ has an inhibitory effect on the muscle by contributing to a tension-limiting reflex. Because the Golgi tendon organs are in series alignment with the contracting muscle fibers, they become activated with tension or stretch within the muscle. Upon activation, sensory impulses are transmitted to the central nervous system. These sensory impulses cause an inhibition of the alpha motor neurons of the contracting muscle and its synergists, thereby limiting the amount of force produced. With a concentric muscle contraction, the activity of the muscle spindle is reduced because the surrounding muscle fibers are shortening. During an eccentric muscle contraction, the muscle stretch reflex generates more tension in the lengthening muscle. When the tension within the muscle reaches a potentially harmful level, the Golgi tendon organ fires, thereby reducing the excitation of the muscle. The muscle spindle and Golgi tendon organ systems oppose each other, and increasing force is produced. The descending neural pathways from the brain help to balance these forces and ultimately control which reflex will dominate.[26]

The degree of muscle fiber elongation is dependent upon three physiologic factors. Fiber length is proportional to the amount of stretching force applied to the muscle. The ultimate elongation or deformation is also dependent upon the absolute strength of the individual muscle fibers. The stronger the tensile strength, the less elongation that will occur. The last factor for elongation is the ability of the muscle spindle to produce a neurophysiologic response. A muscle spindle with a low sensitivity level will result in a difficulty in overcoming the rapid elongation and therefore produce a less powerful response. Plyometric training will assist in enhancing muscular control within the neurologic system.

The increased force production seen during the stretch–shortening cycle is due to the combined effects of the storage of elastic energy and the myotatic reflex activation of the muscle.[2,4,8,9,23,27] The percentage of contribution from each component is unknown.[4] The increased amount of force production is dependent upon the time frame between the eccentric and concentric contractions.[9] This time frame can be defined as the amortization phase.[13] The amortization phase is the electromechanical delay between eccentric and concentric contraction, during which time the muscle must switch from overcoming work to acceleration in the opposite direction. Komi found that the greatest amount of tension developed within the muscle during the stretch–shortening cycle occurred during the phase of muscle lengthening just before the concentric contraction.[21] The conclusion from this study was that increased time in the amortization phase would lead to a decrease in force production.

Physiologic performance can be improved by several mechanisms with plyometric training. Although there has been documented evidence of increased speed of the stretch reflex, the increased intensity of the subsequent muscle contraction might be best attributed to better recruitment of additional motor units.[11] The force–velocity relationship states that the faster a muscle is loaded or lengthened eccentrically, the greater the resultant force output. Eccentric lengthening will also place a load on the elastic components of the muscle fibers. The stretch reflex might also increase the stiffness of the muscular spring by recruiting additional muscle fibers.[11] This additional stiffness might allow the muscular system to use more external stress in the form of elastic recoil.[11]

Another possible mechanism by which plyometric training can increase the force or power output involves the inhibitory effect of the Golgi tendon organs on force production. Because the Golgi tendon organ serves as a tension-limiting reflex, restricting the amount of force that can be produced, the stimulation threshold for the Golgi tendon organ becomes a limiting factor. Bosco and Komi have suggested that plyometric training can desensitize the Golgi tendon organ, thereby raising the level of inhibition.[5] If the level of inhibition is raised, a greater amount of force production and load can be applied to the musculoskeletal system.

Neuromuscular Coordination

The last mechanism in which plyometric training might improve muscular performance centers around neuromuscular coordination (see Chapter 8). The speed of muscular contraction can be limited by neuromuscular coordination. In other words, the body can move only within a set speed range, no matter how strong the muscles are. Training with an explosive prestretch of the muscle can improve the neural efficiency, thereby increasing neuromuscular performance. Plyometric training can promote changes within the neuromuscular system that allow the individual to have better control of the contracting muscle and its synergists, yielding a greater net force even in the absence of morphologic adaptation of the muscle. This neural adaptation can increase performance by enhancing the nervous system to become more automatic.

In summary, effective plyometric training relies more on the rate of stretch than on the length of stretch. Emphasis should center on the reduction of the amortization phase. If the amortization phase is slow, the elastic energy is lost as heat and the stretch reflex is not activated. Conversely, the quicker the individual is able to switch from yielding eccentric work to overcoming concentric work, the more powerful the response.

PROGRAM DEVELOPMENT

Specificity is the key concept in any training program. Sport-specific activities should be analyzed and broken down into basic movement patterns. These specific movement patterns should then be stressed in a gradual fashion, based upon individual tolerance to these activities. Development of a plyometric program should begin by establishing an adequate strength base that will allow the body to withstand the large stress that will be placed upon it. A greater strength base will allow for greater force production due to increased muscular cross-sectional area. Additionally, a larger cross-sectional area can contribute to the SEC and subsequently store a greater amount of elastic energy.

Plyometric exercises can be characterized as rapid eccentric loading of the musculoskeletal complex.[11] This type of exercise trains the neuromuscular system by teaching it to more readily accept the increased strength loads.[3] Also, the nervous system is more readily able to react with maximal speed to the lengthening muscle by exploiting the stretch reflex. Plyometric training attempts to fine tune the neuromuscular system, so all training programs should be designed with specificity in mind.[25] This goal will help to ensure that the body is prepared to accept the stress that will be placed upon it during return to function.

Plyometric Prerequisites

BIOMECHANICAL EXAMINATION

Before beginning a plyometric training program, a cursory biomechanical examination and a battery of functional tests should be performed to identify potential contraindications or precautions. Lower-quarter biomechanics should be sound to help ensure a stable base of support and normal force transmission. Biomechanical abnormalities of the lower quarter are not contraindications for plyometrics but can contribute to stress failure–overuse injury if not addressed. Before initiating plyometric training, an adequate strength base of the stabilizing musculature must be present. Functional tests are very effective to screen for an adequate strength base before initiating plyometrics. Poor strength in the lower extremities will result in a loss of stability when landing and also increase the amount of stress that is absorbed by the weight-bearing tissues with high-impact forces, which will reduce performance and increase the risk of injury. The Eastern European countries arbitrarily placed a one-repetition maximum in the squat at 1.5 to 2 times the individual's body weight before initiating lower-quarter plyometrics.[3] If this were to hold true, a 200-pound individual would have to squat 400 pounds before beginning plyometrics. Unfortunately, not many individuals would meet this minimal criteria. Clinical and practical experience has demonstrated that plyometrics can be started without that kind of leg strength.[11] A simple functional parameter to use in determining whether an individual is strong enough to initiate a plyometric training program has been advocated by Chu.[10] Power squat testing with a weight equal to 60 percent of the individual's body weight is used. The individual is asked to perform five squat repetitions in 5 seconds. If the individual cannot perform this task, emphasis in the training program should again center on strength training to develop an adequate base.

Because eccentric muscle strength is an important component to plyometric training, it is especially important to ensure an adequate eccentric strength base is present. Before an individual is allowed to begin a plyometric regimen, a program of closed-chain stability training that focuses on eccentric

Plyometric Static Stability Testing

- Single-Leg Stance — 30 sec
  - Eyes open
  - Eyes closed

- Single-Leg 25% Squat — 30 sec
  - Eyes open
  - Eyes closed

- Single-Leg 50% Squat — 30 sec
  - Eyes open
  - Eyes closed

F I G U R E　1 1 - 2

Static stability testing.

lower-quarter strength should be initiated. In addition to strengthening in a functional manner, closed-chain weight-bearing exercises also allow the individual to use functional movement patterns. Once cleared to participate in the plyometric program, precautionary safety tips should be adhered to.

STABILITY TESTING

Stability testing before initiating plyometric training can be divided into two subcategories: static stability and dynamic movement testing. Static stability testing determines the individual's ability to stabilize and control the body. The muscles of postural support must be strong enough to withstand the stress of explosive training. Static stability testing (Fig. 11-2) should begin with simple movements of low motor complexity and progress to more difficult high motor skills. The basis for lower-quarter stability centers around single-leg strength. Difficulty can be increased by having the individual close the eyes. The basic static tests are one-leg standing and single-leg quarter squats that are held for 30 seconds. An individual should be able to perform one-leg standing for 30 seconds with eyes open and closed before the initiation of plyometric training. The individual should be observed for shaking or wobbling of the extremity joints. If there is more movement of a weight-bearing joint in one direction than the other, the musculature producing the movement in the opposite direction needs to be assessed for specific weakness. If weakness is determined, the individual's program should be limited and emphasis placed on isolated strengthening of the weak muscles. For dynamic jump exercises to be initiated, there should be no wobbling of the support leg during the quarter knee squats.

After an individual has satisfactorily demonstrated both single-leg static stance and a single-leg quarter squat, more dynamic tests of eccentric capabilities can be initiated. Once an individual has stabilization strength, the concern shifts toward developing and evaluating eccentric strength. The limiting factor in high-intensity, high-volume plyometrics is eccentric capabilities. Eccentric strength can be assessed with stabilization jump tests. If an individual has an excessively long amortization phase or a slow switching from eccentric to concentric contractions, the eccentric strength levels are insufficient.

Chu's Plyometric Categories

- In-place jumping
- Standing jumps
- Multiple-response jumps and hops
- In-depth jumping and box drills
- Bounding
- High-stress sport-specific drills

F I G U R E　1 1 - 3

Six categories of plyometric training.

DYNAMIC MOVEMENT TESTING

Dynamic movement testing will assess the individual's ability to produce explosive, coordinated movement. Vertical or single-leg jumping for distance can be used for the lower quarter. Researchers have investigated the use of single-leg hop for distance and a determinant for return to play after knee injury. A passing score on their test is 85 percent in regard to symmetry. The involved leg is tested twice, and the average between the two trials is recorded. The noninvolved leg is tested in the same fashion, and then the scores of the noninvolved leg are divided by the scores of the involved leg and multiplied by 100. This provides the symmetry index score. Another functional test that can be used to determine whether an individual is ready for plyometric training is the ability to long jump a distance equal to the individual's height. In the upper quarter, the medicine ball toss is used as a functional assessment.

FLEXIBILITY

Another important prerequisite for plyometric training is general and specific flexibility, because a high amount of stress is applied to the musculoskeletal system. Therefore all plyometric training sessions should begin with a general warm-up and flexibility exercise program. The warm-up should produce mild sweating.[19] The flexibility exercise program should address muscle groups involved in the plyometric program and should include static and short dynamic stretching techniques.[18]

When individuals can demonstrate static and dynamic control of their body weight with single-leg squats, low-intensity in-place plyometrics can be initiated. Plyometric training should consist of low-intensity drills, and should progress slowly in deliberate fashion. As skill and strength foundation increase, moderate-intensity plyometrics can be introduced. Mature athletes with strong weight-training backgrounds can be introduced to ballistic–reactive plyometric exercises of high intensity.[10] Once the individual has been classified as beginner, intermediate, or advanced, the plyometric program can be planned and initiated. Chu[11–13] has divided lower-quarter plyometric training into six categories (Fig. 11-3).

PLYOMETRIC PROGRAM DESIGN

As with any conditioning program, the plyometric training program can be manipulated through training variables: direction of body movement, weight of the athlete, speed of the execution, external load, intensity, volume, frequency, training age, and recovery.

Direction of Body Movement

Horizontal body movement is less stressful than vertical movement. This is dependent upon the weight of the athlete and the technical proficiency demonstrated during the jumps.

Weight of the Athlete

The heavier the athlete, the greater the training demand placed on the athlete. What might be a low-demand in-place jump for a lightweight athlete might be a high-demand activity for a heavyweight athlete.

Speed of Execution of the Exercise

Increased speed of execution on exercises like single-leg hops or alternate-leg bounding raises the training demand on the individual.

External Load

Adding an external load can significantly raise the training demand. Do not raise the external load to a level that will significantly slow the speed of movement.

Intensity

Intensity can be defined as the amount of effort exerted. With traditional weight lifting, intensity can be modified by changing the amount of weight that is lifted. With plyometric training, intensity can be controlled by the type of exercise that is performed. Double-leg jumping is less stressful than single-leg jumping. As with all functional exercise, the plyometric exercise program should progress from simple to complex activities. Intensity can be further increased by altering the specific exercises. The addition of external weight or raising the height of the step or box will also increase the exercise intensity.

Volume

Volume is the total amount of work that is performed in a single workout session. With weight training, volume would be recorded as the total amount of weight that was lifted (weight times repetitions). Volume of plyometric training is measured by counting the total number of foot contacts. The recommended volume of foot contacts in any one session will vary inversely with the intensity of the exercise. A beginner should start with low-intensity exercise with a volume of approximately 75 to 100 foot contacts. As ability is increased, the volume

is increased to 200 to 250 foot contacts of low to moderate intensity.

Frequency

Frequency is the number of times an exercise session is performed during a training cycle. With weight training, the frequency of exercise has typically been three times weekly. Unfortunately, research on the frequency of plyometric exercise has not been conducted. Therefore the optimum frequency for increased performance is not known. It has been suggested that 48 to 72 hours of rest are necessary for full recovery before the next training stimulus.[10] Intensity, however, plays a major role in determining the frequency of training. If an adequate recovery period does not occur, muscle fatigue will result with a corresponding increase in neuromuscular reaction times. The beginner should allow at least 48 hours between training sessions.

Training Age

Training age is the number of years an athlete has been in a formal training program. At younger training ages, the overall training demand should be kept low.

Recovery

Recovery is the rest time used between exercise sets. Manipulation of this variable will depend on whether the goal is to increase power or muscular endurance. Because plyometric training is anaerobic in nature, a longer recovery period should be used to allow restoration of metabolic stores. With power training, a work–rest ratio of 1:3 or 1:4 should be used. This time frame will allow maximal recovery between sets. For endurance training, this work–rest ratio can be shortened to 1:1 or 1:2. Endurance training typically uses circuit training, where the individual moves from one exercise set to another with minimal rest in between.

The beginning plyometric program should emphasize the importance of eccentric versus concentric muscle contractions. The relevance of the stretch–shortening cycle with decreased amortization time should be stressed. Initiation of lower-quarter plyometric training begins with low-intensity in-place and multiple-response jumps. The individual should be instructed in proper exercise technique. The feet should be nearly flat in all landings, and the individual should be encouraged to "touch and go." An analogy would be landing on a hot bed of coals. The goal is to reverse the landing as quickly as possible, spending only a minimal amount of time on the ground.

Success of the plyometric program will depend on how well the training variables are controlled, modified, and manipulated. In general, as the intensity of the exercise is increased, the volume is decreased. The corollary to this is that as volume increases, the intensity is decreased. The overall key to successfully controlling these variables is to be flexible and listen to what the athlete's body is telling you. The body's response to the program will dictate the speed of progression. Whenever in doubt as to the exercise intensity or volume, it is better to underestimate to prevent injury.

Before implementing a plyometric program, the sports therapist should assess the type of athlete that is being rehabilitated and whether plyometrics are suitable for that individual. In most cases, plyometrics should be used in the latter phases of rehabilitation, starting in the advanced strengthening phase once the athlete has obtained an appropriate strength base.[31,34] When using plyometric training in the uninjured athlete, the application of plyometric exercise should follow the concept of periodization.[32] The concept of periodization refers to the year-round sequence and progression of strength training, conditioning, and sport-specific skills.[34] There are four specific phases in the year-round periodization model: the competitive season, postseason training, the preparation phase, and the

transitional phase.[32] Plyometric exercises should be performed in the latter stages of the preparation phase and during the transitional phase for optimal results and safety. To obtain the benefits of a plyometric program, the athlete should (1) be well conditioned with sufficient strength and endurance, (2) exhibit athletic abilities, (3) exhibit coordination and proprioceptive abilities, and (4) be free of pain from any physical injury or condition.

Remember that the plyometric program is not designed to be an exclusive training program for the athlete. Rather, it should be one part of a well-structured training program that includes strength training, flexibility training, cardiovascular fitness, and sport-specific training for skill enhancement and coordination. By combining the plyometric program with other training techniques, the effects of training are greatly enhanced.

Tables 11-1 and 11-2 suggest upper-extremity and lower-extremity plyometric drills.

TABLE 11-1

Upper-Extremity Plyometric Drills

I. WARM-UP DRILLS

Plyoball trunk rotation
Plyoball side bends
Plyoball wood chops
ER/IR with tubing
PNF D2 pattern with tubing

II. THROWING MOVEMENTS—STANDING POSITION

Two-hand chest pass
Two-hand overhead soccer throw
Two-hand side throw overhead
Tubing ER/IR (Both at side & 90° abduction)
Tubing PNF D2 pattern
One-hand baseball throw
One-hand IR side throw
One-hand ER side throw
Plyo push-up (against wall)

III. THROWING MOVEMENTS—SEATED POSITION

Two-hand overhead soccer throw
Two-hand side-to-side throw
Two-hand chest pass
One-hand baseball throw

IV. TRUNK DRILLS

Plyoball sit-ups
Plyoball sit-up and throw
Plyoball back extension
Plyoball long sitting side throws

V. PARTNER DRILLS

Overhead soccer throw
Plyoball back-to-back twists
Overhead pullover throw
Kneeling side throw
Backward throw
Chest pass throw

VI. WALL DRILLS

Two-hand chest throw
Two-hand overhead soccer throw
Two-hand underhand side-to-side throw
One-hand baseball throw
One-hand wall dribble

VII. ENDURANCE DRILLS

One-hand wall dribble
Around-the-back circles
Figure eight through the legs
Single-arm ball flips

TABLE 11-2

Lower-Extremity Plyometric Drills

I. WARM-UP DRILLS

Double-leg squats
Double-leg leg press
Double-leg squat-jumps
Jumping jacks

II. ENTRY-LEVEL DRILLS—TWO-LEGGED

Two-legged drills
  Side to side (floor/line)
  Diagonal jumps (floor/4 corners)
  Diagonal jumps (4 spots)
  Diagonal zig/zag (6 spots)
  Plyo leg press
  Plyo leg press (4 corners)

III. INTERMEDIATE-LEVEL DRILLS

Two-legged box jumps
  One-box side jump
  Two-box side jumps
  Two-box side jumps with foam
  Four-box diagonal jumps
  Two-box with rotation
  One/two-box with catch
  One/two-box with catch (foam)
Single-leg movements
  Single-leg plyo leg press
  Single-leg side jumps (floor)
  Single-leg side-to-side jumps (floor/4 corners)
  Single-leg diagonal jumps (floor/4 corners)

IV. ADVANCED-LEVEL DRILLS

Single-leg box jumps
  One-box side jumps
  Two-box side jumps
  Single-leg plyo leg press (4 corners)
  Two-box side jumps with foam
  Four-box diagonal jumps
  One-box side jumps with rotation
  Two-box side jumps with rotation
  One-box side jump with catch
  One-box side jump rotation with catch
  Two-box side jump with catch
  Two-box side jump rotation with catch

V. ENDURANCE/AGILITY PLYOMETRICS

  Side-to-side bounding (20 feet)
  Side jump lunges (cone)
  Side jump lunges (cone with foam)
  Altering rapid step-up (forward)
  Lateral step-overs
  High stepping (forward)
  High stepping (backwards)
  Depth jump with rebound jump
  Depth jump with catch
  Jump and catch (plyoball)

GUIDELINES FOR PLYOMETRIC PROGRAMS

The proper execution of the plyometric exercise program must continually be stressed. A sound technical foundation from which higher-intensity work can build should be established. It must be remembered that jumping is a continuous interchange between force reduction and force production. This interchange takes place throughout the entire body: ankle, knee, hip, trunk, and arms. The timing and coordination of these body segments yields a positive ground reaction that will result in a high rate of force production.

As the plyometric program is initiated, the individual must be made aware of several guidelines.[32] Any deviation from these guidelines will result in minimal improvement and increased risk for injury. These guidelines include the following:

1. Plyometric training should be specific to the individual goals of the athlete. Activity-specific movement patterns should be trained. These sport-specific skills should be broken down and trained in their smaller components and then rebuilt into a coordinated activity-specific movement pattern.

2. The quality of work is more important than the quantity of work. The intensity of the exercise should be kept at a maximal level.

3. The greater the exercise intensity level, the greater the recovery time.

4. Plyometric training can have its greatest benefit at the conclusion of the normal workout. This pattern will best replicate exercise under a partial to total fatigue environment that is specific to activity. Only low- to medium-stress plyometrics should be used at the conclusion of a workout, because of the increased potential of injury with high-stress drills.

5. When proper technique can no longer be demonstrated, maximum volume has been achieved and the exercise must

be stopped. Training improperly or with fatigue can lead to injury.

6. The plyometric training program should be progressive in nature. The volume and intensity can be modified in several ways:

Increase the number of exercises.

Increase the number of repetitions and sets.

Decrease the rest period between sets of exercises.

7. Plyometric training sessions should be conducted no more than three times weekly in the preseason phase of training. During this phase, volume should prevail. During the competitive season, the frequency of plyometric training should be reduced to twice weekly, with the intensity of the exercise becoming more important.

8. Dynamic testing of the individual on a regular basis will provide important progression and motivational feedback.

The key element in the execution of proper technique is the eccentric or landing phase. The shock of landing from a jump is not absorbed exclusively by the foot but rather is a combination of the ankle, knee, and hip joints all working together to absorb the shock of landing and then transferring the force.

INTEGRATING PLYOMETRICS INTO THE REHABILITATION PROGRAM: CLINICAL CONCERNS

When used judiciously, plyometrics are a valuable asset in the sports rehabilitation program. As previously stated, the majority of lower-quarter sport function occurs in the closed-kinetic chain. Lower-extremity plyometrics are an effective functional closed-chain exercise that can be incorporated into the sports rehabilitation program. According to Davis's law, soft tissue responds to stress imparted upon it to become more resilient along these same lines of stress. As previously mentioned, through the eccentric prestretch, plyometrics places added stress on the tendinous portion of the contractile unit. Eccentric loading is beneficial in the management of tendinitis.[33] Through a gradually progressed eccentric loading program, healing tendinous tissue is stressed, yielding an increase in ultimate tensile strength. This eccentric load can be applied through jump-downs (Fig. 11-4).

Clinical plyometrics can be categorized according to the loads applied to the healing tissue. These activities include (1) medial/lateral loading, (2) rotational loading, and (3) shock absorption/deceleration loading. In addition, plyometric drills will be divided into (1) in-place activities (activities that can be performed in essentially the same or small amount of space); (2) dynamic distance drills (activities that occur across a given distance); and (3) depth jumping (jumping down from a predetermined height and performing a variety of activities upon landing). Simple jumping drills (bilateral activities) can be progressed to hopping (unilateral activities).

FIGURE 11-4

Jump-down exercises.

Medial–Lateral Loading

Virtually all sporting activities involve cutting maneuvers. Inherent to cutting activities is adequate function in the medial and lateral directions. A plyometric program designed to stress the athlete's ability to accept weight on the involved lower extremity and then perform cutting activities off that leg is imperative. Individuals who have suffered sprains to the medial or lateral capsular and ligamentous complex of the ankle and knee, as well as strains of the hip abductor/adductor and ankle invertor/evertor muscles, are candidates for medial–lateral plyometric loading. Medial–lateral loading drills should be implemented following injury to the medial soft tissue around the knee after a valgus stress. By gradually imparting progressive valgus loads, tissue tensile strength is augmented.[36] In the rehabilitation setting, bilateral support drills can be progressed to unilateral valgus loading efforts. Specifically, lateral jumping drills are progressed to lateral hopping activities. However, the medial structures must also be trained to accept greater valgus loads sustained during cutting activities. As a prerequisite to full-speed cutting, lateral bounding drills should be performed (Fig. 11-5). These efforts are progressed to activities that add acceleration,

FIGURE   1 1 - 5

Lateral bounding drills.

FIGURE   1 1 - 6

Lateral sliding activities.

deceleration, and momentum. Lateral sliding activities that require the individual to cover a greater distance can be performed on a slide board. If a slide board is not available, the same movement pattern can be stressed with plyometrics (Fig. 11-6).

IN-PLACE ACTIVITIES
- Lateral bounding (quick step valgus loading)
- Slide bounds

DYNAMIC DISTANCE DRILLS
- Crossovers

Rotational Loading

Because rotation in the knee is controlled by the cruciate ligaments, menisci, and capsule, plyometric activities with a rotational component are instrumental in the rehabilitation program after injury to any of these structures. As previously discussed, care must be taken not to exceed healing time constraints when using plyometric training.

IN-PLACE ACTIVITIES
- Spin jumps

DYNAMIC DISTANCE DRILLS
- Lateral hopping

Shock Absorption (Deceleration Loading)

Perhaps some of the most physically demanding plyometric activities are shock-absorption activities, which place a tremendous amount of stress upon muscle, tendon, and articular cartilage. Therefore, in the final preparation for a return to sports involving repetitive jumping and hopping, shock-absorption drills should be included in the rehabilitation program.

One way to prepare the athlete for shock absorption drills is to gradually maximize the effects of gravity, such as beginning in a gravity-minimized position and progressing to performance against gravity. Popular activities to minimize gravity include water activities or assisted efforts through unloading.

IN-PLACE ACTIVITIES
- Cycle jumps
- Five-dot drill

DEPTH JUMPING PREPARATION
- Jump downs

The activities listed are a good starting point from which to develop a clinical plyometric program. Manipulations of volume, frequency, and intensity can advance the program appropriately. Proper progression is of prime importance when using plyometrics in the rehabilitation program. These progressive activities are reinjuries waiting to happen if the progression does not allow for adequate healing or development of an adequate strength base. A close working relationship fostering open communication and acute observation skills is vital in helping ensure that the program is not overly aggressive.

SUMMARY

- Although the effects of plyometric training are not yet fully understood, it still remains a widely used form of combining strength with speed training to functionally increase power. Although the research is somewhat contradictory, the neurophysiologic concept of plyometric training is on a sound foundation.
- A successful plyometric training program should be carefully designed and implemented after establishing an adequate strength base.
- The effects of this type of high-intensity training can be achieved safely if the individual is supervised by a knowledgeable person who uses common sense and follows the prescribed training regimen.
- The plyometric training program should use a large variety of different exercises, because year-round training often results in boredom and a lack of motivation.
- Program variety can be manipulated with different types of equipment or kinds of movement performed.
- Continued motivation and an organized progression are the keys to successful training.
- Plyometrics are also a valuable asset in the rehabilitation program after a sport injury.
- Used after lower-quarter injury, plyometrics are effective in facilitating joint awareness, strengthening tissue during the healing process, and increasing sport-specific strength and power.
- The most important considerations in the plyometric program are common sense and experience.

REFERENCES

1. Adams T. An investigation of selected plyometric training exercises on muscular leg strength and power. *Track Field Q Rev* 84:36–40, 1984.
2. Asmussen E, Bonde-Peterson F. Storage of elastic energy in skeletal muscles in man. *Acta Physiol Scand* 91:385, 1974.
3. Bielik E, Chu D, Costello F, et al. Roundtable: 1. Practical considerations for utilizing plyometrics. *Natl Strength Conditioning Assoc J* 8:14, 1986.
4. Bosco C, Komi PV. Muscle elasticity in athletes. In: Komi PV, ed. *Exercise and Sports Biology.* Champaign, IL, Human Kinetics, 1982.
5. Bosco C, Komi PV. Potentiation of the mechanical behavior of the human skeletal muscle through prestretching. *Acta Physiol Scand* 106:467, 1979.
6. Bosco C, Tarkka J, Komi PV. Effect of elastic energy and myoelectric potentiation of triceps surea during stretch-shortening cycle exercise. *Int J Sports Med* 2:137, 1982.
7. Bosco C, Tihanyia J, Komi PV, et al. Store and recoil of elastic energy in slow and fast types of human skeletal muscles. *Acta Physiol Scand* 116:343, 1987.
8. Cavagna GA, Dusman B, Margaria R. Positive work done by a previously stretched muscle. *J Appl Physiol* 24:21, 1968.
9. Cavagna G, Saibene E, Margaria R. Effect of negative work on the amount of positive work performed by an isolated muscle. *J Appl Physiol* 20:157, 1965.
10. Chu D. *Jumping into Plyometrics.* Champaign, IL, Leisure Press, 1992.
11. Chu D. *Conditioning/plyometrics.* Paper presented at 10th annual sports medicine team concept conference. San Francisco. December 1989.
12. Chu D. Plyometric exercise. *Natl Strength Conditioning Assoc J* 6:56, 1984.
13. Chu D, Plummer L. The language of plyometrics. *Natl Strength Conditioning Assoc J* 6:30, 1984.
14. Curwin S, Stannish WD. *Tendinitis: Its Etiology and Treatment.* Lexington, MA, Collamore Press, 1984.
15. Dunsenev CI. Strength training of jumpers. *Track Field Q* 82:4, 1982.
16. Dunsenev CI. Strength training for jumpers. *Soviet Sports Rev* 14:2, 1979.
17. Enoka RM. *Neuromechanical Basis of Kinesiology.* Champaign, IL, Human Kinetics, 1989.
18. Javorek I. Plyometrics. *Natl Strength Conditioning Assoc* 11:52, 1989.
19. Jensen C. Pertinent facts about warming. *Athletic J* 56:72, 1975.
20. Katchajov S, Gomberaze K, Revson A. Rebound jumps. *Modern Athlete Coach* 14:23, 1976.
21. Komi PV. Physiological and biomechanical correlates of muscle function: Effects of muscle structure and stretch-shortening cycle on force and speed. In: Terjung RL, ed. *Exercise and Sports Sciences Review.* Lexington, MA, Collamore Press, 1984.
22. Komi PV, Bosco C. Utilization of stored elastic energy in leg extensor muscles by men and women. *Med Sci Sports Exerc* 10:261, 1978.
23. Komi PV, Buskirk E. Effects of eccentric and concentric muscle conditioning on tension and electrical activity of human muscle. *Ergonomics* 15:417, 1972.
24. Lundon P. A review of plyometric training. *Natl Strength Conditioning Assoc* 7:69, 1985.
25. Rach PJ, Grabiner MD, Gregor RJ, et al. *Kinesiology and Applied Anatomy,* 7th ed. Philadelphia, Lea & Febiger, 1989.
26. Rowinski M. *The Role of Eccentric Exercise.* Shirley, NY, Biodex, Pro Clinica, 1988.
27. Thomas DW. Plyometrics—More than the stretch reflex. *Natl Strength Conditioning Assoc J* 10:49, 1988.
28. Verkhoshanski Y. Are depth jumps useful? *Yesis Rev Soviet Phys Ed Sports* 4:74–79, 1969.
29. Verkhoshanski Y. Perspectives in the improvement of

speed-strength preparation of jumpers. *Yesis Rev Soviet Phys Ed Sports* 4:28–29, 1969.

30. Verkhoshanski Y, Chornonson G. Jump exercises in sprint training. *Track Field Q* 9:1909, 1967.

31. Voight M, Bradley D. Plyometrics. In: Davies GJ, ed. *A Compendium of Isokinetics in Clinical Usage and Rehabilitation Techniques,* 4th ed. Onalaska, WI, S & S, 1994.

32. Voight M, Draovitch P. Plyometrics. In: Albert M, ed. *Eccentric Muscle Training in Sports and Orthopedics.* New York, Churchill Livingstone, 1991.

33. Von Arx F. Power development in the high jump. *Track Technique* 88:2818–2819, 1989.

34. Wilk KE, Voight ML, Keirns MA. Stretch-shortening drills for the upper extremities: Theory and clinical application. *J Orthopaed Sports Phys Ther J* 17:225–239, 1993.

35. Wilt F. Plyometrics—What it is and how it works. *Athletic J* 55b:76, 1975.

36. Woo SL, Inoue M, McGurk-Burleson E, et al. Treatment of the medial collateral ligament injury: Structure and function of canine knees in response to differing treatment regimens. *Am J Sports Med* 15:22–29, 1987.

CHAPTER 12

Open- Versus Closed-Kinetic Chain Exercises in Rehabilitation

William E. Prentice

OBJECTIVES

After completing this chapter, the student therapist should be able to do the following:

- Differentiate between the concepts of the open- and closed-kinetic chains.
- Discuss the advantages and disadvantages of using open- versus closed-kinetic chain exercise.
- Discuss how closed-kinetic chain exercises can be used to regain neuromuscular control.
- Describe the biomechanics of closed-kinetic chain exercise in the lower extremity.
- Discuss how both open- and closed-kinetic chain exercises should be used in rehabilitation of the lower extremity.
- Identify the various closed-kinetic chain exercises for the lower extremity.
- Describe the biomechanics of closed-kinetic chain exercise in the upper extremity.
- Explain how closed-kinetic chain exercises are used in rehabilitation of the upper extremity.
- Describe the various types of closed-kinetic chain exercises for the upper extremity.

In recent years the concept of **closed-kinetic chain exercise** has received considerable attention as a useful and effective rehabilitation technique, particularly for injuries involving the lower extremity.[45] The ankle, knee, and hip joints comprise the kinetic chain for the lower extremity. When the distal segment of the lower extremity is stabilized or fixed, as is the case when the foot is weight-bearing on the ground, the kinetic chain is said to be closed. Conversely, in an **open-kinetic chain,** the distal segment is mobile and is not fixed. Traditionally, rehabilitation strengthening protocols have used open-kinetic chain exercises such as knee flexion and extension on a knee machine.

Although closed-kinetic chain exercises are used more often in rehabilitation of injuries to the lower extremity, they are also useful in rehabilitation protocols for certain upper-extremity activities as well. For the most part, the upper extremity functions in an open-kinetic chain with the hand moving freely. But there are a number of activities in which the upper extremity functions in a closed-kinetic chain.

Despite the recent popularity of closed-kinetic chain exercises, it must be stressed that both open- and closed-kinetic chain exercises have their place in the rehabilitative process. This chapter will attempt to clarify the role of both open- and closed-kinetic chain exercises in that process.

CONCEPT OF THE KINETIC CHAIN

The concept of the kinetic chain was first proposed in the 1970s and was initially referred to as the "link system" by mechanical engineers.[38] In this link system, pin joints connect a series of overlapping, rigid segments (Fig. 12-1). If both ends of the system are connected to an immovable frame, there is no movement of either the proximal or distal ends. In this closed-link system, each moving body segment receives forces from and transfers forces to adjacent body segments, and thus either affects or is affected by the motion of those components.[17] In a closed-link system, movement at one joint produces predictable movement at all other joints.[38] In reality, this type of closed-link system does not exist in either the upper or lower extremities. However, when the distal segment in an extremity (that is, the foot or hand) meets resistance or is fixed, muscle recruitment patterns and joint movements are different than when the distal segment moves freely.[38] Thus two systems, a closed system and an open system, have been proposed.

Whenever the foot or the hand meets resistance or is fixed, as is the case in a closed-kinetic chain, movement of the more proximal segments occurs in a predictable pattern. If the foot or

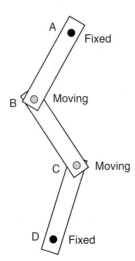

FIGURE 12-1

The link system. If both ends of a link system are fixed, movement at one joint produces predictable movement at all other joints.

hand moves freely in space as in an open-kinetic chain, movements occuring in other segments within the chain are not necessarily predictable.[6]

To a large extent the term "closed-kinetic chain" exercise has come to mean "weight-bearing" exercise. Although all weight-bearing exercises involve some elements of closed-kinetic chain activities, not all closed-kinetic chain activities are weight-bearing.[36]

Muscle Actions in the Kinetic Chain

Muscle actions that occur during open-kinetic chain activities are usually reversed during closed-kinetic chain activities. In open-kinetic chain exercise, the origin is fixed and muscle contraction produces movement at the insertion. Conversely, in closed-kinetic chain exercise, the insertion is fixed and the muscle acts to move the origin. Although this may be important biomechanically, physiologically the muscle can lengthen, shorten, or remain the same length, and thus it makes little difference whether the origin or insertion is moving in terms of the way the muscle contracts.

Concurrent Shift in a Kinetic Chain

The concept of the **concurrent shift** applies to biarticular muscles that have distinctive muscle actions within the kinetic chain during weight-bearing activities. For example, the rectus femoris shortens as the knee flexes and lengthens as the hip extends. Thus the muscle length changes very little even though significant motion is occuring at both the hip and knee. Also, the rectus femoris is exhibiting distinct muscle actions involving simultaneous eccentric contraction at the hip and concentric contraction at the knee. This concurrent shift occurs only during closed-kinetic chain exercises.

The concepts of the reversibility of muscle actions and the concurrent shift are hallmarks of closed-kinetic chain exercises.[36]

OPEN- VERSUS CLOSED-KINETIC CHAIN EXERCISES

Open- and closed-kinetic chain exercises offer distinct advantages and disadvantages in the rehabilitation process. The choice to use one or the other depends on the desired treatment goal. Characteristics of closed-kinetic chain exercises include increased joint compressive forces, increased joint congruency and thus stability, decreased shear forces, decreased acceleration forces, large resistance forces, stimulation of proprioceptors, and enhanced dynamic stability. All of these characteristics are associated with weight-bearing. Characteristics of open-kinetic chain exercises include increased acceleration forces, decreased resistance forces, increased distraction and rotational forces, increased deformation of joint and muscle mechanoreceptors, concentric acceleration and eccentric deceleration forces, and promotion of functional activity. These are characteristics typical of nonweight-bearing activities.[25]

From a biomechanical perspective, it has been suggested that closed-kinetic chain exercises are safer and produce stresses and forces that are potentially less of a threat to healing structures than open-kinetic chain exercises.[35] Coactivation or **co-contraction** of agonist and antagonist muscles must occur during normal movements to provide joint stabilization. Co-contraction, which occurs during closed-kinetic chain exercise, decreases the shear forces acting on the joint, thus protecting healing soft-tissue structures that may otherwise be damaged by open-chain exercises.[17] Additionally, weight-bearing activity increases joint compressive forces, further enhancing joint stability.

It has also been suggested that closed-kinetic chain exercises, particularly those involving the lower extremity, tend to be more functional than open-kinetic chain exercises because they involve weight-bearing activities.[44] The majority of activities performed in daily living, such as walking, climbing, and rising to a standing position, as well as in most sports activities, involve a closed-kinetic chain system. Because the foot is usually in contact with the ground, activities that make use of this closed system are said to be more functional. With the exception of a kicking movement, there is no question that closed-kinetic chain exercises are more sport- or activity-specific, involving exercise that more closely approximates the desired activity.[36]

With open-kinetic chain exercises, motion is usually isolated to a single joint. Open-kinetic chain activities may include exercises to improve strength or range of motion.[19] They may be applied to a single joint manually, as in proprioceptive neuromuscular facilitation or joint mobilization techniques, or through some external resistance using an exercise machine.

Isolation-type exercises typically use a contraction of a specific muscle or group of muscles, which usually produces single-plane and occasionally multiplanar movement. Isokinetic exercise and testing is usually done in an open-kinetic chain and can provide important information relative to the torque production capability of that isolated joint.

When there is some dysfunction associated with injury, the predictable pattern of movement that occurs during closed-kinetic chain activity may not be possible due to pain, swelling, muscle weakness, or limited range of motion. Thus movement compensations result that interfere with normal motion and muscle activity. If only closed-kinetic chain exercise is used, the joints proximal or distal to the injury may not show an existing deficit. Without using open-kinetic chain exercises that isolate specific joint movements, the deficit may go uncorrected, thus interfering with total rehabilitation.[11] The therapist should use the most appropriate open- or closed-kinetic chain exercise for the given situation.

Closed-kinetic chain exercises use varying combinations of isometric, concentric, and eccentric contractions that must occur simultaneously in different muscle groups, creating multiplanar motion at each of the joints within the kinetic chain. Closed-kinetic chain activities require synchronicity of more complex agonist and antagonist muscle actions.[15]

USING CLOSED-KINETIC CHAIN EXERCISES TO REGAIN NEUROMUSCULAR CONTROL

In Chapter 8 it was stressed that proprioception, joint position sense, and kinesthesia are critical to the neuromuscular control of body segments within the kinetic chain. To perform a motor skill, muscular forces, occuring at the correct moment and magnitude, interact to move body parts in a coordinated manner.[33] Coordinated movement is controlled by the central nervous system, which integrates input from joint and muscle mechanoreceptors acting within the kinetic chain. Smooth coordinated movement requires constant integration of receptor, feedback, and control center information.[33]

In the lower extremity, a functional weight-bearing activity requires muscles and joints to work in synchrony and in synergy with one another. For example, taking a single step requires concentric, eccentric, and isometric muscle contractions to produce supination and pronation in the foot; ankle dorsiflexion and plantarflexion; knee flexion, extension, and rotation; and hip flexion, extension, and rotation. Lack of normal motion secondary to injury in one joint will affect the way another joint or segment moves.[33]

To perform this single step in a coordinated manner requires that all of the joints and muscles work together. Thus exercises that act to integrate, rather than isolate, all of these functioning elements would seem to be the most appropriate. Closed-kinetic chain exercises that recruit foot, ankle, knee, and hip muscles in a manner that reproduces normal loading and movement forces in all of the joints within the kinetic chain are similar to functional mechanics and would appear to be most useful.[33]

Quite often, open-kinetic chain exercises are used primarily to develop muscular strength while little attention is given to the importance of including exercises that reestablish proprioception and joint position sense.[1] Closed-kinetic chain activities facilitate the integration of proprioceptive feedback coming from pacinian corpuscles, Ruffini endings, Golgi–Mazzoni corpuscles, Golgi-tendon organs, and Golgi-ligament endings through the functional use of multijoint and multiplanar movements.[6]

BIOMECHANICS OF OPEN- AND CLOSED-KINETIC CHAIN ACTIVITIES IN THE LOWER EXTREMITY

Open- and closed-kinetic chain exercises have different biomechanical effects on the joints of the lower extremity. Walking and running along with the ability to change direction require coordinated joint motion and a complex series of well-timed muscle activations. Biomechanically, shock absorption, foot flexibility, foot stabilization, acceleration and deceleration, multiplanar motion, and joint stabilization must occur in each of the joints in the lower extremity for normal function.[33] Some understanding of how these biomechanical events occur during both open- and closed-kinetic chain activities is essential for the therapist.

Foot and Ankle

The foot's function in the support phase of weight-bearing during gait is twofold. At heel strike, the foot must act as a shock absorber to the impact or ground reaction forces and then adapt to the uneven surfaces. Subsequently, at push-off, the foot functions as a rigid lever to transmit the explosive force from the lower extremity to the ground.[42]

As the foot becomes weight-bearing at heel strike, creating a closed-kinetic chain, the subtalar joint moves into a pronated position in which the talus adducts and plantarflexes while the calcaneus everts. Pronation of the foot unlocks the midtarsal joint and allows the foot to assist in shock absorption. It is important during initial impact to reduce the ground reaction forces and to distribute the load evenly on many different anatomic structures throughout the lower-extremity kinetic chain. As pronation occurs at the subtalar joint, there is obligatory internal rotation of the tibia and slight flexion at the knee. The dorsiflexors contract eccentrically to decelerate plantarflexion. In an open-kinetic chain, when the foot pronates, the talus is stationary while the foot everts, abducts, and dorsiflexes. The muscles that evert the foot appear to be most active.[42]

The foot changes its function from being a shock absorber to a rigid lever system as the foot begins to push off the ground. In weight bearing in a closed-kinetic chain, supination consists of the talus abducting and dorsiflexing on the calcaneus while the calcaneus inverts on the talus. The tibia externally rotates and produces knee extension. During supination, the plantar flexors stabilize the foot, decelerate the tibia, and flex the knee. In an open-kinetic chain, supination consists of the calcaneus inverting as the talus adducts and plantarflexes. The foot moves into adduction and plantarflexion around the stabilized talus.[42]

Knee Joint

It is essential for the therapist to understand forces that occur around the knee joint. Palmitier et al have proposed a biomechanical model of the lower extremity that quantifies two critical forces at the knee joint (Fig. 12-2).[30] A **shear force** occurs in a posterior direction that would cause the tibia to translate anteriorly if not checked by soft-tissue constraints (primarily the anterior cruciate ligament).[7] The second force is a **compressive force** directed along a longitudinal axis of the tibia. Weight-bearing exercises increase joint compression, which enhances joint stability.

In an open-kinetic chain seated knee-joint exercise, as a resistive force is applied to the distal tibia, the shear and compressive forces would be maximized (Fig. 12-3A). When a resistive force is applied more proximally, shear force is significantly

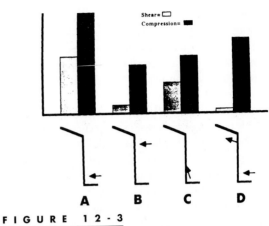

F I G U R E   1 2 - 3

Resistive forces. Resistive forces applied in different positions alter the magnitude of the shear and compressive forces. **A,** Resistive force applied distally. **B,** Resistive force applied proximally. **C,** Resistive force applied axially. **D,** Resistive force applied distally with hamstring co-contraction.

reduced, as is the compressive force (Fig. 12-3B). If the resistive force is applied in a more axial direction, the shear force is also smaller (Fig. 12-3C). If a hamstring co-contraction occurs, the shear force is minimized (Fig. 12-3D).[39]

Closed-kinetic chain exercises induce hamstring contraction by creating a flexion moment at both the hip and knee, with the contracting hamstrings stabilizing the hip and the quadriceps stabilizing the knee. A **moment** is the product of force and distance from the axis of rotation. Also referred to as torque, it describes the turning effect produced when a force is exerted on the body that is pivoted about some fixed point (Fig. 12-4). Co-contraction of the hamstring muscles helps to counteract the tendency of the quadriceps to cause anterior tibial translation. Co-contraction of the hamstrings is most efficient in reducing shear force when the resistive force is directed in an axial orientation relative to the tibia, as is the case in a weight-bearing exercise.[30] Several studies have shown that co-contraction is useful in stabilizing the knee joint and decreasing shear forces.[22,31,37]

The tension in the hamstrings can be further enhanced with slight anterior flexion of the trunk. Trunk flexion moves the center of gravity anteriorly, decreasing the knee flexion moment and thus reducing knee shear force and decreasing patellofemoral compression forces.[29] Closed-kinetic chain exercises try to minimize the flexion moment at the knee while increasing the flexion moment at the hip.

A flexion moment is also created at the ankle when the resistive force is applied to the bottom of the foot. The soleus stabilizes ankle flexion and creates a knee extension moment, which again helps to neutralize anterior shear force (Fig. 12-4). Thus the entire lower-extremity kinetic chain is recruited by applying an axial force at the distal segment.

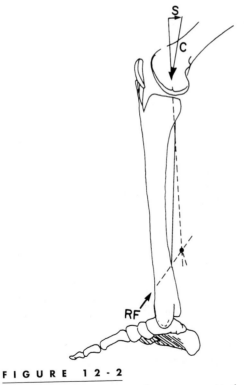

F I G U R E   1 2 - 2

Shear and compressive force vectors. Mathematical model showing shear and compressive force vectors. (RF, resistive force; S, shear; C, compressive.)

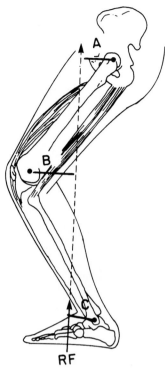

FIGURE 12-4

Closed-kinetic chain exercises. Closed-kinetic chain exercises induce hamstring contraction by creating a flexion moment at **A**, hip; **B**, knee; and **C**, ankle.

In an open-kinetic chain exercise involving seated leg extensions, the resistive force is applied to the distal tibia, creating a flexion moment at the knee only. This negates the effects of a hamstring co-contraction and thus produces maximal shear force at the knee joint. Shear forces created by isometric open-kinetic chain knee flexion and extension at 30 and 60 degrees of knee flexion are greater than with closed-kinetic chain exercises.[26] Decreased anterior tibial displacement during isometric closed-kinetic chain knee flexion at 30 degrees when measured by knee arthrometry has also been demonstrated.[43]

PATELLOFEMORAL JOINT

The effects of open- versus closed-kinetic chain exercises on the patellofemoral joint must also be considered. In open-kinetic chain knee extension exercise, the flexion moment increases as the knee extends from 90 degrees of flexion to full extension, increasing tension in the quadriceps and patellar tendon. Thus the patellofemoral joint reaction forces are increased with peak force occurring at 36 degrees of joint flexion.[13] As the knee moves toward full extension, the patellofemoral contact area decreases, causing increased contact stress per unit area.[3,20]

In closed-kinetic chain exercise, the flexion moment increases as the knee flexes, once again causing increased quadriceps and patellar tendon tension and thus an increase in patellofemoral joint reaction forces. However, the patella has a much

larger surface contact area with the femur, and contact stress is minimized.[3,13,20] Closed-kinetic chain exercises may be better tolerated in the patellofemoral joint because contact stress is minimized.

CLOSED-KINETIC CHAIN EXERCISES FOR REHABILITATION OF LOWER-EXTREMITY INJURIES

For many years, therapists have made use of open-kinetic chain exercises for lower-extremity strengthening. This practice has been due in part to design constraints of existing resistive exercise machines. However, the current popularity of closed-kinetic chain exercises may be attributed primarily to a better understanding of the kinesiology and biomechanics along with the neuromuscular control factors involved in rehabilitation of lower-extremity injuries.

For example, the course of rehabilitation after injury to the anterior cruciate ligament (ACL) has changed drastically in recent years. (Specific rehabilitation protocols will be discussed in detail in Chapter 29.) Technologic advances have created significant improvement in surgical techniques, which has allowed therapists to change their philosophy of rehabilitation. The current literature provides a great deal of support for accelerated rehabilitation programs that recommend the extensive use of closed-kinetic chain exercises.[4,8,12,13,27,35,41,47]

Because of the biomechanical and functional advantages of closed-kinetic chain exercises described earlier, these activities are perhaps best suited to rehabilitation of the ACL. The majority of these studies also indicate that closed-kinetic chain exercises may be safely incorporated into the rehabilitation protocols very early. Some therapists recommend beginning within the first few days after surgery.

SPECIFIC CLOSED-KINETIC CHAIN STRENGTHENING EXERCISES FOR THE LOWER EXTREMITY

In rehabilitation, several different closed-kinetic chain exercises have gained popularity and have been incorporated into rehabilitation protocols.[23] Among those exercises commonly used are the mini-squat, wall slides, lunges, leg press, stair-climbing machines, lateral step-up, terminal knee extension using tubing, and stationary bicycling, slide boards, BAPS boards, and the Fitter.

Mini-Squats, Wall Slides, and Lunges

The mini-squat (Fig. 12-5) or wall slide (Fig. 12-6) involves simultaneous hip and knee extension and is performed in a 0- to 40-degree range.[47] As the hip extends, the rectus femoris

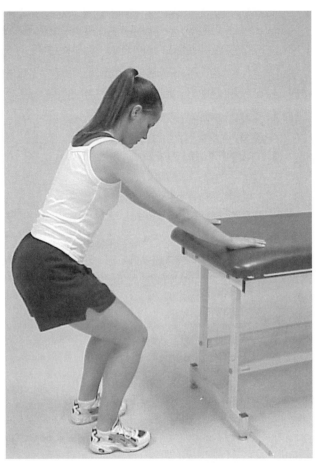

FIGURE 1 2 - 5

Mini-squat performed in 0- to 40-degree range.

FIGURE 1 2 - 6

Standing wall slide.

contracts eccentrically while the hamstrings contract concentrically. Concurrently, as the knee extends, the hamstrings contract eccentrically while the rectus femoris contracts concentrically. Both concentric and eccentric contractions occur simultaneously at either end of both muscles, producing a concurrent shift contraction. This type of contraction is necessary during weight-bearing activities. It will be elicited with all closed-kinetic chain exercise and is impossible with isolation exercises.[38]

These concurrent shift contractions minimize the flexion moment at the knee. The eccentric contraction of the hamstrings helps to neutralize the effects of a concentric quadriceps contraction in producing anterior translation of the tibia. Henning et al found that the half-squat produced significantly less anterior shear at the knee than did an open-chain exercise in full extension.[18] A full squat markedly increases the flexion moment at the knee and thus increases anterior shear of the tibia. As mentioned previously, slightly flexing the trunk anteriorly will also increase the hip flexion moment and decrease the knee moment.

Lunges should be used later in a rehabilitation program to facilitate eccentric strengthening of the quadriceps to act as a decelerator (Fig. 12-7).[46] Like the mini-squat and wall slide, it facilitates co-contraction of the hamstring muscles.

Leg Press

Theoretically the leg press takes full advantage of the kinetic chain and at the same time provides stability, which decreases strain on the low back.[24] It also allows exercise with resistance lower than body weight and the capability of exercising each leg independently (Fig. 12-8).[30] It has been recommended that leg press exercises be performed in a 0- to 60-degree range of knee flexion.[47]

It has also been recommended that leg press machines allow full hip extension to take maximum advantage of the kinetic chain. Full hip extension can only be achieved in a supine position. In this position, full hip and knee flexion and extension can occur, thus reproducing the concurrent shift and ensuring appropriate hamstring recruitment.[30]

The foot plates should also be designed to move in an arc of motion rather than in a straight line. This movement

F I G U R E   1 2 - 7

Lunges are done to strengthen quadriceps eccentrically.

would facilitate hamstring recruitment by increasing the hip flexion moment and decreasing the knee moment. Foot plates should be fixed perpendicular to the frontal plane of the hip to maximize the knee extension moment created by the soleus.

Stair Climbing

Stair-climbing machines have gained a great deal of popularity not only as a closed-kinetic chain exercise device useful in rehabilitation but also as a means of improving cardiorespiratory endurance (Fig. 12-9). Stair-climbing machines have two basic designs: one involves a series of rotating steps similar to a department store escalator; the other uses two foot plates that move up and down to simulate a stepping type movement. With the latter type of stair climber, also sometimes referred to as a stepping machine, the foot never leaves the foot plate, making it a true closed-kinetic chain exercise device.

Stair climbing involves many of the same biomechanical principles identified with the leg press exercise. When exercising on the stair climber, the body should be held erect with only slight trunk flexion, thus maximizing hamstring recruitment

F I G U R E   1 2 - 8

Leg press exercise.

through concurrent shift contractions while increasing the hip flexion moment and decreasing the knee flexion moment.

Exercise on a stepping machine produces increased electromyogram (EMG) activity in the gastrocnemius. Because the gastrocnemius attaches to the posterior aspect of the femoral

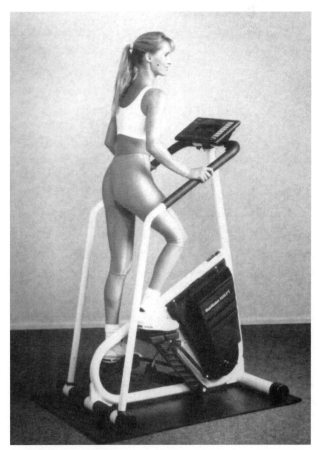

F I G U R E   1 2 - 9

Stairmaster stepping machine.

FIGURE 12-10

Lateral step-ups.

FIGURE 12-11

Terminal knee extensions using surgical tubing resistance.

condyles, increased activity of this muscle could produce a flexion moment of the femur on the tibia. This motion would cause posterior translation of the femur on the tibia, increasing strain on the ACL. Peak firing of the quadriceps may offset the effects of increased EMG activity in the gastrocnemius.[10]

Lateral Step-Ups

Lateral step-ups are another widely used closed-kinetic chain exercise (Fig. 12-10). Lateral step-ups seem to be used more often clinically than do forward step-ups. Step height can be adjusted to patient capabilities and generally progress up to about 8 inches. Heights greater than 8 inches create a large flexion moment at the knee, increasing anterior shear force and making hamstring co-contraction more difficult.[5,10]

Lateral step-ups elicit significantly greater mean quadriceps EMG activity than does a stepping machine. When performing a step-up, the entire body weight must be raised and lowered, while on the stepping machine the center of gravity is maintained at a relatively constant height. The lateral step-up may produce increased muscle and joint shear forces compared to stepping exercise.[10] Caution should be exercised by the therapist in using the lateral step-up in cases where minimizing anterior shear forces is essential. Contraction of the hamstrings appears

to be of insufficient magnitude to neutralize the shear force produced by the quadriceps.[5] In situations where strengthening of the quadriceps is the goal, the lateral step-up has been recommended as a beneficial exercise. However, lateral stepping exercises have failed to increase isokinetic strength of the quadriceps muscle.

Terminal Knee Extensions Using Surgical Tubing

It has been reported in numerous studies that the greatest amount of anterior tibial translation occurs between 0 and 30 degrees of flexion during open-kinetic chain exercise.[14,16,21,28,31,32,47] Avoiding terminal knee extension after surgery became a well-accepted rule among therapists. Unfortunately, this practice led to quadriceps weakness, flexion contracture, and patellofemoral pain.[34]

Closed-kinetic chain terminal knee extensions using surgical tubing resistance have created a means of safely strengthening terminal knee extension (Fig. 12-11). Application of resistance anteriorly at the femur produces anterior shear of the femur, which eliminates any anterior translation of the tibia. This type of exercise performed in the 0- to 30-degree range also minimizes the knee flexion moment, further reducing anterior

FIGURE   12-12

Stationary bicycling.

FIGURE   12-13

BAPS board exercise.

shear of the tibia. The use of rubber tubing produces an eccentric contraction of the quadriceps when moving into knee flexion.

Stationary Bicycling

The stationary bicycle has been routinely used in rehabilitation, primarily for conditioning purposes when the injured patient cannot engage in running activities (Fig. 12-12). However, it also can be of significant value as a closed-kinetic chain exercise device.

The advantage of stationary bicycling over other closed-kinetic chain exercises for rehabilitation is that the amount of the weight-bearing force exerted by the injured lower extremity can be adapted within patient limitations. The seat height should be carefully adjusted to minimize the knee flexion moment on the downstroke. However, if the stationary bike is being used to regain range of motion in flexion, the seat height should be adjusted to a lowered position using passive motion of the injured extremity. Toe clips will facilitate hamstring contractions on the upstroke.

BAPS Board and Mini-Tramp

The BAPS board (Fig. 12-13) and mini-tramp (Fig. 12-14) both provide an unstable base of support, which helps to facilitate reestablishing proprioception and joint position sense in addition to strengthening. Working on the BAPS board allows the therapist to provide stress to the lower extremity in a progressive and controlled manner.[6] It allows the patient to work simultaneously on strengthening and range of motion, while trying to regain neuromuscular control and balance.

The mini-tramp may be used to accomplish the same goals but can also be used for more advanced plyometric training.

Slide Boards and Fitter

Shifting the body weight from side to side during a more functional activity on either a slide board (Fig. 12-15) or a Fitter (Fig. 12-16) helps to reestablish dynamic control as well as improve cardiorespiratory fitness.[6] These motions produce valgus and varus stresses and strains to the joint, which are somewhat unique to these two pieces of equipment.

FIGURE 1 2 - 1 5

Slide board training.

FIGURE 1 2 - 1 4

Mini-tramp provides an unstable base of support to which other functional plyometric activities may be added.

BIOMECHANICS OF OPEN- AND CLOSED-KINETIC CHAIN ACTIVITIES IN THE UPPER EXTREMITY

Although it is true that closed-kinetic chain exercises are most often used in rehabilitation of lower-extremity injuries, there are many injury situations where closed-kinetic chain exercises should be incorporated into upper-extremity rehabilitation protocols. Unlike the lower extremity, the upper extremity is most functional as an open-kinetic chain system. Most activities involve movement of the upper extremity in which the hand moves freely. In these movements, the proximal segments of the kinetic chain are used for stabilization while the distal segments have a high degree of mobility.

Push-ups or chinning exercises are examples of closed-kinetic chain activities in the upper extremity. In these cases, the hand is stabilized, and muscular contractions around the more proximal segments, the elbow and shoulder, function to raise and lower the body. Still other activities, such as swimming and

FIGURE 1 2 - 1 6

The Fitter is useful for weight shifting.

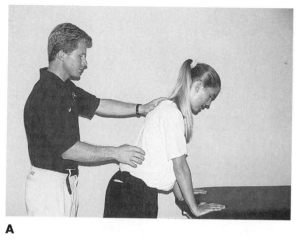

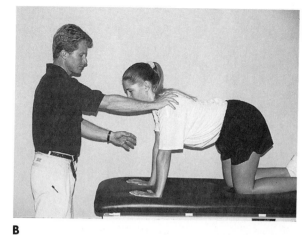

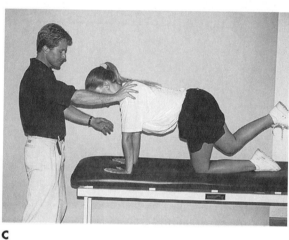

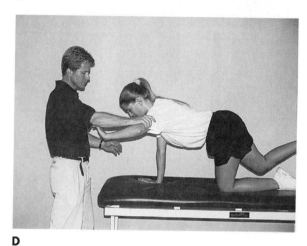

FIGURE 12-17

Weight shifting **A,** Standing. **B,** Quadruped. **C,** Tripod. **D,** Opposite knee and arm.

cross-country skiing, involve rapid successions of alternating open- and closed-kinetic chain movements in much the same way that running does in the lower extremity.[48]

For the most part in rehabilitation, closed-kinetic chain exercises are used primarily for strengthening and establishing neuromuscular control of those muscles that act to stabilize the shoulder girdle. In particular the scapular stabilizers and the rotator cuff muscles function at one time or another to control movements about the shoulder. It is essential to develop both strength and neuromuscular control in these muscle groups, thus allowing them to provide a stable base for more mobile and dynamic movements that occur in the distal segments.

Shoulder Joint Complex

Closed-kinetic chain weight-bearing activities can be used to both promote and enhance dynamic joint stability. Most often closed-kinetic chain exercises are used with the hand fixed and thus no motion occuring. The resistance is then applied either axially or rotationally. These exercises produce both joint com-

pression and approximation, which act to enhance muscular co-contraction about the joint, producing dynamic stability.[48]

Two essential force couples must be reestablished around the glenohumeral joint: the anterior deltoid along with the infraspinatus and teres minor in the frontal plane, and the subscapularis counterbalanced by the infraspinatus and teres minor in the transverse plane. These opposing muscles act to stabilize the glenohumeral joint by compressing the humeral head within the glenoid via muscular co-contraction.

The scapular muscles function to dynamically position the glenoid relative to the position of the moving humerus, resulting in a normal scapulohumeral rhythm of movement. However, they must also provide a stable base on which the highly mobile humerus can function. If the scapula is hypermobile, the function of the entire upper extremity will be impaired. Thus force couples between the inferior trapezius counterbalanced by the upper trapezius and levator scapula, and the rhomboids and middle trapezius counterbalanced by the serratus anterior, are critical in maintaining scapular stability. Again, closed-kinetic chain activities done with the hand fixed should be used to enhance scapular stability.

FIGURE 12-18

A, BAPS board. **B,** wobble board. **C,** KAT system. **D,** plyoball.

Elbow

The elbow is a hinged joint that is capable of 145 degrees of flexion from a fully extended position. In some cases of joint hyperelasticity, the joint may hyperextend a few degrees beyond neutral. The elbow consists of the humeroulnar, humeroradial, and radioulnar articulations. The concave radial head articulates with the convex surface of the capitellum of the distal humerus and is connected to the proximal ulna via the annular ligament. The proximal radioulnar joint constitutes the forearm, which when working in conjunction with the elbow joint permits approximately 90 degrees of pronation and 80 degrees of supination. Depending on the activity, the elbow must perform several functions in an open-kinetic chain.

OPEN- AND CLOSED-KINETIC CHAIN EXERCISES FOR REHABILITATION OF UPPER-EXTREMITY INJURIES

Most typically, closed-kinetic chain glenohumeral joint exercises are used during the early phases of a rehabilitation pro-

gram, particularly in the case of an unstable shoulder, to promote co-contraction and muscle recruitment in addition to preventing shutdown of the rotator cuff secondary to pain or inflammation.[2] Likewise, closed-kinetic chain exercise should be used during the late phases of a rehabilitation program to promote muscular endurance of muscles surrounding the glenohumeral and scapulothoracic joints. They may also be used during the later stages of rehabilitation in conjunction with open-kinetic chain activities to enhance some degree of stability, on which highly dynamic and ballistic motions may be superimposed. At some point during the middle stages of the rehabilitation program, traditional open-kinetic chain strengthening exercises for the rotator cuff, deltoid, and other glenohumeral and scapular muscles must be incorporated.[19,48]

In the elbow, exercises should also be designed to enhance muscular balance and neuromuscular control of the surrounding agonists and antagonists. Closed-kinetic chain exercise should be used to improve dynamic stability of the more proximal muscles surrounding the elbow in those activities where the elbow must provide some degree of proximal stability. Open-kinetic chain exercises for strengthening flexion, extension, pronation, and supination are essential to regain

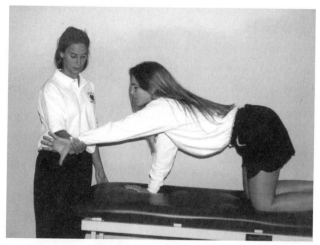

F I G U R E   1 2 - 1 9

D2 pattern in a tripod to produce stabilization in the contralateral support limb.

F I G U R E   1 2 - 2 1

Push-ups done on a plyoball.

high-velocity dynamic movements of the elbow necessary in throwing-type activities.

Weight Shifting

A variety of weight-shifting exercises can be done to assist in facilitating glenohumeral and scapulothoracic dynamic stability through the use of axial compression.[9] Weight shifting may be done in standing, quadruped, tripod, or biped (opposite leg and arm) positions, with weight supported on a stable surface such as the wall or a treatment table (Fig. 12-17) or on a moveable, unstable surface such as a BAPS board, wobble board, KAT system, or plyoball (Fig. 12-18). Shifting may be done side to side, forward and backward, or on a diagonal. Hand position may be adjusted from a wide base of support to one hand placed on top of the other to increase difficulty. The patient can adjust the amount of weight being supported as tolerated. The therapist can provide manual force or resistance in a random manner to

which the patient must rhythmically stabilize and adapt. A D2 PNF pattern may be used in a tripod to force the contralateral support limb to produce a co-contraction and thus stabilization (Fig. 12-19).[48] Rhythmic stabilization can also be used to regain neuromuscular control of the scapular muscles with the hand in a closed-kinetic chain and random pressure applied to the scapular borders (Fig. 12-20).

Push-ups, Push-ups-With-a-Plus, Press-ups, Step-Ups

Push-ups and/or press-ups are also done to reestablish neuromuscular control. Push-ups done on an unstable suface, such as on a plyoball, require a good deal of strength in addition to providing an axial load that requires co-contraction of agonist and antagonist force couples around the glenohumeral and scapulothoracic joints while the distal part of the extremity has some limited movement (Fig. 12-21). A variation of a standard push-up would be to have the patient use reciprocating contractions on a stair climber (Fig. 12-22) or do single-arm lateral set-ups

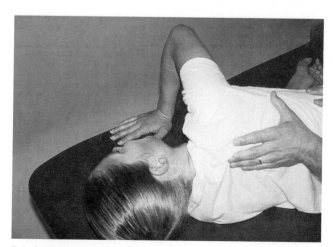

F I G U R E   1 2 - 2 0

Rhythmic stabilization for the scapular muscles.

F I G U R E   1 2 - 2 2

Push-ups done on a stair climber.

F I G U R E   1 2 - 2 3

Single-arm lateral step-ups.

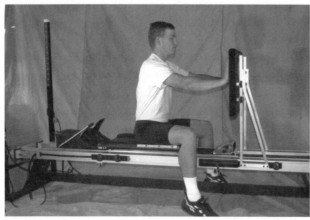

F I G U R E   1 2 - 2 4

Push-ups may be done in a variety of positions on a Shuttle 2000.

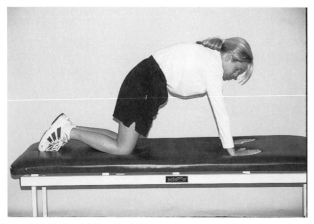

F I G U R E   1 2 - 2 5

Push-ups with a plus.

F I G U R E   1 2 - 2 6

Press-ups.

onto a step (Fig. 12-23). Also, the patient may perform push-ups in a variety of positions including the overhead position on the Shuttle 2000 (Fig. 12-24).[40] Push-ups-with-a-plus are done to strengthen the serratus anterior, which is critical for scapular dynamic stability in overhead activities (Fig. 12-25). Press-ups invole an isometric contraction of the glenohumeral stabilizers (Fig. 12-26).

Slide Board

Upper-extremity closed-kinetic chain exercises performed on a slide board are useful not only for promoting strength and stability but also for improving muscular endurance.[40,48] With the patient in a kneeling position, use a reciprocating motion sliding the hands forward and backward, side to side, in a "wax on–wax off" circular pattern, or both hands laterally (Fig. 12-27). It is also possible to do wall slides in a standing position.

Isokinetic Closed-Kinetic Chain Exercise

Biodex manufactures an attachment for existing equipment that will allow for isokinetic conditioning and testing of the lower extremity in a closed-kinetic chain seated position (Fig. 12-28).

FIGURE 12-27
Slide board strengthening exercise.

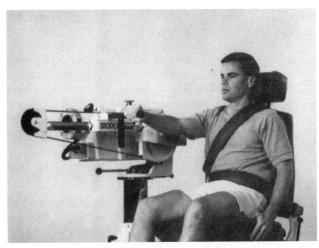

FIGURE 12-28
Biodex upper-extremity closed-kinetic chain exercise system.

Data on reliability, validity, and effectiveness of the particular piece of equipment are not yet available.

SUMMARY

- A closed-kinetic chain exercise is one in which the distal segment of the extremity is fixed or stabilized. In an open-kinetic chain, the distal segment is mobile and is not fixed.
- Both open- and closed-kinetic chain exercises have their place in the rehabilitative process.
- The concepts of the reversibility of muscle actions and the concurrent shift are hallmarks of closed-kinetic chain exercises.
- Open- and closed-kinetic chain exercises offer distinct advantages and disadvantages in the rehabilitation process. The choice to use one or the other depends on the desired treatment goal.
- It has been suggested that closed-kinetic chain exercises are safer due to muscle co-contraction and joint compression; that closed-kinetic chain exercises tend to be more functional; and that they more effectively facilitate the integration of proprioceptive and joint position sense feedback than open-kinetic chain exercises.
- Open- and closed-kinetic chain exercises have different biomechanical effects on the joints of the lower extremity.
- Closed-kinetic chain exercises in the lower extremity decrease the shear forces, reducing anterior tibial translation, and increase the compressive forces, which increases stability around the knee joint.
- Mini-squat, wall slides, lunges, leg press, stair-climbing machines, lateral step-up, terminal knee extension using tubing, stationary bicycling, slide boards, BAPS boards, and the Fitter are all examples of closed-kinetic chain activities for the lower extremity.
- Although it is true that closed-kinetic chain exercises are most often used in rehabilitation of lower-extremity injuries, there are many injury situations where closed-kinetic chain exercises should be incorporated into upper-extremity rehabilitation protocols.
- Closed-kinetic chain exercises in the upper extremity are used primarily for strengthening and establishing neuromuscular control of those muscles that act to stabilize the shoulder girdle.
- Closed-kinetic chain activities, such as push-ups, press-ups, weight shifting, and slide board exercises, are strengthening exercises used primarily for improving shoulder stabilization in the upper extremity.

REFERENCES

1. Andersen S, Terwilliger D, Denegar C. Comparison of open versus closed kinetic chain test postions for

measuring joint position sense. *J Sports Rehab* 4:165–171, 1995.

2. Andrews J, Dennison J, Wilk K. The significance of closed chain kinetics in upper extremity injuries from a physician's perspective. *J Sports Rehab* 5:64–70, 1995.

3. Baratta R, Solomonow M, Zhou B. Muscular coactivation: The role of the antagonist musculature in maintaining knee stability. *Am J Sports Med* 16:113–122, 1988.

4. Blair D, Willis R. Rapid rehabilitation following anterior cruciate ligament reconstruction. *J Athl Train* 26:32–43, 1991.

5. Brask B, Lueke R, Soderberg G. Electromyographic analysis of selected muscles during the lateral step-up. *Phys Ther* 64:324–329, 1984.

6. Bunton E, Pitney W, Kane A. The role of limb torque, muscle action and proprioception during closed kinetic chain rehabilitation of the lower extremity. *J Athl Train* 28:10–20, 1993.

7. Butler D, Noyes F, Grood E. Ligamentous restraints to anterior-posterior drawer in the human knee: A biomechanical study. *J Bone Joint Surg* 62A:259–270, 1980.

8. Case J, DePalma B, Zelko R. Knee rehabilitation following anterior cruciate ligament repair/reconstruction: An update. *J Athl Train* 26:22–31, 1991.

9. Cipriani D. Open and closed chain rehabilitation for the shoulder complex. In: Andrews J, Wilk K, eds. *The Patient's Shoulder*. New York, Churchill-Livingston, 1994.

10. Cook T, Zimmerman C, Lux K, et al. EMG comparison of lateral step-up and stepping machine exercise. *J Orthop Sports Phys Ther* 16:108–113, 1992.

11. Davies G. The need for critical thinking in rehabilitation. *J Sports Rehab* 4:1–22, 1995.

12. DeCarlo M, Shelbourne D, McCarroll J, et al. A traditional vs. accelerated rehabilitation following ACL reconstruction: A one-year follow-up. *J Orthop Sports Phys Ther* 15:309–316, 1992.

13. Fu F, Woo S, Irrgang J. Current concepts for rehabilitation following anterior cruciate ligament reconstruction. *J Orthop Sports Phys Ther* 15:270–278, 1992.

14. Fukubayashi T, Torzilli P, Sherman M. An in-vitro biomechanical evaluation of anterior/posterior motion of the knee. Tibial displacement, rotation, and torque. *J Bone Joint Surg* 64B:258–264, 1982.

15. Grahm V, Gehlsen G, Edwards J. Electromyographic evaluation of closed and open kinetic chain knee rehabilitation exercises. *J Athl Train* 28:23–33, 1993.

16. Grood E, Suntag W, Noyes F, et al. Biomechanics of knee extension exercise. *J Bone Joint Surg* 66A:725–733, 1984.

17. Harter R. Clinical rationale for closed kinetic chain activities in functional testing and rehabilitation of ankle pathologies. *J Sports Rehab* 5:13–24, 1995.

18. Henning S, Lench M, Glick K. An in-vivo strain gauge study of elongation of the anterior cruciate ligament. *Am J Sports Med* 13:22–26, 1985.

19. Hillman S. Principles and techniques of open kinetic chain rehabilitation: The upper extremity. *J Sports Rehab* 3:319–330, 1994.

20. Hungerford D, Barry M. Biomechanics of the patellofemoral joint. *Clin Orthop* 144:9–15, 1979.

21. Jurist K, Otis V. Anteroposterior tibiofemoral displacements during isometric extension efforts. The roles of external load and knee flexion angle. *Am J Sports Med* 13:254–258, 1985.

22. Kaland S, Sinkjaer T, Arendt-Neilsen L, et al. Altered timing of hamstring muscle action in anterior cruciate ligament deficient patients. *Am J Sports Med* 18:245–248, 1990.

23. Kleiner D, Drudge T, Ricard M. An electromyographic comparison of popular open and closed kinetic chain knee rehabilitation exercises. *J Athl Train* 29:156–157, 1994.

24. LaFree J, Mozingo A, Worrell T. Comparison of open kinetic chain knee and hip extension to closed kinetic chain leg press performance. *J Sports Rehab* 3:99–107, 1995.

25. Lepart S, Henry T. The physiological basis for open and closed kinetic chain rehabilitation for the upper extremity. *J Sports Rehab* 5:71–87, 1995.

26. Lutz G, Stuart M, Franklin H. Rehabilitative techniques for patients after reconstruction of the anterior cruciate ligament. *Mayo Clin Proc* 65:1322–1329, 1990.

27. Malone T, Garrett W. Commentary and historical perspective of anterior cruciate ligament rehabilitation. *J Orthop Sports Phys Ther* 15:265–269, 1992.

28. Nisell R, Ericson M, Nemeth G, et al. Tibiofemoral joint forces during isokinetic knee extension. *Am J Sports Med* 17:49–54, 1989.

29. Ohkoshi Y, Yasuda K, Kaneda K, et al. Biomechanical analysis of rehabilitation in the standing position. *Am J Sports Med* 19:605–611, 1991.

30. Palmitier R, Kai-Nan A, Scott S, et al. Kinetic chain exercise in knee rehabilitation. *Sports Med* 11:402–413, 1991.

31. Renstrom P, Arms S, Stanwyck T, et al. Strain within the anterior cruciate ligament during hamstring and quadriceps activity. *Am J Sports Med* 14:83–87, 1986.

32. Reynolds N, Worrell T, Perrin D. Effect of lateral step-up exercise protocol on quadriceps isokinetic peak torque values and thigh girth. *J Orthop Sports Phys Ther* 15:151, 1992.

33. Rivera J. Open versus closed kinetic chain rehabilitation of the lower extremity: A functional and biomechanical analysis. *J Sports Rehab* 3:154–167, 1994.

34. Sachs R, Daniel D, Stone M, et al. Patellofemoral problems after anterior cruciate ligament reconstruction. *Am J Sports Med* 17:760–765, 1989.

35. Shellbourne D, Nitz P. Accelerated rehabilitation after anterior cruciate ligament reconstruction. *Am J Sports Med* 18:292–299, 1990.

36. Snyder-Mackler L. Scientific rationale and physiological

basis for the use of closed kinetic chain exercise in the lower extremity. *J Sports Rehab* 5:2–12, 1995.

37. Solomonow M, Baratta R, Zhou B, et al. The synergistic action of the anterior cruciate ligament and thigh muscles in maintaining joint stability. *Am J Sports Med* 15:207–213, 1987.

38. Steindler A. *Kinesiology of the Human Body Under Normal and Pathological Conditions.* Springfield, IL, Thomas, 1977.

39. Stiene H, Brosky T, Reinking M. A comparison of closed kinetic chain and isokinetic joint isolation exercise in patients with patellofemoral dysfunction. *J Orthop Sports Phys Ther* 24:136–141, 1996.

40. Stone J, Lueken J, Partin N. Closed kinetic chain rehabilitation of the glenohumeral joint. *J Athl Train* 28:34–37, 1993.

41. Tovin B, Tovin T, Tovin M. Surgical and biomechanical considerations in rehabilitation of patients with intra-articular ACL reconstructions. *J Orthop Sports Phys Ther* 15:317–322, 1992.

42. Valmassey R. *Clinical Biomechanics of the Lower Extremities.* St. Louis, Mosby, 1996.

43. Voight M, Bell S, Rhodes D. Instrumented testing of tibial translation during a positive Lachman's test and selected closed chain activities in anterior cruciate deficient knees. *J Orthop Sports Phys Ther* 15:49, 1992.

44. Voight M, Cook G. Clinical application of closed chain exercise. *J Sports Rehab* 5:25–44, 1995.

45. Voight M, Tippett S. Closed-kinetic chain. Presented at 41st annual clinical symposium of the National Athletic Trainers Association, Indianapolis, June 1990.

46. Wawrzyniak J, Tracy J, Catizone P. Effect of closed chain exercise on quadriceps femoris peak torque and functional performance. *J Athl Train* 31:335–345, 1996.

47. Wilk K, Andrews J. Current concepts in the treatment of anterior cruciate ligament disruption. *J Orthop Sports Phys Ther* 15:279–293, 1992.

48. Wilk K, Arrigo C, Andrews J. Closed and open kinetic chain exercise for the upper extremity. *J Sports Rehab* 5:88–102, 1995.

C H A P T E R   1 3

Proprioceptive Neuromuscular Facilitation Techniques in Rehabilitation

William E. Prentice

O B J E C T I V E S

After completing this chapter, the student therapist should be able to do the following:

- Explain the neurophysiologic basis of PNF techniques.
- Discuss the rationale for use of the techniques.
- Discuss the basic principles of using PNF in rehabilitation.
- Identify the various PNF strengthening and stretching techniques.
- Describe PNF patterns for the upper and lower extremity, for the upper and lower trunk, and for the neck.

Proprioceptive neuromuscular facilitation (PNF) is an approach to therapeutic exercise based on the principles of functional human anatomy and neurophysiology. It uses proprioceptive, cutaneous, and auditory input to produce functional improvement in motor output, and can be a vital element in the rehabilitation process of many sports-related injuries. These techniques have long been recommended for increasing strength, flexibility, and range of motion.[7,10,13,18,19,26] It is apparent that PNF techniques are also useful for enhancing neuromuscular control.[25] This discussion should guide the therapist using the principles and techniques of PNF as a component of a rehabilitation program.

NEUROPHYSIOLOGIC BASIS OF PNF

The therapeutic techniques of PNF were first used in the treatment of patients with paralysis and neuromuscular disorders. Most of the principles underlying modern therapeutic exercise techniques can be attributed to the work of Sherrington,[23] who first defined the concepts of facilitation and inhibition.

An impulse traveling down the corticospinal tract, or an afferent impulse traveling up from peripheral receptors in the muscle, causes an impulse volley, which results in the discharge of a limited number of specific motor neurons as well as the discharge of additional surrounding (anatomically close) motor neurons in the subliminal fringe area. An impulse causing the recruitment and discharge of additional motor neurons within the subliminal fringe is said to be facilitatory. Conversely, any stimulus that causes motor neurons to drop out of the discharge zone and away from the subliminal fringe is said to be inhibitory.[12] Facilitation results in increased excitability, and inhibition results in decreased excitability of motor neurons.[28] Thus the function of weak muscles would be aided by facilitation, and muscle spasticity would be decreased by inhibition.[9]

Sherrington attributed the impulses transmitted from the peripheral stretch receptors via the afferent system as being the strongest influence on the alpha motor neurons.[23] Therefore the therapist should be able to modify the input from the peripheral receptors and thus influence the excitability of the alpha motor neurons. The discharge of motor neurons can be facilitated by peripheral stimulation, which causes afferent impulses to make contact with excitatory neurons and results in increased muscle tone or strength of voluntary contraction. Motor neurons can also be inhibited by peripheral stimulation, which causes afferent impulses to make contact with inhibitory neurons, thus resulting in muscle relaxation and allowing for stretching of the muscle.[23] To indicate any technique in which input from peripheral receptors is used to facilitate or inhibit, PNF should be used.[9]

The principles and techniques of PNF described here are based primarily on the neurophysiologic mechanisms involving the stretch reflex. The stretch reflex involves two types of

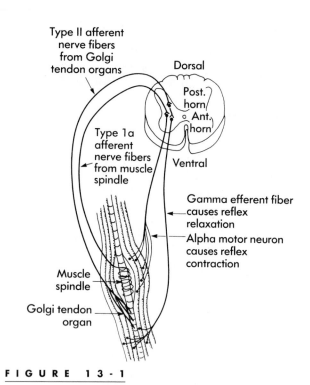

FIGURE   13-1

Diagrammatical representation of the stretch reflex. (Reproduced, with permission, from Prentice WE. *Therapeutic Modalities for Allied Health Professionals.* New York, McGraw-Hill, 1998.)

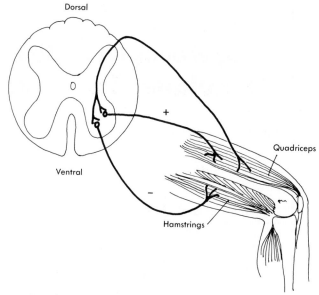

FIGURE   13-2

Diagrammatical representation of reciprocal inhibition. (Reproduced, with permission, from Prentice WE. *Therapeutic Modalities for Allied Health Professionals.* New York, McGraw-Hill, 1998.)

receptors: (1) muscle spindles that are sensitive to a change in length, as well as the rate of change in length of the muscle fiber; and (2) Golgi tendon organs that detect changes in tension (Fig. 13-1).

Stretching a given muscle causes an increase in the frequency of impulses transmitted to the spinal cord from the muscle spindle, which in turn produces an increase in the frequency of motor nerve impulses returning to that same muscle, thus reflexively resisting the stretch. However, the development of excessive tension within the muscle activates the Golgi tendon organs, whose sensory impulses are carried back to the spinal cord. These impulses have an inhibitory effect on the motor impulses returning to the muscles and thus cause that muscle to relax.

Two neurophysiologic phenomena help to explain facilitation and inhibition of the neuromuscular systems. The first is known as autogenic inhibition and is defined as inhibition that is mediated by afferent fibers from a stretched muscle acting on the alpha motor neurons supplying that muscle, thus causing it to relax. When a muscle is stretched, motor neurons supplying that muscle receive both excitatory and inhibitory impulses from the receptors. If the stretch is continued for a slightly extended period of time, the inhibitory signals from the Golgi tendon organs eventually override the excitatory impulses and therefore cause relaxation. Because inhibitory motor neurons receive impulses from the Golgi tendon organs while

the muscle spindle creates an initial reflex excitation leading to contraction, the Golgi tendon organs apparently send inhibitory impulses that last for the duration of increased tension (resulting from either passive stretch or active contraction) and eventually dominate the weaker impulses from the muscle spindle. This inhibition seems to protect the muscle against injury from reflex contractions resulting from excessive stretch.

A second mechanism known as reciprocal inhibition deals with the relationships of the agonist and antagonist muscles (Fig. 13-2). The muscles that contract to produce joint motion are referred to as agonists, and the resulting movement is called an agonistic pattern. The muscles that stretch to allow the agonist pattern to occur are referred to as antagonists. Movement that occurs directly opposite to the agonist pattern is called the antagonist pattern.

When motor neurons of the agonist muscle receive excitatory impulses from afferent nerves, the motor neurons that supply the antagonist muscles are inhibited by afferent impulses.[2] Thus contraction or extended stretch of the agonist muscle must elicit relaxation or inhibit the antagonist. Likewise, a quick stretch of the antagonist muscle facilitates a contraction of the agonist. For facilitating or inhibiting motion, PNF relies heavily on the actions of these agonist and antagonist muscle groups.

A final point of clarification should be made regarding autogenic and reciprocal inhibition. The motor neurons of the spinal cord always receive a combination of inhibitory and excitatory impulses from the afferent nerves. Whether these motor neurons will be excited or inhibited depends on the ratio of these incoming impulses.

Several different approaches to therapeutic exercise based on the principles of facilitation and inhibition have been proposed. Among these are the Bobath method,[3] Brunnstrom method,[4] Rood method,[21] and Knott and Voss method.[11] Although each of these techniques is important and useful, the approach of Knott and Voss, which they called proprioceptive neuromuscular facilitation, probably makes the most explicit use of proprioceptive stimulation.[11]

RATIONALE FOR USE

As a positive approach to injury rehabilitation, PNF is aimed at what the patient can do physically within the limitations of the injury. It is perhaps best used to decrease deficiencies in strength, flexibility, and coordination in response to demands that are placed on the neuromuscular system. The emphasis is on selective reeducation of individual motor elements through development of neuromuscular control, joint stability, and coordinated mobility. Each movement is learned and then reinforced through repetition in an appropriately demanding and intense rehabilitative program.[22]

The body tends to respond to the demands placed on it. The principles of PNF attempt to provide a maximal response for increasing strength, flexibility, and coordination. These principles should be applied with consideration of their appropriateness in achieving a particular goal. That continued activity during a rehabilitation program is essential for maintaining or improving strength or flexibility is well accepted. Therefore an intense program should offer the greatest potential for recovery.

The PNF approach is holistic, integrating sensory, motor, and psychological aspects of a rehabilitation program. It incorporates reflex activities from the spinal levels and upward, either inhibiting or facilitating them as appropriate.

The brain recognizes only gross joint movement and not individual muscle action. Moreover, the strength of a muscle contraction is directly proportional to the activated motor units. Therefore to increase the strength of a muscle, the maximum number of motor units must be stimulated to strengthen the remaining muscle fibers.[10,11] This "irradiation," or overflow effect, can occur when the stronger muscle groups help the weaker groups in completing a particular movement. This cooperation leads to the rehabilitation goal of return to optimal function.[2,11] The following principles of PNF should be applied to reach that ultimate goal.

BASIC PRINCIPLES

Knott and Voss, in their text on PNF,[11] emphasized the importance of the principles rather than specific techniques in a rehabilitation program. These principles are the basis of PNF that must be superimposed on any specific technique. The prin-

ciples of PNF are based on sound neurophysiologic and kinesiologic principles and clinical experience.[22] Application of the following principles may assist in promoting a desired response in the patient being treated.

1. The patient must be taught the PNF patterns regarding the sequential movements from starting position to terminal position. The therapist has to keep instructions brief and simple. It is sometimes helpful for the therapist to passively move the patient through the desired movement pattern to demonstrate precisely what is to be done. The patterns should be used along with the techniques to increase the effects of the treatment.

2. When learning the patterns, the patient is often helped by looking at the moving limb. This visual stimulus offers the patient feedback for directional and positional control.

3. Verbal cues are used to coordinate voluntary effort with reflex responses. Commands should be firm and simple. Commands most commonly used with PNF techniques are "push" and "pull," which ask for an isotonic contraction; "hold," which asks for an isometric or stabilizing contraction; and "relax."

4. Manual contact with appropriate pressure is essential for influencing direction of motion and facilitating a maximal response because reflex responses are greatly affected by pressure receptors. Manual contact should be firm and confident to give the patient a feeling of security. The manner in which the therapist touches the patient influences patient confidence as well as the appropriateness of the motor response or relaxation.[22] A movement response may be facilitated by the hand over the muscle being contracted to facilitate a movement or a stabilizing contraction.

5. Proper mechanics and body positioning of the therapist are essential in applying pressure and resistance. The therapist should stand in a position that is in line with the direction of movement in the diagonal movement pattern. The knees should be bent and close to the patient such that the direction of resistance can easily be applied or altered appropriately throughout the range.

6. The amount of resistance given should facilitate a maximal response that allows smooth, coordinated motion. The appropriate resistance depends to a large extent on the capabilities of the patient. It may also change at different points throughout the range of motion. Maximal resistance may be used with those techniques that use isometric contractions to restrict motion to a specific point; it may also be used in isotonic contractions throughout a full range of movement.

7. Rotational movement is a critical component in all of the PNF patterns, because maximal contraction is impossible without it.

8. Normal timing is the sequence of muscle contraction that occurs in any normal motor activity resulting in coordinated movement.[11] The distal movements of the

patterns should occur first. The distal movement components should be completed by no later than halfway through the total PNF pattern. To accomplish this, appropriate verbal commands should be timed with manual commands. Normal timing may be used with maximal resistance or without resistance from the therapist.

9. Timing for emphasis is used primarily with isotonic contractions. This principle superimposes maximal resistance, at specific points in the range, upon the patterns of facilitation, allowing overflow or irradiation to the weaker components of a movement pattern. Thus the stronger components are emphasized to facilitate the weaker components of a movement pattern.

10. Specific joints may be facilitated by using traction or approximation. Traction spreads apart the joint articulations, and approximation presses them together. Both techniques stimulate the joint proprioceptors. Traction increases the muscular response, promotes movement, assists isotonic contractions, and is used with most flexion antigravity movements. Traction must be maintained throughout the pattern. Approximation increases the muscular response, promotes stability, assists isometric contractions, and is used most with extension (gravity-assisted) movements. Approximation may be quick or gradual and may be repeated during a pattern.

11. Giving a quick stretch to the muscle before muscle contraction facilitates a muscle to respond with greater force through the mechanisms of the stretch reflex. It is most effective if all the components of a movement are stretched simultaneously. However, this quick stretch may be contraindicated in many orthopedic conditions because the extensibility limits of a damaged musculotendinous unit or joint structure may be exceeded, thus exacerbating the injury.

TECHNIQUES

Each of the principles just described should be applied to the specific techniques of PNF. These techniques may be used in a rehabilitation program either to strengthen or facilitate a particular agonistic muscle group or to stretch or inhibit the antagonistic group. The choice of a specific technique depends on the deficits of a particular patient. Specific techniques or combinations of techniques should be selected on the basis of the patient's problem.

Strengthening Techniques

The following techniques are most appropriately used for the development of muscular strength, endurance, and coordination.

The **rhythmic initiation** technique involves a progression of initial passive, then active-assistive, followed by active move-

ment against resistance through the agonist pattern. Movement is slow, goes through the available range of motion, and avoids activation of a quick stretch. It is used for patients who are unable to initiate movement and who have a limited range of motion because of increased tone. It may also be used to teach the patient a movement pattern.

Repeated contraction is useful when a patient has weakness either at a specific point or throughout the entire range. It is used to correct imbalances that occur within the range by repeating the weakest portion of the total range. The patient moves isotonically against maximal resistance repeatedly until fatigue is evidenced in the weaker components of the motion. When fatigue of the weak components becomes apparent, a stretch at that point in the range should facilitate the weaker muscles and result in a smoother, more coordinated motion. Again, quick stretch may be contraindicated with some musculoskeletal injuries. The amount of resistance to motion given by the therapist should be modified to accommodate the strength of the muscle group. The patient is commanded to push by using the agonist concentrically and eccentrically throughout the range.

Slow reversal involves an isotonic contraction of the agonist followed immediately by an isotonic contraction of the antagonist. The initial contraction of the agonist muscle group facilitates the succeeding contraction of the antagonist muscles. The slow reversal technique can be used for developing active range of motion of the agonists and normal reciprocal timing between the antagonists and agonists, which is critical for normal coordinated motion. The patient should be commanded to push against maximal resistance by using the antagonist and then to pull by using the agonist. The initial agonistic push facilitates the succeeding antagonist contraction.

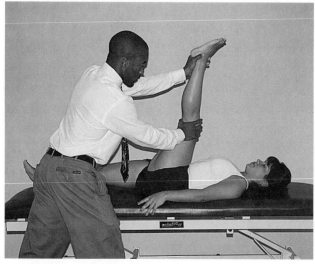

FIGURE   13-3

PNF stretching technique. (Reproduced, with permission, from Prentice WE. *Therapeutic Modalities for Allied Health Professionals.* New York, McGraw-Hill, 1998.)

Slow reversal–hold is an isotonic contraction of the agonist followed immediately by an isometric contraction, with a hold command given at the end of each active movement. The direction of the pattern is reversed by using the same sequence of contraction with no relaxation before shifting to the antagonistic pattern. This technique can be especially useful in developing strength at a specific point in the range of motion.

Rhythmic stabilization uses an isometric contraction of the agonist, followed by an isometric contraction of the antagonist to produce co-contraction and stability of the two opposing muscle groups. The command given is always "hold," and movement is resisted in each direction. Rhythmic stabilization results in an increase in the holding power to a point where the position cannot be broken. Holding should emphasize co-contraction of agonists and antagonists.

Stretching Techniques

The following techniques should be used to increase range of motion, relaxation, and inhibition.

Contract–relax is a stretching technique that moves the body part passively into the agonist pattern. The patient is instructed to push by contracting the antagonist (muscle that will be stretched) isotonically against the resistance of the therapist. The patient then relaxes the antagonist while the therapist

moves the part passively through as much range as possible to the point where limitation is again felt. This contract–relax technique is beneficial when range of motion is limited by muscle tightness.

Hold–relax is very similar to the contract–relax technique. It begins with an isometric contraction of the antagonist (muscle that will be stretched) against resistance, followed by a concentric contraction of the agonist muscle combined with light pressure from the therapist to produce maximal stretch of the antagonist. This technique is appropriate when there is muscle tension on one side of a joint and may be used with either the agonist or antagonist.

Slow reversal–hold–relax begins with an isotonic contraction of the agonist, which often limits range of motion in the agonist pattern, followed by an isometric contraction of the antagonist (muscle that will be stretched) during the push phase. During the relax phase, the antagonists are relaxed while the agonists are contracting, causing movement in the direction of the agonist pattern and thus stretching the antagonist. The technique, like the contract–relax and hold–relax techniques, is useful for increasing range of motion when the primary limiting factor is the antagonistic muscle group.

Because the goal of rehabilitation in most injuries is restoration of strength through a full, nonrestricted range of motion, several of these techniques are sometimes combined in sequence to accomplish this goal. Figure 13-3 shows a PNF stretching

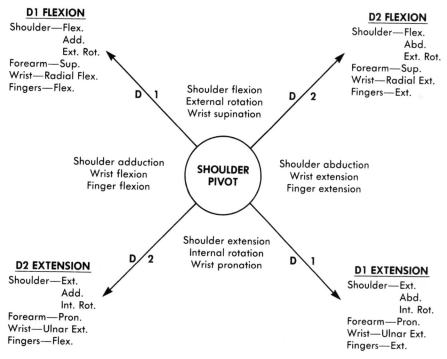

D1 FLEXION
Shoulder—Flex.
　　　Add.
　　　Ext. Rot.
Forearm—Sup.
Wrist—Radial Flex.
Fingers—Flex.

D2 FLEXION
Shoulder—Flex.
　　　Abd.
　　　Ext. Rot.
Forearm—Sup.
Wrist—Radial Ext.
Fingers—Ext.

D 1
Shoulder flexion
External rotation
Wrist supination

D 2

Shoulder adduction
Wrist flexion
Finger flexion

SHOULDER PIVOT

Shoulder abduction
Wrist extension
Finger extension

D 2
Shoulder extension
Internal rotation
Wrist pronation

D 1

D2 EXTENSION
Shoulder—Ext.
　　　Add.
　　　Int. Rot.
Forearm—Pron.
Wrist—Ulnar Ext.
Fingers—Flex.

D1 EXTENSION
Shoulder—Ext.
　　　Abd.
　　　Int. Rot.
Forearm—Pron.
Wrist—Ulnar Ext.
Fingers—Ext.

F I G U R E   1 3 - 4

PNF patterns of the upper extremity. (Reproduced, with permission, from Prentice WE. *Therapeutic Modalities for Allied Health Professionals.* New York, McGraw-Hill, 1998.)

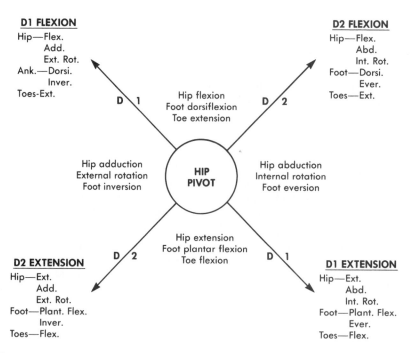

D1 FLEXION
Hip—Flex.
Add.
Ext. Rot.
Ank.—Dorsi.
Inver.
Toes-Ext.

D2 FLEXION
Hip—Flex.
Abd.
Int. Rot.
Foot—Dorsi.
Ever.
Toes—Ext.

Hip flexion
Foot dorsiflexion
Toe extension

Hip adduction
External rotation
Foot inversion

HIP PIVOT

Hip abduction
Internal rotation
Foot eversion

Hip extension
Foot plantar flexion
Toe flexion

D2 EXTENSION
Hip—Ext.
Add.
Ext. Rot.
Foot—Plant. Flex.
Inver.
Toes—Flex.

D1 EXTENSION
Hip—Ext.
Abd.
Int. Rot.
Foot—Plant. Flex.
Ever.
Toes—Flex.

FIGURE 13-5

PNF patterns of the lower extremity. (Reproduced, with permission, from Prentice WE. *Therapeutic Modalities for Allied Health Professionals.* New York, McGraw-Hill, 1998.)

technique in which the therapist is stretching the injured patient.

Treating Specific Problems with PNF Techniques

PNF strengthening and stretching techniques may be useful in a variety of different conditions. To some extent the choice of the most effective technique to use in a given situation will be dictated by the state of the existing condition and by the capabilities and limitations of the individual patient. There are some advantages to using PNF techniques in general.

Relative to strengthening, the PNF techniques are not encumbered by the design constraints of commercially designed exercise machines. With the PNF patterns, movement can

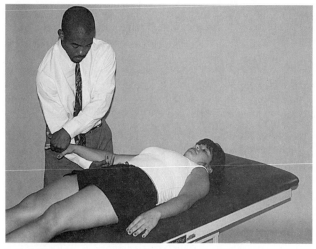

FIGURE 13-6

D1 upper extremity movement pattern moving into flexion. Starting position. (Reproduced, with permission, from Prentice WE. *Therapeutic Modalities for Allied Health Professionals.* New York, McGraw-Hill, 1998.)

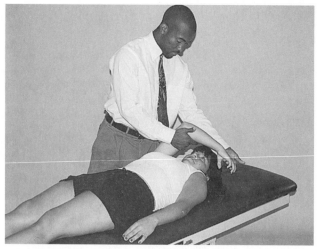

FIGURE 13-7

D1 upper extremity movement pattern moving into flexion. Terminal position. (Reproduced, with permission, from Prentice WE. *Therapeutic Modalities for Allied Health Professionals.* New York, McGraw-Hill, 1998.)

TABLE 13-1

D1 Upper Extremity Movement Patterns

BODY PART	MOVING INTO FLEXION		MOVING INTO EXTENSION	
	STARTING POSITION (FIG. 13-6)	TERMINAL POSITION (FIG. 13-7)	STARTING POSITION (FIG. 13-8)	TERMINAL POSITION (FIG. 13-9)
Shoulder	Extended Abducted Internally rotated	Flexed Adducted Externally rotated	Flexed Adducted Externally rotated	Extended Abducted Internally rotated
Scapula	Depressed Retracted Downwardly rotated	Flexed Protracted Upwardly rotated	Elevated Protracted Upwardly rotated	Depressed Retracted Downwardly rotated
Forearm	Pronated	Supinated	Supinated	Pronated
Wrist	Ulnar extended	Radially flexed	Radially flexed	Ulnar extended
Finger and thumb	Extended Abducted	Flexed Adducted	Flexed Adducted	Extended Abducted
Hand position for sports therapist[a]	Left and inside volar surface of hand. Right hand underneath arm in cubital fossa of elbow.		Left hand on back of elbow on humerus. Right hand on dorsum of hand.	
Verbal command	Pull		Push	

[a]For athlete's right arm.

(Reproduced, with permission, from Prentice WE. *Therapeutic Modalities for Allied Health Professionals.* New York, McGraw-Hill, 1998, p. 489.)

TABLE 13-2

D2 Upper Extremity Movement Patterns

BODY PART	MOVING INTO FLEXION		MOVING INTO EXTENSION	
	STARTING POSITION (FIG. 13-10)	TERMINAL POSITION (FIG. 13-11)	STARTING POSITION (FIG. 13-12)	TERMINAL POSITION (FIG. 13-13)
Shoulder	Extended Adducted Internally rotated	Flexed Abducted Externally rotated	Flexed Abducted Externally rotated	Extended Adducted Internally rotated
Scapula	Depressed Protracted Downwardly rotated	Elevated Retracted Upwardly rotated	Elevated Retracted Upwardly rotated	Depressed Protracted Downwardly rotated
Forearm	Pronated	Supinated	Supinated	Pronated
Wrist	Ulnar flexed	Radially extended	Radially extended	Ulnar flexed
Finger and thumb	Flexed Adducted	Extended Abducted	Extended Abducted	Flexed Adducted
Hand position for sports therapist[a]	Left hand on back of humerus. Right hand on dorsum of hand.		Left hand on volar surface of humerus. Right hand on cubital fossa of elbow.	
Verbal command	Push		Pull	

[a]For athlete's right arm.

(Reproduced, with permission, from Prentice WE. *Therapeutic Modalities for Allied Health Professionals.* New York, McGraw-Hill, 1998, p. 490.)

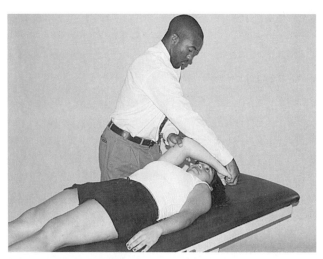

FIGURE 13-8

D1 upper extremity movement pattern moving into extension. Starting position. (Reproduced, with permission, from Prentice WE. *Therapeutic Modalities for Allied Health Professionals.* New York, McGraw-Hill, 1998.)

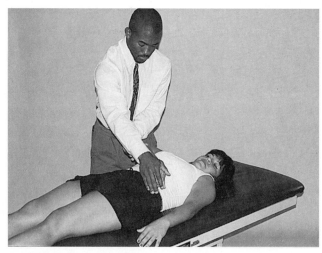

FIGURE 13-10

D2 upper extremity movement pattern moving into flexion. Starting position. (Reproduced, with permission, from Prentice WE. *Therapeutic Modalities for Allied Health Professionals.* New York, McGraw-Hill, 1998.)

occur in three planes simultaneously, thus more closely resembling a functional movement pattern. The amount of resistance applied by the therapist can be easily adjusted and altered at different points through the range of motion to meet patient capabilities. The therapist can choose to concentrate on the strengthening through the entire range of motion or through a very specific range. Combinations of several strengthening techniques can be used concurrently within the same PNF pattern.[15] Rhythmic initiation is useful in the early stages of rehabilitation when the patient is having difficulty in moving actively

through a pain-free arc. Passive movement can allow the patient to maintain a full range while using an active contraction to move through the available pain-free range. Slow reversal should be used to help improve muscular endurance. Slow reversal hold is used to correct existing weakness at specific points in the range of motion through isometric strengthening.

Rhythmic stabilization is used to achieve stability and neuromuscular control about a joint.[8] This technique requires co-contraction of opposing muscle groups and is useful in creating a balance in the existing force couples.

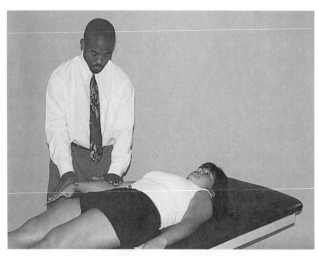

FIGURE 13-9

D1 upper extremity movement pattern moving into extension. Terminal position. (Reproduced, with permission, from Prentice WE. *Therapeutic Modalities for Allied Health Professionals.* New York, McGraw-Hill, 1998.)

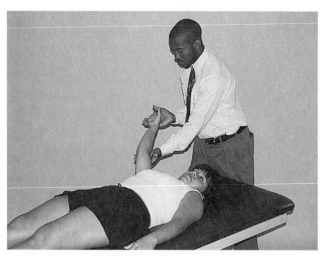

FIGURE 13-11

D2 upper extremity movement pattern moving into flexion. Terminal position. (Reproduced, with permission, from Prentice WE. *Therapeutic Modalities for Allied Health Professionals.* New York, McGraw-Hill, 1998.)

TABLE 13-3

D1 Lower Extremity Movement Patterns

BODY PART	MOVING INTO FLEXION		MOVING INTO EXTENSION	
	STARTING POSITION (FIG. 13-14)	TERMINAL POSITION (FIG. 13-15)	STARTING POSITION (FIG. 13-16)	TERMINAL POSITION (FIG. 13-17)
Hip	Extended Abducted Internally rotated	Flexed Adducted Externally rotated	Flexed Adducted Externally rotated	Extended Abducted Internally rotated
Knee	Extended	Flexed	Flexed	Extended
Position of tibia	Externally rotated	Internally rotated	Internally rotated	Externally rotated
Ankle and foot	Plantar flexed Everted	Dorsiflexed Inverted	Dorsiflexed Inverted	Plantar flexed Everted
Toes	Flexed	Extended	Extended	Flexed
Hand position for sports therapist[a]	Right hand on dorsimedial surface of foot. Left hand on anteromedial thigh near patella.		Right hand on lateralplantar surface of foot. Left hand on posteriolateral thigh near popliteal crease.	
Verbal command	Pull		Push	

[a]For athlete's right leg.

(Reproduced, with permission, from Prentice WE. *Therapeutic Modalities for Allied Health Professionals*. New York, McGraw-Hill, 1998, p. 493.)

PNF PATTERNS

The PNF patterns are concerned with gross movement as opposed to specific muscle actions. The techniques identified previously may be superimposed on any of the PNF patterns. The techniques of PNF are composed of both rotational and diagonal exercise patterns that are similar to the motions required in most sports and in normal daily activities.

The exercise patterns are three component movements: flexion–extension, abduction–adduction, and internal–external

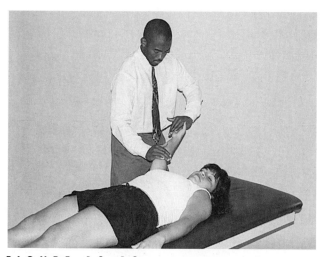

FIGURE 13-12

D2 upper extremity movement pattern moving into extension. Starting position. (Reproduced, with permission, from Prentice WE. *Therapeutic Modalities for Allied Health Professionals*. New York, McGraw-Hill, 1998.)

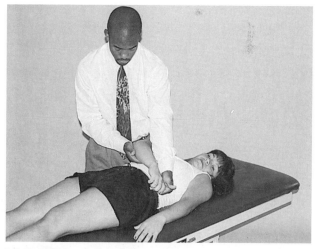

FIGURE 13-13

D2 upper extremity movement pattern moving into extension. Terminal position. (Reproduced, with permission, from Prentice WE. *Therapeutic Modalities for Allied Health Professionals*. New York, McGraw-Hill, 1998.)

T A B L E   1 3 - 4

D2 Lower Extremity Movement Patterns

BODY PART	MOVING INTO FLEXION		MOVING INTO EXTENSION	
	STARTING POSITION (FIG. 13-18)	TERMINAL POSITION (FIG. 13-19)	STARTING POSITION (FIG. 13-20)	TERMINAL POSITION (FIG. 13-21)
Hip	Extended Adducted Externally rotated	Flexed Abducted Internally rotated	Flexed Abducted Internally rotated	Extended Adducted Externally rotated
Knee	Extended	Flexed	Flexed	Extended
Position of tibia	Externally rotated	Internally rotated	Internally rotated	Externally rotated
Ankle and foot	Plantar flexed Inverted	Dorsiflexed Everted	Dorsiflexed Everted	Plantar flexed Inverted
Toes	Flexed	Extended	Extended	Flexed
Hand position for sports therapist[a]	Right hand on dorsilateral surface of foot. Left hand on anterolateral thigh near patella.		Right hand on medialplantar surface of foot. Left hand on posteriomedial thigh near popliteal crease.	
Verbal command	Pull		Push	

[a]For athlete's right leg. (Reproduced, with permission, from Prentice WE. *Therapeutic Modalities for Allied Health Professionals.* New York, McGraw-Hill, 1998, p. 493.)

rotation. Human movement is patterned and rarely involves straight motion because all muscles are spiral in nature and lie in diagonal directions.

The PNF patterns described by Knott and Voss[11] involve distinct diagonal and rotational movements of the upper extremity, lower extremity, upper trunk, lower trunk, and neck.

The exercise pattern is initiated with the muscle groups in the lengthened or stretched position. The muscle group is then contracted, moving the body part through the range of motion to a shortened position.

The upper and lower extremities each have two separate patterns of diagonal movement for each part of the body, which

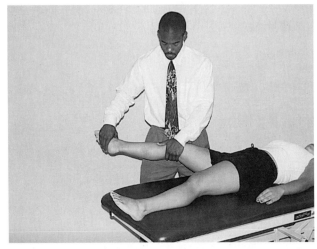

F I G U R E   1 3 - 1 4

D1 lower extremity movement pattern moving into flexion. Starting position. (Reproduced, with permission, from Prentice WE. *Therapeutic Modalities for Allied Health Professionals.* New York, McGraw-Hill, 1998.)

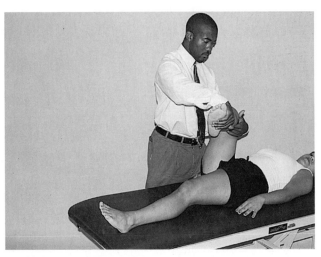

F I G U R E   1 3 - 1 5

D1 lower extremity movement pattern moving into flexion. Terminal position. (Reproduced, with permission, from Prentice WE. *Therapeutic Modalities for Allied Health Professionals.* New York, McGraw-Hill, 1998.)

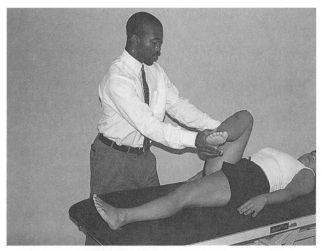

FIGURE 13-16

D1 lower extremity movement pattern moving into extension. Starting position. (Reproduced, with permission, from Prentice WE. *Therapeutic Modalities for Allied Health Professionals.* New York, McGraw-Hill, 1998.)

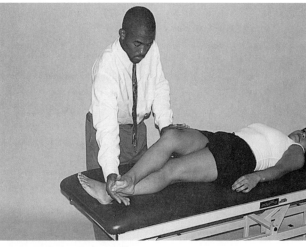

FIGURE 13-18

D2 lower extremity movement pattern moving into flexion. Starting position. (Reproduced, with permission, from Prentice WE. *Therapeutic Modalities for Allied Health Professionals.* New York, McGraw-Hill, 1998.)

are referred to as the diagonal 1 (D1) and diagonal 2 (D2) patterns. These diagonal patterns are subdivided into D1 moving into flexion, D1 moving into extension, D2 moving into flexion, and D2 moving into extension. Figures 13-4 and 13-5 diagram the PNF patterns for the upper and lower extremities, respectively. The patterns are named according to the proximal pivots at either the shoulder or the hip (for example, the glenohumeral joint or femoroacetabular joint).

Tables 13-1 and 13-2 describe specific movements in the D1 and D2 patterns for the upper extremities. Figures 13-6

to 13-13 show starting and terminal positions for each of the diagonal patterns in the upper extremity.

Tables 13-3 and 13-4 describe specific movements in the D1 and D2 patterns for the lower extremities. Figures 13-14 to 13-21 show the starting and terminal positions for each of the diagonal patterns in the lower extremity.

Table 13-5 describes the rotational movement of the upper trunk moving into extension (also called chopping) and moving into flexion (also called lifting). Figures 13-22 and 13-23 show the starting and terminal positions of the upper extremity

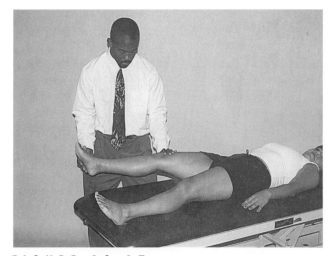

FIGURE 13-17

D1 lower extremity movement pattern moving into extension. Terminal position. (Reproduced, with permission, from Prentice WE. *Therapeutic Modalities for Allied Health Professionals.* New York, McGraw-Hill, 1998.)

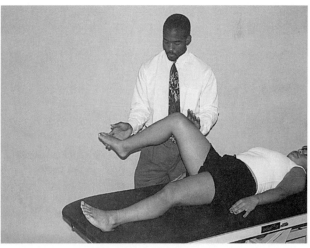

FIGURE 13-19

D2 lower extremity movement pattern moving into flexion. Terminal position. (Reproduced, with permission, from Prentice WE. *Therapeutic Modalities for Allied Health Professionals.* New York, McGraw-Hill, 1998.)

TABLE   13-5
Upper Trunk Movement Patterns

| BODY PART | MOVING INTO EXTENSION (CHOPPING)[a] | | MOVING INTO FLEXION (LIFTING)[a] | |
	STARTING POSITION (FIG. 13-22)	TERMINAL POSITION (FIG. 13-23)	STARTING POSITION (FIG. 13-24)	TERMINAL POSITION (FIG. 13-25)
Right upper extremity	Flexed Adducted Internally rotated	Extended Abducted Externally rotated	Extended Adducted Internally rotated	Flexed Abducted Externally rotated
Left upper extremity (left hand grasps right forearm)	Flexed Abducted Externally rotated	Extended Adducted Internally rotated	Extended Abducted Externally rotated	Flexed Adducted Internally rotated
Trunk	Rotated and extended to left	Rotated and flexed to right	Rotated and flexed to left	Rotated and extended to right
Head	Rotated and extended to left	Rotated and flexed to right	Rotated and flexed to left	Rotated and extended to right
Hand position of sports therapist	Left hand on right anterolateral surface of forehead. Right hand on dorsum of right hand.		Right hand on dorsum of right hand. Left hand on posteriolateral surface of head.	
Verbal command	Pull down		Push up	

[a]Athlete's rotation is to the right.

(Reproduced, with permission, from Prentice WE. *Therapeutic Modalities for Allied Health Professionals.* New York, McGraw-Hill, 1998, p. 496.)

chopping pattern moving into extension to the right. Figures 13-24 and 13-25 show the starting and terminal positions for the upper-extremity lifting pattern moving into flexion to the right.

Table 13-6 describes rotational movement of the lower extremities moving into positions of flexion and extension. Figures 13-26 and 13-27 show the lower-extremity pattern moving into flexion to the left. Figures 13-28 and 13-29 show the lower-extremity pattern moving into extension of the left.

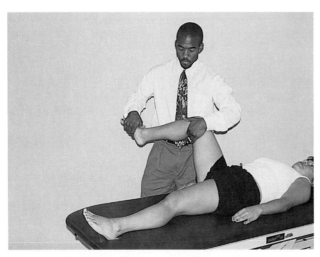

FIGURE   13-20

D2 lower extremity movement pattern moving into extension. Starting position. (Reproduced, with permission, from Prentice WE. *Therapeutic Modalities for Allied Health Professionals.* New York, McGraw-Hill, 1998.)

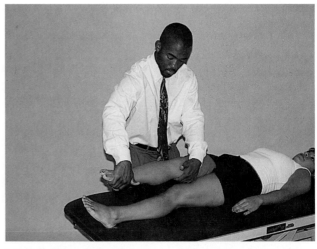

FIGURE   13-21

D2 lower extremity movement pattern moving into extension. Terminal position. (Reproduced, with permission, from Prentice WE. *Therapeutic Modalities for Allied Health Professionals.* New York, McGraw-Hill, 1998.)

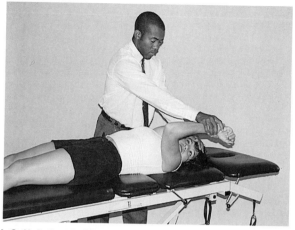

FIGURE 13-22

Upper trunk pattern moving into extension or chopping. Starting position. (Reproduced, with permission, from Prentice WE. *Therapeutic Modalities for Allied Health Professionals.* New York, McGraw-Hill, 1998.)

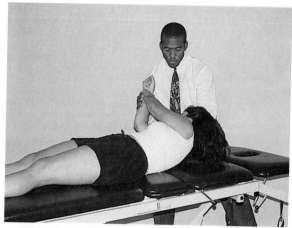

FIGURE 13-25

Upper trunk pattern moving into flexion or lifting. Terminal position. (Reproduced, with permission, from Prentice WE. *Therapeutic Modalities for Allied Health Professionals.* New York, McGraw-Hill, 1998.)

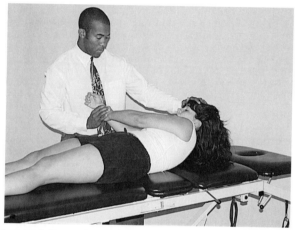

FIGURE 13-23

Upper trunk pattern moving into extension or chopping. Terminal position. (Reproduced, with permission, from Prentice WE. *Therapeutic Modalities for Allied Health Professionals.* New York, McGraw-Hill, 1998.)

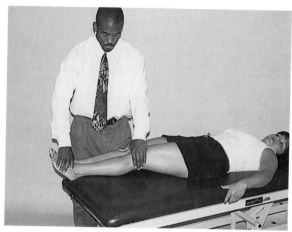

FIGURE 13-26

Lower trunk pattern moving into flexion to the left. Starting position. (Reproduced, with permission, from Prentice WE. *Therapeutic Modalities for Allied Health Professionals.* New York, McGraw-Hill, 1998.)

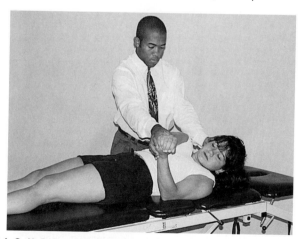

FIGURE 13-24

Upper trunk pattern moving into flexion or lifting. Starting position. (Reproduced, with permission, from Prentice WE. *Therapeutic Modalities for Allied Health Professionals.* New York, McGraw-Hill, 1998.)

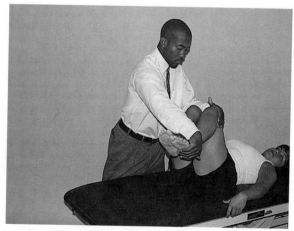

FIGURE 13-27

Lower trunk pattern moving into flexion to the left. Terminal position. (Reproduced, with permission, from Prentice WE. *Therapeutic Modalities for Allied Health Professionals.* New York, McGraw-Hill, 1998.)

T A B L E   1 3 - 6

Lower Trunk Movement Patterns

BODY PART	MOVING INTO FLEXION[a]		MOVING INTO EXTENSION[b]	
	STARTING POSITION (FIG. 13-26)	TERMINAL POSITION (FIG. 13-27)	STARTING POSITION (FIG. 13-28)	TERMINAL POSITION (FIG. 13-29)
Right hip	Extended Abducted Externally rotated	Flexed Adducted Internally rotated	Flexed Adducted Internally rotated	Extended Abducted Externally rotated
Left hip	Extended Adducted Internally rotated	Flexed Abducted Externally rotated	Flexed Abducted Externally rotated	Extended Adducted Internally rotated
Ankles	Plantar flexed	Dorsiflexed	Dorsiflexed	Plantar flexed
Toes	Flexed	Extended	Extended	Flexed
Hand position of sports therapist	Right hand on dorsum of feet. Left hand on anterolateral surface of left knee.		Right hand on plantar surface of foot. Left hand on posteriolateral surface of right knee.	
Verbal command	Pull up and in		Push down and out	

[a]Athlete's rotation is to the left in flexion.

[b]Athlete's rotation is to the right in extension.

(Reproduced, with permission, from Prentice WE. *Therapeutic Modalities for Allied Health Professionals.* New York, McGraw-Hill, 1998, p. 498.)

The neck patterns involve simply flexion and rotation to one side (Figs. 13-30 and 13-31) with extension and rotation to the opposite side (Figs. 13-32 and 13-33). The patient should follow the direction of the movement with the eyes.

The principles and techniques of PNF, when used appropriately with specific patterns, can be an extremely effective tool for rehabilitation of injury.[24] They may be used to strengthen weak muscles or muscle groups and to improve the range of motion about an injured joint. Specific techniques selected for use should depend on individual patient needs and may be modified accordingly.[5,6]

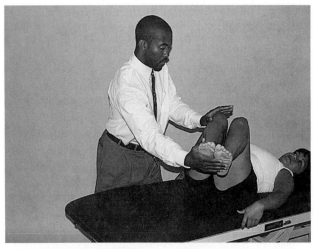

F I G U R E   1 3 - 2 8

Lower trunk pattern moving into extension to the left. Starting position. (Reproduced, with permission, from Prentice WE. *Therapeutic Modalities for Allied Health Professionals.* New York, McGraw-Hill, 1998.)

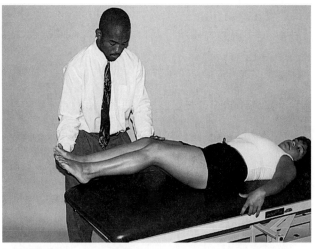

F I G U R E   1 3 - 2 9

Lower trunk pattern moving into extension to the left. Terminal position. (Reproduced, with permission, from Prentice WE. *Therapeutic Modalities for Allied Health Professionals.* New York, McGraw-Hill, 1998.)

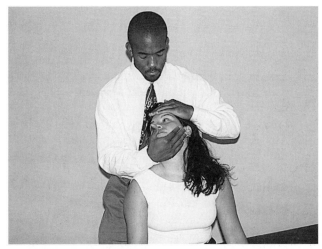

FIGURE 1 3 - 3 0

Neck flexion and rotation to the left. Starting position. (Reproduced, with permission, from Prentice WE. *Therapeutic Modalities for Allied Health Professionals.* New York, McGraw-Hill, 1998.)

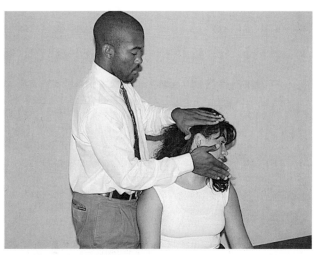

FIGURE 1 3 - 3 2

Neck extension and rotation to the right. Starting position. (Reproduced, with permission, from Prentice WE. *Therapeutic Modalities for Allied Health Professionals.* New York, McGraw-Hill, 1998.)

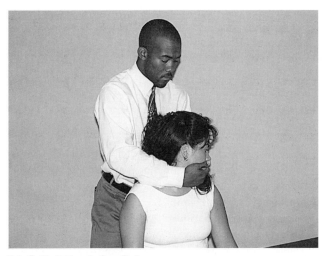

FIGURE 1 3 - 3 1

Neck flexion and rotation to the left. Terminal position. (Reproduced, with permission, from Prentice WE. *Therapeutic Modalities for Allied Health Professionals.* New York, McGraw-Hill, 1998.)

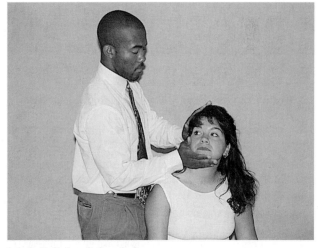

FIGURE 1 3 - 3 3

Neck extension and rotation to the right. Terminal position. (Reproduced, with permission, from Prentice WE. *Therapeutic Modalities for Allied Health Professionals.* New York, McGraw-Hill, 1998.)

SUMMARY

- The PNF techniques may be used to increase both strength and range of motion and are based on the neurophysiology of the stretch reflex.
- The motor neurons of the spinal cord always receive a combination of inhibitory and excitatory impulses from the afferent nerves. Whether these motor neurons will be excited or inhibited depends on the ratio of the two types of incoming impulses.

- The PNF techniques emphasize specific principles that may be superimposed on any of the specific techniques.
- The PNF strengthening techniques include repeated contraction, slow reversal, slow reversal–hold, rhythmic stabilization, and rhythmic initiation.
- The PNF stretching techniques include contract–relax, hold–relax, and slow reversal–hold–relax.
- The techniques of PNF are rotational and diagonal movements in the upper extremity, lower extremity, upper trunk, and head and neck.

REFERENCES

1. Barak T, Rosen E, Sofer R. Mobility: Passive orthopedic manual therapy. In: Gould J, Davies G, eds. *Orthopedic and Sports Physical Therapy.* St. Louis, Mosby, 1985.

2. Basmajian J. *Therapeutic Exercise.* Baltimore, Williams & Wilkins, 1978.

3. Bobath B. The treatment of motor disorders of pyramidal and extrapyramidal tracts by reflex inhibition and by facilitation of movement. *Physiotherapy* 41:146, 1955.

4. Brunnstrom S. *Movement Therapy in Hemiplegia.* New York, Harper & Row, 1970.

5. Cookson J. Orthopedic manual therapy: An overview. II. The spine. *J Am Phys Ther Assoc* 59:259, 1979.

6. Cookson J, Kent B. Orthopedic manual therapy: An overview. I. The extremities. *J Am Phys Ther Assoc* 59:176, 1979.

7. Cornelius W, Jackson A. The effects of cryotherapy and PNF on hip extension flexibility. *Athl Train* 19:184, 1984.

8. Engle R, Canner G. Proprioceptive neuromuscular facilitation (PNF) and modified procedures for anterior cruciate ligament (ACL) instability. *J Orthop Sports Phys Ther* 11:230–236, 1989.

9. Harris F. Facilitation techniques and therapeutic exercise. In: Basmajian J, ed. *Therapeutic Exercise.* Baltimore, Williams & Wilkins, 1978.

10. Hollis M. *Practical Exercise.* Oxford, Blackwell Scientific, 1981.

11. Knott M, Voss D. *Proprioceptive Neuromuscular Facilitation: Patterns and Techniques.* New York, Harper & Row, 1968.

12. Lloyd D. Facilitation and inhibition of spinal motorneurons. *J Neurophysiol* 9:421, 1946.

13. Markos P. Ipsilateral and contralateral effects of proprioceptive neuromuscular facilitation techniques on hip motion and electromyographic activity. *Phys Ther* 59:1766–1773, 1979.

14. Osternig L, Robertson R, Troxel R. et al. Differential responses to proprioceptive neuromuscular facilitation stretch techniques. *Med Sci Sports Exerc* 22:106–111, 1990.

15. Osternig L, Robertson R, Troxel R, Hansen P. Muscle activation during proprioceptive neuromuscular facilitation (PNF) stretching techniques: Stretch–relax (SR), contract–relax (CR) and agonist contract–relax (ACR). *Am J Phys Med* 66:298–307, 1987.

16. Prentice W. Proprioceptive neuromuscular facilitation (videotape). St. Louis, Mosby, 1993.

17. Prentice W. A manual resistance technique for strengthening tibial rotation. *Athl Train* 23:230–233, 1988.

18. Prentice W. A comparison of static stretching and PNF stretching for improving hip joint flexibility. *Athl Train* 18:56–59, 1983.

19. Prentice W. An electromyographic analysis of heat and cold and stretching for inducing muscular relaxation. *J Orthop Sports Phys Ther* 3:173–140, 1982.

20. Prentice W, Kooima E. The use of proprioceptive neuromuscular facilitation techniques in the rehabilitation of sport-related injuries. *Athl Train* 21:26–31, 1986.

21. Rood M. Neurophysiologic reactions as a basis of physical therapy. *Phys Ther Rev* 34:444, 1954.

22. Saliba V, Johnson G, Wardlaw C. Proprioceptive neuromuscular facilitation. In: Basmajian J, Nyberg R, eds. *Rational Manual Therapies.* Baltimore, Williams & Wilkins, 1993.

23. Sherrington C. *The Integrative Action of the Nervous System.* New Haven. Yale University Press, 1947.

24. Surberg P. Neuromuscular facilitation techniques in sports medicine. *Phys Ther Rev* 34:444, 1954.

25. Surberg P, Schrader J. Proprioceptive neuromuscular facilitation techniques: A reassessment. *J Athl Train* 32:34–39, 1997.

26. Taniqawa M. Comparison of the hold–relax procedure and passive mobilization on increasing muscle length. *Phys Ther* 52:725–735, 1972.

27. Worrell T, Smith T, Winegardner J. Effect of hamstring stretching on hamstring muscle performance. *J Orthop Sports Phys Ther* 20:154–159, 1994.

28. Zohn D, Mennell J. *Musculoskeletal Pain: Diagnosis and Physical Treatment.* Boston, Little, Brown, 1976.

SUGGESTED READINGS

Blakely R, Palmer M. Analysis of shoulder rotation accompanying a proprioceptive neuromuscular facilitation approach. *Phys Ther* 66:1224–1227, 1986.

Cornelius W, Craft-Hamm K. Proprioceptive neuromuscular facilitation flexibility techniques: Acute effects on arterial blood pressure. *Phys Ther Sports Med* 16:152, 1988.

Engle R, Canner G. Proprioceptive neuromuscular facilitation (PNF) and modified procedures for anterior cruciate ligament (ACL) instability. *J Orthop Sports Phys Ther* 11:230–236, 1989.

Osternig L, Robertson R, Troxel R, Hansen P. Muscle activation during proprioceptive neuromuscular facilitation (PNF) stretching techniques: Stretch–relax (SR), contract–relax (CR) and agonist contract–relax (ACR). *Am J Phys Med* 66:298–307, 1987.

Segal R. Depression of Hoffmann reflexes following voluntary contraction and implications for proprioceptive neuromuscular facilitation therapy. *Phys Ther* 71:329–331, 1991.

Sundquist R, Harter R. Comparative effects of static and proprioceptive neuromuscular facilitation stretching techniques in increasing hip flexion range of motion. *J Athl Train* 31 (suppl):S5, 1996.

Svendsen D, Matyas T. Facilitation of the isometric maximum voluntary contraction with traction: A test of PNF predictions. Proprioceptive neuromuscular facilitation. *Am J Phys Med* 62:27–37, 1983.

Waddington P. Proprioceptive neuromuscular facilitation techniques and plasticity. *Physiotherapy* 70:295–296, 1984.

Wang R. Effect of proprioceptive neuromuscular facilitation on the gait of patients with hemiplegia of long and short duration. *Phys Ther* 74:1108–1115, 1994.

CHAPTER 14

Muscle Energy Techniques in Rehabilitation

Michael A. Clark

OBJECTIVES

After completing this chapter, the student therapist should be able to do the following:

- Discuss the the functional relationships of the myofascial, neuromuscular, and articular components of the kinetic chain.
- Discuss the various factors that can contribute to muscle dysfunction.
- Define muscle energy techniques.
- Discuss the neuromuscular basis for using muscle energy techniques.
- Identify the various assessment procedures for each muscle group.
- Describe how muscle energy techniques for specific muscles can be used by the clinician.

FUNCTIONAL RELATIONSHIPS

The kinetic chain is a very complex, well-orchestrated system of interrelated and interdependent myofascial, neuromuscular, and articular components. The functional integration of each system allows for optimal neuromuscular efficiency during functional activities. Optimal functioning of all contributing components of the kinetic chain results in appropriate length–tension relationships, optimal force–couple relationships, precise arthrokinematics, and optimal neuromuscular control.[2,18–20,26] Efficiency and longevity of the kinetic chain requires optimal integration of each system.

Injury to the kinetic chain rarely involves only one structure. The kinetic chain functions as an integrated unit. Dysfunction in one system leads to compensations and adaptations in other systems. The myofascial, neuromuscular, and articular systems all play a significant role in the functional pathology of the kinetic chain.[1–3,6] Concepts of muscle imbalances, myofascial adhesions, altered arthrokinematics, and abnormal neuromuscular control need to be addressed by the clinician when developing a comprehensive evaluation and treatment program.[2,8–10]

INTRODUCTION TO MOVEMENT DYSFUNCTION

Alterations in joint arthrokinematics, muscular balance, and neuromuscular control affect the optimal functioning of the entire kinetic chain, leading to abnormal compensations and adaptations.[2,4,5,9,12,13,15,16]

Joint hypomobility is one of the most frequently treated causes of pain. However, the etiology is usually from faulty posture, muscular imbalances, and abnormal neuromuscular control.[2–4,18–20] Once a particular joint has lost its normal arthrokinematics, the muscles around that joint attempt to minimize the stress at that involved segment. Certain muscles become tight and hypertonic to prevent additional joint translation. If one muscle becomes tight or changes its degree of activation, than synergists, stabilizers, and neutralizers have to compensate, leading to the formation of complex neuromusculoskeletal dysfunctions.[2,4,5,12–20]

Muscle tightness and hypertonicity have a significant impact on neuromuscular control. Muscle tightness affects the normal length–tension relationships.[26] When one muscle in a force couple becomes tight or hypertonic, it alters the normal arthrokinematics of the involved joint. This affects the synergistic function of the entire kinetic chain, leading to abnormal joint stress, soft tissue dysfunction, neural compromise, and vascular/lymphatic stasis.[2,16]

Muscle tightness also causes reciprocal inhibition[4,5,12,20] Increased muscle spindle activity in a specific muscle will cause decreased neural drive to that muscle's functional antagonist. This alters the normal force–couple activity, which in turn affects the normal arthrokinematics of the involved segment.[12,13,15,16] For example, if a patient has tightness or hypertonicity in the psoas, then the functional antagonist (gluteus maximus) can be inhibited (decreased neural drive), causing decreased neuromuscular control.[14,17–20] This in turn leads to synergistic dominance. Synergistic dominance is the neuromuscular phenomenon that occurs when synergists compensate for a weak and/or inhibited muscle to maintain force-production capabilities. This process alters the normal force–couple relationships, which in turn creates a chain reaction.

It has been demonstrated that muscle tightness alters neuromuscular control. Alterations in recruitment strategies and stabilization strength result. Such compensations and adaptations affect neuromuscular efficiency throughout the kinetic chain.[2,14,19,26] Decreased neuromuscular control alters the activation sequence or firing order of different muscles involved, and a specific movement is disturbed. Prime movers may be slow to activate, while synergists, stabilizers, and neutralizers substitute and become overactive.[2] When this is the case, new joint stresses will be encountered. For example, if the psoas is tight or hyperactive, then the gluteus maximus will have decreased neural drive. If the gluteus maximus (prime mover during hip extension) has decreased neural drive, than synergists (hamstrings), stabilizers (erector spinae), and neutralizers (piriformis) substitute and become overactive (synergistic dominance). This creates abnormal joint stress and decreased neuromuscular control during functional movements.[18–20]

Several authors have demonstrated specific movement system imbalances in patients with altered neuromuscular control secondary to muscle imbalances.[13,16,26] They have found increased neural drive in the tight or hyperactive muscle and decreased neural drive in the inhibited or hypoactive muscle (Tables 14-1).

Development of Muscle Imbalances

Several factors can lead to the development of muscle imbalances and soft-tissue dysfunction including postural stress,

T A B L E   1 4 - 1

Neural Drive

CHARACTERISTICS OF INCREASED NEURAL DRIVE

1. Early and excessive recruitment of prime movers
2. Decreased neural drive of functional antagonists
3. Decreased neural drive of stabilizers and neutralizers
4. Altered force–couple relationships
5. Altered joint arthrokinematics

CHARACTERISTICS OF DECREASED NEURAL DRIVE

1. Decreased neural drive to stabilizers and neutralizers
2. Decreased activation of postural muscles
3. Delayed motor unit synchronization
4. Altered rate coding
5. Altered intramuscular coordination
6. Altered force–couple activity
7. Altered joint arthrokinematics

T A B L E   1 4 - 2

Muscle Group Characteristics

MOVEMENT GROUP CHARACTERISTICS

1. Prone to develop tightness
2. Prone to develop hypertonicity
3. Readily activated in most functional movement patterns
4. Dominate in fatigue situations
5. Dominate in new movement situations
6. Generally cross two joints

STABILIZATION GROUP

1. Prone to weakness
2. Prone to myokinematic inhibition
3. Prone to arthrokinematic inhibition
4. Fatigue easily
5. Primarily cross one joint

poor neuromuscular efficiency, pattern overload, overtraining, and poor technical efficiency. When a kinetic chain reaction develops in which certain key muscles become shortened and other muscles weaken, predictable patterns of dysfunction develop.[2,5,12,13,16,19,20,26]

Janda[12,13] has developed a system for evaluation of muscular imbalances based on common patterns of kinetic chain dysfunction. Janda has divided the muscular system into two functional divisions: movement group and stabilization group (Tables 14-2 and 14-3).

Treatment of Muscle Imbalances

There are many manual therapy techniques used to treat articular and soft-tissue dysfunction. Muscle energy is one technique that has been established to treat complex kinetic chain dysfunction. (Please refer to Figures 14-20 to 14-35 for specific muscle energy techniques.) **Muscle energy techniques (MET)** are manually applied stretching techniques that use principles of neurophysiology to relax overactive muscles and/or stretch chronically shortened muscles.[4,5,7,11] It is important not to commence strengthening too soon because tight, overactive muscles reflexively inhibit their functional antagonists, thereby altering neuromuscular control.[19,20,26] Researchers[27] have found that competitive basketball and volleyball players often develop patellar tendinitis as a result of abnormal stress and decreased neuromuscular control created from muscle imbalances. The jumping ability of these athletes was studied cinematographically. It was found that the combination of tightness of the psoas and rectus femoris along with weakness of the gluteus maximus and hamstrings resulted in decreased hip extension and concomitant hyperextension at the knee joint. It was found that treating the muscle imbalance with manual

TABLE 14-3

Functional Division of Muscle Groups

MOVEMENT GROUP: MUSCLES PRONE TO DEVELOP TIGHTNESS

1. Gastrocnemius
2. Soleus
3. Hip adductors
4. Hamstrings
5. Rectus femoris
6. Psoas
7. TFL
8. Piriformis
9. Erector spinae
10. Quadratus lumborum
11. Pectoralis minor
12. Upper trapezius
13. Levator scapulae
14. SCM
15. Scalenes

STABILIZATION GROUP: MUSCLES PRONE TO INHIBITION

1. Peroneals
2. Anterior tibialis
3. Posterior tibialis
4. Gluteus maximus
5. Gluteus medius
6. Abdominals
7. Serratus anterior
8. Rhomboids
9. Lower trapezius
10. Deep cervical flexors

TABLE 14-4

Assessment of Muscle Imbalances: Specific Questions

1. What muscles are tight?
2. Is the evident restriction in a specific soft-tissue structure related to neuromuscular influence or tightness secondary to connective tissue fibrosis?
3. Which muscles have become significantly weaker?
4. What kinetic chain substitutions, compensations, and adaptations have occurred?
5. What joint reactions are associated with the soft-tissue dysfunction?
6. What compensatory postural patterns have been created as an adaptive functional strategy?
7. Which symptoms are related to tender/trigger point activity?

therapy prior to strengthening was more effective than a strength program that was initiated before improving the kinetic chain dysfunction.[27]

NEUROMUSCULAR BASIS OF MUSCLE ENERGY TECHNIQUES

MET have the ability to relax overactive muscles or stretch tight muscles and their associated fascial components when connective tissue or viscoelastic changes have occurred.[4,19,20] When using MET, it is important to relax/inhibit the neuromuscular component before attempting to stretch the involved musculature. Two fundamental neurophysiologic principles account for the neuromuscular inhibition that occurs with MET. The first neurophysiologic principle of MET is postcontraction inhibition (*autogenic inhibition*). After a muscle contracts, it is automatically in a relaxed state for a brief latent period. Measurements of the Hoffman reflex (representative of the excitability

of the alpha motor neuron pool) show that activity is decreased for 25 to 30 seconds following MET, whereas inhibition from static stretching lasts only 3 to 5 seconds. These effects are neurophysiologically mediated. The second neurophysiologic principle that MET uses is the principle of *reciprocal inhibition*. When one muscle is contracted (agonist), its antagonist is reciprocally inhibited. This is explained by Sherrington's law of reciprocal inhibition.[4,15,16,19,20]

Symptom Assessment

There are several specific questions that the clinician should try to answer during the assessment of muscle balance (Table 14-4). It is very important to conceptualize muscular function and dysfunction as something other than a local event. We must never forget the complex interrelationships between muscle, fascia, tendon, ligament, bone, neural, lymphatic, and vascular structures.

HOW TO USE MUSCLE ENERGY TECHNIQUES

Finding the resistance barrier is the first step when performing MET. The term "resistance barrier" does not signify "pathologic," but instead represents the first sign of resistance during assessment of muscle length. The resistance barrier is the point in the range of motion where tissues require some degree of passive effort to continue to move. This will be the starting point for MET.[4,19,20] (Please refer to Figures 14-1 to 14-19 for specific assessment procedures.)

Once the resistance barrier is established, MET can begin. The patient is asked to contract the agonist muscle with approximately 20 to 25 percent of his or her available strength. The therapist should give enough resistance to match the patient's isometric contraction. The isometric contraction should

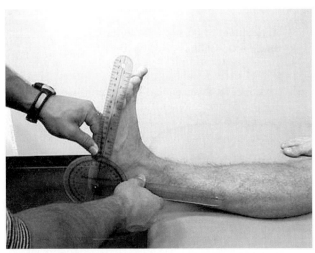

F I G U R E   1 4 - 1

Gastrocnemius muscle assessment.

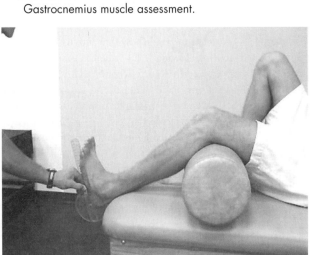

F I G U R E   1 4 - 2

Soleus muscle assessment.

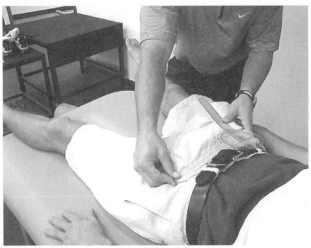

F I G U R E   1 4 - 3

Adductor muscle group assessment.

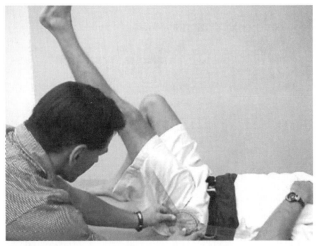

F I G U R E   1 4 - 4

Straight leg raise hamstring assessment.

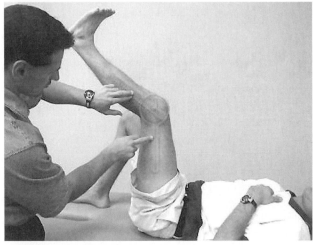

F I G U R E   1 4 - 5

90°/90° hamstring assessment.

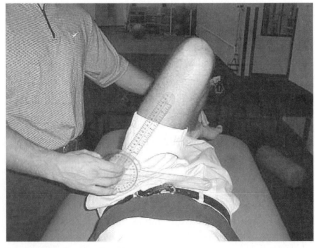

F I G U R E   1 4 - 6

Piriformis muscle assessment.

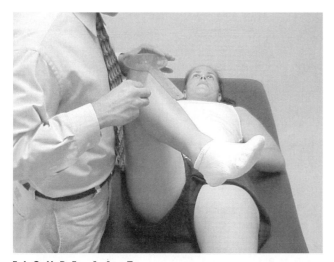

FIGURE 14-7

Piriformis muscle assessment.

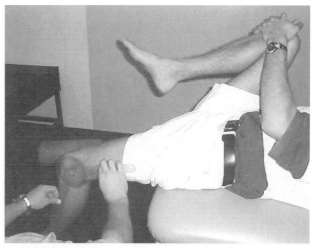

FIGURE 14-10

Rectus femoris muscle assessment.

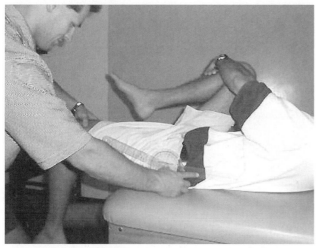

FIGURE 14-8

Psoas muscle assessment.

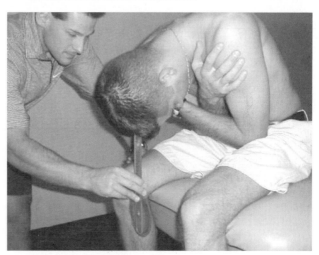

FIGURE 14-11

Erector spinae muscle assessment.

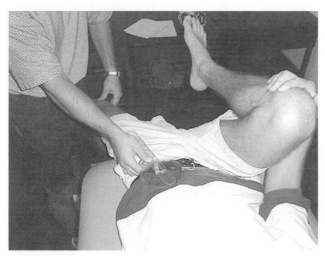

FIGURE 14-9

Tensor fascia latae assessment.

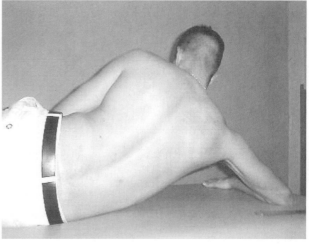

FIGURE 14-12

Quadratus lumborum assessment.

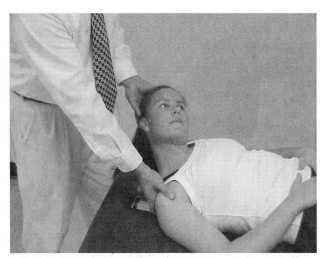

F I G U R E   1 4 - 1 3

Upper trapezius muscle assessment.

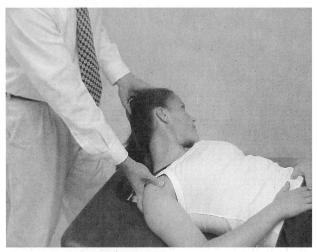

F I G U R E   1 4 - 1 4

Levator scapulae assessment.

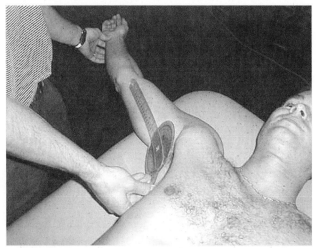

F I G U R E   1 4 - 1 5

Pectoralis major muscle assessment.

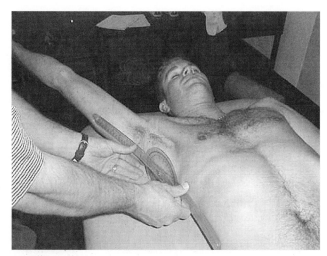

F I G U R E   1 4 - 1 6

Latissimus dorsi muscle assessment.

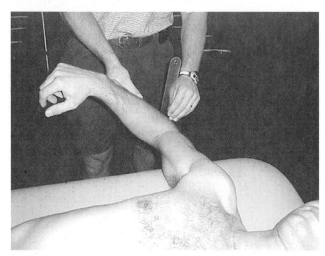

F I G U R E   1 4 - 1 7

Subscapularis muscle assessment.

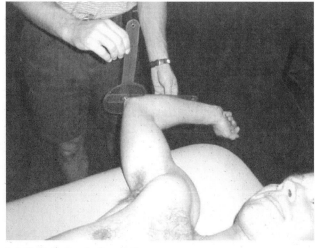

F I G U R E   1 4 - 1 8

Infraspinatus muscle assessment.

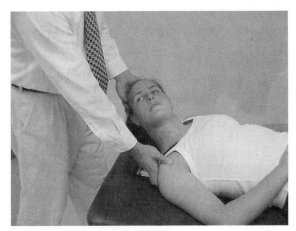

FIGURE 14-19

Scalene muscle assessment.

TABLE 14-5

Common Errors While Performing MET

PATIENT ERRORS

Contraction is too intense
Contraction in the wrong direction
Contraction is not sustained long enough
Lack of full relaxation following the technique
Beginning subsequent contraction too soon

CLINICIAN ERRORS

Inaccurate control
Inadequate counterforce
Counterforce applied in the wrong direction
Moving to the new barrier too soon

be held for 10 seconds. This is the time required to stimulate the excitatory threshold of the Golgi tendon organ, which has a neurophysiologic inhibitory effect on the muscle spindle. This provides the opportunity to take the muscle into a new range of motion.[4] Following the isometric contraction, there is a latency period of approximately 25 to 30 seconds, during which the muscle can be stretched. The patient can be instructed to use the antagonist muscle to pull the area being treated into a new range of motion. This uses the concept of reciprocal inhibition. Otherwise, the segment can be passively moved to the new resistance barrier (see Figures 14-20 to 14-35.) There are several errors that can occur when performing MET (Table 14-5).

The patient should perform neuromuscular stabilization exercises and core stabilization exercises following MET in order to gain neuromuscular control and structural and functional efficiency in the new range of motion.[4,19,20] The patient should also be given self-stretching techniques to maintain the newly acquired range of motion.

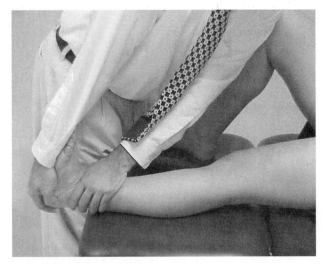

FIGURE 14-20

Gastrocnemius soleus stretch.

MUSCLE ASSESSMENT TECHNIQUES

A. Gastrocnemius (Fig. 14-1)
   1. Patient supine, with knee straight
   2. Measure dorsiflexion with the STJ in neutral
   3. Prevent abnormal compensations (eversion)
   4. Normal = 20 degrees

B. Soleus (Fig. 14-2)
   1. Patient supine, with knee bent to 30 degrees
   2. Measure dorsiflexion with the STJ in neutral
   3. Prevent abnormal compensation
   4. Normal = 20 degrees

C. Adductors (Fig. 14-3)
   1. Patient supine, near the side edge of the table
   2. Place the foot in your hand to prevent ER
   3. Abduct the athlete's leg to the first resistance barrier
   4. Normal = 45 degrees

D. Hamstring (straight leg) (Fig. 14-4)
   1. Patient supine with nontested leg bent to 90 degrees
   2. Grasp the heel with one hand and place the other hand over the ASIS to monitor for movement
   3. Raise the leg until there is movement in the ASIS
   4. Normal = 80 degrees

E. Hamstring (90°/90°) (Fig. 14-5)
   1. Patient supine, with test leg flexed at 90°/90°
   2. Straighten the leg until the first resistance barrier
   3. Normal = 80 degrees

F. Piriformis (Fig. 14-6)
   1. Patient supine on the table with the hip and knee flexed to 90°/90°
   2. Internally rotate the femur to the first resistance barrier, while monitoring for pelvic movement
   3. Normal = 45 degrees

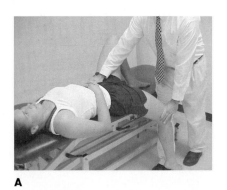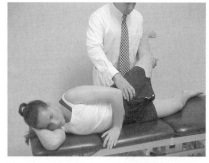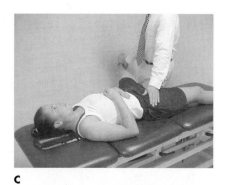

A   B   C

FIGURE 14-21

A, Short adductors stretch. **B,** Sidelying adductors stretch. **C,** Adductor stretch.

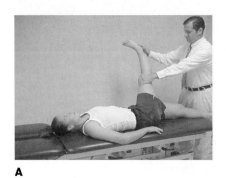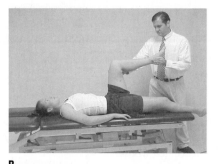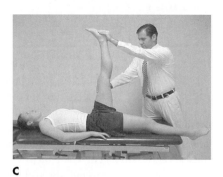

A   B   C

D   E

FIGURE 14-22

A, SL hamstring with adduction stretch. **B,** 90°/90° hamstring stretch (start). **C,** 90°/90° hamstring stretch (end). **D,** Straight leg raise hamstring stretch. **E,** Straight leg hamstring with abduction stretch.

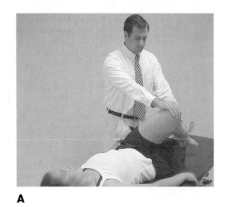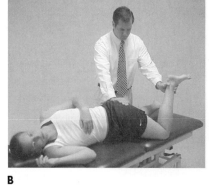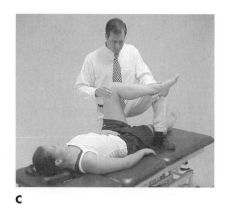

A   B   C

FIGURE 14-23

A, Piriformis stretch supine. **B,** Piriformis stretch sidelying. **C,** Piriformis with hip external rotation stretch.

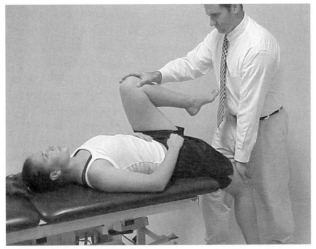

FIGURE 14-24

Psoas muscle stretch.

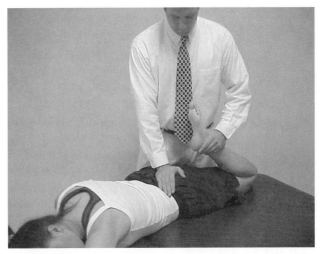

FIGURE 14-26

Prone quadriceps stretch.

G. Piriformis (Fig. 14-7)
   1. Patient supine with the hip flexed to 60 degrees
   2. Provide maximal longitudinal compression through the femur
   3. Maximally adduct the athlete's hip
   4. IR and ER the femur
   5. IR stresses the superior fibers and ER stresses the inferior fibers
   6. Normal = 45 degrees
H. Psoas (Fig. 14-8)
   1. Patient supine in a Thomas test position
   2. Patient holds one knee to the chest
   3. Passively lower the test leg toward the floor, while monitoring the ASIS for movement
   4. Normal = −5/10 degrees (past neutral)

I. Tensor fascia latae (Fig. 14-9)
   1. Patient supine in a Thomas test position
   2. Patient holds one knee to the chest
   3. Passively lower the test leg to the first resistance barrier and then maximally adduct the femur
   4. Monitor the ASIS for movement
   5. Normal = 20 degrees
J. Rectus femoris (Fig. 14-10)
   1. Patient supine in a Thomas test position
   2. Patient holds one knee to the chest
   3. Passively lower the test leg to the first resistance barrier and then flex the athlete's knee to the first resistance barrier
   4. Monitor the ASIS for movement
   5. Normal = 100 to 110 degrees

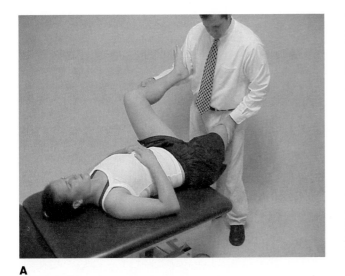

A   B

FIGURE 14-25

A, Tensor fascia latae stretch. **B,** Supine iliotibial tract stretch.

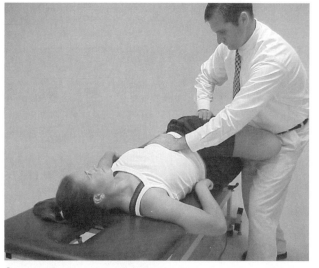

A

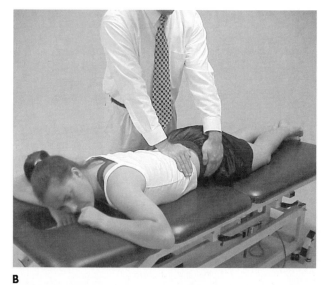

B

FIGURE 14-27

A, Erector spinae stretch. **B,** Erector spinae stretch.

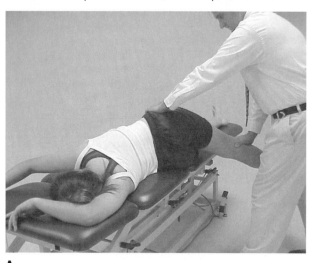

A

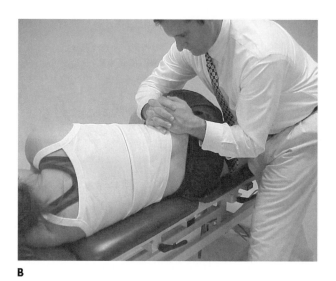

B

FIGURE 14-28

A, Quadratus lumborum muscle stretch. **B,** Quadratus distraction stretch.

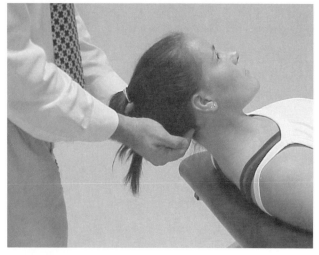

FIGURE 14-29

Suboccipital stretch.

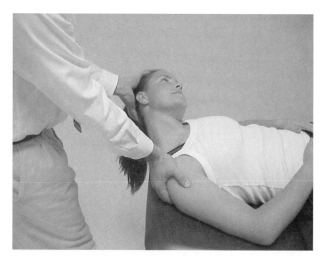

FIGURE 14-30

Upper trapezius stretch.

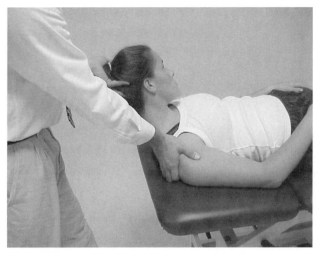

FIGURE 14-31

Levator scapulae stretch.

K. Erector spinae (Fig. 14-11)
   1. Patient long sitting or short sitting (tight hamstrings)
   2. Have athlete place the hands on the hips, while bending forward trying to approximate the forehead to the knees
   3. Monitor the PSIS for movement
   4. Normal = 10 cm (forehead to knees)
L. Quadratus lumborum (Fig. 14-12)
   1. Patient sidelying, they push themselves into lateral flexion
   2. Monitor for rotation/flexion/extension
   3. Normal = 45 degrees
M. Upper trapezius (Fig. 14-13)
   1. Patient supine, with the head supported
   2. Maximally flex the patient's head, contralateral lateral flexion, and ipsilateral rotation
   3. Depress the shoulder while assessing for muscle tightness
   4. Normal = 45 degrees

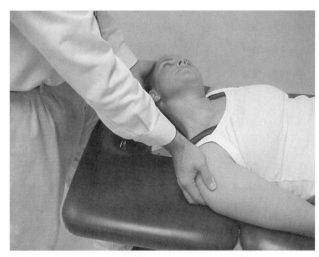

FIGURE 14-32

Scalene muscle stretch.

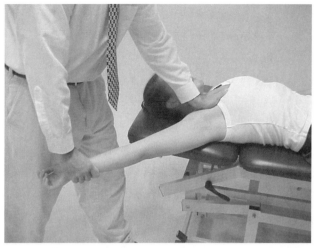

FIGURE 14-33

Pectoralis major stretch.

N. Levator scapulae (Fig. 14-14)
   1. Patient supine, with the head supported
   2. Maximally flex the patient's head, contralateral rotation, and contralateral lateral flexion
   3. Normal = 45 degrees
O. Pectoralis major (Fig. 14-15)
   1. Patient supine while the upper extremity is elevated in the scapular plane
   2. Normal = 150 degrees
P. Latissimus dorsi (Fig. 14-16)
   1. Patient supine while the upper extremity is elevated in the sagittal plane
   2. Monitor the lateral scapular border for movement
   3. Monitor lumbar spine for extension
   4. Normal = 165 degrees
Q. Subscapularis (Fig. 14-17)
   1. Patient supine with the upper arm at 90°/90°
   2. Externally rotate the athlete's arm until the resistance barrier is determined
   3. Normal = 90 degrees
R. Infraspinatus/teres minor (Fig. 14-18)
   1. Patient supine with the upper arm at 90°/90°
   2. Internally rotate the athlete's arm, while monitoring for protraction
   3. Normal = 80 degrees
S. Scalene (Fig. 14-19)
   1. Patient supine
   2. Side bend the head to contralateral side
   3. Apply pressure to shoulder
   4. Normal = 45 degrees

MUSCLE ENERGY TREATMENT TECHNIQUES

A. Gastrocnemius (Fig. 14-20)
   1. Referred pain = posterior knee, Achilles, medial arch

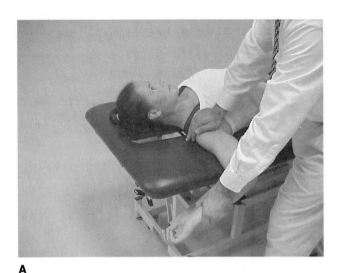

A

B

FIGURE 14-34

A, Subscapularis pectoralis major stretch. **B,** Subscapularis and latissimus stretch.

2. Chronic tightness = Achilles tendinitis, LBP, plantar fasciitis
3. Causes of tightness
   a. STJ dysfunction
   b. TTJ dysfunction
   c. Ankle sprain
   d. Poor gait/running mechanics
   e. High heels
4. Trigger point location = proximal medial/lateral border
5. Periosteal points = medial/lateral femoral condyle, calcaneus
6. Evaluation for overactivity = PF with knee flexion during hip extension
7. Evaluation for tightness = see Muscle Assessment Techniques

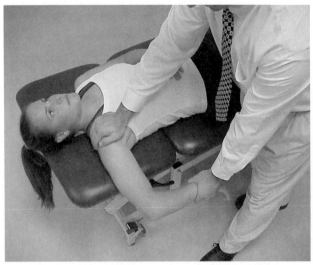

FIGURE 14-35

Teres minor-infraspinatus stretch.

8. Associated joint dysfunction
   a. STJ
   b. TTJ
   c. Proximal TFJ
   d. SI joint
   e. Lumbar spine
9. Muscle energy technique
   a. Patient supine with knee extended
   b. Place STJ in neutral
   c. DF the foot to point of first resistance
   d. Patient actively PF foot against clinician's equal resistance
   e. Contract for 10 seconds, have athlete actively DF, and bring to new point of first resistance
   f. Perform 3 to 5 repetitions
B. Soleus (see Fig. 14-20)
   1. Referred pain = posterior calcaneus, posterior calf
   2. Chronic tightness = forefoot pronation, valgus/IR stress at knee, SI joint stress
   3. Causes of tightness
      a. Excessive running
      b. Ankle/foot arthrokinematic dysfunction
      c. Weak posterior tibialis
      d. Weak quadricep
   4. Trigger point location = inferior/medial aspect of muscle
   5. Periosteal points = posterior tibia, calcaneus
   6. Evaluation for overactivity = elevation of heels with squatting
   7. Evaluation for tightness = see Muscle Assessment Techniques
   8. Associated joint dysfunction
      a. STJ
      b. TTJ
      c. Proximal TFJ

d. SI joint

e. First MTP joint

9. Corrective action

　a. Regular flexibility

　b. Functional conditioning of the entire kinetic chain

10. Muscle energy technique

　a. Prone with knee flexed to 90 degrees

　b. Put STJ in neutral

　c. Maximally DF foot to resistance barrier

　d. Athlete should actively PF against clinician's equal and opposite force (hold 10 seconds)

　e. Athlete and clinician DF foot to new resistance barrier

　f. Perform 3 to 5 sets

C. Adductors (Fig. 14-21)

1. Referred pain = anterolateral hip, groin, medial thigh, medial tibia, anterior knee

2. Chronic tightness

　a. Inhibits gluteus medius

　b. Decreases frontal plane stability

　c. Creates SI joint dysfunction

　d. Creates pubosymphyseal joint dysfunction

　e. ITB tendinitis

　f. Anterior knee pain

　g. Pes anserine tendinitis

3. Causes of tightness

　a. Weak gluteus medius

　b. SI joint dysfunction

　c. TTJ dysfunction

　d. STJ dysfunction

　e. Tight pubofemoral ligament

　f. Posture

　g. Technical inefficiency

4. Trigger point location = superior muscle belly

5. Periosteal points = pubic symphysis, tibial tubercle

6. Evaluation for overactivity

　a. Increased frontal plane compensation during SLS

7. Evaluation for tightness = see Muscle Assessment Techniques

8. Associated joint dysfunction

　a. Iliofemoral joint

　b. Iliosacral joint

　c. Sacroiliac joint

　d. Pubic symphyseal joint

　e. Tibiofemoral joint

　f. STJ

　g. TTJ

　h. First MTP

9. Muscle energy technique

　a. Patient supine or sidelying with leg abducted

　b. Leg straight (2 joint adductors) or bent (1 joint adductor)

　c. Athlete's leg is taken into abduction to resistance barrier

d. The athlete is instructed to attempt adduction against the clinician's equal and opposite force for 10 seconds

e. Perform 3 to 5 repetitions

D. Hamstring (Fig. 14-22)

1. Referred pain = low back, lower buttock, upper calf, medial/lateral knee

2. Chronic tightness

　a. Alters lumbo-pelvic-hip stability

　b. Leads to anterior knee pain

　c. Alters extensor mechanism function

　d. Leads to chronic strains

3. Causes of tightness

　a. Substitution for weak abdominals

　b. Substitution for weak gluteals

　c. Substitution for weak gastrocnemius

　d. Substitution for weak quadriceps

　e. Compensation for tight psoas

　f. STJ dysfunction

　g. TTJ dysfunction

　h. ISJ dysfunction

　i. SIJ dysfunction

　j. PTFJ dysfunction

4. Trigger point location = midbelly

5. Periosteal points = ischial tuberosity, fibular head

6. Evaluation for overactivity

　a. Knee flexion during prone hip extension

　b. Early activation during prone hip extension

7. Evaluation for tightness = see Muscle Assessment Techniques

8. Associated joint dysfunction

　a. First MTP joint

　b. STJ

　c. TTJ

　d. PTFJ

　e. TFJ

　f. IS joint

　g. SI joint

　h. Lumbar spine (L5-S1)

9. Muscle energy technique

　a. Lower hamstrings

　　(1) Athlete supine with opposite knee bent to 90 degrees

　　(2) Flex hip to resistance barrier

　　(3) Athlete extends hip and PF ankle while clinician provides equal and opposite resistance for 10 seconds

　　(4) Athlete then actively flexes hip and DF ankle to the new range of motion with assistance from the clinician

　　(5) This can be performed with abduction/IR (medial hamstrings) and adduction/ER (lateral hamstrings)

　　(6) Repeat 3 to 5 times

b. Upper hamstrings
   (1) Athlete supine with opposite knee bent to 90 degrees
   (2) Hip and knee at 90°/90°
   (3) Athlete flexes knee and PF ankle while the clinician provides equal and opposite resistance for 10 seconds
   (4) Athlete then actively extends knee and DF ankle to the new resistance barrier with assistance from the clinician
   (5) This can be performed with tibial IR (bicep femoris) and tibial ER (semitendinosus/membranosus)
   (6) Repeat 3 to 5 times

E. Piriformis (Fig. 14-23)
  1. Referred pain = posterior thigh, buttock, SI joint
  2. Chronic tightness
    a. LBP
    b. SI joint dysfunction
    c. Entrapment neuropathy
    d. Compressive pathology
    e. ITB tendinitis
  3. Causes of tightness
    a. Substitution for weak gluteus maximus
    b. Substitution for weak gluteus medius
    c. Substitution for weak biceps femoris
    d. SI joint dysfunction
    e. Short leg
  4. Trigger point location = muscle belly, sciatic notch
  5. Evaluation for overactivity
    a. ER during gait
    b. ER during sidelying hip ABD
  6. Evaluation for tightness = see Muscle Assessment Techniques
  7. Associated joint dysfunction
    a. Lumbar spine
    b. SI joint
    c. First MTP
    d. STJ
    e. TTJ
  8. Muscle energy technique
    a. Patient supine with leg flexed and adducted over non-test leg
    b. Clinician stabilizes the pelvis at the ASIS while applying longitudinal compression into the femur
    c. Athlete attempts to ABD/ER femur and lower leg while clinician applies equal and opposite resistance for 10 seconds
    d. Athlete then adducts and IR the femur with assistance from the clinician
    e. Repeat 3 to 5 times
    f. Prone/supine technique

F. Psoas (Fig. 14-24)
  1. Referred pain = low back, SI joint, patellar tendon
  2. Chronic tightness

    a. Inhibits MFS, TA, IO, DES
    b. Inhibits gluteus maximus
    c. Leads to extensor mechanism dysfunction
    d. Causes patellar tendinitis
    e. Causes hamstring strains
    f. Leads to piriformis syndrome
    g. Leads to SI joint/lumbar facet syndrome
  3. Causes of tightness
    a. Weak lower abdominals
    b. Weak gluteals
    c. Weak intrinsic LPHC stabilizers
    d. Prolonged sitting
    e. Prolonged biking
    f. Poor NMC of LPHC
    g. SI joint dysfunction
  4. Trigger point location = muscle belly
  5. Evaluation for overactivity
    a. Lumbar spine extension during hip extension tests
  6. Evaluation for tightness = see Muscle Assessment Techniques
  7. Associated joint dysfunction
    a. Lumbar spine (T10-L1)
    b. SI joint
    c. IS joint
  8. Muscle energy technique
    a. Athlete in a Thomas test position
    b. Clinician extends the hip to resistance barrier while stabilizing the opposite leg in maximal hip and knee flexion
    c. Athlete attempts to flex the hip against equal and opposite resistance from the clinician for 10 seconds
    d. Athlete then attempts to extend the hip with assistance from the clinician
    e. Repeat 3 to 5 times
    f. Prone technique

G. Tensor fascia latae (Fig. 14-25)
  1. Referred pain = lateral aspect of knee
  2. Chronic tightness
    a. ITB tendinitis
    b. Knee extensor mechanism dysfunction
    c. SI joint dysfunction
    d. Piriformis syndrome
    e. Achilles tendinitis
    f. Adductor strains
    g. Hamstring strains
    h. Low back pain
    i. Ankle sprains
  3. Causes of tightness
    a. Substitution for weak gluteus medius
    b. Compensation for weak gluteus maximus
    c. Adaptation for first MTP, STJ, TTJ, PTFJ dysfunction
    d. Adaptation for quadratus dysfunction
    e. Adaptation for psoas tightness
    f. Prolonged sitting

g. Lateral pelvic shift

h. Forefoot instability

4. Trigger point location = superior and midmuscle belly

5. Periosteal points = fibular head, lateral TF joint line, Gerdy's tubercle

6. Evaluation for overactivity

   a. Hip flexion during sidelying ABD test

7. Evaluation for tightness = see Muscle Assessment Techniques

8. Associated joint dysfunction

   a. SI joint

   b. IS joint

   c. Lumbar spine (L5-S1)

   d. PTFJ

   e. TFJ

   f. First MTP, STJ, TTJ

9. Muscle energy technique

   a. Technique I

      (1) Athlete supine in a Thomas test position

      (2) Clinician extends hip to resistance barrier and then adducts femur to resistance barrier

      (3) Athlete is instructed to flex and abduct the hip against the clinician's equal and opposite resistance for 10 seconds

      (4) Athlete then extends and adducts the hip with assistance from the clinician to the new resistance barrier

      (5) Repeat 3 to 5 times

   b. Technique II

      (1) Athlete sidelying with the stretch leg uppermost

      (2) Clinician extends and adducts the femur to the resistance barrier

      (3) Athlete is instructed to flex and abduct the femur against the equal and opposite force of the clinician for 10 seconds

      (4) Athlete then extends and adducts the femur to the new resistance barrier with assistance from the clinician

      (5) Repeat 3 to 5 times

H. Rectus femoris (Fig. 14-26)

1. Referred pain = anterior knee

2. Chronic tightness

   a. ISJ dysfunction

   b. SI joint dysfunction

   c. Hamstring strains

   d. Patellar tendinitis

   e. Post tibialis tendinitis

   f. LBP

3. Causes of tightness

   a. Prolonged sitting

   b. Compensation for weak lower abs

   c. Adaptation for weak gluteus medius

4. Trigger point location = muscle belly

5. Evaluation for tightness = see Muscle Assessment Techniques

6. Associated joint dysfunction

   a. IS joint

   b. SI joint

   c. Lumbar spine

   d. TFJ

   e. PTFJ

7. Muscle energy technique

   a. Athlete supine in a Thomas test position

   b. Clinician extends hip and flexes knee to resistance barrier

   c. Athlete is instructed to flex hip and extend knee against equal and opposite resistance for 10 seconds

   d. Athlete actively moves hip into extension and knee into flexion with assistance from the clinician

   e. Technique II

      (1) Athlete prone, clinician flexes knee to resistance barrier and extends hip to resistance barrier

      (2) Athlete is instructed to extend knee and flex hip against equal and opposite resistance from clinician for 10 seconds

      (3) Athlete then actively flexes knee and extends hip with assistance from clinician

      (4) Repeat 3 to 5 times

I. Erector spinae (Fig. 14-27)

1. Referred pain = SI joint, LB, buttock

2. Chronic tightness

   a. LBP

   b. SI joint dysfunction

   c. Hamstring strains

   d. Inhibition of deep lumbo-pelvic-hip stabilizers

3. Causes of tightness

   a. Compensation for weak gluteus maximus

   b. Compensation for weak hamstrings

   c. Compensation for weak abdominals

   d. Compensation for weak multifidus

   e. Adaptation for tight psoas

   f. Postural dysfunction

   g. Pattern overload

4. Trigger point location

   a. Muscle belly

   b. Spinous process

   c. Transverse process

5. Evaluation for overactivity

   a. Early and excessive erector spinae activity during hip extension test

   b. Lack of normal flexion–relaxation response during forward bending

6. Evaluation for tightness = see Muscle Assessment Technique

7. Associated joint dysfunction

   a. SI joint

   b. Lumbar spine

   c. IS joint

8. Muscle energy technique
   a. Athlete sidelying with involved side up, bottom arm is behind the athlete and off the table, while the upper torso is rotated forward
   b. The upper arm is hanging off the table in front
   c. Bottom leg is flexed to 90°/90°, while uppermost leg is extended and adducted off the table
   d. The clinician is standing in front of the athlete
   e. Athlete is instructed to attempt to rotate the spine into extension and rotation against equal and opposite resistance from the clinician for 10 seconds
   f. Athlete then rotates in the opposite direction and flexes the spine with assistance from the clinician
   g. Repeat 3 to 5 times

J. Quadratus lumborum (Fig. 14-28)
   1. Referred pain
      a. Lateral fibers = iliac crest and lateral hip
      b. Medial fibers = SI joint, deep in buttock
   2. Chronic tightness
      a. LBP
      b. SI joint dysfunction
      c. Abnormal frontal plane gait dysfunction
   3. Causes of tightness
      a. SI joint dysfunction
      b. Lumbar spine dysfunction
      c. IS joint dysfunction
      d. 12th rib dysfunction
      e. Compensation for weak gluteus medius
      f. Pattern overload
   4. Trigger point location = inferior to ES and lateral to transverse process
   5. Evaluation for overactivity
      a. Early and excessive pelvic elevation during sidelying hip abduction
   6. Evaluation for tightness = see Muscle Assessment Techniques
   7. Associated joint dysfunction
      a. SI joint
      b. Lumbar spine
      c. IS joint
   8. Muscle energy technique
      a. Athlete sidelying with bottom arm behind and off the table. The bottom leg is flexed and the top leg is extended and adducted. The uppermost arm is forward and hanging off the table
      b. Clinician adducts the femur and rotates the trunk anteriorly
      c. Athlete is instructed to abduct the femur and elevate the pelvis against equal and opposite resistance from the clinician for 10 seconds
      d. The clinician moves to the new resistance barrier
      e. Repeat 3 to 5 times

K. Rectus capitus (Fig. 14-29)
   1. Referred pain

a. Suboccipitals
b. Forehead
c. Upper shoulders

2. Chronic tightness
   a. Cervical headaches
   b. Cervical facet syndrome
   c. Neck, shoulder, arm pain
3. Causes of tightness
   a. Poor posture
   b. Trauma
   c. Weak deep neck flexors
4. Trigger points
   a. Base of occiput
5. Periosteal points
   a. Transverse process of atlas
6. Associated joint dysfunction
   a. C0-C1 to midcervical
7. Evaluation for tightness
8. MET treatment
   a. With the client supine, the clinician flexes the neck to the first resistance barrier
   b. The client is asked to push the head back into flexion against equal and opposite resistance from the clinician for 10 seconds
   c. Repeat 3 to 5 times

L. Upper trapezius (Fig. 14-30)
   1. Referred pain
      a. Mastoid, along the posterolateral neck and occiput to the forehead
   2. Chronic tightness
      a. Headaches
      b. Neck pain
      c. Altered scapulohumeral rhythm (shoulder impingement)
   3. Causes of tightness
      a. Occupational stress
      b. Compensation for weak lower trapezius
      c. Poor posture
      d. Carrying heavy purse/bag
      e. Compensation for anatomic/functional short leg
      f. Emotional stress
   4. Trigger points
      a. Midbelly, anterior, lateral
   5. Associated joint dysfunction
      a. C0-C1, C1-C2, other cervical facet joints, and cervicothoracic junction
   6. Evaluation for tightness
      a. See Figure 14-13
   7. MET treatment
      a. Client is supine with the head flexed, rotated toward and laterally flexed away from the side of stretch
      b. Clinician stabilizes the client's head with one hand, while the other hand is placed on the client's shoulder

c. Client is instructed to elevate the shoulder toward the ear against equal and opposite resistance from the clinician for 10 seconds

d. The clinician moves to the new resistance barrier

e. Repeat 3 to 5 times

M. Levator scapulae (Fig. 14-31)

1. Referred pain
   a. Vertebral border of the scapula
   b. Midcervical spine

2. Chronic tightness
   a. Pain on the same side as rotation
   b. Altered scapulohumeral rhythm (shoulder pathology)

3. Causes of tightness
   a. Poor posture
   b. Occupational stress
   c. Compensation for weak lower trapezius and rhomboids

4. Trigger points
   a. Superiomedial border of the scapula

5. Periosteal points
   a. Lateral surface of the spinous process of C2

6. Associated joint dysfunction
   a. C1-C2, C2-C3
   b. Cervicothoracic dysfunction

7. Evaluation for tightness
   a. See Figure 14-14

8. MET techniques
   a. Client is supine with the cervical spine flexed, lateral flexed and rotated away from the side to be stretched
   b. Clinician stabilizes the head with one hand, while the other hand contacts the client's shoulder
   c. Client is instructed to elevate the shoulder complex against equal and opposite resistance from the clinician for 10 seconds
   d. Repeat 3 to 5 times

N. Scalenes (Fig. 14-32)

1. Referred pain
   a. Pectoralis muscle, upper arm, hand, and rhomboids

2. Chronic tightness
   a. Cervicobrachial plexopathy

3. Causes of tightness
   a. Poor posture (forward head posture)
   b. Stress
   c. Emotional tension
   d. Poor breathing habits

4. Trigger points
   a. Anywhere along the anterior, medial, or posterior muscle belly
   b. Palpate the scalenes cautiously because of the proximity of sensitive neurovascular structures

5. Associated joint dysfunction
   a. First rib
   b. Flexion dysfunction of the cervical spine

6. Evaluation for tightness
   a. See Figure 14-19

7. MET techniques
   a. Client is supine, head laterally flexed to opposite side and slightly extended
      (1) Anterior fibers = rotate head to involved side
      (2) Medial fibers = no rotation is added
      (3) Posterior fibers = rotate head away from the involved side
   b. Clinician stabilizes the head with one hand and depresses the shoulder girdle with the opposite hand
   c. Client is instructed to laterally flex away from the stretch against equal and opposite resistance from the clinician for 10 seconds
   d. Clinician moves to new resistance barrier with assistance from the client
   e. Repeat 3 to 5 times

O. Pectoralis major (Fig. 14-33)

1. Referred pain
   a. Anterior chest, forearm

2. Chronic tightness
   a. Creates anterior migration of the humeral head
   b. Reciprocal inhibition of the rhomboids

3. Causes of tightness
   a. Poor posture
   b. Weak scapular stabilizers
   c. Pattern overload

4. Trigger points
   a. Anywhere along the muscle belly

5. Periosteal points
   a. Rib head attachments

6. Associated joint dysfunction
   a. Upper ribs

7. Evaluation for tightness
   a. See Figure 14-15

8. MET techniques
   a. Client supine, with the arm abducted 90 degrees and externally rotated maximally
   b. Clinician grasps the client's arm with one arm while stabilizing the muscle against the chest wall with the other arm
   c. Client is asked to horizontally adduct the arm against equal and opposite resistance from the clinician for 10 seconds
   d. Clinician takes the arm to the new resistance barrier with assistance from the client
   e. Repeat 3 to 5 times

P. Subscapularis (Fig. 14-34)

1. Referred pain
   a. Posterior deltoid and posterior arm

2. Chronic tightness
   a. Decreased functional ROM
   b. Inhibits posterior rotator cuff
   c. Creates an anterior migration of the humeral head, leading to GH impingement and microinstability

3. Causes of tightness
   a. Pattern overload (throwers)
   b. Poor posture
   c. Muscle imbalances
4. Trigger points
   a. Ventral scapula
5. Associated joint dysfunction
   a. Glenohumeral joint
6. Evaluation for tightness
   a. See Figure 14-17
7. MET techniques
   a. Client is supine with the arm at 90°/90° (abduction/flexion)
   b. Clinician takes the arm into external rotation to the resistance barrier
   c. Client is asked to internally rotate the arm against equal and opposite resistance from the clinician for 10 seconds
   d. Clinician takes the arm further into ER with assistance from the client to the new resistance barrier
   e. Repeat 3 to 5 times
Q. Infraspinatus/teres minor (Fig. 14-35)
   1. Referred pain
      a. Anterior deltoid
   2. Chronic tightness
      a. Difficulty performing functional shoulder movements
      b. Pain with overhead activities
   3. Causes of tightness
      a. Altered scapulohumeral rhythm
      b. Pattern overload
   4. Trigger points
      a. Infraspinous fossa
   5. Associated joint dysfunction
      a. Glenohumeral joint
   6. Evaluation for tightness
      a. See Figure 14-18
   7. MET techniques
      a. Client is supine with arm flexed and abducted to 90 degrees
      b. Clinician internally rotates the GH joint to the resistance barrier, while stabilizing against the anterior deltoid to prevent excessive protraction
      c. Client is instructed to externally rotate the arm against equal and opposite resistance from the clinician for 10 seconds
      d. Clinician moves to the new resistance barrier with assistance from the client
      e. Repeat 3 to 5 times

SUMMARY

• Optimal functioning of all contributing components of the kinetic chain result in appropriate length–tension relation-

ships, optimal force–couple relationships, precise arthrokinematics, and optimal neuromuscular control.

• Alterations in joint arthrokinematics, muscular imbalance, and neuromuscular control affect the function of the entire kinetic chain, leading to abnormal compensations and adaptations.

• Factors that can lead to the development of muscle imbalances and soft tissue dysfunction include postural stress, poor neuromuscular efficiency, pattern overload, overtraining, and poor technical efficiency.

• Muscle energy techniques are manually applied stretching techniques that use principles of neurophysiology to relax overactive muscles and/or stretch chronically shortened muscles.

• The resistance barrier is the point in the range of motion where tissues require some degree of passive effort to continue to move. Once the resistance barrier is established, MET can begin.

• The patient is asked to isometrically contract the agonist muscle against resistance for 10 seconds. Following the isometric contraction, there is a latency period of approximately 25 to 30 seconds, during which the muscle can be stretched. The patient can be instructed to use the antagonist muscle to pull the area being treated into a new range of motion. This uses the concept of reciprocal inhibition. Otherwise, the segment can be passively moved to the new resistance barrier.

REFERENCES

1. Basmajian J. *Muscles Alive.* Baltimore, Williams & Wilkins, 1974.
2. Bullock-Saxton J. *Muscles and Joint: Inter-relationships with Pain and Movement Dysfunction.* Unpublished course manual, November 1997.
3. Calliet R. *Low Back Pain Syndrome.* Oxford, Blackwell, 1962.
4. Chaitow L. *Muscle Energy Techniques.* New York, Churchill Livingstone, 1997.
5. Chaitow L. *Soft Tissue Manipulation.* Rochester, Healing Arts Press, 1991.
6. Dvorak J, Dvorak V. *Manual Medicine Diagnostics.* New York, George Theim Verlag, 1984.
7. Evjenth O. *Muscle Stretching in Manual Therapy.* Sweden, Alfta Rehab, 1984.
8. Fryette. *Principles of Manual Medicine. Yearbook of the Academy of Applied Osteopathy,* 1954.
9. Greenman P. *Principles of Manual Medicine.* 2nd ed. Baltimore, Williams & Wilkins, 1991.
10. Greenman P. *Principles of Manual Medicine.* Baltimore, Williams & Wilkins, 1989.
11. Holt LE. *Scientific Stretching for Sport.* Halifax, Dalhousie University Press, 1976.
12. Janda V. Physical therapy of the cervical and thoracic

spine. In: Grant R, ed. New York, Churchill Livingstone, 1988.

13. Janda V. *Muscle Function Testing.* London, Butterworth, 1983.

14. Lewit K. *Manipulative Therapy in Rehabilitation of the Locomotor System.* 2nd ed. London, Butterworth, 1992.

15. Lewit K. *Manipulative Therapy in Rehabilitation of the Locomotor System.* London, Butterworth, 1985.

16. Lewit K. Muscular and articular factors in movement restriction. *Manual Med* 1:83–85, 1984.

17. Lewit K, Simons D. Myofascial pain: Relief by postisometric relaxation. *Arch Phys Med Rehabil* 65:452, 1984.

18. Liebenson CL. *Rehabilitation of the Spine.* Baltimore, Williams & Wilkins, 1996.

19. Liebenson CL. Active muscle relaxation techniques: Part II. Clinical application. *J Manipulative Physiol Ther* 13:2–6, 1990.

20. Liebenson CL. Active muscle relaxation techniques: Part I. Basic principles and methods. *J Manipulative Physiol Ther* 12:446–454, 1989.

21. Menell J. *Back Pain.* Boston, T&A Churchill, 1964.

22. Moore M. EMG investigation of manual muscle stretching techniques. *Med Sci Sports Exerc* 12:322–329, 1980.

23. Retzlaff E. The piriformis syndrome. *J Am Osteopath Assn* 173:799–807, 1974.

24. Rolf I. *Rolfing: Integration of Human Structures.* New York, Harper & Row, 1977.

25. Ruddy T. Osteopathic resistive technique. *Academy of Applied Osteopathy Yearbook,* 1962.

26. Sarhmann S. *Diagnosis and Treatment of Muscle Imbalances and Musculoskeletal Pain Syndromes.* Course manual, 1997.

27. Sommer HM. Patellar chondropathy and apicitis, and muscle imbalances of the lower extremities in competitive sports. *Sports Med* 5:386–394, 1988.

CHAPTER 15

Joint Mobilization and Traction Techniques in Rehabilitation

William E. Prentice

OBJECTIVES

After completing this chapter, the student therapist should be able to do the following:

- Differentiate between physiologic movements and accessory motions.
- Discuss joint arthrokinematics.
- Discuss how specific joint positions can enhance the effectiveness of the treatment technique.
- Discuss the basic techniques of joint mobilization.
- Identify Maitland's five oscillation grades.
- Discuss indications and contraindications for mobilization.
- Discuss the use of various traction grades in treating pain and joint hypomobility.
- Explain why traction and mobilization techniques should be used simultaneously.
- Demonstrate specific techniques of mobilization and traction for various joints.

Following injury to a joint, there will almost always be some associated loss of motion. That loss of movement may be attributed to a number of pathologic factors including contracture of inert connective tissue (for example, ligaments and joint capsule); resistance of the contractile tissue or the musculotendinous unit (for example, muscle, tendon, and fascia) to stretch; or some combination of the two.[5] If left untreated, the joint will become hypomobile and will eventually begin to show signs of degeneration.[20]

Joint mobilization and traction are manual therapy techniques that are slow, passive movements of articulating surfaces. They are used to regain normal active joint range of motion, restore normal passive motions that occur about a joint, reposition or realign a joint, regain a normal distribution of forces and stresses about a joint, or reduce pain—all of which will collectively improve joint function.[17] Joint mobilization and traction are two extremely effective and widely used techniques in injury rehabilitation.

RELATIONSHIP BETWEEN PHYSIOLOGIC AND ACCESSORY MOTIONS

For the therapist supervising a rehabilitation program, some understanding of the biomechanics of joint movement is essential.

There are basically two types of movement that govern motion about a joint. Perhaps the better known of the two types of movement are the **physiologic movements** that result from either concentric or eccentric active muscle contractions that move a bone or a joint. This type of motion is referred to as **osteokinematic motion.** A bone can move about an axis of rotation, or a joint into flexion, extension, abduction, adduction, and rotation. The second type of motion is **accessory motion.** Accessory motions refer to the manner in which one articulating joint surface moves relative to another. Physiologic movement is voluntary, while accessory movements normally accompany physiologic movement.[2] The two occur simultaneously. Although accessory movements cannot occur independently, they may be produced by some external force. Normal accessory component motions must occur for full-range physiologic movement to take place. If any of the accessory component motions are restricted, normal physiologic cardinal plane movements will not occur.[14,15] A muscle cannot be fully rehabilitated if the joint is not free to move and vice versa.[20]

Traditionally in rehabilitation programs we have tended to concentrate more on passive physiologic movements without paying much attention to accessory motions. The question is always being asked, "How much flexion or extension is this patient lacking?" Rarely will anyone ask "How much is rolling or gliding restricted?"

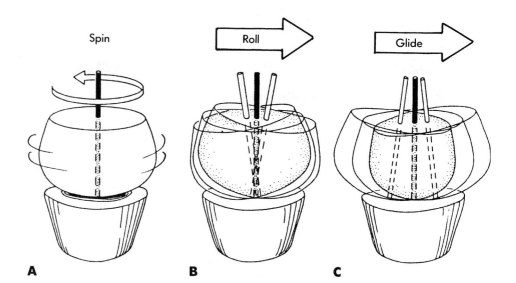

Spin   Roll   Glide

FIGURE 15-1

Joint arthrokinematics.
A, Spin. **B,** Roll.
C, Glide. (Reproduced
with permission from
Prentice 1998.[19A])

A   B   C

It is critical for the therapist to closely evaluate the injured joint to determine whether motion is limited by physiologic movement constraints involving musculotendinous units or by limitation in accessory motion involving the joint capsule and ligaments. If physiologic movement is restricted, the patient should engage in stretching activities designed to improve flexibility. Stretching exercises should be used whenever there is resistance of the contractile or musculotendinous elements to stretch. Stretching techniques are most effective at the end of physiologic range of movement; they are limited to one direction, and they require some element of discomfort if additional range of motion is to be achieved. Stretching techniques make use of long-lever arms to apply stretch to a given muscle.[9]

If accessory motion is limited by some restriction of the joint capsule or the ligaments, the therapist should incorporate mobilization techniques into the treatment program. Mobilization techniques should be used whenever there are tight inert or noncontractile articular structures; they can be used effectively at any point in the range of motion, and they can be used in any direction in which movement is restricted. Mobilization techniques use a short-lever arm to stretch ligaments and joint capsules, placing less stress on these structures, and consequently are somewhat safer to use than stretching techniques.[3]

JOINT ARTHROKINEMATICS

Accessory motions are also referred to as **joint arthrokinematics,** which include **spin, roll,** and **glide** (Fig. 15-1).[1,10,12]

Spin occurs around some stationary longitudinal mechanical axis and may be in either a clockwise or counterclockwise direction. An example of spinning is motion of the radial head at the humeroradial joint as occurs in forearm pronation/supination (Fig. 15-1A).

Rolling occurs when a series of points on one articulating surface come in contact with a series of points on another

articulating surface. An analogy would be to picture a rocker of a rocking chair rolling on the flat surface of the floor. An anatomic example would be the rounded femoral condyles rolling over a stationary flat tibial plateau (Fig. 15-1B).

Gliding occurs when a specific point on one articulating surface comes in contact with a series of points on another surface. Returning to the rocking chair analogy, the rocker slides across the flat surface of the floor without any rocking at all. Gliding is sometimes referred to as **translation.** Anatomically, gliding or translation would occur during an anterior drawer test at the knee when the flat tibial plateau slides anteriorly relative to the fixed rounded femoral condyles (Fig. 15-1C).

Pure gliding can occur only if the two articulating surfaces are congruent, where either both are flat or both are curved. Since virtually all articulating joint surfaces are incongruent, meaning that one is usually flat while the other is more curved, it is more likely that gliding will occur simultaneously with a rolling motion. Rolling does not occur alone because this would result in compression or perhaps dislocation of the joint.

Although rolling and gliding usually occur together, they are not necessarily in similar proportion, nor are they always in the same direction. If the articulating surfaces are more congruent, more gliding will occur, whereas if they are less congruent, more rolling will occur. Rolling will always occur in the same direction as the movement. For example, in the knee joint when the foot is fixed on the ground, the femur will always roll in an anterior direction when moving into knee extension and conversely will roll posteriorly when moving into flexion (Fig. 15-2).

The direction of the gliding component of motion is determined by the shape of the articulating surface that is moving. If you consider the shape of two articulating surfaces, one joint surface can be determined to be convex in shape while the other may be considered to be concave in shape. In the knee, the femoral condyles would be considered the convex joint surface, while the tibial plateau would be the concave joint surface. In the glenohumeral joint, the humeral head would be the

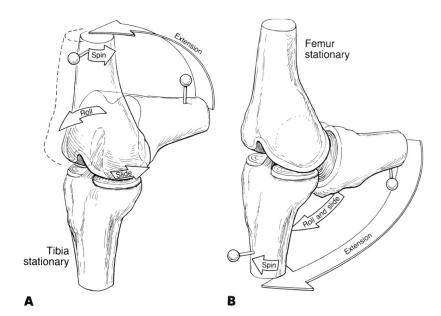

FIGURE 15-2

Convex–concave rule. **A,** Convex moving on concave. **B,** Concave moving on convex. (Reproduced with permission from Prentice 1998.[19A])

convex surface, while the glenoid fossa would be the concave surface.

This relationship between the shape of articulating joint surfaces and the direction of gliding is defined by the **convex–concave rule.** If the concave joint surface is moving on a stationary convex surface, gliding will occur in the same direction as the rolling motion. Conversely, if the convex surface is moving on a stationary concave surface, gliding will occur in an opposite direction to rolling. Hypomobile joints are treated by using a gliding technique. Thus it is critical to know the appropriate direction to use for gliding.

JOINT POSITIONS

Each joint in the body has a position in which the joint capsule and the ligaments are most relaxed, allowing for a maximum amount of **joint play.**[10,11] This position is called the **resting position.** It is essential to know specifically where the resting position is, because testing for joint play during an evaluation, and treatment of the hypomobile joint using either mobilization or traction, are usually performed in this position. Table 15-1 summarizes the appropriate resting positions for many of the major joints.

Placing the joint capsule in the resting position allows the joint to assume a **loose-packed position** in which the articulating joint surfaces are maximally separated. A **close-packed position** is one in which there is maximal contact of the articulating surfaces of bones with the capsule and ligaments tight or tense. In a loose-packed position, the joint will exhibit the greatest amount of joint play, while the close-packed position allows for no joint play. Thus the loose-packed position is most appropriate for mobilization and traction (Fig. 15-3).

Both mobilization and traction techniques use a translational movement of one joint surface relative to the other. This translation may be either perpendicular or parallel to the **treatment plane.** The treatment plane falls perpendicular to, or at a right angle to, a line running from the axis of rotation in the convex surface to the center of the concave articular surface. (Fig. 15-4).[10,11] Thus the treatment plane lies within the concave surface. If the convex segment moves, the treatment plane remains fixed. However, the treatment plane will move along with the concave segment. Mobilization techniques use glides that translate one articulating surface along a line parallel with the treatment plane. Traction techniques translate one of the articulating surfaces in a perpendicular direction to the treatment plane. Both techniques use a loose-packed joint position.[10]

FIGURE 15-3

Joint capsule resting position.
A, Loose-packed position.
B, Close-packed position.
(Reproduced with permission from Prentice 1998.[19A])

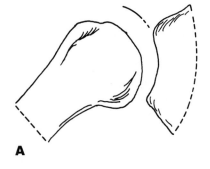
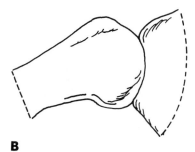

T A B L E   1 5 - 1

Shape, Resting Position, and Treatment Planes of Various Joints

JOINT	CONVEX SURFACE	CONCAVE SURFACE	RESTING POSITION	TREATMENT PLANE
Sternoclavicular	Clavicle[a]	Sternum[a]	Anatomic position	In sternum
Acromioclavicular	Clavicle	Acromion	Anatomic position, in horizontal plane at 60 degrees to sagittal plane	In acromion
Glenohumeral	Humerus	Glenoid	Shoulder abducted 55 degrees, horizontally adducted 30 degrees, rotated so forearm is in horizontal plane	In glenoid fossa in scapular plane
Humeroradial	Humerus	Radius	Elbow extended, forearm supinated	In radial head perpendicular to long axis of radius
Humeroulnar	Humerus	Ulna	Elbow flexed 70 degrees, forearm supinated 10 degrees	In olecranon fossa, 45 degrees to long axis of ulna
Radioulnar (proximal)	Radius	Ulna	Elbow flexed 70 degrees, forearm supinated 35 degrees	In radial notch of ulna, parallel to long axis of ulna
Radioulnar (distal)	Ulna	Radius	Supinated 10 degrees	In radius, parallel to long axis of radius
Radiocarpal	Proximal carpal bones	Radius	Line through radius and third metacarpal	In radius, perpendicular to long axis of radius
Metacarpophalangeal	Metacarpal	Proximal phalanx	Slight flexion	In proximal phalanx
Interphalangeal	Proximal phalanx	Distal phalanx	Slight flexion	In proximal phalanx
Hip	Femur	Acetabulum	Hip flexed 30 degrees, abducted 30 degrees, slight external rotation	In acetabulum
Tibiofemoral	Femur	Tibia	Flexed 25 degrees	On surface of tibial plateau
Patellofemoral	Patella	Femur	Knee in full extension	Along femoral groove
Talocrural	Talus	Mortise	Plantarflexed 10 degrees	In the mortise in anterior/posterior direction
Subtalar	Calcaneus	Talus	Subtalar neutral between inversion/eversion	In talus, parallel to foot surface
Intertarsal	Proximal articulating surface	Distal articulating surface	Foot relaxed	In distal segment
Metatarsophalangeal	Tarsal bone	Proximal phalanx	Slight extension	In proximal phalanx
Interphalangeal	Proximal phalanx	Distal phalanx	Slight flexion	In distal phalanx

[a] In the sternoclavicular joint the clavicle surface is convex in a superior/inferior direction and concave in an anterior/posterior direction.
(Reproduced, with permission, from Prentice WE. *Therapeutic Modalities for Allied Health Professionals.* New York, McGraw-Hill, 1998, p. 447.)

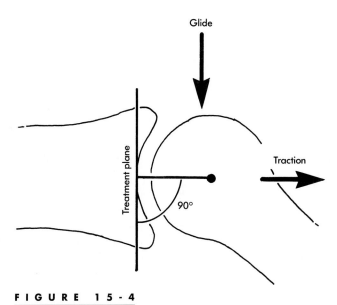

FIGURE 15-4

Treatment plane. The treatment plane is perpendicular to a line drawn from the axis of rotation to the center of the articulating surface of the concave segment.
(Reproduced with permission from Prentice 1998.[19A])

JOINT MOBILIZATION TECHNIQUES

The techniques of joint mobilization are used to improve joint mobility or to decrease joint pain by restoring accessory movements to the joint and thus allowing full, nonrestricted, pain-free range of motion.[16,23]

Mobilization techniques may be used to attain a variety of either mechanical or neurophysiologic treatment goals: reducing pain; decreasing muscle guarding; stretching or lengthening tissue surrounding a joint, in particular capsular and ligamentous tissue; reflexogenic effects that either inhibit or facilitate muscle tone or stretch reflex; and proprioceptive effects to improve postural and kinesthetic awareness.[1,8,14,18,20]

Movement throughout a range of motion can be quantified with various measurement techniques. Physiologic movement is measured with a goniometer and composes the major portion of the range. Accessory motion is thought of in millimeters, although precise measurement is difficult.

Accessory movements may be hypomobile, normal, or hypermobile.[4] Each joint has a range of motion continuum with an anatomic limit (AL) to motion that is determined by both bony arrangement and surrounding soft tissue (Fig. 15-5). In a hypomobile joint, motion stops at some point referred to as a pathologic point of limitation (PL), short of the anatomic limit caused by pain, spasm, or tissue resistance. A hypermobile joint moves beyond its anatomic limit because of laxity of the surrounding structures. A hypomobile joint should respond well to techniques of mobilization and traction. A hypermobile joint should be treated with strengthening exercises, stability exercises, and if indicated, taping, splinting, or bracing.[19,20]

In a hypomobile joint, as mobilization techniques are used into the range-of-motion restriction, some deformation of soft-tissue capsular or ligamentous structures occurs. If a tissue is stretched only into its elastic range, no permenant structural changes will occur. However, if that tissue is stretched into its plastic range, permanent structural changes will occur. Thus, mobilization and traction can be used to stretch tissue and break adhesions. If used inappropriately, they can also damage tissue and cause sprains of the joint.[20]

Treatment techniques designed to improve accessory movement are generally slow, small-amplitude movements, the amplitude being the distance that the joint is moved passively within its total range. Mobilization techniques use these small-amplitude oscillating motions that glide or slide one of the articulating joint surfaces in an appropriate direction within a specific part of the range.

Maitland has described various grades of oscillation for joint mobilization. The amplitude of each oscillation grade falls within the range of motion continuum between some beginning point (BP) and the AL.[14,15] Figure 15-5 shows the various grades of oscillation that are used in a joint with some limitation of motion. As the severity of the movement restriction increases, the PL will move to the left, away from the AL. However, the relationships that exist among the five grades in

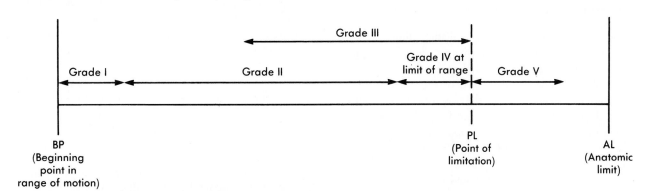

FIGURE 15-5

Maitland's five grades of motion. (PL, point of limitation; AL, anatomic limit.)
(Reproduced with permission from Prentice 1998.[19A])

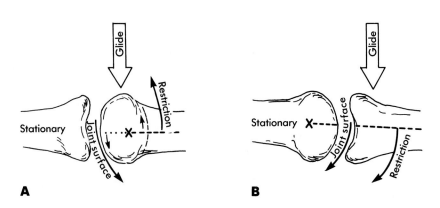

terms of their positions within the range of motion remain the same. The five mobilization grades are defined as follows:

- Grade I. A small-amplitude movement at the beginning of the range of movement. Used when pain and spasm limit movement early in the range of motion.[25]
- Grade II. A large-amplitude movement within the midrange of movement. Used when spasm limits movement sooner with a quick oscillation than with a slow one, or when slowly increasing pain restricts movement halfway into the range.
- Grade III. A large-amplitude movement up to the PL in the range of movement. Used when pain and resistance from spasm, inert tissue tension, or tissue compression limit movement near the end of the range.
- Grade IV. A small-amplitude movement at the very end of the range of movement. Used when resistance limits movement in the absence of pain and spasm.
- Grade V. A small-amplitude, quick thrust delivered at the end of the range of movement, usually accompanied by a popping sound, which is called a manipulation. Used when minimal resistance limits the end of the range. Manipulation is most effectively accomplished by the velocity of the thrust rather than by the force of the thrust.[21] Most authorities agree that manipulation should be used only by individuals trained specifically in these techniques, because a great deal of skill and judgment is necessary for safe and effective treatment.[22]

Joint mobilization uses these oscillating gliding motions of one articulating joint surface in whatever direction is appropriate for the existing restriction. The appropriate direction for these oscillating glides is determined by the convex–concave rule, described previously. When the concave surface is stationary and the convex surface is mobilized, a glide of the convex segment should be in the direction opposite to the restriction of joint movement (Fig. 15-6A).[10,11,24] If the convex articular surface is stationary and the concave surface is mobilized, gliding of the concave segment should be in the same direction as the restriction of joint movement (Fig. 15-6B). For example, the glenohumeral joint would be considered to be a convex joint with the convex humeral head moving on the concave glenoid. If shoulder abduction is restricted, the humerus should be glided in an inferior direction relative to the glenoid to

alleviate the motion restriction. When mobilizing the knee joint, the concave tibia should be glided anteriorly in cases where knee extension is restricted. If mobilization in the appropriate direction exacerbates complaints of pain or stiffness, the therapist should apply the technique in the opposite direction until the patient can tolerate the appropriate direction.[24]

Typical mobilization of a joint may involve a series of 3 to 6 sets of oscillations lasting between 20 and 60 seconds each, with 1 to 3 oscillations per second.[14,15]

Indications for Mobilization

In Maitland's system, grades I and II are used primarily for treatment of pain, and grades III and IV are used for treating stiffness. Pain must be treated first and stiffness second.[14] Painful conditions should be treated on a daily basis. The purpose of the small-amplitude oscillations is to stimulate mechanoreceptors within the joint that can limit the transmission of pain perception at the spinal cord or brainstem levels.

Joints that are stiff or hypomobile and have restricted movement should be treated 3 to 4 times per week on alternating days with active motion exercise. The therapist must continuously reevaluate the joint to determine appropriate progression from one oscillation grade to another.

Indications for specific mobilization grades are relatively straightforward. If the patient complains of pain before the therapist can apply any resistance to movement, it is too early, and all mobilization techniques should be avoided. If pain is elicited when resistance to motion is applied, mobilization using grades I and II is appropriate. If resistance can be applied before pain is elicited, mobilization can be progressed to grades III and IV. Mobilization should be done with both the patient and the therapist positioned in a comfortable and relaxed manner. The therapist should mobilize one joint at a time. The joint should be stabilized as near one articulating surface as possible, while moving the other segment with a firm, confident grasp.

Contraindications for Mobilization

Techniques of mobilization and manipulation should not be used haphazardly. These techniques should generally not be used in cases of inflammatory arthritis, malignancy, bone disease, neurologic involvement, bone fracture, congenital bone

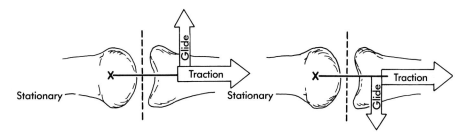

F I G U R E   1 5 - 7

Traction versus glides. Traction should be perpendicular to the treatment plane, while glides are parallel to the treatment plane. (Reproduced with permission from Prentice 1998.[19A])

deformities, and vascular disorders of the vertebral artery. Again, manipulation should be performed only by those therapists specifically trained in the procedure, because some special knowledge and judgment are required for effective treatment.[24]

JOINT TRACTION TECHNIQUES

Traction refers to a technique involving pulling on one articulating segment to produce some separation of the two joint surfaces. While mobilization glides are done parallel to the treatment plane, traction is performed perpendicular to the treatment plane (see Fig. 15-7). Like mobilization techniques, traction may be used either to decrease pain or to reduce joint hypomobility.[26]

Kaltenborn has proposed a system using traction combined with mobilization as a means of reducing pain or mobilizing hypomobile joints.[10] As discussed earlier, all joints have a certain amount of joint play or looseness. Kaltenborn referred to this looseness as **slack.** Some degree of slack is necessary for normal joint motion. Kaltenborn's three traction grades are defined as follows (Fig. 15-8):

- Grade I traction (loosen). Traction that neutralizes pressure in the joint without actual separation of the joint surfaces. The purpose is to produce pain relief by reducing the compressive forces of articular surfaces during mobilization and is used with all mobilization grades.

- Grade II traction (tighten or "take up the slack"). Traction that effectively separates the articulating surfaces and takes up the slack or eliminates play in the joint capsule. Grade II is used in initial treatment to determine joint sensitivity.
- Grade III traction (stretch). Traction that involves actual stretching of the soft tissue surrounding the joint to increase mobility in a hypomobile joint.

Grade I traction should be used in the initial treatment to reduce the chance of a painful reaction. It is recommended that 10-second intermittent grades I and II traction be used, distracting the joint surfaces up to a grade III traction and then releasing distraction until the joint returns to its resting position.

Kaltenborn emphasizes that grade III traction should be used in conjunction with mobilization glides to treat joint hypomobility (Fig. 15-9).[10] Grade III traction stretches the joint capsule and increases the space between the articulating surfaces, placing the joint in a loose-packed position. Applying grades III and IV oscillations within the patient's pain limitations should maximally improve joint mobility.

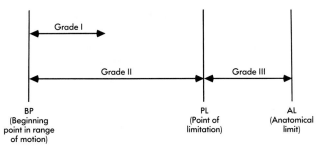

F I G U R E   1 5 - 8

Kaltenborn's grades of traction. (PL, point of limitation; AL, anatomic limit.) (Reproduced with permission from Prentice 1998.[19A])

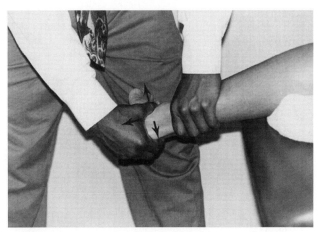

F I G U R E   1 5 - 9

Traction and mobilization. Traction and mobilization should be used together. (Reproduced with permission from Prentice 1998.[19A])

MOBILIZATION AND TRACTION TECHNIQUES

Figures 15-10 through 15-73 provide descriptions and illustrations of various mobilization and traction techniques. These figures should be used to determine appropriate hand positioning, stabilization (S), and the correct direction for gliding (G), traction (T), and/or rotation (R). The information presented in this chapter should be used as a reference base for appropriately incorporating joint mobilization and traction techniques into the rehabilitation program.

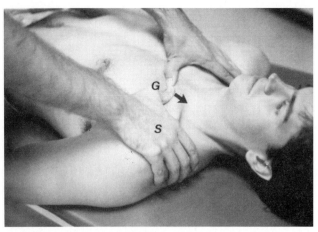

FIGURE 15-10

Posterior and superior clavicular glides. When posterior or superior clavicular glides are done at the sternoclavicular joint, use the thumbs to glide the clavicle. Posterior glides are used to increase clavicular retraction, and superior glides increase clavicular retraction and clavicular depression. (Reproduced with permission from Prentice 1998.[19A])

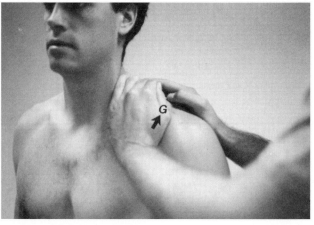

FIGURE 15-12

Posterior clavicular glides. Posterior clavicular glides done at the acromioclavicular (AC) joint apply posterior pressure on the clavicle while stabilizing the scapula with the opposite hand. They increase mobility of the AC joint. (Reproduced with permission from Prentice 1998.[19A])

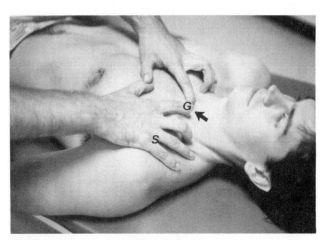

FIGURE 15-11

Inferior clavicular glides. Inferior clavicular glides at the sternoclavicular joint use the index fingers to mobilize the clavicle, which increases clavicular elevation. (Reproduced with permission from Prentice 1998.[19A])

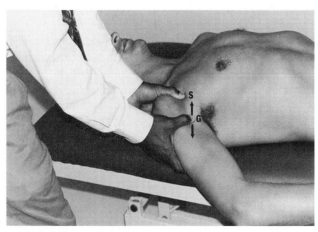

FIGURE 15-13

Anterior/posterior glenohumeral glides. Anterior/posterior glenohumeral glides are done with one hand stabilizing the scapula and the other gliding the humeral head. They initiate motion in the painful shoulder. (Reproduced with permission from Prentice 1998.[19A])

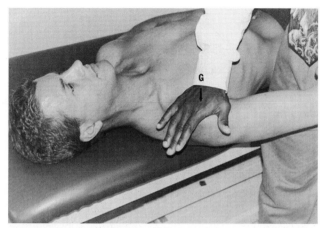

FIGURE 15-14

Posterior humeral glides. Posterior humeral glides use one hand to stabilize the humerus at the elbow and the other to glide the humeral head. They increase flexion and medial rotation. (Reproduced with permission from Prentice 1998.[19A])

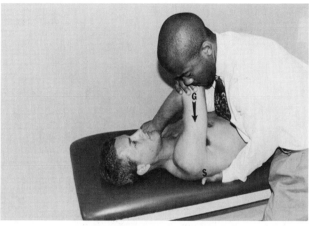

FIGURE 15-16

Posterior humeral glides. Posterior humeral glides may also be done with the shoulder at 90 degrees. With the patient in supine position, one hand stabilizes the scapula underneath, while the patient's elbow is secured at the therapist's shoulder. Glides are directed downward through the humerus. They increase horizontal adduction. (Reproduced with permission from Prentice 1998.[19A])

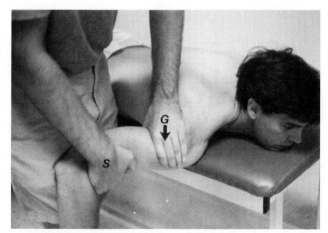

FIGURE 15-15

Anterior humeral glides. In anterior humeral glides the patient is prone. One hand stabilizes the humerus at the elbow, and the other glides the humeral head. They increase extension and lateral rotation. (Reproduced with permission from Prentice 1998.[19A])

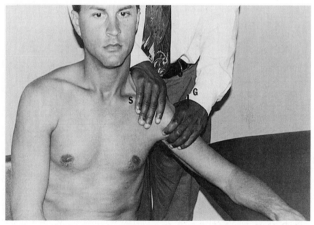

FIGURE 15-17

Inferior humeral glides. For inferior humeral glides the patient is in the sitting position with the elbow resting on the treatment table. One hand stabilizes the scapula, and the other glides the humeral head inferiorly. These glides increase shoulder abduction. (Reproduced with permission from Prentice 1998.[19A])

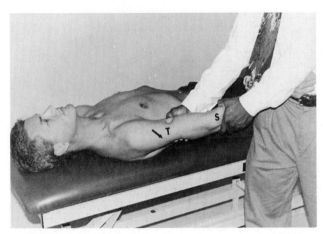

FIGURE   15-18

Lateral glenohumeral joint traction. Lateral glenohumeral joint traction is used for initial testing of joint mobility and for decreasing pain. One hand stabilizes the elbow while the other applies lateral traction at the upper humerus. (Reproduced with permission from Prentice 1998.[19A])

FIGURE   15-20

General scapular glides. General scapular glides may be done in all directions, applying pressure at either the medial, inferior, lateral, or superior border of the scapula. Scapular glides increase general scapulothoracic mobility. (Reproduced with permission from Prentice 1998.[19A])

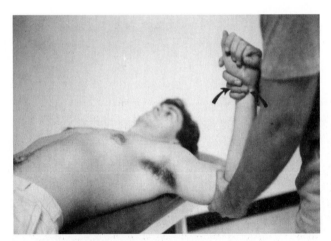

FIGURE   15-19

Medial and lateral rotation oscillations. Medial and lateral rotation oscillations with the shoulder abducted at 90 degrees can increase medial and lateral rotation in a progressive manner according to patient tolerance. (Reproduced with permission from Prentice 1998.[19A])

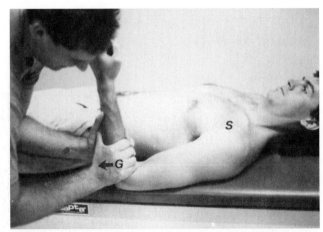

FIGURE   15-21

Inferior humeroulnar glides. Inferior humeroulnar glides increase elbow flexion and extension. They are performed using the body weight to stabilize proximally with the hand grasping the ulna and gliding inferiorly. (Reproduced with permission from Prentice 1998.[19A])

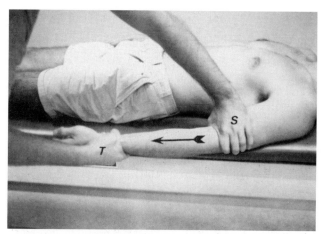

FIGURE 15-22

Humeroradial inferior glides. Humeroradial inferior glides increase the joint space and improve flexion and extension. One hand stabilizes the humerus above the elbow; the other grasps the distal forearm and glides the radius inferiorly. (Reproduced with permission from Prentice 1998.[19A])

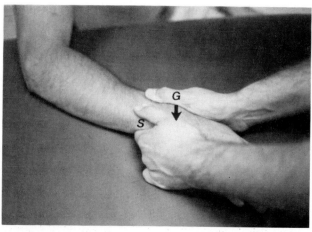

FIGURE 15-24

Distal anterior/posterior radial glides. Distal anterior/posterior radial glides are done with one hand stabilizing the ulna and the other gliding the radius. These glides increase pronation. (Reproduced with permission from Prentice 1998.[19A])

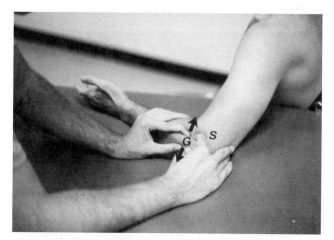

FIGURE 15-23

Proximal anterior/posterior radial glides. Proximal anterior/posterior radial glides use the thumbs and index fingers to glide the radial head. Anterior glides increase flexion, while posterior glides increase extension. (Reproduced with permission from Prentice 1998.[19A])

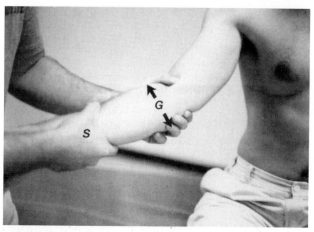

FIGURE 15-25

Medial and lateral ulnar oscillations. Medial and lateral ulnar oscillations increase flexion and extension. Valgus and varus forces are used with a short-lever arm. (Reproduced with permission from Prentice 1998.[19A])

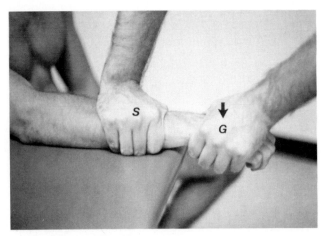

F I G U R E   1 5 - 2 6

Radiocarpal joint anterior glides. Radiocarpal joint anterior glides increase wrist extension. (Reproduced with permission from Prentice 1998.[19A])

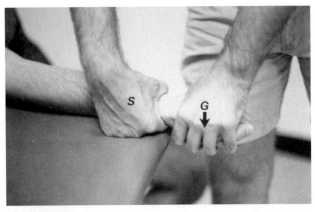

F I G U R E   1 5 - 2 7

Radiocarpal joint posterior glides. Radiocarpal joint posterior glides increase wrist flexion. (Reproduced with permission from Prentice 1998.[19A])

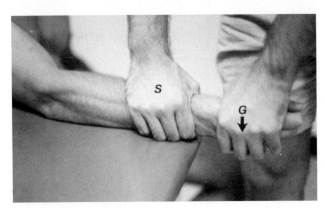

F I G U R E   1 5 - 2 8

Radiocarpal joint ulnar glides. Radiocarpal joint ulnar glides increase radial deviation. (Reproduced with permission from Prentice 1998.[19A])

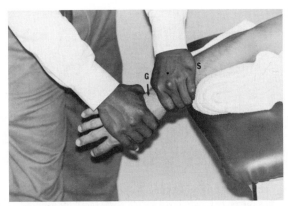

F I G U R E   1 5 - 2 9

Radiocarpal joint radial glides. Radiocarpal joint radial glides increase ulnar deviation. (Reproduced with permission from Prentice 1998.[19A])

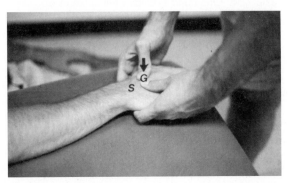

F I G U R E   1 5 - 3 0

Carpometacarpal joint anterior/posterior glides. Carpometacarpal joint anterior/posterior glides increase mobility of the hand. (Reproduced with permission from Prentice 1998.[19A])

F I G U R E   1 5 - 3 1

Metacarpophalangeal (MP) joint anterior/posterior glides. In metacarpophalangeal MP joint anterior or posterior glides, the proximal segment, in this case the metacarpal, is stabilized and the distal segment is mobilized. Anterior glides increase flexion of the MP joint. Posterior glides increase extension. (Reproduced with permission from Prentice 1998.[19A])

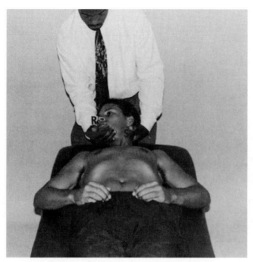

F I G U R E   1 5 - 3 2

Cervical vertebrae rotation oscillations. Cervical vertebrae rotation oscillations are done with one hand supporting the weight of the head and the other rotating the head in the direction of the restriction. These oscillations treat pain or stiffness when there is some resistance in the same direction as the rotation. (Reproduced with permission from Prentice 1998.[19A])

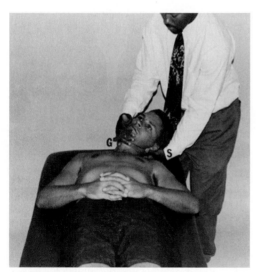

F I G U R E   1 5 - 3 3

Cervical vertebrae sidebending. Cervical vertebrae sidebending may be used to treat pain or stiffness with resistance when sidebending the neck. (Reproduced with permission from Prentice 1998.[19A])

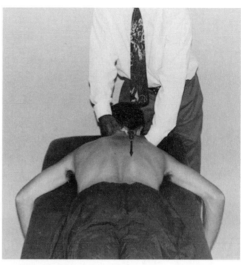

F I G U R E   1 5 - 3 4

Unilateral cervical facet anterior/posterior glides. Unilateral cervical facet anterior/posterior glides are done using pressure from the thumbs over individual facets. They increase rotation or flexion of the neck toward the side where the technique is used. (Reproduced with permission from Prentice 1998.[19A])

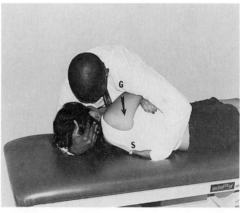

F I G U R E   1 5 - 3 5

Thoracic vertebral facet rotations. Thoracic vertebral facet rotations are accomplished with one hand underneath the patient providing stabilization, and the weight of the body pressing downward through the rib cage to rotate an individual thoracic vertebra. Rotation of the thoracic vertebra is minimal, and most of the movement with this mobilization involves the rib facet joint. (Reproduced with permission from Prentice 1998.[19A])

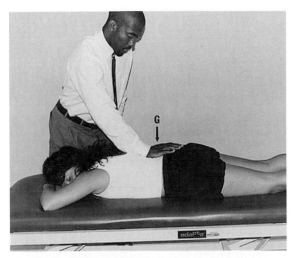

F I G U R E   1 5 - 3 6

Anterior/posterior lumbar vertebral glides. In the lumbar region, anterior/posterior lumbar vertebral glides may be accomplished at individual segments using pressure on the spinous process through the pisiform in the hand. These decrease pain or increase mobility of individual lumbar vertebrae. (Reproduced with permission from Prentice 1998.[19A])

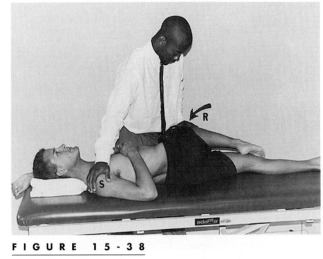

F I G U R E   1 5 - 3 8

Lumbar vertebral rotations. Lumbar vertebral rotations decrease pain and increase mobility in lumbar vertebrae. These rotations should be done in a sidelying position. (Reproduced with permission from Prentice 1998.[19A])

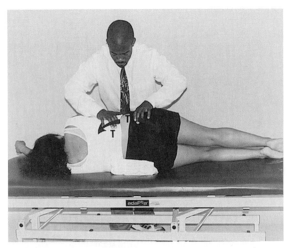

F I G U R E   1 5 - 3 7

Lumbar lateral distraction. Lumbar lateral distraction increases the space between transverse processes and increases the opening of the intervertebral foramen. This position is achieved by lying over a support, flexing the patient's upper knee to a point where there is gapping in the appropriate spinal segment, then rotating the upper trunk to place the segment in a close-packed position. Then finger and forearm pressure are used to separate individual spaces. This pressure is used for reducing pain in the lumbar vertebrae associated with some compression of a spinal nerve. (Reproduced with permission from Prentice 1998.[19A])

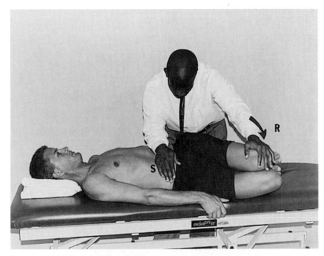

F I G U R E   1 5 - 3 9

Lateral lumbar rotations. Lateral lumbar rotations may be done with the patient in supine position. In this position, one hand must stabilize the upper trunk, while the other produces rotation. (Reproduced with permission from Prentice 1998.[19A])

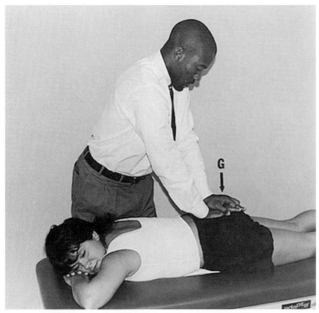

FIGURE 15-40

Anterior sacral glides. Anterior sacral glides decrease pain and reduce muscle guarding around the sacroiliac joint. (Reproduced with permission from Prentice 1998.[19A])

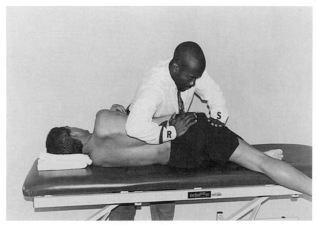

FIGURE 15-42

Anterior innominate rotation. An anterior innominate rotation in a sidelying position is accomplished by extending the leg on the affected side, and then stabilizing with one hand on the front of the thigh while the other applies pressure anteriorly over the posterosuperior iliac spine to produce an anterior rotation. This technique will correct a unilateral posterior rotation. (Reproduced with permission from Prentice 1998.[19A])

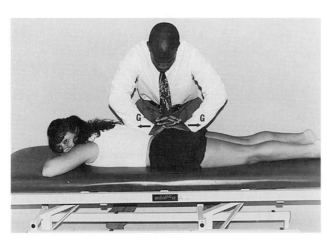

FIGURE 15-41

Superior/inferior sacral glides. Superior/inferior sacral glides decrease pain and reduce muscle guarding around the sacroiliac joint. (Reproduced with permission from Prentice 1998.[19A])

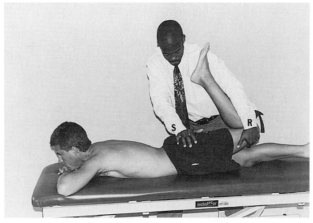

FIGURE 15-43

Anterior innominate rotation. An anterior innominate rotation may also be accomplished by extending the hip, applying upward force on the upper thigh, and stabilizing over the posterosuperior iliac spine. This technique is once again used to correct a posterior unilateral innominate rotation. (Reproduced with permission from Prentice 1998.[19A])

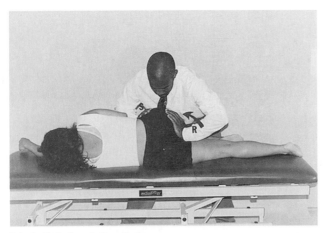

FIGURE 15 - 4 4

Posterior innominate rotation. A posterior innominate rotation with the patient in sidelying position is done by flexing the hip, stabilizing the anterosuperior iliac spine, and applying pressure to the ischium in an anterior direction. (Reproduced with permission from Prentice 1998.[19A])

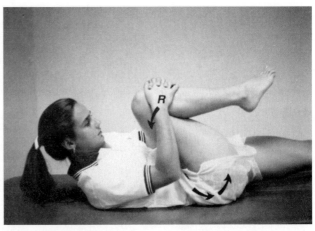

FIGURE 15 - 4 6

Posterior innominate rotation self-mobilization (supine). Posterior innominate rotation may be easily accomplished using self-mobilization. In a supine position, the patient grasps behind the flexed knee and gently rocks the innominate in a posterior direction. (Reproduced with permission from Prentice 1998.[19A])

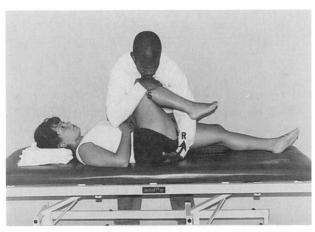

FIGURE 15 - 4 5

Posterior innominate rotation. Another posterior innominate rotation with the hip flexed at 90 degrees stabilizes the knee and rotates the innominate anteriorly through upward pressure on the ischium. (Reproduced with permission from Prentice 1998.[19A])

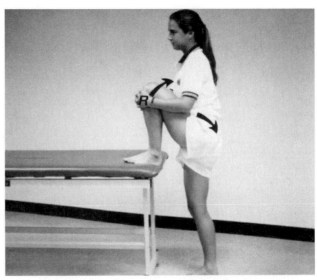

FIGURE 15 - 4 7

Posterior rotation self-mobilization (standing). In a standing position, the patient can perform a posterior rotation self-mobilization by pulling on the knee and rocking forward. (Reproduced with permission from Prentice 1998.[19A])

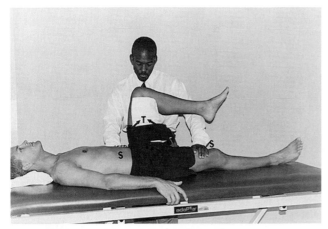

FIGURE 15-48

Lateral hip traction. Because the hip is a very strong, stable joint, it may be necessary to use body weight to produce effective joint mobilization or traction. An example of this would be in lateral hip traction. One strap should be used to secure the patient to the treatment table. A second strap is secured around the patient's thigh and around the therapist's hips. Lateral traction is applied to the femur by leaning back away from the patient. This technique is used to reduce pain and increase hip mobility. (Reproduced with permission from Prentice 1998.[19A])

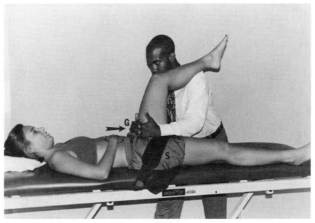

FIGURE 15-50

Inferior femoral glides. Inferior femoral glides at 90 degrees of hip flexion may also be used to increase abduction and flexion. (Reproduced with permission from Prentice 1998.[19A])

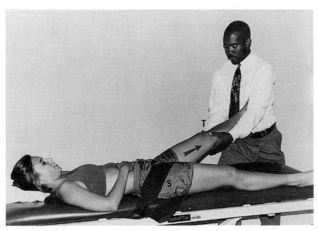

FIGURE 15-49

Femoral traction. Femoral traction with the hip at 0 degrees reduces pain and increases hip mobility. Inferior femoral glides in this position should be used to increase flexion and abduction. (Reproduced with permission from Prentice 1998.[19A])

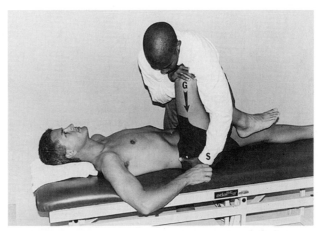

FIGURE 15-51

Posterior femoral glides. With the patient supine, a posterior femoral glide can be done by stabilizing underneath the pelvis and using the body weight applied through the femur to glide posteriorly. Posterior glides are used to increase hip flexion. (Reproduced with permission from Prentice 1998.[19A])

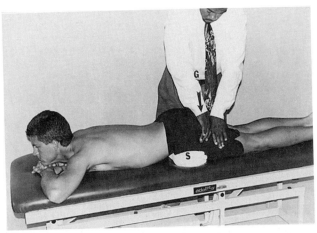

FIGURE   15-52

Anterior femoral glides. Anterior femoral glides increase extension and are accomplished by using some support to stabilize under the pelvis and applying an anterior glide posteriorly on the femur. (Reproduced with permission from Prentice 1998.[19A])

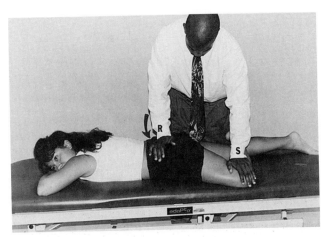

FIGURE   15-54

Lateral femoral rotation. Lateral femoral rotation is done by stabilizing a bent knee in the figure 4 position and applying rotational force to the ischium. This technique increases lateral femoral rotation. (Reproduced with permission from Prentice 1998.[19A])

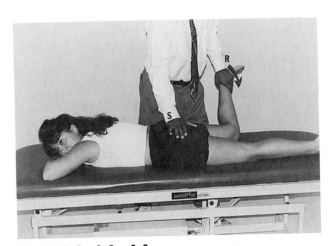

FIGURE   15-53

Medial femoral rotations. Medial femoral rotations may be used for increasing medial rotation and are done by stabilizing the opposite innominate while internally rotating the hip through the flexed knee. (Reproduced with permission from Prentice 1998.[19A])

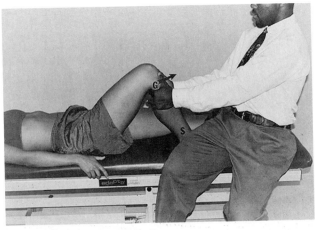

FIGURE   15-55

Anterior tibial glides. Anterior tibial glides are appropriate for the patient lacking full extension. Anterior glides should be done in prone position with the femur stabilized. Pressure is applied to the posterior tibia to glide anteriorly. (Reproduced with permission from Prentice 1998.[19A])

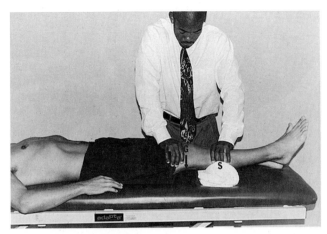

FIGURE 15-56

Posterior femoral glides. Posterior femoral glides are appropriate for the patient lacking full extension. Posterior femoral glides should be done in supine position with the tibia stabilized. Pressure is applied to the anterior femur to glide posteriorly. (Reproduced with permission from Prentice 1998.[19A])

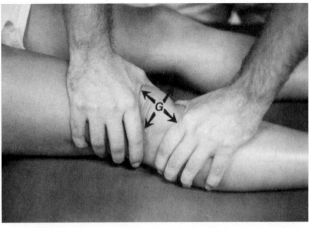

FIGURE 15-58

Patellar glides. Superior patellar glides increase knee extension. Inferior glides increase knee flexion. Medial glides stretch the lateral retinaculum. Lateral glides stretch tight medial structures. (Reproduced with permission from Prentice 1998.[19A])

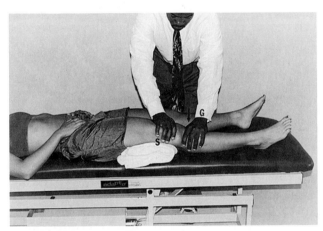

FIGURE 15-57

Posterior tibial glides. Posterior tibial glides increase flexion. With the patient in supine position, stabilize the femur, and glide the tibia posteriorly. (Reproduced with permission from Prentice 1998.[19A])

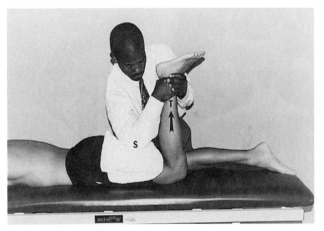

FIGURE 15-59

Tibiofemoral joint traction. Tibiofemoral joint traction reduces pain and hypomobility. It may be done with the patient prone and the knee flexed at 90 degrees. The elbow should stabilize the thigh while traction is applied through the tibia. (Reproduced with permission from Prentice 1998.[19A])

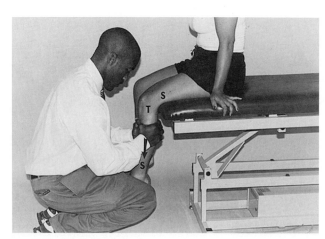

FIGURE 15-60

Alternative techniques for tibiofemoral joint traction. In very large individuals an alternative technique for tibiofemoral joint traction uses body weight of the sports therapist to distract the joint once again for reducing pain and hypomobility. (Reproduced with permission from Prentice 1998.[19A])

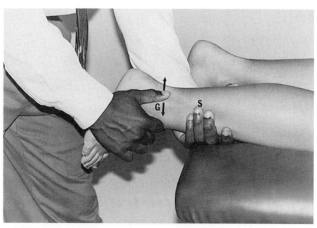

FIGURE 15-62

Distal anterior and posterior fibular glides. Anterior and posterior glides of the fibula may be done distally. The tibia should be stabilized, and the fibular malleolus is mobilized in an anterior or posterior direction. (Reproduced with permission from Prentice 1998.[19A])

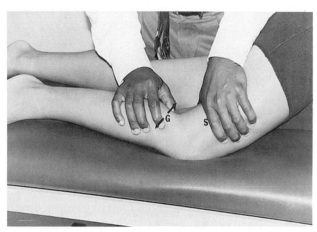

FIGURE 15-61

Proximal anterior and posterior glides of the fibula. Anterior and posterior glides of the fibula may be done proximally. They increase mobility of the fibular head and reduce pain. The femur should be stabilized. With the knee slightly flexed, grasp the head of the femur, and glide it both anteriorly and posteriorly. (Reproduced with permission from Prentice 1998.[19A])

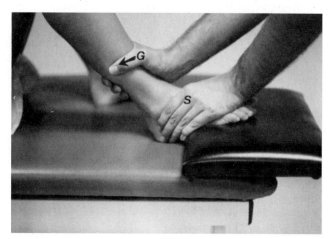

FIGURE 15-63

Posterior tibial glides. Posterior tibial glides increase plantarflexion. The foot should be stabilized, and pressure on the anterior tibia produces a posterior glide. (Reproduced with permission from Prentice 1998.[19A])

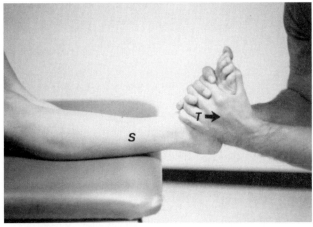

FIGURE 15-64

Talocrural joint traction. Talocrural joint traction is performed using the patient's body weight to stabilize the lower leg and applying traction to the midtarsal portion of the foot. Traction reduces pain and increases dorsiflexion and plantarflexion. (Reproduced with permission from Prentice 1998.[19A])

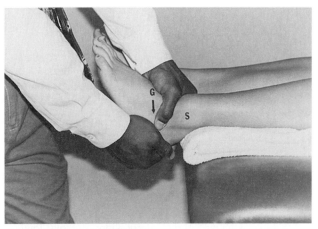

FIGURE 15-66

Posterior talar glides. Posterior talar glides may be used for increasing dorsiflexion. With the patient supine, the tibia is stabilized on the table, and pressure is applied to the anterior aspect of the talus to glide it posteriorly. (Reproduced with permission from Prentice 1998.[19A])

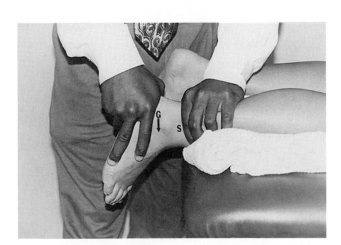

FIGURE 15-65

Anterior talar glides. Plantarflexion may also be increased by using an anterior talar glide. With the patient prone, the tibia is stabilized on the table, and pressure is applied to the posterior aspect of the talus to glide it anteriorly. (Reproduced with permission from Prentice 1998.[19A])

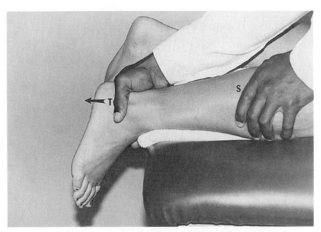

FIGURE 15-67

Subtalar joint traction. Subtalar joint traction reduces pain and increases inversion and eversion. The lower leg is stabilized on the table, and traction is applied by grasping the posterior aspect of the calcaneus. (Reproduced with permission from Prentice 1998.[19A])

FIGURE 15-68

Subtalar joint medial and lateral glides. Subtalar joint medial and lateral glides increase eversion and inversion. The talus must be stabilized while the calcaneus is mobilized medially to increase inversion and laterally to increase eversion. (Reproduced with permission from Prentice 1998.[19A])

FIGURE 15-69

Anterior/posterior calcaneocuboid glides. Anterior/posterior calcaneocuboid glides may be used for increasing adduction and abduction. The calcaneus should be stabilized while the cuboid is mobilized. (Reproduced with permission from Prentice 1998.[19A])

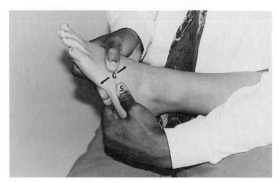

FIGURE 15-70

Anterior/posterior cuboidmetatarsal glides. Anterior/posterior cuboidmetatarsal glides are done with one hand stabilizing the cuboid and the other gliding the base of the fifth metatarsal. They are used for increasing mobility of the fifth metatarsal. (Reproduced with permission from Prentice 1998.[19A])

FIGURE 15-71

Anterior/posterior carpometacarpal glides. Anterior/posterior carpometacarpal glides decrease hypomobility of the metacarpals. (Reproduced with permission from Prentice 1998.[19A])

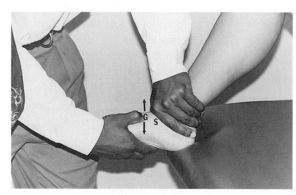

FIGURE 15-72

Anterior/posterior talonavicular glides. Anterior/posterior talonavicular glides also increase adduction and abduction. One hand stabilizes the talus while the other mobilizes the navicular bone. (Reproduced with permission from Prentice 1998.[19A])

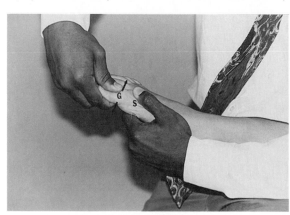

FIGURE 15-73

Anterior/posterior metacarpophalangeal glides. With anterior/posterior metacarpophalangeal glides, the anterior glides increase extension, and posterior glides increase flexion. Mobilizations are accomplished by isolating individual segments. (Reproduced with permission from Prentice 1998.[19A])

SUMMARY

- Mobilization and traction techniques increase joint mobility or decrease pain by restoring accessory movements to the joint.
- Physiologic movements result from an active muscle contraction that moves an extremity through traditional cardinal planes.
- Accessory motions refer to the manner in which one articulating joint surface moves relative to another.
- Normal accessory component motions must occur for full-range physiologic movement to take place.
- Accessory motions are also referred to as joint arthrokinematics, which include spin, roll, and glide.
- The convex–concave rule states that if the concave joint surface is moving on the stationary convex surface, gliding will occur in the same direction as the rolling motion. Conversely, if the convex surface is moving on a stationary concave surface, gliding will occur in an opposite direction to rolling.
- The resting position is one in which the joint capsule and the ligaments are most relaxed, allowing for a maximum amount of joint play.
- The treatment plane falls perpendicular to a line running from the axis of rotation in the convex surface to the center of the concave articular surface.
- Maitland has proposed a series of five graded movements or oscillations in the range of motion to treat pain and stiffness.
- Kaltenborn uses three grades of traction to reduce pain and stiffness.
- Kaltenborn emphasizes that traction should be used in conjunction with mobilization glides to treat joint hypomobility.

REFERENCES

1. Barak T, Rosen E, Sofer R. Mobility: Passive orthopedic manual therapy. In: Gould J, Davies G, eds. *Orthopedic and Sports Physical Therapy.* St. Louis, Mosby, 1990.
2. Basmajian J. *Therapeutic Exercise.* Baltimore, Williams & Wilkins, 1978.
3. Cookson J. Orthopedic manual therapy: An overview. II. The spine. *J Am Phys Ther Assoc* 59:259, 1979.
4. Cookson J, Kent B. Orthopedic manual therapy: An overview. I. The extremities. *J Am Phys Ther Assoc* 59:136, 1979.
5. Cyriax J. *Textbook of Orthopedic Medicine: Treatment by Manipulation, Massage, and Injection,* vol 2. Baltimore, Williams & Wilkins, 1974.
6. Donatelli R, Owens-Burkhart H. Effects of immobilization on the extensibility of periarticular connective tissue. *J Orthop Sports Phys Ther* 3:67, 1981.
7. Edmond S. *Manipulation and Mobilization: Extremity and Spinal Techniques.* St. Louis, Mosby, 1993.
8. Grimsby O. *Fundamentals of Manual Therapy: A Course Workbook.* Vagsbygd, Norway, Sorlandets Fysikalske Institutt, 1981.
9. Hollis M. *Practical Exercise.* Oxford, Blackwell Scientific, 1981.
10. Kaltenborn F. *Mobilization of the Extremity Joints: Examination and Basic Treatment Techniques.* Norway, Olaf Norlis Bokhandel, 1980.
11. Kisner C, Colby L. *Therapeutic Exercise: Foundations and Techniques.* Philadelphia, Davis, 1997.
12. MacConaill M, Basmajian J. *Muscles and Movements: A Basis for Kinesiology.* Baltimore, Williams & Wilkins, 1969.
13. Maigne R. *Orthopedic Medicine.* Springfield, IL, Thomas, 1976.
14. Maitland G. *Vertebral Manipulation.* London, Butterworth, 1978.
15. Maitland G. *Extremity Manipulation.* London, Butterworth, 1977.
16. Mennell J. *Joint Pain and Diagnosis Using Manipulative Techniques.* New York, Little, Brown, 1964.
17. Nygard R. Manipulation: Definition, types, application. In: Basmajian J, Nyberg R, eds. *Rational Manual Therapies.* Baltimore, Williams & Wilkins, 1993.
18. Paris S. *The Spine: Course Notebook.* Atlanta, Institute Press, 1979.
19. Paris S. Mobilization of the spine. *Phys Ther* 59:988, 1979.
19A. Prentice WE. *Therapeutic Modalities for Allied Health Professionals.* New York, McGraw Hill, 1998.
20. Saunders D. *Evaluation, Treatment and Prevention of Musculoskeletal Disorders.* Bloomington, MN, Educational Opportunities, 1985.
21. Schiotz E, Cyriax J. *Manipulation Past and Present.* London, Willian Heinemann Medical Books, 1978.
22. Stoddard A. *Manual of Osteopathic Practice.* London, Hutchinson Ross, 1969.
23. Taniqawa M. Comparison of the hold–relax procedure and passive mobilization on increasing muscle length. *Phys Ther* 52:725–735, 1972.
24. Wadsworth C. *Manual Examination and Treatment of the Spine and Extremities.* Baltimore, William & Wilkins, 1988.
25. Zohn D, Mennell J. *Musculoskeletal Pain: Diagnosis and Physical Treatment.* Boston, Little, Brown, 1976.
26. Zusman M. Reappraisal of a proposed neurophysiological mechanism for the relief of joint pain with passive joint movements. *Physiother Pract* 1:61–70, 1985.

SUGGESTED READINGS

Bukowski E. Assessing joint mobility. *Clin Management* 11:48–56, 1991.

Cibulka M, Rose S, Delitto A. Hamstring muscle strain treated by mobilizing the sacroiliac joint. *Phys Ther* 66:1220–1223, 1986.

Cochrane C. Joint mobilization principles: Considerations for use in the child with central nervous system dysfunction. *Phys Ther* 67:1105–1109, 1987.

DonTigny R. Measuring PSIS movement. *Clin Management* 10:43–44, 1990.

Eiff M, Smith A, Smith G. Early mobilization versus immobilization in the treatment of lateral ankle sprains. *Am J Sports Med* 22:83–88, 1994.

Gibson H, Ross J, Allen J. The effect of mobilization on forward bending range. *J Manual Manipulative Ther* 1:142–147, 1993.

Gratton P. Early active mobilization after flexor tendon repairs. *J Hand Ther* 6:285–289, 1993.

Harris S, Lundgren B. Joint mobilization for children with central nervous system disorders: Indications and precautions. *Phys Ther* 71:890–896, 1991.

Lee M, Latimer J, Maher C. Manipulation: Investigation of a proposed mechanism. *Clin Biomechan* 8:302–306, 1993.

Lee R, Evans J. Towards a better understanding of spinal posteroanterior mobilisation. *Physiotherapy* 80:68–73, 1994.

Levin S. Early mobilization speeds recovery. *Phys Sports Med* 21:70–74, 1993.

Maitland G. Treatment of the glenohumeral joint by passive movement. *Physiotherapy* 69:3–7, 1983.

May E. Controlled mobilization after flexor tendon repair in the hand: Techniques, methods and results. *Aust Occupational Ther J* 41:143, 1994.

McCollam R, Benson C. Effects of postero-anterior mobilization on lumbar extension and flexion. *J Manual Manipulative Ther* 1:134–141, 1993.

Mulligan B. Mobilisations with movement (MWM's). *J Manual Manipulative Ther* 1:154–156, 1993.

Mulligan B. Extremity joint mobilisations combined with movements. *NZ J Physiother* 20:28–29, 1992.

Nield S, Davis K, Latimer J. The effect of manipulation on the range of movement at the ankle joint. *Scand J Rehab Med* 25:161–166, 1993.

Ottenbacher K, Difabio R. Efficacy of spinal manipulation/mobilization therapy: A meta-analysis. *Spine* 10:833–837, 1985.

Petersen P, Sites S, Grossman I. Clinical evidence for the utilisation and efficacy of upper extremity mobilisation. *Br J Occupational Ther* 55:112–116, 1992.

Prentice W. Techniques of manual therapy for the knee. *J Sport Rehab* 1:249–257, 1992.

Quillen W, Halle J, Rouillier L. Manual therapy: Mobilization of the motion-restricted shoulder. *J Sport Rehab* 1:237–248, 1992.

Randall T, Portney L, Harris B. Effects of joint mobilization on joint stiffness and active motion of the metacarpal-phalangeal joint. *J Orthop Sports Phys Ther* 16:30–36, 1992.

Schoensee S, Jensen G, Nicholson G. The effect of mobilization on cervical headaches. *J Orthop Sports Phys Ther* 21:184–196, 1995.

Smith R, Sebastian B, Gajdosik R. Effect of sacroiliac joint mobilization on the standing position of the pelvis in healthy men. *J Orthop Sports Phys Ther* 10:77–84, 1988.

Stuberg W. Manual therapy in pediatrics: Some considerations. *PT—Magazine Phys Ther* 1:54–56, 1993.

Taylor N, Bennell K. The effectiveness of passive joint mobilisation on the return of active wrist extension following Colles' fracture: A clinical trial. *NZ J Physiother* 22:24–28, 1994.

Wilson F. Manual therapy versus traditional exercises in mobilisation of the ankle post-ankle fracture: A pilot study. *NZ J Physiother* 19:11–16, 1991.

Wise P. Mobilisation technique improves neural mobility. *Aust J Physiother* 40:51–54, 1994.

Zito M. Joint mobilization: Stretch specificity using a distraction. *J Orthop Sports Phys Ther* 23:65, 1996.

CHAPTER 16

Core Stabilization Training in Rehabilitation

Michael A. Clark

O B J E C T I V E S

After completing this chapter, the student therapist should be able to do the following:

- Describe the functional approach to kinetic chain rehabilitation.
- Define the concept of the core.
- Discuss the anatomic relationships between the musculature components of the core.
- Explain how the core functions to maintain postural alignment and dynamic postural equilibrium during functional activities.
- Describe procedure for assessing the core.
- Discuss the rationale for core stabilization training.
- Discuss the guidelines for core stabilization training.
- Identify appropriate exercises for each of the four levels in core stabilization training.

To stay on the cutting edge of research, science, and practical application, the clinician needs to follow a comprehensive, systematic, and integrated functional approach when rehabilitating a patient. To develop a comprehensive rehabilitation program, the clinician must fully understand the functional kinetic chain. In order to understand the kinetic chain, the clinician must first understand the definition of function. **Function** is integrated, multiplanar movement that requires acceleration, deceleration, and stabilization.[34,42,58] Functional kinetic chain rehabilitation is a comprehensive approach that strives to improve all components necessary to allow a patient to return to a high level of function. The clinician must understand that the kinetic chain operates as an integrated functional unit. Functional kinetic chain rehabilitation must therefore address each link in the kinetic chain and strive to develop functional strength and neuromuscular efficiency. Functional strength is the ability of the neuromuscular system to reduce force, produce force, and dynamically stabilize the kinetic chain during functional movements upon demand in a smooth coordinated fashion.[2] Neuromuscular efficiency is the ability of the CNS to allow agonists, antagonists, synergists, stabilizers, and neutralizers to work efficiently and interdependently during dynamic kinetic chain activities.[2]

Traditionally, rehabilitation has focused on isolated absolute strength gains, in isolated muscles, using single planes of motion. However, all functional activities are multiplanar and require acceleration, deceleration, and dynamic stabilization.[32,42,58] Movement may appear to be one plane dominant, but the other planes need to be dynamically stabilized to allow for optimal neuromuscular efficiency.[2] Understanding that functional movements require a highly complex, integrated system allows the clinician to make a paradigm shift. The paradigm shift focuses on training the entire kinetic chain using all planes of movement, and establishing high levels of functional strength and neuromuscular efficiency.[16,64,69,71,81,92] The paradigm shift dictates that we train force reduction, force production, and dynamic stabilization to occur efficiently during all kinetic chain activities.[12,34]

A dynamic, core stabilization training program is an important component of all comprehensive functional closed-kinetic chain rehabilitation programs.[10,15,26,27,34,42,58] A core stabilization program will improve dynamic postural control, ensure appropriate muscular balance and joint arthrokinematics around the lumbo-pelvic-hip complex, allow for the expression of dynamic functional strength, and improve neuromuscular efficiency throughout the entire kinetic chain.[2,12,16,34,36,42,61,64,68,71−73,92,93]

WHAT IS THE CORE?

The **core** is defined as the lumbo-pelvic-hip complex.[2,34] The core is where our center of gravity is located and where all movement begins.[46,47,81,82] There are 29 muscles that have an attachment to the lumbo-pelvic-hip complex.[7,8,34,86] An efficient core allows for maintenance of the normal length–tension relationship of functional agonists and antagonists, which allows for the maintenance of the normal force–couple relationships in the lumbo-pelvic-hip complex. Maintaining the normal length–tension relationships and force–couple relationships allows for the maintenance of optimal arthrokinematics in the lumbo-pelvic-hip complex during functional kinetic-chain movements.[92,93,98] This provides optimal neuromuscular efficiency in the entire kinetic chain, allowing for optimal acceleration, deceleration, and dynamic stabilization of the entire kinetic chain during functional movements. It also provides proximal stability for efficient lower-extremity movements.[2,34,46,47,53,58,81,82,92,93]

The core operates as an integrated functional unit, whereby the entire kinetic chain works synergistically to produce force, reduce force, and dynamically stabilize against abnormal force.[2] In an efficient state, each structural component distributes weight, absorbs force, and transfers ground reaction forces.[2] This integrated, interdependent system needs to be trained appropriately to allow it to function efficiently during dynamic kinetic-chain activities.

CORE STABILIZATION TRAINING CONCEPTS

Many individuals have developed the functional strength, power, neuromuscular control, and muscular endurance in specific muscles that enable them to perform functional activities.[2,34,54,58] However, few people have developed the muscles required for spinal stabilization.[53−55] The body's stabilization system has to be functioning optimally to effectively use the strength, power, neuromuscular control, and muscular endurance developed in the prime movers. If the extremity muscles are strong and the core is weak, then there will not be enough force created to produce efficient movements. A weak core is a fundamental problem of inefficient movements that leads to injury.[53−55,58]

The core musculature is an integral component of the protective mechanism that relieves the spine of deleterious forces inherent during functional activities.[16] A core stabilization training program is designed to help an individual gain strength, neuromuscular control, power, and muscle endurance of the lumbo-pelvic-hip complex. This approach facilitates a balanced

muscular functioning of the entire kinetic chain.[2] Greater neuromuscular control and stabilization strength will offer a more biomechanically efficient position for the entire kinetic chain, therefore allowing optimal neuromuscular efficiency throughout the kinetic chain.

Neuromuscular efficiency is established by the appropriate combination of postural alignment (static/dynamic) and stability strength, which allows the body to decelerate gravity, ground reaction forces, and momentum at the right joint, in the right plane, and at the right time.[12,42,64] If the neuromuscular system is not efficient, it will be unable to respond to the demands placed on it during functional activities.[2] As the efficiency of the neuromuscular system decreases, the ability of the kinetic chain to maintain appropriate forces and dynamic stabilization decreases significantly. This decreased neuromuscular efficiency leads to compensation and substitution patterns, as well as poor posture during functional activities.[36,92,93] This leads to increased mechanical stress on the contractile and non-contractile tissue, leading to repetitive microtrauma, abnormal biomechanics, and injury.[18,36,69,70]

REVIEW OF FUNCTIONAL ANATOMY

To fully understand functional core stabilization training and rehabilitation, the clinician must fully understand functional anatomy, lumbo-pelvic-hip complex stabilization mechanisms, and normal force–couple relationships.[5,7,8,86]

A review of the key lumbo-pelvic-hip complex musculature will allow the clinician to understand functional anatomy and therefore develop a comprehensive kinetic-chain rehabilitation program. The key lumbar spine muscles include the transversospinalis group, erector spinae, quadratus lumborum, and latissimus dorsi (Fig. 16-1). The key abdominal muscles include the rectus abdominus, external oblique, internal oblique, and transverse abdominus (Fig. 16-2). The key hip musculature includes the gluteus maximus, gluteus medius, and psoas (Fig. 16-3).

The transversospinalis group includes the rotatores, interspinales, intertransversarii, semispinalis, and multifidus. These muscles are small and have a poor mechanical advantage for contributing to motion.[32,86] They contain primarily type I muscle fibers, and are therefore designed mainly for stabilization.[32,86] Researchers[86] have found that the transversospinalis muscle group contains two to six times the number of muscle spindles found in larger muscles. Therefore, it has been established that this group is primarily responsible for providing the CNS with proprioceptive information.[86] This group is also responsible for inter/intrasegmental stabilization and segmental eccentric deceleration of flexion and rotation of the spinal unit during functional movements.[5,86] The transversospinalis group is constantly put under a variety of compressive and tensile forces during functional movements, and therefore needs to be trained adequately to allow dynamic postural stabilization and

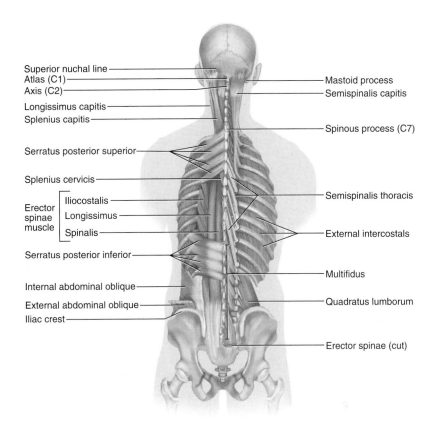

Superior nuchal line
Atlas (C1)
Axis (C2)
Longissimus capitis
Splenius capitis

Serratus posterior superior

Splenius cervicis

Erector spinae muscle — Iliocostalis / Longissimus / Spinalis

Serratus posterior inferior

Internal abdominal oblique

External abdominal oblique

Iliac crest

Mastoid process
Semispinalis capitis

Spinous process (C7)

Semispinalis thoracis

External intercostals

Multifidus

Quadratus lumborum

Erector spinae (cut)

FIGURE 16-1

Spinal muscles. (Reproduced, with permission, from Saladin KS. *Anatomy and Physiology.* New York, WCB/McGraw-Hill, 1998, p. 346.)

optimal neuromuscular efficiency of the entire kinetic chain.[86] The multifidus is the most important of the transversospinalis muscles. It has the ability to provide intrasegmental stabilization to the lumbar spine in all positions.[32,99] Wilke et al[99] found increased segmental stiffness at L4-L5 with activation of the multifidus.

The key back muscles include the erector spinae, quadratus lumborum, and the latissimus dorsi. The erector spinae muscle group functions to provide dynamic intersegmental stabilization and eccentric deceleration of trunk flexion and rotation during kinetic-chain activities.[86] The quadratus lumborum muscle functions primarily as a frontal plane stabilizer that works synergistically with the gluteus medius and tensor fascia lata. The latissimus dorsi has the largest moment arm of all back muscles and therefore has the greatest effect on the lumbo-pelvic-hip complex. The latissimus dorsi is the bridge between the upper extremity and the lumbo-pelvic-hip complex. Any functional upper extremity kinetic chain rehabilitation pay particular attention to the latissimus and its function on the lumbo-pelvic-hip complex.[86]

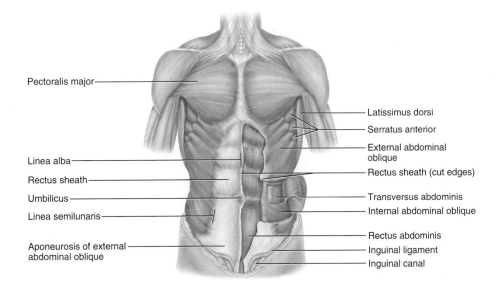

Pectoralis major

Linea alba
Rectus sheath
Umbilicus
Linea semilunaris

Aponeurosis of external abdominal oblique

Latissimus dorsi
Serratus anterior
External abdominal oblique
Rectus sheath (cut edges)
Transversus abdominis
Internal abdominal oblique
Rectus abdominis
Inguinal ligament
Inguinal canal

FIGURE 16-2

Abdominal muscles. (Reproduced, with permission, from Saladin KS. *Anatomy and Physiology.* New York, WCB/McGraw-Hill, 1998, p. 345.)

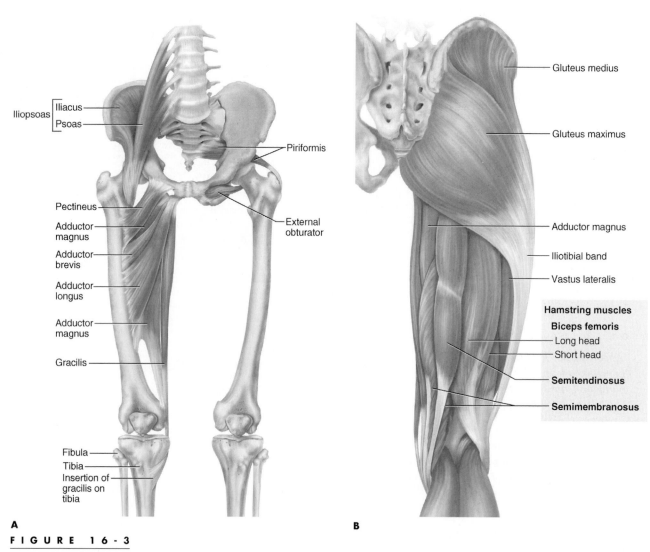

FIGURE 16-3

Hip muscles **A,** Anterior. **B,** Posterior. (Reproduced, with permission, from Saladin KS. *Anatomy and Physiology.* New York, WCB/McGraw-Hill, 1998, pp. 363 and 367.)

The abdominals are made up of four muscles: rectus abdominus, external oblique, internal oblique, and transverse abdominus.[86] The abdominals operate as an integrated functional unit, which helps maintain optimal spinal kinematics.[5,7,8,86] When working efficiently, the abdominals offer sagittal, frontal, and transverse plane stabilization by controlling forces that reach the lumbo-pelvic-hip complex.[86] The rectus abdominus eccentrically decelerates trunk extension and lateral flexion, as well as providing dynamic stabilization during functional movements. The external obliques work concentrically to produce contralateral rotation and ipsilateral lateral flexion, and work eccentrically to decelerate trunk extension, rotation, and lateral flexion during functional movements.[86] The internal oblique works concentrically to produce ipsilateral rotation and lateral flexion, and works eccentrically to decelerate extension, rotation, and lateral flexion. The internal oblique attaches to the posterior layer of the thoracolumbar fascia. Contraction of the internal oblique creates a lateral tension force on the thoracolumbar fascia, which creates intrinsic translational and rotational stabilization of the spinal unit.[47,53] The transverse abdominus (TA) is probably the most important of the abdominal muscles. The TA functions to increase intra-abdominal pressure, provide dynamic stabilization against rotational and translational stress in the lumbar spine, and provide optimal neuromuscular efficiency to the entire lumbo-pelvic-hip complex.[53–56,66] Research has demonstrated that the TA works in a feed-forward mechanism.[53] Researchers have demonstrated that contraction of the TA precedes the initiation of limb movement and all other abdominal muscles, regardless of the direction of reactive forces.[31,53] Cresswell et al [30,31] demonstrated that like the multifidus, the TA is active during all trunk movements, suggesting this muscle has an important role in dynamic stabilization.[54]

Key hip muscles include the psoas, gluteus medius, gluteus maximus, and hamstrings.[7,8,86] The psoas produces hip flexion and external rotation in the open chain position. The psoas produces hip flexion, lumbar extension, lateral flexion, and rotation in the closed chain position. The psoas eccentrically decelerates hip extension and internal rotation, as well as trunk extension, lateral flexion, and rotation. The psoas works synergistically with the superficial erector spinae and creates an anterior shear force at L4-L5.[86] The deep erector spinae, multifidus, and deep abdominal wall (transverse, internal oblique, and external oblique)[86] counteract this force. It is extremely common for clients to develop tightness in their psoas. A tight psoas increases the anterior shear force and compressive force at the L4-L5 junction.[86] A tight psoas also causes reciprocal inhibition of the gluteus maximus, multifidus, deep erector spinae, internal oblique, and transverse abdominus. This leads to extensor mechanism dysfunction during functional movement patterns.[61,68,70,72,73,86,93] Lack of lumbo-pelvic-hip complex stabilization prevents appropriate movement sequencing and leads to synergistic dominance by the hamstrings and superficial erector spinae during hip extension. This complex movement dysfunction also decreases the ability of the gluteus maximus to decelerate femoral internal rotation during heel strike, which predisposes an individual with a knee ligament injury to abnormal forces and repetitive microtrauma.[16,20,61,72,73]

The gluteus medius functions as the primary frontal plane stabilizer during functional movements.[86] During closed-chain movements, the gluteus medius decelerates femoral adduction and internal rotation.[86] A weak gluteus medius increases frontal and transverse plane stress at the patellofemoral joint and the tibiofemoral joint.[86] A weak gluteus medius leads to synergistic dominance of the tensor fascia latae and the quadratus lumborum.[20,61,63] This leads to tightness in the iliotibial band and the lumbar spine. This will affect the normal biomechanics of the lumbo-pelvic-hip complex and the tibiofemoral joint as well as the patellofemoral joint. Research by Beckman and Buchanan[9] has demonstrated decreased EMG activity of the gluteus medius following an ankle sprain. Clinicians must address the altered hip muscle recruitment patterns or accept this recruitment pattern as an injury-adaptive strategy and thus accept the unknown long-term consequences of premature muscle activation and synergistic dominance.[9,36]

The gluteus maximus functions concentrically in the open chain to accelerate hip extension and external rotation. It functions eccentrically to decelerate hip flexion and femoral internal rotation.[86] It also functions through the ITB to decelerate tibial internal rotation.[86] The gluteus maximus is a major dynamic stabilizer of the SI joint. It has the greatest capacity to provide increased compressive forces at the SI joint secondary to its anatomic attachment at the sacrotuberous ligament.[86] It has been demonstrated by Bullock-Saxton[17,18] that the EMG activity of the gluteus maximus is decreased following an ankle sprain. Lack of proper gluteus maximus activity during functional activities leads to pelvic instability and decreased neuromuscular control. This can eventually lead to the development of muscle imbalances, poor movement patterns, and injury.

The hamstrings work concentrically to flex the knee, extend the hip, and rotate the tibia. They work eccentrically to decelerate knee extension, hip flexion, and tibial rotation. The hamstrings work synergistically with the ACL.[86]

All of the muscles mentioned play an integral role in the kinetic chain by providing dynamic stabilization and optimal neuromuscular control of the entire lumbo-pelvic-hip complex. These muscles have been reviewed so the clinician realizes that muscles not only produce force (concentric contractions) in one plane of motion, but also reduce force (eccentric contractions) and provide dynamic stabilization in all planes of movement during functional activities. When isolated, these muscles do not effectively achieve stabilization of the lumbo-pelvic-hip complex. It is the synergistic, interdependent functioning of the entire lumbo-pelvic hip complex that enhances the stability and neuromuscular control throughout the entire kinetic chain.

POSTURAL CONSIDERATIONS

The core functions to maintain postural alignment and dynamic postural equilibrium during functional activities. Optimal alignment of each body part is a cornerstone to a functional training and rehabilitation program. Optimal posture and alignment will allow for maximal neuromuscular efficiency because the normal length–tension relationship, force–couple relationship, and arthrokinematics will be maintained during functional movement patterns.[16,34,36,58,60,61,63,66,69,71,92,93] If one segment in the kinetic chain is out of alignment, it will create predictable patterns of dysfunction throughout the entire kinetic chain. These predictable patterns of dysfunction are referred to as **serial distortion patterns.**[34] Serial distortion patterns represent the state in which the body's structural integrity is compromised because segments in the kinetic chain are out of alignment. This leads to abnormal distorting forces being placed on the segments in the kinetic chain that are above and below the dysfunctional segment.[16,34,36,58] To avoid serial distortion patterns and the chain reaction that one misaligned segment creates, we must emphasize stable positions to maintain the structural integrity of the entire kinetic chain.[18,34,58,72,73] A comprehensive core stabilization program will prevent the development of serial distortion patterns and provide optimal dynamic postural control during functional movements.

MUSCULAR IMBALANCES

An optimally functioning core helps to prevent the development of muscle imbalances and synergistic dominance. The human movement system is a well-orchestrated system of interrelated and interdependent components.[18,68] The functional interaction of each component in the human movement system allows for optimal neuromuscular efficiency. Alterations in joint arthrokinematics, muscular balance, and neuromuscular control affect the optimal functioning of the entire kinetic chain.[18,92,93] Dysfunction of the kinetic chain is rarely an isolated event. Typically any pathology of the kinetic chain is part of a chain reaction involving some key links in the kinetic chain with numerous compensations and adaptations developing.[68] The interplay of many muscles about a joint is responsible for the coordinated control of movement. If the core is weak, normal arthrokinematics are altered. This changes the normal length–tension relationship and the normal force–couple relationship, which in turn affects neuromuscular control. If one muscle becomes weak, tight, or changes its degree of activation, then synergists, stabilizers, and neutralizers have to compensate.[18,36,68,71–73,92,93] Muscle tightness has a significant impact on the kinetic chain. Muscle tightness affects the normal length–tension relationship.[93] This impacts the normal force–couple relationship. When one muscle in a force couple becomes tight, it changes the normal arthrokinematics of two articular partners.[16,68,93] Altered arthrokinematics affect the synergistic function of the kinetic chain.[16,36,68,93] This leads to abnormal pressure distribution over articular surfaces and soft tissues. Muscle tightness also leads to reciprocal inhibition.[16,36,60–63,68,94,98] Therefore, if one develops muscle imbalances throughout the lumbo-pelvic-hip complex, it can affect the entire kinetic chain. For example, a tight psoas causes reciprocal inhibition of the gluteus maximus, transverse abdominus, internal oblique, and multifidus.[55,61,63,80,86] This muscle imbalance pattern may decrease normal lumbo-pelvic-hip stability. Specific substitution patterns develop to compensate for the lack of stabilization, including tightness in the iliotibial band.[36] This muscle imbalance pattern will lead to increased frontal and transverse plane stress at the knee. A strong core with optimal neuromuscular efficiency can help to prevent the development of muscle imbalances. Therefore, a comprehensive core stabilization training program should be an integral component of all rehabilitation programs.

NEUROMUSCULAR CONSIDERATIONS

A strong and stable core can improve optimal neuromuscular efficiency throughout the entire kinetic chain by helping to improve dynamic postural control.[51,53,55,65,88,92,93] A number of authors have demonstrated kinetic-chain imbalances in individuals with altered neuromuscular control.[9,16–18,53–56,60–64,68–73,79,80,88,92] Research has demonstrated that people with low back pain have an abnormal neuromotor response of the trunk stabilizers accompanying limb movement.[54,55,80] It has been demonstrated that individuals with low back pain had significantly greater postural sway and decreased limits of stability. Research has also demonstrated that approximately 70% of patients suffer from recurrent episodes of back pain. Furthermore, it has been demonstrated that individuals have decreased dynamic postural stability in the proximal stabilizers of the lumbo-pelvic-hip complex following lower-extremity ligamentous injuries.[9,16–18] It has also been

demonstrated that joint and ligamentous injury can lead to decreased muscle activity.[33,36,94,98] Joint and ligament injury can lead to joint effusion, which in turn leads to muscle inhibition.[33] This leads to altered neuromuscular control in other segments of the kinetic chain secondary to altered proprioception and kinesthesia.[9,17] Therefore, when an individual with a knee ligament injury has joint effusion, all of the muscles that cross the knee can be inhibited. Several muscles that cross the knee joint are attached to the lumbo-pelvic-hip complex.[86] Therefore, a comprehensive rehabilitation approach should focus on reestablishing optimal core function.

Research has also demonstrated that muscles can be inhibited from an arthrokinetic reflex.[16,68,94,98] This is referred to as athrogenic muscle inhibition. Arthrokinetic reflexes are mediated by joint receptor activity. If an individual has abnormal arthrokinematics, the muscles that move the joint will be inhibited. For example, if an individual has a sacral torsion, the multifidus and the gluteus medius can be inhibited.[52] This will lead to abnormal movement in the kinetic chain. The tensor fascia latae will become synergistically dominant and become the primary frontal plane stabilizer.[86] This can lead to tightness in the iliotibial band. This can also decrease the frontal and transverse plane control at the knee. Furthermore, if the multifidus is inhibited,[52] the erector spinae and the psoas become facilitated. This will further inhibit the lower abdominals (internal oblique and transverse abdominus) and the gluteus maximus.[53,54] This also decreases frontal and transverse plane stability at the knee. As previously mentioned, an efficient core will improve neuromuscular efficiency of the entire kinetic chain by providing dynamic stabilization of the lumbo-pelvic-hip complex and therefore improve pelvofemoral biomechanics. This is yet another reason that all rehabilitation programs should include a comprehensive core stabilization training program.

ASSESSMENT OF THE CORE

Before a comprehensive core stabilization program is implemented, an individual must undergo a comprehensive assessment to determine muscle imbalances, arthrokinematic deficits, core strength, core neuromuscular control, core muscle endurance, core power, and overall function of the lower-extremity kinetic chain.

It has been previously stated that muscle imbalances and arthrokinematic deficits can cause abnormal movement patterns to develop throughout the entire kinetic chain. It is therefore extremely important to thoroughly assess each individual with a kinetic-chain dysfunction for muscle imbalances and arthrokinematic deficits. It is recommended that the interested reader use the reference list to explain a comprehensive muscle imbalance assessment procedure thoroughly.[2,16,20,26,27,34,56,58,62,64,71,92,93,98]

Core strength can be assessed by using the straight leg-lowering test (Fig. 16-4).[4,56,66,79,92,93] The individual is placed

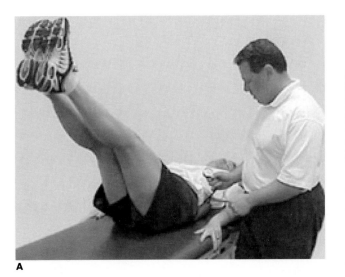

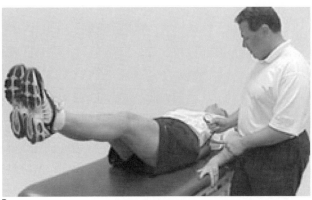

A   B

FIGURE 16-4

Core strength can be assessed by using the straight leg-lowering test.

supine. A blood pressure cuff is placed under the lumbar spine at approximately L4-L5. The cuff pressure is raised to 40 mm Hg. The individual's legs are maintained in full extension while flexing the hips to 90 degrees. The individual is instructed to perform a drawing-in maneuver (pull belly button to spine) and then flatten the back maximally into the table and pressure cuff. The individual is instructed to lower the legs toward the table while maintaining the back flat. The test is over when the pressure in the cuff decreases. The hip angle is then measured with a goniometer to determine the angle. Table 16-1 gives an approximation of an individual's lower abdominal strength.

Lower abdominal neuromuscular control is assessed in a similar fashion (Fig. 16-5).[4,56] The individual is supine with the knees and hips flexed to 90 degrees. The pressure cuff is placed under the lumbar spine at L4-L5 and inflated to 40 mm Hg. The individual is instructed to perform a drawing-in maneuver to stabilize the lumbar spine. The individual is instructed to slowly lower the legs until the pressure in the cuff decreases. This indicates the ability of the lower abdominal wall to preferentially stabilize the lumbo-pelvic-hip complex. When the lumbar spine

begins to move into extension, the hip flexors begin to work as stabilizers. This increases anterior shear forces and compressive forces at the L4-L5 lumbar segments and inhibits the transverse abdominus, internal oblique, and multifidus.

It has been demonstrated that approximately 80 to 85 percent of the general population suffers from low back pain.[4] It has also been demonstrated that individuals with low back pain have decreased muscle endurance in the erector spinae muscle group.[4,13,17,46,47] This leads to abnormal dynamic stabilization and movement during functional activities. This will lead to abnormal neuromuscular control. Therefore, all individuals should undergo an assessment of muscle endurance in the lumbar spine. Erector spinae performance can be assessed by having the individual lying prone on a treatment table, hands crossed behind the head. The axilla is used as a reference for the axis of a goniometer. The adjustable arm is aligned with the lateral side of the body and chin while the stationary arm is parallel to the table. The individual is instructed to extend at the lumbar spine to 30 degrees and hold the position for as long as possible while the clinician times the test.[4]

Power of the core musculature needs to be assessed as well. Power production of the core musculature can be assessed by performing an overhead medicine ball throw.[45] The individual is instructed to hold a 4-kg medicine ball between the legs as the patient squats down. The patient is instructed to jump as high as possible while simultaneously throwing the medicine ball backward over their head. The distance is measured from a starting line to the point where the medicine ball stops. This is an assessment of total body power production with an emphasis on the core.

A lower-extremity functional profile should also be carried out on all individuals with kinetic-chain deficits.[48] These tests

---

TABLE 16-1

Guidelines for Core Stabilization Training Program

1. Base program on science
2. Program should be systematic, progressive, and functional
3. Program should begin in the most challenging environment an athlete can control
4. The program should be performed in a proprioceptively enriched environment

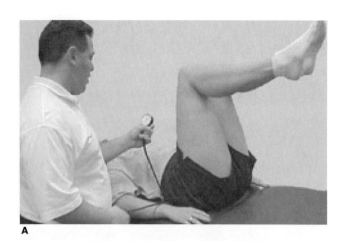
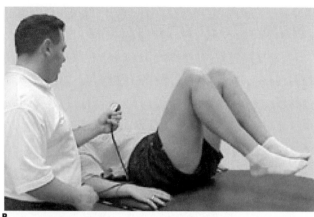

A
B

FIGURE 16-5

Lower abdominal neuromuscular assessment: **A,** Beginning. **B,** Ending.

should include isokinetic tests, balance tests, jump tests, power tests, and sports-specific functional tests.

SCIENTIFIC RATIONALE FOR CORE STABILIZATION TRAINING

Most individuals train their core stabilizers inadequately compared to other muscle groups.[2] Although adequate strength, power, muscle endurance, and neuromuscular control are important for lumbo-pelvic-hip stabilization, performing exercises incorrectly or that are too advanced is detrimental. Several authors have found decreased firing of the transverse abdominus, internal oblique, multifidus, and deep erector spinae in individuals with chronic low back pain.[53-56,80,87] Performing core training with inhibition of these key stabilizers leads to the development of muscle imbalances and inefficient neuromuscular control in the kinetic chain. It has been demonstrated that abdominal training without proper pelvic stabilization increases intradiscal pressure and compressive forces in the lumbar spine.[4,10,53-56,77,78] Furthermore, it has been demonstrated that hyperextension training without proper pelvic stabilization can increase intradiscal pressure to dangerous levels, cause buckling of the ligamentum flavum, and lead to narrowing of the intervertebral foramen.[4,10,78]

Research has also demonstrated decreased stabilization endurance in individuals with chronic low back pain.[10,19,46,47] The core stabilizers are primarily type I slow-twitch muscle fibers.[46,47,81,82] These muscles respond best to time under tension. Time under tension is a method of contraction that lasts for 6 to 20 seconds and emphasizes hypercontractions at end ranges of motion. This method improves intramuscular coordination, which improves static and dynamic stabilization. To get the appropriate training stimulus, you must prescribe the appropriate speed of movement for all aspects of exercises.[26,27] Core

strength endurance must be trained appropriately to allow an individual to maintain dynamic postural control for prolonged periods of time.[4]

Research has demonstrated decreased cross-sectional area of the multifidus in subjects with LBP and that there was not spontaneous recovery of the multifidus following resolution of symptoms.[52] It has also been demonstrated that the traditional curl-up increases intradiscal pressure and increases compressive forces at L2-L3.[4,10,77,78]

Additional research has demonstrated increased EMG activity and increased pelvic stabilization when an abdominal drawing-in maneuver was performed prior to initiating core training.[4,10,15,27,50,51,56,76,79,88] Also, maintaining the cervical spine in a neutral position during core training will improve posture, muscle balance, and stabilization. If the head protracts during movement, then the sternocleidomastoid is preferentially recruited. This increases the compressive forces at the C0-C1 vertebral junction. This can also lead to pelvic instability and muscle imbalances secondary to the pelvo-occular reflex. This reflex is important to maintain the eyes level.[68,69] If the sternocleidomastoid muscle is hyperactive and extends the upper cervical spine, then the pelvis will rotate anteriorly to realign the eyes. This can lead to muscle imbalances and decreased pelvic stabilization.[68,69]

GUIDELINES FOR CORE STABILIZATION TRAINING

Prior to performing a comprehensive core stabilization program, each individual must undergo a comprehensive evaluation to determine the following: muscle imbalances, myokinematic deficits, arthrokinematic deficits, core strength/neuromuscular control/power, and overall kinetic-chain function. All muscle imbalances and arthrokinematic deficits need to be

T A B L E   1 6 - 2

Program Variation

1. Plane of motion
2. Range of motion
3. Loading parameter
4. Body position
5. Speed of movement
6. Amount of control
7. Duration
8. Frequency

corrected prior to initiating an aggressive core training program.

A comprehensive core stabilization training program should be systematic, progressive, and functional. The rehabilitation program should emphasize the entire muscle contraction spectrum, focusing on force production (concentric contractions), force reduction (eccentric contractions), and dynamic stabilization (isometric contractions). The core stabilization program should begin in the most challenging environment the individual can control. A progressive continuum of function should be followed to systematically progress the individual. The program should be manipulated regularly by changing any of the following variables: plane of motion, range of motion, loading parameters (physioball, medicine ball, bodyblade, power sports trainer, weight vest, dumbbell, tubing), body position, amount of control, speed of execution, amount of feedback, duration (sets, reps, tempo, time under tension), and frequency. [2,10,12,15,18,23,26,27,29,34,42,45,50,56,58,59,64,65,71,74–76, 78,79,87–92] Please refer to Tables 16-1 to 16-5.

Specific Core Stabilization Guidelines

When designing a functional core stabilization training program, the clinician should create a proprioceptively enriched environment and select the appropriate exercises to elicit a maximal training response. The exercises must be safe and challenging, stress multiple planes, incorporate a multisensory environment, be derived from fundamental movement skills, and be activity specific (Tables 16-2 and 16-3).

The clinician should follow a progressive functional continuum to allow optimal adaptations.[34,42,50,58] The following are key concepts for proper exercise progression: slow to fast,

T A B L E   1 6 - 3

Exercise Selection

1. Safe
2. Challenging
3. Stress multiple planes
4. Proprioceptively enriched
5. Activity specific

T A B L E   1 6 - 4

Exercise Progression

1. Slow to fast
2. Simple to complex
3. Stable to unstable
4. Low force to high force
5. General to specific
6. Correct execution to increased intensity

simple to complex, known to unknown, low force to high force, eyes open to eyes closed, static to dynamic, and correct execution to increased reps/sets/intensity (Table 16-4).[26,27,34,42,50,58]

The goal of core stabilization should be to develop optimal levels of functional strength and dynamic stabilization.[2,10] Neural adaptations become the focus of the program instead of striving for absolute strength gains.[16,34,53,64,79] Increasing proprioceptive demand by utilizing a multisensory, multimodal (tubing, bodyblade, physioball, medicine ball, power sports trainer, weight vest, cobra belt, dumbbell) environment becomes more important then increasing the external resistance. The concept of quality before quantity is stressed. Core stabilization training is specifically designed to improve core stabilization and neuromuscular efficiency. You must be concerned with the sensory information that is stimulating your CNS. If you train with poor technique and poor neuromuscular control, then you develop poor motor patterns and poor stabilization.[34,58] The focus of your program must be on function. To determine if your program is functional, answer the following questions: Is it dynamic? Is it multiplanar? Is it multidimensional? Is it proprioceptively challenging? Is it systematic? Is it progressive? Is it based on functional anatomy and science? Is it activity specific? (See Table 16-5.)[34,42,58]

CORE STABILIZATION TRAINING PROGRAM

Please refer to Figures 16-6 to 16-34 for those exercises used in a comprehensive core stabilization training program. There are four levels to the program: level I, stabilization (Figs. 16-6 to 16-12); level II, stabilization and strength (Figs. 16-13 to

T A B L E   1 6 - 5

**Guidelines for a Functional
Core Stabilization Program**

1. Is it dynamic?
2. Is it multiplanar?
3. Is it proprioceptively enriched?
4. Is it systematic?
5. Is it progressive?
6. Is it activity-specific?

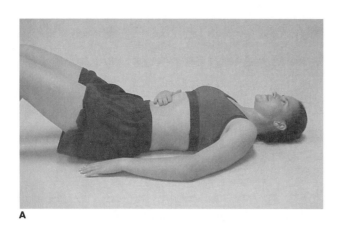

A

B

F I G U R E   1 6 - 6

(**A**) Lower abdominal drawing-in maneuver. (**B**) Quadriped drawing-in maneuver.

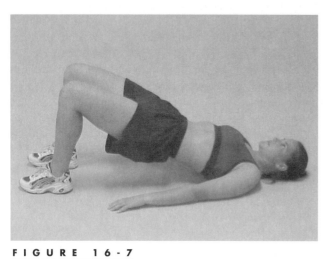

F I G U R E   1 6 - 7

Bridging.

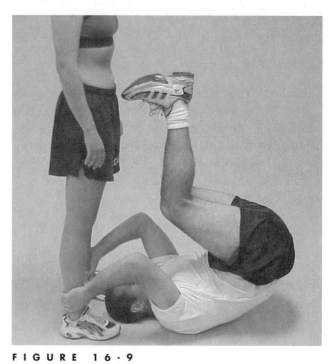

F I G U R E   1 6 - 9

Reverse crunch.

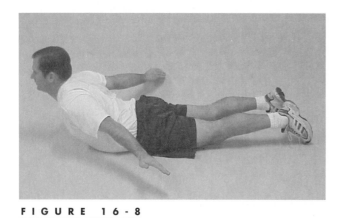

F I G U R E   1 6 - 8

Prone cobra.

F I G U R E   1 6 - 1 0

Prone iso-abdominal.

FIGURE 16-11

Side-lying iso-abdominal.

FIGURE 16-12

Quadraped opposite arm/leg raise.

FIGURE 16-13

Stability ball bridging.

FIGURE 16-14

Stability ball rotation with a power ball.

A

B

FIGURE 16-15

(**A**) Stability ball diagonal long-lever crunch. (**B**) Stability ball crunch.

FIGURE 16-16

Stability ball push-up.

FIGURE 16-18

Stability ball hamstring curl.

FIGURE 16-17

Stability ball PNF with a power ball.

FIGURE 16-19

Stability ball bridge.

FIGURE 16-20

Integrated body blade stabilization.

FIGURE 16-22

Stagger stance medicine ball chest pass.

FIGURE 16-21

Body-blade PNF.

FIGURE 16-23

Medicine ball rotation chest pass.

FIGURE 16-24

Medicine ball side oblique pass.

FIGURE 16-26

Medicine ball pullover on a stability ball.

A

B

FIGURE 16-25

(**A**) Power ball dynamic flexion/extension. (**B**) Power ball dynamic flexion/extension.

F I G U R E   1 6 - 2 7

Medicine ball throw and catch with a sagittal plane lunge.

F I G U R E   1 6 - 2 8

Medicine ball throw and catch with a frontal plane lunge.

F I G U R E   1 6 - 2 9

Medicine ball long jump with stabilization.

A

B

F I G U R E   1 6 - 3 0

(A) Dynamic PNF with power ball. **(B)** Another view of dynamic PNF with power ball.

A

B

FIGURE 16-31

(A) Dynamic medicine ball flexion/extension with a squat jump. (B) Another view of dynamic medicine ball flexion/extension with a squat jump.

A

B

FIGURE 16-32

(A) Medicine ball PNF throw. (B) Medicine ball PNF throw.

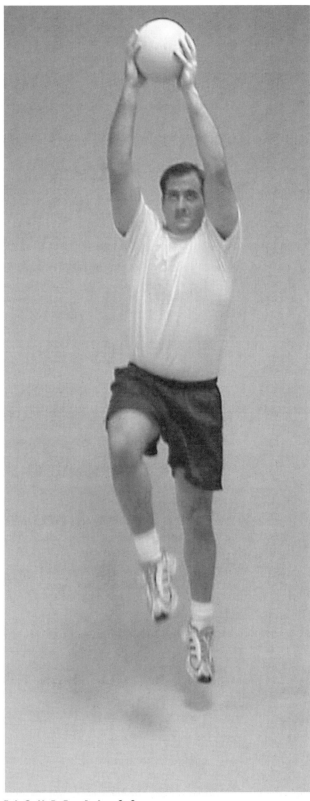

FIGURE 16-33

Medicine ball single-by-squat jump.

FIGURE 16-34

Medicine ball overhead throw.

16-20); level III, integrated stabilization and strength (Figs. 16-21 to 16-26); and level IV, explosive stabilization (Figs. 16-27 to 16-34). The individual is started with the exercises at the highest level at which they can maintain stability and optimal neuromuscular control. They are progressed through the program when they achieve mastery of the exercises in the previous level.[1,2,4,10,12,15,16,18,22,23,26,27,29,34,39,42–48,53,56,58,64,65,71,78,79,90,91]

SUMMARY

- Functional kinetic-chain rehabilitation must address each link in the kinetic chain and strive to develop functional strength and neuromuscular efficiency.

- A core stabilization program should be an integral component for all individuals participating in a closed kinetic chain rehabilitation program.
- A core stabilization training program will allow an individual to gain optimal neuromuscular control of the lumbo-pelvic-hip complex and allow the individual with a kinetic-chain dysfunction to return to activity much faster and safer.

REFERENCES

1. Aaron G. *Clinical Guideline Manual for Spine.* Birmingham, Healthsouth Corporation, 1996.
2. Aaron G. The use of stabilization training in the rehabilitation of the athlete. *Sports Physical Therapy Home Study Course,* 1996.
3. Aruin AS, Latash ML. Directional specificity of postural muscles in feed-forward postural reactions during fast voluntary arm movements. *Exp Brain Res* 103:323–332, 1995.
4. Ashmen KJ, Swanik CB, Lephart SM. Strength and flexibility characteristics of athletes with chronic low back pain. *J Sports Rehab* 5:275–286, 1996.
5. Aspden RM. Review of the functional anatomy of the spinal ligaments and the erector spinae muscles. *Clin Anat* 5:372–387, 1992.
6. Axler CT, McGill SM. Low back loads over a variety of abdominal exercises: Searching for the safest abdominal challenge. *Med Sci Sports Exerc* 29:804–810, 1997.
7. Basmajian J. *Muscles Alive: Their Functions Revealed by EMG,* 5th ed. Baltimore, Williams & Wilkins, 1985.
8. Basmajian J. *Muscles Alive.* Baltimore, Williams & Wilkins, 1974.
9. Beckman SM, Buchanan TS. Ankle inversion and hypermobility: Effect on hip and ankle muscle electromyography onset latency. *Arch Phys Med Rehabil* 76:1138–1143, 1995.
10. Beim G, Giraldo JL, Pincivero DM, et al. Abdominal strengthening exercises: A comparative EMG study. *J Sports Rehab* 6:11–20, 1997.
11. Beimborn DS, Morrissey MC. A review of the literature related to trunk muscle performance. *Spine* 13:665–670, 1988.
12. Blievernicht J. *Balance.* Course manual. Chicago, 1996.
13. Boduk N, Twomey L. *Clinical Anatomy of the Lumbar Spine.* New York, Churchill Livingstone, 1987.
14. Bousiett S, Zattara M. A sequence of postural adjustments precedes voluntary movement. *Neurosci Lett* 22:263–270, 1981.
15. Bittenham D, Brittenham G. Stronger abs and back. *Human Kinetics.* Champaign, IL, 1997.
16. Bullock-Saxton JE. Muscles and joint: Inter-relationships with pain and movement dysfunction. Course manual. 1997.
17. Bullock-Saxton JE. Local sensation changes and altered hip muscle function following severe ankle sprain. *Phys Ther* 74:17–23, 1994.
18. Bullock-Saxton JE, Janda V, Bullock M. Reflex activation of gluteal muscles in walking: An approach to restoration of muscle function for patients with low back pain. *Spine* 18:704–708, 1993.
19. Calliet R. *Low Back Pain Syndrome.* Oxford, Blackwell, 1962.
20. Chaitow L. *Muscle Energy Techniques.* New York, Churchill Livingstone, 1997.
21. Chaitow L. *Soft Tissue Manipulation.* Rochester, Healing Arts Press, 1991.
22. Chek P. *Dynamic Medicine Ball Training.* Correspondence course. La Jolla, CA, Paul Chek Seminars, 1996.
23. Chek P. *Swiss Ball Training.* Correspondence course. La Jolla, CA, Paul Chek Seminars. 1996.
24. Chek P. *Program Design.* Correspondence course. La Jolla, CA, Paul Chek Seminars, 1995.
25. Chek P. *Strong and Stable.* 3-volume video series. La Jolla, CA, Paul Chek Seminars, 1995.
26. Chek P. *Scientific Back Training.* Correspondence course. La Jolla, CA, Paul Chek Seminars, 1994.
27. Chek P. *Scientific Abdominal Training.* Correspondence course. La Jolla, CA, Paul Chek Seminars, 1992.
28. Cook G, Fields K. Functional training for the torso. *WWW.Funct.html,* 1998.
29. Creager C. Therapeutic exercise using foam rollers. *Executive Physical Therapy.* Berthoud, CO, 1996.
30. Cresswell AG, Grundstrom H, Thorstensson A. Observations on intra-abdominal pressure and patterns of abdominal intra-muscular activity in man. *Acta Physiol Scand* 144:409–418, 1992.
31. Cresswell AG, Oddson L, Thorstensson A. The influence of sudden perturbations on trunk muscle activity and intra-abdominal pressure while standing. *Exp Brain Res* 98:336–341, 1994.
32. Crisco J, Panjabi MM. The intersegmental and multisegmental muscles of the lumbar spine. *Spine* 16:793–799, 1991.
33. DeAndre JR, Grant C, Dixon ASJ. Joint distension and reflex muscle inhibition in the knee. *J Bone Joint Surg (Am)* 47:313–322, 1965.
34. Dominguez RH. *Total Body Training.* East Dundee, II, Moving Force Systems, 1982.
35. Dvorak J, Dvorak V. *Manual Medicine: Diagnostics.* New York, George Theim Verlag, 1984.
36. Edgerton VR, Wolf S, Roy RR. Theoreical basis for patterning EMG amplitudes to assess muscle dysfunction. *Med Sci Sports Exerc* 28:744–751, 1996.
37. Evjenth O. *Muscle Stretching in Manual Therapy.* Sweden, Alfta Rehab, 1984.
38. Fairbank JCT, O'Brien JP. The abdominal cavity and the thoracolumbar fascia as stabilizers of the lumbar spine in patients with low back pain. *Engineering Aspects of the Spine.* London, 1980.

39. Freeman MAR. Coordination exercises in the treatment of functional instability of the foot. *Phys Ther* 44:393–395, 1964.

40. Friedeli WG, Cohen L, Hallet M, et al. Postural adjustments associated with rapid arm movements. II: Biomechanical analysis.

41. Freyette. *Principles of Osteopathic Technique.* Yearbook of the Academy of Applied Osteopathy, 1954.

42. Gambetta V. *Building the Complete Athlete.* Course manual. Chicago, 1996.

43. Gambetta V. Everything in balance. *Training Conditioning* 1:15–21, 1996.

44. Gambetta V. Following a functional path. *Training Conditioning* 5:25–30, 1995.

45. Gambetta V. *The Complete Guide to Medicine Ball Training.* Sarasota, FL, Optimum Sports Training, 1991.

46. Gracovetsky S, Farfan H. The optimum spine. *Spine* 11:543–573, 1986.

47. Gracovetsky S, Farfan H, Heuller C. The abdominal mechanism. *Spine* 10:317–324, 1985.

48. Gray GW. *Chain Reaction Festival.* Course manual. Chicago, 1996.

49. Greenman PE. *Principles of Manual Medicine.* Baltimore, Williams & Wilkins, 1991.

50. Gustavsen R, Streeck R. *Training Therapy: Prophylaxis and Rehabilitation.* New York, Thieme, 1993.

51. Hall T, David A, Geere J, Salvenson K. Relative recruitment of the abdominal muscles during three levels of exertion during abdominal hollowing. Manipulative Physiotherapists Association of Australia, 1995.

52. Hides JA, Stokes MJ, Saide M, et al. Evidence of lumbar multifidus wasting ipsilateral to symptoms in subjects with acute/subacute low back pain. *Spine* 19:165–177, 1994.

53. Hodges PW, Richardson CA. Contraction of the abdominal muscles associated with movement of the lower limb. *Phys Ther* 77:132, 1997.

54. Hodges PW, Richardson CA. Inefficient muscular stabilization of the lumbar spine associated with low back pain. *Spine* 21:2640–2650, 1996.

55. Hodges PW, Richardson CA. Neuromotor dysfunction of the trunk musculature in low back pain patients. In: *Proceedings of the International Congress of the World Confederation of Physical Therapists,* Washington, DC, 1995.

56. Hodges PW, Richardson CA, Jull G. Evaluation of the relationship between laboratory and clinical tests of transverse abdominus function. *Physiother Res Int* 1:30–40, 1996.

57. Holt LE. *Scientific Stretching for Sport.* Halifax, Dalhouise University Press, 1976.

58. Jesse J. *Hidden Causes of Injury, Prevention, and Correction for Running Athletes.* Pasadena, Athletic Press, 1977.

59. Kennedy B. An Australian program for management of back problems. *Physiotherapy* 66:108–111, 1980.

60. Janda V. Physical therapy of the cervical and thoracic spine. In: Grant R, ed. *Physical Therapy of the Cervical and Thoracic Spine.* New York, Churchill Livingstone, 1988.

61. Janda V. Muscle weakness and inhibition in back pain syndromes. In: Grieve GP. *Modern Manual Therapy of the Vertebral Column.* New York, Churchill Linvingstone, 1986.

62. Janda V. *Muscle Function Testing.* London, Butterworths, 1983.

63. Janda V. Muscles, central nervous system regulation and back problems. In: Korr IM, ed. *Neurobiologic Mechanisms in Manipulative Therapy.* New York, Plenum, 1978.

64. Janda V, Vavrova M. *Sensory Motor Stimulation* (video). Brisbane, Body Control Systems, 1990.

65. Jull G, Richardson CA, Comerford M. Strategies for the initial activation of dynamic lumbar stabilization. *Proceedings of Manipulative Physiotherapists Association of Australia,* 1991.

66. Jull G, Richardson CA, Hamilton C, et al. Towards the validation of a clinical test for the deep abdominal muscles in back pain patients. Manipulative Physiotherapists Association of Australia, 1995.

67. Lavender SA, Tsuang YH, Andersson GBJ. Trunk muscle activation and co-contraction while resisting movements in a twisted posture. *Ergonomics* 36:1145–1157, 1993.

68. Lewit K. Muscular and articular factors in movement restriction. *Manual Medicine* 1:83–85, 1998.

69. Lewit K. *Manipulative Therapy in the Rehabilitation of the Locomotor System.* London, Butterworths, 1985.

70. Lewit K. Myofascial pain: Relief by post-isometric relaxation. *Arch Phys Med Rehabil* 65:452, 1984.

71. Liebenson CL. *Rehabilitation of the Spine.* Baltimore, Williams & Wilkins, 1996.

72. Liebenson CL. Active muscle relaxation techniques. Part I. Basic principles and methods. *J Manipulative Physiol Ther* 12:446–454, 1989.

73. Liebenson CL. Active muscle relaxation techniques. Part II. Clinical application. *J Manipulative Physiol Ther* 13, 1989.

74. Mayer TG, Gatchel RJ. *Functional Restoration for Spinal Disorders. The Sports Medicine Approach.* Philadelphia, Lea & Febiger, 1988.

75. Mayer-Posner J. *Swiss Ball Applications for Orthopedic and Sports Medicine.* Denver, Ball Dynamics International, 1995.

76. Miller MI, Medeiros JM. Recruitment of the internal oblique and transverse abdominus muscles on the eccentric phase of the curl-up. *Phys Ther* 67:1213–1217, 1987.

77. Nachemson A. The load on the lumbar discs in different positions of the body. *Clin Orthop* 45:107–122, 1966.

78. Norris CM. Abdominal muscle training in sports. *Br J Sports Med* 27:19–27, 1993.

79. O'Sullivan PE, Twomey L, Allison G. Evaluation of specific stabilizing exercises in the treatment of chronic low back pain with radiological diagnosis of spondylolisthesis. Manipulative Physiotherapists Association of Australia, 1995.

80. O'Sullivan PE, Twomey L, Allison G, et al. Altered patterns of abdominal muscle activation in patients with chronic low back pain. *Aust J Physiother* 43:91–98, 1997.

81. Panjabi MM. The stabilizing system of the spine. Part I: Function, dysfunction, adaptation, and enhancement. *J Spinal Disord* 5:383–389, 1992.

82. Panjabi MM, Tech D, White AA. Basic biomechanics of the spine. *Neurosurgery* 7:76–93, 1980.

83. Paquet N, Malouin F, Richards CL. Hip–spine movement interaction and muscle activation patterns during sagittal trunk movements in low back pain patients. *Spine* 19:596–603, 1994.

84. Peck D, Buxton DF, Nitz AJ. A comparison of spindle concentrations in large and small muscles acting in parallel combinations. *J Morphol* 180:243–252, 1984.

85. Pope M, Frymoyer J, Krag M. Diagnosing instability. *Clin Orthop Rel Res* 296:60–67, 1992.

86. Porterfield JA, DeRosa C. *Mechanical Low Back Pain: Perspectives in Functional Anatomy.* Philadelphia, Saunders, 1991.

87. Richardson CA, Jull G. Muscle control—pain control. What exercises would you prescribe? *Manual Med* 1:2–10,

88. Richardson CA, Jull G, Toppenberg R, Comerford M. Techniques for active lumbar stabilization for spinal protection. *Aust J Physiother* 38:105–112, 1992.

89. Robinson R. The new back school prescription: Stabilization training. Part I. *Occupational Med* 7:17–31, 1992.

90. Saal JA. The new back school prescription: Stabilization training part II. *Occupational Med* 7:33–42, 1993.

91. Saal JA. Nonoperative treatment of herniated disc: An outcome study. *Spine* 14:431–437, 1989.

92. Sahrmann S. *Diagnosis and Treatment of Muscle Imbalances and Musculoskeletal Pain Syndrome.* Continuing education course. St. Louis, 1997.

93. Sahrmann S. Posture and muscle imbalance: Faulty lumbo-pelvic alignment and associated musculolskeletal pain syndromes. *Orthop Div Rev—Can Phys Ther* 12:13–20, 1992.

94. Stokes M, Young A. The contribution of reflex inhibition to arthrogenous muscle weakness. *Clin Sci* 67:7–14, 1984.

95. Strohl K, Mead J, Banzett R, et al. Regional differences in abominal activity during various maneuvers in humans. *J Appl Physiol* 51:1471–1476, 1981.

96. Tesh KM, ShawDunn J, Evans JH. The abdominal muscles and vertebral stability. *Spine* 12:501–508, 1987.

97. Throstensson A, Ardidson A. Trunk strength and low back pain. *Scand J Rehabil Med* 14:69–75, 1982.

98. Warmerdam ALA. *Arthrokinetic Therapy: Manual Therapy to Improve Muscle and Joint Functioning.* Continuing education course. Marshfield, WI, 1996.

99. Wilke HJ, Wolf S, Claes LE. Stability increase of the lumbar spine with different muscle groups: A biomechanical in vitro study. *Spine* 20:192–198, 1995.

Aquatic Therapy in Rehabilitation

Gina Martin

O B J E C T I V E S

After completing this chapter, the student therapist should be able to do the following:

- Explain the principles of buoyancy and specific gravity and the role they have in the aquatic environment.
- Identify and describe the three major resistive forces at work in the aquatic environment.
- Discuss the advantages and disadvantages of aquatic therapy in relation to traditional land exercises.
- Identify and describe the two prominent techniques of aquatic therapy.

In the past decade, widespread interest has developed in aquatic therapy as a tool for rehabilitation. It has rapidly become a popular rehabilitation technique among therapists, with numerous research efforts undertaken to evaluate its effectiveness as a therapeutic modality. Current research shows aquatic therapy to be beneficial in the treatment of everything from orthopedic injuries to spinal cord damage, chronic pain, cerebral palsy, multiple sclerosis, and many other conditions, making it useful in a variety of settings.[23] It is also gaining acceptance as a preventative maintenance tool to facilitate overall fitness for healthy patients.[19,21] Movement skills, conditioning, and strength can each be enhanced by aquatic therapy.[12]

Water healing techniques have been traced back through history as early as 2400 BC, but it was not until the late nineteenth century that more traditional water-exercise types of aquatic therapy came into existence. The development of the Hubbard tank in 1920 sparked the initiation of present-day therapeutic water exercise by allowing aquatic therapy to be conducted in a highly controlled, clinical setting.[6] Loeman and Roen took this a step further in 1924 and stimulated actual pool therapy interest. Only recently, however, has water come into its own as a therapeutic exercise medium.[25]

Aquatic therapy is believed to be successful because it lowers pain levels by decreasing joint compression forces. The perception of weightlessness experienced in the water seems to eliminate or drastically reduce the body's protective muscular guarding. This effect results in decreased muscular spasm and pain that may carry over into the patient's daily functional activities.[31] The primary goal of aquatic therapy is to teach the patient how to use water as a modality for improving movement and fitness. Then, along with other therapeutic modalities and treatments, aquatic therapy can become one more link in the patient's recovery chain.

PHYSICAL PROPERTIES AND RESISTIVE FORCES

The therapist must understand several physical properties of the water before designing an aquatic therapy program. Land exercise cannot always be converted to aquatic exercise, because buoyancy rather than gravity is the major force governing movement. A thorough understanding of buoyancy, specific gravity, the resistive forces of water, and their relationships must be the groundwork of any aquatics program. The program must also be specific and individualized to the patient's particular injury if it is to be successful.

Buoyancy

Buoyancy is one of the primary forces involved in aquatic therapy. All objects, on land or in the water, are subjected to the downward pull of Earth's gravity. In the water, however, this force is counteracted to some degree by the upward buoyant force. According to Archimedes' principle, any object submerged or floating in water is buoyed upward by a counterforce that helps support the submerged or partially submerged object against the downward pull of gravity. In other words, the

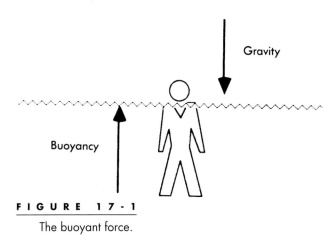

FIGURE 17-1

The buoyant force.

buoyant force assists motion toward the water's surface and resists motion away from the surface.[15] Because of this buoyant force, a person entering the water experiences an apparent loss of weight.[10] The weight loss experienced is nearly equal to the weight of the liquid that is displaced when the object enters the water (Fig. 17-1).

For example, a 100-pound individual, when almost completely submerged, displaces a volume of water that weighs nearly 95 pounds, and therefore feels as though he or she weighs less than 5 pounds. This sensation occurs because when partially submerged, the individual only bears the weight of what is above the water. With immersion to the level of the seventh cervical vertebra, both males and females only bear approximately 6 to 10 percent of their total body weight (TBW). The percentages increase to 25 to 31 percent TBW for females and 30 to 37 percent TBW for males at the xiphisternal level, and 40 to 51 percent TBW for females and 50 to 56 percent TBW for males at the anterosuperior iliac spine (ASIS) level (Table 17-1).[16] The percentages differ for males and females due to the differences in centers of gravity. Males carry a higher percentage of their weight in the upper body, while females carry a higher percentage of their weight in the lower body. The center of gravity on land corresponds with a center of buoyancy in the water.[25] Also, variations of build and body type only minimally effect weight-bearing values. Due to the decreased percentage of weight bearing, each joint that is below the water is decompressed. This allows ambulation and vigorous exercise to be performed with little impact

TABLE   17-1

Weight-Bearing Percentages

BODY LEVEL	PERCENTAGE OF WEIGHT BEARING	
	MALE	FEMALE
C7	8%	8%
Xiphisternal	28%	35%
ASIS	47%	54%

and drastically reduced friction between joint articular surfaces.

Specific Gravity

Buoyancy is partially dependent on body weight. However, the weight of different parts of the body is not a constant. Therefore, the buoyant values of different body parts will also vary. Buoyant values can be determined by several factors. The bone to muscle weight, the amount and distribution of fat, and the depth and expansion of the chest all play a role. Together, these factors determine the specific gravity of the individual body part. On average, humans have a specific gravity slightly less than that of water. Any object with a specific gravity less than that of water will float. A specific gravity greater than that of water will cause the object to sink. However, as with buoyant values, the specific gravity of all body parts is not uniform. Therefore, even with a total body-specific gravity of less than the specific gravity of water, the individual may not float horizontally in the water. Additionally, the lungs, when filled with air, can further decrease the specific gravity of the chest area. This allows the head and chest to float higher in the water than the heavier, denser extremities. Therefore, compensation with flotation devices at the extremities may be necessary for some treatments.

Resistive Forces

When an object moves in the water, just as on land, several resistive forces are at work that must be overcome. These forces include the cohesive force, the bow force, and the drag force.

COHESIVE FORCE

There is a slight but easily overcome cohesive force that runs in a parallel direction to the water surface. This resistance is formed by the water molecules loosely binding together, creating a surface tension. Surface tension can be seen in still water, because the water remains motionless with the cohesive force intact unless disturbed.

BOW FORCE

A second force is the bow force, or the force that is generated at the front of the object during movement. When the object moves, the bow force causes an increase in the water pressure at the front of the object and a decrease in the water pressure at the rear of the object. This pressure change causes a movement of water from the high-pressure area in the front to the low-pressure area behind the object. As the water enters the low-pressure area, it swirls into the low-pressure zone and forms eddies, or small whirlpool turbulences.[9] These eddies impede flow by creating a backward force, or drag force (Fig. 17-2).

DRAG FORCE

This third force, the drag force, is very important in aquatic therapy. The bow force, and therefore also the drag force, on an

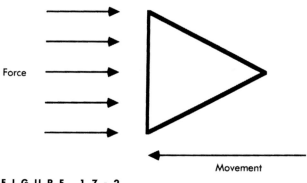

F I G U R E   1 7 - 2

The bow force.

object can be controlled by changing the shape of the object or the speed of its movement (Fig. 17-3).

Frictional resistance can be decreased by making the object more streamlined. This change minimizes the surface area at the front of the object. Less surface area causes less bow force and less of a change in pressure between the front and rear of the object, resulting in less drag force. In a streamlined flow, the resistance is proportional to the velocity of the object. Therefore, to assist a weak patient, exercises should be performed slowly in the most streamlined position possible in order to decrease resistance to movement (Fig. 17-4).

On the other hand, if the object is not streamlined, a turbulent situation exists. In a turbulent situation, drag is a function of the velocity squared. Therefore by increasing the speed of movement 2 times, the resistance the object must overcome is increased 4 times.[10] This provides a method to increase resistance progressively during aquatic rehabilitation. However, increases in speed also affect stability adversely. Single-limb movements are generally not as affected as trunk exercise by this loss of stability. Considerable turbulence can be generated when the speed of movement is increased, causing the muscles to work harder to keep the movement going. This is especially true when changes of direction take place. Therefore, by simply changing the shape of a limb through the addition of rehabil-

itation equipment or increasing the speed of movement, the therapist can modify the patient's workout intensity to match strength increases (Fig. 17-5).

ADVANTAGES OF AQUATIC REHABILITATION

The addition of an aquatic therapy program can offer many advantages to a patient's therapy. The buoyancy of the water allows active exercise while providing a sense of security and causing little discomfort.[28] Using a combination of the water's buoyancy, resistance, and warmth, the patient can typically achieve more in the aquatic environment than is possible on land.[21] Early in the rehabilitation process, aquatic therapy is useful in restoring range of motion and flexibility. As normal function is restored, resistance training and sport-specific activities can be added.

Following an injury, the aquatic experience provides a medium where early motion can be performed in a supportive environment. The slow-motion effect of moving through water provides extra time to control movement, which allows the patient to experience multiple movement errors without severe consequences.[27] This is especially helpful in lower-extremity injuries where balance and proprioception are impaired. The increased amount of time to react, combined with a medium in which the fear of falling is removed, assists the patient's ability to regain proprioception. Additionally, tactile stimulation from the turbulence generated during movement provides feedback that aids in the return of proprioception and balance. Also, the warmth of the water aids in inducing muscular relaxation. The stimulation from the aquatic environment may act as a gating mechanism, decreasing pain. This allows greater pain-free range of motion. There is also an often overlooked benefit of edema reduction due to hydrostatic pressure. This would benefit pain reduction and increase range of motion.

Using the buoyant principles, the aquatic environment can provide a gradual transition from nonweight-bearing to full weight-bearing land exercises. This gradual increase in percent weight bearing helps provide a return to smooth, coordinated movements that are pain free. By using the buoyant force to decrease apparent weight and joint compressive forces, locomotor activities can begin much earlier following an injury to the lower extremity. This provides an enormous advantage to the athletic population. The ability to work out hard without the fear of damaging the recent injury provides a psychological boost to the patient. This helps keep motivation high and may aid in speeding the patient's return to normal function.[21] Psychologically, aquatic therapy increases confidence, because the patient experiences increased success at locomotor, stretching, or strengthening activities in the water. Tension and anxiety are decreased and patient morale increases, as well as postexercise vigor.[9,10,25]

Through careful use of Archimedes' principle, a gradual increase in the percentage of weight bearing can be undertaken. Initially, the patient would begin nonweight bearing in the deep

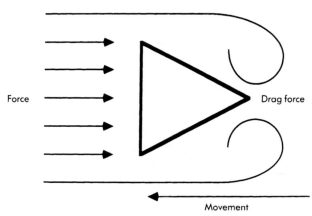

F I G U R E   1 7 - 3

Drag force.

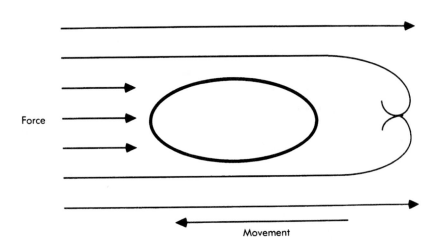

FIGURE 17-4

Streamlined movement. This creates less drag force and less turbulence.

end of the pool. A wet vest or similar buoyant device might be used to help the patient remain afloat for the desired exercises (Fig. 17-6). If such a device is unavailable, empty plastic milk jugs held in each hand are also a quite effective and very inexpensive method of flotation (Fig. 17-7).

Once therapy has progressed, the patient could be moved to neck-deep water to begin light weight bearing. Gradual increases in the percentage of weight bearing are accomplished by systematically moving the patient to more shallow water. Even when in waist-deep water, both male and female patients are only bearing approximately 50 percent of their TBW. By placing a sinkable bench or chair in the shallow water, step-ups can then be initiated under partial weight-bearing conditions long before the patient is capable of performing the same exercise in full weight bearing on land. Thus the advantages of low weight bearing are coupled with the proprioceptive benefits of closed-kinetic chain exercise, making aquatic therapy an excellent functional rehabilitation activity.

Muscular strengthening and reeducation can also be accomplished through aquatic therapy. Progressive resistance exercises can be increased in extremely small increments by using combinations of different resistive forces. The intensity of exercise can be controlled by manipulating the body's position or through the addition of exercise equipment. Then individuals

with minimal muscle contraction capabilities, therefore, are capable of doing work and seeing improvement. Yet the aquatic environment can still provide a challenging resistive workout to a patient nearing full recovery. Additionally, the water serves as an accommodating resistance medium. This allows the muscles to be maximally stressed through the full range of motion available. One drawback to this, however, is that the extent of strength gained depends largely on the effort exerted by the patient, which is not easily quantified. Strength gains through aquatic exercises are also brought about by the increased energy needs of the body working in an aquatic environment. Studies have shown that aquatic exercise requires a higher energy expenditure than the same exercise performed on land. The patient not only has to perform the activity but must also maintain a level of buoyancy and overcome the resistive forces of the water. For example, the energy cost for water running is four times greater than running the same distance on land.[9,10,20]

A simulated run in either shallow or deep water assisted by a tether or flotation devices can be an effective means of alternate fitness training for the injured patient. Not only does the patient benefit from early intervention, but the aquatic exercise helps prevent cardiorespiratory deconditioning through alterations in cardiovascular dynamics as a result of hydrostatic forces.[5,17,29] The heart actually functions more efficiently in

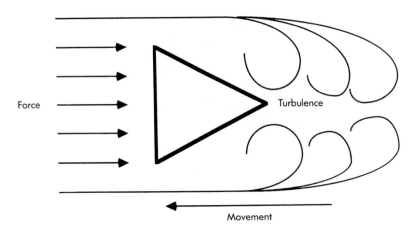

FIGURE 17-5

Turbulent flow.

FIGURE 17-6

Wet vest in deep water.

the water. Hydrostatic pressure enhances venous return, leading to a greater stroke volume and reduced heart rate needed to maintain cardiac output. There is also a decrease in ventilations and an increase in central blood volume. This means that the injured patient can maintain a near-normal maximum aerobic capacity with aquatic exercise.[11,24] Due to the hydrostatic effects

on heart efficiency, it has been suggested that an environment-specific exercise prescription is necessary.[19,29,32] Some research suggests the use of perceived exertion as a method for controlling exercise intensity. Other research continues to use target heart rate values as with land exercise, but compensates for the hydrostatic changes by setting target range at 10% lower than would be expected for land exercise. Regardless of the method used, the keys to successful use of aquatic therapy are supervision and monitoring of the patient during activity and good communication between patient and therapist.

DISADVANTAGES OF AQUATIC REHABILITATION

As with any therapeutic modality, aquatic therapy has its disadvantages. The cost of building and maintaining a rehabilitation pool, if there is no access to an existing facility, can be very high. Also, qualified pool attendants must be present, and the therapist involved in the treatment must be trained in aquatic safety and therapy procedures.[7,20]

A patient who requires high stabilization will be more challenging to work with, because stabilization in the water is considerably more difficult than on land. Stabilization of the therapist is just as important as stabilization of the injured patient. A wide stance in the water will help provide a solid base and better support of the patient by the therapist. Flotation devices placed at the neck, hips, and extremities can also help support the patient in the water (Fig. 17-8).

The presence of any open wounds or sores on the patient is a contraindication to aquatic therapy, as are contagious skin diseases. This restriction is obvious for health reasons to reduce the chance of infection of the patient or of others who use the pool.[18,23] Because of this risk, all surgical wounds must be completely healed before the pool is accessed. An excessive fear of the water would also be a reason to keep a patient out of an

FIGURE 17-7

Milk jugs in water for flotation.

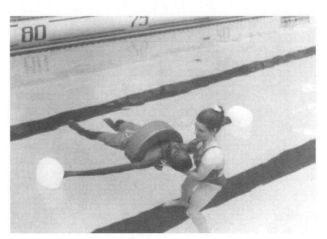

FIGURE 17-8

Patient and therapist using shallow water with floats.

aquatic exercise program. Fever, urinary tract infections, allergies to the pool chemicals, cardiac problems, and uncontrolled seizures are also contraindications.

FACILITIES AND EQUIPMENT

When considering an existing facility or when planning to build one, certain characteristics of the pool should be taken into consideration. The pool should not be smaller than 10 feet by 12 feet. It can be in-ground or aboveground as long as access for the patient is well planned. Both a shallow ($2\frac{1}{2}$ feet) and a deep (5 feet plus) area should be present to allow standing exercise and swimming or nonstanding exercise. The pool bottom should be flat and the depth gradations clearly marked. Water temperature will vary depending on the activity. For water exercise, 92 to 95°F water temperature is appropriate; however, lower temperatures of 85 to 90°F are more suitable for active swimming.[25] Temperature is an important factor, because water that is too warm can lead to fatigue or even heat exhaustion, and water that is too cool can cause shivering, increased muscular tension, or hypothermia.

Some prefabricated pools come with an in-water treadmill or current-producing device (Fig. 17-9). These devices can be beneficial but are not essential to treatment. Rescue tubes, inner tubes, or wet vests can be purchased to assist in flotation activities such as deep-water running. Hand paddles and pull buoys are effective in strengthening the upper extremity, while kickboards and fins are useful for strengthening the lower extremity. Most of these products can be purchased from local sporting goods stores with no special ordering required. Equipment for aquatic therapy, or so-called "pool toys," is limited only by the imagination of the therapist. Plastic milk jugs, balls, and other

FIGURE 17-9

The SwimEx pool. This pool's even, controllable water flow allows for the application of individualized prescriptive exercise and therapeutic programs. Up to three patients can be treated simultaneously.

FIGURE 17-10

Aquatic exercise equipment. Kickboard, fins, pull buoys, paddles, wet vest, and rescue tube are common forms of exercise equipment.

common items can be substituted for the more expensive commercial equipment with comparable results (Fig. 17-10). What is important is to stimulate interest in therapy and to keep in mind what goals are to be accomplished.

TECHNIQUES

Designing an aquatic therapy program is very similar to designing a program for land exercises. A thorough history and evaluation of the injury is the first step. Once contraindications have been ruled out, the patient's water safety skills and swimming ability should be evaluated, as well as the general comfort level in the water. The patient must be supervised at all times and should not be left unattended for any reason. From this point, an aquatic program that is specific and individualized can be developed using the principles of aquatic therapy techniques.

Buoyancy Technique

Several popular aquatic therapy approaches are currently being used. The most common aquatic therapy technique seems to be the buoyancy technique. This technique is actually a three-part progression moving from buoyancy-assisted exercises to buoyancy-supported and finally to buoyancy-resisted exercises.[6] A rehabilitation progression would begin with the therapist assisting the patient in the water through passive range of motion in any plane. Then the patient could move actively from below the water toward the surface in the buoyancy-assisted phase. The next phase would be to move parallel to the water surface while at the buoyant level. In this phase, only the cohesive force is resisting motion. This would be a buoyancy-supported position. An intermediate stage would have movement start at the buoyant level and continue toward the surface. This stage is limited in use because some individuals' buoyant level is already at the surface. Therefore no movement would be possible. In the buoyancy-resisted phase, the patient would move downward from the buoyant level against the upward buoyant force. Finally, flotation devices could be used to increase the difficulty of moving against the buoyant force.[25] Thus every joint could be moved either actively or passively and with or without resistance or assistance through its full range of motion. Increasing the speed of movement or decreasing the streamline by changing the body positioning or adding rehabilitation equipment increases the drag force resistance as the patient gets stronger, making workouts more challenging.[23]

An example of a shoulder progression for flexion using this approach would begin with the therapist and the patient together in neck-deep water. Passive range of motion of the injured extremity would be initiated in the flexion pattern by the therapist. In the next stage, the therapist would place the extremity below the buoyant level and allow the buoyant force to assist the patient's active shoulder flexion. To accomplish this stage the patient stands upright while the arm is passively moved to the patient's side by the therapist. Then the patient actively flexes the shoulder until the arm reaches the water surface. The flexion pattern for the next phase, the buoyancy-supported stage, begins with the patient sidelying with the injured shoulder closest to the pool bottom. Support with floats would be needed at the feet, hips, and neck, as well as additional support from the therapist at the torso. In this position, the patient could work both flexion and extension while only encountering resistance from the cohesive force, allowing an excellent opportunity to increase active range of motion. Generally, 2 to 3 sets of 10 repetitions are appropriate, depending on the patient's tolerance.

In the strengthening phase, the buoyancy-resisted stage, the patient is standing once again. Active flexion and extension of the shoulder begins at a starting position parallel to the water surface and progresses to the side of the thigh. From the thigh, the assistance of the buoyant force is resisted while the arm is returned to the starting position. When 2 to 3 sets of 10 repetitions can be completed without pain, equipment may be added to increase the difficulty. Hand paddles provide a greater surface area and therefore more resistance and a higher intensity. Plastic milk jugs partially filled with water are another excellent way to increase resistance. By placing less water in the jug, its buoyancy is increased, and the resistance on the arm increases correspondingly (Fig. 17-11). It is important to remember to keep the shoulder and upper arm under the water during upper-extremity exercise. This is to avoid sudden shoulder overload and impingement, as the arm can weigh up to eight times its original weight at 90 degrees abduction or flexion. The forearm, however, may come above the water to allow full rotation range of motion.[28]

Bad Ragaz Technique

A second common technique in aquatic therapy is Bad Ragaz. In this method, buoyancy is used for flotation purposes only and not to assist or resist movement. The bow force ahead and drag force behind are the means for providing resistance. Three

FIGURE 17-11

Milk jugs used for resistance.

main positions apply in this method. The therapist should be in waist-deep water to maintain optimal stability. In the first position, the patient actively moves while being fixated by the therapist (isokinetic). The patient determines the resistance by controlling the speed of movement. For example, to work on knee flexion, the patient could be stabilized sidelying with the involved leg closest to the surface. The buoyant force will act on that leg, and movement occurs, resulting in bow and drag forces. The bow force pushes the knee into flexion while the drag force pulls the knee in the same direction.

A second position has the patient and therapist moving together in the direction of the desired motion (isotonic). To work on knee flexion in this position, the patient is pushed forward, either sidelying or backlying. This position facilitates movement of the knee into flexion, since the bow force helps the patient's active contraction to push the knee into flexion. This position decreases the streamline of the leg and increases the drag force that also assists by pulling the knee into flexion. In this situation, the therapist controls the speed and therefore the resistance. The third position in this technique has the patient holding a fixed position while being pushed by the therapist (isometric). In this position, the patient holds an isometric contraction against the bow and drag forces (Fig. 17-12).

Hold–relax, repeated contraction, and other PNF techniques can also be used in the water (see Chapter 13). They are very similar to those done on land but are performed in a buoyancy-assisted position to enhance results.[6,9] PNF techniques should be done carefully since research by Hurley and Turner[18] suggests the patient may have a reduced perception of stretch in the water. Once again, as the patient's strength increases, resistive equipment should be added to make the workouts more challenging.

The aquatic therapist is limited only by the imagination when using aquatic therapy principles as a basis for workouts in the water. This additional method of therapy can help stimulate interest and motivation in the patient helping to supplement traditional exercise and return the patient to normal function and competition.

FIGURE 17-12

Bad Ragaz technique.

SUMMARY

- The buoyant force counteracts the force of gravity as it assists motion toward the water's surface and resists motion away from the surface.
- Because of differences in the specific gravity of the body, the head and chest tend to float higher in the water than the heavier, denser extremities, making compensation with flotation devices necessary.
- The three forces that oppose movement in the water are the cohesive force, bow force, and drag force.
- Aquatic therapy allows for fine gradation of exercise, increased control over the percentage of weight bearing, increased range of motion and strength, decreased pain, and increased confidence.
- Cost, decreased stabilization, and patient contraindications are some disadvantages of aquatic therapy.
- Pool size, water temperature, and equipment will vary depending on the population using the facility.
- The buoyancy technique consists of buoyancy-assisted, buoyancy-supported, and buoyancy-resisted phases.
- The Bad Ragaz technique uses isokinetic, isotonic, and isometric holding positions.
- Aquatic therapy is meant to complement, not replace, traditional land exercise.

REFERENCES

1. Arrigo C, ed. Aquatic rehabilitation. *Sports Med Update* 7, 1992.
2. Arrigo C, Fuller CS, Wilk KE. Aquatic rehabilitation following ACL-PTG reconstruction, *Sports Med Update* 7:22–27, 1992.
3. Bolton F, Goodwin D. *Pool Exercises.* Edinburgh, Churchill Livingstone, 1974.
4. Broach E, Groff D, Yaffe R, et al. Effects of aquatics therapy on physical behavior of adult with multiple sclerosis. 1995 Leisure Research Symposium, San Antonio, 1995. *http://www.indiana.edu/~Irs/Irs95/ebroach95.html* (1/27/97).
5. Butts NK, Tucker M, Greening C. Physiologic responses to maximal treadmill and deep water running in men and women. *Am J Sports Med* 19:612–614, 1991.
6. Campion MR. *Adult Hydrotherapy: A Practical Approach.* Oxford, Heineman Medical, 1990.
7. Dioffenbach L. Aquatic therapy services. *Clin Management* 11:14–19, 1991.
8. Doughterty NJ. Risk management in aquatics, JOHPERD May/June, 46–48, 1990.
9. Duffield NH. *Exercise in Water.* London, Bailliere Tindall, 1976.
10. Edlich RF, Towler MA, Goitz RJ, et al. Bioengineering principles of hydrotherapy. *J Burn Care Rehab* 8:580–584, 1987.
11. Eyestone ED, Fellingham G, George J, Fisher G. Effect of water running and cycling on maximum oxygen consumption and 2 mile run performance. *Am J Sports Med* 21:41–44, 1993.
12. Fawcett CW. Principles of aquatic rehab: A new look at hydrotherapy. *Sports Med Update* 7:6–9, 1992.
13. Genuario SE, Vegso JJ. The use of a swimming pool in the rehabilitation and reconditioning of athletic injuries. *Contemp Orthop* 20:381–387, 1990.
14. Golland A. Basic hydrotherapy. *Physiotherapy* 67:258–262, 1961.
15. Haralson KM. Therapeutic pool programs. *Clin Management* 5:10–13, 1985.
16. Harrison R, Bulstrode S. Percentage weight bearing during partial immersion in the hydrotherapy pool. *Physiother Pract* 3:60–63, 1987.
17. Hertler L, Provost-Craig M, Sestili D, et al. Water running and the maintenance of maximal oxygen consumption and leg strength in runners. *Med Sci Sports Exerc* 24:S23, 1992.
18. Hurley R, Turner C. Neurology and aquatic therapy. *Clin Management* 11:26–27, 1991.
19. Koszuta LE. From sweats to swimsuits: Is water exercise the wave of the future? *Phys Sports Med* 17:203–206, 1989.
20. Kolb ME. Principles of underwater exercise. *Phys Ther Rev* 27:361–364, 1957.
21. Levin S. Aquatic therapy. *Phys Sports Med* 19:119–126, 1991.
22. McWaters JG. For faster recovery just add water. *Sports Med Update* 7:4–5, 1992.
23. Meyer RI. Practice settings for kinesiotherapy-aquatics. *Clin Kinesiol* 44:12–13, 1990.
24. Michaud TL, Brennean DK, Wilder RP, Sherman NW. Aquarun training and changes in treadmill running maximal oxygen consumption. *Med Sci Sports Exerc* 24:S23, 1992.
25. Moor FB, Peterson SC, Manueall EM, et al. *Manual of Hydrotherapy and Massage.* Mountain View, CA, Pacific Press, 1964.

26. Nolte-Heuritsch I. *Aqua Rhythmics: Exercises for the Swimming Pool.* New York, Sterling, 1979.

27. Simmons V, Hansen PD. Effectiveness of water exercise on postural mobility in the well elderly: An experimental study on balance enhancement. *J Gerontol* 51A:M233–M238, 1996.

28. Speer K, Cavanaugh JT, Warren RF, et al. A role for hydrotherapy in shoulder rehabilitation. *Am J Sports Med* 21:850–853, 1993.

29. Svendenhag J, Seger J. Running on land and in water: Comparative exercise physiology. *Med Sci Sports Exerc* 24:1155–1160, 1992.

30. Town GP, Bradley SS. Maximal metabolic responses of deep and shallow water running in trained runners. *Med Sci Sport Exerc* 23:238–241, 1991.

31. Triggs M. Orthopedic aquatic therapy. *Clin Management* 11:30–31, 1991.

32. Wilder RP, Brennan D, Schotte D. A standard measure for exercise prescription and aqua running. *Am J Sports Med* 21:45–48, 1993.

Using Therapeutic Modalities in Rehabilitation

William E. Prentice

O B J E C T I V E S

After completing this chapter, the student therapist should be able to do the following:

- Describe the approach of the therapist in using therapeutic modalities.
- Discuss the physiologic effects of thermotherapy and cryotherapy techniques.
- Discuss the use of ultrasound as a deep-heating modality.
- Discuss the use of diathermy in rehabilitation.
- Discuss the potential physiologic responses of biologic tissue to electrical stimulating currents.
- Describe the possible uses for the low-power laser.
- Explain how intermittent compression can be used to decrease swelling.
- Discuss how the various massage techniques may be used clinically.
- Discuss the progression of modality use as the healing process progresses through the different phases of healing.
- List indications and contraindications for the use of the various modalities.
- Discuss the physiologic effects associated with the use of the different modalities.

Therapeutic modalities, when used appropriately, can be extremely useful tools in the rehabilitation of the injured patient. Like any other tool, their effectiveness is limited by the knowledge, skill, and experience of the clinician using them. For the therapist, decisions regarding how and when a modality may best be used should be based on a combination of theoretical knowledge and practical experience. Modalities should not be used at random, nor should their use be based on what has always been done before. Instead, consideration must always be given to what should work best in a specific clinical situation. In any program of rehabilitation, modalities should be used primarily as adjuncts to therapeutic exercise and certainly not to the exclusion of range-of-motion and strengthening exercises.[25]

There are many different approaches and ideas regarding the use of modalities in injury rehabilitation. Therefore no "cookbook" exists for modality use. Instead, therapists should make their own decision from the options in a given clinical situation about which modality will be most effective.

SUPERFICIAL HEATING AND COOLING MODALITIES (INFRARED)

The superficial heating and cooling modalities (more correctly referred to as **infrared** modalities) used in a clinical setting are all classified as infrared modalities.[26] Heating modalities are referred to as **thermotherapy.** Thermotherapy is used when a rise in tissue temperature is the goal of treatment. The use of cold, or **cryotherapy,** is most effective in the acute stages of the healing process immediately after injury when tissue temperature loss is the goal of therapy (Fig. 18-1). Cold applications can be continued into the reconditioning state of injury management. The term **hydrotherapy** can be applied to any cryotherapy or

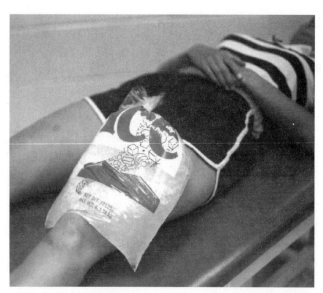

FIGURE 18-1

Cryotherapy is a superficial therapeutic technique used to decrease tissue temperature.

thermotherapy technique that uses water as the medium for heat transfer.[37]

Clinical Use of Heat and Cold

The physiologic effects of heat and cold are rarely the result of direct absorption of infrared energy. There is general agreement that no form of infrared energy can have a depth of penetration greater than 1 centimeter. Thus the effects of the infrared modalities are primarily superficial and directly affect the cutaneous blood vessels and the cutaneous nerve receptors.[26]

Absorption of infrared energy cutaneously increases and decreases circulation subcutaneously in both the muscle and fat layers. If the energy is absorbed cutaneously over a long enough period to raise the temperature of the circulating blood, the hypothalamus will reflexively increase blood flow to the underlying tissue. Likewise, absorption of cold cutaneously can decrease blood flow via a similar mechanism in the area of treatment.[21]

Thus if the primary treatment goal is a tissue temperature increase with corresponding increase in blood flow to the deeper tissues, a wiser choice is perhaps a modality, such as diathermy or ultrasound, that produces energy that can penetrate the cutaneous tissues and be directly absorbed by the deep tissues.[26] If the primary treatment goal is to reduce tissue temperature and decrease blood flow to an injured area, the superficial application of ice or cold is the only modality capable of producing such a response.

Perhaps the most effective use of the infrared modalities is for **analgesia,** that is, reducing the sensation of pain associated with injury. The infrared modalities primarily stimulate the cutaneous nerve receptors. Through one of the mechanisms of pain modulation, most likely the gate control theory,

hyperstimulation of these nerve receptors by heating or cooling reduces pain. Within the philosophy of an aggressive program of rehabilitation, as is standard in most clinical settings, the reduction of pain as a means of facilitating therapeutic exercise is a common practice. As emphasized earlier, therapeutic modalities are perhaps best used as an adjunct to therapeutic exercise. Certainly, this should be a prime consideration when selecting an infrared modality for use in any treatment program.[26]

Cryotherapy

Cryotherapy is the use of cold to treat acute trauma and subacute injury and to decrease discomfort after athletic reconditioning and rehabilitation.[22] Tools of cryotherapy include ice packs, cold whirlpool, ice whirlpool, ice massage, commercial chemical cold spray, and contrast baths. Application of cryotherapy produces a three- to four-stage sensation. The first sensation of cold is followed by a stinging, then a burning or aching feeling, and finally numbness. Each stage is related to the nerve endings as they temporarily cease to function as a result of decreased blood flow. The time required for this sequence varies from 5 to 15 minutes. After 12 to 15 minutes, a reflex deep-tissue vasodilation called the **hunting response** has been said to occur with intense cold (10°C or 50°F). However, this response appears to occur only in the distal extremities, and its value as a protective mechanism is debatable.[16] A minimum of 15 minutes is necessary to achieve extreme analgesic effects.

Application of ice is safe, simple, and inexpensive. Cryotherapy is contraindicated in patients with cold allergies (hives, joint pain, nausea), Raynaud's phenomenon (arterial spasm), and some rheumatoid conditions.[22]

Depth of penetration depends on the amount of cold and the length of the treatment time. The body is well equipped to maintain skin and subcutaneous tissue viability through the capillary bed by reflex vasodilation of up to four times normal blood flow. The body can decrease blood flow to the body segment that is supposedly losing too much body heat by shunting the blood flow. Depth of penetration is also related to intensity and duration of cold application and the circulatory response to the body segment exposed. If the person has normal circulatory responses, frostbite should not be a concern. Even so, caution should be exercised when applying intense cold directly to the skin. If deeper penetration is desired, ice therapy is most effective with ice towels, ice packs, ice massage, and whirlpools.[22] Patients should be advised of the four stages of cryotherapy and the discomfort they will experience. The therapist should explain this sequence and advise the patient of the expected outcome, which may include a rapid decrease in pain.[26]

Thermotherapy

Heat is still used as a universal treatment for pain and discomfort.[19] Much of the benefit is derived because the treatment simply feels good. In the early stages after injury, however, heat causes increased capillary blood pressure and increased cellular permeability, which results in additional swelling or edema accumulation.[26] No patient with edema should be treated with any heat modality until the reasons for edema are determined. The therapist should use cryotherapy techniques or contrast baths to reduce the edema before heat applications. Superficial heat applications seem to feel more comfortable for complaints of the neck, back, low back, and pelvic areas and may be most appropriate for the patient who exhibits some allergic response to cold application. However, the tissues in these areas are absolutely no different from those in the extremities. Thus the same physiologic responses to the use of heat or cold are elicited in all body areas.

Primary goals of thermotherapy include increased blood flow and muscle temperature to stimulate analgesia, increased nutrition to the cellular level, reduction of edema, and removal of metabolites and other products of the inflammatory process.[26]

Continued investigation and research into the use of heat and cold is warranted to provide useful data for the clinician. Heat and cold applications, when used properly and efficiently, provide the therapist with tools to enhance recovery and provide the patient with optimal health care management. Thermotherapy and cryotherapy are only two of the tools available to assist in the well-being and reconditioning of the injured patient.

ULTRASOUND

Ultrasound is defined as inaudible, acoustic vibrations of high frequency that may produce either thermal or nonthermal physiologic effects.[27] It has traditionally been classified as a "deep heating modality" and used primarily for the purpose of elevating tissue temperatures (Fig. 18-2).[4]

The main piece of equipment for delivering therapeutic ultrasound is a high-frequency generator, which provides an electrical current through a coaxial cable to a transducer contained within an applicator. Ultrasound is produced by a piezoelectric

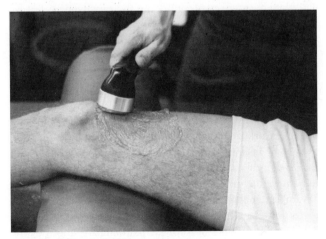

FIGURE 18-2

Technique for applying ultrasound.

crystal within the transducer that converts electrical energy to acoustic energy through mechanical deformation via the piezo-electric effect.[35]

Ultrasound energy travels within the tissues as a highly focused collimated beam with a nonuniform intensity distribution. The intensity of the ultrasound beam is determined by the amount of energy delivered to the sound head (applicator). It is expressed in the number of watts per square centimeter (W/cm^2). As a therapeutic modality used in sports medicine, it ranges from 0.1 to 3 W/cm^2.[38]

As the ultrasound wave is transmitted through the various tissues, there will be **attenuation** or a decrease in energy intensity due to either absorption of energy by the tissues or dispersion and scattering of the sound wave. Tissue penetration depends on impedance or acoustic properties of the media that are proportional to tissue density. Therapeutic ultrasound has a frequency range between 0.75 and 3.0 MHz (megahertz). Ultrasound energy generated at 1 MHz is transmitted through the more superficial tissues and absorbed primarily in the deeper tissues. A 1-MHz frequency is most useful in individuals with a high percentage of body fat cutaneously, and whenever the desired effects are in the deeper structures.[27] At 3 MHz the energy is absorbed in the more superficial tissues.

Virtually all therapeutic ultrasound generators can emit either continuous or pulsed ultrasound waves. Continuous ultrasound is most commonly used when the desired effect is to produce thermal effects. The clinical effects of using ultrasound to heat the tissues are similar to other forms of superficial heat, which have already been discussed. Whenever ultrasound is used to produce thermal changes, nonthermal changes will also occur simultaneously. However, if appropriate treatment parameters are selected, nonthermal effects can occur with minimal thermal effects. The use of pulsed ultrasound results in a reduced average heating of the tissues. Pulsed ultrasound or continuous ultrasound at a low intensity will produce nonthermal or mechanical effects, which may be associated with soft-tissue healing.[27]

The nonthermal effects of therapeutic ultrasound include cavitation and acoustic microstreaming. Cavitation is the formation of gas-filled bubbles that expand and compress due to ultrasonically induced pressure changes in tissue fluids.[7] Cavitation results in an increased flow in the fluid around these vibrating bubbles. Microstreaming is the unidirectional movement of fluids along the boundaries of cell membranes resulting from the mechanical pressure wave in an ultrasonic field.[27] Microstreaming can alter cell membrane structure and function due to changes in cell membrane permeability to sodium and calcium ions important in the healing process. As long as the cell membrane is not damaged, microstreaming can be of therapeutic value in accelerating the healing process.[27] The nonthermal effects of therapeutic ultrasound in the treatment of injured tissues may be as important if not more important than the thermal effects. The nonthermal effects of cavitation and microstreaming can be maximized while minimizing the thermal effects by using an intensity of 0.1 to 0.2 W/cm^2 with continuous ultrasound.

Application Technique

Therapeutic ultrasound is most effective when an appropriate coupling medium and technique using either direct contact, immersion, or a bladder is combined with a moving transducer. The purpose of a coupling medium is to provide an airtight contact with the skin and a slick, friction-proof surface for the ultrasound head to glide over. Coupling mediums for direct contact include mineral oil, water-soluble creams, and gels. Underwater administration of ultrasound is suggested for irregular body parts such as the wrist, hand, elbow, ankle, and foot. Another technique for treating irregular surfaces has been recommended in which a water-filled balloon is placed between the transducer and the treatment area with sufficient amounts of coupling gel to ensure good contact.[27]

Moving the transducer in a circular pattern or a stroking pattern during treatment leads to a more even distribution of energy within the treatment area and can reduce the likelihood of developing hot spots. The transducer should be moved slowly at approximately 4 cm per second. The transducer should be kept in maximum contact with the skin via some coupling agent throughout the treatment.

Dosage of ultrasound varies according to the depth of the tissue treated and the state of injury, such as subacute or chronic. Basically, 0.1 to 0.3 W/cm^2 is regarded as low intensity, 0.4 to 1.5 W/cm^2 is medium intensity, and 1.5 to 3 W/cm^2 is high intensity. The duration of treatment time ranges from 5 to 10 minutes.[27]

Therapeutic Uses

Therapeutic ultrasound when applied to biologic tissue may induce clinically significant responses in cells, tissues, and organs through both thermal effects, which produce a tissue temperature increase, and nonthermal effects, which include cavitation and microstreaming.[10] Even though there is relatively little documented evidence concerning the efficacy of ultrasound, it is most often used for soft-tissue healing and repair; with scar tissue and joint contracture; for chronic inflammation; for bone healing; with plantar warts; and for placebo effects.

It is generally accepted that acute conditions require more frequent treatments over a shorter period of time while more chronic conditions require fewer treatments over a longer period of time.[27] Ultrasound treatments should begin as soon as possible following injury, ideally within hours but definitely within 48 hours, to maximize effects on the healing process.[27] Acute conditions may be treated using low-intensity ultrasound once or even twice daily for 6 to 8 days until acute symptoms such as pain and swelling subside. In chronic conditions, when acute symptoms have subsided, treatment may be done on alternating days for a total of 10 to 12 treatments.[11]

It is not uncommon to combine modalities to accomplish a specific treatment goal. Ultrasound is frequently used with other modalities including hot packs, cold packs, and electrical stimulating currents.[11]

Phonophoresis

Phonophoresis is a technique in which ultrasound is used to drive molecules of a topically applied medication, usually either anti-inflammatories or analgesics, into the tissues.[30] Like iontophoresis, it is designed to move medication into injured tissues. However, phonophoresis is not as likely to damage or burn skin. Also the depth of penetration with phonophoresis is substantially greater than with iontophoresis.

The most widespread use of the phonophoresis technique has been to deliver hydrocortisone, which has anti-inflammatory effects. This technique has been successful in treating painful trigger points, tendinitis, and bursitis.[38] Salicylates have also been used to evoke a number of pharmacologic effects including analgesia and decreased inflammation. Lidocaine is a commonly used local anesthetic drug. The use of phonophoresis with lidocaine was found to be effective in treating a series of trigger points.[27]

In phonophoresis, coupling can be either direct or using immersion. The medication in preparation is rubbed directly into the surface of the skin over the treatment area. With the direct technique, transmission gel should be applied, and with immersion the treatment area with the preparation applied is simply treated underwater.

Both pulsed and continuous ultrasound have been used in phonophoresis. Continuous ultrasound at an intensity great enough to produce thermal effects may induce a pro-inflammatory response.[7]

DIATHERMY

Diathermy is the application of high-frequency electromagnetic energy that is primarily used to generate heat in body tissues (Fig. 18-3).

Diathermy as a therapeutic agent may be classified as two distinct modalities, **shortwave diathermy** and **microwave diathermy.** Shortwave diathermy may be continuous or pulsed. The physiologic effects of continuous shortwave and microwave diathermy are primarily thermal, resulting from high-frequency vibration of molecules. However, pulsed shortwave diathermy has been used for its nonthermal effects in the treatment of soft-tissue injuries and wounds.[28] Clinically the use of the diathermies, particularly shortwave pulsed diathermy, is once again on the rise.

A shortwave diathermy unit that generates a high-frequency electrical current will produce both an electrical field and a magnetic field in the tissues. The ratio of the electrical field to the magnetic field depends on the characteristics of the different units as well as on the characteristics of electrodes or applicators. The capacitance technique, using capacitor electrodes (airspace plates and pad electrodes), creates a strong electrical field that is essentially the lines of force exerted on charged ions by the electrodes that cause charged particles to move from one pole to the other. The inductance technique, using induction electrodes

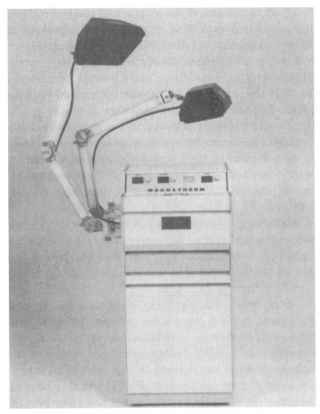

FIGURE   18 - 3

Shortwave diathermy unit. Magnatherm is an example of a shortwave diathermy unit.

(cable electrodes and drum electrodes), creates a strong magnetic field when current is passed through a coiled cable. It affects surrounding tissues by inducing localized secondary currents, called eddy currents, within the tissues.[28]

Pulsed diathermy is created by simply interrupting the output of continuous shortwave diathermy at consistant intervals. Generators that deliver pulsed shortwave diathermy typically use a drum type of electrode to induce energy in the treatment area via the production of a magnetic field. Pulsed diathermy is claimed to have therapeutic value and to produce nonthermal effects with minimal thermal physiologic effects, depending on the intensity of the application.[15] When pulsed diathermy is used in intensities that create an increase in tissue temperature, its effects are no different from those of continuous shortwave diathermy. Successful treatments have largely resulted from the application of higher intensities and longer treatment times.

Microwave diathermy units generate a strong electrical field and relatively little magnetic field through either circular-shaped or rectangular-shaped applicators that beam energy to the treatment area. With microwave diathermy, the energy can be focused toward the body part to be treated. This focus allows for greater penetration because more of the energy strikes the skin perpendicularly. Scatter of the energy is minimized, and absorption is maximized. Because microwave energy can be

focused, therapeutic tissue temperature increases can occur up to a depth of 5 centimeters, and microwave diathermy is probably as effective as shortwave diathermy in producing deep-tissue temperature rise.

The diathermies have been used in the treatment of a variety of musculoskeletal conditions including muscle strains, contusions, ligament sprains, tendinitis, tenosynovitis, bursitis, joint contractures, and myofascial trigger points.[33] There are probably more treatment precautions and contraindications for the use of either shortwave or microwave diathermy than for any of the other physical agents. Effective treatments using the diathermies require practice in application and adjustment of techniques to the individual patient.

ELECTRICAL STIMULATING CURRENTS

Electrical stimulating currents are among the therapeutic modalities most often used by the therapist (Fig. 18-4).[12] The effects of electrical current passing through biologic tissues may be physiologic, chemical, or thermal. All biologic tissue has some response to this current flow. The type and extent of the response depends on (1) the type of tissue and physiologic response characteristics and (2) the parameters of the electrical current applied, that is, its intensity, duration, waveform, modulation, and polarity. Biologic tissue responds to electrical energy in a manner similar to how it normally functions and grows.

Clinically, the therapist uses electrical currents for several purposes: (1) producing muscle contraction through stimulation of nerve muscle, (2) stimulating sensory nerves to help treat pain, (3) creating an electrical field on the skin surface to drive ions into tissues (iontophoresis), and (4) creating an electrical field within the tissues to stimulate or alter the healing process (medical galvanism). The major therapeutic uses of

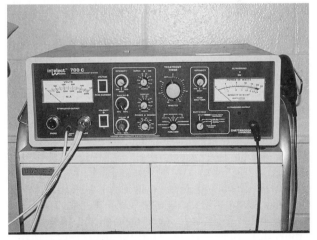

FIGURE   18 - 4

Electrical stimulating current. Depending on the treatment parameters selected, the physiologic effects may involve sensory or motor nerves or chemical changes.

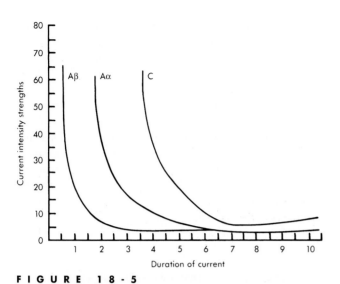

FIGURE 18 - 5

Strength–duration curves. Curves represent the thresholds for depolarization of the various types of nerve fibers. (Aβ, sensory nerves; Aα, motor fibers; C, pain fibers.)

electricity center on muscle contraction, sensory stimulation, and ion transfer.[12]

To produce any physiologic response in the nerve and muscle fibers, an electrical current must be of sufficient intensity and last long enough to equal or exceed the nerve membrane's basic threshold for excitation. When this occurs, depolarization of the nerve fiber results in an action potential.[34]

Different types (sizes) of nerves have different thresholds for depolarization. The **strength–duration curves** in Figure 18-5 represent graphically the thresholds for depolarization of sensory (Aβ), motor (Aα), and pain (C) nerve fibers. If current intensity or duration is increased to a level great enough to reach the minimal threshold for depolarization of Aβ fibers, the electrical current can be felt. If current intensity or duration is increased further, a muscle contraction may be elicited by reaching the threshold for depolarization of the Aα fibers. If the intensity and/or duration continues to increase, eventually a level is reached that causes depolarization of the C fibers and pain. By simply changing current intensity, current duration, or some combination of the two, very different physiologic responses can be achieved.[12]

Traditionally, various types of electric currents have been classified by attaching specific names, such as high-volt, low-volt, alternating, direct, pulsed, interferential, Russian, and microamperage (MENS or LIS). Electrical stimulators that output any of these varieties of current (with the possible exception of some new LIS or MENS units in which the intensity is not great enough) can produce any of these physiologic responses if the current parameters are adjusted appropriately.[23]

Electrical stimulators are designed to deliver pulses with a waveform that generally differs depending on the manufacturer. Electrical currents are either direct (DC), alternating (AC), or pulsed and may take on sine, square, or triangular waveforms.[23]

Various claims concerning the effectiveness of specific waveforms have been made by manufacturers, and although one type of waveform may be more effective for a particular patient, generalizations are difficult to make. These waveforms refer to the waveform produced by the stimulator and delivered to the patient and not the waveform of the current used to drive the generator.

The electrical stimulating units are connected via electrodes placed on the skin surface generally in or over the area of pain. Electrodes placed at the painful region may be within the dermatome, on a specific point, or over a peripheral nerve supplying the painful region. Spinal cord segments that give rise to a specific nerve root conveying nociceptive input provide another choice for electrode placement. Electrodes are often placed along vertebrae or between spinous processes in conjunction with electrodes placed over specific dermatomal regions.[12]

Stimulation of Sensory Nerves

Transcutaneous electrical nerve stimulation (TENS) has been traditionally defined as a technique used to stimulate sensory nerve fibers with electrodes placed on the skin specifically to relieve either chronic or acute pain. TENS is an effective, noninvasive, nonpharmacologic method of pain modulation.[36]

Peripheral nerves are actually bundles of a large number of large- and small-diameter sensory and motor nerve fibers, innervating skin, muscle, and visceral structures. As previously mentioned, different-sized nerve fibers have characteristic strength–duration curves. The large-diameter sensory fibers (Aβ) are more easily excited by an electrical stimulus than smaller fibers. As stimulus intensity (or duration) is increased, large-diameter afferent motor fibers (Aα) are excited (or recruited) before smaller sensory fibers. If the intensity or duration of the stimulus is increased sufficiently, both motor (Aα) and small-diameter sensory or pain fibers (C) are excited. With conventional TENS, the objective is to maximally stimulate the large-diameter afferent or Aβ fibers without concomitant motor nerve responses or pain.[12]

MECHANISMS OF PAIN RELIEF

The mechanism by which TENS produces pain relief is a matter for debate. There are several different models that attempt to explain pain modulation (discussed in detail in Chapter 4). It must be stressed that these models of pain control are not mutually exclusive but rather the result of overlapping processes.[5]

Stimulation of Motor Nerves

Electrical stimulation of motor nerve fibers (Aδ) at sufficient intensity and duration to produce depolarization results in muscular contraction. Once a stimulus reaches the depolarizing threshold, an increase in the intensity of the stimulus does not alter the quality of the contraction. However, as the frequency of stimulation is increased, the time for repolarization of the muscle fiber is decreased, and thus the contractions tend to summate.

When the stimulation frequency reaches 50 pulses/second or greater, the muscle exhibits a tetanic contraction.

Several therapeutic gains can be accomplished by electrically stimulating muscle contraction. Electrically induced **muscle pumping** contractions can facilitate circulation by pumping fluid and blood through the venous and lymphatic channels away from an area of swelling.[12]

Muscular inhibition after periods of immobilization or surgery, or as a result of swelling, is an indication for muscle reeducation. Electrically stimulating the muscle to contract produces an increase in the sensory input from the muscle and assists the patient in **relearning a muscular response** or pattern.[12]

Muscular strengthening may be accomplished using high-frequency AC current in conjunction with voluntary muscle contractions.[12] The exclusive use of electrical current does not appear to increase muscle strength. Electrically stimulating the muscle to contract during periods of immobilization retards muscle atrophy and may potentially reduce the time required for rehabilitation after immobilization.

Electrical currents may also assist in **increasing range of motion** about a joint where contractures are limiting motion. Repeated contraction over an extended time appears to make the contracted joint structures and muscle modify and lengthen.[34]

Interferential Currents

Interferential current is a nonmodulated sine waveform alternating current produced by two simultaneously applied electrical generators that each produce this current at different frequencies. When the two currents intersect, the pulse intensities combine, and the difference in frequency produces a low-frequency "beat" pattern. Individual beats produce a physiologic response that is essentially identical to a single pulse produced by a conventional electrical stimulator.

Proponents of interferential currents claim that this beating pulse lowers skin resistance and produces a more comfortable stimulation with a greater depth of penetration than other stimulators. However, they fail to realize that higher voltages also reduce tissue impedance; thus the relative comfort is no different than with high-volt stimulators. Interferential currents are simply a different electrical approach to achieve the same excitatory responses that traditional high-volt stimulators produce. The disadvantages of interferential units are that they are expensive and not as versatile as other high-volt generators. They can be used for pain modulation, edema reduction, and muscle relaxation. They are not suitable for muscle reeducation because there is no interrupt mode or modulation.[34]

Low-Intensity Stimulation (LIS)

Low-intensity stimulation (LIS) was in the past referred to as microcurrent electrical neuromuscular stimulation (MENS).[12] LIS is one of the newer types of electrical stimulating currents currently being used by the therapist. Certainly, the type of current being produced by these LIS generators is no different

than current produced by other electrical stimulator generators. The majority of other electrical stimulating devices are capable of producing microcurrent. The only difference is that with LIS treatment the intensity of the current is at subsensory levels (below 1000 microamps) at a frequency of less than 1 pulse per second.[3]

The majority of the literature dealing with microcurrents centers around research into stimulation of the healing process in fractures and skin wounds, and in pain modulation. The mechanism of their effectiveness is thought to be based on changes that occur at the cellular level rather than having to do with the effects of depolarization of sensory and motor nerve fibers.[12] Microcurrent treatment may well be a useful addition to the electrical therapies. However, to date they are untested clinically, and claims of their effectiveness are based primarily on empirical rather than experimental evidence.[12]

Russian Current

Russian current is another relatively new type of current used by therapists. It uses an AC current at a high frequency (2500 to 10,000 PPS) produced in a series of "bursts." By putting the current in bursts, a greater intensity of current can be used, and the patient will have a high tolerance to the current. As intensity of stimulation increases, more muscle fibers are stimulated and a stronger contraction occurs.[2]

When used for muscle strengthening, this current is most effective when combined with active muscle contraction against resistance.

Iontophoresis

Electrical stimulating currents may also be used to produce chemical changes. Electricity is used in the clinic to cause chemical change in two important ways. The first is **iontophoresis** or **ion transfer,** defined as the introduction of chemical ions into superficial body tissues for medicinal purposes with the use of direct current. For iontophoresis to work, the chemical substance must be in an ionic form. Because like charges repel, chemical substances with a positive charge are introduced through the skin with the positive electrode, or anode, and substances with a negative charge must be introduced with the negative electrode, or cathode.[24]

The Phoresor is an electrical stimulating device designed specifically for iontophoresis. During recent years, this technique has gained significant popularity as a treatment modality. If the drug is in solution form, it is generally applied to a gauze pad that is placed directly over the area to be treated. The active electrode of the same polarity as the charge of the ion is then placed on top of the drug-soaked gauze and secured firmly in place. The dispersive or indifferent electrode is generally placed at a remote area of the same extremity. Drugs in paste form are usually rubbed onto the skin surface, and a moist electrode with the proper polarity is then secured. In general, intensity is adjusted to tolerance. Treatment time is generally indicated by the physician, but 10 to 15 minutes is a typical time.

Some care must be taken with very potent drugs that could potentially have deleterious systemic effects. However, iontophoretically applied medicinal ions generally do not migrate far below the surface of the skin or mucous membranes.

Some of the more common substances that may be iontophoretically applied are the following[24]:

1. Heavy metal ions, such as zinc and copper, to fight certain types of skin infections.
2. Chloride ions to loosen superficial scars.
3. Local anesthetics.
4. Vasodilating drugs.
5. Magnesium ions for plantar warts.

Medical Galvanism

The other major use of direct current that may be included under the general category of chemical effects has been termed **medical galvanism,** defined as the use of low-voltage galvanic or direct current for therapeutic purposes without the introduction of pharmacologic substances. The therapeutic benefit is thought to result largely from local ionic changes that result in increased circulation to body parts between the electrodes. Presumably the improved circulation speeds up absorption of inflammatory products, such as accumulated metabolites, with subsequent pain relief. Low-volt electrical currents may speed wound healing, decrease edema, and help fight localized infection. Some conditions for which galvanic current has been used effectively include contusions, sprains, myositis, acute edema, certain forms of arthritis, tenosynovitis, and neuritis.[23]

Some other effects of long-duration, low-volt current, which seem to be polarity specific and result from local ionic and electrical changes are as follows: Positive pole (anode) current produces hardening of tissues and decreases nerve excitability; and negative pole (cathode) current produces softening of tissues and increases nerve excitability.

LOW-POWER LASER

Laser is an acronym that stands for Light Amplification of Stimulated Emissions of Radiation.[32] Lasers are relatively new to the medical community and are certainly the newest of the modalities used by therapists. The principles of physics under which laser energy is produced are complex. Basically, an atom is excited when energy is applied and raises an orbiting electron to a higher orbit. When the electron return to its original orbit, it releases energy (photons) through **spontaneous emission.** Stimulated emission occurs when the photon is released from the excited atom, and it promotes the release of an identical photon to be released from a similarly excited atom. For lasers to operate, a medium of excited atoms must be generated. This is termed **population inversion** and results when

an external energy source or pumping device is applied to the medium.[32]

Laser light differs from conventional light in that laser light is monochromic (single color or wavelength), coherent (in phase), and collimated (minimal divergence). Laser can be thermal (hot) or nonthermal (low-power, soft, cold). The categories include solid-state (glass or crystal), gas, semiconductor, dye, and chemical lasers.[32]

Helium–neon (HeNe gas) and gallium arsenide (GaAs semiconductor) lasers are two low-power lasers currently being investigated by the FDA for potential application in physical medicine. The HeNe lasers deliver a characteristic red beam with a wavelength of 632.8 nanometers. They are delivered in a continuous wave and have a direct penetration of 2 to 5 millimeters and an indirect penetration of 10 to 15 millimeters. The GaAs laser is invisible, with a wavelength of 904 nanometers. It is delivered in a pulse mode at a very low power output. It has a direct penetration of 1 to 2 centimeters and an indirect penetration of 5 centimeters.[8]

The proposed therapeutic applications of lasers in physical medicine include acceleration of collagen synthesis, decrease in microorganisms, increase in vascularization, and reduction of pain and inflammation.[32]

Laser application is ideally done with light contact to the surface and should be perpendicular to the target surface. Dosage appears to be the critical factor in eliciting a response, but exact dosages have not been determined. Dosage is altered by varying the pulse frequency and the treatment times. The treatment is applied by developing an imaginary grid over the target area. The grid comprises 1-cm squares, and the laser is applied to each square for a predetermined time. Trigger or acupuncture points are also treated for painful conditions.

The FDA considers low-power lasers as low-risk devices. Although no deleterious effects have been reported, certain precautions and contraindications exist, including lasing over cancerous tissue, directly into the eyes, and during the first trimester of pregnancy. Initial pain increases, and episodes of syncope have been reported but do not warrant treatment cessation.

INTERMITTENT COMPRESSION

Intermittent compression units are used to control or reduce swelling after acute injury or pitting edema, which tends to develop in the injured area several hours after injury. Intermittent compression uses a nylon pneumatic inflatable sleeve applied around the injured extremity (Fig. 18-6). The sleeve can be inflated to a specific pressure that forces excessive fluid accumulated in the interstitial spaces into vascular and lymphatic channels, through which it is removed from the area of injury. Compression facilitates the movement of lymphatic fluid, which helps to eliminate the by-products of the injury process.[13]

Intermittent compression devices have essentially three parameters that may be adjusted: on–off time, inflation pressures,

FIGURE 18-6

Jobst full-leg sleeve. Intermittent compression is generally used to reduce swelling.

and treatment time. Recommended treatment protocols have been established through clinical trial and error with little experimental data currently available to support any protocol.[31] On–off times include 1 minute on and 2 minutes off, 2 minutes on and 1 minute off, and 4 minutes on and 1 minute off. These recommendations are not based on research. Thus patient comfort should be the primary guide. Recommended inflation pressures have been loosely correlated with blood pressures. The Jobst Institute recommends that pressure be set at 30 to 50 mmHg for the upper extremity and at 30 to 60 mmHg for the lower extremity. Because arterial capillary pressures are approximately 30 mmHg, any pressure that exceeds this rate should encourage the absorption of edema and the flow of lymphatic fluid.[13] Clinical studies have demonstrated a significant reduction in limb volume after 30 minutes of compression. Thus a 30-minute treatment time seems to be efficient in reducing edema.

Some intermittent compression units can combine cold along with compression. Electrical stimulating currents may also be used to produce muscle pumping and thus facilitate lymphatic flow.[1]

MASSAGE

Massage is a mechanical stimulation of the tissues by means of rhythmically applied pressure and stretching (Fig. 18-7).[9] Over the years many claims have been made relative to the therapeutic benefits of massage in the athletic population, although few are based on well-controlled and well-designed studies. Therapists have used massage to increase flexibility and coordination as well as to increase pain threshold; to decrease neuromuscular excitability in the muscle being massaged; to stimulate circulation, thus improving energy transport to the muscle; to facilitate healing and restore joint mobility; and to remove lactic acid, thus alleviating muscle cramps.[29] Conclusive evidence of the efficacy of massage as an ergogenic aid in the athletic population is lacking.

How these effects may be accomplished is determined by the specific approaches used with massage techniques and how they are applied. Generally the effects of massage may be either reflexive or mechanical. The effect of massage on the nervous system will differ greatly according to the method employed, pressure exerted, and duration of applications. Through the reflex mechanism, sedation is induced. Slow, gentle, rhythmical, and superficial **effleurage** may relieve tension and soothe, rendering the muscles more relaxed. This indicates an effect on sensory and motor nerves locally and some central nervous system response. The mechanical approach seeks to make mechanical or histologic changes in myofascial structures through direct force applied superficially.[29]

Among the most widely used massage techniques are the following[29]:

1. *Hoffa massage.* The classic form of massage, which uses strokes that include effleurage, petrissage, percussion or tapotement, and vibration.
2. *Friction massage.* Used to increase the inflammatory response, particularly in cases of chronic tendinitis or tenosynovitis.
3. *Acupressure/Shiatsu.* Massage of acupuncture and trigger points used to reduce pain and irritation in anatomic areas known to be associated with specific points.
4. *Connective tissue massage.* A stroking technique done on layers of connective tissue, which is a relatively new form of treatment in the United States that has its primary effects on circulatory pathologies.
5. *Myofascial release.* A massage technique used for the purpose of relieving soft tissue from the abnormal grip of tight fascia.
6. *Rolfing.* A system devised to correct inefficient structure by balancing the body within a gravitational field through a technique involving manual soft-tissue manipulation.
7. *Trager.* A technique that attempts to establish neuromuscular control so that more normal movement patterns can be routinely performed.

INJURY MANAGEMENT USING MODALITIES

Traditionally in a clinical setting, injuries have been classified as being either acute injuries that result from trauma or chronic injuries that result primarily from overuse. This operational definition is not necessarily correct. If active inflammation is present—which includes the classic symptoms of tenderness, swelling, redness, and so on—the injury should be considered acute and must be treated accordingly, using rest, compression, and elevation. Even if active inflammation persists for months after initial injury, it should still be considered acute. The point is that classification of an injury should be made according to the

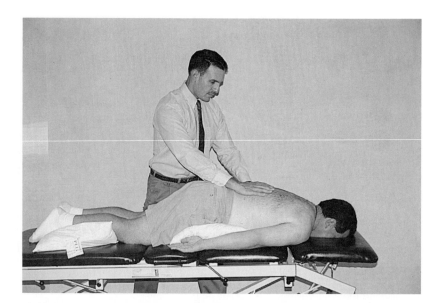

FIGURE 18-7

Therapeutic massage. (Reproduced, with permission, from Prentice WE. *Therapeutic Modalities for Allied Health Professionals.* New York, McGraw-Hill, 1998.)

existing signs and symptoms that indicate the various stages of the healing process and not according to time frames or mechanisms of injury. Once the signs of acute inflammation are no longer present, the injury may be considered to be chronic. As discussed in Chapter 3, inflammation may be considered chronic when the normal cellular response in the inflammatory process is altered by replacing leukocytes with macrophages and plasma cells, along with degeneration of the injured structure. Based on these definitions of acute and chronic injury, the rehabilitation progression after injury may be loosely classified in four phases: initial acute injury, acute inflammatory response, fibroblastic repair, and maturation–remodeling. These phases overlap, and the estimated time frame for each phase shows extreme variability between patients. Table 18-1 summarizes the various modalities that may be used in each of the four phases.

Initial Acute-Injury Phase

Modality use in the initial treatment phase should be directed toward limiting the amount of swelling and reducing pain that occurs acutely. The acute phase is marked by swelling, pain when touched, and pain on both active and passive motion. In general, the less initial swelling, the less the time required for rehabilitation. Traditionally, the modality of choice has been and still is **ice.**

Cryotherapy produces vasoconstriction, at least superficially and perhaps indirectly in the deeper tissues, and thus limits the bleeding that always occurs with injury. Ice bags, cold packs, and ice massage may all be used effectively. Cold baths should be avoided because the foot is placed in the gravity-dependent position. Cold whirlpools also place the foot in the gravity-dependent position and produce a massaging action that is likely to retard clotting. The importance of cryotherapy techniques for reducing acute swelling has probably been exaggerated. Cryotherapy is perhaps best used for producing analgesia, which most likely results from stimulation of sensory cutaneous nerves that, via the gating mechanism, blocks or reduces pain.

Compression is perhaps the most critical element in controlling swelling initially. An intermittent compression device may be used to provide even pressure around an injured extremity. The pressurized sleeve mechanically reduces the amount of space available for swelling to accumulate. Units that combine both compression and cold are extremely useful in this phase. Regardless of the specific techniques selected, cold and compression should always be combined with elevation to avoid any additional pooling of blood in the injured area from the effects of gravity.

Electrical stimulating currents may also be used in the initial phase for pain reduction. Parameters should be adjusted to maximally stimulate sensory cutaneous nerve fibers, again to take advantage of the gate control mechanism of pain modulation. Intensities that produce muscle contraction should be avoided initially because they may increase clotting time.

Low-intensity ultrasound with an intensity of less than 0.2 W/cm^2 may be used immediately following injury to take advantage of the nonthermal physiologic effects that are thought to have a positive effect on the healing process. However, caution must be applied since the moving transducer may tend to interfere with clotting, once again due to the massage effect. It is perhaps best to wait at least 24 hours following injury until clotting is firmly established.

The low-power laser has also been demonstrated to be effective in pain modulation through the stimulation of trigger points and may be used acutely.

The injured part should be rested and protected for at least the first 24 to 48 hours to allow the inflammatory phase of the healing process to do what it is supposed to.

Inflammatory-Response Phase

The inflammatory-response phase begins immediately following injury and may last as long as day 6 after injury, depending on severity. Clinically, swelling begins to subside and eventually stops altogether. The injured area may feel warm to the touch,

TABLE 18-1

Clinical Decision Making on the Use of Various Therapeutic Modalities in Treatment of Acute Injury

PHASE	APPROXIMATE TIME FRAME	CLINICAL PICTURE	POSSIBLE MODALITIES USED	RATIONALE FOR USE
Initial acute	Injury–day 3	Swelling, pain to touch, pain on motion	CRYO ESC IC LPL Rest	↓ Swelling, ↓ pain ↓ Pain ↓ Swelling ↓ Pain
Inflammatory response	Day 1–day 6	Swelling subsides, warm to touch, discoloration, pain to touch, pain on motion	CRYO ESC IC LPL Range of motion	↓ Swelling, ↓ pain ↓ Pain ↓ Swelling ↓ Pain
Fibroblastic repair	Day 4–day 10	Pain to touch, pain on motion, swollen	THERMO ESC LPL IC Range of motion Strengthening	Mildly ↑ circulation ↓ Pain-muscle pumping ↓ Pain Facilitate lymphatic flow
Maturation-remodeling	Day 7–recovery	Swollen, no more pain to touch, decreasing pain on motion	ULTRA ESC LPL SWD MWD Range of motion Strengthening Functional activities	Deep heating to ↑ circulation ↑ Range of motion, ↑ strength ↓ Pain ↓ Pain Deep heating to ↑ circulation Deep heating to ↑ circulation

CRYO, Cryotherapy; *ESC*, electrical stimulating currents; *IC*, intermittent compression; *LPL*, low-power laser; *MWD*, microwave diathermy; *SWD*, short-wave diathermy; *THERMO*, thermotherapy; *ULTRA*, ultrasound; ↓ decrease; ↑ increase.

and some discoloration is usually apparent. The injury is still painful to the touch, and pain is elicited on movement of the injured part. As in the initial injury stage, modalities should be used to control pain and reduce swelling. Cryotherapy should still be used during the inflammatory stage. Ice bags, cold packs, or ice massages provide analgesic effects. The use of cold also reduces the likelihood of swelling, which may continue during this stage. The acute process of swelling should likely subside completely by the end of this phase.

It must be emphasized that heating an injury too soon is a bigger mistake than using ice on an injury for too long. Many therapists elect to stay with cryotherapy for weeks after injury; some never switch to the superficial heating techniques. This procedure is simply a matter of personal preference that should be dictated by experience. Once swelling has stopped, the therapist may elect to begin contrast baths with a longer cold-to-hot ratio.[20]

An intermittent compression device may be used to decrease swelling by facilitating resorption of the by-products of injury by the lymphatic system. Electrical stimulating currents

and low-power laser can be used to help reduce pain. Low-intensity ultrasound is still useful for facilitating healing.

After the initial stage, the patient should begin to work on active and passive range of motion. Decisions regarding how rapidly to progress exercise should be determined by the response of the injury to that exercise. If exercise produces additional swelling and markedly exacerbates pain, then the level or intensity of the exercise is too great and should be reduced. Therapists should be aggressive in their approach to rehabilitation, but the approach will always be limited by the healing process.

Fibroblastic-Repair Phase

Once the inflammatory response has subsided, the fibroblastic-repair phase begins. During this phase of the healing process, fibroblastic cells lay down a matrix of collagen fibers and form scar tissue. This stage may begin as early as 4 days after the injury and may last for several weeks. At this point, swelling has stopped completely. The injury is still tender to the touch but is not as painful as during the last stage. There is also less pain on active and passive motion.

Treatments may change during this stage from cold to heat, once again using increased swelling as a precautionary indicator. Thermotherapy techniques, including hydrocollator packs, paraffin, or eventually warm whirlpool, may be safely used. The purpose of thermotherapy is to increase circulation to the injured area to promote healing. These modalities can also produce some degree of analgesia.

Intermittent compression can once again be used to facilitate removal of injury by-products from the area. Electrical stimulating currents can be used to assist this process by eliciting a muscle contraction and thus inducing a muscle pumping action. This aids in facilitating lymphatic flow. Electrical currents can once again be used for modulation of pain, as can stimulation of trigger points with the low-powered laser.

The therapist must continue to stress the importance of range-of-motion and strengthening exercises and progress them appropriately during this phase.

Maturation–Remodeling Phase

The maturation–remodeling phase is the longest of the four phases and may last for several years, depending on the severity of the injury. The ultimate goal during this maturation stage of the healing process is return to activity. The injury is no longer painful to the touch, although some progressively decreasing pain may still be felt on motion. The collagen fibers must be realigned according to tensile stresses and strains placed upon them. Virtually all modalities may be safely used during this stage; thus decisions should be based on what seems to work most effectively in a given situation.

At this point some type of heating modality is beneficial to the healing process. The deep-heating modalities, ultrasound or shortwave and microwave diathermy, should be used to increase circulation to the deeper tissues. Increased blood flow delivers the essential nutrients to the injured area to promote healing, and increased lymphatic flow assists in breakdown and removal of waste products. The superficial heating modalities are certainly less effective at this point.

Electrical stimulating currents can be used for a number of purposes. As before, they may be used in pain modulation. They may also be used to assist in increasing range of motion or muscular strength. Low-power laser can also assist in modulating pain. If pain is reduced, therapeutic exercises may be progressed more quickly. Range-of-motion and strengthening exercises can be increased relatively quickly and progress toward a full, pain-free return to levels required for successful participation in sports activities.

Other Considerations in Treating Injury

During the rehabilitation period after injury, patients must alter their physical activities to allow the injury to heal sufficiently. The therapist must not neglect maintenance of aerobic capacity in designing a rehabilitation program. Consideration must be given to maintaining levels of strength, flexibility, and cardiorespiratory endurance.

Modality use should be combined with anti-inflammatory medication, particularly during the initial acute and acute inflammatory phases of rehabilitation. A complete discussion of the effects of various medications on the rehabilitation process appears in Chapter 23.

INDICATIONS AND CONTRAINDICATIONS

Table 18-2 is a summary list of indications, contraindications, and precautions in using the various modalities. This list should aid the therapist in making decisions regarding the appropriate use of a therapeutic modality in a given clinical situation.

SUMMARY

- Modalities are best used by the therapist as adjuncts to other forms of therapeutic exercise. Decisions on how a particular modality may best be used should be based on both theoretical knowledge and practical experience.
- The effects of thermotherapy and cryotherapy are primarily superficial. These modalities are perhaps most effectively used to produce analgesia. They also have an indirect effect on circulation in the deeper tissues.
- Ultrasound is vibrational acoustic energy that causes a tissue temperature increase in addition to other physiologic effects that aid healing.
- Shortwave and microwave diathermy units use extremely high-frequency electrical currents to produce a tissue temperature increase in the deeper tissues.
- Electrical stimulating currents may be used to stimulate sensory nerves to modulate pain, stimulate motor nerves to elicit a muscle contraction, introduce chemical ions into superficial tissues for medicinal purposes, and create an electrical field in the tissues to stimulate or alter the healing process.
- The physiologic response of the biologic tissues to electrical stimulating currents is to a great extent determined by the treatment parameters of the current selected by the therapist.
- Low-powered lasers are the newest modality used in clinical settings, primarily to promote wound healing and also pain modulation through stimulation of acupuncture and trigger points.
- Massage is the mechanical stimulation of tissue by means of rhythmically applied pressure and stretching. It allows the therapist, as a health care provider, to assist a patient to overcome pain and to relax through the application of the therapeutic massage techniques.
- Modality use in the initial acute injury phase should be directed toward one goal, that being to reduce the amount of

TABLE 18-2

Indications and Contraindications for Therapeutic Modalities

THERAPEUTIC MODALITY	PHYSIOLOGIC RESPONSES (INDICATIONS FOR USE)	CONTRAINDICATIONS AND PRECAUTIONS
Electrical stimulating currents— high voltage	Pain modulation Muscle reeducation Muscle pumping contractions Retard atrophy Muscle strengthening Increase range of motion Fracture healing Acute injury	Pacemakers Thrombophlebitis Superficial skin lesions
Electrical stimulating currents— low voltage	Wound healing Fracture healing Iontophoresis	Malignancy Skin hypersensitivities Allergies to certain drugs
Electrical stimulating currents— interferential	Pain modulation Muscle reeducation Muscle pumping contractions Fracture healing Increase range of motion	Same as high-voltage
Electrical stimulating currents— Russian	Muscle strengthening	Pacemakers
Electrical stimulating currents— MENS	Fracture healing Wound healing	Malignancy Infections
Shortwave diathermy and microwave diathermy	Increase deep circulation Increase metabolic activity Reduce muscle guarding/spasm Reduce inflammation Facilitate wound healing Analgesia Increase tissue temperatures over a large area	Metal implants Pacemakers Malignancy Wet dressings Anesthetized areas Pregnancy Acute injury and inflammation Eyes Areas of reduced blood flow Anesthetized areas
Cryotherapy—cold packs, ice massage	Acute injury Vasoconstriction—decreased blood flow Analgesia Reduce inflammation Reduce muscle guarding/spasm	Allergy to cold Circulatory impairments Wound healing Hypertension
Thermotherapy—hot whirlpool, paraffin, hydrocollator, infrared lamps	Vasodilation—increased blood flow Analgesia Reduce muscle guarding/spasm Reduce inflammation Increase metabolic activity Facilitate tissue healing	Acute and postacute trauma Poor circulation Circulatory impairments Malignancy
Low-power laser	Pain modulation (trigger points) Facilitate wound healing	Pregnancy Eyes
Ultraviolet	Acne Aseptic wounds Folliculitis	Psoriasis Eczema Herpes

(Continued)

T A B L E   1 8 - 2

(Continued)

THERAPEUTIC MODALITY	PHYSIOLOGIC RESPONSES (INDICATIONS FOR USE)	CONTRAINDICATIONS AND PRECAUTIONS
	Pityriasis rosea	Diabetes
	Tinea	Pellagra
	Septic wounds	Lupus erythematosus
	Sinusitis	Hyperthyroidism
	Increase calcium metabolism	Renal and hepatic insufficiency
		Generalized dermatitis
		Advanced atherosclerosis
Ultrasound	Increase connective tissue extensibility	Infection
	Deep heat	Acute and postacute injury
	Increased circulation	Epiphyseal areas
	Treatment of most soft tissue injuries	Pregnancy
	Reduce inflammation	Thrombophlebitis
	Reduce muscle spasm	Impaired sensation
		Eyes
Intermittent compression	Decrease acute bleeding	Circulatory impairment
	Decrease edema	

swelling that occurs. The less the amount of initial swelling, the less time will be required for rehabilitation.

- During the inflammatory-response stage of healing, modalities should be used to reduce pain and limit the amount of swelling. The injured part should be rested to allow the healing process to work.
- During the fibroblastic-repair phase, thermotherapy may be used to increase blood flow to the injured area. Also during this time, strengthening and range-of-motion exercises should begin.
- The maturation–remodeling phase is a long-term process during which the patient returns to activity. Deep-heating modalities that increase blood flow and assist in the breakdown and removal of the by-products of the healing process should be used. The quantity and intensity of therapeutic exercise should be progressively increased during this phase of healing.

REFERENCES

1. Angus J, Prentice W, Hooker D. A comparison of two external intermittent compression devices and their effect on post acute ankle edema. *J Athl Train* 29:178, 1994.
2. Baker L, McNeal D, Benton L. *Neuromuscular Electrical Stimulation.* Downey, CA, Rancho Los Amigos Medical Center, 1993.
3. Brown S. The effect of microcurrent on edema, range of motion, and pain in treatment of lateral ankle sprains. *J Orthop Sports Phys Ther* 19:55, 1994. Abstract.
4. Castel C, Draper D, Castel D. Rate of temperature increase during ultrasound treatments: are traditional times long enough? *J Athl Train* 29:156, 1994.
5. DeVahl J. Neuromuscular electrical stimulation (NMES) in rehabilitation. In: Gersh M, ed. *Electrotherpy in Rehabilitation.* Philadelphia, Davis, 1992.
6. Draper D, Schulthies S, Sorvisto P. The effect of cooling the tissue prior to ultrasound treatment. *J Athl Train* 29:154, 1994.
7. Dyson M. The use of ultrasound in sports physiotherapy. In: Grisogono V, ed. *Sports Injuries, International Perspectives in Physiotherapy.* Edinburgh, Churchill Livingstone, 1989.
8. Enwemeka C. Laser biostimulation of healing wounds: Specific effects and mechanisms of action. *J Orthop Sports Phys Ther* 9:333–338, 1988.
9. Fritz S. *Fundamentals of Therapeutic Massage.* St. Louis, Mosby, 1995.
10. Geick J, et al. Therapeutic ultrasound: Technology, performance standards, biological effect, and clinical application. HSH publication, FOA 84-XXXX, August 1984.
11. Harris S, Draper D, Schulthies S. The effect of ultrasound on temperature rise in preheated human muscle. *J Athl Train* 30:S42, 1995.
12. Hooker D. Electrical stimulating currents. In: Prentice W, ed. *Therapeutic Modalities in Sports Medicine.* Dubuque, WCB/McGraw-Hill, 1999.
13. Hooker D. Intermittent compression devices. In: Prentice W, ed. *Therapeutic Modalities in Sports Medicine.* Dubuque, WCB/McGraw-Hill, 1999.

14. Hooker D. Traction as a specialized modality. In: Prentice W, ed. *Therapeutic Modalities in Sports Medicine.* Dubuque, WCB/McGraw-Hill, 1999.

15. Kloth L. Shortwave and microwave diathermy. In: Michlovitz SL, ed. *Thermal Agents in Rehabilitation.* Philadelphia, Davis, 1996.

16. Knight K. *Cryotherapy in Sport Injury Management.* Champaign, IL, Human Kinertics, 1995.

17. Krumholz A, Gelfand B, O'Cooner P. Therapeutic modalities. In: Nicholas J, Hershman EB, eds. *The Lower Extremity and Spine in Sports Medicine,* vol 1. St. Louis, Mosby-Year Book, 1995.

18. Lehmann JF, DeLateur BJ. Cryotherapy. In: Lehmann JF, ed. *Therapeutic Heat and Cold,* 3rd ed. Baltimore, Williams & Wilkins, 1982.

19. Lehmann JF, DeLateur BJ. Therapeutic heat. In: Lehmann JF, ed. *Therapeutic Heat and Cold,* 3rd ed. Baltimore, Williams & Wilkins, 1982.

20. Meyer J, Draper D, Durrant E. Contrast therapy and intramuscular temperature in the leg. *J Athl Train* 29:318–324, 1994.

21. Michlovitz SL. Biophysical principles of heating and superficial heat agents. In: Michlovitz SL, ed. *Thermal Agents in Rehabilitation.* Philadelphia, Davis, 1996.

22. Michlovitz SL. Cryotherapy: The use of cold as a therapeutic agent In: Michlovitz SL, ed. *Thermal Agents in Rehabilitation.* Philadelphia, Davis, 1996.

23. Prentice W. Basic principles of electricity. In: Prentice W, ed. *Therapeutic Modalities in Sports Medicine.* Dubuque, WCB/McGraw-Hill, 1999.

24. Prentice W. Iontophoresis. In: Prentice W, ed. *Therapeutic Modalities in Sports Medicine.* Dubuque, WCB/McGraw-Hill, 1999.

25. Prentice W. Preface. In: Prentice W, ed. *Therapeutic Modalities in Sports Medicine.* Dubuque, WCB/McGraw-Hill, 1999.

26. Prentice W, Bell G. Infrared modalities. In: Prentice W, ed. *Therapeutic Modalities in Sports Medicine.* Dubuque, WCB/McGraw-Hill, 1999.

27. Prentice W, Draper D. Therapeutic ultrasound. In: Prentice W, ed. *Therapeutic Modalities in Sports Medicine.* Dubuque, WCB/McGraw-Hill, 1999.

28. Prentice W, Draper D, Donley P. Shortwave and microwave diathermy. In: Prentice W, ed. *Therapeutic Modalities in Sports Medicine.* Dubuque, WCB/McGraw-Hill, 1999.

29. Prentice W, Lehn C. Therapeutic massage. In: Prentice W, ed. *Therapeutic Modalities in Sports Medicine.* Dubuque, WCB/McGraw-Hill, 1999.

30. Quillin WS. Ultrasonic phonophoresis. *Phys Sports Med* 10:211, 1982.

31. Rucinski T, Prentice W, Hooker D, et al. The effects of intermittent compression on edema in postacute ankle sprains. *J Orthop Sports Phys Ther* 13, 1991.

32. Saliba E, Foreman S. Low-power laser. In: Prentice W, ed. *Therapeutic Modalities in Sports Medicine.* Dubuque, WCB/McGraw-Hill, 1999.

33. Schliephakle E. Carrying out treatment. In: Throm H, ed. *Introduction to Shortwave and Microwave Therapy,* 3rd ed. Springfield, IL, Thomas, 1966.

34. Snyder-Mackler L, Robinson A. *Clinical Electrophysiology: Electrotherapy and Electrophysiology.* Baltimore, Williams & Wilkins, 1997.

35. Ter Harr C. Basic physics of therapeutic ultrasound. *Physiotherapy* 73:110–113, 1987.

36. Thorsteinsson G. Electrical stimulation for analgesia. In: Stillwell GK, ed. *Therapeutic Electricity and Ultraviolet Radiation,* 7th ed. Baltimore, Williams & Wilkins, 1983.

37. Walsh M. Hydrotherapy. The use of water as a therapeutic agent. In: Michlovitz SL, ed. *Thermal Agents in Rehabilitation.* Philadelphia, Davis, 1997.

38. Ziskin MC, Michlovitz SL. Therapeutic ultrasound In: Michlovitz SL, ed. *Thermal Agents in Rehabilitation.* Philadelphia, Davis, 1997.

CHAPTER 19

Using Biofeedback in Rehabilitation

William E. Prentice

After completing this chapter, the student therapist should be able to do the following:

- Define biofeedback and identify its uses in a clinical setting.
- Discuss the various types of biofeedback instruments.
- Explain physiologically how the electrical activity generated by a muscle contraction can be measured using EMG.
- Explain how the electrical activity picked up by the electrodes is amplified, processed, and converted to meaningful information by the EMG unit.
- Differentiate between visual and auditory feedback.
- Discuss the equipment setup and clinical applications for EMG biofeedback.

Electromyographic (EMG) biofeedback is a modality that has become widely used in musculoskeletal rehabilitation. It is a therapeutic procedure that uses electronic or electromechanical instruments to accurately measure, process, and feed back reinforcing information via auditory or visual signals.[21] In clinical practice, it is used to help the patient develop greater voluntary control in terms of either neuromuscular relaxation or muscle reeducation following injury.

THE ROLE OF BIOFEEDBACK

The term "biofeedback" should be familiar because all therapists routinely serve as instruments of biofeedback when teaching a therapeutic exercise or in coaching a movement pattern. Using feedback can help the patient to regain function of a muscle that may have been lost or forgotten following injury.[11] Feedback includes information related to the sensations associated with movement itself as well as information related to the result of the action relative to some goal or objective. Feedback refers to the intrinsic information inherent to movement including kinesthetic, visual, cutaneous, vestibular, and auditory signals collectively termed "response-produced feedback." But feedback also refers to extrinsic information or some knowledge of results that is presented verbally, mechanically, or electronically to indicate the outcome of some movement performance.

Therefore feedback is ongoing, in a temporal sense, occuring before, during, and after any motor or movement task. Feedback from some measuring instrument that provides moment-to-moment information about a biologic function is referred to as biofeedback.[18]

Perhaps the biggest advantage of biofeedback is that it provides the patient with a chance to correct small changes in performance that are immediately noted and rewarded so that eventually larger changes or improvements in performance can be accomplished. The goal is to train patients to perceive these changes without the use of the measuring instrument, so that they can practice by themselves. Therefore patients learn early in the rehabilitation process to do something for themselves and not to totally rely on the therapist. This will help to build confidence and increase feelings of self-efficacy. Treatments using biofeedback would be useful particularly in patients who have difficulty in perceiving the initial small correct responses, or who may have a faulty perception of what they are doing. Hopefully, the rehabilitating patient will be motivated and encouraged by seeing early signs of slight progress, thus to some extent relieving their feelings of helplessness and reducing injury-related stress.[18]

To process feedback information, the patient makes use of a complicated series of interrelated feedback loops involving very complex anatomic and neurophysiologic components.[29] Our focus will be oriented toward how biofeedback may best be incorporated in a treatment program.

BIOFEEDBACK INSTRUMENTATION

Biofeedback instruments are designed to monitor some physiologic event, objectively quantify these monitorings, and then interpret the measurements as meaningful information.[22] There are several different types of biofeedback modalities available for use in rehabilitation. These biofeedback units cannot directly measure a physiologic event. Instead, they record some aspect that is highly correlated with the physiologic event. Thus the biofeedback reading should be taken as a convenient indication of a physiologic/process but not confused with the physiologic process itself.[22]

The most commonly used instruments include those that record **peripheral skin temperatures** indicating the extent of vasoconstriction or vasodilation; **finger phototransmission units (photoplethysmograph)** that also measure vasoconstriction and vasodilation; units that record **skin conductance activity** indicating sweat gland activity; and units that measure **electromyographic (EMG) activity** indicating amount of electrical activity during muscle contraction. Other types of biofeedback units available include electroencephalographs (EEGs), pressure transducers, and electrogoniometers.

Peripheral Skin Temperature

Peripheral skin temperature is an indirect measure of the diameter of peripheral blood vessels. As vessels dilate, more warm blood is delivered to a particular area, thus increasing the temperature in that area. This effect is easily seen in the fingers and toes where the surrounding tissue warms and cools rapidly. Variations in skin temperature seem to be correlated with affective states, with a decrease occuring in response to stress or fear. Temperature changes are usually measured in degrees Farenheit.[22]

Finger Phototransmission

The degree of peripheral vasoconstriction can also be measured indirectly using a photoplethysmograph. This instrument monitors the amount of light that can pass through a finger or toe, reflect off a bone, and pass back though the soft tissue to a light sensor. As the volume of blood in a given area increases, the amount of light detected by the sensor decreases, thus giving some indication of blood volume. Only changes in blood volume can be detected, because there are no standardized units of measure. These instruments are used most often to monitor pulse.[14]

Skin Conductance Activity

Sweat gland activity can be indirectly measured by determining electrodermal activity most commonly referred to as the "galvanic skin response." Sweat contains salt, which increases electrical conductivity. Thus sweaty skin is more conductive than dry skin. This instrument applies a very small electrical voltage to the skin, usually on the palmar surface of the hand or the volar surface of the fingers where there are a lot of sweat glands, and measures the impedance of the electrical current in micro-ohm units. Measuring skin conductance is a technique useful in objectively assessing psychophysiologic arousal and is most often used in "lie detector" testing.[22]

EMG BIOFEEDBACK

EMG biofeedback is certainly the most typically used of all the biofeedback modalities in a clinical setting. Muscle contraction results from the more or less synchronous contraction of individual muscle fibers that compose a muscle. Individual muscle fibers are innervated by nerves that collectively comprise a motor unit. The axon of that motor unit conducts an action potential to the neuromuscular junction, where a neurotransmitter substance (acetylcholine) is released. As this neurotransmitter binds to receptor sites on the sarcolemma, depolarization of that muscle fiber occurs, moving in both directions along the muscle fiber, creating movement of ions and thus an electrochemical gradient around the muscle fiber. Changes in potential difference or voltage associated with depolarization can be detected by an electrode placed in close proximity (Fig. 19-1).

Motor Unit Recruitment

The amount of tension developed in a muscle is determined by the number of active motor units. As more motor units are recruited and as the frequency of discharge increases, muscle tension increases.

The pattern of motor unit recruitment varies depending on the inherent properties of specific motorneurons, the force required during the activity, and the speed of contraction. Smaller motor units are recruited first and are somewhat limited in their ability to generate tension. Larger motor units generate greater tension because more muscle fibers are recruited.

Motor units are recruited based on the force required in an activity and not on the type of contraction performed. Thus the firing rate and recruitment of the motor units is dependent on the external force required. The speed of contraction also influences motor unit recruitment. Fast contractions tend to excite larger motor units and depress the smaller motor units.

Measuring Electrical Activity

Despite the fact that EMG is used to determine muscle activity, it does not measure muscle contraction directly. Instead it measures electrical activity associated with muscle contraction. Movement of ions across the membrane creates a depolarization of the muscle membranes, resulting in a reversal in polarity, followed by repolarization. The various stages of membrane activity generate a triphasic electrical signal.[4] Electrical activity of

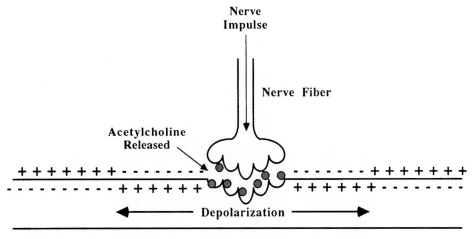

Nerve Impulse

Nerve Fiber

Acetylcholine Released

$+ + + + + + + - - - - - - - - - - - - - - + + + + + +$

$- - - - - - - - - - + + + + + + - - - - - - - + + + + + + + - - - - - - - - -$

← **Depolarization** →

Muscle Fiber

FIGURE 19-1

The nerve fiber conducts an impulse to the neuromuscular junction, where acetylcholine binds to receptor sites on the sarcolemma inducing a depolarization of the muscle fiber, which creates movement of ions and thus an electrochemical gradient around the muscle fiber. (Reproduced, with permission, from Prentice WE. *Therapeutic Modalities for Allied Health Professionals*. New York, McGraw-Hill, 1998.)

the muscle is measured in volts, or more precisely in microvolts (1V = 1,000,000 μV).

Measurement of electrical activity is made in standard quantitative units. Monitoring is useful in detecting changes in electrical activity, although changes cannot be quantified. The advantage of measurement over monitoring is that an objective scale is used on which comparisons can be made between different individuals, occasions, and instruments. Measurement allows procedures to be replicated.

Unfortunately, with EMG biofeedback units there is no universally accepted standardized measurement scale. Each brand of EMG unit serves as its own reference standard.

Different brands of EMG equipment may give different readings for the same degree of muscle contraction. Consequently, EMG readings can be compared only when the same equipment is used for all readings.[22]

The EMG biofeedback unit receives small amounts of electrical energy generated during muscle contraction through some type of electrode. It then separates or filters this electrical energy from other extraneous electrical activity on the the skin and amplifies the EMG electrical energy. The amplified EMG activity is then converted to some type of information that has meaning to the user. Figure 19-2 is a diagram of the various components of an EMG biofeedback unit.

FIGURE 19-2

The anatomy of a typical EMG biofeedback unit. (Reproduced, with permission, from Prentice WE. *Therapeutic Modalities for Allied Health Professionals*. New York, McGraw-Hill, 1998.)

Differential Amplifier → Band-width Filter → Rectifier → Smoothing Filter →

Strip Recorder Output

Meter

Tone Generator → Tone Output

Light Display

Raw EMG

Integrator

Time

Average EMG Activity (microvolts)

Active + | Reference | Active −

Muscle

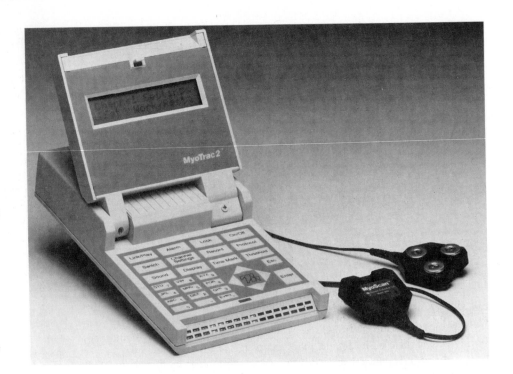

FIGURE 19-3

The biofeedback unit is connected via a series of electrodes to the skin over the contracting muscle. (Reproduced, with permission, from Prentice WE. *Therapeutic Modalities for Allied Health Professionals.* New York, McGraw-Hill, 1998.)

ELECTRODES

Skin surface electrodes are most often used in EMG biofeedback. Fine-wire indwelling electrodes may also be used, which permit localized highly accurate measurement of electrical activity. However, these electrodes must be inserted percutaneously, and thus are relatively impractical in a clinical setting.

Various types of surface electrodes are available for use with EMG biofeedback units. Electrodes are most often made of stainless steel or nickel-plated brass recessed in a plastic holder. These less expensive electrodes are effective in EMG biofeedback applications. More expensive electrodes made of gold or silver/silver chloride have also been used.[28]

The size of the electrodes may range from 4 mm in diameter for recording small muscle activity to 12.5 mm for use with larger muscle groups. Increasing the size of the electrode will not cause an increase in the amplitude of the signal.[17]

Regardless of whether electrodes are disposable on nondisposable, some type of conducting gel, paste, or cream with high salt content is necessary to establish a highly conductive connection with the skin. Disposable electrodes come with the appropriate amount of gel and an adhesive ring already applied, so that the electrode can be easily connected to the skin. Nondisposable electrodes need to have a double-sided adhesive ring applied. Then enough conducting gel must be added such that it is level with the surface of the adhesive ring before the electrode is applied to the skin.

Prior to attachment of the surface electrodes, the skin must be appropriately prepared by removing oil and dead skin along with excessive hair from the surface to reduce skin impedance. Scrubbing with an alcohol-soaked prep pad is recommended.[28]

However, if the skin is cleaned until it becomes irritated, it may interfere with EMG recording.

Some surface electrodes are permanently attached to cable wires while others may snap onto the wire. Some biofeedback units include a set of three electrodes preplaced on a Velcro band that may be easily attached to the skin.

ELECTRODE PLACEMENT   The electrodes should be placed as near to the muscle being monitored as possible to minimize recording extraneous electrical activity. They should be secured with the body part in the position in which it will be monitored, so that movement of the skin will not alter the positioning of the electrodes over a particular muscle (Fig. 19-3).[28]

The electrodes should be parallel to the direction of the muscle fibers to ensure that a better sample of muscle activity is monitored while reducing extraneous electrical activity.

Spacing of the electrodes is also a critical consideration. Electrodes generally detect measurable signals from a distance equal to that of the interelectrode spacing. Therefore as the distance between the electrodes increases, the EMG signal will include electrical activity not only from muscles directly under the electrodes but also from other nearby muscles.[4]

SEPARATION AND AMPLIFICATION OF EMG ACTIVITY

Once the electrical activity is detected by the electrodes, the extraneous electrical activity, or **noise,** must be eliminated before the EMG activity is amplified and subsequently objectified. This is accomplished by using two **active electrodes** and a single ground or **reference electrode** in a **bipolar arrangement** to create three separate pathways from the skin to the biofeedback

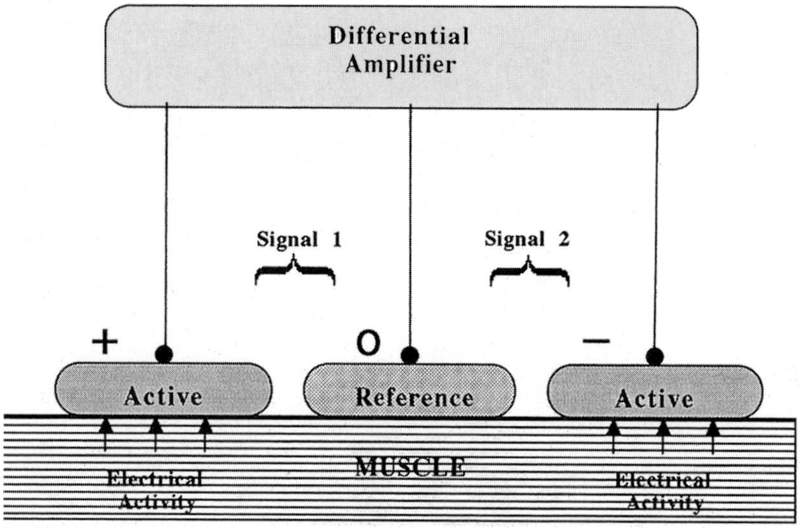

FIGURE 19-4

The differential amplifier monitors the two separate signals from the active electrodes and amplifies the difference, thus eliminating extraneous noise. (Reproduced, with permission, from Prentice WE. *Therapeutic Modalities for Allied Health Professionals.* New York, McGraw-Hill, 1998.)

unit (Fig. 19-4). The active electrodes should be placed in close proximity to one another while the reference electrode may be placed anywhere on the body. Typically in biofeedback, the reference electrode is placed between the two active electrodes.

The active electrodes pick up electrical activity from motor units firing in the muscles beneath the electrodes. The magnitude of the small voltages detected by each active electrode will differ with respect to the reference electrode, creating two separate signals. These two signals are then fed to a **differential amplifier,** which basically subtracts the signal from one active electrode from the other active electrode. This in effect cancels out or rejects any components that the two signals coming from the active electrodes have in common, thus amplifying the difference between the signals. The differential amplifier uses the reference electrode to compare the signals of the two active or recording electrodes (Fig. 19-4).

There will always be some degree of extraneous electrical activity created by power lines, motors, lights, appliances, and so forth, which is picked up by the body and eventually is detected by the surface electrodes on the skin. Assuming that this extraneous "noise" is detected equally by both active electrodes, the differential amplifier will subtract the noise detected by one active electrode from the noise detected by the other active electrode, leaving only the true difference between the active electrodes. The ability of the differential amplifier to eliminate the common noise between the active electrodes is called the **common mode rejection ratio (CMRR).**

External noise can be further reduced by using **filters,** which essentially make the amplifier more sensitive to some incoming frequencies and less sensitive to others. Therefore the amplifier will pick up signals only at those frequencies produced by electrical activity in the muscle within a specific frequency range or **bandwidth.** In general, the wider the bandwidth, the higher the EMG and noise readings.

It must be noted that the therapist is interested in measuring the electrical activity within the muscle. An excessive

external noise that is not eliminated by the biofeedback instrument will mask true EMG activity and will significantly decrease the reliability of the information being generated by that device.

Converting EMG Activity to Meaningful Information

After amplification and filtering, the EMG signal is indicative of the true electrical activity within the muscles being monitored. This is referred to as **raw EMG** activity. Raw EMG is an alternating voltage, which means that the direction or polarity is constantly reversing (Fig. 19-5A). The amplitude of the oscillations increases to a maximum and then diminishes. Biofeedback measures the overall increase and decrease in electrical activity. To obtain this measurement, the deflection toward the negative pole must be flipped upward toward the positive pole; otherwise the sum of their deflections would cancel one another out (Fig. 19-5B). This process is referred to as **rectification,** which essentially creates a pulsed direct current (DC).

PROCESSING THE EMG SIGNAL

The rectified EMG signal can be **smoothed** and **integrated.** Smoothing the EMG signal means eliminating the peaks and valleys or eliminating the high-frequency fluctuations that are produced with a changing electrical signal (Fig. 19-5C). Once the EMG has been smoothed, the signal may be integrated by measuring the area under the curve for a specified period of time. Integration forms the basis for quantification of EMG activity (Fig. 19-5D).

At this point it is necessary to take this rectified, smoothed, and integrated EMG signal and display the information in a form that has some meaning. Biofeedback units generally provide either visual or auditory feedback relative to the quantity of electrical activity. Some biofeedback units can provide both

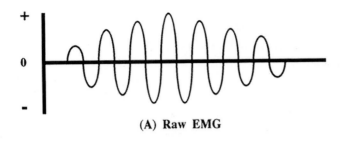

(A) Raw EMG

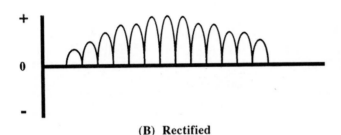

(B) Rectified

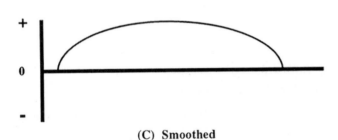

(C) Smoothed

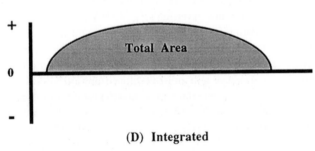

(D) Integrated

FIGURE   19-5

Processing an EMG signal involves taking **(A)** raw EMG and then **(B)** rectifying, **(C)** smoothing, and **(D)** integrating it so that the information can be presented in some meaningful format. (Reproduced, with permission, from Prentice WE. *Therapeutic Modalities for Allied Health Professionals.* New York, McGraw-Hill, 1998.)

visual and auditory feedback, depending on the output mode selected.

VISUAL FEEDBACK

Raw EMG activity is usually displayed visually on an oscilloscope. On most biofeedback units, integrated EMG activity is visually presented as a line traveling across a monitor, as a light or series of lights that go on and off, or as a bar graph that changes dimension—all of which change in response to the incoming integrated signal. Some of the newer EMG units have incorporated video games as part of their visual feedback system. If a biofeedback unit uses some type of meter, it may either be calibrated in objective units such as microvolts, or it may simply give some relative scale of measure.[28]

Meters can also be either analog or digital. Analog meters have a continuous scale and a needle that indicates the level of electrical activity within a particular range. Digital meters display only a number. They are very simple and easy to read. However, the disadvantage of a digital meter is that it is more difficult to tell where in a given range the signal falls.

AUDIO FEEDBACK

On some biofeedback units, raw EMG activity can be listened to and is one type of audio feedback. The majority of biofeedback units have audio feedback that produces some tone, such as buzzing, beeping, or clicking. An increase in the pitch of a tone, buzz, or beep, or an increase in the frequency of clicking, indicates an increase in the level of EMG activity. This would be most useful for individuals who need to strengthen muscle contractions. Conversely, decreases in pitch or frequency indicating a decrease in EMG activity would be most useful in teaching patients to relax.

SETTING SENSITIVITY

Signal sensitivity or **signal gain** may be set by the therapist on many biofeedback units. If a high gain is chosen, the biofeedback unit will have a high sensitivity for the muscle activity signal. Sensitivity may be set at 1 μV, 10 μV, or 100 μV. A 1-μV setting is sensitive enough to detect the smallest amounts of electrical activity and thus has the highest signal gain. High-sensitivity levels should be used during relaxation training. Comparatively lower sensitivity levels would be more useful in muscle reeducation, during which the patient may produce several hundred μV of EMG activity. Generally, when adjusting the sensitivity range it should be set at the lowest level that does not elicit feedback at rest.

EQUIPMENT SETUP AND APPLICATION

It is imperative that the therapist has some understanding of how biofeedback units monitor and record the electrical activity being produced in a muscle before attempting to set up and use the biofeedback unit in treatment of a patient. Specific treatment protocols involve skin preparation, application of electrodes, selection of feedback or output modes, and selection of sensitivity settings, all of which have been previously discussed. Once these are complete, the therapist should choose to have the patient sitting, lying, or occasionally standing in a comfortable position depending on the treatment objectives. Generally the therapist should begin with easier tasks and progressively make the activities more difficult. Teaching the patient how to appropriately use the biofeedback unit and briefly explaining what is being measured is essential. In most cases, it is recommended that the therapist attach the biofeedback unit to themselves and then demonstrate to the patient exactly what is to be done during the treatment.[17]

CLINICAL APPLICATIONS FOR BIOFEEDBACK

There are a number of clinical conditions for which biofeedback would be useful as a therapeutic modality. The primary applications for using biofeedback include muscle reeducation, which involves regaining neuromuscular control and/or increasing strength of a muscle; relaxation of muscle spasm or muscle guarding; and pain reduction.

Muscle Reeducation

The goal in muscle reeducation is to provide feedback that will reestablish neuromuscular control or promote the ability of a muscle or group of muscles to contract. It may also be used to regain normal agonist/antagonist muscle action and for postural control retraining. EMG biofeedback is used to indicate the electrical activity associated with that of muscle contraction.

When biofeedback is being used to elicit a muscle contraction, the sensitivity setting should be chosen by having the patient perform a maximum isometric contraction of the target muscle. Then the gain should be adjusted such that the patient will be able to achieve the maximum on about two-thirds of the muscle contractions. If the patient cannot produce a muscle contraction, the therapist should attempt to facilitate a contraction by stroking or tapping the target muscle. It is also helpful to have the patient look at the muscle when trying to contract. It may be necessary to move the active electrodes to the contralateral limb and have the patient "practice" the muscle contraction you hope to achieve on the opposite side.

The patient should maximally contract the target muscle isometrically for 6 to 10 seconds. During this contraction, the visual or auditory feedback should be at a maximum and should be closely monitored by both the therapist and the patient. Between each contraction, the patient should be instructed to completely relax the muscle such that the feedback mode returns to baseline or zero prior to initiating another contraction. A period of 5 to 10 minutes working with a single muscle or muscle group is most desirable, because longer periods tend to produce fatigue and boredom, neither of which is conducive to optimal learning.[16]

As increases in EMG activity occur, the patient should develop the ability to rapidly activate motor units. This can be accomplished by setting the sensitivity level to 60 to 80 percent of maximum isometric activity and instructing the patient to reach that level as many times as possible during a given time period (e.g., 10 or 30 seconds). Again, total relaxation must occur between contractions.

For the patient it is essential that the treatment be functionally relevant. Attention to mobility and muscle power cannot be neglected in favor of biofeedback therapy.[16] The therapist should have the patient perform functional movements while simultaneously observing body mechanics and the related EMG activity. Then recommendations can be made as to how movements can be altered to elicit normal EMG responses.[8] Biofeedback is useful in patients who perform poorly on manual muscle tests. If the patient can only elicit a fair, trace, or zero grade, then biofeedback should be incorporated. Stronger muscles should generally be given resistive exercises rather than biofeedback,[16] although biofeedback has been recommended for increasing the strength of healthy muscle.[10]

Relaxation of Muscle Guarding

Often in a clinical setting, patients demonstrate a protective response in muscle that occurs due to pain or fear of movement that is most accurately described as **muscle guarding.** Muscle guarding must be differentiated from those neuromuscular problems arising from central nervous system deficits that result in a clinical condition known as **muscle spasticity.** For the therapist treating patients exhibiting muscle guarding, the goal is to induce relaxation of the muscle by reducing EMG activity through the use of biofeedback.[16]

Because muscle guarding most often involves fear of pain that may result when the muscle moves, perhaps the most important goal in treatment is to modulate pain. This is best accomplished through the use of other modalities such as ice or electrical stimulation.

Biofeedback treatments should be designed so that the patient experiences success from the first treatment. The patient is now attempting to reduce the visual or auditory feedback to zero. Initially, positioning of the patient in a comfortable relaxed position is critical to reduction in muscle guarding. A high-sensitivity setting should be selected so that any electrical activity in the muscle will be easily detected.

During relaxation training the patient should be given verbal cues that will enhance relaxation of either individual muscles, muscle groups, or body segments. For example, with individual muscles or small muscle groups, the patient may be instructed to contract and then relax a specific muscle or to imagine a feeling of warmth within the muscle. For larger muscle groups, using mental imagery or deep breathing exercises may be useful.

As relaxation progresses, the spacing between the electrodes should be increased. Also, the sensitivity setting should move from low to high. Both of these changes will require the patient to relax more muscles, thus achieving greater relaxation. The patient must then apply this newly learned relaxation technique in different positions that are potentially more uncomfortable.

Again, the goal is to eliminate muscle guarding during functional activities.[16]

Pain Reduction

A number of therapeutic modalities can be used for the purpose of reducing or modulating pain. As mentioned in the section on muscle guarding, biofeedback can be used to relax muscles that are tense secondary to fear of pain on movement. If the muscle can be relaxed, then chances are that pain will also be reduced by breaking the "pain–guarding–pain" cycle. Biofeedback has been experimentally demonstrated to reduce pain in headaches[2,7,9] and low back pain.[8,20,25] Pain modulation is often associated with techniques of imagery and progressive relaxation.

Treating Neurologic Conditions

Biofeedback has been identified as an effective technique for treating a variety of neurologic conditions including hemiplegia following stroke,[12,19,24] spinal cord injury,[6,15] spasticity,[1,23] cerebral palsy,[3] facial paralysis,[5] urinary incontinence,[26] and fecal incontinence.[27]

SUMMARY

- Biofeedback is a therapeutic procedure that uses electronic or electromechanical instruments to accurately measure, process, and feed back reinforcing information via auditory or visual signals.

- Perhaps the biggest advantage of biofeedback is that it provides the patient with a chance to make small changes in performance that are immediately noted and rewarded so that eventually larger changes or improvements in performance can be accomplished.

- Several different types of biofeedback modalities are available for use in rehabilitation, with EMG biofeedback being the most widely used in a clinical setting.

- An EMG biofeedback unit measures the electrical activity produced by depolarization of a muscle fiber as an indicator of the quality of a muscle contraction.

- The EMG biofeedback unit receives small amounts of electrical energy generated during muscle contraction through active electrodes, then separates or filters extraneous electrical energy via a differential amplifier before it is processed and subsequently converted to some type of information that has meaning to the user.

- Biofeedback information is displayed either visually using lights or meters, or auditorily using tones, beeps, buzzers, or clicks.

- High sensitivity levels should be used during relaxation training, while comparatively lower sensitivity levels would be more useful in muscle reeducation.

- In a clinical setting, biofeedback is most typically used for muscle reeducation, to decrease muscle guarding, or for pain reduction.

REFERENCES

1. Amato A, Hermomeyer C, Kleinman K. Use of electromyographic feedback to increase control of spastic muscles. *Phys Ther* 53:1063, 1973.
2. Arena J, Bruno G, Hannah S. A comparison of frontal electromyographic biofeedback training, trapezius electromyographic biofeedback training, and progressive muscle relaxation therapy in the treatment of tension headache. *Headache* 35:411–419, 1995.
3. Asato H, Twiggs D, Ellison S. EMG biofeedback training for a mentally retarded individual with cerebral palsy. *Phys Ther* 61:1447–1451, 1981.
4. Basmajian J. Description and analysis of EMG signal. In: Basmajian J, Deluca C, eds. *Muscles Alive. Their Functions Revealed by Electromyography*. Baltimore, Williams & Wilkins, 1985.
5. Brown D, Nahai F, Wolf S. Electromyographic feedback in the re-education of facial palsy. *Am J Phys Med* 57:183–190, 1978.
6. Brucker B, Bulaeva N. Biofeedback effect on electromyography responses in patients with spinal cord injury. *Arch Phys Med Rehab* 77:133–137, 1996.
7. Budzynski D. Biofeedback strategies in headache treatment. In: Basmajian J, ed. *Biofeedback Principles and Practice for Clinicians*. Baltimore, Williams & Wilkins, 1989.
8. Bush C, Ditto B, Feuerstein M. Controlled evaluation of paraspinal EMG biofeedback in the treatment of chronic low back pain. *Health Psychol* 4:307–321, 1985.
9. Chapman S. A review and clinical perspective on the use of EMG and thermal biofeedback for chronic headaches. *Pain* 27:1, 1986.
10. Croce R. The effects of EMG biofeedback on strength acquisition. *Biofeedback Self Regul* 9:395, 1986.
11. Draper V. Electromyographic feedback and recovery in quadriceps femoris muscle function following anterior cruciate ligament reconstruction. *Phys Ther* 70:25, 1990.
12. Engardt M. Term effects of auditory feedback training on relearned symmetrical body weight distribution in stroke patients. A follow-up study. *Scand J Rehab Med* 26:65–69, 1994.
13. Fogel E. Biofeedback-assisted musculoskeletal therapy and neuromuscular re-education. In: Schwartz MS, ed. *Biofeedback: A Practitioners Guide*. New York, Guilford Press, 1987.
14. Jennings J, Tahmoush A, Redmond D. Non-invasive measurement of peripheral vascular activity. In: Martin I, Venables PH, eds. *Techniques in Psychophysiology*. New York, Wiley, 1980.
15. Klose K, Needham B, Schmidt D. An assessment of the contribution of electromyographic biofeedback as a therapy in the physical training of spinal cord injured persons. *Arch Phys Med Rehab* 74:453–456, 1993.
16. Krebs D. Neuromuscular re-education and gait training.

In: Schwartz M, ed. *Biofeedback: A Practitioners Guide.* New York, Guilford Press, 1987.

17. LeCraw D, Wolf S. Electromyographic biofeedback (EMGBF) for neuromuscular relaxation and reeducation. In: Gersh M, ed. *Electrotherapy in Rehabilitation.* Philadelphia, Davis, 1992.

18. Miller N. Biomedical foundations for biofeedback as a part of behavioral medicine. In: Basmajian J, ed. *Biofeedback Principles and Practice for Clinicians.* Baltimore, Williams & Wilkins, 1989.

19. Moreland J, Thompson M. Efficacy of EMG biofeedback compared with conventional physical therapy for upper extremity function in patients following stroke: A research overview and meta-analysis. *Phys Ther* 74:534–543, 1994.

20. Nouwen A, Bush C. The relationship between paraspinal EMG and chronic low back pain. *Pain* 20:109–123, 1984.

21. Olson R. Definitions of biofeedback. In: Schwartz M, ed. *Biofeedback: A Practitioner's Guide.* New York, Guilford Press, 1987.

22. Peek C. A primer of biofeedback instrumentation. In: Schwartz M, ed. *Biofeedback: A Practitioner's Guide.* New York, Guilford Press, 1987.

23. Regenos E, Wolf S. Involuntary single motor unit discharges in spastic muscles during EMG biofeedback training. *Arch Phys Med Rehab* 60:72–73, 1979.

24. Schleenbaker R, Mainous A. Electromyographic biofeedback for neuromuscular reeducation in the hemiplegic stroke patient: A meta-analysis. *Arch Phys Med Rehab* 74:1301–1304, 1993.

25. Studkey S, Jacobs A, Goldfarb J. EMG biofeedback training, relaxation training, and placebo for the relief of chronic back pain. *Percept Motor Skills* 63:1023, 1986.

26. Sugar E, Firlit C. Urodynamic feedback: A new therapeutic approach to childhood incontinence/infection. *J Urol* 128:1253, 1982.

27. Whitehead W. Treatment of fecal incontinence in children with spina bifida: Comparison of biofeedback and behavior modification. *Arch Phys Med Rehab* 67:218, 1986.

28. Wolf S. Treatment of neuromuscular problems, treatment of musculoskeletal problems. In: Sandweiss J, ed. *Biofeedback Review Seminars.* Los Angeles: University of California, 1982.

29. Wolf S, Binder-Macleod S. Electromyographic feedback in the physical therapy clinic. In: Basmajian JV, ed. *Biofeedback Principles and Practice for Clinicians.* Baltimore, Williams & Wilkins, 1989.

30. Wolf S, Binder-Macleod S. Neurophysiological factors in electromyographic feedback for neuromotor disturbances. In: Basmajian JV, ed. *Biofeedback Principles and Practice for Clinicians.* Baltimore, Williams & Wilkins, 1989.

Functional Progressions and Functional Testing in Rehabilitation

Turner A. Blackburn, Jr., and John A. Guido, Jr.

O B J E C T I V E S

After completing this chapter, the student therapist should be able to do the following:

- Define what functional exercise progression is.
- Define the SAID principle.
- Outline the need for functional progression and testing.
- Describe the continuum of functional progression for low- and high-level patients.
- Outline a functional progression program for the lower extremity.
- Outline a functional progression program for the upper extremity.
- Outline a functional progression program for the spine.
- Discuss major functional testing research.

The physical therapist plays an important role in helping individuals return to their preinjury level of function. While working to achieve clinically based goals, functional testing is employed to gauge readiness to move through the rehabilitation program and to return to activity. A functional exercise progression can be initiated prior to functional testing or following these results. In either case, the testing or the progression should not exceed the healing constraints of the injured tissue. By breaking down functional activities into basic tasks, a safe and effective rehabilitation program can be designed. This chapter examines functional exercise testing and functional exercise progression and provides examples for some common upper- and lower-extremity disorders as well as a sample spine program.

WHAT IS FUNCTIONAL TESTING AND FUNCTIONAL EXERCISE PROGRESSION?

The ultimate goal of any rehabilitation program is to return an individual to the preinjury level of function as quickly and safely as possible. Decreasing pain and swelling—and restoring normal range of motion, strength, proprioception, and balance—are only part of the plan. Functional testing and a functional exercise progression will complete the rehabilitation program.

Functional testing encompasses measuring various activities to provide a baseline for determining progress or to provide normative data with which to compare performance. A functional exercise progression can be defined as a series of activities that have been ordered from basic to complex, simple to difficult, that allows for the reacquisition of a specific task. Many of the exercises in the functional progression may be used for functional testing. Functional testing and functional exercise progression allow the clinician to bridge the gap between basic rehabilitation and a full return to activity.

HOW DO WE PERFORM FUNCTIONAL TESTING?

Functional testing and functional exercise progression are used in a variety of physical therapy settings but in very different capacities. Physical therapists practicing in outpatient orthopedic settings use these techniques to help their patients return to activities of daily living, work, and sports. In the rehabilitation and nursing home settings, functional testing and functional exercise progression take on a different meaning, being geared more toward activities of daily living, transfers, and ambulating on level and unlevel surfaces.

Despite these differences, the principles that guide functional testing and exercise progression are the same regardless of the practice setting and level of the patient. Some patients will move further through the program than others, based on their specific rehabilitation goals. There is little basic science and research to guide the physical therapist in designing a functional exercise progression. Rather, common sense prevails and is employed along with the information available regarding healing constraints of various musculoskeletal disorders or the precautions that must be heeded for various medical conditions.

A complete discussion of collagen healing is beyond the scope of this chapter, but in general, many of the injuries encountered in the outpatient setting will heal in 3 to 6 weeks.[10] In the early phases of the rehabilitation program, appropriate stress must be placed on the healing tissues to ensure proper healing. Our bodies heal according to the SAID principle, *s*pecific *a*daptation to an *i*mposed *d*emand.[6] The imposed demand is therapeutic exercise in the form of a functional progression that will stress the injured tissue to allow it to heal at an adequate length and strength. This enables the individual to handle the demands of return to full function without reinjuring the area. If the functional progression is employed incorrectly, the stress imparted will cause reinjury and impede the patient's progress. Healing constraints may be exceeded or new injuries created during functional testing or exercise progression, and the therapist should be acutely aware of the individual's response to activity. The presence or absence of the cardinal signs of inflammation as well as muscle weakness, loss of motion, and instability of the injured joint should alert the clinician to reassess the activity being performed. The culprit may be one activity that is above the abilities of the patient at that time, or that the overall volume exceeds the ability of the healing structures to accommodate to the stress.

Early in the rehabilitation program, therapeutic techniques will be employed to meet the various clinical goals such as eliminating pain and swelling and restoring full range of motion, strength, proprioception, balance, and normal ambulation without deviations or assistive devices. Normal range of motion can be assessed with a goniometer by comparing established norms or the range of the uninvolved opposite extremity. Swelling can be assessed via tape measure for circumferential measurements, or with volumetric measures of water displacement. Pain levels can be determined with a visual analog scale.

Strength testing poses a challenge to the clinician. A 5/5 manual muscle test grade may not show true deficits in strength and endurance of the musculature. Isokinetic testing, if available, may be a better alternative and has been shown to correlate with function despite being performed in an open-chain fashion.[13] The authors recommend less than a 30 percent deficit in the strength and endurance of the involved versus the uninvolved extremity prior to initiating functional testing activities. This form of testing will not be available to all clinicians and not all patients will need to undergo an isokinetic evaluation. Basic manual muscle testing or the use of a hand-held dynamometer to increase objectivity will suffice in many cases. Proprioception at a given joint can be assessed through basic joint repositioning tasks, or can be measured using the electrogoniometer on the Biodex Multi-Joint System. Balance testing can be performed with or without high-technology equipment. At a minimum, performing a single-leg stance activity for total duration, or counting the number of touchdowns with the opposite lower extremity, can be assessed with a second hand on a watch. There are several excellent balance screens such as the Berg Balance Scale, the Clinical Test of Sensory Interaction for Balance (CTSIB), and the Functional Reach Test. There are also several excellent testing devices on the market that will give the clinician information regarding the postural sway envelope and directions of movement such as the Biodex Stability System and the NeuroCom Balance System.

When an individual has no pain or swelling, and has reached sufficient range of motion, strength, balance, and ambulation without deviations, the clinician can determine if functional testing is appropriate. In some cases, functional testing may be used prior to meeting the clinical goals, provided the individual is not placed at risk for reinjury based on the healing constraints of the injured tissue. The information gained will be valuable to the clinician and the individual in planning further treatment.

SPECIFICS

How do we measure function? Functional testing is a onetime, maximal effort that is performed to assess performance.[12] The key is that the test must re-create the activity that the individual will be performing, and must be completed in a controlled environment. The purpose of functional testing is to determine an individual's readiness to return to the preinjury level of function. The information gained will allow the clinician to point out deficits that must be overcome, and to progress the rehabilitation program. Functional testing, like the functional exercise progression, must begin with simple tasks and progress to highly coordinated tasks. At the lowest level, for an individual to perform a sit to stand transfer, the leg press or bilateral minisquats can be performed for repetitions or a length of time. This will re-create an individual's daily activities, in this case rising from a chair, commode, or car seat. Testing can be performed through various ranges of motion to re-create the seat heights the individual will encounter. The clinician can also use ambulation itself as a functional test. Ambulation for distance is an important determinant to see if the patient can function in the community. Ambulation measured for time will determine if the patient can cross a street safely or exit an elevator before the door closes.

Lastly, let's examine a patient's ability to climb stairs. How would we create a functional test to assess this skill? Front or lateral step-ups or step-downs can be used to determine an individual's readiness to complete this task. This test is also easily standardized. Step-ups can be performed with only the heel of the opposite limb touching the ground. A step height can be chosen that equals heights that will be encountered at home, the office, or in the community. Repetitions are counted, or the number of repetitions in a set time can be measured. The results are compared with the uninvolved limb or established norms. Rosenthal et al[11] reported an intraclass correlation coefficient of .99 for the lateral step-up test. Functional testing can be as simple as performing minisquats, ambulation, or lateral step-ups for repetitions, distance, or time.

At the highest level of functional testing in the lower extremity, an athlete may have to complete complex movements such as hop tests, shuttle runs, and agility drills. Unfortunately, our training leaves us slightly behind other health care professionals, particularly athletic trainers, when it comes to functional testing of an athlete or weekend warrior. This part of the rehabilitation process is an integral part of the athletic trainer's daily routine, but we can easily incorporate this form of functional testing to meet our patients' needs in the clinic. The results of functional testing in this case will determine when they can return to play. Daniel et al[3] described the one-leg hop for distance test. It is easy to see how important this activity is in terms of a return to athletic competition. This is an ideal test to determine the individual's willingness to accept weight on the involved leg after injury.[12] The one-leg hop for distance and the one-leg timed hop, predominantly used with athletes, have also shown good reliability.[3] A single-leg hop does have its limitations, in that it only describes one movement, whereas most sports require a series of complex maneuvers. Therefore, many authors have attempted to create even higher-level tests to determine readiness to play. Lephart et al[7] examined three functional testing procedures for the anterior cruciate-deficient athlete. These included the co-contraction maneuver (a shuffling maneuver around a semicircle while tethered to surgical tubing), a carioca (cross-over stepping), and a shuttle run (an acceleration and deceleration test). In lieu of these tests, the physical therapist can have the patient run through a series of progressively difficult tasks such as running straight ahead and backpedaling, performing figure-eight runs, cutting maneuvers, and finally sports-specific tasks.

In the upper extremity, the clinician needs to be more creative to re-create the functional demands an individual may encounter during ADLs or sports. Functional testing can include push-ups for an athlete or overhead activities performed in a specially designed apparatus for an electrician or carpenter. Again, at the lowest level, simple reaching tests can re-create ADLs such as removing items from overhead cabinets. To standardize this, we can use a goniometer to measure range of motion at the glenohumeral joint, or a finger ladder to document reach height. A tape measure can be used to measure reach distance. At the highest levels, activities that re-create job tasks, as alluded to, can be performed in the clinic. Measures of specific skills, duration of overhead activity, or speed of activity provide objective evidence of functional ability. For the athlete, both open-chain (throwing activities) and closed-chain (for football or wrestling) activities can be reproduced in the clinic. The clinician is only limited by his or her imagination.

Whether testing the upper or lower extremity, begin with bilateral support drills and progress to more demanding unilateral support drills. Always observe for substitution and poor technique, which may signify that the activity is too difficult for the patient at that time, or that the stress is too great on the healing structures. Through functional testing, the therapist can assess speed, strength, agility, and power which when combined equal function.[12] Functional testing can be adapted to meet the needs of every patient with whom we come into contact. Physical therapists have always performed functional testing with their patients, although they may not have placed these activities under this heading. In the acute care or rehabilitation hospital, as well as in the nursing home, most activities have a functional component and can be used to document functional status. Everything from bed mobility and transfers, to ambulation on level and unlevel surfaces can be measured fairly objectively. In the outpatient setting, the activities required for functional testing may be more dynamic, but the principles and goals of treatment are the same. We take for granted the ease with which we perform our activities of daily living. A functional test can be performed to document limitations in ADL tasks, and a functional exercise progression can be implemented to meet the specific needs of the patient. It is imperative to enable individuals to return to their maximum level of function or their preinjury status.

WHAT NOW?

Now that we've completed our functional testing procedure at the appropriate time in the rehabilitation process, where do we go from here? When the functional testing is completed, the clinician must be able to use this information to determine the next step in the rehabilitation process. In one scenario, if the individual completes the tasks adequately, return to work or activities of daily living without restrictions may be recommended. In another scenario, if the individual is not able to complete the tasks, the clinician must determine where the breakdown occurred. Return to full function is restricted until these tasks can be completed and it is safe for the individual to return to the preinjury activity level. This is where the functional exercise progression should dominate the rehabilitation program. Up until now, the patient may have been working on and achieved the majority of the clinical goals, but from the results of the functional testing, the patient may not be ready to return to full function.

If we keep in mind the goal activity, whether it is a return to sports or ADLs, we can break it down into small segments that can be performed in the clinic. Once the specific activity has been broken down into required fundamental movements, the individual's injured body part is stressed progressively until function is adequate for a return to work, ADLs, or sports-specific demands.[12] Removing the "conscious mind" from the activity will make the movement pattern more automatic and natural. Some suggestions include throwing a ball for the patient

TABLE   20-1

Knee Functional Progression

| FUNCTIONAL ACTIVITY | CRITERIA FOR RETURN | | |
	STRENGTH	ROM	OTHER
Sit to stand	3/5 MMT quad	90 degrees one knee	Sitting balance
	3/5 MMT ham		
	3/5 MMT gastroc	120 degrees hip flexion	Stand balance
Assistive free gait	5/5 MMT quad	Full extension	No pain
	4/5 MMT ham	100 degrees flexion	No swelling
	Lift body wt one leg with heel lift	10 degrees dorsifexion	Nonantalgic gait
	Motor control of knee		Adequate balance
Ascend/descend			10 side-step-downs
Stairs (step over step)			10 side-step-downs
Running	70% quad/ham	full flexion	30 mins bike
		15 degrees dorsiflexion	50 side-step-downs
			2 miles walking
Sprinting	90% quad/ham		2 miles running
Agility			Successful sprinting
Sports activity			Functional progression of activity

to catch during the activity or having the patient count the fingers held up on your hand. Functional exercises that meet the specific needs of the patient can truly be termed "functional."

The concept of open- versus closed-chain exercise becomes a moot point when discussing functional exercise progression because everything we do is a combination of these two types of activity. Walking requires a combination of movements (the swing phase is open chain, the stance phase is closed chain), as does picking an object up off the floor (the individual braces the body with the uninvolved extremity on a table, which is closed chain, and reaches for the object, which is open chain). The hallmark of closed-chain activities, however, is that they are more closely related to function, incorporating movements that mimic daily activities. Both open- and closed-chain exercise can create concentric, isometric, and eccentric muscular contractions, which are all used for functional tasks. These exercises can also include acceleration and deceleration, which are extremely important principles when discussing functional tasks. Attempting to cross a busy intersection requires acceleration to get across safely. Descending an inclined walkway requires deceleration to prevent falls. An advantage that closed-chain exercises have is the addition of appropriate proprioceptive feedback from the mechanoreceptors. Discontinuing the rehabilitation program when the clinical-based rehabilitation goals alone are achieved may be appropriate for some individuals, but this will surely be a disservice to those patients returning to higher levels of function. These patients will have an increased risk for reinjury when they attempt to return to their preinjury level of function without completing a functional exercise progression.

EXAMPLES

Let's illustrate this point by discussing some examples of specific patients frequently encountered in the outpatient setting. Assume you are treating a police officer who has suffered a sprain of the medial compartment of his right knee. After valgus stress testing at 30 degrees of flexion and an anterior drawer test with the tibia in external rotation, you determine that there is a slight opening of the joint space—in other words, a grade III ligament sprain with 1+ instability. Functional testing may be appropriate initially in the form of lateral step-ups or minisquats, provided these activities do not cause too great a stress on the healing medial compartment. This will tell you if the individual can perform sit-to-stand transfers from various heights, and climb stairs, important aspects of ADL. Table 20-1 describes lower extremity criteria needed for return to various functional activities.

Initially, starting the patient on a regimen of knee isometrics, modalities as needed to control pain and swelling, and flexibility training is an appropriate course. From an earlier discussion, we know that adequate collagen healing will occur in 3 to 6 weeks. This particular patient will need to return to high-level functional activities such as chasing and apprehending suspects. The second phase of the rehabilitation program must employ a functional exercise progression to progressively load the injured body part. In relation to Davis' Law,[5] the medial compartment will heal along the lines of stress. So, to enable it to heal strong and at an adequate length, activities that involve a valgus stress

TABLE 20-2

Lower-Quarter Functional Progression and Testing Template

LEVELS	SUPPORT	STABILITY	PLANE	RESPONSE	DIRECTION	EXAMPLES
1	Bilateral	Stable	Single	Single	Vertical	Leg press Shuttle Mini-squat
2	Bilateral	Unstable	Single	Single	Vertical	DynaDisc Foam roller Biodex stability
3	Unilateral	Stable	Single	Single	Vertical	Leg press Shuttle Mini-squat Step-up
4	Unilateral	Unstable	Single	Single	Vertical	Leg press Shuttle Mini-squat Step-up
5	Bilateral nonsupport	Stable	Single, multiple	Single, multiple	Vertical, horizontal	Jumping "5 dot drill" Spin hops
6	Unilateral nonsupport	Stable	Single, multiple	Single, multiple	Vertical, horizontal	Jumping "5 dot drill" Spin hops
7	Acceleration, deceleration	Stable				"Suicide" "T-drill" "SEMO" Co-contraction Lateral power hop

must be included. To strengthen the surrounding musculature, open-chain exercises are incorporated. However, we are unable to apply a controlled valgus stress to the knee in the open chain. Therefore, closed-chain exercises are a must. These may include the testing activities themselves, minisquats and lateral step-ups with a valgus stress, the BAPS board, profitter, and the balance-testing devices. Table 20-2 describes sample lower extremity functional exercise progression and testing activities.

Once the clinic-based goals have been achieved and the patient is able to ambulate on level and unlevel surfaces without deviation or an assistive device, functional testing is again performed to determine where the patient stands in relation to return to work. Due to the high-level demands this patient will encounter upon his return to full duty as a police officer, we need to perform higher-level functional testing, beginning with a hop test. This test is performed with the individual standing on both limbs. He is asked to jump as far as possible in a horizontal fashion (a standing broad jump) and to stick to the landing. The individual should be able to jump a distance equal to his height (or $1\frac{1}{2}$ times his height).[12] If this task is completed, a single-leg hop can be performed as described by Daniel. Noyes et al[9] suggest that two types of one-leg hopping tests—for distance and for time—be used to rule out the instability caused

by ACL rupture. Table 20-3 describes current functional testing research and conclusions related to functional activity.

If this task is completed and there is less than a 10 percent deficit between limbs, higher-level functional testing can be performed. This will include jogging and backpedaling in a straight line at 25, 50, 75, and 100 percent effort. Then, figure-eight drills are employed. Finally, cutting activities are performed, and in this case, emphasizing an open cut (side-step cut) to stress the medial compartment. In the late stages of knee rehabilitation, low-level plyometric activities could be incorporated, such as hopping drills in place, in diagonal patterns, and lateral hops to stress the medial compartment. If these tasks are completed without signs and symptoms of inflammation or hesitancy on the patient's part, a recommendation to return to tactical training and full duty will follow. Clinical outcomes can measure the effectiveness of the clinician's functional exercise progression. Table 20-4 describes various scoring systems that can be employed with knee injuries to document clinical outcomes.

In the upper extremity, we may have a patient who has suffered an anterior glenohumeral shoulder dislocation. Table 20-5 describes a sample progression of activities with criteria for advancement. Assume that this individual is an artist and

T A B L E   2 0 - 3

Functional Test Research

FUNCTIONAL TEST	RESEARCH
Lateral step-up	ICC.99 (Rosenthal, 1994)
One-leg hop for distance	ICC.99 (Worrell, 1994)
	ICC.96 (Boigia, 1997)
One-leg hop timed	ICC.77 (Worrell, 1994)
	ICC.66 (Boigia, 1997)
One-leg hop triple	ICC.95 (Boigia, 1997)
One-leg hop crossover	ICC.96 (Boigia, 1997)
Four-point run	ICC.98 (Boigia, 1997)
Lateral power hop	ICC.91–92 (Tippett, 1996)
Decreased one-leg timed hop without ACL	Positive correlation (Mangine, 1989)
Decreased one-leg hop distance without ACL	Positive correlation (Barber, 1990)
Decreased one-leg hop distance in post ACL reconstruction	Positive correlation (Sekiya, 1998)
One-leg hop distance and time postlateral ankle sprain	No correlation (Worrell, 1994)
Objective scoring system with postlateral ankle reconstruction	Positive correlation (Kaikkonen, 1994)
One-leg hop distance with decreased quad strength without ACL	Positive correlation (Friden, 1990)
One-leg hop distance with decreased quad strength without ACL	No correlation (Gauffin, 1990)
One-leg hop distance without ACL with a strengthening and coordination program	Positive correlation (Friden, 1991)
One-leg hop distance in reconstructed ACL and laxity	No correlation (Jonsson, 1992)
Co-contraction test and isokinetic strength and power	No correlation (Lephart, 1992)
Co-contraction test and ACL laxity	No correlation (Lephart, 1992)

painting is her medium. Special testing may include an anterior apprehension sign, in this case positive, along with the standard measures of range of motion, strength, pain level, and proprioception in the form of joint repositioning. Angular repositioning has been advocated at the glenohumeral joint to determine the input from the mechanoreceptors about the shoulder joint.[2,4]

Functional testing at this early stage may include reaching to a certain height for a specific number of repetitions, or holding the upper extremity at a certain angle for a specific length of time. Both of these activities will re-create the functional demands of painting. In the first stage of the rehabilitation process, just as for the lower-extremity problem, the focus is on decreasing pain and swelling through modalities, increasing range of motion as tolerated, and increasing strength through the use of shoulder isometrics. Functional exercise in this phase may take the form of rhythmic stabilization at 90 degrees of flexion and at 45 degrees of abduction. This technique will increase the stability of the shoulder joint by firing the dynamic stabilizers.

Also in this phase, total shoulder girdle strengthening, as tolerated, may begin with emphasis on the scapular stabilizers and rotator cuff musculature. There have been several EMG studies documenting various exercises for these muscle groups. The authors use a combination of exercises recommended by Mosely et al[8] for the scapula and Blackburn et al[1] for the rotator cuff. The core exercises for the scapula consist of rows, seated press-ups, scaption, and push-ups with a plus (scapula protraction).[8] The core exercises for the rotator cuff include prone extension with external rotation, prone horizontal abduction with external rotation, and prone external rotation at 90 degrees of abduction.[1] It is up to the clinician to determine the appropriate application of these core strengthening exercises.

In the second phase of the functional exercise progression, increased emphasis is placed on raising the upper extremity in the plane of the scapula initially, to raising the arm in the sagittal plane. The patient is questioned regarding the duration of time that she spends painting and an estimation can be made as to how many times she must lift her arm each session. For other individuals, the application of closed-chain exercises for the glenohumeral joint may be appropriate. Closed-chain exercises can be employed to increase the proprioceptive input of the joint mechanoreceptors, which will enhance motor control. Moving a ball on a wall and weight shifting on a table may be low-level activities that are easily implemented. A functional exercise progression may include quadruped activities, the use of the profitter, and even the stairmaster for higher-level tasks. The use of the Bodyblade at this stage may also help increase the endurance of the shoulder girdle musculature while enhancing dynamic stability in the sagittal plane. In the final stage of the rehabilitation process for this individual, large muscle group strengthening and endurance exercises are added for the deltoid, pectoralis major, and latissimus dorsi. Final functional testing

TABLE 20-4
Knee Scoring Systems

KNEE SCORING SYSTEM	
Lysholm Scale	Developed in 1986 by Lysholm 100-point scale Assesses support with ambulation, limp, stairs, squatting, pain, swelling, atrophy, and instability with walking, running, and jumping Very specific to ADLs
Cincinnati Scale	Developed in 1984 by Noyes Preinjury/surgery to postinjury/surgery comparison Assesses walking, stairs, running, jumping, twisting, sports/work activity level More specific to sports
Methodist Hospital Scale	Developed in 1986 by Shelbourne Assesses 1-mile walk, stairs, jogging, heavy work, ADLs, repetitive jumping, recreational and competitive sports More specific to sports
International Knee Society Scale	Developed in 1986 by the IKDC Assigns an A–D group grading based upon patient subjective assessment, pain, swelling, giving way, ROM, laxity, crepitus, and one-leg hop More specific to ADLs
Combined Rating System	Developed in 1995 by Karlson Cincinnati, HSS, Lysholm, IKDC Assesses pain, swelling, giving way, walk, stairs, squat, run, jump, twist, decelerate, sports, ADLs, locking, function, limp, activity, brace, crutches
Knee Outcome Survey (KOS)	Scale for disability during ADLs Scale for disability during sports

TABLE 20-5
Shoulder Functional Progression

| FUNCTIONAL ACTIVITY | CRITERIA FOR ADVANCEMENT | | |
	STRENGTH	ROM	OTHER
Active/passive ROM after surgery			Depends on healing restraints
Isometric strengthening	As tolerated	As tolerated	Depends on healing restraints
Elevation of arm after surgery	Successful gravity eliminated	As tolerated	Depends on healing restraints
Elevation of arm with weights	Successful elevation with no weights over 3 sets of 10 reps	As tolerated	Protect healing tissue as necessary
Motor control: Blade, tubing, plyoballs	Successful elevation with no weights over 3 sets of 10 reps	As tolerated	Protect healing tissue as necessary
Weight machines/full-body weight	Successful elevation with 3 pounds, 3 sets of 10 reps 5/5 MMT	As tolerated	Isokinetics as tolerated
Free weights	Successful weight machine program	As tolerated	
Sports activities	5/5 MMT Isokinetic test WNL	Enough for sport activity	Sufficient healing time No pain, swelling with progressive activity

T A B L E   2 0 - 6

Lumbar Stabilization Progression

FUNCTIONAL ACTIVITY	CRITERIA FOR ADVANCEMENT: LUMBAR STABILIZATION ACTIVITIES
Supine	Abdominal bracing Latissimus dorsi sets Gluteal sets Hip extensions sets "Marching " (hip flexions) "Dying bug" (unilateral hip and arm movement) Pelvic ant/post tilt
Prone	Quadruped with arm flexion Quadruped with hip extensions Quadruped with contralateral limb elevation Prone extensions
Seated	Gym ball "Marching" "Dying bug"
Standing	Trunk rotation stabilization with surgical tubing Horizontal adduction and abduction Flexion and extension
Lifting	Table to table Carrying objects Floor to table Table to overhead shelf

can be performed to determine whether the patient has the endurance and strength to hold the upper extremity at approximately 90 degrees for repetitions or time.

For the majority of patients seen in the outpatient setting with low back dysfunction, functional testing and a functional exercise progression can return them to their preinjury level of function (Table 20-6). For example, a patient with a bulging disk may present with pain, decreased range of motion, and decreased functional status. Functional testing may include lifting tasks or sitting or walking for duration, depending on the individual's occupation. A functional exercise progression in this case would include lumbar stabilization exercises in the supine, sitting, and, ultimately, standing positions.

To provide one more example, suppose you have a new mother who has suffered a sprain/strain of the lumbar region while picking up her child. The immediate postinjury care is dedicated to relieving the pain, inflammation, and muscle spasm, and to restoring range of motion. Proper instruction in posture and body mechanics can also begin. The second phase of the program can be initiated quickly, usually within the first 2 weeks, and activities are designed around lifting tasks. A functional exercise program may progress to mini-squats to increase lower-extremity strength and endurance, to lifting tasks from various heights, to carrying objects around the clinic. Functional testing, when appropriate, is geared toward lifting an object of equal or greater weight than the infant, from the floor to the table and vice versa. Carrying for distances and holding for time will mimic feeding and nurturing tasks.

SUMMARY

- Functional exercise progression and functional testing are important components of a complete rehabilitation program.
- Taking into account the patient's medical condition, the healing constraints of that condition, and the external environment that must be overcome, tasks can be designed to re-create the functional demands of each individual.
- When the patient is able to perform the goal activity without physical assistance or verbal cueing from the therapist, the entire activity is attempted and practiced.
- The entire formal rehabilitation program does not have to be completed prior to performing functional testing or initiating a functional exercise progression.
- Activities that are compatible with the patient's physical status may be implemented at any time. These techniques are employed by physical therapists regardless of setting and patient diagnosis.

- The use of functional testing and functional exercise progression will enable the patient to return to preinjury level of function as quickly and safely as possible.

REFERENCES

1. Blackburn TA, McLeod WD, White B, et al. EMG analysis of posterior rotator cuff exercises. *Athl Train* 25:40–45, 1990.

2. Borsa PA, Lephart SM, Kocher MS, et al. Functional assessment and rehabilitation of shoulder proprioception for glenohumeral instability. *J Sport Rehab* 3:84–104, 1994.

3. Daniel DM, Malcom L, Stone ML, et al. Quantification of knee stability and function. *Contemp Orthop* 5:83–91, 1982.

4. Davies GJ, Dickoff-Hoffman S. Neuromuscular testing and rehabilitation of the shoulder complex. *J Orthop Sports Phys Ther* 18:449–458, 1993.

5. Gould J, Davies G, eds. *Orthopedic and Sports Physical Therapy.* St. Louis, Mosby, 1985.

6. Kegerreis S. The construction and implementation of functional progression as a component of athletic rehabilitation. *J Orthop Sports Phys Ther* 5:14–19, 1983.

7. Lephart SM, Perrin DN, Fu FH, et al. Functional performance tests for the ACL insufficient athlete. *J Athl Train* 26:44–50, 1991.

8. Mosely BJ, Jobe FW, Pink M, et al. EMG analysis of the scapula muscles during a rehabilitation program. *Am J Sports Med* 20:128–134, 1992.

9. Noyes FR, Barber SD, Mangine RE. Abnormal lower limb symmetry determined by functional hop tests after anterior cruciate ligament rupture. *Am J Sports Med* 19:513–518, 1992.

10. Reed BV. Wound healing and the use of thermal agents. In: Michovitz S, ed. *Thermal Agents in Rehabilitation.* Philadelphia, Davis, 1996, pp. 3–29.

11. Rosenthal MD, Baer LL, Griffith PP, et al. Comparability of work output measures as determined by isokinetic dynamometry and a closed chain kinetic exercise. *J Sport Rehab* 3:218–227, 1994.

12. Tippett SR, Voight ML. *Functional Progressions for Sports Rehabilitation.* Champaign, IL, Human Kinetics, 1995.

13. Wilk KE, Romaniello WT, Soscia SM, et al. The relationship between subjective knee scores, isokinetic testing and functional testing in the ACL reconstructed knee. *J Orthop Sports Phys Ther* 20:60–73, 1994.

14. Worrell TW, Booher LD, Hench KM. Closed kinetic chain assessment following inversion ankle sprain. *J Sport Rehab* 3:197–203, 1994.

C H A P T E R 2 1

Orthotics in Rehabilitation

Robert S. Gailey

O B J E C T I V E S

After completing this chapter, the student therapist should be able to do the following:

- Explain the basic mechanical principles that are the foundation for orthotic design.
- Describe the functional considerations for an orthoses based on the client's diagnosis.
- Justify indications, contraindications, advantages, and disadvantages of various orthotic devices.
- Differentiate between materials used in the fabrication of orthotics; this includes the basis for selection of materials for specific purposes.
- Identify various designs of shoewear, lower limb, upper limb and spinal orthotics and discuss the function of their principle components.

The use of orthotic intervention in rehabilitation spans the history of humans, from the first crude fracture splint made from sticks in the forest, to the sophisticated modern day dynamic orthoses fabricated from hybrid materials. Many of the principles have remained the same through time, however, the new materials and structural designs, and breadth of application to a greater number of medical conditions have contributed to the expansive utilization of orthotic intervention. The use of orthotics can be found in almost every aspect of rehabilitation today. With the appreciation and understanding of terminology, principles, materials, generic designs, and the application of orthotics, clinicians can enhance the delivery of healthcare to their clients.

TERMINOLOGY

The terminology related to medical appliances is fairly straight-forward. The prefix "ortho" means to "straighten or correct," with the suffix "tic" referring to the "systematic pursuit of." The term orthosis refers to an exoskeletal appliance applied to a body part, and has replaced the traditional term, "bracing."[24] A brace is considered to be an appliance that allows movement at the joint, whereas a splint does not allow movement at a joint. Through the years, the term "splint" has been used, especially in the area of hand therapy, to mean a short-term orthosis and splints have been described as both static and dynamic. As a result, the terms orthosis, brace, and splint have become interchangeable across many allied health professions.

The orthotist is the person who designs, fabricates, and repairs the orthotic appliance, however, physical and occupational therapists, as well as physicians, may fabricate low temperature thermoplastic orthotics.

The American Academy of Orthopaedic Surgeons and the American Orthotic and Prosthetic Association developed a standard of nomenclature for orthotic devices.[24,5] The acronyms used for the generic are listed in Table 21-1.

BIOMECHANICAL PRINCIPLES OF ORTHOTIC DESIGN

The biomechanical principles of orthotic design assist in promoting control, correction, stabilization, or dynamic movement. All orthotic designs are based on three relatively simple principles: (1) pressure, (2) equilibrium and (3) the lever arm principle.[21] However, the complexities of these principles can increase when applied to the human anatomy. These considerations include and are not limited to: the forces at the interface between the orthotic materials and the skin, the degrees-of-freedom of each joint, the number of joint segments, the neuromuscular control of a segment, including strength and tone, the material selected for orthotic fabrication, and the activity level of the client. As a result, the following principles do indeed provide the foundation for all orthotic design and can assist the clinician in visualizing the effects an orthosis will have on a body segment, keeping in mind that the more complicated the

T A B L E   2 1 - 1

Orthotic Acronyms

LOWER LIMB ORTHOSES			
		AFO	Ankle-Foot Orthosis
FO	Foot Orthosis	KAFO	Knee-Ankle-Foot Orthosis
KO	Knee Orthosis	HKAFO	Hip-Knee-Ankle-Foot Orthosis
HO	Hip Orthosis	RGO	Reciprocal Gait Orthosis
SPINAL ORTHOSES			
CO	Cervical Orthosis	CTO	Cervical-Thoracic Orthosis
TO	Thoracic Orthosis	CTLSO	Cervicothoraciclumbrosacral Orthosis
SO	Sacral Orthosis	TLSO	Thoraciclumbrosacral Orthosis
SIO	Sacroiliac Orthosis	LSO	Lumbrosacral Orthosis
UPPER EXTREMITY ORTHOSES			
HdO	Hand Orthosis	WHO	Wrist-Hand Orthosis
WO	Wrist Orthosis	EWHO	Elbow-Wrist-Hand Orthosis
EO	Elbow Orthosis	SEO	Shoulder-Elbow Orthosis
SO	Shoulder Orthosis	SEWHO	Shoulder-Elbow-Wrist-Hand Orthosis

orthotic application, the more confounded the various principles become.

1. The **pressure principle** states that: Pressure is equal to the total force per unit area. Clinically, what this means is that the greater the area of a pad or the plastic shell of an orthosis, the less force will be placed on the skin. Therefore, any material that creates a force against the skin should be of a dimension to minimize the forces on the tissues.

$$P = \frac{Force}{Area\ of\ application}$$

2. The **equilibrium principle** states that: The sum of the forces and the bending moments created must be equal to zero. The practical application is best explained by the most commonly used loading system in orthotics, the three-point pressure system (Fig. 21-1). The three-point pressure or loading system occurs when three forces are applied to a segment in such a way that a single primary force is applied between two additional counterforces with the sum of all three forces equaling zero. The primary force is of a magnitude and located at a point where movement is either inhibited or facilitated, depending on the functional design of the orthosis.

$$\Sigma F = 0$$

3. The **lever arm principle** states that: The farther the point of force from the joint, the greater the moment arm and the smaller the magnitude of force required to produce a given torque at the joint. This is why most orthoses are

designed with long metal bars or plastic shells that are the length of an adjacent segment. The greater the length of the supporting orthotic structure, the greater the moment or torque that can be placed on the joint or unstable segment.

$$M = F \times d \ or \ T = F \times d$$

Collectively, these three principles rarely, if ever, act independently of each other. Ideally, when designing or evaluating an orthotic appliance, the clinician should check that (1) there is adequate padding covering the greatest area possible for comfort; (2) The total forces acting on the involved segment is equal to zero or there is equal pressure throughout the orthosis and no areas of irritation to the skin; and (3) the length of the orthosis is suitable to provide an adequate force to create the desired effect and to avoid increased transmission of shear forces against the anatomic tissues.

ORTHOTIC CONSIDERATIONS

The goal of orthotic fitting is to meet the functional requirements of the client with minimal restriction. To meet this goal, the rehabilitation team must evaluate each client individually without preconceived ideas of routine orthotic prescription based purely on the diagnosis. It must be determined whether the appliance will be a temporary device to protect or assist the client until further restorative therapies have been progressed, or in other cases, it might be a permanent or definitive orthosis fabricated for long-term use. The functional considerations for an orthoses typically include one or more of the following.

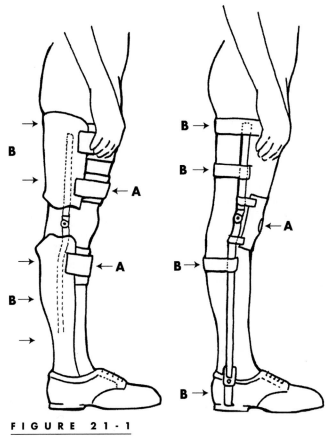

FIGURE 21-1

The three-point pressure system. **A,** The primary force. **B,** The counterforce application. The sum of all forces will equal zero.

1. *Alignment:* the correction of a deformity or maintenance of a body segment.
   Clinical examples:
   a) Musculoskeletal considerations
      i. Milwaukee brace for scoliosis
      ii. dynamic splint to prevent scar shortening in clients with burns
   b) Neurologic considerations
      i. Tone reducing AFOs in pediatric clients with cerebral palsy
      ii. CTLSO to prevent motion of the cervical region
2. *Movement:* a joint requires assistance with motion or resistance to excessive motion.
   Clinical examples:
   A. Assistance with joint motion
   a) Musculoskeletal considerations
      i. AFO with dorsiflexion assist for dorsiflexor weakness
      ii. Wheelchair to assist with propulsion
   b) Neurologic considerations
      i. RGO to assist clients with spinal cord injury with ambulation
      ii. Tenodesis splint to assist clients with spinal cord injury

B. Resistance of joint motion
   a) Musculoskeletal considerations
      i. Shoe insert for a diabetic patient with foot deformity
      ii. Finger splints for arthritic hands
   b) Neurologic considerations
      i. Swedish knee cage for unstable knee
      ii. Arm sling for neurologic shoulder
3. *Weight-bearing:* to reduce axial loading and reduce the forces placed on a joint.
   Clinical examples:
   a) Musculoskeletal considerations
      i. Shoe insert with metatarsal pad for a diabetic patient with foot deformity
      ii. Rocker bottom on the outsole to prevent excessive weight over the metatarsals
   b) Neurologic considerations
      i. Patella tendon bearing (PTB) orthosis for Charcot joints
      ii. Heel wedge for the pronated foot of a child with cerebral palsy
4. *Protection:* support or protect a segment against further injury or pain.
   Clinical examples:
   a) Musculoskeletal considerations
      i. Functional knee brace
      ii. Infrapatella strap
   b) Neurologic considerations
      i. Cock-up splints post spinal cord injury
      ii. Long leg brace for clients with cerebral palsy

There are only a few contraindications for orthotic application: (1) the orthosis cannot provide the required amount of motion, (2) when greater stabilization is required than can be provided, (3) the orthosis actually limits function, therefore, the client is more functional without the appliance, and (4) abnormal pressures from the orthosis would result in injury to the skin and other tissues.

Materials

Over the years several materials have been introduced which offer great strength at reduced weight and, in many cases, are easier to work with during the fabrication process. As a result, the client is fitted with an orthotic appliance that is both functional and, in most cases, cosmetically acceptable. Selecting the appropriate material characteristics for the fabrication of an orthotic device requires careful consideration of a number of factors.[24,22]

1. *Strength:* the maximum external load that can be sustained by a material. The strength of a material is determined by stress, which relates to the magnitude of the applied forces and the amount of material resisting the forces. Depending on the way that a force is applied, stress can be subdivided into several types: tensile, compressive, shear, and flexural (bending) stress. Because the strength of a material can be multidirectional, both the direction and the magnitude

of the forces that will be placed on a material must be determined prior to selecting a material.

2. **Stiffness:** the stress-strain or force-to-displacement ratio of a material or simply the amount of bending or compression that occurs under stress. A tension test can be performed on a material to determine the stress–strain curve that reflects the mechanical properties of a material. The stiffness or flexibility of a material is determined by the elasticity and the amount of residual deformation remaining after being placed under tension. Creep is referred to as the deformation that follows initial loading of a viscoelastic material that occurs over time. Clinically, when greater support is required, a stiffer material is used; when a more dynamic orthosis is desired, a more flexible material is used.

3. **Durability** (fatigue resistance): the ability of a material to withstand repeated cycles of loading and unloading. Fatigue stresses, which are the result of repeated low loads rather than the application of a high load, are the main cause of material breakage. As a result, all materials and many orthotic products are subjected to cyclic testing to determine fatigue strength. Selection of a material for orthotic appliances is frequently based on the ability of the material to withstand the day-to-day stresses of each individual client.

4. **Density:** the material's weight per unit volume. Generally, the greater the volume or thicker a material the more rigid and more durable it will be, however, this usually increases the overall weight of the finished orthosis. Some synthetic materials will utilize the arrangement or orientation of the material's properties to increase strength rather than just increasing the volume of material in an effort to minimize the additional weight, yet still increase stiffness.

5. **Corrosion resistance:** the vulnerability of the material to chemical degradation. Most materials will exhibit corrosion over time, metals will rust and plastics will become brittle. Contact with human perspiration and environmental elements such as dirt, temperatures, and water accelerate the wearing effect on materials. Knowing the client's daily environment can assist in material selection.

6. **Ease of fabrication:** the equipment and resources available to work with materials are also very important. Some materials require expensive equipment and familiarity with the properties of the material, such as shrinkage when heated. Others are relatively easy to use with little equipment but may not offer the strength and durability of the more complex materials.

LOWER LIMB ORTHOTICS

Footwear

Shoes are often considered to be the foundation of an orthosis and may also be a corrective device by design. Footwear can be modified to redistribute weight-bearing not only throughout the foot and ankle but also can alter the forces transmitted throughout the lower limb. Although consumers often select shoes based on cosmetic or fashion concerns, clinicians should regard a client's footwear as the device that forms the base on which they stand and as a result can have a significant effect on skin, lower limb joints, and posture. Consequently, understanding the components of footwear and the relationship each component may have to the human anatomy is important when evaluating a client.

Often a simple change in footwear style or replacing a worn pair of shoes can benefit a person. If further intervention is necessary, modification to shoes is frequently easily performed and inexpensive. If warranted, custom shoes can be made. Well-designed shoes can frequently promote healing, prevent further injury, and provide an adequate foundation for lower limb orthotics. The basic components of a shoe are illustrated in Figure 21-2. Athletic shoes and custom-designed shoes typically have additional components that are important to athletes and may also prove beneficial to clients in some cases.[20]

Shoe Components

A. Outersole: the hard out layer that protects the plantar surface of the foot and contacts the floor.

B. Innersole: the softer inner layer that interfaces with the plantar surface of the foot.

C. Ball: the widest part of the sole located below the metatarsal heads.

D. Upper: divided into three parts that covers the dorsum of the foot.
   a) Vamp: covers the anterior foot.
   b) Tongue: an extension of the vamp that protects the foot from the eyelet rows and laces.
   c) Quarters: medial and lateral quarters extend posteriorly, under the malleolus in low shoes or covers the malleolus in high shoes, and join at the heel.

E. Eyelet (stays) rows: the laces are contained within the eyelet stays.

F. Closures or throat styles: the portion of the upper that influences the ease of donning and internal adjustability of the shoe (Fig. 21-3).
   a) Balmore (Bal): the tongue is separated from the vamp.
   b) Blucher: the tongue is an extension of the vamp, permitting wider opening.
   c) Lace-to-toe: the eyelet stays and tongue extend to the toe, permitting the widest opening for donning and may have a high or low quarter.

G. Heel: located posteriorly beneath the outer sole under the anatomic heel. A low broad heel provides the greatest stability and assists in evenly distributing the weight between the rear and forefoot.

H. Heel counter: a reinforcement cup incorporated into the rear of the upper that helps maintain the anatomic heel in neutral and controls excessive movement.

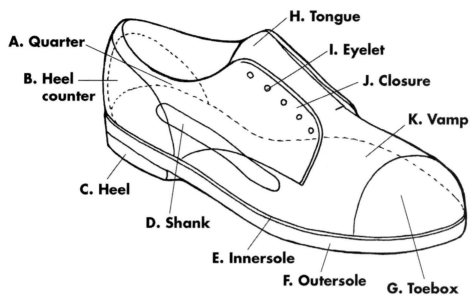

FIGURE 21-2

The anatomy of a shoe. **A,** Quarter. **B,** Heel counter. **C,** Heel. **D,** Shank. **E,** Innersole. **F,** Outersole. **G,** Toe box. **H,** Tongue. **I,** Eyelet. **J,** Closure. **K,** Vamp.

I. Toe box: a reinforcement material inserted in the vamp to maintain the height of the shoe protecting the anatomic toes.

J. Shank: a reinforcement material between the ball and heel of the shoe.

K. Lasts: shoes are constructed over a model of the foot stylized from wood, plaster, plastic, or a computer-generated design called a last. The last determines the fit, walking progression, and the outward appearance of the shoe (Fig. 21-4).
   a) Medial or inflared last
   b) Straight last
   c) Lateral or outflared last

Foot Orthoses

Foot orthoses can be classified into three general categories, soft, semirigid, and rigid, depending on the material properties or the degree of flexibility.

1. **Soft:** flexible foam type materials provide cushioning, improve shock absorption, decrease shear forces, and are used to redistribute plantar pressures affording comfort with limited joint control.

2. **Semirigid:** combination of soft and rigid materials including cork, rubber, or plastics providing some flexibility and shock absorption, however, designed to balance or control the foot.

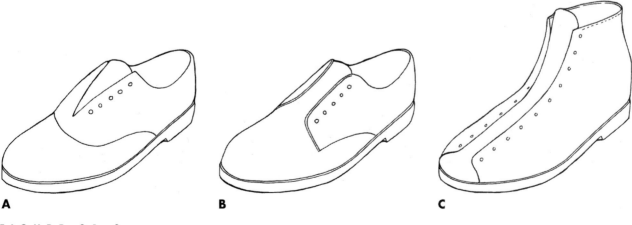

A   **B**   **C**

FIGURE 21-3

Closures or throat styles of a shoe. **A,** Balmore (Bal). **B,** Blucher. **C,** Lace-to-toe.

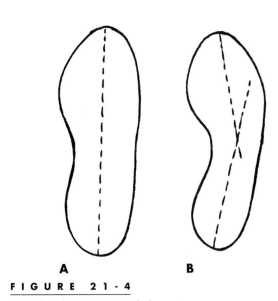

FIGURE   21-4

Shoe lasts. **A,** Straight last.
B, Medical or inflared last.

3. ***Rigid:*** strong, stiff, and durable materials such as plastics or metals are used to assist with transfer of weight, stabilize flexible deformities, and to control abnormal motion.

Shoe Modifications

Shoe modifications can be either an internal modification where the corrective adaptation is affixed inside the shoe or an external modification, which is attached to the outside of the shoe. Medial supports are incorporated either internally or externally to the shoe with the intention of supporting the anatomic medial longitudinal arch of the foot and shifting the body weight more laterally, decreasing the valgus deformity of the foot, and restraining the depression of the subtalar joint. Conversely, lateral supports are designed to decrease varus deformity of the foot. The lateral aspect of the shoe is reinforced to support the lateral aspect of the foot to shift the body weight more medially.[17]

INTERNAL MODIFICATIONS (FIGURE 21-5)

1. ***Medial longitudinal arch support*** (cookie/scaphoid pad): a rubber or leather pad often used in conjunction with a medial longitudinal counter to prevent depression of the subtalar joint by posting the sustentaculum tali and the navicular tuberosity.
2. ***Metatarsal pad:*** a rubber or semisoft pad that is placed at the apex of the metatarsal shafts, relieving the metatarsal heads from excessive pressure and supporting the collapsed transverse metatarsal arch.
3. ***Heel cushion:*** a viscoelastic material placed in the heel cup of an orthosis or directly into the shoe to accommodate for the inability to achieve a neutral position in the sagittal plane, shock attenuation, and to relieve calcaneal stress fractures or heel pain.

EXTERNAL MODIFICATIONS

Heel Corrections (Figure 21-6)

1. ***Medial heel wedge:*** a leather wedged insert incorporated into the heel, used to elevate and maintain the medial margin of shoe to decrease hyperpronation, and designed to shift the weight laterally.
2. ***Lateral heel wedge:*** a leather wedged insert incorporated into the heel, used to elevate and maintain the lateral margin of shoe to decrease supination, and designed to shift the weight medially.
3. ***Thomas heel:*** The heel of the shoe extends anteriorly 1 inch on the medial aspect to assist with balance, support the longitudinal arch, and assist in maintaining the subtalar joint in a neutral position. The Thomas heel is often coupled with medial heel wedges to assist with stability during ambulation.
4. ***Reversed Thomas heel:*** opposite of the Thomas heel, the heel is extended 1 inch on the lateral aspect to assist with balance, subtalar joint alignment, and is used in conjunction with lateral heel wedges.

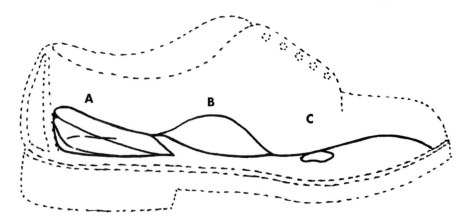

FIGURE   21-5

Internal modifications. **A,** Heel cushion. **B,** Medial longitudinal arch support (cookie/scaphoid pad). **C,** Metatarsal pad.

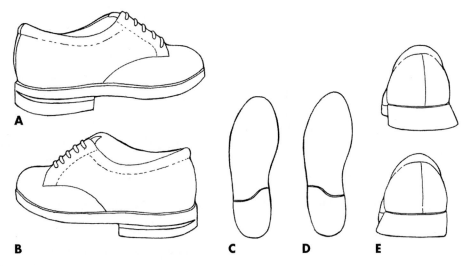

FIGURE 21-6

External modifications, heel corrections. **A,** Medial heel wedge. **B,** Lateral heel wedge.
C, Thomas heel. **D,** Reversed Thomas heel. **E,** Heel flares.

5. *Heel flares:* either medial or lateral extension of the shoe heel that broadens the base of support for greater stability.

Outsole Corrections (Figure 21-7)

1. *Medial sole wedges:* a crepe or leather wedge used to correct forefoot eversion and promote inversion.
2. *Lateral sole wedge:* a leather wedge used to correct forefoot inversion and promote eversion.
3. *Rocker bottom:* a crepe or leather convex buildup under the posterior to the metatarsal heads, intended to redistribute body weight over the entire plantar surface, reduce stress to the forefoot, and assist with rollover during ambulation.
4. *Metatarsal bar:* a flat strip of leather positioned just posterior to the metatarsal heads, designed to transfer the forces from the metatarsophalangeal joints to the metatarsal shafts.

Custom Molded Inserts

1. *University of California Berkeley (UCB) insert:* a molded plastic design that covers the heel (providing a heel counter for subtalar joint control) that extends to the midfoot, providing support to the medial longitudinal arch (Fig. 21-8).
2. *Custom inserts:* there are a remarkable number of custom or biomechanical inserts available to clinicians today. Some require casting; others use foam impression, and a few use computer imaging. Regardless of how the image of the foot and deformity are obtained, most use semirigid and soft materials to fabricate the insert. Rigid materials are used when maximal control is required. The foot is divided into the rear foot and forefoot. The foot deformity is altered by positioning the rear or forefoot with a technique called posting, whereby specific structures of the foot are raised by padding under the soft orthotic shell. Excessive pronation or supination of the foot is corrected by controlling for rear

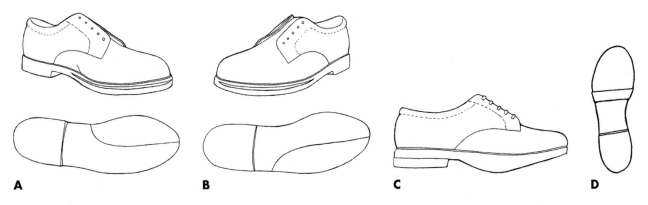

FIGURE 21-7

External modifications, outersole corrections. **A,** Medial sole wedges. **B,** Lateral sole.
C, Rocker bottom wedge. **D,** Metatarsal bar.

FIGURE   21-8

University of California Berkeley (UCB) insert.

and forefoot varus or valgus. The length of the insert varies from posterior to the metatarsal heads to running the full length of the foot.

Ankle-Foot Orthoses

Ankle-foot orthoses are designed to control the rate and direction of tibial advancement and to maintain an adequate base of support while meeting the specific demands for acceptable gait. There are several designs of AFO constructed from a wide variety of materials with the express purpose of meeting the individual needs of each client. Frequently, standard designs of AFOs are modified for an individual based on the specific requirements of the orthotic prescription. Because of the large variety of AFOs and custom designs, understanding the standard designs and the individual components provides the clinician with a sound foundation for the majority of clients.

SHOE AND FOOT ATTACHMENTS (FIG. 21-9)

1. ***Stirrup (solid):*** a one-piece attachment with a solid metal plate riveted to the sole of the shoe, creating a U-shaped frame that forms the medial and lateral upright.

2. ***Stirrup (split):*** a two-piece attachment with a metal plate riveted to sole of shoe has two channels to permit donning and doffing of the removable metal uprights. The split stirrup permits use of multiple shoes, providing that the shoes have the receptacle attachment.

3. ***Caliper:*** very similar to the split stirrup with a metal plate riveted to sole of shoe, however, the uprights are slightly lighter and round.

4. ***Molded shoe insert:*** a plastic custom-formed footplate attaches directly to the metal uprights with a calf band for proximal support.

ANKLE JOINTS AND CONTROLS

Stops (Fig. 21-10)

1. ***Plantarflexion stop:*** a posterior stop restricting plantarflexion but allowing full dorsiflexion.

2. ***Dorsiflexion stop:*** an anterior stop that restricts dorsiflexion but allows full plantarflexion.

3. ***Limited motion stop:*** an ankle joint that limits motion in all directions.

4. ***Free motion joint:*** an ankle joint that provides medial lateral stability from the uprights while permitting full plantar/dorsiflexion. Plastic AFOs use lightweight joints, such as the Gillette or Gaffney joints, that permit free motion, but other mechanisms fabricated into the AFO design, such as posterior stops, have the ability to control motion.

Assists (Fig. 21-11)

1. ***Dorsiflexion assist:*** a posterior spring assists with dorsiflexion and permits full plantar flexion, which compresses the spring during early stance phase of gait; as the limb

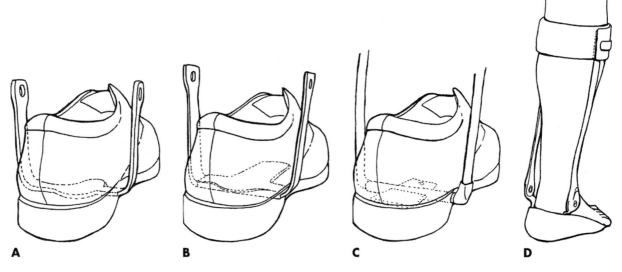

A   **B**   **C**   **D**

FIGURE   21-9

Shoe and foot attachments. **A,** Stirrup (solid). **B,** Stirrup (split). **C,** Caliper. **D,** Molded shoe insert.

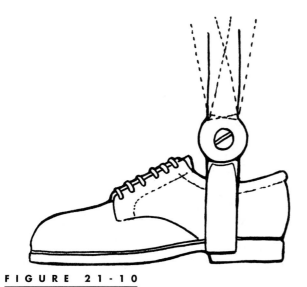

FIGURE 21-10

Ankle joints and controls. Stops:
A, Plantarflexion and dorsiflexion limited
motion stop.

moves into swing phase the spring promotes dorsiflexion. The spring resistance can be adjusted.

2. ***Dorsiflexion, plantarflexion assist (dual channel) or bichannel adjustable ankle locks (BiCAAL):*** joints with anterior and posterior springs that assist with both plantar and dorsiflexion to varying degrees according to the adjusted settings of the springs. Pins may also be used to replace the spring to limit or control motion in the sagittal plane.

VARUS AND VALGUS CORRECTION (FIG. 21-12)

1. ***Medial T-strap:*** the leather strap arises from the shoe quarter covering the medial malleolus and buckles to the lateral upright, pushing laterally to correct a valgus (eversion) deformity.

2. ***Lateral T-strap:*** the leather strap arises from the shoe quarter, covers the lateral malleolus and buckles to the medial upright, pushing medially to correct a varus (inversion) deformity.

3. ***Supramalleolar orthoses (SMO):*** a low-profile supramalleolar design for subtalar joint control to limit varus or valgus. The ankle joint also assists with dorsiflexion during swing. The footplate can be molded for greater rear or forefoot control.

Custom Molded Thermoplastic Ankle-Foot Orthoses

The vast majority of AFOs are custom fitted with high temperature thermoplastic materials such as polyethylene or polypropylene plastic. Plastic AFO designs tend to offer a more intimate fit and can be molded around bony prominence and other anatomic structures, offering greater control of the foot and ankle. The footplates can also be fabricated with arches, postings, counters, and other modifications to support the architecture of the foot and, in the case of central nervous system involvement, potentially reduce tone or spasticity.

The degree of rigidity of the AFO can also be varied by the chemical composition of the plastic or hybrid materials, such as metals or carbon fiber composites, that can be incorporated into the appliance. The thickness of the materials can also determine the stiffness of the AFO. Finally, the shape of the AFO can have an effect. The more anterior the trim lines, the greater the stability. In fact, if an anterior closure is included in the design, a complete cylinder is created, offering maximal control of the tibia over the ankle (Fig. 21-13)[8].

The components of an AFO include the shoe insert, which is often referred to as the footplate. The calf shell runs the length of the posterior leg. If the calf shell is narrow enough to permit bending of the plastic, it is called a posterior leaf spring in that

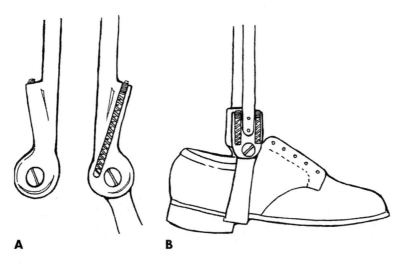

FIGURE 21-11

Ankle joints and controls. Assists. **A,** Dorsiflexion assist. **B,** Dorsiflexion and plantarflexion assist (dual channel).

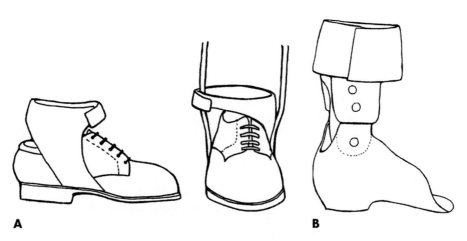

FIGURE 21-12

Varus and valgus correction. **A,** Medial T-strap. **B,** Supramalleolar orthoses (SMO).

even though movement may take place during weight bearing, the ankle will return to a neutral position when unweighted. The position of the calf shell in relation to the footplate can also have an effect on the knee joint, where the greater the ankle dorsiflexion, the more knee flexion that will occur. Conversely, the greater the plantarflexion at the ankle, the more that knee extension is promoted. The proximal portion of the AFO has the calf strap, which is typically a Velcro closure to secure the orthosis and provide some stability (Fig. 21-14).

1. ***Floor Reaction Orthosis (FRO) AFO:*** this design utilizes the joint moments that result from the ground reaction force to create stability at the knee. By placing the ankle in slight plantar flexion, an extension moment is created at

the knee. The length and rigidity of the footplate coupled with the plantarflexion angle of ankle, as well as the proximal anterior shell, prevent the tibia from progressing over the foot and promotes extension.

2. ***Articulating or hinged AFO:*** a variety of mechanical ankle joints as just described are available. The type of joint and design of the foot insert and calf shell control the degree of ankle movement.

3. ***Patella tendon bearing (PTB) AFO:*** to reduce the body weight and ground reaction forces transmitted through the ankle, a rigid proximal shell is incorporated to offer a patella tendon bar that rests just inferior to the patella. The ankle is set in slight plantarflexion so weight is borne through the patella tendon, therefore reducing the weight-bearing

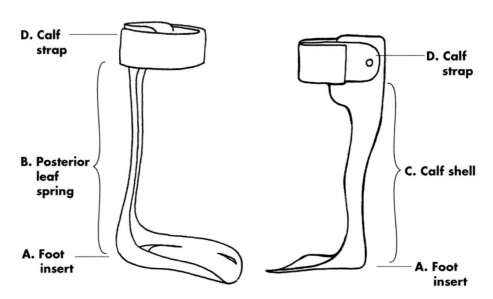

FIGURE 21-13

Ankle-foot orthosis (AFO). **A,** Foot insert. **B,** Calf shell. **C,** Posterior leaf spring. **D,** Calf strap.

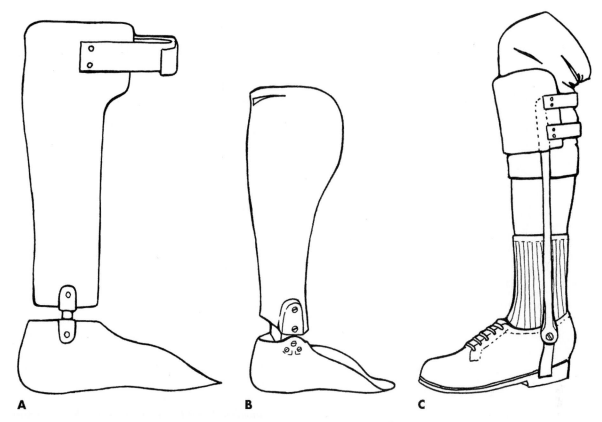

FIGURE 21-14

Custom molded ankle-foot orthosis (AFO). **A,** Floor reaction orthosis (FRO) AFO.
B, articulating or hinged AFO. **C,** Patella tendon–bearing (PTB) AFO.

forces at the ankle. This design is often prescribed for degenerative joints such as Charcot joint and arthritic ankles.

KNEE-ANKLE-FOOT ORTHOTICS

The primary purpose of most knee orthotic devices is to provide knee control in one or more planes. Typically, the shoe is the foundation for the KAFO with or without a foot insert and ankle joints as described previously. A pair of metal uprights or plastic calf shell connects the foot/ankle components to the mechanical knee joint. The orthosis is suspended by the stabilizing structures, such as the calf bands or shells distally and thigh bands or shells proximally.

Knee Joints (Fig. 21-15)

1. *Single axis joint:* designed to behave like a hinge, preventing movement in the coronal plane, providing medial/lateral stability, while permitting movement in the sagittal plane. Free motion joints allow full knee flexion and extension yet prevent hyperextension. Prescribed for genu varum and valgum.

2. *Offset axis joint:* a single axis joint design with the axis set further posterior from the weight line than the standard

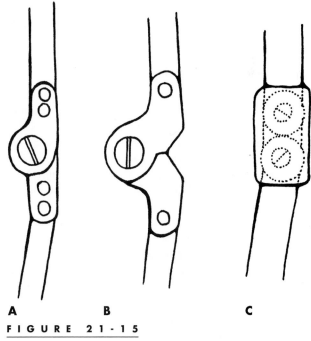

FIGURE 21-15

Knee joints. **A,** Single axis joint. **B,** Offset axis joint.
C, Polycentric axis joint.

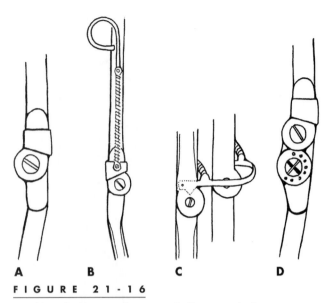

FIGURE 21-16

Knee locking mechanisms. **A,** Drop-ring locks.
B, Spring-load pull rod. **C,** Pawl or bail locks.
D, Adjustable knee lock.

single axis joint, promoting maximal knee extension during weight bearing without having to use a mechanical lock. The offset joint is prescribed when greater stability than is offered with a single axis joint is warranted.

3. *Polycentric axis joint:* designed to mimic the instantaneous center of rotation present in the anatomic knee, the two-geared mechanical joint is still confined to a uniplanar path. The gliding and rolling motion emulated with the polycentric joint is intended to reduce excessive motion and slippage and to provide greater comfort than conventional single axis joints afford.

Knee Locking Mechanism (Fig. 21-16)

1. *Drop-ring locks:* the most common locking system. It has small rings that slide down over the proximal portion of a single axis knee joint to maintain full knee extension during standing and may be raised manually to release for sitting or free knee flexion and extension.

2. *Spring-load pull rod:* a spring system with a control rod that can be extended to a height for convenient reach permits easier release of locking mechanism. Often prescribed for clients with poor balance or dexterity issues that preclude them from using standard locking systems.

3. *Pawl or bail locks:* levers posterior to the knee provide easy release of the locking mechanism for sitting. Clients who have extreme balance disturbances or cannot free their hands to operate a locking system during sitting benefit from this type of locking mechanism.

4. *Adjustable knee lock:* a variety of mechanisms are available to preset the knee lock range of motion (ROM), allowing clinicians to establish the specific knee flexion and extension range to prevent reinjury. As greater knee ROM is

permitted during the course of rehabilitation, the preset ROM of the knee mechanism can be adjusted to accommodate progress or prevent further injury.

KNEE ORTHOTICS

1. *Rigid KO (knee cage):* commonly referred to as the "Swedish" knee cage, the prefabricated device has a metal frame with canvas or heavy elastic thigh, and calf straps are designed to prevent recuvatum and provide some medial and lateral support. Frequently used with clients having knee instability, preventing further damage or internal derangement to inert structures of the knee while strength is returning.

2. *Knee/Immobilizer and two phase/breakdown braces:* fabricated from a variety of fabrics and metal inserts for stability, these orthoses are designed to comfortably restrict all motions of the knee. More sophisticated versions are known as two-phase/breakdown braces, can be either custom-fitted or prefabricated, and are usually used during the immobilization phase of an acute injury and prior to or after surgery. They include knee joints to limit motion as necessary with adjustable hinges and to gradually increase ROM as the person progresses through rehabilitation.

3. *Functional knee braces:* individuals who have returned to activity and require or feel the need for additional stability to protect the knee wear functional knee braces. Although a topic of controversy with regards to prophylactic ability of these braces, the major attributes cited for their use are: (1) satisfactory primary and secondary ligament restraint, (2) static compressive joint forces with dynamic forces resulting from muscular contraction, and (3) proprioceptive and neuromuscular input to integrate co-contraction. The negative aspects of wearing functional knee braces during activity have been identified as: (1) brace slippage, (2) bulkiness and weight, (3) heat retention and irritation, (4) excessive medial condylar tightness, (5) calf strap tightness, (6) brace hinge malalignment with the femoral condyles or knee joint.[20]

4. *Patellofemoral joint:* the primary goals of these braces are to minimize patella compression, assist in guiding patella tracking, and prevent excessive lateral shift. There are a number of brace designs targeted at one or all three of the stated goals for the patellofemoral joint. Generically, there are two types of patellofemoral orthotics (Fig. 21-17).

   • *Elastic sleeves:* running the length of the mid-thigh to mid-calf, this type of brace provides medial dynamic tension and attempts to counterbalance the lateral displacement of the patella. The stabilizing component of the brace can be either a series of three adjustable straps, horseshoe-shaped felt, or rubber pads or pneumatic chambers.

   • *Infrapatella straps:* a fabric strap with Velcro closure is worn over the patella tendon to support the distal patella, to alter patellofemoral joint mechanics, and

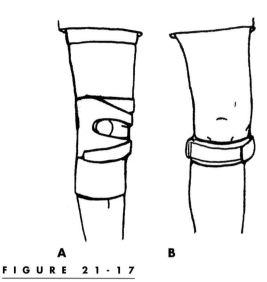

FIGURE 21-17

Knee orthotics (KO). **A,** Elastic
sleeves. **B,** Infrapatella straps.

facilitate improved tracking to relieve compressive forces
between articular forces.
- *Patellar tapping:* one other popular intervention, patella
tapping, is used to assist in correcting patellar orientation
and control tracking while decreasing pain and facilitating vastus medialis obliqus.[20]

HIP-KNEE-ANKLE-FOOT ORTHOSES

Hip Joints (Fig. 21-18)

1. *Single axis:* most commonly, hip joints are single axis joints
   permitting flexion and extension, restricting abduction,
   adduction, and rotation.
2. *Double axis:* if hip abduction and adduction are desired
   in addition to flexion and extension, the double axis locks
   offer two planes of motion with adjustable stops to set
   limits as needed in each direction.

Hip Locks (Fig. 21-19)

1. *Drop locks:* similar to knee drop lock, a small ring slides
   down over the axis to lock the joint in extension while
   standing.
2. *Two-position hip locks:* designed to lock in full extension
   and 90 degrees of hip flexion, this locking system proves
   to be a great asset when poor sitting balance is present,
   especially in children.

Pelvic Bands

1. *Unilateral band:* when a single limb orthosis requires
   proximal stability, a rigid band can be incorporated that
   encircles the pelvis between the iliac crest and greater trochanter, with a flexible belt that continues around the
   waist.

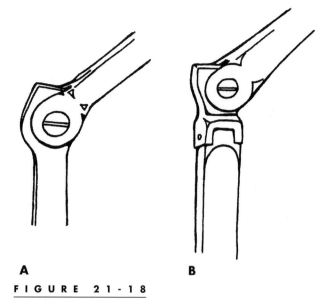

A   **B**

FIGURE 21-18

Hip joints. **A,** Single axis joint. **B,** Double axis joint.

2. *Bilateral band:* most commonly the bilateral pelvic band
   is used for bilateral HKAFOs where the padded metal band
   encompasses the pelvis just above the buttock with the
   posterior band positioned over the sacrum.
3. *Double or pelvic girdle:* when maximal control is required, the entire proximal pelvis is encapsulated from
   the iliac crest to just proximal to the greater trochanter
   with varying posteriorly depending on strength and pelvis

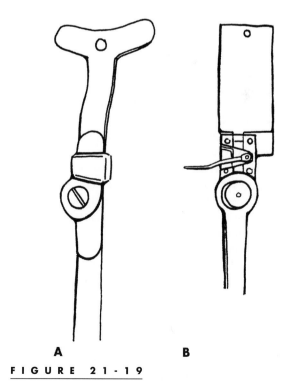

A   **B**

FIGURE 21-19

Hip locks. **A,** Drop locks. **B,** Two-postion
hip locks.

stability. High-temperature thermoplastics are typically used and custom-molded to each client, ensuring optimal fit.

4. **Silesian belt:** a flexible strap that attaches to proximal portion of the orthosis and encircles the pelvis, assisting in stabilizing the orthosis and providing suspension. Although more comfortable than rigid pelvic bands, some stability is sacrificed because of flexible nature of the belt.

Bilateral KAFOs

Often referred to as Craig Scott or long leg braces (LLBs), these orthoses are intended for standing or ambulation in people with spinal cord lesions from the level of L1–T12 to T9–L1-2. A swing-through gait is required because the person must keep their hips extended as they "hang on" or the iliofemoral ligaments limit further extension, with crutches in front of body.

Reciprocal Gait Orthoses

As the name implies, RGOs are designed to permit a reciprocal gait as opposed to the traditional swing-through gait used with HKAFOs. The patient selection criterion requires stability of the spine, adequate upper extremity and shoulder girdle strength and endurance, and a cardiovascular and respiratory system that is free of disease and provides adequate endurance. The types of disabilities often associated with RGO prescription include people with spinal cord injuries levels as high as C8 to T12–L1, however, use of RGOs with the higher levels are rare and most commonly T9 to L1 are candidates. Other diagnoses: myelodyplasia, osteogenesis imperfecta, spinal bifida, paraplegia, muscular dystrophy (not Duchenne type), and cerebral palsy. The three most outstanding contraindications are obesity, hip flexion contractures, and genu varum greater than 15 degrees.

The passive reciprocal motion is facilitated by a variety of mechanisms depending on the individual design. Currently, the three most widely used basic designs are: (1) the Louisiana State University (LSU) RGOs, which have a cable system coupling the passive hip flexion and extension movements that advance the lower limbs in a reciprocal fashion, (2) the isocentric system, which uses a bar balance system located at the lumbrosacral level of the orthosis, providing the reciprocating hip flexion action; and (3) the ARGO system, which utilizes a low profile push–pull cable system that not only provides the reciprocating motion at the hip but also assists with standing through a hip and knee extension assist mechanism. Other RGO systems and variations of the aforementioned orthoses are also used throughout the world.

The suggested advantages of RGOs include: increased walking velocity, smoothness of gait, decreased energy expenditure, improved control of lumbar lordosis and hip flexion with a decrease in the risk of flexion contractures, less weight-bearing demand on the shoulder joints from crutch use, improved bowel and bladder function, improved cardiopulmonary mechanics, increased bone density, psychological benefits of standing, and the ability to look eye to eye during personal encounters, as well as increased mobility within narrow confines and on steps.

Disadvantages that have been described include: the need for high motivation by the parent and child or the adult patient, excessive perspiration in warm climates, skin irritation, spinal deformity, poor cosmesis, difficult donning/doffing procedures, high metabolic demand, decreased velocity (typically one-fifth of normal walking speed) as compared to using a wheelchair, and multiple orthotist visits and cost.

SPINAL ORTHOTICS

The use of spinal orthotics for back pain, restriction of spinal motion, or postural care has long been a standard of care. Normally, the spinal orthosis is used to augment other therapies as the client progresses through his or her rehabilitation.[3] There are two general classifications of spinal orthosis: flexible and rigid. Flexible orthotics or corsets are typically constructed out of strong fabrics or elastic materials with a variety of stiffer supports incorporated, as necessary, for the prescription. A rigid spinal orthotic is used when greater control of motion or posture is required. Fabricated from high-temperature thermoplastics or lightweight metals, with a broad selection of pads and coverings, a wide variety designs are available to meet the majority of clinical diagnoses.

Flexible corsets and rigid orthoses may offer a combination of the following therapeutic benefits.

1. **Intraabdominal pressure:** although somewhat controversial,[11,12] the pressure exerted on the abdomen by the corset or rigid orthosis creates a cylinder effect, which in turn, raises the intracavitary pressure,[15,16] and is believed to reduce the intradiscal pressure, especially during forward bending.[18,19]

2. **Muscle relaxation:** the use of a spinal orthosis reduces the need for abdominal contractions as the cylinder effect to support the vertebral column is created passively, therefore relaxing the abdominal and erector spinae muscles.[14] Performing abdominal muscle contractions can create a flexion moment on the spine that must be restrained by the back extensors, and as a result, increase disk compression.[1,15,16] Decreasing the need for contractile support of the vertebral column may relax the muscles and reduce existing pain.

3. **Restriction of motion:** the primary method employed for motion control is the three-point pressure system. A rigid system is used when cervical, thoracic, and lumbrosacral motions are sought to be limited to the greatest possible degree. The amount of limitation varies between the various designs, however, a reduction in the motion at respective intervertebral segments has been linked to a reduction in pain and spinal instability with the intention of promoting healing.[23] Postoperative spinal orthotics not only limit motion by virtue of the mechanical restraint but, additionally, offer constant proprioceptive feedback, reinforcing positive behaviors.

4. *Postural realignment:* increased intraabdominal pressure, relaxation of muscle in spasm,[12] and restriction of movement[9] can assist in facilitating improved posture and reduce compensatory postures related to pain. In the case of scoliosis, the use of orthotic intervention may prevent the progression of a spinal curve, stabilize the curvature, and, in many instances, offer some degree of curvature correction, providing the client is compliant.[2]

Flexible Orthoses or Corsets

1. *Sacroiliac corset (binder):* numerous prefabricated designs are available made from a combination of fabric, elastic, laces, and Velcro, offering multiple adjustments. Encircling the waist from the iliac crest to the greater trochanter, and extending anteriorly to the symphysis pubis, they are offered in a variety of widths. Depending on the specific design, intraabdominal pressure and posture reinforcement promote stability for clients with postpartum or sacroiliac instability. Some versions include a moldable plastic insert for low back pain.

2. *Lumbrosacral corset:* Constructed from heavy fabrics with laces and hooks for multiple adjustments throughout the garment, the LSO corset is designed to encompass the torso and pelvis. The anterior and lateral truk containment elevate the intracavitary pressure. Most manufacturers include rigid stays, maintaining a three-point pressure system to restrict motion, or as a reminder to limit motion. The primary use is for back pain clients (Fig. 21-20).

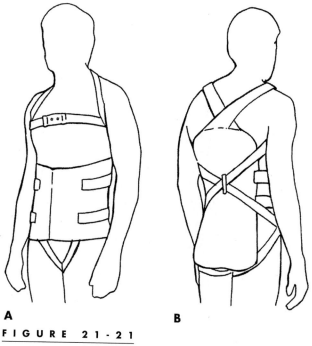

A   **B**
FIGURE   21-21
Thoracolumbrosacral corset (TLSO). **A,** Front view.
B, Rear view.

3. *Thoracolumbrosacral corset:* relatively the same construction and function as the LSO corset except the TLSO includes a shoulder strap to restrict spinal motion to the thoracic region as well as to the lumbar spine (Fig. 21-21).

Rigid Orthoses

1. *Lumbrosacral orthoses (Williams) (Extension-lateral control):* fabricated from lightweight materials, such as leather and vinyl, a single three-point pressure system limits trunk extension in the lumbar spine and increases intraabdominal pressure. Lordosis is decreased to limit lumbar extension while the pelvic and thoracic bands exert a medial force that tends to limit lateral trunk motions. There is no limitation of trunk flexion, therefore permitting light flexion exercises to increase abdominal strength while wearing the orthosis (Fig. 21-22).

2. *Thoracic-lumbrosacral orthoses*
   * *Taylor (flexion/extension control):* a pelvic band connects with two posterior uprights terminating at the midscapular level of the thoracic region, with an anterior abdominal closure and axillary straps. Two three-point pressure systems are coupled together to limit both flexion and extension of the lumbar and thoracic spine.
   * *Jewett (flexion control):* a three-point pressure system is created with two pads, one across the sternum and one at the symphysis pubis, providing the counterforce with a single pad posteriorly to promote hyperextension and thus restricting forward flexion (Fig. 21-23).

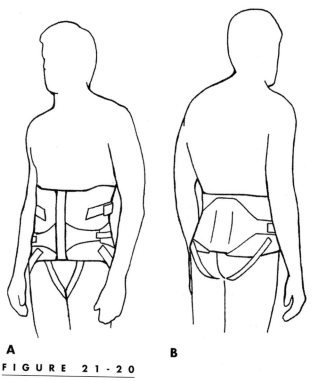

A   **B**
FIGURE   21-20
Lumbrosacral corset (LSO). **A,** Front view. **B,** Rear view.

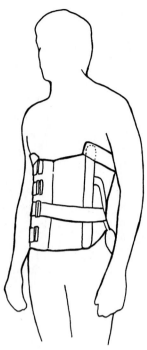

FIGURE 21-22

*Lumbrosacral orthoses
(LSO) (Williams)
(extension-lateral
control).*

- *Plastic body jacket (flexion-extension-lateral-rotary control):* typically fabricated with high-temperature copolymer plastics, a well-fitted body jacket will restrict motion in all planes. Anterior and lateral trunk containment elevate intracavitary pressure, and decrease demands on the vertebral disks. Body jackets are frequently used postsurgically or during an acute trauma. A variety of modifications can be made for comfort such as anterior chest cutouts and altering pelvic trim lines depending on the diagnosis (Fig. 21-24).

CERVICAL ORTHOSES

1. *Soft collar:* made from soft foam, the collar provides mechanical restraint for cervical flexion and extension and, to a lesser degree, lateral flexion and rotation. Although the soft collar provides minimal restriction of movement, it is a good transitional appliance from more rigid orthoses, and acts as a proprioceptive reminder to the wearer to limit head and neck motions (Fig. 21-25).
2. *Hard collars (Philadelphia collar):* constructed from semirigid and rigid plastics, depending on the manufacturer. Hard collars provide more rigid stabilization of the cervical spine and typically offer some type of chin and occipital support, with the inferior collar extending to the sternal notch anteriorly and to the T3 spinous process posteriorly. Generally, hard collars such as the Philadelphia

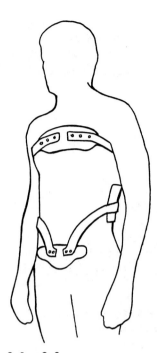

FIGURE 21-23

Jewett (flexion control).

collar limit motion much more than soft collars, but on average still permit 40 to 50 percent of normal cervical ROM, depending on the motion (Fig. 21-25).[6]

3. *Cervicothoracic orthoses (Sterno-occipital mandibular immobilizer [SOMI]):* the SOMI is one of the most

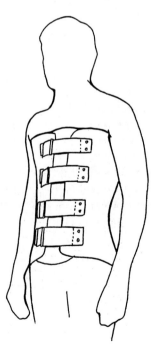

FIGURE 21-24

Plastic body jacker
(flexion-extension-lateral-
rotary control).

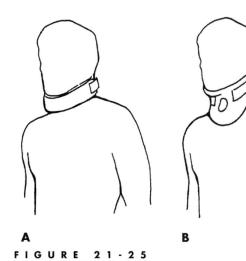

A   **B**

FIGURE 21-25

Cervical orthoses
(CO). **A,** Soft collar.
B, Hard collars
(Philadelphia collar).

common postsurgical appliances. It consists of a rigid metal frame with a chin and occipital rest connected to a chest and back plate, with padded shoulder and trunk straps. The added chest and back plates help to reduce cervical motion by an average of 55 to 75 percent, depending on the motion (Fig. 21-26).[6]

4. ***Halo-cervical orthosis:*** the greatest reduction in cervical mobilization occurs with the halo-vest appliance. A cranial ring is secured to the skull using four metal pins. The ring is attached by four metal bars to a plastic vest and is worn continuously. The estimated reduction in all cervical motions is 90 to 95 percent.[6] It also has the ability to provide distracting forces that aid in the spinal stabilization and in reducing the load of the head on the cervical spine.

Cervicothoraciclumbra sacral Orthosis

The CTLSO is most commonly used for the treatment of scoliosis and kyphosis. Although a number of designs are used for a variety of clients, the Milwaukee brace is without question the most popular. There is extensive literature describing the etiology, clinical findings, and treatments of scoliosis and kyphosis that extends far beyond the scope of this chapter. Suffice it to say that the Milwaukee brace is designed with a neck ring and occipital pad, connected to four metal upright bars secured to a plastic TLSO, which extends distally, forming a molded pelvic section.

The advantage of the Milwaukee brace is that each component pelvic, thoracic, and cervical can be molded or adjusted to slow, or even in some cases, correct scoliotic curve. In the case of idiopathic scoliosis the average 1-year follow-up showed an average 20 percent correction for thoracic curves.[1] The disadvantage to this treatment is that the brace must be worn for 12 to 18 months, 23 hours a day, with the child being out of the brace only for exercise or athletic activity. The psychological

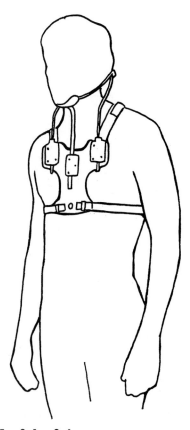

FIGURE 21-26

*Cervicothoracic orthoses
(CTO)* (Sterno-occipital
mandibular immobilizer
[SOMI]).

issues and poor acceptance by clients and physicians leads to rejection of scoliotic bracing, even with the more cosmetic, low-profile TLSOs.[4]

UPPER EXTREMITY ORTHOTICS

Architecture of the Hand

The hand is an extremely complex anatomic structure that requires muscular contractions and joint movement to act in concert with incredible accuracy, coordination, and power. The ability to manipulate the hand to perform the infinite number of functional patterns has, in part, to do with the command of opposition and prehension, two functions that are directly related to the three arches of the hand. The intrinsic muscles and ligaments of the hand and wrist are responsible for maintaining the integrity of the arches of the hand.

Arches of the Hand

1. ***Proximal transverse (carpal) arch:*** formed by the carpal bones, the capitate bone is considered to be the keystone

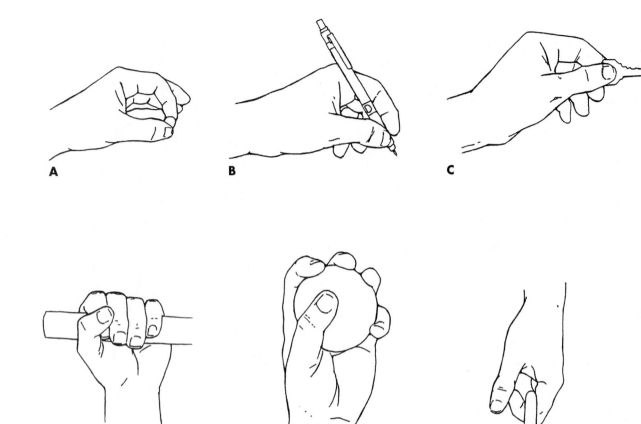

FIGURE 21-27

Prehension. **1.** *Pinch:* **A,** Tip. **B,** Palmar (three-jaw chuck). **C,** Lateral. **2.** *Grasp:*
D, Cylindrical. **E,** Spherical. **3.** *Hook:* **F,** Hook.

for this arch, as the annular ligaments secure the bony structures together, providing the stability through the wrist, and a mechanical advantage for strength of finger flexors.[7]

2. ***Distal transverse (metacarpal) arch:*** the intermetacarpal and metaphalangeal volar ligaments along with the metacarpal bones form the distal transverse arch, permitting thumb opposition to the other fingers, and rounding of the hand.[7]

3. ***Longitudinal (carpometacarpophalangeal) arch:*** formed by the intrinsic muscles of the hand and the carpal, metacarpal, and phalanges of each digit, the longitudinal arch is the basis for the three-jaw chuck position of the hand. Two other longitudinal arches, sometimes described are the oblique arch, where the thumb and fifth digit create an arch during opposition, and when the thumb and index finger form another arch with the web space.[7]

The hand typically functions in four phases: (1) reach, frequently recruiting the motions of the shoulder, the hand is extended as it is about to grasp or manipulate an object. (2) prehension, three patterns of prehension occur: pinch, grasp,

and hook, allowing humans to capture objects in their hands. (3) carry, the ability to move an object from one point to another. (4) release, the ability to discard or place an object at a specific point or time. The three phases of prehension can be further subdivided into more precise categories (Fig. 21-27).[10]

PINCH

Tip	Index finger to thumb (OK)
Palmer	Index and middle finger to thumb (three-jaw chuck)
Lateral	Thumb to lateral index finger (key grip)

GRASP

Cylindrical	Hand around cylinder
Spherical	Holding a ball

HOOK

Hook	PIP joints without thumb (link grip)

UPPER EXTREMITY ORTHOTICS

As stated earlier, when describing upper extremity orthotics it is very common, especially in the case of the hand, to use the term "splint" or "splinting." The use of orthoses and splints are interchangeable in this area.[13] There are two general classifications of splints or orthotics. The first: static orthoses, which do not permit motion and are often referred to as resting or positional splints, are used to position or to hold the wrist and hand. Static splints are commonly fabricated from low-temperature thermoplastics, or, if a permanent orthosis is required, high-temperature copolymer plastics are used. Dynamic orthoses permit movement and are splints that provide a dynamic force, generally using energy-storing materials like rubber bands, spring steel, wound coiled wire, or plastic with memory.

The design variations of upper limb orthoses are quite extensive and require considerable detail and explanation. The orthoses presented are single examples from selected categories of orthoses and are not an attempt to be all inclusive. Because of the complexity of the hand in terms of anatomy, function, and associated complications with each diagnosis, hand splinting or orthotic fabrication is clearly a specialty that requires careful examination of each client and, in many cases, frequent modifications to the orthosis to meet his or her individual needs.

Hand and Wrist Orthoses

HAND ORTHOSIS (BASIC OR SHORT OPPONENS) (FIG. 21-28)

Fabricated from low-temperature thermoplastics, this orthosis is designed to immobilize the first carpometacarpal (CMC) and metacarpophalangeal (MCP) joints and position the thumb in opposition and abduction to maintain the web space and the architecture of the hand for future procedures. There is no orthotic wrist control, therefore strong wrist flexor and extensors are required for functional use. Positioning of the hand can be functional for grasp (three-jaw chuck).
Indications include:

- Inflammation or injury of the thumb
- Median nerve lesions
- C6–7 spinal cord lesions
- Hemiplegia with loss of thumb opposition

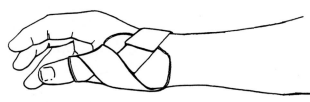

F I G U R E   2 1 - 2 8

Hand orthosis (HdO) (basic or short opponens).

F I G U R E   2 1 - 2 9

Wrist-hand orthosis (WHO) (long opponens splint or volar forearm wrist orthosis).

WRIST-HAND ORTHOSIS (LONG OPPONENS SPLINT OR VOLAR FOREARM WRIST ORTHOSIS) (FIG. 21-29)

Constructed from low-temperature thermoplastics, like the short opponens splint, the first CMC and MCP joints are immobilized with the thumb in extension and opposition, preserving the web space. The addition of wrist immobilization with a volar wrist control design, maintaining neutral or slight extension, offers less tension to the inflamed tendons, with reduction of movement to the thumb in general. Basically, this splint is a short opponens with wrist control.
Indications include:

- DeQuervains's tenosynovitis
- Median and ulnar nerve lesions
- C5–6 spinal cord lesions
- Wrist or thumb instability
- Degenerative or inflamed wrist thumb joint
- Scaphoid or Bennett's fracture-dislocation

VOLAR FOREARM STATIC WRIST HAND ORTHOSIS (RESTING HAND SPRINT) (FIG. 21-30)

Commonly referred to as a resting hand splint, the objective of this splint is to place the hand and wrist in a neutral, functional, or lumbrical position, with the MCP joints flexed to 60 to 90 degrees, and the PIP and DIP joints flexed to 0 to 45 degrees. The wrist is in slight extension to neutral. This position maintains the web space, preventing a flat hand or flexion contractures of the hand and is also used to reduce pain and inflammation.
Indications include:

- Flaccid hand due to paralysis
- Burns or healing skin grafts
- Dupuytren's release

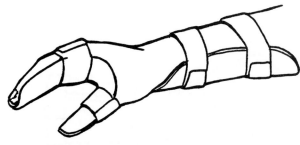

F I G U R E   2 1 - 3 0

Volar forearm static wrist-hand orthosis (resting hand sprint).

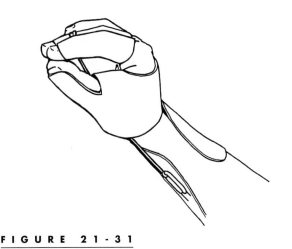

FIGURE 21-31

Wrist driven prehension orthosis (tenodesis orthosis).

- Degenerative or inflamed joints
- Volkman's ischemia
- Trauma to hand or wrist

WRIST DRIVEN PREHENSION ORTHOSIS (TENODESIS ORTHOSIS) (FIG. 21-31)

Several designs with a variety of materials from low-temperature thermoplastics to lightweight metals are used to fabricate these orthoses. Designed specifically for clients with spinal cord injury at the C6–7 level and who have the $3^-/5$ to $3^+/5$ extensor carpi radialis muscle strength, necessary to facilitate the passive flexion of the thumb index and middle fingers, to create passive three-jaw chuck hand position, or protect the hand for functional tenodesis. The orthotic assist for this motion depends on the design and the required assistance due to weakness. Some clients have the strength, or increase their strength, so that the orthosis is no longer mandatory.

UTENSIL HOLDERS (ADL CUFF, UNIVERSAL SPLINT) (FIG. 21-32)

A custom or prefabricated splint frequently fabricated from leather and flexible metal. A small sleeve or pouch is located within the palmar aspect, permitting the placement of eating utensils, grooming aids, and writing implements. Active shoulder motions and elbow flexion are required to manipulate the objects placed in the splint.

Indications include:

- C5–6 spinal cord leions
- Hemiplegia

EXTERNALLY POWERED PREHENSION ORTHOSIS (EPPO)

Ratchet Orthosis (Pawl Lever) (Fig. 21-33)

Generally indicated for clients with C5 tetraplegia, or when the extensor muscles of the hand are less than a 3/5 strength grade, a manually controlled orthosis can be used to provide pinch in the three-jaw chuck position. Operation of the orthosis is controlled by a ratchet bar located on the radial side of the splint. By tapping the knob with the other hand, or on another stable object, a simple gear system closes the fingers in discrete increments. A second ratchet button releases the spring-loaded gear system to open the hand. Many feeding, hygiene, and functional activities that otherwise would be impossible can be performed with this orthosis.

EXTERNALLY POWERED PREHENSION UNIT (EPPU)

The battery-driven externally powered prehension unit (EPPU) is another alternative that allows clients with paralysis or severe weakness to have hand function with the use of a WHO. The rechargeable battery power source drives the mechanical closing and opening of the hand. Gross movements of the upper extremity operate the rocker type electrical switch, producing pronation to produce prehension and supination to open the hand.

Mobile Arm Support (MAS)

When shoulder and elbow weakness limits upper limb mobility, the mobile arm support (MAS) orthotic system becomes a viable aid. The appliance clamps to a table, wheelchair, attaches to body jacket, or can be mounted on the iliac crest with ambulatory patients. The client must have $2^+/5$ strength of the shoulder or trunk to depress the elbow, thus elevating the hand by using a ball-bearing forearm component that permits movement of the flaccid upper extremity and permits horizontal arm adduction and abduction of the shoulder.

Indications include:

- Spinal cord lesion
- Guillain-Barré syndrome
- Amyotrophic lateral sclerosis
- Muscular dystrophy
- Poliomyelitis

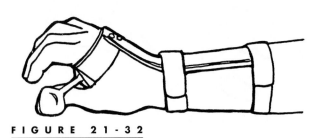

FIGURE 21-32

Utensil holders (ADL cuff, universal splint).

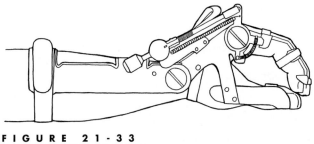

FIGURE 21-33

Ratchet orthosis (Pawl lever) orthosis.

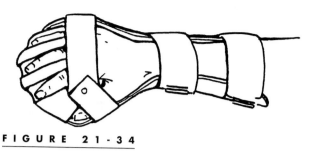

FIGURE 21-34

Tone-reducing orthosis.

TONE-REDUCING ORTHOSES (FIG. 21-34)

Tone-reducing or antispasticity splints are prescribed when hypertonicity is present. The primary objective is to reduce flexor tone, reduce the incidence of contractures, and maintain the arches by placing the hand and fingers in an extended and abducted position, creating firm pressure to the palmar surface of the hand. Care must be taken to avoid areas of pressure and potential skin irritation. The splints are typically worn with a 2-hour on, 2-hour off wearing schedule throughout the day. A variety of designs include: antispasticity ball splint, Snook splint, Cone splint (Rood splint), Bobath splint, finger abduction splint, and dynafoam wrist–hand splint.

Elbow Orthosis

STATIC ORTHOSES (SPLINTS)

Frequently custom-fabricated from low-temperature thermoplastics, these splints are formed over the volar surface of the elbow for the purpose of restricting motion and promoting tissue healing. These splints can be removed for topical treatments and hygiene. As ROM returns, the angle of the splint can be adjusted by reforming the plastic shell, a process similar to that of serial casting. Indications for the static splints include: burns, fractures, tendon, nerve, vascular repairs, and cubital tunnel syndrome.

DYNAMIC ORTHOSES (SPLINTS)

When ROM is lost and there is a need to increase the resting length of the elbow, dynamic splints provide a low load with prolonged stretch, with the intent of stretching the soft tissues and skin over time. The mechanical or dynamic splints may be utilized in the same fashion as serial casting techniques. This type of splint is used for clients with burns and elbow contractures.

Shoulder Orthoses

Arm Slings

Commonly made of fabric, an assortment of designs include the figure eight, universal sling, cuff sling, orthopedic sling, bandana sling, and flail arm sling. They are used to immobilize and promote healing of tissue immediately after injury. For the neurologically involved client who presents with hemiplegia, there are designs such as the hemi arm sling, worn to prevent subluxation of the shoulder while the arm is flaccid.

SHOULDER-ELBOW-WRIST ORTHOSES (AIRPLANE SPLINT)

Shoulder-elbow-wrist orthoses, more commonly referred to as airplane splints, are used to protect the soft tissues of the shoulder and prevent contractures. Most frequently custom fit to the client, although prefabricated kits are available, the shoulder is abducted 70 to 90 degrees, with the majority of body weight borne on the iliac crest and lateral trunk. Custom fabrication permits specific placement of joint angles and can be adjusted as healing progresses throughout rehabilitation.

Illustrations (Figs. 21-1 through 21-34) by Frank Angulo. Reproduced with permission of Advanced Rehabilitation Therapy, Inc.

REFERENCES

1. Bartelink DL. The role of abdominal pressure in relieving the pressure on the lumbar intervertebral discs. *J Bone Joint Surg* 39B:718–725, 1957.
2. Blount WP, Moe JH. *The Milwaukee Brace.* Baltimore, MD, Williams & Wilkins Co, 1973.
3. Cailliet R. Biomechanics of the spine. *Phys Med Rehabil Clin North Am* 3:1–28, 1992.
4. Emans JB, et al: The Boston bracing system for idiopathic scoliosis: Follow-up results in 295 patients. *Spine* 11:172, 1986.
5. Goldberg B, Hsu JD, eds. *Atlas of Orthoses and Assistive Devices/American Academy of Orthopaedic Surgeons.* 3rd ed. St. Louis, Mosby-Year Book, Inc., 1985.
6. Johnson RM, et al: Cervical orthosis: A study comparing their effectiveness in restricting cervical motion in normal subjects. *J Bone Joint Surg* 59A:332–339, 1977
7. Kapandji IA. *The Physiology of the Joints: Vol. I.* Upper Limb. 2nd ed. Edinburgh, Churchill Livingstone, 1970.
8. Kottke FJ, Lehmann JF, eds. *Krusen's Handbook of Physical Medicine and Rehabilitation.* 4th ed. Philadelphia, WB Saunders Co., 1990.
9. Lantz SA, Schultz AB. Lumbar spine orthosis wearing: I. Restriction of gross body motion. *Spine* 11:834–837, 1986.
10. Lusardi MM, Nielsen CC. *Orthotics and Prosthetics in Rehabilitation.* Woburn, MA, Butterworth-Heinemann, 2000.
11. McGill SM, Norman RW. Reassessment of the role of intra-abdominal pressure in spinal compression. *Ergonomics* 30:1565–1588, 1987.
12. McGill SM, Norman RW, Sharratt MT. The effect of an abdominal belt on trunk muscle activity and intra-abdominal pressure during squat lifts. *Ergonomics* 33:147–160, 1990.
13. McKee P, Morgan L. *Orthotics in Rehabilitation: Splinting*

the Hand and Body. Philadelphia, F.A. Davis Co., 1998.

14. McKenzie AR, Lipscomb PR. Corsets on and off. *J Bone Joint Surg,* 61B:384, 1979.

15. Morris JM. Biomechanics of the spine. *Arch Surg* 107:418–423, 1973.

16. Morris JM. Low back bracing. *Clin Orthop* 102:126–132, 1974.

17. Myers RS, ed. *Saunders Manual of Physical Therapy Practice.* Ist ed. Philadelphia, WB Saunders Co., 1995.

18. Nachemson A, Morris JM. In vivo measurement of intradiscal pressure: Discometry, a method for determining pressure in the lower lumbar discs. *J Bone Joint Surg* A: 1077–1092, 1964.

19. Nachemson A, Schultz A, Andersson G. Mechanical effectiveness studies of lumbar spine orthosis. *Scand J Rehabil Med* (suppl 9):139–149, 1983.

20. Nawoczenski DA, Epler ME, eds. *Orthotics in Functional Rehabilitation of the Lower Limb.* Philadelphia, WB Saunders Co., 1997.

21. New York University Medical Center. Lower-limb orthotics. New York, *NYU Post-graduate Medical School, Prosthetics and Orthotics* January 1986.

22. Redford JB, Basmajian JV, Trautman P, eds. *Orthotics: Clinical Practice and Rehabilitation Technology.* New York, Churchill Livingstone, 1995.

23. Russek AS. Biomechanical and physiological basis for ambulatory treatment of low back pain. 4:21–26, 1976.

24. Shurr DG, Cook TM. *Prosthetics and Orthotics.* Norwalk, CT, Appleton & Lange, 1990.

Using Assistive Gait Devices in Rehabilitation

Kevin Robinson and Sussette Robinson

O B J E C T I V E S

After completing this chapter, the student therapist should be able to do the following:

- Identify the different types of assistive devices.
- Explain the advantages and disadvantages of the different types of assistive devices.
- Discuss the physiologic demands of ambulation with assistive gait devices.
- Identify the muscles needed to be strength-tested prior to ambulating with assistive gait devices.
- Discuss the safety precautions that need to be followed before and during ambulation with assistive gait devices.
- Determine the appropriate assistive device for a patient.
- Instruct a patient in the proper use of assistive gait devices.

Many of the patients you will work with will need to use an assistive device for ambulation. Some of the reasons for using an assistive gait device are poor balance, inability to bear weight on a lower extremity due to fracture or other injury, paralysis involving one or both lower extremities, or amputation of a lower extremity. There are many advantages to early ambulation following an injury. Some of the advantages include aiding in circulation, preventing calcium loss in bones, and aiding the pulmonary and renal systems.[1] (See Fig. 22-1.)

It is important for the patient to be carefully evaluated in order to select the appropriate assistive device to meet the patient's needs. The therapist must be aware of the patient's total medical condition, prior ambulatory status, obstacles the patient will encounter in the home environment (e.g., stairs, family support), and weight-bearing status of the involved extremity when considering which type of assistive device to use with the patient. For example, your patient may be taking medications that could adversely effect balance and coordination. Another consideration is whether your patient has been on prolonged bed rest. If this is the case, caution must be taken when assisting these patients to an upright position. A sudden decrease in blood pressure, a condition known as orthostatic hypotension, could result, causing the patient to feel faint or lose consciousness.

PRIOR TO SEEING THE PATIENT

Prior to seeing the patient, the therapist should determine the patient's current medical status, surgeries that have been performed, weight-bearing restrictions (if applicable), medications being taken, past medical history, sensory deficits (poor vision or hearing), and prior functional status. Once the therapist has an overview of the patient's condition, then they are ready to see the patient.

INITIAL PATIENT ENCOUNTER

During the initial interview with the patient, the therapist thoroughly explains any weight-bearing precautions the physician has ordered and other safety precautions in terms the patient will understand. The clinician should also assess the patient's ability to follow instructions and to comprehend what he or she is saying. The therapist will need to determine the range of motion of the extremities and the strength of the primary muscles required for ambulation. The specific techniques to determine joint range of motion and muscle strength are beyond the scope of this chapter. The primary muscles required for

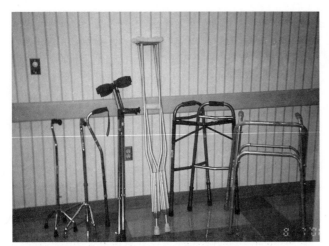

FIGURE 22-1

Examples of different types of assistive devices. From left to right: two types of quad canes, a straight cane, forearm (Loftstrand) crutches, axillary crutches, folding walker, and a standard walker.

ambulation with axillary crutches, using a three-point (non-weight bearing on one lower extremity) crutch gait pattern, are the scapula stabilizers, shoulder depressors, shoulder extensors, elbow extensors, and finger flexors for the upper extremity. The patient must press downward on the assistive gait device in order to move the body forward. When using axillary crutches and a three-point gait pattern, studies have shown that between 44.4 and 49 percent of the patient's body weight is transmitted through the upper extremities.[7,17] The scapular, shoulder, and elbow musculature supports the body's weight while the nonaffected lower extremity is moved forward. The finger flexors hold the handpiece of the assistive gait device.

The primary lower-extremity muscles in the weight-bearing lower extremity are the hip extensors, hip abductors, knee extensors, knee flexors, and ankle dorsiflexors.[14] While the patient is standing on the unaffected lower extremity, the muscles of the hip and knee provide stability. The ankle dorsiflexors position the foot so that it can clear the floor when the limb is swinging forward.[14,17]

Next, the therapist determines the appropriate assistive device and gait pattern based upon assessment and treatment goals. Prepare the patient for ambulation by thoroughly explaining and demonstrating how to use the assistive device and the appropriate gait pattern. The therapist should be sure that all of the patient's questions have been answered. It is very common for patients to be anxious and display a fear of falling when first learning how to use an assistive gait device.

Clear the area of obstacles prior to beginning ambulation. If the patient is in a hospital bed or a wheelchair, the therapist should make sure the wheels are locked prior to standing (Fig. 22-2). The patient should have proper footwear. Do not allow the patient to ambulate while wearing slippers, socks, or no shoes at all. This can lead to falls and additional injury.

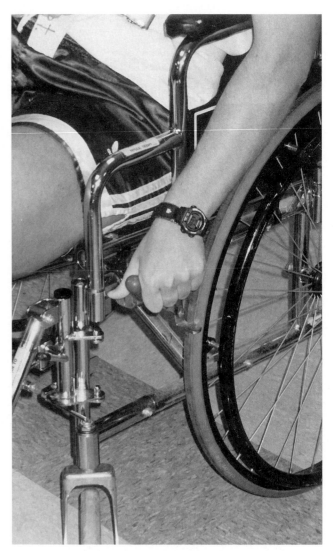

FIGURE 22-2

Make sure the wheels of the wheelchair are locked prior to assisting your patient to stand.

Proper footwear fits securely, has a nonskid sole, and has an enclosed heel.

In order to assist the patient from a sitting to a standing position, have the patient first slide to the edge of the seat or bed. The therapist should then apply a gait belt snugly around the patient's waist. The gait belt will be used to assist the patient if he or she has a lapse in balance. Next, the patient should be instructed to lean the body weight forward, over the lower extremities, and push down on the armrest or the bed with the hands. Once standing, the patient will then grasp the assistive gait device. The therapist should make sure the assistive gait device fits the patient properly. If it does not, then the patient should be assisted to a sitting position before the equipment is readjusted.

While the patient is ambulating, continually monitor the patient to determine if he or she is placing the appropriate amount of weight on the affected lower extremity. Make sure the patient is performing the gait pattern correctly. Observe the patient's physiologic response to ambulation. Frequently evaluate the patient's vital signs, general appearance, and mental alertness during and following the activity. Ambulating with an assistive gait device is less efficient and requires greater energy than normal ambulation.[2,5–7,16,18,19] In a study of three-point crutch ambulation in patients with lower-extremity fractures, Waters et al found that after 5 minutes of crutch ambulation, the rate of oxygen uptake was 32 percent greater and the heart rate was 53 percent greater than the value for normal walking. The researchers concluded that a three-point crutch gait pattern was "a severe exercise challenge requiring strenuous arm and shoulder exertion under anaerobic conditions."[19]

TYPES OF ASSISTIVE GAIT DEVICES

When choosing an assistive gait device, the therapist considers the amount of support the patient will need and the patient's ability to manipulate the device. The selection of an assistive gait device is based on the patient's disability, coordination, and stability. For example, you may have two patients with the same type of fracture. One of the patients may use crutches if he or she has adequate stability and coordination to safely use them. The other patient may require a walker due to poor stability and coordination. As the patients' abilities improve, they may advance to an assistive device providing less stability and support for easier maneuverability

Assistive gait devices are designed to improve the patient's stability by increasing the base of support. The categories of assistive ambulation devices, in order from greatest to least amount of support, are parallel bars, walkers, axillary crutches, forearm (Loftstrand) crutches, two canes, and one cane.[11,15] All categories of assistive gait devices are adjustable and come in tall, adult, and child sizes. Additionally, a special platform can be attached to walkers or axillary crutches for patients who are unable to bear weight through the hand, wrist, or forearm (Fig. 22-3).

Parallel Bars

Parallel bars are used when maximal patient support and stability are required. The gait pattern can be practiced in parallel bars and the fit of the assistive device can be checked. The parallel bars limit mobility. So once the patient becomes proficient with the appropriate gait pattern, the patient must be progressed to another assistive gait device to be mobile.[15] Care must be taken so that the patient does not become dependent on the parallel bars.

The parallel bar height needs to be adjusted to provide 15 to 20 degrees of elbow flexion when the patient is standing erect and is grasping the bars about 6 inches anterior to the hips.[15] The bars need to be approximately 2 inches wider than the patient's hips when the patient is centered between the bars.

Walkers

Walkers provide maximum stability and support and allow the patient to be mobile. Walkers are designed in many styles, but

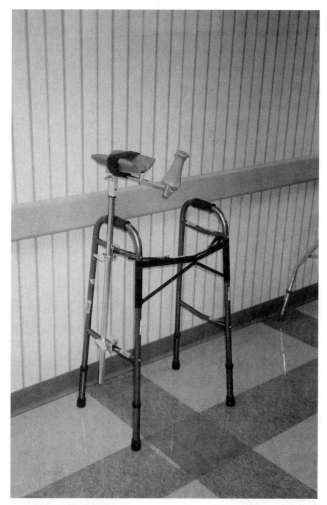

FIGURE 22-3
Folding walker with platform attachment.

all have four legs. Some may have two or four wheels. Wheels allow the patient to gently push the device forward as opposed to picking the walker up to move it forward. Another variation in the design of the walker is the ability to fold the walker when it is not being used. This feature allows for easier transportation in a car and for storage.

Disadvantages of using walkers are the following:

1. Walkers are cumbersome and difficult to store and transport.
2. Walkers are very difficult to use on stairs.
3. Walkers reduce the speed of ambulation.
4. By using a walker, the patient is unable to use a normal gait pattern.

To properly fit a patient with a walker, adjust the height of the walker so that the patient has between 15 and 25 degrees of elbow flexion when grasping the handles of the walker. Another way of adjusting the walker is to align the top of the handgrip with the patient's ulnar styloid process while the patient is standing with the arm relaxed at the patient's side.[11,15]

Axillary Crutches

Axillary crutches are used with patients who do not require as much stability or support as provided by a walker. Axillary crutches allow the patient to perform a greater variety of gait patterns and ambulate at a faster pace.

The disadvantages of axillary crutches include the following:

1. Axillary crutches are less stable than a walker.
2. Improper use of axillary crutches can cause injury to the neurovascular structures in the axillary region.[7] (See Fig. 22-4)
3. Axillary crutches require good standing balance by the patient.
4. Geriatric patients may feel insecure or may not have the necessary upper-body strength to use axillary crutches.

To properly fit a patient with axillary crutches, both the length of the crutches and the height of the handpiece must be properly adjusted. The length of the axillary crutch should be adjusted so the therapist can fit two or three fingers between the top of the axillary crutch and the patient's axilla. When standing, the tips of the crutches should be approximately 6 inches from the toes of the patient's shoes at a 45-degree angle.[7,11,15–17,20] Goh et al found when axillary crutches were used improperly, 34 percent of the patient's body weight was carried by the underarm.[7]

The handpiece of the axillary crutch should be adjusted so the patient has 15 to 25 degrees of elbow flexion.[7,11,15–17,20] Reisman and colleagues, performing a biomechanical analysis of subjects using axillary crutches, found increasing the elbow flexion angle above 30 degrees resulted in a 100% increase in elbow extension moment.[16]

Forearm Crutches

Forearm crutches, also referred to as Loftstrand or Canadian crutches, are used when the patient is going to need crutches permanently, or for long periods of time. People who use Loftstrand crutches must have the stability and coordination to use them.[11] Using forearm crutches requires no more energy, increased oxygen consumption or heart rate, than axillary crutches.[6,11,18] This type of crutch has the advantage of being easily stored and transported. There is no risk of injury to the neurovascular structures in the axillary region when using this type of crutches.[6,15,18]

The disadvantages of forearm crutches are the following:

1. Forearm crutches are less stable than a walker.
2. They require good standing balance and upper-body strength.
3. Geriatric patients sometimes feel insecure with these crutches. They may not have the necessary upper-body strength to use forearm crutches.

To fit the patient with forearm crutches, have the patient stand with arms hanging loosely by the side. Place the crutch parallel to the lateral aspect of the tibia and femur. Adjust the height of the handpiece so that it is level with the ulnar styloid process. This will insure the elbow is flexed between 15 and 25 degrees. The top of the forearm cuff should be adjusted so that it is located 1 to 1.5 inches distal to the olecranon process of the elbow while the patient is grasping the handpiece of the crutch with the wrist in neutral flexion-extension.[6,11,15,18] (See Fig. 22-5.)

Canes

Canes are used to compensate for impaired balance or to increase stability while ambulating. There are several styles of canes, but the standard is known as the J cane.[11,15] A cane is functional on stairs and in confined areas. It is also easily stored and transported. The disadvantage of a cane is that it provides limited support due to its small base of support.

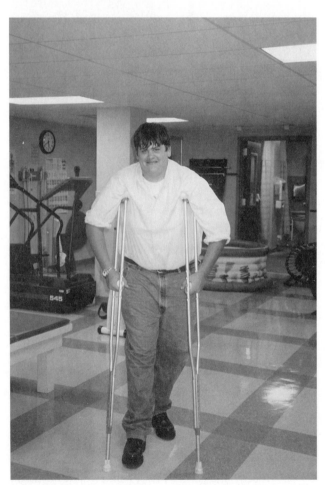

FIGURE 22-4

Improper use of axillary crutches. In this case, the crutches are too long for this patient, causing excessive pressure in the axilla. This could lead to damage of the neurovascular structures in this region.

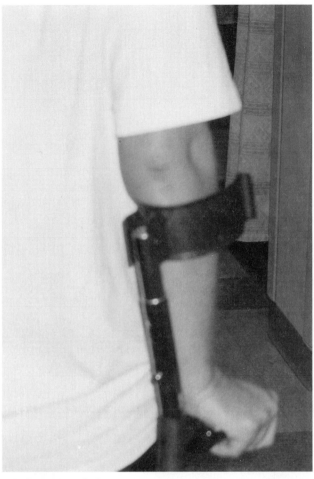

FIGURE 22-5

The top of the forearm crutch should be 1 to 1.5 inches distal to the olecranon process of the elbow while the patient is grasping the handpiece of the crutch with the wrist in neutral flexion-extension.

To fit a patient with a cane, have the patient stand and place the cane parallel to the lateral aspect of the tibia and femur. Adjust the handpiece of the cane so it is level with the ulnar styloid process. This will provide 15 to 25 degrees of elbow flexion when the patient grasps the handle of the cane.

BASIC GAIT PATTERNS

The selection of the proper gait pattern is dependent upon the patient's balance, strength, coordination, functional needs, and weight-bearing status.

Four-Point Pattern

A four-point gait pattern is used when the patient requires maximum assistance with balance. It requires the use of bilateral assistive gait devices (canes or crutches). The pattern begins with the forward movement of one of the assistive gait devices, and then the contralateral lower extremity, the other assistive gait device, and finally the opposite lower extremity (e.g., right cane, then left foot; left cane, then right foot). This is a slow gait pattern, but a stable one.[10,11,15]

Two-Point Pattern

The two-point gait pattern requires the use of bilateral assistive gait devices. This pattern is faster than the four-point gait, and according to McDonough and Razza-Doherty, the two-point gait pattern closely approximates a normal gait pattern and should be encouraged.[10] This pattern does require the patient to coordinate moving an assistive gait device and the contralateral lower extremity at the same time. This pattern is less stable than the four-point pattern.

Modified Four-Point and Two-Point Gait Patterns

The modified four-point and two-point gait patterns require only one assistive gait device. These patterns are used with patients who have only one functional upper extremity or who use only one assistive device. These patterns are also commonly referred to as a "hemi" gait or "hemi" pattern.[15] The assistive device is used with the opposite upper extremity to the involved lower extremity, if possible. This widens the base of support. Additionally, studies looking at the biomechanical aspects of ambulation with canes show that patients using the cane on the contralateral side of the involved lower extremity have greater stride lengths, cadence, and walking velocities than when using the cane on the same side as the involved lower extremity.[3,4,8]

Three-Point Gait Pattern

The three-point gait pattern requires two crutches or a walker, but it cannot be performed with two canes. This pattern is used when the patient is only able to bear full weight on one lower extremity. As mentioned earlier in this chapter, when using axillary crutches and a three-point gait pattern, studies have shown that between 44.4 and 49 percent of the patient's body weight is transmitted through the upper extremities.[7,17] So the strength of the upper extremities and uninvolved lower extremity must be assessed prior to attempting ambulation. Additionally, studies have also shown that the energy cost (oxygen consumption) for this type of gait is about twice as high as normal walking.[6] After 5 minutes of crutch ambulation, using a three-point pattern, the rate of oxygen consumption was 32 percent higher and the heart rate was 53 percent higher than normal values for walking.[5–7,19,20] The walker or crutches are moved forward first. Next, the involved lower extremity is advanced. Then the patient presses down on the assistive gait device and advances the uninvolved lower extremity. If the uninvolved lower extremity is advanced to where it is parallel to the involved

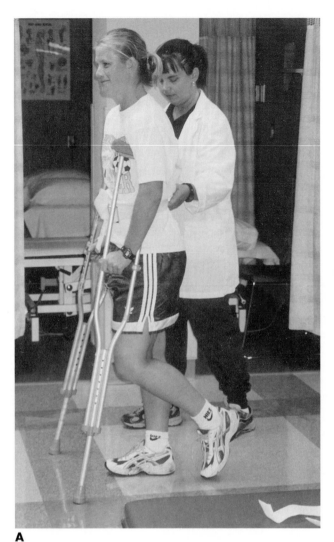

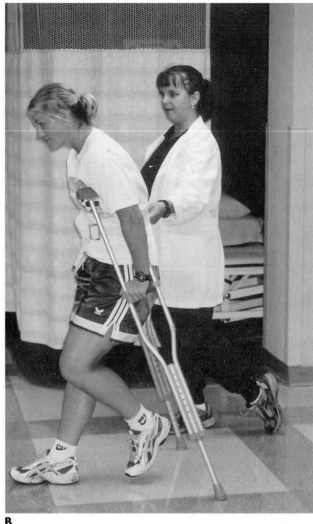

A   **B**

FIGURE 22-6

Example of a patient (nonweight bearing on the left lower extremity) using a
swing-through gait pattern. (A) The crutches are advanced forward. (B) The patient
presses down on the handpieces and advances her right (noninvolved) lower extremity
forward.

lower extremity, then this would be a "swing to" pattern. If
the uninvolved lower extremity is advanced ahead of the uninvolved lower extremity, then this would be a "swing through"
pattern.[7,15,18–20] See Fig. 22-6.

Modified Three-Point Gait Pattern

The modified three-point gait pattern requires two crutches or
a walker. This pattern is used when the patient can bear full
weight with one lower extremity but is only allowed to touch
the involved lower extremity to the floor. This is known as
touchdown weight bearing (TDWB). The term "partial weight
bearing" (PWB) refers to when the involved lower extremity
is allowed only part of the patient's weight to be transferred
through it.

In this pattern, the walker or crutches are advanced first,
and then the involved lower extremity is advanced forward. The
patient presses down on the assistive gait device and advances
the uninvolved lower extremity using either a "swing to" or
"swing through" pattern (Fig. 22-7).

FUNCTIONAL ACTIVITIES WITH ASSISTIVE GAIT DEVICES

Once an assistive gait device and the appropriate gait pattern
have been chosen, the patient will need instruction in their
use as well as how to perform functional activities with the
devices.

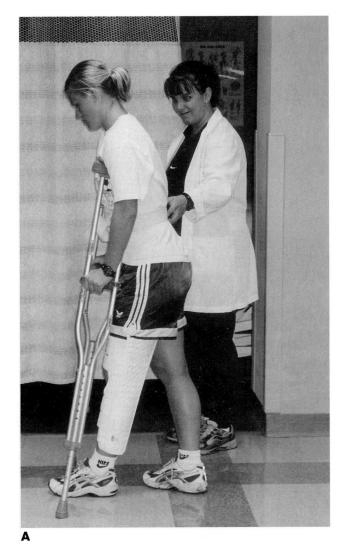

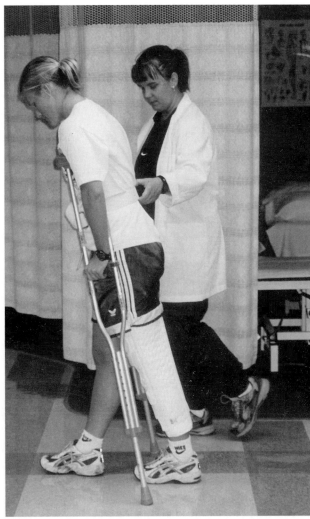

A   B

FIGURE 22-7

Example of a patient (partial weight bearing on the left lower extremity) using a swing-through gait pattern. (A) The crutches are advanced forward, followed by the involved lower extremity. (B) The patient presses down on the handpieces and advances her right (noninvolved) lower extremity forward.

Helping the Patient Come From Sit to Stand

When assisting the patient to come from sit to stand, the therapist stands on the involved side of the patient.

WALKER

Before the patient can begin ambulation with a walker, the patient must first learn to safely come from a sitting position to a standing position. Care must be taken to assure that the wheels of the bed or the wheelchair are locked before attempting to stand. Once the wheels of the bed or wheelchair have been locked, apply a gait belt around the patient's waist. This will allow the therapist to assist if the patient has a lapse in balance without grabbing hold of the patient's arms or clothing, which could lead to further injury. Enable the patient to sit on the front edge of the chair or bed. Sitting forward on the bed or in the chair places the center of gravity closer to the center of the patient's base of support. This will make it easier for the patient to stand. Remind the patient of any weight-bearing restrictions. Have the patient lean forward and push up with the hands from the bed or armrests. Once up, the patient should grasp the handpieces of the walker and begin to ambulate. Do not allow the patient to try to pull forward on the walker. This may cause the walker to tip forward, resulting in loss of balance.

CRUTCHES

If the patient is using crutches, assist the patient to the edge of the chair or bed as described above. Apply a gait belt and remind the patient of any weight-bearing restrictions. The patient holds both crutches with the hand on the same side as the involved lower extremity. The patient then presses down on the handpieces of the crutches, the armrest or bed, and with the uninvolved lower extremity to stand. Once standing, the patient then moves the crutches into position and begins to ambulate.

CANES

If the patient is using one or two canes, assist the patient to the edge of the chair or bed as described above. Apply a gait belt and remind the patient of any weight-bearing restrictions. Place the handpiece of the cane or canes on the armrest of the chair or lean them against the edge of the bed. Then have the patient lean forward and push up with the hands from the bed or armrests. Once standing, the patient should grasp the handpiece(s) of the cane(s) with the appropriate hand and begin to ambulate.

Sitting Down

WALKER

In order for the patient to sit down using a walker, the patient must first back up against the front edge of the bed or chair. If the patient has difficulty bending the knee of the involved lower extremity, have the patient slowly advance the lower extremity forward. Next, have the patient reach for the bed or armrest with both hands and slowly sit down.

CRUTCHES

In order for the patient to sit down with crutches, the patient must first back up against the front edge of the bed or chair. If the patient has difficulty bending the knee of the involved lower extremity, have the patient slowly advance the lower extremity forward. Next, the patient moves both crutches to the hand on the side of the involved lower extremity. With that hand holding onto both hand pieces of the crutches, have the patient reach back for the bed or armrest with the other hand and then slowly sit down. Do not allow the patient to try to sit down with the axillary crutches still under the axilla. This could cause injury to the neurovascular structures in the axilla and/or lead to the patient falling.

CANES

When sitting with one or two canes, the patient should back up against the front edge of the bed or chair. If the patient has difficulty bending the knee of the involved lower extremity, have the patient slowly advance the lower extremity forward. The patient should place the handpiece of the cane against the edge of the chair or bed. Next, the patient should reach back for the bed or armrest and slowly sit down.

Ascending Stairs

WALKER

In order to ascend steps with a walker, the patient must first move to the front edge of the step. The walker will have to be turned sideways and placed on the opposite side of the handrail or wall. The patient will then grasp the handrail, if available, with one hand and the top handpiece of the walker with the other. Next, the patient will press down on the walker and handrail, and advance the uninvolved lower extremity on top of the first step. The patient will then advance the uninvolved lower extremity to the first step and then move the walker forward. This process is repeated as the patient moves up the steps. Due to the narrowness of most residential steps, this author does not recommend the use of a walker with more then three steps. When there are more than three steps involved, the walker frame can not be properly balanced and increases the risk of falls (Figs. 22-8 and 22-9).

CRUTCHES

To ascend steps or stairs with crutches, the patient moves to the front edge of the steps. If there is a handrail, the patient should use the handrail and turn the crutch sideways, grasping both the crutch and handrail with one hand. If the patient is unable to grasp both the crutch and handrail with one hand, or if the handrail is not stable, then the patient should use both crutches only. Once the patient is at the front edge of the step, the patient will press down on the crutches and handrail, if applicable, and advance the uninvolved lower extremity to the first step. The patient will then stand erect and advance the involved lower extremity and finally the crutches. This process is repeated for the remaining steps (Figs. 22-10 and 22-11).

CANES

To ascend steps or stairs with one or two canes, the patient moves to the front edge of the steps. If there is a handrail, the patient should use the handrail and turn the cane sideways, grasping both the cane and handrail with one hand. If the patient is unable to grasp both the cane and handrail with one hand, or if the handrail is not stable, then the patient should use the cane(s) only. Once the patient is at the front edge of the step, the patient will press down on the cane or handrail, if applicable, and advance the uninvolved lower extremity to the first step. The patient will then stand erect and advance the involved lower extremity. This process is repeated for the remaining steps.

Descending Stairs

WALKER

In order to descend steps with a walker, the patient must first move to the front edge of the step. The walker will have to be turned sideways and placed on the opposite side of the handrail or wall. The patient will then grasp the handrail, if available, with one hand and the top handpiece of the walker with the other. Next, the patient will lower the involved lower extremity down to the first step. Then the patient will press down on the walker and handrail and advance the uninvolved lower extremity down the first step. This process is repeated as the patient moves down the steps. Due to the narrowness of most

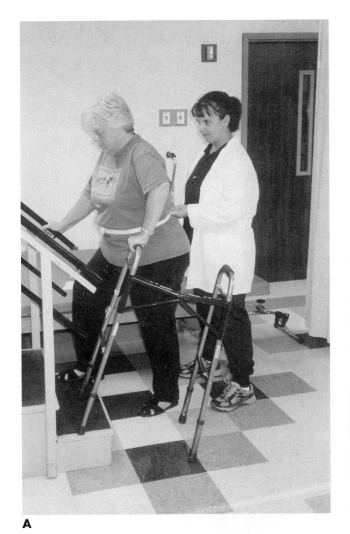

A

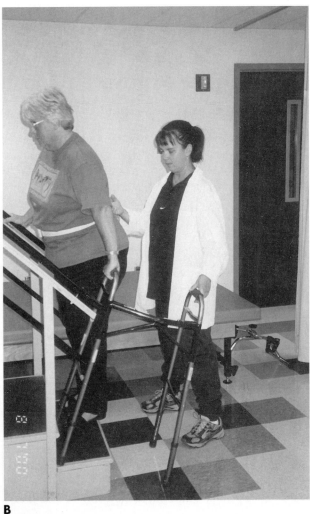

B

FIGURE 22-8

Example of a patient ascending and descending steps using a walker. (A) The walker is turned sideways and two of its legs are advanced to the next step. Then the patient will press down on the top edge of the walker and handrail (if available) to advance their noninvolved lower extremity to the next step, and the process is repeated for subsequent steps.

residential steps, the authors do not recommend the use of a walker with more than three steps. The reason for this is that with more than three steps, the walker's frame is not able to be properly balanced and increases the risk of falls.

CRUTCHES

To descend steps or stairs with crutches, the patient moves to the front edge of the steps. If there is a handrail, the patient should use the handrail and turn the crutch sideways, grasping both the crutch and handrail with one hand. If the patient is unable to grasp both the crutch and handrail with one hand, or if the handrail is not stable, then the patient should use both crutches only. Once the patient is at the front edge of the step, the patient will lower the involved lower extremity down to the first step. Next, the patient will press down on the crutches

and handrail, if applicable, and advance the uninvolved lower extremity down to the first step. This process is repeated for the remaining steps.

CANES

To descend steps or stairs with one or two canes, the patient moves to the front edge of the steps. If there is a handrail, the patient should use the handrail and turn the cane sideways, grasping both the cane and handrail with one hand. If the patient is unable to grasp both the cane and handrail with one hand, or if the handrail is not stable, then the patient should use cane or canes only. Once the patient is at the front edge of the step, the patient will lower the involved lower extremity down to the first step. Next, the patient will press down on the cane(s) and handrail, if applicable, and advance the uninvolved

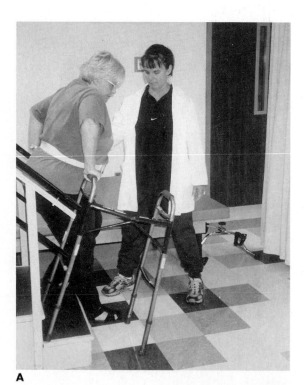
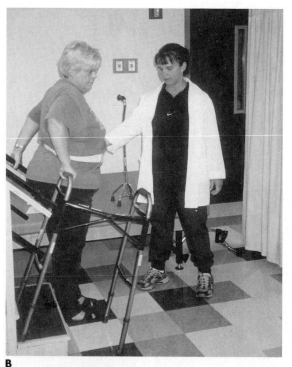

A

B

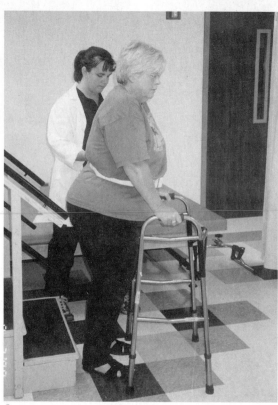

C

FIGURE 22-9

In order to descend steps with a walker, the process is reversed. (A) With two legs of
the walker placed on the lower level, the patient presses down on the top edge of the
walker and handrail if (available) to advance their involved lower extremity down to the
next step. (B) The patient then advances the noninvolved lower extremity down. (C) The
walker is then turned and placed in front of the patient for ambulation.

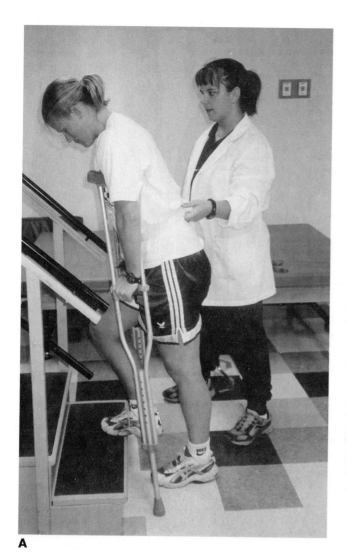
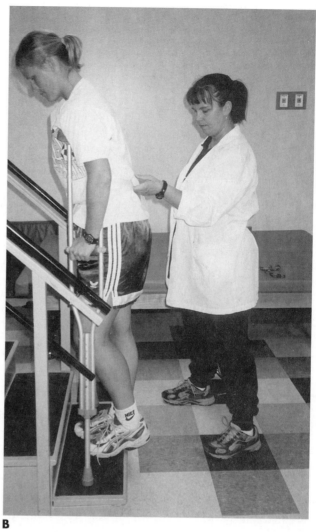

A   B

FIGURE 22-10

Ascending stairs with axillary crutches. (A) The patient pushes down on the handpieces of the crutches and advances the noninvolved lower extremity ot the next step. (B) Then the involved lower extremity is advanced and finally the crutches.

lower extremity down to the first step. This process is repeated for the remaining steps.

GUARDING A PATIENT USING AN ASSISTIVE GAIT DEVICE

The therapist will need to provide physical support and instruction while working with a patient using an assistive gait device. The therapist will need to stand on the involved side of the patient, holding the gait belt, while the patient is moving from a sitting to standing position. This way the therapist will be able to assist the patient on the side where the patient will most likely have difficulty.

When ambulating with a patient, the therapist should be just behind the patient, standing toward the involved side. The

therapist should hold the gait belt with a supinated grip. If the patient has a lapse in balance, the therapist will have a strong grip on the belt in order to assist the patient or possibly help lower the patient to the floor. The therapist should not try to "catch" or pick up a falling patient. By doing so, the therapist may injure himself or herself or drop the patient. Instead, if the patient loses balance, slowly lower the patient to the floor. Then request assistance from another coworker or family member when moving the patient from the floor.

When instructing the patient on ascending and descending the stairs, the therapist should hold onto the gait belt with one hand and the stair rail with the other. The therapist should always be on the lower step than the patient. This way, if the patient loses balance, the therapist can prevent the patient from falling down the steps. If the therapist is on the step above the patient and the patient loses balance, the therapist and patient are at risk of falling down the stairs.

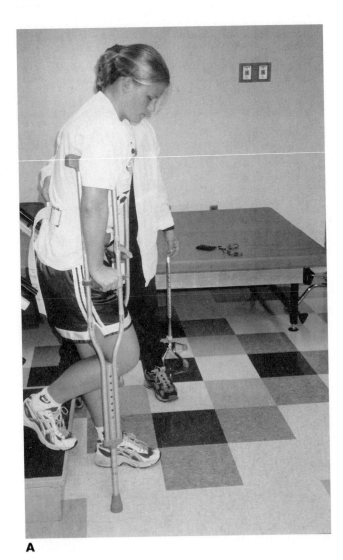
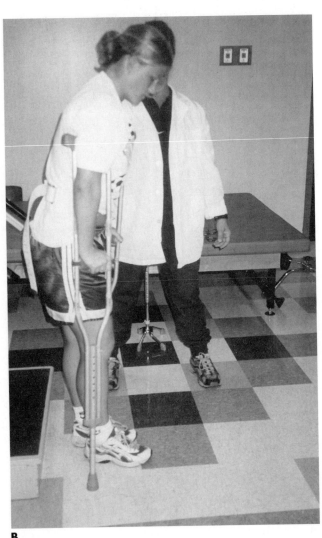

A   B

FIGURE 22-11

Descending stairs with axillary crutches. (A) The patient pushes down on the
handpieces of the crutches and lowers the involved lower extremity to the lower step.
(B) Then the noninvolved lower extremity is advanced and finally the crutches.

HOME INSTRUCTIONS

Provide written and illustrated instructions for using the assistive gait device your patient takes home. These instructions
should also include a telephone number the patient can call
with questions. Make sure your patient understands any weight-
bearing precautions the patient may have. Additionally, the
therapist will need to be sure the patient understands how to
maneuver any physical barriers in the home such as steps. Instruct the patient to avoid having throw rugs in the home while
using an assistive device. A throw rug may cause the assistive
device to slip out from under the patient. Other obstacles to
avoid are spilled liquids on tile or wooden floors or using assistive gait devices outside in inclement weather such as sleet

or snow. Finally, remind the patient not to be in a rush while
ambulating with an assistive gait device. These devices are built
for stability, not speed.

SUMMARY

- Assistive devices are commonly used in orthopedic rehabilitation. Reasons for use include: poor balance, inability to
  bear weight secondary to injury, paralysis, and lower extremity amputation.
- Prior to seeing the patient, the rehabilitation specialist should
  obtain a thorough overview of the patient's condition, including: medical status, weight-bearing restrictions, medications, and prior functional status.

- When employing the use of assistive devices, the rehabilitation specialist must be aware of any physiological concerns that may affect performance.
- The type of assistive gait device and the gait pattern utilized should be chosen depending on the amount of support the patient will need and the ability of the patient to manipulate the device within their environment.

REFERENCES

1. Bruno J. Some considerations and guidelines for crutch walking. *Clin Podiatry* 1:291, 1984.
2. Dounis E, Wilson RS, Steventon RD. A comparison of efficiency of three types of crutches using oxygen consumption. *Rheumatol Rehabil* 19:252, 1980.
3. Edwards BG. Contralateral and ipsilateral cane usage by patients with total knee or hip replacements. *Arch Phys Med Rehabil* 67:734, 1986.
4. Ely DD, Smidt GL. Effect of cane on variables of gait for patients with hip disorders. *Phys Ther* 57:507, 1977.
5. Fischer SV, Gullickson G Jr. Energy cost of ambulation in health and disability: A literature review. *Arch Phys Med Rehabil* 59:124, 1978.
6. Fisher SV, Patterson RP. Energy cost of ambulation with crutches. *Arch Phys Med Rehabil* 62:250, 1981.
7. Goh JC, Toh SL, Bose K. Biomechanical study on axillary crutches during single-leg swing through gait. *Prosthetic Orthotic Int* 10:89, 1986.
8. Joyce BM, Kirby RL. Canes, crutches, and walkers. *Am Fam Physician* 43:535, 1991.
9. Kalchthaler T, Bascon RA, Quintos V. Falls in the institutionalized elderly. *J Geriatr Soc* 26:424, 1978.
10. McDonough AL, Razza-Doherty M. Some biomechanical aspects of crutch and cane walking: The relationship between forward symmetry, and efficiency—a case report. *Clin Podiatry Med Surg* 5:677, 1988.
11. Minor DML, Minor SD. Ambulation with assistive devices. In: Minor MAD, ed. *Patient Care Skills.* Norwalk, CT, Appleton & Lange, 1990.
12. Nielson DH, Harris JM, Minton YM, et al. Energy cost, exercise intensity, and gait efficiency of standard versus rocker-bottom axillary crutch walking. *Phys Ther* 70:487, 1990.
13. Noreau L, Richards CL, Comeau F, Tardif D. Biomechanical analysis of swing-through gait in paraplegic and non-disabled individuals. *J Biomechanics* 28:689, 1995.
14. Perry J. *Gait Analysis: Normal and Pathological Function.* Thorofare, NJ, Slack, 1992.
15. Pierson FM. Ambulation aids, patterns, and activities. In: Pierson FM, ed. *Principles and Techniques of Patient Care.* Philadelphia, Saunders, 1994.
16. Reisman M, Burdett RG, Simon SR, Norkin C. Elbow moment and forces at the hands during swing-through axillary crutch gait. *Phys Ther* 65:601, 1985.
17. Shiokawa K. Dynamic roles of the upper extremity during axillary crutch gait. *Nippon Seikeigeka Gakkai Zasshi* 67:1014, 1993.
18. Stallard J, Sankarankutty M, Rose GK. A comparison of axillary, elbow, and Canadian crutches. *Rheumatol Rehabil* 17:237, 1978.
19. Waters RL, Campbell J, Perry J. Energy cost of three-point crutch ambulation in fracture patients. *J Orthopa Trauma* 1:170, 1987.
20. Wilson JF, Gilbert JA. Dynamic body forces on axillary crutch walkers during swing-through gait. *Am J Phys Med* 61:85, 1982.
21. Waters RL, Yakura JS, Adkins R, Barnes G. Determinants of gait performance following spinal cord injury. *Arch Phys Med Rehabil* 70:811, 1989.

CHAPTER 23

Using Pharmacologic Agents in Rehabilitation

Patsy Huff and William E. Prentice

O B J E C T I V E S

After completing this chapter, the student therapist should be able to do the following:

- Discuss the various methods by which drugs can be administered.
- Discuss pharmacokinetics relative to absorption, distribution, metabolism, and excretion.
- Explain the difference between administering and dispensing medications.
- Discuss legal concerns for administering medications.
- Discuss the various drugs that can be used to treat infection, reduce pain and inflammation, relax muscles, treat gastrointestinal disorders, treat colds and congestion, and control bleeding.

For the therapist supervising a program of rehabilitation, some knowledge of the potential effects of certain types of drugs during the rehabilitation program is essential.[6] On occasion, the therapist must make decisions regarding the appropriate use of medications. The therapist must be cognizant of the potential effects and side effects of over-the-counter and prescription medications on the patient during rehabilitation.

WHAT IS A DRUG?

A drug is a chemical agent used in the prevention, treatment, or diagnosis of disease.[12] The use of substances for the express purpose of treating some infirmity or disease dates back to early history. The ancient Egyptians were highly skilled in making and using medications, treating a wide range of external and internal conditions.

Many of our common drugs, such as aspirin and penicillin, are derived from natural sources. Historically, medications were composed of roots, herbs, leaves, or other natural materials when they were identified or believed to have medicinal properties. Today many medications that originally came from nature are produced synthetically.

PHARMACOKINETICS

Pharmacokinetics refers to the method by which drugs are absorbed, distributed, metabolized, and eliminated or excreted by the body. The term *pharmacodynamics* is often confused with pharmacokinetics. Pharmacodynamics refers to the actions or the effects of a drug on the body.[9,14]

Administration of Drugs

To be effective therapeutically, a drug must first get into the system, and then reach a receptor in a target tissue.[1] The administration of medications can be either internal or external and is based on the type of local or general response desired. Drugs and medications can be taken internally through inhalation, or they may be administered intradermally, intramuscularly, intranasally, intraspinally, intravenously, orally, rectally, or sublingually. Medications administered externally include inunctions, ointments, pastes, plasters, and solutions.

DRUG VEHICLES

A *drug vehicle* is a therapeutically inactive substance that transports a drug. A drug is housed in a vehicle that may be either a solid or a liquid.

Absorption

Once a drug is in the system, the drug must be dissolved before it can be absorbed. The rate and extent of absorption is determined by the chemical characteristics of the drug, the dosage form (e.g., tablet or solution), and the gastric emptying time. The fastest absorption rate is with solutions in which the drug is already dissolved, and the slowest rate is with time-release medications.[9]

Bioavailability refers to how completely a particular drug is absorbed by the system. Bioavailability is most dependent on the characterisitcs of the drug and not on the dosage form, whereas absorption rate is largely determined by dosage form.

DISTRIBUTION

Once absorbed, the drug is transported through the blood to a specific target tissue. In addition, the drug will be distributed to other parts of the body. The *volume of distribution* is the volume of fluid through which the drug would have to be distributed to reach a therapeutic level of concentration. The *efficacy* of a drug is the capability of producing a specific therapeutic effect once the drug reaches a particular receptor site in a target tissue. *Potency* is the dose of the drug that is required to produce a desired therapeutic effect.[9]

METABOLISM

The *biotransformation* of drugs into water-soluble compounds that can be excreted is referred to as metabolism. Most of the metabolism takes place in the liver, with some occuring in the kidneys and blood. Metabolism of drugs in the liver transforms most active drugs into inactive compounds. Occasionally, when an active drug is metabolized, the metabolites may be toxic.[9]

EXCRETION

Excretion of a drug or its metabolites is controlled by the kidneys. Drugs are filtered through the kidneys and are usually excreted in the urine, although some may be reabsorbed. Some drugs may also be excreted in saliva, sweat, and feces.[9]

Drug Half-life

The rate at which a drug disappears from the body, through metabolism, excretion, or a combination, is called the *half-life*. It is the amount of time required for half of the drug that is in the body to be eliminated. For most drugs, the half-life is measured in hours, but for some it is measured in minutes or days. Knowing the half-life of a drug is critical in determining how often and in what dosage a drug must be administered to achieve and maintain therapeutic levels of concentration. The dosage interval or time between administration of individual doses is equal to the half-life of that particular drug.[9]

In determining how a drug will be administered, a *steady state* will be reached when the amount that is taken is equal to the amount that is excreted. A steady state is usually reached after five half-lives of the drug have occurred. Drugs with long half-lives may take several days to weeks to reach a steady state.[9]

Effects of Physical Activity on Pharmacokinetics

In general, exercise decreases the absorption after oral administration of a drug, while absorption is increased after intramuscular or subcutaneous administration due to an increased blood flow in the muscle.[14] Thus, exercise has an influence on the amount of a drug that reaches a receptor site, which significantly affects the pharmacodynamic activity of that drug.[11]

LEGAL CONCERNS IN ADMINISTERING VERSUS DISPENSING DRUGS

Administering a drug is defined as providing a single dose of medication for immediate use by the patient. Dispensing refers to providing the patient with a drug in a quantity sufficient to be used for multiple doses.

Dispensing Prescription Drugs

At no time can anyone other than a person licensed by law legally prescribe or dispense prescription drugs. A therapist, unless specifically allowed by state licensure, is not permitted to dispense a prescription drug. Failure to heed this requirement can be a violation of federal laws and state statutes.

Administering Over-the-Counter Drugs

The situation is not so clear-cut for nonprescription drugs. Basically, the therapist may be allowed to administer a single dose of a nonprescription medication.

Record-Keeping

Those involved in any health care profession are acutely aware of the necessity of maintaining complete, up-to-date medical records. If medications are administered by a therapist, maintaining accurate records of the types of medications administered is just as important as recording progress notes, treatments given, and rehabilitation plans. The therapist should include the following information on the medication administration log: name of the patient, complaint or symptoms, current medications, any known drug allergies, name of medication given, lot number if available, expiration date, quantity of medication given, method of administration, and date and time of administration.[7,13]

Every therapist should be aware of state regulations and laws that pertain to the ordering, prescribing, distributing, storing, and dispensing or administering of medications. Obtaining legal counsel, working with the state board of pharmacy, working in cooperation with a physician, and establishing strict written policies can all minimize the chances of violating state laws that regulate the use of medications.[7,13]

LABELING REQUIREMENTS

Over-the-counter drugs are required to have adequate directions for use, precautions, and adequate readability. The Federal

Seven-Point Label for nonprescription drugs requires the following information:

- Name of the product.
- Name and address of the manufacturer, packer, or distributor.
- Net contents of the package.
- Established name of all active ingredients, and the quantity of certain other ingredients, whether active or not.
- Name of any habit-forming drug contained in the preparation.
- Cautions and warnings needed to protect the consumer.
- Adequate directions for safe and effective use.

Nonprescription drugs may not be repackaged without meeting labeling criteria. All drugs dispensed from the athletic training room must be properly labeled. Legal violations may occur if a portion of a nonprescription drug is removed from an original properly labeled package and dispensed to a patient. This practice carries the same liability as dispensing prescription drugs, because the patient is not given the opportunity to review the label for name, contents, precautions, directions, and other information considered essential for the safe use of the product. Liability for any adverse patient outcome is therefore transferred to the dispenser of the improperly labeled over-the-counter drug.[7]

Safety of Pharmaceutical Drugs

As stated many times, no drug can be considered completely safe and harmless. If a drug is potent enough to effect some physiologic action, it is also strong enough, under some conditions, to be dangerous. All persons react individually to any drug. A given amount of a specific medication may result in no adverse reaction in one patient, whereas another person may experience a pronounced adverse response. Both the patient and the therapist should be fully aware of any untoward effect a drug may have. It is essential that the patient be instructed clearly about when specifically to take medications, with meals or not, and what not to combine with the drug, such as other drugs or specific foods. Some drugs can nullify the effect of another drug or can cause a serious antagonistic reaction.

DRUG RESPONSES

Individuals react differently to the same medication, and different conditions may alter the effect of a drug on the patient. Drugs themselves can be changed through age or improper preservation, as well as through the manner in which they are administered. Response variations also result from differences in each individual's size or age.

Alcohol should not be ingested with a wide variety of drugs, both prescription and nonprescription. A fatty diet may decrease a drug's effectiveness by interfering with its absorption. Excessively acid foods such as fruits, carbonated drinks, or vegetable juice may cause adverse drug reactions.[4] The possibility of an adverse drug reaction is ever present and requires continual education and vigilance.

Buying Medications

A pharmacist can assist in the selection and purchase of nonprescription drugs, can save money by suggesting the lower-priced generic drugs, and can act as a general advisor on what drugs are most effective, the dose of a medicine, and even the inherent dangers of a specific drug.

All pharmaceuticals must be properly labeled, clearly indicating the content, expiration date, and any dangers or contraindications for use. Pharmaceutical manufacturers place the expiration date on drugs, and it is up to the therapist to locate this date on the package. Individuals buying medications should always learn the best ways to store them, including the correct temperature and moisture and the amount of light that may be tolerated.[13]

SELECTED THERAPEUTIC DRUGS

The use of drugs and medicine is widespread throughout society in general. There are thousands of drugs, both prescription and nonperscription (over the counter), available for physicians and consumers to choose from, with new drugs being constantly developed. Pharmaceutical laboratories develop compounds in vitro, and then test, retest, and refine the drug in vivo before submitting it for Food and Drug Administration (FDA) approval.

A number of texts and databases (e.g., *Physician's Desk Reference, Drug Facts and Comparisons*) are available and are widely used as references for comparison of *bioequivalent* (producing similar biologic effects) drugs relative to their appropriateness and effectiveness in treating a specific condition or illness. Table 23-1 summarizes the various classifications of drugs available.

The following discussion includes both prescription and nonprescription drugs, with emphasis on what should most concern the therapist and what the medications or materials are designed to accomplish.

Drugs that Inhibit Pain and Inflammation

PAIN RELIEVERS

Controlling pain can involve innumerable drugs and procedures. As discussed in Chapter 4, why pain is positively affected by certain methods is not clearly understood; however, some of the possible reasons are as follows:

The excitatory effect of an individual impulse is depressed.
An individual impulse is inhibited.
The perceived impulse is decreased.
Anxiety created by the pain or impending pain is decreased.

T A B L E   2 3 - 1

Pharmaceutical Classifications

DRUG	DESCRIPTION
Analgesics (anodynes)	Pain-relieving drugs
Anesthetics	Agents that produce local or general numbness to touch, pain, or stimulation
Antacids	Substances that neutralize acidity; commonly used in the digestive tract
Anticoagulants	Agents that prevent coagulation of blood
Antidotes	Substances that prevent or counteract the action of a poison
Antipruritics	Agents that relieve itching
Antiseptics	Agents that kill bacteria or inhibit their growth and that can be applied to living tissue
Antispasmodics	Agents that relieve muscle spasm
Antitussives	Agents that inhibit or prevent coughing
Astringents	Agents that cause contraction or puckering action
Bacteriostatics and fungistatics	Agents that retard or inhibit the growth of bacteria or fungi
Carminatives	Agents that relieve flatulence (caused by gases) in the intestinal tract
Cathartics	Agents used to evacuate substances from the bowels; active purgatives
Caustics	Burning agents, capable of destroying living tissue
Counterirritants	Agents applied locally to produce an inflammatory reaction for the relief of a deeper inflammation
Depressants	Agents that diminish body functions or nerve activity
Disinfectants	Agents that kill or inhibit the growth of microorganisms; should be applied only to nonliving materials
Diuretics	Agents that increase the secretion of urine
Emetics	Agents that cause vomiting
Expectorants	Agents that suppress coughing
Hemostatics	Substances that either slow down or stop bleeding or hemorrhage
Irritants	Agents that cause irritation
Narcotics	Drugs that produce analgesic and hypnotic effects
Sedatives	Agents that relieve anxiety
Skeletal muscle relaxants	Drugs that depress neural activity within skeletal muscles
Stimulants	Agents that excite the central nervous system
Vasoconstrictors and vasodilators	Drugs that constrict or dilate blood vessels, respectively

COUNTERIRRITANTS AND LOCAL ANESTHETICS

Analgesics give relief by causing a systemic and topical analgesia. Many chemical reactions on the skin can inhibit pain sensations through rapid evaporation, which causes a cooling action, or by counterirritating the skin. Irritating and counterirritating substances used in sports act as rubefacients (skin reddeners) and skin stimulants, although their popularity has decreased in recent years. Their application causes a local increase in blood circulation, redness, and a rise in skin temperature. Frequently, mild pain can be reduced by a counterirritant, which produces a stimulus to the skin of such intensity that the patient is no longer aware of the pain. Some examples of counterirritants include liniments, analgesic balms, heat, and cold.

Spray Coolants

Spray coolants, because of their rapid evaporation, act as topical anesthetics to the skin. Several commercial coolants are presently on the market. Chloromethane is one of the most popular spray coolants currently used in a sports setting. Cooling results so quickly that superficial freezing takes place, inhibiting pain impulses for a short time. Experts disagree on the effectiveness of spray coolants. Some use them extensively for strains, sprains, and contusions. In most cases, spray coolants are useful only when other analgesics are not available.

Alcohol

Alcohol evaporates rapidly when applied to the skin, causing a refreshingly cool effect that gives a temporary analgesia.

Menthol

Menthol is an alcohol taken from mint oils and is principally used as a local analgesic, counterirritant, and antiseptic. Most often it is used with a petroleum base for treating cold symptoms and in analgesic balms.

Cold

Cold applications also immediately act to constrict blood vessels and to numb sensory nerve endings. Applications of ice packs or submersion of a part in ice water may completely anesthetize an area. If extreme cold is used, caution must be taken that tissue damage does not result.

Local Anesthetics

Local anesthetics are usually injected by the physician in and around injury sites for minor surgical procedures or to alleviate the pain of movement. Lydocaine hydrochloride is used extensively as a local anesthetic.

NARCOTIC ANALGESICS

Most narcotics used in medicine are derived directly from opium or are synthetic opiates. They depress pain impulses and the individual's respiratory center. The two most often used derivatives are codeine and morphine.

Codeine

Codeine resembles morphine in its action but is less potent. Codeine is effective in combination with nonnarcotic analgesics. In small doses it is a cough suppressant found in many cough medicines.

Propoxyphene Hydrochloride

Propoxyphene hydrochloride (Darvon) is a mild analgesic narcotic that is slightly stronger than aspirin in its pain relief. It is not an anti-inflammatory drug. It is addictive, and when combined with alcohol, tranquilizers, or other sedatives or depressants, it can be fatal.

Morphine

Morphine depresses pain sensations to a greater extent than any other drug. It is also the most dangerous drug because of its ability to depress respiration and because of its habit-forming qualities. Morphine is never used in the following situations: before a diagnosis has been made by the physician; when the subject is unconscious; when there is a head injury; or when there is a decreased rate of breathing. It is never repeated within 2 hours.

Meperidine

Meperidine (Demerol) is used as a substitute for morphine for the relief of mild or moderate pain, and is effective only when given intravenously or intramuscularly.

NONNARCOTIC ANALGESICS AND ANTIPYRETICS

Nonnarcotic analgesics are those drugs designed to suppress all but the most severe pain, without the patient's losing consciousness. In most cases these drugs also act as antipyretics, regulating the temperature-control centers.

Acetaminophen

Acetaminophen (Tylenol) is an effective analgesic and antipyretic but has no anti-inflammatory activity. Because it does not irritate the gastrointestinal system, it is often a replacement for aspirin in noninflammatory conditions. Overingestion

could lead to liver damage. Chronic heavy alcohol users may be at risk for liver damage when taking more than the recommended dose of acetaminophen.

Drugs to Reduce Inflammation

Physicians have a wide choice of drugs at their disposal for treatment of inflammation. There is also a great variety of over-the-counter drugs that claim to deal effectively with inflammation of the musculoskeletal system. The problem of proper drug selection is tenuous, even for a physician, because of new drugs continually coming to the forefront. The situation is compounded by highly advertised over-the-counter preparations. Any drug selection, especially drugs designed to treat the inflammatory process, must be effective, must be appropriate for the highly physical patient, and must not create any adverse reactions. With these points in mind, the more generally accepted anti-inflammatory drugs are discussed.

ACETYLSALICYLIC ACID (ASPIRIN)

Aspirin is one of the most widely used analgesics, anti-inflammatories, and antipyretics. It is also one of the most abused drugs in use today. A number of medications that have salicylates act in reducing pain, fever, and inflammation. Aspirin has been associated with various adverse reactions that are primarily centered in the gastrointestinal region. They include difficulty in food digestion (dyspepsia), nausea, vomiting, and gastric bleeding.

Overingestion of aspirin can lead to serious side effects. Adverse reactions to aspirin, especially in high doses, are ear ringing or buzzing (tinnitus) and dizziness. A major problem that can arise in individuals under 18 years of age is Reye's syndrome. The administration of aspirin to a child during chicken pox or influenza can induce Reye's syndrome. Its etiology is unknown.

Severe allergic response resulting in an anaphylactic reaction can occur in individuals who have an intolerance to aspirin. Asthmatic patients may be at greater risk for allergic reactions to aspirin. Aspirin use should be avoided by patients in contact sports, because it prolongs blood-clotting time.

NONSTEROIDAL ANTI-INFLAMMATORY DRUGS (NSAIDs)

Nonsteroidal drugs have anti-inflammatory, antipyretic, and analgesic properties. They are strong inhibitors of prostaglandin synthesis and are effective for such chronic problems as rheumatoid arthritis and osteoarthritis.[3] Nonsteroidal anti-inflammatory drugs (NSAIDs) are used primarily for reducing the pain, stiffness, swelling, redness, and fever associated with localized inflammation. Their anti-inflammatory capabilities are thought to be equal to those of aspirin, with the advantage of fewer side effects and relatively longer duration of action. They are effective for patients who cannot tolerate aspirin because of gastrointestinal distress associated with aspirin use. Even though NSAIDs have analgesic and antipyretic capabilities, they should not be used in cases of mild headache or increased body temperature in place of aspirin or acetaminophen. However, they can be

T A B L E   2 3 - 2

Commonly Used NSAIDs

DRUG	INITIAL DOSE (MG)	MAXIMUM DAILY DOSE (MG)
Aspirin	325–650 every 4 hours	4000
Voltaren[a]	50–75 twice a day	200
Catatlam		
Dolobid	500–1000 followed by 250–500, 2 or 3 times a day	1500
Nalfon[a]	300–600, 3 or 4 times a day	3200
Motrin,[a] Rufin	400–800, 3 or 4 times a day	3200
Indocin[a]	75–150 a day in 3 or 4 divided doses	200
Orudis,[a] Orudis KT, Actron, Oruvail	75, 3 times a day or 50, 4 times a day	300
Ponstel	500, followed by 250 every 6 hours	1000
Naprosyn[a]	250–500 twice a day	1250
Anaprox[a]	550, followed by 275 every 6–8 hours	1375
Feldene[a]	20 a day	20
Clinoril[a]	200 twice a day	400
Tolectin[a]	400, 3 or 4 times a day	1800
Relafen	1000 once or twice a day	2000
Ansaid	50–100, 2 or 3 times a day	300
Toradol[a,b]	10 every 4–6 hours for pain	40
Lodine	200–400 every 6–8 hours for pain	1200
Vioxx	12.5 once per day (osteoarthritis)	25
	50 once per day (acute pain)	50
Celebrex	100 twice per day or 200 per day (osteoarthritis)	200
	100–200 twice per day (rheumatoid arthritis)	400

[a] Available generically.

[b] Not to be used for more than 5 days.

used to relieve many other mild to moderately painful somatic conditions such as menstrual cramps and soft-tissue injury. Table 23-2 lists the most commonly used NSAIDs.

The anti-inflammatory effect of NSAIDs is due primarily to inhibition of the enzyme cyclooxygenase (COX), which is required for synthesis of prostaglandins. There are two COX isoforms. COX-1 is available in most tissues and is thought to protect the gastric mucosa. COX-2 is induced primarily at sites of inflammation. The older NSAIDs block both COX isoforms. Two new NSAIDs inhibit COX-2, but not COX-1, thus maintaining protection of the gastric mucosa. Rofecoxib (Vioxx) is FDA approved for treatment of osteoarthritis, acute pain, and menstrual pain. Celecoxib (Celebrex) is approved for treatment of osteoarthritis and rheumatoid arthritis. Neither is approved for patients under 18 years of age.

The NSAIDs can produce adverse reactions and should be used cautiously. Patients who have the aspirin allergy triad of nasal polyps, associated bronchospasm or asthma, and history of anaphylaxis should not receive any NSAID. The NSAIDs can cause gastrointestinal tract reactions, headache, dizziness, depression, tinnitus, and a variety of other systemic reactions. Taking ibuprofen with heavy alcohol use may increase the risk of stomach bleeding.

CORTICOSTEROIDS

Corticosteroids, of which cortisone is the most common, are used primarily for chronic inflammation of musculoskeletal and joint regions. Cortisone is a synthetic glucocorticoid that is usually given orally or by injection. Increasingly, more caution is taken in the use of corticosteroids than was practiced in the past. Prolonged use of corticosteroids can produce the following serious complications:

- Fluid and electrolyte disturbances (e.g., water retention caused by excess sodium levels).
- Musculoskeletal and joint impairments (e.g., bone thinning and muscle and tendon weakness).
- Dermatologic problems (e.g., delayed wound healing).
- Neurologic impairments (e.g., vertigo, headache, convulsions).
- Endocrine dysfunctions (e.g., menstrual irregularities).
- Ophthalmic conditions (e.g., glaucoma).
- Metabolic impairments (e.g., negative nitrogen balance, muscle wasting).

Cortisone is primarily administered by injection. Other ways are iontophoresis and phonophoresis (see Chapter 17). Studies have indicated that cortisone injected directly into tendons, ligaments, and joint spaces can lead to weakness and degeneration. Strenuous activity may predispose the treated part to rupturing.

Drugs that Produce Skeletal Muscle Relaxation

Drugs that produce skeletal muscle relaxation include methocarbamol (Robaxin) and carisoprodol (Soma). Because centrally acting muscle relaxants also act as sedatives or tranquilizers on the higher brain centers, there is growing speculation among physicians that these drugs are less specific to muscle relaxation than was once believed. Another major side effect is that they cause drowsiness.

Muscle spasm and guarding accompany many musculoskeletal injuries. Elimination of spasm and guarding should facilitate programs of rehabilitation. In many situations, centrally acting oral muscle relaxants are used to reduce spasm and guarding. However, to date, the efficacy of using muscle relaxants has not been substantiated, and they do not appear to be superior to analgesics or sedatives in either acute or chronic conditions.

Drugs to Combat Infection

Combating infection, especially skin infection, is of major importance. Serious infection can cause countless hours of lost time and has even been the indirect cause of death.

LOCAL ANTISEPTICS AND DISINFECTANTS

Antiseptics are substances that can be placed on living tissue for the express purpose of either killing bacteria or inhibiting their growth. Disinfectants are substances that combat microorganisms but should be applied only to nonliving objects. Other general names given to antiseptics and disinfectants are germicides, which are designed to destroy bacteria; fungicides, which kill fungi; sporicides, which destroy spores; and sanitizers, which minimize contamination by microorganisms.

Many agents are used to combat infection. It is critical that agents have a broad spectrum of activity against infective organisms, including the human immunodeficiency virus (HIV).

Alcohol

Alcohol is one of the most widely used skin disinfectants. Ethyl alcohol (70 percent by weight) and isopropyl alcohol (70 percent) are equally effective. They are inexpensive and nonirritating; they kill bacteria immediately, with the exception of spores. However, they have no long-lasting germicidal action. Besides being directly combined with other agents to form tinctures, alcohol acts independently on the skin as an antiseptic and astringent. In a 70-percent solution it can be used for disinfecting instruments. Because of alcohol's rapid rate of evaporation, it produces a mild anesthetic action. Combined with 20-percent benzoin, it is used as a topical skin dressing to provide a protective skin coating and astringent action.

Phenol

Phenol was one of the earliest antiseptics and disinfectants used by the medical profession. From its inception to the present it has been used to control disease organisms, both as an antiseptic and as a disinfectant. It is available in liquids of varying concentrations and emollients. Substances that are derived from phenol and that cause less irritation are now used more extensively. Some of these derivatives are resorcinol, thymol, and the common household disinfectant Lysol.

Halogens

Halogens are chemical substances (chlorine, fluoride, and bromine) that are used for their antiseptic and disinfectant qualities. Iodophors, or halogenated compounds—a combination of iodine and a carrier—create a much less irritating preparation than tincture of iodine. A popular iodophor is povidone-iodine complex (Betadine), which is an excellent germicide commonly used as a surgical scrub by surgeons. Betadine as an antiseptic and germicide has proved extremely effective on skin lesions such as lacerations, abrasions, and floor burns.

Oxidizing Agents

Oxidizing agents, as represented by hydrogen peroxide (3 percent), are commonly used. Hydrogen peroxide is an antiseptic that, because of its oxidation, affects bacteria but readily decomposes in the presence of organic substances such as blood and pus. For this reason it has little effect as an antiseptic. Contact with organic material produces an effervescence, during which no great destruction of bacteria takes place. The chief value of hydrogen peroxide in the care of wounds is its ability to cleanse the infected cutaneous and mucous membranes. Application of hydrogen peroxide to wounds results in the formation of an active effervescent gas that dislodges particles of wound material and debris and, by removing degenerated tissue, eliminates the wound as a likely environment for bacterial breeding. Hydrogen peroxide also possesses compounds that are widely used as antiseptics. Because it is nontoxic, hydrogen peroxide may be used for cleansing mucous membranes. A diluted solution (50 percent water and 50 percent hydrogen peroxide) can be used for treating inflammatory conditions of the mouth and throat.

ANTIFUNGAL AGENTS

Many medicinal agents on the market are designed to treat fungi. The three most common fungi are *Epidermophyton, Trichophyton,* and *Candida albicans.*

In recent years there has been successful development and use of antifungal agents such as ketoconazole (Nizoral), amphotericin B (Fungizone), and griseofulvin. Both ketoconazole and amphotericin B seem to be effective against deep-seated fungus infections such as those caused by *C. albicans.* Ketoconazole, fluconazole, and griseofulvin, all of which can be administered orally, produce an effective fungistatic action against the specific fungus species of *Microsporum, Trichophyton,* and

Epidermophyton, all of which are associated with common "patient's foots."[3] Given over a long period of time, griseofulvin becomes a functioning part of the cutaneous tissues, especially the skin, hair, and nails, producing a prolonged and continuous fungistatic action. Miconazole (Micatin), clotrimazole (Lotrimin), and tolnaftate (Tinactin, which does not treat *Candida* infections) are topical medications for a superficial fungus infection caused by *Trichophyton* and other fungi.

Mechanical antiseptics, usually soaps that provide a cleansing and detergent action, remove pathogens from the skin.

ANTIBIOTICS

Antibiotics are chemical agents that are produced by microorganisms. Their useful action is primarily a result of their interfering with the necessary metabolic processes of pathogenic microorganisms. They may be used by a physician as either topical dressings or systemic medications. The indiscriminate use of antibiotics can produce extreme hypersensitivity or idiosyncrasies and can prevent the development of natural immunity or resistance to subsequent infections. The use of any antibiotic must be carefully controlled by the physician, who selects the drug on the basis of the most desirable type of administration and the least amount of toxicity to the patient.

The antibiotics mentioned here are just a few of the many available. New types continue to be developed, mainly because, over a period of time, microorganisms often become resistant to a particular antibiotic, especially if it is indiscriminately used. Some of the more common antibiotics are penicillin, streptomycin, bacitracin, tetracycline, erythromycin, and the sulfonamides.[4]

Penicillin

Penicillin as a prescription medication is probably the most important of the antibiotics; it is useful in a variety of skin and systemic infections. In general, penicillin interferes with the metabolism of the bacteria.

Bacitracin

Bacitracin has a broad spectrum of effectiveness as an antibacterial agent. Bacitracin plus polymixin (Polysporin) also has a broad spectrum of effectiveness as an antibacterial agent. Adding neomycin to the product (Neosporin) does not increase effectiveness, and some individuals are allergic to neomycin.

Tetracycline

Tetracyclines consist of a wide group of antibiotics that have a broad antibacterial spectrum. Their application, which is usually oral, modifies the infection rather than eradicating it completely.

Erythromycin

Erythromycin is most often used for streptococcal infection and *Mycoplasma pneumoniae.* It has the same general spectrum as penicillin and is a useful alternative in the penicillin-allergic patient.

Sulfonamides

Sulfonamides are a group of synthetic antibiotics. In general, sulfonamides make pathogens vulnerable to phagocytes by inhibiting certain enzymatic actions.

Quinolones

Quinolones are a relatively new group of antibiotics. They have a broad spectrum of activity. Patients taking these must be carefully monitored for adverse effects.

Drugs for Asthma

Asthma is a chronic inflammatory lung disorder that is characterized by obstruction of the airways as a result of complex inflammatory processes, smooth muscle spasm, and hyperresponsiveness to a variety of stimuli.[5,10] Asthma triggers may include exercise, viral infection, animal exposure, dust mites, mold, air pollutants, weather, and NSAIDS as well as other drugs. The National Asthma Education and Prevention Program (NAEPP) has established international guidelines for the diagnosis and management of asthma.[9,10] The goals of asthma therapy are to prevent chronic and troublesome symptoms, maintain normal lung function and activity levels, prevent asthma exacerbations, provide optimal pharmacotherapy with minimal adverse effects, and meet patients' expectation of and satisfaction with asthma care.

Exercise-induced bronchospasm (EIB) is a limiting and disruptive experience. Any asthma patient may be subject to EIB. A bronchospastic event caused by loss of heat, water, or both from lungs during exercise or exertion, EIB results from hyperventilation of air that is cooler and dryer than that in the respiratory tract.[2] EIB may occur during or minutes after physical activity, reaches its peak in 5 to 10 minutes after stopping the activity, and usually resolves in 20 to 30 minutes. In some asthma patients, exercise may be the only precipitating factor.

It is important that the patient who has asthma be monitored carefully. The NAEPP recommends measurements of the following: asthma signs and symptoms, pulmonary function (peak flow or spirometry), quality of life/functional status, history of asthma exacerbations, and pharmacotherapy.

Drugs Used to Treat Gastrointestinal Disorders

Disorders of the gastrointestinal tract include upset stomach or formation of gas because of food incompatibilities and acute or chronic hyperacidity, which leads to inflammation of the mucous membrane of the intestinal tract. Poor eating habits may lead to digestive tract problems such as diarrhea or constipation. Drugs that elicit responses within the gastrointestinal tract include antacids, antiemetics, carminatives, cathartics, laxatives, and antidiarrheals.

ANTACIDS

The primary function of an antacid is to neutralize acidity in the upper gastrointestinal tract by raising the pH, inhibiting the activity of the digestive enzyme pepsin, and thus reducing its action on the gastric mucosal nerve endings. Antacids are effective not only for relief of acid indigestion and heartburn but also in the treatment of peptic ulcer. Antacids available in the market possess a wide range of acid-neutralizing capabilities and side effects.

One of the most commonly used antacid preparations is sodium bicarbonate, or baking soda. Other antacids include alkaline salts, which again neutralize hyperacidity but are not easily absorbed in the blood. Ingestion of antacids containing magnesium tends to have a laxative effect. Those containing aluminum or calcium seem to cause constipation. Consequently, many antacid liquids or tablets are combinations of magnesium and either aluminum or calcium hydroxides. Overuse can cause electrolyte imbalance and other adverse effects.

ANTIEMETICS

Antiemetics are used to treat the nausea and vomiting that may result from a variety of causes. Antiemetics are classified as acting either locally or centrally. The locally acting drugs, such as most over-the-counter medications (e.g., Pepto-Bismol), reportedly affect the mucosal lining of the stomach. However, the effects of soothing an upset stomach may be more of a placebo effect. The centrally acting drugs affect the brain by making it less sensitive to irritating nerve impulses from the inner ear or stomach. A variety of prescription antiemetics can be used for controlling nausea and vomiting, including phenothiazines (Phenegran), antihistamines, anticholinergic drugs for preventing motion sickness, and sedative drugs. The primary side effect of these medications is drowsiness.

CARMINATIVES

Carminatives are drugs that give relief from flatulence (gas). Their action on the digestive canal is to inhibit gas formation and aid in its expulsion. Simethicone is the most commonly used carminative.

CATHARTICS (LAXATIVES)

The use of laxatives should always be under the direction of a physician. Constipation may be symptomatic of a serious disease condition. Indiscriminant use of laxatives may render the patient unable to have normal bowel movements. It may also lead to electrolyte imbalance. There is seldom need for healthy, active individuals to rely on artificial means for stool evacuation.

ANTIDIARRHEALS

Diarrhea may result from many causes, but it is generally considered to be a symptom rather than a disease. It can occur as a result of emotional stress, allergies to food or drugs, adverse drug reactions, or many different types of intestinal problems. Diarrhea may be acute or chronic. Acute diarrhea, the most common, comes on suddenly and may be accompanied by nausea, vomiting, chills, and intense abdominal pain. It typically runs its course rapidly, and symptoms subside once the irritating agent is removed from the system. Chronic diarrhea, which may last for weeks, may result from more serious disease states.

Medications used for control of diarrhea are either locally acting or systemic. The locally acting medications most typically contain kaolin, which absorbs other chemicals, and pectin, which soothes irritated bowel. Some contain substances that add bulk to the stool. The systemic agents, which are generally antiperistaltic or antispasmodic medications, are considered to be much more effective in relieving symptoms of diarrhea, but most, except loperamide (Imodium AD), are prescription drugs. The systemic medications are either opiate derivatives or anticholinergic agents, both of which reduce peristalsis. Common side effects of the systemic antidiarrheals include drowsiness, nausea, dry mouth, and constipation. It is not advisable to treat antibiotic-induced diarrhea because diarrhea may be a protective symptom in antibiotic-induced pseudomembranous colitis.

HISTAMINE-2 BLOCKERS (H_2 BLOCKERS)

The H_2 blockers reduce stomach acid output by blocking the action of histamine on certain cells in the stomach. They are used to treat peptic and gastric ulcers and other gastrointestinal hypersecretory conditions. Cimetidine (Tagamet) and ranitidine (Zantac) are examples.

Drugs Used to Treat Colds and Allergies

Drugs on the market designed to affect colds and allergies are almost too numerous to count. In general, they fall into three basic categories, all of which deal with the symptoms of the condition and not the cause. They are drugs dealing with nasal congestion, histamine reactions, and cough.

NASAL DECONGESTANTS

Topical nasal decongestants that contain mild vasoconstricting agents such as oxymetazoline (Afrin) and xylometazoline (Otivin) are on the market. These agents are relatively safe. However, prolonged use can cause rebound congestion and dependency.

An effective oral decongestant is psuedoephedrine hydrochloride (Sudafed). Repeated dosing does not lead to rebound congestion.

ANTIHISTAMINES

Antihistamines are often added to nasal decongestants. Histamine is a protein substance contained in animal tissues that, when released into the general circulation, causes the reactions of an allergy. Histamine causes dilation of arteries and capillaries, skin flushing, and a rise in temperature. An antihistamine is a substance that opposes histamine action. Antihistamines offer little benefit in treating the common cold. They are beneficial in allergies. Examples are terfenadine (Seldane), diphenhydramine hydrochloride (Benadryl), and chlorphenerimine (Chlor-Trimeton).

Antihistamines, as well as decongestants and diuretics, can decrease the peripheral mechanisms of sweating, impairing the body's ability to dissipate heat and thus predisposing the patient to heat-related illness.

COUGH MEDICINES

Cough medicines either suppress the cough (antitussives) or increase the fluid content to increase the production of fluid in the respiratory system (expectorants). Antitussives are available in liquid, capsule, troche, or spray form. Narcotic antitussives contain codeine (Robitussin AC); nonnarcotic antitussives contain diphenhydramine (Benylin cough syrup), dextromethorphan (Benylin DM, Sucrets), or benzonatate (Tessalon). The advantage of nonnarcotic antitussives is that they have few side effects and are not addictive. There is little evidence that expectorants (guaifenesin) are any more effective in controlling coughing than simply drinking water.

SYMPATHOMIMETICS

Exercise-induced bronchospasm involves spasm of smooth muscle in the bronchioles and shortness of breath. Drugs used to treat exercise-induced bronchospasm are called sympathomimetics. An example is albuterol (Proventil, Ventolin). Bronchodilators generally reverse the symptoms. Sympathomimetics may cause heat-related problems if used in a hot environment.

Epinephrine

In some states, the therpist may receive instructions and certification for the administration of epinephrine via an Epipen to treat anaphylaxis resulting from insect stings. Once it is clear that a patient is having an anaphylactic reaction, the Epipen can be used to safely and easily inject medication into the thigh.

Drugs Used to Control Bleeding

Various drugs and medicines cause selective actions on the circulatory system, including vasoconstrictors and anticoagulants.

VASOCONSTRICTORS

Vasoconstrictors are most often administered externally to sites of profuse bleeding. The drug most commonly used for this purpose is epinephrine (adrenaline), which is applied directly to a hemorrhaging area. It acts immediately to constrict damaged blood vessels and is extremely valuable in cases of epistaxis (nosebleed) in which normal procedures are inadequate.

HEMOSTATIC AGENTS

Drugs that immediately inhibit bleeding are currently being investigated. Hemostatic agents such as thrombin may prove to be useful; however, specific drug recommendations are not available at this time.

ANTICOAGULANTS

The most common anticoagulants used by physicians are heparin and coumarin derivatives. Heparin prolongs the clotting time of blood but will not dissolve a clot once it has developed. Heparin is used primarily to control extension of a thrombus that is already present. Coumarin derivatives act by suppressing the formation of prothrombin in the liver. Given orally, they are used to slow clotting time in certain vascular disorders.

SUMMARY

- A drug is a chemical agent used in the prevention, treatment, or diagnosis of disease that may be administered either internally or externally. It is transported in an inactive substance called a vehicle.
- Pharmacokinetics refers to the method by which drugs are absorbed, distributed, metabolized, and eliminated or excreted by the body.
- Administering a drug is defined as providing a single dose of medication for immediate use by the patient. Dispensing refers to providing the patient with a drug in a quantity sufficient to be used for multiple doses. At no time can anyone other than a person licensed by law legally prescribe or dispense drugs for a patient.
- Drugs used to inhibit pain or inflammation include counterirritants and local anesthetics, narcotic analgesics, nonnarcotic analgesics and antipyretics, acetylsalicylic acid (aspirin), nonsteroidal anti-inflammatory drugs, and corticosteroids.
- Drugs used to combat infection include local antiseptics and disinfectants, antifungal agents, and antibiotics.
- Drugs used to treat gastrointestinal disorders include antacids, antiemetics, carminatives, carthartics or laxatives, and antidiarrheals.
- Drugs used to treat colds and allergies include nasal decongestants, antihistamines, cough suppressants, and asthma drugs.
- Drugs used to control bleeding include vasoconstrictors, hemostatic agents, and anticoagulants.

REFERENCES

1. Almekinders L. Athletic injuries and the use of medication. In: Torg J, Shepard R, eds. *Current Therapy in Sports Medicine.* St. Louis, Mosby, 1995.
2. Barnes P. Is immunotherapy for asthma worthwhile? *N Engl J Med* 334:531–532, 1996.
3. Blood K. Nonmedical substance use among patients at a small liberal arts college. *Athl Train* 25:335, 1990.
4. Clark W. *Goth's Medical Pharmacology,* 13th ed. St. Louis, Mosby, 1992.
5. Fuentes R, Rosenberg J, Davis A. *Allen and Hanbury's Athletic Drug Reference.* Durham, NC, Galaxo, 1995.
6. Hepler CD, Strand LM. Opportunities and responsibilities in pharmaceutical care. *Am J Hosp Pharm* 4:533–543, 1990.
7. Huff P. Drug distribution in the training room. *Clin Sports Med* 17:214, 1998.
8. National Asthma Education and Prevention Coordinating

Committee, National Heart Lung and Blood Institute, and World Health Organization. *Global Initiative for Asthma.* Bethesda, National Institutes of Health, 1995, publication no. NIH-95-3659.

9. Poe TE. Pharmacology. In: Malone T, ed. *Physical and Occupational Therapy: Drug Implications for Practice.* Philadelphia, Lippincott, 1989.

10. Second Expert Panel on the Management of Asthma. National Heart, Lung, and Blood Institute. *Highlights of Expert Panel Report 2: Guidelines for the Dignosis and Management of Asthma.* Bethesda, National Institutes of Health, 1997, publication no. NIH 97-4051A.

11. Somani SM, Kamimori GH. The effects of exercise on absorption, distribution, metabolism, excretion, and pharmacokinetics of drugs. In: Somain SM, ed. *Pharmacology in Exercise and Sports.* Boca Raton, CRC Press, 1996.

12. U.S. Olympic Committee. *Drug Education Handbook 1993–1996.* Colorado Springs, USOC, 1993.

13. Whitehill W, Wright K, Robinson J. Guidelines for dispensing medications. *J Athl Train* 27:20, 1992.

14. Young LL, Koda-Kimble MA. *Applied Therapeutics: The Clinical Use of Drugs.* Vancouver, Applied Therapeutics, 1995.

C H A P T E R   2 4

Designing Home Exercise Programs

John S. Halle and Brian C. Thomson

O B J E C T I V E S

After completing this chapter, the student therapist should be able to do the following:

- List and briefly discuss four ways that utilization of a home exercise program improves the overall quality of patient care provided by a therapist.

- Identify two patient barriers to exercise program compliance and design a strategy to address each of the identified barriers.

- Using the health belief model as a framework, discuss why there has traditionally been poor compliance with prescribed medical regimes.

- List the five elements associated with an "exercise prescription" and discuss the role of each when designing a home exercise program.

- List and discuss six pitfalls commonly found in prescribed home exercise programs.

- Given a mock patient with a musculoskeletal injury, design an appropriate home exercise program prescription that incorporates the key elements discussed in this chapter.

The role of a physical therapist has changed over the years, in response to advances in our understanding of pathology and in technology, and due to changes in the way that health care is delivered. While the profession grew from the need for "hands-on" intervention to assist with maximizing potential associated with neuromusculoskeletal problems and movement disorders, in today's world it is also essential that all therapists are accomplished educators to reach the patient's potential. The increased emphasis on the role of educator is based on two very basic assumptions that are part of any treatment intervention program: (1) the time that a patient is able to spend in a clinical setting under the direct supervision of a therapist is limited, compared to the time that will be spent at home or work; and (2) reimbursement limitations associated with managed care have cut the number of visits that can be employed to rehabilitate a patient.[13] Therefore, the therapist of today spends a larger portion of his or her time and effort designing programs that the patient can use at home or work to reach their personal goals. These programs need to be clear, concise, and conveyed in a way that the patient can understand. They need to be flexible enough that they can be performed in environments ranging from home to the local fitness club or YMCA. Any program prescribed also needs to have a clear progression based on objective criteria, so the patient knows when to progress and, as importantly, when something is wrong and they need to seek additional help. To convey all of this in the course of one or several patient visits is an ambitious undertaking, yet it is the reality that accompanies the contemporary practice of the physical therapy profession.

The purpose of this chapter is to provide an overview of the fundamentals associated with designing home exercise programs. The emphasis of the chapter will be on examining what can be done to educate the patient so that effective therapy will be conducted both within and outside the clinic. To that end, a range of suggestions will be offered along with the research findings associated with clinical instruction. Because individuals have various learning styles, approaches will be overviewed that recognize that people learn in different ways. The "home exercise program prescription" will be covered, along with the potential role that technological advances such as computer software, E-mail, and videocassette recorders (VCRs) can have in assisting with education. The chapter will conclude with a listing of some of the commercial products available to assist the busy clinician.

THE IMPACT OF MANAGED CARE

Managed care has changed the way that medicine is practiced, in part by working to decrease the amount of time that a patient spends with a health care provider to reduce costs. Perhaps the best known example of this change is associated with childbirth, with hospital stays shortened to the point that legislation was enacted to prohibit payers from restricting "benefits for any hospital length of stay in connection with childbirth of the mother or newborn child, following normal vaginal delivery, to less than 48 hours."[23] To be sure, this trend is not completely fiscally driven, with changes in technology permitting care to be rendered less invasively and thus decreasing hospital and/or clinical time. The bottom line, however, is that the goal of the third-party payer is to keep costs down and provide the patient with the basic elements of care that will allow them to return to a reasonable functional status. The managed care approach rewards health care providers able to "get the patient back" to this reasonable functional level quickly, because those are the individuals that the capitated care environment seeks to employ.

An issue that is intimately related to a rehabilitation approach that seeks to minimize patient visits and still return the patient to a reasonable (if not ideal), functional level, is quality. If an individual has surgery to the knee and is left completely to his or her own devices, it is not unrealistic to assume that over the passage of time, the patient will eventually recover and walk without an assistive device and may be able to resume many previous physical activities. What is perhaps unrealistic is the belief that without some information and guidance, the patient will accomplish rehabilitation in the most efficient way without incurring permanent negative consequences. For example, without rehabilitative care, the patient may walk, but end up with a permanent contracture of the knee, and have the knee "give way" at times due to the inability to achieve full extension.

The scenario just described illustrates that intervention of a rehabilitation specialist is a necessary part of a program of complete medical care. Recognizing this, the "ideal" environment, which gives the clinician the greatest control and maximizes the potential of the patient, is one where regular visits to the clinic are provided for all required rehabilitation. This permits direct supervision, use of therapeutic pieces of equipment and modalities to facilitate improvement, and close monitoring of progress to insure that the mutual goals of the therapist and patient are being met. Although at one end of a continuum, where the greatest degree of control is provided, this situation where all care is performed under direct supervision is not necessarily optimal. Indeed, having a patient perform all care in a clinical environment is not realistic or even desirable. In addition to the therapist needing to work within the constraints of the capitated system, it is good to require the patient to be an active participant and assume a large measure of responsibility for his or her care. The challenge is to develop a plan of care that will render a quality product within the number of patient visits deemed appropriate for a given condition. Because quality typically takes time and

effort, therapists should engage their patients with home programs that both work within the system and push the rehabilitation envelope. This will work to maintain quality, which should not be sacrificed simply because reimbursement and ethical factors make it unrealistic to provide all care in the clinical setting.

PHILOSOPHY ASSOCIATED WITH HOME EXERCISE PROGRAMS

The use of home exercise programs improves the overall quality of care rendered by a therapist. Even if the number of patient visits was not an issue, home exercise programs could be used to the patient's benefit. First, by giving the patient some activities to perform away from the clinic, the patient becomes vested in the rehabilitation. In other words, patients learn to take some responsibility for their own care and are not dependent on the therapist to "fix" them. This promotes active involvement in the process of rehabilitation and lets the patient understand that he or she is ultimately in charge of the final result.

Second is the recognition that many of the elements of therapeutic exercise need to be performed a number of times throughout the day. As mentioned, it is unrealistic to think that all rehabilitation will be done in a clinical setting. Therefore, if rapid return to function at a high level of performance is the hallmark of a job well done, then therapeutic exercises will need to be done throughout the day, over weekends, and on holidays—home exercise programs are the vehicle to accomplish this. Performing exercises several times a day and throughout the week also provides increased continuity of care. Rather than fragmented treatments squeezed in once or twice a week, care is rendered at near-optimal time intervals.

Third, developing a home program for a patient requires communication and education. Bidirectional communication is essential, because the patient needs to outline the goals and measures associated with a successful outcome, and the therapist needs to link the procedures that will allow those to be met. Thus, the process of thinking ahead to the construction of a home exercise program requires that the parties involved develop mutual expectations and then work together to make them a reality. As was alluded to at the beginning of this chapter, this job of being a patient educator has increased in importance to the point where therapists today are as much educators as they are hands-on clinicians.

Fourth, the use of home programs is what is expected by third-party payers and by the profession of physical therapy. For example, the "Guide to Physical Therapy Practice" includes a section on "Patient/Client-Related Instruction" when talking about the types of interventions provided by physical therapists.[2] Managed-care companies have similar expectations, and expect to see home exercise programs annotated in the plan of care. Record audits may look for this element of the treatment program, and failure to provide instructions that can be used at home could result in diminished or denied payment for the clinical visit.

It is good for patients to develop some ownership of their rehabilitation, but the therapist prescribing a home exercise program needs to be aware that there may be a real challenge associated with this goal. Simply because something is good for an individual, or is the right thing to do, does not mean that behavior will change to embrace this positive action. A recent editorial entitled "Why Won't Patients Do Their Home Exercise Programs?" addressed the challenge that all health care practitioners are confronted with when attempting to effect a behavior change.[5] The editorial pointed out that although patients are intelligent and well intentioned, the truth is that it is difficult for anyone to take on a new challenge and stick with it for a period of time. When we each consider the "New Year resolutions" that have been made in the past and the progress or lack thereof that has accompanied those resolutions, the difficulty associated with changing behavior is easily seen. Most adults do not even bother to make resolutions anymore, because they have recognized they will not stick with the task that they "want" to do! Thus, it is clear that in addition to providing guidance, we need to assist with the elimination of barriers and provide motivation to our patients. The next section addresses some research that has been shown to increase the likelihood that the prescribed home exercises may actually be performed.

BEHAVIORAL MODELS AND HOME EXERCISE PROGRAMS

There are a number of behavioral models that attempt to provide an explanation for why an individual is either successful in embracing a change in behavior or falls short of the mark. It appears that the average therapist prescribing home exercise programs is using a very loose interpretation of the health belief model (HBM),[15] believing that if someone becomes aware of what is good for them, then that incentive alone will motivate them sufficiently to change their behavior. Years of research with this model have demonstrated that there remains "widespread failure of people to accept . . . compliance with prescribed medical regimens."[15] This HBM views alterations in behavior as influenced primarily by two variables: "(1) the value placed by an individual on a particular goal, and (2) the individual's estimate of the likelihood that a given action will achieve that goal."[15] Within these two variables, the interplay between four dimensions associated with behavior has been examined for the impact on generating a real change. Those dimensions are (1) perceived susceptibility, (2) perceived severity, (3) perceived benefits, and (4) perceived barriers.[15] Due to this interplay, what is seen across the patient population is a range of behaviors from no willingness to implement an alteration in behavior to individuals who are totally dedicated and motivated.

What is responsible for this differential response? The significance of each of these dimensions on behavior was found in a review article on the HBM to be (in descending order) "barriers" (89 percent), "susceptibility" (81 percent), "benefits"

(78 percent), and "severity" (65 percent).[15] Thus, issues like what barriers exist that would keep a patient from being able to perform an exercise program on a regular basis, or patient belief regarding the amount of benefit the patient will receive, appear to influence behavior. The HBM thus tells us that the success rate with home exercise programs will be largely dependent on how the patient perceives his or her condition and the benefits associated with the recommendations provided. Indeed, within this model, the issue of perceived benefits has been found to be the strongest predictor of compliance in rehabilitation programs where an individual already has a medical problem.[6] "Compliance" is the term traditionally used to describe how well a patient ultimately follows the exercise prescription or other health-related recommendations.[6]

Another very popular model used by psychologists and other health care professionals to explain resistance to behavior change is the transtheoretical model, developed by Prochaska and colleagues.[25] This is the model frequently used when examining health behaviors such as smoking cessation or decreasing fat consumption within the standard diet, and what needs to occur to effect a change. Because it deals with the need of the individual to enact a change, it is often called the "stages of change" model as well. This model recognizes that individuals come to a situation at various levels of willingness to engage in the behavior that is ultimately in their best interest. The various levels outlined in this model are used to identify where an individual is at in terms of acting on a change in behavior. The stages range from "precontemplative," which is a level where no change in behavior is even considered, to "maintenance," where a change has been enacted and sustained for 6 months or longer. (Table 24-1).

For example, it is now clear that smoking is a health hazard, yet many individuals choose to maintain this behavior despite the fact that they recognize it is unhealthy. The argument could be made that smoking is an addictive habit, so the recognition that not all individuals change their behavior is not surprising. Yet the same could be said about the general concept of exercise, where only about 16 percent of Americans engage in vigorous

TABLE 24-1

Transtheoretical Model (Stages of Change)

Precontemplation	No intention to change, or denial of the need to change
Contemplation	Seriously considering change
Preparation	Making small changes
Action	Actively engaged in changing behavior
Maintenance	Continuation of successful change efforts

SOURCE: Marcus BH, Simkin LR. The transtheoretical model: Applications to exercise behavior. *Med Sci Sports Exerc* 26: 1400–1404, 1994.

activity three or more times per week.[36] The statistics that illustrate that 23 percent of Americans are essentially sedentary and another 38 percent engage in less than light to moderate exercise are more revealing, considering that there is little controversy that exercise is essential for a healthy life.[36] Thus, although exercise is cognitively recognized as an important part of a healthy lifestyle, it is not performed regularly by the majority of individuals who will be rehabilitation clients. The transtheoretical model would suggest that the therapist needs to meet the patient wherever he or she is situated in terms of willingness to engage in the activities that appear to be appropriate for the patient's condition. Thus, compliance with this model would dictate that in addition to being an educator, the therapist must also become a mentor and coach. This means finding creative ways to meet patients at their level, and when necessary motivating them to strive for the next level. This needs to be done in a way that is not judgmental and works to accomplish the rehabilitation task at hand.

The transtheoretical model can be a useful tool when dealing with patients because it provides the therapist with the knowledge that patients may move progressively forward from one stage to the next, regress or relapse to a previous stage, or become stuck at a given level.[24,25] Thus, the changes in behavior that are associated with personal implementation of an exercise program are rarely monotonically progressive, and the therapist should be prepared for "positive steps forward" and occasional "steps back." This allows therapists to build checkpoints and rationale into their home program progression, so that they are able to optimally respond to the patient's actual level of involvement. The checkpoints may take the form of identifying the barriers that are keeping the patient from engaging in the program and providing strategies to remove those barriers. Also, the therapist will want to illustrate advantages for the patient to be involved, so that on balance, the scale will tip in favor of being engaged with the exercise program. It is anticipated that when the benefits outweigh the barriers, the person will engage in the changed behavior.[5] Again, as was the case with the HBM, the prevailing view is that when the pros associated with engaging in a recommended behavior exceed the cons, there is increased likelihood that the recommendations will be followed.

An additional aid of the transtheoretical model is that it provides therapists with a continuum where they can recognize and place patients, in terms of patient willingness to be involved in rehabilitation. Then, a program can be designed that coincides with current patient willingness to embrace the behavior change being suggested. If the patient has no interest in being involved in care and is at a precontemplative stage, then the patient will probably not embrace a home program regardless of the clarity of instruction. In this case, the therapist needs to scale back the program and work to educate and move the patient toward the next level within the "stages of change" model (contemplation). In contrast, an individual in the action or maintenance phase of this model, may have to be held back. Thus, in the same way that a therapist cannot approach each patient as having a given clinical condition that

a prefabricated exercise list will address, the therapist cannot assume that all patients are starting at the same point in terms of behavior change. The therapist has to work with the individual at the stage they are at, and provide an intervention that promotes progress. In a study of cardiac patients, exercise time was found to be significantly increased with each progressive stage of change measured, illustrating that compliance is affected by factors such as perceived self-efficacy, perceived benefits of exercise, and the reduction or elimination of perceived barriers.[12] Therefore, part of this job of evaluating, coaching, and motivating patients is to provide them with information that will allow them to accurately evaluate how their actions are related to the final outcome that they may expect.

In summary, the literature surrounding behavior change indicates that the therapist has to do more than simply assign exercises. Barriers need to be discussed, and strategies should be developed to minimize them. Benefits associated with engaging in the program need to be illustrated in ways that are meaningful to the patient. The stage of potential involvement with his or her own care needs to be recognized, and the program tailored to maximize the patient's potential at the current behavioral stage. If participation in the program is not always consistent, recognition by the therapist that this is how most individuals progress may provide understanding that will enable instruction to be given again in a positive light. Employing the suggestions that have emerged from these psychosocial models will hopefully improve compliance as well as provide some understanding of factors that influence a patient's behavior.

LEARNING STYLES AND PATIENT COMPLIANCE

In addition to considering some of the psychological factors that are associated with achieving compliance, it is also important to consider the learning style of your patient.[16,33,39,42] Each individual has a learning style that he or she is most comfortable with and responsive to when information is provided that "meshes" with the individual's preferred mode of reception.[16,33,39,42] A number of categorization schemes are available.[7,21,31,32] One common method uses the labels of "visual," "auditory," and "tactile" learners to describe three prominent styles of information gathering.[37,40,42,44] Although individuals tend to have a preference for one of these styles and learn best when information is obtained via that medium, we all are able to extract information from each of these sources.[14] A visual learner, for example, has a preference for information presented graphically. In spite of this preference, the person will also experience some learning, although the efficiency may be less, through hearing and by interacting with the environment. Due to the differences in the way that we obtain information, home exercise program instruction should be designed to have elements that appeal to all three of these types of learners to "cover all the bases."[14,16,39,42] A brief summary of each of the basic learning styles as outlined by Taylor is provided next.[42]

Visual learning occurs through visual stimulation. The visual learner assimilates information using the eyes as the primary source of input.[45] These are the patients who will intently watch a clinician or concentrate on a picture while a verbal explanation is being conveyed, looking for visual supplementation to what they are hearing. Colorful, organized, and/or moving information is most conducive to their education and should be at the core of the instruction provided for this type of patient.[45] Clinicians should concentrate on providing information to visual learners through pictures and physical demonstrations, and may even consider using videocassettes. This type of learner is especially receptive to the graphical information that can be produced with computer software, described later in this chapter.[45] Where possible, the clinical education of these individuals should include the use of anatomic models and/or pictures. Through visual stimulation, this type of learner may have improved understanding of the nuances of the program, resulting in a better understanding of perceived benefits, which are linked to improved compliance.[15,45]

Auditory learners acquire information best while someone, or some device, explains it to them verbally. This learning style is characterized predominately by individuals who concentrate their attention on what is being said to them.[16,39] Because effective learning is so dependent on what is heard, the clinician should take special care to explain in a manner and on a grade level that the person can easily understand. When this style is recognized, the therapist should try to provide detailed verbal explanations, supplemented with visual and tactile input. These explanations should routinely avoid medical or therapeutic terminology, as the patient may concentrate on trying to determine the meaning of these words or phrases and miss hearing subsequent information that may be important.[39]

Tactile learners are perhaps the most difficult to educate.[16,39] These individuals are "sensors" who have a predisposition to learn through touch and who tend to obtain information about their environment by interacting with it.[44] Anatomic models are very helpful when educating tactile learners. The models can be manipulated and viewed while a verbal explanation is being given. In this way, the manual interaction of the environment complements the auditory information presented to the patient. Additionally, pointing to the structures of interest during the instruction may significantly enhance individuals' understanding of what is being presented to them.[16,39] It is also very important to have tactile learners practice exercises with clinical supervision before they can be expected to perform them independently. Again, using this learning style, it may be possible to improve learning by tactilely stimulating the patient while they are learning the exercise. For example, a common procedure used with proprioceptive neuromuscular facilitation (PNF) is for the therapist to place the hands over the region to be facilitated.[43] The goal with this type of manual stimulation is to communicate to the patient through tactile cues and increase the exchange of information. This type of physical contact, combined with verbal and

TABLE 24-2

Learning Style Suggestions to Increase Compliance

1. Recognize different learning styles and, where possible, accommodate them.[39]
2. Explain tasks in various ways and use models when appropriate.[39]
3. Keep explanations and directions simple.
4. Use examples and analogies where appropriate.[39]
5. Encourage active participation in the setting of goals and development of the program.[16]
6. Nurture success by accentuating the positive—focus on what to do, not what to avoid.[16,37,39]
7. Heighten understanding by providing clear examples.[16]
8. Speak appropriately, on the patient's level, with commonly understood words—minimize using medical terminology.[39]
9. Integrate different teaching methods and activities into the instruction, when feasible.[16]
10. Strive to challenge the learner.[16]
11. Listen actively and attentively.
12. Provide written information sheets—use multimedia when possible.[16,39]
13. End a session with "what else can I answer for you?" (to maximize understanding).[39]

visual instruction, should work to maximize the tactile learner's capabilities.

The key element with this discussion on learning styles is to recognize that not all individuals learn in the same way. When developing patient instruction, therapists should make an attempt to include methodologies that appeal to all three learning styles, because there will not be time in a busy clinic to individually assess a particular individual's preferred learning style.[39] In those cases where the patient has either told you that he or she learns best one way or another, or it is obvious, adjust the instruction accordingly. In the vast majority of cases, however, a good generalist approach that includes elements that will appeal to visual, auditory, and tactile learners is recommended.[14,16,39] An abbreviated list of suggestions that may positively impact learning styles is provided in Table 24-2.

LEVEL OF COMPLIANCE DEMONSTRATED IN PAST RESEARCH

Working to optimize compliance is vitally important, because research has demonstrated that patients who follow the prescribed treatment program generally have more favorable treatment outcomes.[11] Will implementing psychosocial models and considering the patient's learning style pay off with increased compliance? A tentative "yes" appears to be the proper response. The research to date recognizes that there are other elements that factor into this question, but reducing barriers, clearly conveying personal benefits of the program, and explaining the relationship between the medical problem and the course of the treatment, should positively affect compliance.[6,15,35,39]

What level of compliance can be expected, and is this something that health care providers really need to work at to increase? This is not an easy question to answer in black and white, because achieved levels of compliance depend in large part on how the question is asked. For example, in a follow-up of occupational and physical therapy patients, when patients were asked to rate their actual exercise performance on home programs, 74 percent of the 102 persons surveyed reported that they were 100 percent compliant.[6] Having three out of four patients perform their prescribed exercises at a 100 percent level does not sound too bad. If this level of compliance were truly found in all rehabilitation settings, then the emphasis thus far on issues associated with compliance has perhaps been misplaced. When this same group of researchers asked the question in a different way, however—where they compared what the patients were actually doing to what was recorded in their records—they found that only 35 percent were 100 percent compliant.[6]

A similar picture of possibly inflated compliance values emerge in two other studies on this topic. Mulder considered patients "compliant" if they accomplished greater than 75 percent of their exercise goal.[28] Thus, the operational definition of compliance immediately allowed a level of 25 percent noncompliance, while still achieving "success." As a result, the values achieved were not representative of all that had been prescribed, nor could these values be directly compared to the previous research that looked at actual compliance values.[6] In another study, by Henry et al,[13] a similar situation was found. The research examined three groups of subjects who were asked to perform 2, 5, or 8 home exercises. According to their daily logs,

there was no difference in the compliance of the three groups, and the *median* score of self-reported performance was 100 percent.[13] When the researchers assessed actual performance, however, the average scores for the groups tested ranged from 11.4 to 4.4, out of a possible 12-point scoring system.[13] Here again, the subjects' self-perceptions were far better than what was assessed objectively as an outcome measure of compliance.

Other interesting observations associated with these compliance figures included the following: (1) some of the patients had no involvement with their prescribed exercise program, (2) patients did not understand or forgot to mention about 12 percent of the home exercises documented in their charts, and (3) no compliance differences were noted based on gender, marital status, or work status during rehabilitation.[6] Again, the issues of perceived benefits versus barriers, along with self-efficacy of the treatment program (that the individual believes he or she is able to perform the requested behaviors, in this case exercise), were related to the patient's adherence to the prescribed exercise program.[6] The observed relationship to self-efficacy led these investigators to note that "encouraging patients to become actively involved in treatment and increasing their confidence in performing recommendations seems crucial for treatment effectiveness."[6] They also noted that patients with higher expectations regarding their own outcome also tended to be more actively engaged in their own rehabilitation program.[6] Clearly, demonstrated compliance is less than ideal, and there are measures that the clinician can take to maximize the likelihood that the therapeutic program will be performed. Table 24-3 summarizes some of the factors that can be influenced by the involved clinician and that may work to promote increased patient compliance. Other factors that are less likely to be positively affected by the therapist's approach but are nevertheless related to compliance include psychological factors,

TABLE   24-3

Factors That Can Be Employed to Promote Increased Patient Compliance

1. Work to minimize barriers.[5,6,15]
2. Involve patient in treatment planning and goal setting and set realistic short- and long-term goals.[6]
3. Provide clear instruction with appropriate feedback.[10]
4. Keep exercise pain free or with low level of pain.[10]
5. Keep the instruction simple—complex or inconvenient programs hinder performance.[4,13,29]
6. Promote perceived benefits.[15]
7. Increase the patient's perceived self-efficacy.[6,15]
8. Encourage patient problem solving.[6]
9. Project positive attitude. Therapist attitude and involvement play an essential role, particularly with regard to compliance.[10,41]
10. Promote high expectations regarding final outcome.[6]
11. Encourage peer sharing for role modeling.[6]
12. Have regular follow-up built into the program.[27] (Compliance during a 12-week training program was 81%, but after an additional 12 weeks, only half [52%] were still exercising when the regular follow-up was withdrawn.)
13. Brochures alone are inadequate, with over 50 percent of patients instructed this way demonstrating incorrect exercise performance when assessed.[10]

environmental factors (including sociological and family influences, and physiologic factors (characteristics of the illness).[28]

THE HOME EXERCISE PROGRAM PRESCRIPTION

The research examining exercise compliance provides an excellent framework around which the home exercise prescription can be built. The approach taken here will deal with three key elements that will incorporate virtually all of the findings outlined previously with some new material. First, the exercise prescription needs to address the characteristics associated with the exercise itself. This is well known to all groups of health care practitioners as the "exercise prescription," and deals with the elements of intensity, duration, frequency, and specificity. In addition, a new element of "what to watch for" has been added, so that the patient is informed about what to expect both positively and negatively from the exercises. In the vast majority of cases, the program should be customized so that the needs of the individual are kept in mind.

The second key element deals with incorporating the science associated with home exercise programs into the package produced, so that compliance is improved. Issues such as the recognition of potential barriers and strategies to combat them should be incorporated. Additional items addressed within this second block of important points includes increasing the patient's perceived self-efficacy, promoting high expectations, keeping the instructions simple, and setting realistic short-term and long-term goals.

The third piece deals with the stylistic issue of providing a home exercise program that is professional and aesthetically pleasing, while at the same time cost and time effective.

The Exercise Prescription

The exercise prescription has wide application for exercise programs, ranging from musculoskeletal to cardiac problems. The five elements that make up the exercise prescription are intensity, duration, frequency, specificity, and symptoms to watch for. Intensity refers to how hard the patient should work. When this type of prescription is applied to aerobic training, the variable that is normally assessed is heart rate. In a weight training mode, the amount of weight lifted, or thickness of surgical tubing prescribed, is the way that intensity of effort is controlled. Regardless of the situation, a patient should not be sent home without a clear understanding of what is appropriate in terms of the effort that they should be putting into the program. A key element here is that intensity should be high enough to elicit a training effect, but not so hard as to either discourage a patient or result in unintended injury. It is better to ease an individual into a program and build some time into the program for neurologic and morphologic adaptation, than to have the person become discouraged and quit.

The second element deals with duration, or how long the exercise should be performed during a given session. With aerobic training, this is normally reflected with a specific number of minutes that an individual would train at a given heart rate (intensity). In the case of weight training, the duration is the number of repetitions and sets that should be performed. Again, this is an area where it is vitally important to communicate clearly with the patient and give precise guidance. In our Western culture, if a little is good, more is better. Patients will misinterpret the duration employed if a priori steps have not been taken to insure that they know how long they should be involved in the exercise program.

The third element of the exercise program is frequency, or how often the patient should be performing the prescribed regimen. In the case of aerobic training, this is typically interpreted as the number of days a week engaged in training. With weight training, this is also the number of days a week, because the number of sets was included in duration. The frequency should be prescribed based on the physiologic system that the provider is attempting to affect with an appropriate rationale. For example, in traditional aerobic exercise training with the goal of increasing an individual's aerobic capacity, the frequency prescribed has been 3 to 4 days a week. This is based on work that demonstrates that at an appropriate intensity and duration, an appropriate mix has been achieved between significant aerobic gains while at the same time limiting the risk of injury.[34] The same holds for traditional strength training, where recovery time is essential for the morphologic transition of muscle tissue. A slight variant associated with frequency, that is often not well understood by the practitioner prescribing exercises, is how contraction frequency can be used to influence an intact neurologic system. In this case, the frequency may be many times a day, such as performing 10 sets of static quadriceps exercises, spaced throughout the day, every day. The primary goal in this case is to activate the neurologic system and improve the quality of the contraction, enhance the control of the leg, or some other goal that is neurologically based. The very different frequency levels are based on the target systems that need to be considered in all prescriptions. The fact that this is often not well understood by health care practitioners underlines the reality that patients have no idea how frequency may be used in different ways to impact on the various systems of the body. The exercise prescription provides an excellent opportunity for patient education.

Specificity deals with the physiologic fact that we respond best to the type of training that we are performing. Simply stated, if an individual needs to improve the ability to perform wheelchair push-ups, the best activity to prescribe will be wheelchair push-ups. The carryover from other related tasks is only partial. Specificity has been shown to be related to the type of contraction (eccentric, concentric, isometric), the speed of contraction, the angle used when performing a contraction, and a number of other variables.[9] The key point here is that exercises should be designed in a way that closely replicates the mutual goals of the patient and therapist.

The last element, dealing with symptoms that the patient should watch for, is not part of the standard exercise prescription, but it is important from several perspectives. First, by outlining both the positive and potentially negative consequences of the exercise program, a foundation of clear communication has been established between the patient and the health care provider. When the patient knows what to expect and the range of consequences that might be encountered, the patient is more apt to carry out the program. Also, because this is a "home program," it is essential that the individual monitoring the program (the patient) knows when the response to exercise is either positive or negative. If the patient has reached a plateau and needs to progress further, the objective criteria should clearly identify what the next step should be and permit the progression. On the other hand, if the patient has experienced a negative result with the exercise, the patient should be informed enough that this will be recognized and the exercise program adjusted accordingly. Ideally, the patient should leave with some guidance regarding what to do if expected improvement occurs, what to do if there is no change, and what to do if the patient encounters a problem. Thus, clear communication about actions to take in a variety of circumstances should be part of all exercise prescriptions. The interested reader is referred to the works of Pollock et al,[34] Knapik et al,[19] and Jones et al,[17,18] for more information on the interaction between intensity, duration, and frequency, and the rate of musculoskeletal injury that can be anticipated.

An additional consideration for most, but not all, therapeutic exercise programs, is the need to consider warming-up prior to an exercise bout, and cooling-down when the exercise has been completed. Although it is possible that a program that deals with a very specific task, such as passive range-of-motion exercises or low-level isometric contractions, might not require a warm-up and cool-down, these elements will need to be considered in the vast majority of home exercise programs. Certainly any type of traditional aerobic or anaerobic conditioning should be performed within the context of an appropriate warm-up and cool-down. Thus, if this element were added on to the five points already discussed, the entire exercise prescription would include warm-up, the elements of the exercise prescription, and cool-down.

Finally, when dealing with the topic of the exercise prescription, an assumption is made that the practitioner has intuitively based the home program and its progression on the fundamentals associated with therapeutic exercise. Specifically, the assumption is that the following have been considered: (1) the stage of tissue healing, (2) tissue irritability and symptom stability, (3) the patient's time and willingness to participate, and (4) the time between scheduled physical therapy visits.

RESEARCH APPLIED TO THE HOME EXERCISE PROGRAM PRESCRIPTION

Many of the elements shown to positively affect patient compliance with home exercise programs have been discussed previously, and are outlined in Tables 24-2 and 24-3. In an effort to minimize redundancy, only new material or particularly important points will be expanded upon in this subsection of the chapter. Having noted that, the consequent brevity of this section should not be misinterpreted in terms of the importance of these findings. This section should be viewed in light of the material covered earlier in the sections "Behavioral Models and Home Exercise Programs," "Learning Styles and Patient Compliance," and "Level of Compliance Demonstrated in Past Research."

One very important point that is ironically often overlooked in the rush to provide quality care is the previously mentioned examination of the barriers that might keep the patient from performing the exercises. A common barrier is perceived lack of time on the part of the patient. This can be addressed by asking patients how they will work the prescribed exercise program into their day.[28] Often, when dealing with activities that need to be done throughout the day, such as flexibility exercises or neuromuscular training exercises, they can be tied to common tasks. Television is a great example, because the average individual watches several hours a day. If the exercises can be linked to the time taken up by commercials, this serves as a trigger to say that it is time to perform the treatment program. When coupled with other "triggers," such as mealtime or a break-time commonly taken at work, this provides a strategy that the patient can use to implement and gauge compliance with the program. Without a plan, all the patient has when leaving the office is a set of good intentions. Unfortunately, the reality is that many roads to nowhere have been paved with good intentions. Most research studies that have examined why individuals do not perform their prescribed instructions identify unresolved barriers as a key element.[5,6,15]

To overcome barriers, a physical therapist should work with patients to develop short-term and long-term measurable goals and insure that the goals agreed upon are realistic. When patients understand that their care has been customized for them and has been designed to restore the function that is important to them, two important things happen. First, they accept some ownership of the program, because they were involved in the development of the plan. It is a common finding that individuals are more likely to follow a procedure that they can see direct relevance in, and less likely to follow programs that they see as meaningless.[30,41] Second, it provides the patient with a road map to follow. Because the goals are measurable, the patient is able to self-assess, and the plan provides the patient with a means of recognizing when he or she is on the expected glide path. Practically, measurable goals are also a requirement of virtually all documentation systems and are explicitly required in the "Guidelines for Physical Therapy Documentation."[1] The short-term and long-term goals need to be realistic and linked to the problem that they are seeking help for, or the majority of patients will not stick with the program. It is better to have two or three simple exercises that are executed faithfully and correctly than to have an elaborate program that will not be done due to lack of time, understanding, or some other perceived barrier. Thus, another key element that goes hand-in-hand with the development of short-term goals is to keep the instruction simple. The time available to communicate and supervise the performance of a home program is finite, and it is more important to do several items well than to not correctly perform a long laundry list.

Two points that are closely related to goal setting and the level of instruction provided are identifying perceived benefits and working to increase the patient's perceived self-efficacy in terms of the exercise program. If the patient does not understand that there is direct linkage between the program and progress, it is likely that the patient will not make the effort to perform the program.[6,30,41] The challenge for the therapist is to make patients appreciate that what they do on their own time may very well exceed in importance all that is done in the clinical setting. In this regard, the therapist is serving as a coach, and is assisting the athlete with the design of an effective training program. If this analogy is continued, for progress to occur, the training has to be carried out independently by the athlete. The benefit will be a change in functional level that is a direct consequence of the program developed. At the same time, the patient has to be able to picture himself or herself performing the exercise program. If an extremely creative and effective program were developed for a patient that involved modern dance and jazz music, and the patient was someone who had never learned to dance, there is virtually no chance that the program will be followed. There has to be a match between the type of activity that patients can "picture themselves" doing and what the therapist is asking them to do.[28] Another place where this reality confronts health care providers is when an avid athlete is asked to stop all activity and rest. A marathon runner who has run consistently for the past decade will not stop running simply because a health care provider makes that recommendation. The runner cannot "picture" himself or herself as a sedentary individual. A reasonable recommendation in this case is to work with the athlete and to develop a program of "active or relative rest." The athlete is still able to train, but it may be on an upper body ergometer, so that an inflamed patellar ligament can rest. When the benefit of the program and the perception of self-efficacy are both in place, the likelihood that the home exercises will be performed increases significantly.

A final educational concept that can contribute to the design of the program is the Pygmalion concept.[8,22] Succinctly stated, it has been shown that when teachers have been told by an outside source that select students will excel in the program of instruction, those students tend to succeed at a higher level than other students.[3,38] This has occurred even though the teachers never shared their expectations with the students involved. Thus, the influence that a suggestion from an outside source has on ultimate performance occurs at a level other than standard verbal or written communication. Undoubtedly, this set of expectations was conveyed with body language, the way instruction was phrased, and the myriad other ways that we communicate at a subconscious level. This type of influence of expectations has also been shown to be related to exercise compliance.[6] The message that this provides to the clinician is that if you hold high expectations for your patient, and these expectations are communicated in all that you say and do, the ultimate result will probably be improvement.

STYLISTIC HOME EXERCISE PROGRAM ISSUES

It has often been said that both style and substance are required when approaching a problem. What has been discussed thus far with the exercise prescription and research findings associated with exercise compliance has been largely substance. These are the key elements necessary to insure that the home exercise program has the "right stuff," and that the program truly meets the needs of the patient. In addition, the style in which the program is communicated and given to the patient to take home and refer to when questions arise can make the difference between an "adequate" program and a program that "exceeded all expectations." Because one of the goals of this chapter is to provide suggestions to enhance the ultimate quality of care rendered, it is important to consider style. Within this discussion, other practical elements such as time, cost, and flexibility of the medium used to annotate the home exercise program will be discussed.

The simplest home exercise program is one that is written down on a piece of paper and given to the patient. This can be expanded upon slightly by adding a few stick drawings, but the final result is still much the same—a program that the patient can follow, but that also requires the ability to read the therapist's handwriting and understand what a quickly composed sentence means several days later. Certainly a hand-generated home program can be effective, but it does have a number of drawbacks. First, it is time consuming to compose a set of instructions with even cryptic illustrations by hand. Second, as has been alluded to already, the instructions are often difficult to understand at a later point in time, due to the lack of critical review of the material as it is being composed. Educators often hear this truism when students state that they understood it clearly when it was explained in class, but the same issue made no sense to them later in the day when they were looking over their notes. The annotation of the program prescribed needs to be detailed enough and graphic enough that it would trigger all the key elements in the patient's mind. Therefore, although handwritten programs are a possibility, it is recommended that a slightly more advanced technological solution be employed. Handwritten programs do have the advantages of being inexpensive and easily customized, but these advantages are not great enough to overcome the disadvantages.

The next level of home exercise program documentation is the generation of "exercise sheets" that can be handed out to patients with general classes of dysfunction. For example, this method is often employed with low back pain patients, where either William's back flexion exercises or McKenzie's back extension exercises are printed out and kept in a file drawer. Then, when a patient is identified with a given condition, the therapist simply gives the appropriate sheet to the patient and checks off the exercises that should be done. There may be a little annotation regarding the exercise prescription elements—such as intensity, duration, and frequency—but this does provide a very efficient and inexpensive method of dispensing home exercises. Using previously developed sheets also has the advantage of permitting clear graphics and carefully worded descriptions that can be used to insure that the exercise is done appropriately. When customized with the clinic's letterhead, this can even serve a marketing function. Although these are all marked improvements over the handwritten program, there are also a few drawbacks. First, the tendency is to use everything on the sheet rather than to think through what is best for this patient. This is a natural tendency, because everyone is busy and if the exercises that are there are used, the therapist can move on to the next patient. Therefore, it is often the case that a patient is given more exercises than really needed, or the exercises given are not precisely the very best ones for a particular condition. Related to this is the situation where some other exercise should be added that is not on the original sheet. In this case, the therapist is faced with adding a second or third exercise sheet with exercises scratched out, or dropping back to the first method and writing any additional exercises on the existing sheet. In either case, it is clear to the patient that he or she is receiving a slight modification of what is commonly handed out, rather than a customized program for the patient's problem. The impression of a "one size fits all" exercise prescription is compounded if the handouts are reproduced from old copies; and after copies of copies of copies have been made, they are difficult to read. Thus, while better than handwritten notes, this is also not the optimal way to provide stylistically pleasing annotation for your patients.

With the advent of ready access to line art reproduction (photocopiers) and computer-generated graphics, many of the limitations mentioned have been eliminated. When employing sortable cards or computer graphics, true customized programs can be readily made in a very short period of time. Excellent annotation of the exact exercise program given to the patient is improved, and the quality of the graphics and text instruction is typically very professional. The two biggest drawbacks are the learning curve associated with using either the cards or computer programs, and the potential onetime cost of the system selected. Because the majority of these programs are relatively intuitive without exorbitant costs, this "higher-tech approach" appears to be best for the majority of clinical settings today. Additionally, there is some evidence that suggests that home exercise programs designed on computers or generated with the aid of video equipment are more effective in terms of compliance and understanding, than programs produced by traditional methods.[20] A number of these packages and their manufacturers are listed at the end of the chapter.

Other methodologies exist that hold even greater promise for truly customized and individualized home exercise program annotation, yet at this time are limited due to time involvement required and cost. These include the production of videotapes that the patient can view at home, and exercise sheets that use digital photographs of the patient performing the exercise, that can be electronically pasted into a previously drafted narrative. When the digital format is coupled with other mediums like e-mail, the possibility of superb distance interaction with the patient becomes a real possibility. Undoubtedly, with the passage of time and the reduction of costs, new advances in this area will make the digital display of home exercises more attractive.

Summarizing the stylistic issues with home exercise programs, the method selected should be inexpensive, time-efficient, easily customized for each patient, clear both in verbal description and in visual presentation, and easily learned by the therapist, and should require minimal expenditures for equipment that is not already part of the modern therapy clinic. At this point in time, the preferred methodology appears to be the line-art drawings that are easily reproduced by rearranging cards, or generated on a computer. In the next few years, new options will probably supersede this current technology. In any case, whatever methodology is employed, there should be a clear set of instructions sent home with the patient so that they are readily available as a reminder regarding exercises or specific elements of the exercise prescription. The method should also permit a duplicate copy to be placed in the patient's medical folder or record.

PITFALLS TO BE AWARE OF WITH HOME EXERCISE PROGRAMS

Although the emphasis of this chapter has been on positive steps that can be taken to increase the likelihood of success when prescribing home exercises, there are also a number of common mistakes that tend to negatively influence performance. Pitfalls that are frequently part of the home exercise package include (1) too many exercises prescribed at one time,[13] (2) inadequate demonstration of the exercises, (3) inadequate follow-up to assure that the exercises are being done properly, (4) poor illustrations or instructions that patients are not able to follow when they arrive home, (5) failure to clearly communicate "why" this specific set of exercises has been prescribed for this patient and the need for them to be done, and (6) expecting the patient to use equipment of resources not readily available.

Almost all rehabilitation protocols or exercise sheets have a variety of exercises outlined for a given patient problem. The natural tendency when using one of these templates is to give the patient "the works," or at least a healthy dose of what is readily available. This is in accord with the way in which we purchase almost any other commodity, where we obtain our best value when we seek the whole package. With the exercise prescription, however, where it is typically desired that select exercises be performed in a particular fashion,[10] the truth may be that "less is more." In a recent study examining the ability of adults over the age of 65 to perform home exercises, the subjects were randomly assigned to groups that had 2, 5, or 8 exercises to perform.[13] The researchers found a difference in the ability of these three groups to perform their assigned exercises, with the group with only 2 exercises demonstrating significantly better performance than those prescribed 8 exercises.[13] The group that was prescribed 5 exercises fell midway in performance and was not found to be significantly different from the groups that performed 2 or 8 exercises.[13] Although the optimal number of exercises to prescribe at one time is not known—and most certainly depends on a variety of factors (e.g., motivation, subject's intellect, age)—it appears that too many exercises are often prescribed. The recommendation here is to err on the side of too few exercises. The authors of the study cited concluded that "in our experience, we believe that patients are often given more instructions than they can manage, requiring more changes in lifestyle than they are willing to make. In our view, physical therapists should consider the type and frequency of the exercises they prescribe." Start with only 2 or 3 exercises and see how the patient both complies with their performance and physically tolerates the exercises. The challenge for the therapist heeding this advice is to settle on the "best" 2 or 3 exercises to prescribe, and then to closely follow the patient's progress.

A second common pitfall that is associated with the limited time that we have access to each patient is not demonstrating the exercise program adequately. If the home exercise program is left to the last couple of minutes of the treatment session, there may only be enough time to hand the patient the sheet and ask if they have any questions. Human nature dictates that the patient will probably answer "no" at that time, yet not have a clear idea of what to do when he or she arrives home. This type of approach is commonly employed when crutches are given to patients right after an injury, yet when they arrive in the clinic it is clear that they would have benefited from instruction and an overview of potential problems. Research mentioned previously has demonstrated that patients comply better when exercises are demonstrated for them.[10] Health care professionals need to build the time into the treatment session to insure that the exercises are well understood and performed properly, prior to releasing patients to perform the exercises on their own. If the time is not built in, the therapist is implicitly telling the patient that performance of the exercise program properly is really not a high priority.

A truism is that the key to adult learning is repetition. When the patient has a recheck appointment, one integral part of the recheck appointment should be a review of the exercises that the patient has been performing. This provides time to correct mistakes, review techniques, or address questions that have arisen since the last appointment. If the exercise program was important for the patient's recovery, then spending a few minutes and reinforcing what has been done and what should be done in the future is an integral part of the recheck appointment. Ideally, this should take the form of active demonstration of the exercises, rather than simply asking the patient if they have any questions. Observing what the patient has been doing will often provide the therapist with a starting point for conversation regarding subtle nuances that will make the program more effective. A good general rule is to "assume nothing," and evaluate for yourself if the patient is having any problems with the exercises. Unfortunately, due to time demands, this element is often overlooked or ignored completely, and an excellent patient education opportunity is missed.

A fourth pitfall is the documentation that is given to the patient to take home. If the most basic home program of a few exercises scribbled on a piece of paper is given to the patient, the patient may run into a variety of problems, including inability to read the instructions, understand the terms, or recognize the stick drawing. As the handouts or other media (videotapes) become more automated, this becomes less of an issue but should still be considered. Here again, it is probably better to provide clear documentation for only 2 or 3 exercises, than to overwhelm with a small encyclopedia that will only benefit the bookshelf that it is placed on.

The final pitfall mentioned here is making the assumption that if the patient has access to a facility such as the YMCA or gym, that his or her compliance will be enhanced. This may not be the case. Research by Martin and Dubbert[26] has suggested that compliance decreases when patients are asked to exercise at locations that are perceived as inconvenient (e.g., fitness gym located across town). Other references can be found that suggest when exercises are done in the home, performance of the assigned exercises increases.[13] This is another example where "less can be more." Prescribe only those things that can be done easily with the resources that the patient has readily available.

APPENDIX: ABRIDGED LIST OF AUTOMATED RESOURCES

Card Catalog

The Saunders Group
4250 Norex Drive
Chaska, MN 55318-3047
(800) 966-4312

Computer Programs

PTEX

211 Manchonis Road
Wilbraham, MA 01095
(413) 596-5041
URL: *www.ptexsys.com*

Physiovideo

57 Providence Highway
Norwood, MA 02062
(781) 255-2053
URL: *www.physiovideo.com*

PhysioTools North America

250 Montgomery Street, 14th Floor
San Francisco, CA 94104

☐	Based on mutually agreed-upon short- and long-term goals.
☐	Exercises are compatible with stage of tissue healing and standard therapeutic exercise principles.
☐	Determine patient's "stage of change" level and adjust the home exercise program accordingly.
☐	Linkage made between the exercises and patient's condition, when explanation was provided.
☐	Potential barriers identified and attempt made to minimize their impact—discussion included when/how this can be fit into patient's standard day.
☐	Elements of the exercise prescription were implemented (warm-up, intensity, duration, frequency, specificity, symptoms to watch for, cool-down).
☐	Objective guidance given regarding proper progression of the program between clinic appointments (when to advance, when to "ease up," and when to contact the therapist).
☐	Exercise explanation/instruction contained examples for all basic learning styles (visual, auditory, and tactile).
☐	Exercises were properly demonstrated and appropriate feedback given during the clinic appointment.
☐	Customized home exercise program given to the patient (paper form or video). Is the material visually appealing, with clear narrative and illustrations?
☐	Patient provided with an e-mail address or phone number that they can use when questions arise.
☐	Recheck appointment scheduled.
☐	Less is more—has the tendency to prescribe too many exercises been avoided?
☐	Consider significant other involvement, if appropriate—particularly effective with activities such as posture education, where the family member can provide feedback without drawing public attention to the fact that they are communicating about a medical issue.
☐	Safety built in to the program? If there is anything that if misunderstood or improperly performed could actually result in harm, attempt to anticipate the problem and work to prevent it from occurring.

FIGURE 24-1

Checklist of key points to consider when generating a home exercise program.

(888) 564-0639
URL: *www.physiotools.com*

Exercise Pro

BioEx Systems
P.O. Box 684584
Austin, TX 78768
(800) 750-2756
URL: *www.bioexsystems.com*

Exercise Xpress 2.0

The Saunders Group
4250 Norex Drive
Chaska, MN 55318-3047
(800) 966-4312

Fysio Fix

Innovative Rehab Systems
826 Office Park Circle, #104
Lewisville, TX 75057
(972) 420-6954
URL: *www.innovativerehab.com*

Video Systems

Peak Care Video
7388 South Revere Parkway, Suite 707
Englewood, CO 80112
(800) 978-PEAK
URL: *www.peakcare.com*

SUMMARY

Developing a quality home program is not difficult, yet it challenges the therapist to serve as an educator, motivator, facilitator, and mentor. Including a home program as a part of the treatment plan is almost always the right thing to do for the patient, and it is a requirement of contemporary practice.[1]

Often, the exercise intervention will be the vital element in the treatment of a patient that will determine ultimate success or failure. By considering and implementing many of the issues discussed previously—ranging from barriers identified in the transtheoretical model to positive ways to facilitate adherence to the exercise prescription—a great deal can be done to encourage exercise compliance. Figure 24-1 provides a checklist that highlights the key elements discussed in this chapter. If these elements are in place when designing a program, then much will have been done to create an environment for compliance and success. From a substance standpoint, it is hoped that this overview has provided both tangible suggestions and food for future thought. Stylistically, we are approaching a time where if a better way to communicate a block of information to a patient can be imagined, it can also be done. The appendix that follows provides a source list of some of the more common home exercise program aids in use today. Rehabilitation specialists should develop quality home programs, so that both patients and the profession will benefit from the time and thought put into them.

REFERENCES

1. American Physical Therapy Association. Guidelines for physical therapy documentation—guide to physical therapist practice. *Phys Ther* 77:1634–1636,1997.

2. American Physical Therapy Association. What types of interventions do physical therapists provide? Guide to physical therapy practice. *Phys Ther* 77:1213–1226, 1997.

3. Babad E. Pygmalion—25 years after interpersonal expectations in the classroom. In: Blanck PD, ed. *Interpersonal Expectations: Theory, Research, and Applications.* New York, Cambridge University Press, 1993, pp. 125–153.

4. Becker MH. Patient adherence to prescribed therapies. *Med Care* 23:539–555, 1985.

5. Blanpied P. Why won't patients do their home exercise programs? *J Orthop Sports Phys Ther* 25:101–102, 1997. Editorial.

6. Chen CY, Neufeld PS, Feely CA, et al. Factors influencing compliance with home exercise programs among patients with upper-extremity impairment. *Am J Occup Ther* 53:171–180, 1999.

7. Cross DS, Tilson ER. Tools to assess student's learning styles. *Radiol Technol* 69:89–92, 1997.

8. Dvir T, Eden D, Banjo ML. Self-fulfilling prophecy and gender: Can women be Pygmalion and Galatea? *J Appl Psychol* 80:253–270, 1995.

9. Enoka RM. Neural adaptations with chronic physical activity. *J Biomech* 30:447–455, 1997.

10. Friedrich M, Cermak T, Madebacher P. The effect of brochure use versus therapist teaching on patients performing therapeutic exercise and on changes in impairment status. *Phys Ther* 76:1082–1088, 1996.

11. Groth GN, Wilder D, Young VL. The impact of compliance on rehabilitation of mallet finger injuries. *J Hand Ther* 7:21–24, 1994.

12. Hellman EA. Use of the stages of change in exercise adherence model among older adults with a cardiac diagnosis. *J Cardiopulm Rehabil* 17:145–155, 1997.

13. Henry KD, Rosemond C, Eckert LB. Effect of number of home exercises on compliance and performance in adults over 65 years of age. *Phys Ther* 78:270–277, 1998.

14. Hoover TS, Marshall TT. A comparison of learning styles and demographic characteristics of students enrolled in selected animal science courses. *J Animal Sci* 76:3169–3173, 1998.

15. Janz NK, Becker MH. The health belief model: A decade later. *Health Educ Q* 11:1–47, 1984.

16. Johnson DP. Adult educators need to have enthusiasm. *Adult Learning* 9:11–14, 1998.

17. Jones BH, Cowan DN, Knapik JJ. Exercise, training and injuries. *Sports Med* 18:202–214, 1994.

18. Jones BH, Knapik JJ. Physical training and exercise-related injuries. Surveillance, research and injury prevention in military populations. *Sports Med* 27:111–125, 1999.

19. Knapik JJ, Jones BH, Bauman CL, et al. Strength, flexibility and athletic injuries. *Sports Med* 14:277–288, 1992.

20. Koning P. *Barnes-Jewish Hospital Implements "New Millennium" Rehabilitation Patient, Information System.* 1999. Unpublished work.

21. Kosower E, Berman N. Comparison of pediatric resident and faculty learning styles: Implications for medical education. *Am J Med Sci* 312:214–218, 1996.

22. Learman LA, Avorn, J, Everit DE, et al. Pygmalion in the nursing home. The effects of caregiver expectations on patient outcomes. *J Am Geriatr Soc* 38: 797–803, 1990.

23. Mandl KD, Brennan TA, Wise P, et al. Maternal and infant health: Effects of moderate reductions in postpartum length of stay. *Arch Pediatr Adolesc Med* 151:915–921, 1997.

24. Marcus BH, Selby VC, Niaura RS, et al. Self-efficacy and the stages of exercise behavior change. *Res Q Exerc Sport* 63:60–66, 1992.

25. Marcus BH, Simkin LR. The transtheoretical model: Applications to exercise behavior. *Med Sci Sports Exerc* 26:1400–1404, 1994.

26. Martin JE, Dubbert PM. Exercise applications and promotion in behavioral medicine: Current status and future directions. *J Consult Clin Psychol* 50:1004–1007, 1982.

27. Mikesky AE, Topp R, Wigglesworth JK, et al. Efficacy of a home-based training program for older adults using elastic tubing. *Eur J Appl Physiol* 69:316–320, 1994.

28. Mulder JA. Patient compliance to individualized home exercise programs. *J Fam Pract* 12:991–996, 1981.

29. Oldridge NB. Compliance and exercise in primary and secondary prevention of coronary heart disease: A review. *Prev Med* 11:56–70, 1982.

30. Oldridge NB. Compliance in exercise rehabilitation. *Physician Sportsmed* 7:95–103, 1979.

31. Partridge R. Learning styles: A review of selected models. *J Nurs Educ* 22:243–248, 1983.

32. Payton OD, Hueter AE, McDonald ME. Learning style preferences: Physical therapy students in the United States. *Phys Ther* 59:147–152, 1979.

33. Pitney WA. Continuing education in athletic training: An alternative approach based on adult learning theory. *J Athl Train* 33:72–76, 1998.

34. Pollock ML, Gettman LR, Milesis CA, et al. Effects of frequency and duration of training on attrition and incidence of injury. *Med Sci Sports* 9:31–36, 1977.

35. Prochaska JO, Marcus BH. The transtheoretical model: The applications to exercise. In: Dishman RK, ed. *Advances in Exercise Adherence*. Champaign, IL, Human Kinetics, 1994, pp. 161–180.

36. Public Health Service. *Priority Area 1: Physical Activity and Fitness. Healthy People 2000 Review (1998–1999)*. Washington, DC, Public Health Service, 1999, pp. 29–35.

37. Puliyel MM, Puliyel JM, Puliyel U. Drawing on adult learning theory to teach personal and professional values. *Med Teacher* 21:513–523, 1999.

38. Rosenthal R, Jacobson L. *Pygmalion in the Classroom*. New York, Holt, Rinehart & Winston, 1968.

39. Samelson TC. Getting information across to patients. *Med Economics* 74:105–108, 1997.

40. Sharp JE. Applying Kolb learning style theory in the communication classroom. *Business Communication Q* 60:129–134, 1997.

41. Sluijs EM, Kok GJ, van der Zee J. Correlates of exercise: Compliance in physical therapy. *Phys Ther* 73:771–786, 1993.

42. Taylor JA. A practical tool for improved communications. *Supervision* 59:18–19, 1998.

43. Voss DE, Ionta MK, Myers BJ. Techniques for Facilitation. Proprioceptive Neuromuscular Facilitation 3rd ed. Philadelphia, Harper & Row, 1985, pp. 289–314.

44. Washington N, Parnianpour M. Using CAI to accomodate a variety of learning styles in a biomechanics course. *Biomed Sci Instrument* 33:41–46, 1997.

45. Wynn KE. Medical College of Ohio: Learning the art of healing through technology. *Magazine Phys Ther* 6:40–44, 1999.

CHAPTER 25

Essentials of Functional Exercise: A Four-Step Clinical Model for Therapeutic Exercise Prescription

Gray Cook and Michael L. Voight

O B J E C T I V E

After completing this chapter, the student therapist should be able to do the following:

- Demonstrate a four-step model designed to promote the practical systematic thinking requisite for the effective therapeutic exercise prescription and progression.

It is widely accepted that therapeutic exercise encompasses a majority of treatment techniques employed in physical medicine. Although many practitioners of physical medicine, such as psychiatrists, chiropractors, and occupational therapists prescribe or employ physical means to advance and accelerate the rehabilitation process of their patients, the field of physical therapy has always housed a specialized exercise-specific knowledge base. Today's therapist has received instruction and information in general exercise science with emphasis in exercise physiology, kinesiology, and biomechanics. This general knowledge is enhanced by a unique clinical focus on pathologic orthopedic and neurologic states and their functional representation. This special focus charges the therapist to consider evaluation of human movement as a complex multisystem interaction and the logical starting point for exercise prescription. Exercise prescription choices must continually represent the specialized training of the therapist through a consistent and centralized focus on human function. Exercise used at the therapeutic level must refine movement, not simply create general exertion with the hope of increased movement tolerance.[4] Moore and Durstine state: "Unfortunately, exercise training to optimize functional capacity has not been well studied in the context of most chronic diseases or disabilities. As a result, many exercise professionals have used clinical experience to develop their own methods for prescribing exercise."[1]

Experience, self-critique, and specialization produce seasoned clinicians with intuitive evaluation abilities and exercise innovations that are sometimes difficult to follow and even harder to ascertain; however, common characteristics do exist. The clinical expert uses *parallel* (simultaneous) consideration of all factors influencing functional movement. The treatment philosophy is inclusive and adaptable with the ability to address a variety of clinical situations. There also is an understanding that a clinical philosophy is designed to serve, not to be served. The treatment design demonstrates specific attention to the parts (clinical measurements and isolated details) with continual consideration of the whole (restoration of function).[4] Moore and Durstine follow their previous statement by acknowledging that "experience is an acceptable way to guide exercise management, but a systematic approach would be better."[1]

The purpose of this chapter is to demonstrate a four-step model designed to promote the practical systematic thinking requisite for effective therapeutic exercise prescription and progression.[4] The approach will be a *serial* (consecutive) step-by-step method that will, with practice and experience, lead to *parallel* thinking and multilevel problem solving. The intended purpose of this method is to reduce arbitrary trial-and-error exercise attempts and protocol-based thinking. It will give the novice clinician a framework that will guide but not confine clinical exercise prescription. It will provide experienced therapists with a system to observe their particular strengths and weaknesses with respect to exercise dosage and design. Inexperienced and experienced therapists alike will develop practical insight by applying the model and observing the interaction of the systems that produce human movement. The focus is specifically geared to orthopedic physical therapy and the clinical problem-solving strategies used to develop an exercise prescription through an outcome-based goal-setting process.

All considerations for therapeutic exercise prescription will regard conventional orthopedic exercise standards (biomechanical and physiologic parameters) as well as neurophysiologic strategies (motor learning, proprioceptive feedback, and synergistic recruitment principles) with equal importance. This model will create a mechanism that will necessitate interaction between orthopedic exercise approaches and optimal neurophysiologic techniques. The four-step progression will demonstrate the hierarchy and interaction of the founding principles used in physical therapy (both orthopedic and neurologic). For all practical purposes, these four categories help demonstrate efficient and effective continuity necessary in formulation of treatment plan and prompt the therapist to maintain an inclusive open-minded clinical approach.

This chapter is written with the clinic-based practicing therapist in mind. It will help the therapist formulate a clinical exercise philosophy. Some clinicians will discover reasons for success that were intuitive and therefore hard to communicate to other professionals. Others will discover a missing step in the therapeutic exercise-design process. Much of the confusion and frustration encountered by the modern therapist is due to the vast opportunities and treatment options afforded by ever-improving technology and information accessibility. To effectively use the wealth of information the future has yet to bestow, the therapist must adopt an operational framework or personal philosophy regarding therapeutic exercise. If clinical exercise philosophy is based on technology, equipment, or protocols, the scope of problem solving is strictly confined. It will have to continually change, because it has no universal standard or gauge. However, a philosophy based solely on the structure and function of the human body will keep the focus (function) uncorrupted and centralized. Technological developments can only enhance exercise effectiveness as long as the technology, system, or protocol remains true to a holistic functional standard.

The following four principles for exercise prescription are based on human movement and the systems upon which it is constructed. The intention of these four distinct categories is to break down and reconstruct the factors that influence functional movement, and to stimulate inductive reasoning, deductive reasoning, and the critical thinking needed to develop a therapeutic exercise progression. Hopefully, these factors will serve the intended purpose of organization and clarity, thereby giving due respect to the many insightful clinicians who have provided the foundation and substance for the construction of this practical framework.[4]

The four principle considerations for therapeutic exercise prescription are the following:

1.   Functional evaluation and assessment of conditions of dysfunction (disability) and impairment.
2.   Identification and management of motor control.
3.   Identification and management of osteokinematic and arthrokinematic limitations.
4.   Identification of current movement patterns followed by facilitation and integration of synergistic movement patterns.

FUNCTIONAL EVALUATION, ASSESSMENT & DIAGNOSIS

Successful medical intervention is the result of some sort of evaluation or assessment. Physical therapy intervention through exercise prescription is no different. The physical therapy evaluation is the starting point of all exercise recommendations. Saunders states that "Because many different tests, measurements, and sequences for collecting the required data are available, the format chosen largely depends on individual preference. However, a methodical and complete examination is essential."[10] Although each clinician has his or her own individual evaluation style, all must generate the necessary baseline information to proceed with effective treatment choices. Therefore, although one must adhere to a specific evaluation method for personal reliability, that method must provide all the necessary information without a collection or interpretation bias. Clinicians must continually *evaluate* their *evaluations,* because habitual testing and treatment preferences can move the therapist over the line from clinical individuality to personal subjectivity. The functional evaluation is unique in that the primary concern is not signs, symptoms, or structures, as with most medical assessments. In the past, the focus on measuring and altering impairments superceded the more important goals of improving function and reducing disability. A more current emphasis is not on using therapeutic exercise to alter the list of impairments, but rather to use the interventions to improve function and reduce disability that is meaningful to the individual seeking rehabilitation. This type of evaluation process results in a pathomechanical and/or pathoanatomic determination of the problem.

The purpose of the functional evaluation is to identify the current level of function. Consider all the possible reasons for that level of function, and then decide how function can be positively influenced through intervention. Impairments are isolated movement limitations or abnormalities that can be measured by clinical means. Functional limitations represent a restriction in performance of basic tasks. Instead of considering which exercise can be prescribed to improve an impairment, the rehabilitation provider should consider which impairments are related to reduce function for this patient, and which exercises can enhance function by addressing the appropriate impairments. Liebenson states that, "In the majority of soft tissue injuries, functional changes are the only objective findings on which to base treatment and judge progress. Unfortunately, most orthopedic examinations rely on tests that search for structural lesions. Although structural lesions are present in only about 20% of cases, overuse of expensive diagnostic tests is typical in the search to diagnose such structural pathology. The remaining 80% have no identifiable structural pathologic abnormality and require treatment based on the evaluation of functional deficits."[14]

A brief discussion of the information generated through the evaluation process will negate assimilation errors at this vital stage of the rehabilitation process. As with any treatment, therapeutic exercise prescription must be constructed on a solid and objective evaluation base. The evaluation is not simply the automatic result of collected information but rather careful deliberation upon that information. The information is most effectively managed in definable categories. The categories will give significance and hierarchy to information and help create a uniform direction toward attainment of functional goals through outcome-based exercise treatments. A brief discussion of the categories will demonstrate how clear lines between information groups support organized patient management and objective treatment choices. The goal-setting process is a result of the evaluation, which should encompass both medical and functional information. The primary goal of physical therapy intervention is first to evaluate and then to generate a plan of care that restores functional homeostasis. Therefore, we must review and outline the evaluation process before further discussion of exercise is possible. The role of the evaluation in exercise prescription can be better clarified by first defining the roles of the medical evaluation and diagnosis for orthopedic and musculoskeletal conditions compared to the functional diagnosis of the same.[4]

Disablement: The Medical Diagnosis

The medical evaluation and diagnosis is generated by the physician and places the patient in a diagnostic group or category that correlates the anatomic structures, standardized testing procedures, pharmacology, surgery, and so forth. The medical diagnosis along with a medical history usually results in the use of medications or surgery. The medical diagnosis will help the therapist determine *contraindications* affecting therapeutic exercise choices. The "functional diagnosis" is the term that names the primary dysfunction toward which the rehabilitation provider directs treatment. In the rehabilitation model, the therapist examines patients with impairments, functional limitations, and disabilities to determine diagnosis, prognosis, and intervention. If the distinction between the medical and rehabilitation diagnosis is not clear, the process of effective and efficient exercise prescription is not possible. The medical diagnosis does not dictate the type of exercise intervention; it only limits certain types of movement, stress, or physical exertion because of a surgical protocol or anatomic or cellular condition. Because the medical diagnosis is based on physical signs and symptoms and not "functional movement," it cannot provide insight as to specific therapeutic exercise choices. Patients who fall within the same diagnostic categories present a variety of functional movement abilities. This makes it impossible to develop an individualized therapeutic exercise protocol based solely on a medical diagnosis. Of course, medical diagnostic protocols for exercise do exist, but they are usually generalized and not representative of the full potential of modern rehabilitation.

Two main problems are the following:

1. The medical diagnosis is geared toward a specific biomechanical, physiologic, or anatomic abnormality, not a specific function or movement pattern.

2. Medical "diagnostic" exercise protocols are usually time-based, not function-based. For example, many postsurgical protocols set a time line from the surgical date with recommended exercises based on the days and weeks from the surgical procedure.

This does not challenge the postsurgical exercise protocol. These protocols are based on normative standards designed to help, not hinder. Moreover, it is the sole right of the surgeon to recommend a specific exercise course, but once again it is to limit postsurgical stress and reinforce contraindications. It is the therapist's role to work within the confines of that protocol as long as it does not interfere with efficient and effective treatment. Scientifically based innovation and clinical creativity is usually a welcome addition to most standard protocols whether for consideration of an individual requiring isolated protocol modification or for grounds to challenge the protocol. The therapist and surgeon working together is the only conceivable solution. It is usually a surgeon therapist team that sets postsurgical rehabilitation standards and creates the inventiveness behind continual evolution of most modern postsurgical exercise protocols. Dr. Jerome Ciullo states that "Surgery can correct the original problem but the muscles are still out of balance, so in most cases it is not the surgery that cures you. It is the surgery that allows you to go back to your exercise program."[9] Therefore, a medical diagnosis alone cannot create or determine a therapeutic exercise treatment plan—it can only, at best, limit the available options. From this, the therapist will define impairments or abnormalities at the tissue, organ, or body system level. This will help establish the specific causes of the limitation or dysfunction prior to intervention.[4]

Disablement: The Functional Diagnosis

Functional assessment is obviously required to create a functional diagnosis. It is not simply the reproduction, observation, and appraisal of daily life skills, occupational duties, or sports activities, but a perceptive understanding of the basic movements upon which they are constructed. The word "function" has grown in popularity over the last decade without enjoying the same degree of success with respect to professional clarification or practical understanding. The word implies natural, practical, and purposeful movement; but it has also been used to describe exercise methods at a far greater frequency than evaluation methods. This creates a perplexing question. Most medical treatment is based on and defined by the effect it produces on a particular physical parameter (either chemical or mechanical). The effect can only be measured if an evaluation produces a baseline appraisal of that parameter followed by a reappraisal upon cessation of a treatment cycle. Without a central functional evaluation model, the therapist has no standard or universal functional parameter with which to measure the effectiveness of one particular exercise versus another. The common but sad assumption is that if an exercise replicates a specific task or activity, then that exercise by default is therefore functional.

A better way to define functional exercise is by documenting its positive effects on a functional outcome. This refers to the "functional influence" of an exercise as opposed to its observable similarity to a functional activity. When a functional problem is identified, the therapist does not simply recommend that the activity be repeated by manipulating the parameters of frequency, intensity, and duration. This simple approach may change quantitative measures but will rarely improve qualitative measures "since the body will usually sacrifice movement quality for movement quantity."[5,22] The therapist must break down the functional movement into its fundamental submovements. These submovements, like functional movements, are still multisegmental whole-body movements, but because they are simple and distinguished they are more specific to problem identification. They are distinguished by the particular way each represents a level of motor control as well as the normal developmental parameters needed for acquisition of skill. Skill defined by Sullivan et al, in reference to early motor development, is the "highest level of motor control" that "includes two functions: the manipulation and exploration of the environment."[20]

This broad and general description is then more specifically described as those activities where the distal component (the hands and feet) are mobile as the proximal musculature and joints, as well as the musculature of the spine, remain dynamically stable.[20] For the purposes of this model, the aforementioned definition of skill will be considered **general skill,** because it can be considered a common or basic function of most adult orthopedic patients. The definition becomes more specific when applied to individual adult movement patterns. The many demands of sedentary (static postural demands) and laborious jobs (dynamic physical exertion), as well as the vast array of movement specificity needed for sports and hobbies, should be referred to as **specific skill.** All skillful movement is built on a foundation of *fundamental* movements. This foundation can be simply described by cornerstones called mobility and stability, and central pillars called controlled mobility and/or dynamic stability (Fig. 25-1).

The model is constructed to demonstrate the absolute dependence of specific complex movement on its fundamental constituents. Subtle changes in mobility and stability can tilt the entire movement structure.[4] The clinician can assume that functional limitation at a fundamental level is the endowment of the next level. The body and mind, however, are designed to compensate and will absorb the limitation through compensation and substitution. This necessitates the need to return to the most basic level where the limitation remains observable. This may or may not correspond to the level where the limitation first occurred. It also demonstrates that the determinants (mobility, stability, and dynamic stability) of skillful function viewed in isolation sometimes do not appear functional; nevertheless, they are the only unforced paths to restoration of true function. Evaluation and exercise prescription should always consider these as the natural course to skill development and function, as they replicate the normal course of physical development and, more importantly, the primary process of motor learning. "Since normal motor control is acquired during the developmental sequence, when motor control is adversely affected, a recapitulation of the sequence may be the most effective means of reestablishing control."[20]

Functional assessment can be defined as the identification of limitations concerning movement generation or movement control by a deductive process employing both qualitative and quantitative measurements. The ability to test both movement quality and quantity will greatly improve exercise prescription effectiveness. This process involves breaking down the functional movement into the submovements or fundamental movements so the stages of motor control can be viewed and evaluated. This also lends itself nicely to systematic exercise program design. "A functional progression for return to activity can be developed by breaking specific activities down into a hierarchy and then performing them in a sequence that allows for acquisition or reacquisition of skill."[22] Normative data are an essential component to assessment. Developmental specialists have mapped the path to normal motor control, which gives us insight as to the initial sequence of movement abilities and motor learning. "The four major stages of motor control are mobility, stability, controlled mobility and skill."[20] This sequence is helpful and often employed in treatment, but the clinician must also consider available data on normative levels of adult skill or function needed for prognosis and goal setting.

Unfortunately, very little normative data has been gathered on adult populations with specific focus on functional movement *quality*. Quantitative measurements and performance data are helpful, but these data must be balanced and preceded by a quality standard to truly understand and affect (through feedback and treatment) human movement.[11] This is not a new observation. One of the many examples stating a need for more normative quality-based data was by Richter et al in a 1988 physical therapy journal article. The article dealt with rolling movements in normal adults and attempted to describe normal rolling variance and observe if the rolling represented different developmental steps demonstrated in the use of body segments. The authors stated, "Physical therapy for patients with neurologic dysfunction often includes the evaluation and teaching of rolling movements. To determine the quality of the rolling pattern, rolling movements must be evaluated against some standard or norm. To date, no reported research exists describing the movement patterns that adults use to roll. Although specific rolling movements have been recommended for use in treatment, whether these movements are valid representations of healthy individuals' movements is unknown."[18] Likewise, orthopedic patients are given functional exercises that profess to replicate normal movements, but very few normative quality standards are used. One simple reason for limited qualitative, as compared to quantitative, norms, may be the problem with data collection. Quantitative norms are easy to obtain once the tester's reliability with a measuring device is achieved. Qualitative norms require much more from the test design and tester.

F I G U R E   2 5 - 1

All skillful movement is built on a foundation of *fundamental* movements. This foundation can be simply described by cornerstones called mobility and stability, and central pillars called controlled mobility and/or dynamic stability.

However, with adequate training, high levels of reliability can be achieved.[8,18]

The key to qualitative testing for both clinical and normative research data collection is the practical and employable description of movement. The way a movement is described will determine the amount of quality assigned to that particular movement. The rolling article stated, "If less than 85% of exact agreement was obtained within a body region, we refined the movement pattern description to resolve any possible ambiguities."[18] The Functional Movement Screen (FMS) is an attempt at normative data collection in a healthy physically active population with respect to movement quality. It was designed to set normative standards for specific and general physically active populations in an attempt to monitor movement factors influencing performance and injury factors. It was also specifically designed to detect those movement problems that are not detected in the preparticipation (medical) physical by specifically observing functional movement extremes and

predictable limitations. Lastly, it provides a functional baseline in the event of an injury.[8] The Berg Balance Measure (BBM) is another excellent example of a qualitative test. Although the FMS and BBM are geared for two different populations, note the detail of movement description. Distinct lines are drawn between the ability to demonstrate various levels of control.

Whether the physical therapist uses standardized functional testing or creates a new or hybrid test, it is important to understand the need for and contribution of both qualitative and quantitative functional measures. At present, bilateral comparison is a temporary solution for physical therapists who want to employ functional movement patterns for evaluative purposes but are reluctant because of the lack of normative data. Many functional movements and their submovements can be compared in this manner. Consider bilateral qualitative comparison of rolling, single-leg stance, or any fundamental or functional activity that has a right–left component.

The next division of information comes within the physical therapy evaluation itself. This division is between functional evaluation and specific clinical measurements. This will also help to separate and define impairment, functional limitation, and disability. *Impairment* refers to a loss or abnormality at the tissue, organ, or body system level. Functional limitations are restrictions of the ability to perform a physical action, activity, or task in an efficient, typically expected, or competent manner. In contrast, *disability* refers to the inability to perform tasks and activities usually expected in specific social roles that are customary for the individual or expected for one's status or role in the environment. Not all impairments or functional limitations result in disability. It is possible for two individuals with the same disease and similar levels of impairment and functional limitation to have two different levels of disability. One person may remain active in all aspects of life while the other individual may choose to limit social contact, depend on others for care, and to have a job where it is not possible to use adaptive methods to participate in work tasks.

Through functional assessment, the therapist will recognize and classify impairments, functional limitations, and disability using clinical measurements in an attempt to demonstrate the underlying causes by qualifying and quantifying the impairments. The observation of functional movement should, in most cases, precede clinical measurements, and qualitative testing should precede quantitative measurements. Qualitative assessment can establish a desired level of competence or ability, at which time quantitative assessment will allow comparison bilaterally or with norms and other individuals. Qualitative assessment is particularly useful as a formative evaluation because it helps create instructional experiences and feedback, according to Haywood in her text on *Life Span Motor Development*.[11] This improves the deductive component of movement problem solving, thereby directing the focus on whole movement patterns to consider issues such as synergistic movement, compensatory movement, coordination and balance reactions, and daily activities. Functional movements should usually be described in both qualitative and quantitative terms when possible, whereas clinical measurement is usually reported in the form of quantitative documentation. The observation of mass or whole movements can sometimes redirect and broaden the clinical focus by revealing limitations unrelated to the medical diagnosis but still necessary for improvement or restoration of normal function (Fig. 25-2).[4]

Consider the multiple reasons for the differences in the squatting abilities of these subjects. The knee and ankle range of motion is different to some extent. The sum of their limitation or impairment, however, does not account for gross difference in squat function. It is also possible to have no significant differences in hip, knee, and ankle active range of motion between subjects and still have significantly altered squatting ability. One simple explanation is not lower-quarter mobility but trunk dynamic stability. Secondly, timing, coordination, weight shifting, and balance can determine the ability of mul-

tiple joint segments to work together in a functional pattern. A structural or functional asymmetry between limbs can stop a symmetrical pattern altogether instead causing the obvious and predictable weight shift or asymmetrical response, which is more often expected. The squat may not be functional for some lifestyles but it is fundamental to all general and specific skill, because it is a transitional posture and an excellent demonstration of dynamic stability. It is up to the therapists to determine what can be learned from a limitation at this level. Therefore, when possible, a functional or fundamental movement pattern should precede the clinical measurement. Functional and fundamental movement qualitative assessment is the obvious starting point in the deductive reasoning and problem-solving process.

Clinical Measurements

Clinical measurements now use special equipment and/or special test formats to help explain underlying causative factors of dysfunction with greater accuracy than ever before. Balance assessment tools, range-of-motion testing, pain scale testing, and dynamometer-assisted muscle testing may be chosen because of initial qualitative observations by the therapist. The therapist will then use a means of more specific measurement for quantitative testing regarded as reliable and objective. With time, technology will continue to advance the practice of physical therapy. Improvements in clinical measurement and data collection have increased the specificity and convenience of isolated testing. It should not, however, influence the problem-solving process used by the clinician to develop a therapeutic exercise program.

Technological advances will continue to allow the clinician to improve clinical testing and objective data collection. However, the enhanced ability to collect a single piece of data should not change the weight or significance of that data; it should only provide increased sensitivity and objectivity with the same level of importance. This type of mistake is often not intentional but nevertheless a hindrance to problem solving. When one single measurement is favored, the exercise program may be specifically geared toward improving that isolated measure. As the favored measure improves, another equally important parameter may become unmasked, cease to improve, or even decline. A good example of this problem was the introduction of isokinetics. Isokinetics demonstrated a significant advancement in clinical measurement of muscle performance, thereby enabling the therapist to generate data with greater specificity regarding isolated muscle group testing. In addition, this technology also served to improve communication with physicians, because the charts and graphs resembled familiar lab results. Objectivity, reliability, and convenience served to confirm the popularity of isokinetics. However, the simple fact remains that it is only one tool for a clinical measurement of a single parameter or impairment. Isolated strength testing does not have the ability to measure function or independently generate a functional diagnosis.

Subject 1

Clinical measurements of hip flexion do not correlate with hip flexion in functional movement. Unloaded open chain assessment of active and passive range of motion using a goniometer is not representative of the functional movement utilized in squatting.

Subject 2

Clinical measurements of hip flexion seem to correlate with hip flexion in functional movement. Unloaded open chain assessment of active and passive hip using a goniometer is representative of the functional movement of squatting.

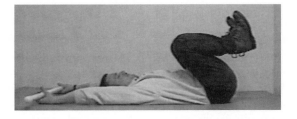

FIGURE 25-2

Unloaded versus loaded lower extremity AROM demonstrated through deep squatting with arms elevated.

This popular clinical measurement tool may have changed the magnitude of muscle testing and given it greater clinical significance than other equally important forms of testing. This is in part due to the fact that manual joint assessment, muscle length testing, postural analysis, trigger point observation, balance and proprioception testing, and other tests lacked the flash and cold reliability of the dynamometer. Because of this, isolated muscle testing may have been weighted with greater significance than other isolated clinical measurements. This error should have been evident long before the research stated that "current literature suggests that a poor correlation exists between the performance of an open kinetic chain strength test and the ability of an individual to perform weight-bearing activities."[16] The lesson is that when greater objectivity is gained on one level (a simple clinical measurement of impairment), it is sometimes lost at a much higher level (functional movement assessment for the purpose of a functional diagnosis).

The last point to be made concerning clinical measurement is the application of two fundamental principles of orthopedic medicine. The first is bilateral comparison, which needs no explanation but should be applied to both structure and function in all cases when possible. Although the information is highly individualized, it is invaluable to the problem-solving process. Nationally published norms and standards are informative, but individualized clinical treatment requires specific attention to a single system. The second principle is just as simple and obvious but often forgotten. It is the complete assessment and clearing of the joints and muscular structures above and below the area in question. Any dysfunction or limitation can greatly influence the rehabilitation process. The clinician may not have control over these limitations but nevertheless needs to be aware of the factors that can potentially limit outcomes. In most cases the proximal and distal joints should also be compared bilaterally as well.

The systematic application of clinical measurements complements the problem-solving process needed for functional evaluation and diagnosis and effective exercise prescription. The previous information may seem oversimplified, but breakdowns of information will improve clinical self-analysis. Most clinicians will agree with this process but may not adhere to it in all clinical situations. Routine case review with these ideas in mind will only improve problem-solving skills.

Pain and Subjective Complaint

Although pain and subjective complaint are significant considerations in exercise prescription, they were intentionally placed after objective functional assessment and clinical measurements (with the exception of the mention of objective pain scale measurement). Subjective complaints are identified while taking the patient's history as well as during functional assessment and clinical measurements. Physical therapists are as close to the subjective complaints of the patient as a health care professional can get. This close proximity can often distort the functional picture. Subjective and objective information must be weighted separately for clarity and precision during the evaluation purposes. The separation will allow comparison and correlation of information and allow the therapist to observe the interaction of pain and function. It is seldom possible to observe a continuous linear relationship between pain and function. The lack of this linear relationship does not automatically indicate magnification or malingering behavior, nor does it suggest denial of symptoms. Physical therapy is unique in that patients do not just passively discuss their pain and symptoms; they actively confront these problems through movement with supervision and guidance supported by education. When function is discussed with the patient, the therapist must consider which activities and positions directly affect symptoms and which ones produce some degree of fear or apprehension reported as symptoms. Fear, apprehension, and pain are all strong influences on both temporary and long-term function, and should never be discounted.[3,12] Practical explanations and analogies, along with demonstrations, can usually minimize the effect of this common response.

Liebenson emphasizes that, "During functional testing, the effects of movement and position on the behavior of pain, the painful or pain-free range, and the effects of repeated testing should be determined. Sensitivity to various movements and positions, along with any weight-bearing intolerance, should also be determined."[14] However, it is the relationship and interaction of function and symptoms, and not simply the degree of symptomatic response to movement, that should dictate exercise choices. "If the clinician is unable to correlate or match the findings in the various test positions, then the source of the syndrome may be non-mechanical."[17] This could simply implicate acute or subacute chemical irritation or a more involved behavioral or perceptual problem. In chronic cases, if no observable correlation in pain and function can be established, the patient and referral source must be made aware of special circumstances because the scope of physical therapy treatment no longer has a functional or objective goal outside of symptom management.

Lastly, therapeutic exercise, like most forms of manual therapy, should not produce pain (unless special circumstances are present and have been discussed with all involved—such as burns). A reproduction of pain, especially during exercise, goes against the natural instincts of human movement as well as the patient's common sense. Those who discuss pain and gain in the same sentence (usually in a fitness setting) are obviously only concerned with exercise quantities, not exercise quality (which is not possible in the presence of pain). Posture, muscle tone, synergistic movements, agonist/antagonist relationships, proprioception, motor learning, and numerous other functional movement determinants are affected when unnecessary and avoidable pain enters the picture. A thorough functional orthopedic physical therapy evaluation will often provoke symptoms (to some degree) to outline both chemical and mechanical irritability of structures. According to Porterfield and DeRosa, "Two of the main goals of the functional assessment are reproducing the pain syndrome with applied stresses, and having the clinician and patient mutually understand the pain pattern".[17] Exercise prescription can then be implemented in such a way as to not provoke symptoms. A review of the principles of chemical and mechanical pain will assist the therapist in the formulation of a ratio of rest to exercise that will best suit the state of the tissue and the attitude of the patient during each stage of recovery. Because of this fact, exercise focus usually takes on one of two general paths, to restore or improve tissue metabolism or to stimulate mechanical efficiency and motor control. It is important to clearly choose one path or the other initially, and assess the response and adaptation behavior accordingly.

EVOLUTION OF A CLINICAL EXERCISE PHILOSOPHY

Technological advances will refine objective data, but they will not change the inherent systematic reasoning needed for clinical practice. A comprehensive functional evaluation philosophy will help reduce confusion created by differing physical therapy evaluation and exercise methods. The variety of techniques available to the modern physical therapist in some ways has reduced cohesion and communication in the profession as a whole. Many debates have resulted between therapists because of differing views about exercise treatments. These debates cannot be truly settled until a central evaluation based on functional outcomes is used as a universal standard. A review of the current literature reveals two distinct problems, both relating to functional movement. The following two examples will discuss range of motion and flexibility as a simple example and use cases for debate and consideration.

Examples

EXAMPLE ONE: THE LACK OF NORMATIVE FUNCTIONAL DATA

First there is a profound lack of normative data regarding functional movement quality. This lack of normal data can possibly allow clinicians to make assumptions about populations based on a small clinical sample or personal experience. The two most common assumptions regarding function concern age and medical diagnosis. Any assumption about a functional limitation without complete qualitative and quantitative evaluation of that limitation will greatly inhibit the ability of the therapist to effectively consider all available exercise options.

First Assumption

"Direct correlation exists between age and function." It is not uncommon to presume that a direct linear correlation is present between age and functional movement. However, research suggests that activity and lifestyle are significant considerations and may play an equal if not greater role than simply considering chronological age.[1,3,11,12] Most geriatric physical therapists do not consider deep squatting (heels flat, thighs below parallel) beneficial or necessary in the treatment of the elderly orthopedic patient. This assumption over time, however, may lead to the notion that deep squatting beyond a certain age is not even possible. Just because deep squatting is not practical does not automatically indicate that it is not possible. The excessive motion of deep squatting may very well be contraindicated for many orthopedic conditions. Nevertheless, it is a fundamental step in the developmental progression and a precursor to ambulation. It is a transitional movement that demonstrates dynamic stability. Dynamic stability precedes ambulation, which is considered a skill. The developmental progression of postures and transitions should be considered on an individual basis and deleted

through selective program design and not through age-related functional assumptions. This will maintain an unprejudiced and flexible exercise philosophy based solely on individual function. An enlightening trip abroad will reveal that deep squatting is often preferred to sitting for both work and recreation by young and old alike. Therefore, lack of deep squatting in all likelihood may be cultural and activity-based and not simply a result of age. Researchers indicate that "the greatest losses (in flexibility) occurred in movements an individual does not habitually perform" and "inactivity is certainly a major factor that may contribute to flexibility decline in old age." Most of these changes are reversible.[11]

Second Assumption

"Diagnosis correlates directly with function." Patients (as well as some medical professionals) usually view the common diagnosis of osteoarthritis as the cause, and not the result, of poor movement patterns. Functional abilities cannot be predicted with any degree of accuracy by only considering structural changes. The clinician cannot assume in cases of nontraumatic arthritis that structural changes preceded functional changes. Consider the words of two physicians on this often oversimplified clinical matter. Janda observes the profound effect of compromised movement relative to an irritant (such as a common sprain or strain) when he states that "joint pain is not a local problem, but affects the entire motor system. Impaired relations within the motor system outlast the elimination of the painful cause." Therefore, "impairment of central motor control results in defective or uneconomical movement patterns which is one of the main causes of joint dysfunction. Poor movement patterns appear in conjunction with joint dysfunction and alter pressure on joints, therefore leading to further overstrain. Chronic or severe pain may lead to fixation of certain 'pain-motor' patterns. Movement patterns can change due to altered CNS function from stress, anxiety, depression or fatigue."[12] Cailliet makes a similar point when he discusses that "normal use and normal movement place no stress upon soft tissues. Excessive use, abuse, and misuse can cause irritation with resultant pain and disability. Once the neuromuscular pattern is altered, the normal biomechanics of the part is altered and the soft tissue is abused and damaged."[3]

EXAMPLE TWO: QUESTIONABLE VALIDITY OF CURRENT NORMATIVE FUNCTIONAL DATA

The second problem questions the current database available for use. Tests are carried out in the name of function, creating implications that can be prejudiced or incorrect.

Flexibility

Researchers will place individuals in a functional category of either flexible or inflexible based on a single test such as the sit and reach. This test is not representative of an individual's total movement patterns and even less representative of realistic practical movement.[2] When discussing functional categories such as individuals grouped as flexible or inflexible, many factors need to be considered. Significant differences in static and dynamic flexibility, as well as differences in loaded compared to unloaded movements, must be considered.

Stress or Efficiency Testing

Some cardiovascular function tests are conducted without any appropriate *qualitative* biomechanical screen. Posing a question to the validity of the test: Is poor biomechanical efficiency or cardiovascular capacity the major limiting factor of the test? The test does in fact measure physical output, endurance, and work, but if a limitation is detected, it is not qualified because all the parameters affecting efficient movement are not addressed. If a defect or poor score is demonstrated, the tester may automatically assume the problem is cardiovascular and therefore prescribe the associated exercise regimen. If, however, the deficit is simply poor biomechanics with a significant loss of movement efficiency, then the major limiting factor of the test has gone unnoticed. A significant improvement in test results could be demonstrated by simply resolving the limiting biomechanical component. This would improve mechanical efficiency and economy, which may change the stress factors on the cardiorespiratory system. Normative data concerning cardiovascular output can possibly be skewed by the unintentional detection of musculoskeletal mechanical dysfunction in the attempt to identify metabolic dysfunction. Brown reminds us that "anatomical changes in the heart (atrophy, lipofuscin accumulation, increased fat and connective tissue) do occur with age but they do not explain the declines in function that have been observed."[1] When testing, one must consider the relationship of cardiac output measured and the work or power produced. This relationship demonstrates efficiency. *Work* is defined as force x distance and *power* is defined as force x distance/time.[2] Therefore, force and distance are important factors in determining efficiency, necessitating the qualitative and quantitative measurement of those structures producing force (muscles) and allowing distance (joints and connective tissue) prior to the calculation and determination of efficiency problems.

Balance Testing

The popular topic of balance testing in the elderly may need to consider that when range of motion is not optimal, proprioception cannot be optional. Simple restrictions in joint mobility can cause alternative balance strategies and compensations. Often researchers will define functional parameters for the system they are currently studying without full consideration of the functional status of other systems or the comprehensive interaction of multiple systems, which can magnify a small problem in one system.

Four Considerations for Clinical Exercise Philosophy

(1) Some of the greatest advancements in the physical therapy profession have first developed more appropriate evaluations that eventually led to superior treatment options. A brief historical perspective of orthopedic physical therapy will demonstrate the contributions of James Cyriax and Florence Kendall[7,13]. Both greatly advanced the quality of the physical

therapy evaluation process. Their work is so ingrained in the profession that most forms of muscle or joint assessment owe some common trait to their early observations. The Kendalls demonstrated how, through postural assessment and specialized manual muscle testing, a more specific evaluation and exercise prescription could be generated. Cyriax, an orthopedic physician, helped devise a basic methodology for differentiating contractile and noncontractile problems about a joint, which greatly refined the soft-tissue diagnostic process. Both created testing that improved the categorization and communication of functional information with respect to the structure and function relationship.

Since that time, the orthopedic physical therapy evaluation has become highly mechanized and specialized. This has greatly expanded the therapist's ability to evaluate, monitor, communicate, and affect changes in human function. The growth in physical therapy research has produced a wealth of quantitative testing data. This has helped develop many quantitative standards and norms. Much of this data is highly specific. This is the obvious direction for research, because it offers fewer variables and greater specificity. Yet the need for more general functional norms and standards continues to grow. More specifically, the need for qualitative functional norms may be even greater, because qualitative testing lends itself to treatment and education and helps explain the causes for variations in quantitative measurements of performance. Quantitative testing is good for general ranking purposes but offers little insight on the underlying factors influencing the raw score.

(2) It is interesting to observe how normal human movement is appreciated and evaluated throughout the life span. From birth until 2 years of age, the development of movement is considered to proceed along a predictable course.[19] Most agree that a continuum, sequence, or stage model is observable, and this progression is clearly defined for clinical purposes. "The developmental sequence has provided the most consistent base for almost all treatment approaches used by physical therapists."[19] Because most of the stages or steps toward the development of posture and movement are defined by clear descriptions, the evaluation of these stages is qualitative in nature. These stages are defined as representations of mobility and stability, and the transitional activities that demonstrate the interaction of the two. Various nonweight-bearing, weight-shifting, and weight-bearing movements display milestones of achievement. As we age, we rank ourselves through more and more quantitative observations. There is a significant quality component to special populations like dance, martial arts, and the skill positions in sport. However, general populations are rarely ranked according to functional movement quality. This has a profound influence on the physical therapy profession, because restoration of qualitative and quantitative function is a primary concern.

A brief contrast between orthopedic and neurologic physical therapy will demonstrate the differences in the initial approach of the evaluation process. More specifically, the neurologic therapist working with infants and toddlers has an obvious advantage from a qualitative evaluation standpoint, because the developmental sequence and progression is a qualitative standard. Of course, the comparison is unfair, considering the greater variability of the general orthopedic caseload. However, the contrast in theory still serves as a good analogy of qualitative and quantitative evaluation methods. Orthopedic physical therapy does not currently have a centralized or universal, quality-based functional assessment. This may be the central cause of minor divisions in orthopedic physical therapy as a profession. Highly specialized orthopedic physical therapists have honed their skills and improved their training on technique-based philosophies that hold themselves to extremely high standards. However, there is not a functional standard of measurement (qualitative and quantitative combination) that would allow objective comparison of all techniques. In contrast, the neurologic physical therapist uses a quality-based functional assessment to monitor and evaluate growth and motor development. The infant, toddler, and child must achieve developmental milestones with respect to mobility, stability, controlled mobility, and skill. A goniometer is not used, and strength tests are not needed to demonstrate success or failure. The patient either achieves a functional milestone or does not. Reasons for pass and fail can be evaluated separately with more specific clinical measurements, but the patient is now in a functional category. The functional category is the logical starting point for functional diagnosis and treatment.

Orthopedic medicine measures the parts with accuracy and reliability and must strive to observe the whole both quantitatively and qualitatively. Observations in science and nature demonstrate that the whole often is not represented by the sum of its parts. Measuring the parts is very scientific and can be tracked with quantitative values. Developmental milestones seem to be pass/fail with ranges of normalcy and require a trained eye to discuss the quality of movement. It is this quality-based assessment tool that sets physical therapists apart from other individuals prescribing exercise. Most individuals with rudimentary exercise training can quantify values such as range of motion, strength, and endurance. The discerning clinician can demonstrate how three different individuals achieving the same quantitative value of a particular performance parameter can do so with varying degrees of quality. The ability to create an equal balance and appreciation for these two forms of movement assessment is, and will continue to be, the defining factor of physical therapy exercise prescription. An analogy for human movement can be observed in today's modern computer. Historically, orthopedics was concerned with hardware (musculoskeletal system) while neurologic physical therapy observed and attempted to modify software (motor control). Today the therapist understands that the human hardware can be changed or improved, but if the human software remains the same, movement efficiency is rarely changed or maintained.

(3) Orthopedic manual therapy has contributed greatly to advances in exercise. McKenzie, Kaltenborn, Maitland, Paris, and many others have increased our awareness of joint assessment considering the established osteokinematic model and providing practical treatment options involving arthrokinematic movement. Modern physical therapists have bridged the gap between passive mobilization and active movement, using a combination of mobilization and exercise techniques to achieve accelerated restoration of functional movement. Mulligan has created mobilization techniques that involve a manual mobilizing (sometimes stabilizing) force in the presence of active movement followed by passive stretch. This creative new work demonstrates the disappearing line between mobilization and exercise.[15] Likewise, the new techniques for taping the spine and extremities have moved the science of taping from protective and restrictive to facilitory and dynamic. The focus is now placed on proprioception, and complements exercise by not simply reducing symptoms but by providing continuous tactile feedback.[4] Taping has now moved out of sport-specific applications and is now commonplace for the innovative and aggressive therapist. Taping should be considered an extension of manual therapy by providing mechanical feedback and facilitation as the patient progresses. Taping is complementary to exercise as well. It should follow arthrokinematic rules and replicate anatomy whenever possible.[4]

(4) Kabat and Knott demonstrated in their early work, called proprioceptive neuromuscular facilitation (PNF), how the brain has an affinity for synergistic movements encompassing both spiral and diagonal patterns without consideration of isolated muscle activity or single-plane joint motion. It is unfortunate that many exercise protocols do not employ the inspired theme of proprioceptive neuromuscular facilitation at any point in the entire protocol. They go from open-chain, fixed-axis, fitness-styled exercise equipment and recycled home exercises to functional movement patterns without ever first using PNF techniques to refine and stimulate the natural synergistic patterns of movement. PNF has often been considered a hands-on treatment approach, but the idea that a proprioceptive reaction can be improved with movement input rather than visual and auditory input is gaining popularity with hands-off exercise as well (see Chapter 8).[6,22] When clinicians become familiar and comfortable with the techniques of PNF, their exercise skills will improve and their understanding of practical motor learning will be greatly advanced.

INCORPORATION OF FOUR PRINCIPLES

- *Functional evaluation and assessment.* The evaluation must identify a functional problem or limitation resulting in a functional diagnosis. The observation of whole movement patterns, tempered with practical knowledge of key stress points and common compensatory patterns, will improve evaluation efficiency.
- *Identification of motor control.* Orthopedic and sports physical therapy could be greatly advanced by understanding functional milestones and fundamental movements such as those demonstrated during the positions and postures paramount to growth and development. These milestones serve as key representations of functional mobility and

control. They also play a role in the initial setup and design of the exercise program.

- *Identification of osteokinematic and arthrokinematic limitations.* The skills and techniques of orthopedic manual therapy are beneficial in identification of specific arthrokinematic restrictions that would limit movement or impede the motor learning process. Management of myofascial structures will improve osteokinematic movement as well as balance muscle tone between the agonist and antagonist. This will also help the therapist understand the dynamics of the impairment.

- *Integration of synergistic movement patterns.* Once those restrictions and limitations are managed and gross motion is restored, the application of PNF-type patterning will further improve neuromuscular function and control. Considering synergistic movement is the final step in the restoration of function by focusing on coordination, timing, and motor learning.

The application of all four principles in the appropriate sequence will allow the clinician to understand a starting point, consistent progression, and end point for each exercise prescription. This sequence is achieved by using functional activities and fundamental movement patterns as goals. By proceeding in this fashion, the physical therapist will have the ability to evaluate the whole above the parts and then discuss the parts as they apply. The true art of physical therapy is to understand the whole of synergistic functional movement and those therapeutic techniques that will have the greatest positive effect on that movement in the least amount of time. The system is designed to produce musculoskeletal and neuromuscular changes while creating a more favorable motor learning environment.

THE FOUR Ps

The four Ps are actually four simple words starting with the letter "P" that represents the four principles previously mentioned. They serve as quick reminders of the hierarchy, interaction, and application of each principle. The questions of what, when, where, and how with respect to functional movement assessment and exercise prescription are answered in the appropriate order.

1. *Purpose.* Functional evaluation and assessment.
2. *Posture.* Identification of motor control.
3. *Position.* Identification of osteokinematic and arthrokinematic limitations.
4. *Pattern.* Integration of synergistic movement patterns.

Purpose

PRIMARY QUESTIONS

1. *What* functional activity is limited?
2. *What* does the limitation appear to be—a mobility problem or a stability problem?

3. *What* is the dysfunction or disability?
4. *What* fundamental movement is limited?
5. *What* is the impairment?

The word "purpose" is simply a cue to be used both during the evaluation process and the exercise prescription process to keep the clinician intently focused on the greatest single limiting factor of function. It is not uncommon for the therapist to attempt to resolve multiple problems with the initial exercise prescription. However, the practice of identifying the single greatest limiting factor will reduce frustration and also not overwhelm the patient. There may be other factors that have also been identified in the evaluation; however, a major limiting factor or a single weak link should stand out and be the focus of initial therapeutic intervention regarding exercise. Alterations in the limiting factor may produce positive changes elsewhere that can be identified and considered prior to the next exercise progression.

The functional evaluation process should take on three distinct layers or levels. Each of the three levels should involve qualitative observations followed by quantitative documentation when possible. The levels are functional activity assessment, functional or fundamental movement assessment, and specific clinical measurement. Normative data is helpful but bilateral comparison is also effective and serves to demonstrate the functional problem to the patient at each level. Until the physical therapy evaluation, many patients think the problem is simply symptomatic and structural in nature and have no example of dysfunction outside of pain with movement. Moffroid and Zimny suggest that, "Muscle strength of the right and left sides is more similar in the proximal muscles whereas we accept a 10% to 15% difference in strength of the distal muscles. . . . With joint flexibility, we accept a 5% difference between goniometric measurements of the right and left sides."[19]

FUNCTIONAL ACTIVITY ASSESSMENT

This is a reproduction of combined movements common to the patient's lifestyle and occupation. They usually fit the definition of general or specific skill. The therapist must have the patient demonstrate a variety of positions and not just those positions that correspond to symptom reproduction. This includes static postural assessment as well as dynamic activity. The quality of control and movement are assessed. Specific measurement of bilateral differences is difficult, but demonstration and observation is helpful for the patient. The therapist should note the positions and activities that provoke symptoms as well as the activities that illustrate poor body mechanics, poor alignment, right–left asymmetries, and inappropriate weight shifting. When the therapist has observed gross movement quality it may be necessary to also quantify movement performance. Repetition of the activity for endurance comparison, symptom reproduction, or rapidly declining quality will create a functional baseline for bilateral comparison and documentation.

FUNCTIONAL OR FUNDAMENTAL MOVEMENT ASSESSMENT

The therapist must take what is learned through the observation of functional activity and break those movements down to the static and transitional postures seen in the normal developmental sequence. This will reduce activities to the many underlying mobilizing and stabilizing actions and reactions that constitute the functional activity. More simply stated, the activity is broken down into a sequence of primary movements that can be observed independently. It must be noted that these movements still involve multiple joints and muscles. Individual joint and muscle group assessment will be performed during clinical measurements. Martin notes, "The developmental sequence has provided the most consistent base for almost all approaches used by physical therapists."[19] This is a powerful statement and, because true qualitative measurements of normal movement in adult populations are limited, the therapist must look for universal movement similarities. Changes in fundamental movements can affect significant and prompt changes in function and therefore must be considered functional as well. Because the movement patterns of most adults are habitual and specific and therefore not representative of a full or optimal movement spectrum, the clinician must first consider the nonspecific basic movement patterns common to all individuals during growth and development. The developmental sequence is predictable and universal in the first 2 years of life. There are individual differences in rate and quality of the progression. The differences are minimal compared to the variations seen in the adult population with their many habits, occupations, and lifestyles. In addition to diverse movement patterns, the adult population has the consequential complicating factor of a previous medical and injury history. Each medical problem and injury has had some degree of influence on activity and movement. So evaluation of functional activities alone may hide many uneconomical movement patterns, compensations, and asymmetries that when integrated into functional activities are not readily obvious to the clinician. By using the fundamental movements of the developmental progression, the clinician can view mobility and static and dynamic stability problems in a more isolated setting.

Although enormous variations of functional movement quality and quantity exist between specific adult patient populations, most individuals have the developmental sequence in common. The movements used in normal motor development are the building blocks of skill and function. Many of these building blocks can be lost while the skill is maintained or retained at some level (although rarely optimal). We will refer to these movement building blocks as fundamental movements and consider them as precursors to a higher function. Bilateral comparison is helpful when identifying qualitative differences between right and left sides. These movements (like functional activities) can be compared quantitatively as well. Repetition of movement for endurance comparison, symptom reproduction, or rapidly declining quality will create a functional baseline for comparison and documentation.

CLINICAL MEASUREMENTS TO IDENTIFY SPECIFIC PROBLEMS

Clinical measurements should be used to identify specific problems that contribute to limitation of motion or limitation of control. Clinical measurements will first classify a patient through qualitative assessment. The parameters that define that classification must then be quantified to reveal impairment. These classifications are called hypermobility and hypomobility, and help to create treatment guides considering the functional status, anatomic structures, and severity of symptoms. The therapist should not proceed into exercise prescription without proper identification of one of these general categories. The success or failure of a particular exercise treatment regime is probably more dependent on this classification than the choice of exercise technique or protocol (Fig. 25-3). Janda then provides greater depth of insight to the classification process by identifying muscle groups with common traits and placing them into a functional division. Janda proposes that muscular imbalance progresses in a predictable fashion. "Postural muscles tend to tightness while phasic muscles tend to weakness" (Fig. 25-4).[21]

Once the appropriate clinical classification is produced, specific quantitative measurements will define the level of involvement within the classification and set a baseline for exercise treatment. Periodic reassessments may identify a different major limiting factor or weak link that may require reclassification followed by specific measurement. The new problem or limitation would then be inserted as the purpose for a new exercise intervention. A simple diagram (Fig. 25-5) will help the clinician separate the different levels of function so that intervention and purpose will always be at the appropriate level and assist with clinical decision making relative to exercise prescription.[8]

Functional performance deals with specific parameters that are more extrinsic and achievement-based. It is concerned with repetition of and recovery from a given movement. These are quantitative measures that represent interaction with the environment and a demonstration of work, speed, power, coordination, agility, balance, strength, energy expenditure, and efficiency. The tests employ basic movements previously defined as fundamental (dynamic stability), but basic locomotion (lower extremities) and manipulation (upper extremities), seen as skill by motor development specialists, can also be used. However, the movements should be common so general comparisons of volume and intensity can be observed.

The last category for consideration is specific skill function. For the athlete, this would mean sport-specific analysis as well as position-specific demands. For the industrial patient, it would consider job site ergonomics, job description and responsibilities, as well as norms and averages of production. Other considerations for general populations demonstrate ADL function and specific training for the use of assistive devices and equipment as well as movement for special circumstances. Before entering into specific exercise recommendations, the therapist should demonstrate the specific purpose of exercise intervention. The patient's responses and questions will help the

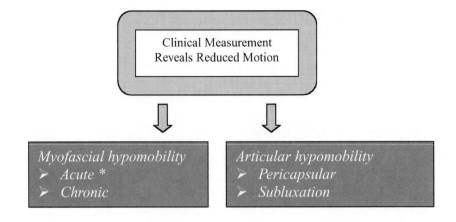

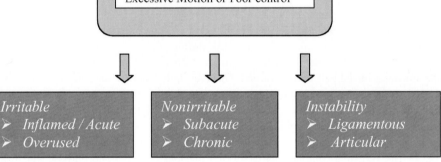

F I G U R E   2 5 - 3

Biomechancial assessment
and treatment (Source:
Cook G. *Meadows Manual
Therapy: Biomechanical
Assessment and Treatment.*
NAIOMT Course Notes.)

Muscles Prone to Tightness	Muscles Prone to Weakness
• Gastroc/soleus • Tibialis posterior • Short hip adductors • Hamstrings • Rectus femoris • Iliopsoas • Tensor fasciae latae • Piriformis • Erector spinae (especially lumbar, thoracolumbar, and cervical portions) • Quadratus lumborum • Pectoralis major • Upper portion of trapezius • Levator scapulae • Scalenes • Flexors of the upper limb	• Peronei • Tibialis anterior • Vastus medialis and lateralis • Gluteus maximus, medius, and minimus • Rectus abdominis • Serratus anterior • Rhomboids • Lower portion of the trapezius • Short cervical flexors • Extensors of the upper limb

F I G U R E   2 5 - 4

Janda's functional
division of muscle groups.

Specific Skill

Since both functional movement and functional performance have been appropriately addressed, the restoration of skill becomes a process of sensory motor learning techniques and positive feedback experiences.

Functional Performance & General Skill Performance

Only consider if all functional movement quality and quantity is within normal or functional limits. If structural or physiological barriers (that cannot be addressed) limit movement, then proceed into performance and consider current fundamental movement as an acceptable plateau.

Functional or Fundamental Movement

This is always the first consideration for all functional evaluation and exercise intervention. This involves restoring movement by addressing the clinical classification and level of involvement. The isolated improvement is then integrated into the fundamental movement and reassessed.

FIGURE 25-5

Levels of function.

therapist understand the level with which the patient can appreciate the problem. It is helpful to verbally describe the problem, visually demonstrate the problem, and then let the patient experience dysfunction by performing a movement that illustrates the problem. This will provide an educational experience that involves visual auditory and kinesthetic feedback. Motor learning usually occurs in the presence of three conditions: need or necessity, repetition, and reinforcement. By demonstrating the functional problem through three different sensory examples, the patient might better understand the purpose and necessity of the exercise prescription. Appropriate exercise dosage will enable the patient to perform the volume of exercise needed for repetition with unnecessary stress. The appropriate progression and sequence of exercise will create reinforcement through positive feedback and success. The exercise program should be designed around a predetermined success model with steps designed for the individual's motivation and ability.

Posture

PRIMARY QUESTIONS

1. *When* in the development sequence is the impairment obvious?

2. *When* do the substitutions and compensations occur?
3. *When* in the developmental sequence does the patient demonstrate success?
4. *When* in the developmental sequence does the patient experience difficulty?
5. *When* is the best possible starting point for exercise with respect to posture?

"Posture" is a word to help the therapist consider a much more holistic approach to exercise prescription. Janda creates an interesting point when discussing posture and the muscles responsible for its maintenance. Most discussions regarding posture and postural musculature generally refer to erect standing. However, "erect standing position is so well balanced that little or no activity is necessary to maintain it."[21] Therefore, "basic human posture should be derived from the principle movement pattern, namely gait. Since we stand on one leg for the most of the time during walking, the stance on one leg should be considered to be the typical posture in man; the postural muscles are those which maintain this posture." Janda reports the ratio of single- to double-leg stance in gait at 85 to 15 percent. "The muscles which maintain erect posture in standing on one leg are exactly those which show a striking tendency to get tight" (Fig. 25-4).[21] Infants and toddlers use tonic holding before normal motor development, and maturation produces abilities for the use of co-contraction as a means of effective support. "Tonic holding is the ability of tonic postural muscle to maintain a contraction in their shortened range against gravitational or manual resistance."[20] The adult orthopedic patient may revert to some level of tonic holding following injury or in the presence of pain and altered proprioception. Likewise, those adults who have habitual postures and limited activity may adopt tonic holding for some postures.

Just as Janda uses single-leg stance to observe postural function with greater specificity in contrast to a more conventional double leg erect standing, the developmental progression can give even greater understanding by looking at the precursors of single-leg stance.[4] As stated previously, fundamental movements are basic representations of mobility, stability, and dynamic stability and include the transitional postures used in growth and development. This approach will help the therapist consider how the mobility or stability problem, which was isolated in the evaluation, has been (temporarily) integrated by substitution and compensation of other body parts. The therapist must remember that motor learning is a survival mechanism. The principles that the therapist will use in rehabilitation to produce motor learning have already been activated by the functional response to the impairment. Necessity or affinity, repetition, and reinforcement have been used to avoid pain or produce alternative movements since the onset of symptoms. Therefore, a new motor program has been activated to manage the impairment and produce some level of function that is usually viewed as dysfunction. It should be considered a natural and appropriate response of the body reacting to limitation or symptoms. The body will sacrifice movement quality to maintain a degree of movement quantity. Considering this, two distinct needs are presented.

POSTURE FOR PROTECTION AND INHIBITION

The therapist must restrict or inhibit the inappropriate motor program. In the case of a control or stability problem, the patient must have some form of support, protection, or facilitation. Otherwise, the inappropriate program will take over in an attempt to protect and respond to the postural demand. Although nearly all adult patients function at the skill level upon evaluation, many qualitative problems are noted. Inappropriate joint loading and locking, poor tonic responses, or even tonic holding can be observed with simple activities. Some joint movements are used excessively while other joint movements are unconsciously avoided. Many primary stability problems exist in the presence of underlying secondary mobility problems. Moreover, in some cases the mobility problem preceded the stability problem. This is a common explanation for microtraumatic and overuse injuries. It is also why bilateral comparison and assessment of proximal and distal structures is mandatory in the evaluative process. In the case of a mobility problem, a joint is not used appropriately due to weakness or restriction. The primary mobility problem may be the result of compromised stability elsewhere. Motor programs have been created to allow the patient to push on in the presence of the mobility or stability problem. The problems can be managed by mechanical consideration of the mobility and stability status of the patient in the fundamental postures.

- Primary stability problems must be mechanically supported or assisted in some way. This can be done simply by a reduction of partial or complete stress through postural variations. This may include nonweight-bearing or partial weight bearing of the spine and extremities or temporary bracing. If the stability problem is only in a particular range of movement, then that movement must be managed. If there is an underlying mobility problem, then it must be managed and temporarily taken out of the initial exercise movement. The alteration of posture can effectively limit complete or partial motion with little need for active control by the patient. The stability problem must be trained independently of the mobility problem or at a great mechanical advantage to avoid compensation. The secondary mobility problem, once managed, should be reintroduced in a nonstressful manner so the previous compensatory pattern is not activated.
- The primary mobility problem must be assisted and managed by manual articular and soft-tissue techniques, when appropriate, and followed by movement to integrate any improved range and benefit from more appropriate tone. If the mobility limitation seems to be the result of weakness, then make sure the proximal structures can demonstrate the requisite amount of stability prior to strengthening. Then proceed with strengthening or endurance activities with a focus on recruitment, relaxation, timing, coordi-

nation, and reproducibility. Note that the word "resistance" was not used initially. Resistance is not synonymous with strengthening, and is only one of many techniques used to improve functional movement in early movement reeducation. However, the subsequent sections on position and pattern will address resistance in greater detail. Use posture to mechanically block or restrict substitution of stronger segments and improve quality at the segment being exercised.

POSTURE FOR RECRUITMENT AND FACILITATION

The therapist must facilitate or stimulate the correct motor program, coordination, and sequence of movement. Although verbal and visual feedback are helpful through demonstration and cueing, kinesthetic feedback is paramount to motor learning.[22] Correct body position or posture will improve feedback. Posture and movement that are early in the developmental sequence will require a less complex motor task and activate a more basic motor program. This will create positive feedback and reinforcement and mark the point (posture) where appropriate and inappropriate actions and reactions meet. From this point, the therapist can manipulate frequency, intensity, and duration or advance to a more difficult posture in the appropriate sequence.

The therapist must also consider developmental biomechanics that divides the movement ability into two categories, internal forces and external forces. "Internal forces include the center of gravity, base of support, and line of gravity." "External forces include gravity, inertia of the body segment, and ground reaction."[6] Considering this, the therapist should evaluate the patient's abilities in the same manner by first observing management of the mass of the body over the particular base provided by the posture. Then progress the patient toward more external stresses like inertia, gravity, and ground reaction forces. This interaction will require various degrees of acceleration production, deceleration control, anticipatory weight shifting, and increased proprioception. Resistance and movement can stress static and dynamic postures, but the therapist should also understand that resistance and movement could be used to refine movement and stimulate appropriate reactions.[22] Postures must be chosen to reduce compensation and allow the patient to exercise below the level where the impairment hinders movement or control. This is easily accomplished by creating "self-limiting" exercises.[4] These exercises require passive or active "locking" by limiting movement of the area the patient will most likely use to substitute or "cheat" with during exercise.

To review, posture identifies the fundamental movements used in growth and development. These movements serve as steps toward skill that are also helpful in the presence of skill when quality is questionable. A few examples are:

- Supine bridging movements.
- Rolling to side-lying, rolling to prone, rolling to supine.
- Prone on elbows to rolling or reaching, prone press-up.
- Quadruped positions, static, dynamic.
- Transitions to and from sitting, sitting and reaching.

- Kneeling, tall kneeling, half kneeling, add reaching movements.
- Squatting movement variations.
- Lunging movement variations.
- Single-leg stance, static, dynamic.

By following this natural sequence of movement, the therapist can observe where a mobility or stability problem will first limit the quality of a whole movement pattern. A patient with a mild knee sprain or even a total knee replacement may demonstrate segmental rolling to one side but "log roll" to the other simply to avoid using a flexion adduction medial rotation movement pattern with the involved lower extremity. The therapist has now identified where success and failure meet in the developmental sequence. The knee problem creates a dynamic stability problem in the developmental sequence long before partial or full weight bearing is an issue. It therefore must be addressed at that level. The patient is provided with an example of how limited knee mobility can greatly affect movement patterns (like rolling) that seem to require little of the knee. The clinician must define postural levels of success and failure to identify the postural level where therapeutic exercise intervention should start. Otherwise, the therapist could potentially prescribe exercise at a postural level where the patient is creating significant amounts of compensation, substitution, and frustration during exercise. The example of the knee patient is actually a common occurrence and often goes unnoticed. However, by restoring bilateral segmental rolling function, many gait problems will be affected with measurable qualitative and quantitative observations. By using a postural progression, the earliest level of functional limitation can be easily identified and incorporated into the exercise program. Limitations can also be placed on the posture and movement (the self-limiting concept) to limit postural compensation and focus.

Position

PRIMARY QUESTIONS

1. *Where* is the impairment located?
2. *Where* among the structures (myofascial or articular) does the impairment have its greatest effect?
3. *Where* in the ROM does the impairment have the greatest effect?
4. *Where* is the most beneficial position for the exercise?

The word "position" describes not only the location of the anatomic structure (joint, muscle group, ligament) where impairment has been identified but also the positions (with respect to movement and load) that the greatest and least limitations occur. The limitations can be either reduced strength and control or restricted movement. Orthopedic manual assessment of joints and muscles in various functional positions will demonstrate the influence of the impairment and symptoms throughout the range of movement. The clinician will identify various deficits. Each will be qualified or quantified through assessment

and objective testing and then addressed through the appropriate dosage and positioning for exercise.

To better understand the role of position, consider the single-leg bridge exercise progression. Purpose and posture are clearly defined. Purpose is the obvious reason for exercise intervention while posture describes the orientation of the body in space. Position refers to the specific mobilizing or stabilizing segment. In the case of the single-leg bridge, the hip is moving toward extension. If range of motion were broken down into thirds, it would only involve the extension third of movement. The flexion third and middle third of movement are not needed, because no impairment was identified in those respective ranges. Not only was the hip in extension, but also the knee was in flexion. This is important, because the hamstring muscle will try to assist hip extension in the end range of movement when gluteal strength is not optimal. However, the hamstrings cannot assist hip extension to any significant degree because of "active insufficiency." Likewise, the lumbar extensors cannot assist the extension pattern due to the passive stretch placed upon them via maximal passive hip flexion on the opposite side. The hip extension proprioception is now void of any inappropriate patterning or compensation from the hamstrings or spinal erectors through the positional use of active and passive insufficiency.[4,13]

Qualitative measures will provide specific information regarding exercise start position, finish position, movement speed and direction, open- and closed-chain considerations, and the need for cueing and feedback. Close observation of osteokinematic and arthrokinematic relationships respecting movement and bilateral comparison is the obvious starting point. Specific identification of the structure and position represent mobility observed by selective tension (active, passive, and resisted movements), and "end feel" of the joint structures would provide specific information about the mechanical nature of limitations and symptoms.[7] Assessment of positional static and dynamic control will describe stability limitations and provide a more specific starting point for exercise. The therapist should map the specific limitations of a segment (muscle/joint complex). The terms "hypermobility" and "hypomobility" create clear *structure* and *function*-based categories (Fig. 25-3). Quantitative measures will reveal a degree of defect, which can be recorded in the form of a percentage through bilateral comparison and compared to normative data when possible. Range of motion, strength, endurance, and recovery time should be considered along with many other (quantitative) clinical parameters to describe isolated or positional function. This will provide clear communication and specific documentation for goals as well as a tracking device for treatment effectiveness. This information will help define the baseline for initial exercise considerations.

As previously stated, any limitation in mobility or stability will require a bilateral comparison as well as clearing of the joints above and below. The proximal and distal structures must also be compared to their contralateral counterparts. This central point of physical examination is often overlooked. Cyriax noted, "Positive signs must always be balanced by corroborative negative signs." If a lesion appears to lie at or near one joint,

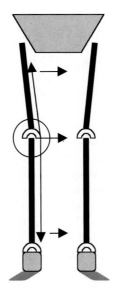

1. Assess right knee
2. Compare to left knee
3. Assess right hip
4. Compare to left hip
5. Assess right ankle
6. Compare to left ankle

FIGURE 25-6

Right knee positional comparison.

this region must be examined for signs identifying its site. It is equally essential for the adjacent joints and the structures about them to be examined so that, by contrast, their normality can be established. These negative findings then reinforce the positive findings emanating elsewhere; only then can the diagnosis be regarded and established"[7] (Fig. 25-6).

Once position and movement options have been established, a trial exercise session should be used to observe and quantify performance prior to prescription. Variables including intensity and duration can be used to establish strength or endurance baselines. Bilateral comparison should be used to document a performance deficit, which is also recorded as percentage. A maximum repetition test (with or without resistance) to fatigue, onset of symptoms, or loss of exercise quality are common examples. This will allow close tracking of home exercise compliance and help establish a rate of improvement. All other factors being addressed, the rate of improvement should be quite large. This is the benefit of correct dosage with regards to prescription of exercise position and appropriate workload. Most of the significant improvement is not due to training volume, tissue metabolism, or muscle hypertrophy. It is the efficient adaptive response of "neural factors."[2] These factors can include motor recruitment efficiency, improved timing, increased proprioceptive awareness, improved agonist/antagonist coordination, appropriate phasic and tonic response to activity, task familiarity, and motor learning as well as psychological factors. Usually the greater the deficit, the more drastic the improvement. Treatments should be geared to stimulate these changes whenever possible.[5]

Pattern

PRIMARY QUESTIONS

1. *How* is the movement pattern different upon bilateral comparison?
2. *How* can synergistic movement, coordination, recruitment and timing be facilitated?
3. *How* will this affect the movement limitation?
4. *How* will this affect function?

The word "pattern" will serve as a cue to the clinician to continually consider the functional movements of the human body that occur in unified patterns that occupy three-dimensional space and cross three planes (frontal, sagittal, and transverse).[6] Sometimes this is not easily ascertained by observing the design and usage of fixed axis exercise equipment and the movement patterns suggested in some rehabilitation protocols. The basic patterns of PNF, for both the extremities and the spine, are excellent examples of how the brain groups movement. Muscles of the trunk and extremities are recruited in the most advantageous sequence (proprioception) to create movement (mobility) or control (stability) movement. Not only does this provide efficient and economical function but it also effectively protects the respective joints and muscles from undue stress and strain. Voss et al clearly and eloquently state this: "The mass movements patterns of facilitation are spiral and diagonal in character and closely resemble the movements used in sports and work activities. The spiral and diagonal character is in keeping with the spiral rotatory characteristics of the skeletal system of bones and joints and the ligamentous structures. This type of motion is also in harmony with the topographical alignment of the muscles from origin to insertion and with the structural characteristics of the individual muscles."[23]

When a structure within the sequence is limited by impairment, the entire pattern is limited in some way. The therapist should document the limited pattern as well as the isolated segment causing the pattern to be limited. The isolated segment is usually identified in the evaluation process and outlined in the "position" considerations. The resultant effect on one or more movement patterns must also be investigated. A review of the basic PNF patterns can be beneficial to the orthopedic therapist. Once a structure is evaluated, look at the basic PNF patterns involving that structure. Multiple patterns can be limited in some way, but usually one pattern in particular will demonstrate significantly reduced function. Obviously, poor function in a muscle group or joint can limit the strength, endurance, and range of motion of an entire PNF pattern to some degree. However, the clinician must not simply view reduced PNF pattern function as an output problem. It should be equally viewed as an input problem. When muscle and joint function are not optimal, mechanoreceptor and muscle spindle are not optimal. This can create an input or proprioceptive problem and greatly distort joint position and muscle tension information. This distorts initial information (before movement is initiated) as well as feedback (once movement is in progress). Therefore, the therapist cannot only consider functional output.

Altered proprioception, if not properly identified and outlined, can unintentionally become part of the recommended exercises and therefore be reinforced. The therapist must focus on synergistic and integrated function at all levels of rehabilitation. The orthopedic outpatient cannot afford to have a problem simply isolated three times a week for 30 minutes only to reintegrate the same problem at a subconscious level during necessary daily activities throughout the remaining week. PNF-style movement pattern exercise can often be taught as easily as an isolated movement at a significantly greater benefit. Therapeutic exercise is no longer limited by sets as repetitions of the same activity. Successive intervals of increasing difficulty (although not physically stressful) building on the accomplish-

ment of an earlier task will reinforce one level of function and continually challenge the next. A simple movement set focused on isolation of a problem can be quickly followed by a pattern that will improve integration. The integration can be followed by a familiar fundamental movement or functional activity, which may reduce the amount of conscious and deliberate movement and give the therapist a chance to observe subcortical control of mobility and stability as well as appropriate use of phasic and tonic responses (see Chapter 8). By continuously

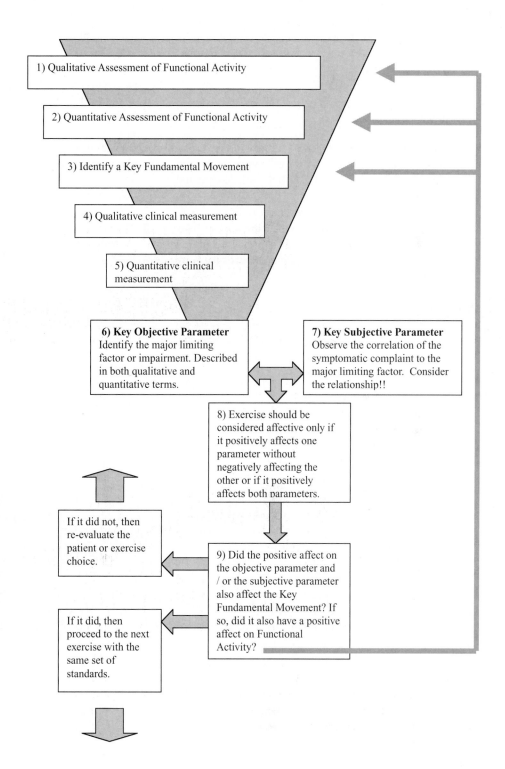

FIGURE   25-7

The deductive process of exercise prescription.

considering the pattern options as well as pattern limitations, the therapist will be able to refine the exercise prescription and reduce unnecessary supplemental movements that could easily be incorporated into pattern-based exercise.

Direction, speed, and amount of resistance (or assistance) will be used to produce more refined patterns. Manual resistance, weighted cable or elastic resistance, weight-shifting activities, and even proprioceptive taping can improve recruitment and facilitate coordination. The therapist should refrain from initially discussing specific structural control like "pelvic tilting" or "scapular retraction." Instead, the therapist should use posture and position to set the initial movement and design proprioceptive feedback to produce a more normal pattern whenever possible (Chapter 8).

SUMMARY

- Hopefully the mastery of functional evaluation and exercise prescription will remain in the rehabilitative domain (Fig. 25-7). This chapter was designed to both describe and define some of the most effective and efficient considerations for functional exercise prescription and progression. Although exercise prescription falls within the scope of many modern health care and fitness professionals, the physical therapist is unique. The four principles in particular serve to describe this distinction.

- In review, the four Ps are actually four simple words starting with the letter "P" that represent each of the four principles. They serve as quick reminders of the hierarchy, interaction, and application of each principle. The questions of what, when, where, and how with respect to functional movement assessment and exercise prescription are answered in the appropriate order.
  - ➢ Functional evaluation and assessment = Purpose.
  - ➢ Identification of motor control = Posture.
  - ➢ Identification of osteokinematic and arthrokinematic limitations = Position.
  - ➢ Integration of synergistic movement patterns = Pattern.

- Current information has been synchronized to produce a new perspective. This new perspective was specifically designed to improve treatment efficiency and effectiveness. These four principles attempt to assist problem solving by providing a framework that categorizes clinical information in a hierarchy. The information groups are then linked together to demonstrate a natural flow from problem to solution to outcome.

- It is best to first apply the four principles and their primary questions to a case review. This will demonstrate assimilation or sequencing errors related to initial exercise prescription or progression. Likewise, it may also demonstrate individual clinical affinity resulting in efficient use of resources and treatment consistency.

- Once the four principles have been applied to previous cases,

the clinician can incorporate all four principles or one principle at a time into his or her current caseload or clinical research. With experience, self-critique, and continued education, the therapist may see the four principles vanish. The clinician will eventually assimilate and implement the four principles in parallel, which refers to simultaneous consideration of the major factors influencing function. The need for a serial step-by-step deduction process is no longer necessary. The steps are still used, but the human mind now has an operative framework and the practical experiences that produce higher and higher levels of intercommunication. This will allow the clinician to move smoothly from evaluation to exercise prescription, progression, and re-evaluation, demonstrating objective improvement in both clinical measurements and functional movement.

- Clinical wisdom is the result of experience and applied knowledge. Intense familiarity and practical observation improve application. To be of benefit, available knowledge must be organized and tempered by an objective and inclusive framework. Hopefully, this framework will provide a starting point and to better organize and apply each clinician's knowledge and experience of functional exercise prescription. In the words of Eden Phillpotts (1862–1960): "The universe is full of magical things patiently waiting for our wits to grow sharper."

REFERENCES

1. American College of Sports Medicine. Exercise *Management for Persons with Chronic Diseases and Disabilities.* Champaign, IL, Human Kinetics, 1997.
2. Baechle TR. *Essentials of Strength Training and Conditioning.* Champaign, IL, Human Kinetics, 1994.
3. Cailliet R. *Soft Tissue Pain and Disability.* Philadelphia, Davis, 1977.
4. Cook G. *The Four Ps (Exercise Prescription). Functional Exercise Training Course Manual.* North American Sports Medicine Institute, ACE, 1997–present
5. Cook G, Burton L, Fields K. Reactive neuromuscular training for the anterior cruciate ligament-deficient knee: A case report. *J Athl Train* 34:194–201, 1999.
6. Cook G, Fields K. Functional Training for the Torso, National Strength & Conditioning Association, April 1997; 14–19.
7. Cyriax J. *Textbook of Orthopaedic Medicine,* 8th ed. Vol I: *Diagnosis of Soft Tissue Lesions.* Bailliere Tindall, 1982.
8. *FMS Manual.* Danville, VA, ATS, 1998.
9. Glassman S. Advances in treating shoulder injuries. *Adv Phys Ther* 8:11, 19 xy.
10. Gould JA III. *Orthopaedic and Sports Physical Therapy,* 2nd ed. St. Louis, Mosby, 1990, p. 169.
11. Haywood KM. *Life Span Motor Development,* 2nd ed. Champaign, IL, Human Kinetics, 1993.
12. Janda V. Pain in the locomotor system. Paper presented

at second annual interdisciplinary symposium on rehabilitation in chronic low back disorders, Los Angeles, 1988.

13. Kendall FP, McCreaary KE, Provance PG. *Muscle Testing and Function*, 4th ed. Baltimore, Williams & Wilkins, 1993.

14. Liebenson C. *Rehabilitation of the Spine: A Practitioner's Manual.* Media, PA, Williams & Wilkins, 1996.

15. Mulligan B. *Manual Therapy, "NAGS", "SNAGS", "MWM."* Wellington, NZ, Plane View Services, 19 xy.

16. Munich H et al. The test–retest reliability of an inclined squat strength test protocol. *J Orthop Sports Phys Ther* 26: 209–213, 1997.

17. Porterfield JA, DeRosa C. *Mechanical Low Back Pain: Perspectives in Functional Anatomy*, 2nd ed. Philadelphia, Saunders, 1998, Chapter 5.

18. Richter R, VanSant A, Newton R. Description of adult rolling movements and hypothesis of developmental sequences. *Phys Ther* 69:63–76, 1989.

19. Scully R, Barnes M. *Physical Therapy.* Philadelphia, Lippincott, 1989.

20. Sullivan PE, Markos PD, Minor MD. *An Integrated Approach to Therapeutic Exercise: Theory and Clinical Application.* Reston, VA, Reston Publishing Company, 1982.

21. Twomey L, ed. Physical therapy of the low back. In: Janda V, ed. *Muscles and Motor Control in Low Back Pain: Assessment and Management.* New York, Churchill Livingstone, 1987, pp. 253–278.

22. Voight M, Cook G. *Clinical application of closed kinetic chain exercise. J Sport Rehabil* 5:25–44, 1996.

23. Voss DE, Ionta MK, Myers BJ. *Proprioceptive Neuromuscular Facilitation: Patterns and Techniques*, 3rd ed. Philadelphia, Harper & Row, 1985.

P A R T   4
Intervention Strategies for Specific Injuries

Rehabilitation of the Shoulder

Rob Schneider and William E. Prentice

O B J E C T I V E S

After completing this chapter, the student therapist should be able to do the following:

- Discuss the functional anatomy and biomechanics associated with normal function of the shoulder joint complex.
- Discuss the various rehabilitative strengthening techniques for the shoulder, including both open- and closed-kinetic chain isotonic, plyometric, isokinetic, and PNF exercises.
- Identify the various techniques for regaining range of motion, including stretching exercises and joint mobilizations.
- Discuss exercises that may be used to reestablish neuromuscular control.
- Relate biomechanical principles to the rehabilitation of various shoulder injuries/pathologies.
- Discuss criteria for progression of the rehabilitation program for different shoulder injuries/pathologies.
- Describe and explain the rationale for various treatment techniques in the management of shoulder injuries.

FUNCTIONAL ANATOMY AND BIOMECHANICS

The anatomy of the shoulder joint complex allows for tremendous range of motion. This wide range of motion of the shoulder complex proximally permits precise positioning of the hand distally, creating both gross and skilled movements. However, the high degree of mobility requires some compromise in stability, which in turn increases the vulnerability of the shoulder joint to injury, particularly in dynamic overhead activities.

The shoulder girdle complex is composed of three bones: the scapula, clavicle, and humerus. These bones are connected to one another or to the axial skeleton or trunk via the glenohumeral, acromioclavicular, sternoclavicular, and scapulothoracic joints (Fig. 26-1). Dynamic movement as well as stabilization of the shoulder complex requires integrated function of all four articulations if normal motion is to occur.

Sternoclavicular Joint

The clavicle articulates with the manubrium of the sternum to form the sternoclavicular joint (SC joint), the only direct skeletal connection between the upper extremity and the trunk. The sternal articulating surface is larger than the sternum, causing the clavicle to rise much higher than the sternum. A fibrocartilaginous disk is interposed between the two articulating surfaces. It functions as a shock absorber against the medial forces and also helps to prevent any displacement upward. The articular disk is placed so that the clavicle moves on the disk, and the disk, in turn, moves separately on the sternum. The clavicle is permitted to move up and down, forward and backward, in combination, and in rotation.

The sternoclavicular joint is extremely weak because of its bony arrangement, but it is held securely by strong ligaments that tend to pull the sternal end of the clavicle downward and toward the sternum, in effect anchoring it. The main ligaments are the anterior sternoclavicular, which prevents upward displacement of the clavicle; the posterior sternoclavicular, which also prevents upward displacement of the clavicle; the interclavicular, which prevents lateral displacement of the clavicle; and the costoclavicular, which prevents lateral and upward displacement of the clavicle.[3]

It should also be noted that for the scapula to abduct and upward rotate throughout 180 degrees of humeral abduction,

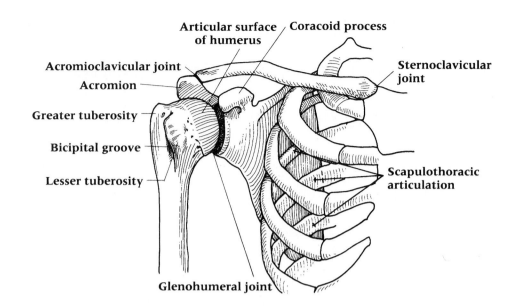

Articular surface / Coracoid process
of humerus

Acromioclavicular joint

Sternoclavicular
joint

Acromion

Greater tuberosity

Bicipital groove

Scapulothoracic
articulation

Lesser tuberosity

Glenohumeral joint

FIGURE 26-1

Skeletal anatomy of the
shoulder complex.

clavicular movement must occur at both the sternoclavicular
and acromioclavicular joints. The clavicle must elevate approximately 40 degrees to allow upward scapular rotation.[51]

Acromioclavicular Joint

The acromioclavicular joint (AC joint) is a gliding articulation
of the lateral end of the clavicle with the acromion process.
This is a rather weak joint. A fibrocartilaginous disk seperates
the two articulating surfaces. A thin, fibrous capsule surrounds
the joint.

The acromioclavicular ligament consists of anterior, posterior, superior, and inferior portions. In addition to the acromioclavicular ligament, the coracoclavicular ligament joins the coracoid process and the clavicle and helps to maintain the position
of the clavicle relative to the acromion. The coracoclavicular
ligament is further divided into the trapezoid ligament, which
prevents overriding of the clavicle on the acromion, and the
conoid ligament, which limits upward movement of the
clavicle on the acromion. As the arm moves into an elevated
position there is a posterior rotation of the clavicle on its long
axis, which permits the scapula to continue rotating, thus
allowing full elevation. The clavicle must rotate approximately
50 degrees for full elevation to occur; otherwise elevation would
be limited to approximately 110 degrees.[51]

CORACOACROMIAL ARCH

The coracoacromial ligament connects the coracoid to the
acromion. This ligament, along with the acromion and the
coracoid, forms the coracoacromial arch over the glenohumeral
joint. In the subacromial space between the coracoacromial arch
superiorly and the humeral head inferiorly, lie the supraspinatus tendon, long head of the biceps tendon, and subacromial
bursa. Each of these structures is subject to irritation and
inflammation resulting either from excessive humeral head trans-

lation or from impingement during repeated overhead activities. In asymptomatic individuals the optimal subacromial space
appears to be about 9 to 10 mm.[52]

Glenohumeral Joint

The glenohumeral joint is an enarthrodial, or ball-and-socket,
synovial joint in which the round head of the humerus articulates with the shallow glenoid cavity of the scapula. The cavity is
deepened slightly by a fibrocartilaginous rim called the glenoid
labrum. The humeral head is larger than the glenoid, and at any
point during elevation, only 25 to 30 percent of the humeral
head is in contact with the glenoid.[25] The glenohumeral joint
is maintained by both static and dynamic restraints. Position
is maintained statically by the glenoid labrum and the capsular ligaments, and dynamically by the deltoid and rotator cuff
muscles.

Surrounding the articulation is a loose, articular capsule
that is attached to the labrum. This capsule is strongly reinforced
by the superior, middle, and inferior glenohumeral ligaments
and by the tough coracohumeral ligament, which attaches to the
coracoid process and to the greater tuberosity of the humerus.[47]

The long tendon of the biceps muscle passes superiorly
across the head of the humerus and then through the bicipital
groove. In the anatomic position, the long head of the biceps
moves in close relationship with the humerus. The transverse
humeral ligament maintains the long head of the biceps tendon
within the bicipital groove by passing over it from the lesser and
the greater tuberosities, converting the bicipital groove into a
canal.

Scapulothoracic Joint

The scapulothoracic joint is not a true joint; however, the movement of the scapula on the wall of the thoracic cage is critical
to shoulder joint motion. Contraction of the scapular muscles,

which attach the scapula to the axial skeleton, is essential in stabilizing the scapula, thus providing a base on which a highly mobile joint can function.

Stability in the Shoulder Joint

Maintaining stability while the four articulations of the shoulder complex collectively allow for a high degree of mobility is critical in normal function of the shoulder joint. Instability is very often the cause of many of the specific injuries to the shoulder, which will be discussed later in this chapter. In the glenohumeral joint, the rounded humeral head articulates with a relatively flat glenoid on the scapula. Thus during movement of the shoulder joint, it is essential to maintain the positioning of the humeral head relative to the glenoid. Likewise it is also critical for the glenoid to adjust its position relative to the moving humeral head while simultaneously maintaining a stable base. The glenohumeral joint is inherently unstable and stability depends on the coordinated and synchronus function of both dynamic and static stabilizers.[41]

DYNAMIC STABILIZERS OF THE GLENOHUMERAL JOINT

The muscles that cross the glenohumeral joint produce motion and function to establish dynamic stability to compensate for a bony and ligamentous arrangement that allows for a great deal of mobility. Movements at the glenohumeral joint include flexion, extension, abduction, adduction, circumduction, and rotation.

The muscles acting on the glenohumeral joint may be separated into two groups. The first group consists of muscles that originate on the axial skeleton and attach to the humerus, including latissimus dorsi and pectoralis major. The second group originates on the scapula and attaches to the humerus, including the deltoid, teres major, coracobrachialis, subscapularis, supraspinatus, infraspinatus, and teres minor. These muscles constitute the short rotator muscles whose tendons insert into the articular capsule and serve as reinforcing structures. The biceps and triceps muscles attach on the glenoid and effect elbow motion.

The muscles of the rotator cuff—subscapularis, infraspinatus, supraspinatus, and teres minor—along with the long head of the biceps, function to provide dynamic stability to control the position and prevent excessive displacement or translation of the humeral head relative to the position of the glenoid.[8]

Stabilization of the humeral head occurs through co-contraction of the rotator cuff muscles, which creates a series of force couples that act to compress the humeral head into the glenoid, thus minimizing humeral head translation. A force couple involves the action of two opposing forces acting in opposite directions to impose rotation about an axis. These force couples can establish dynamic equilibrium of the glenohumeral joint regardless of the position of the humerus. If an imbalance exists between the muscular components that create these force couples, abnormal glenohumeral mechanics occur.

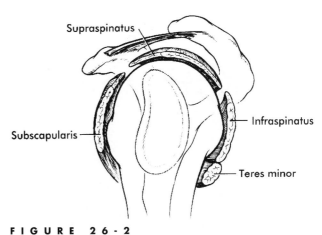

F I G U R E   2 6 - 2

Transverse plane force couples.

In the transverse plane, a force couple exists between subscapularis anteriorly and infraspinatus and teres minor posteriorly (Fig. 26-2). Co-contraction of the infraspinatus, teres minor, and subscapularis muscles act to both depress and compress the humeral head during overhead movements.

In the coronal plane, there is a critical force couple between the deltoid and inferior rotator cuff muscles (Fig. 26-3). With the arm fully adducted, contraction of the deltoid produces a vertical force in a superior direction, causing an upward translation of the humeral head relative to the glenoid. Co-contraction of the inferior rotator cuff muscles produces both a compressive force and a downward translation of the humerus, which counterbalances the force of the deltoid, thus stabilizing the humeral head. The supraspinatus compresses the humeral head into the glenoid, and along with the deltoid initiates abduction on this stable base. Dynamic stability is created by an increase in joint compression forces from contraction of the supraspinatus and by humeral head depression from contraction of the inferior rotator cuff muscles.[14]

The long head of the biceps tendon also contributes to dynamic stability by limiting superior translation of the humerus during elbow flexion and supination.

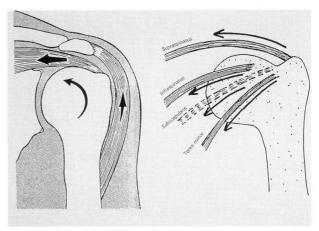

F I G U R E   2 6 - 3

Coronal plane force couples.

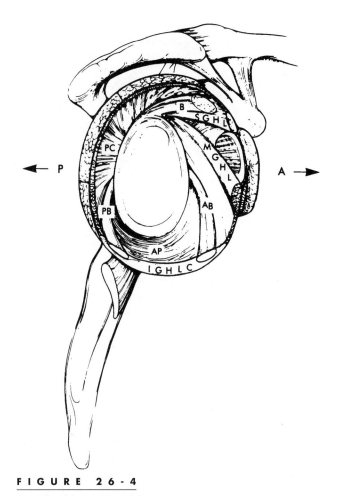

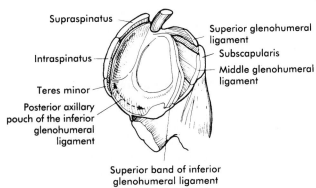

F I G U R E   2 6 - 5

Rotator cuff tendons blend into the joint capsule.

humeral head (Fig. 26-5). Thus as these muscles contract, tension is produced, dynamically tightening the capsule and helping to center the humeral head in the glenoid fossa. This creates both static and dynamic control of humeral head movement.

The posterior capsule is tight when the shoulder is in flexion, abduction, internal rotation, or in any combination of these. The superior and middle segment of the posterior capsule has the greatest tension while the shoulder is internally rotated.

The bones and articular surfaces within the shoulder are positioned to contribute to static stability. The glenoid labrum, which is tighty attached to the bottom half of the glenoid and loosely attached at the top, increases the glenoid depth approximately two times, enhancing glenohumeral stability.[37] The scapula faces 30 degrees anteriorly to the chest wall and is tilted upward 3 degrees to enable easier movement on the anterior frontal plane and movements above the shoulder.[25] The glenoid is tilted upward 5 degrees to help control inferior instability.[39]

F I G U R E   2 6 - 4

Shoulder static stabilizers.

STATIC STABILIZERS

The primary static stabilizers of the glenohumeral joint are the glenohumeral ligaments, posterior capsule, and glenoid labrum (Fig. 26-4).

The glenohumeral ligaments appear to produce a major restraint in shoulder flexion, extension, and rotation. The anterior glenohumeral ligament is tight when the shoulder is in extension, abduction, and/or external rotation. The posterior glenohumeral ligament is tight in flexion with internal rotation. The inferior glenohumeral ligament is tight when the shoulder is abducted, extended, and/or externally rotated. The middle glenohumeral ligament is tight when in flexion and external rotation. Additionally, the middle glenohumeral ligament along with the subscapularis tendon limit lateral rotation from 45 to 75 degrees of abduction and are important anterior stabilizers of the glenohumeral joint.[3] The inferior glenohumeral ligament is a primary check against both anterior and posterior dislocation of the humeral head and is the most important stabilizing structure of the shoulder in patients engaging in overhead activities.[3]

The tendons of the rotator cuff muscles blend into the glenohumeral joint capsule at their insertions about the

SCAPULAR STABILITY AND MOBILITY

Like the glenohumeral muscles, the scapular muscles play a critical role in normal function of the shoulder. The scapular muscles produce movement of the scapula on the thorax and help to dynamically position the glenoid relative to the moving humerus. They include the levator scapula and upper trapezius, which elevate the scapula; the middle trapezius and rhomboids, which adduct the scapula; the lower trapezius, which adducts and depresses the scapula; pectoralis minor, which depresses the scapula, and serratus anterior, which abducts and upward rotates the scapula. Collectively they function to maintain a consistent length–tension relationship with the scapulohumeral muscles.[43]

The only attachment of the scapula to the thorax is through these muscles. Thus the muscle stabilizers must fix the position of the scapula on the thorax, providing a stable base for the rotator cuff to perform its intended function on the humerus. It has been suggested that the serratus anterior moves the scapula while the other scapular muscles function to provide scapular stability.[34] The scapular muscles may act isometrically, concentrically, or eccentrically, depending on the movement desired and whether the movement is speeding up or slowing down.[39]

Scapulohumeral Rhythm

Scapulohumeral rhythm describes the movement of the scapula relative to the movement of the humerus throughout a full range of abduction. As the humerus elevates to 30 degrees there is no movement of the scapula. This is referred to as the setting phase, during which a stable base is being established on the thoracic wall. From 30 to 90 degrees, the scapula abducts and upward rotates 1 degree for every 2 degrees of humeral elevation. From 90 degrees to full abduction, the scapula abducts and upward rotates 1 degree for each 1 degree of humeral elevation. If normal scapulohumeral rhythm is compromised, normal shoulder joint function in moving to a fully elevated position cannot occur, and adaptive compensatory motions may predispose the patient to injury.[50]

Plane of the Scapula

The concept of the plane of the scapula refers to the angle of the scapula in its resting position, usually 35 to 45 degrees anterior to the frontal plane toward the sagittal plane. When the limb is positioned in the plane of the scapula, the mechanical axis of the glenohumeral joint is in line with the mechanical axis of the scapula. Thus the glenohumeral joint capsule is lax, and the deltoid and supraspinatus muscles are optimally positioned to elevate the humerus. Movement of the humerus in this plane is less restricted than in the frontal or sagittal planes, because the glenohumeral capsule is not twisted.[19] Because the rotator cuff muscles originate on the scapula and attach to the humerus, repositioning the humerus into the plane of the scapula increases the length of those muscles, thus improving the length–tension relationship. This is likely to increase muscle force.[19] It has been recommended that many strengthening exercises for the shoulder joint complex be done in the scapular plane.[19,70,71]

REHABILITATION TECHNIQUES FOR SPECIFIC INJURIES

Sternoclavicular Joint Sprains

PATHOMECHANICS

Although sternoclavicular joint sprains are relatively uncommon, the joint's complexity and integral interaction with the other joints of the shoulder complex warrant a discussion. The SC joint has multiple axes of rotation and articulates with the manubrium with an interposed fibrocartilaginous disk. Pathology of this joint can include injury to the fibrocartilage and sprains of the sternoclavicular and/or costoclavicular ligaments.[27]

As stated earlier in this chapter, the sternoclavicular joint is extremely weak because of its bony arrangement. It is held in place by its strong ligaments, which tend to pull the sternal end of the clavicle downward and toward the sternum. A sprain of these ligaments often results in either a subluxing or a dislocated SC joint. This can be a significant occurrence due to

the joint's integral role in scapular motion through the clavicle's articulation with the scapula. Combined movements at both the acromioclavicular and sternoclavicular joints have been reported to account for up to 60 degrees of upward scapular rotation inherent in glenohumeral abduction.[3]

When this joint incurs an injury, a resultant inflammatory process occurs. The inflammatory process can cause an increase in the joint capsule pressure as well as a stiffening of the joint due to the collagen tissue being produced for the healing tissues. The pathogenesis of this inflammatory process can cause an alteration of the joint mechanics as well as an increase in pain felt at the joint. This often has adverse results on the shoulder complex.[59]

INJURY MECHANISM

Next to motor vehicle accidents, the most common source of injuries to the sternoclavicular joint is in sports.[48] The SC joint may be injured by direct or indirect forces, resulting in sprains, dislocations, or physeal injuries.[27] Direct-force injuries are usually the result of a blow to the anteromedial aspect of the clavicle and produce a posterior dislocation.[27] Indirect-force injuries can occur in many different sporting events. This usually occurs when the patient falls, landing with an outstretched arm in either a flexed and adducted position or extended and adducted position of the upper extremity. The flexed position causes an anterior lateral compression force to the adducted arm, producing a posterior dislocation. The extended position causes a posterior lateral compression force to the adducted arm, leading to an anterior dislocation. Lesser forces can also lead to varying degrees of sprains to the SC joint. Additionally, there have been reports of repetitive microtrauma to this joint in sports such as golf, gymnastics, and rowing.[53,59]

REHABILITATION CONCERNS

In addressing the rehabilitation of a patient with a sternoclavicular joint injury, it is important to address the function of the joint on shoulder complex movement. The sternoclavicular joint acts as the sole passive attachment of the shoulder complex to the axial skeleton. As noted earlier in the chapter, the clavicle must elevate approximately 40 degrees to allow upward scapular rotation.[51]

In most cases the primary problem reported by the injured patient is discomfort associated with end-range movement of the shoulder complex. It is important to identify the cause of the pain—ligamentous instability, disk degeneration, or ligamentous trauma.

In cases where there is ligamentous instability as well as disk degeneration, the rehabilitation should focus on strengthening the muscles attached to the clavicle in a range that does not put further stress on the joint. Muscles such as pectoralis minor, sternal fibers of pectoralis major, and upper trapezius are strengthened to aid in controlling the motion of the clavicle during motion of the shoulder complex. Exercises include the seated press-up, shoulder shrugs, and incline bench in a limited range of motion (Exercises 26-3, 26-16, and 26-23). In addition to addressing the dynamic supports of the sternoclavicular joint, the therapist should employ the appropriate modalities necessary to control pain and the inflammatory process. It is also noteworthy in cases where dislocation or subluxation has occurred to consider the structures in close proximity to the sternoclavicular joint. In the case of a posterior dislocation, signs of circulatory vessel compromise, nerve tissue impingement, and difficulty swallowing may be seen. It is important to avoid these symptoms and communicate any lasting symptoms to the patient's physician.[59]

When dealing with ligamentous trauma that lacks instability, the therapist should also address the associated pain with the appropriate modalities and use exercise that strengthen muscle with clavicular attachments. In all of the above scenarios it is important to address the role of the SC joint on shoulder complex movement. A full evaluation of the shoulder complex should be performed to address issues related to scapular elevation. The superman, rhomboid, bent over row, and push-ups with a plus exercises should be included to help control upward rotation of the scapula (Exercises 26-17 to 26-20). Appropriate progression should be followed while addressing the healing stages for the appropriate tissues.

REHABILITATION PROGRESSION

In the initial stages of rehabilitation, the primary goal is to minimize pain and inflammation associated with shoulder complex motion. The therapist should limit the range of activities to midrange exercises and incorporate the use of therapeutic modalities along with the use of NSAID intervention from the physician. Ultrasound is often useful for increasing blood flow as well as for facilitating the process of healing. Occasionally a shoulder sling or figure-8 strap can help minimize stress at the joint. During this phase of the rehabilitation progression, the therapist should identify the specific needs of the patient in order to tailor the later rehabilitation phases to the patient's demands. The patient should also continue to work on exercises that maintain cardiorespiratory fitness.

As the pain and inflammation are controlled, the patient should gradually engage in a controlled increase of stress to the tissues of the joint. This is a good time to begin low-grade joint mobilizations, and to start resisted exercises for the muscles attaching to the clavicle. Exercises in this phase are best done in the midrange to minimize pain. As the patient's tolerance increases, the resistance and range of motion can be increased. During this phase it is also important to address any limitations there may be in the patient's range of motion. Emphasis should be placed on restoring the normal mechanics of the shoulder complex during shoulder movements.

Acromioclavicular Joint Sprains

PATHOMECHANICS

The acromioclavicular joint is composed of a bony articulation between the clavicle and the scapula. The soft tissues included in the joint are the hyaline cartilage coating the ends of the bony articulations, a fibrocartilaginous disk between the two bones, the acromioclavicular ligaments, and the costoclavicular ligaments. There have been two conflicting papers regarding the motion available at the joint. Codman reported little movement at the joint while Inman et al reported exactly the opposite.[12,26] Multiple authors have reported degenerative changes at the AC joint by age 40 in the average healthy adult.[16,57]

The acromioclavicular joint provides the bridge between the clavicle and the scapula. When an injury occurs to the joint, all soft tissue should be considered in the rehabilitation process. An elaborate grading system has been reported to categorize injuries based on the soft tissue that is involved in the injury (Table 26-1).[55] Through evaluation by X ray, the patient's injury should be categorized in order to provide the therapist with a guideline for rehabilitation.

INJURY MECHANISM

Type I or II acromioclavicular joint sprains are most commonly seen due to a direct fall on the point of the shoulder with the arm at the side in an adducted position, or falling on an outstretched arm. The injury mechanism for type III and IV sprains usually involves a direct impact that forces the acromion process downward, backward, and inward while the clavicle is pushed down against the rib cage. The impact can produce a number of injuries: (1) a fracture of the clavicle, (2) AC joint sprain, (3) AC and coracoclavicular joint sprain, or (4) a combination of the previous injury with concomitant muscle tearing of the deltoid and trapezius at their clavicular attachments.[3] Another possible mechanism for injury to the acromioclavicular joint is repetitive compression of the joint, often seen in weight training.[59]

REHABILITATION CONCERNS

Management of acromioclavicular injuries is dependent on the type of injury that is inflicted upon the patient.[20] Age, level of play, and the demand on the patient may also factor into the management of this injury. In general, most physicians prefer to handle type I and II injuries conservatively. Although conservative management is presently the treatment of choice for these injuries, some authors have suggested that type I and II injuries may cause further problems to the patient later in life.[5,13] These injuries may require surgical excision of the distal 2 cm of the clavicle. When developing a treatment plan, the therapist should consider the stability of the AC joint, the amount of time the patient was immobilized, the level of pain as a guide for the type of exercises to use, and the soft tissue that was involved in the type of injury. Rehabilitation of these injuries should focus on strengthening the deltoid and trapezius muscles. Additional strengthening of the clavicular fibers of pectoralis major should also be done. Other muscles that help restore the proper mechanics to the shoulder complex should also be addressed.

TABLE 26-1

Acromioclavicular Sprain Classification

TYPE I

- Sprain of the acromioclavicular ligaments.
- Acromioclavicular ligament intact.
- Coracoclavicular ligament, deltoid, and trapezius muscles intact.

TYPE II

- Acromioclavicular joint is disrupted with tearing of the acromioclavicular ligament.
- Coracoclavicular ligament is sprained.
- Deltoid and trapezius muscles are intact.

TYPE III

- Acromioclavicular ligament is disrupted.
- Acromioclavicular joint displaced and the shoulder complex displaced inferiorly.
- Coracoclavicular ligament disrupted with a coracoclavicular interspace 26 to 100 percent greater than the normal shoulder.
- Deltoid and trapezius muscles usually detached from distal end of the clavicle.

TYPE IV

- Acromioclavicular ligaments disrupted with the acromioclavicular joint displaced and the clavicle anatomically displaced posteriorly through the trapezius muscle.
- Coracoclavicular ligaments disrupted with wider interspace.
- Deltoid and trapezius muscles detached.

TYPE V

- Acromioclavicular and coracoclavicular ligaments disrupted.
- Acromioclavicular joint is dislocated and gross displacement between the clavicle and the scapula.
- Deltoid and trapezius muscles detached from distal end of the clavicle.

TYPE VI

- Acromioclavicular and coracoclavicular ligaments disrupted.
- Distal clavicle is inferior to the acromion or the coracoid process.
- Deltoid and trapezius muscles detached from distal end of the clavicle.

Type I

Treatment for the type I injury consists of ice to relieve pain and a sling to support the extremity for several days. The amount of time in the sling is usually dependent on the patient's ability to tolerate pain and to begin carrying the involved extremity with the appropriate posture. The therapist can have the patient begin active assisted range of motion immediately and then incorporate isometric exercises to the muscles with clavicular attachments. This will aid in restoring the appropriate carrying posture for the involved upper extremity. When the patient is able to remove the sling, the therapist should increase the exercise program to incorporate PRE exercises for the muscles with clavicular attachments and add exercise to encourage appropriate scapular motion. This will help prevent the possibility of related shoulder discomfort due to poor glenohumeral mechanics after return to activity.

Type II

The treatment for type II injuries is also nonsurgical. Because this type of injury to the AC joint involves complete disruption of the acromioclavicular ligaments, immobilization plays a greater role in the treatment of these patients. There is no consensus to the time of immobilization. Some authors have recommended 7 to 14 days, and others have suggested using a sling that not only supports the upper extremity but depresses the clavicle.[1,59] This debate is fueled by the time it takes the body to produce collagen and bridge the gap left from the injury. It has been reported that tissue mobilized too early shows a greater amount of type III collagen than the stronger type I collagen.[31] The time of healing for the soft tissues involved in this injury needs to be considered prior to beginning exercises that stress the injury. Heavy lifting should be avoided for 8 to 12 weeks.

Type III

Many authors have recommended a nonoperative approach for type III injury. Most agree that a sling is adequate for allowing the patient to rest comfortably.[3] Use of this nonoperative technique has been reported to have limited success. Cox reported improved results without support of the arm in 62 percent of patients, whereas only 26 percent had relief after 3 to 6 weeks of immobilization and a sling.[13]

Operative management options for this type of injury include the following:

- Stabilization of clavicle to coracoid with a screw.
- Resection of distal clavicle.
- Transarticular acromioclavicular fixation with pins.
- Use of coracoclavicular ligament as a substitute acromioclavicular ligament.

Taft et al found superior results with coracoclavicular fixation. They found that patients with acromioclavicular fixation had a higher rate of posttraumatic arthritis than those managed with a coracoclavicular screw.[62]

Types IV to VI

Type IV, V, and VI injuries require open reduction and internal fixation. Operative procedures are designed to attempt realignment of the clavicle with the scapula. The immobilization for this type of injury is longer and therefore the rehabilitation time is longer. After immobilization, the concerns are similar to those previously discussed.

REHABILITATION PROGRESSION

Early in the rehabilitation progression the therapist should be concerned with application of cold therapy and pressure for the first 24 to 48 hours to control local hemorrhage. Fitting the patient for a sling is also important to control the patient's pain. The time in the sling depends on the severity of the injury. After the patient has been seen by a physician for differential diagnosis, the rehabilitation progression should be tailored to the type of sprain given the diagnosis.

Type I, II, and III sprains should be handled similarly at first, with the time of progression accelerated with less severe sprains. Exercises should begin with encouraging the patient to use the involved extremity for ADL activities and gentle range-of-motion exercises. Return of normal range of motion in the patient's shoulder is the first objective goal. The patient can also begin isometric exercises to maintain or restore muscle function in the shoulder while he or she is in the sling. Once the sling is removed, pendulum exercises can be started to encourage movement. In type III sprains, the therapist should hold off doing passive ROM exercises in the end ranges of shoulder elevation for the first 7 days. The patient should have full passive ROM by 2 to 3 weeks. Once the patient has full active range of motion, a program of progressive resistive exercises should begin. Strengthening of the deltoid and upper trapezius muscles should be emphasized. The therapist should evaluate the patient's shoulder mechanics to identify problems with neuromuscular control and address specific deficiencies as noted. As the patient regains strength in the involved extremity, functional exercises should be incorporated into the rehabilitation program.

In the case of type IV, V, and VI acromioclavicular sprains, a postsurgical progression should be followed. The therapist should design a program that is broken down into four phases of rehabilitation with the goal of returning the patient to normal activity as quickly as possible.[3] Contact with the physician is important to determine the time frame in which each phase may begin. Common surgeries for this injury include open reduction with pin or screw fixation and/or acromioplasty.

The early stage of rehabilitation should be designed with the goal of reestablishing pain-free range of motion, preventing muscle atrophy, and decreasing pain and inflammation. Range-of-motion exercises may include Codman's exercises (Exercise 26-45), rope and pulley exercises (Exercise 26-48), L-bar exercises (Exercises 26-50 to 26-55), and self-capsular stretches (Exercises 26-57 and 26-58). Strengthening exercises in this phase may include isometrics in all of the cardinal planes and isometrics for medial and lateral rotation of the glenohumeral joint at 0 degrees of elevation (Exercise 26-1).

As rehabilitation progresses, the therapist has the goal of regaining and improving muscle strength, normalizing arthrokinematics, and improving neuromuscular control of the shoulder complex. The patient should have full ROM, minimal pain and tenderness, and a 4/5 manual muscle test for internal rotation, external rotation, and flexion prior to advancing to this phase. Initiation of isotonic PRE exercises should begin. Shoulder medial and lateral rotation (Exercises 26-12 and 26-13), shoulder flexion and abduction to 90 degrees (Exercises 26-7 and 26-9), scaption (Exercise 26-14), bicep curls, and tricep extensions should be included. Additionally, a program of scapular stabilizing exercises should begin. Exercises should include superman exercises (Exercise 26-17), rhomboid exercises (Exercise 26-19), shoulder shrugs (Exercise 26-16), and seated push-ups (Exercise 26-23). To help normalize arthrokinematics of the shoulder complex, joint mobilization techniques should be used for the glenohumeral, acromioclavicular, sternoclavicular, and scapulothoracic joints (Exercises 26-59 to 26-69). To complete this phase, the patient should begin neuromuscular control exercises (Exercises 26-70 to 26-79) and trunk exercises, and should begin a low-impact aerobic exercise program.

During the advanced strengthening phase of rehabilitation, the goals should be to improve strength, power, and endurance of muscles as well as to improve neuromuscular control of the shoulder complex, and to prepare the patient to return to functional activities. Before advancing to this phase, the therapist should use criteria of full pain-free range of motion, no pain or tenderness, and strength of 70 percent of the uninvolved shoulder. The emphasis in this phase is on high-speed strengthening, eccentric exercises, and multiplanar motions. The patient should advance to surgical tubing exercises (Exercise 26-26), plyometric-style exercises (Exercises 26-27 to 26-32), PNF-style diagonal strengthening (Exercises 26-34 to 26-39), and isokinetic strengthening exercises (Exercise 26-33).

Clavicle Fractures

PATHOMECHANICS

The clavicle acts as a strut connecting the upper extremity to the trunk of the human body.[18] Forces acting on the clavicle are most likely to cause a fracture of the bone medial to the attachment of the coracoclavicular ligaments.[4] Intact acromioclavicular and coracoclavicular ligaments aid in keeping fractures nondisplaced and stabilized.

INJURY MECHANISM

The mechanism of injury for a clavicle fracture may be direct or indirect. Fractures may result from a fall on an outstretched arm, a fall or blow to the point of the shoulder, or less commonly, a direct blow.[53]

REHABILITATION CONCERNS

Early identification of the fracture is an important factor in rehabilitation. If stabilization occurs early, with minimal damage and irritation to the surrounding structures, the likelihood of an uncomplicated recovery is increased. Other factors influencing the likelihood of complications are injuries to the acromioclavicular, coracoclavicular, and sternoclavicular ligaments. Treatment for clavicle fractures includes approximation of the fracture and immobilization for 6 to 8 weeks. Most commonly, a figure-8 wrap is used with the involved arm in a sling.

When designing a rehabilitation program for a patient who has sustained a clavicle fracture, the therapist should consider the function of the clavicle. The clavicle acts as a strut, offering shoulder girdle stability and allowing the upper extremity to move more freely about the thorax by positioning the extremity away from the body axis.[22] Mobility of the clavicle is therefore very important to normal shoulder mechanics. Joint mobilization techniques are started immediately after the immobilization period in order to restore normal arthrokinematics. The clavicle also serves as an insertion point for the deltoid, upper trapezius, and pectoralis major muscles, providing stability

and aiding in neuromuscular control of the shoulder complex. It is important to address these muscles with the appropriate exercises in order to restore normal shoulder mechanics.

REHABILITATION PROGRESSION

For the first 6 to 8 weeks the patient is immobilized in the figure-8 brace and sling. If good approximation and healing of the fracture is occurring at 6 weeks, the patient may begin gentle isometric exercises for the upper extremity. Utilization of the involved extremity below 90 degrees of elevation should be encouraged to prevent excessive loss of glenohumeral ROM and muscle atrophy. After the immobilization period, the patient should begin a program to regain full active and passive ROM. Joint mobilization techniques are used to restore normal arthrokinematics (Exercises 26-59 to 26-61). The patient may continue to wear the sling for the next 3 to 4 weeks while the patient regains the ability to carry the arm in an appropriate posture without the figure-8 brace. The patient should begin a strengthening program utilizing progressive resistance as range of motion improves. Once full ROM is achieved, the patient should begin resisted diagonal PNF exercises and continue to increase strength of the shoulder complex muscle including the periscapular muscles to enable normal neuromuscular control of the shoulder.

Glenohumeral Dislocations/Instabilities (Surgical Versus Nonsurgical Rehabilitation)

PATHOMECHANICS

Dislocations of the glenohumeral joint involve the temporary displacement of the humeral head from its normal position in the glenoid labral fossa. From a biomechanical perspective, the resultant force vector is directed outside the arc of contact in the glenoid fossa, creating a dislocating moment of the humeral head by pivoting about the labral rim.[17]

Shoulder dislocations account for up to 50 percent of all dislocations. The inherent instability of the shoulder joint necessary for extreme mobility of this joint make the glenohumeral joint susceptible to dislocation. The most common kind of dislocation is that occurring anteriorly. Posterior dislocations account for only 1 to 4.3 percent of all shoulder dislocations. Inferior dislocations are extremely rare. Of dislocations caused by direct trauma, 85 to 90 percent are reccurring.[58]

In an anterior glenohumeral dislocation, the head of the humerus is forced out of its anterior capsule in an anterior direction past the glenoid labrum and then downward to rest under the coracoid process. The pathology that ensues is extensive, with torn capsular and ligamentous tissue, possibly tendonous avulsion of the rotator cuff muscles, and profuse hemorrhage. A tear or detachment of the glenoid labrum may also be present. Healing is usually slow, and the detached labrum and capsule can produce a permanent anterior defect on the glenoid labrum called a Bankart lesion. Another defect that may occur with anterior dislocation can be found on the posterior lateral aspect of the humeral head, called a Hill–Sachs lesion. This is caused by compressive forces between the humeral head and the glenoid rim while the humeral head rests in the dislocated position. Additional complications may arise if the head of the humerus comes into contact with and injures the brachial nerves and vessels. Rotator cuff tears may also arise as a result of the dislocation. The bicipital tendon may also sublux from its canal as the result of a rupture of the transverse ligament.[58]

Posterior dislocations may also result in significant soft-tissue damage. Tears of the posterior glenoid labrum are common in posterior dislocation. A fracture of the lesser tubercle may occur if the subscapularis tendon avulses its attachment.

Glenohumeral dislocation is usually a very disabling phenomenon. The patient assumes an obvious disabled posture and the deformity itself is obvious. A positive sulcus sign is usually present at the time of the dislocation, and the deformity can be easily recognized on an X ray. As detailed above, the damage can be extensive to the soft tissue.

INJURY MECHANISM

When discussing the mechanism of injury for dislocations of the glenohumeral joint, it is necessary to categorize the injury by traumatic versus atraumatic, and anterior versus posterior. An anterior dislocation of the glenohumeral joint may result from the direct impact to the posterior or posterolateral aspect of the shoulder. The most common mechanism is forced abduction, external rotation, and extension that forces the humeral head out of the glenoid cavity.[40] The injury mechanism for a posterior glenohumeral dislocation is usually forced adduction and internal rotation of the shoulder or a fall on an extended and internally rotated arm.

The two mechanisms described for anterior dislocation can be categorized into traumatic or atraumatic. The TUBS and AMBRI acronyms have been described to summarize the two mechanisms: *t*raumatic, *u*nidirectional, *b*ankart lesion, *s*urgery required; or *a*traumatic, *m*ultidirectional, *b*ilateral involvement, *r*ehabilitation effective, *i*nferior capsular shift recommended.[33]

The AMBRI group can be characterized by subluxation or dislocation episodes without trauma, resulting in a stretched capsuloligamentous complex that lacks end-range stabilizing ability. Several authors report a high rate of recurrence for dislocations, especially those in the TUBS category.[56]

REHABILITATION CONCERNS

Management of shoulder dislocation depends on a number of different factors that need to be identified. Mechanism, chronology, and direction of instability all need to be considered in the development of a conservatively managed rehabilitation program. No single rehabilitation program is an absolute solution for success in the treatment of a shoulder dislocation. The therapist should thoroughly evaluate the injury and discuss the objective findings of the evaluation along with the physician's findings. The initial concern in rehabilitation focuses on the maintenance of appropriate reduction of the glenohumeral joint. The patient is immobilized in a reduced position for a

period of time dependent on the type of management used in the reduction (surgical versus nonsurgical). For the purpose of this section, the discussion will continue with conservative management in mind. The principles of rehabilitation, however, remain constant regardless of whether the physician's management is surgical or nonsurgical. Surgical rehabilitation should be based on the healing time of tissue affected by the surgery. The limitations of motion in the early stages of rehabilitation should also be based on surgical fixation. It is extremely important, because of this, that the therapist and physician communicate prior to rehabilitation initiation.

After the immobilization period, the rehabilitation program should be focused on restoring the appropriate axis of rotation for the glenohumeral joint, optimizing the stabilizing muscles' length–tension relationship, and restoring proper neuromuscular control to the shoulder complex. In the uninjured shoulder complex with intact capsuloligamentous structures, the glenohumeral joint maintains a tight axis of rotation within the glenoid fossa. This is accomplished dynamically with complex neuromuscular control of the periscapular muscles, rotator cuff muscles, and the intact passive structures of the joint. Because the extent of damage in this type of injury is variable, the exercises employed to restore these normal mechanics must be adjusted accordingly.[55] As the therapist aids the patient in regaining full range of motion, a safe zone of positioning should be followed. Starting in the plane of the scapula is a safe place to begin, because the axis of rotation for forces acting on the joint fall in the center of this plane. The least provocative position is somewhere between 20 and 55 degrees of scapular plane abduction. Keeping the humerus below 55 degrees prevents subacromial impingement, while avoiding full adduction minimizes excessive tension across the supraspinatus/coracohumeral and/or capsuloligamentous complex.

As range of motion improves, the therapist should progress the exercise program to positions outside the safe zone, accommodating to the demand that the patient will need to meet. Specific strengthening should be given to address the muscles of the shoulder complex responsible for maintaining the axis of rotation, such as the supraspinatus and rotator cuff muscles. The periscapular muscles should also be addressed in order to provide the rotator cuff muscles with their optimal length–tension relationship for more efficient usage. In the later stages of rehabilitation, neuromuscular control exercises are incorporated with specific exercises to prepare the patient for functional return.[33]

REHABILITATION PROGRESSION

The first essential to a successful rehabilitation program is removing the patient from activities that risk reinjury to the glenohumeral joint. A reasonable time frame for resuming normal activity is approximately 12 weeks, with unrestricted activity coming closer to 20 weeks. This is variable depending on the extent of soft-tissue damage and type of intervention chosen by the patient and physician. Some exercises previously used by the patient may produce undesired forces on noncontractile

TABLE 26-2

Exercise Modification According to Direction of Instability

DIRECTION OF INSTABILITY	POSITION TO AVOID	EXERCISES TO MODIFY OR AVOID
Anterior	Combined position of external rotation and abduction	Fly, pull-down, push-up, bench press, military press
Posterior	Combined position of internal rotation, horizontal adduction, and flexion	Fly, push-up, bench press, weight-bearing exercises
Inferior	Full elevation, dependent arm	Shrugs, elbow curls, military press

tissues and need to be modified to be performed safely. Push-ups, pull-downs, and the bench press are performed with the hands in close and avoiding the last 10 to 20 degrees of shoulder extension. Pull-downs and military press performed with widegrips are kept in front rather than behind the head. Supine fly exercises are limited to −30 degrees in the coronal plane while maintaining glenohumeral internal rotation. See Table 26-2 for further modifications dependent on directional instability.[3]

During phase I, the patient is immobilized in a sling. This lasts for up to 3 weeks with first-time dislocations. The goal of this phase is to limit the inflammatory process, decrease pain, and retard muscle atrophy. Passive range-of-motion exercises can be initiated along with low-grade joint-mobilization techniques to encourage relaxation of the shoulder musculature. Isometric exercises are also started, with the patient starting with submaximal contractions and increasing to maximal contractions for as long as 8 seconds. The protective phase is a good time to initiate a scapulothoracic exercise program, avoiding elevated positions of the upper extremity that put stability at risk. Patients should begin an aerobic training regime with the lower extremity like stationary biking.

Phase II begins after the patient has been removed from the sling. This phase lasts from 3 to 8 weeks postinjury and focuses on full return of active range of motion. The program begins with the use of an L-bar performing active assistive ROM (Exercises 26-50 to 26-55). Manual therapy techniques can also begin using PNF techniques to help reestablish neuromuscular control (Exercises 26-34 to 26-39). Exercises with the hands on the ground can help begin strengthening the scapular stabilizers more aggressively. These exercises should begin on a stable surface like a table, progressing the amount of weight bearing by advancing from the table to the ground (Exercise 26-70). Advancing to a less stable surface like a BAPS board (Exercise 26-74) or Swiss ball (Exercise 26-75) will also help reestablish neuromuscular control.

Between 6 and 12 weeks the therapist should gradually enter phase III of the rehabilitation progression. The goal of this phase is to restore normal strength and neuromuscular control. Prophylactic stretching is done, as full range of motion should already be present. Scapular and rotator cuff exercises should focus on strength and endurance. Weight-bearing exercises should become more challenging by adding motion

to the demands of the stabilization. Scapular exercises should be performed with guidance from the therapist to meet the challenge of the patient's strength. Weight shifting on a Fitter (Exercise 26-72) and closed kinetic strengthening on a stair climber (Exercise 26-25) for endurance are started. Strengthening exercises progress from PRE to plyometric. The use of surgical tubing for rotator cuff exercises with emphasis on eccentrics is added.[2] Progression to multiangle exercises and sports-specific positioning is started. The Body Blade is a good rehabilitation tool for this phase of rehabilitation (Exercise 26-79), progressing from static to dynamic stabilization and from single position to multiangular dynamic exercises.

Phase IV is the functional progression. Patients are gradually returned to their sport with interval training and progressive activity increasing the demands on endurance and stability. This can last as long as 20 weeks depending on the patient's shoulder strength, lack of pain, and the ability to protect the involved shoulder. Between 20 and 26 weeks will be required for rehabilitation. Some therapist and physicians recommend use of a protective shoulder harness while participating in athletic activities.

Multidirectional Instabilities of the Glenohumeral Joint

PATHOMECHANICS

Multidirectional instabilities are an inherent risk of the glenohumeral joint. The shoulder has the greatest range of motion of all the joints in the human body. The bony restraints are minimal, and the forces that can be generated in dynamic overhead motions far exceed the strength of the static restraints of the joint. Attenuation of force is multifactorial, with time, distance, and speed determining forces applied to the joint. Thus, stability of the joint must be evaluated based on the patient's ability to dynamically control all of these factors in order to have a stable joint. In cases of multidirectional instability, there are two catagories for pathology, atraumatic and traumatic. The atraumatic category includes patients who may have congenitally loose joints and patients who have increased the demands on their shoulder prior to having the muscular maturity to meet these demands. When forces are generated at the glenohumeral joint that the stabilizing muscles are unable to handle, the humeral head has a tendency to translate anterior and inferiorly into the capsuloligamentous structures. Over time, repetitive microtrauma causes these structures to stretch. In a paper presented by Lephart et al, the importance of tension in the anterior capsule of the glenohumeral joint was documented to be an essential part as a protective mechanism against excessive strain in these capsuloligamentous structures.[36] They theorized that the loss of this protective reflex joint stabilization can increase the potential for continuing shoulder injury. Increased translation of the humeral head also increases the demand on the posterior structures of the glenohumeral joint, leading to repetitive microtrauma and breakdown of those soft tissues. In this type of instability there will usually be some inferior laxity, leading to a positive sulcus sign. Although the anterior glenoid labrum is usually intact during the early stages of this instability, splitting and partial detachment can develop.[3] The patient usually has some pain and clicking when the arm is held by the side. Any symptoms and signs associated with anterior or posterior recurrent instability may be present.

INJURY MECHANISM

It is generally believed that the cause of multidirectional instability is excessive joint volume with laxity of the capsuloligamentous complex. This laxity may be an inherent condition that becomes more pronounced with trauma. This type of instability may also occur due to extensive capsulolabral trauma in patients who do not appear to have laxity of other joints.[53]

REHABILITATION CONCERNS

The rehabilitation concerns for multidirectional instability are similar to those already discussed in the previous section related to shoulder instabilities. The complexity of this program is increased due to the addition of inferior instability. The success of the program is often determined by both the patient's tissue status and by compliance.[61] Additionally, emphasis in this program is put on the anterior and posterior musculature. These muscles working together are referred to as force couples and are believed to be essential stabilizers of the joint. The rehabilitation program should also address the neuromuscular control of these muscles to promote dynamic stability.[23] Compliance is often an extremely important factor in maintaining good results with this type of instability. The patient must continue to do the exercise program even after symptoms have subsided. If the patient doesn't, subluxation usually reoccurs. If conservative treatment is not successful, Neer recommended an inferior capsular shift surgical procedure that has proven successful in restoring joint stability when used in conjuction with a rehabilitation program.[45]

REHABILITATION PROGRESSION

The rehabilitation program should begin with reestablishing muscle tone and proper scapulothoracic posture. This helps provide a steady base with appropriate length–tension relationships for the anterior and posterior muscles of the shoulder complex acting as force couples. Strengthening of the rotator cuff muscles in the plane of the scapula should progress to higher resistance starting at 0 degrees of shoulder elevation. As the patient becomes asymptomatic, the therapist should incorporate an emphasis on neuromuscular control exercises like PNF, rhythmic stabilization, and weight-bearing activity to establish co-contraction at the glenohumeral joint. For successful results, the patient may have to continue a program of maintenance for neuromuscular control as long as the patient wishes to be asymptomatic. Burkhead et al reported an 80 percent success rate using a conservative approach with patients who had atraumatic multidirectional instability.[10,55]

Shoulder Impingement

PATHOMECHANICS

Shoulder impingement syndrome was first identified by Dr. Charles Neer, who observed that impingement involves a mechanical compression of the supraspinatus tendon, the subacromial bursa, and the long head of the biceps tendon, all of which are located under the coracoacromial arch. This syndrome has been described as a continuum during which repetitive compression eventually leads to irritation and inflammation that progresses to fibrosis and eventually to rupture of the rotator cuff. Neer has identified three stages of shoulder impingement.

Stage I

- Seen in patients under 25 years of age with report of repetitive overhead activity.
- Localized hemorrhage and edema with tenderness at supraspinatus insertion and anterior acromion.
- Painful are between 60 and 119 degrees; increased with resistance at 90 degrees.
- Muscle test reveals weakness secondary to pain.
- Positive Neer or Hawkins–Kennedy Impingement signs (Figs. 26-6 and 26-7).
- Radiographs are typically normal.
- Reversible; usually resolves with rest, activity modification, and rehabilitation program.

Stage II

- Seen in patients 26 to 40 years of age with report of repetitive overhead activity.
- Many of the same clinical findings as in stage I.
- Severity of symptoms worse than stage I, progressing to pain with activity and night pain.
- More soft-tissue crepitus or catching at 100 degrees.
- Restriction in passive ROM due to fibrosis.
- Radiographs may show osteophytes under acromion, degenerative AC joint changes.
- No longer reversible with rest; long-term rehabilitation program may help.

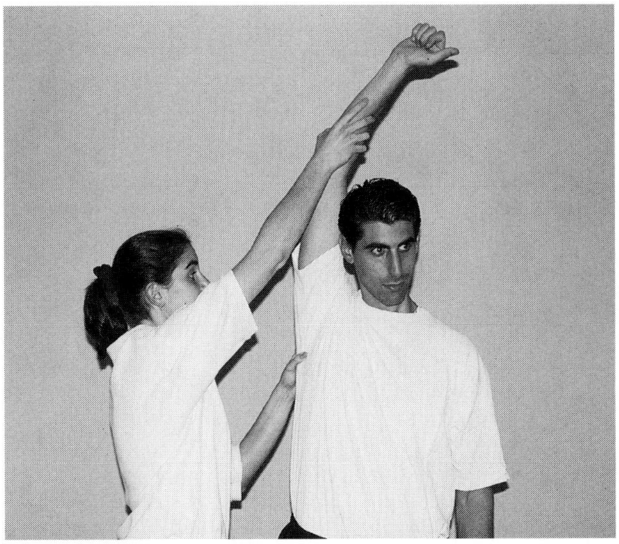

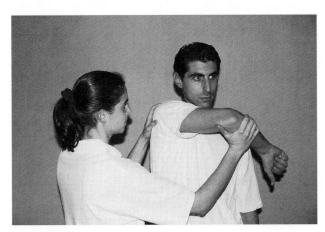

FIGURE 26-6

Neer impingement test.

Stage III

- Seen in patients older than 40 years of age with history of chronic tendinitis and prolonged pain.
- Many of the same clinical findings as stage II.
- Tear in rotator cuff usually less than 1 cm.
- More limitation in active and passive ROM.
- May have prominent capsular laxity with multidirectional instability seen on radiograph.
- Atrophy of infraspinatus and supraspinatus due to disuse.
- Treatment typically surgical following a failed conservative approach.

Neer's impingement theory was based primarily on the treatment of older, nonathletic patients. The older population will likely exhibit what has been referred to as "outside" or "outlet" impingement.[7,45] In outside impingement there is contact of the rotator cuff with the coracoacromial ligament or the acromion with fraying, abrasion, inflammation, fibrosis, and

FIGURE 26-7

Hawkins–Kennedy impingement test.

degeneration of the superior surface of the cuff within the subacromial space. There may also be evidence of degererative processes including spurring, decreased joint space due to fibrotic changes, and decreased vascularity.

"Inside" or "nonoutlet" impingement is more likely to occur in the younger overhead patient. With inside impingement the subacromial space appears relatively normal. With forced humeral elevation and internal rotation, the rotator cuff can be impinged on the posterior superior glenoid labrum and the humeral head, potentially producing inflammation on the undersurface of the rotator cuff tendon, posterior superior tears in the glenoid labrum, and lesions in the posterior humeral head (Bankart lesion).

The mechanical impingement syndrome as originally proposed by Neer has been referred to as primary impingement. Jobe and Kvnite have proposed that an unstable shoulder permits excessive translation of the humeral head in an anterior and superior direction, resulting in what has been termed secondary impingement.[28] Based on the relationship of shoulder instability to shoulder impingement, Jobe and Kvnite have proposed an alternative system of classification[28]:

Group IA

- Found in recreational patients older than 35 years with pure mechanical impingement and no instability.
- Positive impingement signs.
- Lesions on the superior surface of the rotator cuff, possibly with subacromial spurring.
- There may be some arthritic changes in the glenohumeral joint.

Group IB

- Found in recreational patients older than 35 years who demonstrate instability with impingement secondary to mechanical trauma.
- Positive impingement signs.
- Lesions found on the undersurface of the rotator cuff, superior glenoid, and humeral head.

Group II

- Overhead activity patients younger than 35 years who demonstrate instability and impingement secondary to repetitive microtrauma.
- Positive impingement signs with excessive anterior translation of humeral head.
- Lesions on the posterior superior glenoid rim, posterior humeral head, or anterior inferior capsule.
- Lesions on the undersurface of the rotator cuff.

Group III

- Overhead activity patients younger than 35 years.
- Positive impingement signs with atraumatic multidirectional, usually bilateral humeral instabilities.
- Demonstrate generalized laxity in all joints.
- Humeral head lesions as in group II but less severe.

Group IV

- Overhead activity patients younger than 35 years with anterior instability resulting from a traumatic event but without impingement.
- Posterior defect in the humeral head.
- Damage in the posterior glenoid labrum.

It has also been proposed that wear of the rotator cuff is due to intrinsic tendon pathology including tendinopathy and partial or small complete tears with age-related thinning, degeneration, and weakening. This permits superior migration of the humeral head, leading to secondary impingement, thus creating a cycle that may ultimately lead to full-thickness tears.[66]

A "critical zone" of vascular insufficiency has been proposed to exist in the tendon of the supraspinatus at about 1 cm proximal to its distal insertion on the humerus. It has been hypothesized that when the humerus is adducted and internally rotated, a "wringing out" of the blood supply occurs in this tendon. Should this occur repetitively, such as in the recovery phase on a swimming stroke, ultimately irriation and inflammation may lead to partial or complete rotator cuff tears.[54]

It is likely that some as yet unidentified combination of mechanical, traumatic, degenerative, and vascular processes collectively leads to pathology in the rotator cuff.

INJURY MECHANISM

Shoulder impingement syndrome occurs when there is compromise of the subacromial space under the coracoacromial arch. When the dynamic and static stabilizers of the shoulder complex fail for one reason or another to maintain this subacromial space, the soft-tissue structures are compressed, leading to irritation and inflammation. Impingement most often occurs in repetitive overhead activities. There is ongoing controversy and disagreement regarding the specific mechanisms that cause shoulder impingement syndrome. It has been proposed that mechanical impingement may result from either structural or functional causes. Structural causes may be attributed to existing congenital abnormalities or to degenerative changes under the coracoacromial arch, and may include the following:

- An abnormally shaped acromion (Fig. 26-8). Patients with a type III or hook-shaped acromion are approximately 70 percent more likely to exhibit signs of impingement than those with a flat or slightly curved acromion.[6]
- Inherent capsular laxity compromises the ability of the glenohumeral joint capsule to act as both a static and dynamic stabilizer.[28]
- Ongoing or recurring tendinitis or subacromial bursitis causes a loss of space under the coracoacromial arch, which can potentially lead to irritation of other uninflamed structures, thus setting up a vicious degenerative cycle.[59]
- Laxity in the anterior capsule due to recurrent subluxation or dislocation can allow an anterior migration of the humeral head, which can cause impingement under the coracoid process.[69]

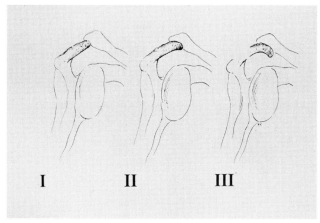

F I G U R E   2 6 - 8

Acromion Shapes. Type I, flat; type II, curved; type III, hooked.

- Postural malalignments such as a forward head, round shoulders, and an increased kyphotic curve, which cause the scapular glenoid to be positioned such that the space under the coracoacromial arch is decreased, can also contribute to impingement.

Functional causes include adaptive changes that occur with repetitive overhead activities, thus altering the normal biomechanical function of the shoulder complex. These include the following:

- Failure of the rotator cuff to dynamically stabilize the humeral head relative to the glenoid, thus producing excessive translation and instability. The inferior rotator cuff muscles (infraspinatus, teres minor, subscapularis) should act collectively to both depress and compress the humeral head. In the overhead or throwing patient, the internal rotators must be capable of producing humeral rotation on the order of 7000 degrees per second.[64] Thus subscapularis tends to be stronger than infraspinatus and teres minor, creating a strength imbalance in the existing force couple in the transverse plane. This imbalance produces excessive anterior translation of the humeral head. Furthermore, weakness in the inferior rotator cuff muscles creates an imbalance in the existing force couple with the deltoid in the coronal plane. The deltoid produces excessive superior translation of the humeral head, thus decreasing subacromial space. Weakness in supraspinatus, which normally functions to compress the humeral head into the glenoid, allows for excessive superior translation of the humeral head.[67]
- Because the tendons of the rotator cuff blend into the joint capsule, we rely on tension created in the capsule by contraction of the rotator cuff to both statically and dynamically center the humeral head relative to the glenoid. Tightness in the posterior and inferior portions of the glenohumeral joint capsule causes an anterosuperior migration of the humeral head, again decreasing the subacromial

space. In patients who engage in overhead activities, range of motion in internal rotation is usually limited by tightness of both the muscles that externally rotate and the posterior capsule. There tends to be excessive external rotation primarily due to laxity in the anterior joint capsule.[9]

- The scapular muscles function to dynamically position the glenoid relative to the humeral head, therefore maintaining a normal length–tension relationship with the rotator cuff. As the humerus moves into elevation, the scapula should also move, so that the glenoid is able to adjust regardless of the position of the elevating humerus. Weakness in the serratus anterior, which elevates, upward rotates, and abducts the scapula; or weakness in the levator scapula or upper trapezius, which elevate the scapula, will compromise positioning of the glenoid during humeral elevation, thus interfering with normal scapulohumeral rhythm.

- It is critical for the scapula to maintain a stable base on which the highly mobile humerus can move. Weakness in the rhomboids and/or middle trapezius, which function eccentrically to decelerate the scapula in high-velocity throwing motions, can contribute to scapular hypermobility. Likewise, weakness in the inferior trapezius creates an imbalance in the force couple with the upper trapezius and levator scapula, thus contributing to scapular hypermobility.

- An injury that affects normal arthrokinematic motion at either the sternoclavicular joint or the acromioclavicular joint can also contribute to shoulder impingement. Any limitation in posterior-superior clavicular rotation and/or clavicular elevation will prevent normal upward rotation of the scapula during humeral elevation, thus compromising the subacromial space.

REHABILITATION CONCERNS

Management of shoulder impingement involves gradually restoring normal biomechanics to the shoulder joint in an effort to maintain space under the coracoacromial arch during overhead activities.[63] The therapist should address the pathomechanics and the adaptive changes that most often occur with overhead activities.

Overhead activities that involve humeral elevation (full abduction or forward flexion), or a position of humeral flexion, horizontal adduction, and internal rotation, are likely to increase the pain.[38] The patient complains of diffuse pain around the acromion or glenohumeral joint. Palpation of the subacromial space increases the pain.

Exercises should concentrate on strengthening the dynamic stabilizers, the rotator cuff muscles, which act to both compress and depress the humeral head relative to the glenoid (Exercises 26-12 and 26-13).[32,44,63] The inferior rotator cuff muscles in particular should be strengthened to re-create a balance in the force couple with the deltoid in the coronal plane. Supraspinatus should be strengthened to assist in compression of the humeral head into the glenoid (Exercises 26-14 and 26-15). The external rotators, infraspinatus and teres minor, are generally weaker concentrically but stronger eccentrically than the internal rotators, and should be strengthened to re-create a balance in the force couple with subscapularis in the transverse plane.

The external rotators and the posterior portion of the joint capsule are tight and tend to limit internal rotation and should be stretched (Exercises 26-54, 26-56, and 26-58). There is excessive external rotation due to laxity in the anterior portion of the joint capsule, and thus stretching should be avoided. There may be some tightness in both the inferior and posterior portions of the joint capsule, which can be decreased by using posterior and inferior glenohumeral joint mobilizations (Exercises 26-63 and 26-65 to 26-67).

Strengthening of those muscles that abduct, elevate, and upward rotate the scapula—which include serratus anterior, upper trapezius, and levator scapula—should also be incorporated (Exercises 26-16 and 26-20). The middle trapezius and rhomboids should be strengthened eccentrically to help decelerate the scapula during throwing activities (Exercises 26-18 and 26-19). The inferior trapezius should also be strengthened to re-create a balance in the force couple with the upper trapezius, facilitating scapular stability (Exercise 26-17).

Anterior, posterior, inferior, and superior joint mobilizations at both the sternoclavicular and acromioclavicualr joints should be done to assure normal arthrokinematic motion at these joints (Exercises 26-59 to 26-61).

Strengthening of the lower extremity and trunk muscles to provide core stability is essential for reducing the stresses and strains placed on the shoulder and arm is also important for overhead activites (Exercise 26-27).

REHABILITATION PROGRESSION

In the early stages of a rehabilitation program, the primary goal of the therapist is to try and minimize pain associated with impingement syndrome. This may be accomplished by some combination of activity modification, therapeutic modalities, and the appropriate use of NSAIDs.

Once existing performance techniques have been corrected, the therapist must make some decision about limiting the activity that caused the problem in the first place. Activity limitation does not, however, mean immobilization. Instead, a baseline of tolerable activity should be established. The key is to initially control the frequency and level of the load on the rotator cuff, and then to gradually and systematically increase the level and the frequency of that activity. It may be necessary to initially restrict activity, avoiding any exercise that places the shoulder in the impingement position, to allow the inflammation a chance to subside. During this period of restricted activity, the patient should continue to engage in exercises to maintain cardiorespiratory fitness. Working on an upper extremity erogometer will help to improve both cardiorespiratory fitness as well as muscular endurance in the shoulder complex.

Therapeutic modalities such as electrical stimulating currents and hot and cold therapy may be used to modulate pain. Ultrasound or the diathermies are most useful for elevating tissue temperatures and increasing blood flow as well as for facilitating the process of healing. NSAIDs prescribed by the physician are useful not only as an analgesic but for their long-lasting anti-inflammatory capabilities.

Once pain and inflammation have been controlled, exercises should concentrate on strengthening of the dynamic stabilizers of the glenohumeral joint, stretching of the inferior and posterior portions of the joint capsule, strengthening of the scapular muscles that collectively produce normal scapulohumeral rhythm, and maintainence of normal arthrokinematic motions of the acromioclavicular and sternoclavicular joints.

Strengthening exercises are done to establish neuormuscular control of the humerus and the scapula (Exercises 26-70 to 26-76). Strengthening exercises should progress from isometric pain-free contractions to isotonic full range pain-free contractions. Humeral control exercises should be used to strengthen the rotator cuff to restrict migration of the humeral head and to regain voluntary control of the humeral head positioning through rotator cuff stabilization.[72] Scapular control exercises should be used to maintain a normal relationship between the glenohumeral and scapulothoracic joints.[38]

Closed-chain exercises for the shoulder should be primarily eccentric. They tend to compress the joint, providing stability, and are perhaps best used for establishing scapular stability and control.[39]

Gradually, the duration and intensity of the exercise may be progressed within individual patient tolerance limitations, using increased pain or stiffness as a guide for progression, eventually progressing to full-range overhead activities.

Rotator Cuff Tendinitis and Tears

PATHOMECHANICS

Rotator cuff injury has often been considered part of the continuum starting with impingement of the tendon that, through repetitive compression, eventually leads to irritation and inflammation and ultimately fibrosis of the rotator cuff tendon. This idea began with the work of Codman in 1934, when he identified a critical zone near the insertion of the supraspinatus tendon.[12] Since then, many researchers have studied this area and have expanded the information base, identifying other causative factors.[29,49] Neer is also credited with developing a system of classification for rotator cuff disease. This system seemed to be appropriate until sports medicine professionals began dealing with overhead patients as a separate entity due to the acceleration of repetitive stresses applied to the shoulder. Impairment usually results from failure due to one or both chronic stresses, repetitive tension or compression of the tissue. We now regard rotator cuff injury as an accumulation of microtrauma to both the static and dynamic stabilizers of the shoulder complex. In 1993, Meister and Andrews classified these causative traumas based on the pathophysiology of events leading to rotator cuff failure. The five categories of classification for modes of

failure are primary compressive, secondary compressive, primary tensile overload, secondary tensile overload, and macrotraumatic injuries.[42]

INJURY MECHANISM

Because rotator cuff tendonopathy is a gradation of tendon failure, it is important to identify the causative factors. The following classification system helps group injury mechanisms to better aid the therapist in developing a rehabilitation plan.

Primary compressive disease results from direct compression of the cuff tissue. This occurs when something interferes with the gliding of the cuff tendon in the already tight space of the subacromial space. A predisposing factor in this category is a type III hooked acromion process, a common factor seen in younger patients with rotator cuff disease. Other factors in younger patients include a congenitally thick coracoacromial ligament and the presence of an os acromiale. In younger patients, a primary impingement without one of these associated factors is rare. In middle-aged patients, degenerative spurring on the undersurface of the acromion process can cause irritation of the tendon and eventually lead to complete tearing of the tendon.

Secondary compressive disease is a primary result of glenohumeral instability. The high forces generated by overhead activities can cause chronic repetitive trauma to the glenoid labrum and capsuloligamentous structures, leading to subtle instability. Patients with inherent multidirectional instability are also at risk. The additional volume created in the glenohumeral capsule allows for extraneous movement of the humeral head, leading to compressive forces in the subacromial space.

Primary tensile overload can also cause tendon irritation and failure as the rotator cuff resists horizontal adduction, internal rotation, anterior translation of the humeral head, and distraction forces in the deceleration phase of throwing and overhead activities. The repetitive high forces generated by eccentric activity in the rotator cuff while attempting to maintain a central axis of rotation can cause microtrauma to the tendon and eventually lead to tendon failure. This type of mechanism is not associated with previous instability of the joint. Causes for this mechanism often are found when evaluating the patient's mechanics and taking a complete history during the evaluation. The therapist may find that the throwing patient had a history of injury to another area of the body where the muscles are used in the deceleration phase of overhead motion (for example, a right-handed pitcher who sprained his left ankle).

Secondary tensile disease is often a result of primary tensile overload. In this case, the repetitive irritation and weakening of the rotator cuff allows for subtle instability. In contrast to secondary compressive disease of the tendon, the rotator cuff tendon experiences greater distractive and tensile forces because the humeral head is allowed to translate anteriorly. Over time, the increased tensile force causes failure of the tendon.

Macrotraumatic failure occurs as a direct result of one distinct traumatic event. The mechanism for this is often a fall on an outstretched arm. This is rarely seen in patients with normal, healthy rotator cuff tendons. For this to occur, forces generated by the fall must be greater than the tensile strength of the tendon. Because the tensile strength of bone is less than the young healthy tendon, it is rare to see this in a young healthy patient. It is more common to see a longitudinal tear in the tendon with an avulsion of the greater tubercle.

REHABILITATION CONCERNS

When designing a rehabilitation program for rotator cuff tendonopathy, the basic concerns remain the same regardless of the extent to which the tendon is damaged. Instead, the rehabilitation concerns are based on why and how the tendon has been damaged. Once the cause of the tendonopathy and the extent of secondary factors involved are identified, a comprehensive program can be designed. If a comprehensive rehabilitation program does not relieve the painful shoulder, surgical repair of the tendon and alteration of the glenohumeral joint are performed. Surgical rehabilitation is similar to the nonsurgical plan with the time of progression altered, based on tissue healing and tendon histology.

Conservative Management

Stage I of the rehabilitation process is focused on reducing inflammation and removing the patient from the activity that caused pain. Pain should not be a part of the rehabilitation process. The therapist may employ therapeutic modalities to aid in patient comfort. A course of NSIADs is usually followed during this stage of rehabilitation. Range-of-motion exercises begin, avoiding further irritation of the tendon. Attention is paid to restoring appropriate arthrokinematics to the shoulder complex. If the injury is a result of a compressive disease to the tendon, capsular stretching may be done (Exercises 26-59 to 26-69). Active strengthening of the glenohumeral joint should begin, concentrating on the force couples active around the joint. Begin with isometric exercises for the medial and lateral rotators of the joint (Exercise 26-1), and progress to isotonic exercises if the patient does not experience pain (Exercises 26-12 and 26-13). A towel roll under the patient's arm can help initiate co-contraction of the shoulder muscles, increasing joint stability. Exercises may need to be altered to limit translational forces of the humeral head. Strengthening of supraspinatus may begin if 90 degrees of elevation in the scapular plane is available (Exercises 26-14 and 26-15). Aggressive pain-free strengthening of the periscapular muscle should also start, as the restoration of normal scapular control will be essential to removal of abnormal stresses of the rotator cuff tendon in later stages. The therapist may want to begin with manual resistance first (Exercise 26-21), progressing to free weight exercises (Exercises 26-16 to 26-20).

In stage II, the healing process progresses and range of motion will need to be restored. The therapist may need to be more aggressive in stretching techniques, addressing capsular tightness as it develops. The prone on elbows position is a good technique for self-mobilization (Exercise 26-57). This

position should be avoided if compressive disease was part of the irritation. If pain continues to be absent, strengthening gets increasingly aggressive. Isokinetic exercises at speeds greater than 200 degrees per second for shoulder medial and lateral rotation may begin (Exercise 26-33).

Aggressive neuromuscular control exercises are started in this stage. Quick reversals during PNF diagonal patterns, starting with manual resistance from the therapist and advancing to resistance applied by surgical tubing (Exercises 26-40 and 26-41). A Body Blade may also be used for rhythmic stabilization (Exercise 26-42).

The exercise program should now progress to free weights, and eccentric exercises of the rotator cuff should be emphasized to meet the demands of the shoulder in overhead activities. Strengthening of the deltoid and upper trapezius muscles can begin above 90 degrees of elevation. Exercises include military press (Exercise 26-5), shoulder flexion (Exercise 26-7), and reverse flys (Exercise 26-11). Push-ups can also be added; restricting range of motion so the body does not go below the elbow may be necessary to prevent excessive translation of the glenohumeral joint. This author prefers combining this exercise with serratus anterior strengthening in a modified push-up with a plus (Exercise 26-20).

In the later part of stage II, exercises should progress to plyometric strengthening. Surgical tubing is used to allow the patient to exercise in 90 degrees of elevation with the elbow bent to 90 degrees (Exercise 26-26). Plyoball exercises are initiated (Exercises 26-27 and 26-28). The weight and distance of the exercises can be altered to increase demands. The Shuttle 2000-1 is an excellent exercise to increase eccentric strength in a plyometric fashion (Exercise 26-31).

Stage III of the rehabilitation focuses on specific functional activities. Total body conditioning, return of strength, and increased endurance are the emphasis. The patient should remain pain-free as specific functional activities are advanced.

Postsurgical Management

If conservative management is insufficient, surgical repair is often indicated. The type of repair done is dependent on the classification of the injury. Subacromial decompression has been described by Neer as a method to stimulate tissue healing and increase the subacromial space.[45] Additional procedures may be done as open repairs of the tendon along with a capsular tightening procedure. One example is a modified Bankart procedure and capsulolabral reconstruction.[27]

Stage I is often begun with some form of immobilization. This does not mean complete lack of movement. Instead it refers to restricting positions based on the surgical repair. In open repairs, flexion and abduction may be restricted for as long as 4 weeks. When the repair addresses the capsulolabral complex, the patient may spend up to 2 weeks in an airplane splint (Fig. 26-9).

Pain control and prevention of muscle atrophy are addressed in this stage. Shoulder shrugs, isometrics, and joint mobilization for pain control can be done. Later in the stage, active

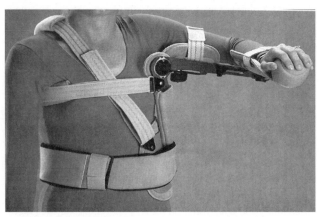

FIGURE 26-9

Airplane splint.

assistive exercises with the L-bar and multiangle isometrics are done in the pain-free range of motion.

In stage II, collagen and elastin components have begun to stabilize. Healing tissue should have a decreased level of elastin and increased level of collagen by now.[59] Regaining full range of motion and increasing the stress to healing tissue for better collagen alignment is important in this stage. Having the patient hang from an overhead bar (Exercise 26-44) or using a rope-and-pulley system (Exercise 26-48) can help achieve desired ROM.

Active range-of-motion exercises are added, progressing from no resistance to resistance with surgical tubing. If a primary repair has been done to the tendon, resisted supraspinatus exercises should be avoided until 10 weeks.

The restoration of normal arthrokinematics and scapulothoracic rhythm is addressed with exercises emphasizing neuromuscular control. The patient can use a mirror to judge progress.

Stage III remains similar to that of conservative management; however, the time frame may lag getting to this stage.

REHABILITATION PROGRESSION

The rehabilitation progression for conservatively managed rotator cuff injury should follow along with the progression outlined in the section on impingement syndrome. The following progression is the authors' preference for postsurgical progression. The principles followed for rehabilitation progression are based on the dynamics of healing tissue. Depending on the surgical procedure, the time frame for this progression may be altered. A simple way to stage the rehabilitation of the postsurgical patient is by following the rule of six. During the first 6 weeks after the surgery, the goal is to decrease pain, address inflammation, and prevent muscle atrophy. Use of therapeutic modalities and gentle ROM are initiated.

The second 6-week period (6 to 12 weeks) begins the stage of rehabilitation, where full active and passive range of motion need to be achieved prior to maturation of the healing tissue. Other emphasis is placed on regaining normal static and

dynamic joint mechanics. Proprioceptive and neuromuscular exercises are used to achieve this goal.

During the last 6 weeks (12 to 18 weeks), the repair should be mature enough to tolerate progression to activities that prepare the patient for return to normal activity. Increase the speed and control of resisted exercises. Plyometric training and interval progression to specific functional activities are used. This stage ends with the patient's return to normal activity.

Adhesive Capsulitis (Frozen Shoulder)

PATHOMECHANICS

Adhesive capsulitis is characterized by the loss of motion at the glenohumeral joint. The cause of this arthrofibrosis is not well defined. One set of criteria used for diagnosis of a frozen shoulder included (1) decreased glenohumeral motion and loss of synchronous shoulder girdle motion, (2) restricted elevation (less than 135 or 90 degrees depending on the author), (3) external rotation 50 to 60 percent of normal, and (4) arthrogram findings of 5 to 10 mL volume with obliteration of the normal axillary fold.[30] Other authors have identified histologic changes in different areas surrounding the glenohumeral joint.[59] Travell and Simons explained that a reflex autonomic reaction could be the underlying cause due to the presence of subscapularis trigger points.[65] The result is a chronic inflammation with fibrosis and rotator cuff muscles that are tight and inelastic.

INJURY MECHANISM

For the purposes of this chapter, we will separate this diagnosis into two categories: primary versus secondary frozen shoulder. Adhesive capsulitis may be considered primary when it develops spontaneously, and is considered secondary when a known underlying condition is present (e.g., fractured humeral head).

Primary frozen shoulder usually has an insidious onset. The patient often describes a sequence of painful restriction in the shoulder, followed by a gradual stiffness with less pain. Factors that have been found to predispose a patient to idiopathic capsulitis include diabetes, hypothyroidism, and underlying cardiopulmonary involvement.[59] These factors were identified through epidemiologic studies and may have more to do with characteristic personalities of these patients.

Secondary frozen shoulder has been associated with many different underlying diagnoses. Rockwood and Matsen listed eight categories of conditions that should be considered in the differential diagnosis of frozen shoulder: trauma, other soft-tissue disorders about the shoulder, joint disorders, bone disorders, cervical spine disorders, intrathoracic disorders, abdominal disorders, and psychogenic disorder (Table 26-3).[55]

REHABILITATION CONCERNS

The primary concern for rehabilitation is proper differential diagnosis. Attempting to progress the patient into the strength or functional activities portion of a rehabilitation program can

TABLE 26-3

Differential Diagnosis of Frozen Shoulder

TRAUMA

Fractures of the shoulder region
Fractures anywhere in the upper extremity
Missed diagnosed posterior shoulder dislocation
Hemarthrosis of shoulder secondary to trauma

OTHER SOFT-TISSUE DISORDERS ABOUT THE SHOULDER

Tendonitis of the rotator cuff
Tendonitis of the long head of biceps
Subacromial bursitis
Impingement
Suprascapular nerve impingement
Thoracic outlet syndrome

JOINT DISORDERS

Degenerative arthritis of the AC joint
Degenerative arthritis of the glenohumeral joint
Septic arthritis
Other painful forms of arthritis

BONE DISORDERS

Avascular necrosis of the humeral head
Metastatic cancer
Paget's disease
Primary bone tumor
Hyperparathyroidism

CERVICAL SPINE DISORDERS

Cervical spondylosis
Cervical disc herniation
Infection

INTRATHORACIC DISORDER

Diaphragmatic irritation
Pancoast tumor
Myocardial infarction

ABDOMINAL DISORDER

Gastric ulcer
Cholecystitis
Subphrenic abscess

PSYCHOGENIC

Reproduced, with permission, from Rockwood CA, Matsen FA. *The Shoulder.* Philadelphia, Saunders, 1990.

lead to exacerbation of the motion restriction. The single best treatment for adhesive capsulitis is prevention.

Depending on the stage of pathology when intervention is started, the rehabilitation program time frame can be shortened. In all cases, the goals of rehabilitation are the same: first relieving the pain in the acute stages of the disorder, gradually restoring proper arthrokinematic, gradual restoration of range of motion, and strengthening the muscles of the shoulder complex.

REHABILITATION PROGRESSION

In the acute phase, Codman's exercises and low-grade joint mobilization techniques can be used to relieve pain. This may be accompanied by therapeutic modalities and passive stretching of the upper trapezius and levator scapulae muscles. The therapist may also want to suggest that the patient sleep with a pillow under the involved arm to prevent internal rotation during sleep.

In the subacute phase, range of motion is more aggressively addressed. Incorporating PNF techniques such as hold–relax can be helpful. Progressive demands should be placed on the patient with rhythmic stabilization techniques. Wall climbing (Exercise 26-47) and wall/corner stretches (Exercise 26-49) are also good additions to the rehabilitation program. As ROM returns, the program should start to address strengthening. Isometric exercises for the shoulder are often the best way to begin. Progressive strengthening will continue in the next phase.

The final phase of rehabilitation is a progressive strengthening of the shoulder complex. Exercises for maintenance of ROM continue, and a series of strengthening exercises should be added. The rehabilitation program should be tailored to meet the needs of the patient based on the differential diagnosis.

Thoracic Outlet Syndrome

PATHOMECHANICS

Thoracic outlet syndrome is the compression of neurovascular structures within the thoracic outlet. The thoracic outlet is a conical-shaped passage, with the greater circumferential opening proximal to the spine and the narrow end passing into the distal extremity. On the proximal end, the cone is bordered anteriorly by the anterior scalene muscles, and posteriorly by the middle and posterior scalene muscles. Anatomic structures traveling through the thoracic outlet are the brachial plexus, subclavian artery and vein, and axillary vessels. The neurovascular structures pass distally under the clavicle and subclavius muscle. Beneath the neurovascular bundle is the first rib. At the narrow end of the cone, the bundle passes under the coracoid process of the scapula and into the upper extremity through the axilla. The distal end is bordered anteriorly by the pectoralis minor and posteriorly by the scapula.

Based on the anatomy of the thoracic outlet, there are several areas where neurovascular compression may occur.

Therefore, pathology of the thoracic outlet syndrome is dependent on the structures being compressed.

INJURY MECHANISM

In 60 percent of the population affected by thoracic outlet syndrome, there is no report from the patient of an inciting episode.[35] Some of the theories presented by authors regarding the etiology of thoracic outlet syndrome include trauma, postural components, shortening of the pectoralis minor, shortening of the scalenes, and muscle hypertrophy.

There are four areas of vulnerability to compressive forces:

- The superior thoracic outlet, where the brachial plexus passes over the first rib.
- The scalene triangle, at the proximal end of the thoracic outlet, where there may be overlapping insertions of the anterior and middle scalenes onto the first rib.
- The costoclavicular interval, which is the space between the first rib and clavicle where the neurovascular bundle passes. The space may be narrowed by poor posture, inferior laxity of the glenohumeral joint, or an exostosis from a fracture of the clavicle.
- Under the coracoid process, where the brachial plexus passes and is bordered anteriorly by the pectoralis minor.[59]

REHABILITATION CONCERNS

As described, thoracic outlet syndrome is an anatomically based problem. It involves compressive forces applied to the neurovascular bundle. Conservative management of thoracic outlet syndrome is moderately successful, resulting in decreased symptoms 50 to 90 percent of the time. As the first course of treatment, rehabilitation should be based on encouraging the least provocative posture. Leffert advocated a detailed history and evaluation of the patient's activities and lifestyle to help identify where and when postural deficiency is occurring.[35]

Through a detailed history and evaluation of a patient's activity, the therapist can identify the cause of compression in the thoracic outlet. The rehabilitation program should be tailored to encourage good posture throughout the patient's day. Therapeutic exercises should be used to strengthen postural muscles, such as the rhomboids (Exercise 26-19), middle trapezius (Exercise 26-18), and upper trapezius (Exercise 26-16). Flexibility exercises are also used to increase the space in the thoracic outlet. Scalene stretches and wall/corner stretches (Exercise 26-49) are used to decrease the incidence of muscle impinging on the neurovascular bundle. Proper breathing technique should also be reviewed with the patient. The scalene muscles act as accessory breathing muscles, and improper breathing technique can lead to tightening of these muscles.

REHABILITATION PROGRESSION

The rehabilitation process begins by detailed evaluation of the patient's activities and symptoms. First, the patient is removed from activities exacerbating the neurovascular symptoms until the patient can maintain a symptom-free posture. During

TABLE 26-4

Trigger Points of the Shoulder

POSTERIOR SHOULDER PAIN

Deltoid
Levator scapulae
Supraspinatus
Subscapularis
Teres minor
Teres major
Serratus posterior superior
Triceps
Trapezius

ANTERIOR SHOULDER PAIN

Infraspinatus
Deltoid
Scalene
Supraspinatus
Pectoralis major
Pectoralis minor
Biceps
Coracobrachialis

SOURCE: Travell JG, Simons, DG. *Myofascial Pain and Dysfunction. The Trigger Point Manual.* Baltimore, Williams & Wilkins, 1983.

this time, an erect posture is encouraged using stretching and strengthening exercises. Encourage the patient to maintain a pain-free posture. This helps build endurance of the postural muscles. Exercising on an upper-body ergometer, by pedaling backward, can help build endurance.

If the patient fails to respond to therapy, and functionally significant pain and weakness persist, surgical intervention may be indicated. Surgical procedure is dependent on the anatomic basis for the patient's symptoms.

Brachial Plexus Injuries (Stinger or Burner)

PATHOMECHANICS

The brachial plexus begins at cervical nerve roots C5 through C8 and thoracic nerve root T1. The ventral rami of these roots are formed from a dorsal (sensory) and ventral (motor) root. The ventral rami join to form the brachial plexus. The ventral rami lie between the anterior and middle scalene muscles, where they run adjacent to the subclavian artery. The plexus continues distally, passing over the first rib. It is deep to the sternocleidomastoid muscle in the neck.[46] Just caudal to the clavicle and subclavius muscle, the five ventral rami unite to form the three trunks of the plexus: superior, middle, and inferior. The superior trunk is composed of the C5 and C6 ventral roots. The middle trunk is formed by the C7 root, and the inferior trunk is formed by C8 and T1 ventral roots. After passing under the clavicle, the three trunks divide into three divisions, which eventually contribute to the three cords of the brachial plexus.

The typical picture of a brachial plexus injury is that of a traction injury. This syndrome is commonly referred to as burner or stinger syndrome. These injuries usually involve the C5 to C6 nerve roots. The patient will complain of a sharp, burning pain in the shoulder that radiates down the arm into the hand. Weakness in the muscles supplied by C5 and C6 (deltoid, biceps, supraspinatus, and infraspinatus) accompanies the pain. Burning and pain is often transient, but weakness may last a few minutes or indefinitely.

Clancy et al have classified brachial plexus injuries into three categories.[11] A grade I injury results in a transient loss of motor and sensory function, which usually resolves completely within minutes. A grade II injury results in significant motor weakness and sensory loss that may last from 6 weeks to 4 months. EMG evaluation after 2 weeks will demonstrate abnormalities. Grade III lesions are characterized by motor and sensory loss for at least 1 year in duration.

INJURY MECHANISM

The structure of the brachial plexus is such that it winds its way through the musculoskeletal anatomy of the upper extremity, as described. Clancy et al identified neck rotation, neck lateral flexion, shoulder abduction, shoulder external rotation, and simultaneous scapular and clavicular depression as potential mechanisms of injury.[11]

During neck rotation and lateral flexion to one side, the brachial plexus and the subclavius muscle on the opposite side are put on stretch and the clavicle is slightly elevated about its AP axis. If the arm is not elevated, the superior trunk of the plexus will assume the greatest amount of tension. If the shoulder is abducted and externally rotated, the brachial plexus migrates superiorly toward the coracoid process and the scapula retracts, putting the pectoralis minor on stretch. As the shoulder is moved into full abduction, a condition similar to a movable pulley is formed, where the coracoid process of the scapula acts as the pulley. In full abduction, the majority of stress falls on the lower cords of the brachial plexus.[60] The addition of clavicular and scapula depression to these scenarios would produce a downward force on the pulley system, bringing the brachial plexus in contact with the clavicle, and the coracoid process. The portion of the plexus that recieves the greatest amount of tensile stress depends on the position of the upper extremity during a collision.

REHABILITATION CONCERNS

Management of brachial plexus injuries begins with the gradual restoration of the patient's cervical range of motion. Muscle tightness caused by the direct trauma and reflexive guarding that occurs because of pain needs to be addressed. Gentle passive range-of-motion exercises, and stretching for the upper trapezius, levator scapulae, and scalene muscles should be done. The therapist should be careful not to cause sensory symptoms.

Strengthening of the involved muscles is also addressed in the rehabilitation program. Supraspinatus strengthening exercises like scaption (Exercise 26-14) and alternative suprapinatus exercises (Exercise 26-15) should be done. Other exercises for involved musculature are shoulder lateral rotation (Exercise 26-13) for infraspinatus, forward flexion and abduction to 90 degrees (Exercises 26-7 to 26-9) to strengthen the deltoid, and bicep curls for elbow flexion.

REHABILITATION PROGRESSION

Removing the patient from activity is done immediately after the injury. The rehabilitation progression should begin with the restoration of both active and passive range of motion at the neck and shoulder. As the patient gets return of range of motion, strengthening of the neck and shoulder are incorporated into the rehabilitation program. Strengthening should progress from PRE-type strengthening with free weights to exercises that emphasize power and endurance. Functional progression begins with teaching proper technique for specific demands that mimic the position of injury.

Myofascial Trigger Points

PATHOLOGY

Clinically, a trigger point (TP) is defined as a hyperirritable focus in muscle or fascia that is tender to palpation and may, upon compression, result in referred pain or tenderness in a characteristic "zone," which is distinct from myotomes, dermatomes, schlerotomes, or peripheral nerve distribution. TPs are identified via palpation of taut bands of muscle or discrete nodules or adhesions. Snapping of a taut band will usually initiate a local twitch response.[59]

Physiologically, the definition of a trigger point is not as clear. Muscles with myofascial trigger points reveal no diagnostic abnormalities upon EMG examination. Routine laboratory tests show no abnormalities or significant changes attributable to TPs. Normal serum enzyme concentrations have been reported with a shift in the distribution of LDH isoenzymes. Skin temperature over active TPs may be higher in a 5- to 10-cm diameter.[65]

Travell and Simons classify TPs as follows:

- Active TPs. Symptomatic at rest, with referral pain and tenderness upon direct compression. Associated weakness and contracture are often present.
- Latent TPs. Pain is not present unless direct compression is applied. May show up on clinical exam as stiffness and/or weakness in the region of tenderness.
- Primary TPs. Located in specific muscles.
- Associated TPs. Located within the referral zone of a primary TP's muscle or in a muscle that is functionally overloaded in compensation for a primary TP.[65]

Pathology of a myofascial trigger point is identified with (1) history of sudden onset during or shortly after an acute overload stress or chronic overload of the affected muscle, (2) characteristic patterns of pain in a muscle's referral zone, (3) weakness and restriction in the end range of motion of the affected muscle, (4) a taut, palpable band in the affected muscle, (5) focal tenderness to direct compression in the band of taut muscle fibers, (6) a local twitch response elicited by snapping of the tender spot, and (7) reproduction of the patient's pain through pressure on the tender spot.

INJURY MECHANISM

The most common injury mechanism for myofascial trigger points in the shoulder region is acute muscle strain. The damaged muscle tissue causes tearing of the sarcoplasmic reticulum and release of its stored calcium, with loss of the ability of that portion of the muscle to remove calcium ions. The chronic stress of sustained muscle contraction can cause continued muscle damage, repeating the above cycle of damage. The combined presence of the normal muscle ATP supplies and excessive calcium initiate and maintain a sustained muscle band contracture. This produces a region of the muscle with an uncontrolled metabolism, to which the body responds with local vasoconstriction. This region of increased metabolism and decreased local circulation, with muscle fibers passing through that area, causes muscle shortening independent of local motor-unit action potentials. This taut band may be palpated in the muscle.

REHABILITATION CONCERNS

Because the principle mechanism of myofascial trigger points is related to muscular overload and fatigue, the primary concern is identification of the incriminating activity. The therapist should take a detailed history of the patient's daily activity demands as well as changing demands of sport activities.

The cyclic nature of TPs requires interruption of the cycle for successful treatment. Interrupting the shortening of the muscle fibers and prevention of further breakdown of the muscle tissue components should be attempted using modified hold–relax techniques and postisometric stretching. Travell and Simons advocate a spray and stretch method, where vapocoolant spray is applied and passive stretching follows. Theoretically, when the muscle is placed in a stretched position and the skin receptors are cooled, a reflexive inhibition of the contracted muscle is facilitated, allowing for increased passive stretching.[65]

After a treatment session where passive range of motion has been achieved, the muscle must be activated to stimulate normal actin and myosin cross-bridging. Gentle active range-of-motion exercises or active assistive exercises with the L-bar may be a good activity to use as posttreatment activity. Normal muscle activity and endurance must be encouraged after range of motion is restored. A gradual progression of shoulder exercises with an endurance emphasis should be used.

REHABILITATION PROGRESSION

Treatment progression for TPs should begin with temporary removal from activities that overload the contracted tissue. The patient is then treated with myofascial stretching techniques to increase the length of the contracted tissue. Immediate use of the extended range of motion should be emphasized. Strengthening exercises are added once the patient can maintain the normal muscle length without initiating the return of the contracted myofascial band. As strength and function of the involved muscles return, the patient may gradually return to normal activity.

The patient may return to normal activity in a relatively short period of time if he or she can demonstrate the ability to function without reinitiating the myofascial trigger points and associated taut bands. Early return without meeting this criterion may lead to greater regionalization of the symptoms.

EXERCISES

REHABILITATION TECHNIQUES FOR THE SHOULDER

Strengthening Techniques

ISOMETRIC AND ISOTONIC OPEN-KINETIC CHAIN EXERCISES

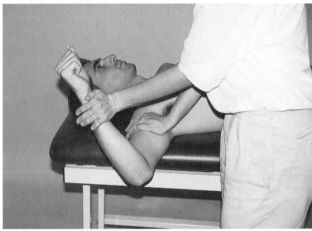

A

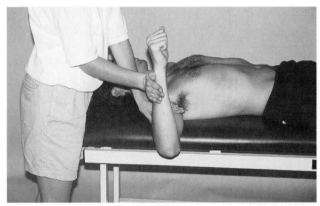

B

EXERCISE 26-1

A, Isometric medial rotation, and **B,** isometric lateral rotation, are useful in the early stages of a shoulder rehabilitation program when full ROM isotonic exercise is likely to exacerbate a problem. The towel under the arm is used to help establish neuromuscular control and help facilitate scapular stability.

EXERCISE 26-2

Bench press. Used to strengthen pectoralis major, anterior deltoid, and triceps; and secondarily the coracobrachialis muscles. Performing this exercise with the feet on the bench serves to flatten the low back and helps to isolate these muscles.

EXERCISE 26-3

Incline bench press. Used to strengthen pectoralis major (upper fibers), triceps, middle and anterior deltoid; and secondarily the coracobrachialis, upper trapezius, and levator scapula muscles.

E X E R C I S E   2 6 - 4

Decline bench press. Used to strengthen pectoralis major (lower fibers), triceps, anterior deltoid, coracobrachialis, and latissimus dorsi.

A

B

E X E R C I S E   2 6 - 5

Military press. Used to strengthen middle deltoid, upper trapezius, levator scapula, and triceps.

E X E R C I S E   2 6 - 6

Lat pull-downs. Used to strengthen primarily latissimus dorsi, teres major, and pectoralis minor; and secondarily the biceps. This exercise may be done by pulling the bar down in front of the head or behind the neck. Pulling the bar down behind the neck requires contraction of the rhomboids and middle trapezius. Pull-ups done on a chinning bar can also be used as an alternative strengthening technique.

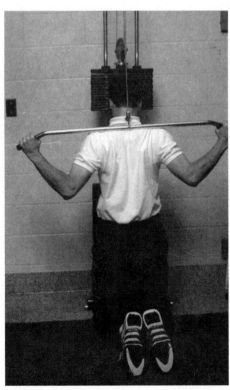

E X E R C I S E 2 6 - 7

Shoulder flexion. Used to strengthen primarily the anterior deltoid, and coracobrachialis; and secondarily the middle deltoid; pectoralis major, and biceps brachii. Note that the thumb should point upward.

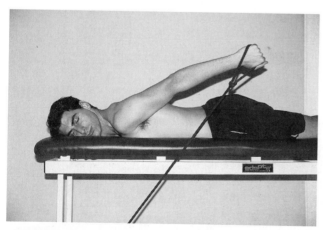

E X E R C I S E 2 6 - 8

Shoulder extension. Used to strengthen primarily latissimus dorsi, teres major, and posterior deltoid; and secondarily teres minor and the long head of the triceps. Note that the thumb should point down. May be done standing using a dumbbell or lying prone using surgical tubing.

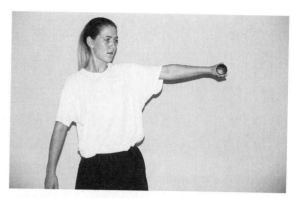

E X E R C I S E 2 6 - 9

Shoulder abduction to 90 degrees. Used to strengthen primarily the middle deltoid and supraspinatus; and secondarily the anterior and posterior deltoid and serratus anterior. Note that the thumb is in a neutral position.

A

B

E X E R C I S E 2 6 - 1 0

Flys (shoulder horizontal adduction). Used to strengthen primarily pectoralis major and secondarily the anterior deltoid. Note that the elbow may be slightly flexed. May be done in a supine position or standing with surgical tubing or wall pulleys behind.

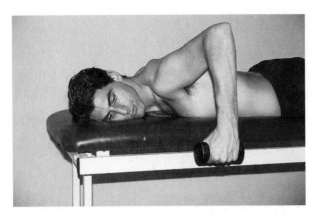

EXERCISE 26-11

Reverse flys (shoulder horizontal abduction). Used to strengthen primarily the posterior deltoid; and secondarily infraspinatus, teres minor, the rhomboids, and middle trapezius muscles. May be done lying prone using either dumbbells or tubing. Note that with the thumb pointed upward the middle trapezius is more active, and with the thumb pointed down the rhomboids are more active.

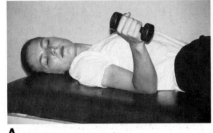  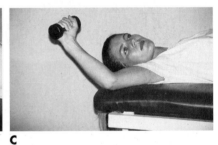

A   B   C

EXERCISE 26-12

Shoulder medial rotation. Used to strengthen primarily subscapularis, pectoralis major, latissimus dorsi, and teres major; and secondarily the anterior deltoid. This exercise may be done isometrically or isotonically either lying supine using a dumbbell or standing using tubing. Strengthening should be done with the arm fully adducted at 0 degrees, and also in 90 degrees and 135 degrees of abduction.

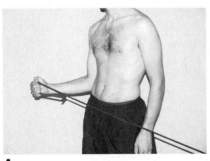  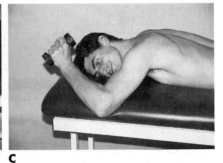

A   B   C

EXERCISE 26-13

Shoulder lateral rotation. Used to strengthen primarily infraspinatus and teres minor; and secondarily the posterior deltoid. This exercise may be done isometrically or isotonically either lying prone using a dumbbell or standing using tubing. Strengthening should be done with the arm fully adducted at 0 degrees, and also in 90 degrees and 135 degrees of abduction.

EXERCISE 26-14

Scaption. Used to strengthen primarily supraspinatus in the plane of the scapula; and secondarily the anterior and middle deltoid. This exercise should be done standing with arm horizontally adducted to 45 degrees and the thumb pointing downward.

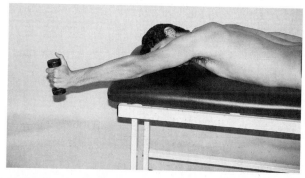

EXERCISE 26-15

Alternative supraspinatus exercise. Used to strengthen primarily supraspinatus and secondarily the posterior deltoid. In the prone position with the arm abducted to 100 degrees, the arm is horizonally abducted in extreme lateral rotation. Note that the thumb should point upward.

EXERCISE 26-16

Shoulder shrugs. Used to strengthen primarily the upper trapezius and the levator scapula; and secondarily the rhomboids.

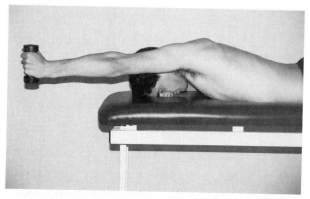

EXERCISE 26-17

Superman. Used to strengthen primarily the inferior trapezius and secondarily the middle trapezius. May be done lying prone using either dumbbells or tubing. Note that the thumb is in a neutral position.

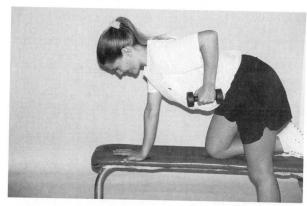

EXERCISE 26-18

Bent-over rows. Used to strengthen primarily the middle trapezius and rhomboids. Done standing in bent-over position with one knee supported on a bench.

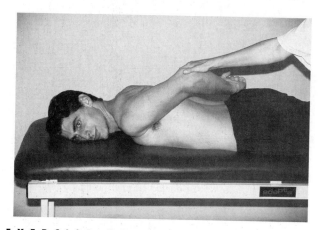

EXERCISE 26-19

Rhomboids exercise. Used to strengthen primarily the rhomboids and secondarily the inferior trapezius. Should be done lying prone with manual resistance applied at the elbow.

A   **B**

EXERCISE 26-20

Push-ups with a plus. Used to strengthen the serratus anterior. There are several variations to this exercise including **A,** regular push-up; **B,** weight-loaded push-up.

CLOSED-KINETIC CHAIN EXERCISES

A

EXERCISE 26-21

Scapular strengthening using a Body Blade. Holding an oscillating Body Blade with both hands, the patient moves from a fully adducted position in front of the body to a fully elevated overhead position.

B

EXERCISE 26-22

Push-ups. May be done with **A,** weight supported on feet, or **B,** modified to support weight on the knees.

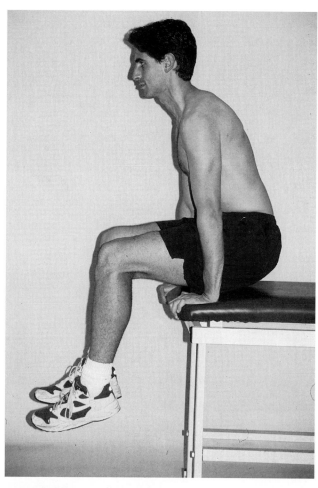

EXERCISE 26-23

Seated push-up. Done sitting on the end of a table. Place hands on the table and lift weight upward off the table isotonically.

EXERCISE 26-24

Biodex upper extremity closed-chain device. One of the only isokinetic closed-kinetic chain exercise devices currently available.

EXERCISE 26-25

Stair climber, feet on chair. An advanced closed-kinetic chain strengthening exercise that places the hands on the footplates of a stair climber with the feet supported on a chair. Requires substantial upper body strength.

PLYOMETRIC STRENGTHENING EXERCISES

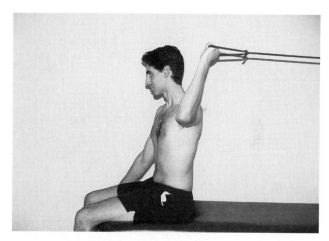

EXERCISE 26-26

Surgical tubing. For example, to strengthen the medial rotators use a quick eccentric stretch of the medial rotators to facilitate a concentric contraction of those muscles.

A

B

C

D

E

F

EXERCISE 26-27

Plyoball. The patient should catch the ball, decelerate it, and then immediately accelerate in the opposite direction. **A,** Single-arm toss. **B,** Two-arm toss with trunk rotation. **C,** Two-arm overhead toss. **D,** Single-arm toss on unstable surface. **E,** Kneeling single arm toss. **F,** Kneeling two-arm toss. The weight of the plyoball should be increased as rapidly as can be tolerated.[73]

E X E R C I S E   2 6 - 2 8

Seated single-arm weighted ball throw. The patient should be seated with the arm abducted to 90 degrees and the elbow supported on a table. The therapist tosses the ball to the hand, creating an overload in lateral rotation, which forces the patient to dynamically stabilize in that position.

E X E R C I S E   2 6 - 3 0

Push-ups on boxes. When performing a plyometric push-up on boxes, the patient can stretch the anterior muscles, which facilitates a concentric contraction.

E X E R C I S E   2 6 - 2 9

Push-ups with a clap. The patient pushes off the ground and then claps the hands and finally catches his or her weight as he or she decelerates.

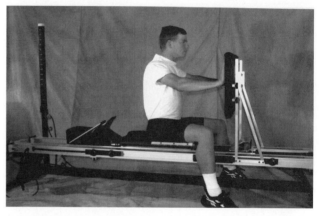

E X E R C I S E   2 6 - 3 1

Shuttle 1900-1. The exercise machine can be used for plyometric exercises in either the upper or lower extremity.

ISOKINETIC STRENGTHENING EXERCISE

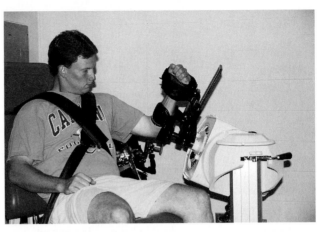

E X E R C I S E   2 6 - 3 3

Isokinetic medial/lateral rotation. When using an isokinetic device for strengthening the shoulder, the patient should be set up such that strengthening may be done in a scapular plane.[21]

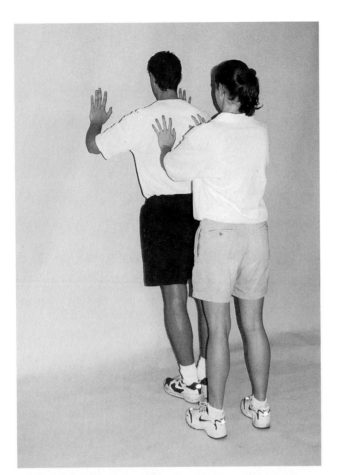

E X E R C I S E   2 6 - 3 2

Push into wall. The therapist stands behind the patient and pushes him or her toward the wall. The patient decelerates the forces and then pushes off the wall immediately.

PNF STRENGTHENING TECHNIQUES

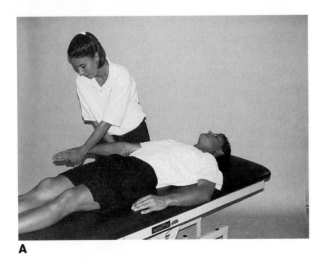

A   **B**

E X E R C I S E   2 6 - 3 4

D1 upper extremity movement pattern moving into flexion. **A,** Starting position. **B,** Terminal position.

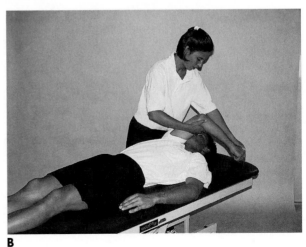

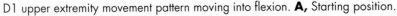

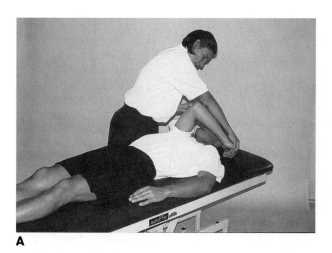

A

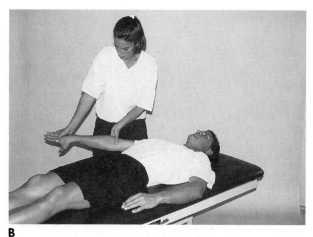

B

EXERCISE 26-35

D1 upper extremity movement pattern moving into extension. **A,** Starting position.
B, Terminal position.

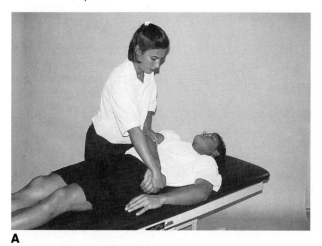

A

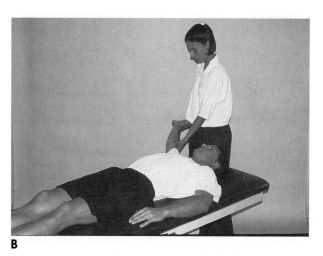

B

EXERCISE 26-36

D2 upper extremity movement pattern moving into flexion. **A,** Starting position.
B, Terminal position.

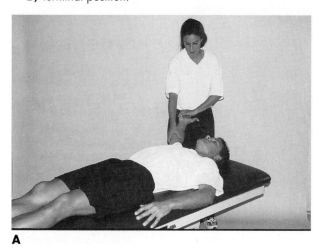

A

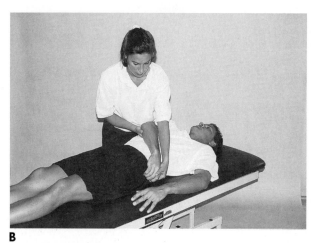

B

EXERCISE 26-37

D2 upper extremity movement pattern moving into extension. **A,** Starting position.
B, Terminal position.

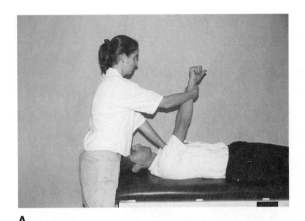

A

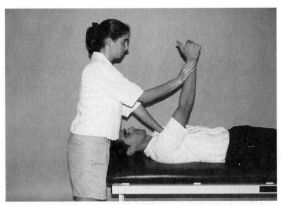

B

EXERCISE 26-38

Rhythmic contraction. Using either a D1 or D2 pattern. **A,** The patient uses an isometric co-contraction to maintain a specific position within the ROM. **B,** The therapist repeatedly changes the direction of passive pressure.

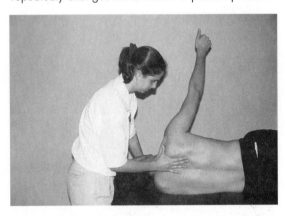

EXERCISE 26-39

PNF technique for scapula. As the patient moves through either a D1 or D2 pattern, the therapist applies resistance at the appropriate scapular border.

EXERCISE 26-40

Using surgical tubing in PNF patterns. The patient can use resistance from tubing through a PNF movement pattern. **A,** D2 pattern starting position. **B,** D2 pattern terminal position.

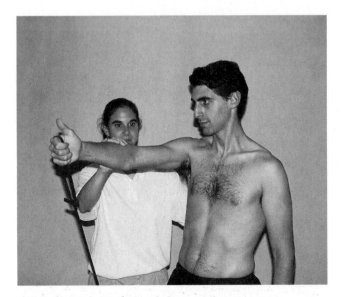

EXERCISE 26-41

PNF using both manual resistance and surgical tubing. Rhythmic stabilization can be performed as the patient isometrically holds a specific position in the ROM with surgical tubing and force applied by the therapist.

EXERCISE 26-42

PNF using a Body Blade. In a standing position the patient moves an oscillating Body Blade through a D2 pattern.

Stretching Exercises

EXERCISE 26-44

Static hanging. Hanging from a chinning bar is a good general stretch for the musculature in the shoulder complex.

EXERCISE 26-43

Surgical tubing may be attached to a tennis racket as the patient practices an overhead serve technique. This is useful as a functional progression technique.

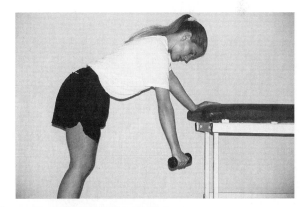

EXERCISE 26-45

Codman's circumduction exercise. The patient holds a dumbbell in the hand and moves the dumbbell in a circular pattern, reversing direction periodically. This technique is useful as a general stretch in the early stages of rehabilitation when motion above 90 degrees is restricted.

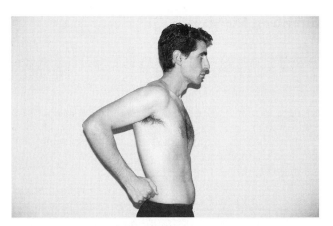

E X E R C I S E   2 6 - 4 6

Sawing. The patient moves the arm forward and backward as if performing a sawing motion. This technique is useful as a general stretch in the early stages of rehabilitation when motion above 90 degrees is restricted.

E X E R C I S E   2 6 - 4 8

Rope and pulley exercise. This exercise may be used as an active-assistive exercise when trying to regain full overhead motion. ROM should be restricted to a pain-free arc.

E X E R C I S E   2 6 - 4 7

Wall climbing. The patient uses the fingers to "walk" the hand up a wall. This technique is useful when attempting to regain full-range elevation. ROM should be restricted to a pain-free arc.

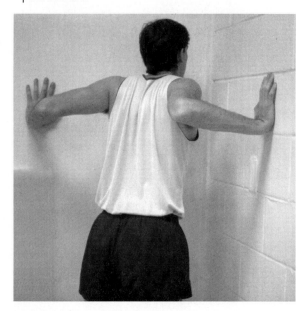

E X E R C I S E   2 6 - 4 9

Wall/corner stretch. Used to stretch pectoralis major and minor, the anterior deltoid, coracobrachialis, and anterior joint capsule.

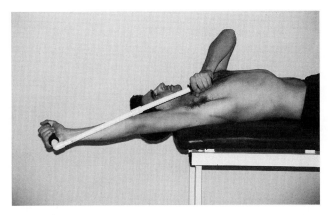

EXERCISE 26-50

Shoulder extensor stretch using an L-bar. Used to stretch latissimus dorsi, teres major and minor, the posterior deltoid, triceps, and inferior joint capsule.

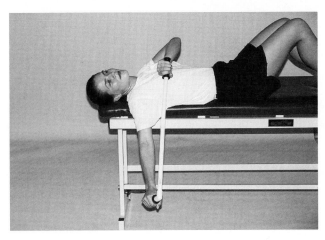

EXERCISE 26-51

Shoulder flexors stretch using an L-bar. Used to stretch the anterior deltoid, coracobrachialis, pectoralis major, biceps, and anterior joint capsule.

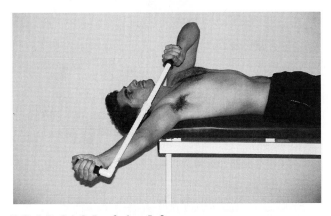

EXERCISE 26-52

Shoulder adductors stretch using an L-bar. Used to stretch latissimus dorsi, teres major and minor, pectoralis major and minor, the posterior deltoid, triceps, and inferior joint capsule.

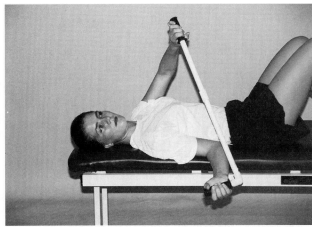

A

B

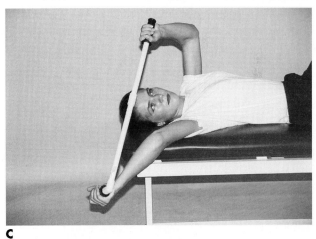

C

EXERCISE 26-53

Shoulder medial rotators stretch using an L-bar. Used to stretch subscapularis, pectoralis major, latissimus dorsi, teres major, anterior deltoid, and anterior joint capsule. This stretch should be done at **A,** 0 degrees; **B,** 90 degrees; and **C,** 135 degrees.

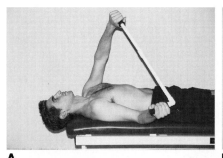
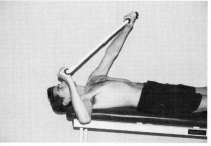
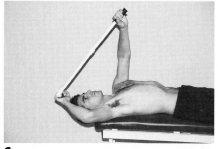

A   **B**   **C**

E X E R C I S E   2 6 - 5 4

Shoulder lateral rotators using an L-bar. Used to stretch infraspinatus, teres minor, posterior deltoid, and posterior joint capsule. This stretch should be done at **A,** 0 degrees; **B,** 90 degrees; and **C,** 135 degrees.

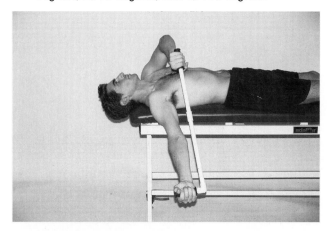

E X E R C I S E   2 6 - 5 5

Horizontal adductors stretch using an L-bar. Used to stretch the pectoralis major, anterior deltoid, long head of the biceps, and anterior joint capsule.

E X E R C I S E   2 6 - 5 7

Anterior capsule stretch. Self-stretch using the wall.

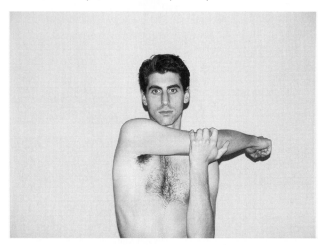

E X E R C I S E   2 6 - 5 6

Horizonal abductors stretch. Used to stretch the posterior deltoid, infraspinatus, teres minor, rhomboids, middle trapezius, and posterior joint capsule. This position may be uncomfortable for patients with shoulder impingement syndrome.

E X E R C I S E   2 6 - 5 8

Inferior capsule stretch. Self-stretch done with the arm in the fully elevated overhead position. This position may be uncomfortable for patients with shoulder impingement syndrome.

Joint Mobilization Techniques

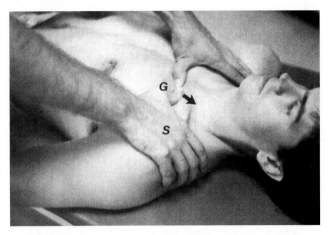

EXERCISE 26-59

Posterior and superior clavicular glides. When posterior or superior clavicular glides are done at the sternoclavicular joint, use the thumbs to glide the clavicle. Posterior glides are used to increase clavicular retraction, and superior glides increase clavicular retraction and clavicular depression.

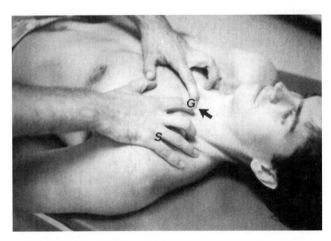

EXERCISE 26-60

Inferior clavicular glides. Inferior clavicular glides at the sternoclavicular joint use the index fingers to mobilize the clavicle, which increases clavicular elevation.

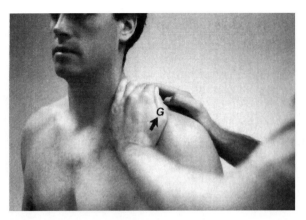

EXERCISE 26-61

Posterior clavicular glides. Posterior clavicular glides done at the acromioclavicular (AC) joint apply posterior pressure on the clavicle while stabilizing the scapula with the opposite hand. They increase mobility of the AC joint.

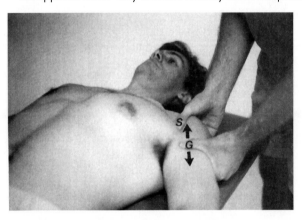

EXERCISE 26-62

Anterior/posterior glenohumeral glides. Anterior/posterior glenohumeral glides are done with one hand stabilizing the scapula and the other gliding the humeral head. They initiate motion in the painful shoulder.

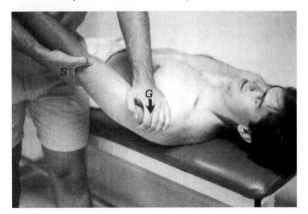

EXERCISE 26-63

Posterior humeral glides. Posterior humeral glides use one hand to stabilize the humerus at the elbow and the other to glide the humeral head. They increase flexion and medial rotation.

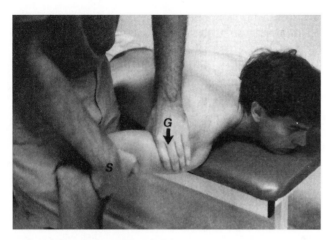

E X E R C I S E   2 6 - 6 4

Anterior humeral glides. In anterior humeral glides the patient is prone. One hand stabilizes the humerus at the elbow, and the other glides the humeral head. They increase extension and lateral rotation.

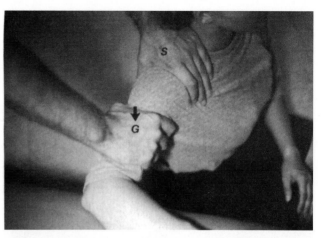

E X E R C I S E   2 6 - 6 6

Inferior humeral glides. For inferior humeral glides the patient is in the sitting position with the elbow resting on the treatment table. One hand stabilizes the scapula, and the other glides the humeral head inferiorly. These glides increase shoulder abduction.

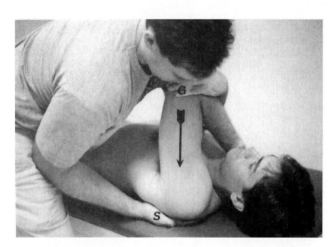

E X E R C I S E   2 6 - 6 5

Posterior humeral glides. Posterior humeral glides may also be done with the shoulder at 90 degrees. With the patient in supine position, one hand stabilizes the scapula underneath while the patient's elbow is secured at the therapist's shoulder. Glides are directed downward through the humerus. They increase horizontal adduction.

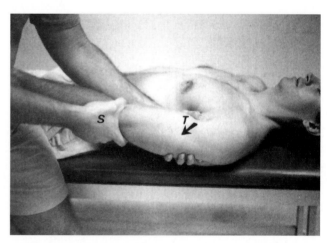

E X E R C I S E   2 6 - 6 7

Lateral glenohumeral joint traction. Lateral glenohumeral joint traction is used for initial testing of joint mobility and for decreasing pain. One hand stabilizes the elbow while the other applies lateral traction at the upper humerus.

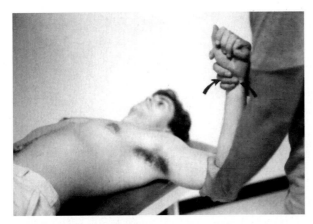

EXERCISE 26 - 68

Medial and lateral rotation oscillations. Medial and lateral rotation oscillations with the shoulder abducted at 90 degrees can increase medial and lateral rotation in a progressive manner according to patient tolerance.

Exercises to Reestablish Neuromuscular Control

EXERCISE 26 - 69

General scapular glides. General scapular glides may be done in all directions, applying pressure at the medial, inferior, lateral, or superior border of the scapula. Scapular glides increase general scapulothoracic mobility.

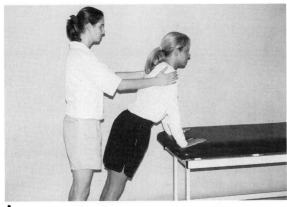

A

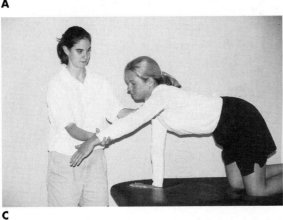

B

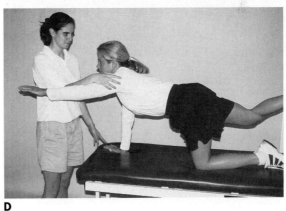

C

D

EXERCISE 26 - 70

Weight shifting on stable surface. May be done **A,** standing with hands supporting weight on table; **B,** kneeling in four-point position; **C,** kneeling in three-point position; or **D,** kneeling in two-point position. The therapist can apply random directional pressure, to which the patient must respond to maintain a static position. In the two- and three-point positions, the arm that is supported in a closed-kinetic chain is using shoulder force couples to maintain neuromuscular control.

E X E R C I S E   2 6 - 7 1

Weight shifting on a ball. In a push-up position with weight supported on a ball, the patient shifts weight from side to side and/or forward and backward. Weight shifting on an unstable surface facilitates co-contraction of the muscles involved in the force couples that collectively maintain dynamic stability.

E X E R C I S E   2 6 - 7 2

Weight shifting on a Fitter. In a kneeling position, the patient shifts weight from side to side using a Fitter. Weight shifting on an unstable surface facilitates co-contraction of the muscles involved in the force couples that collectively maintain dynamic stability.

E X E R C I S E   2 6 - 7 3

Weight shifting on a KAT system. In a kneeling position, the patient shifts weight from side to side and/or backward and forward using a KAT. Weight shifting on an unstable surface facilitates co-contraction of the muscles involved in the force couples that collectively maintain dynamic stability.

E X E R C I S E   2 6 - 7 4

Weight shifting on a BAPS board. In a kneeling position, the patient shifts weight from side to side and/or backward and forward using a BAPS board. Weight shifting on an unstable surface facilitates co-contraction of the muscles involved in the force couples that collectively maintain dynamic stability.

E X E R C I S E   2 6 - 7 5

Weight shifting on a Swiss ball. With the feet supported on a chair, the patient shifts weight from side to side and/or backward and forward using a Swiss ball. Weight shifting on an unstable surface facilitates co-contraction of the muscles involved in the force couples that collectively maintain dynamic stability.

A

B

C

E X E R C I S E   2 6 - 7 6

Slide board exercises. **A,** Forward and backward motion. **B,** Wax-on/wax-off motion. **C,** Hands lateral motion. Patient shifts weight from side to side and/or backward and forward using a BAPS board. Weight shifting on an unstable surface facilitates co-contraction of the muscles involved in the force couples that collectively maintain dynamic stability.

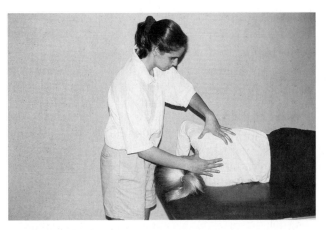

E X E R C I S E   2 6 - 7 7

Scapular neuromuscular control exercises. The patient's hand is placed on the table creating a closed-kinetic chain, and the therapist applies pressure to the scapula in a random direction. The patient moves the scapula isotonically into the direction of resistance.

E X E R C I S E   2 6 - 7 8

Swiss ball exercises. The patient lies in a prone position on the Swiss ball and resists pressures applied by the sports therapist to maintain a stable positon.

E X E R C I S E   2 6 - 7 9

Body Blade exercises. The patient is in a three-point kneeling position holding an oscillating Body Blade in one hand while working on neuromuscular control on the weight-bearing shoulder.

SUMMARY

- The high degree of mobility in the shoulder complex requires some compromise in stability, which in turn increases the vulnerability of the shoulder joint to injury, particularly in dynamic overhead activities.

- In rehabilitation of the sternoclavicular joint, effort should be directed toward regaining normal clavicular motion that will allow the scapula to abduct and upward rotate throughout 180 degrees of humeral abduction. The clavicle must elevate approximately 40 degrees to allow upward scapular rotation.

- Acromioclavicular joint sprains most commonly occur due to a direct fall on the point of the shoulder with the arm at the side in an adducted position or falling on an outstretched arm.

- Management of acromioclavicular injuries is dependent on the type of injury sustained by the patient. Types I and II injuries are usually handled conservatively, focusing on strengthening of the deltoid, trapezius, and the clavicular fibers of pectoralis major. Occasionally, AC injuries may require surgical excision of the distal portion of the clavicle.

- Treatment for clavicle fractures includes approximation of the fracture and immobilization for 6 to 8 weeks, using a figure-8 wrap with the involved arm in a sling. Because mobility of the clavicle is important for normal shoulder mechanics, rehabilitation should focus on joint mobilization and strengthening of the deltoid, upper trapezius, and pectoralis major muscles.

- Following a short immobilization period, the rehabilitation for a dislocated shoulder should focus on restoring the appropriate axis of rotation for the glenohumeral joint, optimizing the stabilizing muscles' length–tension relationship, and restoring proper neuromuscular control of the shoulder complex. Similar rehabilitation strategies are applied in cases of multidirectional instabilities that may occur as a result of recurrent dislocation.

- Management of shoulder impingement involves gradually restoring normal biomechanics to the shoulder joint in an effort to maintain space under the coracoacromial arch during overhead activities. Techniques include strengthening of the rotator cuff muscles; strengthening of those muscles that abduct, elevate, and upward rotate the scapula; and stretching both the inferior and posterior portions of the joint capsule.

- The basic concerns of a rehabilitation program for rotator cuff tendonopathy are based on why and how the tendon has been damaged. If a comprehensive rehabilitation program does not relieve the painful shoulder, surgical repair of the tendon and alteration of the glenohumeral joint are performed. Surgical rehabilitation is similar to the nonsurgical plan with the time of progression altered, based on tissue healing and tendon histology.

- In cases of adhesive capsulitis, the goals of rehabilitation are relieving the pain in the acute stages of the disorder, gradually restoring proper arthrokinematic, gradual restoration of range of motion, and strengthening the muscles of the shoulder complex.

- Rehabilitation for thoracic outlet syndrome should be directed toward encouraging the least provocative posture combined with exercises to strengthen postural muscles (rhomboids, middle trapezius, upper trapezius) and stretching exercises for the scalenes to increase the space in the thoracic outlet, thus reducing muscle impingment on the neurovascular bundle.

- Management of brachial plexus injuries includes the gradual restoration of cervical range of motion and stretching for the upper trapezius, levator scapulae, and scalene muscles.

- After identifing the cause of myofascial trigger points, rehabilitation may include a spray and stretch method with passive stretching, gentle active range-of-motion exercises, or active assistive exercises, encouraging normal muscle activity and endurance and gradual improvement of muscle endurance.

REFERENCES

1. Allman FL. Fractures and ligamentous injuries of the clavicle and its articulations. *J Bone Joint Surg Am* 49:774, 1967.

2. Anderson L, Rush R, Shearer L. The effects of a theraband exercise program on shoulder internal rotation strength. *Phys Ther* 72(suppl):540, 1992.

3. Andrews JR, Wilk KE, eds. *The Athlete's Shoulder.* New York, Churchill Livingstone, 1994.

4. Bateman JE. *The Shoulder and Neck.* Philadelphia, Saunders, 1971.

5. Bergfeld JA, Andrish JT, Clancy WG. Evaluation of the acromioclavicular joint following first and second degree sprains. *Am J Sports Med* 6:153, 1978.

6. Bigliani L, Kimmel J, McCann P. Repair of rotator cuff tears in tennis players. *Am J Sports Med* 20:112–117, 1992.

7. Bigliani L, Morrison D, April E. The morphology of the acromion and its relation to rotator cuff tears, *Orthop Trans* 10:216, 1986.

8. Blackburn T, McCloud W, White B. EMG analysis of posterior rotator cuff exercises. *Athl Train* 26:40–45, 1990.

9. Brewster C, Moynes D. Rehabilitation of the shoulder following rotator cuff injury or surgery. *J Orthop Sports Phys Ther* 18:422–426, 1993.

10. Burkhead W, Rockwood C. Treatment of instability of rotator cuff injuries in the overhead athlete. *J Bone Joint Surg Am* 74:890, 1992.

11. Clancy WG, Brand RI, Bergfeld JA. Upper trunk brachial plexus injuries in contact sports. *Am J Sports Med* 5:209, 1977.

12. Codman EA. Ruptures of the supraspinatus tendon and other lesions in or about the subacromial bursa. In: Codman EA, ed. *The Shoulder.* Boston, Thomas Todd, 1934.

13. Cox JS. The fate of the acromioclavicular joint in athletic injuries. *Am J Sports Med* 9:50, 1981.

14. Culham E, Malcolm P. Functional anatomy of the shoulder complex. *J Orthop Sports Phys Ther* 18:342–350, 1993.

15. Davies G, Dickoff-Hoffman S. Neuromuscular testing and rehabilitation of the shoulder complex. *J Orthop Sports Phys Ther* 18:449–458, 1993.

16. Depalma AF. *Surgery of the Shoulder,* 2nd ed. Philadelphia, Lippincott, 1973.

17. Duncan A. Personal communication, August 1997.

18. Dvir Z, Berme N. The shoulder complex in elevation of the arm: A mechanism approach. *J Biomechanics* 11:219–226, 1978.

19. Greenfield B. Special considerations in shoulder exercises: Plane of the scapula. In: Andrews J, Wilk K, eds. *The Athlete's Shoulder.* New York, Churchill Livingstone, 1993.

20. Gryzlo SM. Bony disorders: Clinical assessment and treatment. In: Jobe FW, ed. *Operative Techniques in Upper Extremity Sports Injuries.* St. Louis, Mosby, 1996.

21. Hageman P, Mason D, Rydlund K. Effects of position and speed on concentric isokinetic testing of the shoulder rotators. *J Orthop Sports Phys Ther* 11:64–69, 1989.

22. Hart DL, Carmichael SW. *Biomechanics of the Shoulder. J Orthop Sports Phys Ther* 6:229–234, 1985.

23. Hawkins R, Bell R. Dynamic EMG analysis of the shoulder muscles during rotational and scapular strengthening exercises. In: Post M, Morey B, Hawkins R, eds. *Surgery of the Shoulder.* St. Louis, Mosby, 1990.

24. Hawkins R, Kennedy J. Impingement syndrome in athletes. *Am J. Sports Med* 8:151, 1980.

25. Howell S, Kraft T. The role of the supraspinatus and infraspinatus muscles in glenohumeral kinematics of anterior shoulder instability. *Clin Orthop* 263:128–134, 1991.

26. Inman VT, Saunders JB, Abbott LC. Observations on the function of the shoulder joint. *J Bone Joint Surg* 26:1, 1944.

27. Jobe FW, ed. *Operative Techniques in Upper Extremity Sports Injuries.* St. Louis, Mosby, 1996.

28. Jobe F, Kvnite R. Shoulder pain in the overhand and throwing athlete: The relationship of anterior instability and rotator cuff impingement. *Orthop Rev* 18:963, 1989.

29. Jobe F, Moynes D. Delineation of diagonistic criteria and a rehabilitation program for rotator cuff injuries. *Am J. Sports Med* 10:336–339, 1982.

30. Jobe FW, Schwab, Wilk KE, Andrews JE. Rehabilitation of the shoulder. In: Brotzman SB, ed. *Clinical Orthopedics Rehabilitation.* St. Louis, Mosby, 1996.

31. Kannus P, Josza L, Renstrom P, et al. The effects of training, immobilization and remobilization on musculoskeletal tissue. 2. Remobilization and prevention of immobilization atrophy. *Scand J Med Sci Sports* 2:164–176, 1992.

32. Keirns M. Conservative management of shoulder impingement. In: Andrews J, Wilk K, eds. *The Athlete's Shoulder.* New York, Churchill Livingstone, 1993.

33. Kelley MJ. Anatomic and biomechanical rationale for rehabilitation of the athlete's shoulder. *J Sports Rehabil* 4:122–154, 1995.

34. Kibbler B. Role of the scapula in the overhead throwing motion. *Contemp Orthop* 22:526–532, 1991.

35. Leffert RD. Neurological problems. In: Rockwood CA, Masten FA, eds. *The Shoulder.* Philadelphia, Saunders, 1990.

36. Lephart SM, Warner JP, Borsa PA, Fu FH. Proprioception of the shoulder joint in healthy, unstable, and surgically repaired shoulders. *J Shoulder Elbow Surg* 3:371–380, 1994.

37. Lew W, Lewis J, Craig E. Stabilization by capsule ligaments and labrum: Stability at the extremes of motion. In: Masten F, Fu F, Hawkins R, eds. *The Shoulder: A Balance of Mobility and Stability.* Rosemont, IL, American Academy of Orthopedic Surgeons, 1993.

38. Litchfield R, Hawkins R, Dillman C. Rehabilitation for the overhead athlete. *J Orthop Sports Phys Ther* 18:433–441, 1993.

39. Magee D, Reid D. Shoulder injuries. In: Zachazewski J, Magee D, Quillen W, eds. *Athletic Injuries and Rehabilitation.* Philadelphia, Saunders, 1995.

40. Matsen FA, Thomas SC, Rockwood CA. Glenohumeral instability. In: Rockwood CA, Matsen FA, eds. *The Shoulder.* Philadelphia, Saunders, 1990.

41. McCarroll J. Golf. In: Pettrone FA, ed. *Athletic Injuries of the Shoulder.* New York, McGraw-Hill, 1995.

42. Meister K, Andrews JR. Classification and treatment of rotator cuff injuries in the overhead athlete. *J Orthop Sports Phys Ther* 18:413–421, 1993.

43. Moseley J, Jobe F, Pink M. EMG analysis of the scapular muscles during a shoulder rehabilitation program. *Am J Sports Med* 20:128–134, 1992.

44. Mulligan E. Conservative management of shoulder impingement syndrome. *Athl Train* 23:348–353, 1988.

45. Neer C. Anterior acromioplasty for the chronic impingement syndrome in the shoulder: A preliminary report. *J Bone Joint Surg Am* 54:41, 1972.

46. Nicholas JA, Hershmann EB, eds. *The Upper Extremity in Sports Medicine.* St. Louis, Mosby, 1990.

47. O'Brien S, Neeves M, Arnoczky A. The anatomy and histology of the inferior glenohumeral ligament complex of the shoulder. *Am J Sports Med* 18:451, 1990.

48. Omer GE. Osteotomy of the clavicle in surgical reduction of anterior sternoclavicular dislocations. *J Trauma* 7:584–590, 1967.

49. Ozaki J, Fujimoto S, Nakagawa Y. Tears of the rotator cuff of the shoulder associated with pathological changes in the acromion: A study of cadavers. *J Bone Joint Surg Am* 70:1224, 1988.

50. Paine R, Voight M. The role of the scapula. *J Orthop Sports Phys Ther* 18:386–391, 1993.

51. Peat M, Culham E. Functional anatomy of the shoulder complex. In: Andrews J, Wilk K, eds. *The Athlete's Shoulder*. New York, Churchill Livingstone, 1993.

52. Petersson C, Redlund-Johnell I. The subacromial space in normal shoulder radiographs. *Acta Orthop Scand* 55:57, 1984.

53. Pettrone FA, ed. *Athletic Injuries of the Shoulder*. New York, McGraw-Hill, 1995.

54. Rathburn J, McNab I. The microvascular pattern of the rotator cuff. *J Bone Joint Surg Br* 52:540, 1970.

55. Rockwood C, Masten F. The Shoulder, (vols. 1 & 2). Philadelphia, Saunders, 1990.

56. Rowe CR. Prognosis in dislocation of the shoulder. *J Bone Joint Surg Am* 38:957, 1956.

57. Salter EG, Shelley BS, Nasca R. A morphological study of the acromioclavicular joint in humans. *Anat Rec* 211:353, 1985. Abstract.

58. Skyhar M, Warren R, Althcheck D. Instability of the shoulder. In: Nicholas JA, Hershmann EB, eds. *The Upper Extremity in Sports Medicine*. St. Louis, Mosby, 1990.

59. Souza TA. *Sports Injuries of the Shoulder: Conservative Management*. New York, Churchill Livingstone, 1994.

60. Stevens JH. The classic brachial plexus paralysis. In: Codman EA, ed. *The Shoulder*. Boston, 1934, pp. 344–350. Privately published.

61. Sutter JS. Conservative treatment of shoulder instability. In: Andrews J, Wilk KE, eds. *The Athlete's Shoulder*. New York, Churchill Livingstone, 1994.

62. Taft TN, Wilson FC, Ogelsby JW. Dislocation of the AC joint, an end result study. *J Bone Joint Surg Am* 69:1045, 1987.

63. Thein L. Impingement syndrome and its conservative management. *J Orthop Sports Phys Ther* 11:183–191, 1989.

64. Townsend H, Jobe F, Pink M. EMG analysis of the glenohumeral muscles during a baseball rehabilitation program. *Am J Sports Med* 19:264–272, 1991.

65. Travell JG, Simons DG. *Myofascial Pain and Dysfunction. The Trigger Point Manual*. Baltimore, Williams & Wilkins, 1983.

66. Uthoff H, Loeher J, Sarkar K. The pathogenesis of rotator cuff tears. In: Takagishi N, ed. *The Shoulder*. Philadelphia, Professional Post Graduate Services, 1987.

67. Warner J, Michili L, Arslanin L. Patterns of flexibility, laxity, and strength in normal shoulders and shoulders with instability and impingement. *Am J Sports Med* 18:366–375, 1990.

68. Warren RF. Neurological injuries in football. In: Jordan BD, Tsiaris P, Warren RF, eds. *Sports Neurology*. Rockville, MD, Aspen, 1989.

69. Wilk K, Andrews J. Rehabilitation following subacromial decompression. *Orthopaedics* 16:349–358, 1993.

70. Wilk K, Arrigo C. Current concepts in the rehabilitation of the athletic shoulder. *J Orthop Sports Phys Ther* 18:365–378, 1993.

71. Wilk K, Arrigo C. Current concepts in rehabilitation of the shoulder. In: Andrews J, Wilk K, eds. *The Athlete's shoulder*. New York, Churchill Livingstone, 1993.

72. Wilk K, Arrigo C. An integrated approach to upper extremity exercises. *Orthop Phys Ther Clin North Am* 9:337–360, 1992.

73. Wilk K, Voight M, Kearns M. Stretch shortening drills for the upper extremity: Theory and application, *J Orthop Sports Phys Ther* 17:226–239, 1993.

CHAPTER 27

Rehabilitation of the Elbow

Pete Zulia and William E. Prentice

OBJECTIVES

After completing this chapter, the student therapist should be able to do the following:

- Discuss the functional anatomy and biomechanics associated with normal function of the elbow.
- Identify the various techniques for regaining range of motion including stretching exercises and joint mobilizations.
- Discuss exercises that may be used to reestablish neuromuscular control.
- Discuss criteria for progression of the rehabilitation program for different elbow injuries.
- Demonstrate the various rehabilitative strengthening techniques for the elbow, including open- and closed-kinetic chain isometric, isotonic, plyometric, isokinetic, and PNF exercises.

FUNCTIONAL ANATOMY AND BIOMECHANICS

Anatomically, the elbow joint is three joints in one. The humeroulnar joint, humeroradial joint, and the proximal radioulnar joint are the articulations that make up the elbow complex (Fig. 27-1). The elbow allows for flexion, extension, pronation, and supination movement patterns about the joint complex. The bony limitations, ligamentous support, and muscular stability will help to protect it from vulnerability of overuse and resultant injury.

The elbow complex is composed of three bones: the distal humerus, proximal ulna, and proximal radius. The articulations between these three bones dictate elbow movement patterns.[32] It is also important to mention that the appropriate strength and function of the upper quarter (cervical spine to the hand) needs to be addressed when evaluating the elbow specifically. The elbow complex has an intricate articulation mechanically between the three separate joints of the upper quarter to allow for function to occur.

In the elbow, the joint capsule plays an important role. The capsule is continuous (Fig. 27-2A) between the three articulations and highly innervated.[19,20] This is important not only for support of the complex but also for proprioception of the joint. The capsule of the elbow will function as a neurologic link between the shoulder and the hand. This has an affect on upper-quarter activity and an obvious aspect of the rehabilitation process if injury does occur.

Humeroulnar Joint

The humeroulnar joint is the articulation between the distal humerus medially and the proximal ulna. The humerus has distinct features distally. The medial aspect has the medial epicondyle and an hourglass-shaped trochlea, located anteromedial on the distal humerus.[1,15] The trochlea extends more distal than the lateral aspect of the humerus. The trochlea will articulate with the trochlear notch of the proximal ulna.

Because of the more distal projection of the humerus medially, the elbow complex will demonstrate a carrying angle that is an abducted position of the elbow in the anatomic position. The normal carrying angle (Fig. 27-3) in females is 10 to 15 degrees and in males 5 degrees.[3] When the elbow is in flexion, the ulna slides forward until the coronoid process of the ulna stops in the floor of the coronoid fossa of the humerus. In extension, the ulna will slide backwards until the olecranon process of the ulna makes contact with the olecranon fossa of the humerus posteriorly.

Humeroradial Joint

The humeroradial joint is the articulation of the laterally distal humerus and the proximal radius. The lateral aspect of the humerus has the lateral epicondyle and the capitellum, which is located anteriolateral on the distal humerus. With flexion, the radius is in contact with the radial fossa of the distal humerus, whereas in extension, the radius and the humerus are not in contact.

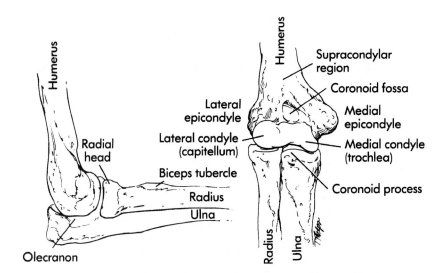

FIGURE 27-1

Bony anatomy of the elbow (anterior).

Proximal Radioulnar Joint

The proximal radioulnar joint is the articulation between the radial notch of the proximal lateral aspect of the ulna, the radial head, and the capitellum of the distal humerus. The proximal and distal radioulnar joints are important for supination and pronation. When evaluating this motion, it is important to look at them as one functionally. The proximal and distal aspects of this joint cannot function without the other. Proximally, the radius articulates with the ulna by the support of the annular ligament, which attaches to the ulnar notch anteriorly and posteriorly. The ligament circles the radial head for support. The interosseous membrane is the connective tissue that functions to complete the interval between the two bones. When there is a fall on the outstretched arm, the interosseous membrane can transmit some forces off the radius, the main weight-bearing bone to the ulna. This can help prevent the radial head from having forceful contact with the capitellum. Distally, the concave

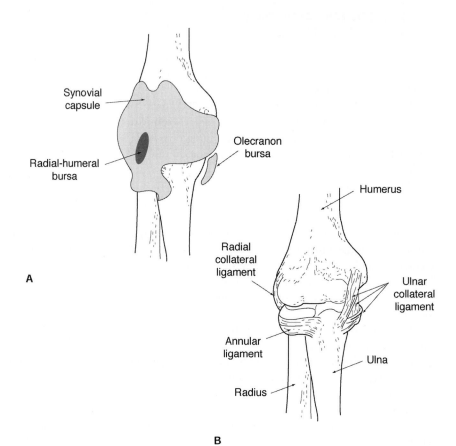

FIGURE 27-2

A, Joint capsule at the elbow joint.
B, Major supporting ligaments of the elbow.

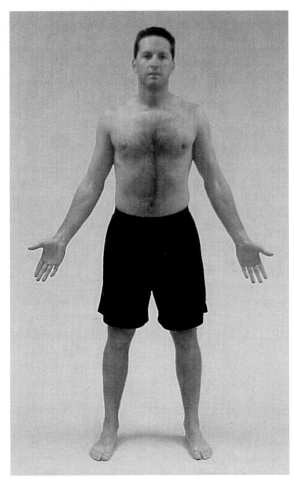

FIGURE 27-3

The elbow carrying angle is an abducted position of the elbow in the anatomic position. The normal carrying angle in females is 10 to 15 degrees and in males 5 degrees.

radius will articulate with the convex ulna. With supination and pronation, the radius will move on the ulna.

Ligamentous Support

The stability of the elbow first starts with the joint capsule that is continuous between all three articulations. The capsule is loose anteriorly and posteriorly to allow for movement in flexion and extension.[38] It is taut medially and laterally due to the added support of the collateral ligaments. The capsule is highly innervated for proprioception, as stated earlier.

The medial (ulnar) collateral ligament is fan shaped in nature and has three aspects (Fig. 27-2B). The anterior aspect of the MCL is the primary stabilizer in the MCL from approximately 20 degrees to 120 degrees of motion.[34] The posterior and the oblique aspect of the MCL add support and assist in stability to the MCL.

The lateral elbow complex consists of four structures. The radial collateral ligament attachments are from the lateral epi-condyle to the annular ligament. The lateral ulnar collateral ligament is the primary lateral stabilizer and passes over the annular ligament into the supinator tubercle. It reinforces the elbow laterally, as well as reenforcing the humeroradial joint.[24,34] The assessory lateral collateral ligament passes from the tubercle of the supinator into the annular ligament. The annular ligament, as previously stated, is the main support of the radial head in the radial notch of the ulna. The interosseous membrane is a syndesmotic condition that connects the ulna and the radius in the forearm. This structure prevents the proximal displacement of the radius on the ulna.

Dynamic Stabilizers of the Elbow Complex

The elbow flexors are the biceps brachii, brachialis, and bra-chioradialis muscles (Fig. 27-4). The biceps brachii originate via two heads proximally at the shoulder. The long head from the supraglenoid tuberosity of the scapula and the short head from the coracoid process of the scapula. The insertion is from a common tendon at the radial tuberosity and lacertus fibrosis to origins of the forearm flexors. The biceps brachii function is flexion of the elbow and supination the forearm.[35] The brachialis originates from the lower two-thirds of the anterior humerus to the cornoid process and tuberosity of the ulna. It functions to flex the elbow. The brachioradialis, which originates from the lower two-thirds of the lateral humerus and attaches to the lateral styloid process of the distal radius, functions as an elbow flexor and semipronator and semisupinator.

The elbow extensors are the triceps brachii and the an-coneus muscles. The triceps brachii has a long, medial and lateral head origination. The long head originates at the infra-glenoid tuberosity of the scapula, the lateral and medial heads to the posterior aspect of the humerus. The insertion is via the common tendon posteriorly at the olecranon. Through this insertion along with the anconeus muscle that assists the triceps, extension of the elbow complex is accomplished.

Elbow in the Upper Quarter

For functional activity to occur in the upper quarter, the elbow will play an important part in the process. Anatomic position places the elbow in full extension and full supination. The function of the elbow will be with flexion, extension, supination, and pronation movement patterns. The elbow allows for approximately 145 degrees of flexion and 90 degrees of both supination and pronation, although normals for range of motion are individual for the involved and for the noninvolved joint.[23] The capsule, as previously stated, is a proprioceptive link of the upper quarter to the hand. Functionally, the relationship between the hand and the shoulder needs the elbow for proper activity to occur. The connection between multijoint muscles that affect the elbow will work proximally and distally in the upper quarter as a whole.

The hand and wrist muscles add to the support of the capsule for stability. Function of the cervical spine and shoulder

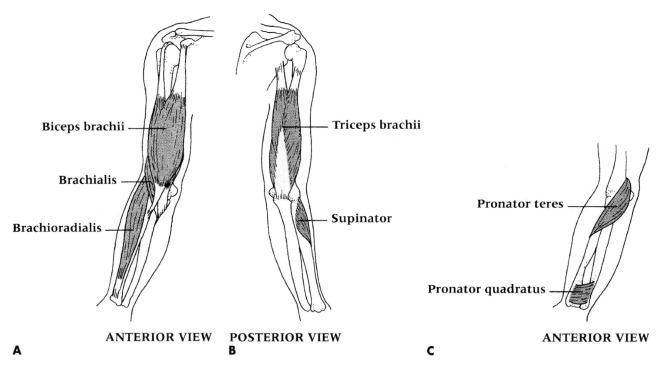

FIGURE 27-4

Dynamic stabilizers of the elbow.

can also affect the elbow. Limitations in motion in either area can have an accommodative effect to the elbow complex. For example, a patient has a decrease in supination due to injury; an accommodation of the injury is an increase in adduction and external rotation at the shoulder and an increased valgus stress to the elbow to allow function to continue. This is why proper knowledge of biomechanics in the elbow complex and associated joints is appropriate for proper assessment of injury and rehabilitation.

REHABILITATION TECHNIQUES FOR SPECIFIC INJURIES

Fractures of the Elbow

PATHOMECHANICS

Fractures to the elbow proper will be specific to one or more bones in the elbow, with effects to the joint as a whole. The fractures seen in the humeral shaft and distal humerus, radial head, and proximal ulna will affect the function of the entire elbow complex as well as the individual bones themselves. There may be associated dislocations that may accompany a fracture in the elbow, which is dependent upon the specific mechanism of injury. With elbow fractures, properly evaluating the neurovascular system is critical. The ulnar, radial, median, and musculocutaneous nerves pass the elbow in various positions

anatomically. The brachial artery has various branches that will provide the blood supply from the proximal elbow to the digits. The radial, ulnar, and the common interosseous arteries (and the collateral and recurrent arteries) specifically provide the circulation off the brachial artery to the structures at and distal to the elbow.

MECHANISM OF INJURY

The fracture of an elbow bone can have various injury mechanisms. The shaft of the humerus can fracture as a result of a direct force, as well as from a rotational component with the hand in a fixed position. There is also evidence that a direct blow can fracture the bones of the elbow.[28] A rotational or twisting mechanism can also occur when pushing off on a fixed hand,[27] and can cause the onset of immediate pain and loss of function. The increased load on the joint structures from a direct blow can increase the possibility of supracondylar fractures. Olecranon process fractures will occur with a fall directly on the tip of the elbow. A forearm fracture will often occur in the shafts of both the radius and ulna. A fracture of one of the forearm bones can result in a dislocation of the other bone.[8,30] Radial head fractures make up one third of all elbow fractures and one fourth of all elbow trauma. They are more common in females compared to males by a 2:1 ratio.[30] The mechanism of injury is when an axial load is placed on a pronated arm. This can occur in skating falls and biking accidents, when the posterolateral aspect of the radius is in contact with the capitellum. This type of stress makes the medial collateral ligament susceptible to injury. A valgus stress can also injure the epiphyseal plate of an adolescent patient, with an avulsion fracture as a possible result.

REHABILITATION CONCERNS

Undisplaced or minimally displaced fractures in adults and children are treated conservatively and require little or no immobilization. Cases managed using open reduction and internal fixation (ORIF) surgical procedures require only slightly longer periods of immobilization. The joint may be aspirated if the swelling is extremely painful. With the elbow flexed 90 degrees, a posterior plaster splint and sling are applied. Early motion is encouraged and the splint is removed in 1 to 2 weeks while a sling is continued for another 1 to 2 weeks as tolerated.

Displaced or comminuted radial head fractures in adults are usually treated by early (24 to 48 hours) surgery, to minimize the liklihood of permanent restriction of joint motion, traumatic arthritis, soft-tissue calcification in the anterior elbow region, and myositis ossificans.

Fractures in children with less than 15 to 30 degrees of angulation are treated as undisplaced fractures. Displaced fractures, or fractures angulated greater than 15 to 30 degrees, are treated by closed or open reduction.

Fractures of the olecranon may be either displaced or undisplaced. The extensor mechanism is intact in undisplaced fractures, and further displacement is unlikely. The undisplaced fracture is treated with a posterior plaster splint for 2 weeks, followed by a sling and progressive range-of-motion exercises. Displaced fractures usually require open reduction and internal flexation to restore the bony alignment and repair the triceps insertion.

Regardless of the method of treatment, some loss of extension at the elbow is very likely; however, little functional impairment usually results.

REHABILITATION PROGRESSION

Immediately following the injury or with ORIF surgical procedures, the goal is to minimize pain and swelling by using cold, compression, and electrical stimulation. Active and passive ROM exercises (see Exercises 27-21 to 27-31) should begin immediately after injury. The goal should be to achieve 15 to 105 degrees of motion by the end of week 2. Within the first week, isometric elbow flexion and extension exercises (see Exercise 27-2), and gentle isometric pronation/supination exercises (see Exercise 27-3), should begin. Isotonic shoulder and wrist exercises should also be used and should continue to progress throughout the rehabilitation program. Joint mobilizations should begin during the second week in an attempt to minimize loss of extension (see Exercises 27-33 to 27-36). Progressive light weight (1 to 2 lb) isotonic elbow flexion exercises (see Exercise 27-4) and elbow extension exercises (see Exercise 27-5) can be incorporated during the third week and should continue for as long as 12 weeks. Active-assisted passive pronation/supination exercises (see Exercise 27-6) should begin at week 6, progressing as tolerated.

Beginning at week 7, eccentric elbow flexion and extension exercises (see Exercises 27-7 and 27-8) along with plyometric exercises can be used. Exercises designed to establish neuromuscular control, including closed-kinetic chain activities, should also be used to help regain dynamic stability about the elbow joint (see Exercises 27-9 to 27-11 and 27-37 to 27-40). Functional training activities will also begin about this time and should progressively incorporate the stresses, strains, and forces that occur during normal activities. Each of these exercises should continue in a progressive manner throughout the rehabilitative period. Rehabilitation will require about 12 weeks.

Osteochondritis Dissecans and Panner's Disease

PATHOMECHANICS

Osteochondritis dissecans and Panner's disease are injuries that affect the lateral aspect of the elbow. In osteochondritis dissecans, a condition that affects the central and/or lateral aspect of the capitellum or radial head, an underlying osteochondral bone fragment becomes detached from the articular surface, forming a loose body in the joint. It may also be found in the knee and ankle joints. Osteochondritis dissecans is considered to be different from osteochondrosis but may represent different stages of the same disease.[29,30] With osteochondritis there is no inflammation. It is the most common cause of loose bodies in adolescents between the ages of 12 and 15.[7,22] The primary cause is thought to be trauma due to a repetitive compressive force between the radial head and the capitellum at the radiocapitular joint with valgus forces that load the joint during throwing.[6]

Some confusion exists as to whether there is any difference between osteochondritis dissecans and Panner's disease. Although Panner's disease may just be a part of the spectrum of osteochondritis dissecans, it is probably better to limit the diagnosis of Panner's disease to children age 10 or younger at the time of onset.[31] Panner's disease is an osteochondrosis of the capitellum in which there is a localized avascular necrosis leading to loss of the subchondral bone of the capitellum that can cause softening and fissuring of articular surfaces of the radiocapitellar joint. If loose bodies develop, Panners disease will produce osteochondritis dissecans.[4]

MECHANISM OF INJURY

Osteochondritis dissecans occurs due to compressive forces at the lateral aspect of the elbow. Panner's disease is an idiopathic condition, which encompasses the entire capitellum.[15,18]

REHABILITATION CONCERNS

Impaired motion and pain to the lateral aspect of the elbow are among the most common complaints. The caution is to avoid excessive and repetitive compression of the joint surfaces, which can lead to degenerative changes and the formation of loose bodies within the joint.[12,18]

Treatment of osteochondritis dissecans is variable. In some cases lesions in the skeletally immature elbow will heal if properly managed. Treatment includes totally avoiding any throwing or impact-loading activities as seen in gymnastics. Pain, tenderness, contracture, and radiographic changes provide objective parameters to determine the activity of the disease. If there is formation of loose bodies or if healing has been incomplete (as is usually the case) and symptoms persist, surgical intervention is necessary. Arthroscopic joint debridement and loose body removal has been advocated.

REHABILITATION PROGRESSION

The functional progression after the injury has been diagnosed should be first and foremost pain free. The injury is articular in nature and a cautious rehabilitation program should be followed. Range-of-motion exercises should be full and pain free (see Exercises 27-21 to 27-29). Strengthening exercises (see Exercises 27-4 to 27-6) will progress at the pain-free level and with restriction from increased pressure between the radius and the capitellum. The patient may have to decrease or modify the activity level to avoid the compressive nature in the joint. A slow, progressive program that gradually increases the load on the injured structure is essential.

Following arthroscopic debridement and removal of loose bodies, the goal is to minimize pain and swelling by using cold, electrical stimulation, and compression using a bulky dressing initially followed by an elastic wrap. Active and passive ROM exercises (see Exercises 27-21 to 27-31) should begin immediately after surgery as tolerated. The goal should be to achieve full ROM within 7 to 14 days after surgery, although the patient must continue to work on ROM throughout the rehabilitation period. Within the first 2 days, isometric elbow flexion and extension exercises (see Exercise 27-2) and isometric pronation/supination exercises (see Exercise 27-3) should begin. Isometric shoulder and wrist exercises (see Exercise 27-1) should also be used and should continue to progress throughout the rehabilitation program.

Progressive light-weight (1 to 2 lb) isotonic elbow flexion exercises (see Exercise 27-4), elbow extension exercises (see Exercise 27-5), and pronation/supination exercises can be incorporated between days 3 and 7. Isotonic shoulder and wrist exercises should begin during this period and continue to progress throughout the rehabilitation program.

At 3 weeks, eccentric elbow flexion and extension exercises (see Exercises 27-7 and 27-8) can be used. Joint mobilizations should begin in an attempt to normalize joint arthrokinematics (see Exercises 27-33 to 27-36).

Beginning at week 5, in addition to continuing strengthening and ROM exercises, activities that progressively incorporate the stresses, strains, and forces that prepare the patient for gradual return to functional activities should begin. Exercises designed to establish neuromuscular control, including closed-kinetic chain activities, should also be used to help regain dynamic stability about the elbow joint (see Exercises 27-9 to 27-11 and 27-37 to 27-40).

In the athletic population, realistically the prognosis for full return to throwing or to loading activities, such as in gymnastics and wrestling, especially at a competitive level, should be cautious. The therapist should educate parents, coaches, and children about this problem so that early recognition and subsequent intervention and referral to medical personnel can reduce the likelihood of surgical intervention. Following an arthoscopic procedure, the patient may be able to return to full throwing activities in 7 to 8 weeks.

Ulnar Collateral Ligament Injuries

PATHOMECHANICS

The medial complex of the elbow is susceptible to various injuries.[5] The repetitive stresses that are placed on the medial elbow increase the possibilities of injury. The ulnar collateral ligament, the medial aspect of the joint capsule, and the ulnar nerve may individually or collectively be stressed when valgus forces are applied to the elbow. The ulnar collateral ligament is composed of three bands: the anterior oblique ligament, which remains tight throughout full ROM; the posterior oblique ligament, which is tight during flexion and loose during extension; and the transverse oblique ligament, which remains tight throughout the range but provides little medial stability.[37] The anterior band of the ulnar collateral ligament has been demonstrated to be the primary structure resisting valgus stress at the elbow, and is tight from 20 to 120 degrees of flexion. The osseous articulation of the elbow contributes little to medial stability with the arm in this position.[14]

The ulnar collateral ligament provides the primary resistance to valgus stresses.[21] On examination the patient typically complains of pain along the medial aspect of the elbow. There is tenderness over the medial collateral ligament, usually at the distal insertion and occasionally in a more diffuse distribution. In some cases the patient may describe associated paresthesias in the distribution of the ulnar nerve with a positive Tinel's sign. When valgus stress is applied to the elbow at 20 to 30 degrees of flexion, local pain, tenderness, and end-point laxity are assessed. On standard X-ray hypertrophy of the humeral condyle and posteromedial aspect of the olecranon, marginal osteophytes of the ulnohumeral or radiocapitellar joints, calcification within the medial collateral ligament, and/or loose bodies in the posterior compartment may be present.[11]

The adolescent elbow will have an increased injury potential due to ligament laxity, which may produce stress on the epiphyseal growth plate and an avulsion fracture of the medial epicondyle from the pull of the medial collateral ligament. This may occur in patients at or around the age of 13.[16]

MECHANISM OF INJURY

The ulnar collateral ligament is most often injured as a result of a valgus force from the repetitive trauma of overhead throwing. In the general population, acute injury to the ulnar collateral ligament rarely results in recurrent instability of the elbow. Stress of the medial complex can also result in ulnar nerve inflammation or impairment, or wrist flexor tendinitis.

Repetitive stresses applied to the medial elbow joint frequently result in ligament failure, tendinitis, or osseous changes. Injuries can vary in degree from an overuse flexor/pronator muscular strain to ligamentous sprains of the ulnar collateral ligament. These injuries can result in elbow flexion contractures or potentially increase the instability of the elbow in adolescents.

REHABILITATION CONCERNS

Conservative treatment of patients with chronic ulnar collateral ligament injury should begin with rest and nonsteroidal anti-inflammatory medication. With resolution of symptoms, rehabilitation should be instituted, with emphasis on strengthening. If periods of rest and rehabilitation fail to result in a resolution of symptoms, surgical intervention may be necessary.

Operative management consists of repair or reconstruction. In the case of an acute rupture, surgical repair can be considered; however, the indications are extremely limited. The avulsed ligament should be without evidence of calcification, and if there is any question as to the quality of the tissue, reconstruction should be performed.

Because the ulnar collateral ligament is the primary stabilizer to valgus stress at the elbow, reconstruction is vital to competitive throwing patients who wish to return to their previous levels of performance. An autograft, using either the palmaris longus or extensor hallucis, is used to reconstruct the ulnar collateral ligament. The graft then simulates function of the ulnar collateral ligament, particularly the anterior oblique portion, providing the primary restraint to valgus stress during throwing. During this surgical procedure, the ulnar nerve is transposed medially and is held in place with fascial slings. Immediate postoperative precautions must be observed, especially in relation to the soft tissue of the fascial slings that stabilize the ulnar nerve.

REHABILITATION PROGRESSION

Following a requisite period of rest and rehabilitation techniques designed to reduce inflammation, the rehabilitation progression for ulnar collateral ligament injuries should concentrate primarily on strengthening of the flexor muscles, particularly the flexor carpi ulnaris and flexor digitorum superficialis, which can help prevent medial injury by providing additional support of to medial elbow structures.[32] Strengthening exercises (see Exercises 27-1 to 27-8) should be done initially in the pain-free midrange of motion, with a gradual increase of forces at the end ranges of motion. Exercises to increase both static and dynamic flexibility of the elbow without producing valgus stress should be incorporated (see Exercises 27-9 to and 27-11). The use of support taping can also assist in the protection for return to activity (see Exercise 27-43).

Following a reconstruction of the ulnar collateral ligament, the initial goal is to decrease pain and swelling (using a compression dressing for 2 to 3 days) and to protect the healing reconstruction. The patient is placed in a 90 degree posterior

splint for 1 week, during which time submaximal isometrics for the wrist musculature (see Exercise 27-1) and the elbow flexors and extensors (see Exercises 27-2 and 27-3) are performed at multiple angles as long as all valgus stress is eliminated. Isometric shoulder exercises except for external rotation along with isometric biceps exercises should be used.

In the second week, the patient is placed into a ROM brace set at 30 to 100 degrees (see Exercise 27-41). Range of motion should be increased by 5 degrees extension and 10 degrees of flexion each week, with full range of motion at 6 to 7 weeks. In addition to the exercises used during the first week, wrist isometrics and elbow flexion and extension isometrics (see Exercises 27-2) should begin.

At 4 weeks, progressive light-weight (1 to 2 lb) isotonic elbow flexion exercises (see Exercise 27-4), elbow extension exercises (see Exercise 27-5) and pronation/supination exercises (see Exercise 27-6) can be incorporated. Isotonic shoulder exercises (avoiding external rotation for 6 weeks) should begin during this period and continue to progress throughout the rehabilitation program. Passive elbow flexion and extension ROM exercises (Exercises 27-28 and 27-29) may begin during this period.

At 6 weeks, isotonic strengthening exercises for the shoulder (now including external rotation), elbow, and wrist should continue to progress.

At 9 weeks, as strength continues to increase, more functional activities can be incorporated, including eccentric elbow flexion and extension exercises (see Exercises 27-7 and 27-8), PNF diagonal strengthening patterns (see Exercises 27-17 to 27-20), and plyometric exercises (see Exercise 27-12). Exercises designed to establish neuromuscular control, including closed-kinetic chain activities, should also be used to help regain dynamic stability about the elbow joint (see Exercises 27-9 to 27-11 and 27-38 to 27-40).

Beginning at week 11, in addition to continuing stregthening and ROM exercises, activities that progressivly incorporate the stresses, strains, and forces that prepare the patient for gradual return to normal activities should begin. Generally the throwing patient can return to competitive levels at about 22 to 26 weeks postsurgery.

Nerve Entrapments

PATHOMECHANICS AND INJURY MECHANISM

The ulnar, median, and radial nerves are susceptible to injury and entrapment in the elbow. The ulnar nerve, which passes through the medial epicondylar groove, can be injured with medial stress to the elbow as previously described. The median nerve, passing between the supracondylar process and the medial epicondyle, can become compressed. The radial nerve passes under the lateral head of the triceps and, if compressed, can cause weakness in the forearm extensors. Whenever nerve compression conditions at the elbow are considered, the therapist should also consider the possibility of compression lesions at other levels such as the cervical spine, brachial plexus, and wrist.

Ulnar Nerve Entrapment

Ulnar nerve compression may occur from a number of causes, including (1) direct trauma, (2) traction due to an increase of laxity in the medial complex that causes a compressive force to be placed on the nerve resulting in a tension neuropathy, (3) compression due to a thickened retinaculum or a hypertrophied flexor carpi ulnaris muscle, (4) recurrent subluxation or dislocation, and (5) osseous degenerative changes.[10] In throwing patients, ulnar nerve irritation is most likely to develop secondary to mechanical factors that occur during the late cocking and early acceleration phases of the throwing motion. In these patients, ulnar neuritis often occurs along with medial instability and medial epicondylitis.[10]

The term **cubital tunnel syndrome** is used to identify a specific anatomic site for entrapment of the ulnar nerve. The ulnar nerve can be compromised by any swelling that occurs within the canal or with inflammatory changes that result in thickening of the fascial sheath.

The patient generally complains of medial elbow pain associated with numbness and tingling in the ulnar nerve distribution. Paresthesias may be present that radiate from the medial epicondyle distally along the ulnar aspect of the forearm into the fourth and fifth fingers. These sensory symptoms usually precede the development of motor deficits. There is tenderness at the cubital tunnel, which may include the medial epicondyle. Tinel's sign is generally present at the cubital tunnel. Subluxation of the ulnar nerve may occur in as many as 16 percent of those patients with symptoms, particularly in those with a shallow medial epicondylar groove. Radiographs may show osteophytes on the humerus and olecranon, calcifications of the medial collateral ligament, and loose bodies.[10]

Median Nerve Entrapment

The median nerve can be compressed under the ligament of Struthers, within the pronator teres muscle and under the superficial head of the flexor digitorum superficialis. The compression can occur as a result of hypertrophy of the proximal forearm muscles, particularly the pronator teres muscle, which occurs with repetitive grip-related activity or pronation and extension of the forearm such as occurs in the racket sports and other grip/hold activities. The patient will usually describe aching pain and fatigue or weakness of the forearm muscles along with paresthesia in the distribution of the median nerve. Symptoms seem to worsen with repetitive pronation. There is usually tenderness of the proximal pronator teres with a positive Tinel's sign. The patient may also complain of increased pain while sleeping.

Radial Nerve Entrapment

Entrapment of the radial nerve, specifically the posterior interosseous nerve, occurs within the radial tunnel and has been referred to as either **radial tunnel syndrome,** in which there is pain with no motor weakness, or **posterior interosseous nerve**

compression, where there is motor weakness in the absence of pain.[10] The radial nerve innervates the brachioradialis as well as the extensor muscles of the proximal forearm. Radial nerve compression occurs in throwing mechanisms and overhead activities. The patient typically complains with lateral elbow pain that is sometimes confused with lateral epicondylitis. There is tenderness distal to the lateral epicondyle over the supinator muscle. The pain is described as an ache that spreads into the extensor muscles and occasionally radiates distally to the wrist. Nocturnal pain may be present.

REHABILITATION CONCERNS

If rehabilitation begins early after onset of symptoms, treatment should include rest, avoiding those activities that seem to exacerbate pain; the use of anti-inflammatory medications; protective padding; and occasionally the use of extension night splints. This should be followed by a rehabilitation program that concentrates on range-of-motion exercises. A concern that will arise and needs to be addressed with regard to nerve entrapments is that of decreased muscle function, which may lead to accommodative activity and possible muscle imbalance. If the patient remains symptomatic despite a conservative program, surgery is generally recommended. It should be noted that, although physical findings other than local tenderness may be minimal and electrodiagnostic tests are rarely positive, good to excellent results may be obtained by surgery. The surgical treatment options include decompression alone and subcutaneous, intramuscular, or submuscular transposition.

REHABILITATION PROGRESSION

Following a course of conservative care involving rest and anti-inflammatory medication, the rehabilitation program should concentrate on strengthening of the involved muscles to maintain a balance between agonist and antagonist muscles (see Exercises 27-1 to 27-8). In addition, maintaining range of motion through aggressive stretching exercises will help to free up entrapped nerves (see Exercises 27-21 to 27-31). Massage techniques that can be used in the affected area can prevent adhesions from developing, thus restricting injured nerves. Mobility of the nerve is critical in reducing nerve entrapment.

Following surgical decompression or transposition of an entrapped nerve, the initial goal is to decrease pain and swelling (using a compression dressing for 2 to 3 days). The patient is placed in a 90 degree posterior splint for 1 week, during which time gripping exercises (see Exercise 27-1), isometric shoulder exercises, and wrist ROM exercises are used. During weeks 2 and 3 the posterior splint ROM is limited to 30 to 90 degrees initially, progressing to 15 to 127 degrees. The splint may be removed for exercise. Isometric flexion and extension exercises (see Exercises 27-2 and 27-3) are begun, and shoulder isometrics continue.

At 3 weeks, the splint can be discontinued. Progressive isotonic elbow flexion exercises (see Exercise 27-4), elbow extension exercises (see Exercise 27-5), and pronation/supination exercises (see Exercise 27-6) can be incorporated. Isotonic shoulder exercises should begin during this period and continue to progress throughout the rehabilitation program. Passive elbow flexion and extension ROM exercises (see Exercises 27-28 and 27-29) continue during this period, with particular emphasis placed on regaining extension.

At 7 weeks, as strength continues to increase, more functional activities can be incorporated, including eccentric elbow flexion and extension exercises (see Exercises 27-7 and 27-8), PNF diagonal strengthening patterns (see Exercises 27-17 to 27-20), and plyometric exercises (see Exercise 27-12). Exercises designed to establish neuromuscular control, including closed-kinetic chain activities, should also be used to help regain dynamic stability about the elbow joint (see Exercises 27-9 to 27-11 and 27-37 to 27-40). The rehabilitative process will require approximately 12 weeks.

Elbow Dislocations

PATHOMECHANICS

Generally elbow dislocations are classified as either anterior or posterior dislocations. Anterior dislocations and radial head dislocations are not common, occuring in only 1 to 2 percent of cases. There are several different types of posterior dislocations, which are defined by the position of the olecranon relative to the humerus: (1) posterior, (2) posterolateral (most common), (3) posteromedial (least common), and (4) lateral. Dislocations can be complete or *perched*. As compared with complete dislocations, perched dislocations have less ligament tearing, and thus they have a more rapid recovery and rehabilitation period.[2,37] In a complete dislocation, there is rupture of the ulnar collateral ligament and a possibility that the anterior capsule will rupture, along with possible ruptures of the lateral collateral ligament, brachialis muscle, or wrist flexor/extensor tendons.[33] Fractures occur in 25 to 50 percent of patients with elbow dislocations, with a fracture of the radial head being most common.

A rupture of the anterior oblique band of ulnar collateral ligament sometimes requires repair in patients if the injury occurs in the dominant arm.

INJURY MECHANISM

Elbow dislocations most frequently occur as a result of elbow hyperextension from a fall on the outstretched or extended arm, although dislocation may occur in flexion. The radius and ulna are most likely to dislocate posterior or posterolateral to the humerus. The olecranon process is forced into the olecranon fossa with such impact that the trochlea is levered over the coronoid process. Flexion dislocation is often associated with radial head fractures.

If the dislocation is simple without associated fractures, reduction may result in a stable elbow if the forearm flexors, extensors, and annular ligament have maintained their continuity. In these cases, early motion is resumed and the ultimate prog-

nosis is good. The injury will present with rapid swelling, severe pain at the elbow, and a deformity with the olecronon in posterior position, giving the appearance of a shortened forearm.

Elbow dislocations that involve fractures of the bony stabilizing forces about the elbow, such as a radial head or capitellar fracture/dislocation, create a significant instability pattern that cannot completely be corrected on either the medial or lateral side of the elbow alone for maximum functional return. These injuries must be treated surgically.

REHABILITATION CONCERNS

Following reduction of an elbow dislocation, the degree of stability present will determine the course of rehabilitation. If the elbow is stable, best results are obtained with a brief period of immobilization followed by rehabilitation focused on restoring early range of motion within the limits of elbow stability. Prolonged immobilization after dislocation has been closely associated with flexion contractures and more increased pain, with no decrease in instability. An unstable dislocation requires surgical repair of the ulnar collateral ligament and thus a longer period of immobilization.

A recurrent elbow dislocation is uncommon, occurring after only 1 to 2 percent of simple dislocations. Recurrent instability is more likely if the initial dislocation involved a fracture or if the first incident took place during childhood.

An overly aggressive rehabilitation program is more likely to result in chronic instability, while being overly conservative can lead to a flexion contracture. Typically, flexion contracture is much more likely. It is not uncommon to have a flexion contracture of 30 degrees at 10 weeks. After 2 years, a 10-degree flexion contracture is often still present.[2] Unfortunately this flexion contracture does not improve with time. For the patient it is most desirable to regain full elbow extension. For physically active patients, it is more important to ensure that the joint structure and ligaments are given sufficient time to heal to decrease the risk of recurrent subluxation or dislocation. Loss of motion, joint stiffness, and heterotopic ossification are more likely complications following dislocation.

REHABILITATION PROGRESSION

The rehabilitation progression will be determined by whether the elbow is stable or unstable following reduction. If the elbow is stable, it should be immobilized in a posterior splint at 90 degrees flexion for 3 to 4 days. During this period, gripping exercises (see Exercise 27-1) and isometric shoulder exercises are used. All exercises that place valgus stress on the elbow should be avoided. Therapeutic modalities should also be used to modulate pain and control swelling. On day 4 or 5, gentle active ROM elbow exercises (see Exercises 27-4 to 27-6) and gentle isometric elbow flexion and extension exercises (see Exercises 27-2 and 27-3) can be done out of the splint. Passive stretching is absolutely avoided because of the tendency toward scarring of the traumatized soft tissue and the possibility of recurrent posterior dislocation. Shoulder and wrist isotonic exercises can be done in the splint Gentle joint mobilizations can be used to regain normal joint arthrokinematics (see Exercises 27-32 to 27-36).

At 10 days, the splint can be discontinued. Passive ROM exercises (see Exercises 27-28 to 27-31) can begin, progressing to stretching exercises (see Exercises 27-21 to 27-25). Progressive isotonic elbow flexion exercises (see Exercise 27-4), elbow extension exercises (see Exercise 27-5), and pronation/supination exercises (see Exercise 27-6) should continue and progress as tolerated. Isotonic shoulder exercises should continue to progress throughout the rehabilitation program. Eccentric elbow flexion and extension exercises (see Exercises 27-7 and 27-8), PNF diagonal strengthening patterns (see Exercises 27-17 to 27-20), and plyometric exercises (see Exercise 27-12) may be incorporated as tolerated. Exercises designed to establish neuromuscular control, including closed-kinetic chain activities, should also be used to help regain dynamic stability about the elbow joint (see Exercises 27-9 to 27-11 and 27-37 to 27-40). The patient should continue to wear the brace or use taping (see Exercise 27-43) to prevent elbow hyperextension and valgus stress during return to normal activities.

For an unstable elbow, the goal during the first 3 to 4 weeks is to protect the healing soft tissue while decreasing pain and swelling. During this period, the protective brace should be set initially at 10 degrees less than the active ROM extension limit. Starting at week 1, a ROM brace preset at 30 to 90 degrees is implemented. Each week, motion in this brace is increased by 5 degrees of extension and 10 degrees of flexion. The brace can be discontinued when full ROM is achieved. During the period, gripping exercises (see Exercise 27-1) and wrist ROM exercises are used. All exercises that place valgus stress on the elbow should be avoided. Shoulder isometric exercises, avoiding internal or external rotation, can be used.

At 4 weeks, progressive light-weight (1 to 2 lb) isotonic elbow flexion exercises (see Exercise 27-4), elbow extension exercises (see Exercise 27-5), and pronation/supination exercises (see Exercise 27-6) can be incorporated. Isotonic shoulder exercises (avoiding internal and external rotation for 6 weeks) should begin during this period and continue to progress throughout the rehabilitation program. Passive elbow flexion and extension ROM exercises (see Exercises 27-28 and 27-29) may begin during this period.

At 6 weeks, isotonic strengthening exercises for the shoulder external and internal rotation should begin and continue to progress.

At 9 weeks, as strength continues to increase, more functional activities can be incorporated, including eccentric elbow flexion and extension exercises (see Exercises 27-7 and 27-8), PNF diagonal strengthening patterns (see Exercises 27-17 to 27-20), and plyometric exercises (see Exercise 27-2). Exercises designed to establish neuromuscular control, including closed-

kinetic chain activities, should also be used to help regain dynamic stability about the elbow joint (see Exercises 27-9 to 27-11 and 27-37 to 27-40).

At 11 weeks, the patient can begin some sport activities as tolerated, while continuing to progress the strengthening program. The protective brace should be worn whenever the patient is engaging in any type of sport activity.

Medial and Lateral Epicondylitis

PATHOMECHANICS AND INJURY MECHANISM

The medial and the lateral epicondyles of the distal humerus are the tendon attachments of the wrist flexors and extensors.[27] The medial epicondyle serves as the attachment for the wrist flexors and the wrist extensors attach to the lateral epicondyle.

Medial Epicondylitis

Medial epicondylitis (*golfer's elbow, racquetball elbow, or swimmer's elbow* in adults, and *Little League elbow* in adolescents) generally occurs as a result of repetitive microtrauma to the pronator teres and the flexor carpi radialis muscles during pronation and flexion of the wrist. The patient usually complains of pain on the medial aspect of the elbow, which is exacerbated when throwing a baseball, serving or hitting a forehand shot in racquetball, pulling during a swimming backstroke, or hitting a golf ball in which case the trail arm is affected. There is tenderness at the medial epicondyle and pain is exacerbated with resisted pronation, resisted volar flexion of the wrist, or passive extention of the wrist with the elbow extended. Associated ulnar neuropathy at the elbow has been reported in 25 to 60 percent of patients with medial epicondylitis.[10]

Lateral Epicondylitis

Lateral epicondylitis (*tennis elbow*) occurs with repetitive microtrauma that results in either concentric or eccentric overload of the wrist extensors and supinators, most commonly, the extensor carpi radialis brevis.[27] There is pain along the lateral aspect of the elbow, particularly at the origin of the extensor carpi radialis brevis. Pain increases with passive flexion of the wrist with the elbow extended, as it does with resisted wrist dorsiflexion. Pain with resisted wrist extension and full elbow extension indicates involvement of the extensor carpi radialis longus. Lateral epicondylitis usually results from repeated forceful wrist hyperextension, as often occurs in hitting a backhand stroke in tennis. For beginning tennis players, the backhand stroke is somewhat unnatural, and to get enough power to hit the ball over the net there is a tendency to use forced wrist hyperextension. In more advanced players, lateral epicondylitis can develop in a number of ways, including hitting a topspin backhand stroke using a "flick" of the wrist instead of a long follow-through; hitting a serve with the wrist in pronation and "snapping" the wrist to impart spin; using a racquet that is strung with too much tension (55 to 60 lbs is recommended); using a grip size that is too small; and hitting a heavy wet ball.[30] It must be emphasized that any activity that involves repeated forceful wrist extension can result in lateral epicondylitis.

REHABILITATION CONCERNS

Medial and lateral epicondylitis—but particularly lateral epicondylitis—can be lingering, limiting, and frustrating painful pathologic conditions for both the patient and the therapist. Perhaps the first step in treating these conditions is altering faulty performance mechanics to minimize the repetitive stress created by these activities. The stressful components of high-level activities may also be alleviated by altering the frequency, intensity, or duration of play.[25]

Two rehabilitation approaches may be taken in treating medial and lateral epicondylitis. The first approach involves using all of the normal measures to reduce inflammation and pain. Treatment may include several weeks of rest or at least restricted activity during which painful movements, like gripping activities that aggravate the condition, are avoided; using therapeutic modalities such as cryotherapy, electrical stimulating currents, ultrasound phonophoresis with hydrocortisone, or iontophoresis using dexamethasone; and using nonsteroidal anti-inflammatory drugs. If pain persists, some physicians may recommend a steroid injection, because they feel that the patient may be incapable of progressing in the rehabilitation program. However, more than two or three steroid injections per year are inappropriate and probably harmful, because that may result in potential weakening of the surrounding normal tissues.

A second approach would be to realize that the patient has a chronic inflammation. For one reason or another, the inflammatory phase of the healing process has not accomplished what it is supposed to and thus the inflammatory process is in effect "stuck." The goal in this approach is to "jump-start" the inflammatory process, using techniques that are likely to increase the inflammatory response, with the idea that increasing inflammation might allow healing to progress as normal to the fibroblastic and remodeling phases. To increase the inflammatory response, transverse friction massage can be used. This technique involves firm pressure massage over the point of maximum tenderness at the epicondyle in a direction perpendicular to the muscle fibers. This massage will be painful for the patient, so it is recommended that a 5-minute ice treatment be used prior to the massage to minimize pain. Transverse friction massage should be done for 5 to 7 minutes every other day, using a maximum of 5 treatments. It is our experience that if the symptoms do not begin to resolve in a week to 10 days, it is likely that this approach is

not going to eliminate the problem. It must also be emphasized that during this treatment period, all measures previously described to reduce inflammation should be avoided. Remember that the idea is to increase the inflammatory response.

In those individuals who have persistent pain that does not resolve after 1 year of conservative treatment, surgery should be considered.

REHABILITATION PROGRESSION

Rehabilitation time frames will be somewhat different depending on which of the two approaches are used in the early treatment of medial and lateral epicondylitis. Regardless of which of the two techniques is used, some submaximal exercise can begin during this period as long as exercise does not cause pain. If rest and anti-inflammatory measures are used, a 2- to 3-week period of restricted activity with very limited or no submaximal exercise may be necessary to control pain and inflammation. If the more aggressive approach, which uses a transverse friction massage, is chosen, submaximal exercises can begin immediately within pain-free limits.

Exercise intensity should be based on patient tolerance but should adhere to an exercise progression. Throughout the rehabilitation process, pain should always be used as a guide for progression. Each of the following exercises should continue in a progressive manner throughout the rehabilitative period: gentle active and passive ROM exercises for both the elbow and wrist (see Exercises 27-21 to 27-31), gentle isometric elbow flexion and extension exercises (see Exercise 27-2), gentle isometric pronation/supination exercises (see Exercise 27-3), progressive isotonic elbow flexion exercises (see Exercise 27-4), elbow extension exercises (see Exercise 27-5), and pronation/supination exercises (see Exercise 27-6) beginning with light weight (1 to 2 lb); lateral counterforce bracing should be used as a supplement to muscular strengthening exercises (see Exercise 27-42), with the patient gradually weaning from use as appropriate. Eccentric elbow flexion and extension exercises should be used (see Exercises 27-7 and 27-8), along with plyometric exercises (see Exercise 27-12) and functional training activities that should progressively incorporate the stresses, strains, and forces that occur during normal activities, gradually increasing the frequency, intensity, and duration of exercise.

Perhaps the biggest mistake made with epicondylitis is trying to progress too quickly in the exercise program and rushing full return to activity. The therapist should counsel the patient about doing too much too soon, cautioning that rapid increases in activity levels often exacerbate the condition. The involved muscles must regain appropriate strength, flexibility, and endurance with reduced inflammation and pain. Functional activity needs to progress slowly to prepare the patient for the return without restrictions.

EXERCISES

REHABILITATION TECHNIQUES OF THE ELBOW COMPLEX

Isotonic Open-Kinetic Chain Strengthening Exercises

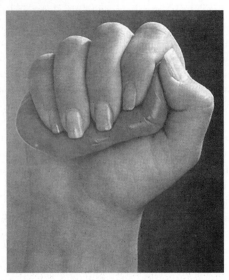

E X E R C I S E   2 7 - 1

Gripping exercise. Used to strengthen the wrist flexors as well as the intrinsic muscles of the hand.

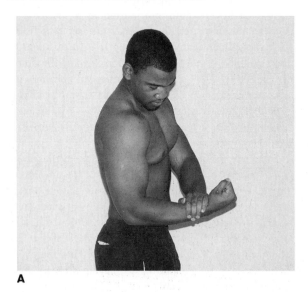
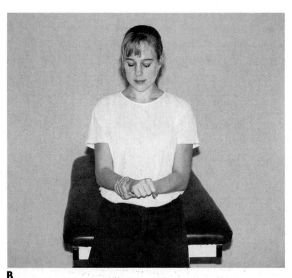

A   **B**

E X E R C I S E   2 7 - 2

A, Isometric elbow flexion; resist elbow flexion with the opposite hand. **B,** Isometric elbow extension; resist elbow extension with the opposite hand. The reeducation that the isometric contractions provide is a safe technique for the early stages of rehabilitation. Contractions can be performed in various angles prior to isotonic exercise.

 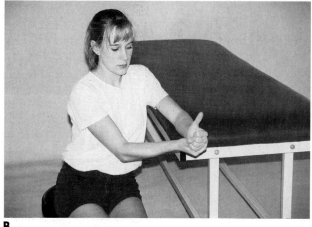

A **B**

EXERCISE 27-3

A, Isometric wrist supination; resist supination with the opposite hand. **B,** Isometric wrist pronation; resist pronation with the opposite hand. This exercise is performed with the same benefits for safe muscle reeducation in the early rehabilitation stages. Resistance can be performed in various angles prior to isotonic exercise.

A **B** **C**

EXERCISE 27-4

Isotonic elbow flexion. The biceps brachii, brachialis, and brachioradialis are used when moving the elbow from full extension into full flexion. **A,** Used in the standing position. **B,** In the seated position, with the proximal humerus resting on the opposite forearm. **C,** With the use of tension band.

 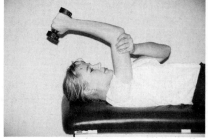 

A **B** **C**

EXERCISE 27-5

Isotonic elbow extension. The triceps brachii muscle moves the arm from full flexion to full extension. **A,** Standing position. **B,** Supine position. **C,** With the use of tension band (patient is standing on the band that is over the shoulder).

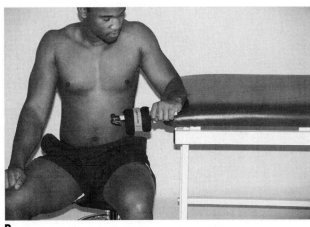

A   **B**

E X E R C I S E   2 7 - 6

Isotonic wrist supination/pronation. The forearm is in a stable position on the table and the elbow is in a 90-degree position. **A,** Supinate the forearm while holding onto a hammer. **B,** Pronate the forearm while holding a hammer.

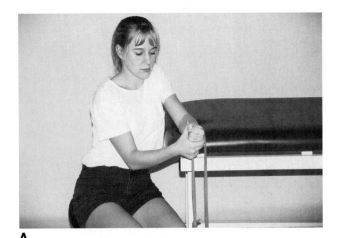

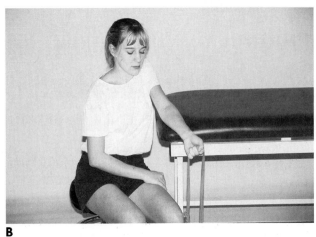

A   **B**

E X E R C I S E   2 7 - 7

Concentric/eccentric flexion with the use of tension band. For the benefits of maximum load on the muscle. **A,** Concentric: This is done slow at first, and then the speed is increased to mimic functional activity. **B,** Eccentric: This is done by pulling the muscle into a shortened position, and then allowing a lengthening contraction to take place by lowering the hand in control. Increased speed is introduced when proficiency is obtained.

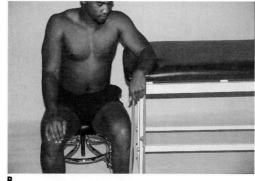

A   **B**

EXERCISE 27-8

Concentric/eccentric extension with the use of tension band. For the benefits of maximum load on the muscle. **A,** Concentric: This is done slow at first, and then the speed is increased to mimic functional activity. **B,** Eccentric: This is done by pulling the muscle into a shortened position, and then allowing a lengthening contraction to take place by lowering the hand in control. Increased speed is introduced when proficiency is obtained.

Closed-Chain Exercises

EXERCISE 27-9

Closed-chain static hold. The body weight is over the elbow in varying degrees for the purpose of bearing weight and initiating kinesthetic awareness in the elbow joint.

EXERCISE 27-10

Gymnastic ball exercise. Used for activities that require closed-chain activity. There is stimulation of the joint receptors.

A

B

EXERCISE 27-11

Push-ups. **A,** Standing. **B,** Prone.

Plyometric Exercises

A

B

C

D

E

E X E R C I S E   2 7 - 1 2

Plyometric exercise drills. Plyometric exercise working on a Plyoback has three phases: a quick eccentric load (stretch), a brief amortization phase; and a concentric contraction. **A,** Elbow extensors. **B,** Two-hand, overhead toss. **C,** Two-hand side throws. **D,** Side-to-side throws. **E,** One-arm overhead throw.

Isokinetic Exercises

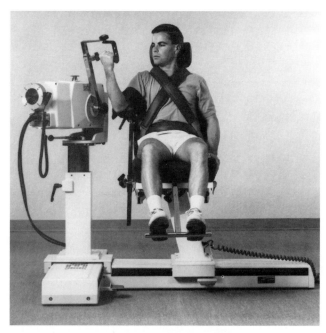

EXERCISE 27-13

Isokinetic elbow flexion (hand positioned in supination).

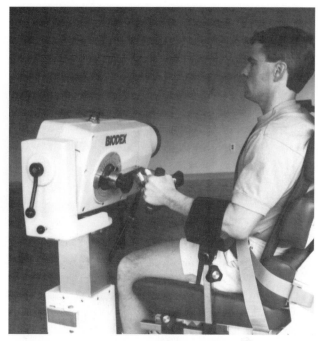

EXERCISE 27-15

Isokinetic wrist supination/pronation.

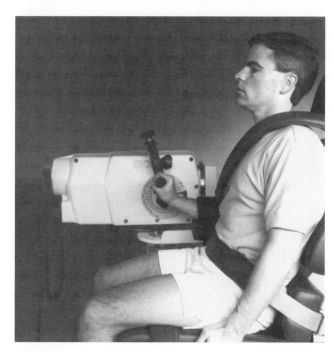

EXERCISE 27-14

Isokinetic wrist flexion/extension.

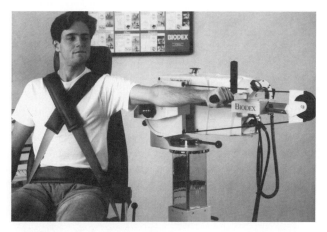

EXERCISE 27-16

Isokinetic elbow flexion/extension with scapular retraction/protraction.

PNF Strengthening Exercises

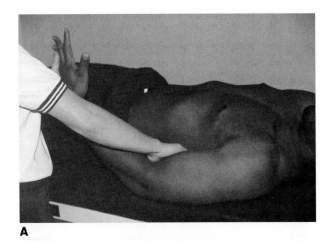

A

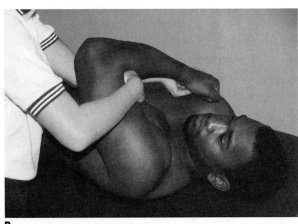

B

E X E R C I S E   2 7 - 1 7

    D1 pattern moving into flexion. **A,** Starting position. **B,** Terminal position.

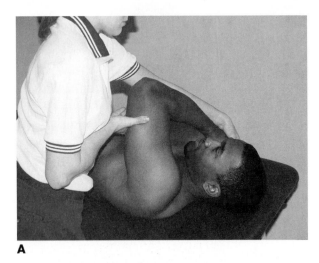

A

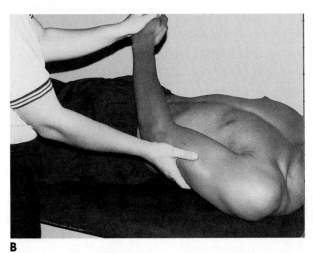

B

E X E R C I S E   2 7 - 1 8

    D1 pattern moving into extension. **A,** Starting position. **B,** Terminal position.

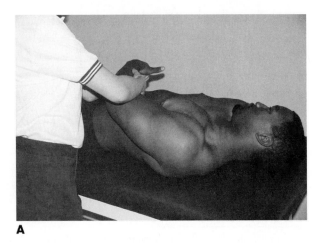

A

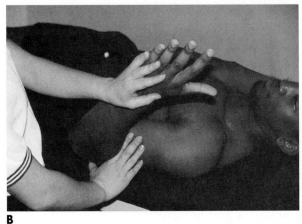

B

E X E R C I S E   2 7 - 1 9

    D2 pattern moving into flexion. **A,** Starting position. **B,** Terminal position.

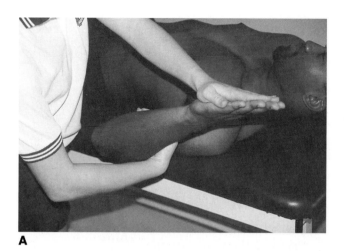

A

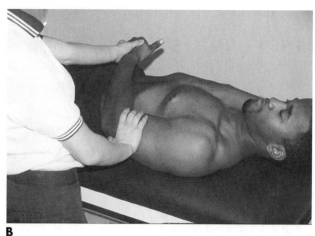

B

EXERCISE   27-20

D2 pattern moving into extension. **A,** Starting position. **B,** Terminal position.

Stretching Exercises

EXERCISE   27-21

Stretching of the elbow and wrist flexors. The elbow is extended with the wrist in extension, and force is applied to stretch the brachialis and brachioradialis.

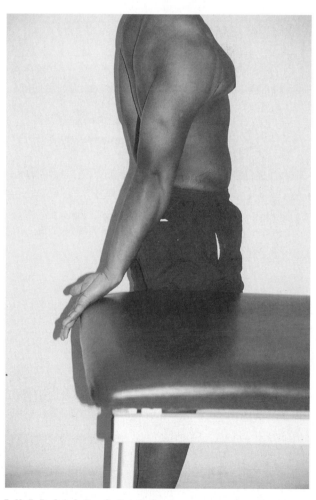

EXERCISE   27-22

Stretching of the biceps brachii. Extend the elbow and pronate the wrist, bring the arm into extension.

E X E R C I S E   2 7 - 2 3

Stretching of the triceps brachii. Flex arm with the elbow in flexion, passive force is applied by pulling the arm into flexion.

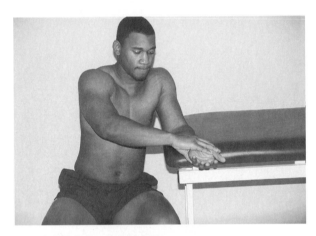

E X E R C I S E   2 7 - 2 4

Stretching of the pronators of the elbow. Place the forearm on a table. With the opposite hand pull the wrist into supination.

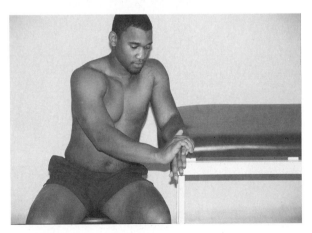

E X E R C I S E   2 7 - 2 5

Stretching of the supinators of the elbow. Place the forearm on a table. To stretch the supinators, pull the wrist into pronation.

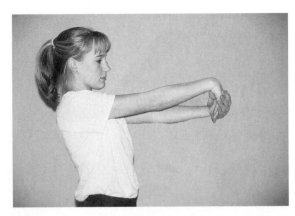

E X E R C I S E   2 7 - 2 6

Stretching of the wrist extensors.

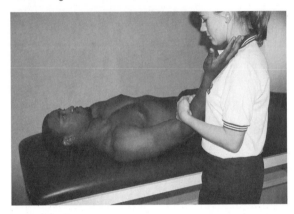

E X E R C I S E   2 7 - 2 7

Passive distraction. Elbow is at 90 degrees while the patient is supine, and the arm is in the plane of the body, hands are clasped while a pull on the proximal radius and ulna is performed. Used to increase elasticity of the adhesed joint capsule to enhance range of motion in all planes of motion.

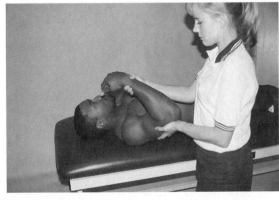

E X E R C I S E   2 7 - 2 8

Passive flexion. While the patient is supine and the arm is in the plane of the body, a push of the forearm toward the shoulder is performed to increase the angle of the elbow toward a straight position. Used to increase elasticity of the adhesed joint capsule to enhance range of motion in all planes of motion.

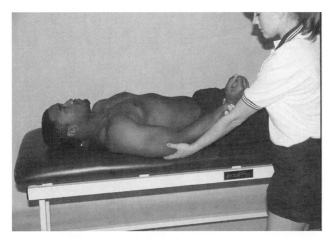

EXERCISE 27-29

Passive extension; while the patient is supine and the arm is in the plane of the body, a push of the forearm away from the shoulder is performed to decrease the angle of the elbow toward a straight position. Used to increase elasticity of the adhesed joint capsule to enhance range of motion in all planes of motion.

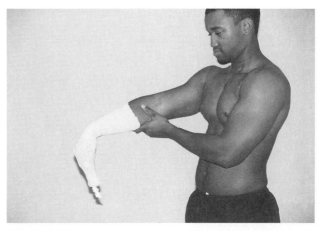

EXERCISE 27-31

Long-duration, low-intensity stretching to increase flexibility to the wrist extensors. (Can be used for wrist flexors by supinating wrist.) This is done using a tube sock or nylon with a 2-3 pound weight inside.

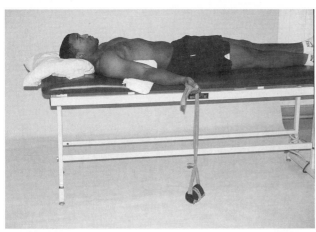

A

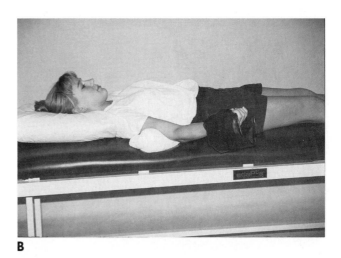

B

EXERCISE 27-30

Long-duration, low-intensity passive range of motion. **A,** with the use of tension band (The weight should be almost resting on the floor as a safety precaution; if the patient feels pain, the weight can simply be dropped). **B,** cuff weight at the wrist. This will increase range of motion by stretching the joint capsule while the patient is supine and the arm is in anatomic position at the shoulder and the wrist.

Joint Mobilization Techniques

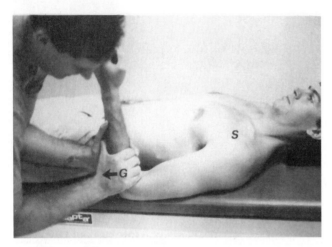

Inferior humeroulnar glides. Inferior humeroulnar glides increase elbow flexion and extension. They are performed using the body weight to stabilize proximally with the hand grasping the ulna and gliding inferiorly.

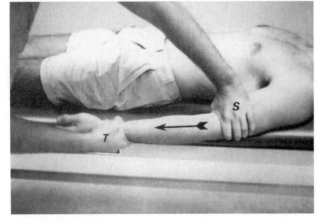

EXERCISE   27-33

Humeroradial inferior glides. Humeroradial inferior glides increase the joint space and improve flexion and extension. One hand stabilizes the humerus above the elbow; the other grasps the distal forearm and glides the radius inferiorly.

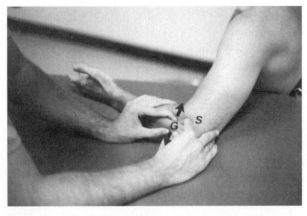

EXERCISE   27-34

Proximal anterior/posterior radial glides. Proximal anterior/posterior radial glides use the thumbs and index fingers to glide the radial head. Anterior glides increase flexion, while posterior glides increase extension.

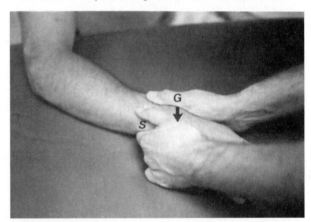

EXERCISE   27-35

Distal anterior/posterior radial glides. Distal anterior/ posterior radial glides are done with one hand stabilizing the ulna and the other gliding the radius. These glides increase pronation.

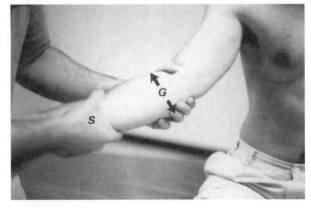

EXERCISE   27-36

Medial and lateral ulnar oscillations. Medial and lateral ulnar oscillations increase flexion and extension. Valgus and varus forces are used with a short lever arm.

Exercises to Reestablish Neuromuscular Control

EXERCISE 27-37

Slide board exercises. The closed chain patterns as shown incorporate joint awareness and movement for proprioceptive benefits. Stress to the patient the importance of developing the weight over the upper quarter while movement patterns are worked.

EXERCISE 27-39

Kinesthetic Training for Timing. The use of this device is for the purpose of proprioception/timing with functional activity. The pulling of the handle causes the weight to move and, with the benefit of inertia, proprioceptive and kinesthetic awareness can improve.

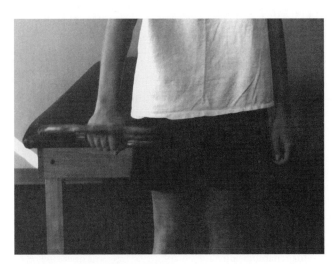

EXERCISE 27-38

Proprioceptive oscillation. This is for kinesthetic/proprioceptive exercises for the elbow and the entire upper quarter. An upper quarter exercise tool, there are three metal balls in the ring that move when the upper extremity generates the movement. This can be performed in various positions to mimic arm positioning in sport.

EXERCISE 27-40

Surgical Tubing Exercises done in the scapular plane to mimic the throwing motion using internal and external rotation.

BRACING AND TAPING

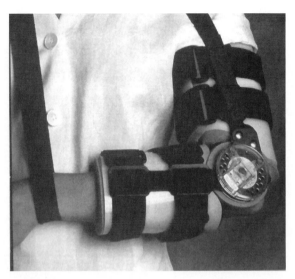

Brace to protect the medial elbow structures; this brace is used when injury stress has occurred to the medial aspect of the elbow. The hinge design is developed for valgus and also varus stress, and can have limits on range of motion as well.

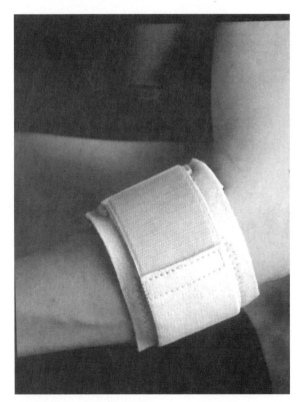

Elbow brace for lateral epicondylitis. This brace is used to decrease the tension of the extensor muscles at the elbow. The brace is applied over the extensor muscles just distal to the elbow joint.

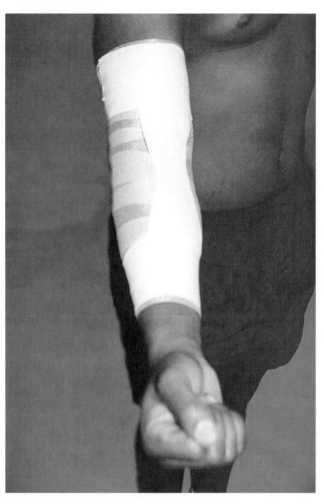

Elbow taping for hyperextension of the elbow uses a checkrein to limit extension in the joint.

SUMMARY

- The elbow joint is composed of the humeroulnar joint, humeroradial joint, and the proximal radioulnar joint. Motions in the elbow complex include flexion, extension, pronation, and supination.
- Fractures in the elbow may occur from a direct blow or from falling on an outstretched hand. They may be treated by casting or in some cases by surgical reduction and fixation. Following surgical fixation, the patient may require 12 weeks for rehabilitation.
- Osteochondritis dissecans and Panner's disease are injuries that affect the lateral aspect of the elbow. Osteochondritis dissecans is associated with a loose body in the joint while Panner's disease is an osteochondrosis of the capitellum.
- The ulnar collateral ligament is injured as a result of a repetitive valgus force. Reconstruction is vital to competitive throwing patients, and rehabilitation may require as long as 22 to 27 weeks.

- In the case of entrapment of the ulnar, median, and radial nerves, mobility of the nerve is critical in reducing nerve entrapment. Rehabilitation should concentrate primarily on stretching to free up the nerve. If conservative treatment fails, surgical release may be indicated.
- Elbow dislocations result from elbow hyperextension from a fall on an extended arm, with the radius and ulna dislocating posteriorly. The degree of stability present will determine the course of rehabilitation. If the elbow is stable, a brief period of immobilization is followed by rehabilitation. An unstable dislocation requires surgical repair and thus a longer period of immobilization.
- Medial epicondylitis (*golfer's elbow, racquetball elbow, swimmer's elbow, Little League elbow*) result from repetitive microtrauma to flexor carpi radialis muscles during pronation and flexion of the wrist. Lateral epicondylitis (*tennis elbow*) occurs with concentric or eccentric overload of the wrist extensors and supinators, most commonly the extensor carpi radialis brevis.

REFERENCES

1. An KN, Morrey BF. Biomechanics of the elbow. In: Morrey BF, ed. *The Elbow and Its Disorders*. Philadelphia, Saunders, 1993.

2. Andrews JR, Wilk KE, Groh D. Elbow rehabilitation. In: Brotzman B. *Clinical Orthopaedic Rehabilitation*. St. Louis, Mosby, 1996.

3. Andrews JR, Wilk KE, Satterwhite YE, Tedder JL. Physical examination of the throwers elbow. *J Obstet Sports Phys Ther* 17:296–304, 1993.

4. Andrich J. Upper extremity injuries in the skeletally immature athlete. In: Nicholas J, Hershman E. *The Upper Extremity in Sports Medicine*. St. Louis, Mosby, 1995.

5. Azar FM, Wilk KE. Nonoperative treatment of the elbow in throwers. *Operative Techniques Sports Med* 4:91–99, 1996.

6. Bauer M, Jonsson K, Josefsson PO, Linden B. Osteochondritis dissecans of the elbow. A long-term follow-up study. *Clin Orthop Rel Res* 284:156–160, 1992.

7. Brown R, Blazina ME, Kerlan K. Osteochondritis of the capitellum. *J Sports Med* 2:27–46, 1974.

8. Bruckner JD, Alexander AH, Lichtman DM. Acute dislocations of the distal radioulnar joint. *Instructional Course Lectures* 45:27–36, 1996.

9. Byron P. Restoring function. *J Hand Ther* 10:334–337, 1997.

10. Cordasco F, Parkes J. Overuse injuries of the elbow. In: Nicholas J, Hershman E. *The Upper Extremity in Sports Medicine*. St. Louis, Mosby, 1995.

11. Davidson PA, Pink M, Perry J, Jobe FW. Functional anatomy of the flexor pronator muscle group in relation to the medial collateral ligament of the elbow. *Am J Sports Med* 23:245–250, 1995.

12. Ferlic DC, Morrey BF. Evaluation of the painful elbow: The problem elbow. In: Morrey BF, ed. *The Elbow and Its Disorders*, 2nd ed. Philadelphia, Saunders, 1993.

13. Fyfe I, Stanish WD. The use of eccentric training and stretching in the treatment and prevention of tendon injuries. *Clin Sports Med* 3:601–624, 1992.

14. Gore RM, Rogers LF, Bowerman J, et al. Osseus manifestations of elbow stress associated with sports. *AJR* 134:971–977, 1980.

15. Guerra JJ, Timmerman LA. Clinical anatomy, histology, & pathomechanics of the elbow in sports. *Operative Techniques Sports Med* 4:69–76, 1996.

16. Harrelson GL. Elbow rehabilitation. In: Andrews J, Harrelson GL, eds. *Physical Rehabilitation of the Injured Athlete*. Philadelphia, Saunders, 1991.

17. Kao JT, Pink M, Jobe FW, Perry J. Electromyographic analysis of the scapular muscles during a golfswing. *Am J Sports Med* 23:19–23, 1995.

18. Lindholm TS, Osterman K, Vankka E. Osteochondritis dissecans of the elbow, ankle, and hip: A comprehensive survey. *Clin Orthop* 148:245–253, 1980.

19. Magee DJ. Elbow. In: Magee DJ, ed. *Orthopedic Physical Assessment*. Philadelphia, Saunders, 1997.

20. Morrey BF. Anatomy of the elbow joint. In: Morrey BF, ed. *The Elbow and Its Disorders,* 2nd ed. Philadelphia, Saunders, 1993.

21. Morrey BF, An KN. Articular and ligamentous contributions to the stability of the elbow joint. *Am J Sports Med* 11:315–318, 1983.

22. Morrey BF, An KN, Stormont TJ. Force transmissions through the radial head. *J Bone Joint Surg Am* 70:250–256, 1988.

23. Norkin CC, Levangie PK. Function: Humeroulnar and humeroradial joints. In: Norkin CC, ed. *Joint Structure and Function,* 2nd ed. Philadelphia, Davis, 1992.

24. Olsen BS, Sojbjerg JO, Dalstra M, Sneppen O. Kinematics of the lateral ligamentous constraints of the elbow joint. *J Shoulder Elbow Surg* 5:333–341, 1996.

25. Plancher KD, Halbrecht J, Lourie GM. Medial and lateral epicondylitis in the athlete. *Clin Sports Med* 15:283–305, 1996.

26. Priest JD. Elbow injuries in gymnastics. *Clin Sports Med* 4:73–84, 1985.

27. Roetert EP, Brody H, Dillman CJ, et al. The biomechanics of tennis elbow. An integrated approach. *Clin Sports Med* 14:47–57, 1995.

28. Saliba E. The upper arm, elbow, and forearm. In: Hunter LY, ed. *AAOS Athletic Training and Sports Medicine,* 2nd ed. Park Ridge, IL, American Academy of Orthopedic Surgeons, 1991.

29. Singer KM, Roy SP. Osteochondrosis of the humeral capitellum. *Am J Sports Med* 12:351–360, 1984.

30. Sobel J, Nirschl RP. Elbow injuries. In: Zachewski J, Magee D, Quillen W: *Athletic Injuries and Rehabilitation*. Philadelphia, Saunders, 1996.

31. Stoane JM, Poplausky MR, Haller JO, Berdon WE. Panner's disease: X-ray, MR imaging findings and review of the literature. *Comput Med Imaging Graphics.* 19:473–476, 1995.

32. Stroyan M, Wilk KE. The functional anatomy of the elbow complex. *J Orthop Sports Med Phys Ther* 17:279–288, 1993.

33. Thomas PJ, Noellert RC. Brachial artery disruption after closed posterior dislocation of the elbow. *Am J Orthop* 24:558–560, 1995.

34. Tullos HS, Ryan WJ. Functional anatomy of the elbow. In: Zarins B, Andres JR, Carson WD, eds. *Injuries to the Throwing Arm.* Philadelphia, Saunders, 1985.

35. Warfel JH. Muscles of the arm. In: *The Extremities, Muscles, and Motor Points.* Philadelphia, Lea & Febinger, 1993.

36. Wilk KE, Arrigo C, Andrews JR. Rehabilitation of the elbow in the throwing athlete. *J Orthop Sports Phys Ther* 17:305–317, 1993.

37. Williams PL, Warwick R, Dyson M, Bannister L, eds. *Gray's Anatomy,* 37th ed. London, Churchill Livingstone, 1989.

CHAPTER 28

Rehabilitation of the Wrist, Hand, and Fingers

Anne Marie Schneider

OBJECTIVES

After completing this chapter, the student therapist should be able to do the following:

- Discuss the functional anatomy and biomechanics associated with normal function of the wrist and hand.
- Identify techniques for improving range of motion, including stretching exercises.
- Relate biomechanical and tissue-healing principles to the rehabilitation of various wrist and hand injuries.
- Discuss criteria for progression of the rehabilitation program for different hand and wrist injuries.
- Describe and explain the rationale for various treatment techniques in the management of wrist and hand injuries.
- Demonstrate the various rehabilitative strengthening techniques for the wrist and hand.

FUNCTIONAL ANATOMY AND BIOMECHANICS

The hand is an intricate balance of muscles, tendons, and joints working in unison. Hands are almost always exposed, and for that reason may be especially prone to injuries. Changing the mechanics can greatly alter the function and appearance of the hand.

The Wrist

The wrist is the connecting link between the hand and forearm.[52] The wrist joint is comprised of eight carpal bones and their articulations with the radius and ulna proximally, and the metacarpals distally.

There is an intricate relationship between the carpal bones. They are connected by ligaments to each other, and to the radius and ulna. The palmar ligaments from the proximal carpal row to the radius are strongest, followed by the dorsal ligaments (scaphoid-triquetrum, and distal radius to lunate and triquetrum), with intrinsic ligaments (scapholunate and lunotriquetral) being the weakest.[7] The carpal bones are arranged in two rows, proximal and distal, with the scaphoid acting as the

functional link between the two.[52] The distal carpal row determines the position of the scaphoid and thus the lunate. With radial deviation, the distal row is displaced radially while the proximal row moves ulnarly. The distal portion of the scaphoid must shift to avoid the radial styloid. The scaphoid palmar flexes. This is reversed in ulnar deviation.[46] The total arc of motion for radial and ulnar deviation averages approximately 50 degrees, 15 degrees radially and 35 degrees ulnarly.[46] The uneven division is due to the buttressing effect of the radial styloid.[46]

Flexion and extension occur through synchronous movement of proximal and distal rows. The total excursion is equally distributed between the midcarpal and radiocarpal joints.[7] The arc of motion for flexion and extension is 121 degrees.[38]

There are no collateral ligaments in the wrist. Their presence would impede radial and ulnar deviation, allowing only flexion and extension. Cross sections through the wrist reveal that tendons of the extensor carpi ulnaris (ECU) at the ulnar aspect of the wrist, and the extensor pollicus brevis (EPB) and abductor pollicus longus (APL) on the radial side, are in "collateral" position.[23] EMG studies have been performed and show ECU, EPB, and APL were active in wrist flexion and extension.[23] These muscles show only small displacement with flexion and extension so they are in an isometric position.[23]

Their function can be described as an adjustable collateral system. The ECU shows activity in ulnar deviation and the APL and EPB in radial deviation.[23]

Stability of the ulnar side of the wrist is provided by the triangular fibrocartilage complex (TFCC).[52] This ligament arises from the radius, inserts into the base of the ulnar styloid, the ulnar carpus, and the base of the fifth metacarpal.[52] This ligament complex is the major stabilizer of the distal radioulnar joint (DRUJ) and is a load-bearing column between the distal ulna and ulnar carpus.[52]

There are no muscular or tendinous insertions on any carpal bones except the flexor carpi ulnaris (FCU) into the pisiform.[52] Muscles that move the wrist and fingers cross the wrist and insert on the appropriate bones. There is a dorsal retinaculum (fascia) with six vertical septa that attach to the distal radius and partition the first five dorsal compartments.[37] These define fibroosseous tunnels that position and maintain extensor tendons and their synovial sheaths relative to the axis of wrist motion.[37] The sixth compartment, which houses the ECU, is a separate tunnel formed from infratendinous retinaculum. This allows unrestricted ulnar rotation during pronation and supination.[37] The retinaculum prevents bowstringing of the tendons during wrist extension.

Volarly, the long finger flexors, long thumb flexor, median nerve, and radial artery pass through the carpal tunnel. Bowstringing is prevented by the thick transverse carpal ligament.

The Hand

The metacarpal phalangeal (MCP) joints allow for multiplanar motion, but the primary function is flexion and extension.[52] The metacarpal head has a convex shape, which fits with a shallow concave proximal phalanx. The stability of the MCP joint is provided by its capsule, collateral ligaments, accessory collateral ligaments, volar plate, and musculotendinous units.[52] The collateral ligaments are laterally positioned and are dorsal to the axis of rotation. In extension, the collateral ligament is lax; in flexion it is taut.[22] This is important to remember if immobilizing the MCP joint. If the joint is casted or splinted in extension, the lax collateral ligament will tighten, which will then prevent flexion once mobilization has begun. The accessory collateral ligament is volar to the axis of rotation and is taut in extension and lax in flexion.

The volar plate helps prevent hyperextension of the MCP joint. It forms the dorsal wall of the flexor tendon sheath and the A1 pulley.[52]

Several muscles cross the MCP joints. On the flexor surface, the flexor digitorum superficialis (FDS) and flexor digitorum profundus (FDP) are held close to the bones by pulleys. These pulleys prevent bowstringing during finger flexion. The FDS flexes the proximal interphalangeal (PIP) joint, and the FDP flexes the distal interphalangeal (DIP) joint. The interosseous muscles are lateral to the MCP joints and are responsible for abduction and adduction of the MCP joints. The lumbrical muscles are volar to the axis of rotation of the MCP joint, but

then insert into the lateral bands and are dorsal to the PIP and DIP joints. Their function is MCP joint flexion and IP joint extension. (This is also the reason you can have IP extension with a radial nerve palsy.) Dorsally, the extensor mechanism crosses the MCP joint. The tendon is held centrally by the sagittal bands.

The Fingers

The IP joints are bicondylar hinge joints allowing flexion and extension. Collateral and accessory collateral ligaments stabilize the joints on the lateral aspect. The collateral ligament is taut in extension and lax in flexion. This is important when splinting the PIP joint. If it is not a contraindication with the injury (as with PIP fracture dislocation), the joint should be splinted in full extension to help prevent flexion contractures.

On the flexor surface the FDS bifurcates proximal to the PIP joint, allowing the FDP to become more superficial as it continues to insert on the distal phalanx, allowing DIP flexion. The FDS inserts on the middle phalanx for PIP flexion. Five annular pulleys and three cruciate pulleys between the MCP and DIP joints prevent bowstringing of the tendons and help provide nutrition to the tendons.

On the extensor surface, the common extensor tendon crosses the MCP joint and then divides into three slips. The central slip inserts on the dorsal middle phalanx, allowing for PIP extension. The two lateral slips, called the lateral bands, get attachments from the lumbricals, travel dorsal and lateral to the PIP joint, rejoin after the PIP joint, and insert as the terminal extensor into the DIP joint. This is a delicately balanced system to extend the IP joints. Disruption of this system greatly alters the balance, and thus the dynamic function of the hand.

REHABILITATION TECHNIQUES FOR SPECIFIC INJURIES

Distal Radius Fractures

PATHOMECHANICS

Fractures of the distal radius can be described in many different ways, by several classification systems. Of importance in treatment is to be able to describe the fracture and X ray. Is the fracture intraarticular or extraarticular? Displaced or nondisplaced? Simple or comminuted? Open or closed? Is the radius shortened? Is the ulna also fractured? Answers to these questions will help guide your treatment and expected outcomes.

Simple, extraarticular, nondisplaced fractures tend to heal without incident with immobilization with full (or close to it) motion expected following treatment. As the fractures become more involved, either intraarticular or comminuted, chances of full return of motion are decreased.

The normal anatomic radius is tilted volarly. If in a fracture the volar tilt becomes dorsal, motion will be affected. It may also lead to midcarpal instability, decreased strength, increased ulnar loading, and a dysfunctional DRUJ.[17]

The normal anatomic radius is longer than the ulna. If in a comminuted fracture the radius is shortened, this is the most disabling.[17,18] Radial shortening may lead to DRUJ problems, decreased mobility, and decreased power (strength). Articular displacement correction is critical. Radial shortening needs to be corrected via external fixation.

The external fixator will attach to the midradius and to the second metacarpal shaft. Length may be restored and held with the traction bars of the external fixator. If the fixator was not in place and the fracture was not reduced, the weight and anatomy of the carpal bones, and the force of the muscles, would cause loss of reduction and shortening of the radius. The type of fracture, size of the fragments, and displacement determine initial (cast versus fixator) treatment. Once reduced, the fractures need to be closely monitored to be sure reduction is being maintained.

Rehabilitation following a distal radius fracture is similar regardless of method of fixation (cast, ORIF, or ex fix). Range-of-motion and edema control of noninvolved joints is essential so that when immobilization is discontinued, rehabilitation can be concentrated on the wrist and forearm rather than also on the fingers, elbow, and shoulder.

INJURY MECHANISM

As is true of most wrist injuries, distal radius fractures occur from a fall on an outstretched hand. It may be a high-impact event, but does not always have to be.

REHABILITATION CONCERNS

Early and proper reduction and immobilization is of utmost importance. The fracture must be closely watched initially to be sure reduction is being maintained. Early ROM to noninvolved joints is imperative. This helps prevent muscle atrophy, aids in muscle pumping to decrease edema, and most importantly, maintains motion so treatment can focus on the wrist once fracture is healed and fixation is removed.

Other concerns include complications of carpal tunnel or reflex sympathetic dystrophy (RSD).[26] If present and first noted in the therapy clinic, referral should be made back to the physician as soon as possible. One other complication, which usually occurs late in a seemingly inconsequential nondisplaced distal radius fracture, is an extensor pollicis longus (EPL) rupture.[26] It is thought that this occurs from the EPL rubbing around the fracture site near Lister's tubercle. The patient would be unable to extend the thumb IP joint. This would need to be surgically repaired.

REHABILITATION PROGRESSION

Rehabilitation may be initiated while the wrist is immobilized. This should include shoulder ROM in all planes, elbow flexion and extension, and finger flexion and extension. Finger exercises should include isolated MCP flexion, composite flexion (full fist), and intrinsic minus fisting (MCP extension with IP flexion) (see Exercise 28-14). Coban or an isotoner glove may be used for edema control if necessary.

If a fixator or pins are present, pin site care may be performed, depending on physician preference. Most physicians that this author works with prefer hydrogen peroxide with a cotton applicator to remove the crusted areas from around the pins. A different applicator should be used on each pin to prevent possible spread of infection. Some physicians allow patients to shower with the fixator in place (not soaking while bathing); other physicians prefer a plastic bag, leaving the pin sites alone.

Once immobilization is discontinued (approximately 6 weeks for casting, 8 weeks with an external fixator, or 2 weeks if ORIF with plate and screws), ROM to the wrist is begun. Active motion is begun immediately. Wrist flexion, extension, and radial and ulnar deviation are evaluated, and then instructed. Wrist extension should be taught with finger (especially MCP) flexion (see Exercise 28-1). This isolates the wrist extensors rather than "cheating" using the extensor digitorum communis (EDC). The importance of wrist extensor isolation is for hand function. If a person is using the EDC to extend the wrist, as soon as he or she grasps something, flexing the fingers, the wrist will also flex, tenodesis will extend the fingers, and the object will be dropped. Isolating wrist extension should be the emphasis of treatment on the first visit.

Passive ROM may be dependent on physician preference. Many let PROM begin immediately; others prefer waiting 1 to 2 weeks (see Exercises 28-1 and 28-2) for passive stretching exercises. Forearm rotation (supination and pronation) must not be ignored. AROM and PROM are important. When stretching rotation passively, pressure should be applied at the distal radius, proximal to the wrist, not at the hand. This will help apply pressure where the limitations are and not put unnecessary torque across the carpus (see Exercises 28-5 and 28-26).

Active motion can be progressed to strengthening. Light weights, theraband, or tubing may be graded for all wrist and forearm motions. This can be in conjunction with weight-bearing, wall push-ups to countertop to mat to floor progression (see Exercises 28-8 to 28-10). Push-ups on a ball may be the next progression (Exercise 28-26), along with lying prone over a large ball and "walking" out and back on extended wrists (see Exercise 28-27).

Putty for grip strengthening can be begun and graded to harder putty beginning about 1 week after immobilization. This also helps to strengthen wrist musculature (see Exercise 28-7).

Plyometric exercises for wrist and general upper extremity strength are next. Activities are graded from playground-type ball to large gym ball to weighted balls. Activities can be done supine, against a wall, or if available, using a rebounder. Specific return to sport exercises and activities must also be done.

If the fracture is nondisplaced, rehabilitation may require 2 to 3 weeks. If a nondisplaced fracture is treated by ORIF with plate-and-screw fixation, rehabilitation may require a total of 6 weeks. If the fracture was displaced, the patient may require 8 to 12 weeks for rehabilitation. Athletes, particularly those in

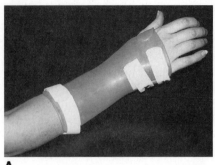
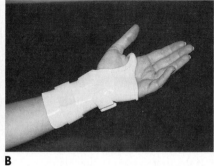
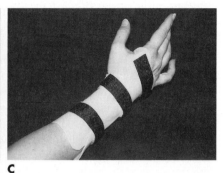

A   **B**   **C**

FIGURE 28-1

Wrist splint. This may be made (**A**) dorsally, (**B**) volarly, or (**C**) circumferentially depending on support needs and type of injury. These splints may be used for tendinitis, wrist fractures, wrist sprains, or carpal tunnel syndrome.

contact sports, require additional padding and protection as they resume athletic activity (see Figures 28-1 and 28-2).

Wrist Sprain

PATHOMECHANICS

The term "wrist sprain" is often seen when patients complain of pain and have a history of minor trauma. The diagnosis should be one of exclusion. Injuries that must be ruled out include scaphoid fracture, traumatic instability patterns, lunate fractures, dorsal chip fractures, other carpal fractures and injuries, and ligament tears.[17]

INJURY MECHANISM

The injury is usually a minor trauma—a fall landing on an outstretched hand, a twisting motion, or some impact such as striking the ground with a club.

REHABILITATION CONCERNS

The primary concern is ruling out more serious injury. Once other diagnoses are ruled out, treatment is focused on edema control, pain control, and maintaining (or increasing) active and passive ROM to the wrist and other noninvolved joints. If necessary, splint immobilization (Fig. 28-1) may also be tried for pain relief. If activities increase pain, those activities should be examined to determine if modifications can be made to decrease pain and increase activity level.

REHABILITATION PROGRESSION

Following decrease in pain and edema, and return of ROM, strengthening should be performed to all wrist motions, and if necessary, to grip strength and the entire arm. Refer to the distal radius fracture section for specific exercises (see Exercises 28-1 to 28-10, 28-26, and 28-27). Joint mobilizations for the wrist can certainly help improve joint arthrokinematics and ROM (see Exercises 28-19 to 28-24). Taping the wrist (Fig. 28-2) may help provide support and help to decrease pain.

Scaphoid Fracture

PATHOMECHANICS

Fractures of the scaphoid account for 60 percent of all carpal injuries.[3] The prognosis is related to the site of the fracture, obliquity, displacement, and promptness of diagnosis and treatment.[17] The blood supply of the scaphoid comes distal to proximal. Fracture through the waist of the proximal one third of the scaphoid may result in delayed union or avascular necrosis secondary to poor blood supply. It may take 20 weeks for a proximal one-thirdfracture to heal, versus 5 to 6 weeks at the scaphoid tuberosity.[17] Displacement of the fracture occurs at the time of injury and must be treated early using ORIF.

Ninety percent of scaphoid fractures heal without complications if treated early and properly.[28] If the fracture does go on to nonunion, whether symptomatic or not it should be treated. Not treating will lead to carpal instability and periscaphoid arthritis.[34,44]

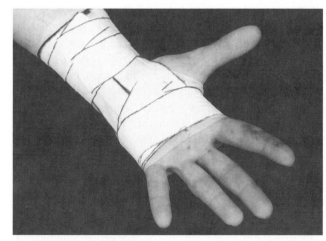

FIGURE 28-2

Wrist taping may be done when extra support is needed but hard plastic splinting is inappropriate.

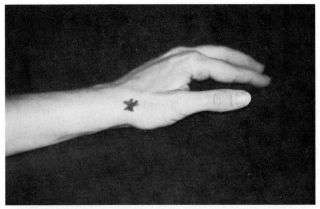

FIGURE 28-3

The * indicates the anatomic snuffbox under which the scaphoid is positioned. This area will be painful to palpation with scaphoid fracture or scapholunate ligament injury.

Diagnosis is made by X ray. Patients will have wrist pain, especially in the anatomic snuffbox (Fig. 28-3).

INJURY MECHANISM

Scaphoid fractures result from a fall on an outstretched hand. The radial styloid may impact against the scaphoid waist, causing a fracture.[7] The scaphoid fails in tension when the palmar surface experiences an excessive bending movement.[45] Because the scaphoid blocks wrist extension, it is at risk for injury.[17]

REHABILITATION CONCERNS

Of primary concern is proper diagnosis. If the patient has a history of a fall on an outstretched hand and has pain in the anatomic snuffbox, but the initial X ray is negative, the patient should be treated conservatively in a thumb spica cast for 2 weeks, then be X-rayed again.[9,29] If the X ray is negative after 2 weeks, the cast may be removed and ROM begun.

Another concern is nonunions that may lead to carpal instability or periscaphoid arthritis. ROM of noninjured and noncasted joints must be maintained during prolonged periods of immobilization.

REHABILITATION PROGRESSIONS

Treatment of the nondisplaced scaphoid is casting. Following casting, an additional 2 to 4 weeks of splinting (Fig. 28-4) may be used, with the removal of splint for the exercise program. AROM exercises of wrist flexion, wrist extension (with finger flexion to isolate wrist extensors), and radial and ulnar deviation are initiated following immobilization (see Exercises 28-1 to 28-4). Thumb flexion and extension, abduction and adduction, and opposition to each finger are also initiated. After approximately 2 weeks (sooner if cleared by a physician), PROM to the same motion is begun. Gentle strengthening with weights and or putty may be started around the same time frame. Strengthening is progressed over the next several weeks to

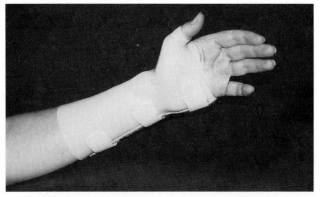

FIGURE 28-4

A thumb spica splint is circumferential and includes the thumb and wrist. It may or may not include the thumb IP joint. It is most commonly used for a scaphoid or thumb metacarpal fracture.

include weight-bearing activities, plyometrics, and general arm conditioning to return to sport-specific activity (see Exercises 28-8 to 28-10, 28-26, and 28-27).

Surgical repair rehabilitation is the same progression as nonsurgical. The time frame of immobilization may be less because of the repair of the scaphoid with rigid fixation.

If the fracture is nondisplaced and is treated by casting, a padded protective cast should be worn for 6 to 12 weeks. When the arm stops hurting, there are early signs of healing, and there is no pain with a blow to the cast, a physically active patient may return to activity, depending on the activity, with protection. Rehabilitation once a cast is removed can take 4 to 6 weeks.

If the nondisplaced fracture has undergone ORIF, the patient requires about 2 to 3 weeks for rehabilitation without additional protection unless the patient is an athlete competing in a contact sport. If the fracture is displaced and surgically repaired, the time for rehabilitation may be longer.

Lunate Dislocations

PATHOMECHANICS

Stability of the carpus is dependent upon the maintenance of bony architecture interlaced with ligaments.[17] Most carpal dislocations are the dorsal perilunate type, with many people believing that a lunate dislocation is the end of a perilunate dislocation.[17] The lunate dislocates palmarly with the loss of ligamentous stability. It may be reduced if seen early by placing the wrist in extension and putting pressure on the lunate (Fig. 28-5). The wrist is then brought into flexion and immobilized. It is very common for reduction to be lost over time with this injury, so percutaneous pinning or ORIF is recommended.[17]

Median nerve compression is frequently caused by this injury. The palmarly displaced lunate puts pressure on the nerve. Symptoms may continue for several weeks following reduction of the lunate secondary to swelling and contusion of the nerve.

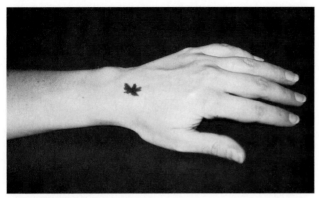

FIGURE   28-5

The * indicates the position of the lunate and location of pain with lunate, or scapholunate ligament injuries.

INJURY MECHANISM

A violent hyperextension of the wrist is the injury mechanism.[7,17] A fall on the outstretched hand produces a translational compressive force when the lunate is caught between the capitate and the dorsal aspect of the distal radius articular surface.[17] If the lunate does not fracture, a periscaphoid or lunate dislocation may occur.

REHABILITATION CONCERNS

Primary concern is early surgical repair. Complications if this is not surgically corrected include pain, weakness, wrist clicking, and bones slipping.[7] Carpal tunnel syndrome, if present, must be addressed at the time of surgery. ROM of noninvolved joints must be maintained during immobilization.

REHABILITATION PROGRESSIONS

Progression is very similar to the rehabilitation of distal radius fractures and other wrist injuries. Following cast and pin (if applicable) removal, AROM is begun. This is progressed to passive stretching and gentle strengthening. Strengthening becomes more aggressive with free weights, weight-bearing activities, and plyometric activities. Motions that need to be addressed for ROM and strengthening are flexion, extension, radial deviation, ulnar deviation, supination, and pronation (see Exercises 28-1 to 28-10, 28-26, and 28-27).

The severity of this injury and need for ORIF secondary to frequent loss of reduction if not repaired will require at least 8 weeks for rehabilitation. At 8 weeks, the wrist may be taped for support and protection (see Fig. 28-2).

Hamate Fractures

PATHOMECHANICS

Hook of the hamate fractures are more common than hamate body fractures.[4] The hook is the attachment for the pisohamate ligament, short flexor, and opponens to the small finger and the transverse carpal ligament.[52] Because of these attachments, if there is a hamate hook fracture, there are deforming forces on

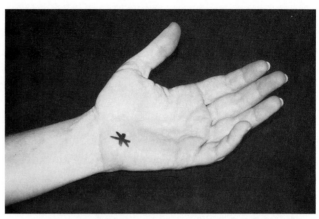

FIGURE   28-6

The * indicates the point that will elicit pain with palpation (especially deep) for a hamate hook fracture. Some pain may also be referred to the ulnar wrist.

the fragment with intermittent tension. This makes it nearly impossible to align and immobilize the fracture, and as a result they often do not heal.[52] The hook can be palpated on the volar surface of the hand at the base of the hypothenar eminence deep and radial to the pisiform.

The hamate is in close proximity to the ulnar nerve and artery on the ulnar side, and flexor tendons to the ring and small finger in the carpal canal on the radial side (Fig. 28-6). There is a possibility of an ulnar neuropathy, tendinitis, or tendon rupture with this injury.[10,40,41]

INJURY MECHANISM

The suspected injury mechanism is a shearing force transmitted from a handle of a club to the hamate. It will often occur when striking an unexpected object, for example a rock or tree root by a golfer. It most frequently occurs in golfers but may occur in any stick sport such as baseball or field hockey. There is also a possibility of a stress fracture from tension from ligament and muscle attachments; however, this is rare.[7]

REHABILITATION CONCERNS

Of first concern is diagnosis. Patients may have felt a snap or pop. They will have localized tenderness over the hamate hook, ulnar-sided wrist pain, and weakness of grip that increases over time. A carpal tunnel view X ray will confirm the diagnosis. The therapist must also watch for signs of ulnar neuritis or neuropathy and flexor tendon rupture.

REHABILITATION PROGRESSIONS

Treatment has been described as casting an acute hamate hook fracture[2,31] or bone grafting a nonunion.[47] However, as described previously, these fractures do not usually heal secondary to forces applied to the fracture fragment. Treatment of symptomatic hamate fractures is fragment excision.[40,41]

Treatment following excision is edema control, scar massage (3 to 5 minutes, 5 times/day), and grip strengthening if necessary.

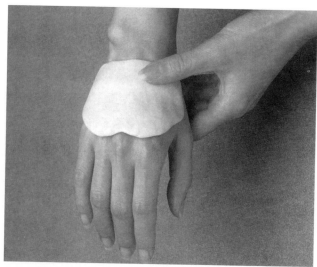

FIGURE 28-7

Otoform is used as a scar control pad. It comes in varying size containers out of which you get the "putty" to the size that is needed. A catalyst is then added and mixed, and applied directly to the scar area. Once it hardens, in 1 to 2 minutes, it can be rinsed and applied with Coban or other similar object. It is usually worn 23 hours per day for scar control. It does need to be removed as it does not breathe and skin can become macerated, or a rash may develop. It may also be worn during sport activity for additional protection to a sensitive area.

CRITERIA FOR RETURN

Acute injuries need to be treated symptomatically. Tape or padding, if allowed, may be placed in the palm. Chronic fractures may be treated symptomatically initially with pain being the limiting factor. Eventually, surgical excision will be necessary. Once the fragment has been excised, the patient should use a small splint, padding, or scar control pad such as Topigel or Otoform (Fig. 28-7), which may be helpful initially for scar control and to decrease hypersensitivity around the incision area.

Carpal Tunnel Syndrome

PATHOMECHANICS

Carpal tunnel syndrome is compression of the median nerve at the level of the wrist. The carpal tunnel is made of the carpal bones dorsally and transverse carpal ligament volarly. Located in the carpal tunnel are the FDS and FDP to all digits, FPL, median nerve, and median artery.[19] If tendons get inflamed, the space within the carpal tunnel is decreased and the nerve gets compressed. Excessive wrist flexion or extension will also increase pressure in the carpal tunnel. Symptoms of classic carpal tunnel are numbness and tingling in thumb through radial half of ring finger, pain or waking at night, and clumsiness or weak-

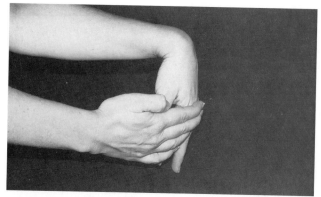

FIGURE 28-8

Phalen's test for carpal tunnel syndrome is extreme wrist flexion, which narrows the space in the carpal canal. Test is positive if there is numbness and tingling in the median nerve distribution within 60 seconds. Do not flex elbows or rest elbows on the table, as this may elicit ulnar nerve symptoms.

ness in the hand. Symptoms may increase with static positioning (e.g., driving or reading a newspaper).[19] Diagnosis is made by history, Phalen's test (Fig. 28-8), Tinel's sign, nerve conduction studies, direct pressure over the carpal tunnel (Fig. 28-9), and EMGs. Injection may help confirm diagnosis and may relieve symptoms.

INJURY MECHANISM

Conditions and injuries that have been associated with carpal tunnel syndrome include tenosynovitis from overuse or from rheumatoid arthritis, external or internal pressure such as lipoma, diabetes, and pregnancy.[48] Acute carpal tunnel syndrome may occur following a fracture or other trauma by either edema or fracture fragment pressing on the median nerve.

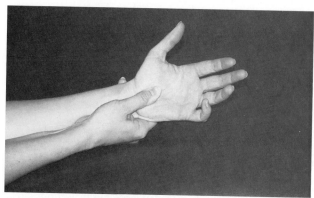

FIGURE 28-9

Firm pressure over the carpal tunnel may elicit numbness or tingling in the median nerve distribution. It alone is not indicative of carpal tunnel syndrome, but it provides more information.

The incidence of carpal tunnel in the athletic population is extremely low,[33] but may be found occasionally in cyclists, throwers, or tennis players.[35] Pressure from resting on handlebars may cause symptoms. Sustained grip and repetitive action of throwers and racquet sports may also increase symptoms.

REHABILITATION CONCERNS

Conservative treatment is tried first and consists of night splinting with the wrist in neutral position, (see Fig. 28-1), anti-inflammatory medication, and relative rest from aggravating source (if known). Occasionally physicians will recommend full-time wrist splinting. This author prefers that wrist splints are not worn during the day, as this leads to muscle weakness and arm pain from distribution of forces to new areas. Injections may be done by the physician for symptom relief—this is also diagnostic. If the symptoms disappear with injection, the diagnosis is correct. Symptoms may recur. Nerve gliding exercises described by Butler[6] (see Exercise 28-13) and myofascial release may also help relieve symptoms. Activity analysis and biomechanical analysis of activities that increase symptoms should be done to see if change in technique will decrease symptoms.

If conservative treatment fails, a carpal tunnel release may be performed. Rehabilitation following release consists of wound care, if necessary; scar massage; and ROM exercises. Tendon gliding exercises are done to improve ROM and isolation of tendons. Start with full finger extension, and then hook fist to maximize FDP pull-through in relation to FDS, and then long fist to maximize FDS pull-through, and then composite fist. Full extension should be performed between each position (see Exercise 28-14). Wrist ROM should also be performed (see Exercises 28-1 and 28-2).

REHABILITATION PROGRESSIONS

Progression for carpal tunnel release includes grip strengthening. Start slowly to not increase the symptoms. Wrist strengthening may also be performed. Strengthening is generally begun 2 to 4 weeks postsurgery. Speak with the individual physician regarding his or her preference. If conservative treatment fails and a release is performed, patients can typically return to normal activity once sutures are removed.

Ganglion Cysts

PATHOLOGY

A ganglion cyst is the most common soft-tissue tumor in the hand.[5] It is a synovial cyst arising from the synovial lining of a tendon sheath or joint. The etiology is unclear. They are most common on the dorsal radial wrist, but may also be volar (Fig. 28-10). They originate deep in the joint and may be symptomatic before they appear at the surface. The usual origin is from the area of the scapholunate ligament.[5] Ganglion cysts are translucent, which can help confirm the diagnosis.

Treatment is aspiration of the cyst. Results of recurrence are variable. In adults, multiple aspirations are suggested, with suc-

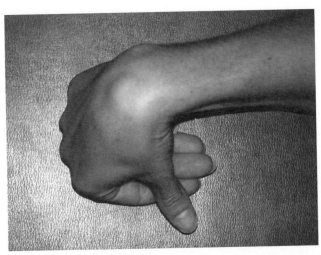

FIGURE 28-10
This is a dorsal wrist ganglion. They vary in size or shape. They will transilluminate.

cess rates of 51 percent[53] to 85 percent.[25] If multiple aspirations are not successful and cysts recur, they may be surgically excised.

INJURY MECHANISM

It appears that ganglions most often form with repeated forceful hyperextension of the wrist. Pain is indication for treatment.

REHABILITATION CONCERNS

These patients do not need to be seen for rehabilitation once diagnosed and aspirated. The aspiration usually decreases pain and allows for full ROM. Following ganglion cyst excision, patients may need to be seen for ROM, passive stretching, strengthening, and scar control. ROM emphasis should be on wrist flexion and extension and finger flexion and extension (see Exercises 28-1, 21-2, and 28-14). Scar massage and desensitization may be done with lotion, rubbing on scar, tapping on scar, and performing vibration to scar. Less noxious stimuli should be done first, with increasing difficulty being added to program. Scar control pads such as Otoform (see Fig. 28-7) or Topigel sheeting may also be used, held in place with Coban.

REHABILITATION PROGRESSIONS

Activity is limited by pain. Patients may continue normal activity with a ganglion if is not symptomatic. If symptomatic, it may be aspirated with immediate return to activity. If it recurs it may be aspirated again. If excised, patients may begin normal activities once sutures are removed, at approximately 10 days. Following excision and return of ROM, strengthening may be done as necessary for grip, wrist flexion and extension, and general upper extremity return to play exercises.

Boxer's Fracture

PATHOMECHANICS

A boxer's fracture is a fracture of the fifth metacarpal neck. It is the most commonly fractured metacarpal.[21] It will frequently shorten and angulate on impact. There is a large amount of movement of the fifth metacarpal. For this reason, perfect anatomic reduction is not necessary. It should be noted, however, that excess angulation may lead to either to an imbalance between intrinsic and extrinsic muscles of the hand leading to clawing, or to a mass in the palm.[32]

INJURY MECHANISM

This injury occurs most frequently from contact against an object with a closed fist. The impact is usually through the 5th metacarpal head.

REHABILITATION CONCERNS

Of concern is skin integrity. The injuries frequently occur as a result of a fight and pieces of tooth may be in an open wound. If the injury is closed, concern is for proper immobilization, edema control, and ROM of noninvolved joints—especially the IP joints of the small finger. Occasionally, ORIF is required. Edema control is critical. AROM may be initiated 72 hours after the ORIF.[32]

Treatment is immobilization in a plaster gutter splint, or in a thermoplastic splint fabricated by a hand therapist (Fig. 28-11). The latter is often preferred, as it allows for skin hygiene, wrist ROM, and IP joint ROM. The splint only immobilizes the ring and small finger MCP joints. The splint is also easily remolded if necessary as edema decreases. Splinting is continued for approximately 4 weeks.

REHABILITATION PROGRESSION

During time of immobilization, ROM to noninvolved joints is maintained by active and passive exercises. At approximately 4 weeks the splint is discontinued and ROM to MCP joints is begun. Buddy taping may be done to encourage ROM. A patient may resume normal activity when there is a sign of healing fracture, it feels stable, and there is no pain with fracture or movement. Between 4 and 6 weeks, gentle resistance may be performed, with vigorous activities at about 6 weeks.

DeQuervain's Tenosynovitis and Tendinitis

PATHOMECHANICS

Tendinitis, most simply put, is inflammation of a tendon. It may occur on the dorsal wrist, volar wrist, or thumb. Symptoms are pain along muscle, or pain with resisted motions, or swelling. It is frequently caused by overuse. Injections may be helpful for relief of symptoms and to help confirm diagnosis.

DeQuervain's tenosynovitis is an inflammation in the first dorsal compartment; abductor pollicus longus (APL) and extensor pollicus brevis (EPB) are affected.[1] The third dorsal compartment is usually not affected, and as such the IP joint of the thumb does not need to be included in any splint. It can be aggravated by excessive wrist radial and ulnar deviation, flexion and adduction of the thumb, or adduction of the thumb.[24] Finklestein's test,[15] passive thumb flexion into the palm with passive wrist ulnar deviation, will be positive for pain (Fig. 28-12). Always compare to the noninjured side as this test can be uncomfortable normally.

INJURY MECHANISM

Tendinitis is usually caused by overuse. It may also be caused by weakness, poor body mechanics, or abnormal postures. DeQuervain's tenosynovitis can be caused by repeated wrist radial and ulnar deviation. Less frequent causes include a direct blow to the radial styloid, acute strain as in lifting, or a ganglion in the first dorsal compartment.[24]

REHABILITATION CONCERNS

Initial treatment is anti-inflammatory medication and rest from aggravating activities. Modalities for edema reduction and pain control—such as ultrasound, iontophoresis, or ice—may be effective. Analysis of activity should be done to see if poor mechanics are aggravating symptoms.

Splinting for wrist tendinitis includes the wrist only (Fig. 28-1). Splinting for DeQuervain's tenosynovitis includes

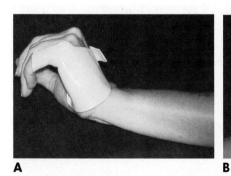
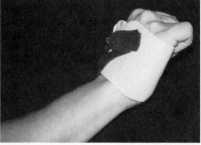
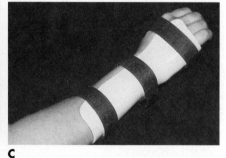

A   B   C

FIGURE 28-11

A boxer's fracture splint protects the ring and small finger proximal phalanxes and metacarpals, including the MCP joint. The splint may be modified for a different neck fracture (immobilizing the involved MCP joint), metacarpal shaft fracture (may need only the metacarpal in the splint leaving the wrist and MCP joints free), or metacarpal base fracture (may need to include the wrist, usually leave the MCP joints free).

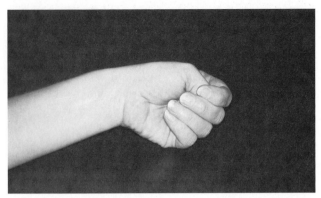

FIGURE   28-12

Finklestein's test will be positive for pain in DeQuervain's tenosynovitis. Passive flexion of the thumb with wrist ulnar deviation is the provocative position. Always compare to the noninvolved side, as this test can be uncomfortable normally.

the thumb MCP and CMC joints, and wrist, usually in a radial gutter fashion (Fig. 28-13). Splinting is usually full time except for hygiene for the first 2 to 3 weeks; then if symptoms are subsiding, slowly decrease the wearing time while increasing activity. If pain is persistent, continue with splinting.

REHABILITATION PROGRESSIONS

Stretching of affected areas in a pain-free range (see Exercises 28-11 and 28-12) three times per day should begin immediately with rest (splinting) and anti-inflammatory medication. Once pain has decreased, strengthening of grip and wrist musculature may begin. If strengthening is begun too early, symptoms will be reexacerbated. If tendinitis is a result of muscle imbalance, the weak muscle groups must be strengthened. If symptoms do not subside, and injections are helpful but do not cure the symptoms, a release of the first dorsal compartment may need to be performed.

Pain and strength are limiting factors for return to normal activity. Patients should have pain-free ROM in the affected part. Strength should be significant to prevent reinjury. If a release is performed, the patient can resume normal activities when comfortable, as early as 10 days postsurgery. Strength should be sufficient to prevent reinjury, aggravating forces should have been addressed, and support may be needed initially.

Ulnar Collateral Ligament Sprian (Gamekeeper's Thumb)

PATHOMECHANICS

The ulnar collateral ligament (UCL) injury to the MCP joint of the thumb is the most common ligament injury.[36,39,50] The injury can be classified as grade I or II, in which the majority of the ligament remains intact. Grade III is a complete disruption of the UCL and surgical repair is recommended. It is most often the distal attachment of the ligament where the rupture occurs (Fig. 28-14).[20,30]

The patient will complain of pain or tenderness on the ulnar side of the MCP joint. X rays should be taken to rule out fracture. Following X rays, the MCP joint stability should be evaluated at full extension and at 30 degrees of flexion. These two positions will test the accessory collateral ligament and the proper collateral ligament, respectively. Angulation greater than 35 degrees, or 15 degrees greater than the noninjured side, indicates instability and surgery is recommended.[20]

If the ligament is completely torn, one must also worry about a Stener lesion. This is where the torn UCL protrudes beneath the adductor aponeurosis. This places the aponeurosis between the ligament and its insertion. If this occurs, reattachment will not occur and surgery is needed.[43]

A more appropriate term for this injury in a patient would be skier's thumb. Initially, when Campbell described the gamekeeper's injury, it was from chronic repeated stress on the

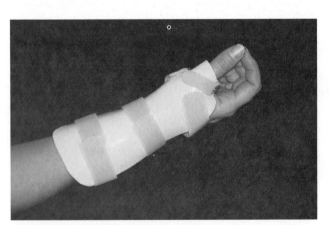

FIGURE   28-13

A DeQuervain's tenosynovitis splint is a radial gutter thumb splint. It supports the wrist and thumb CMC and MCP joints. It is used to rest the thumb and wrist.

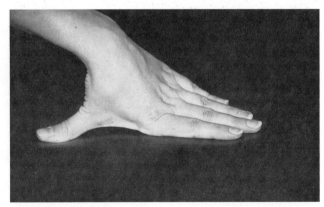

FIGURE   28-14

The ulnar collateral ligament provides support for the ulnar MCP joint. A fall on an abducted thumb may cause injury or rupture.

UCL.[8] It was not an acute injury as it most commonly is in sports.

INJURY MECHANISM

UCL injuries occur when a torsional load is applied to the thumb.[7] It frequently occurs in pole sports (e.g., skiing) where the thumb is abducted to hold the pole (or stick in other sports) and the patient falls and tries to catch himself or herself on an outstretched hand, landing on an abducted thumb.[30,36,50] Defensive backs in football may sustain this injury while abducting the thumb before making a tackle.[30]

REHABILITATION CONCERNS

Early diagnosis and treatment are important. An unstable thumb or Stener lesion, if not treated, will become chronically and painfully unstable with weak pinch and arthritis as sequelae.[20]

Treatment for incomplete (grade I or II) tears is immobilization in a thumb spica cast (see Fig. 28-4) for 3 weeks, with additional protective splinting for 2 weeks (Fig. 28-15). AROM to flexion and extension may be performed following the first 3 weeks.

Treatment for complete (grade III, unstable MCP joint) should be surgical repair. Late reconstruction is not as successful as early surgery, so early operative treatment is recommended.[30] Postoperatively, a thumb spica cast or splint is worn for 3 weeks, with an additional 2 weeks of splinting except for exercise sessions of active flexion and extension.

Concerns during the initial 5 to 6 weeks postinjury include protective immobilization, controlling edema, and maintaining motion in all noninvolved joints. Additional concern is, once movement is begun, to not place radial stress on the thumb to stretch the UCL.

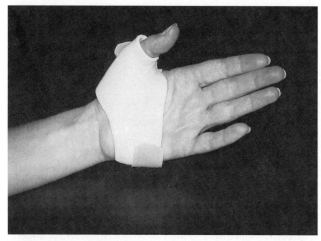

FIGURE 28-15

A gamekeeper's splint may also be called a hand-based thumb spica splint. It always includes the thumb MCP joint and may include the CMC or IP joint depending on the injury or sport.

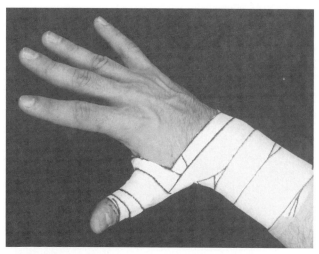

FIGURE 28-16

Thumb spica taping may be used when additional support is needed to the wrist and thumb. Tendinitis, gamekeepers injuries, or healed fractures are some indications.

REHABILITATION PROGRESSION

After protective splinting is discontinued, exercises are upgraded from AROM of flexion and extension to active assistive and passive exercises. Care should be taken not to apply abduction stress to the MCP joint during the first 2 to 6 weeks following immobilization. Putty exercises for strength may be performed at approximately 8 weeks postinjury. When measuring thumb ROM, always compare to the noninjured side. There is a large amount of variation in MCP and IP ROM from person to person.

For nonoperative treatment, a cast or splint (Fig. 28-16) to prevent reinjury from extension and abduction should be fabricated by a hand therapist to provide protection and should be continued for 4 to 8 weeks until pain and swelling subside and the patient has complete pain-free ROM (approximately 5 to 6 weeks).[30] If surgical repair is performed, the patient will need a minimum of 2 weeks for the incision to heal and 4 to 6 weeks will usually be necessary for rehabilitation.[36]

Finger Joint Dislocations

PATHOMECHANICS

Dislocation of the MCP joint is very infrequent. The force is dissipated by the joint mobility.[49] These injuries can be a simple dorsal subluxation, in which the proximal phalanx may rotate on the metacarpal head and lock the joint in 60 degrees of hyperextension; or an irreducible dorsal dislocation, where the volar plate is interposed dorsal to the metacarpal head and prevents reduction. When simple, after reduction some physicians splint the MCP joints in 50 degrees of flexion for 7–10 days[49];

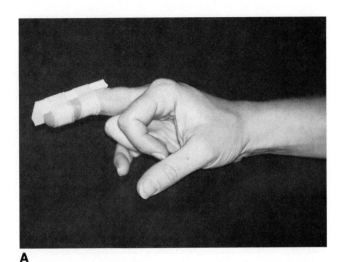

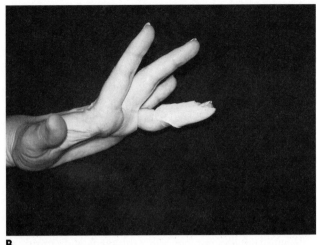

A   B

FIGURE 28-17

A mallet finger splint must hold the DIP in neutral to slight hyperextension. It may be
dorsally based, volarly based, or circumferential. A dorsal **(A)** splint, made from
Alumafoam, or **(B)** a stack-type splint are usually preferred as they rarely impede PIP
motxion.

others buddy tape and allow full motion immediately. If the
fracture is irreducible, it must be openly reduced with the volar
plate retracted. The MCP joints are then splinted at 50 degrees
or greater of flexion.

Dislocation of the PIP joint volarly is very rare and is usually a grade III irreducible fracture. It requires open reduction.
Because it is very complex and rare in patients, it will not be
covered in depth in this chapter.

Dorsal dislocations are much more common in sports.
The patient may not even bring the injury to the attention of
the therapist; rather, they just pull the finger back in place independently. If a finger PIP is dorsally dislocated, immediate
reduction (usually by physician) is preferred. X rays should
be taken to be sure there is no fracture. If there is no fracture, and the PIP joint is reduced and stable, the finger should
be wrapped in Coban for edema control and buddy taped to
the adjacent finger. ROM is begun immediately (see Exercises
28-14 to 28-17). These injuries do not need to be splinted; do
not overtreat.

DIP joint dislocations are more rare than PIP dislocations.[13] Dorsal dislocations occur more frequently than
volar. If the injury is closed, it is usually reducible. X rays
should be taken to rule out fracture. If the joint is reduced and
there is no fracture, splint the DIP only in neutral for 1 to
2 weeks (Fig. 28-17). If the DIP dislocation is open (and it
frequently is) or is irreducible, it needs to be surgically
addressed.[49]

INJURY MECHANISM

The mechanism for all finger dislocations is a hyperextension
force or a compressive load force.[7]

REHABILITATION CONCERNS

Of initial concern is ruling out a fracture and relocating the injured joint. If the joint is not reducible, appropriate surgical intervention is needed. Once reduced, Coban (Fig. 28-18) should
be applied to decrease edema. Protective splinting or buddy taping is also applied. In PIP dorsal dislocations without fracture,
immediate ROM is important to decrease stiffness. Complications of finger dislocations include pain, swelling, stiffness, and
loss of reduction.

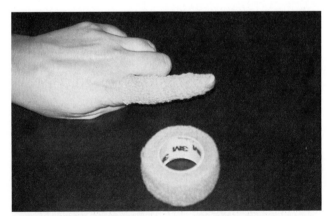

FIGURE 28-18

Coban is similar to Ace wrap in that it is elastic. It sticks
to itself, so there is no need for clips. It comes in varying
widths from 1 to 3 inches. One inch is perfect for fingers.
Start wrapping from distal to proximal, pulling slightly
but still leaving some wrinkles. Check circulation
following application. Coban is perfect to help prevent
swelling in finger injuries, especially PIP dislocations,
immediately following injury.

REHABILITATION PROGRESSIONS

Simple dorsal subluxation of the MCP joints is reduced and splinted in 50 degrees of flexion for 7 to 10 days. Following splinting, AROM is begun. Because the joints are immobilized in flexion, the collateral ligaments remain taut and full MCP flexion should be maintained. Extension is not lost at the MCP joints with this injury. Progression is full ROM, to gentle strengthening, to more aggressive strengthening.

If the MCP joint dislocation is irreducible, it will require open reduction. Pins may be placed holding MCP joints in flexion. If not, the hand needs to be splinted with MCP joints in flexion. Once motion is allowed, active flexion and extension are initiated. Stiffness can be a problem, as can tendon adherence in scar. Rehabilitation may be difficult and require consultation with a hand therapist for splinting to regain motion. ROM is progressed to ADLs, strengthening, and functional return to activities.

PIP dislocations without fractures, once reduced, need to be wrapped in Coban for edema control (Fig. 28-18) and started on early motion. Exercises include composite flexion and extension, and blocked PIP and DIP flexion exercises (see Exercises 28-14 to 28-16). Buddy taping is often helpful to encourage ROM and provide protection. This is frequently enough to maintain motion and strength. If stiffness does occur, a referral to a hand therapist may be necessary for dynamic splinting or aggressive strength and motion program.

If the DIP is dislocated, closed, and easily reduced, it should be splinted in neutral to slight flexion for 1 to 2 weeks. AROM begins at 2 to 3 weeks, with protective splinting continued between exercise sessions for 4 to 6 weeks.[49] At that time putty for strengthening (see Exercise 28-7) and blocked DIP exercises (see Exercise 28-16) may begin.

Open or irreducible fractures require surgical wound care with debridement to prevent infection. These injuries are then treated like mallet fingers and progressed accordingly.[49]

For all finger joint dislocations, the length of time for rehabilitation is dependent upon the complexity of the dislocation and whether a fracture has occurred. If the MCP joints have a simple dislocation and are easily reduced, and remain reduced, the affected finger may be buddy taped, Coban wrapped for edema control, and protective splinted for pain control if necessary, with return to activity immediately or within the first few days after injury. If it is a complex dislocation and surgery is necessary, the patient will be unable to use the hand for a minimum of 2 to 3 weeks.

For PIP joint dorsal dislocations without fracture, once the joint is reduced and stable, the finger should be Coban wrapped and buddy taped. A dorsal Alumafoam splint is optional for pain control. The patient may resume normal activity immediately.

For DIP joint dislocations that are easily reduced, the patient may return immediately with Coban and splint. If open or irreducible, the patient can usually return to normal activities once sutures are removed after surgery, at about 10 days, with protective splinting. The criteria for the DIP joint is very similar to the mallet finger.

Flexor Digitorum Profundus Avulsion (Jersey Finger)

PATHOMECHANICS

Jersey finger is a rupture of the flexor digitorum profundus (FDP) tendon from its insertion on the distal phalanx. It most frequently occurs in the ring finger. It may be avulsed with or without bone. If avulsed with bone, depending on size of fragment, the tendon will usually not retract back into the palm, as it gets "caught" on the pulley system of the finger. If no bone, or only very small fleck of bone is avulsed, the tendon will retract back into the palm. This is the most common.[50] Each time the patient tries to flex the finger, the muscle contracts but the insertion is not attached. This brings the insertion closer to its origin.

The way to isolate the FDP to evaluate function and integrity is to hold the MCP and PIP joints of affected finger in full extension, and then have the patient attempt to flex the DIP joint. If it flexes, it is intact. If not, it is ruptured (see Exercise 28-16).

If the tendon is ruptured there are two options. The first is to do nothing. If the tendon is not repaired, the patient will be unable to flex the DIP joint, may have decreased grip strength, and may have tenderness at the site of tendon retraction, but functionally should not have difficulty.[50] The second option is to have the tendon surgically repaired. If repaired, the patient should be informed that this is a labor-intensive operation and rehabilitation, there is a risk of scarring with poor tendon glide, and there is a risk of tendon rupture. The patient will not have full activity level for approximately 12 weeks after surgery. The repair should be done within 10 days of injury for the best results.

INJURY MECHANISM

Forceful hyperextension of the fingers while tightly gripping into flexion is the injury mechanism (Fig. 28-19).[50]

REHABILITATION CONCERNS

This can be a very difficult injury to treat if surgically repaired. The surgery should be performed by an experienced hand surgeon,[11] with rehabilitation by an experienced hand therapist. Close communication between the hand surgeon and the hand therapist is a must. All protocols are guidelines and as such may need to be altered if complications such as infection, poor tendon glide, or excellent tendon glide occur. With this injury, unlike most others, the better a person is doing (full active tendon glide), the more they are held back and protected. Good tendon glide is indicative of less scar, which means there is less scar holding the repaired tendon together, and thus less tensile strength and increased chance of rupture. If a tendon is ruptured, it must be repaired again and the prognosis is poorer.

Proper patient education is a must. Instruction in what to expect, reasons for specific exercises, and consequences must be conveyed.

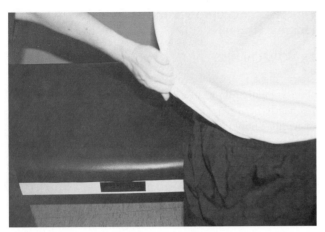

FIGURE 28-19

A jersey finger (FDP avulsion) injury is named for the injury mechanism—forced hyperextension with finger flexion—as in trying to grab a shirt during a tackle in the sport of football. The position of the DIP joint after injury will be extension or hyperextension.

REHABILITATION PROGRESSIONS

The following are guidelines. They are not all inclusive, nor are they an indication that anyone can treat this injury. For more specific information on the protocol, readers are encouraged to read and review the Evans article on zone I flexor tendon rehabilitation.[14]

Between 2 and 5 days postoperative the bulky dressing should be removed with a dorsal splint fabricated to hold the wrist in neutral, MCP joints in 30 degrees of flexion, and IP joints with full extension with the hood extending to the fingertips for protection (Fig. 28-20). The affected DIP joint is splinted at 45 degrees of flexion with a second dorsal splint that extends from the PIP joint to the fingertip, held on with tape at the middle phalanx only. Exercises for the first three weeks are: (1) passive DIP flexion; (2) full composite passive flexion, then extend MCP joints passively to a modified hook position; (3) hyperflexion of MCP joints with active extension of PIP joints to 0 degrees; and (4) strap or hold noninvolved fingers to the top of the splint. Position PIP joint in flexion passively, then actively hold the joint in flexion (see Exercise 28-18). All exercises should be done with the splint on, at a frequency of 10 repetitions every waking hour. The patients should not use their injured hand for anything, extend the wrist or fingers with the splint off, or actively flex the fingers. All of the preceding could cause tendon rupture. In addition, during the first weeks, Coban (see Fig. 28-18) can be used for edema control and scar control. Scar massage may be performed in the splint. The dressing may be changed at home, but the DIP splint should remain in place at all times for 3 weeks.

Between 3 and 4 weeks postrepair, the digital splint is discontinued, passive fist and hold is begun for composite flexion, and dorsal protective splinting is continued. Between 4 and 6 weeks, active hook fist and active composite fisting is begun,

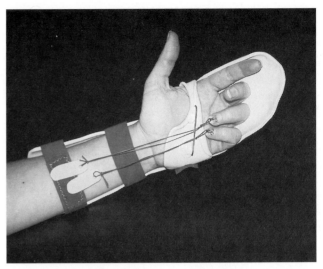

FIGURE 28-20

Flexor tendon splint. Usually applied within 5 days postoperative, the splint is dorsally based, and includes wrist in neutral to slight flexion, MCP joint flexion, and IP joint extension. Depending on location of injury, the amount of flexion may be increased or decreased, and rubberband traction may be applied from fingernails to forearm strap.

wrist ROM is begun, and gentle isolated profundus exercises are initiated (see Exercises 28-14 to 28-16). The splint may be discontinued if poor tendon glide is present.

At 6 to 8 weeks the splint is discontinued, ADLs may be done with the injured hand, and tendon gliding exercises and blocked DIP exercises are continued. Light resistive exercises (putty; see Exercise 28-7) may be initiated. Graded resistive exercises are begun if poor tendon glide. Be very careful during this time—it is a prime time for tendon ruptures. Patients are excited to be out of their splints and may overdo. Graded resistive exercises and dynamic splinting if necessary are initiated at 8 to 10 weeks.

Between 10 and 12 weeks, strengthening is begun. By 12 weeks patients should be back with full tendon glide and good tendon strength to return to all normal activities. Activities and sports in which a sudden surprise force may pull on flexed fingers—such as rock climbing, windsurfing, water skiing, or dog walking—should not be done until 14 to 16 weeks postoperative.

Mallet Finger

PATHOMECHANICS

A mallet finger is the avulsion of the terminal extensor tendon, which is responsible for extension of the DIP joint.[37] It may occur with or without fracture of bone. If there is a large fracture fragment where the fracture fragment is displaced greater than 2 mm, or the DIP joint has volar subluxation on X ray, the injury will require ORIF.

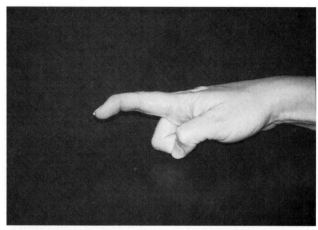

FIGURE 28-21

A mallet finger deformity with DIP flexion. There may or may not be redness dorsally.

There is no other mechanism for extending the DIP joint. Presenting complaint is inability to extend the DIP joint (Fig. 28-21).

Treatment is splinting the DIP joint in neutral to slight hyperextension (Fig. 28-17) for 6 to 8 weeks with no flexion of the DIP joint.[12,42] If the DIP joint is flexed even once during that period, the 6 weeks starts again at that time.

INJURY MECHANISM

Injury mechanism is forced flexion of the DIP joint while it is held in full extension.[49] It frequently happens when the end of the finger is struck by a ball or some other object while fully extended.

REHABILITATION CONCERNS

Rehabilitation of the mallet finger is minimal. A splint may be custom made or prefabricated, such as a stack splint or Alumafoam. It should hold the DIP joint in neutral to slight hyperextension. Skin integrity needs to be monitored with splint being modified or redesigned if breakdown occurs. ROM of noninvolved fingers and joints should be maintained. PIP flexion with the DIP splinted will not put tension on the injury and should be encouraged.

REHABILITATION PROGRESSIONS

Once the tendon is healed, approximately 6 to 8 weeks, splinting may be discontinued. If an extensor lag is present, splinting may be continued longer. Night splinting is often continued for 2 weeks after full-time splinting is discontinued. AROM to DIP joint is started following splint removal. No attempts to passively flex the finger to regain ROM should be attempted for 4 weeks after splinting is discontinued. Blocked DIP flexion exercises are most important. Full ROM is usually gained through blocked exercises (see Exercise 28-16) and regular functional hand use. Athletes should wear a finger splint for no less than 8 weeks.

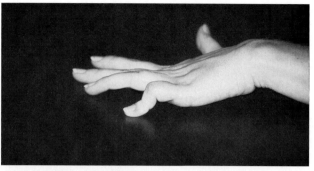

FIGURE 28-22

A boutonnière deformity may start as a PIP contracture. It will in time cause hyperextension of the DIP joint.

Boutonnière Deformity

PATHOMECHANICS

The posture of a finger with a boutonnière deformity is PIP joint flexion and DIP joint hyperextension (Fig. 28-22). It is caused by interruption of the central slip. Normally the central slip will initiate extension of flexed PIP joints. The lateral bands cannot initiate PIP joint extension but can maintain extension if passively positioned because they are dorsal to the axis of motion. When the central slip is disrupted, the extensor muscle displaces proximally and shifts the lateral bands volarly. The FDS is unopposed without an intact central slip and will flex the PIP joint. As the length of time postinjury increases, the lateral bands displace volarly and may become fixed to the joint capsule or collateral ligament. This then makes passive correction very difficult. The DIP joint hyperextends because all the force to extend the PIP is transmitted to the DIP joint.[37]

Once a fixed deformity is present it is much more difficult to treat; however, many patients do not seek immediate medical attention, feeling that the finger was "jammed" and would be fine in several days or weeks.

Treatment for the acute injury is uninterrupted splinting of the PIP joint in full extension for 6 weeks (Fig. 28-23). The DIP joint is left free with motion encouraged. This will synergistically relax the extrinsic and intrinsic extensor tendon muscles and also exercises the oblique retinacular ligament.[37]

Following 6 weeks of immobilization, gentle careful flexion of the PIP joint is begun. Continue splinting 2 to 4 weeks when not exercising. When full PIP joint extension can be maintained throughout the day, then night splinting only is appropriate. Length of treatment and splinting may be several months.

INJURY MECHANISM

Injury occurs when the extended finger is forcibly flexed, such as when being hit by a ball or as a result of a fall with striking the finger on another object.[50]

REHABILITATION CONCERNS

Of primary concern is early and proper diagnosis and treatment. X rays should be taken to rule out fracture or PIP joint

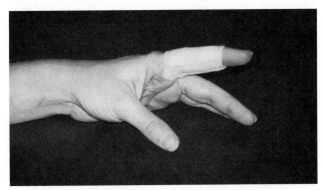

FIGURE   28-23

A boutonnière splint needs to immobilize the PIP joint in full extension, leaving the MCP and DIP joints free. The author makes these in two pieces, overlapping slightly, holding on with tape.

dislocation. It is also very important to splint the PIP in full extension. If edema is present when initially splinted, as edema decreases the splint gets loose and full extension is no longer achieved. Passive flexion should not be performed to the PIP joint following removal of the splint. Blocked PIP ROM exercises are appropriate to isolate flexion (see Exercise 28-15). If diagnosis is made late and there is a fixed PIP flexion contracture, serial casting may be necessary to restore extension. Following return of full extension, the finger is then splinted for 8 weeks. One other factor to keep in mind is that initially a central slip injury does not present as a boutonnière, but rather a PIP flexor contracture. DIP hyperextension comes later.

REHABILITATION PROGRESSIONS

Progression is increasing ROM following splint removal. Strengthening of grip may also be performed if needed at 10 to 12 weeks following acute injury (approximately 4 weeks following splinting).

The patient may return to normal activity when the finger is comfortable with the affected finger splinted at all times in full extension. The finger splint should be worn for no less than 8 weeks.

EXERCISES

REHABILITATION TECHNIQUES

Strengthening Techniques

OPEN-KINETIC CHAIN STRENGTHENING EXERCISES

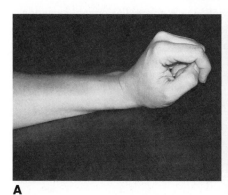 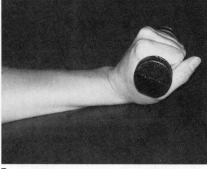 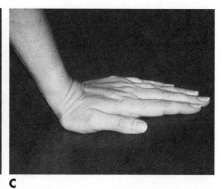

A   B   C

E X E R C I S E   2 8 - 1

A, Wrist extension should be done in pronation to work against gravity. This exercise encourages strength and motion of the common wrist extensor tendons (ECRL, ECRB, ECU). MCP flexion should be maintained to eliminate EDC contribution and isolate wrist musculature. **B,** This position can be graded by adding weights. **C,** Passive wrist extension helps regain motion in the wrist that then needs to be maintained actively.

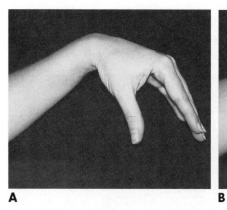  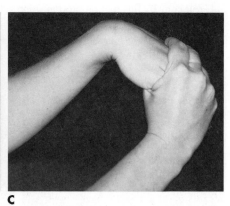

A   B   C

E X E R C I S E   2 8 - 2

A, Wrist flexion actively works on FCR and FCU. It may be done in pronation as gravity assist or in supination with gravity. **B,** Position may be graded by adding weights. **C,** Passive wrist flexion should be done first by pulling out or distracting the wrist, and then flexing.

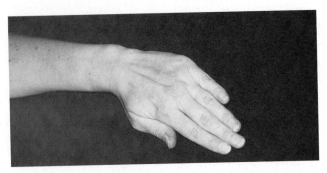

EXERCISE   28 - 3

Wrist radial deviation with neutral flexion and extension will exercise the FCR and ECRL. It may be performed with palm flat on a table, or with arm in neutral over the edge of a table. It may be graded to include weights.

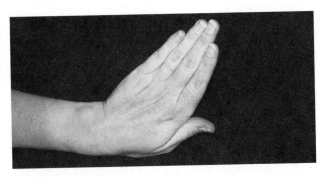

EXERCISE   28 - 4

Wrist ulnar deviation with neutral flexion and extension will exercise the ECU and FCU. It may be performed in neutral rotation with gravity assisted, or with palm on the table. It is difficult to position for against gravity. It can be graded to include weights.

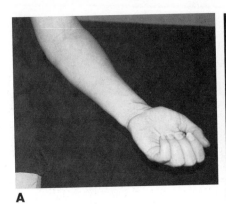

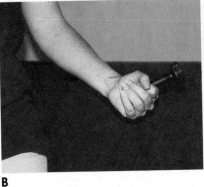

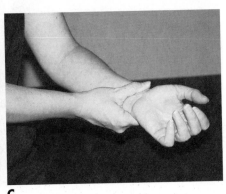

A   B   C

EXERCISE   28 - 5

A, Active supination exercises the supinator and the biceps. It should be done with elbow at 90 degrees of flexion with the humerus by the side. This eliminates shoulder rotation. **B,** This can be graded using a hammer or weights for strengthening. The hammer with lever action being heavier on one end will also assist with passive motion. **C,** Passive stretching should be done in the same position, with force applied proximal to the wrist, applying pressure over the radius rather than torquing the wrist.

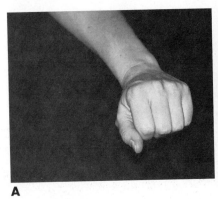

A   B   C

EXERCISE   28 - 6

A, Active pronation exercises the pronator. It should be done with elbow flexed to 90 degrees with the humerus by the side. This eliminates shoulder rotation. **B,** This can be done with a hammer or weights for strengthening. **C,** Passive stretching should be done in the same position with the pressure applied proximal to the wrist.

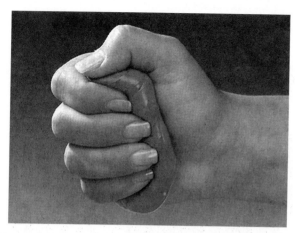

Putty exercises are for grip strengthening and wrist stabilization. It tends to be more effective than a ball because it gives resistance throughout the entire range of motion. Putty can be used for gross grasp, pinch, or extension.

CLOSED-KINETIC CHAIN STRENGTHENING EXERCISES

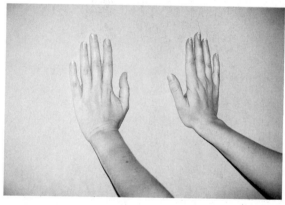

EXERCISE 28-8

Wall push-ups encourage wrist motion and general upper body strengthening. They also encourage weight bearing and closed-chain activities.

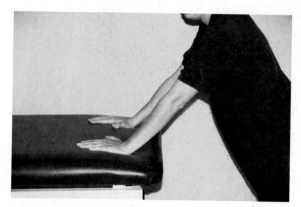

EXERCISE 28-9

Push-ups can be progressed from the wall to a table or countertop. This encourages increased weight but not full weight of floor push-ups.

EXERCISE 28-10

Push-ups on the floor requires full or close to full wrist motion. It encourages full upper body weight bearing on the wrist.

STRETCHING AND RANGE-OF-MOTION EXERCISES

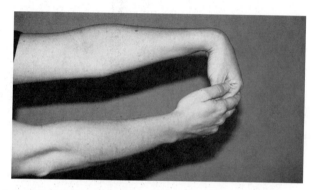

EXERCISE 28-11

Stretching wrist extensor musculature is appropriate when tendinitis is present. The greatest stretch will occur with the elbow at full extension and the arm at shoulder height. If this stretch is too great, increase elbow flexion to a comfortable stretch point. Do not bounce at the end of a stretch.

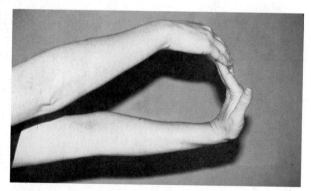

EXERCISE 28-12

Stretching wrist flexor musculature is appropriate with flexor tendinitis. Again, the largest stretch will occur with full elbow extension. Modify elbow flexion as necessary. Stretching should not be painful.

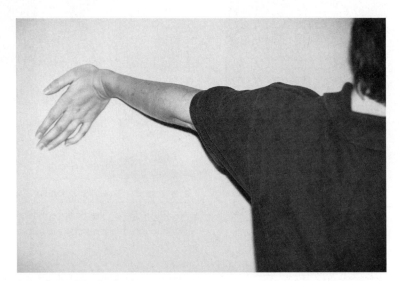

E X E R C I S E   2 8 - 1 3

Butler describes median nerve gliding exercises to be done in the clinic. It is also
important to teach patients to stretch on their own. This is a median nerve glide that
patients can perform on their own against a wall. Start with arm at shoulder height,
elbow extended, and wrist extension with palm against the wall. Rotate shoulder
externally. Turn away from the wall so as to be perpendicular. The last step is to add
lateral neck flexion. Stop at any point along this progression where numbness or
burning is felt along the arm.

TENDON-MOBILIZATION EXERCISES

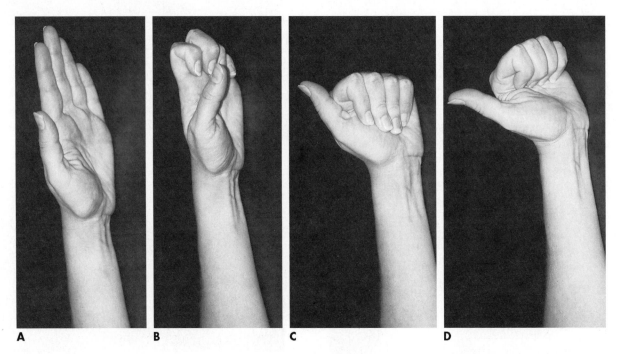

E X E R C I S E   2 8 - 1 4

Tendon gliding exercises allow for maximum gliding of the FDS and FDP independent of
each other. **A,** Start with full composite finger extension. **B,** Move to hook fisting, which
gives the maximum glide of the FDP. **C,** Return to extension, move to long fisting with
MCP and PIP flexion and DIP extension for maximum FDS glide. **D,** Return to extension,
and then to composite flexion with full fisting.

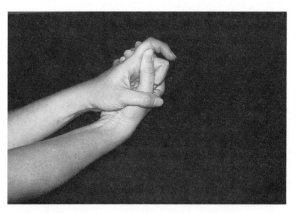

EXERCISE 28-15

Blocked PIP exercises encourage FDS pull-through. Stabilizing the proximal phalanx then allows the flexion force to act at the PIP joint. It is most often used with tendon injuries or finger fractures.

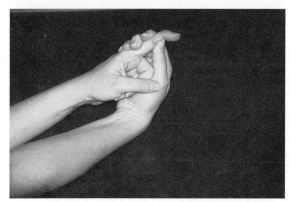

EXERCISE 28-16

Blocked DIP exercises encourage FDP pull-through. Stabilizing the middle phalanx allows the flexion force to concentrate at the DIP joint. These are most often done with flexor tendon injuries, extensor tendon injuries, or finger fractures.

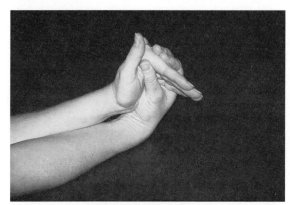

EXERCISE 28-17

MCP flexion with IP extension exercises the intrinsic muscles of the hand. It may help with edema control and muscle pumping. This is most often done with distal radius fractures or MCP joint injuries. Performing IP extension with the MCP joints blocked in flexion concentrates the extension force at the IP joints. This is beneficial during IP joint injuries or tendon injuries.

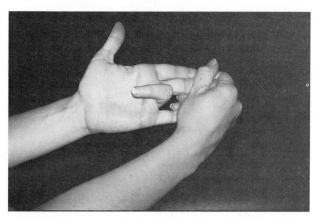

EXERCISE 28-18

Isolated superficialis exercises are done for tendon gliding of the FDS. Noninvolved fingers should be help in full extension, allowing only the involved finger to flex. This is most helpful during flexor tendon lacerations.

JOINT MOBILIZATIONS

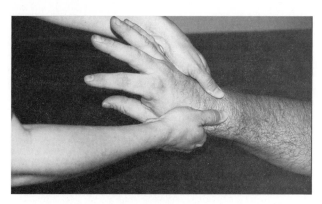

EXERCISE 28-19

Distal anterior/posterior radial glides. Distal anterior/posterior radial glides are done with one hand stabilizing the ulna and the other gliding the radius. These glides increase pronation.

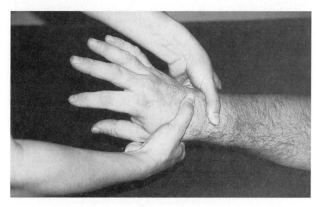

EXERCISE 28-20

Radiocarpal joint anterior glides. Radiocarpal joint anterior glides increase wrist extension.

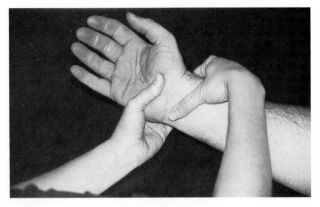

E X E R C I S E   2 8 - 2 1

Radiocarpal joint posterior glides. Radiocarpal joint posterior glides increase wrist flexion.

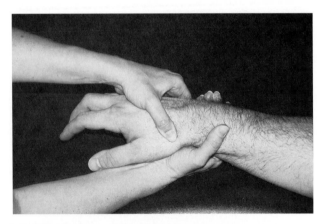

E X E R C I S E   2 8 - 2 2

Radiocarpal joint ulnar glides. Radiocarpal joint ulnar glides increase radial deviation.

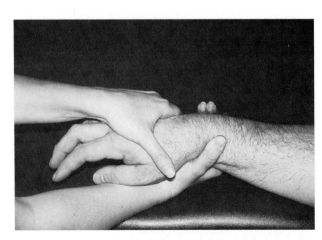

E X E R C I S E   2 8 - 2 3

Radiocarpal joint radial glides. Radiocarpal joint radial glides increase ulnar deviation.

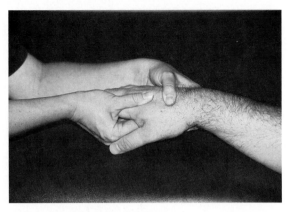

E X E R C I S E   2 8 - 2 4

Carpometacarpal joint anterior/posterior glides. Carpometacarpal joint anterior/posterior glides increase mobility of the hand.

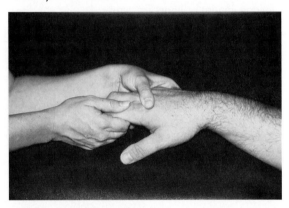

E X E R C I S E   2 8 - 2 5

Metacarpophalangeal joint anterior/posterior glides. In metacarpophalangeal joint anterior or posterior glides, the proximal segment, in this case the metacarpal, is stabilized, and the distal segment is mobilized. Anterior glides increase flexion of the MP joint. Posterior glides increase extension.

EXERCISES FOR REESTABLISHING NEUROMUSCULAR CONTROL

E X E R C I S E   2 8 - 2 6

Push-ups on a ball allow for an unstable surface to encourage strengthening and upper extremity control. Overhead plyometric activities encourage endurance and strength of entire upper extremity.

EXERCISE 28-27

Prone over a large gym ball allows for weight bearing throughout the upper extremity, weight shifting, and balance activities.

SUMMARY

- Distraction of the wrist while performing passive range of motion after fracture may help to increase motion and decrease pain during stretching.
- Wrist sprains are a diagnosis of exclusion. All other pathology must be ruled out prior to return to sport or other heavy activity.
- Scaphoid fractures may not be seen on initial X ray. If suspected, but the X ray is negative, the patient should be treated as if a fracture is present with X rays repeated in 2 weeks to confirm diagnosis. Early proper immobilization is important in long-term outcome.
- Lunate dislocations are serious injuries that will require ORIF and possible lengthy rehabilitation.
- Hamate hook fractures are not seen on regular X ray views. A carpal tunnel view will confirm the diagnosis; then treat symptomatically.
- Carpal tunnel syndrome occurs due to repeated flexion of the wrist and is usually treated initially by rest, anti-inflammatories, and night splints.
- Ganglion cysts need only be treated if symptomatic. Multiple aspirations can be performed during the season with excision postseason if necessary. There are usually few rehabilitation needs.
- Boxer's fractures tend to heal without incident with full return of motion in 4 to 6 weeks. Splint immobilization should leave the PIP joint and wrist free to move.
- Tendinitis and DeQuervain's tenosynovitis should be immobilized for 2 to 3 weeks with gentle pain-free range of motion performed daily to maintain mobility. Increase activity and pain decreases.
- The goal in the treatment of ulnar collateral ligament injuries (gamekeeper's thumb) is stability of the MCP joint. Patients will be stiff following immobilization—do not passively push motion initially.

- Dislocations of the MCP joints are very rare and are often complicated. Dorsal PIP dislocations without fracture are common and need early range-of-motion and edema control. Splinting is not necessary unless the dislocation is unstable. DIP dislocations are frequently open and require surgery. They are treated like a mallet finger.
- Flexor tendon injuries are very labor-intensive significant injuries. Be sure an experienced hand surgeon and hand therapist are involved in the care, and be sure the patient is aware of what to expect.
- The mallet finger must be splinted in full extension uninterrupted for 6 to 8 weeks. If the DIP joint is flexed, even once, any healing is disrupted and the 6 to 8 weeks begins again.
- Early treatment of the boutonnière deformity is essential, as is proper splint position. The PIP joint should be fully extended with the DIP joint free.

The author wishes to thank Dr. Wallace Andrew of Raleigh Orthopaedic Clinic for his support, knowledge, and willingness to answer my countless questions.

REFERENCES

1. Baxter-Petralia P, Penney V. Cumulative trauma. In: Stanley BG, Tribuzi SM, eds. *Concepts in Hand Rehabilitation.* Philadelphia, Davis, 1992.
2. Bishop AT, Beckenbaugh RD. *Fracture of the Hamate Hook. J. Hand Surg Am* 13:135–139, 1988.
3. Bohler L. *The Treatment of Fractures,* 4th ed. Baltimore, William Wood, 1942.
4. Bryan RS, Dobyns JH. Less commonly fractured carpal bones. *Clin Orthop Rel Res* 149:108–109, 1980.
5. Bush DC. Soft-tissue tumors of the hand. In: Hunter JM, Mackin EJ, Callahan AD, eds. *Rehabilitation of the Hand: Surgery and Therapy,* 4th ed. St. Louis, Mosby, 1995.
6. Butler DS. *Mobilisation of the Nervous System.* Melbourne, Churchill Livingstone, 1991.
7. Cahalan TD, Cooney WP. Biomechanics. In: Jobe FW, Pink MM, Glousman RE, et al, eds. *Operative Techniques in Upper Extremity Sports Injuries.* St. Louis, Mosby, 1996.
8. Campbell CS. Gamekeeper's thumb. *J Bone Joint Surg Br* 37:148–149, 1955.
9. Cooney WP. Sports injuries in the upper extremity. *Postgrad Med* 76:45–50, 1984.
10. Crosby EB, Linscheid RI. Rupture of the flexor profundus tendon of the ring finger secondary to ancient fracture of the hook of the hamate: Review of the literature and report of two cases. *J Bone Joint Surg Am* 56:1076–1078, 1974.
11. Culp RW, Taras JS. Primary care of flexor tendon injuries. In: Hunter JM, Mackin EJ, Callahan AD, eds. *Rehabilitation of the Hand: Surgery and Therapy,* 4th ed. St. Louis, Mosby, 1995.

12. Doyle JR. Extensor tendons—acute injuries. In: Green DP, ed. *Operative Hand Surgery,* 2nd ed. New York, Churchill Livingstone, 1988.

13. Dray GJ, Eaton RG. Dislocations and ligament injuries in the digits. In: Green DP, ed. *Operative Hand Surgery,* 3rd ed, vol. 1. New York, Churchill Livingstone, 1993.

14. Evans R. A study of the zone I flexor tendon injury and implications for treatment. *J Hand Ther* 3:133, 1990.

15. Finklestein H. Stenosing tendovaginitis at the radial styloid process. *J Bone Joint Surg* 12:509, 1930.

16. Frykman G. Fracture of the distal radius including sequelae—shoulder-hand-finger syndrome, disturbance in the distal radioulnar joint, and impairment of nerve function: A clinical and experimental study. *Acta Orthop Scand Suppl* 108:1, 1967.

17. Frykman GK, Kropp WE. Fractures and traumatic conditions of the wrist. In: Hunter JM, Mackin EJ, Callahan AD, eds. *Rehabilitation of the Hand: Surgery and Therapy,* 4th ed. St. Louis, Mosby, 1995.

18. Gartland JJ, Werley CW. Evaluation of healed Colles' fractures. *J Bone Joint Surg Br* 43:245, 1961.

19. Hunter JM, Davlin LB, Fedus LM. Major neuropathies of the upper extremity: The median nerve. In: Hunter JM, Mackin EJ, Callahan, AD, eds. *Rehabilitation of the Hand: Surgery and Therapy,* 4th ed. St. Louis, Mosby, 1995.

20. Husband JB, McPherson SA. Bony skier's thumb injuries. *Clin Orthop Rel Res* 327:79–84, 1996.

21. Jupiter JB, Belsky MR. Fractures and dislocations of the hand. In: Browner BD, Jupiter JB, Levine AM, Trafton PG, eds. *Skeletal Trauma.* Philadelphia, Saunders, 1992.

22. Kaplan EM. *Joints and Ligaments in Functional and Surgical Anatomy of the Hand.* Philadelphia, Lippincott, 1965.

23. Kauer JM. Functional anatomy of the wrist. *Clin Orthop Rel Res* 149:9–20, 1980.

24. Kirkpatrick WH, Lisser S. Soft-tissue conditions: Trigger fingers and DeQuervain's disease. In: Hunter JM, Mackin EJ, Callahan AD, eds. *Rehabilitation of the Hand: Surgery and Therapy,* 4th ed. St. Louis, Mosby, 1995.

25. Korman J, Pearl R, Hentz VR. Efficacy of immobilization following aspiration of carpal and digital ganglion. *J Hand Surg* 17; 1097, 1992.

26. Kozin SH, Wood MB. Early soft tissue complications after fractures of the distal part of the radius. *J Bone Joint Surg Am* 75:144, 1993.

27. London PS. The broken scaphoid bones: The case against pessimism. *J Bone Joint Surg Br* 42:237, 1961.

28. Mazet R, Hohl M. Fractures of the carpal navicular: Analysis of 91 cases and review of the literature. *J Bone Joint Surg Am* 45:82, 1967.

29. McCue FC. The elbow, wrist and hand. In: Kulund D, ed. *The Injured Patient,* 2nd ed. Philadelphia, Lippincott, 1988.

30. McCue FC, Nelson WE. Ulnar collateral ligament injuries of the thumb. *Physician Sports Med* 21:67–80, 1993.

31. McCue FC, Bougher WN, Kulund DN, Gieck JH. Hand and wrist injuries in the patient. *Am J Sports Med* 7:275–286, 1979.

32. Meyer FN, Wilson RL. Management of nonarticular fractures of the hand. In: Hunter JM, Mackin EJ, Callahan AD, eds. *Rehabilitation of the Hand: Surgery and Therapy,* 4th ed., St. Louis, Mosby, 1995.

33. Mosher FJ. Peripheral nerve injuries and entrapments of the forearm and wrist. In: Pettrone FA, ed. *American Academy of Orthopaedic Surgeons Symposium on Upper Extremity Injuries in Patients.* St. Louis, Mosby, 1986.

34. Palmer AK, Dobyns JH, Linscheid RL. Management of post-traumatic instability of the wrist secondary to ligament rupture. *J Hand Surg* 3:507, 1978.

35. Pianka G, Hershman EB. Neurovascular injuries. In: Nicholas JA, Hershman EB, eds. *Upper Extremity in Sports Medicine.* St. Louis, Mosby, 1990.

36. Rettig AC. Current concepts in management of football injuries of the hand and wrist. *J Hand Ther* 4 (2):42–50, 1991.

37. Rosenthal EA. The extensor tendons: Anatomy and management. In: Hunter JM, Mackin EJ, Callahan AD, eds. *Rehabilitation of the Hand: Surgery and Therapy,* 4th ed. St. Louis, Mosby, 1995.

38. Sarrafian S, Melamed JL, Goshgarian GM. Study of wrist motion in flexion and extension. *Clin Orthop* 126:153, 1977.

39. Smith RJ. Posttraumatic instability of the metacarpophalangeal joint of the thumb. *J Bone Joint Surg* 59:14–21, 1977.

40. Stark HH, Jabe FW, Boyes JH, Ashworth CR. Fracture of the hook of the hamate in patients. *J Bone Joint Surg Am* 59:575–582, 1977.

41. Stark HH, Chow E, Zemel NP, Rickard TA, Ashworth CR. Fracture of the hook of the hamate. *J Bone Joint Surg Am* 71:1202–1207, 1989.

42. Stark HH, Bayer JH, Wilson JN. Mallet finger. *J Bone Joint Surg* 44:1061, 1962.

43. Stener B. Displacement of the ruptured ulnar collateral ligament of the metacarpophalangeal joint of the thumb. *J Bone Joint Surg Br* 44:869–879, 1962.

44. Vender MI. Degenerative changes in symptomatic scaphoid non-union. *J Hand Surg Am* 12:514, 1987.

45. Viegas SF, Patterson RM, Hillman GR, Peterson PD, Crossley M, Foster R. Simulated scaphoid proximal pole fracture. *J Hand Surg Am* 16:485–500, 1991.

46. Volz RG, Lieb M, Benjamin J. Biomechanics of the wrist. *Clin Orthop Rel Res* 149:112–117, 1980.

47. Watson HK, Rogers WD. Nonunion of the hook of the hamate, an argument for bone grafting the nonunion. *J Hand Surg Am* 14:486–490, 1989.

48. Weinstein SM, Herring SA. Nerve problems and compartment syndromes in the hand, wrist, and forearm. *Clin Sports Med* 11, 1992.

49. Wilson RL, Hazen J. Management of joint injuries and intraarticular fractures of the hand. In: Hunter JM, Mackin EJ, Callahan AD, eds. *Rehabilitation of the Hand: Surgery and Therapy,* 4th ed. St. Louis, Mosby, 1995.

50. Wright HH, Retting AC. Management of common sports injuries. In: Hunter JM, Mackin EJ, Callahan AD, eds. *Rehabilitation of the Hand: Surgery and Therapy,* 4th ed. St. Louis, Mosby, 1995.

51. Zemel NP. Anatomy and surgical approaches: Hand, wrist and forearm. In: Jobe FW, Pink MM, Glousman RE, eds. *Operative Techniques in Upper Extremity Sports Injuries.* St. Louis, Mosby, 1996.

52. Zemel NP. Fractures and ligament injuries of the wrist. In: Jobe FW, Pink MM, Glousman RE, eds. *Operative Techniques in Upper Extremity Sports Injuries.* St. Louis, Mosby, 1996.

53. Zubowicz VN, Ishii CH. Management of ganglion cysts by simple aspiration. *J Hand Surg* 12:618, 1987.

Rehabilitation of the Groin, Hip, and Thigh

Bernie DePalma

After completing this chapter, the student therapist should be able to do the following:

- Discuss the functional anatomy and biomechanics of the groin, hip, and thigh.
- Discuss injuries to the groin, hip, and thigh, and describe the biomechanical changes occurring during and after injury.
- Discuss and describe functional injury evaluation, using biomechanical changes, to the groin, hip, and thigh.
- Recognize abnormal gait patterns as they relate to specific groin, hip, and thigh injuries, and use this knowledge during the evaluation process and rehabilitation program.
- Demonstrate the various rehabilitation techniques used for specific groin, hip, and thigh injuries including open- and closed-kinetic chain strengthening exercises, stretching exercises, and plyometric, isokinetic, and PNF exercises.

This chapter describes functional rehabilitation programs that follow groin, hip, and thigh injuries. The therapist and patient, together, should develop the rehabilitation program with an emphasis on injury mechanism, the therapist's functional and biomechanical evaluation, and clinical findings. Each exercise program should be presented to the patient in terms of short-term goals. One objective for the therapist is to make the rehabilitation experience challenging for the patient to promote adherence to the rehabilitation program.

FUNCTIONAL ANATOMY AND BIOMECHANICS

The pelvis and hip are made up of the pelvic girdle and the articulation of the femoral head to the bony socket of the pelvic girdle, the acetabulum, forming a ball-in-socket joint.[14] This joint connects the lower extremity to the pelvic girdle.[6] The angle of inclination and angle of declination are used to describe the position of the femoral head and neck with respect to the shaft of the femur.[6] The frontal projection of the angle formed by the femoral shaft and neck is the angle of inclination. The angle of declination is sometimes referred to as the angle of anteversion.[6] This is the angle formed by the femoral neck down through the femur to the femoral condyles. Changes in

both these angles could cause changes in rotation of the femoral head within the acetabulum that predispose the patient to stress fractures and overuse hip injuries, as well as hip subluxation.

The pelvis itself moves in three directions: anteroposterior tilting, lateral tilting, and rotation. The iliopsoas muscle and other hip flexors, as well as extensors of the lumbar spine, perform anterior tilting in the sagittal plane and facilitates lumbar lordosis. The rectus abdominus, obliques, gluteus maximus, and hamstrings posteriorly tilt the pelvis and cause a decrease in lumbar lordosis.[6] During lateral tilting in the frontal plane, the hip joint acts as the center of rotation.[6] Hip abduction or adduction is a result of pelvic lateral tilting. The hip abductors control lateral tilting by contracting isometrically or eccentrically.[6] Pelvic rotation occurs in the transverse plane, again using the hip joint as the axis of rotation. The gluteal muscles, external rotators, adductors, pectineus, and iliopsoas all act together to perform this movement in the transverse plane.[6] These movements of the pelvis play an important role when analyzing gait, evaluating an injury, and teaching correct gait.

The hip joint is a true ball-in-socket joint and has intrinsic stability not found in other joints.[6] This intrinsic stability does not prevent the hip joint from retaining great mobility.[6] During normal gait, the hip joint moves in all three planes—sagittal, frontal, and transverse. To participate in athletic activities, a greater range of motion is needed. With the increased range of motion, the hip is capable of performing a wide range of combined movements. Forces at the hip joint have been increased to five times the body weight during running. These forces can also contribute to injuries, both muscular and bony.

The most frequently injured structures of the groin, hip, pelvis, and thigh are the muscles and tendons that perform the movements. The majority of these muscles originate on the pelvis or the proximal femur. The iliac crest serves as the attachment site for the abdominal muscles, the ilium serves as the attachment for the gluteals, and then the gluteals insert to the proximal femur. The pubis serves as the attachment for the adductors, and the iliopsoas inserts distally to the lesser trochanter of the proximal femur.[6] Due to all the attachments in a small area, injury to these structures can be very disabling and difficult to distinguish.[6]

The quadriceps inserts by a common tendon to the proximal patella. The rectus femoris is the only quadriceps muscle that crosses the hip joint, which not only extends the knee but also flexes the hip. This is very important in differentiating hip flexor strains (iliopsoas vs. rectus femoris) and the ensuing treatment and rehabilitation programs.

The hamstrings all cross the knee joint posteriorly, and all except the short head of the biceps cross the hip joint. These biarticular muscles produce forces dependent upon the position of both the knee joint and the hip joint. The position of the hip and knee during movement, and the injury mechanism, play a very important role and provide information to use when rehabilitating and preventing hamstring injuries.

REHABILITATION TECHNIQUES FOR SPECIFIC INJURIES

Hip Pointer

PATHOMECHANICS

A hip pointer can best be described as a subcutaneous contusion. In most cases, the contusion can cause separation or tearing of the origins or insertions of the muscles that attach to the prominent bony sites.[18] Usually the patient has no immediate concern, but within hours of the injury, bleeding, swelling, and pain can severely limit the patient's movement. In rare cases, a fracture of the crest may occur.[1] More serious injuries must be ruled out. One patient who reported the signs and symptoms of a hip pointer later was determined to have a ruptured spleen.

INJURY MECHANISM

A hip pointer is usually caused by a direct blow to the iliac crest or the anterosuperior iliac spine. A strain of the abdominal muscles at their attachment to the anterior and inferior iliac crest can be differentiated from a contusion by obtaining a good history of the mechanism of injury at the time it occurs. A forceful contraction of the abdominal muscles while the trunk

is being passively forced to the opposite side may cause a strain of the muscles at their insertion on the iliac bone.[32]

REHABILITATION CONCERNS

An x-ray film should be taken to rule out iliac crest fractures or avulsion fractures, especially in younger patients.[18] If the hip pointer is not treated early, within approximately 2 to 4 hours, the patient may experience severe pain and limited range of motion of the trunk because of the muscle attachments involved.

As in most contusions, the hip pointer is graded. A patient with a grade I hip pointer may have both normal gait cycle and normal posture. The patient may complain of slight pain on palpation with little or no swelling. This patient may also present with full range of motion of the trunk, especially when checking for lateral side-bending to the opposite side of the injury.

A patient with a grade II hip pointer may have moderate to severe pain on palpation, noticeable swelling, and an abnormal gait cycle. The gait cycle may be changed because of a short swing-through phase on the affected side; the patient may take a short step and be reluctant to keep the foot off the ground. The patient's pelvis and therefore posture may be slightly tilted to the side of the injury. Active hip and trunk flexion may cause pain, especially if the anterosuperior iliac spine is involved because of the insertion of the sartorius muscle. Range of motion may be limited, especially lateral side bending to the opposite side of the injury and trunk rotation in both directions.

A patient with a grade III hip pointer may have severe pain on palpation, noticeable swelling, and possible discoloration. The patient's gait cycle could be abnormal, with very slow, deliberate ambulation and extremely short stride length and swing-through phase. The patient's posture may present a severe lateral tilt to the affected side. Trunk range of motion may be limited in all directions. Active hip and trunk flexion may reproduce pain.

With all hip pointers, continue with ice, compression, and rest. Subcutaneous steroid injection has been known to decrease inflammation and enable early range-of-motion exercises. Oral anti-inflammatory medication is also beneficial in the early stages to reduce pain and inflammation and facilitate early range of motion. Transcutaneous electrical nerve stimulation (TENS) may be helpful on the day of injury to decrease pain and allow early range-of-motion exercises. To regain normal function and speed recovery, use ice massage with pain-free trunk range-of-motion exercises at the same time. Concentrate on lateral side bending to the opposite side of the injury (see Exercise 29-34). Other modalities such as ultrasound and electric stimulation are beneficial for increasing range of motion and functional movement. Pain-free active and active resistance range-of-motion exercises are vital to the functional recovery process. Active motion helps promote healing and decreases the time the patient is prohibited from practice and competition. Exercises as shown in Exercises 29-1 to 29-7, 29-14, and 29-15 should be used to progress the patient. Trunk strengthening exercises may also be added.

REHABILITATION PROGRESSION

A grade I hip pointer usually does not prevent the patient from normal activity. A patient with a grade II hip pointer could be functionally limited for 5 to 14 days and a patient with a grade III hip pointer could be functionally limited for 14 to 21 days. With grade II and III hip pointers, the patient can progress to active resistive strengthening exercises, if pain free, after the initial 2 days of ice, compression, and active range of motion.

Injury to the Anterosuperior and Anteroinferior Iliac Spine

PATHOMECHANICS

Pain at the site of the anterosuperior iliac spine may indicate contusion or apophysitis, an inflammatory response to overuse.[1] Severe pain associated with disability requires an x-ray to rule out an avulsion fracture.[1]

As with the anterosuperior iliac spine, the anteroinferior iliac spine may also present apophysitis or a contusion. An avulsion fracture should also be ruled out with severe pain. These injuries are seen more often in younger patients.[34]

INJURY MECHANISM

The anterosuperior iliac spine serves as an attachment for the sartorius, and the anteroinferior iliac spine serves as an attachment for the rectus femoris. In both cases a violent, forceful passive stretch of the hip into extension or a violent, forceful active contraction into flexion can cause injury to these sites.[38] Apophysitis or a contusion to these two sites may accompany a hip pointer to the iliac crest.

REHABILITATION CONCERNS AND PROGRESSION

After ruling out an avulsion fracture, these injuries should follow the same treatment and rehabilitation guidelines as a hip pointer.

Posterosuperior Iliac Spine Contusion

PATHOMECHANICS

Contusions to the posterosuperior iliac spine must be differentiated from vertebral fractures and more serious internal organ injuries.[1] Depending upon the patient's pain and range of motion, an x-ray should be taken to rule out vertebral fractures, vertebral transverse process fractures, and fractures of the posterosuperior iliac spine. Other injuries to this area are not common because of the lack of muscle attachments.[23] Avulsion fractures are rare in this area, although a fracture of the posterosuperior iliac spine should be ruled out. The injury may be painful but usually does not cause disability.

INJURY MECHANISM AND REHABILITATION CONCERNS

A contusion to the posterosuperior iliac spine is usually caused by a blow or fall. A patient with a contusion may complain of pain on palpation and have swelling that is usually not extensive. The patient's gait cycle may look normal except in severe cases, when the patient may take short, choppy steps to avoid the pain associated with landing at heel strike. In severe cases, the patient's posture may show a slight forward flexion tilt of the trunk. This patient may show full active range of motion of the trunk, with mild discomfort. In moderate to severe cases, up to 3 days of rest may be needed before return to normal activity.

REHABILITATION PROGRESSION

The same treatment can be followed that is used for hip pointers. Pain-free active and passive range-of-motion exercises of the trunk and hip can be used in sets and repetitions with stretches held for 20 to 30 seconds for each repetition. Time required for rehabilitation is the same as for a hip pointer, and protective padding is recommended.

Piriformis Syndrome (Sciatica)

PATHOMECHANICS

The sciatic nerve is a continuation of the sacral plexus as it passes through the greater sciatic notch and descends deeply through the back of the thigh.[25] Hip and buttock pain is often diagnosed as sciatic nerve irritation. The sciatic nerve may be irritated by a low back problem, but it is also subject to trauma where the nerve passes underneath or through the piriformis muscle, in which case sciatic nerve irritation is also called piriformis syndrome.[1,20] In approximately 15 percent of the population, the sciatic nerve passes through the piriformis muscle, separating it in two. This condition is seen in more women than men, and the cause of piriformis syndrome may be a tight piriformis muscle.[22]

Injury to the hamstring muscles may also cause sciatic nerve irritation, as can irritation from ischial bursitis.[22] In a traumatic accident that causes posterior dislocation of the femoral head, the sciatic nerve may be crushed or severed and require surgery.[22]

INJURY MECHANISM

The most common cause of sciatic nerve irritation involves a direct blow to the buttock. Because of the large muscle mass, this injury is not usually disabling when the sciatic nerve is not involved. When the sciatic nerve is involved, however, the patient may experience pain in the buttock, extending down the back of the thigh, possibly into the lateral calf and foot. Sciatic pain is usually a burning sensation.[32]

REHABILITATION CONCERNS

With sciatica, the therapist must rule out disk disease before starting any exercise rehabilitation program. Stretching exercises that are indicated for sciatica, such as trunk and hip flexion, may be contraindicated for disk disease. To differentiate low back problems (disk disease) from piriformis syndrome as the cause of sciatica, determine if the patient has low back pain with radiation into the extremity. Back pain is most likely midline, exacerbated by trunk flexion and relieved by rest.[13] Coughing and straining may also increase back pain and possibly the radiation. Muscle weakness and sensory numbness may also be found in a patient with disk disease.[13] Patients with piriformis syndrome may have the same symptoms without the low back pain and without the low back pain being reproduced with coughing and straining. If, after treatment and rehabilitation, the patient still maintains neurologic deficits, further evaluation to rule out disk disease is necessary.

In the case of piriformis syndrome, the patient may report a deep pain in the buttock without low back pain and possibly radiating pain in the back of the thigh, lateral calf, and foot, also indicating sciatica.[22] The therapist evaluation should include the low back, as well as the hip and thigh. The patient's gait cycle could include lack of heel strike, landing in the foot-flat phase, a shortening of the stride, and possible ambulation with a flexed knee to relieve the stretch on the sciatic nerve. The patient's posture, in severe cases, shows a flexed knee with the leg externally rotated. Palpation in the sciatic notch could also produce pain.

With the patient lying prone and the hip in a neutral position with the knee in extension or flexion, active resistive external rotation and passive internal rotation of the hip may reproduce the pain (Exercise 29-47).[22] Straight leg raises performed passively or actively may also cause symptoms. With the patient in the same position as above and the knee in extension and relaxed, a decrease in passive internal rotation of the hip joint as compared to the uninjured side may indicate piriformis tightness.

REHABILITATION PROGRESSION

Severe sciatica caused by piriformis syndrome may keep the patient out of normal activity for 2 to 3 weeks or longer. If the sciatic nerve is irritated and the patient complains of radiation into the extremity, the first 3 to 5 days should consist of rest and modalities to decrease the pain associated with sciatica.

After the acute pain has been controlled, the patient may perform pain-free stretching exercises for the low back and hamstring muscles, as long as disk disease has been ruled out. Stretching exercises (Exercises 29-38 to 29-40, 29-45, and 29-48) can be used to treat piriformis syndrome. Piriformis strengthening may be accomplished through resistive external rotation of the hip (Exercise 29-7).

Reviewing a normal gait cycle may also aid in gaining range of motion if the patient has been ambulating with a flexed knee. The hamstrings, as well as the sciatic nerve, may have shortened in this case.

The patient should be capable of performing pain-free activity, such as running and cutting, without neurologic symptoms, before returning to normal activities (see Exercises 29-4 to 29-13). Participating with constant radiation into the extremity poses a risk for developing chronic problems. The best method of treatment is prevention by instituting a good flexibility program for all patients.

Trochanteric Bursitis

PATHOMECHANICS

The most commonly diagnosed hip bursitis is greater trochanteric bursitis. The greater trochanteric bursa lies between the gluteus maximus and the surface of the greater trochanter.[22,37]

Bursitis and other disorders of the bursa are often mistaken for other injuries because of the location of numerous other structures around the bursa. The bursa is a structure that normally lies within the area of a joint and produces a fluid that lubricates the two surfaces between which it lies.[16] It also may attach, very loosely, to the joint capsule, tendons, ligaments, and skin. Therefore, it is indirectly involved with other close structures.[16] The function of the bursa is to dissipate friction caused by two or more structures moving against one another.

Bursitis associated with bleeding into the bursa is the most disabling form. With hemorrhagic bursitis, swelling and pain may limit motion.[27] The therapist must also consider the possibility of an infected bursa. If it is suspected, the patient should be referred for a medical evaluation.

INJURY MECHANISM

Bursitis in general is usually caused by direct trauma or overuse stress. One possible cause for trochanteric bursitis may be irritation caused by the iliotibial band where the gluteus maximus inserts into it.[22] Repetitive irritation, such as running with one leg slightly adducted (as on the side of a road), may cause trochanteric bursitis on the adducted side.

Trochanteric bursitis caused by overuse is mostly seen in women runners who have an increased Q angle with or without a leg-length discrepancy.[1] Tight adductors may cause a runner's feet to cross over the midline, resulting in excessive tilting of the pelvis in the frontal plane, and consequently place an exceptional amount of force on the trochanteric bursa.[18]

Lateral heel wear in running shoes may also cause excessive hip adduction, which may indirectly result in trochanteric bursitis. A direct blow may result in a hemorrhagic bursitis, which could be extremely painful to the patient.[16]

REHABILITATION CONCERNS

Traumatic trochanteric bursitis is more easily diagnosed than overuse trochanteric bursitis. Palpation produces pain over the lateral hip area and greater trochanter. In both cases the patient's gait cycle may be slightly abducted on the affected side to relieve pressure on the bursa. A patient's attempt to remove weight from the affected extremity may cause a shortened weight-bearing phase. The patient may report an increase in pain on activity, and active resistive hip abduction may also reproduce the pain.

A complete history must be taken to determine the cause of trochanteric bursitis. The patient's gait cycle, posture, flexibility, and running shoes should be examined. Oral anti-inflammatory medication usually helps decrease pain and inflammation initially. After the initial treatment of ice, compression, and modalities, the patient can use various stretching exercises (see Exercises 29-35, 29-38 to 29-46, and 29-48).

REHABILITATION PROGRESSION

An orthotic evaluation should be performed to check for any malalignment that may have caused dysfunction, excessive adduction, or leg-length discrepancy. Progressive resistive strengthening exercises in hip abduction may be performed when the patient is free of pain. Also see treatment for all hip bursitis injuries.

    The patient could require 3 to 5 days for rehabilitation, depending on the severity of the bursitis. For contact sports, a protective pad should be worn upon return to competition after the patient can perform the sport-specific functional tests.

Ischial Bursitis

PATHOMECHANICS AND INJURY MECHANISM

The ischial bursa lies between the ischial tuberosity and gluteus maximus (see also "Pathomechanics" under "Trochanteric Bursitis" earlier in the chapter). Ischial bursitis is often seen in people who sit for long periods.[22] Ischial bursitis may also be caused by direct trauma, such as falling or a direct hit when the hip is in a flexed position that exposes the ischial area.

REHABILITATION CONCERNS

The patient may report trauma to the area. With the hip in a flexed position, palpation over the ischial tuberosity may reproduce the pain. The patient may experience pain on ambulation when the hip is flexed during the gait cycle. Also, stair climbing, uphill walking and running may reproduce pain.

REHABILITATION PROGRESSION

Treatment for ischial bursitis consists of positioning the patient with the hip in a flexed position to expose the ischial area. After the initial phase of treatment with ice and anti-inflammatory medication, the patient may begin a pain-free stretching program (Exercises 29-38 to 29-46 and 29-48).

    Depending on injury severity, this patient needs a long period for rehabilitation. Avoiding direct trauma to the area usually allows healing within 3 to 5 days. For contact sports, a protective pad should be worn (see treatment for all hip bursitis injuries).

Iliopectineal Bursitis

PATHOMECHANICS AND INJURY MECHANISM

Iliopectineal bursitis may often be mistaken for a strain of the iliopsoas muscle and can be difficult to differentiate. Although rare, iliopectineal bursitis could potentially be caused by a tight iliopsoas muscle.[22] Osteoarthritis of the hip may also cause iliopectineal bursitis.[22]

REHABILITATION CONCERNS

Resistive hip flexion—sitting with the knee bent or lying supine with the knee extended—may reproduce the pain associated with iliopectineal bursitis. Also, passive hip extension with the knee extended may produce pain. Palpable pain in the inguinal area may also help in evaluating the patient. In some cases, the nearby femoral nerve may become inflamed and cause radiation into the front of the thigh and knee.[22] Osteoarthritis must be ruled out in evaluating iliopectineal bursitis.

REHABILITATION PROGRESSION

Oral anti-inflammatory medication may be helpful initially. A form of deep heat or ice massage may be used to aid in decreasing inflammation and pain. The iliopsoas tendon must be stretched (see Exercises 29-35 to 29-37) and hip flexion strengthening exercises are performed pain free with the knee straight (see Exercises 29-1, 29-2, and 29-14).

Snapping or Clicking Hip Syndrome

PATHOMECHANICS AND INJURY MECHANISM

Clinically, snapping hip syndrome is secondary to what could be a number of causes.[6] Excessive repetitive movement has been linked to snapping hip syndrome in dancers or in athletes where a muscle imbalance develops.[1] The most common causes of the "snapping" when muscle is involved, is the iliotibial band over the greater trochanter resulting in trochanteric bursitis (see trochanteric bursitis) and the iliopsoas tendon over the iliopectineal eminence.[6] Other extra-articular causes of the "snapping" are the iliofemoral ligaments over the femoral head, and the long head of the biceps femoris over the ischial tuberosity.[6] Extraarticular causes commonly occur when the hip is externally rotated and flexed. Other causes or anatomic structures that can predispose to "snapping hip" are a narrow pelvic width, abnormal increases in abduction range of motion, and lack of range of motion into external rotation or tight internal rotators.[1] Intraarticular causes are less likely but may consist of loose bodies, synovial chondromatosis, osteocartilaginous exostosis, and possibly subluxation of the hip joint itself.[6]

REHABILITATION CONCERNS

Due to the extraarticular causes, the hip joint capsule, ligaments, and muscles become loosened and allow the hip to become unstable. The patient will complain of a "snapping" and this snapping may be accompanied by severe pain and disability upon each "snap."

    The key to treating and rehabilitating the snapping hip syndrome is to decrease pain and inflammation with ice, anti-inflammatory medication, and other modalities such as ultrasound. This could significantly decrease the pain initially so that the patient can begin a stretching and strengthening program. The most important aspect of the evaluation process is to find the source of the imbalance (which muscles are tight and which are weak).

REHABILITATION PROGRESSION

In the case of the iliopsoas muscle snapping over the iliopectineal eminence, the following stretches should be used (see Exercises 29-35 to 29-37 and 29-49). Strengthening should take into account the entire hip, especially the hip extensors and internal and external rotators (see Exercises 29-3, 29-6, 29-7, and 29-14).

After pain has subsided and the patient can actively flex the hip pain free, the patient can begin strengthening exercises for the hip flexor (see Exercises 29-1, 29-2, and 29-14) flexion with the knee straight. After the first 3 to 5 days, the patient can begin functional activities including jogging.

Osteitis Pubis

PATHOMECHANICS

Pain in the area of the pubic symphysis may be difficult to diagnose. Unless the patient reports being hit or experiencing some kind of direct trauma, pubic pain may be caused by osteitis pubis, fractures of the inferior ramus (stress fractures and avulsion fractures), and groin strains.[1]

Because an overuse situation and rapid repetitive changing in directions predisposes a patient to this injury, osteitis pubis is seen mostly in distance running or other activities where constant movement of the symphysis produces inflammation and pain.

INJURY MECHANISM

Repetitive stress on the pubic symphysis, caused by the insertion of muscles to the area, creates a chronic inflammation.[1] Direct trauma to the symphysis may also cause periostitis. Symptoms develop gradually, and may be mistaken for muscle strains. Exercises that aid muscle strains may cause more irritation to the symphysis; thus early active exercises are contraindicated.[18]

REHABILITATION CONCERNS

Referral to a physician to rule out hernia problems, infection, and prostatitis may be helpful in evaluating osteitis pubis.[18] Changes in x-ray films may take 4 to 6 weeks to show. The patient should be treated symptomatically.

A patient with osteitis pubis may have pain in the groin area and may complain of an increase in pain with running, sit-ups, and squatting.[1] The patient may also complain of lower abdominal pain with radiation into the inner thigh. Differentiating osteitis pubis from a muscle strain is difficult.

Palpation over the pubic symphysis may reproduce pain. In severe cases the patient may show a waddling gait because of the shear forces at the symphysis.[1] Rest is the main course of treatment, with modalities and anti-inflammatory medication to ease pain. As soon as pain permits, the patient should begin pain-free adductor stretching exercises as shown in Exercises 29-41 and 29-42. Also, pain-free abdominal strengthening, low back strengthening, and open-chain hip abductor, adductor, flexor, and extensor strengthening can be started (see Exercises 29-1 to 29-5). Because excessive movement that causes shear forces at the symphysis is the main cause of pain, stabilization exercises that concentrate on tightening the muscles around the pubic symphysis are recommended. The patient is asked to concentrate on tightening the buttock, groin, abdomen, and low back (the entire pelvic area) as the patient performs a closed-chain exercise such as the leg press as (see Exercise 29-16) and lunges (see Exercise 29-19). This stabilization techniques helps to control excessive movement at the pubic symphysis while the patient performs movements at other joints. These closed-chain exercises may be started, for stabilization purposes, and may actually be pain free before the start of open-chain exercises.

The lower body must be protected from shear forces to the symphysis area. In most cases, the patient may need 3 to 5 days for recovery. In severe cases, from 3 weeks up to 3 months and possibly 6 months of rest and treatment may be necessary.

Fractures of the Inferior Ramus

PATHOMECHANICS

Stress and avulsion fractures should be ruled out before treating the pubic area for injury. The extent of an avulsion fracture must be diagnosed by x-ray. In some cases, a palpable mass may be detected under the skin. Stress fractures may be diagnosed with the same symptoms as in osteitis pubis. With a stress fracture, an x-ray may appear normal until the third or fourth week. Obtaining a good history may aid in diagnosing a stress fracture.

INJURY MECHANISM

Avulsion fracture of the inferior ramus is usually caused by a violent, forceful contraction of the hip adductor muscles or forceful passive movement into hip abduction, as in a split. Stress fractures may occur from overuse (see treatment for femoral stress fractures later in the chapter).

REHABILITATION CONCERNS AND PROGRESSION

Rest is the key in treating fractures of the inferior ramus. Hip stretching and strengthening exercises may be performed, as in pubic injuries, within a pain-free range of motion. An avulsion fracture may require up to 3 months for rehabilitation. A patient with a stress fracture may require 3 to 6 weeks for healing. Activities that cause muscle contraction forces at the inferior ramus should be avoided and closed-chain stabilization exercises as described in pubic symphysis injury rehabilitation should be used. Return to activity should be gradual and deliberate and must be pain free.

Groin and Hip Flexor Strain

PATHOMECHANICS

A groin strain may occur to any muscle in the inner hip area. Whether it is to the sartoris, rectus femoris, the adductors, or the iliopsoas, the muscle and degree of injury must be determined and the injury treated accordingly.[5]

Discomfort may start as mild but develop into moderate to severe pain with disability if not treated correctly. A chronic strain may cause bleeding into the groin muscles resulting in myositis ossificans (see the section on myositis ossificans later in the chapter). If a groin strain is treated acutely, myositis ossificans can be avoided.

INJURY MECHANISM AND REHABILITATION CONCERNS

A groin strain may develop from overextending and externally rotating the hip or from forcefully contracting the muscles into flexion and internal rotation as involved in running, jumping, twisting, and kicking. Differential diagnosis and treatment may be difficult because of the number of muscles in the area.

With a grade I groin strain, the patient may complain of mild discomfort with no loss of function and full range of motion and strength. Point tenderness may be minimal, with negative swelling. The gait cycle may be normal.

With a grade II groin strain, palpation may reproduce pain and show a minimal to moderate defect. Swelling may also be detected. This patient may show an abnormal gait cycle. Ambulation may be slow, and the stride length may be shortened on the affected side. The patient may tend to hike the hip and tilt the pelvis in the frontal plane rather then drive the knee through during the swing-through phase. Range of motion may be severely limited, and resistance could cause an increase in pain. When the iliopsoas is involved the patient may experience severe pain after the initial injury. This is thought to be caused by spasm of the iliopsoas muscle, which tilts the pelvis in the frontal plane. The patient will walk with a flexed hip and knee and will be unable to extend the hip during the push-off phase of the gait cycle due to the muscle spasm not allowing hip extension and active hip flexion during swing-through. This patient will also externally rotate the hip in order to use the hip adductors for the swing-through phase.

A patient with a grade III groin strain may need crutches to ambulate. A moderate to severe defect may be detected in the involved muscle or tendon. Point tenderness may be severe, with noticeable swelling. Range of motion is severely limited, especially if the iliopsoas is involved. The patient may splint the legs together and be apprehensive about allowing movement in abduction. Resistance may not be tolerated.

Differentiating a hip adductor strain from a hip flexor strain is the first step in treating this injury. Resistive adduction while lying supine with the knee in extension may significantly increase pain if the hip adductors are involved. Flexing the hip and knee and resisting hip adduction may also increase pain. If the injury is a pure hip adductor strain, the supine position with the knee extended may reproduce more discomfort than flexing the hip and knee. If resistive adduction with the hip and knee flexed produces more discomfort, the hip flexor may also be involved.

With the patient lying supine, more pain on resistive hip flexion with the knee in extension (straight leg raise) tests for iliopsoas involvement. More pain on resistive hip flexion with the knee flexed tests for rectus femoris involvement. After de-

termining the muscle or muscle groups involved and the degree of the injury, treatment and rehabilitation is the next step.

REHABILITATION PROGRESSION

With a grade I strain, modalities and pain-free hip stretching exercises can begin immediately (see Exercises 29-35 to 29-37, 29-41, 29-42, 29-45, and 29-46). Pain-free progressive strengthening exercises may also be performed (see Exercises 29-1, 29-2, 29-4, 29-6, 29-7, and 29-14), progressing to flexion with knee straight and bent and adduction (see Exercises 29-15, 29-19, 29-22, and 29-23), and PNF exercises (see Exercises 29-30 and 29-32). Depending upon the severity of the injury, this patient can be quickly progressed to the slide board (see Exercise 29-24), plyometrics (see Exercises 29-27 to 29-29), and functional activities as soon as pain allows.

A patient with a grade II strain should be started immediately with gentle, pain-free, active range-of-motion exercises of the hip. When the iliopsoas is involved, it has been found that lying supine on a treatment table with the leg and hip hanging over the end of the table, with the hip in a passively extended position, while applying ice for 15 to 20 minutes has helped eliminate muscle spasm and pain (see Exercises 29-37). Electrical muscle stimulation modalities can be very useful in the early stages to decrease inflammation, pain, and spasm and to promote range of motion.[29] Isometrics should also be performed as soon as they can be managed without pain. If crutches are used, a normal gait cycle is taught. The patient can begin pain-free stretching as soon as possible (see Exercises 29-35 to 29-37, 29-41, 29-42, 29-45, and 29-46). As soon as pain allows, the patient can begin pain-free strengthening exercises (see Exercises 29-1, 29-2, 29-4, 29-6, 29-7, 29-13, and 29-14), flexion and adduction strengthening exercises (see Exercises 29-15, 29-19, 29-22, and 29-23), and PNF (see Exercises 29-30 and 29-32). After approximately one week the patient can begin pain-free slide board (see Exercise 29-24) and plyometrics (see Exercises 29-27 to 29-29) as well as functional activities. This patient may require 3 to 14 days of rehabilitation, depending on the severity of injury. Hip adductor strains usually take longer to treat and rehabilitate than hip flexor strains of the same grade, especially if the muscle spasm involved with a hip flexor is eliminated as soon as possible. Treatment and rehabilitation should be modified accordingly.

A patient with a grade III strain should be iced, compressed, immobilized, and nonweight bearing. Electrical muscle stimulation modalities are useful in the acute stage to decrease inflammation and pain and to promote range of motion. Rest for 1 to 3 days is recommended, with compression at all times. If the iliopsoas is involved, you can begin passive stretching with ice (see Exercise 29-37) after the third day.

If surgery is ruled out, the patient may perform pain-free isometric exercises between days 3 and 5. Slow, pain-free active range-of-motion exercises may also be performed between days 3 and 5. A normal gait cycle should be emphasized using crutches. Crutches should not be eliminated until the patient can ambulate with a normal, pain-free gait cycle. Between days

7 and 10, the patient may perform pain-free stretching exercises (see Exercises 29-35 to 29-37, 29-41, 29-42, 29-45, and 29-46) and can begin progressive resistive strengthening exercises without pain, progressing in weight and motion (see Exercises 29-1, 29-2, 29-4, 29-6, 29-7, 29-13, and 29-14), flexion and adduction (see Exercises 29-15, 29-19, 29-22, and 29-23), and PNF (see Exercises 29-30 and 29-32). The patient needs to achieve a good strength level, usually within 10 days after starting progressive resistive strengthening exercises, to perform pain-free slide board (see Exercise 29-24) and plyometrics (see Exercises 29-27 to 29-29) as well as functional activities.

Treatment and rehabilitation timetables may be modified. The modifications should be based on the degree of injury within the grade presented. This patient could potentially require 3 weeks to 3 months for rehabilitation.

Hip Dislocation

PATHOMECHANICS

Dislocation of the hip joint is extremely rare and takes a considerable amount of force because of the deep-seated ball-in-socket joint.[26,33] Fractures and avascular necrosis, which is a degenerative condition of the head of the femur caused by a disruption of blood supply during dislocation, should always be considered.[1,12] If dislocation should occur, it should be treated as a medical emergency. The patient should be checked for distal pulses and sensation. The sciatic nerve should be examined to see if it has been crushed or severed.[1] Do this by checking sensation and foot and toe movements. If the sciatic nerve is damaged, knee, ankle, and toe weakness may be pronounced.

INJURY MECHANISM

A hip dislocation is generally a posterior dislocation that takes place with the knee and hip in a flexed position. The patient may be totally disabled, in severe pain, and usually unwilling to allow movement of the extremity. The trochanter may appear larger than normal with the extremity in internal rotation, flexed, and adducted.[32] X-ray studies should be performed before anesthetized reduction.[26]

REHABILITATION PROGRESSION

Two or three weeks (and in some cases, longer) of immobilization are initially needed. Rehabilitation of the thigh, knee, and ankle may be included at this time. Pain-free hip isometric exercises should be performed. Electrical muscle stimulation modalities may be used initially to promote muscle reeducation and retard muscle atrophy.[32] At approximately 3 to 6 weeks, pain-free active range-of-motion exercises can be performed (see Exercises 29-1 to 29-7) with no resistance/weight. Crutch walking is progressed and performed until the patient can ambulate with a normal gait cycle and without pain. At approximately 6 weeks, the patient may perform gentle progressive resistive strengthening exercises with a weight cuff or weight boot. All six movements of the hip should be included in the progres-

sive resistive strengthening exercises (hip flexion, abduction, extension, adduction, internal rotation, and external rotation) (see Exercises 29-1 to 29-7 and 29-14), and PNF exercises (see Exercises 29-30 to 29-33). Pain-free stretching exercises should not be performed for 8 to 12 weeks (see Exercises 29-35, 29-36, and 29-38 to 29-49). At approximately 12 weeks, the patient may begin closed-chain exercises (see Exercises 29-16 to 29-22) as well as open-chain exercises (see Exercise 29-15). At 16 to 20 weeks, the patient may progress to pain-free slide board (see Exercise 29-24), plyometric exercises (see Exercises 29-27 to 29-29), and functional activities. If pain returns, the patient must eliminate plyometrics and functional activities until they can be performed pain free. This patient may require 6 to 12 months for rehabilitation if there have not been any delays and the patient is pain free with all activity.

Hamstring Strain and Avulsion Fracture of the Ischial Tuberosity

PATHOMECHANICS

The ischial tuberosity is a common site of injury to the hamstring muscle group (the biceps femoris, semitendinosus, and semimembranosus). All three hamstring muscles originate from the ischial tuberosity. The most common ischial injury, as it relates to the hamstring group, is an avulsion fracture of the tuberosity.[2,28]

INJURY MECHANISM

This injury usually results from a violent, forceful flexion of the hip, with the knee in extension.[1] A less severe irritation of the hamstring origin at the ischial tuberosity may also develop.

REHABILITATION CONCERNS, REHABILITATION PROGRESSION, AND CRITERIA FOR FULL RETURN (STRAIN)

A patient with a less severe injury or irritation of the hamstring origin at the ischial tuberosity may complain of discomfort on sitting for extended periods and discomfort on palpation. This patient may also complain of pain while walking up stairs or uphill. The patient may ambulate with a normal gait cycle. Also, the patient may be able to jog normally, but pain may be present with attempts at sprinting. Resistive knee flexion and resistive hip extension with the knee in an extended position may reproduce the pain. Passive hip flexion with the knee in extension may also cause discomfort.

After the initial treatment phase of ice and other modalities, the patient may begin gentle, pain-free hamstring stretching exercises (see Exercises 29-38 to 29-40). To isolate the hamstring muscle while stretching, the patient should maintain a lordotic curve in the lumbar back area while flexing at the trunk to stretch the hamstrings (see Exercise 29-39). Pain-free hamstring muscle progressive resistive strengthening exercises may also be performed, as soon as possible (see Exercises 29-3, 29-8 to 29-10, and 29-14), and closed-chain extension exercises (see Exercises 29-16 to 29-22) and PNF exercises (see Exercises

29-31 and 29-33). This patient can be progressed functionally as tolerated.

REHABILITATION CONCERNS (AVULSION FRACTURE)

The more severe ischial tuberosity avulsion fracture presents a different clinical picture. Palpation may produce moderate to severe pain, and the patient may be in moderate to severe pain with a very abnormal gait cycle. The patient's gait cycle may lack a heel-strike phase and have a very short swing-through phase.[2] The patient may attempt to keep the injured extremity behind or below the body to avoid hip flexion during the gait cycle. Resistive knee flexion and hip extension with the knee in an extended or flexed position may reproduce the pain. Passive hip flexion with the knee extended and with the knee flexed may cause moderate to severe pain at the ischial tuberosity. X-rays may or may not show the injury.[32]

After week 3 and the initial acute phase of treatment with modalities, the patient may begin pain-free active range of motion lying prone and supine. Pain-free hamstring stretching exercises (see Exercises 29-38 to 29-40) may also be performed. Regaining full range of motion during the rehabilitation program is very important. Many patients never gain full hip flexion range of motion after this injury.

Weeks 6 through 12 are a progressive phase for pain-free hamstring progressive resistive strengthening exercises (see Exercises 29-3, 29-8 to 29-10, and 29-14), closed-chain extension exercises (see Exercises 29-16, 29-17, 29-20, and 29-22), isokinetics (see Exercises 29-25 and 29-26), and PNF exercises (see Exercises 29-31 and 29-33). After 2 to 3 weeks you can add exercises as shown in Exercises 29-19 to 29-22).

REHABILITATION PROGRESSION (AVULSION FRACTURE)

Surgery is usually not necessary. Immobilization and limiting physical activity are usually enough to allow healing. Ice and limited physical activity that involves hip flexion and forceful hip extension and knee flexion for the first 3 weeks is usually all that is necessary. Crutches should be used until normal gait is taught. During the 6- to 12-week phase, the patient will begin activities such as swimming, biking, and jogging, but the patient should avoid forceful knee and hip flexion and forceful hip extension. After week 12, the patient, without pain, may progress to the slide board (see Exercise 29-24), plyometrics (see Exercises 29-27 to 29-29), and functional activities.

Hamstring Strains

PATHOMECHANICS

Hamstring strains are common, and the causes are numerous.[40] The ability of the hamstring muscles and quadriceps muscles to work together is very complex because the hamstrings cross two joints.[20] This produces forces and therefore stresses on the hamstrings dependent upon the positions of the hip and knee.[6] Some research has shown, through dissections, that there is consistent overlap of tendon vertically, over the course of the muscle

with the exception of the semitendinosus.[6] With research showing the musculotendinous junction as the main injury site, then anywhere along the muscle/tendon is susceptible to injury.[6]

The patient may report a "pop" Palpation is the easiest way to identify the site and extent of injury. Even though bleeding (ecchymosis) may be present, some people believe that this isn't associated with the degree or severity of injury.[6]

A patient with a grade I hamstring strain will complain of sore hamstring muscles, with some pain on palpation and possibly minimal swelling. A patient with a grade II hamstring strain may report having heard or felt a "pop" during the activity. At the first or second day, moderate ecchymosis may be observed. Palpation may produce moderate to severe pain, and even though a defect and noticeable swelling in the muscle belly may be evident, the grade II hamstring strain most likely occurs at the musculotendinous junction, either mid to high semimembranosus/tendinosis or lower lateral biceps femoris. A patient with a grade III strain may report having heard or felt a "pop" during the activity. The therapist may detect swelling and severe pain on palpation. A noticeable defect may be present, again at the musculotendinous junction as described above. After the first through third days, moderate to severe ecchymosis may be observed.

INJURY MECHANISM

A quick, explosive contraction that involves a rapid activity could lead to a strain of the hamstring muscles. Many theories try to explain the cause of hamstring strains. Imbalance with the quadriceps is one theory, according to which the hamstring muscles should have 60 to 70 percent of the quadriceps muscles' strength. Other possibilities are hamstring muscle fatigue, running posture and gait, leg-length discrepancy, decreased hamstring range of motion, and an imbalance between the medial and lateral hamstring muscle.[1]

Another factor that plays a role in injury as well as in rehabilitation, is that the semitendinosus, semimembranosus, and long head of the biceps femoris are innervated from the tibial branch of the sciatic nerve, while the short head of the biceps femoris is innervated by the peroneal branch of the sciatic nerve.[6] This innervation difference makes the short head a completely separate muscle, "a factor implicated in the etiology of hamstring muscle strains" as described by DeLee and Drez.[6]

Two phases of the running gait described in DeLee and Drez show that the support phase and the recovery phase may predispose the patient to hamstring strains. During the support phase, foot strike, midsupport, and take-off occurs.[6] During recovery phase, follow-through, forward swing, and foot descent occurs.[6] The two portions of these two phases that are implicated in hamstring strains are the late forward swing segment of the recovery phase and the take-off phase of the support phase. EMG data show that the semimembranosus is very active during the late forward swing segment and that the biceps femoris is inactive.[6] At take-off of the support phase, the biceps femoris shows maximal activity.[6] This shows that the mid to high semimembranosus and semitendinosus strains may occur during the deceleration portion of the running cycle while the lower lateral biceps femoris strains are occurring at the take-off or push-off portion of the running cycle. The rehabilitation implications are connected to the position of the hip and knee while rehabilitating in order to isolate and identify the specific muscle involved.[4] Using the correct biomechanical positions during rehabilitation, based on the EMG findings presented above, will enhance rehabilitation and improve preventive programs.

REHABILITATION CONCERNS

A patient with a grade I hamstring strain may have a normal gait cycle. Hip flexion range of motion is probably normal, with a tight feeling reported at the extreme range of hip flexion. Resistive knee flexion, and hip extension with the knee extended, are probably free of pain of possibly produce a tight feeling with good strength present.

A patient with a grade II hamstring strain usually ambulates with an abnormal gait cycle. The patient may lack heel strike and land during the foot-flat phase of the gait cycle. The swing-through phase may be limited because of the patient's unwillingness to flex the hip and knee. The patient may tend to ambulate with a flexed knee. Resistive knee flexion and hip extension with the knee extended may cause moderate to severe pain. The patient may also have a noticeable weakness on resistive knee flexion and hip extension with the knee extended and flexed. Resistive hip extension with the knee flexed also tests the strength of the gluteus maximus muscle. Passive hip flexion with the knee extended may also produce moderate to severe pain. The patient's range of motion may be moderately to severely limited in hip flexion with the knee extended and moderately limited in hip flexion with the knee flexed.

A patient with a grade III hamstring strain may be unable to ambulate without the aid of crutches. The patient may have poor strength and be unable to resist knee flexion and hip extension with the knee extended. The patient may have fair strength upon resistive hip extension with the knee flexed because of the gluteus maximus muscle. Resisting these motions usually causes pain. Passive hip flexion, with the knee extended, may not be tolerated because of pain. Passive hip flexion, knee flexed, may be moderately to severely limited.

Because most hamstring injuries occur due to a rapid activity that involves an explosive concentric contraction during toe-off or a strong eccentric contraction during deceleration swing-through, it is this author's belief that the hamstring should be rehabilitated in a rapid-activity fashion with high intensity and a high volume of exercises. After the initial treatment of ice, rest, compression, and active range of motion, the following exercises, in the order given and with a load that does not produce pain, should be instituted. Alternating a single-joint open-chain exercise with a multijoint closed-chain exercise, with 30 seconds rest between sets and

actual exercises, has been shown to facilitate rapid healing and earlier return to normal function as well as to present preventive advantages (all exercises are performed pain free and in the order given). The first are the bike, stairmaster, and stretch (see Exercises 29-38, 29-39 to 29-42, 29-45, 29-46, and 29-48). Stretching is followed by pain-free progressive strengthening exercises in the following order: extension knee straight to bent for mid/high semimembranosus/tendinosis strains, and knee bent to straight for lower/lateral biceps femoris strains (see Exercises 29-8, 29-16, and 29-14); followed by heavy negatives (two legs up, one leg down), 1 set of 8 each leg (see Exercises 29-9 and 29-19); feet in front for mid/high strain (see Exercise 29-17); feet in back for lower/lateral strain (see Exercise 29-18); for mid/high strain (see Exercises 29-10, 29-21, 29-23, and 29-25); for lower/lateral strain (see Exercise 29-26); and PNF stretching (see Exercises 29-31 and 29-33).

REHABILITATION PROGRESSION

Each exercise done in the order given and sets, repetitions, and suggested rest periods should be progressed based on daily evaluation that involves pain, range of motion, muscle strength from previous workout session, and how the patient subjectively feels. Days between strengthening exercise sessions should be used for aerobic conditioning such as biking, stairmaster, and aquatic therapy, as well as slide board activity (see Exercise 29-24) followed by stretching as described above.

A pain-free normal gait cycle should be taught as soon as possible, and crutches should be used to accomplish a normal gait cycle. Ice, compression, and gentle, pain-free hamstring stretching exercises—making sure the patient maintains a lumbar lordotic curve to isolate the hamstring muscles—are performed on day 1. Electrical muscle stimulation modalities may be used to promote range of motion and to decrease pain and spasm.[20] Active knee and hip range of motion while lying prone may also be performed between days 1 and 3, if the patient can do so without pain. Hamstring isometric exercises are taught as soon as possible, again within pain-free limits. Starting pain-free active range of motion, as soon as possible, is very important and usually decreases the length of time a patient misses competition. At approximately day 3, the patient may begin heat in the form of hot packs and whirlpool, combined with pain-free stretching exercises described earlier. If pain free, the above strengthening program may be started between days 3 and 7.

A patient with a grade I hamstring strain may continue normal activities as much as possible but should be monitored for exacerbation of the existing injury. The rehabilitation program described should begin immediately to avoid further injury. A patient with a grade II hamstring strain could require 5 to 21 days for rehabilitation. A patient with a grade III hamstring strain could require 3 to 12 weeks for rehabilitation. In all situations the patient should not be discharged until plyometrics (see Exercises 29-27 to 29-29) and functional activities can be performed pain free.

Hamstring Tendon Strains

PATHOMECHANICS

Another injury that occurs to the hamstring muscles is a strain of the hamstring tendons near their attachments to the tibia and fibula. This injury has also been diagnosed as tendinitis. Injury to the gastrocnemius muscle tendons in the same area must be ruled out.

INJURY MECHANISM

The patient may report pain but may not experience disability. A patient with a hamstring tendon strain or tendinitis may present a history of overuse and chronic pain for a few days with no specific mechanism of injury.

REHABILITATION CONCERNS, REHABILITATION PROGRESSION, AND CRITERIA FOR FULL RETURN

Palpation helps to isolate which tendon or tendons are involved, and resistive knee flexion, with the tibia in internal and external rotation, aids in the evaluation. If resistive ankle plantar flexion with the knee in extension does not reproduce symptoms, gastrocnemius involvement may be ruled out.

A patient who presents with this condition responds well to 1 to 2 days rest with oral anti-inflammatory medication. Ice massage and ultrasound are helpful in decreasing inflammation and pain. Gentle hamstring stretching exercises (see Exercises 29-38 and 29-39) with the hip in internal and external rotation help to isolate the tendon or tendons involved, and PNF stretching (see Exercise 29-40) should be performed on day 1. Hamstring progressive resistive strengthening exercises, which isolate the hamstring muscles, can be performed on day 1 (see Exercises 29-3, 29-8 to 29-10, and 29-14) along with extensions (see Exercise 29-21), if they can be performed without pain.

Femoral Stress Fractures

PATHOMECHANICS AND INJURY MECHANISM

Stress fractures, often described as a partial or incomplete fracture of the femur, may be seen because of repetitive microtrauma or cumulative stress overload to a localized area of the bone.[9,41] Young patients are more likely to develop this injury. The patient may complain of pinpoint pain that increases during activity. The initial X ray film is usually negative. Obtaining a good history is very important and should include activities, change in activities and surfaces, and running gait analysis.[41]

The basic biomechanics and biodynamics of normal bone are very important in understanding the mechanism of stress fractures. A process of bone resorption, followed by new bone formation, in normal bone, is constantly occurring by turning over and remodeling by the dynamic organ itself.[41] This remodeling occurs in response to weight-bearing and muscular contractions that cause stresses. Responses by the bone to these loads allow the bone to become as strong as it has to be to with-

stand the stresses placed upon it during the required activity.[10,41] Because bone is a dynamic tissue, there is a cell system in place that carries out the process of constant bone breakdown and bone repair for the task at hand.[41] There are two types of bone cells responsible for this dynamic procedure: osteoclasts, which resorb bone, and osteoblasts, which produce new bone to fill the areas that have been resorbed.[41] When stress is applied, the osteoblasts produce new bone at a rate comparable to the osteoclasts. When the stress is applied over time, as in overuse, the osteoclasts work at a faster rate than the osteoblasts, and a stress fracture occurs. Some studies have shown that this stress reaction occurs during approximately the third week of a workout session.[11] This becomes very important when developing a rehabilitation program in reference to using the advantages of bone physiology within the rehabilitation program to facilitate new bone formation.

REHABILITATION CONCERNS

As with all stress fractures, finding the cause is the first step in treatment and rehabilitation.[35] The patient may perform pain-free thigh strengthening and stretching exercises and progress as shown in the sections on hamstring and quadriceps rehabilitation programs.

The most important treatment for stress fractures is rest, especially from the activity that caused the fracture. In a period of 6 to 12 weeks, most femoral stress fractures heal clinically if the specific cause is discontinued.[41] The resorptive process will slow down and the reparative process will catch up with simple rest from the activity that caused the problem. Rest should be "active," which allows the patient to exercise pain free, and helps prevent muscle atrophy and deconditioning. Except in special "problem" fractures, immobilization in a cast or brace is usually unnecessary. When there is excessive pain or motion of the part, casts or braces may be used. In unreliable patients, a cast or some form of immobilization may be recommended. Nonweight-bearing or partial weight-bearing with crutches is highly recommended as the process of ambulating with a normal gait, while using crutches, may actually facilitate bone formation at the fracture site.[24]

Once normal activities are pain free with no tenderness or edema over the fracture site, and there are no abnormal gait patterns during ambulation, pain-free rehabilitation should start immediately and continue throughout the recovery period with a slow progressive return to activity. With recurrence of any symptoms, all activity should be discontinued immediately.[41]

REHABILITATION PROGRESSION

The first phase of the rehabilitation program begins at the time the stress fracture is diagnosed. This phase consists of modalities to decrease pain and swelling and increase or maintain active range of motion to the hip, knee, and ankle joints.[41] The second phase of rehabilitation begins as acute pain subsides. This phase consists of functional rehabilitation and conditioning in a progression of sport-specific training. Keeping in mind bone physiology as described, the patient is advised not to run, jump, or force activity during the third week after two weeks of vigorous "normal" exercise or rehabilitation and conditioning. This cycle is repeated—two weeks of vigorous "normal" activity, followed by one week of either eliminating running and jumping or at least cutting it back to half the "normal" activity level. This cycling of activities, every third week, facilitates osteoblast function (bone formation) and, therefore, new bone growth at the fracture site as the osteoblasts are able to keep pace with and actually work faster than the osteoclasts.

Rehabilitation and treatment should be an ongoing process as described above, with general physical conditioning as part of the "active rest" period. Aquatic exercise and conditioning—such as swimming, treading water, running in a swimming pool, biking, stairmaster, and the slide board (see Exercise 29-24), should be started as soon as they are pain free. These activities could come under the umbrella of "normal" exercise or rehabilitation and conditioning. Upper-body ergometers may also be utilized. A patient with a femoral stress fracture should also be evaluated for lower extremity deformities and foot malalignments.[41] Orthotics can be very useful in treating a femoral stress fracture if a malalignment is found.

Avulsion Fracture of the Femoral Trochanter

PATHOMECHANICS AND INJURY MECHANISM

Patients may suffer an isolated avulsion fracture of the femoral trochanters. When the greater trochanter is involved, the cause is usually a violent, forceful contraction of the hip abductor muscles. An avulsion fracture of the lesser trochanter occurs because of a violent, forceful contraction of the iliopsoas muscle.[30]

Palpation may produce pain and possibly a noticeable defect of the greater trochanter. Resistive movements and passive range of motion of the hip may reproduce pain. X-rays must be taken to confirm the injury. Immobilization may be the treatment of choice for an incomplete avulsion fracture. With a complete avulsion fracture, internal fixation is usually required.

REHABILITATION CONCERNS AND PROGRESSION

During the initial immobilization period, as prescribed by the physician, the patient with a femoral avulsion fracture should perform isometric hip exercises on the first day of rehabilitation, with isometric quadriceps and hamstring exercises and ankle strengthening exercises. Crutches should be used for the first 6 weeks until a pain-free normal gait cycle can be accomplished. After 6 weeks, the patient may perform pain-free active range-of-motion exercises, as well as pain-free stretching exercises (see Exercises 29-35 to 29-42). When pain allows, the patient may add stretching (see Exercises 29-43 to 29-46 and 29-48). The patient may also begin pain-free straight-leg raise exercises (see Exercises 29-2 to 29-4), and progress to hip abduction and rotation (see Exercises 29-5 to 29-7). During approximately week 8, the patient may perform hip progressive resistive exercises in

all four directions (see Exercise 29-14). Swimming can be added as soon as pain allows, and biking is performed when sufficient range of motion is attained. The patient is then progressed to closed-chain weight-bearing lifting activities (see Exercises 29-16, 29-17, 29-19, 29-20, 29-22, and 29-23). Jogging, plyometrics (see Exercises 29-27 to 29-29), slide board (see Exercise 29-24), and functional activities can be started as soon as the patient is pain free and has the necessary strength base.

TRAUMATIC FEMORAL FRACTURES

PATHOMECHANICS AND INJURY MECHANISM

A femoral neck fracture is often associated with osteoporosis.[16,36] A twisting motion combined with a fall may produce this fracture. Because the femoral neck fracture may disrupt the blood supply to the head of the femur, avascular necrosis is often seen later. This injury must receive proper treatment.

REHABILITATION CONCERNS AND PROGRESSION

After surgery or during immobilization, isometric hip exercises are started immediately. Patients, especially younger patients, are progressed slowly. A normal gait cycle should be taught to the patient as soon as possible. If osteoporosis is known to be involved, in some cases, exercise has been shown to increase bone density and reverse the rate of osteoporosis. Progress the patient with functional range of motion and functional strength; aquatic therapy and biking, if pain free. Within 6 to 8 weeks, gentle active hip range-of-motion exercises with no weight can be performed (see Exercises 29-1 to 29-7). Stretching exercises are performed at approximately week 8 (see Exercises 29-35 to 29-44 and 29-49); progress to stretches for hip rotation and the piriformis (see Exercises 29-45, 29-46, and 29-48). Progressive resistive muscle-strengthening exercises should be started after 2 to 4 weeks of active range-of-motion and stretching exercises. At approximately week 12, weight can be added to Exercises 29-1 to 29-7, and the exercises shown in Exercises 29-9, 29-12, and 29-14 can be added, along with closed-chain exercises (see Exercises 29-16, 29-17, 29-19, 29-20, 29-22, and 29-23).

After the patient's strength level has reached the "norm" the patient may begin pain-free slide board (see Exercise 29-24), plyometrics (see Exercises 29-27 to 29-29), and functional activities.

Quadriceps Muscle Strain

PATHOMECHANICS

A strain to the large quadriceps muscles in the front of the thigh may be very disabling, especially when the rectus femoris muscle is involved due to its involvement at two joints.[17] The four quadriceps muscles share the same innervation and tendon of insertion.[6] The rectus femoris is the only quadriceps muscle that crosses the hip joint; therefore is considered a biarticular

the knee bent over the end of a table may cause mild discomfort with good strength present.

A patient with a grade III contusion may herniate the muscle through the fascia to cause a marked defect, severe bleeding, and disability. The patient may not be able to ambulate without crutches. Pain, severe swelling, and a bulge of muscle tissue may be present on palpation. When the patient is lying prone, knee flexion active range of motion may be severely limited. Active resistive knee extension while the patient is sitting and lying supine with the knee bent over the end of a table may not be tolerated, and severe weakness may be present.

Grade III lateral quadriceps contusions are very rare due to the lack of muscle belly tissue. If a grade III lateral quadriceps contusion is diagnosed, a femoral contusion and possible fracture should be ruled out.

REHABILITATION CONCERNS AND PROGRESSION

A patient with a grade I quadriceps contusion should begin ice and 24-hour compression immediately. Twenty-four hour compression should be continued until all signs and symptoms are absent. Gentle, pain-free quadriceps stretching exercises (see Exercises 29-35, 29-36, and 29-49) may be performed on the first day. Quadriceps progressive resistive strengthening exercises may also be performed as soon as possible, usually on the second day, in the order given and pain free (see Exercises 29-2 and 29-11 to 29-14), flexion with knee both extended and flexed (see Exercises 29-16 to 29-20 and 29-22), and isokinetics (see Exercises 29-25 and 29-26). This patient's active range of motion should be carefully monitored. A patient with a grade I quadriceps contusion may try to continue normal activities, but compression and protective padding should be worn until the patient is symptom free. If motion decreases, the injury should be updated to a grade II contusion and treated as such.

A patient with a grade II contusion should be treated very conservatively. Crutches should be used until a normal gait can be accomplished free of pain. Ice, 24-hour compression, and electrical muscle stimulation modalities may be started immediately to decrease swelling, inflammation, and pain and to promote range of motion.[29] Compression should be applied at all times to minimize bleeding into the area. Pain-free quadriceps isometric exercises may be performed as soon as possible, usually within the first 3 days. Between days 3 and 5, ice is continued with pain-free active range of motion, while the patient is sitting and lying prone. Active range of motion lying supine with the knee bent over the end of a table can be added. Passive stretching is not used until the later phases of rehabilitation. Massage and heat modalities are also contraindicated in the early phases because of the possibility of promoting bleeding and eventually myositis ossificans. At approximately day 5, the patient may perform straight leg raises without weights and then progress to weights, pain free (see Exercise 29-2). As active range of motion increases and approaches 95 to 100 degrees of knee flexion, swimming, aquatic therapy, and biking may be performed if the seat height is adjusted to the patient's available range of motion. Between

days 7 and 10, heat in the form of hot packs, ultrasound, or whirlpool may be used, as long as swelling is negative and the patient is approaching full active range of motion while lying prone. Pain-free quadriceps progressive resistive strengthening exercises may be performed in the order given (see Exercises 29-2 and 29-11 to 29-14), flexion with knee both extended and flexed (see Exercises 29-16 to 29-20 and 29-22), and isokinetics (see Exercises 29-25 and 29-26). Ice or heat modalities, with active range of motion, should be continued before all exercises as a warm-up. Pain-free quadriceps stretching exercises should not be rushed and can be started between 10 and 14 days as needed (see Exercises 29-35, 29-36, and 29-49). A patient with a grade II quadriceps contusion may require 3 to 21 days for rehabilitation, depending upon the severity of the injury. Jogging, slide board (see Exercise 29-24), plyometrics (see Exercises 29-27 to 29-29), and functional activities may be used after the 14th day. Compression and protective padding should be worn during physical activity until the patient is symptom free. A patient with a grade II quadriceps contusion to the lateral thigh area may not need a long period for rehabilitation but should wear compression and protective padding during participation.

A patient with a grade III quadriceps contusion should use crutches, rest, ice, 24-hour compression, and electrical muscle stimulation modalities immediately to decrease pain, bleeding, and swelling and counteract atrophy.[29] The patient may begin pain-free isometric quadriceps exercises between days 5 and 7. Ice and 24-hour compression should be continued from the very first day through day 7, with pain-free active range-of-motion exercises, while the patient is sitting and lying prone, are added about day 7. Active range of motion lying supine with the knee bent over the end of a table can also be added. At approximately day 10, the patient may perform straight leg raises without weights and then progress to weights by day 14 (see Exercise 29-2). Electrical muscle stimulation may be very helpful in this phase to counteract muscle atrophy and reeducate muscle contraction. Again, as active range of motion increases and approaches 95 to 100 degrees of knee flexion, swimming, aquatic therapy, and biking may be performed if the seat height is adjusted to the patient's available range of motion. After day 14, the patient may use heat in the form of hot packs or whirlpool, as long as the swelling has decreased and the patient has gained active range of motion. At approximately the third week of rehabilitation, pain-free quadriceps progressive resistive strengthening exercises may be performed in the order presented (see Exercises 29-2 and 29-11 to 29-14), flexion with knee both extended and flexed (see Exercises 29-16 to 29-20 and 29-22), and isokinetics (see Exercises 29-25 and 29-26). Pain-free quadriceps stretching may also be performed (see Exercises 29-35, 29-36, and 29-49) if the patient is careful not to overstretch the quadriceps muscles. A patient with a grade III quadriceps contusion may require 3 weeks to 3 months for rehabilitation. In general, at approximately week 3, the patient may begin jogging, slide board (see Exercise 29-24), plyometrics (see Exercises 29-27 and 29-29), and functional activities. Again, compression and protective padding should be worn during all competition until the patient is symptom free.

Myositis Ossificans

PATHOMECHANICS AND INJURY MECHANISM

With a severe direct blow or repetitive direct blows to the quadriceps muscles that cause muscle tissue damage, bleeding, and injury to the periosteum of the femur, ectopic bone production may occur.[1,21] In 3 to 6 weeks, calcium formation may be seen on x-ray films. If the trauma was to the quadriceps muscles only and not the femur, a smaller bony mass may be seen on x-ray films.[1]

If quadriceps contusion and strain are properly treated and rehabilitated, myositis ossificans can be prevented. Myositis ossificans can be caused by trying to "play through" a grade II or III quadriceps contusion or strain and by early use of massage, stretching exercises into pain, ultrasound, and other heat modalities.[1]

REHABILITATION CONCERNS AND PROGRESSION

After 1 year, surgical removal of the bony mass may be helpful. If the bony mass is removed too early, the trauma caused by the surgery may actually enhance the condition.

After diagnosis by x-ray film, treatment and rehabilitation should follow that of a grade II or III quadriceps contusion or quadriceps strain (see treatment and rehabilitation for grade II and III quadriceps contusions and strains). The bony mass usually stabilizes after the sixth month.[18] If the mass does not cause disability, the patient should be closely monitored and follow the treatment and rehabilitation programs outlined in grade II and III quadriceps contusions and strains. It has also been recommended that myositis be treated using acetic acid with iontophoresis.[39]

EXERCISES

REHABILITATION TECHNIQUES FOR THE GROIN, HIP, AND THIGH

Preferred treatment and rehabilitation of these injuries are broken down into phases. During the early phase of rehabilitation, ice, compression, and modalities are used with pain-free active range of motion as early as possible. Try to avoid any movement that causes pain, especially passive range of motion started too early. After the acute phase, the therapist should use modalities in combination with active range of motion and the beginning of active resistive pain-free strengthening exercises, both open chain and closed chain, as well as concentric and eccentric contractions. Pain-free stretching is also started in this phase. During the late phase, the therapist should progress the patient into plyometric activities, activity-specific functional training with agility, and ground/power-based activities. Keep in mind that the time sequences for programs and phases are approximations and need to be adjusted depending upon the degree of injury, the activity level, and the patient.

Strengthening Exercises

ISOTONIC OPEN-KINETIC CHAIN STRENGTHENING EXERCISES

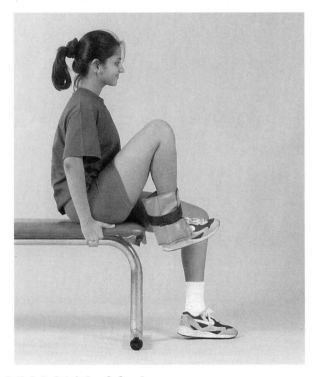

EXERCISE 29-1

Pain-free hip flexion iliopsoas progressive resistive strengthening exercises: 4 sets of 10 to 15 repetitions daily.

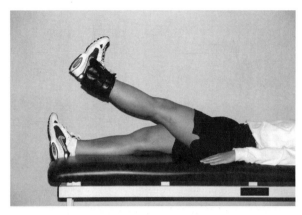

EXERCISE 29-2

Straight leg raises (quadriceps and iliopsoas): 4 sets of 10 repetitions daily.

EXERCISE 29-3

Pain-free hip extension (gluteus maximus and hamstring) progressive resistive strengthening exercises: 4 sets of 10 to 15 repetitions daily.

EXERCISE 29-4

Pain-free hip adduction (adductor magnus, brevis, longus, pectineus, and gracilis) progressive resistive strengthening exercises: 4 sets of 10 to 15 repetitions daily.

E X E R C I S E   2 9 - 5

Pain-free hip abduction (gluteus medius, gluteus maximus, and tensor fasciae latae) progressive resistive strengthening exercises: 4 sets of 10 to 15 repetitions daily.

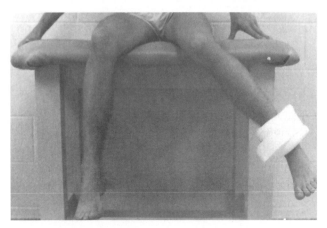

E X E R C I S E   2 9 - 6

Pain-free hip internal rotation (gluteus minimus, tensor fasciae latae, semitendinosis, and semimembranosis) progressive resistive strengthening exercises: 4 sets of 10 to 15 repetitions daily.

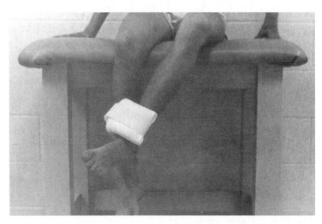

E X E R C I S E   2 9 - 7

Pain-free hip external rotation (piriformis and gluteus maximus) progressive resistive strengthening exercises: 4 sets of 10 to 15 repetitions daily.

E X E R C I S E   2 9 - 8

Pain-free seated hamstring progressive resistive strengthening exercises (maintain lordotic lumbar curve). Isotonics performed on the NK table, 4 sets of 10 repetitions, 2 or 3 days/week.

E X E R C I S E   2 9 - 9

Pain-free prone hamstring single-leg progressive resistive strengthening exercises: 4 sets of 12 repetitions, 2 or 3 days/week.

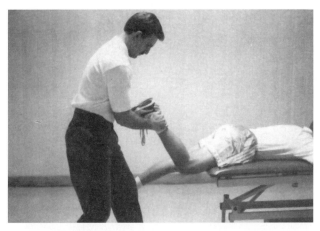

EXERCISE 29-10

Manual resistance hamstring strengthening to fatigue. Patient lies prone with knee over the edge of treatment table. With the patient in full knee extension, resistance is applied to the back of the heels as the patient contracts concentrically to full knee flexion for a count of 5 seconds. After a 2-second pause at full flexion, resistance is applied into extension for a count of 5 as the patient contracts the hamstrings eccentrically. This is repeated, contracting as fast as possible, for 2 or 3 sets of 10 to 12 repetitions or until failure, 1 or 2 days/week.

EXERCISE 29-12

Pain-free seated quadriceps progressive resistive strengthening exercises single leg, 3 or 4 sets of 10 to 12 repetitions, 1 or 2 days/week.

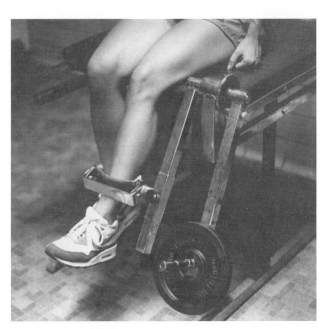

EXERCISE 29-11

Pain-free seated quadriceps progressive resistive strengthening exercises. Isotonics using the NK table, 4 sets of 10 repetitions, 2 or 3 days/week.

EXERCISE 29-13

Pain-free supine quadriceps progressive resistive strengthening exercises single leg (lying supine), to isolate rectus femoris, 2 or 3 sets of 10 to 12 repetitions, 1 or 2 days/week.

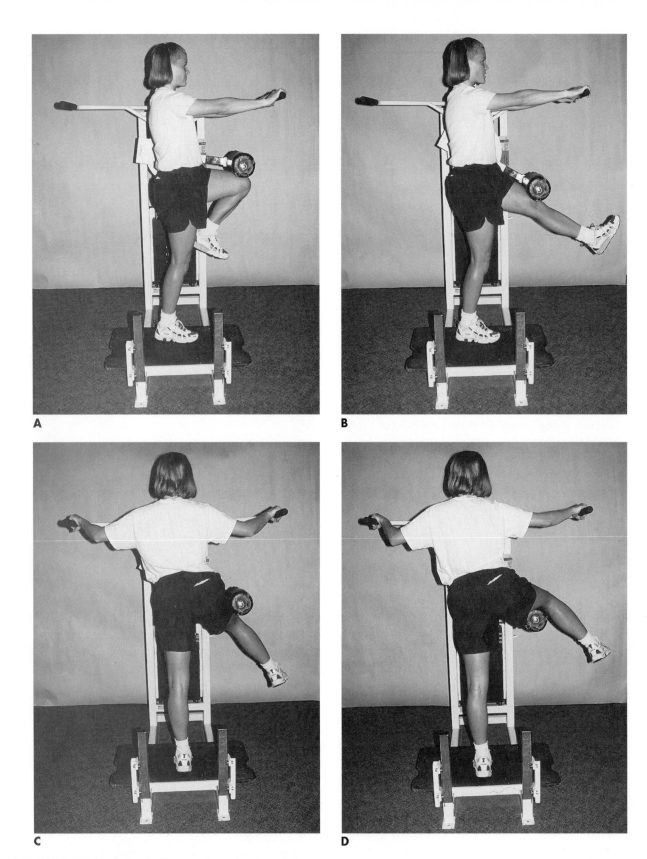

A

B

C

D

EXERCISE 29-14

Pain-free multihip progressive resistive strengthening exercises in all four directions, 2 sets of 15 repetitions, 1 or 2 days/week: **(A)** Flexion with knee flexed (rectus femoris) and **(B)** knee extended (iliopsoas), **(C)** abduction, adduction, extension with knee extended start position to knee. **(D)** Bent terminal position (semimembranosis, tendinosis, and gluteus maximus) and (on the next page) **(E)** knee bent start position to knee extended terminal position (biceps femoris and gluteus maximus).

E

EXERCISE 29-14

Continued

A

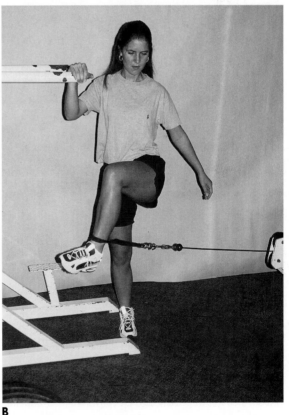

B

EXERCISE 29-15

A, Pain-free low-cable column starting position of hip abduction, extension, and external rotation to **B,** terminal position of adduction, flexion, and internal rotation: 3 sets of 15 repetitions, 1 or 2 days/week.

CLOSED-KINETIC CHAIN STRENGTHENING EXERCISES

E X E R C I S E   2 9 - 1 6

Leg press with feet high on the footplate and shoulder width apart to work the upper hamstring while keeping knees over the feet (not over the toes or in front of the toes). Seat setting should be close, so that at the bottom of the motion the hips are lower than the knees. (Quadriceps, upper hamstrings, and gluteus maximus.) Perform 3 sets of 12 repetitions, 2 days/week.

E X E R C I S E   2 9 - 1 8

Smith press squats with feet behind the patient's center of gravity and hip in extension (as on a hip sled) (quadriceps, lower lateral hamstring, and gluteus maximus). The patient descends while keeping a lordotic curve in the low back. Perform 3 sets of 12 repetitions, 2 days/week.

E X E R C I S E   2 9 - 1 7

Smith press squats with feet placement forward of the patient's center of gravity and close (within 1 to 2 inches of each other) or hack squat (quadriceps, upper hamstrings, and gluteus maximus). The patient descends keeping a lordotic curve in the low back until the hip joints break parallel (lower than the knee joints). Perform 3 sets of 12 repetitions, 2 days/week.

E X E R C I S E   2 9 - 1 9

Lunges (quadriceps, hamstrings, gluteus maximus, groin muscles, and iliopsoas) stepping onto 4- to 6-inch step height. Once the foot hits the step, the patient should bend the back knee straight down towards the floor to work the upper hamstring of the front leg and the hip flexors of the back leg. Perform 2 sets of 12 to 15 repetitions, 2 days/week.

EXERCISE 29-20

Standard squats below parallel (quadriceps, upper hamstrings, groin muscles, and gluteus maximus): 3 sets of 12 repetitions, 2 days/week.

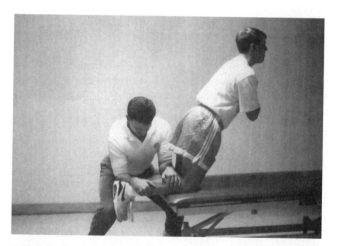

EXERCISE 29-21

Hamstring leans—kneeling eccentric hamstring lowering exercises. With the patient kneeling on a treatment table and feet hanging over the end, the therapist stabilizes the lower legs as the patient lowers the body to the prone position, eccentrically contracting the hamstrings. The patient should maintain a lumbar lordotic curve and stay completely erect, avoiding any hip flexion. The patient should perform 2 sets of 8 to 10 repetitions or until failure, 1 or 2 days/week.

EXERCISE 29-22

Lateral step-ups (quadriceps, hamstrings, gluteus maximus, gluteus medius, and tensor fasciae latae) using repetitions and sets, or time, 2 or 3 days/week.

A   **B**

E X E R C I S E   2 9 - 2 3

A, Standing running pattern, manual resistance starting position, 2 sets of 20 repetitions, 1 or 2 days/week. Resistance is applied to the back of the heel, resisting hip flexion and knee flexion to terminal position, and then resisting hip extension and knee extension back down to starting position. The patient contracts as fast as possible through the entire range of running motion. **B,** Standing running pattern, terminal position.

ISOKINETICS EXERCISES

E X E R C I S E   2 9 - 2 4

Slide board or fitter keeping knees bent and maintaining a squat position for the entire workout (increases hamstring activity). Use sets and repetitions or time, 1 or 2 days/week.

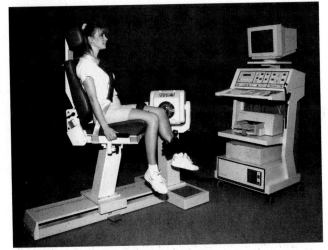

E X E R C I S E   2 9 - 2 5

Seated isokinetic hamstring and quadriceps strengthening. Three speed settings, 2 sets of 15 to 20 repetitions each setting, each leg, 1 or 2 days/week.

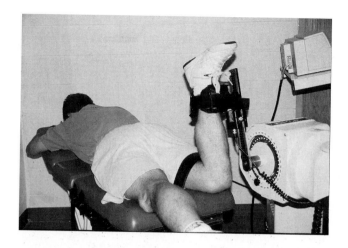

EXERCISE 29-26

Prone lying single-leg isokinetic hamstring and quadriceps strengthening. Three speed settings, 2 sets of 15 to 20 repetitions each setting, for each leg, 1 or 2 days/week.

PLYOMETRIC EXERCISES

EXERCISE 29-27

Jump-down exercises (sets and repetitions or time), 1 or 2 days/week.

EXERCISE 29-28

Lateral bounding (sets and repetitions or time), 1 or 2 days/week.

EXERCISE 29-29

Lateral sliding (sets and repetitions or time), 1 or 2 days/week.

PNF STRENGTHENING

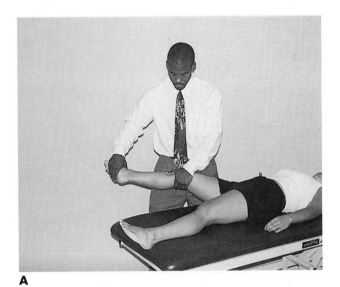

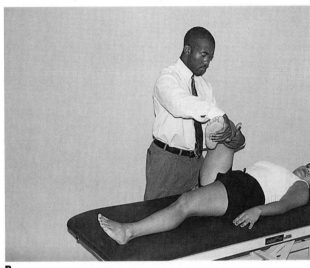

A

B

EXERCISE 29-30

A, D1 Movement pattern into flexion, starting position, 2 sets of 12 to 15 repetitions, 2 or 3 days/week. **B,** Movement pattern into flexion, terminal position.

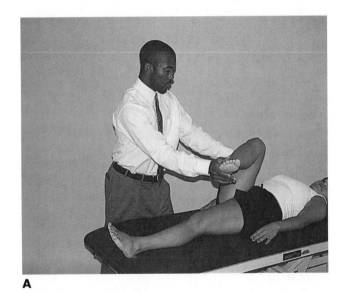

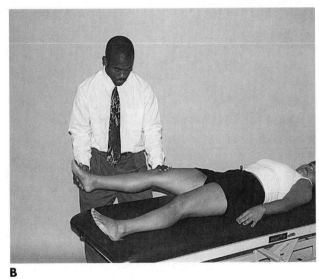

A

B

EXERCISE 29-31

A, D1 Movement pattern into extension, starting position, 2 sets of 12 to 15 repetitions, 2 or 3 days/week. **B,** Movement pattern into extension, terminal position.

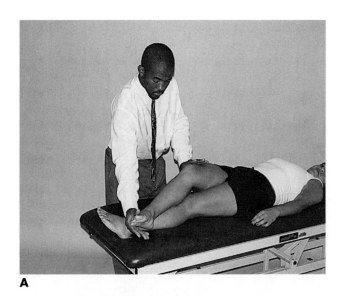
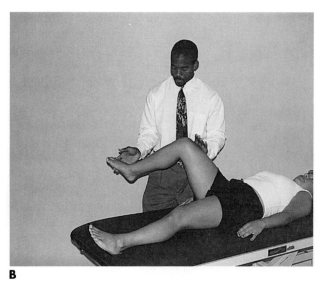

A   B

EXERCISE 29-32

A, D2 Movement pattern into flexion, starting position, 2 sets of 12 to 15 repetitions, 2 or 3 days/week. **B,** Movement pattern into flexion, terminal position.

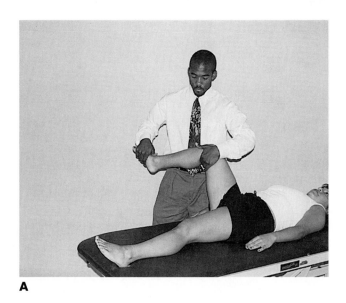
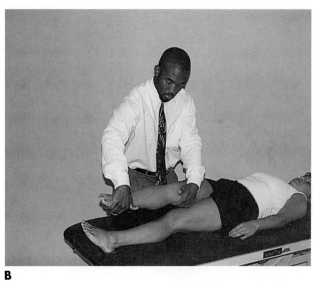

A   B

EXERCISE 29-33

A, D2 Movement pattern into extension, starting position, 2 sets of 12 to 15 repetitions, 2 or 3 days/week. **B,** Movement pattern into extension, terminal position.

STRETCHING EXERCISES

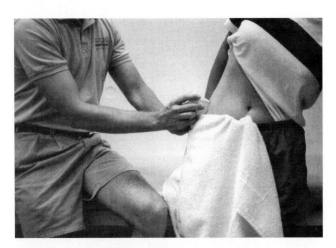

E X E R C I S E   2 9 - 3 4

Hip pointer stretching with ice.

E X E R C I S E   2 9 - 3 6

Hip flexor stretch with knee flexed to isolate the rectus femoris.

E X E R C I S E   2 9 - 3 5

Hip flexor stretch.

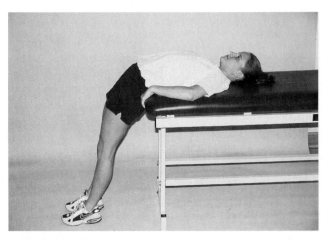

E X E R C I S E   2 9 - 3 7

Passive static stretch over end of table with hip extended (using ice or heat for 15 to 20 minutes).

A

B

E X E R C I S E 2 9 - 3 8

A, Hamstring and **B,** gluteus stretch.

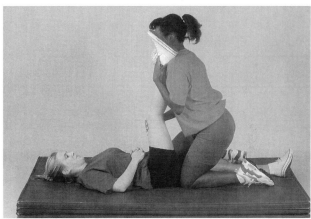

E X E R C I S E 2 9 - 4 0

PNF hamstring stretching.

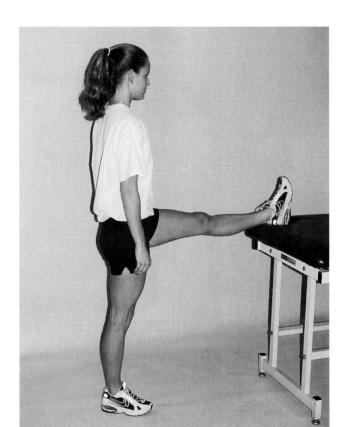

E X E R C I S E 2 9 - 3 9

Hamstring stretch maintaining lordotic curve.

E X E R C I S E 2 9 - 4 1

Hip adductor stretch.

EXERCISE 29-42

Standing hip adductor stretch.

EXERCISE 29-43

Hip abductor stretch.

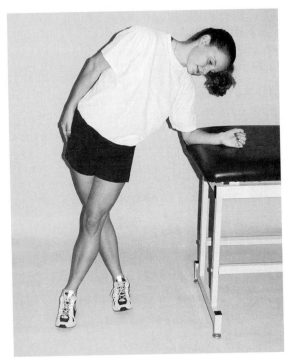

EXERCISE 29-44

Standing hip abductor stretch.

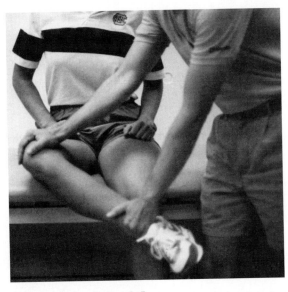

EXERCISE 29-45

Hip internal rotator stretch.

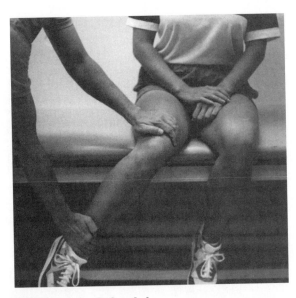

EXERCISE 29-46

Hip external rotator stretch.

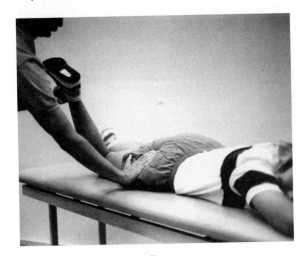

EXERCISE 29-47

Piriformis stretch.

A

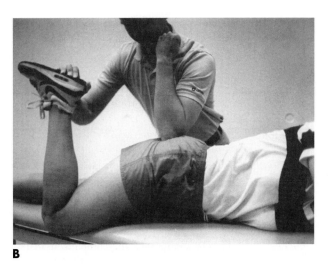

B

EXERCISE 29-48

Alternate piriformis stretches.

SUMMARY

- Injuries to the groin, hip, and thigh can be extremely disabling and often require a substantial amount of time for rehabilitation.
- Hip pointers are contusions of the soft tissue in the area of the iliac crest and must be treated aggressively during the first 2 to 4 hours after injury.
- Piriformis syndrome sciatica should be specifically differentiated from other problems that produce low back or radiating pain in the buttocks and leg. Rehabilitation programs are extremely variable for different conditions and may even be harmful if used inappropriately.
- Trochanteric bursitis is relatively common in patients, as is ischial bursitis. Treatment involves efforts directed at protection and reduction of inflammation in the affected area.
- Snapping or clicking hip syndrome most often occurs when the iliotibial band snaps over the greater trochanter causing trochanteric bursitis.
- Osteitis pubis and fractures of the inferior ramus both produce pain at the pubic symphysis and are best treated with rest.
- Hip dislocations are rare and require between 6 to 12 months of rehabilitation before the patient can return to full activity.
- Strains of the groin musculature, the hamstring, and the quadriceps muscles can require long periods of rehabilitation for the patient. Early return often exacerbates the problem.
- The femur is subject to stress fractures, avulsion fractures of the lesser trochanter, and traumatic fractures of the femoral neck.
- Protection is the key to treatment and rehabilitation of quadriceps contusions and accompanying myositis ossificans.

I would like to thank Jim Case, MA, ATC, Assistant Athletic Trainer at Cornell University, for his contribution to various portions of this chapter.

REFERENCES

1. Arnheim DD, Prentice WE. *Principles of Athletic Training*, New York, McGraw-Hill, 2000.
2. Berry JM. Fracture of the tuberosity of the ischium due to muscular action, *JAMA* 59:1450, 1992.
3. Brunet M, Hontas R. The thigh. In: DeLee JC, Drez D, eds. *Orthopaedic Sports Medicine*, vol. 2. Philadelphia, Saunders, 1994.
4. Coole WG, Gieck JH. An analysis of hamstring strains and their rehabilitation. *J Orthop Sports Phys Ther* 9:77–85, 1987.
5. Daniels L, Worthingham C. *Muscle Testing, Techniques of Manual Examination.* Philadelphia, Saunders, 1996.
6. DeLee JC, Drez D. *Orthopaedic Sports Medicine*, vol. 2. Philadelphia, Saunders, 1994.
7. DeLorme TI, Watkins AI. *Progressive Resistive Exercise Technique and Medical Application.* New York, Appleton-Century-Crofts, 1952.
8. DePalma BF, Zelko RR. Knee rehabilitation following anterior cruciate ligament injury or surgery. *Athl Train* 21:3, 1986.
9. Devas MB. *Stress Fractures.* New York, Longman, 1975.
10. Frost H. *Laws of Bone Structures.* Springfield, IL, Thomas, 1964.
11. Gilbert RS, Johnson HA. Stress fractures in military recruits—A review of 12 years' experiences. *Mil Med* 131:716–721, 1966.
12. Gordon EJ. Diagnosis and treatment of common hip disorders. *Med Tra Tech Q* 28:443, 1981.

13. Harvey J, ed. *Rehabilitation of the Injured Athlete: Clinics in Sports Medicine.* Philadelphia, Saunders, 1985.

14. Hollinshead WH. *Functional Anatomy of the Limbs and Back.* Philadelphia, Saunders, 1976.

15. Hoppenfield S. *Physical Examination of the Spine and Extremities.* New York, Appleton-Century-Crofts, 1976.

16. Hunter-Griffen L, ed. *Overuse Injuries: Clinics in Sports Medicine.* Philadelphia, Saunders, 1987.

17. Jaivin J, Fox J. Thigh injuries. In: Nicholas J, Hershman E. *The Lower Extremtiy and Spine in Sports Medicine.* St. Louis, Mosby, 1995.

18. Kuland DN. *The Injured Athlete.* Philadelphia, Lippincott, 1982.

19. Lewinneck G. The significance and comparison analysis of the epidemiology of hip fractures. *Clin Orthop* 152:35, 1980.

20. Lewis A. *Normal Human Locomotion.* Hamden, CT, Quinnipiac College, 1977.

21. Lipscomb AB. Treatment of myositis ossificans traumatica in athletes. *J Sports Med* 4:61,1976.

22. Malone T et al. *Orthopedic and Sports Physical Therapy.* St. Louis, Mosby, 1996.

23. Magee DJ. *Orthopedic Physical Assessment.* Philadelphia, Saunders, 1997.

24. Mendez A, Eyster R. Displaced nonunion stress fracture of the femoral neck treated with internal fixation and bone graft. *Am J Sports Med* 20:220–223, 1992.

25. Moore KL. *Clinical Oriented Anatomy.* Baltimore, Williams & Wilkins, 1985.

26. Nadkarni J. Simultaneous anterior and posterior dislocation of the hip. *J Postgrad Ed* 37:117–118, 1991.

27. Norkin L, LeVange P. *Joint Structure and Function.* Philadelphia, Davis, 1983.

28. Orava S, Kujala U. Rupture of the ischial origin of the hamstrings. *Am J Sports Med* 22:702–705, 1995.

29. Prentice WE. *Therapeutic Modalities in Sports Medicine.* Dubuque, WC Brown/McGraw-Hill, 1999.

30. Pruner R, Johnston C. Avulsion fracture of the ischial tuberosity. *Pediatr Orthop* 13:357–358, 1991.

31. Ryan J, Wheeler J, Hopkinson W. Quadriceps contusion: West Point update. *Am J Sports Med* 19:299–303, 1991.

32. Sanders B, Nemeth W. Hip and thigh injuries. In: Zachazewski J, Magee D, Quillen S. *Athletic Injuries and Rehabilitation.* Philadelphia, Saunders, 1996.

33. Schlickewei W, Elsasser B. Hip dislocation without fracture. *Injury* 24:27–31, 1993.

34. Sim F, Rock M, Scott S. Pelvis and hip injuries in athlete: Anatomy and function. In: Nicholas J, Hershman E, eds. *The Lower Extremity and Spine in Sports Medicine.* St. Louis, Mosby, 1995.

35. Stanitski CL, McMaster JH, Scranton PE. On the nature of stress fractures. *Am J Sports Med* 6:391–396, 1978.

36. Stevens J. The incidence of osteoporosis in patients with femoral neck fractures. *J Bone Joint Surg* 44:520, 1962.

37. Tinker R, ed. *Ramamurti's Orthopaedics in Primary Care.* Baltimore, Williams & Wilkins, 1979.

38. Torg J, Vegso J, Torg P. *Rehabilitation of Athletic Injuries: A Guide to Therapeutic Exercise.* St. Louis, Mosby, 1987.

39. Wieder D. Treatment of traumatic myositis ossificans with acetic acid and iontophoresis. *Phys Ther* 72:133–137, 1992.

40. Worrell T, Perrin D. Hamstring muscle injury: The influence of strength, flexibility, warmup and fatigue. *J Orthop Sports Phys Ther* 16:12–18, 1992.

41. Zelko RR, DePalma BF. *Stress Fractures in Athletes: Diagnosis and Treatment.* Forum Medicus, Postgraduate Advances in Sports Medicine, I-XI, 1986.

CHAPTER 30

Rehabilitation of the Knee

William E. Prentice and Marc Davis

OBJECTIVES

After completing this chapter, the student therapist should be able to do the following:

- Discuss the functional anatomy and biomechanics associated with normal function of the knee joint.
- Identify the various techniques for regaining range of motion, including stretching exercises and joint mobilizations.
- Discuss exercises that can be used to reestablish neuromuscular control.
- Discuss the rehabilitation progressions for various ligamentous and meniscal injuries.
- Describe and explain the rationale for various treatment techniques in the management of injuries to the patellofemoral joint and the extensor mechanism.
- Demonstrate the various rehabilitative strengthening techniques for the knee, including both open- and closed-kinetic chain isotonic, plyometric, isokinetic, and PNF exercises.

FUNCTIONAL ANATOMY AND BIOMECHANICS

The knee is part of the kinetic chain and is directly affected by motions and forces occurring and being transmitted from the foot, ankle, and lower leg. In turn, the knee must transmit forces to the thigh, hip, pelvis, and spine. Abnormal forces that cannot be distributed must be absorbed by the tissues. In a closed-kinetic chain, forces must either be transmitted to proximal segments or be absorbed in a more distal joint. The inability of this closed system to dissipate these forces typically leads to a breakdown in some part of the system. Certainly, as part of the kinetic chain, the knee joint is susceptible to injury resulting from absorption of these forces.

The knee is commonly considered a hinge joint because its two principal movements are flexion and extension (Fig. 30-1). Because rotation of the tibia is an essential component of knee movement, however, the knee is not a true hinge joint. The stability of the knee joint depends primarily on the ligaments, the joint capsule, and muscles that surround the joint. The knee is primarily designed to provide stability in weight bearing and mobility in locomotion; however, it is especially unstable laterally and medially.

Movement between the tibia and the femur involves the physiologic motions of flexion, extension, and rotation, as well as arthrokinematic motions, including rolling and gliding. As the tibia extends on the femur the tibia glides and rolls anteriorly. If the femur is extending on the tibia, gliding occurs in an anterior direction, whereas rolling occurs posteriorly.

Axial rotation of the tibia relative to the femur is an important component of knee motion. In the "screw home" mechanism of the knee, as the knee extends the tibia externally rotates. Rotation occurs because the medial femoral condyle is larger than the lateral condyle. Thus, when weight bearing, the tibia must rotate externally to achieve full extension. The rotational component gives a great deal of stability to the knee in full extension. When weight bearing, the popliteus muscle must contract and externally rotate the femur to "unlock" the knee so that flexion can occur.

Collateral Ligaments

The medial collateral ligament (MCL) is divided into two parts, the stronger superficial portion and the thinner and weaker "deep" medial ligament or capsular ligament, with its accompanying attachment to the medial meniscus.[85] The superficial position of the MCL is separate from the deeper capsular ligament

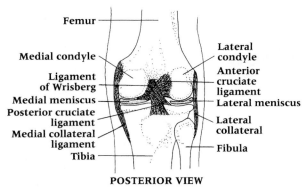

POSTERIOR VIEW

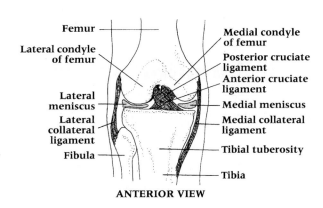

ANTERIOR VIEW

FIGURE 30-1

Anatomy of the knee.

at the joint line. The posterior aspect of the ligament blends into the deep posterior capsular ligament and semimembranous muscle. Fibers of the semimembranous muscle go through the capsule and attach to the posterior aspect of the medial meniscus, pulling it backward during knee flexion. The MCL functions as the primary static stabilizer against valgus stress. The MCL is taut at full extension and begins to relax between 20 to 30 degrees of flexion and comes under tension again at 60 to 70 degrees of flexion, although a portion of the ligament is taut through the range of motion.[42,85] Its major purpose is to prevent the knee from valgus and external rotating forces.

The medial collateral ligament was thought to be the principal stabilizer of the knee in a valgus position when combined with rotation. In the normal knee, valgus loading is greatest during the push-off phase of gait when the foot is planted and the tibia is externally rotated relative to the femur. It is now known that the anterior cruciate ligament plays an equal or greater part in this function.[82]

The lateral (fibular) collateral ligament is a round, fibrous cord shaped like a pencil. It is attached to the lateral epicondyle of the femur and to the head of the fibula. The lateral collateral ligament (LCL) functions with the iliotibial band, the popliteous tendon, the arcuate ligament complex, and the biceps tendons to support the lateral aspect of the knee. The LCL is under constant tensile loading, and the thick, firm configuration of the ligament is well designed to withstand this constant stress.[42] The lateral collateral ligament is taut during knee extension but relaxed during flexion.

Capsular Ligaments

The deep medial capsular ligament is divided into three parts: the anterior, medial, and posterior capsular ligaments. The anterior capsular ligament connects with the extensor mechanism and the medial meniscus through the coronary ligaments. It relaxes during knee extension and tightens during knee flexion. The primary purposes of the medial capsular ligaments are to attach the medial meniscus to the femur and to allow the tibia to move on the meniscus inferiorly. The posterior capsular ligament is called the posterior oblique ligament. It attaches to

the posterior medial aspect of the meniscus and intersperses with the semimembranous muscle. Along with the MCL, the pes anserinus tendons, and the semimembranosus, the posterior oblique ligament reinforces the posteromedial joint capsule.

The arcuate ligament is formed by a thickening of the posteriorlateral capsule. Its posterior aspect attaches to the fascia of the popliteal muscle and the posterior horn of the lateral meniscus. This arcuate ligament along with the the iliotibial band, the popliteus, the biceps femoris, and the LCL reinforce the posteriorlateral joint capsule.

The iliotibial band becomes taut during both extension and flexion. The popliteal muscle stabilizes the knee during flexion and, when contracting, protects the lateral meniscus by pulling it posteriorly. The biceps femoris muscle also stabilizes the knee laterally by inserting into the fibular head, iliotibial band, and capsule.

Cruciate Ligaments

The anterior cruciate ligament prevents the femur from moving posteriorly during weight bearing, stabilizes the knee in full extension, and prevents hyperextension. It also stabilizes the tibia against excessive internal rotation and serves as a secondary restraint for valgus/varus stress with collateral ligament damage. The anterior cruciate ligament works in conjunction with the thigh muscles, especially the hamstring muscle group, to stabilize the knee joint.

During extension there is external rotation of the tibia during the last 15 degrees of which the anterior cruciate ligament unwinds. In full extension the anterior cruciate ligament is tightest, and it loosens during flexion. When the knee is fully extended, the posterolateral portion of the anterior cruciate ligament is tight. In flexion, the posterolateral fibers loosen and the anteromedial fibers tighten.

Some portion of the posterior cruciate ligament is taut throughout the full range of motion. As the femur glides on the tibia, the posterior cruciate ligament becomes taut and prevents further gliding. In general, the posterior cruciate ligament prevents excessive internal rotation. Hyperextension of the knee guides the knee in flexion, and acts as a drag during the initial glide phase of flexion.

Menisci

The medial and lateral menisci function to improve the stability of the knee, increase shock absorption, and distribute weight over a larger surface area. The menisci help to stabilize the knee, especially the medial meniscus, when the knee is flexed at 90 degrees. The menisci transmit one half of the contact force in the medial compartment and even a higher percentage of the contact load in the lateral compartment.

During flexion, the menisci move posteriorly and during extension, they move anteriorly. This is primarily due to attachments of the medial meniscus to the semimembranosus, and the lateral meniscus to the popliteus tendon. During internal rotation the medial meniscus moves anteriorly relative to the medial tibial plateau, and the lateral meniscus moves posterior relative to the lateral tibial plateau. In internal rotation, the movements are reversed.

Function of Patella

Collectively, the quadriceps muscle group, the quadriceps tendon, the patella, and the patellar tendon form the extensor mechanism. The patella aids the knee during extension by lengthening the lever arm of the quadriceps muscle. It distributes the compressive stresses on the femur by increasing the contact area between the patellar tendon and the femur.[65] It also protects the patellar tendon against friction. Tracking within this groove depends on the pull of the quadriceps muscle, patellar tendon, depth of the femoral condyles, and shape of the patella.

During full extension, the patella lies slightly lateral and proximal to the trochlea. At 20 degrees of knee flexion, there is tibial rotation and the patella moves into the trochlea. At 30 degrees, the patella is most prominent. At 30 degrees and more, the patella moves deeper into the trochlea. At 90 degrees, the patella again becomes positioned laterally. When knee flexion is 135 degrees, the patella has moved laterally beyond the trochlea.[65]

Muscle Actions

For the knee to function properly, a number of muscles must work together in a highly complex fashion. The following is a list of knee actions and the muscles that initiate them:

- Knee flexion is executed by the biceps femoris, semitendinous, semimembranous, gracilis, sartorius, gastrocnemius and popliteus, and plantaris muscles.
- Knee extension is executed by the quadriceps muscle of the thigh, consisting of three vasti—the vastus medialis, vastus lateralis, and vastus intermedius—and by the rectus femoris.
- External rotation of the tibia is controlled by the biceps femoris. The bony anatomy also produces external tibial rotation as the knee moves into extension.
- Internal rotation is accomplished by the popliteus, semitendinous, semimembranous, sartorius, and gracilis muscles. Rotation of the tibia is limited and can occur only when the knee is in a flexed position.
- The iliotibial band on the lateral side primarily functions as a dynamic lateral stabilizer.

REHABILITATION TECHNIQUES FOR LIGAMENTOUS AND MENISCAL INJURIES

Medial Collateral Ligament Sprain

PATHOMECHANICS

The medial collateral ligament (MCL) is the most commonly injured ligament in the knee.[57] About 65 percent of MCL sprains occur at the proximal insertion site on the femur. Individuals with proximal injuries tend to have more stiffness but less residual laxity than those with injuries nearer the tibial insertion. Tears of the medial meniscus are occasionally associated with grades 1 and 2 MCL sprains but almost never occur with grade 3 sprains.

Diagnosis of MCL sprains can usually always be made by physical evaluation and do not generally require MRI. The grade of ligament injury is usually determined by the amount of joint laxity. In a grade 1 sprain the MCL is tender due to microtears, however, there is no increased laxity and a firm endpoint. A grade 2 sprain involves an incomplete tear with some increased laxity with valgus stress at 30 degrees of flexion and minimal laxity in full extension, yet there is still a firm endpoint. There is tenderness to palapation, hemorrhage, and pain on valgus stress test. A grade 3 sprain is a complete tear with significant laxity on valgus stress in full extension. No endpoint is evident and pain is generally less than with grades 1 or 2. Significant laxity with valgus stress testing in full extension indicates injury to the medial joint capsule and to the cruciate ligaments as well.[37]

INJURY MECHANISM

An MCL sprain usually occurs with contact from a laterally applied valgus force to the knee that is sufficient to exceed the strength of the ligament. This is especially true with grade 3 sprains. Very rarely, an MCL sprain can occur with noncontact and may result in an isolated MCL tear. It has also been suggested that the majority of grade 2 sprains occur through indirect rotational forces associated with valgus movement of the knee.[76] The patient will usually explain that the knee was hit on the lateral side with the foot planted and that there was immediate pain on the medial side of the knee that felt more like a "pulling" or "tearing" than a "pop." Swelling occurs immediately and it is likely that some ecchymosis will appear over the site of injury within 3 days.

REHABILITATION CONCERNS

Since the early 1990s, the treatment of MCL sprains has changed considerably. Typically, grade 3 MCL sprains were treated surgically to repair the torn ligament and then immobilized for 6 weeks. Several studies have demonstrated that treating patients with isolated MCL sprains nonoperatively with immobilization is as effective as treating them surgically regardless of the grade of injury, the age of the patient, or the activity level.[36] This was especially true with isolated MCL tears where the ACL is intact.[1,83] Patients with a combined MCL–ACL injury will most likely have an ACL reconstruction without MCL repair and this procedure appears to provide sufficient functional stability. Three conditions must be met for healing to occur at the MCL: (1) the ligament fibers must remain in continuity or within a well-vascularized soft-tissue bed; (2) there must be enough stress to stimulate and direct the healing process; and (3) there must be protection from harmful stresses.[85]

With grades 2 and 3 sprains there will be some residual laxity because the ligament has been stretched, but this does not seem to have much of an effect on knee function. Patients with grades 1 and 2 sprains may be treated symptomatically and may be full weight bearing as soon as tolerated. It is possible that a patient with a grade 1 and, occasionally, even a grade 2 sprain can continue to play. With grade 3 sprains the patient should not be allowed to play and a rehabilitative brace should be worn for 4 to 6 weeks set from 0 degrees to 90 degrees to control valgus stress (Fig. 30-2).

REHABILIATION PROGRESSION

Initially, cold, compression, elevation, and electrical stimulation can be used to control swelling, inflammation, and pain. It may be necessary to have the patient on crutches initially, progressing to full weight bearing as soon as tolerated. The patient should use crutches until full extension without an extension lag can be demonstrated and the patient can walk normally without

gait deviation. For patient comfort a knee immobilizer may be worn for a few days to a week following injury with grade 2 sprains requiring 7 to 14 days in either an immobilizer or a brace.

The patient with a grade 1 sprain can begin on the second day following injury with quad sets (see Exercise 30-3) and straight leg raising (see Exercise 30-4). Early pain-free range-of-motion exercises should be incorporated with grade 1 sprains, whereas grade 2 sprains may require 4–5 days for inflammation to subside. With grade 1 and 2 sprains, the patient may begin by doing knee slides on a treatment table (see Exercise 30-29), wall slides (see Exercise 30-30), active assistive slides (see Exercise 30-31), or riding an exercise bike with the seat adjusted to the appropriate height to permit as much knee flexion as can be tolerated (see Exercise 30-14).

As pain subsides and ROM improves the patient may incorporate isotonic open chain flexion and extension exercises (see Exercises 30-3 and 30-4), but the patient should concentrate on closed chain strengthening exercises as tolerated throughtout the rehabilitation process (see Exercises 30-8 through 30-17). Functional PNF patterns stressing tibial rotation should be incorporated for strengthening with resistance increasing as the patient becomes stronger (see Exercises 30-25 through 30-29). As strength improves, the patient should engage in plyometric exercises (see Exercises 30-15 through 30-17) and functional activities to enhance the dynamic stability of the knee. With a grade 1 sprain the patient should be able to return to full activity in 3 to 5 weeks.

With a grade 3 sprain the patient will be in a brace for 2 to 3 weeks with the brace locked from 0 to 45 degrees and at 0 to 90 degrees for another 2 to 3 weeks, during which time isometric quad sets and SLR strengthening exercises may be performed as tolerated.[12] The patient should remain nonweight bearing with crutches for 3 weeks. The strengthening program should progress as with grades 1 and 2 sprains, with return to activity at about 3 months.[12,81]

Lateral Collateral Ligament Sprains

PATHOMECHANICS

Fortunately, the lateral aspect of the knee is well supported by secondary stabilizers. Thus, isolated injury to the LCL is rare in athletics and when it does occur, it is critical to rule out other ligamentous injuries.[76] Most LCL sprains in the athletic population result from a stress placed on the lateral aspect of the knee. Isolated sprain of the LCL is the least common of all knee ligament sprains.[57] LCL sprains result in disruption at the fibular head either with or without avulsion in approximately 75 percent of the cases, with 20 percent occurring at the femur, and only 5 percent as midsubstance tears.[82] It is not uncommon to see associated injuries of the peroneal nerve because the nerve courses around the head of the fibula. A complete disruption of the LCL often involves injury to the posterolateral joint capsule as well as the PCL and, occasionally, the ACL.[19,42,49]

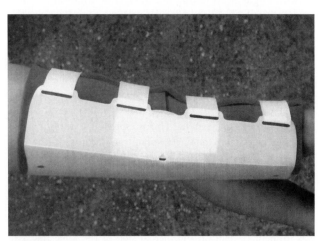

F I G U R E   3 0 - 2

A knee immobilizer can be used for comfort following injury.

The extent of laxity determines the severity of the injury. In a grade 1 sprain the LCL is tender due to microtears, with some hemorrhage and tenderness to palpation; however, there is no increased laxity and a firm endpoint. A grade 2 sprain involves an incomplete tear with some increased laxity, with varus stress at 30 degrees of flexion and minimal laxity in full extension, yet there is still a firm endpoint. There is tenderness to palpation, hemorrhage, and pain on varus stress test. A grade 3 sprain is a complete tear with significant laxity on varus stress in 30 degrees of flexion and in full extension when compared to the opposite knee. No endpoint is evident and pain is generally less than with grades 1 or 2. Significant laxity with varus stress testing in full extension indicates injury to the posterolateral joint capsule, the PCL, and, perhaps, the ACL.

INJURY MECHANISM

An isolated MCL injury is almost always the result of a varus stress applied to the medial aspect of the knee. Occasionally, a varus stress may occur during weight bearing when weight is shifted away from the side of injury creating stress on the lateral structures.[39] Patients who sustain a LCL sprain will report that they heard or felt a "pop" and that there was immediate lateral pain. Swelling will be immediate and extraarticular, with no joint effusion unless there is an associated menicus or capsular injury.

REHABILITATION CONCERNS

Patients with grades 1 and 2 sprains that exhibit stability to varus stress may be treated symptomatically and may be full weight bearing as soon as tolerated. For patient comfort a knee immobilizer may be worn for a few days to a week following injury, however, the use of a brace is not necessary. It is possible that a patient with a grade 1 and, occasionally, even a grade 2 sprain can continue to play. With grades 2 and 3 sprains, there will be some residual laxity because the ligament has been stretched. Grade 3 sprains may be managed nonoperatively with bracing for 4 to 6 weeks limited to 0 to 90 degrees of motion; however grade 3 MCL tears with associated ligamentous injuries that result in rotational instabilities are usually managed by surgical repair or reconstruction. This is certainly the case if the patient has chronic varus laxity and intends to continue participation in athletics, or if there is a displaced avulsion.

REHABILITATION PROGRESSION

The rehabilitation progression following LCL sprains should follow the same course as was previously described for MCL sprains. In the case of a grade 3 LCL sprain that involves multiple ligamentous injury with associated instability that is surgically repaired or reconstructed, the patient should be placed in a postoperative brace with partial weight bearing for 4 to 6 weeks. At 6 weeks, a rehabilitation program involving a carefully monitored gradual sport-specific functional progression should begin. In general, the patient may return to full activity at about 6 months.[39]

Anterior Cruciate Ligament Sprain

PATHOMECHANICS

The ACL is perhaps the most commonly injured ligament in the knee. In simple terms, the ACL functions as a primary stabilizer to prevent anterior translation of the tibia on the fixed femur and posterior translation of the femur if the tibia is fixed as in a closed chain. It also serves as a secondary stabilizer to prevent external and internal rotation as well as valgus and varus stress. It works in conjunction with the posterior cruciate ligament to control the gliding and rolling of the tibia on the femur during normal flexion and extension, limiting hyperextension. The twisted configuration of the fibers of the ACL causes the ligament to be under some degree of tension in all positions of knee motion, with lesser tension present from 30 to 90 degrees.[39,40,42]

Injury to the ACL most often occurs as a result of sport-related activities that place significant stress on the knee joint, such as is the case in cutting or jumping.[39] It appears that females tend to have a higher incidence of ACL injury than do males.[51] Recently, there seems to be increasing evidence that individuals with a narrow intracondylar notch width may be at greater risk for ACL injury.[46,79] This is particularly evident in patients with noncontact injuries. It has also been suggested that poor conditioning results in increased physiologic laxity, although this has never been demonstrated experimentally.

Tears of the ACL occur in the midsubstance of the ligament about 75 percent of the time, with 20 percent of the tears at the femur and 5 percent at the tibia.[38] As with MCL and LCL sprains, the severity of the injury is indicated by the degree of laxity or instability. A grade 1 sprain of the ACL results in partial microtears with some hemorrhage, however, there is no increased laxity and a firm endpoint. A grade 2 sprain involves an incomplete tear with hemorrhage, some loss of function, and increased anterior translation, yet there is still a firm endpoint. A grade 2 sprain is painful and pain increases with Lachman's and anterior drawer stress tests.

A grade 3 sprain is a complete tear with significant laxity with Lachman's and anterior drawer stress tests. There is also rotational instability as indicated by a positive pivot shift. No endpoint is evident. The patient will most often report feeling and hearing a "pop" and a feeling that the knee "gave out." There is significant pain initially, but pain decreases substantially within several minutes. A complete ACL tear will result in significant hemarthrosis occurring within 1 to 2 hours.

The term "anterior cruciate deficient knee" refers to a grade 3 sprain in which there is a complete tear of the ACL. It is generally accepted that a torn ACL will not heal.[78] An ACL deficient knee will exhibit rotational instability, which may eventually cause functional disability in the patient. Additionally, rotational instability may lead to tears of the meniscus and subsequent degenerative changes in the joint.

INJURY MECHANISM

The ACL may be injured in several different ways. By far the most common mechanism of injury involves a noncontact injury twisting motion in which the foot is planted and the patient is attempting to change direction creating deceleration, valgus stress, and external rotation of the knee. Occasionally, the mechanism of injury involves deceleration, valgus stress, and internal rotation.[87] Knee hyperextension combined with internal rotation can also produce a tear of the ACL.

It is possible that the ACL can be torn with contact involving a valgus force that can produce a tear of the ACL, MCL, and, possibly, a detachment of the medial meniscus as originally described by O'Donohue, which he referred to as the "unhappy triad."[60]

REHABILITATION CONCERNS

After the diagnosis of injury of the ACL, the patient, the physician, the therapist, and the patient's family are faced with various treatment options. The conservative approach is to allow the acute phase of the injury to pass and to then implement a vigorous rehabilitation program. If it becomes apparent that normal function cannot be recovered with rehabilitation, and if the knee remains unstable even with normal strengthening and hamstring retraining, then reconstructive surgery is considered. For a sedentary individual, this approach may be acceptable, but most patients prefer a more aggressive approach.

The older and more sedentary the individual, the less appropriate a reconstruction. This individual may not have the inclination or the time for an extensive rehabilitation program and may not be greatly inconvenienced by some degree of knee instability. Conversely, the ideal patient is a young, motivated, and skilled patient who is willing to make the personal sacrifices necessary to successfully complete the rehabilitation process. Wilk and Andrews state that any active individual with a goal of returning to stressful pivoting activities should undergo surgical ACL reconstruction.[84] Thus, successful surgical repair and reconstruction of the ACL-deficient knee is dependent to a large extent upon patient selection.[40] The following would be indications for deciding to surgically repair/reconstruct the injured knee.

- The ACL injury involves a highly athletic individual.
- An unwillingness on the part of an active person to alter his or her lifestyle.
- There is rotational instability and a feeling of the knee "giving way" in normal activities.
- There is injury to other ligaments and/or the menisci.
- Recurrent effusions.
- Failure at rehabilitation and instability after 6 months of intensive rehabilitation.[40]
- Surgery is necessary to prevent the early onset of degenerative changes within the knee.[42]

In the case of a partially torn ligament, the medical community is split on treatment approach. Some feel that a partially damaged ACL is incompetent and that the knee should be viewed as if the ligament were completely gone. Others prefer a prolonged initial period of immobilization and limited motion, hoping that the ligament will heal and remain functional. Decisions to treat a patient nonoperatively should be based on the individual's preinjury status and a willingness of that patient to engage only in activities such as jogging, swimming, or cycling that will not place the knee at high risk.[58] This is clearly a case where the patient may wisely seek several opinions before choosing the treatment course.

The most widely accepted opinion seems to be that when more than one major ligament is disrupted and there is functional disability, surgery is indicated. The surgical approach to ACL pathology is either repair or reconstruction. With a surgical repair, the damaged ligament is sutured if the tear is in the midsubstance of the ligament or the bony fragment is reattached in the case of an avulsion injury. However, it is generally felt that direct repair of an isolated ACL tear will tend to have a poor result.[1] In the case of suturing, the repair may be augmented with an internal splint or an extraarticular reconstruction, which seems to be more successful than a direct repair.[73]

Surgical reconstruction is performed using either an extraarticular or intraarticular technique. An extraarticular reconstruction involves taking a structure that lies outside of the joint capsule and moving it so that it can affect the mechanics of the knee in a manner that mimics normal ACL function. The iliotibial band is the most commonly used structure. This procedure is effective in reducing the pivot shift phenomena that is found in anterolateral rotational instability but cannot match the normal biomechanics of the ACL.[40,49] Isolated extraarticular reconstructions may be effective in patients with mild-to-moderate instability. Also, it may be the treatment of choice in patients who cannot afford the commitment of time and resources for an intraarticular reconstruction.[40] The rehabilitation after an extraarticular reconstruction is aggressive and permits an earlier return to functional activities; however as an isolated procedure, it is not recommended for high-level patients.

Intraarticular reconstruction involves placing a structure within the knee that will roughly follow the course of the ACL and will functionally replace the ACL. Bone–patellar tendon–bone grafts are the current state of the art, using human autografts/allografts.[22,25,40,71,84] Semitendinosis or gracilis autografts and Achilles tendon allografts also have been used. Procedures that use synthetic replacements have generally not produced favorable results. The major problem with an autograft is avascularity of the tissue, which results in a progressive decrease in strength of the graft, resulting in possible failure.[25] The main problems with allografts are disease transmission and rejection of the tissue. It has been demonstrated that at 6 months postsurgery, allografts show a prolonged inflammatory response, and a more significant decrease in their structural properties.[41] Thus, rehabilitation following an allograft reconstruction should be less aggressive than with an autograft reconstruction.[39]

Surgical technique is crucial to a successful outcome. The improper placement of the tendon graft by only a few millimeters can prevent the return of normal motion.

In cases where there is reconstruction of the ACL along with a repair of a torn meniscus, the time required for rehabilitation will be slightly longer. This is discussed in detail under the section dealing with meniscus tears.

REHABILITATION PROGRESSION

Nonoperative Rehabilitation

If the ACL-deficient knee is to be treated nonoperatively, it is critical to rule out any other existing problems (i.e., torn meniscus, loose bodies, etc.) and correct those problems before proceeding with rehabilitation.[58] Initial treatment should involve controlling swelling, pain, and inflammation through the use of cold, compression, and electrical stimulation. If necessary, the knee can be placed in an immobilizer for the first few days for comfort and minimal protection, with the patient ambulating on crutches until he or she regains full extension and can walk without an extension lag. The patient can begin immediately following injury with quad sets (see Exercise 30-3) and straight leg raising (see Exercise 30-4) to regain motor control and minimize atrophy. Early pain-free range-of-motion exercises using knee slides on a treatment table (see Exercise 30-29), wall slides (see Exercise 30-30), active assistive slides (see Exercise 30-31), or riding an exercise bike with the seat adjusted to the appropriate height to permit as much knee flexion as can be tolerated (see Exercise 30-14).

As pain subsides and ROM improves, the patient may incorporate isotonic open-chain flexion and extension exercises (see Exercises 30-5 and 30-6). With open chain strengthening exercises, it has been recommended that extension be restricted initially to 0 to 45 degrees for as long as 8 to 12 weeks (6 to 9 weeks minimum) to minimize stress on the ACL.[58] Strengthening exercises should be emphasized for both the hamstrings and gastrocnemius muscles (see Exercise 30-7), which act to translate the tibia posteriorly, minimizing anterior translation. Closed chain strengthening exercises (see Exercises 30-8 through 30-17) are thought to be safer because they minimize anterior translation of the tibia. Closed chain exercises are used to regain neuromuscular control by enhancing dynamic stabilization through co-contraction of the hamstrings and quadriceps (see Exercises 30-47 through 30-50). Closed chain exercises also minimize the possibility of developing patellofemoral pain. A goal of these strengthening exercises should be to achieve a quadriceps/hamstring strength ratio of 1:1.

It is important to incorporate PNF strengthening patterns that stress tibial rotation (see Exercises 30-25 through 30-28). These manually resisted PNF patterns are essentially the only way to concentrate on strengthening of the rotational component of knee motion, which is essential to normal function of the knee. Unfortunately, many of the more widely known and used rehabilitation protocols fail to address this critical rotational component.

FIGURE 30-3

A functional knee brace can provide some protection to the injured knee.

The use of functional knee braces for a patient with either a partial ACL tear or with an ACL-deficient knee is controversial (Fig. 30-3). These braces have not been shown to control translation, especially at functional loads.[6,67] There may, however, be some benefit in terms of increased joint position sense through stimulation of cutaneous sensory receptors, which may enhance both conscious and subconscious awareness of the existing injury.[47]

It is incumbent on the therapist to council the patient with regard to the precautions that must be exercised when engaging in physical activity with an ACL-deficient knee. Nonoperative treatment is appropriate for an individual who does not plan on engaging in the types of activities than can potentially create stresses that can further damage the supporting structures of that joint. If the patient is not willing to make lifestyle changes relative to those activities, then surgical intervention may be a better treatment alternative.

Surgical Reconstruction

There is great debate as to the course of rehabilitation following ACL reconstruction. Traditionally, rehabilitation has been conservative and there are a great number of physicians and therapists who maintain this basic traditional philosophy. In recent years, however the trend has been to become more aggressive in rehabilitation of the reconstructed ACL primarily as a result of the reports of success by Shelbourne and Nitz.[77] This has been referred to as an accelerated protocol. They have demonstrated that this program returns the patient to normal function early, results in fewer patellofemoral problems, and reduces the number of surgeries to obtain extension, all without compromising stability.[77] The accelerated rehabilitation protocol is not without its detractors. Some clinicians feel that it places too much stress on vulnerable tissues and that there are not sufficient scientific data to justify the protocol.[25,59,64,84]

The traditional protocol emphasizes the following.

- Slow progression to regain flexion and extension.
- Partial or nonweight bearing postoperatively.
- Closed chain exercises at 3 to 4 weeks postoperatively.
- Return to activity at 6 to 9 months.[20,25,84]

The accelerated protocol emphasizes the following.

- Immediate motion, including full extension.
- Immediate weight bearing within tolerance.
- Early closed chain exercise for strengthening and neuromuscular control.
- Return to activity at 2 months and to competition at 5 to 6 months.[77]

PREOPERATIVE PERIOD   Regardless of the various recommended time frames for rehabilitation, the rehabilitative process begins immediately following injury in what has been referred to as the preoperative phase. There is general agreement that surgical reconstruction be delayed until pain, swelling, and inflammation have subsided and range of motion, quadriceps muscle control, and a normal gait pattern have been regained during this preoperative phase. This appears to occur at about 2 to 3 weeks postinjury.[33,75] It also appears that delaying surgery decreases the incidence of postoperative arthrofibrosis.[75]

POSTOPERATIVE PERIOD   Perhaps the single most important rehabilitation consideration postoperatively has to do with the initial strength of the graft and how the graft heals and matures. It has been demonstrated that the tensile strength of a 10 mm central third patellar tendon graft is approximately 107 percent of the normal ACL initially. It has been predicted that the strength is at 57 percent at 3 months, 56 percent at 6 months, and 87 percent at 9 months.[15] Thus stress on the graft should be minimized during the period of graft necrosis (6 weeks), revascularization (8 to 16 weeks), and remodeling (16 weeks).[84] Assuming that the surgical technique for reconstruction is technically sound, the graft is at its strongest immediately following surgery, thus rehabilitation can be very aggressive early in the process. Also it appears that an aggressive rehabilitation program minimizes complications and maximizes restoration of function following ACL reconstruction.[39]

CONTROLLING SWELLING   Immediately following surgery, the goal is to minimize pain and swelling by using cold, compression and electrical stimulation. A Cryo-cuff is widely used for this purpose. Significant swelling can initially inhibit firing of the quadriceps.

FIGURE 30 - 4

In a rehabilitative brace the range of movement can be restricted and changed whenever appropriate.

BRACING   The patient is placed in a rehabilitative brace and most often locked in either full extension,[77] or 0 to 90 degrees passive with 40 to 90 degrees active ROM, for the first 2 weeks (Fig. 30-4). The brace will be worn from 4 to 6 weeks or until knee flexion exceeds the limits of the brace, and may be removed for exercise and for bathing. Shelbourne and Nitz recommend that a knee immobilizer be used for the first 2 weeks but that the patient be fitted for a functional brace at the end of the first week, which should be worn for protection throughout the rehabilitation process.[77] There does not appear to be a general consensus among physicians as to the value of wearing a functional brace during return to activity. Decisions should be made on an individual basis.

WEIGHT BEARING   Generally, the patient is placed on crutches with either 50 weight bearing,[64] or progressed to full weight bearing as tolerated[77] for the first 2 weeks. The patient can get off the crutches when there is minimal swelling, no extension lag, and sufficient quadriceps strength to allow for nearly normal gait. This may take anywhere from 2 to 6 weeks.

RANGE OF MOTION   Range-of-motion exercises can begin immediately. Some clinicians advocate the judicious use of continuous passive motion (CPM) machines, which may be applied immediately after surgery (Fig. 30-5).[59,61,72] Others prefer that the patient engage in active range-of-motion exercises as soon as possible (see Exercises 30-29 through 30-31). Certainly, current research is sparse regarding the efficacy of CPM.

In their accelerated rehabilitation program, Shelbourne and Nitz emphasize the importance of early restoration of full

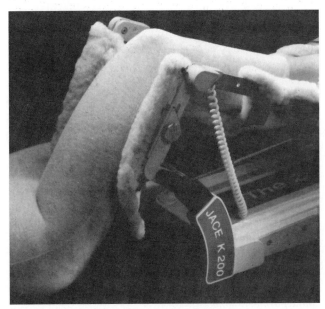

FIGURE 30-5

A CPM device may be used to help regain ROM.

knee extension.[77] Full extension can be achieved using knee extension on a rolled up towel (see Exercise 30-32) or prone leg hangs (see Exercise 30-33). Exercises to maintain full extension should be emphasized throughout the rehabilitation process. Active knee extension should be limited to 60 to 90 degrees to minimize anterior tibial translation, whereas knee flexion should reach 90 degrees by the end of the second week. Full flexion (135 degrees) should be achieved at 5 to 6 weeks. Once knee flexion reaches 100 to 110 degrees, the patient may begin stationary cycling to help with regaining ROM (see Exercise 30-17).

During the second week the therapist should teach the patient self-mobilization techniques for the patella (see Exercise 30-43). Restriction of patellar motion can interfere with regaining both flexion and extension. The grade of mobilization used should be based on the degree of inflammation, and should avoid creating additional pain and swelling.[68]

STRENGTHENING   Initially, strengthening exercises should avoid placing high levels of stress on the graft. Quad sets (see Exercise 30-3) and straight leg raises (see Exercise 30-4) using co-contraction of the hamstrings should begin immediately to prevent shutdown of the quadriceps. Progressive resistive exercise can begin during the second week for hamstrings (see Exercise 30-5), hip adductors (see Exercise 30-2), hip abductors (see Exercise 30-1), and gastrocnemius muscles (see Exercise 30-7). Strengthening exercises for all of these muscle groups, particularly emphasising strengthening of the hamstrings, should continue throughout rehabilitation.

The rationale and biomechanical advantages for using closed-kinetic chain strengthening exercises in the rehabilitation of various knee injuries was discussed in detail in Chapter 12. When using the different closed-kinetic chain exercises, it is es-

sential to emphasize co-contraction of the hamstrings both to stabilize the knee and to provide a posterior translational force to counteract the anterior shear force created by the quadriceps during knee extension. Once flexion reaches 90 degrees, which should generally be during 1 to 2 weeks, the patient can begin closed-kinetic chain minisquats in the 40 to 90 degrees range (Exercise 30-8), lateral step-ups (Exercise 30-12), standing wall slides Exercise 30-7, or leg press (Exercise 30-11).

Open-kinetic chain quadriceps strengthening exercises should be completely avoided in the early stages of rehabilitation due to anterior shear forces, which are greatest from 30 degrees of flexion to full extension. At some point in the later stages of rehabilitation, however, open-kinetic chain quardiceps strengthening exercises may be safely incorporated (see Exercise 30-6).

It should be reemphasized that the strength of the graft is at its weakest between weeks 8 to 14 during the period of revascularization. Therefore, caution should be exercised relative to strengthening exercises during this period. The accelerated program has recommended isokinetic testing begin at about 2 months, although other programs recommend that testing be delayed until 4 to 5 months. This should be done only using an antishear device with a 20-degree terminal extension block.[44,76] Isokinetic strengthening exercises may be safely incorporated at about 4 months (see Exercises 30-21 through 30-23).

PNF strengthening patterns that stress tibial rotation may also be used. These manually resisted PNF patterns are essentially the only way to concentrate on strengthening of the rotational component of knee motion, which is essential to normal function of the knee. Because the PNF patterns are done in an open-kinetic chain, they should only involve active contraction through the functional movement pattern. Progressively resisted patterns can be used beginning at about 5 months (see Exercises 30-25 through 30-28).

REESTABLISHING NEUROMUSCULAR CONTROL   Along with the early controlled weight bearing and closed chain exercises, which act to stimulate muscle and joint mechanoreceptors, seated BAPS board exercises to reestablish balance and neuromuscular control should also begin early in the rehabilitation process (see Exercise 30-47B). Balance training using a standing BAPS board (see Exercise 30-47A), and lateral shifting for strengthening and agility using the Fitter (see Exercise 30-50) may be incorporated at 6 weeks.

CARDIORESPIRATORY ENDURANCE   Cycling on an upper extremity ergometer may begin during the first week. Cycling on a stationary bike can begin as early as possible when the patient achieves about 100 to 110 degrees of flexion (see Exercise 30-17). Walking with full weight bearing on a treadmill can usually begin at about 3 weeks using forward walking initially, then progressing to retro walking. Swimming is considered to be a safe activity at 4 to 5 weeks. Stair climbing (see Exercise 30-16) or cross-country skiing can begin as early as week 6 or 7. Recommendations for progressing to jogging/running are as early 4 months in the accelerated program but are more often closer to 6 months.

FUNCTIONAL TRAINING   Functional training should progressively incorporate the stresses, strains, and forces that occur during normal running, jumping, and cutting activities in a controlled environment.[12,23] Exercises such as single- and double-leg hopping, carioca, shuttle runs, vertical jumping, rope skipping, and co-contraction activities (most of which were described in Chapter 20) should be incorporated. In the more traditional programs, these activities may begin at about 4 months, although in the accelerated program they may begin as early as 5 to 6 weeks.

Physicians typically have varying criteria for full return of the patient following injury to the anterior cruciate. Perhaps the greatest variability exists in the recommended time frames required for rehabilitation. Among the more widely used protocols are the following recommendations.

Shelbourne and Nitz	4–6 months
Andrews and Wilk	5–6 months
Fu and Irrgang	6–9 months
Campbell Clinic	6–12 months
Paulos and Stern	9 months
Kerlan and Jobe	9 months

In general, the following criteria appear to be the most widely accepted: (1) no joint effusion; (2) full ROM; (3) isokinetic testing indicates that strength of the quadriceps and hamstrings are between 85% to 100% of the uninvolved leg; (4) satisfactory ligament stability testing using a KT-1000 arthrometer; (5) successful progression from walking to running; and (6) successful performance during functional testing (i.e., hop tests, agility runs, etc.).

Posterior Cruciate Ligament Sprain

PATHOMECHANICS

Isolated tears of the posterior cruciate ligament (PCL) are not common but certainly do occur in patients. It is more likely that the PCL is injured concurrently with the ACL, MCL, LCL, or menisci. The PCL is the strongest ligament in the knee and functions with the ACL to control the rolling and gliding of the tibiofemoral joint and has been called the primary stabilizer of the knee. More specifically, the PCL prevents 85% to 90% of the posterior translational force of the tibia on the femur. This is evident in the PCL-deficient knee when, upon descending an incline, the force of gravity works to increase the anterior glide of the femur on the tibia, and, without the PCL, the femur will sublux on the tibia from mid-stance to toe-off where the quadriceps are less effective in controlling the anterior motion of the femur on the tibia.[50,52]

The majority of PCL tears occur on the tibia (70 percent), whereas 15 percent occur on femur and 15 percent are midsubstance tears.[82] In the PCL-deficient knee, there is an increased likelihood of meniscus lesions and chondral defects most often involving the medial side.[29]

The extent of laxity determines the severity of the injury. In a grade 1 sprain, the PCL is tender due to microtears with some hemorrhage and tenderness to palpation; however, there is no increased laxity and a firm endpoint. A grade 2 sprain involves an incomplete tear, with some increased laxity in a positive posterior drawer test, yet there is still a firm endpoint. There is tenderness to palaption, hemorrhage, and pain on posterior drawer test. A grade 3 sprain is a complete tear with significant posterior laxity in posterior drawer, posterior sag, and reverse pivot shift tests when compared to the opposite knee. No endpoint is evident and pain is generally less than with grades 1 or 2.

INJURY MECHANISM

In athletics, the most common mechanism of injury to the PCL is with the knee in a position of forced hyperflexion with the foot plantar flexed. The PCL may also be injured when the tibia is forced posteriorly on the fixed femur or the femur is forced anteriorly on the fixed tibia.[49] It is also possible to injure the PCL when the knee is hyperflexed and a downward force is applied to the thigh.

Forced hyperextension will usually result in injury to both the PCL and ACL. If an anteromedial force is applied to a hyperextended knee, the posterolateral joint capsule may also be injured. If enough valgus or varus force is applied to the fully extended knee to rupture either collateral ligament, it is possible that the PCL may also be torn.

The patient will indicate that he or she felt and heard a "pop" but will often feel that the injury was minor and that he or she can return to activity immediately. There will be mild to moderate swelling occurring within 2 to 6 hours.

REHABILITATION CONCERNS

Perhaps the greatest concern in rehabilitating a patient with an injured PCL is the fact that the arthrokinematics of the joint are altered, and this change can eventually lead to degeneration of both the medial compartment and the patellofemoral joint.[39]

The decision as to whether the PCL-deficient knee is best treated nonoperatively or surgically is controversial. This is primarily due to the relative lack of data-based information in the literature regarding the normal history of PCL tears. Many patients with an isolated PCL tear do not seem to exhibit any functional performance limitations and can continue to compete athletically, whereas others occasionally are limited in performing normal daily activities.[29]

Parolie and Bergfield reported a success rate of over 80 percent with nonoperative treatment.[62] Conversely, Clancy reported a high incidence of femoral condylar articular injury involving degenerative changes, which may eventually result in arthritis in patients 4 years after PCL injury. Thus, surgical reconstruction has been advocated.[16,52]

It is generally felt that the surgical treatment of PCL tears is technically difficult. Surgery to reconstruct a PCL-deficient knee is most often indicated with avulsion injuries. Techniques involving a reconstructive procedure using the semitendinous tendon, the tendon of the medial gastrocnemius, the Achilles tendon, the patellar tendon, or synthetic material to replace the lost PCL have been recommended.[39] Both autografts and allografts have been used.

REHABILITATION PROGRESSION

Nonoperative Rehabilitation

If the PCL-deficient knee is to be treated nonoperatively, initial treatment should involve controlling swelling, pain, and inflammation through the use of cold, compression, and electrical stimulation. If necessary, the knee can be placed in an immobilizer for the first few days for comfort and minimal protection, with the patient ambulating on crutches until he or she regains full extension and can walk without an extension lag. Because there is often little functional limitation, the patient may progress rapidly through the rehabilitative process, the rate of progression limited only by pain and swelling.

The patient can begin immediately following injury with quad sets (see Exercise 30-3) and straight leg raising (see Exercise 30-4) to regain motor control and minimize atrophy. Early pain-free range-of-motion exercises can begin using knee slides on a treatment table (see Exercise 30-29), wall slides, (see Exercise 30-30) active assistive slides, (see Exercise 30-31) or riding an exercise bike with the seat adjusted to the appropriate height to permit as much knee flexion as can be tolerated (see Exercise 30-14). Hamstring exercises should be avoided initially to minimize posterior laxity.

Nonoperative rehabilitation should focus primarily on quadriceps strengthening. As pain subsides and ROM improves, the patient may incorporate isotonic open chain extension exercises (see Exercise 30-6). With open chain quadriceps strengthening exercises, it has been recommended that extension be restricted initially to the 45 to 20 degree range to avoid developing patellofemoral pain.[35] It has also been recommended that quadriceps strength in the PCL-deficient knee be greater than 100 percent of the uninjured knee, particularly in patients attempting to fully return to sport activity.[62]

Open chain hamstring strengthening exercises using knee flexion, which increase posterior translation of the tibia, should be avoided. Posterior tibial translation may be minimized by strengthening the hamstrings using open chain hip extension with the knee fully extended (see Exercise 29-3). Closed chain exercises (see Exercises 30-8 through 30-17) that use a co-contraction of the quadriceps to reduce posterior tibial translation and also minimize the possibility of developing patellofemoral pain may be safely used to strengthen the hamstrings.

The use of functional knee braces for a patient with a PCL-deficient knee is generally not recommended because functional braces are designed primarily for ACL-deficient knees. There may be some benefit in terms of increased joint position sense through stimulation of cutaneous sensory receptors, which may enhance both conscious and subconscious awareness of the existing injury.[47]

Because of the tendency toward progressive degeneration of the medial aspect of the knee with a PCL-deficient knee, it is incumbent on the therapist to counsel the patient with regard to avoiding repetitive activities that produce pain or swelling.[39]

Surgical Rehabilitation

The time frame of the maturation and healing process for a PCL graft has not been documented in the literature as has been the case with ACL grafts. Thus, the course of rehabilitation following surgical reconstruction of the PCL is not well defined, and recommended rehabilitation protocols are difficult to find. Clancy has perhaps the largest study of operative PCL reconstructions using a pattelar tendon graft.[16]

Immediately following surgery, the goal is to minimize pain and swelling by using cold, compression, and electrical stimulation. A Cryo-cuff may be used to accomplish this. The patient is placed in a rehabilitative brace and locked in 0 degrees extension at all times for the first week (Fig. 30-3). During the second week, the brace may be unlocked for ambulation and passive ROM exercises. The brace will be worn for 4 to 6 weeks until the patient can achieve 90 to 100 degrees of flexion. Generally, the patient is placed on crutches with full weight bearing as soon as possible, but he or she should stay on crutches for 4 to 6 weeks until full extension is achieved.

Quad sets (see Exercise 30-3) and straight leg raises (see Exercise 30-4) done in the brace can begin at 2 to 4 weeks. Resisted exercise can begin during the second week for hip adductors (see Exercise 30-2), and hip abductors (see Exercise 30-1). After surgical reconstruction of the PCL, it is important to limit hamstring function to reduce the posterior translational forces.[50] Thus, strengthening exercises for the hamstrings should be avoided initially because they tend to place stress on the graft. At 4 to 6 weeks, closed chain exercises from 0 to 45 degrees of flexion are initiated. Resisted terminal knee extensions in a closed chain should also be used (see Exercise 30-13).

Along with the early controlled weight bearing and closed chain exercises begun at about 6 weeks (which act to stimulate muscle and joint mechanoreceptors), seated BAPS board exercises to reestablish balance and neuromuscular control should also begin early in the rehabilitation process (see Exercise 30-47B).

Cycling on a stationary bike can begin at 6 weeks when the patient achieves about 100 to 110 degrees of flexion (see Exercise 30-17). Walking with full weight bearing on a treadmill can begin when the patient has no extension lag and sufficient quadriceps strength to allow for nearly normal gait. Recommendations for progressing to jogging/running is generally not recommended until 9 months. Functional training should progressively incorporate the stresses, strains, and forces that occur during normal running, jumping, and cutting activities in a controlled environment.

Meniscal Injury

PATHOMECHANICS

The menisci function to aid in joint lubrication; to distribute weight-bearing forces; to increase joint congruency, which aids in stability; to act as a secondary restraint in checking tibiofemoral motion; and to act as a shock absorber.[13,48]

The medial meniscus has a much higher incidence of injury than the lateral meniscus. The higher number of medial meniscal lesions may be attributed to the coronary ligaments that attach the meniscus peripherally to the tibia and also to the capsular ligament. The lateral meniscus does not attach to the capsular ligament and is more mobile during knee movement. Because of the attachment to the medial structures, the medial meniscus is prone to disruption from valgus and torsional forces.

A meniscus tear may result in immediate joint-line pain localized to either the medial or lateral side of the knee. Effusion develops gradually over 48 to 72 hours, although a tear at the periphery may produce a more acute hemarthrosis. Initially, pain is described as a "giving-way" feeling but the knee may be "locked" near full extension due to displacement of the meniscus. A knee that is locked at 10 to 30 degrees of flexion may indicate a tear of the medial meniscus, whereas a knee that is locked at 70 degrees or more may indicate a tear of the posterior portion of the lateral meniscus.[18] A positive McMurray's test usually indicates a tear in the posterior horn of the meniscus. The knee that is locked by a displaced meniscus may require unlocking with the patient under anesthesia so that a detailed examination can be conducted. If discomfort, disability, and locking of the knee continue, arthroscopic surgery may be required to remove a portion of the meniscus. If the knee is not locked but shows indications of a tear, the physician might initially obtain an MRI. A diagnostic arthroscopic examination may also be performed. Diagnosis of meniscal injuries should be made immediately after the injury has occurred and before muscle guarding and swelling obscure the normal shape of the knee.

INJURY MECHANISM

The most common mechanism of meniscal injury is weight bearing combined with internal or external rotation while extending or flexing the knee. It is also possible that a valgus or varus force sufficient to cause disruption of the MCL or LCL may produce an ACL tear as well as a meniscus tear. A large number of medial meniscus lesions are the outcome of a sudden, strong internal rotation of the femur with a partially flexed knee while the foot is firmly planted such as would be the case in a cutting motion. As a result of the force of this action, the medial meniscus is detached and pinched between the femoral condyles.

Meniscal lesions can be longitudinal, oblique, or transverse. Stretching of the anterior and posterior horns of the meniscus can produce a vertical-longitudinal or "bucket-handle" tear. A longitudinal tear may also occur by forcefully extending the knee from a flexed position while the femur is internally rotated. During extension, the medial meniscus is suddenly pulled back, causing the tear. In contrast, the lateral meniscus can sustain an oblique tear by a forceful knee extension with the femur externally rotated.

REHABILITATION CONCERNS

Quite often the choice is to initially treat meniscus tears conservatively, which means that the course of rehabilitation takes

on a "wait and see" approach. Occasionally, the patient will choose to simply "deal" with the associated symptoms of a torn meniscus to see how he or she can do in the long run. In some individuals the symptoms may resolve and there is no longer a need for surgery.

The problem is that once a meniscal tear occurs, the ruptured edges harden and may eventually atrophy. On occasion, portions of the meniscus may become detached and wedge themselves between the articulating surfaces of the tibia and femur, thus imposing a chronic locking, "catching," or "giving way" of the joint. Chronic meniscal lesions may also display recurrent swelling and obvious muscle atrophy around the knee. The patient may complain of an inability to perform a full squat or to change direction quickly when running without pain, a sense of the knee collapsing, or a "popping" sensation. Displaced meniscal tears can eventually lead to serious articular degeneration with major impairment and disability. Such symptoms and signs usually warrant surgical intervention.

Three surgical treatment choices are possible for the patient with a damaged meniscus: partial meniscectomy, meniscal repair, and meniscal transplantation. It was not too long ago that the accepted surgical treatment for a torn meniscus involved total removal of the damaged meniscus. However, total meniscectomy has been shown to cause premature degenerative arthritis. With the advent of arthroscopic surgery, the need for total meniscectomy has been virtually eliminated. Surgical management of meniscal tears should include every effort to minimize loss of any portion of the meniscus.

The location of the meniscal tear often dictates whether surgical treatment will involve a partial meniscectomy or a meniscal repair. Tears that occur within the inner one-third of the meniscus will have to be resected because they are unlikely to heal, even with surgical repair, due to avascularity. Tears in the middle one-third of the meniscus, and particularly in the outer one-third, may heal well following surgical repair because they have a good vascular supply. Partial meniscectomy of a torn meniscus is much more common than meniscal repair.

REHABILITATION PROGRESSIONS

Nonoperative Management

If a consensus decision is made by the physician, the patient, and the therapist to treat a meniscus tear nonoperatively, the patient may return to full activity as soon as the initial signs and symptoms resolve. Rehabilitation efforts should be directed primarily at minimizing pain and controlling swelling, in addition to getting the patient back to functional activities as soon as possible. Generally, the patient may require 3 to 5 days of limited activity to allow for resolution of symptoms.

Partial Meniscectomy

Postsurgical management for a partial meniscectomy that is not accompanied by degenerative change or injury to other ligaments initially involves controlling swelling, pain, and inflammation through the use of cold, compression, and electrical stimulation. The patient should ambulate on crutches for 1 to

3 days, progressing to full weight bearing as soon as tolerated until he or she regains full extension and can walk without a limp or an extension lag. Early pain-free range-of-motion exercises using knee slides on a treatment table (see Exercise 30-29), wall slides, (see Exercise 30-30), active assistive slides (see Exercise 30-31), and stationary cycling (see Exercise 30-17) can begin immediately along with quad sets (see Exercise 30-3) and straight leg raising (see Exercise 30-4), which are used to regain motor control and minimize atrophy. As pain subsides and ROM improves, the patient may incorporate isotonic open and closed chain exercises (see Exercises 30-5, 30-6, and 30-8 through 30-17). Functional activity training may begin as soon as the patient feels that he or she is ready. It is not uncommon in the athletic population for functional activity training to begin within 3 to 6 days following partial menisectomy, although it is more likely that full return will require about 2 weeks.

Meniscal Repair

The repair of a damaged meniscus involves the use of absorbable sutures, vascular access channels drilled from vascular to non-vascular areas, and the insertion of a fibrin clot.[14] Rehabilitation after arthroscopic surgery for partial menisectomy with no associated capsular damage is rapid, and the likelihood of complications is minimal.

Rehabilitation after either meniscal repair or menicus transplant requires that joint motion be limited and is more prolonged than for partial menisectomy. Thus, for the patient, it is essential that some type of cardiorespiratory endurance conditioning be incorporated throughout the period of immobilization. Because of the limitation of the rehabilitative brace, an upper extremity ergometer is perhaps the most effective for maintaining endurance.

The patient is placed in a rehabilitative brace locked in full extension for the first 2 weeks both for protection and to prevent flexion contractures (Fig. 30-3). During this period, there is partial weight bearing on crutches. Submaximal isometric quad sets are performed in the brace along with hip abduction and adduction strengthening exercises (see Exercises 30-1 and 30-2).

From 2 to 4 weeks, motion in the brace is limited to 20 to 90 degrees of flexion; and from 4 to 6 weeks, motion is limited in the 0- to 90-degree range. Hip exercises and isometric quad sets should continue. Range-of-motion exercises using knee slides (see Exercise 30-29), wall slides (see Exercise 30-30), and active assistive slides (see Exercise 30-31) should all be done in the brace within the protected range. Partial weight bearing on crutches should progress to full weight bearing after 6 weeks.

At 6 weeks, the brace can be removed and the knee rehabilitation progressions described previously may be incorporated as the patient can tolerate to regain full range of motion and normal muscle strength. Generally, the patient can return to full activity at about 3 months.

If a patient has also had an ACL reconstruction in addition to a meniscal repair, the healing constraints associated with meniscal repair must be taken into consideration in the rehabilitation plan.[81] Range-of-motion exercises, strengthening exercises, and weight bearing all have some mechanical impact on the meniscus. If the rehabilitation protocols for other ligament injuries are more aggressive or accelerated, the guidelines for meniscus repair healing must be incorporated into the treatment plan.

Meniscal Transplant

Meniscus transplants using either allografts or synthetic material have been recommended.[28,80] Although reports of the efficacy of these procedures have been inconsistent,[18] generally, the preference seems to be an allograft using bone plugs and suturing to the capsule at the periphery of the graft.[28] The use of meniscus transplants is markedly less common than either menisectomy or repair.

It is recommended that following transplantation, a rehabilitative brace be locked in full extension for 6 weeks. However the brace may be unlocked during this period to allow passive range-of-motion exercises in the 0- to 90-degree range. Isometric quad sets and hip exercises are performed throughout this 6-week period. Also only partial weight bearing on crutches is allowed.

At 6 weeks, the brace is unlocked and there should be progression to full weight bearing. Use of the brace may be discontinued at 8 weeks or whenever the patient can achieve full extension, flexion to 100 degrees, and a normal gait.[39] At that point, progressive strengthening, range of motion, and functional training techniques as described previously can be incorporated when appropriate. Full return is expected in 9 to 12 months.

REHABILITATION TECHNIQUES FOR PATELLOFEMORAL AND EXTENSOR MECHANISM INJURIES

Complaints of pain and disability associated with the patellofemoral joint and the extensor mechanism are exceedingly common. The terminology used to describe this anterior knee pain has been a source of some confusion and requires some clarification. Until recently, it was not uncommon for every patient who walked into a clinic complaining of anterior knee pain to be diagnosed as having condromalacia patella. However, there can be many other causes of anterior knee pain, and chondromalacia patella is only one of these causes. The term patellofemoral arthralgia is a catch-all term used to describe anterior knee pain. Chondromalacia patella, along with patellofemoral stress syndrome, patellar tendinitis, patellar bursitis, chronic patellar subluxation, acute patellar dislocation, and a synovial plica are all conditions that can cause anterior knee pain. The treatment and rehabilitation of patients complaining of anterior knee pain can be very frustrating for the therapist. The more conservative approach to treatment of patellofemoral pain described as follows should be used initially. If this approach fails, surgical intervention may be required.

Patellofemoral Stress Syndrome

PATHOMECHANICS

Patients presenting with patellofemoral pain typically exhibit relatively common symptoms. They complain of nonspecific pain in the anterior portion of the knee. It is difficult to place one finger on a specific spot and be certain that the pain is there. Pain seems to be increased when either ascending or descending stairs or when moving from a squatting to a standing position. Patients also complain of pain when sitting for long periods of time. This has occasionally been referred to as the "movie-goer's sign." Reports of the knee "giving away" are likely, although typically no instability is associated with this problem. When evaluating the pathomechanics of the patellofemoral joint, the therapist must assess static alignment, dynamic alignment, and patellar orientation.

Static Alignment

Static stabilizers of the patellofemoral joint act to maintain the appropriate alignment of the patella when no motion is occurring (Fig. 30-6). The superior static stabilizers are the quadriceps muscles (vastus lateralis, vastus intermedius, vastus medialis, rectus femoris). Laterally, static stabilizers include the lateral retinaculum, vastus lateralis, and iliotibial band. Medially, the medial retinaculum and the vastus medialis are the static stabilizers. Inferiorly, the patellar tendon stabilizes the patella.

Dynamic Alignment

Dynamic alignment of the patella must be assessed during functional activities. It is critical to look at the tracking of the patella from an anterior view during normal gait. Muscle control should be observed while the patient engages in other functional activities, including stepping, bilateral squats, or one-legged squats.

There are a number of different anatomic factors that can affect dynamic alignment. It is essential to understand that both static and dynamic structures must create a balance of forces about the knee. Any change in this balance may produce improper tracking of the patella and patellofemoral pain.

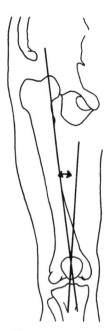

Measuring the Q-angle.

INCREASED Q-ANGLE   The Q-angle (Fig. 30-7) is formed by drawing a line from the anterosuperior iliac spine to the center of the patella. A second line drawn from the tibial tubercle to the center of the patella that intersects the first line forms the Q-angle. A normal Q-angle falls between 10 to 12 degrees in the male and 15 to 17 degrees in the female. Q-angle may be increased by lateral displacement of the tibial tubercle, external tibial torsion, or femoral neck anteversion. The Q-angle is a static measurement that may have no direct correlation with patellofemoral pain.[26] Dynamically, however, this increased Q-angle may increase the lateral valgus vector force, thus encouraging lateral tracking, resulting in patellofemoral pain (Fig. 30-8).[45]

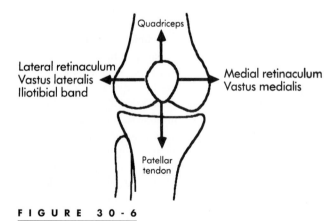

F I G U R E   3 0 - 6
Static and dynamic patellar stabilizers.

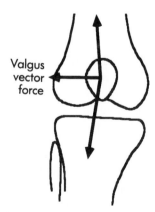

F I G U R E   3 0 - 8
A lateral valgus vector force created when the quadriceps is contracted.

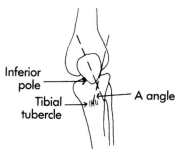

FIGURE 30-9

Measurement of the A-angle.

A-ANGLE The A-angle (Fig. 30-9) measures the patellar orientation to the tibial tubercle. It is created by the intersection of lines drawn bisecting the patella longitudinally and from the tibial tubercle to the apex of the inferior pole of the patella. An angle of 35 degrees or greater has been correlated with patellofemoral pathomechanics, which results in patellofemoral pain.[3]

ILIOTIBIAL BAND The distal portion of the iliotibial band interdigitates with both the deep transverse retinaculum and the superficial oblique retinaculum. As the knee moves into flexion, the iliotibial band moves posteriorly, causing the patella to tilt and track laterally.[27]

VASTUS MEDIALIS OBLIQUE INSUFFICIENCY The vastus medialis oblique (VMO) functions as an active and dynamic stabilizer of the patella. Anatomically, it arises from the tendon of the adductor magnus.[10] Normally, the VMO is tonically active electromyographically throughout the range of motion. In individuals with patellofemoral pain, it is phasically active, and it tends to lose fatigue resistant capabilities.[70] The VMO is innervated by a separate branch of the femoral nerve; therefore, it can be activated as a single motor unit.[4] In normal individuals, the VMO to vastus lateralis (VL) ratio has been shown to be 1:1.[69] However, in individuals who complain of patellofemoral pain, the VMO to VL ratio is less than 1:1.

VASTUS LATERALIS The vastus lateralis interdigitates with fibers of the superficial lateral retinaculum. Again, if this retinaculum is tight or if a muscle imbalance exists between the vastus lateralis and the vastus medialis with the lateralis being more active, lateral tilt or tracking of the patella may occur dynamically.[26]

EXCESSIVE PRONATION Excessive pronation may result from existing structural deformities in the foot. With overpronation, there is excessive subtalar eversion and adduction with an obligatory internal rotation of the tibia, increased internal rotation of the femur, and thus an increased lateral valgus vector force at the knee that encourages lateral tracking.[32] Various structural deformities in the feet that may cause knee pain should be corrected biomechanically according to techniques recommended in Chapter 32.

TIGHT HAMSTRING MUSCLES Tight hamstring muscles cause an increase in knee flexion. When the heel strikes the ground, there must be increased dorsiflexion at the talocrural joint. Excessive subtalar joint motion may occur to allow for necessary dorsiflexion. As stated previously, this produces excessive pronation with concomitant increased internal tibial rotation and a resultant increase in the lateral valgus vector force.

TIGHT GASTROCNEMIUS MUSCLE A tight gastrocnemius muscle will not allow for the 10 degrees of dorsiflexion necessary for normal gait. Once again, this produces excessive subtalar motion, increased internal tibial rotation, and increased lateral valgus vector force.[32]

PATELLA ALTA In patella alta, the ratio of patellar tendon length to the height of the patella is greater than the normal 1:1 ratio. In patella alta, the length of the patellar tendon is 20 percent greater than the height of the patella. This creates a situation where greater flexion is necessary before the patella assumes a stable position within the trochlear groove, and thus there is an increased tendency toward lateral subluxation.[38]

Patellar Orientation

Patellar orientation refers to the positioning of the patella relative to the tibia. Assessment should be done with the patient in supine position. Four components should be assessed when looking at patellar orientation: the glide component, the tilt component, rotation component, and the anteroposterior tilt component.

GLIDE COMPONENT This component assesses the lateral or medial deviation of the patella relative to the trochlear groove of the femur. Glide should be assessed both statically and dynamically. Figure 30-10 provides an example of a positive lateral glide.

TILT COMPONENT Tilt is determined by comparing the height of the medial patellar border with the lateral patellar border. Figure 30-11 shows an example of a positive lateral tilt.

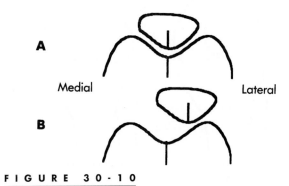

FIGURE 30-10

Positive lateral glide. **A,** Normal positioning. **B,** Positive lateral glide component.

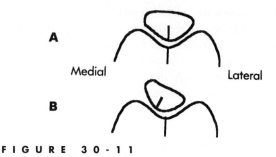

F I G U R E   3 0 - 1 1

Positive lateral tilt. **A,** Normal Positioning. **B,** Positive lateral tilt component.

ROTATIONAL COMPONENT   Rotation is identified by assessing the deviation of the longitudinal axis (line drawn from superior pole to inferior pole) of the patella relative to the femur. The point of reference is the inferior pole. Thus if the inferior pole is more lateral than the superior pole, a positive external rotation exists (Fig. 30-12).

ANTEROPOSTERIOR TILT COMPONENT   This must be assessed laterally to determine if a line drawn from the inferior patellar pole to the superior patellar pole, is parallel to the long axis of the femur. If the inferior pole is posterior to the superior pole, the patient has a positive anteroposterior tilt component (Fig. 30-13).

REHABILITATION CONCERNS

Traditionally, rehabilitation techniques for patients complaining of patellofemoral pain tended to concentrate on avoiding those activities that exacerbated pain (for example, squatting or stair climbing), occasional immobilization, and strengthening of the quadriceps group using open-kinetic chain exercises. The current treatment approach has a new direction and focus that includes strengthening of the quadriceps through closed-kinetic chain exercise, regaining optimal patellar positioning and tracking, and regaining neuromuscular control to improve lower limb mechanics.

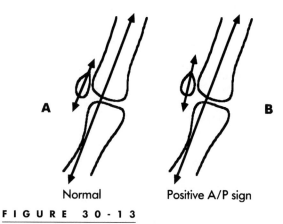

F I G U R E   3 0 - 1 3

Positive inferior anteroposterior tilt. **A,** Normal positioning. **B,** Positive inferior anteroposterior tilt component.

Strengthening Techniques

Earlier in this chapter, closed-kinetic chain exercises were recommended for strengthening in the rehabilitation of ligamentous knee injuries. These same exercises are also useful in the rehabilitation of patellofemoral pain, not because anterior shear is reduced, but because of how they affect patellofemoral joint reaction force (PFJRF).

More traditional rehabilitation techniques focused on reducing the compressive forces of the patella against the femur and reducing PFJRF. PFJRF increases when the angle between the patellar tendon and the quadriceps tendon decreases (Fig. 30-14). PFJRF also increases when the quadriceps tension increases to resist the flexion moment created by the lever arms; however PFJRF can be minimized by maximizing the area of surface contact of the patella on the femur. As the knee moves into greater degrees of flexion, the area of surface contact increases, distributing the forces associated with increased compression over a larger area (Fig. 30-15). Therefore, the compressive forces per unit area are minimized.[31]

Rehabilitation techniques involving closed-kinetic chain exercises try to maximize the area of surface contact. With

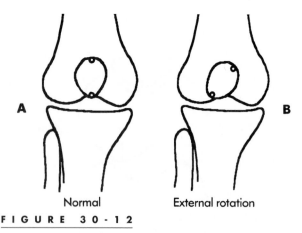

F I G U R E   3 0 - 1 2

Positive external rotation. **A,** Normal positioning. **B,** Positive external rotation.

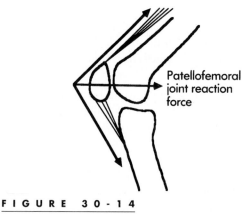

F I G U R E   3 0 - 1 4

Patellofemoral joint reaction force (PFJRF).

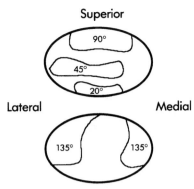

FIGURE 30-15

Compression force and contact stress. Even though compression forces increase with increasing knee flexion, the amount of contact stress per unit area decreases.

closed-kinetic chain exercises, as the angle of knee flexion decreases, the flexion moment acting on the knee increases. This requires greater quadriceps and patellar tendon tension to counteract the effects of the increased flexion moment arm, resulting in an increase in PFJRF as flexion increases. The force is distributed over a larger patellofemoral contact area, however minimizing the increase in contact stress per unit area. Therefore, it appears that closed-kinetic chain exercises may be better tolerated by the patellofemoral joint than open-kinetic chain exercises.

Closed-kinetic chain exercises were discussed in detail in Chapter 12. In the case of patellofemoral rehabilitation, minisquats from 0 to 40 degrees (see Exercise 30-8), leg press from 0 to 60 degrees (see Exercise 30-11), lateral step-ups using an 8-inch step (see Exercise 30-12), a stepping machine (see Exercise 30-16), a stationary bike (see Exercise 30-17), slide board exercises (see Exercise 30-14), and a Fitter (see Exercise 30-15) are all examples of closed-kinetic chain strengthening exercises that may be used in patellofemoral rehabilitation.

Regaining Optimal Patellar Positioning and Tracking

This second goal in our current treatment approach is based on the work of an Australian physiotherapist, Jenny McConnell.[30,55] This goal may be accomplished by stretching the tight lateral structures, correcting patellar orientation, and improving the timing and force of the VMO contraction.

STRETCHING Successfully stretching the tight lateral structures involves a combination of both active and passive stretching techniques. Active stretching techniques include joint mobilization techniques as discussed in Chapter 15. Specific techniques should involve medial patellar glides and medial patellar tilts along the longitudinal axis of the patella (see Exercise 30-43). Passive stretch is accomplished through a long duration stretch created by the use of very specific taping techniques to alter patellar alignment and orientation.

CORRECTING PATELLAR ORIENTATION After a thorough assessment of patellofemoral mechanics as described earlier, the therapist should have the patient perform an activity that produces patellofemoral pain, such as step-ups or double- or single-leg squats, to establish a baseline for comparison.

From the beginning of this discussion, it should be stressed that not all individuals who complain of patellofemoral pain exhibit some positive patellar orientation component. In those patients who do, patellofemoral orientation may be corrected to some degree by using tape. Correction of patellar positioning and tracking is accomplished by using passive taping of the patella in a more biomechanically correct position. In addition to correcting the orientation of the patella, the tape provides a prolonged stretch to the soft tissue structures that affect patellar movement.

Taping should be done using two separate types of highly adhesive tape available from several different manufacturers. A base layer using white tape is applied directly to the skin from the lateral femoral condyle to just posterior to the medial femoral condyle, making certain that the patella is completely covered by the base layer (Fig. 30-16). This tape is used as a base to which the other tape is adhered to correct patellar alignment. The glide component should always be corrected first, followed by the component found to be the most excessive. If no positive glide exists, begin with the most pronounced component found.

The glide component should always be corrected with the knee in full extension. To correct a positive lateral glide, attach the tape one thumb's breadth from the lateral patellar border, push the patella medially, gather the soft tissue over the medial

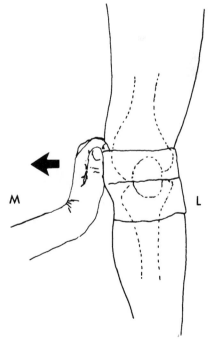

FIGURE 30-16

Application of base tape.

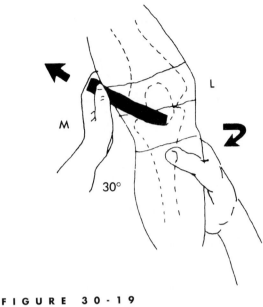

FIGURE 30-19

Taping to correct positive external rotation.

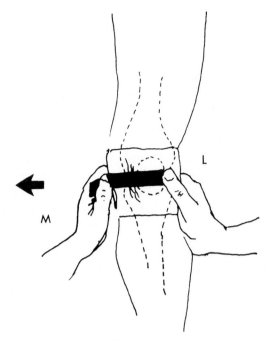

FIGURE 30-17

Taping to correct positive lateral glide.

condyle, push toward the condyle, and adhere to the medial condyle (Fig. 30-17).

The tilt component should be corrected with the knee flexed 30 to 45 degrees. To correct a positive lateral tilt, from the middle of the patella pull medially to lift the lateral border. Again, gather the skin underneath, and adhere to the medial condyle (Fig. 30-18).

The rotational component is corrected in 30 to 40 degrees of flexion. To correct a positive external rotation, from the middle of the inferior border pull upward and medially while rotating the superior pole externally (Fig. 30-19).

To correct a positive anteroposterior inferior tilt, place the knee in full extension. Adhere a 6-inch strip of tape over the upper half of the patella, and press directly posterior, adhering with equal pressure on both sides (Fig. 30-20).

One piece of tape may be used to correct two components simultaneously. For example, when correcting a lateral glide along with an anteroposterior inferior tilt, follow the same taping procedure for the glide component, except the tape should be applied to the upper half of the patella.

After this taping procedure, the therapist should reassess the activity that caused the patient's pain. In many cases, the patient will indicate improvement almost immediately. If not, the order of the taping or the way the patella is taped may have

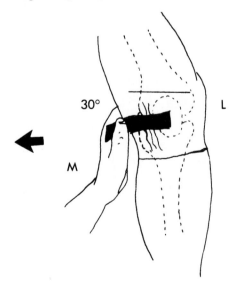

FIGURE 30-18

Taping to correct positive lateral tilt.

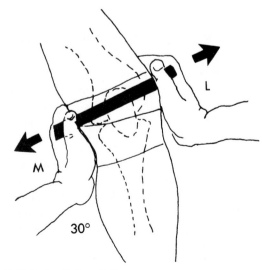

FIGURE 30-20

Taping to correct positive inferior anteroposterior tilt.

to be changed considerably. The tape should be worn 24 hours a day initially, and the therapist should instruct the patient on how to adjust and tighten the tape as necessary.

It is important to understand that taping changes the forces acting on the patella and thus the kinematics of the knee joint. Taping essentially attempts to decrease the lateral pull on the patella. This, when combined with an increase in the force and timing of the VMO contraction, will result in alteration of the balance of forces on the patella. Interestingly, a study by Bockrath et al demonstrated that patellar taping reduced pain in patients with anterior knee pain, but radiographic studies before and after taping revealed no change in patellofemoral congruency or patellar rotational angles. Hence, the reduction in pain was not associated with positional change of the patella.[8]

Reestablishing Neuromuscular Control

Establishing neuromuscular control involves improving the timing and force of VMO contraction. It is perhaps most important for the therapist to emphasize the quality rather than the quantity of the contraction. This means that training the VMO should concentrate more on motor skill acquisition rather than on strengthening activities. Strengthening should occur concomitantly with improvement in motor skill.

As mentioned previously, the VMO to VL strength ratio should be 1:1. In patients who have a VMO to VL ratio of less than 1:1 with patellofemoral pain, training efforts should focus on selectively strengthening the VMO. Isolating and training the VMO selectively requires concentration on the part of the patient. Techniques of facilitation, such as manually stroking or taping the VMO or the use of biofeedback, are recommended. The use of a dual channel biofeedback unit capable of monitoring both VMO and VL electromyographic activity can help the patient gain neuromuscular control over both the force of contraction and timing for the firing of the VMO.

Because the VMO is a tonic muscle that acts to stabilize the patella both statically and dynamically, it should be active throughout the range of motion. Training goals should be directed toward increasing the force of the VMO contraction both concentrically and eccentrically throughout the range of motion. Because the VMO arises from the adductor magnus tendon, adduction exercises may be used to facilitate VMO contraction. The VMO should be trained to respond to a new length–tension relationship between the agonist (VMO) and the antagonist (VL).

Several sources have indicated that the VMO has a separate nerve supply from the rest of the quadriceps, although this is in our opinion somewhat debatable.[4,10,24] Nevertheless, assuming this is the case, the patient should be taught to fire the VMO before the VL. Neuromuscular control of the VMO firing should help the patient maintain appropriate patellar alignment. VMO exercises should concentrate on controlling the firing of the VMO. Exercises should be performed slowly and with concentration to selectively activate muscles. The therapist should address concentric and eccentric control in a variety of functional tasks and positions. Mini-squats, step-ups or

step-downs, and leg presses are good exercises for establishing concentric and eccentric control. Training on a BAPS board is useful for proprioceptive training (see Exercise 30-47). It is extremely important to concentrate on VMO control during gait training activities.

Taping should continue throughout the VMO training period. Again, tape should initially be worn 24 hours per day. The patient may be weaned from tape progressively when he or she demonstrates VMO control. Examples of functional criteria for weaning would be when the patient can keep the VMO activated for 5 minutes during a walking gait and when the patient can fire the VMO either before or simultaneously with the vastus lateralis consistently in step-downs for 1 minute. At this point, tape may be left off every third day for 1 week, then every second day for 1 week, then worn only during activity, and finally worn only if pain is present. Taping may be eliminated altogether when the patient can perform step-downs for 5 minutes with appropriate timing and when he or she can sustain a one fourth to half squat for 1 minute without VMO loss.

Chondromalacia Patella

PATHOMECHANICS AND INJURY MECHANISM

Chondromalacia patella may occur either as a consequence of patellofemoral stress syndrome or from a direct impact to the patella. It is a softening and deterioration of the articular cartilage on the back of the patella that has been described as undergoing three stages: swelling and softening of the articular cartilage; fissuring of the softened articular cartilage; and deformation of the surface of the articular cartilage caused by fragmentation.[13]

The exact cause of chondromalacia is unknown. As indicated previously, abnormal patellar tracking could be a major etiologic factor. However, individuals with normal tracking have acquired chondromalacia, and some individuals with abnormal tracking are free of it.[9]

The patient may experience pain in the anterior aspect of the knee while walking, running, ascending and descending stairs, or squatting. There may be recurrent swelling around the kneecap and a grating sensation when flexing and extending the knee. There may also be crepitation and pain during a patellar grind test. During palpation, there may be pain on the inferior border of the patella or when the patella is compressed within the femoral groove while the knee is passively flexed and extended. Degenerative arthritis occurs on the lateral facet of the patella, which makes contact with the femur when the patient performs a full squat.[9] Degeneration first occurs in the deeper portions of the articular cartilage, followed by blistering and fissuring that stems from the subchondral bone and appears on the surface of the patella.[9,13]

REHABILITATION CONCERNS

Chondromalacia patella is initially treated conservatively using the same rehabilitation plan as was described with patellofemoral stress syndrome.[54] If conservative measures fail to help, surgery may be the only alternative. Some of the following surgical measures have been recommended[9]: realignment procedures such as lateral release of the retinaculum; moving the insertion of the vastus medialis muscle forward; shaving and smoothing the irregular surfaces of the patella and/or femoral condyle; in cases of degenerative arthritis, removing the lesion through drilling; elevating the tibial tubercle; or, as a last resort, completely removing the patella.

REHABILITATION PROGRESSION

Chondromalacia patella is a degenerative process that, unfortunately, does not tend to get better or resolve with time. There are times when the knee is painful and times when it is not. Perhaps the key to managing chondromalacia is to maintain strength of the quadriceps muscle group and, in particular, the VMO. Closed chain exercises are recommeneded because they tend to decrease the patellofemoral joint reaction forces. The patient must be consistent in his or her strengthening efforts.

Irritating activities that tend to exacerbate pain, such as stair climbing, squatting, and long periods of sitting, should be avoided. Isometric exercises or closed chain isotonics performed through a pain-free arc to strengthen the quadriceps and hamstring muscles should be routinely done. The use of oral anti-inflammatory agents and small doses of aspirin may help to modulate pain. Wearing a neoprene knee sleeve helps certain patients but does absolutely nothing for others. Use of an orthotic device to correct pronation and reduce tibial torsion is helpful in many instances.

As long as the patient can tolerate the pain and discomfort that occurs with chondromalacia patella, he or she can continue to train and compete. Again, the key is essentially to "play games" with this condition, training normally when there is no pain and backing off when the knee is painful.

Acute Patellar Subluxation or Dislocation

PATHOMECHANICS

As it tracks superiorly and inferiorly in the femoral groove, the patella can be subject to direct trauma or degenerative changes, leading to chronic pain and disability.[34] Of major importance among patients are those conditions that stem from abnormal patellar tracking within the femoral groove. Improper patellar tracking leading to patellar subluxation or dislocation may result from a number of different biomechanical factors, including femoral anteversion with increased internal femoral rotation; genu valgum with a concommitant increase in the Q angle; a shallow femoral groove; flat lateral femoral condyles; patella alta; weakness of the vastus medialis muscle realtive to the vastus lateralis; ligamentous laxity with genu recurvatum; excessive external rotation of the tibia; pronated feet; a tight lateral retinaculum; and a patella with a positive lateral tilt. Each of these factors was discussed in detail earlier in this chapter.

INJURY MECHANISM

When the patient plants the foot, decelerates, and simultaneously cuts in an opposite direction from the weight-bearing foot, the thigh rotates internally while the lower leg rotates externally, causing a forced knee valgus. The quadriceps muscle attempts to pull in a straight line and as a result pulls the patella laterally, creating a force that may sublux the patella. As a rule, displacement takes place laterally, with the patella shifting over the lateral condyle.

A chronically subluxing patella places abnormal stress on the patellofemoral joint and the medial restraints. The knee may be swollen and painful. Pain is a result of swelling but also results because the medial capsular tissue has been stretched and torn. Because of the associated swelling, the knee is restricted in flexion and extension. There may also be a palpable tenderness over the adductor tubercle where the medial retinaculum (patellar femoral ligament) attaches.

Acute patellar dislocation most often occurs when the foot is planted and there is contact with another patient on the medial surface of the patella, forcing it to dislocate laterally. The patient reports a painful "giving way" episode. The patient experiences a complete loss of knee function, pain, and swelling, with the patella remaining in an abnormal lateral position. A physician should immediately reduce the dislocation by applying mild pressure on the patella with the knee extended as much as possible. If a period of time has elapsed before reduction, a general anesthetic may have to be used. After aspiration of the joint hematoma, ice is applied, and the joint is immobilized. A first-time patellar dislocation is sometimes associated with loose bodies from a chondral or osteochondral fracture as well as articular cartilage lesions. Thus, some physicians advocate arthroscopic examination following patellar dislocation.[74]

REHABILITATION PROGRESSION

Chronic Patellar Subluxation

Rehabilitation for a chronically subluxing patella should focus on addressing each of the potential biomechanical factors that either individually or collectively contribute to the pathomechanics. It is important to regain a balance in strength of all musculature associated with the knee joint. Postural malalignments must be corrected as much as possible. Shoe orthotic devices may be used to reduce foot pronation, tibial internal rotation, and subsequently, reduce stress to the patellofemoral joint.

Particular attention should address strengthening of the quadriceps through closed-kinetic chain exercises; strengthening of the hip abductors (see Exercise 30-1), hip adductors (see Exercise 30-2), and gastrocnemius (see Exercise 30-7); stretching the tight lateral structures, which, using a combination of patellar mobilization glides (see Exercise 30-43) and medial patellar, tilts along the longitudinal axis of the patella, as well as a stretching for the iliotibial band (see Exercise 30-35) and biceps femoris (see Exercise 30-38); correcting patellar orientation;

and establishing neuromuscular control by improving the timing and force of the VMO contraction.

If the patient does not respond to extensive efforts by the therapist to correct the pathomechanics and subluxation remains a recurrent problem, surgical intervention may be necessary: however, a surgical release of the lateral retinacular ligaments does not appear to be a particularly effective procedure and should only be done after failure of more conservative treatment.

Acute Patellar Dislocation

In the case of acute patellar dislocation, following reduction the knee should be placed in an immobilizer immediately and it is recommended that it remain in place from 3 to 6 weeks with the patient ambulating on crutches until he or she regains full extension and can walk without an extension lag. The patient can begin immediately following the dislocation with isometric quad sets (see Exercise 30-3) and straight leg raising (see Exercise 30-4), always paying close attention to achieving a good contraction of the VMO. Early pain-free range-of-motion exercises including knee slides on a treatment table (see Exercise 30-29), wall slides (see Exercise 30-30), or active assistive slides, (see Exercise 30-31), can be used.

As pain subsides and ROM improves, the patient should incorporate closed chain strengthening exercises (see Exercises 30-8 through 30-17) to minimize stress on the patellofemoral joint. Strengthening should be directed toward increasing the force of the VMO contraction both concentrically and eccentrically throughout the range of motion. Neuromuscular control of the VMO firing should help the patient maintain appropriate patellar alignment. It is also important to concentrate on VMO control during gait training activities.

After 3 to 6 weeks, when immobilization is discontinued, the patient should wear a neoprene knee sleeve with a lateral horseshoe-shaped felt pad, which helps the patella track medially (Fig. 30-21).

Patellar Tendinitis (Jumper's Knee)

PATHOMECHANICS AND INJURY MECHANISM

Jumper's knee occurs when chronic inflammation develops in the patellar tendon either at the superior patellar pole (usually referred to as quadriceps tendinitis), the tibial tubercle, or most commonly, at the distal pole of the patella (patellar tendinitis). It usually develops in patients involved in activities that require repetitive jumping; hence the name. Point tenderness on the posterior aspect of the inferior pole of the patella is the hallmark of patellar tendinitis. This condition is felt to be related to the shock-absorbing function (an eccentric contraction) that the quadriceps provides upon landing from a jump. Initially, the patient complains of a dull aching pain after jumping or running following repetitive jumping activities. Pain usually disappears with rest but returns with activity. Pain becomes progressively

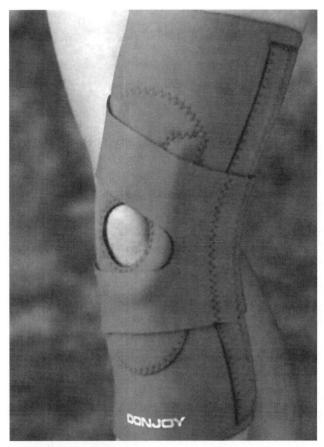

F I G U R E   3 0 - 2 1

A brace that can help limit patellar dislocation and/or subluxation should have a felt horseshoe applied laterally.

worse until the patient is unable to continue. There are also reports of difficulty in stair climbing and an occasional feeling of "giving way."

REHABILITATION CONCERNS

Because jumper's knee involves a chronic inflammation, rehabilitation strategies may take one of two courses. The therapist may choose to use traditional techniques designed to reduce the inflammation, which include rest, anti-inflammatory medication, ice, and ultrasound. Another more aggressive approach would be to use a transverse friction massage technique designed to exacerbate the acute inflammation, so that the healing process is no longer "stuck" in the inflammatory-response phase, and can move on to the fibroblastic repair phase. The technique involves a 5 to 7 minute friction massage at the inferior pole of the patella in a direction perpendicular to the direction of the tendon fibers, performed every other day for approximately 1 week. During this treatment, all other medicative or modality efforts to reduce inflammation should be eliminated. It is our experience that if pain is not decreased after 4 to 5 treatments, it is unlikely that this technique will resolve the problem.

Ruptures of the patellar tendon are rare in young patients but increase in incidence with age. A sudden powerful contraction of the quadriceps muscle with the weight of the body applied to the affected leg can cause a rupture of the patellar tendon.[86] The rupture may occur to the quadriceps tendon or to the patellar tendon. Usually, rupture does not occur unless there has been a prolonged period of inflammation of the patellar tendon, causing weakening of the tendon. Seldom does a rupture occur in the middle of the tendon, but usually it is torn from its attachment. The quadriceps tendon ruptures from the superior pole of the patella, whereas the patellar tendon ruptures from the inferior pole of the patella. A rupture of the patellar tendon usually requires surgical repair.

REHABILITATION PROGRESSION

Regardless of which of the two treatment approaches is used, once the problem begins to resolve, the patient should engage in a thorough warm-up prior to activity. Strengthening of the quadriceps is critical during rehabilitation. Success has been reported using eccentric strengthening exercises for both the quadriceps and the ankle dorsiflexors.[17,42,56] Curwin and Stanish have theorized that a graded program of eccentric stress will stimulate the tendon to heal.[17] They feel that rest does not stimulate healing, whereas low-to-moderate level eccentric exercise will. Their program consists of five parts: warm-up, stretching, eccentric squatting, stretching, and ice.[5,17] The eccentric squats, called drop squats, are performed with the patient moving slowly from standing to a squat position and return. To increase stress, the speed of the drop is increased until a mild level of pain is experienced (Fig. 30-22). The goal is to perform 3 sets of 10 repetitions at a speed that causes mild pain during the last set. The presence of mild pain is indicative of the mild stress.

Jensen and DiFabio have suggested treating patellar tendinitis with a program of isokinetic eccentric quadriceps training (see Exercise 30-21).[43] The program begins with 6 sets of 5 repetitions at 30 degrees per second 3 times per week progressing over an 8-week period to 4 sets of 5 repetitions each at 30/50/70 degrees per second.[43] Vigorous quadriceps and hamstring stretching precede and follow each workout (see Exercise 30-37 and 30-38).

The use of a tenodesis strap or brace worn about the patellar tendon has also been recommended for patellar tendinitis (Fig. 30-23). It appears that the effectiveness of this strap in reducing pain is variable from one patient to another.

The injection of cortisone into the tendon to reduce inflammation is not recommended because it will tend to weaken the tendon and may predispose the patient to patellar tendon rupture.

Bursitis

PATHOPHYSIOLOGY

Bursitis in the knee can be acute, chronic, or recurrent. Although any one of the numerous knee bursae can become inflamed,

FIGURE 30-22

Drop squats are performed with the patient moving slowly from standing to a squat position and return.

anteriorly the prepatellar, deep infrapatellar, and suprapatellar bursae have the highest incidence of irritation in sports. The pathophysiologic reaction that occurs with bursitis follows the normal course of the inflammatory response as described in Chapter 3.

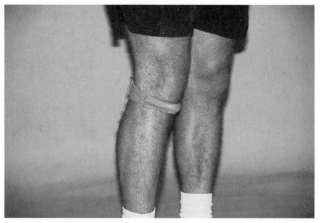

FIGURE 30-23

A tendonesis strap can be used to help control patellar tendonitis.

Swelling patterns can often help in differentiating bursitis from other conditions in the injured knee. With bursitis, swelling is localized to the bursa. For example, prepatellar bursitis results in localized swelling above the knee that is ballottable. In the more severe cases, it may seem to extend over the lower portion of the vastus medialis. Swelling is not intraarticular and there may be some redness and increased temperature. In acute prepatellar bursitis, the range of motion of the knee is not restricted except in the last degrees of flexion when pain-producing pressure is felt in the bursa, whereas a true hemarthrosis or synovitis of the knee joint most frequently shows a more significant limitation of terminal flexion and extension of the joint.[9]

Injuries to the ligaments of the knee and also fractures of the patella may occur along with acute prepatellar bursitis. Patellar fractures may occur either from a direct blow to the patella, with the knee held in flexion, or a violent contraction of the quadriceps mechanism may produce transverse patellar fractures, which should be ruled out with radiographs. Infection of the infrapatellar bursa can be similarly difficult to diagnosis because of its deep location. It is a rare condition and requires aspiration for diagnosis.

Swelling posteriorly in the popliteal fossa does not necessarily indicate bursitis but could instead be a sign of Baker's cyst. A Baker's cyst is connected to the joint, which swells because of a problem in the joint and not due to bursitis. A Baker's cyst is often asymptomatic, causing little or no discomfort or disability.

INJURY MECHANISM

The cause of prepatellar bursitis can involve either a single trauma, as would occur in falling on a flexed knee, or it may result from repetitive crawling or kneeling on the knee, although acute or posttraumatic inflammation is not uncommon. The prepatellar bursa is more likely to become inflamed from continued kneeling, whereas the deep infrapatellar becomes irritated from repetitive stress to the patellar tendon, as is the case in jumper's knee.

REHABILITATION CONCERNS AND PROGRESSION

Acute prepatellar bursitis should be treated conservatively, and the rehabilitative process should begin with ice, compression, anti-inflammatory medication, and, possibly, a brief period of immobilization in a knee splint. If necessary, the patient should walk on crutches until he or she has regained quadriceps control and can ambulate without a limp. The compression wrap should be applied from the foot upward to the middle of the thigh in a manner that maintains constant pressure on the bursa. The leg should be elevated as much as possible. The patient should begin with quad sets (see Exercise 30-3) and straight leg raising (see Exercise 30-4), both to maintain function of the quadriceps and to use active muscle contractions to help facilitate resorption of fluid. On the second day, the patient may begin ROM exercises doing knee slides on a treatment table (Exercise 30-29),

wall slides (Exercise 30-30), or active assistive slides (Exercise 30-31). The compression wrap should be left in place until there is no evidence of fluid reaccumulation.

Occasionally, a physician may choose to aspirate the bursa to relieve the pressure and speed up the recovery period. If so, it is essential to take necessary precautions to prevent contamination and subsequent infection. If infection does occur it should be treated with antibiotics.

In cases of chronic bursitis, the techniques for controlling swelling listed previously should be used. A compression wrap needs to be worn constantly. Unfortunately, there will generally not be complete resolution. Chronic bursitis becomes a recurrent problem, with thickening of the bursa and reaccumulation of fluid. In these cases, injection with a corticosteriod or surgical excision of the bursa may be necessary.

Iliotibial Band Friction Syndrome

PATHOMECHANICS

The iliotibial band is a tendinous extension of the fascia covering the gluteus maximus and tensor fasciae latae muscles proximally which attaches distally at Gerdy's tubercle on the proximal portion of the lateral tibial. As the patient flexes and extends the knee, the tendon glides anteriorly and posteriorly over the lateral femoral condyle. This repetitive motion, as typically occurs in walking or running, may produce irritation and inflammation of the tendon.

Iliotibial band friction syndrome involves localized pain about 2 cm above the joint line over the lateral femoral condyle when the knee is in 30 degrees of flexion. Pain appears to radiate toward the lateral joint line and down toward the proximal tibia, becoming increasingly severe as the patient continues to run. Eventually, it becomes so symptomatic that the activity must be discontinued. The patient has tenderness, crepitus, and an area of swelling over the lateral condyle. In some instances, patients with iliotibial band friction syndrome also give a history of having had trochanteric bursitis and pain along the iliac crest at the origin at the tensor fasciae latae.

Leg length discrepancies, contractures of the tensor fasciae latae and gluteus maximus, tightness of the hamstrings and quadriceps, genu varum, excessive pronation leading to increased internal tibial torsion, and a tight heel cord can individually or collectively increase the tension of the iliotibial band across the femoral condyle. Ober's test to detect tightness in this muscle group will be positive.

INJURY MECHANISM

As is the case in many injuries associated with overuse, there is often a history of poor training techniques that may include running on irregular surfaces such as on the side of the road, downhill running, or running long distances without gradually building up to that level. Symptoms frequently develop in patients who do not have an adequate stretching program.

REHABILITATION CONCERNS AND PROGRESSION

Initial treatment for iliotibial band friction syndrome is directed at reducing the local inflammatory reaction by using rest, ice, ultrasound, and oral anti-inflammatory medications. Rehabilitation should focus on correcting the underlying biomechanical factors that may cause the problem. If the Ober test is positive, stretching exercises to correct this static contracture should be used (Exercise 30-35). Some patients also have hip flexion contractures with a positive Thomas test and require stretching of the iliopsoas and the anterior capsule, as well as the tensor fasciae latae.

During normal gait, pronation leads to an obligatory internal rotation of the tibia. Orthotics may help reduce this pronation and relieve symptoms at the knee. Generally, 4 to 6 weeks of conservative treatment is required to control the symptoms of iliotibial band syndrome. Although conservative treatment is usually effective in controlling symptoms, occasionally, cases of iliotibial band syndrome do not respond and require surgical treatment.

As was the case with patellar tendinitis, transverse friction massage used to increase the inflammatory response appears to be effective in treating iliotibial band friction syndrome. A 5- to 7-minute friction massage to the iliotibial band over the lateral femoral condyle in a direction perpendicular to the direction of the tendon fibers should be done every other day for approximately 1 week. During this treatment, all other medicative or modality efforts to reduce inflammation should be eliminated.

When the local tenderness over the lateral epicondyle has subsided, the patient may resume running but should avoid prolonged workouts and running on hills and irregular surfaces. If it is necessary to run on the side of the road, it is essential that the patient alternate sides of the road during workouts. Shortening the stride and applying ice after running may also be beneficial.

Patellar Plica

PATHOMECHANICS

A plica is a fold in the synovial lining of the knee, which is a remnant from the embryological development within the knee. The most common synovial fold is the infrapatellar plica, which originates from the infrapatellar fat pad and extends superiorly in a fanlike manner. The second most common synovial fold is the suprapatellar plica, located in the suprapatellar pouch. The least common, but most subject to injury, is the mediopatellar plica, which is bandlike, begins on the medial wall of the knee joint, and extends downward to insert into the synovial tissue that covers the infrapatellar fat pad.[7] The mediopatellar plica can bowstring across the anteromedial femoral condyle impinging between the articular cartilage and the medial facet of the patella with increasing flexion. A plica is often associated with a torn meniscus, patellar malalignment, or osteoarthritis. Because most synovial plicae are pliable, most are asymptomatic; however, the mediopatellar plica may be thick, nonyielding, and fibrotic, causing a number of symptoms.

INJURY MECHANISM

The patient may or may not have a history of knee injury. If symptoms are preceded by trauma, it is usually one of blunt force, such as falling on the knee or of twisting with the foot planted, either of which may lead to inflammation and hemorrhage. Inflammation leads to fibrosis and thickening with a loss of extensibility.

As the knee passes 15 to 20 degrees of flexion, a snap may be felt or heard. Internal and external tibial rotation can also produce this snapping. The mediopatellar plica can snap over the medial femoral condyle, contributing to the development of chondromalacia.[7] A major complaint is recurrent episodes of painful pseudolocking of the knee when sitting for a period of time. Such characteristics of locking and snapping could be misinterpreted as a torn meniscus. The patient complains of pain while ascending or descending stairs or when squatting. Unlike meniscal injuries, there is little or no swelling and no ligamentous laxity.

REHABILITATION CONCERNS AND PROGRESSION

Initially, a plica should be treated conservatively to control inflammation with rest, anti-inflammatory agents, and local heat. If the plica is associated with improper patellar tracking, the pathomechanics should be corrected as previously discussed. If conservative treatment is unsuccessful, the plica may be surgically excised, usually with good results.[21]

Osgood–Schlatter Disease

PATHOMECHANICS AND INJURY MECHANISM

Two conditions common to the immature adolescent's knee are Osgood–Schlatter disease and Larsen–Johansson disease. Osgood–Schlatter disease is characterized by pain and swelling over the tibial tuberosity that increases with activity and decreases with rest. Traditionally, Osgood–Schlatter disease was described as either a partial avulsion of the tibial tubercle or an avascular necrosis of the same. Current thinking views it more as an apophysitis characterized by pain at the attachment of the patellar tendon at the tibial tubercle with associated extensor mechanism problems. The most commonly accepted cause of Osgood–Schlatter disease is repeated stress of the patellar tendon at the apophysis of the tibial tubercle. Complete avulsion of the patellar tendon is an uncommon complication of Osgood–Schlatter disease.

This condition first appears in adolescents and usually resolves when the patient reaches the age of 18 or 19. The only remnant is an enlarged tibial tubercle. Repeated irritation causes swelling, hemorrhage, and gradual degeneration of the apophysis as a result of impaired circulation. The patient complains of severe pain when kneeling, jumping, and running. There is point tenderness over the anterior proximal tibial tubercle.

Larsen–Johansson disease, although much less common, is similar to Osgood–Schlatter disease, but it occurs at the inferior pole of the patella. As with Osgood–Schlatter disease, the cause is believed to be excessive repeated strain on the patellar tendon. Swelling, pain, and point tenderness characterize Larsen–Johansson disease. Later, degeneration can be noted during X-ray examination.

REHABILITATION CONCERNS AND PROGRESSION

Management is usually conservative and includes the following: stressful activities are decreased until the apophyseal union occurs usually within 6 months to 1 year; ice is applied to the knee before and after activities; isometric strengthening of quadriceps and hamstring muscles is performed; and severe cases may require a cylindrical cast.

Treatment is symptomatic with emphasis placed on icing, quadriceps strengthening, hamstring stretching, and activity modification. Only in extreme cases is immobilization necessary.

EXERCISES

E X E R C I S E   3 0 - 2

Hip adduction. Used to strengthen the adductor magnus, longus, and brevis; the pectineus; and the gracilis. The gracilis is the only one of the hip adductors to cross the knee joint.

REHABILITATION TECHNIQUES

Strengthening Exercises

A primary goal in knee rehabilitation is the return of normal strength to the musculature surrounding the knee. Along with the return of muscular strength, it is also important to improve muscular endurance and power.

It is critically important to understand that strength will be gained only if the muscle is subjected to overload. However, it is also essential to remember that healing tissues may be further damaged by overloading the injured structure too aggressively. Especially during the early phases of rehabilitation, muscular overload needs to be carefully applied to protect the damaged structures. The recovering knee needs protection, and the high-resistance, low-repetition program designed to strengthen a healthy knee may compromise the integrity of the injured knee.[49] The strengthening phase of rehabilitation must be gently progressive and will generally progress from isometric to isotonic to isokinetic to plyometric to functional exercise.

For years, open-kinetic chain exercises were the treatment of choice. However more recently, closed-kinetic chain exercises have been widely used and recommended in the rehabilitation of the injured knee. Closed-kinetic chain exercises may be safely introduced early in the rehabilitation process for virtually all types of knee injury.[11,22,76,77,84] Closed-kinetic chain activities may involve isometric, isotonic, plyometric, and even isokinetic techniques.

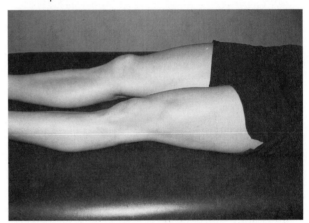

E X E R C I S E   3 0 - 3

Quad Sets are done isometrically with the knee in full extension to help the patient relearn how to contract the quadriceps following injury or surgery.

ISOTONIC OPEN-KINETIC CHAIN EXERCISES

E X E R C I S E   3 0 - 1

Hip abduction. Used to strengthen the gluteus medius and tensor fascia lata which share a commen tendon, the iliotibial band. The IT band serves as a weak knee flexor and helps to provide stability laterally.

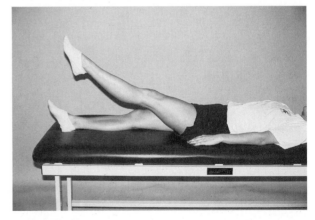

E X E R C I S E   3 0 - 4

Straight leg raising is done early in the rehabilitation for active contraction of the quadriceps.

E X E R C I S E   3 0 - 5

Knee flexion. Primary muscles: Biceps femoris, semimembranous, semitendinous. Secondary muscles: Gracilis, gastrocnemius, sartorius, popliteus. NOTE: Biceps femoris is best strengthened with tibia rotated externally, semimembranous and semitendinous muscles are best strengthened with tibia rotated internally.

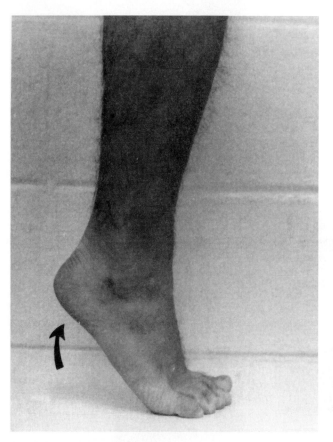

E X E R C I S E   3 0 - 7

Ankle plantarflexion. Used to strengthen the gastrocnemius which serves as a knee flexor.

E X E R C I S E   3 0 - 6

Knee extension. Primary muscles: Rectus femoris, vastus lateralis, vastus intermedialis, vastus medialis.

CLOSED-KINETIC CHAIN STRENGTHENING EXERCISES

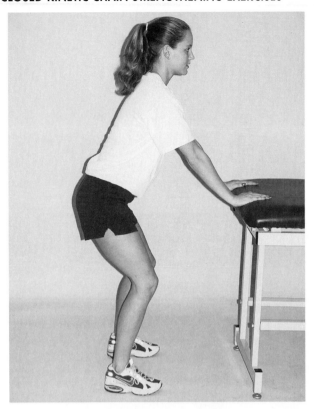

E X E R C I S E   3 0 - 8

Mini-squat performed in 0 to 40 degree range.

E X E R C I S E   3 0 - 1 0

Lunges are done to strengthen quadriceps eccentrically.

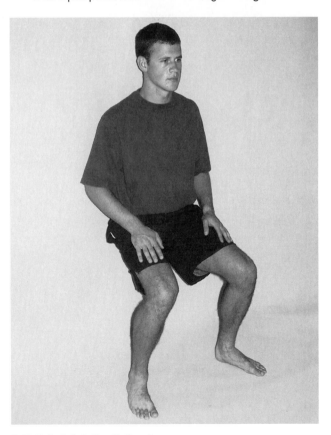

E X E R C I S E   3 0 - 9

Standing wall slide are done to strengthen the quadriceps.

E X E R C I S E   3 0 - 1 1

Leg press exercise. The seat may be adjusted to whatever knew joint angle is appropriate.

EXERCISE 30-12

Lateral step-ups as well as forward step-ups may be done using different stepping heights.

EXERCISE 30-13

Terminal knee extensions using surgical tubing resistance for strengthening primarily the vastus medialis.

A

B

E X E R C I S E   3 0 - 1 4

Slide board exercises are used in side to side training.

E X E R C I S E   3 0 - 1 6

Stairmaster stepping machine allows the patient to maintain constant contact with the step.

E X E R C I S E   3 0 - 1 5

The Fitter is useful in side to side functional training.

E X E R C I S E   3 0 - 1 7

Stationary bicycling is good for regaining ROM by adjusting the seat to the appropriate height but also for maintaining cardiorespiratory endurance.

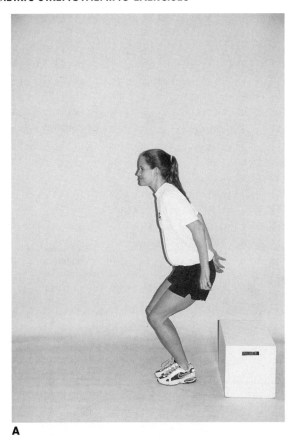

A

B

EXERCISE 30-18

Box jumps. The patient should jump off a box at heights ranging from 6″ to 24″ **(A)** and then immediately jump again as soon as contact is made with the floor **(B)**.

A

B

EXERCISE 30-19

Single-leg **(A)** and double-leg **(B)** bounding hops.

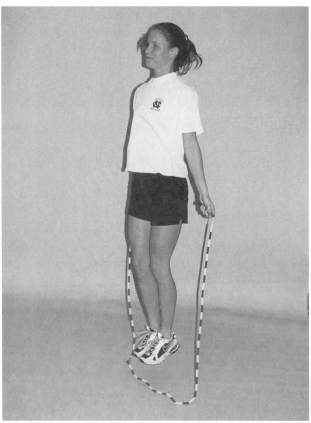

EXERCISE   30-20

Rope skipping is a plyometric exercise which is also good for improving cardiorespiratory endurance.

ISOKINETIC STRENGTHENING EXERCISES

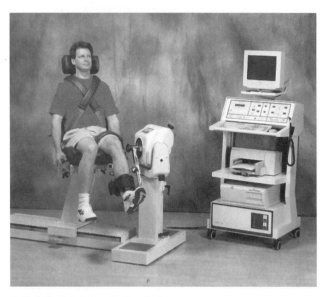

EXERCISE   30-21

Knee Extension set-up to strengthen the quadriceps.

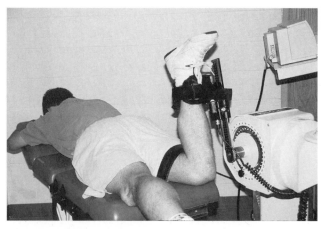

EXERCISE   30-22

Knee Flexion set-up to strengthen the hamstrings.

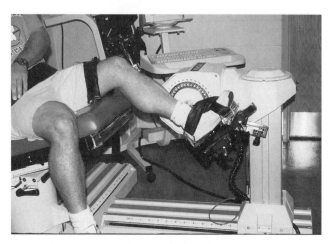

EXERCISE   30-23

Tibial rotation is done with resistance at the ankle joint and is an extremely important though often neglected aspect of knee rehabilitation.

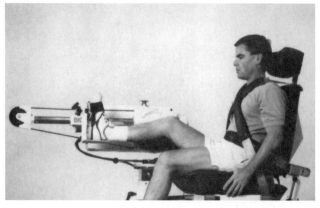

EXERCISE   30-24

Biodex manufactures an isokinetic closed chain exercise device.

PNF STRENGTHENING EXERCISES

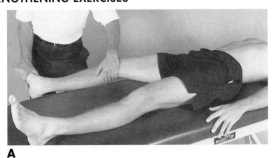

A

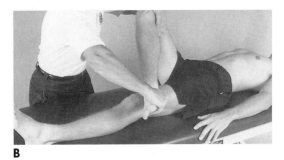

B

EXERCISE 30-25

D1 lower extremity movement pattern moving into flexion. **A.** Starting position.
B. Terminal position.

A

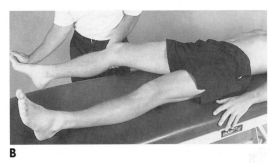

B

EXERCISE 30-26

D1 lower extremity movement pattern moving into extension. **A.** Starting position,
B. Terminal position.

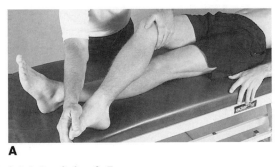

A

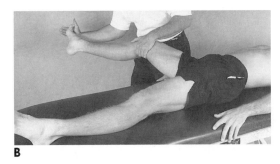

B

EXERCISE 30-27

D2 lower extremity movement pattern moving into flexion. **A.** Starting position.
B. Terminal position.

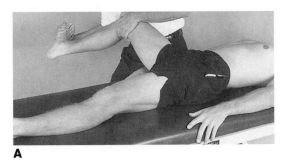

A

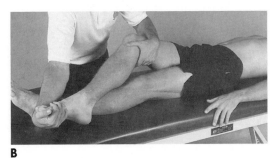

B

EXERCISE 30-28

D2 lower extremity movement pattern moving into extension. **A.** Starting position,
B. Terminal position.

Range-of-Motion Exercises

After injury to the knee, some loss of motion is likely. This loss may be caused by the effects of the injury, the trauma of surgery, or the effects of immobilization. Waiting for ligaments to heal completely is a luxury that cannot be afforded in an effective rehabilitation program. Ligaments do not heal completely for 18 to 24 months, yet periarticular tissue changes can begin within 4 to 6 weeks of immobilization.[40] This is marked histologically by a decrease in water content in collagen and by an increase in collagen cross linkage.[40] The initiation of an early range-of-motion program can minimize these harmful changes. Controlled movement should be initiated early in the recovery process and progress based on healing constraints and patient tolerance toward a normal range of approximately 0 to 130 degrees.

Pitfalls that can slow or prevent regaining normal range of motion include imperfect surgical technique (improper placement of an anterior cruciate replacement), development of joint capsule or ligament contracture, and muscular resistance caused by pain.[32,40,45] The surgeon must address motion lost from technique, but the therapist can successfully deal with motion lost from soft tissue contracture or muscular resistance.

To effectively alleviate lost motion, the cause of the limitation must be identified. An experienced therapist can detect soft tissue resistance to motion by the quality of the feel of the resistance at the end of the range. Muscular resistance, which restricts normal physiologic movement, has a firm end feel and can best be treated by using PNF stretching techniques in combination with appropriate therapeutic modalities (that is, heat, ice, electrical stimulation, etc.).[66]

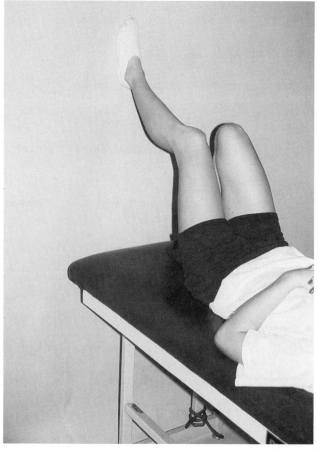

EXERCISE   30-30

Wall slides are done to regain flexion and extension.

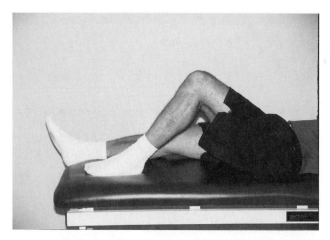

EXERCISE   30-29

Knee slides are done on a treatment table by sliding a foot in a sock forward and backward flexing and extending the knee through a pain free range.

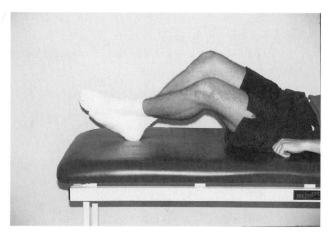

EXERCISE   30-31

Active assistive knee slides use the good leg supporting the injured knee to regain flexion and extension.

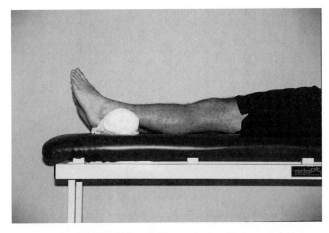

EXERCISE 30-32

Knee extension with the foot supported on a rolled up towel is used to regain knee extension.

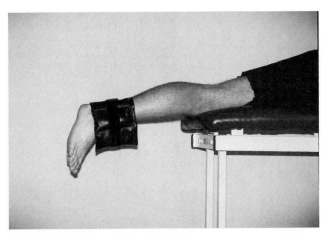

EXERCISE 30-33

Knee extension in prone with an ankle weight around the foot is used to regain extension.

EXERCISE 30-34

Groin stretch. Muscles: Adductor magnus, longus, and brevis; pectineus; gracilis.

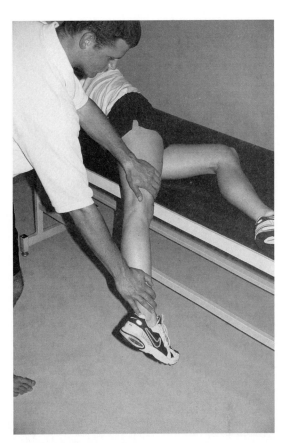

EXERCISE 30-35

Iliotibial band stretch. The iliotibial band may be stretched in a variety of ways that use a scissoring position with extreme hip adduction. The major problem with these techniques is the lack of stabilization of the pelvis and therefore loss of stretch force transmission to the iliotibial band. To maximize the stretch the pelvis must be manually stabilized to prevent lateral pelvic tilt. If the tensor fascia lata portion is tight, the hip should be flexed, abducted, extended, and adducted, in sequence, to position the tensor fascia lata fibers directly over the trochanter (rather than anterior to it) to produce maximal stretch.

EXERCISE 30-36

Kneeling thrusts. Muscles: Rectus femoris.

EXERCISE 30-37

Knee extensors stretch. Muscles: Quadriceps.

EXERCISE 30-38

Knee flexors stretch. Muscles: Hamstrings. NOTE: Externally rotated tibia stretches semimembranous and semitendinous; internally rotated tibia stretches biceps femoris.

A

B

EXERCISE 30-39

Ankle plantarflexors stretch. Muscles: Gastrocnemius.

Joint Mobilization Techniques

Joint capsule or ligamentous contractures have a leathery end feel and may not respond to conventional simple passive, active-assistive, and active motion exercises.[32] These contractures can limit the accessory motions of the joint, and until the accessory motions are restored, conventional exercises will not produce positive results. Accessory motions in the knee joint must occur between the patella and femur, the femur and tibia, and the tibia and fibula. Restriction in any or all of these accessory motions must be addressed early in the rehabilitation program.

Mobilization of a knee that is restricted by soft tissue constraints may be accomplished by specifically applying graded oscillations to the restricted soft tissue as discussed in Chapter 12. In doing so, the therapist is addressing a specific limiting structure rather than assaulting the entire joint with a "crank till you cry" technique. After the release of the soft tissue contracture, accessory motion should improve, and thus so should physiologic motion.

E X E R C I S E   3 0 - 4 0

Anterior tibial glides. Anterior tibial glides are appropriate for the patient lacking full extension. Anterior glides should be done in prone position with the femur stabilized. Pressure is applied to the posterior tibia to glide anteriorly.

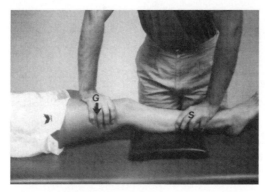

E X E R C I S E   3 0 - 4 1

Posterior femoral glides. Posterior femoral glides are appropriate for the patient lacking full extension. Posterior femoral glides should be done in supine position with the tibia stabilized. Pressure is applied to the anterior femur to glide posteriorly.

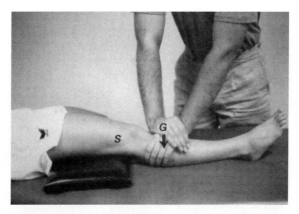

E X E R C I S E   3 0 - 4 2

Posterior tibial glides. Posterior tibial glides increase flexion. With the patient in supine position, stabilize the femur, and glide the tibia posteriorly.

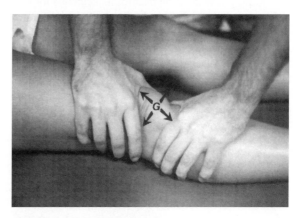

E X E R C I S E   3 0 - 4 3

Patellar glides. Superior patellar glides increase knee extension. Inferior glides increase knee flexion. Medial glides stretch the lateral retinaculum. Lateral glides stretch tight medial structures.

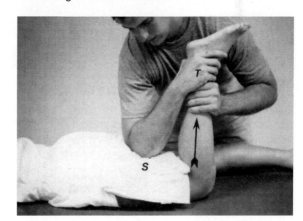

E X E R C I S E   3 0 - 4 4

Tibiofemoral joint traction. Tibiofemoral joint traction reduces pain and hypomobility. It may be done with the patient prone and the knee flexed at 90 degrees. The elbow should stabilize the thigh while traction is applied through the tibia.

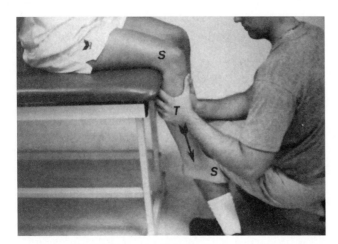

E X E R C I S E   3 0 - 4 5

Alternative techniques for tibiofemoral joint traction. In very large individuals an alternative technique for tibiofemoral joint traction uses body weight of the therapist to distract the joint once again for reducing pain and hypomobility.

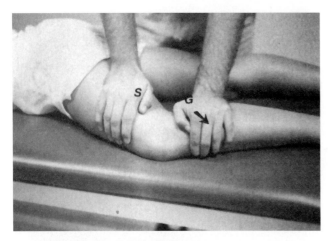

E X E R C I S E   3 0 - 4 6

Proximal anterior and posterior glides of the fibula. Anterior and posterior glides of the fibula may be done proximally. They increase mobility of the fibular head and reduce pain. The femur should be stabilized. With the knee slightly flexed, grasp the head of the femur, and glide it both anteriorly and posteriorly.

EXERCISES TO REESTABLISH NEUROMUSCULAR CONTROL

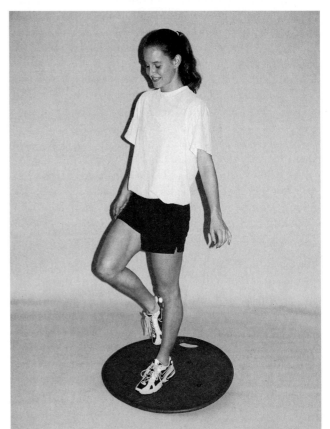

A

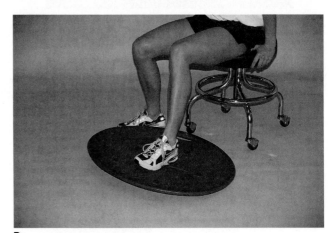

B

E X E R C I S E   3 0 - 4 7

BAPS Board Exercise **A.** Standing, **B.** Sitting.

EXERCISE 30-48

Mini-tramp provides an unstable base of support to which other functional plyometric activities may be added.

EXERCISE 30-50

Biofeedback units can be used to help the patient learn how to fire a specific muscle or muscle group.

EXERCISE 30-49

Slide board training.

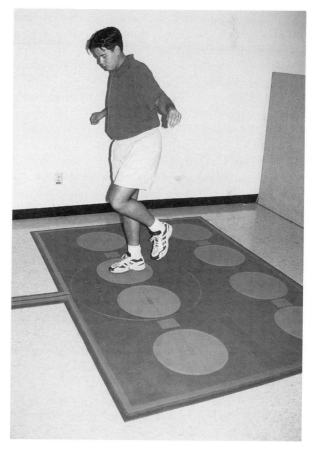

EXERCISE 30-51

FASTEX is a useful device for functional neuromuscular training.

SUMMARY

- To be effective in a knee rehabilitation program, the therapist must have a good understanding of functional anatomy and the biomechanics of knee joint motion.
- Techniques of strengthening involving closed-kinetic chain, isometric, isotonic, isokinetic, and plyometric exercises are recommended after injury to the knee because of their safety and because they are more functional than open chain exercises.
- Range of motion may be restricted by lack of either physiologic motion, which may be corrected by stretching; or by lack of accessory motions, which may be corrected by patellar mobilization techniques. Constant passive motion may be used postoperatively to assist the patient in regaining range of motion.
- PCL, MCL, and LCL injuries are generally treated nonoperatively and the patient is progressed back into activity rapidly within his or her limitations.
- The current surgical procedure of choice for ACL reconstruction uses an intraarticular patellar tendon graft.
- Recent trends in rehabilitation after ACL reconstruction are toward an aggressive, accelerated program that emphasizes immediate motion, immediate weight bearing, early closed chain strengthening exercises, and early return to activity.
- The current trend in treating meniscal tears is to surgically repair the defect if possible or perform a partial meniscectomy arthroscopically. Repaired menisci should be immobilized nonweight bearing for 4 to 6 weeks.
- It is critical to assess the mechanics of the patellofemoral joint in terms of static alignment, dynamic alignment, and patellar orientation to determine what specifically is causing pain.
- Rehabilitation of patellofemoral pain concentrates on strengthening of the quadriceps through closed-kinetic chain exercises, regaining optimal patellar positioning and tracking, and regaining neuromuscular control to improve lower limb mechanics.

REFERENCES

1. Anderson C, Gillquist J. Treatment of acute isolated and combined ruptures of the ACL. A long term follow-up study. *Am J Sports Med* 20:7–12, 1992.
2. Anderson A, Snyder R, Federspiel C. Instrumented evaluation of knee laxity: A comparison of five arthrometers. *Am J Sports Med* 20:135–140, 1992.
3. Arno S. The A-angle: A quantitative measurement of patellar alignment and realignment. *J Orthop Sports Phys Ther* 12:237–242, 1990.
4. Basmajian J, DeLuca C. *Muscles Alive: Their Functions Revealed by Electromyography.* Baltimore, Williams & Wilkins, 1985.
5. Bennet J, Stauber W. Evaluation and treatment of anterior knee pain using eccentric exercise. *Med Sci Sports Exerc* 18, 1986.
6. Black K, Raasch W. Knee braces in sports. In: Nicholas J, Hershman E, eds. *The Lower Extremity and Spine in Sports Medicine.* St. Louis, Mosby, 1995.
7. Blackburn T. An introduction to the plica. *J Orthop Sports Phys Ther* 3:171, 1982.
8. Bockrath K. Effect of patellar taping on patellar position and perceived pain. Poster presentation, APTA combined sections, San Antonio, 1993.
9. Boland A, Hulstyn M. Soft tissue inuries of the knee. In: Nicholas J, Hershman E, eds. *The Lower Extremity and Spine in Sports Medicine.* St. Louis, Mosby, 1995.
10. Bose K, Kanagasuntheram R, Osman M. Vastus medialis oblique: An anatomic and physiologic study. *Orthopaedics* 3:880–883, 1980.
11. Brewster C, Moynes D, Jobe F. Rehabilitation for the anterior cruciate reconstruction. *J Orthop Sports Phys Ther* 5:121–126, 1983.
12. Brotzman B, Head P. The knee. In: Brotzman B, ed. *Clinical Orthopedic Rehabilitation.* St. Louis, Mosby, 1996.
13. Calliet R. *Knee Pain and Disability.* Philadelphia, Davis, 1983.
14. Cavenaugh J. Rehabilitation following meniscal surgery. In: Engle R, ed. *Knee Ligament Rehabilitation.* New York, Churchill Livingstone, 1991.
15. Clancy W, Nelson D, Reider B. Anterior cruciate ligament reconstruction using one third of the patellar ligament augmented by extra-articular tendon transfers. *J Bone Joint Surg Am* 62:352, 1982.
16. Clancy W, Narechania R, Rosenberg T. Anterior and posterior cruciate ligament reconstruction in rhesus monkeys. *J Bone Joint Surg Am* 63:1270–1284, 1981.
17. Curwin S, Stanish WD. *Tendinitis: Its Etiology and Treatment.* New York, Collamore Press, 1984.
18. DeHaven K, Bronstein R. Injuries to the meniscii in the knee. In: Nicholas J, Hershman E, eds. *The Lower Extremity and Spine in Sports Medicine.* St. Louis, Mosby, 1995.
19. DeLee J, Riley M, Rockwood C. Acute straight lateral instability of the knee. *Am J Sports Med* 11:404–411, 1983.
20. DePalma B, Zelko R. Knee rehabilitation following anterior cruciate injury or surgery. *JNATA* 21:200–206, 1986.
21. Dorchak J. Arthroscopic treatment of symptomatic synovial plica of the knee. *Am J Sports Med* 19:503, 1991.
22. Engle R, Giesen D. ACL reconstruction rehabilitation. In: Engle R, ed. *Knee Ligament Rehabilitation.* New York, Churchill Livingstone, 1991.
23. Ferguson D. Return to functional activities. *Sports Med Update* 3:6–9, 1988.
24. Ficat P, Hungerford D. *Disorders of the Patellofemoral Joint.* Baltimore, Williams & Wilkins, 1977.
25. Fu F, Woo S, Irrgang J, et al. Current concepts for rehabilitation following ACL reconstruction. *J Orthop Sports Phys Ther* 15:270–278, 1992.

26. Fulkerson J. Evaluation of peripatellar soft tissues and retinaculum in patients with patellofemoral pain. *Clin Sports Med* 8:197–202, 1989.

27. Fulkerson J, Hungerford D. *Disorders of the Patellofemoral Joint.* Baltimore, Williams & Wilkins, 1990.

28. Garret J, Stevensen R. Meniscal transplantation in the human knee: A preliminary report. *Arthroscopy* 7:57–62, 1991.

29. Geissler W, Whipple T. Intraarticular abnormalities in association with PCL injuries. *Am J Sports Med* 21:846–849, 1993.

30. Gerrard B. The patellofemoral pain syndrome: A clinical trial of the McConnell program. *Aust J Physiother* 35:71–80, 1989.

31. Goodfellow J, Hungerford D, Woods C. Patellofemoral mechanics and pathology. II. Chondromalacia patella. *J Bone Joint Surg Br* 58:287, 1976.

32. Gould J, Davies G. *Orthopaedic and Sports Physical Therapy.* St. Louis, Mosby, 1990.

33. Harner C, Irrgang J, Paul J. Loss of motion after ACL reconstruction. *Am J Sports Med* 20:99–506, 1992.

34. Hughston J, Walsh W, Puddu G. *Patellar Subluxation and Dislocation.* Philadelphia, Saunders, 1984.

35. Hungerford D, Barry M. Biomechanics of the patellofemoral joint. *Clin Orthop* 144:9–15, 1979.

36. Indelicato P, Hermansdorfer J, Huegel M. Non-operative management of incomplete tears of the MCL of the knee in intercollegiate football players. *Clin Orthop* 256:174–177, 1990.

37. Inoue M. Treatment of MCL injury: The importance of the ACL ligament on varus-valgus knee laxity. *Am J Sports Med* 15:15, 1987.

38. Insall J. Chondromalacia patella: Patellar malalignment syndromes. *Orthop Clin North Am* 10:117–125, 1979.

39. Irrgang J, Safran M, Fu F. The knee: Ligamentous and meniscal injuries. In: Zachazewski J, Magee D, Quillen W, eds. *Athletic Injuries and Rehabilitation.* Philadelphia, Saunders, 1995.

40. Jackson D, Drez D. *The Anterior Cruciate Deficient Knee.* St. Louis, Mosby, 1987.

41. Jackson D, Grood E, Goldstein J. A comparison of patellar tendon autograft and allograft used for ACL reconstruction in the goat model. *Am J Sports Med* 21:176–181, 1993.

42. Jenkins D. *Ligament Injuries and Their Treatment.* Rockville, MD, Aspen, 1985.

43. Jensen J, DiFabio R. Evaluation of eccentric exercise in the treatment of patellar tendinitis. *Phys Ther* 69:211–216, 1989.

44. Johnson D. Controlling anterior shear during isokinetic knee exercise. *J Orthop Sports Phys Ther* 4:27, 1982.

45. Kramer P. Patellar malalignment syndrome: Rationale to reduce lateral pressure. *J Orthop Sports Phys Ther* 8:301, 1983.

46. LaPrade R, Burnett Q. Femoral intercondylar notch stenosis and correlation to anterior cruciate ligament injuries: A prospective study. *Am J Sports Med* 22:198–202, 1994.

47. Lephart S, Kocher M, Fu F. Proprioception following anterior cruciate ligament reconstruction. *J Sports Rehab* 1:188–196, 1992.

48. Lutz G, Warren R. Meniscal injuries. In: Griffin L., eds. *Rehabilitation of the Injured Knee.* St. Louis, Mosby, 1995.

49. Mangine R. *Physical Therapy of the Knee.* New York, Churchill Livingstone, 1988.

50. Mangine R, Eifert-Mangine M. Postoperative PCL reconstruction rehabilitation. In: Engle R, ed. *Knee Ligament Rehabilitation.* New York, Churchill Livingstone, 1991.

51. Malone T. Relationship of gender in ACL injuries of NCAA division I basketball players. Presented at specialty day meeting of AOSSM, Washington, DC, February 1992.

52. Mansmann K. PCL reconstruction. In: Engle R, ed. *Knee Ligament Rehabilitation.* New York, Churchill Livingstone, 1991.

53. McCarthy M, Yates C, Anderson J, et al. The effects of immediate CPM on pain during the inflammatory phase of soft tissue healing following ACL reconstruction. *J Orthop Sports Phys Ther* 17:96–101, 1993.

54. McConnell J. The management of chondromalacia patella: A long-term solution. *Aust J Physiother* 32:215–223, 1986.

55. McConnell J, Fulkerson J. The knee: Patellofemoral and soft tissue injuries, In: Zachazewski J, Magee D, Quillen W, eds. *Athletic Injuries and Rehabilitation.* Philadelphia, Saunders, 1995.

56. Mellion M, ed. *Office Management of Sports Injury and Athletic Problems.* Philadelphia, Hanley & Belfus, 1987.

57. Miyasaka, Daniel D, Stone M. The incidence of knee ligament injuries in the population. *Am J Knee Surg* 4:3–8, 1991.

58. Nichols C, Johnson R. Cruciate ligament injuries: Non-operative treatment. In: Scott N. *Ligament and Extensor Mechanism Injuries of the Knee.* St. Louis, Mosby, 1991.

59. Noyes F, Mangine R, Barber S. Early knee motion after open and arthroscopic anterior cruciate ligament reconstruction. *Am J Sports Med* 15:149, 1987.

60. O'Donohue D. *Treatment of Injuries to Patients.* Philadelphia, Saunders, 1970.

61. O'Driscoll S, Keely F, Salter R. The chondrogenic potential of free autogenous periosteal grafts for biological resurfacing of major full-thickness defects in joint surfaces under the influence of continuous passive motion: An experimental investigation in the rabbit. *J Bone Joint Surg Am* 68:1017, 1986.

62. Parolie J, Bergfeld J. Long-term results of non-operative treatment of PCL injuries in the patient. *Am J Sports Med* 14:35–38, 1986.

63. Paulos L, Noyes F, Grood E. Knee rehabilitation after

anterior cruciate ligament reconstruction and repair. *Am J Sports Med* 9:140–149, 1981.

64. Paulos L, Stern J. Rehabilitation after anterior cruciate ligament surgery. In: Jackson D, ed. *The Anterior Cruciate Ligament.* New York, Raven, 1993.

65. Pittman M, Frankel V. Biomechanics of the knee in athletics. In: Nicholas J, Hershman E, eds. *The Lower Extremity and Spine in Sports Medicine.* St. Louis, Mosby, 1995.

66. Prentice W. A manual resistance technique for strengthening tibial rotation. *JNATA* 23:230-233, 1988.

67. Prentice W, Toriscelli T. The effects of lateral knee stabilizing braces on running speed and agility. *Athl Train* 23:230, 1988.

68. Quillen W. Gieck J. Manual therapy: Mobilization of the motion restricted knee. *JNATA* 23:123–130, 1988.

69. Reynold L, Levin T, Medoiros J, et al. EMG activity of the vastus medialis oblique and the vastus lateralis and their role in patellar alignment. *Am J Phys Med* 62:61–71, 1983.

70. Richardson C. The role of the knee musculature in high speed oscillating movements of the knee. MTAA fourth biennial conference proceedings, Brisbane, Australia, 1985.

71. Saal J, ed. *Physical Medicine and Rehabilitation: Rehabilitation of Sports Injuries.* Philadelphia, Hanley & Belfus, 1987.

72. Salter R. Clinical applications for basic research on continuous passive motion for disorders and injuries of synovial joints: A preliminary report of a feasibility study. *J Orthop Res* 3:325, 1983.

73. Sgaglione N, Warren R, Wickiewicz T. Primary repair with semitendinosis augmentation of acute ACL injuries. *Am J Sports Med* 18:64–73, 1990.

74. Shea K, Fulkerson J. Patellofemoral joint injuries. In: Griffin L. *Rehabilitation of the Knee.* St. Louis, Mosby, 1995.

75. Shelbourne K, Wilckens J, Mollabashy A. Arthrofibrosis in acute anterior cruciate ligament reconstruction: The effect of timing on reconstruction and rehabilitation. *Am J Sports Med* 19:322–336, 1991.

76. Shelbourne K, Klootwyk T, DeCarlo M. Ligamentous injuries. In: Griffin L, ed. *Rehabilitation of the Knee.* St. Louis, Mosby, 1995.

77. Shelbourne K, Nitz P. Accelerated rehabilitation after ACL reconstruction. *J. Orthop Sports Phys Ther* 15:256–264, 1992.

78. Sommerlath K, Lysholm J, Gillquiost J. The long-term course of treatment of acute ACL ruptures. A 9 to 16-year follow-up. *Am J Sports Med* 19:156–162, 1991.

79. Souryal T, Freeman T, Evans J. Intercondylar notch size and ACL injuries in patients. A prospective study. *Am J Sports Med* 21:535–539, 1993.

80. Stone K, Rosenberg T. Surgical technique of meniscal transplantation. *Arthroscopy* 9:234–237, 1993.

81. Sweitzer R, Sweitzer D, Sarantini A. Rehabilitation for ligament and extensor mechanism injuries. In Scott N, ed. *Ligament and Extensor Mechanism Injuries of the Knee.* St. Louis, Mosby, 1991.

82. Tria A, Klein K. *An Illustrated Guide to the Knee.* New York, Churchill Livingstone, 1991.

83. Weiss J, Woo S, Ohland K. Evaluation of a new injury model to study MCL healing: Primary repair vs. non-operative treatment. *J Orthop Res* 9:516–528, 1991.

84. Wilk K, Andrews J. Current concepts in treatment of ACL disruption. *J Orthop Sports Phys Ther* 15:279–293, 1992.

85. Wilk K, Clancey W. Medial collateral ligament injuries: Diagnosis, treatment, and rehabilitation. In: Engle R, ed. *Knee Ligament Rehabilitation.* New York, Churchill Livingstone, 1991.

86. Woodall W, Welsh J. A biomechanical basis for rehabilitation programs involving the knee joint. *J Orthop Sports Phys Ther* 11:535, 1991.

87. Zarins B, Fish D. Knee ligament injury. In: Nicholas J, Hershman E, eds. *The Lower Extremity and Spine in Sports Medicine.* St. Louis, Mosby, 1995.

C H A P T E R   3 1

Rehabilitation of the Lower Leg

Christopher J. Hirth

O B J E C T I V E S

After completing this chapter, the student therapist should be able to do the following:

- Discuss the functional anatomy and biomechanics of the lower leg during open-chain and weight-bearing activities such as walking and running.
- Identify common causes of various lower-leg injuries and provide a rationale for treatment of those injuries.
- Discuss criteria for progression of the rehabilitation program for various lower-leg injuries.
- Describe and explain the rationale for various treatment techniques in the management of lower-leg injuries.
- Identify the various techniques for regaining range of motion including stretching exercises and joint mobilizations.
- Demonstrate the various rehabilitative strengthening techniques including open- and closed-kinetic chain isotonic exercise, balance/proprioceptive exercises, and isokinetic exercise for dysfunction of the lower leg.

FUNCTIONAL ANATOMY AND BIOMECHANICS

The lower leg consists of the tibia and fibula and four muscular compartments that either originate or traverse various points along these bones. Distally the tibia and fibula articulate with the talus to form the talocrural joint. Because of the close approximation of the talus within the mortise, movement of the leg will be dictated by the foot, especially upon ground contact. This becomes important when examining the effects of repetitive stresses placed upon the leg with excessive compensatory pronation secondary to various structural lower-extremity malalignments.[53,54] Proximally the tibia articulates with the femur to form the tibiofemoral joint as well as serving as an attachment site for the patellar tendon, the distal soft-tissue component of the extensor mechanism. The lower leg serves to transmit ground reaction forces to the knee as well as rotatory forces proximally along the lower extremity that may be a source of pain, especially with athletic activities.[54]

Compartments of the Lower Leg

The muscular components are divided anatomically into four compartments. In an open-kinetic chain position, these muscle groups are responsible for movements of the foot, primarily in a single plane. When the foot is in contact with the ground, these muscle-tendon units work both concentrically and eccentrically to absorb ground reaction forces, to control excessive movements of the foot and ankle to adapt to the terrain, and ideally to provide a stable base to propel the limb forward during walking and running.

The anterior compartment is primarily responsible for dorsiflexion of the foot in an open-kinetic chain position. Functionally these muscles are active in the early and midstance phases of gait with increased eccentric muscle activity directly after heel strike to control plantarflexion of the foot and pronation of the forefoot.[11] EMG studies have noted that the tibialis anterior is active in more than 85 percent of the gait cycle during running.[35]

The deep posterior compartment is made up of the tibialis posterior and the long toe flexors, and is responsible for inversion of the foot and ankle in an open-kinetic chain. These muscles assist in controlling pronation at the subtalar joint and internal rotation of the lower leg.[11,35] Along with the soleus, the tibialis posterior will help decelerate the forward momentum of the tibia during the midstance phase of gait.

The lateral compartment is made up of the peroneus longus and brevis, which are responsible for eversion of the foot in an open-kinetic chain. Functionally the peroneus longus plantar flexes the first ray at heel-off, while the peroneus brevis counteracts the supinating forces of the tibialis posterior to provide osseous stability of the subtalar and midtarsal joints during the propulsive phase of gait. EMG studies of running report an increase in peroneus brevis activity when the pace of running is increased.[35]

The superficial posterior compartment is made up of the gastrocnemius and soleus muscles, which in an open-kinetic chain position are responsible primarily for plantarflexion of the foot. Functionally these muscles are responsible for acting eccentrically, controlling pronation of the subtalar joint and internal rotation of the leg in the midstance phase of gait and activated concentrically during the push-off phase of gait.[11,35]

REHABILITATION TECHNIQUES FOR SPECIFIC INJURIES

Tibial and Fibular Fractures

PATHOMECHANICS

The tibia and fibula constitute the bony components of the lower leg and are primarily responsible for weight bearing and muscle attachment. The tibia is the most commonly fractured long bone in the body, and fracture is usually the result of either direct trauma to the area or indirect trauma such as a combination rotatory/compressive force. Fractures of the fibula are usually seen in combination with a tibial fracture or as a result of direct trauma to the area. Tibial fractures will present with immediate pain, swelling, and possible deformity and may be open or closed in nature. Fibular fractures alone are usually closed and present with pain to palpation and with ambulation. Treatment of these fractures is immediate medical referral and most likely a period of immobilization and restricted weight bearing for weeks to possibly months depending on the severity and involvement of the injury. Surgery—such as open reduction with internal fixation (ORIF) of the bone, usually of the tibia— is common.

INJURY MECHANISM

The two mechanisms of a traumatic lower-leg fracture are either a direct insult to the bone or indirectly through a combined rotatory/compressive force. Direct impact to the long bone such as from a projectile object or the top of a ski boot can produce enough damaging force to fracture a bone. Indirect trauma from a combination of rotatory and compressive forces can be manifested in situations when a patient's foot is planted and the proximal segments are rotated with a large compressive force. A fibular fracture may accompany the tibial fracture.

REHABILITATION CONCERNS

Tibial and fibular fractures are usually immobilized and placed on a restricted weight-bearing status for a period of time to facilitate fracture healing. Immobilization and restricted weight bearing of a bone, its proximal and distal joints, and surrounding musculature will lead to functional deficits once the fracture is healed. Depending on the severity of the fracture, there also may be postsurgical considerations such as an incision and hardware within the bone. Complications following immobilization include joint stiffness of any joints immobilized, muscle atrophy of the lower leg and possibly the proximal thigh and hip musculature, as well as an abnormal gait pattern. It is important that the therapist perform a comprehensive evaluation of the patient to determine all potential rehabilitation problems including range of motion, joint mobility, muscle flexibility, strength and endurance of the entire involved lower extremity, balance, proprioception, and gait. The therapist must also determine the functional demands that will be placed on the patient and set up short- and long-term goals accordingly. Upon cast removal it is important to address ROM deficits. This can be managed with PROM/AROM exercises in a supportive medium such as a warm whirlpool. (See Exercises 31-1 to 31-4, 31-9, 31-14, 31-15, 31-20, and 31-22). Joint stiffness can be addressed via joint mobilization to any joint that was immobilized (see Chapter 32). It is possible to have posttraumatic edema in the foot and ankle after cast removal that can be reduced with massage. Strengthening exercises can help facilitate muscle firing, strength, and endurance (see Exercises 31-5 to 31-8 and 31-10 to 31-13). Balance and proprioception can be improved with single-leg standing activities and balance-board activities (see Exercises 31-24 to 31-27). Cardiovascular endurance can be addressed with pool activities including swimming and pool running with a flotation device, stationary cycling, and the use of an upper-body ergometer (see Exercises 31-16, 31-17, 31-28, and 31-29). A stair stepper is also an excellent way to address cardiovascular needs as well as lower-extremity strength, endurance, and weight bearing (see Exercise 31-17).

REHABILITATION PROGRESSION

Management of a postimmobilization fracture will require good communication with the physician to determine progression of weight-bearing status; any assistive devices to be used during the rehabilitation process, such as a walker boot; and any other pertinent information that will influence the rehabilitation process. It is important to address ROM deficits immediately with AROM, passive stretching, and skilled joint mobilization. Isometric strengthening can be initiated and progressed to isotonic exercises once ROM has been normalized. After weight-bearing status is determined, gait training to normalize walking should be initiated. Assistive devices should be used as needed. Strengthening of the involved lower extremity can be incorporated into the rehabilitation process, especially for the hip and thigh musculature. Balance and proprioceptive exercises can begin once there is full pain-free weight-bearing on the involved lower extremity.

As ROM, strength, and walking gait are normalized, the patient can be progressed to a walking/jogging progression. It must be realized that the rate of rehabilitation progression will be different depending on the severity of the fracture, any surgical involvement, and length of immobilization. The average healing time for uncomplicated nondisplaced tibial fractures is 10 to 13 weeks; for displaced, open, or comminuted tibial fractures it is 16 to 26 weeks.[45]

Fibular fractures may be immobilized for 4 to 6 weeks. Again, an open line of communication with the physician is required to facilitate a safe rehabilitation progression for the patient.

Tibial and Fibular Stress Fractures

PATHOMECHANICS

Stress fractures of the tibia and fibula are common in sports. Studies indicate that tibial stress fractures occur at a higher rate than those of the fibula.[3,4,32] Stress fractures in the lower leg are usually the result of the bone's inability to adapt to the repetitive loading response during training and conditioning of the patient. The bone attempts to adapt to the applied loads initially through osteoclastic activity, which will break down the bone. Osteoblastic activity, or the laying down of new bone, will soon follow.[34,52] If the applied loads are not reduced during this process, stuctural irregularities will develop within the bone, which will further reduce the bone's ability to absorb stress and will eventually lead to a stress fracture.[4,14,17] Stress fractures in the tibial shaft mainly occur in the midanterior aspect and the posteromedial aspect.[3,32,36,52] Anterior tibial stress fractures usually present in patients involved in repetitive jumping activities with localized pain directly over the midanterior tibia. The patient will complain of pain with activity that is relieved with rest. The pain may affect ADLs if activity is not modified. Vibration testing using a tuning fork will reproduce the symptoms, as will hopping on the involved extremity. A triple-phase technetium[99] bone scan can confirm the diagnosis faster than an X ray, which may take a minimum of 3 weeks to demonstrate radiographic changes.[34,36,52] Posteromedial tibial pain usually occurs over the distal one third of the bone with a gradual onset of symptoms.

Focal point tenderness on the bone will help differentiate a stress fracture from medial tibial stress syndrome (MTSS), which is located in the same area but is more diffuse upon palpation. The procedures listed above will be positive and will implicate the stress fracture as the source of pain. Fibular stress fractures usually occur in the distal one third of the bone with the same symptomatology as tibial stress fractures. Although less common, stress fractures of the proximal fibula are noted in the literature.[32,49,59]

INJURY MECHANISM

Anterior tibial stress fractures are prevalent in patients involved with jumping. Several authors have noted that the tibia will bow anteriorly with the convexity on the anterior aspect.[9,34,38,52] This places the anterior aspect of the tibia under tension, which is less than ideal for the healing of bone, which prefers compressive forces. Repetitive jumping will place greater tension on this area, which has minimal musculotendinous support and blood supply. Other biomechanical factors may be involved including excessive compensatory pronation at the subtalar joint to accommodate lower extremity structural alignments such as forefoot varus, tibial varum, and femoral anteversion. This excessive pronation may not affect the leg during ADLs or with moderate activity, but may become a factor with increases in training intensity, duration, and frequency even with sufficient recovery time.[21,52] Increased training may affect the surrounding muscle-tendon unit's ability to absorb the impact of each applied load, which places more stress on the bone. Stress fractures of the distal posteromedial tibia will also arise from the same problems as above with the exception of repetitive jumping as a potential cause. Excessive compensatory pronation may play a greater role with this type of injury. This hyperpronation can be accentuated when running on a crowned road, such as the case of the uphill leg.[40] Also running on a track with a small radius and tight curves will tend to increase pronatory stresses on the leg that is closer to the inside of the track.[40] Excessive pronation may also play a role with fibular stress fractures. The repeated activity of the ankle evertors and calf musculature pulling on the bone may be a source of this type of stress fracture.[34] Training errors of increased duration and intensity, along with worn-out shoes, will only accentuate these problems.[40] Other factors including menstrual irregularities, diet, bone density, increased hip external rotation, tibial width, and calf girth have also been identified as contributing to stress fractures.[4,20]

REHABILITATION CONCERNS

Immediate elimination of the offending activity is most important. The patient must be educated on the importance of this to prevent further damage to the bone. Many patients will express concerns about fitness level with loss of activity. Stationary cycling and running in the deep end of the pool with a flotation device can serve as excellent ways to maintain cardiovascular fitness (see Exercises 31-16 and 31-28). Eyestone et al demonstrated only a small but statistically significant decrease in maximum aerobic capacity when water running was substituted for regular running.[13] This was also true with using a stationary bike.[13] These authors recommend that the intensity, duration, and frequency be equivalent to the regular training. Wilder et al noted that water provides a resistance that is proportional to the effort exerted.[56] These authors found that cadence, via a metronome, gave a quantitative external cue that with increased rate showed high correlation with heart rate.[56] Thus nonimpact activity in the pool or on the bike will help maintain aerobic endurance and allow proper bone healing.

Proper footware that matches the needs of the foot is also important. For example, a high arched or pes cavus foot type will require a shoe with good shock-absorbing qualities. A pes planus foot type or more pronated foot will require a shoe with good motion control characteristics. A detailed biomechanical exam of the lower extremity both statically and dynamically may reveal problems that require the use of a custom foot orthotic. Stretching and strengthening exercises can be incorporated into the rehabilitation process. The use of ice and electrical stimulation to control pain is also recommended. The use of an Aircast with patients who have diagnosed stress fractures has obtained positive results.[10] Dickson and Kichline speculate that the Aircast unloads the tibia and fibula enough to allow healing of the stress fracture with continued participation.[10]

Fibular and posterior medial tibial stress fractures will usually heal without residual problems if the above-mentioned concerns are addressed. Stress fractures of the midanterior tibia may take much longer, and residual problems may exist months to years after the initial diagnosis with attempts at increased activity.[9,12,36,38] Initial treatment may include a short leg cast and nonweight-bearing for 6 to 8 weeks. Rettig et al used rest from the offending activity as well as electrical stimulation in the form of a pulsed electromagnetic field for a period of 10 to 12 hours per day. The authors noted an average of 12.7 months from the onset of symptoms to return to full activity with this regimen.[38] They recommended using this program for 3 to 6 months before considering surgical intervention.[38] Chang and Harris noted good to excellent results with a surgical procedure involving intramedullary nailing of the tibia with individuals with delayed union of this type of stress fracture.[9] Surgical procedures involving bone grafting have also been recommended to improve healing of this type of stress fracture.

REHABILITATION PROGRESSION

After diagnosis of the stress fracture, the patient may be placed on crutches depending on the amount of discomfort with ambulation. Ice can be used to reduce local inflammation and pain. The patient can immediately begin pool running with the same training parameters as the patient's regular regimen. Stretching exercises for the gastrocnemius–soleus musculature can be performed 2 to 3 times per day (see Exercise 31-21). Isotonic strengthening exercises with rubber tubing can begin as soon as tolerated on an every-other-day basis with an increase in repetitions and sets as the therapist sees fit (see Exercises 31-5 to 31-8). Strengthening of the gastrocnemius can be done initially in an open chain and eventually be progressed to a closed chain (see Exercises 31-5, 31-12, and 31-13). The patient should wear supportive shoes during the day and avoid shoes with a heel, which may cause adaptive shortening of the gastrocnemius–soleus complex and increase strain on the healing bone. Custom foot orthotics can be fabricated for motion control in order to prevent excessive pronation for those patients

who need it. Foot orthotics can also be fabricated for a high arched foot to increase stress distribution throughout the plantar aspect of the whole foot versus the heel and the metatarsal heads. Shock-absorbing materials can augment these orthotics to help reduce ground reaction forces. As the symptoms subside over a period of 3 to 4 weeks and X rays confirm that good callous formation is occurring, the patient may be progressed to a walking/jogging progression on a surface suitable to patient needs. A quality track or grass surface may be the best choice to begin this progression. The patient may be instructed to jog for 1 minute, and then walk for 30 seconds, for 10 to 15 repetitions. This can be performed on an every-other-day basis with high-intensity/long-duration cardiovascular training occurring in the pool or on the bike in a daily fashion. The patient should be reminded that the purpose of the walk/jog progression is to provide a gradual increase in stress to the healing bone in a controlled manner. If tolerated, the jogging time can be increased by 30 seconds every 2 to 3 training sessions until the patient is running 5 minutes without walking. The above progression serves as a guideline and can be modified for each individual based on his or her specific needs. Experimentation with the use of an air cast is recommended to determine its effectiveness with each individual. Initially, it may be used with ADLs to allow pain relief and eventually for activity.

Compartment Syndromes

PATHOMECHANICS AND INJURY MECHANISM

Compartment syndrome is a condition in which increased pressure, within a fixed osseofascial compartment, causes compression of muscular and neurovascular structures within the compartment. As compartment pressures increase, the venous outflow of fluid decreases and eventually stops, which causes further fluid leakage from the capillaries into the compartment. Eventually arterial blood inflow also ceases secondary to rising intracompartmental pressures.[55] Compartment syndrome can be divided into three categories: acute compartment syndrome, acute exertional compartment syndrome, and chronic compartment syndrome.

Acute compartment syndrome occurs secondary to direct trauma to the area and is a medical emergency.[26,50,55] The patient will complain of a deep-seated aching pain, tightness, and swelling of the involved compartment. Reproduction of the pain will occur with passive stretching of the involved muscles. Reduction in pedal pulses and sensory changes of the involved nerve can be present but are not reliable signs.[55,58] Intracompartmental pressure measurements will confirm the diagnosis, with emergency fasciotomy being the definitive treatment.

Acute exertional compartment syndrome occurs without any precipitating trauma. Cases have been cited in the literature in which acute compartment syndrome has evolved with minimal to moderate activity and if not diagnosed and treated properly, can lead to a poor functional outcome for the patient.[14,58] Again, intracompartmental pressures will confirm the diagnosis, with emergency fasciotomy being the treatment of choice.

Chronic compartment syndrome (CCS) is activity-related in that the symptoms arise rather consistently at a certain point in the activity. The patient complains of a sensation of pain, tightness, and swelling of the affected compartment, which resolves upon stopping the activity. Studies indicate that the anterior and deep posterior compartments are usually involved.[2,37,43,51,57] Upon presentation of these symptoms, intracompartmental pressure measurements will further define the severity of the condition. Pedowitz et al have developed modified criteria using a slit catheter measurement of the intra-compartmental pressures. These authors consider one or more of the following intramuscular pressure criteria as diagnostic of CCS: (1) preexercise pressure greater than 15 mm Hg, (2) 1-minute postexercise pressure of 30 mm Hg, and (3) 5-minute postexercise pressure greater than 20 mm Hg.[33]

REHABILITATION CONCERNS

Management of CCS is initially conservative with activity modification, icing, and stretching of the anterior compartment and gastrocnemius–soleus complex (see Exercises 31-21 to 31-23). A lower-quarter structural examination along with gait analysis may reveal a structural variation that may be causing excessive compensatory pronation, which may benefit with the use of foot orthotics and proper footwear. But these measures will not address the issue of increased compartment pressures with activity. Stationary cycling has been shown to be an acceptable alternative in preventing increased anterior compartment pressures when compared to running, and can be used to maintain cardiovascular fitness.[2] If conservative measures fail, fasciotomy of the affected compartments has shown favorable results in a return to higher-level activity.[37,41,55,57]

REHABILITATION PROGRESSION

Following fasciotomy for CCS, the immediate goals are to decrease postsurgical pain and swelling with RICE and assisted ambulation with the use of crutches. After suture removal and soft-tissue healing of the incision has progressed, AROM and flexibility exercises should be initiated (see Exercises 31-1 to 31-4, and 31-20 to 31-23). Weight bearing will be progressed as ROM improves. Gait training should be incorporated to prevent abnormal movements in the gait pattern secondary to joint and soft-tissue stiffness or muscle guarding. AROM exercises should be progressed to open-chain exercises with rubber tubing (see Exercises 31-5 to 31-8). Closed-kinetic chain activities can also be initiated to incorporate strength, balance, and proprioception that may have been affected by the surgical procedure (see Exercises 31-12 to 31-15 and 31-24 to 31-27). Lower-extremity structural variations that lead to excessive compensatory pronation during gait should be addressed with foot orthotics and proper shoeware after walking gait has been normalized. These measures should help control excessive movements at the subtalar joint/lower leg and thus theoretically decrease muscular activity of the deep posterior compart-

ment, which is highly active in controlling pronation during running.[35] Aerobic endurance can be maintained and improved with stationary cycling and running in the deep end of a pool with a flotation device (see Exercises 31-16 and 31-28). When ROM, strength, and walking gait have normalized, a walking/jogging progression can be initiated.

It should be noted that patients undergoing anterior compartment fasciotomy may require 8 to 12 weeks for rehabilitation after surgery, while rehabilitation for patients undergoing deep posterior compartment fasciotomy may take 3 to 4 months postsurgery.[28,41]

Muscle Strains

PATHOMECHANICS

The majority of muscle strains in the lower leg occur in the medial head of the gastrocnemius at the musculotendinous junction. The injury is more common in middle-aged patients and occur in activities requiring ballistic movement such as tennis and basketball. The patient may feel or hear a pop as if being kicked in the back of the leg. Depending on the severity of the strain, the patient may be unable to walk secondary to decreased ankle dorsiflexion in a closed-kinetic chain that passively stretches the injured muscle and causes pain during the push-off phase of gait. Palpation will elicit tenderness at the site of the strain, and a palpable divot may be present depending on the severity of the injury and how soon it is evaluated.

INJURY MECHANISM

Strains of the medial head of the gastrocnemius usually occur during sudden ballistic movements. A common scenario may be when a patient is lunging with the knee extended and the ankle dorsiflexed. The ankle plantarflexors, in this case the medial head of the gastrocnemius, will be activated to assist in push-off of the foot. The muscle will be placed in an elongated position and activated in a very short period of time. This will place the musculotendinous junction of the gastrocnemius under excessive tensile stress. The musculotendinous junction, a transition area of one homogenous tissue to another, will not be able to endure the tensile loads nearly as well as the homogenous tissue itself, and thus tearing of the tissue at the junction will occur.

REHABILITATION CONCERNS

The initial management of a gastrocnemius strain is ICE. It is important for the patient to pay special attention to compression and elevation of the lower extremity to avoid edema in the foot and ankle, which can further limit ROM and prolong the rehabilitation process. Gentle stretching of the muscle-tendon unit should be initiated early in the rehabilitation process (see Exercise 31-20). Ankle plantarflexor strengthening with rubber tubing can also be initiated when tolerated (see Exercise 31-5). Weight bearing may be limited to a weight-bearing-as-tolerated status with crutches. The foot/ankle will prefer a plantarflexed position, and closed-kinetic chain dorsiflexion of the foot/ankle, which is required during walking, will stress the muscle and cause pain. Pulsed ultrasound can be used early in the rehabilitation process and eventually progressed to continuous ultrasound for its thermal effects. A stationary cycle can be used for an active warmup as well as for maintaining aerobic endurance. A heel lift may be placed in both shoes to gradually increase dorsiflexion of the foot/ankle as the patient is progressed off crutches. Standing, stretching, and strengthening can be added as soft-tissue healing occurs and ROM/strength improve. Eventually the patient can be progressed to a walking/jogging program. It is important that the patient warm up and stretch properly before activity so as not to have a recurrence of the injury.

REHABILITATION PROGRESSION

Early management of a medial head gastrocnemius strain focuses on pain and swelling reduction with ICE and modified weight bearing. The patient is encouraged to perform gentle towel stretching for the affected muscle group several times per day (see Exercise 31-20). AROM of the foot and ankle in all planes will also facilitate movement and act to stretch the muscle (see Exercises 31-1 to 31-4). With mild muscle strains, the patient may be off crutches and performing standing calf stretches and strengthening exercises by about 7 to 10 days with a normal gait pattern (see Exercises 31-21, 31-12, and 31-13). Moderate to severe strains may take 2 to 4 weeks before normalization of ROM and gait occur. This is usually due to the excessive edema in the foot and ankle. Strengthening can be progressed from open to closed-chain activity as the soft-tissue healing occurs (see Exercises 31-14, 31-15, and 31-24 to 31-27). As walking gait is normalized, the patient is encouraged to begin a graduated walking or jogging program in which distance and speed are modulated throughout the progression. Most soft-tissue injuries demonstrate good healing by 14 to 21 days postinjury. In the case of mild muscle strain, as the patient becomes more comfortable with jogging/running, plyometric activities can be added to the rehabilitation process. Plyometric activities should be introduced in a controlled fashion with at least 1 to 2 days of rest between activities to allow muscular soreness to diminish. Care should be taken to save sudden, ballistic activities for when the patient is warmed up and the gastrocnemius is well stretched.

Medial Tibial Stress Syndrome

PATHOMECHANICS

Medial tibial stress syndrome (MTSS) is a condition that involves increasing pain about the distal two thirds of the posterior medial aspect of the tibial.[17,47] The soleus and tibialis posterior have been implicated as muscular forces that may stress the fascia and periosteum of the distal tibia during running activities.[1,16,43] Pain is usually diffuse about the distal medial tibia and the surrounding soft tissues and can arise secondary to excessive pronation, improper shoeware, and poor fitness

level.[7,44] Initially, the area is diffusely tender and may only hurt after an intense workout. As the condition worsens, daily ambulation may be painful, and morning pain and stiffness may be present. Rehabilitation of this condition must be comprehensive and address the musculoskeletal factors, factors associated with training and conditioning, and proper shoeware and orthotics intervention.

INJURY MECHANISM

Many sources have linked excessive compensatory pronation as a primary cause of MTSS.[7,16,43,47] Subtalar joint pronation serves to dissipate ground reaction forces upon foot strike in order to reduce the impact to proximal structures. If the amount of pronation is excessive, occurs too quickly, or occurs at the wrong time in the stance phase of gait, greater tensile loads will be placed on the muscle-tendon units that assist in controlling this complex triplanar movement.[22,53] Lower-extremity structural variations such as a rearfoot and forefoot varus can cause the subtalar joint to pronate excessively in order to get the medial aspect of the forefoot in contact with the ground for push-off.[47] The magnitude of these forces will increase during running, especially with a rearfoot striker. Sprinters may present with similar symptoms but with a different cause—overuse of the plantarflexors secondary to being on their toes during their event. Training surfaces, including embankments and crowned roads, can place increased tensile loads on the distal medial tibia, and modifications should be made whenever possible.

REHABILITATION CONCERNS

Management of this condition should include physician referral to rule out the possibility of stress fracture via the use of bone scan and plain films. Activity modification along with measures to maintain aerobic endurance are set in place immediately. Correction of abnormal pronation during walking and running must also be addressed with shoes and, if needed, custom foot orthotics. Ice massage to the area may be helpful in the reduction of localized pain and inflammation. A flexibility program for the gastrocnemius–soleus musculature should be initiated.

REHABILITATION PROGRESSION

Running and jumping activities may need to be completely eliminated for the first 7 to 10 days after diagnosis. Pool workouts with a flotation device will help to maintain cardiovascular fitness during the healing process. Gastrocnemius–soleus flexibility is improved with static stretching (see Exercise 31-21). Ice and electrical stimulation can be used to reduce inflammation and modulate pain in the early stages. As the condition improves, general strengthening of the ankle musculature with rubber tubing can be performed along with calf muscle strengthening (see Exercises 31-5 to 31-8, 31-12, and 31-13). These exercises may cause muscle fatigue but should not increase the patient's symptoms. An isokinetic strengthening program of the ankle invertors and evertors can be used to improve strength and has been shown to reduce pronation during treadmill running (see Exercise 31-18).[15] As mentioned previously, it is imperative that all structural deviations that cause pronation be addressed with a foot orthotic or at least proper motion-control shoes. As pain to palpation of the distal tibia resolves, the patient should be progressed to a jogging/running program on grass with proper footwear. This may involve beginning with a 10- to 15-minute run and progressing by 10 percent every week. In the case of track patients, a pool or bike workout can be implemented for 20 to 30 minutes after the run to complement a full workout. The patient needs to be compliant with a gradual progression and should be educated in avoiding doing too much, too soon, which could lead to a recurrence of the condition or possibly a stress fracture.

Achilles Tendinitis

PATHOMECHANICS

Achilles tendinitis is an inflammatory condition that involves the Achilles tendon and/or its tendon sheath, the paratenon. Often there is excessive tensile stress placed on the tendon in a repetitive nature, such as with walking or running activities that overload the tendon, especially on its medial aspect.[29,42] This condition can be divided into Achilles paratenonitis or peritendinitis, which is an inflammation of the paratenon or tissue that surrounds the tendon; and tendinosus, which denotes tears within the tendon.[18,39] The patient often complains of generalized pain and stiffness about the Achilles tendon region, which when localized is usually 2 to 6 cm proximal to the calcaneal insertion. Uphill walking will usually aggravate the condition. There may be reduced gastrocnemius and soleus muscle flexibility in general that may worsen as the condition progresses and adaptive shortening occurs. Muscle testing of the above muscles may be within normal limits but painful, and a true deficit may be observed when performing toe raises to fatigue as compared to the uninvolved extremity.

INJURY MECHANISM

Achilles tendinitis will often present with a gradual onset over a period of time. Initially the patient may ignore the symptoms that may present at the beginning of activity and resolve as the activity progresses. Symptoms may progress to morning stiffness and discomfort with walking after periods of prolonged sitting. Repetitive weight-bearing activities such as walking or running, in which the duration and intensity are increased too quickly and with insufficient recovery time, will worsen the condition. Excessive compensatory pronation of the subtalar joint with concomitant internal rotation of the lower leg secondary to a forefoot varus, tibial varum, or femoral anterversion will increase the tensile load about the medial aspect of the Achilles tendon.[18,23,39] Decreased gastrocnemius and soleus complex flexibility can also increase subtalar joint pronation to compensate for the decreased closed-kinetic chain dorsiflexion needed during the early and midstance phases of gait. If this stress continues, the tendon will become further inflamed, and the gastrocnemius–soleus musculature will become less efficient secondary to pain inhibition. The tendon may be warm and painful to palpation, as well as thickened, which may indicate the chronicity of the condition. Crepitace may be palpated with AROM plantar and dorsiflexion and pain will be elicited with passive dorsiflexion.

REHABILITATION CONCERNS

Achilles tendinitis may be resistant to a quick resolution secondary to the slower healing response of tendinous tissue. It has also been noted that an area of hypovascularity exists within the tendon that may further impede the healing response. It is important to create a proper healing environment by reducing the offending activity and replacing it with an activity that will reduce strain on the tendon. Addressing structural faults that may lead to excessive pronation or supination should be done through proper shoeware and foot orthotics as well as flexibility exercises for the gastrocnemius–soleus complex. Modalities such as ice can help reduce pain and inflammation early on, and ultrasound can facilitate an increased blood flow to the tendon in the later stages of rehabilitation. Cross-friction massage may be used to break down adhesions that may have formed during the healing response and further improve the gliding ability of the paratenon. Strengthening of the gastrocnemius–soleus musculature must be progressed carefully so as not to cause a recurrence of the symptoms. Lastly, a gradual progression must be made for a safe return to activity to avoid the condition becoming chronic.

REHABILITATION PROGRESSION

Activity modification is necessary to allow the Achilles tendon to begin the healing process. Swimming, pool running with a flotation device, stationary cycling, and upper-body ergometer (UBE) are all possible alternative activities for cardiovascular maintenance (see Exercises 31-16, 31-28, and 31-29). It is important to reduce stresses on the Achilles tendon that may occur with daily ambulation. Proper footwear with a slight heel lift can reduce stress on the tendon during gait. Structural biomechanical abnormalities that manifest with excessive pronation/supination should be addressed with a custom foot orthotic. Placing a heel lift in the shoe or building it into the orthotic can reduce stress on the Achilles tendon initially, but should be gradually reduced so as not to cause an adaptive shortening of the muscle-tendon unit. Gentle pain-free stretching can be performed several times per day and can be done after an active or passive warm-up with exercise or modalities such as superficial heat or ultrasound (see Exercises 31-20 and 31-21). Open-kinetic chain strengthening with rubber tubing can begin early in the rehabilitation process and should be progressed to closed-kinetic chain strengthening in a concentric and eccentric fashion using the patient's body weight with modification of sets, repetitions, and speed of exercise to facilitate a more intense rehabilitation session (see Exercises 31-5, 31-12, and 31-13). A walking/jogging progression on a firm but forgiving surface can be initiated when the symptoms have resolved and ROM, strength, endurance, and flexibility have been normalized to the uninvolved extremity. The patient must be reminded that this progression is designed to improve the affected tendon's ability to tolerate stress in a controlled fashion and not to improve fitness level. Studies have shown that aerobic endurance can be maintained with biking and swimming.[13] Finally, it is important to educate the patient on the nature of the condition, in order to set realistic expectations for a safe return without recurrence.

Achilles Tendon Rupture

PATHOMECHANICS

The Achilles tendon is the largest tendon in the human body. It serves to transmit force from the gastrocnemius and soleus musculature to the calcaneus. Rupture of the Achilles tendon usually occurs in an area 2 to 6 cm proximal to the calcaneal insertion, which has been implicated as an avascular site prone to degenerative changes.[8,25,27] The injury presents after a sudden plantarflexion of the ankle such as with jumping or accelerating. The patient will often feel or hear a pop and note a sensation of being kicked in the back of the leg. The ability to plantarflex the ankle will be painful and limited but still possible with the assistance of the tibialis posterior and the peroneals. A palpable defect will be noted along the length of the tendon, and the Thompson test will be positive. The patient will require the use of crutches to continue ambulation without an obvious limp.

INJURY MECHANISM

Achilles tendon rupture is usually caused by a sudden forceful plantarflexion of the ankle. It has been theorized that the area of rupture has undergone degenerative changes and is more prone to rupture when placed under higher levels of tensile loading.[25] The degenerative changes may be due to excessive compensatory pronation at the subtalar joint to accomodate for structural deviations of the forefoot, rearfoot, and lower leg during walking and running. This pronation may place an increased tensile stress on the medial aspect of the Achilles tendon. Also a chronically inflexible gastrocnemius–soleus complex will reduce the available amount of dorsiflexion at the ankle joint and excessive subtalar joint pronation will assist in accommodating this loss. The above mechanisms may result in tendinitis symptoms that precede the tendon rupture, but this is not always the case. Fatigue of the sedentary patient or weekend warrior may also contribute to tendon rupture, as well as improper warm-up prior to ballistic activities such as basketball or racket sports.[24]

REHABILITATION CONCERNS

After an Achilles tendon rupture, the question of surgical repair versus cast immobilization will arise. Cetti et al report that surgical repair of the tendon is recommended in allowing the patient to return to previous levels of activity.[8] Surgical repair of the Achilles tendon may require a period of immobilization for 6 to 8 weeks to allow for proper tendon healing.[6,25,31]

The deleterious effects of this lengthy immobilization include muscle atrophy, joint stiffness including intraarticular adhesions and capsular stiffness of the involved joints, disorganization of the ligament substance, and possible disuse osteoporosis of the bone.[6] Isokinetic strength deficits for the ankle plantarflexors, especially at lower speeds, have been documented with periods of cast immobilization of 6 weeks.[31] Steele et al noted significant deficits isokinetically of ankle plantarflexor strength after 8 weeks of immobilization.[48] These authors feel that the primary limiting factor that influences functional outcome may be the duration of postsurgical immobilization.[48] Thus, several studies have been done using early controlled ankle motion and progressive weight bearing without immobilization.[6,25,31,46] It is important not only to regain full ROM without harming the repair, but also to regain normal muscle function through controlled progressive strengthening. This can be performed through a variety of exercises including isometrics, isotonics, and isokinetics (see Exercises 31-1 to 31-13). Open- and closed-kinetic chain activities can be incorporated into the progression to gradually increase weight-bearing stress on the tendon repair as well as to improve proprioception (see Exercises 31-11, 31-14, 31-15, and 31-24 to 31-27). Aerobic endurance can be maintained with stationary biking and pool running with a flotation device. Gait normalization for walking and running can be performed using a treadmill.

REHABILITATION PROGRESSION

It is important for the therapist to have an open line of communication with the physician in charge of the surgical repair. Decisions about length and type of immobilization, weight-bearing progression, allowable ROM, and progressive strengthening should be discussed with the physician thoroughly. Recent literature demonstrates excellent results with early and controlled mobilization with the use of a splint that allows early plantarflexion ROM and that slowly increases ankle dorsiflexion to neutral and full dorsiflexion over a 6- to 8-week period of time.[6,25] Controlled progressive weight bearing based on percentages of the patient's body weight can be done over a 6- to 8-week period postoperatively with full weight bearing by the end of this time frame. During the early stages of rehabilitation, ICE is used to decrease swelling. A variety of ROM exercises are done to increase ankle ROM in all planes as well as initiate activation of the surrounding muscles (see Exercises 31-1 to 31-4, 31-9, 31-10, 31-14, 31-15, 31-20, and 31-22).

By 4 to 6 weeks postoperatively, strengthening exercises with rubber tubing can be progressed to closed-chain exercises using a percentage of the patient's body weight with heel raises on a Total Gym apparatus (see Exercises 31-5, 31-8, and 31-11). It is important to do more concentric than eccentric loading initially so as not to place excessive stress on the repair. Gradual increases in eccentric loading can occur from 10 to 12 weeks postoperatively. Also at this time, isokinetic exercise can be introduced with submaximal high-speed exercise and progressed to lower concentric speeds gradually over time (see Exercise 31-19).

By 3 months, full weight-bearing heel raises can be performed (see Exercises 31-12 and 31-13). At the same time, a walking/jogging program can be initiated. Isokinetic strength testing can be done between 3 and 4 months to determine if any deficits in ankle plantarflexor strength exist (see Exercise 31-19). The number of single-leg heel raises performed in a specified amount of time as compared to the uninvolved extremity can also be used to determine functional plantarflexor strength and endurance. Functional activities can be initiated at 3 months along with a progressive jogging program. Complete rehabilitation may require 6 months.

Retrocalcaneal Bursitis

PATHOMECHANICS

The retrocalcaneal bursa lies between the Achilles tendon and the superior tuberosity of the calcaneus.[5] The patient will report a gradual onset of pain that may be associated with Achilles tendinitis. Careful palpation anterior to the Achilles tendon will rule out involvement of the tendon. Pain is increased with AROM/PROM ankle dorsiflexion and relieved with plantarflexion. Depending on the severity and swelling associated, it may be painful to walk, especially when attempting to attain full closed-kinetic chain ankle dorsiflexion during the midstance phase of gait.

INJURY MECHANISM

Loading the foot and ankle in repeated dorsiflexion, such as with walking or running uphill, can be a cause of this condition. When the foot is dorsiflexed, the distance between the posterior/superior calcaneus and the Achilles tendon will be reduced, thus resulting in a repeated mechanical compression of the retrocalcaneal bursa. Also structural abnormalities of the foot may lead to excessive compensatory movements at the subtalar joint, which may cause friction of the Achilles tendon on the bursa with running.

REHABILITATION CONCERNS

Because of the close proximity of other structures, it is important to rule out involvement of the calcaneus and Achilles tendon with careful palpation of the area. Rest and activity modification in order to reduce swelling and inflammation is necessary. If walking is painful, then use of crutches with weight bearing as tolerated is recommended for a brief period. Gentle but progressive stretching and strengthening should be added as tolerated, with care being taken not to increase pain with gastrocnemius–soleus stretching (see Exercises 31-5, 31-12, 31-13, 31-20, and 31-21). If excessive compensatory pronation is noted during gait analysis, recommendations on proper footwear should be made, especially in regards to the heel counter, and foot orthotics should be considered.

REHABILITATION PROGRESSION

The early management of this condition requires all measures to reduce pain and inflammation including ice, rest from offending activity, proper shoeware, and modified weight bearing with crutches if necessary. Aerobic endurance can be maintained with pool running with a flotation device. Gentle stretching of the gastrocnemius–soleus needs to be introduced slowly, because this will tend to increase compression of the retrocalcaneal bursa. As pain resolves and ROM and walking gait are normalized, the patient may begin a progressive walking/jogging program. The patient can progress back to activity as the condition allows. Heel lifts in both shoes may be necessary in the early return to activity, with gradual weaning away from them as AROM/PROM dorsiflexion improves. The condition may allow full return in 10 days to 2 weeks if treated early enough. If the condition persists, 6 to 8 weeks of rest, activity modification, and treatment may be needed before a successful result is attained with conservative care.

EXERCISES

REHABILITATION TECHNIQUES FOR THE LOWER LEG

Strengthening Techniques

ISOTONIC OPEN-KINETIC CHAIN EXERCISES

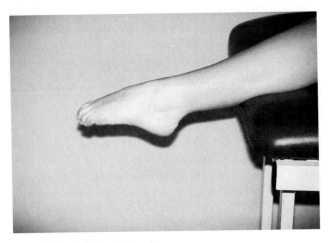

EXERCISE 31-1

AROM ankle plantarflexion. Used to activate the primary and secondary ankle plantarflexer muscle-tendon units after a period of immobilization or disuse. This exercise can be performed in a supportive medium such as a whirlpool.

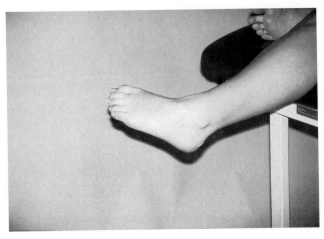

EXERCISE 31-3

AROM ankle inversion. Used to activate the tibialis posterior, flexor hallucis longus, and flexor digitorum longus muscle-tendon units after a period of immobilization or disuse.

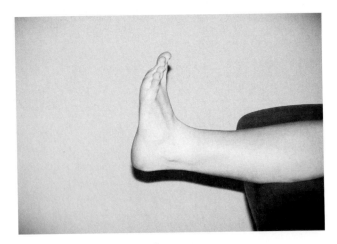

EXERCISE 31-2

AROM ankle dorsiflexion. Used to activate the tibialis anterior, extensor hallucis longus, and extensor digitorum longus muscle-tendon units after a period of immobilization or disuse.

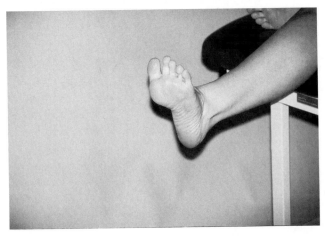

EXERCISE 31-4

AROM ankle eversion. Used to activate the peroneus longus and brevis muscle-tendon units after a period of immobilization or disuse.

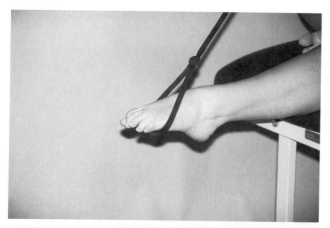

E X E R C I S E   3 1 - 5

RROM ankle plantarflexion with rubber tubing. Used to strengthen the gastrocnemius, soleus, and secondary ankle plantarflexors including the peroneals, flexor hallucis longus, flexor digitorum longus, and tibialis posterior in an open-chain fashion. This exercise will also place a controlled concentric and eccentric load on the Achilles tendon.

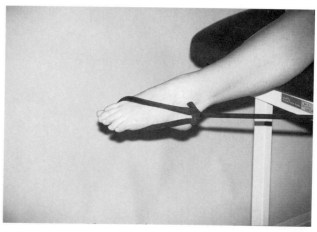

E X E R C I S E   3 1 - 7

RROM ankle inversion with rubber tubing. Used to isolate and strengthen the ankle invertors including the tibialis posterior, flexor hallucis longus, and flexor digitorum longus in an open-chain fashion.

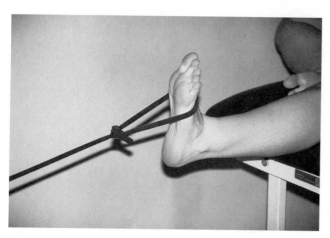

E X E R C I S E   3 1 - 6

RROM ankle dorsiflexion with rubber tubing. Used to isolate and strengthen the ankle dorsiflexors including the tibialis anterior, extensor hallucis longus, and extensor digitorum longus in an open-chain fashion.

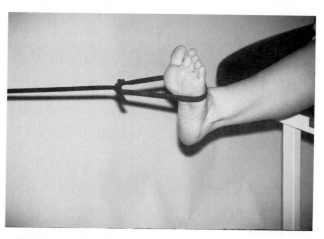

E X E R C I S E   3 1 - 8

RROM ankle eversion with rubber tubing. Used to isolate and strengthen the ankle evertors including the peroneus longus and peroneus brevis in an open-chain fashion.

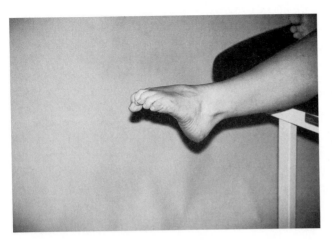

EXERCISE 31 - 9

AROM toe flexion/extension. Used to activate the long toe flexors, extensors, and foot intrinsic musculature. This exercise will also help to improve the tendon gliding ability of the extensor hallucis longus, extensor digitorum longus, flexor hallucis longus, and flexor digitorum longus tendons after a period of immobilization.

CLOSED-KINETIC CHAIN STRENGTHENING EXERCISES

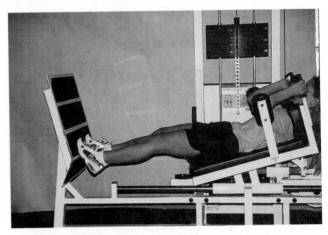

EXERCISE 31 - 11

Heel raises. Used to strengthen the gastrocnemius musculature. Will also directly load the Achilles tendon with a percentage of the patient's body weight depending on the angle of the carriage relative to the ground.

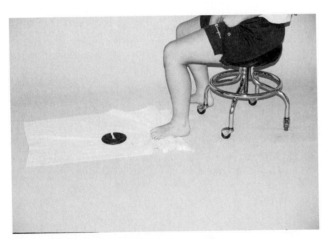

EXERCISE 31 - 10

Towel-gathering exercise. Used to strengthen the foot intrinsics and long toe flexor and extensor muscle-tendon units. A weight can be placed on the end of the towel, which will require more force production by the muscle-tendon unit as ROM and strength improve.

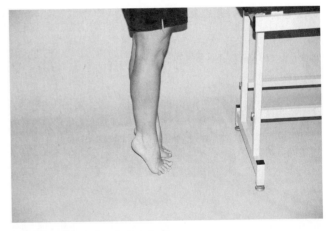

EXERCISE 31 - 12

Two-legged heel raise. Used to strengthen the gastrocnemius when the knee is extended and the soleus when the knees are flexed. The flexor hallucis longus, flexor digitorum longus, tibialis posterior, and peroneals will also be activated during this activity. The patient can modify concentric/eccentric activity depending on the type and severity of the condition. For example, if an eccentric load is not desired on the involved side, the patient can raise up on both feet and lower down on the uninvolved side until eccentric loading is tolerated on the involved side.

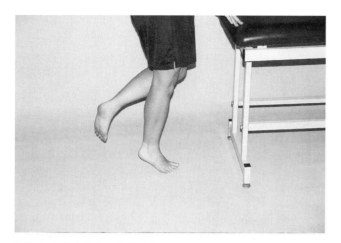

EXERCISE   31-13

One-legged heel raise. Used to strengthen the gastrocnemius and soleus muscles when the knee is extended and flexed respectively. This can be used as a progression from the two-legged heel raise.

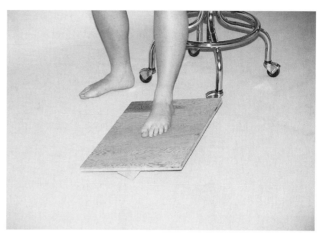

EXERCISE   31-15

Seated closed-chain ankle inversion/eversion AROM. Used to activate the ankle invertor/evertor musculature in a closed-chain position.

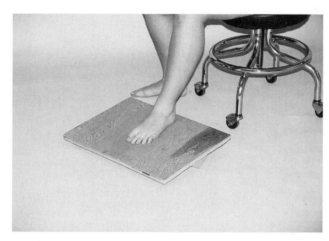

EXERCISE   31-14

Seated closed-chain ankle dorsiflexor/plantarflexor AROM. Used to activate the ankle dorsiflexor/plantarflexor musculature in a closed-chain position.

EXERCISE   31-16

Stationary cycle. Used to reduce impact weight-bearing forces on the lower extremity while also maintaining cardiovascular fitness levels.

ISOKINETIC EXERCISES

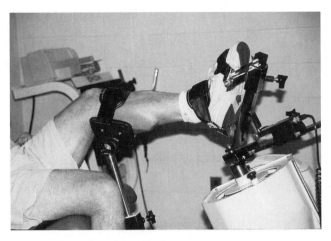

E X E R C I S E   3 1 - 1 8

Isokinetic ankle inversion/eversion RROM. Used to improve the strength and endurance of the ankle invertors and evertors in an open chain. Also can provide an objective measurement of muscular torque production.

E X E R C I S E   3 1 - 1 7

Stair-stepping machine. Used to progressively load the lower extremity in a closed kinetic fashion as well as maintain and improve cardiovascular fitness.

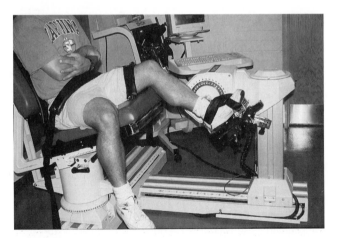

E X E R C I S E   3 1 - 1 9

Isokinetic ankle plantarflexion/dorsiflexion RROM. Used to improve the strength and endurance of the ankle dorsiflexors and plantarflexors in an open chain. Also can provide an objective measurement of torque production.

Stretching Exercises

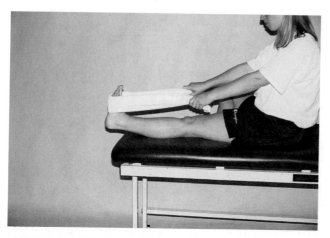 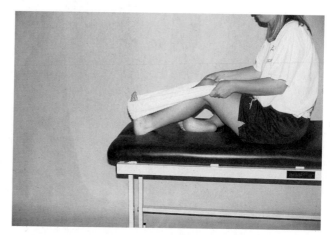

EXERCISE 31-20

Ankle plantarflexion towel stretch. Used to stretch the gastrocnemius when the knee is extended and the soleus when the knee is flexed. The Achilles tendon will be stretched with both positions. The patient can hold the stretch for 20 to 31 seconds.

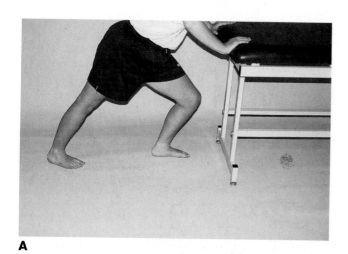 

A

B

EXERCISE 31-21

A, Standing gastrocnemius stretch. Used to stretch the gastrocnemius muscle. The Achilles tendon will also be stretched. The stretch is held for 20 to 31 seconds.
B, Standing soleus stretch. Used to stretch the soleus muscle. The Achilles tendon will also be stretched. The stretch is held for 20 to 31 seconds.

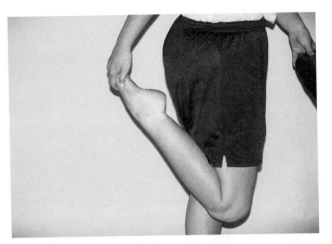

EXERCISE 31-22

Standing ankle dorsiflexor stretch. Used to stretch the extensor hallucis longus, extensor digitorum longus, tibialis anterior, and anterior ankle capsule. The stretch is held for 20 to 31 seconds.

Exercises to Reestablish Neuromuscular Control

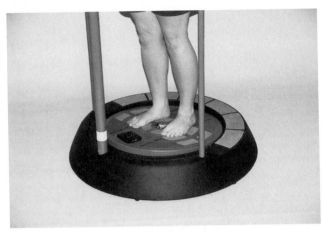

EXERCISE 31-24

Standing double-leg balance board activity. Used to activate the lower-leg musculature and improve balance and proprioception of the lower extremity.

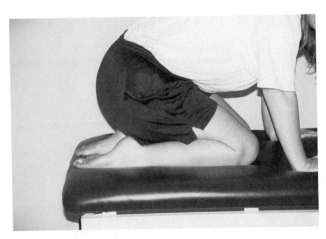

EXERCISE 31-23

Kneeling ankle dorsiflexor stretch. Used to stretch the extensor hallucis longus, extensor digitorum longus, tibialis anterior, and anterior ankle capsule. This is an aggressive stretch that can be used in the later stages of the rehabilitation process to gain end ROM ankle dorsiflexion.

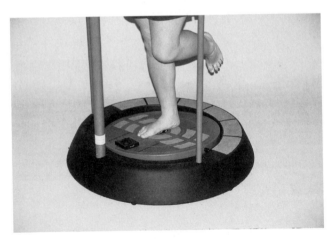

EXERCISE 31-25

Standing single-leg balance board activity. Used to activate the lower-leg musculature and improve balance and proprioception of the involved extremity.

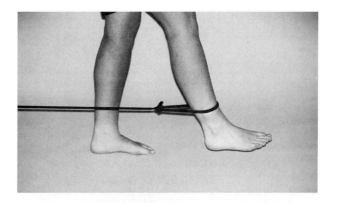

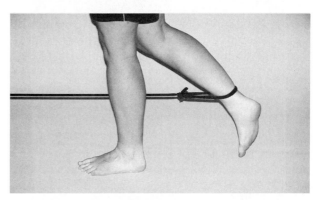

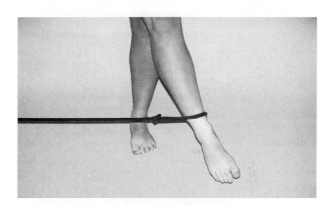

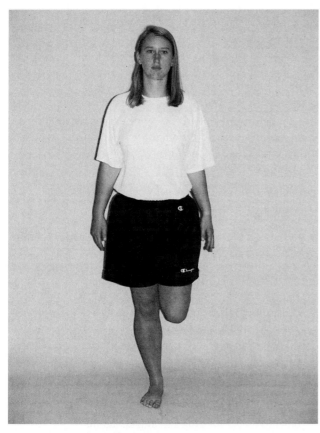

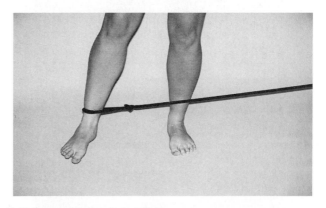

EXERCISE 31-26

Static single-leg standing balance progression. Used to improve balance and proprioception of the lower extremity. This activity can be made more difficult with the following progression: (1) single-leg stand, eyes open; (2) single-leg stand, eyes closed; (3) single-leg stand, eyes open, toes extended so only the heel and metatarsal heads are in contact with the ground; and (4) single-leg stand, eyes closed, toes extended.

EXERCISE 31-27

Single-leg standing rubber tubing kicks. Used to improve muscle activation of the lower leg to maintain single-leg standing on the involved extremity while kicking against the resistance of the rubber tubing.

Exercises to Improve Cardiorespiratory Endurance

E X E R C I S E   3 1 - 2 8

Pool running with flotation device. Used to reduce impact weight-bearing forces on the lower extremity while maintaining cardiovascular fitness level and running form.

E X E R C I S E   3 1 - 2 9

Upper-body ergometer. Used to maintain cardiovascular fitness when lower?

SUMMARY

- Although some injuries that occur in the region of the lower leg are acute, the majority of injuries seen result from overuse, most often from running.
- Tibial fractures can create long-term problems for the patient if inappropriately managed, while fibular fractures generally require much shorter periods for immobilization. Treatment of these fractures is immediate medical referral and most likely a period of immobilization and restricted weight bearing.
- Stress fractures in the lower leg are usually the result of the bone's inability to adapt to the repetitive loading response during training and conditioning of the patient and are more likely to occur in the tibia.
- Chronic compartment syndromes can occur from acute trauma or repetitive trauma of overuse. They can occur in any of the four compartments, but are most likely in the anterior or deep posterior compartments.
- Rehabilitation of medial tibial stress syndrome must be comprehensive and address musculoskeletal factors, training and conditioning, and proper footwear and orthotics intervention.
- Achilles tendinitis will often present with a gradual onset over a period of time and may be resistant to a quick resolution secondary to the slower healing response of tendinous tissue.
- Perhaps the greatest question after an Achilles tendon rupture is whether surgical repair versus cast immobilization is the best method of treatment. Regardless, the time required for rehabilitation is significant.
- With retrocalcaneal bursitis the patient will report a gradual onset of pain that may be associated with Achilles tendinitis. Treatment should include rest and activity modification in order to reduce swelling and inflammation.

REFERENCES

1. Andrish J, Work J. How I mangage shin splints. *Phys Sports Med* 18:113–114, 1990.
2. Beckham S, Grana W, Buckley P, et al. A comparison of anterior compartment pressures in competitive runners and cyclists. *Am J Sports Med* 21:36–40, 1993.
3. Bennell K, Malcolm S, Thomas S, et al. The incidence and distribution of stress fractures in competitive track and field patients: A twelve-month prospective study. *Am J Sports Med* 24:211–217, 1996.
4. Bennell K, Malcolm S, Thomas S, et al. Risk factors for stress fractures in track and field patients: A twelve-month prospective study. *Am J Sports Med* 24:810–817, 1996.
5. Bordelon R. The heel. In: DeLee J, Drez D, eds. *Orthopaedic and Sports Medicine: Principles and Practice.* Philadelphia, Saunders, 1994.

6. Carter T, Fowler P, Blokker C. Functional postoperative treatment of Achilles tendon repair. *Am J Sports Med* 20:459–462, 1992.

7. Case W. Relieving the pain of shin splints. *Phys Sports Med* 22:31–32, 1994.

8. Cetti R, Christensen S, Ejsted R, et al. Operative versus nonoperative treatment of Achilles tendon rupture: A prospective randomized study and review of the literature. *Am J Sports Med* 21:791–799, 1993.

9. Chang P, Harris R. Intramedullary nailing for chronic tibial stress fractures: A review of five cases. *Am J Sports Med* 24:688–692, 1996.

10. Dickson T, Kichline P. Functional management of stress fractures in female patients using a pneumatic leg brace. *Am J Sports Med* 15:86–89, 1987.

11. Donatelli R. Normal anatomy and biomechanics. In: Donatelli R, Wolf S, eds. *The Biomechanics of the Foot and Ankle,* 1st ed. Philadelphia, Davis, 1990.

12. Ekenman I, Tsai-Fellander L, Westblad P, et al. A study of instrinsic factors in patients with stress fractures of the tibia. *Foot Ankle* 17:477–482, 1996.

13. Eyestone E, Fellingham G, George J, Fisher G. Effect of water running and cycling on maximum oxygen consumption and 2-mile run performance. *Am J Sports Med* 21:41–44, 1993.

14. Fehlandt A, Micheli L. Acute exertional anterior compartment syndrome in an adolescent female. *Med Sci Sports Exerc* 27:3–7, 1995.

15. Feltner M, Macrae H, Macrae P, et al. Strength training effects on rearfoot motion in running. *Med Sci Sports Exerc* 26:102–107, 1994.

16. Fick D, Albright J, Murray B. Relieving painful shin splints. *Phys Sports Med* 20:105–113, 1992.

17. Fredericson M, Bergman A, Hoffman K, Dillingham M. Tibial stress reaction in runners. A correlation of clinical symptoms and scintigraphy with a new magnetic resonance imaging grading system. *Am J Sports Med* 23:472–481, 1995.

18. Galloway M, Jokl P, Dayton W. Achilles tendon overuse injuries. *Clin Sports Med* 11:771–782, 1992.

19. Garrick J, Couzens G. Tennis leg. How I manage gastrocnemius strains. *Phys Sports Med* 20:203–207, 1992.

20. Giladi M, Milgrom C, Simkin A, et al. Stress fractures. Identifiable risk factors. *Am J Sports Med* 19:647–652, 1991.

21. Goldberg B, Pecora C. Stress fractures. A risk of increased training in freshman. *Phys Sports Med* 22:68–78, 1994.

22. Gross M. Lower quarter screening for skeletal malalignment: Suggestions for orthotics and shoeware. *J Orthop Sports Phys Ther* 21:389–405, 1995.

23. Gross M. Chronic tendinitis: Pathomechanics of injury factors affecting the healing response, and treatment. *J Orthop Sports Phys Ther* 16:248–261, 1992.

24. Hamel R. Achilles tendon ruptures. Making the diagnosis. *Phys Sports Med* 20:189–200, 1992.

25. Heinrichs K, Haney C. Rehabilitation of the surgically repaired Achilles tendon using a dorsal functional orthosis: A preliminary report. *J Sport Rehabil* 3:292–303, 1994.

26. Kaper B, Carr C, Shirreffs T. Compartment syndrome after arthroscopic surgery of knee. A report of two cases managed nonoperatively. *Am J Sports Med* 25:123–125, 1997.

27. Karjalainen P, Aronen H, Pihlajamaki H, et al. Magnetic resonance imaging during healing of surgically repaired Achilles tendon ruptures. *Am J Sports Med* 25:164–171, 1997.

28. Kohn H. Shin pain and compartment syndromes in running. In: Guten G, ed. *Running Injuries.* Philadelphia, Saunders, 1997.

29. Leach R, Schepsis A, Takai H. Achilles tendinitis. Don't let it be a patient's downfall. *Phys Sports Med* 19:87–92, 1991.

30. Leppilahti J, Siira P, Vanharanta H, et al. Isokinetic evaluation of calf muscle performance after Achilles rupture repair. *Int J Sports Med* 17:619–623, 1996.

31. Mandelbaum B, Myerson M, Forster R. Achilles tendon ruptures. A new method of repair, early range of motion, and functional rehabilitation. *Am J Sports Med* 23:392–395, 1995.

32. Matheson G, Clement B, McKenzie C, et al. Stress fractures in patients. A study of 320 cases. *Am J Sports Med* 15:46–58, 1987.

33. Pedowitz R, Hargens A, Mubarek S, et al. Modified criteria for the objective diagnosis of chronic compartment syndrome of the leg. *Am J Sports Med* 18:35–40, 1990.

34. Puddu G, Cerullo G, Selvanetti A, DePaulis F. Stress fractures, In: Harries M, Williams C, Stanish W, Micheli L, eds. *Oxford Textbook of Sports Medicine.* New York, Oxford, 1994.

35. Reber L, Perry J, Pink M. Muscular control of the ankle in running. *Am J Sports Med* 21:805–810, 1993.

36. Reeder M, Dick B, Atkins J, et al. Stress fractures. Current concepts of diagnosis and treatment. *Sports Med* 22:198–212, 1996.

37. Rettig A, McCarroll J, Hahn R. Chronic compartment syndrome. Surgical intervention in 12 cases. *Phys Sports Med* 19:63–70, 1991.

38. Rettig A, Shelbourne K, McCarrol J, et al. The natural history and treatment of delayed union stress fractures of the anterior cortex of the tibia. *Am J Sports Med* 16:250–255, 1988.

39. Reynolds N, Worrell T. Chronic Achilles peritendinitis: Etiology, pathophysiology, and treatment. *J Orthop Sports Phys Ther* 13:171–176, 1991.

40. Sallade J, Koch S. Training errors in long distance runners. *J Athl Train* 27:50–53, 1992.

41. Schepsis A, Martini D, Corbett M. Surgical management of exertional compartment syndrome of the lower leg. Long term follow-up. *Am J Sports Med* 21:811–817, 1993.

42. Schepsis A, Wagner C, Leach R. Surgical management of

Achilles tendon overuse injuries. A long-term follow-up study. *Am J Sports Med* 22:611–619, 1994.

43. Schon L, Baxter D, Clanton T. Chronic exercise-induced leg pain in active people. More than just shin splints. *Phys Sports Med* 20:100–114, 1992.

44. Shwayhat A, Linenger J, Hofher L, et al. Profiles of exercise history and overuse injuries among United States Navy sea, air, and land (SEAL) recruits. *Am J Sports Med* 22:835–840, 1994.

45. Simon R. The tibial and fibular shaft. In: Simon R, Koenigshnecht S, eds. *Emergency Orthopedics, The Extremities,* 3rd ed. Norwalk, CT, Appleton & Lange, 1995.

46. Solveborn S, Moberg A. Immediate free ankle motion after surgical repair of acute Achilles tendon ruptures. *Am J Sports Med* 22:607–610, 1994.

47. Sommer H, Vallentyne S. Effect of foot posture on the incidence of medial tibial stress syndrome. *Med Sci Sports Exerc* 27:800–804, 1995.

48. Steele G, Harter R, Ting A. Comparison of functional ability following percutaneous and open surgical repairs of acutely ruptured tendons, *J Sport Rehabil* 2:115–127, 1993.

49. Strudwick W, Stuart G. Proximal fibular stress fracture in an aerobic dancer. A case report. *Am J Sports Med* 20:481–482, 1992.

50. Stuart M, Karaharju T. Acute compartment syndrome. Recognizing the progressive signs and symptoms. *Phys Sports Med* 22:91–95, 1994.

51. Styf J, Nakhostine M, Gershuni D. Functional knee braces increase intramuscular pressures in the anterior compartment of the leg. *Am J Sports Med* 20:46–49, 1992.

52. Taube R, Wadsworth L. Managing tibial stress fractures. *Phys Sports Med* 21:123–130, 1993.

53. Tiberio D. Pathomechanics of structural foot deformities. *Phys Ther* 68:1840–1849, 1988.

54. Tiberio D. The effect of excessive subtalar joint pronation on patellofemoral mechanics: A theoretical model. *J Orthop Phys Ther* 9:160–165, 1987.

55. Vincent N. Compartment Syndromes. In: Harries M, Williams C, Stanish W, Micheli L, eds. *Oxford Textbook of Sports Medicine.* New York, Oxford, 1994.

56. Wilder R, Brennan D, Schotte D. A standard measure for exercise prescription for aqua running. *Am J Sports Med* 21:45–48, 1993.

57. Wiley J, Clement D, Doyle D, et al. A primary care perspective of chronic compartment syndrome of the leg. *Phys Sports Med* 15:111–120, 1987.

58. Willy C, Becker B, Evers H. Unusual development of acute exertional compartment syndrome due to delayed diagnosis. A case report. *Int J Sports Med* 17:458–461, 1996.

59. Yasuda T, Miyazaki K, Tada K, et al. Stress fracture of the right distal femur following bilateral fractures of the proximal fibulas. A case report. *Am J Sports Med* 20:771–774, 1992.

CHAPTER 32

Rehabilitation of the Ankle and Foot

Skip Hunter and William E. Prentice

OBJECTIVES

After completing this chapter, the student therapist should be able to do the following:

- Discuss the biomechanics and functional anatomy of the foot and ankle.
- Discuss the various injuries that occur at the ankle joint.
- Discuss the various treatment options for rehabilitating the ankle sprain.
- Discuss the effect of forefoot varus, forefoot valgus, and rearfoot varus on the foot and lower extremity.
- Describe the biomechanical examination of the foot.
- Describe techniques for orthotic fabrication.
- Identify problems associated with the foot and the treatment options for each.

FUNCTIONAL ANATOMY AND BIOMECHANICS

Talocrural Joint

The ankle or talocrural joint is a hinge joint formed by articular facets on the distal tibia, the medial malleolus, and the lateral malleolus, which articulate with the talus. The talus is the second largest tarsal bone and is the main weight-bearing bone of the articulation linking the lower leg to the foot. The relatively square shape of the talus allows the ankle only two movements about the transverse axis: plantarflexion and dorsiflexion. Because the talus is wider on the anterior aspect than posteriorly, the most stable position of the ankle is dorsiflexion, because the talus fits tighter between the malleoli. By contrast, as the ankle moves into plantarflexion, the wider portion of the tibia is brought into contact with the narrower posterior aspect of the talus, creating a less stable position than dorsiflexion.[2]

The lateral malleolus of the fibula extends further distally so that the bony stability of the lateral aspect of the ankle is more stable than the medial. Motion at the talocrural joint ranges from 20 degrees of dorsiflexion to 50 degrees of plantarflexion, depending on the patient. A normal foot requires 20 degrees of plantarflexion and 10 degrees of dorsiflexion with the knee extended for a normal gait.

TALOCRURAL JOINT LIGAMENTS

The ligamentous support of the ankle consists of the articular capsule, three lateral ligaments, two ligaments that connect the tibia and fibula, and the medial or deltoid ligament (Fig. 32-1). The three lateral ligaments include the anterior talofibular, posterior talofibular, and calcaneofibular ligaments. The anterior and posterior tibiofibular ligaments bridge the tibia and fibula and form the distal portion of the interosseous membrane. The thick deltoid ligament provides primary resistance to foot eversion. A thin articular capsule encases the ankle joint.

TALOCRURAL JOINT MUSCLES

The muscles passing posterior to the lateral malleolus will produce ankle plantarflexion along with toe flexion. Anterior muscles serve to dorsiflex the ankle and to produce toe extension. The anterior muscles include the extensor hallucis longus, the extensor digitorum longus, the peroneus tertius, and the tibialis anterior. The posterior muscle group falls into three layers: at the superficial layer is the gastrocnemius; the middle layer includes the soleus and the plantaris; and the deep layer contains the tibialis posterior, flexor digitorum longus, and flexor hallucis longus.[2]

Subtalar Joint

The subtalar joint consists of the articulation between the talus and the calcaneus (Fig. 32-2).[67] Supination and pronation are

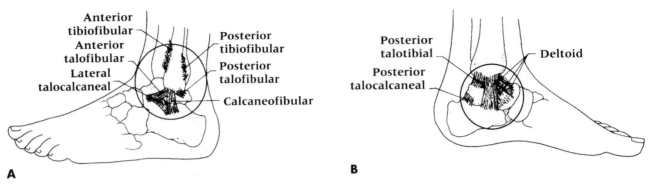

F I G U R E   3 2 - 1

F I G U R E   3 2 - 1

Ligaments of the talocrural joint **A,** Lateral aspect. **B,** Medial aspect.

normal movements that occur at the subtalar joint. These movements are triplanar movements—that is, movements that occur in all three planes simultaneously.[20,53,60] In weight bearing, the subtalar joint acts as a torque convertor to translate the pronation/supination into leg rotation.[76,83] The movements of the talus during pronation and supination have profound effects on the lower extremity both proximally and distally.

In weight bearing, supination causes the talus to abduct and dorsiflex on the calcaneus (relative calcaneal inversion), while pronation occurs when the talus adducts and plantarflexes on the calcaneus (calcaneal inversion). In supination, the foot moves into adduction, plantarflexion, and inversion. In pronation, the foot moves into abduction, dorsiflexion, and eversion.[20,53]

Midtarsal Joint

The midtarsal joint consists of two distinct joints: the calcaneocuboid and the talonavicular joints. The midtarsal joint depends mainly on ligamentous and muscular tension to maintain position and integrity. Midtarsal joint stability is directly related to the position of the subtalar joint. If the subtalar joint is pronated, the talonavicular and calcaneocuboid joints become

hypermobile. If the subtalar joint is supinated, the midtarsal joint becomes hypomobile. As the midtarsal joint becomes more or less mobile, it affects the distal portion of the foot because of the articulations at the tarsometatarsal joint.[55]

EFFECTS OF MIDTARSAL JOINT POSITION DURING PRONATION

During pronation, the talus adducts and plantarflexes and makes the joint articulations of the midtarsal joint more congruous. The long axes of the talonavicular and calcaneocuboid joints are more parallel and thus allow more motion. The resulting foot is often referred to as a "loose bag of bones."[20,67]

As more motion occurs at the midtarsal joint, the lesser tarsal bones, particularly the first metatarsal and first cuneiform, become more mobile. These bones comprise a functional unit known as the first ray. With pronation of the midtarsal joint, the first ray is more mobile because of its articulations with that joint. One of the original descriptions was Morton's paper describing the now classic Morton's toe.[56] The first ray is also stabilized by the attachment of the long peroneal tendon, which attaches to the base of the first metatarsal. The long peroneal tendon passes posteriorly around the base of the lateral malleolus and then through a notch in the cuboid to cross the foot to the

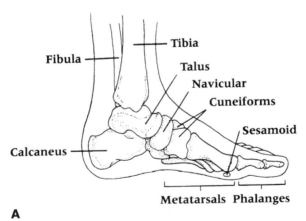

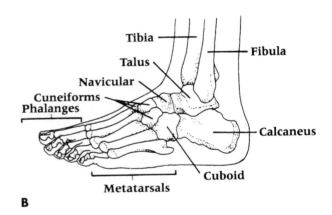

F I G U R E   3 2 - 2

Bones of the foot. **A,** Medial aspect. **B,** Lateral aspect.

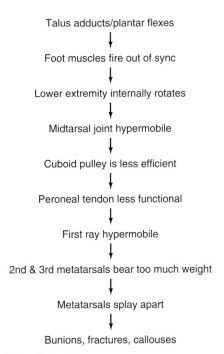

Talus adducts/plantar flexes

↓

Foot muscles fire out of sync

↓

Lower extremity internally rotates

↓

Midtarsal joint hypermobile

↓

Cuboid pulley is less efficient

↓

Peroneal tendon less functional

↓

First ray hypermobile

↓

2nd & 3rd metatarsals bear too much weight

↓

Metatarsals splay apart

↓

Bunions, fractures, callouses

FIGURE 32-3

Effects of a forefoot varus.

first metatarsal. The cuboid functions as a pulley to increase the mechanical advantage of the peroneal tendon. Stability of the cuboid is essential in this process. In the pronated position, the cuboid loses much of its mechanical advantage as a pulley; therefore the peroneal tendon no longer stabilizes the first ray effectively. This condition creates hypermobility of the first ray and increased pressure on the other metatarsals (Fig. 32-3).

EFFECTS OF MIDTARSAL JOINT POSITION DURING SUPINATION

During supination, the talus abducts and dorsiflexes, which raises the level of the talonavicular joint superior to that of the calcaneocuboid joint and allows less congruency of both joint articulations.[66] Also the long axes of the joints become more oblique. Both allow less motion to occur at this joint, making the foot very rigid and tight. Because less movement occurs at the calcaneocuboid joint, the cuboid becomes hypomobile. The long peroneal tendon has a greater amount of tension because the cuboid has less mobility and thus will not allow hypermobility of the first ray. In this case the majority of the weight is borne by the first and fifth metatarsals (Fig. 32-4).

Tarsometatarsal Joint

The tarsometatarsal joint is comprised of the cuboid; first, second, and third cuneiforms; and the bases of the metatarsal bones. These bones allow for rotational forces when engaged in weight-bearing activities. They move as a unit, depending on the position of the midtarsal and subtalar joints. Also known

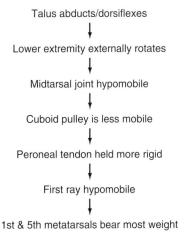

Talus abducts/dorsiflexes

↓

Lower extremity externally rotates

↓

Midtarsal joint hypomobile

↓

Cuboid pulley is less mobile

↓

Peroneal tendon held more rigid

↓

First ray hypomobile

↓

1st & 5th metatarsals bear most weight

FIGURE 32-4

Effects of a forefoot valgus.

as Lisfranc's joint, the tarsometatarsal joint provides a locking device that enhances foot stability.

Metatarsal Joints

Together with subtalar, talonavicular, and tarsometatarsal interrelationships, foot stabilization depends on the interaction between the metatarsal joints. The first ray moves independently from the other metatarsal bones. As a main weight bearer, the first ray is concerned with body propulsion. Stabilization depends on the peroneus longus muscle, which attaches on the medial aspect of the first ray. As with the other segments of the foot, stability of the first metatarsal bone depends on the relative position of the subtalar and talonavicular joints. The fifth metatarsal bone, like the first metatarsal bone, moves independently. In plantarflexion it moves into adduction and inversion; conversely, in dorsiflexion it moves the foot into abduction and eversion.[34]

Biomechanics of Normal Gait

The action of the lower extremity during gait can be divided into two phases. The first is the stance, or support, phase, which starts with initial contact at heel strike and ends at toe-off. The second is the swing or recovery phase. This represents the time immediately after toe-off in which the leg is moved from behind the body to a position in front of the body in preparation for heel strike.

The foot's function during the support phase of running is twofold. At heel strike, the foot acts as a shock absorber to the impact forces and then adapts to the uneven surfaces. At push-off, the foot functions as a rigid lever to transmit the explosive force from the lower extremity to the running surface. In a heel-strike running gait, initial contact of the foot is on the lateral aspect of the calcaneus with the subtalar joint in supination.[5]

At initial contact, the subtalar joint is supinated. Associated with this supination of the subtalar joint is an obligatory external rotation of the tibia. As the foot is loaded, the subtalar joint moves into a pronated position until the forefoot is in contact with the running surface. The change in subtalar motion occurs between initial heel strike and 20 percent into the support phase of running. As pronation occurs at the subtalar joint, there is obligatory internal rotation of the tibia. Transverse plane rotation occurs at the knee joint because of this tibial rotation.[5] Pronation of the foot unlocks the midtarsal joint and allows the foot to assist in shock absorption and to adapt to uneven surfaces. It is important during initial impact to reduce the ground reaction forces and to distribute the load evenly on many different anatomic structures throughout the foot and leg. Pronation is normal and allows for this distribution of forces on as many structures as possible to avoid excessive loading on just a few structures. The subtalar joint remains in a pronated position until 55 to 85 percent of the support phase with maximum pronation is concurrent with the body's center of gravity passing over the base of support.[2]

The foot begins to resupinate and will approach the neutral subtalar position at 70 to 90 percent of the support phase. In supination, the midtarsal joints are locked and the foot becomes stable and rigid to prepare for push-off. This rigid position allows the foot to exert a great amount of force from the lower extremity to the running surface.[40]

REHABILITATION TECHNIQUES FOR SPECIFIC INJURIES

Ankle Sprains

PATHOMECHANICS AND INJURY MECHANISM

Ankle sprains are among the more common musculoskeletal injuries.[7,18,85] Injuries to the ligaments of the ankle may be classified either according to their location or by the mechanism of injury.

Inversion Sprains

An inversion ankle sprain is the most common and often results in injury to the lateral ligaments. The anterior talofibular ligament is the weakest of the three lateral ligaments. Its major function is to stop forward subluxation of the talus. It is injured in an inverted, plantarflexed, and internally rotated position.[42,78] The calcaneofibular and posterior talofibular ligaments are also likely to be injured in inversion sprains as the force of inversion is increased. Increased inversion force is needed to tear the calcaneofibular ligament. Because the posterior talofibular ligament prevents posterior subluxation of the talus, its injuries are severe, such as complete dislocations.[8]

Eversion Sprains

The eversion ankle sprain is less common than the inversion ankle sprain, largely because of the bony and ligamentous anatomy. As mentioned previously, the fibular malleolus extends further inferiorly than does the tibial malleolus. This, combined with the strength of the thick deltoid ligament, prevents excessive eversion. More often, eversion injuries may involve an avulsion fracture of the tibia before the deltoid ligament tears.[13] The deltoid ligament may also be contused in inversion sprains due to impingement between the fibular malleolus and the calcaneous. Despite the fact that eversion sprains are less common, the severity is such that these sprains may take longer to heal than inversion sprains.[58]

Syndesmodic Sprains

Isolated injuries to the distal tibiofemoral joint are referred to as syndesmodic sprains. The anterior and posterior tibiofibular ligaments are found between the distal tibia and fibula and extend up the lower leg as the interosseous ligament or syndesmodic ligament. Sprains of the ligaments are more common than has been realized in the past. These ligaments are torn with increased external rotational or forced dorsiflexion and are often injured in conjunction with a severe sprain of the medial and lateral ligament complexes.[77] Initial rupture of the ligaments occurs distally at the tibiofibular ligament above the ankle mortise. As the force of disruption is increased, the interosseous ligament is torn more proximally. Sprains of the syndesmodic ligaments are extremely hard to treat and often take months to heal. Treatments for this problem are essentially the same as for medial or lateral sprains, with the difference being an extended period of immobilization. Rehabilitation will likely require a longer period of time than for the inversion or eversion sprains.

Severity of the Sprain

In a grade 1 sprain, there is some stretching or perhaps tearing of the ligamentous fibers, with little or no joint instability. Mild pain, little swelling, and joint stiffness may be apparent. With a grade 2 sprain, there is some tearing and separation of the ligamentous fibers and moderate instability of the joint. Moderate to severe pain, swelling, and joint stiffness should be expected.

Grade 3 sprains involve total rupture of the ligament, manifested primarily by gross instability of the joint. Severe pain may be present initially, followed by little or no pain due to total disruption of nerve fibers. Swelling may be profuse, and thus the joint tends to become very stiff some hours after the injury. A grade 3 sprain with marked instability usually requires some form of immobilization lasting several weeks. Frequently the force producing the ligament injury is so great that other ligaments or structures surrounding the joint may also be injured. With cases in which there is injury to multiple ligaments, surgical repair or reconstruction may be necessary to correct an instability.

REHABILITATION CONCERNS

During the initial phase of ankle rehabilitation, the major goals are reduction of postinjury swelling, bleeding, and pain; and protection of the already healing ligament. As is the case in all acute musculoskeletal injuries, initial treatment efforts should be directed toward limiting the amount of swelling.[62] This is perhaps more true in the case of ankle sprains than with any other injury. Controlling initial swelling is the single most important treatment measure that can be taken during the entire rehabilitation process. Limiting the amount of acute swelling can significantly reduce the time required for rehabilitation. Initial management includes ice, compression, elevation, rest, and protection.

Compression

Immediately following injury and evaluation, a compression wrap should be applied to the sprained ankle. An elastic bandage should be firmly and evenly applied, wrapping distal to proximal. It is also recommended that the elastic bandage be wet to facilitate the passage of cold. To add more compression, a horseshoe-shaped felt pad may be inserted under the wrap over the area of maximum swelling.

Following initial treatment, open Gibney taping may be applied under an elastic wrap to provide additional compression and support. Care should be taken not to compartmentalize this treatment by placing tape across the top and bottom of the open area of the open Gibney (Fig. 32-5). Uneven pressure or uncovered areas over any part of the extremity may allow the swelling to accumulate.

Other devices are available that apply external compression to the ankle to control or reduce swelling. External compression should be used both initially and throughout the rehabilitative process. Most of these devices use either air or cold water within an enclosed bag to provide pressure to reduce swelling. One commonly used device is the intermittent compression unit, such as a Josbt pump or Cryo-cuff (Fig. 32-6).

Ice

The use of ice on acute injuries has been well documented in the literature. Initially, ice and compression should be used together, because this treatment regimine is more effective than ice alone.[72] The initial use of ice has its basis in constricting superficial blood flow to prevent hemorrhage as well as in reducing the hypoxic response to injury by decreasing cellular metabolism. Long-term benefits may be from reduction of pain and guarding.[2] Garrick suggests the use of ice for a minimum of 20 minutes once every 4 waking hours.[26] Ice should not be used longer than 30 minutes, especially over superficial nerves such as the peroneal and ulnar nerves. Prolonged use of ice in such areas may produce transient nerve palsy.[22]

Current literature suggests that ice can be used during all phases of rehabilitation,[45] but is most effective if used immediately after injury.[62] Ice can certainly do no harm if used properly, but heat, if applied too soon after injury, may lead to increased swelling. Often the switch from ice to heat cannot be made for days or weeks.

Elevation

Elevation is an essential part of edema control. Pressure in any vessel below the level of the heart is increased, which may lead to increased edema.[14] Elevation allows gravity to work with the

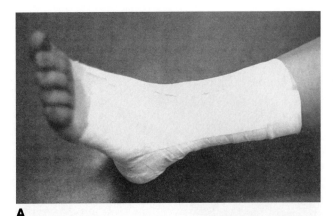

A

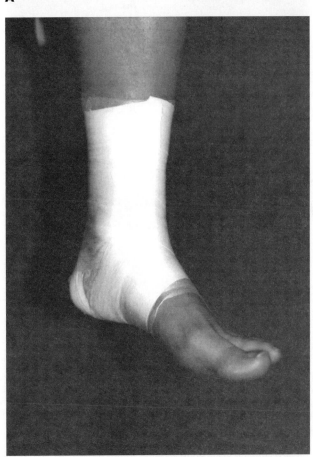

B

FIGURE 32-5

A, Correctly done open Gibney tape. **B,** Closed basketweave tape.

lymphatic system rather than against it. Elevation decreases hydrostatic pressure to decrease fluid loss and also assists venous and lymphatic return through gravity.[62] Patients should be encouraged to maintain an elevated position as often as possible, particularly during the first 24 to 48 hours following injury. An attempt should be made to treat in the elevated position rather than the gravity-dependent position. Any treatment done in the dependent position will allow edema to increase.[62,70]

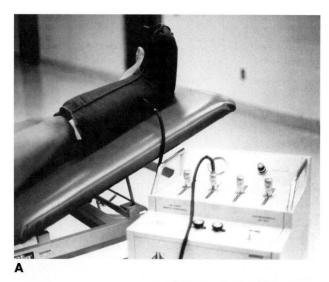

A

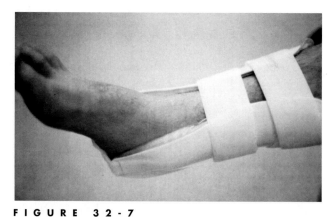

F I G U R E   3 2 - 7

Commercially available Aircast ankle stirrup.

initiated early because they also do not endanger the healing ligament as long as they are done in a pain-free range. Active plantarflexion and dorsiflexion can be done while the patient is iced and elevated. Inversion and eversion are to be avoided, because they might initiate bleeding and further traumatize ligaments.

Protection

Several appliances are available to accomplish this early protected motion. Quillen[63] recommends the ankle stirrup, which allows motion in the sagittal plane while limiting movement of the frontal plane and thus avoids stressing the ligaments through inversion and eversion (Fig. 32-7). Several commercially available braces accomplish this goal and also apply cushioned pressure to help with edema.[73] When a commercially available product is not feasible, a similar protective device may be fashioned from thermoplastic materials such as Hexalite or Orthoplast (Fig. 32-8).

The open Gibney taping technique also provides early medial and lateral protection while allowing plantarflexion and dorsiflexion, in addition to being an excellent mechanism of edema control (Fig. 32-5).

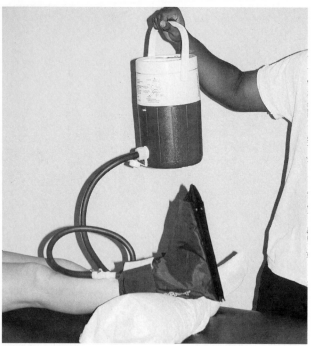

B

F I G U R E   3 2 - 6

A, Jobst intermittent air compression device. **B,** Cryo-cuff.

Rest

It is important to allow the inflammatory process to run its course during the first 24 to 48 hours before incorporating aggressive exercise techniques. However, rest does not mean that the injured patient does nothing. Contralateral exercises may be performed to obtain cross-transfer effects on the muscles of the injured side.[44] Isometric exercises may be performed very early in dorsiflexion, plantarflexion, inversion, and eversion (see Exercises 32-1 to 32-4). These types of exercises may be performed to prevent atrophy without fear of further injury to the ligament. Active plantarflexion and dorsiflexion may be

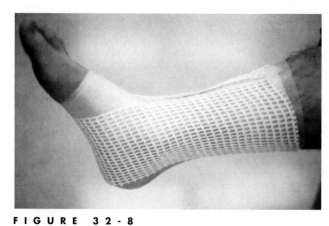

F I G U R E   3 2 - 8

Molded Hexalite ankle stirrup.

Gross et al compared the effectiveness of a number of commercial ankle orthoses and taping in restricting eversion and inversion. All of these support systems significantly reduced inversion and eversion immediately after initial application and following an exercise bout when compared to preapplication measures. Of the orthoses tested, taping provided the least support after exercise.[32] Early application of these devices allows early ambulation.

REHABILITATION PROGRESSION

In the early phase of rehabilitation, vigorous exercise is discouraged. The injured ligament must be maintained in a stable position so that healing can occur. Thus, during the period of maximum protection following injury, the patient should be either nonweight bearing or perhaps partial weight bearing on crutches. Partial weight bearing with crutches helps control several complications to healing. Muscle atrophy, proprioceptive loss, and circulatory stasis are all reduced when even limited weight bearing is allowed. Weight bearing also inhibits contracture of the tendons, which may lead to tendinitis. For these reasons, early ambulation, even if only touchdown weight bearing, is essential.[48] It has been clearly demonstrated that a healing ligament needs a certain amount of stress to heal properly. The literature suggests that early limited stress following the initial period of inflammation may promote faster and stronger healing.[8,59] These studies found that protected motion facilitated proper collagen reorientation and thus increased the strength of the healing ligament.

Once swelling and pain decrease, indicating that ligaments have healed enough to tolerate limited stress, rehabilitation can become more aggressive.

Range of Motion

In the early stages of the rehabilitation, inversion and eversion should be minimized. Light joint mobilization concentrating on dorsiflexion and plantarflexion should be started first.[47] ROM can be improved by manual joint mobilization techniques (see Exercises 32-27 to 32-30). It can also be improved through exercises such as towel stretching for the plantarflexors (see Exercise 32-23) and standing or kneeling stretches for the dorsiflexors (see Exercise 32-24). Patients are encouraged to do these exercises slowly, without pain, and to use high repetitions (2 sets of 40).

As tenderness over the ligament decreases, inversion-eversion exercises may be initiated in conjunction with plantarflexion and dorsiflexion exercises. Early exercises include pulling a towel from one side to the other by alternatively inverting and everting the foot (see Exercise 32-11 B) and alphabet drawing in an ice bath, which should be done in capital letters to ensure that full range is used.

Exercises performed on a BAPS board, wedge board, or KAT (see Exercise 32-39) may be beneficial for range of motion as well as a beginning exercise for regaining neuromuscular control.[79] These exercises should at first be done seated, progressing to standing (see Exercise 32-21). Initially the patient should start in the seated position with a wedge board in the plantarflexion-dorsiflexion direction. As pain decreases and ligament healing progresses, the board may be turned in the inversion-eversion direction. As the patient performs these movements easily, a seated BAPS board may be used for full range-of-motion exercises. When seated exercises are performed with ease, standing balance exercises should be initiated. They may be started on one leg standing without a board. The patient then supports weight with the hands and maintains balance on a wedge board in either plantarflexion-dorsiflexion or inversion-eversion. Next, hand support may be eliminated while the patient balances on the wedge board. The same sequence is then used on the BAPS board. The BAP board is initially used with assistance from the hands. Then balance is practiced on the BAPS board unassisted.

Vigorous heelcord stretching should be initiated as soon as possible (see Exercise 32-22). McCluskey et al[50] found that the heelcord acts as a bowstring when tight and may increase the chance of ankle sprains.

Strengthening

Isometrics may be done in the four major ankle motion planes, frontal and sagittal (see Exercises 32-1 to 32-4). They may be accompanied early in the rehabilitative phase by plantarflexion and dorsiflexion isotonic exercises, which do not endanger the ligaments (see Exercises 32-7 and 32-8). As the ligaments heal further and range of motion increases, strengthening exercises may be begun in all planes of motion (see Exercises 32-5 and 32-6). Care must be taken when exercising the ankle in inversion and eversion to avoid tibial rotation as a substitute movement. Pain should be the basic guideline for deciding when to start inversion-eversion isotonic exercises. Light resistance with high repetitions has fewer detrimental effects on the ligaments (2 to 4 sets of 10 repetitions). Resistive tubing exercises, ankle weights around the foot, or a multidirectional Elgin ankle exerciser (see Exercise 32-9) are excellent methods of strengthening inversion and eversion. Tubing has advantages in that it may be used both eccentrically and concentrically. Isokinetics have advantages in that more functional speeds may be obtained (see Exercises 32-15 and 32-16). PNF strengthening exercises, which isolate the desired motions at the talocrural joint, can also be used (see Exercises 32-17 to 32-20).

Proprioception and Neuromuscular Control

The role of proprioception in repeated ankle trauma has been questioned.[12,23,25,57] The literature suggests that proprioception is certainly a factor in recurrent ankle sprains. Rebman[64] reported that 83 percent of patients experienced a reduction in chronic ankle sprains after a program of proprioceptive exercises. Glencross and Thornton[30] found that the greater the ligamentous disruption, the greater the proprioceptive loss. Early weight bearing has previously been mentioned as a method of reducing proprioceptive loss. During the rehabilitation phase, standing on both feet with closed eyes, with progression to standing on one leg, is an exercise to recoup proprioception (see Exercise 32-38). This exercise may be followed by standing and balancing on a BAPS board, which should be done initially with support from the hands. As a final-stage exercise, the patient can progress to free standing and controlling the board through all ranges (see Exercises 32-39). Other closed-kinetic chain exercises may be beneficial. Leg press (see Exercise 32-42) and mini-squats (see Exercise 32-43) on the involved leg will encourage weight bearing and increase proprioceptive return. Single-leg standing kicks using abduction, adduction, extension, and flexion of the uninvolved side, while weight bearing on the affected side, will increase both strength and proprioception. This may be accomplished either free standing (see Exercise 32-41) or on a machine.

Cardiorespiratory Endurance

Cardiorespiratory conditioning should be maintained during the entire rehabilitation process. Pedaling a stationary bike (see Exercise 32-46) or an upper-extremity ergometer (see Exercise 32-45) with the hands provides excellent cardiovascular exercise without placing stress on the ankle. Pool running using a float vest, or swimming are also good cardiovascular exercises. (see Exercise 32-44).

Functional Progressions

Functional progressions may be as complex or simple as needed. The more severe the injury, the more the need for a detailed functional progression. The typical progression begins early in the rehabilitation process as the patient becomes partially weight bearing. Full weight bearing should be started when ambulation is performed without a limp. Running may be begun as soon as ambulation is pain free. Pain-free hopping on the affected side may also be a guideline to determine when running is appropriate.

Exercising in a pool allows for early running. The patient is placed in the pool in a swim vest that supports the body in water. The patient then runs in place without touching the bottom of the pool. Proper running form should be stressed. Eventually the patient is moved into shallow water so that more weight is placed on the ankle.

Progression is then to running on a smooth, flat surface, ideally a track. Initially the patient should jog the straights and walk the curves, and then progress to jogging the entire track. Speed may be increased to a sprint in a straight line. The cutting sequence should begin with circles of diminishing diameter. Cones may be set up for the patient to run figure-8s as the next cutting progression. The crossover or side step is next.[1] The patient sprints to a predesignated spot and cuts or sidesteps abruptly. When this progression is accomplished, the cut should be done without warning on the command of another person. Jumping and hopping exercises should be started on both legs simultaneously, and gradually reduced to only the injured side.

The patient may perform at different levels for each of these functional sequences. One functional sequence may be done at half speed while another is done at full speed. An example of this is the patient who is running full speed on straights of the track while doing figure-8s at only half speed. Once the upper levels of all the sequences are reached, the patient may return to limited practice, which may include early teaching and fundamental drills.

Estimates are that 30 to 40 percent of all inversion injuries result in reinjury.[23,37,38,49,69] In the past, patients were simply allowed to return to their normal activities once the pain was low enough to tolerate the activity. The rehabilitative process should include a gradual progression of functional activities that slowly increase the stress on the ligament.[43]

It is common practice that some type of ankle support be worn initially. It appears that ankle taping does have a stabilizing effect on unstable ankles,[27,80] without interfering with motor performance.[24,50] McCluskey et al[50] suggest taping the ankle and also taping the shoe onto the foot to make the shoe and ankle function as one unit. High-topped footwear may further stabilize the ankle.[33] An Aircast or some other supportive ankle brace can also be worn for support as a substitute for taping (Fig. 32-7).

Subluxation and Dislocation of the Peroneal Tendons

PATHOMECHANICS

The peroneus brevis and longus tendons pass posterior to the fibula in the peroneal groove under the superior peroneal retinaculum. Peroneal tendon dislocation may occur because of rupture of the superior retinaculum or because the retinaculum strips the periosteum away from the lateral malleolus, creating laxity in the retinaculum. It appears that there is no anatomic correlation between peroneal groove size or shape and instability of the peroneal tendons.[41] An avulsion fracture of the lateral ridge of the distal fibula may also occur with a subluxation or dislocation of the peroneal tendons.

INJURY MECHANISM

Subluxation of peroneal tendons can occur from any mechanism causing sudden and forceful contraction of the peroneal muscles that involves dorsiflexion and eversion of the foot.[41] This forces the tendons anteriorly, rupturing the retinaculum and potentially causing an avulsion fracture of the lateral malleolus. The patient will often hear or feel a "pop." In differentiating peroneal subluxation from a lateral ligament sprain or tear, there will be tenderness over the peroneal tendons and swelling and ecchymosis in the retromalleolar area. During active eversion, the foot subluxation of the peroneal tendons may be observed and palpated. This is easier to observe when acute symptoms have subsided. The patient will typically complain of chronic "giving way" or "popping." If the tendon is dislocated on initial evaluation, it should be reduced using gentle inversion and plantarflexion with pressure on the peroneal tendon.[41]

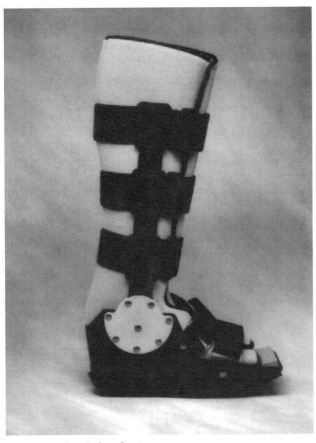

FIGURE 32-9

Short leg walking cast.

REHABILITATION CONCERNS AND PROGRESSION

Following reduction the patient should be initially placed in a compression dressing with a felt pad cut in the shape of a keyhole strapped over the lateral malleolus, placing gentle pressure on the peroneal tendons. Once the acute symptoms abate, the patient should be placed in a short leg cast in slight plantarflexion and nonweight-bearing for 5 to 6 weeks (Fig. 32-9). Aggressive ankle rehabilitation, as previously described, is initiated after cast removal.

In the case of an avulsion injury or when this becomes a chronic problem, conservative treatment is unlikely to be successful and surgery is needed to prevent the problem from recurring. A number of surgical procedures have been recommended, including repair or reconstruction of the superior peroneal retinaculum, deepening of the peroneal groove, or rerouting the tendon. Following surgery, the patient should be placed in a nonweight-bearing short leg cast for about 4 weeks. The course of rehabilitation is similar to that described for ankle fractures with increased emphasis on strengthening of the peroneal tendons in eversion.[41]

The patient may require approximately 10 to 12 weeks for rehabilitation.

Tendinitis

PATHOMECHANICS AND INJURY MECHANISM

Inflammation of the tendons surrounding the ankle joint is common. The tendons most often involved are the posterior tibialis tendon behind the medial malleolus, the anterior tibialis under the extensor retinaculum on the dorsal surface of the ankle, and the peroneal tendons both behind the lateral malleolus and at the base of the fifth metatarsal.[77]

Tendinitis in these tendons may result from one specific cause or from a collection of mechanisms, including faulty foot mechanics, which will be discussed later in this chapter; inappropriate or poor footwear that can create faulty foot mechanics; acute trauma to the tendon; tightness in the heel cord complex; or training errors in the athletic population. Training errors would include training at intensities that are too high or too often, changing training surfaces, or changes in activities within the training program.[77]

Patients who develop tendinitis are likely to complain of pain both with active movement and passive stretching; swelling around the area of the tendon due to inflammation of the tendon and the tendon sheath; creptius on movement; and stiffness and pain following periods of inactivity but particularly in the morning.

REHABILITATION CONCERNS AND PROGRESSION

In the early stages of rehabilitation, exercises are used to produce increased circulation and thus increased lymphatic flow. This will not only facilitate removal of fluid and the by-products of the inflammatory process, but will also increase nutrition to the healing tendon. In addition, exercise should also be used to limit atrophy, which may occur with disuse, and to minimize loss of strength, proprioception, and neuromuscular control.

Techniques should be incorporated into rehabilitation that act to reduce or eliminate inflammation, including rest, using therapeutic modalities (ice, ultrasound, diathermy), and using anti-inflammatory medications.

If faulty foot mechanics are a cause of tendinitis, it may be helpful to construct an appropriate orthotic device to correct the biomechanics. Taping of the foot may also be helpful in reducing stress on the tendons (see Fig. 32-41).

In many instances, if the mechanism causing the irritation and inflammation of the tendon is removed, and the inflammatory process runs its normal course, the tendinitis will often resolve within 10 days to 2 weeks. This is particularly true if rest and treatment are begun as soon as the symptoms begin. Unfortunately, as is most often the case, if treatment does not begin until the symptoms have been present for several weeks or even months, the tendinitis will take much longer to resolve. This is due to the fact that because of long-standing inflammation, the tendon thickens and the period of time required for that tendon to remodel is significantly greater.

In our experience, it is better to allow the patient to rest for a sufficient period of time so that tendon healing can take place.

With tendinitis, an aggressive approach that does not allow the tendon to first eliminate the inflammatory response and then to begin tissue realignment and remodeling will not allow the tendon to heal. This may potentially exacerbate the existing inflammation. Thus, the rehabilitation progression must be slow and controlled, with full return when the patient seems to be free of pain.

Ankle Fractures and Dislocation

PATHOMECHANICS AND INJURY MECHANISM

When dealing with fractures of the ankle or tibial and fibular malleoli, the therapist must always be cautious about suspecting an ankle sprain when a fracture actually exists. A fracture of the malleoli will generally result in immediate swelling. Ankle fractures can occur from several mechanisms that are similar to those seen for ankle sprains. In an inversion injury, medial malleolar fractures are often accompanied by a sprain of the lateral ligaments of the ankle. A fracture of the lateral malleolus is often more likely to occur than a sprain if an eversion force is applied to the ankle. This is due to the fact that the lateral malleolus extends as far as the distal aspect of the talus. With a fracture of the lateral malleolus, however, there may be also be a sprain of the deltoid ligament. Fractures result from either avulsion or compression forces. With avulsion injuries it is often the injured ligaments that prolong the rehabilitation period.[31]

Osteochondral fractures are sometimes seen in the talus. These fractures may also be referred to as dome fractures of the talus. Generally, they will be either undisplaced fractures or compression fractures.[31]

While sprains and fractures are very common, dislocations in the ankle and foot are rare. They most often occur in conjunction with fractures and require open reduction and internal fixation.[68]

REHABILITATION CONCERNS

Generally, undisplaced ankle fractures should be managed with rest and protection until the fracture has healed, while displaced fractures are treated with open reduction and internal fixation. Undisplaced fractures are treated by casting in a short leg walking cast for 6 weeks with early weight bearing. The course of rehabilitation following this period of immobilization is generally the same as for ankle sprains. Following surgery for displaced or unstable fractures, the patient may be placed in a removable walking cast; however it is essential to closely monitor the rehabilitation process to make certain that the patient is compliant.[31]

If an osteochondral fracture is displaced and there is a fragment, surgery is required to remove the fragment. In other cases, if the fragment has not healed within a year, surgery may be considered to remove the fragment.[31]

REHABILITATION PROGRESSION

Following open reduction and internal fixation, a posterior splint with the ankle in neutral should be applied, and the patient should be nonweight-bearing for about 2 weeks. During this period efforts should be directed at controlling swelling and wound management.

At 2 to 3 weeks the patient may be placed in a short leg walking brace (Fig. 32-9), which allows for partial weight bearing, for 6 weeks. Active ROM plantarflexion and dorsiflexion exercises can begin and should be done 2 or 3 times a day, along with general strengthening exercises for the rest of the lower extremity.

At 6 weeks, the patient can be weight bearing in the walking brace and this should continue for 2 to 4 weeks more. Isometric exercises (see Exercises 32-1 to 32-4) can be performed initially without the brace, progressing to isotonic strengthening exercises (see Exercises 32-5 to 32-8), which concentrate on eccentrics. Stretching exercises can also be incorporated (see Exercises 32-21 to 32-24). Joint mobilization exercises should be used to reduce capsular tightness (see Exercises 32-26 to 32-32). Exercises to regain proprioception and neuromuscular control can progress from sitting to standing as tolerated (see Exercises 32-38 to 32-43). As strength and neuromuscular control continue to increase, more functional closed-kinetic chain strengthening activities can begin (see Exercises 32-12 to 32-14).

Excessive Pronation and Supination

PATHOMECHANICS AND INJURY MECHANISM

Often when we hear the terms "pronation" or "supination" we automatically think of some pathologic condition related to gait. It must be reemphasized that pronation and supination of the foot and subtalar joint are normal movements that occur during the support phase of gait. However, if pronation or supination is excessive or prolonged, overuse injuries may develop. Excessive or prolonged supination or pronation at the subtalar joint is likely to result from some structural or functional deformity in the foot or leg. The structural deformity forces the subtalar joint to compensate in a manner that will allow the weight-bearing surfaces of the foot to make stable contact with the ground and get into a weight-bearing position. Thus, excessive pronation or supination is a compensation for an existing structural deformity. Three of the most common structural deformities of the foot are a forefoot varus (Fig. 32-10), forefoot valgus (Fig. 32-11), and rearfoot varus (Fig. 32-12).

Structural forefoot varus and structural rearfoot varus deformities are usually associated with excessive pronation. A structural forefoot valgus causes excessive supination. The deformities usually exist in one plane, but the subtalar joint will interfere with the normal functions of the foot and make it more difficult for it to act as a shock absorber, to adapt to uneven surfaces, and to act as a rigid lever for push-off. The

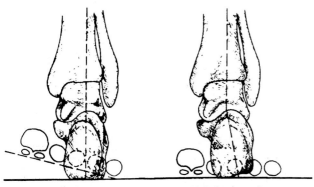

Neutral   **Weight-bearing**

F I G U R E   3 2 - 1 0

Forefoot varus. Comparing neutral and weight-bearing positions.

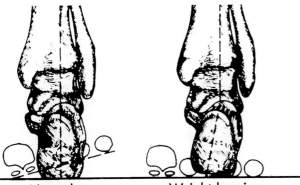

Neutral   **Weight-bearing**

F I G U R E   3 2 - 1 1

Forefoot valgus. Comparing neutral and weight-bearing positions.

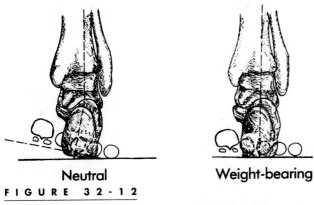

Neutral   **Weight-bearing**

F I G U R E   3 2 - 1 2

Rearfoot varus. Comparing neutral and weight-bearing positions.

compensation rather than the deformity itself usually causes overuse injuries.

Excessive or prolonged pronation of the subtalar joint during the support phase of running is one of the major causes of stress injuries. Overload of specific structures results when

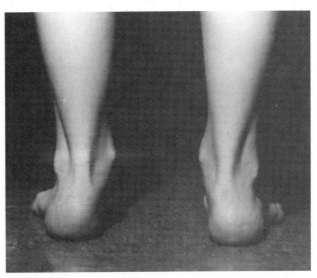

F I G U R E   3 2 - 1 3

Eversion of the calcaneus, indicating pronation.

excessive pronation is produced in the support phase or when pronation is prolonged into the propulsive phase of running. Excessive pronation during the support phase will cause compensatory subtalar joint motion such that the midtarsal joint remains unlocked, resulting in an excessively loose foot. There is also an increase in tibial rotation, which forces the knee joint to absorb more transverse rotation motion. Prolonged pronation of the subtalar joint will not allow the foot to resupinate in time to provide a rigid lever for push-off, resulting in a less powerful and efficient force. Thus, various foot and leg problems will occur with excessive or prolonged pronation during the support phase, including callus formation under the second metatarsal, stress fractures of the second metatarsal, bunions due to hypermobility of the first ray, plantar fascitis, posterior tibial tendinitis, Achilles tendinitis, tibial stress syndrome, and medial knee pain.

Several extrinsic keys may be observed that indicate pronation.[67] Excessive eversion of the calcaneus during the stance phase indicates pronation (Fig. 32-13). Excessive or prolonged internal rotation of the tibia is another sign of pronation. This internal rotation may cause increased symptoms in the shin or knee. A lowering of the medial arch accompanies pronation. It may be measured as the navicular differential,[51] the difference between the height of the navicular tuberosity from the floor in a nonweight-bearing position versus a weight-bearing position (Fig. 32-14). As previously discussed, the talus plantarflexes and adducts with pronation. It may be seen as a medial bulging of the talar head (Fig. 32-15). This same talar adduction causes increased concavity below the lateral malleolus in a posterior view while the calcaneus everts (Fig. 32-16).[53]

At heel strike in prolonged or excessive supination, compensatory movement at the subtalar joint will not allow the midtarsal joint to unlock, causing the foot to remain excessively rigid. Thus, the foot cannot absorb the ground reaction

F I G U R E   3 2 - 1 4

Measurement of the navicular differential.

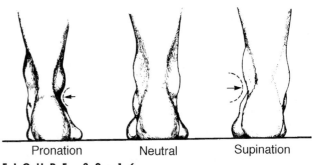

Pronation   Neutral   Supination

F I G U R E   3 2 - 1 6

Concavity below the lateral malleolus, indicating pronation.

forces as efficiently. Excessive supination limits tibial internal rotation. Injuries typically associated with excessive supination include inversion ankle sprains, tibial stress syndrome, peroneal tendinitis, iliotibial band friction syndrome, and trochanteric bursitis.

Structural deformities originating outside the foot also require compensation by the foot for a proper weight-bearing position to be attained. Tibial varum is the common bowleg deformity.[53] The distal tibia is medial to the proximal tibia (Fig. 32-17).[20] This measurement is taken weight bearing with the foot in neutral position.[35] The angle of deviation of the distal tibia from a perpendicular line from the calcaneal midline is considered tibial varum.[28] Tibial varum increases pronation to allow proper foot function.[9] At heel strike the calcaneus must evert to attain a perpendicular position.[76]

Ankle joint equinus is another extrinsic deformity that may require abnormal compensation. It may be considered an extrinsic or intrinsic problem.

During normal gait, the tibia must move anterior to the talar dome.[53] Approximately 10 degrees of dorsiflexion is required for this movement (Fig. 32-18).[53] Lack of dorsiflexion may cause compensatory pronation of the foot with resultant foot and lower extremity pain. Often this lack of dorsiflexion results from tightness of the posterior leg muscles. Other causes include forefoot equinus, in which the plane of the forefoot is below the plane of the rearfoot.[53] It occurs in many high-arched feet. This deformity requires more ankle dorsiflexion. When enough dorsiflexion is not available at the ankle, the additional movement is required at other sites, such as dorsiflexion of the midtarsal joint and rotation of the leg.

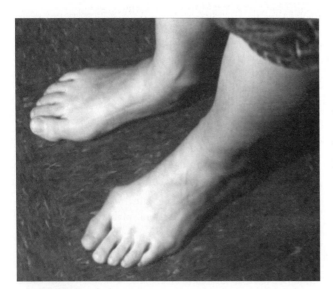

F I G U R E   3 2 - 1 5

Medial bulge of the talar head, indicating pronation.

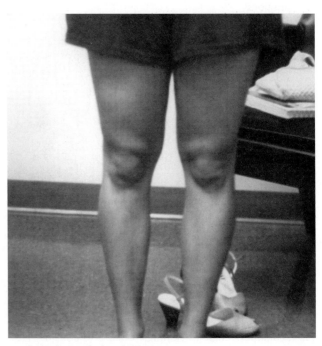

F I G U R E   3 2 - 1 7

Tibial varum or bowleg deformity.

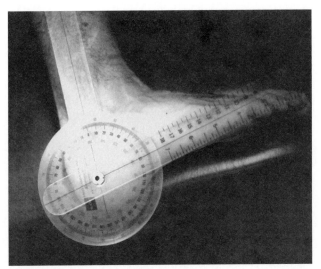

F I G U R E   3 2 - 1 8

Ten degrees of dorsiflexion is necessary for normal gait.

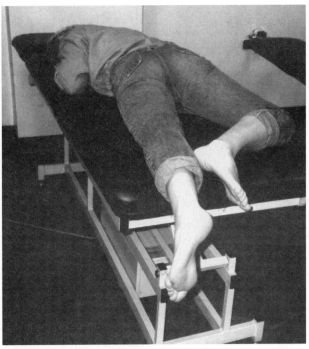

F I G U R E   3 2 - 1 9

Examination position for neutral position.

REHABILITATION CONCERNS

In individuals who excessively pronate or supinate, the goal of treatment is quite simply to correct the faulty biomechanics that occur due to the existing structural deformity. An accurate biomechanical analysis of the foot and lower extremity should identify those deformities that require abnormal compensatory movements. In the majority of cases faulty biomechanics can be corrected by constructing an appropriate orthotic device.

Despite arguments in the literature, the author has found orthotic therapy to be of tremendous value in the treatment of many lower extremity problems. This view is supported in the literature by several clinical studies. Donatelli[20] found that 96 percent of patients reported pain relief from orthotics and that 52 percent would not leave home without the devices in their shoes. McPoil et al found that orthotics were an important treatment for valgus forefoot deformities only.[52] Riegler reported that 80 percent of patients experienced at least a 50 percent improvement with orthotics.[65] This same study reported improvements in sports performance with orthotics. Hunt reported decreased muscular activity with orthotics.[35]

The process for evaluating the foot biomechanically, for constructing an orthotic device, and for selecting the appropriate footwear is detailed below.

Examination

The first step in the evaluation process is to establish a position of subtalar neutral. The patient should be prone with the distal third of the leg hanging off the end of the table (Fig. 32-19). A line should be drawn bisecting the leg from the start of the musculotendinous junction of the gastrocnemius to the distal portion of the calcaneus (Fig. 32-20).[77] With the patient still prone, the therapist palpates the talus while the forefoot is inverted and everted. One finger should palpate the talus at the anterior aspect of the fibula and another finger at the anterior

portion of the medial malleolus (Fig. 32-21). The position at which the talus is equally prominent on both sides is considered neutral subtalar position.[39] Root et al[67] describe this as the position of the subtalar joint where it is neither pronated or supinated. It is the standard position in which the foot should

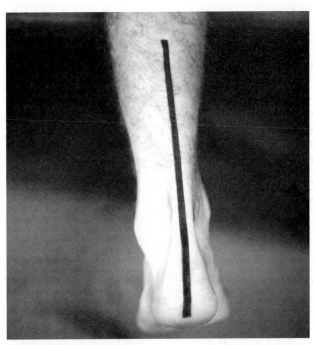

F I G U R E   3 2 - 2 0

Line bisecting the gastrocnemius and posterior calcaneus.

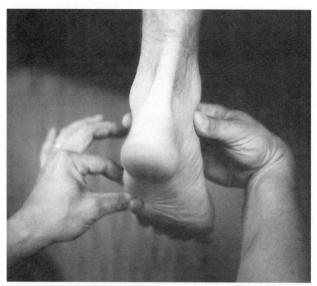

FIGURE 32-21

Palpation of the talus to determine neutral position.

be placed to examine deformities.[60] In this position, the lines on the lower leg and calcaneus should form a straight line. Any variance is considered to be a rearfoot valgus or varus deformity. The most common deformity of the foot is a rearfoot varus deformity.[54] A deviation of 2 to 3 degrees is normal.[82]

Another method of determining subtalar neutral position involves the lines that were drawn previously on the leg and back of the heel. With the patient prone, the heel is swung into full eversion and inversion, with measurements taken at each position. Angles of the two lines are taken at each extreme. Neutral position is considered two-thirds away from maximum inversion or one-third away from maximum eversion. The normal foot pronates 6 to 8 degrees from neutral.[67] For example, from neutral position a foot inverts 27 degrees and everts 3 degrees. The position at which this foot is neither pronated nor supinated is that point at which the calcaneus is inverted 7 degrees.

Once the subtalar joint is placed in a neutral position, mild dorsiflexion should be applied while observing the metatarsal heads in relation to the plantar surface of the calcaneous. Forefoot varus is an osseous deformity in which the medial metatarsal heads are inverted in relation to the plane of the calcaneus (see Fig. 32-10). Forefoot varus is the most common cause of excessive pronation, according to Subotnick.[74] Forefoot valgus is a position in which the lateral metatarsals are everted in relation to the rearfoot (see Fig. 32-11). These forefoot deformities are benign in a nonweight-bearing position, but in stance the foot or metatarsal heads must somehow get to the floor to bear weight. This movement is accomplished by the talus rolling down and in and the calcaneus everting for a forefoot varus. For the forefoot valgus, the calcaneus inverts and the talus abducts and dorsiflexes. McPoil et al[54] report that forefoot valgus is the most common forefoot deformity in their sample group.

In a rearfoot varus deformity, when the foot is in subtalar neutral position nonweight-bearing, the medial metatarsal heads are elevated as in a forefoot varus, and the calcaneous is also in an inverted position. To get to foot flat in weight bearing, the subtalar joint must pronate (see Fig. 32-12). Minimal osseous deformities of the forefoot have little effect on the function of the foot. When either forefoot varus or valgus is too large, the foot compensates through abnormal movements to bear weight.

Constructing Orthotics

Almost any problem of the lower extremity appears at one time to have been treated by orthotic therapy. The use of orthotics in control of foot deformities has been argued for many years.[4,15,17,29,39,66,74,76,83] The normal foot functions most efficiently when no deformities are present that predispose it to injury or exacerbation of existing injuries. Orthotics are used to control abnormal compensatory movements of the foot by "bringing the floor to the foot."[36]

The foot functions most efficiently in neutral position. By providing support so that the foot does not have to move abnormally, an orthotic should help prevent compensatory problems. For problems that have already occurred, the orthotic provides a platform of support so that soft tissues can heal properly without undue stress.

Basically there are three types of orthotics:

1. Pads and soft flexible felt supports (Fig. 32-22). These soft inserts are readily fabricated and are advocated for mild

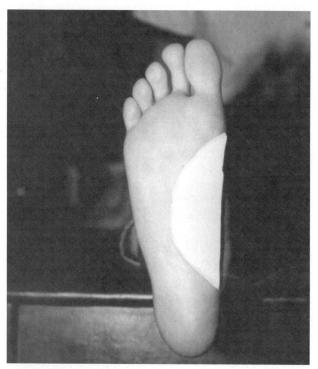

FIGURE 32-22

Felt pads.

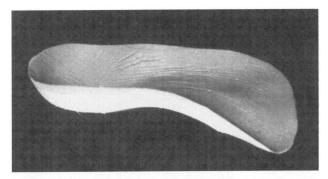

FIGURE 32-23

Semirigid orthotics.

overuse syndromes. Pads are particularly useful in shoes, such as spikes and ski boots, that are too narrow to hold orthotics.

2. Semirigid orthotics made of flexible thermoplastics, rubber, or leather (Fig. 32-23). These orthotics are prescribed for patients who have increased symptoms. These orthotics are molded from a neutral cast. They are well tolerated by patients whose sports require speed or jumping.

3. Functional or rigid orthotics are made from hard plastic and also require neutral casting (Fig. 32-24). These orthotics allow control for most overuse symptoms.[36,46,76]

Many therapists make a neutral mold, put it in a box, mail it to an orthotic laboratory, and several weeks later receive an orthotic back in the mail. Others like to complete the entire orthotic from start to finish, which requires a much more skilled technician than the mail-in method, as well as approximately $1000 in equipment and supplies. The obvious advantage is cost if many orthotics are to be made.

No matter which method is chosen, the first step is the fabrication of the neutral mold, done with the patient in the same position used to determine subtalar neutral position. Once subtalar neutral is found, three layers of plaster splints are applied to the plantar surface and sides of the foot (Fig. 32-25). Subtalar neutral position is maintained as pressure is applied on the fifth metatarsal area in a dorsiflexion direction until the midtarsal joint is locked (Fig. 32-26). This position is held until

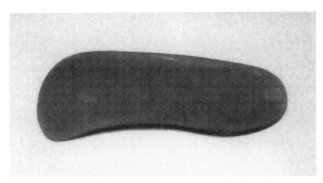

FIGURE 32-24

Hard orthotic.

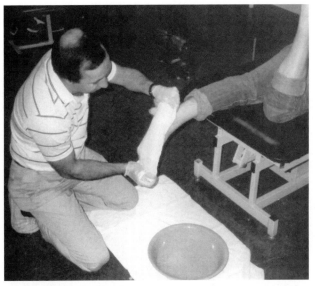

FIGURE 32-25

Three layers of plaster form neutral mold.

the plaster dries. At this point the plaster cast may be sent out to have the orthotic made or it may be finished (Fig. 32-27). If it is mailed out, the appropriate measurements of forefoot and rearfoot positions should be sent, along with any extrinsic measurements. If the orthotic is to be fabricated in-house, the plaster cast should be liberally lined interiorly with talc or powder. Plaster of paris should then be poured into the cast to form a positive mold of the foot (Fig. 32-28).

Many different materials may be used to fabricate an orthotic from the positive mold. The author uses 1/8-inch Aliplast covering (Alimed Inc., Boston) with a 1/4-inch Plastazote

FIGURE 32-26

Mild pressure over the fifth metatarsal to lock the midtarsal joint.

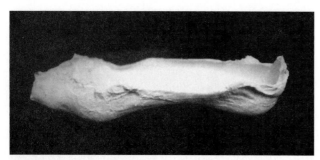

underneath. A rectangular piece of each material large enough to completely encompass the lower third of the mold is cut. These two pieces are placed in a convection oven (Fig. 32-29) at approximately 275°F. At this temperature the two materials bond together and become moldable in about 5 to 7 minutes. At this time the orthotic materials are removed from the oven and placed on the positive mold (Fig. 32-30). Ideally, a form or vacuum press should be used to form the orthotic to the mold.[36]

Once cooled, the uncut orthotic is placed under the foot while the patient sits in a chair (Fig. 32-31). Excess material is then trimmed from the sides of the orthotic with scissors. Any material that can be seen protruding from either side of the foot should be trimmed (Fig. 32-32) to provide the proper width of the orthotic. The length should be trimmed so that the end of the orthotic bisects the metatarsal heads (Fig. 32-33). This style is slightly longer than most orthotics that are made, but the author has found that this length provides better comfort.[36]

Next, a third layer of medial Plastazote may be glued to the arch to fill that area to the floor. Grinding begins with the sides of the orthotic, which should be ground so that the sides

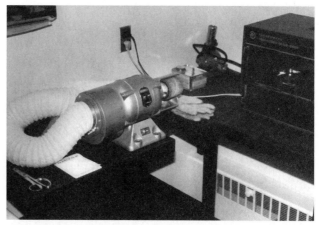

F I G U R E   3 2 - 2 9

Convection oven and grinder.

are slightly beveled inward (Fig. 32-34) to allow better shoe fit. The bottom of the orthotic is leveled so that the surface is perpendicular to the bisection of the calcaneus. Grinding is continued until very little Plastazote remains under the Aliplast at the heel. The forefoot is posted by selectively grinding Plastazote just proximal to the metatarsal heads. Forefoot varus is posted by grinding more laterally than medially. Forefoot valgus requires grinding more medially than laterally. The final step is to grind the distal portion of the orthotic so that only a very thin piece of Aliplast is under the area where the orthotic ends. This prevents discomfort under the forefoot where the orthotic stops. If the patient feels that this area is a problem, a full insole of Spenco or other material may be used to cover the orthotic to the end of the shoe to eliminate the drop-off sometimes felt as the orthotic ends.

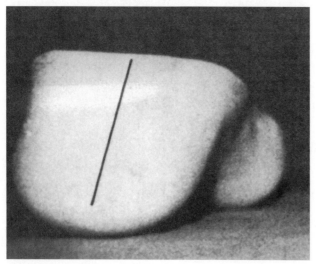

F I G U R E   3 2 - 2 8

Positive mold.

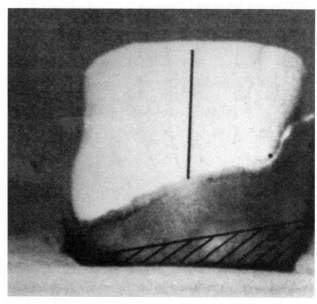

F I G U R E   3 2 - 3 0

Orthotic material on the positive mold.

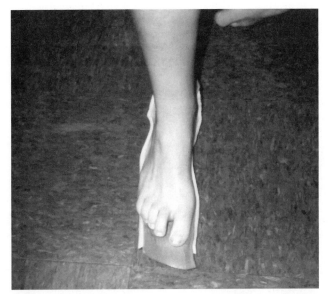

FIGURE 32-31

Orthotic mold under the foot with patient sitting.

Time must be allowed for proper break-in. The patient should wear the orthotic for 3 to 4 hours the first day, 6 to 8 hours the next day, and then all day on the third day. Physical activities should be started with the orthotic only after it has been worn all day for several days.[36]

Shoe Selection

The shoe is one of the biggest considerations in treating a foot problem.[75] Even a properly made orthotic is less effective if placed in a poorly constructed shoe.

As noted, pronation is a problem of hypermobility. Pronated feet need stability and firmness to reduce this excess movement. Research indicates that shoe compression may actually increase pronation versus a barefoot condition.[3] The ideal shoe for a pronated foot is less flexible and has good rearfoot control.

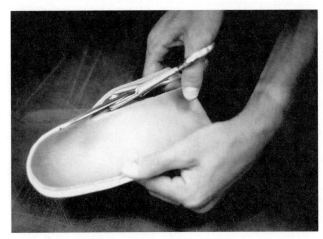

FIGURE 32-32

Trim excess material from orthotic.

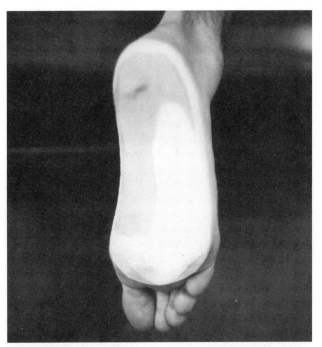

FIGURE 32-33

The length of the orthotic should bisect the metatarsal heads.

Conversely, supinated feet are usually very rigid. Increased cushion and flexibility benefit this type of foot. Several construction factors may influence the firmness and stability of a shoe. The basic form upon which a shoe is built is called the last.[3] The upper is fitted onto a last in several ways. Each method has its own flexibility and control characteristics. A slip-lasted shoe is sewn together like a moccasin (Fig. 32-35) and is very flexible. Board-lasting provides a piece of fiberboard upon which the upper is attached (Fig. 32-36), which provides a very firm, inflexible base for the shoe. A combination-lasted shoe is boarded in the back half of the shoe and slip-lasted in the front (Fig. 32-37), which provides rearfoot stability with forefoot mobility. The shape of the last may also be used in shoe selection. Most patients with excessive pronation perform better in

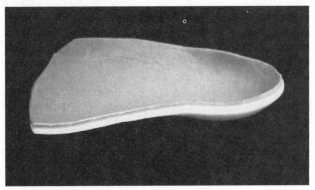

FIGURE 32-34

Sides of the orthotic should be leveled inward.

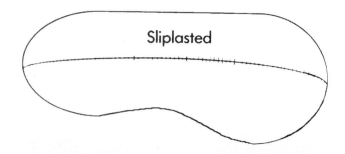

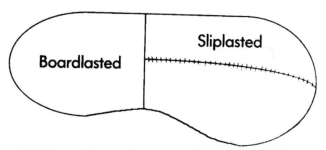

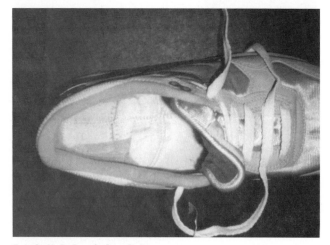

FIGURE 32-35

Slip-lasted shoe.

FIGURE 32-37

Combination-lasted shoe.

a straight-lasted shoe,[3] that is, a shoe in which the forefoot does not curve inward in relation to the rearfoot. Midsole design also affects the stability of a shoe. The midsole separates the upper from the outsole.[11] Ethylene vinyl acetate (EVA) is one of the most commonly used materials in the midsole.[61] Often, denser EVA, which is colored differently to show that it is denser, is placed under the medial aspect of the foot to control pronation (Fig. 32-38).

In an effort to control rearfoot movement, many shoe manufacturers have reinforced the heel counter both internally and

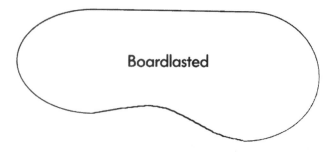

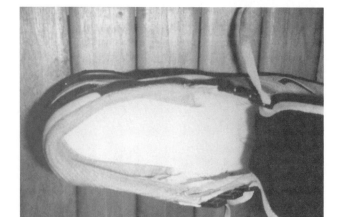

FIGURE 32-36

Board-lasted shoe.

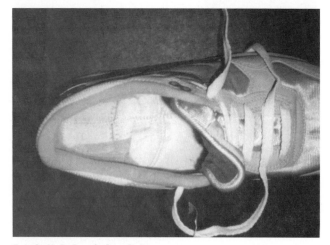

FIGURE 32-38

EVA in a midsole.

FIGURE 32-39

External heel counter.

externally, often in the form of extra plastic along the outside of the heel counter (Fig. 32-39).[51] Other factors that may affect the performance of a shoe are the outsole contour and composition, lacing systems, and forefoot wedges.

Shoe Wear Patterns

Patients with excessive pronation often wear out the front of the running shoe under the second metatarsal (Fig. 32-40). Shoe wear patterns are commonly misinterpreted by patients who think they must be pronators because they wear out the back outside edges of their heels. Actually, most people wear out the back outside edges of their shoes. Just before heelstrike, the anterior tibial muscle fires to prevent the foot from slapping forward. The anterior tibialis muscle not only dorsiflexes the foot but also slightly inverts it, hence the wear pattern on the

FIGURE 32-40

Front forefoot of a running shoe showing the typical wear pattern of a pronator.

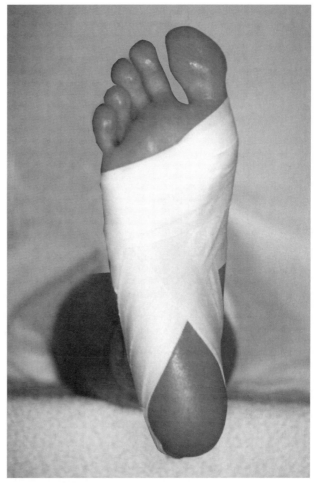

FIGURE 32-41

Low-dye taping for arch support.

back edge of the shoe. The key to inspection of wear patterns on shoes is observation of the heel counter and the forefoot.

Stress Fractures in the Foot

PATHOMECHANICS AND INJURY MECHANISM

The most common stress fractures in the foot involve the navicular, second metatarsal (March fracture), and diaphysis of the fifth metatarsal (Jones fracture). Navicular and second metatarsal stress fractures are likely to occur with excessive foot pronation, while fifth metatarsal stress fractures tend to occur in a more rigid pes cavus foot.

Navicular Stress Fractures

Individuals who excessively pronate during running gait are likely to develop a stress fracture of the navicular. Of the tarsal bones it is the most likely to have a stress fracture.

Second Metatarsal Stress Fractures

Second metatarsal stress fractures occur most often in running and jumping sports. As is the case with other injuries in the foot associated with overuse, the most common causes include rearfoot varus and forefoot varus structural deformities in the foot that result in excessive pronation; training errors; changes in training surfaces; and wearing inappropriate shoes. The base of the second metatarsal extends proximally into the distal row of tarsal bones and is held rigid and stable by the bony architecture and ligament support. In addition, the second metatarsal is particularly subjected to increased stress with excessive pronation, which causes a hypermobile foot. In addition, if the second metatarsal is longer than the first, as seen with a Morton's toe, it is theoretically subjected to greater bone stress during running. A bone scan, as opposed to a standard radiograph, is frequently necessary for diagnosis.

Fifth Metatarsal Stress Fractures

Fifth metatarsal stress fractures can occur from overuse, acute inversion, or high-velocity rotational forces. A Jones fracture occurs at the diaphysis of the fifth metatarsal most often as a sequela of a stress fracture.[68] The patient will complain of a sharp pain on the lateral border of the foot and will usually report hearing a "pop." Because of a history of poor blood supply and delayed healing, a Jones fracture may result in nonunion, requiring an extended period of rehabilitation.

REHABILITATION CONCERNS

Rehabilitation efforts for stress fractures should focus on determining the precipitating cause or causes and alleviating them. Second metatarsal stress fractures tend to do well with modified rest and nonweight-bearing exercises such as pool running (see Exercise 32-44), upper-body ergometer (see Exercise 32-45), or stationary bike (see Exercise 32-46) to maintain the patient's cardiorespiratory fitness for 2 to 4 weeks. This is followed by a progressive return to running and jumping sports over a 2- to 3-week period using appropriately constructed orthotics and appropriate shoes.

Stress fractures of both the navicular of the proximal shaft of the fifth metatarsal usually require more aggressive treatment, requiring nonweight-bearing short leg casts for 6 to 8 weeks for nondisplaced fractures. With cases of delayed union, nonunion, or especially displaced fractures, both the Jones and navicular fractures require internal fixation, with or without bone grafting. In the highly active patient, immediate internal fixation should be recommended.

Plantar Fasciitis

PATHOMECHANICS

Heel pain is a very common problem that may be attributed to several etiologies, including heel spurs, plantar fascia irritation, and bursitis. Plantar fasciitis is a catchall term that is commonly used to describe pain in the proximal arch and heel.

The plantar fascia (plantar aponeurosis) runs the length of the sole of the foot. It is a broad band of dense connective tissue that is attached proximally to the medial surface of the calcaneus. It fans out distally, with fibers and their various small branches attaching to the metatarsophalangeal articulations and merging into the capsular ligaments. Other fibers, arising from well within the aponeurosis, pass between the intrinsic muscles of the foot and the long flexor tendons of the sole and attach themselves to the deep fascia below the bones. The function of the plantar aponeurosis is to assist in maintaining the stability of the foot and in securing or bracing the longitudinal arch.[77]

Tension develops in the plantar fascia both during extension of the toes and during depression of the longitudinal arch as the result of weight bearing. When the weight is principally on the heel, as in ordinary standing, the tension exerted on the fascia is negligible. However, when the weight is shifted to the ball of the foot (on the heads of the metatarsals), fascial tension is increased. In running, because the push-off phase involves both a forceful extension of the toes and a powerful thrust by the ball of the foot (on the heads of the metatarsals), fascial tension is increased to approximately twice the body weight.

Patients who have a mild pes cavus are particularly prone to fascial strain. Modern street shoes, by nature of their design, take on the characteristics of splints and tend to restrict foot action to such an extent that the arch may become somewhat rigid. This occurs because of shortening of the ligaments and other mild abnormalities. The patient, when changing from dress shoes to softer, more flexible athletic shoes, often develops irritation of the plantar fascia. Trauma may also result from poor running technique. Lumbar lordosis, a condition in which an increased forward tilt of the pelvis produces an unfavorable angle of footstrike when there is considerable force exerted on the ball of the foot, can also contribute to this problem.

INJURY MECHANISM

A number of anatomic and biomechanical conditions have been studied as possible causes of plantar fasciitis. They include leg length discrepency, excessive pronation of the subtalar joint, inflexibility of the longitudinal arch, and tightness of the gastrocnemius–soleus unit. Wearing shoes without sufficient arch support, a lengthened stride during running, and running on soft surfaces are also potential causes of plantar fasciitis.

The patient complains of pain in the anterior medial heel, usually at the attachment of the plantar fascia to the calcaneus, that eventually moves more centrally into the central portion of the plantar fascia. This pain is particularly troublesome upon arising in the morning or upon bearing weight after sitting for a long period. However, the pain lessens after a few steps. Pain also will be intensified when the toes and forefoot are forcibly dorsiflexed.

REHABILITATION CONCERNS

Orthotic therapy is very useful in the treatment of this problem. The authors have found that soft orthotics in combination with exercises can significantly reduce the pain level of these patients.

A soft orthotic works better than a hard orthotic. An extra-deep heel cup should be built into the orthotic. The orthotic should be worn at all times, especially upon arising from bed

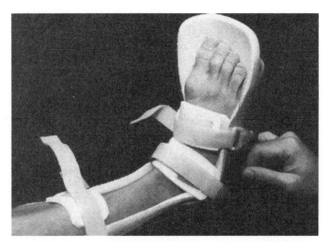

FIGURE 32-42

Night splint for plantar fasciitis.

in the morning. Always have the patient step into the orthotic rather than ambulating barefooted.[10] When soft orthotics are not feasible, taping may reduce the symptoms. A simple arch taping or alternative taping often allows pain-free ambulation.[86] Use of a heel cup compresses the fat pad under the calcaneous, providing a cushion under the area of irritation.

The use of a night splint to maintain a position of static stretch has also been recommended (Fig. 32-42). In some cases it may be necessary to use a short leg walking cast for 4 to 6 weeks.

Vigorous heel-cord stretching should be used, along with an exercise to stretch the plantar fascia in the arch. Exercises that increase dorsiflexion of the great toe also may be of benefit to this problem (see Exercises 32-22 and 32-25). Stretching should be done at least 3 times a day.

Anti-inflammatory medications are recommended. Steroidal injection may be warranted at some point if symptoms fail to resolve.

Management of plantar fasciitis will generally require an extended period of treatment. It is not uncommon for symptoms to persist for as long as 8 to 12 weeks. Persistence on the part of the patient in doing the recommended stretching exercises is critical.

Cuboid Subluxation

PATHOMECHANICS

A condition that often mimics plantar fasciitis is cuboid subluxation. Pronation and trauma have been reported to be prominent causes of this syndrome.[84] This displacement of the cuboid causes pain along the fourth and fifth metatarsals, as well as over the cuboid. The primary reason for pain is the stress placed on the long peroneal muscle when the foot is in pronation. In this position, the long peroneal muscle allows the cuboid bone to move downward medially. This problem often refers pain to the heel area as well. Many times this pain is increased upon arising after a prolonged nonweight-bearing period.

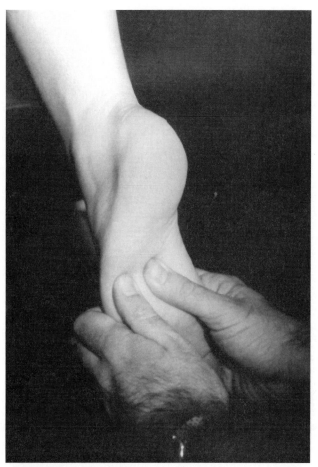

FIGURE 32-43

Prone position for cuboid manipulation.

REHABILITATION CONSIDERATIONS

Dramatic treatment results may be obtained by manipulation technique to restore the cuboid to its natural position. The manipulation is done with the patient prone (Fig. 32-43). The plantar aspect of the forefoot is grasped by the thumbs with the fingers supporting the dorsum of the foot. The thumbs should be over the cuboid. The manipulation should be a thrust downward to move the cuboid into its more dorsal position. Often a pop is felt as the cuboid moves back into place. Once the cuboid is manipulated, an orthotic often helps to support it in its proper position.

If manipulation is successful, quite often the patient can return to normal function immediately with little or no pain. It should be recommended that the patient wear an appropriately constructed orthotic to reduce the chances of recurrence.

Hallux Valgus Deformity (Bunions)

PATHOMECHANICS AND INJURY MECHANISM

A bunion is a deformity of the head of the first metatarsal in which the large toe assumes a valgus position (Fig. 32-44). Commonly it is associated with a structural forefoot varus in which

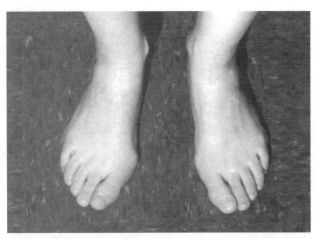

FIGURE 32-44

Hallux valgus deformity with a bunion.

the first ray tends to splay outward, putting pressure on the first metatarsal head. The bursa over the first metatarsophalangeal joint becomes inflamed and eventually thickens. The joint becomes enlarged and the great toe becomes malaligned, moving laterally toward the second toe, sometimes to such an extent that it eventually overlaps the second toe. This type of bunion may also be associated with a depressed or flattened transverse arch. Often the bunion occurs from wearing shoes that are pointed, too narrow, too short, or have high heels.

A bunion is one of the most frequent painful deformities of the great toe. As the bunion is developing there is tenderness, swelling, and enlargement with calcification of the head of the first metatarsal. Poorly fitting shoes increase the irritation and pain.

REHABILITATION CONCERNS

If the condition progresses, a special orthotic device may help normalize foot mechanics. Often an orthotic designed to correct a structural forefoot varus that can help increase stability of the first ray significantly reduces the symptoms and progression of a bunion. Shoe selection may also play an important role in the treatment of bunions. Shoes of the proper width cause less irritation to the bunion. Local therapy, including moist heat, soaks, and ultrasound, may alleviate some of the acute symptoms of a bunion. Protective devices such as wedges, pads, and tape can also be used. Surgery to correct the hallux valgus deformity is very common during the later stages of this condition.

Morton's Neuroma

PATHOMECHANICS

A neuroma is a mass occurring about the nerve sheath of the common plantar nerve while it divides into the two digital branches to adjacent toes. It occurs most commonly between the metatarsal heads and is the most common nerve problem of the lower extremity. A Morton's neuroma is located between the third and fourth metatarsal heads where the nerve is the thickest, receiving both branches from the medial and lateral plantar nerves. The patient complains of severe intermittent pain radiating from the distal metatarsal heads to the tips of the toes and is often relieved when nonweight-bearing. Irritation increases with the collapse of the transverse arch of the foot, putting the transverse metatarsal ligaments under stretch and thus compressing the common digital nerve and vessels. Excessive foot pronation can also be a predisposing factor, with more metatarsal shearing forces occurring with the prolonged forefoot abduction.

The patient complains of a burning paresthesia in the forefoot that is often localized to the third web space and radiating to the toes.[76] Hyperextension of the toes on weight bearing—as in squatting, stair climbing, or running—can increase the symptoms. Wearing shoes with a narrow toe box or high heels can increase the symptoms. If there is prolonged nerve irritation, the pain can become constant. A bone scan is often necessary to rule out a metatarsal stress fracture.

REHABILITATION CONCERNS

Orthotic therapy is essential to reduce the shearing movements of the metatarsal heads. To increase this effect, often either a metatarsal bar is placed just proximal to the metatarsal heads or a teardrop-shaped pad is placed between the heads of the third and fourth metatarsals in an attempt to have these splay apart with weight bearing (Fig. 32-45). It may decrease pressure on the affected area.

Therapeutic modalities can be used to help reduce inflammation. The author has used phonophoresis with hydrocortisone with some success in symptom reduction.

Shoe selection also plays an important role in treatment of neuromas. Narrow shoes, particularly women's shoes that are pointed in the toe area and certain men's boots, may squeeze the metatarsal heads together and exacerbate the problem. A shoe that is wide in the toe box area should be selected. A straight-laced shoe often provides increased space in the toe box.[71] Often, appropriate soft orthotic padding will markedly reduce pain.

On a rare occasion surgical excision may be required.

Turf Toe

PATHOMECHANICS AND INJURY MECHANISM

Turf toe is a hyperextension injury that usually occurs in the athletic population and results in a sprain of the metatarsophalangeal joint of the great toe, either from repetitive overuse or trauma.[81] Typically, this injury occurs on unyielding synthetic turf, although it can occur on grass also. Many of these injuries occur because artificial turf shoes often are more flexible and allow more dorsiflexion of the great toe.

REHABILITATION CONCERNS

Some shoe companies have addressed this problem by adding steel or other materials to the forefoot of their turf shoes to

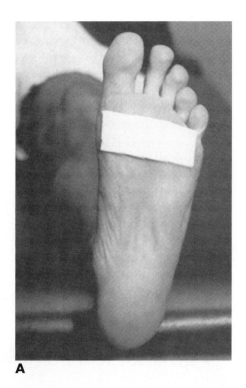
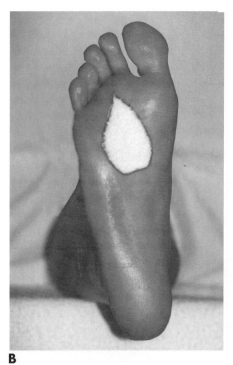

FIGURE 32-45

A, Metatarsal bar. **B,** Teardrop pad.

stiffen them. Flat insoles that have thin sheets of steel under the forefoot are also available. When commercially made products are not available, a thin, flat piece of Orthoplast may be placed under the shoe insole or may be molded to the foot.[81] Taping the toe to prevent dorsiflexion may be done separately or with one of the shoe-stiffening suggestions (Fig. 32-46).

Modalities of choice include ice and ultrasound. One of the major ingredients in any treatment for turf toe is rest.

In less severe cases, patient can continue normal activities with the addition of a rigid insole. With more severe sprains, 3 to 4 weeks may be required for pain to reduce to the point where the patient can push off on the great toe.

Tarsal Tunnel Syndrome

PATHOMECHANICS AND INJURY MECHANISM

The tarsal tunnel is a loosely defined area about the medial malleolus that is bordered by the retinaculum, which binds the tibial nerve.[29] Pronation, overuse problems such as tendinitis, and trauma may cause neurovascular problems in the ankle and foot. Symptoms may vary, with pain, numbness, and paresthesia reported along the medial ankle and into the sole of the foot.[6] Tenderness may be present over the tibial nerve area behind the medial malleolus.

REHABILITATION CONCERNS

Neutral foot control may alleviate symptoms in less involved cases. Surgery is often performed if symptoms do not respond

to conservative treatment or if weakness occurs in the flexors of the toes.[6]

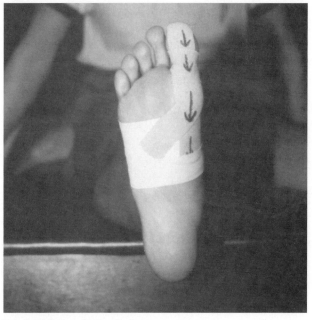

FIGURE 32-46

Turf toe taping.

EXERCISES

REHABILITATION TECHNIQUES

Strengthening Exercises

ISOMETRIC STRENGTHENING EXERCISES

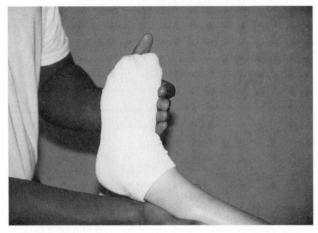

E X E R C I S E   3 2 - 1

Isometric inversion against a stable object. Used to strengthen the posterior tibialis, flexor digitorum longus, and flexor hallucis longus.

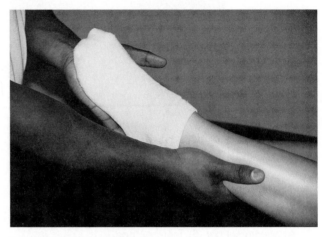

E X E R C I S E   3 2 - 3

Isometric plantarflexion against a stable object. Used to strengthen the gastrocnemius, soleus, posterior tibialis, flexor digitorum longus, flexor hallucis longus, and plantaris.

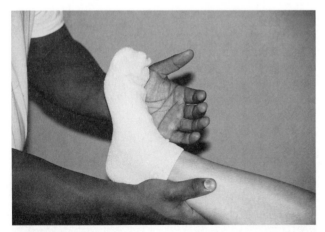

E X E R C I S E   3 2 - 2

Isometric eversion against a stable object. Used to strengthen the peroneus longus, brevis, tertius, and extensor digitorum longus.

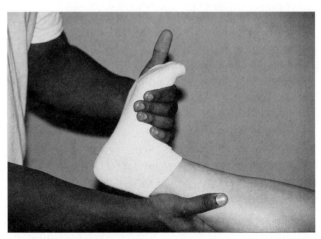

E X E R C I S E   3 2 - 4

Isometric dorsiflexion against a stable object. Used to strengthen the anterior tibialis and peroneus tertius.

ISOTONIC OPEN-CHAIN STRENGTHENING EXERCISES

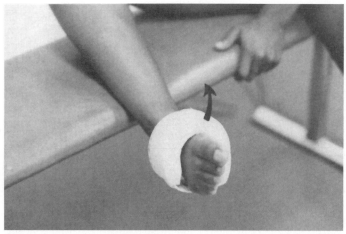

A

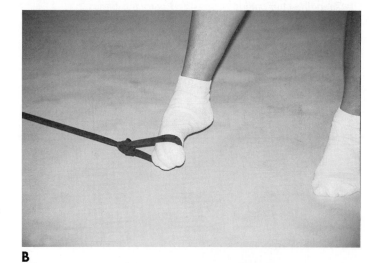

B

EXERCISE 3 2 - 5

Inverion exercise. **A,** Using a weight cuff, **B,** Using resistive tubing. Used to strengthen the posterior tibialis, flexor digitorum longus, and flexor hallucis longus.

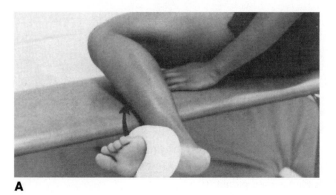

A

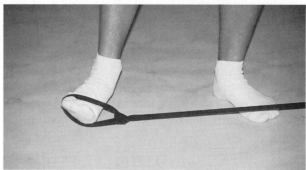

B

EXERCISE 3 2 - 6

Everion exercise. **A,** Using a weight cuff, **B,** Using resistive tubing. Used to strengthen the peroneus longus, brevis, tertius, and extensor digitorum longus.

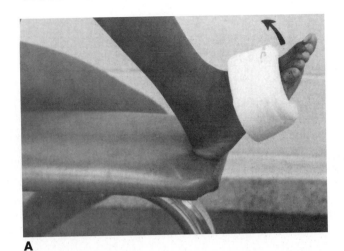
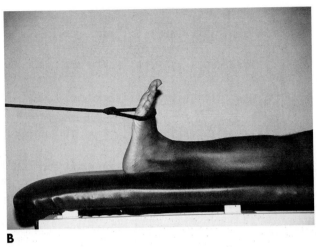

A   B

E X E R C I S E   3 2 - 7

Dorsiflexion exercise. **A,** Using a weight cuff. **B,** Using resistive tubing. Used to strengthen the anterior tibialis and peroneus tertius.

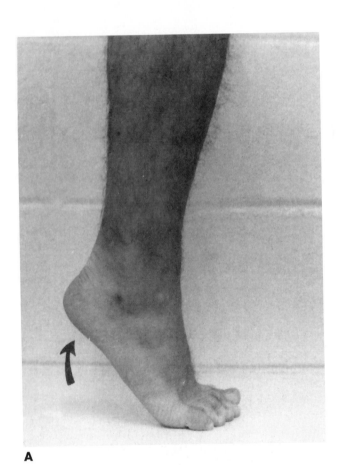
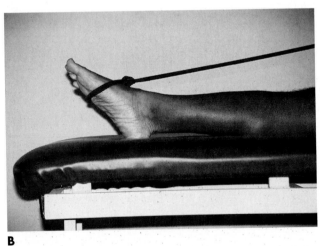

A   B

E X E R C I S E   3 2 - 8

Plantarflexion exercise using surgical tubing. Used to strengthen the gastrocnemius, soleus, posterior tibialis, flexor digitorum longus, flexor hallucis longus, and plantaris.

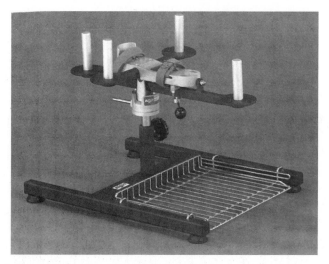

EXERCISE 3 2 - 9

Multidirectional Elgin ankle exerciser.

EXERCISE 3 2 - 1 0

Toe raises. Used to strengthen the gastrocnemius, soleus, posterior tibialis, flexor digitorum longus, flexor hallucis longus, and plantaris. **A,** Toe raises with extended knee strengthens the gastrocnemius. **B,** Toe raises with flexed knee strengthens the soleus.

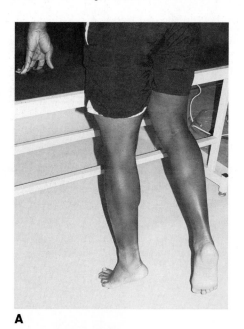

A

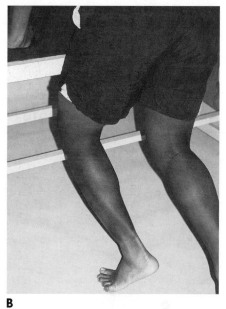

B

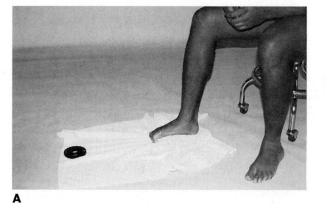

A

B

EXERCISE 3 2 - 1 1

Towel gathering exercise. **A,** Toe flexion. Used to strengthen the flexor digitorum longus and brevis, lumbricales, and flexor hallucis longus. **B,** Inversion/eversion exercises. Used to strengthen the posterior tibialis, flexor digitorum longus, flexor hallucis longus, peroneus longus, brevis, tertius, and extensor digitorum longus.

CLOSED-CHAIN STRENGTHENING EXERCISES

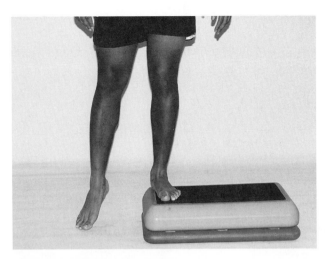

E X E R C I S E   3 2 - 1 2

Lateral step-ups.

E X E R C I S E   3 2 - 1 4

Shuttle exercise machine.

ISOKINETIC STRENGTHENING EXERCISES

E X E R C I S E   3 2 - 1 3

Slide board exercises.

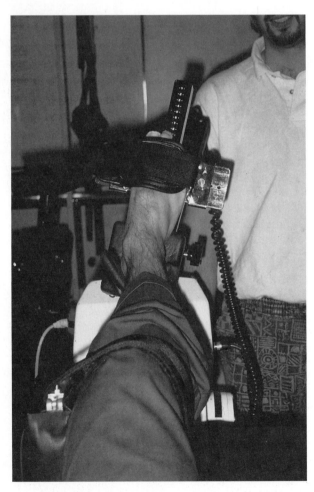

E X E R C I S E   3 2 - 1 5

Isokinetic inverion/eversion exercise. Used to improve the strength and endurance of the ankle inverters and everters in an open chain. Also can provide an objective measurement of muscular torque production.

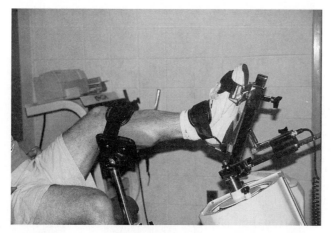

EXERCISE 32-16

Isokinetic plantarflexion/dorsiflexion exercise. Used to improve the strength and endurance of the ankle dorsiflexers and plantarflexers in an open chain. Also can provide an objective measurement of torque production.

PNF STRENGTHENING EXERCISES

EXERCISE 32-17

D1 pattern moving into flexion. **A,** Starting position: ankle plantarflexed, foot everted, toes flexed. **B,** Terminal position: ankle dorsiflexed, foot inverted, toes extended.

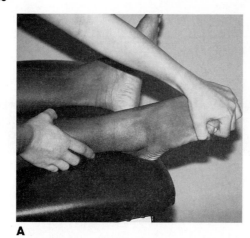

A

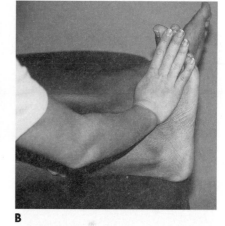

B

EXERCISE 32-18

D1 pattern moving into extension. **A,** Starting position: ankle dorsiflexed, foot inverted, toes extended. **B,** Terminal position: ankle plantarflexed, foot everted, toes flexed.

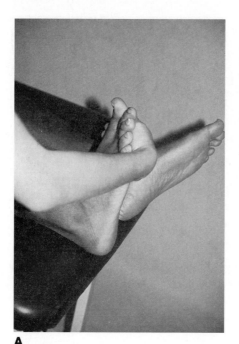

A

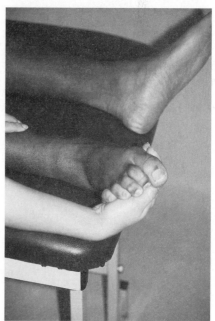

B

EXERCISE 32-19

D2 pattern moving into flexion: **A,** Starting position: ankle plantarflexed, foot inverted, toes flexed. **B,** Terminal position: ankle dorsiflexed, foot everted, toes extended.

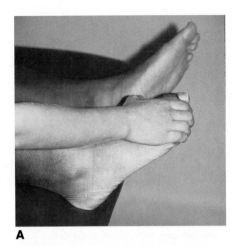

A

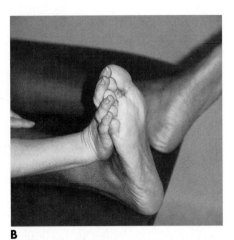

B

EXERCISE 32-20

D2 pattern moving into extension. **A,** Starting position: ankle dorsiflexed, foot everted, toes extended. **B,** Terminal position: ankle plantarflexed, foot inverted, toes flexed.

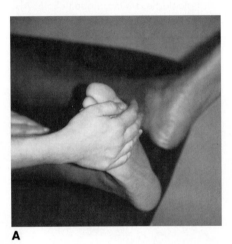

A

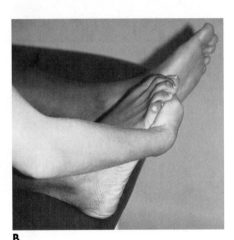

B

Stretching Exercises

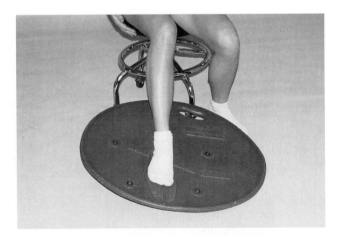

EXERCISE 32-21

Seated BAPS board exercises are an AROM exercise, useful in regaining normal ankle motion.

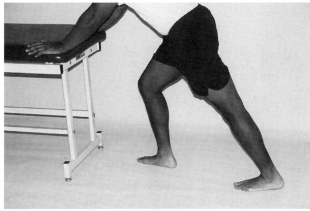

A

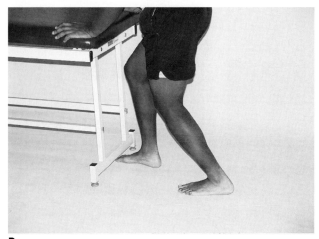

B

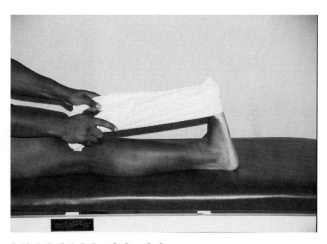

EXERCISE 32-23

Seated ankle plantarflexors stretch using a towel.

C

EXERCISE 32-22

Standing ankle plantar flexors stretch. **A**. Gastrocnemius.
B. Soleus. **C**. Stretching may also be done using a slant
board.

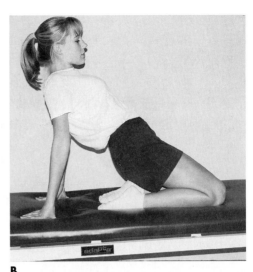

EXERCISE 32-24

Ankle dorsiflexors stretch
for the anterior tibialis. **A**.
Standing. **B**. Kneeling.

A

B

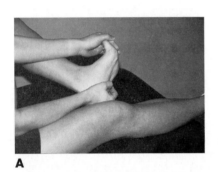

A

B

C

EXERCISE 32-25

Plantar fascia stretches. **A,** Manual. **B,** Floor stretch. **C,**
Prostretch.

Joint Mobilizations

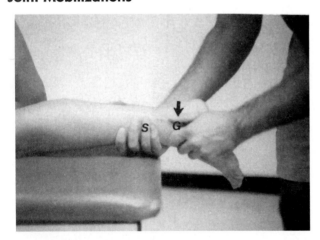

EXERCISE 32-26

Distal anterior and posterior fibular glides. Anterior and
posterior glides of the fibula may be done distally. The
tibia should be stabilized, and the fibular malleolus is
mobilized in an anterior or posterior direction.

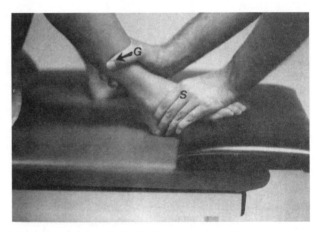

EXERCISE 32-27

Posterior tibial glides. Posterior tibial glides increase
plantarflexion. The foot should be stabilized, and
pressure on the anterior tibia produces a posterior glide.

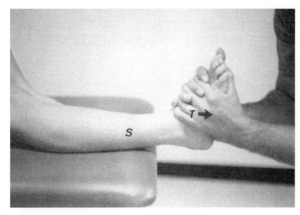

EXERCISE 32-28

Talocrural joint traction. Talocrural joint traction is performed using the patient's body weight to stabilize the lower leg and applying traction to the midtarsal portion of the foot. Traction reduces pain and increases dorsiflexion and plantarflexion.

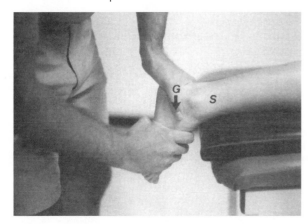

EXERCISE 32-29

Anterior talor glides. Plantarflexion may also be increased by using an anterior talar glide. With the patient prone, the tibia is stabilized on the table, and pressure is applied to the posterior aspect of the talus to glide it anteriorly.

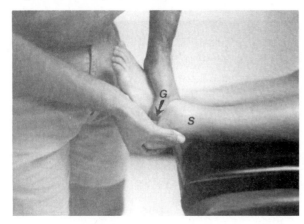

EXERCISE 32-30

Posterior talor glides. Posterior talar glides may be used for increasing dorsiflexion. With the patient supine, the tibia is stabilized on the table, and pressure is applied to the anterior aspect of the talus to glide it posteriorly.

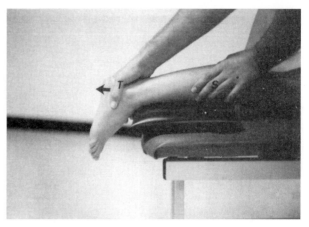

EXERCISE 32-31

Subtalar joint traction. Subtalar joint traction reduces pain and increases inversion and eversion. The lower leg is stabilized on the table, and traction is applied by grasping the posterior aspect of the calcaneus.

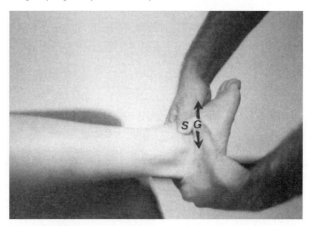

EXERCISE 32-32

Subtalar joint medial and lateral glides. Subtalar joint medial and lateral glides increase eversion and inversion. The talus must be stabilized while the calcaneus is mobilized medially to increase inversion and laterally to increase eversion.

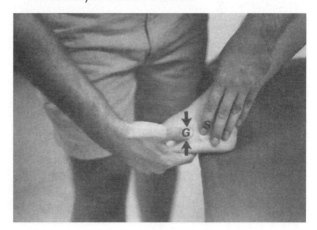

EXERCISE 32-33

Anterior/posterior calcaneocuboid glides. Anterior/posterior calcaneocuboid glides may be used for increasing adduction and abduction. The calcaneus should be stabilized while the cuboid is mobilized.

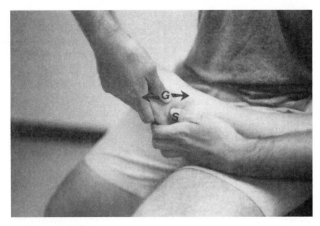

Anterior/posterior cuboid metatarsal glides. Anterior/posterior cuboid metatarsal glides are done with one hand stabilizing the cuboid and the other gliding the base of the fifth metatarsal. They are used for increasing mobility of the fifth metatarsal.

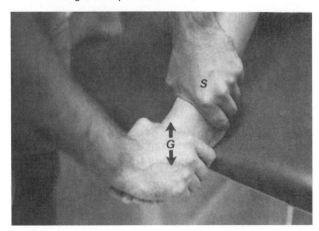

Anterior/posterior carpometacarpal glides. Anterior/posterior carpometacarpal glides decrease hypomobility of the metacarpals.

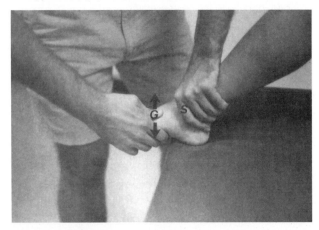

Anterior/posterior talonavicular glides. Anterior/posterior talonavicular glides also increase adduction and abduction. One hand stabilizes the talus while the other mobilizes the navicular bone.

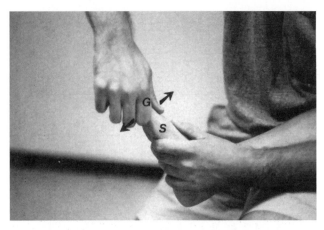

Anterior/posterior metacarpophalangeal glides. With anterior/posterior metacarpophalangeal glides, the anterior glides increase extension, and posterior glides increase flexion. Mobilizations are accomplished by isolating individual segments.

Exercises to Reestablish Neuromuscular Control

Static single standing balance progression. Used to improve balance and proprioception of the lower extremity. This activity can be made more difficult with the following progression: **A,** single leg stand/eyes open: **B,** single leg stand, eyes closed, **C,** single leg stand/eyes open/toes extended so only the heel and metatarsal heads are in contact with the ground, and **D,** single leg stand/eyes closed/toes extended.

A   B   C

EXERCISE 32-39

   Standing single leg balance board activity. Used to activate the lower leg musculature
and improve balance and proprioception of the involved extremity. **A,** BAPS board,
B, Wedge board, **C,** KAT system.

EXERCISE 32-40

   Single leg stance on an unstable surface while
performing functional activities.

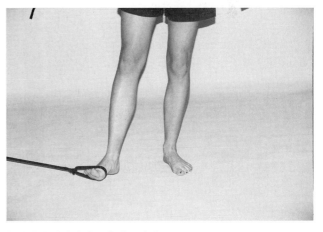

EXERCISE 32-41

Single leg standing rubber tubing kicks. Using kicks
resisted by surgical tubing of the noninvolved side while
weight bearing on the noninvolved side may encourage
neuromuscular control.

EXERCISE   32-42

Leg press.

EXERCISE   32-43

Mini-squats

Exercises to Improve Cardiorespiratory Endurance

EXERCISE   32-44

Pool running with flotation device. Used to reduce the impact of weight-bearing forces on the lower extremity while maintaining cardiovascular fitness level and running form.

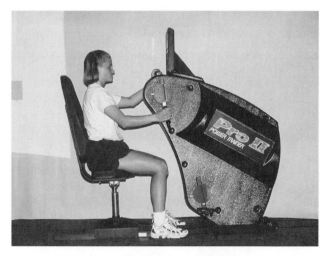

EXERCISE   32-45

Upper body ergometer. Used to maintain cardiovascular fitness when lower extremity ergometer is contraindicated or too difficult for the patient to use.

EXERCISE 32-46

Stationary exercise bike. Used to maintain cardiovascular fitness when lower extremity weight bearing is difficult.

SUMMARY

- The movements that take place at the talocrural joint are ankle plantarflexion and dorsiflexion. Inversion and eversion occur at the subtalar joint.
- The position of the subtalar joint determines whether the midtarsal joints will be hypermobile or hypomobile. Dysfunction at either joint may have a profound effect on the foot and lower extremity.
- Ankle sprains are very common. Inversion sprains usually involve the lateral ligaments of the ankle, and eversion sprains frequently involve the medial ligaments of the ankle. Rotational injuries often involve the tibiofibular and syndesmodic ligaments and may be very severe.
- The early phase of treatment uses ice, compression, elevation, rest, and protection, all of which are critical components in preventing swelling.
- Early weight bearing following ankle sprain is beneficial to the healing process. Rehabilitation may become more aggressive following the acute inflammatory response phase of healing.

- Undisplaced ankle fractures should be managed with rest and protection until the fracture has healed, while displaced fractures are treated with open reduction and internal fixation.
- Subluxation of peroneal tendons can occur from any mechanism causing sudden and forceful contraction of the peroneal muscles that involves dorsiflexion and eversion of the foot. In the case of an avulsion injury or when this becomes a chronic problem, conservative treatment is unlikely to be successful and surgery is needed to prevent the problem from recurring.
- Tendinitis in the posterior tibialis, anterior tibialis, and the peroneal tendons may result from one specific cause or from a collection of mechanisms. Techniques should be incorporated into rehabilitation that act to reduce or eliminate inflammation, including rest, using therapeutic modalities (ice, ultrasound, diathermy), and using anti-inflammatory medications.
- Excessive or prolonged supination or pronation at the subtalar joint is likely to result from some structural or functional deformity, including forefoot varus, a forefoot valgus, or a rearfoot varus, which forces the subtalar joint to compensate in a manner that will allow the weight-bearing surfaces of the foot to make stable contact with the ground and get into a weight-bearing position.
- Orthotics are used to control abnormal compensatory movements of the foot by "bringing the floor to the foot." By providing support so that the foot does not have to move abnormally, an orthotic should help prevent compensatory problems.
- Shoe selection is an important parameter in the treatment of foot problems. The type of foot will dictate specific shoe features.
- The most common stress fractures in the foot involve the navicular, second metatarsal (March fracture), and diaphysis of the fifth metatarsal (Jones fracture). Navicular and second metatarsal stress fractures are likely to occur with excessive foot pronation, while fifth metatarsal stress fractures tend to occur in a more rigid pes cavus foot.
- A number of anatomic and biomechanical conditions have been studied as possible causes of plantar fasciitis. There is pain in the anterior medial heel, usually at the attachment of the plantar fascia to the calcaneus. Orthotics in combination with stretching exercises can significantly reduce pain.
- Subluxation of the cuboid will create symptoms similar to plantar fasciitis and can be corrected with manipulation.
- A bunion is a deformity of the head of the first metatarsal in which the large toe assumes a valgus position that is commonly associated with a structural forefoot varus in which the first ray tends to splay outward, putting pressure on the first metatarsal head.
- In treating a Morton's neuroma, a metatarsal bar is placed just proximal to the metatarsal heads or a teardrop-shaped pad is placed between the heads of the third and fourth

metatarsals in an attempt to have these splay apart with weight bearing.

- Turf toe is a hyperextension injury resulting in a sprain of the metatarsophalangeal joint of the great toe.

REFERENCES

1. Andrews JR, McClod W, Ward T, et al. The cutting mechanism. *Am J Sports Med* 5:111–121, 1977.
2. Arnheim D, Prentice W. *Principles of Athletic Training*. New York, McGraw-Hill, 2000.
3. Baer T. Designing for the long run. *Mech Eng Sept* 1984, 67–75.
4. Bates BT, Osternig L, Mason B, et al. Foot orthotic devices to modify selected aspects of lower extremity mechanics. *Am J Sports Med* 7:338, 1979.
5. Baxter D. *The Foot and Ankle in Sport*. St. Louis, Mosby, 1995.
6. Birnham JS. The Musculoskeletal Manual. New York, Academic Press, 1982.
7. Bosien WR, Staples OS, Russell SW. Residual disability following acute ankle sprains. *J Bone Joint Surg Am* 37:1237, 1955.
8. Bostrum L. Treatment and prognosis in recent ligament ruptures. *Acta Chir Scand* 132:537–550, 1966.
9. Brody DM. Techniques in the evaluation and treatment of the injured runner. *Orthop Clin North Am* 13:541, 1982.
10. Brotzman B, Brasel J. Foot and ankle rehabilitation. In: Brotzman B. *Clinical Orthopaedic Rehabilitation*. St. Louis, Mosby, 1996.
11. Brunwich T, Wischnia B. Battle of the midsoles. *Runner's World*, April 1987, 47.
12. Burgess PR, Wei. J. Signalling of kinesthetic information by peripheral sensory receptors. *Annu Rev Neurosci* 5:171–187, 1982.
13. Calliet R. *Foot and Ankle Pain*. Philadelphia, Davis, 1968.
14. Canoy WF. *Review of Medical Physiology*, 7th ed. Los Altos, Lange, 1975.
15. Cavanaugh PR. An evaluation of the effects of orthotics force distribution and rearfoot movement during running. Paper presented at meeting of American Orthopedic Society for Sports Medicine, Lake Placid, 1978.
16. Choi J. Acute conditions: Incidence and associated disability. *Vital Health Stat* 120:10, 1978.
17. Collona P. Fabrication of a custom molded orthotic using an intrinsic posting technique for a forefoot varus deformity. *Phys Ther Forum* 8:3, 1989.
18. Cutler JM. Lateral ligamentous injuries of the ankle. In: Hamilton WC, ed. *Lateral Ligamentous Injuries of the Ankle*. New York, Springer-Verlag, 1984.
19. Delacerda FG. A study of anatomical factors involved in shinsplints. *J Orthop Sports Phys Ther* 2:55–59, 1980.
20. Donatelli R. Normal biomechanics of the foot and ankle. *J Orthop Sports Phys Ther* 7:91–95, 1985.
21. Donatelli R, Hurlbert C, Conaway D, et al. Biomechanical foot orthotics: A retrospective study. *J Orthop Sports Phys Ther* 10:205–212, 1988.
22. Drez D, Faust D, Evans P. Cryotherapy and nerve palsy. *Am J Sports Med* 9:256–257, 1981.
23. Freeman M, Dean M, Hanhan I. The etiology and prevention of functional instability at the foot. *J Bone Joint Surg Br* 47:678–685, 1965.
24. Fumich RM, Ellison A, Guerin G, et al. The measured effect of taping on combined foot and ankle motion before and after exercise. *Am J Sports Med* 9:165–169, 1981.
25. Garn SN, Newton RA. Kinesthetic awareness in subjects with multiple ankle sprains. *J Am Phys Ther Assoc* 68:1667–1671, 1988.
26. Garrick JG, When can I . . . ? A practical approach to rehabilitation illustrated by treatment of an ankle injury. *Am J Sports Med* 9:67–68, 1981.
27. Garrick JG, Requa RK. Role of external supports in the prevention of ankle sprains. *Med Sci Sports Exerc* 5:200, 1977.
28. Giallonardo LM. Clinical evaluation of foot and ankle dysfunction. *Phys Ther* 68:1850–1856, 1988.
29. Gill E. Orthotics. *Runner's World*, Feb 1985, 55–57.
30. Glencross D, Thornton E. Position sense following joint injury. *J Sport Med Phys Fitness* 21:23–27, 1981.
31. Glick J, Sampson T. Ankle and foot fractures in athletics. In: Nicholas J, Hershman E. *The Lower Extremity and Spine in Sports Medicine*. St. Louis, Mosby, 1996.
32. Gross M, Lapp A, Davis M. Comparison of Swed-O-Universal ankle support and Aircast Sport Stirrup orthoses and ankle tape in restricting eversion–inversion before and after exercise. *J Orthop Sports Phys Ther* 13:11–19, 1991.
33. Hirata I. Proper playing conditions. *J Sports Med* 4:228–234, 1974.
34. Hoppenfield S. *Physical Examination of the Spine and Extremities*. New York, Appleton-Century-Crofts, 1976.
35. Hunt G. Examination of lower extremity dysfunction. In: Gould J, Davies G, ed. *Orthopedic and Sports Physical Therapy*, vol. 2. St. Louis, Mosby, 1985.
36. Hunter S, Dolan M, Davis M. *Foot Orthotics in Therapy and Sports*. Champaign, IL, Human Kinetics, 1996.
37. Isakov E, Mizrahi J, Solzi P, et al. Response of the peroneal muscles to sudden inversion of the ankle during standing. *Int J Sports Biomech* 2:100–109, 1986.
38. Itay S. Clinical and functional status following lateral ankle sprains: Follow-up of 90 young adults treated conservatively. *Orthop Rev* 11:73–76, 1982.
39. James SL. Chondromalacia of the patella in the adolescent. In: Kennedy SC, ed. *The Injured Adolescent*. Baltimore, Williams & Wilkins, 1979.
40. James SL, Bates BT, Osternig LR. Injuries to runners. *Am J Sports Med* 6:43, 1978.
41. Jones D, Singer K. Soft-tissue conditions of the foot and ankle. In: Nicholas J, Hershman E, eds. The Lower

Extremity and Spine in Sports Medicine. St. Louis, Mosby, 1996.

42. Kelikian H, Kelikian AS. *Disorders of the Ankle.* Philadelphia, Saunders, 1985.

43. Kergerris S. The construction and implementation of functional progressions as a component of athletic rehabilitation. *J Orthop Sports Phys Ther* 5:14–19, 1983.

44. Klein KK. A study of cross transfer of muscular strength and endurance resulting from progressive resistive exercises following surgery. *J Assoc Phys Mental Rehabil* 9:5, 1955.

45. Kowal MA. Review of physiologic effects of cryotherapy. *J Orthop Sports Phys Ther* 5:66–73, 1983.

46. Lockard MA. Foot orthoses. *Phys Ther* 68:1866–1873, 1988.

47. Loudin J, Bell S. The foot and ankle: An overview of arthrokinematics and selected joint techniques. *J Athl Train* 31:173–178, 1996.

48. Mandelbaum BR, Finerman G, Grant T, et al. Collegiate football players with recurrent ankle sprains. *Phys Sports Med* 15:57–61, 1987.

49. Mayhew JL, Riner WF. Effects of ankle wrapping on motor performance. *Athl Train* 3:128–130, 1974.

50. McCluskey GM, Blackburn TA, Lewis T. Prevention of ankle sprains. *Am J Sports Med* 4:151–157, 1976.

51. McPoil TG. Footwear. *Phys Ther* 68:1857–1865, 1988.

52. McPoil TG, Adrian M, Pidcoe P. Effects of foot orthoses on center of pressure patterns in women. *Phys Ther* 69:149–154, 1989.

53. McPoil TG, Brocato RS. The foot and ankle: Biomechanical evaluation and treatment. In: Gould J, Davies G, eds. *Orthopedic and Sports Physical Therapy.* St. Louis, Mosby, 1985.

54. McPoil TG, Knecht HG, Schmit D. A survey of foot types in normal females between the ages of 18 and 30 years. *J Orthop Sports Phys Ther* 9:406–409, 1988.

55. Morris JM. Biomechanics of the foot and ankle. *Clin Orthop* 122:10–17, 1977.

56. Morton DJ. Foot disorders in general practice. *JAMA* 109:1112–1119, 1937.

57. Nawoczenski DA, Owen M, Ecker M, et al. Objective evaluation of peroneal response to sudden inversion stress. *J Orthop Sports Phys Ther* 7:107–119, 1985.

58. Nicholas JA, Hershman EB. The lower extremity and spine in sports medicine. St. Louis, Mosby, 1990.

59. Noyes FR. Functional properties of knee ligaments and alterations induced by immobilization: A correlative biomechanical and histological study in primates. *Clin Orthop* 123:210–243, 1977.

60. Oatis CA. Biomechanics of the foot and ankle under static conditions. *Phys Ther* 68:1815–1821, 1988.

61. Pagliano JN. Athletic footwear. *Sports Med Digest* 10:1–2, 1988.

62. Prentice W. *Therapeutic Modalities in Sports Medicine.* Dubuque, WCB/McGraw-Hill, 1999.

63. Quillen S. Alternative management protocol for lateral ankle sprains. *J Orthop Sports Phys Ther* 12:187–190, 1980.

64. Rebman LW. Ankle injuries: Clinical observations. *J. Orthop Sports Phys Ther* 8:153–156, 1986.

65. Riegler HF. Orthotic devices for the foot. *Orthop Rev* 16:293–303, 1987.

66. Rogers MM, LeVeau BF. Effectiveness of foot orthotic devices used to modify pronation in runners. *J Orthop Sports Phys Ther* 4:86–90, 1982.

67. Root ML, Orien WP, Weed JH. Normal and abnormal functions of the foot. Los Angeles, Clinical Biomechanics, 1977.

68. Sammarco JG. *Rehabilitation of the Foot and Ankle.* St. Louis, Mosby, 1995.

69. Sammarco JG. Biomechanics of foot and ankle injuries. *Athl Train* 10:96, 1975.

70. Sims D. Effects of positioning on ankle edema. *J Orthop Sports Phys Ther* 8:30–33, 1986.

71. Sims DS, Cavanaugh PR, Ulbrecht JS. Risk factors in the diabetic foot. *Phys Ther* 68:1887–1901, 1988.

72. Sloan JP, Guddings P, Hain R. Effects of cold and compression on edema. *Phys Sports Med* 16:116–120, 1988.

73. Stover CN, York JM. Air stirrup management of ankle injuries in the patient. *Am J Sports Med* 8:360–365, 1980.

74. Subotnick SI. The flat foot. *Phys Sports Med* 9:85–91, 1981.

75. Subotnick SI. *The Running Foot Doctor.* Mt. Vias, CA, World, 1977.

76. Subotnick SI, Newell SG. *Podiatric Sports Medicine.* Mt. Kisko, NY, Futura, 1975.

77. Tiberio D. Pathomechanics of structural foot deformities. *Phys Ther* 68:1840–1849, 1988.

78. Tippett SR. A case study: The need for evaluation and reevaluation of acute ankle sprains. *J Orthop Sports Phys Ther* 4:44, 1982.

79. Tropp H, Askling C, Gillquist J. Prevention of ankle sprains. *Am J Sports Med* 13:259–266, 1985.

80. Vaes P, DeBoeck H, Handleberg F, et al. Comparative radiologic study of the influence of ankle joint bandages on ankle stability. *Am J Sports Med* 13:46–49, 1985.

81. Visnich AL. A playing orthoses for "turf toe." *Athl Train* 22:215, 1987.

82. Vogelbach WD, Combs LC. A biomechanical approach to the management of chronic lower extremity pathologies as they relate to excessive pronation. *Athl Train* 22:6–16, 1987.

83. Williams JGP. The foot and chondromalacia—a case of biomechanical uncertainty. *J Orthop Sports Phys Ther* 2:50–51, 1980.

84. Woods A, Smith W. Cuboid syndrome and the techniques used for treatment. *Athl Train* 18:64–65, 1983.

85. Yablon IG, Segal D, Leach RE. *Ankle Injuries.* New York, Churchill Livingstone, 1983.

86. Zylks DR. Alternative taping for plantar fasciitis. *Athl Train* 22:317, 1987.

CHAPTER 33

Rehabilitation of Injuries to the Spine

Dan Hooker and William E. Prentice

OBJECTIVES

After completing this chapter, the student therapist should be able to do the following:

- Discuss the functional anatomy and biomechanics of the spine.
- Discuss the rationale for using the different positioning exercises for treating pain in the spine.
- Discuss the importance of a thorough evaluation of the back before developing a rehabilitative plan.
- Explain the importance of using either joint mobilization or dynamic stabilization exercises for treating spine patients.
- Describe the acute versus reinjury chronic stage model for treating low back pain.
- Explain the eclectic approach to specific conditions affecting the low back.
- Discuss the rehabilitation approach to conditions of the cervical spine.

FUNCTIONAL ANATOMY AND BIOMECHANICS

From a biomechanical perspective, the spine is one of the most complex regions of the body, with numerous bones, joints, ligaments, and muscles, all of which are collectively involved in spinal movement. The proximity to and relationship of the spinal cord, nerve roots, and peripheral nerves to the vertebral column adds to the complexity of this region. Injury to the cervical spine has potentially life-threatening implications, and low back pain is one of the most common human ailments.

The 33 vertebrae of the spine are divided into five regions: cervical, thoracic, lumbar, sacral, and coccygeal. Between each of the cervical, thoracic, and lumbar vertebrae lie fibrocartilagenous intervertebral disks, which act as important shock absorbers for the spine.

The design of the spine allows a high degree of flexibility forward and laterally and limited mobility backward. The movements of the vertebral column are flexion and extension, right and left lateral flexion, and rotation to the left and right. The degree of movement differs in the various regions of the vertebral column. The cervical and lumbar regions allow extension, flexion, and rotation around a central axis. Although the thoracic vertebrae have minimal movement, their com-

bined movement between the first and twelfth thoracic vertebrae can account for 20 to 30 degrees of flexion and extension.

As the spinal vertebrae progress downward from the cervical region, they grow increasingly larger to accommodate the upright posture of the body, as well as to contribute in weight bearing. The shape of the vertebrae is irregular, but the vertebrae possess certain characteristics that are common to all. Each vertebra consists of a neural arch through which the spinal cord passes, and several projecting processes that serve as attachments for muscles and ligaments. Each neural arch has two pedicles and two laminae. The pedicles are bony processes that project backward from the body of the vertebrae and connect with the laminae. The laminae are flat bony processes occurring on either side of the neural arch that project backward and inward from the pedicles. With the exception of the first and second cervical vertebrae, each vertebra has a spinous and transverse process for muscular and ligamentous attachment, and all vertebrae have an articular process (Fig. 33-1).

Intervertebral articulations are between vertebral bodies and vertebral arches. Articulation between the bodies is of the symphyseal type. Besides motion at articulations between the bodies of the vertebrae, movement takes place at four articular processes that derive from the pedicles and laminae. The direction of movement of each vertebra is somewhat dependent on the direction in which the articular facets face.

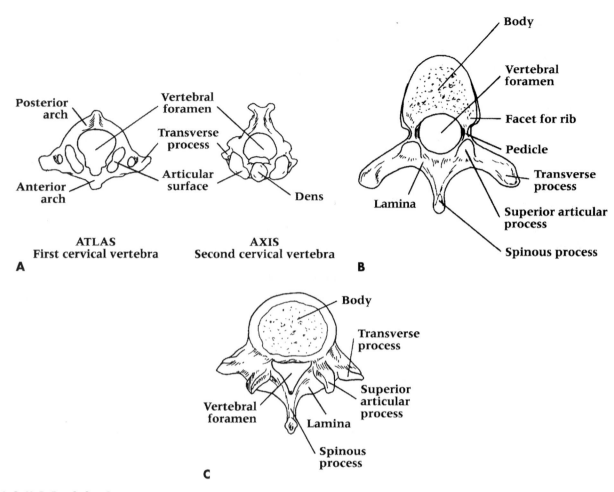

FIGURE 33-1

Anatomy of a vertebrae.

The sacrum articulates with the ilium to form the sacroiliac joint, which has a synovium and is lubricated by synovial fluid.

The major ligaments that join the various vertebral parts are the anterior longitudinal, posterior longitudinal, and supraspinous ligaments. The anterior longitudinal ligament is a wide, strong band that extends the full length of the anterior surface of the vertebral bodies. The posterior longitudinal ligament is contained within the vertebral canal and extends the full length of the posterior aspect of the bodies of the vertebrae. Ligaments connect one lamina to another. The interspinous, supraspinous, and intertransverse ligaments stabilize the transverse and spinous processes, extending between adjacent vertebrae. The sacroiliac joint is maintained by the extremely strong dorsal sacral ligaments. The sacrotuberous and the sacrospinous ligaments attach the sacrum to the ischium.

The muscles that extend the spine and rotate the vertebral column can be classified as either superficial or deep (Fig. 33-2). The superficial muscles extend from the vertebrae to ribs. The erector spinae is a group of superficial paired muscles that is made up of three columns or bands: longissimus group,

iliocostalis group, and spinalis group. Each of these groups is further divided into regions: the cervicis region in the neck, thoracis region in the middle back, and the lumborum region in the low back. Generally, the erector spinae muscles extend the spine. The deep muscles attach one vertebrae to another and function to extend and rotate the spine. The deep muscles include the interspinales, multifidus, rotatores, thoracis, and the semispinalis cervicis.

Flexion of the cervical region is produced primarily by the sternocleidomastoid muscles and the scalene muscle group on the anterior aspect of the neck. The scalenes flex the head and stabilize the cervical spine as the sternocleidomastoids flex the neck. The upper trapezius, semispinalis capitis, splenius capitus, and splenius cervicis muscles extend the neck. Lateral flexion of the neck is accomplished by all of the muscles on one side of the vertebral column contracting unilaterally. Rotation is produced when the sternocleidomastoid, scalenes, semispinalis cervicis, and upper trapezius on the side opposite to the direction of rotation contract in addition to a contraction of the splenius capitus, splenius cervicis, and longissimus capitus on the same side as the direction of rotation.

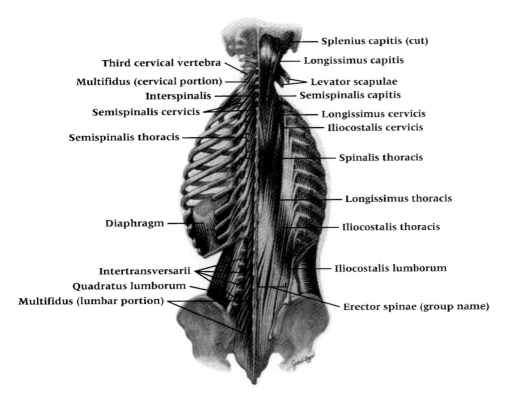

FIGURE 33-2

Deep and superficial muscles of the spine.

Flexion of the trunk primarily involves lengthening of the deep and superficial back muscles and contraction of the abdominal muscles (rectus abdominus, internal oblique, external oblique) and hip flexors (rectus femoris, iliopsoas, tensor faciae lata, sartorius). Seventy-five percent of flexion occurs at the lumbosacral junction (L5-S1), whereas 15 to 70 percent occurs between L4 and L5. The rest of the lumbar vertebrae execute 5 to 10 percent of flexion.[5] Extension involves lengthening of the abdominal muscles and contraction of the erector spinae and the gluteus maximus, which extends the hip. Trunk rotation is produced by the external obliques and the internal obliques. Lateral flexion is produced primarily by the quadratus lumborum muscle, along with the obliques, latissimus dorsi, iliopsoas, and the rectus abdominus on the side of the direction of movement.

The spinal cord is that portion of the central nervous system that is contained within the vertebral canal of the spinal column. Thirty-one pairs of spinal nerves extend from the sides of the spinal cord coursing downward and outward through the intervertebral foramen, passing near the articular facets of the vertebrae. Any abnormal movement of these facets, such as in a dislocation or a fracture, may expose the spinal nerves to injury. Injuries that occur below the third lumbar vertebra usually result in nerve root damage but do not cause spinal cord damage.

The spinal nerve roots combine to form a network of nerves or a plexus. There are five nerve plexuses: cervical, brachial, lumbar, sacral, and coccygeal.

IMPORTANCE OF EVALUATION IN TREATING BACK PAIN

In many instances after referral for medical evaluation, the patient returns to the therapist with a diagnosis of low back pain. Although this is a correct diagnosis, it does not offer the specificity needed to help direct the treatment planning. The therapist planning the treatment would be better served with a more specific diagnosis such as spondylolysis, disk herniation, quadratus lumborum strain, piriformis syndrome, or sacroiliac ligament sprain.

Regardless of the diagnosis or the specificity of the diagnosis, the importance of a thorough evaluation of the patient's back pain is critical to good care. The therapist should become an expert on this individual patient's back. Taking the time to perform a comprehensive evaluation will pay great rewards in the success of treatment and rehabilitation. The major purposes of the evaluation are to

1. Clearly locate areas and tissues that might be part of the problem. The therapist should use this information to direct treatments and exercises.[21]
2. Establish the baseline measurements used to assess progress and guide the treatment progression and help the therapist make specific judgments on the progression of or changes in specific exercises. The improvement in these

measurements also guides the return to practice and play and provides one measure of the success of the rehabilitation plan.[21]

3. Provide some provocative guidance to help patients probe the limits of their condition and help them better understand their problem, present limitations, and the management of their injury.[21]

4. Establish confidence in the therapist and increase the placebo effect of the therapist–patient interaction.[38,39]

5. Decrease the anxiety of the patient, thereby increasing patient comfort, which will increase compliance with the rehabilitation plan; a more positive environment is created, and the therapist and patient avoid the "no one knows what is wrong with me" trap.[8]

6. Provide information for making judgments on pads, braces, and corsets.

Table 33-1 provides a detailed scheme for evaluation of back pain.

T A B L E   3 3 - 1

Lumbar and Sacroiliac Joint Objective Examination

A. Observation
B. Standing position
   1. Posture—alignment
   2. Gait
      a. Patient's trunk frequently bent laterally or hips shifted to one side
      b. Walks with difficulty and limps
   3. Alignment and symmetry
      a. Level of malleoli
      b. Level of popliteal crease
      c. Trochanteric levels
      d. PSIS and ASIS positioning
      e. Levels of iliac crests
         1. If there is sacroiliac dysfunction the iliac crests will be unlevel; the ASIS and the PSIS will also be unlevel but in the opposite direction. Slight changes in leg length are probably insignificant. With shortening of 1/2 inch or more, there is a tendency for the pelvis to try to right the upper sacral surface. In the long leg, the ilium tends to move posterior or the short leg ilium moves anterior
   4. Standing forward bending of trunk—(standing flexion test)
      a. Note extent of cranial movement of the PSIS
         1. If one PSIS moves further cranially, a motion restriction is possibly present on that side of the inominates
         2. If the PSISs move at different times, the side that moves first is usually the side with restriction
   5. Lumbar spine active movements
      a. With sacroiliac dysfunction, the athlete will experience exacerbation of pain with side bending toward painful side
      b. Often a lumbar lesion is present along with sacroiliac dysfunction. Side-bending toward sacroiliac joints will often aggravate this
   6. Single-leg standing backward bending is a provocation test to produce pain from spondylolysis or spondylolisthesis
C. Sitting position
   1. Sitting forward bending trunk test (sitting forward flexion test)
      a. Note extent of cranial movement of PSIS
         1. Involved PSIS moves more cranially
            a. Blocked joint moves solidly as one, while the sacrum on the painless side is free to move through its small range with the lumbar spine
         2. Rotation—Check lumbar spine
         3. Hip internal rotation
            a. Leg on the involved side may reproduce pain. This is thought to be a piriformis irritation pain and is reproduced as the muscle is stretched
            b. Range of motion
         4. Hip external rotation
D. Supine position
   1. Hip external rotation—piriformis contracture may cause exaggerated external rotation posture of involved hip
   2. Palpation of symphysis pubis—for postural deviations and tenderness. Some sacroiliac joint problems create pain

(continues)

and tenderness in this area. Sometimes the presenting subjective symptoms mimic adductor or groin strain, but objective evaluation of muscle strength and tenderness are negative for strain of these groups

3. Straight leg raising (SLR)
    a. Applies stress to sacroiliac joint—can indicate a unilateral torsional stress of the sacroiliac joint; however, could also be a coexisting lumbar problem
    b. Interpretation of SLR:
        1. 30 degrees—hip or very inflamed nerve
        2. 30 to 60 degrees—sciatic nerve involvement
        3. 70 to 90 degrees—sacroiliac joint
        4. Bilateral SLR—lumbar spine problem
        5. Neck flexion—exacerbates symptoms—disk or root irritation
        6. Ankle dorsiflexion or Lasègue sign—usually indicates sciatic nerve or root irritation
4. Sacroiliac compression and distraction tests
    a. Tests useful in excluding joint irritability, hypermobility, and serious disease, usually negative unless classical pathology exists
5. Patrick's test—flexion abduction external rotation (FABER)
    a. When pushed into extension may cause exacerbation of sacroiliac lesion—assess irritable motion
6. Flexion adduction internal rotation (FADIR)—will give iliolumbar ligament stretch
7. Bilateral knees to chest—will usually exacerbate lumbar spine symptoms as the sacroiliac joints move with the sacrum in this maneuver
8. Single knee to chest—if pain is reported to the posterolateral thigh—indicates sacrotuberous irritation
9. Single knee to opposite shoulder—if pain is reported in the PSIS area, this indicates sacroiliac ligament irritation
E. Sidelying—each side
   1. Anterior and posterior pelvic tilt—pain on movement indicates irritation of sacroiliac joint. Also gives direction of movement clues used in treatment
   2. Iliotibial band length—long-standing sacroiliac joint problems sometimes create tightness of iliotibial band
F. Prone position
   1. Palpation
       a. Tenderness medial to or around PSIS that is well localized indicates sacroiliac problem
       b. Gluteus maximus area—sacrotuberous and sacrospinous ligaments are in this area, as well as piriformis and sciatic nerve. Changes in tension, tenderness, springiness can occur from positional changes of ilium
       c. Tenderness or alignment changes from S1 to T10 interspaces indicates lumbar problems
       d. Anteroposterior or rotational stresses to lumbar spinous processes
       e. Sacral provocation tests
           1. Do this series of tests only when applicable: If unable to reproduce signs and symptoms by now, do not do if by previous tests the joint has been found to be hypermobile
               a. Anteroposterior pressure of sacrum at center of its base
               b. Anteroposterior pressure of sacrum on each side of sacrum just medial to PSIS
           2. Hip extension knee flexion stretch will provoke the L3 nerve root. Pain similar to nerve pain down the anterolateral thigh would be a positive finding
G. Manual muscle test—if the lumbar spine or posterior hip muscle is strained, active movement against gravity or resistance should provoke the complaints of similar pain to pain under evaluation
   1. Hip extension—isometric and isotonic
   2. Hip internal rotation
   3. Hip external rotation
   4. Arm and shoulder extension
   5. Arm, shoulder, and neck extension
   6. Resisted trunk extension

EXERCISES

REHABILITATION EXERCISES FOR THE LOW BACK

Positioning and Pain-Relieving Exercises

Most patients with back pain have some fluctuation of their symptoms in response to certain postures and activities. The therapist logically treats this patient by reinforcing pain-reducing postures and motions and by starting specific exercises aimed at specific muscle groups or specific ranges of motion. A general rule in making these decisions is as follows: **Any movement that causes the back pain to radiate or spread over a larger area should not be included during this early phase of treatment.** Movements that centralize or diminish the pain are correct movements to include at this time.[3,25] Including some exercise during initial pain management generally has a positive effect on patients. The exercise encourages them to be active in the rehabilitation plan and helps them to regain lumbar movement.[14,39]

When a patient relieves pain through exercise and attention to proper postural control, he or she is much more likely to adopt these procedures into a daily routine. A patient who has pain relieved via some other passive procedure, and is then taught exercises, will not be able to readily see the connection between relief and exercise.[3]

The types of exercises that may be included in initial pain management include lateral shift corrections, extension exercises, and flexion exercises.

LATERAL SHIFT CORRECTIONS

Lateral shift corrections and extension exercises probably should be discussed together because the indications for use are similar, and extension exercises will immediately follow the lateral shift corrections.

The indications for the use of lateral shift corrections are as follows:

- Subjectively, the patient complains of unilateral pain reference in the lumbar or hip area.
- The typical posture is scoliotic with a hip shift and reduced lumbar lordosis.
- Walking and movements are very guarded and robotic.
- Forward-bending is extremely limited and increases the pain.
- Backward-bending is limited.
- Side-bending toward the painful side is minimal to impossible.
- Side-bending away from the painful side is usually reasonable to normal.

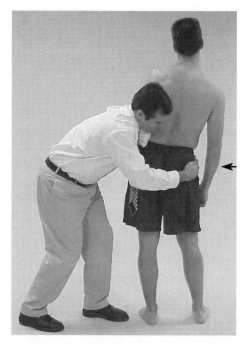

E X E R C I S E   3 3 - 1

Lateral shift correction exercise.

- A test correction of the hip shift either reduces the pain or causes the pain to centralize.
- The neurologic examination may or may not elicit the following positive findings:
  - Straight leg raising may be limited and painful, or it could be unaffected.
  - Sensation may be dull, anesthetic, or unaffected.
  - Manual muscle test may indicate unilateral weakness of specific movements, or the movements may be strong and painless.
  - Reflexes may be diminished or unaffected.[3,25]

The patient will be assisted by the therapist with the initial lateral shift correction. The patient is then instructed in the techniques of self-correction. The lateral shift correction is designed to guide the patient back to a more symmetrical posture. The therapist's pressure should be firm and steady and more guiding than forcing. The use of a mirror to provide visual feedback is recommended for both the therapist-assisted and self-corrected maneuvers. The specific technique guide for therapist-assisted lateral shift correction is as follows (Exercise 33-1):

1. Preset the patient by explaining the correction maneuver and the roles of the patient and the therapist.
   a. The patient is to keep the shoulders level and avoid the urge to side-bend.

b. The patient should allow the hips to move under the trunk and should not resist the pressure from the therapist but allow the hips to shift with the pressure.

c. The patient should keep the therapist informed about the behavior of the back pain.

d. The patient should keep the feet stationary and not move after the hip shift correction until the standing extension part of the correction is completed.

e. The patient should practice the standing extension exercise as part of this initial explanation.

2. The therapist should stand on the patient's side opposite the patient's hip shift. The patient's feet should be a comfortable distance apart, and the therapist should have a comfortable stride stance aligned slightly behind the patient.

3. Padding should be placed around the patient's elbow, on the side next to the therapist, to provide comfortable contact between the patient and therapist.

4. The therapist should contact the patient's elbow with the shoulder and chest, with the head aligned along the patient's back. The therapist's arms should reach around the patient's waist and apply pressure between the iliac crest and the greater trochanter.

5. The therapist should gradually pull the patient's hips toward him or her. If the pain increases, the therapist should ease the pressure and maintain a more comfortable posture for 10 to 20 seconds, and then again pull gently. If the pain increases again, the therapist should again lessen the pull and allow comfort, and then instruct the patient to actively extend gently, pushing the patient's back into and matching the resistance supplied by the therapist. The goal for this maneuver is an overcorrection of the scoliosis, reversing its direction.

6. Once the corrected or overcorrected posture is achieved, the therapist should maintain this posture for 1 to 2 minutes. This procedure may take 2 to 3 minutes to complete, and the first attempt may be less than a total success. Repeated efforts 3 to 4 minutes apart should be attempted during the first treatment effort before the therapist stops the treatment for that episode.

7. The therapist gradually releases pressure on the hip while the patient does a standing extension movement. The patient should complete approximately 6 repetitions of the standing extension movement, holding each 15 to 20 seconds.

8. Once the patient moves the feet and walks even a short distance, the lateral hip shift usually will reoccur, but to a lesser degree. The patient then should be taught the self-correction maneuver. The patient should stand in front of a mirror and place one hand on the hip where the therapist's hands were and the other hand on the lower ribs where the therapist's shoulder was.

9. The patient then pushes the hip under the trunk, watching the mirror to keep the shoulders level and trying to achieve a corrected or overcorrected posture. The patient should hold this posture for 30 to 45 seconds and then follow with several standing extension movements as described in step 7.[3,25]

EXTENSION EXERCISES

The indications for the use of extension exercise are as follows:

- Subjectively, back pain is diminished with lying down and increased with sitting. The location of the pain may be unilateral, bilateral, or central, and there may or may not be radiating pain into either or both legs.
- Forward-bending is extremely limited and increases the pain, or the pain reference location enlarges as the patient bends forward.
- Backward-bending can be limited, but the movement centralizes or diminishes the pain.
- The neurologic examination is the same as outlined for lateral shift correction.[3,24]

The efficacy of extension exercise is theorized to be from one or a combination of the following effects:

- A reduction in the neural tension.
- A reduction of the load on the disk, which in turn decreases disk pressure.
- Increases in the strength and endurance of the extensor muscles.
- Proprioceptive interference with pain perception as the exercises allow self-mobilization of the spinal joints.

Hip shift posture has previously been theoretically correlated to the anatomic location of the disk bulge or nucleus pulposus herniation. Creating a centralizing movement of the nucleus pulposus has been the theoretical emphasis of hip shift correction and extension exercise. This theory has good logic, but research on this phenomenon has not been supportive.[26] However, in explaining the exercises to the patient, the use of this theory may help increase the patient's motivation and compliance with the exercise plan.

End-range hyperextension exercise should be used cautiously when the patient has facet joint degeneration or impingement of the vertebral foramen borders on neural structures. Also, spondylolysis and spondylolisthesis problems should be approached cautiously with any end-range movement exercise using either flexion or hyperextension.

Exercises 33-2 to 33-9 are examples of extension exercises. This list is not exhaustive but is representative of most of the exercises used clinically. The order in which exercises are presented is not significant. Instead, each therapist should base the starting exercises on the evaluative findings. Jackson and Brown, in a review of back exercise, stated "no support was found for the use of a preprogrammed flexion regimen that includes exercises of little value or potential harm and is not specific to the current needs of the patient, as determined by a

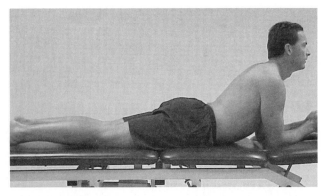

EXERCISE 33-2

Prone on elbows.

thorough back evaluation." The review also included a report of Kendall and Jenkins' study, which stated that one third of the patients for whom hyperextension exercises had been prescribed worsened.[17]

FLEXION EXERCISES

The indications for the use of flexion exercises are as follows:

- Subjectively, back pain is diminished with sitting and increased with lying down or standing. Pain is also increased with walking.
- Repeated or sustained forward-bending eases the pain.
- The patient's lordotic curve does not reverse as the patient bends forward.
- The end range of or sustained backward bending is painful or increases the pain.
- Abdominal tone and strength are poor.

In his approach, Saal elaborates on the thought that, "No one should continue with one particular type of exercise regimen during the entire treatment program."[28] We concur with these thoughts and believe starting with one type of exercise should not preclude rapidly adding other exercises as the patient's pain resolves and other movements become more comfortable.

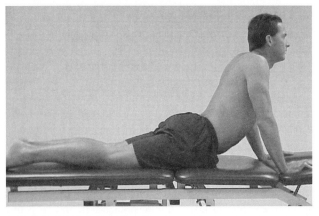

EXERCISE 33-3

Prone on hands.

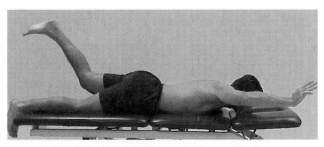

EXERCISE 33-4

Alternate arm and leg.

The efficacy of flexion exercise is theorized to be from one or a combination of the following effects:

- A reduction in the articular stresses on the facet joints.
- Stretching to the dorsolumbar fascia and musculature.
- Opening of the intervertebral foramen.
- Relief of the stenosis of the spinal canal.
- Improvement of the stabilizing effect of the abdominal musculature.
- Increasing the intraabdominal pressure because of increased abdominal muscle strength and tone.
- Proprioceptive interference with pain perception as the exercises allow self-mobilization of the spinal joints.[17]

Flexion exercises should be used cautiously or avoided in most cases of acute disk prolapse and when a laterally shifted posture is present. In patients recovering from disk-related back pain,

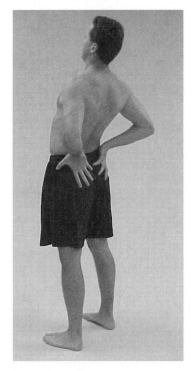

EXERCISE 33-5

Standing extension.

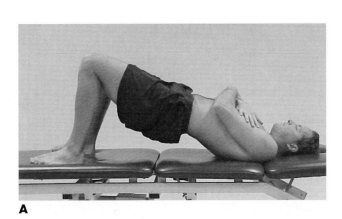

A   **B**

EXERCISE 33-6

Supine hip extension—butt lift or bridge. **A,** Double-leg support. **B,** Single-leg support.

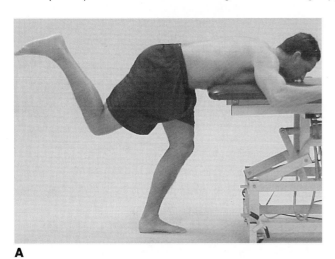

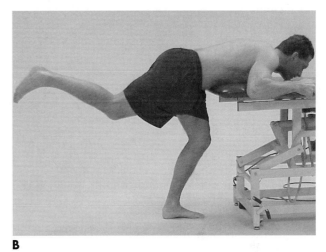

A   **B**

EXERCISE 33-7

Prone single-leg hip extension. **A,** Knee flexed. **B,** Knees extended.

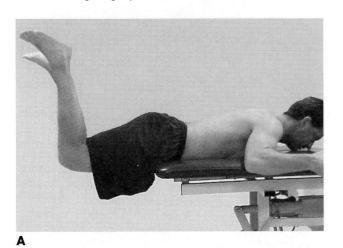

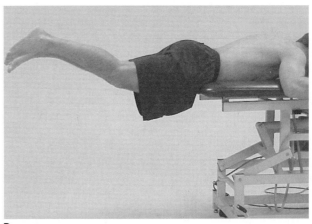

A   **B**

EXERCISE 33-8

Prone double-leg hip extension. **A,** Knees flexed. **B,** Knees extended.

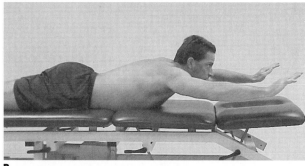

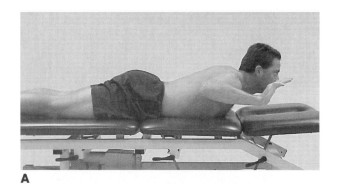

E X E R C I S E   3 3 - 9

Trunk extension—prone. **A,** Hands near head. **B,** Arms extended—superman position.

flexion exercise should not be commenced immediately after a flat-lying rest interval longer than 30 minutes. The disk can become more hydrated in this amount of time, and the patient would be more susceptible to pain with postures that increase disk pressures. Other less stressful exercises should be initiated first and flexion exercise done later in the exercise program.[3,24]

Exercises 33-10 to 33-18 show examples of flexion exercises. Again, this list is not exhaustive but is representative of the exercises used clinically.

Joint Mobilizations

The indications for the use of joint mobilizations are as follows:

- Subjectively, the patient's pain is centered around a specific joint area and increases with activity and decreases with rest.
- The accessory motion available at individual spinal segments is diminished.
- Passive range of motion is diminished.
- Active range of motion is diminished.
- There may be muscular tightness or increased fascial tension in the area of the pain.

E X E R C I S E   3 3 - 1 1

Double knee to chest. **A,** Stretching—holding posture 15 to 20 seconds. **B,** Mobilizing—using a rhythmic rocking motion within a pain-free range of motion.

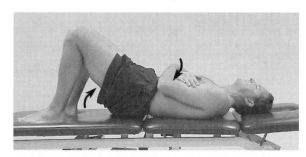

E X E R C I S E   3 3 - 1 2

Posterior pelvic tilt.

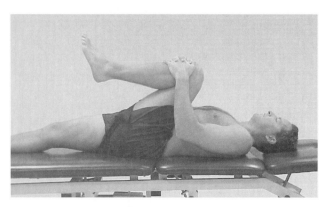

E X E R C I S E   3 3 - 1 0

Single knee to chest. **A,** Stretch, holding 15 to 20 seconds. **B,** Same as step 2.

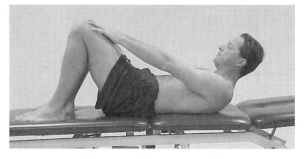

E X E R C I S E   3 3 - 1 3

Partial sit-up.

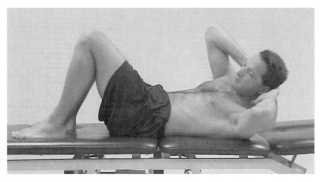

EXERCISE 33-14

Rotation partial sit-up.

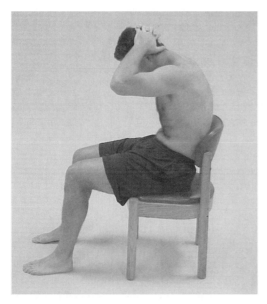

EXERCISE 33-15

Slump sit stretch position.

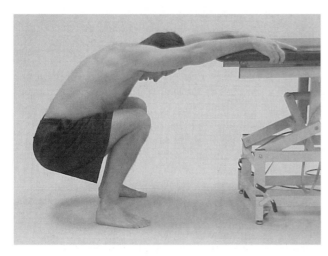

EXERCISE 33-16

Flat-footed squat stretch.

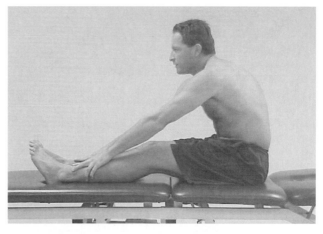

EXERCISE 33-17

Hamstring stretch.

- Back movements are asymmetrical when comparing right and left rotation or side-bending.
- Forward and backward-bending may steer away from the midline.

The efficacy of mobilization is theorized to be from one or a combination of the following effects:

- Tight structures can be stretched to increase the range of motion.
- The joint involved is stimulated by the movement to more normal mechanics, and irritation is reduced because of better nutrient waste exchange.
- Proprioceptive interference occurs with pain perception as the joint movement stimulates normal neural firing whose perception supercedes nociceptive perception.

Mobilization techniques are multidimensional and are easily adapted to any back pain problem. The mobilizations can be active, passive, or assisted by the therapist. All ranges (flexion, extension, side-bending, rotation, and accessory) can be incorporated within the exercise plan. The mobilizations can

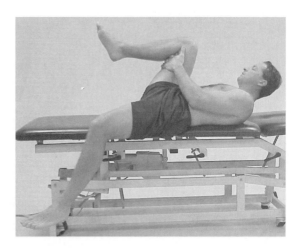

EXERCISE 33-18

Hip flexor stretch.

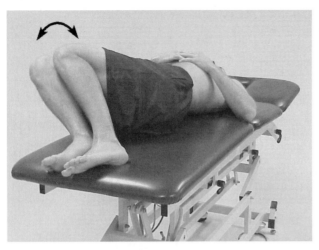

E X E R C I S E   3 3 - 1 9

Knee rocking side to side.

be carried out according to Maitland's grades of oscillation as discussed in Chapter 15. The magnitude of the forces applied can range from grade 1 to grade 4, depending on levels of pain. The theory, technique, and application of the therapist-assisted mobilizations are best gained through guided study with an expert practitioner.[21]

Exercises 33-19 to 33-28 show the various self-mobilization exercises. Exercises 33-29 to 33-38 show joint mobilizations that can be used by the therapist.

Core Stabilization Exercises

Core stabilization training was discussed in detail in Chapter 16. Despite the fact that the patient may have adequate strength and flexibility, there may be difficulty controlling the spine if the patient does not learn to contract the appropriate muscles in a desired sequence. Stabilization, especially during complex functional movements, relies heavily on a learned response by the patient to control the movement. Stabilization exercises for the trunk and spine may help to minimize the cumulative

E X E R C I S E   3 3 - 2 0

Knees toward chest rock.

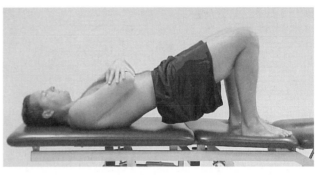

E X E R C I S E   3 3 - 2 1

Supine hip lift-bridge-rock.

effects of repetitive microtrauma to the spine. Spinal stabilization does not mean maintaining a static position. **Dynamic stabilization** involves maintaining a controlled range of motion that varies with the position and the activity being performed. Dynamic stabilization is achieved by conscious repetitive training, which over time eventually becomes an unconscious natural response. Dynamic stabilization techniques are widely used in rehabilitation programs for the low back.[17]

The first step in dynamic stabilization involves learning to control the position of the pelvis in a neutral position. A posterior tilt of the pelvis causes the lumbar curve to flatten and is caused by a simultaneous co-contraction of the abdominal and gluteal muscles (see Exercise 33-12). Once the patient has learned to control pelvic tilt progressively, more advanced movement activities should be incorporated that involve movements of both the spine and extremities while the pelvis is maintained in a neutral position.[17]

Abdominal muscle control is another key to stabilization of the low back (see Exercises 33-13 and 33-14). Abdominal bracing exercises focus attention on motor control of the external oblique muscles in different positions. There should also be co-contraction of the abdominal muscles and lumbar extensors to maintain a "corset" control of the lumbar spine.[13]

The progression of stabilization exercises should go from supine activities (see Exercise 33-4), to prone activities (see Exercises 33-3 and 33-7 to 33-9), to kneeling activities (quadriped to triped to biped), and eventually to weight-bearing activities—all performed while actively stabilizing the trunk. The patient should be taught to perform a stabilization contraction before starting any movement. As the movement begins, the patient will become less aware of the stabilization contraction. The patient may begin by incorporating stabilization into every movement performed in the strengthening exercises. Stabilization contractions can also be used in aerobic conditioning activities. The exercises should include those activities that replicate the functional demands of the patient. The patient should consciously practice the stabilization technique with each exercise. Each individual patient will have a difference in the degree of control and in the speed at which he or she can aquire the skills of dynamic trunk stabilization.[13]

Exercises 33-39 to 33-43 show additional examples of dynamic stabilization exercises.

A   **B**

EXERCISE 33-22

Pelvic tilt or pelvic rock, butt out, tail tuck.

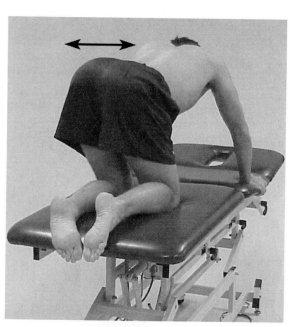

EXERCISE 33-23

Kneeling—dog-tail wags.

EXERCISE 33-24

Sitting or standing rotation.

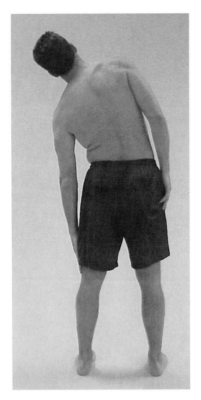

E X E R C I S E   3 3 - 2 5

Sitting or standing
side-bending.

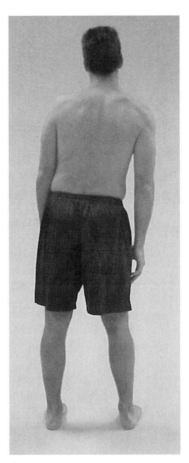

E X E R C I S E   3 3 - 2 6

Standing hip shift side to side.

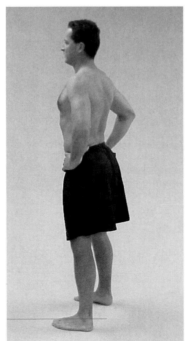

E X E R C I S E   3 3 - 2 7

Standing pelvic rock, butt out,
tail tuck.

A   B

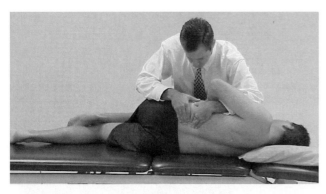

EXERCISE 33-28

Various side-lying and back-lying positions to both stretch and mobilize specific joints areas.

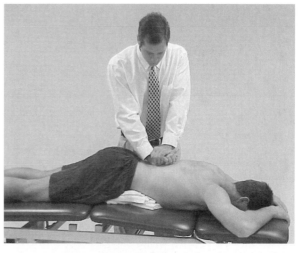

EXERCISE 33-30

Anterior/posterior lumbar vertebral glides. In the lumbar region, anterior/posterior lumbar vertebral glides may be accomplished at individual segments using pressure on the spinous process through the pisiform in the hand. These decrease pain or increase mobility of individual lumbar vertebrae.

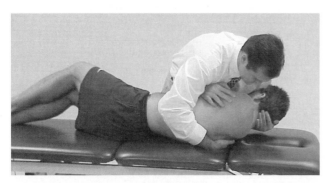

EXERCISE 33-29

Thoracic vertebral facet rotations. Thoracic vertebral facet rotations are accomplished with one hand underneath the patient, providing stabilization and the weight of the body pressing downward through the rib cage to rotate an individual thoracic vertebra. Rotation of the thoracic vertebrae is minimal, and most of the movement with this mobilization involves the rib facet joint.

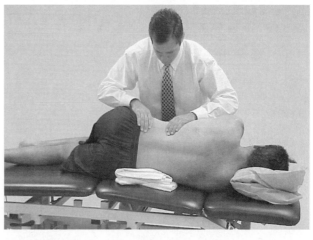

EXERCISE 33-31

Lateral lumbar distraction. Lumbar lateral distraction increases the space between transverse process and increases the opening of the intervertebral foramen. This position is achieved by lying over a support, flexing the patient's upper knee to a point where there is gapping in the appropriate spinal segment, and then rotating the upper trunk to place the segment in a close-packed position. Then finger and forearm pressure are used to separate individual spaces. This pressure is used for reducing pain in the lumbar vertebrae associated with some compression of a spinal nerve.

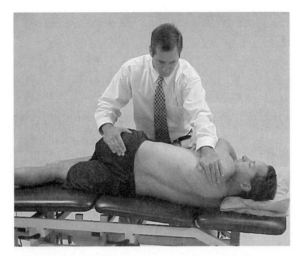

E X E R C I S E   3 3 - 3 2

Lumbar vertebral rotations. Lumbar vertebral rotations decrease pain and increase mobility in lumbar vertebrae. These rotations should be done in a side-lying position.

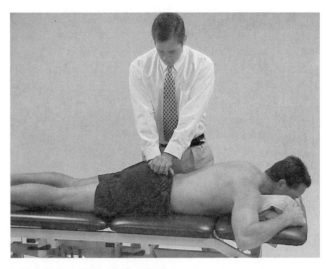

E X E R C I S E   3 3 - 3 4

Anterior sacral glides. Anterior sacral glides decrease pain and reduce muscle guarding around the sacroiliac joint.

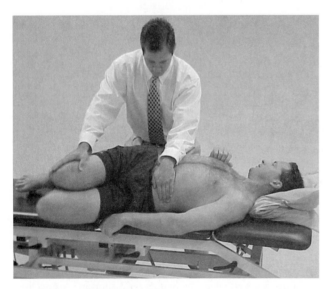

E X E R C I S E   3 3 - 3 3

Lateral lumbar rotations. May be done with the patient in supine position. In this position, one hand must stabilize the upper trunk, while the other produces rotation.

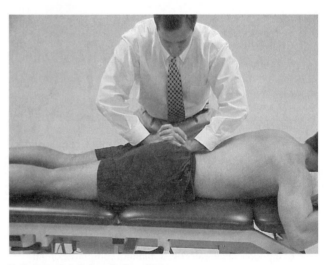

E X E R C I S E   3 3 - 3 5

Superior/inferior sacral glides. Superior/inferior sacral glides decrease pain and reduce muscle guarding around the sacroiliac joint.

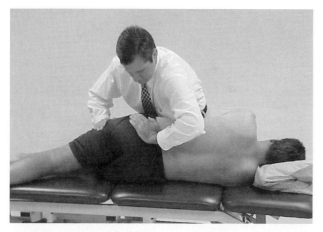

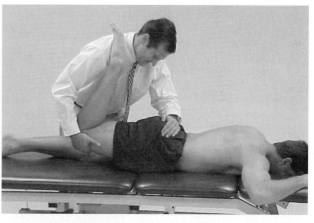

EXERCISE 33-36

Anterior innominate rotation. An anterior innominate rotation in a side-lying position is accomplished by extending the leg on the affected side and then stabilizing with one hand on the front of the thigh while the other applies pressure anteriorly over the posterosuperior iliac spine to produce an anterior rotation. This technique will correct a unilateral posterior rotation.

EXERCISE 33-37

Anterior innominate rotation. An anterior innominate rotation may also be accomplished by extending the hip, applying upward force on the upper thigh, and stabilizing over the posterosuperior iliac spine. This technique is once again used to correct a posterior unilateral innominate rotation.

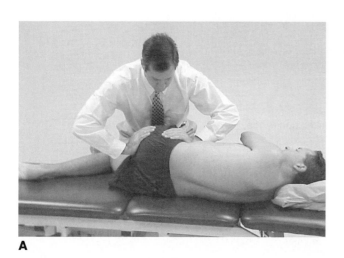

A

B

EXERCISE 33-38

Posterior innominate rotations. **A,** A posterior innominate rotation with the patient in side-lying position is done by flexing the hip, stabilizing the anterosuperior iliac spine, and applying pressure to the ischium in an anterior direction. **B,** Another posterior innominate rotation with the hip flexed at 90 degrees stabilizes the knee and rotates the innominate anteriorly through upward pressure on the ischium.

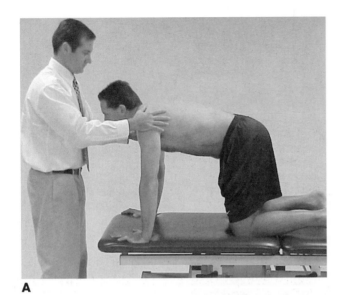

A

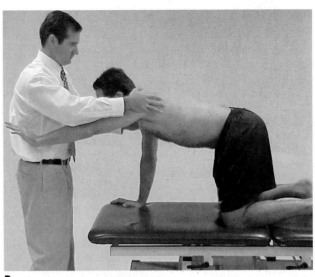

B

C

E X E R C I S E   3 3 - 3 9
Weight-shifting and stabilization exercises should progress from **A,** quadriped, to
B, triped, to **C,** biped.

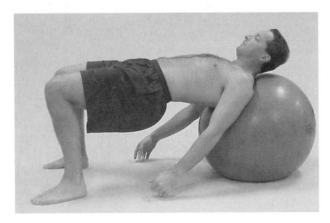

E X E R C I S E   3 3 - 4 0
Bridging exercises on a Swiss ball.

E X E R C I S E   3 3 - 4 1
Alternate arm/leg extension.

EXERCISE 33-42

Lunges.

EXERCISE 33-43

Wall slides.

REHABILITATION TECHNIQUES FOR LOW BACK PAIN

Low Back Pain

PATHOMECHANICS

In the majority of cases involving acute injury, low back pain does not have serious or long-lasting pathology. It is generally accepted that the soft tissues (ligament, fascia, and muscle) can be the initial pain source. The patient's response to the injury and to the provocative stresses of evaluation is usually proportional to the time since the injury and the magnitude of the physical trauma of the injury. The soft tissues of the lumbar region should react according to the biological process of healing, and the time lines for healing should be similar to other body parts. There is no substantiation that acute injury to the low back should cause a pain syndrome whose symptoms last longer than 6 to 8 weeks.[8,28]

INJURY MECHANISM

Back pain can result from one or a combination of problems, including muscle strain, piriformis muscle or quadratus lumborum myofascial pain or strain, myofascial trigger points, lumbar facet joint sprains, hypermobility syndromes, disk-related back problems, and sacroiliac joint dysfunction.

REHABILITATION CONCERNS

Acute Versus Chronic Low Back Pain

The low back pain that patients most often experience is an acute, painful experience rarely lasting longer than 3 weeks. As is the case with many injuries, therapists often go through exercise or treatment fads in trying to rehabilitate the patient with low back pain. The latest fad might involve flexion exercise, extension exercise, joint mobilization, dynamic muscular stabilization, abdominal bracing, myofascial release, electrical stimulation protocols, and so on. To keep perspective as therapists select exercise and modalities, they should keep in mind that 90 percent of people with back pain get resolution of the symptoms in 6 weeks regardless of the care administered.[28,39]

There are patients who have pain persisting beyond 6 weeks. This group of patients will generally have a history of reinjury or exacerbation of previous injury. They describe a low back pain that is similar to their previous back pain experience.

These patients are experiencing an exacerbation or reinjury of previously injured tissues by continuing to apply stresses that may have created their original injury. This group of patients needs a more specific and formal treatment and rehabilitation program.[8,28]

There are also people who have chronic low back pain. This is a very small percentage of the population suffering from low back pain. The difference between the patient with an acute injury or reinjury and a person with chronic pain has been defined by Waddell. He states that "Chronic pain becomes a completely different clinical syndrome from acute pain."[39] Acute and chronic pain are not only different in time scale but are fundamentally different in kind. Acute and experimental pains bear a relatively straightforward relationship to peripheral stimulus, nociception, and tissue damage.

There may be some understandable anxiety about the meaning and consequences of the pain, but acute pain, disability, and illness behavior are generally proportionate to the physical findings. Pharmacologic, physical, and even surgical treatments directed to the underlying physical disorder are generally highly effective in relieving acute pain. Chronic pain, disability, and illness behavior, in contrast, become increasingly dissociated from their original physical basis, and there may be little objective evidence of any remaining nociceptive stimulus. Instead, chronic pain and disability become increasingly associated with emotional distress, depression, failed treatment, and adoption of a sick role. Chronic pain progressively becomes a self-sustaining condition that is resistant to traditional medical management. Physical treatment directed to a supposed but unidentified and possibly nonexistent nociceptive source is not only understandably unsuccessful but may cause additional physical damage. Failed treatment may both reinforce and aggravate pain, distress, disability, and illness behavior.[39]

REHABILITATION PROGRESSION

In discussing the rehabilitation progression for the patient with low back pain, the discussion can be much more specific and meaningful if treatment plans are lumped into two stages. Stage I (acute stage) treatment consists mainly of the modality treatment and pain-relieving exercises. Stage II treatment involves treating patients with a reinjury or exacerbation of a previous problem. The treatment plan in stage II goes beyond pain relief, strengthening, stretching, and mobilization to include trunk stabilization and movement-training sequences and to provide a specific, guided program to return the patient to his or her normal activities.[28]

Stage I (Acute Stage) Treatment

Modulating pain should be the initial focus of the therapist. Progressing rapidly from pain management to specific rehabilitation should be a primary goal of the acute stage of the rehabilitation plan. The most common treatment for pain relief in the acute stage is to use ice for analgesia. Rest, but not total bed rest, is used to allow the injured tissues to begin the healing process without the stresses that created the injury.[9]

Along with rest, during the initial treatment stage, the patient should be taught to increase comfort by using the *appropriate* body-positioning techniques described previously that may involve (1) lateral shift corrections (see Exercise 33-1), (2) extension exercises (see Exercises 33-2 to 33-9), (3) flexion exercises (see Exercises 33-10 to 33-18), or (4) self-mobilization exercises (see Exercises 33-19 to 33-28). Outside support, in

the form of corsets and the use of props or pillows to enhance comfortable positions, also needs to be included in the initial pain-management phase of treatment.[28,39] They should also be taught to avoid positions and movements that increase any sharp, painful episodes. The limits of these movements and positions that provide comfort should be the initial focus of any exercises.

The patient should be encouraged to move through this stage as quickly as comfort will allow. The addition of a supportive corset during this stage should be based mostly on the comfort of the patient. We suggest using an eclectic approach to the selection of the exercises, mixing the various protocols described according to the findings of the patient's evaluation. Rarely will a patient present with classic signs and symptoms that will dictate using one variety of exercise.

Stage II (Reinjury Stage) Treatment

In the reinjury or chronic stage of back rehabilitation, the goals of the treatment and training should again be based on a thorough evaluation of the patient. Identifying the causes of the patient's back problem and reoccurrences is very important in the management of rehabilitation and prevention of reinjury. A goal for this stage of care is to make the patient responsible for management of the back problem. The therapist should identify specific problems and corrections that will help the patient better understand the mechanisms and management of the problem.[28]

Specific goals and exercises should be identified concerning the following:

- Which structures to stretch.
- Which structures to strengthen.
- Incorporating dynamic stabilization into the patient's daily life and exercise routine.
- Which movements need a motor learning approach to control faulty mechanics.[28]

STRETCHING The therapist and the patient need to plan specific exercises to stretch restricted groups, maintain flexibility in normal muscle groups, and identify hypermobility that may be a part of the problem. In planning, instructing, and monitoring each exercise, adequate thought and good instruction must be used to ensure that the intended structures get stretched and areas of hypermobility are protected from overstretching.[10,15] Inadequate stabilization will lead to exercise movements that are so general that the exercise will encourage hyperflexibility at already hypermobile areas. Lack of proper stabilization during stretching may help perpetuate a structural problem that will continue to add to the patient's back pain.

In the therapist's evaluation of the patient with back pain, the following muscle groups should be assessed for flexibility:

- Hip flexors.
- Hamstrings.
- Low back extensors.
- Lumbar rotators.

- Lumbar lateral flexors.
- Hip adductors.
- Hip abductors.
- Hip rotators.[10]

STRENGTHENING   There are numerous techniques for strengthening the muscles of the trunk and hip. Muscles are perhaps best strengthened by using techniques of progressive overload to achieve specific adaptation to imposed demands (SAID principle). The overload can take the form of increased weight load, increased repetition load, or increased stretch load to accomplish physiologic changes in muscle strength, muscle endurance, or flexibility of a body part.[10]

The treatment plan should call for an exercise that the patient can easily accomplish successfully. Rapidly but gradually, the overload should push the patient to challenge the muscle group needing strengthening. The therapist and the patient should monitor continuously for increases in the patient's pain or reoccurrences of previous symptoms. If those changes occur, the exercises should be modified, delayed, or eliminated from the rehabilitation plan.[17,28]

CORE STABILIZATION   Core stabilization, dynamic abdominal bracing, and finding neutral position all describe a technique used to increase the stability of the trunk. This increased stability will enable the patient to maintain the spine and pelvis in the most comfortable and acceptable mechanical position that will control the forces of repetitive microtrauma and protect the structures of the back from further damage. Abdominal muscular control is one key to giving the patient the ability to stabilize the trunk and control posture. Abdominal strengthening routines are rigorous, and the patient must complete them with vigor. However, in their functional activities, patients do not take advantage of abdominal strength to stabilize the trunk and protect the back.[15,22,27]

Kennedy's dynamic abdominal bracing exercises focus attention on the motor control of the external oblique muscles in various positions. Once this control is established, different positions and movements are added.[22] Saal describes this type of exercise as finding and maintaining the neutral position with muscle fusion. He specifically singles out the external oblique muscles as a major factor, but describes a co-contraction of the abdominal and lumbar extensors, including gluteus maximus, to maintain a corseting action on the lumbar spine. Adequate flexibility of hip muscles and other structures is also necessary to accomplish this muscle fusion concept.[28] The concept of increasing trunk stability with muscle contractions that support and limit the extremes of spinal movement is important, regardless of whether muscle fusion or dynamic abdominal bracing are the terms used to describe this action (see Exercises 33-40 to 33-45).

BASIC FUNCTIONAL TRAINING   The patient must be constantly committed to improving body mechanics and trunk control in all postures in the activities of daily living. The therapist needs

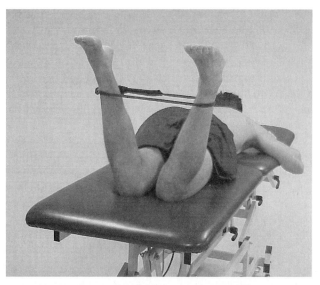

EXERCISE   3 3 - 4 4

Prone-lying hip internal rotation with elastic resistance.

to evaluate the patient's daily patterns and give instruction, practice, and monitoring on the best and least stressful body mechanics in as many activities as possible.

The basic program follows the developmental sequence of posture control, starting with supine and prone extremity movement while actively stabilizing the trunk. The patient is then progressed to all fours, kneeling, and standing. Emphasis on trunk control and stability is maintained as the patient works through this exercise sequence.[15,23,28]

The most critical aspect for developing motor control is repetition of exercise. However, variability in positioning, speed of movement, and changes in movement patterns must also be incorporated. The variability of the exercise will allow the patient to generalize the newly learned trunk control to the constant changes necessary in daily activities. The basic exercise, including a trunk-stabilizing contraction, is the key. Incorporating this stabilization contraction into various activities helps reinforce trunk stabilization and makes trunk control a subconscious automatic response.

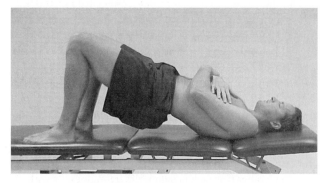

EXERCISE   3 3 - 4 5

Hip lift bridges.

The use of augmented feedback (EMG, palpation) of the trunk-stabilizing contraction may be needed early in the exercise plan to help maximize the results of this exercise. The therapist should have the patient internalize this feedback as quickly as possible to make the patient apparatus-free and more functional. With augmented feedback, it is recommended that the patient be rapidly and progressively weaned from dependency on external feedback.

ADVANCED FUNCTIONAL TRAINING   Each activity that the patient is involved in becomes part of the advanced exercise rehabilitation plan. The usual place to start is with the patient's exercise program. Each step of the program is monitored, and emphasis is placed on trunk stabilization for even the simple task of putting the weights on a bar or getting on and off of exercise equipment. Each exercise in their program should be retaught, and the patient is made aware of the best mechanical position and the proper stabilizing muscular contraction. The strengthening program is patient-specific, attempting to strengthen weak areas and improve strength in specific muscle groups as needed.[28]

Aerobic activities are also included in advanced programs. The same emphasis on technique and stabilization is used as the patient begins aerobic activities. A functional progression should be used so that changes in symptoms can be controlled by working with lower-level exercises and then progressing to more difficult and stressful exercises.[28] Modification of normal aerobic exercises may be an important part of eliminating some of the unnecessary stress from the patient's overall program. Substituting an aquatic conditioning program for jogging or running may keep the patient participating effectively without increasing back pain.

Using exercises designed to incorporate trunk control into specific skills is the next step in the exercise progression. The patient should be taught to start stabilization contraction before starting any movement. This presets the patient's posture and stabilization awareness before the movement takes place. As the movement occurs, the patient will become less aware of the stabilization contraction as the patient attempts to accomplish the drill.

Patients may revert to old postures and habits, so feedback is important. The next step is to incorporate a firmer stabilization contraction during the power phase of the drill. The patient is instructed to contract more firmly during initiation of a jump or push during change in direction. The drills should be constructed to have several changes in contraction strength planned as the patient moves through the drill. Expect that the patient may experience paralysis by analysis as he or she tries to think through stabilizing contraction plus drill execution. Adequate practice time will be necessary before the patient can master this stabilization technique. The patient should find this stabilization control comfortable, efficient, and powerful.

Remember that each patient is different, not only with the individual back problem but also in the ability to gain motor skill. Each patient will have differences in degree of control and in the speed at which the patient acquires these new skills of trunk stabilization.

Reducing stress to the back by using braces, orthotics, shoes, or comfortable supportive furniture (beds, desks, or chairs) is essential to help the patient minimize chronic or overload stresses to the back. The stabilization exercise should be incorporated into activities of daily living.[30] The use of a low back corset or brace may also make the patient more comfortable (Exercise 33-60).

For most low back problems, the stage I treatment and exercise programs will get patients back into their activities quickly. If the pain or dysfunction is pronounced or the problem becomes recurrent, an in-depth evaluation and treatment using stage I and stage II exercise protocols will be necessary. The team approach with patient, physician, and therapist working together will provide the comprehensive approach needed to manage the patient's back problem. Close attention to and emphasis on the patient's progress will provide both the patient and the therapist with the encouragement to continue this program.

Muscular Strains

INJURY MECHANISM

Evaluative findings include a history of sudden or chronic stress that initiates pain in a muscular area during physical activity. There are three points on the physical examination that must be positive to indicate the muscle as the primary problem. There will be tenderness to palpation in the muscular area. The muscular pain will be provoked with contraction and with stretch of the involved muscle.

REHABILITATION PROGRESSION

The treatment should include the standard protection, ice and compression. Ice may be applied in the form of ice massage or ice bags, depending on the area involved. An elastic wrap or corset would protect and compress the back musculature. Additional modalities would include pulsed ultrasound as a biostimulative and electrical stimulation for pain relief and muscle reeducation. The exercises used in rehabilitation should make the involved muscle contract and stretch, starting with very mild exercise and progressively increasing the intensity and repetition loads. In general, this would include active extension exercises such as hip lifts (see Exercises 33-6 to 33-8), alternate arm and leg, hip extension (see Exercise 33-4), trunk extension (see Exercise 33-9), and quadratus hip shift exercises (Exercises 33-53 to 33-55). A good series of abdominal strengthening and stabilization exercises would also be helpful (see Exercises 33-12 and 33-13). Stretching exercises might include the following: knee to chest (see Exercises 33-10 and 33-11), side-lying leg hang to stretch the hip flexors (see Exercise 33-18), slump sitting (see Exercise 33-15), and knee rocking side to side (see Exercise 33-19).

Initially, the patient may wish to continue to use a brace or corset, but should be encouraged to do away with the corset as the back strengthens and performance returns to normal.[10,17]

Piriformis Muscle Strain

PATHOMECHANICS

Piriformis syndrome was discussed in detail in Chapter 29. The piriformis muscle refers pain to the posterior sacroiliac region, to the buttocks, and sometimes down the posterior or posterolateral thigh. The pain is usually described as a deep ache that can get more intense with exercise and with sitting with the hips flexed, adducted, and medially rotated. The pain gets sharper and more intense with activities that require decelerating medial hip and leg rotation during weight bearing.

Tenderness to palpation has a characteristic pattern with tenderness medial and proximal to the greater trochanter and just lateral to the posterosuperior iliac spine. Isometric abduction in the sitting position produces pain in the posterior hip buttock area, and the movement will be weak or hesitant. Passive hip internal rotation in the sitting position will also bring on posterior hip and buttock pain.

REHABILITATION PROGRESSION

Rehabilitation exercises should include both strengthening and stretching. Strengthening exercises should include prone lying hip internal rotation with elastic resistance (Exercise 33-46), hip lift bridges (Exercise 33-47), hand knee position—fire hydrant exercise (Exercise 33-48), side-lying hip abduction straight leg raises (Exercise 33-49), and prone hip extension exercise (Exercise 33-50).

Stretching exercises for the piriformis include long leg sitting with the involved hip and knee flexed and foot crossed over the uninvolved leg (Exercise 33-51); back-lying legs-crossed hip adduction stretch (Exercise 33-52); back-lying with the involved leg crossed over the uninvolved leg, ankle-to-knee position, pulling the uninvolved knee to the chest to create the stretch (Exercise 33-53); and contract–relax–stretch with elbow

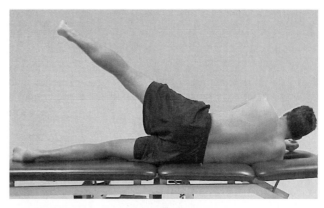

EXERCISE 33-47

Side-lying hip abduction straight leg raises.

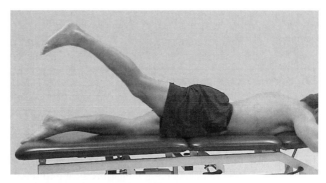

EXERCISE 33-48

Prone hip extension exercise.

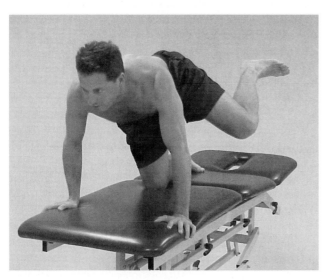

EXERCISE 33-46

Hand, knee position–fire hydrant exercise.

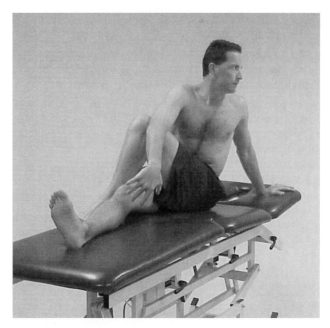

EXERCISE 33-49

Long leg sitting stretch.

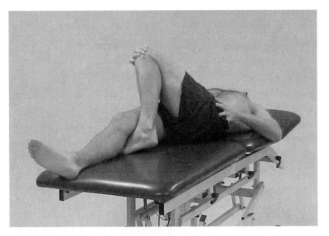

EXERCISE 33-50

Back-lying legs crossed hip adduction stretch.

pressure to the muscle insertion during the relaxation phase (Exercise 33-54).[18,32,35]

Quadratus Lumborum Strain

PATHOMECHANICS

Pain from the quadratus lumborum muscle is described as an aching, sharp pain located in the flank, lateral back area, and near the posterior sacroiliac region and upper buttocks. The patient usually describes pain on moving from sitting to standing, standing for long periods, coughing, sneezing, and walking. Activities requiring trunk rotation or side bending aggravate the pain.

The muscle is tender to palpation near the origin along the lower ribs and along the insertion on the iliac crest. Pain will be aggravated on side bending, and the pain will usually be localized to one side. For example, with a right quadratus problem, side bending right and left would provoke only right-sided pain. Supine hip hiking movements would also provoke the pain.

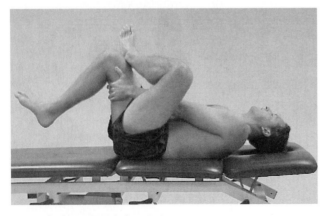

EXERCISE 33-51

Back-lying legs crossed pulling uninvolved knee.

REHABILITATION PROGRESSION

Rehabilitation strengthening exercises should include back-lying hip hike-shifting (Exercise 33-53), standing with one leg on an elevated surface and the other free to move below that level, hip-hiking the free side (Exercise 33-54); and back-lying hip hike resisted by pulling on the involved leg (Exercise 33-55).

Stretching exercises should include side-lying over a pillow roll leg hand stretch (Exercise 33-56), supine self-stretch with legs crossed (Exercise 33-57), hip hike exercise with hand pressure to increase stretch (Exercise 33-58), and standing with one leg on a small book stretch (Exercise 33-59).[35]

Myofascial Pain and Trigger Points

PATHOMECHANICS AND INJURY MECHANISM

The above examples of muscular oriented back pain in both the piriformis and quadratus lumborum could also have a myofascial origin. The major component in successfully changing myofascial pain is stretching the muscle back to a normal resting length. The muscle irritation and congestion that create the trigger points are relieved, and normal blood flow resumes, further reducing the irritants in the area. Stretching through a painful trigger point is difficult. A variety of comfort and counterirritant modalities can be used preliminary to, during, and after the stretching to enhance the effect of the exercise. Some of the methods used successfully are dry needling, local anesthetic injection, ice massage, friction massage, acupressure massage, ultrasound electrical stimulation, and cold sprays.

The indications for treating low back pain with myofascial stretching and treatment techniques are as follows:

1. Subjectively, muscle soreness and fatigue from repetitive motions are common antecedent mechanisms. Patients are also susceptible when fatigue and stress overload specific muscle groups. There may be a history of sudden onset during or shortly after an acute overload stress, or there may be a gradual onset with repetitive or postural overload of the affected muscle.

   The pain may be an incapacitating event in the case of acute onset, but it may also be a nagging, aggravating type of pain with an intensity that varies from an awareness of discomfort to a severe unrelenting type of pain. The pain location is usually a referred pain area, and the actual myofascial trigger point is often remote to the pain area. These trigger points can be present but quiescent until they are activated by overload, fatigue, trauma, or chilling. These points are called *latent trigger points*. This deep, aching pain can be specifically localized, but the patient is not sensitive to palpation in these areas. This pain can often be reproduced by maintaining pressure on a hypersensitive myofascial trigger point.

2. Passive or active stretching of the affected myofascial structure increases pain.

3. The stretch range of muscle is restricted.

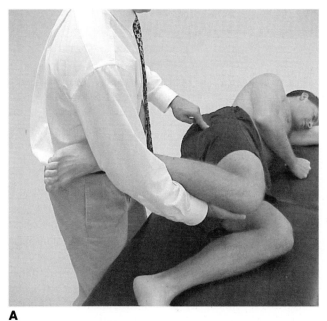

A

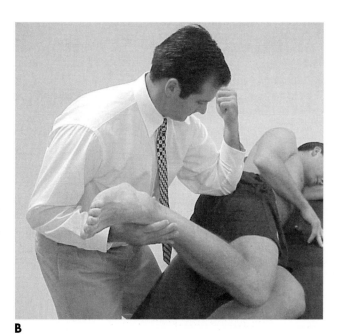

B

EXERCISE 33-52

Piriformis stretch using elbow pressure. **A,** Start-contract. **B,** Relaxation-stretch.

4. The pain is increased when the muscle is contracted against a fixed resistance or the muscle is allowed to contract into a very shortened range. The pain in this case is described as a muscle cramping pain.
5. The muscle may be slightly weak.
6. Trigger points may be located within a taut band of the muscle. If taut bands are found during palpation, explore them for local hypersensitive areas.
7. Pressure on the hypersensitive area will often cause a "jump sign"; as the therapist strums the sensitive area, the patient's muscle involuntarily jumps in response.

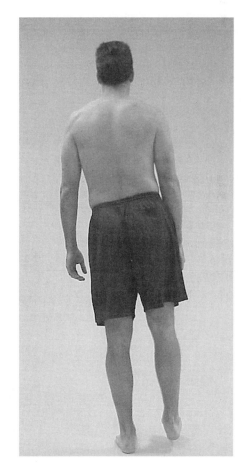

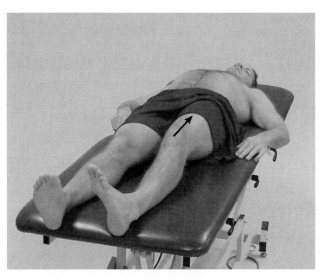

EXERCISE 33-53

Back-lying hip hike shifting.

EXERCISE 33-54

Standing hip hike.

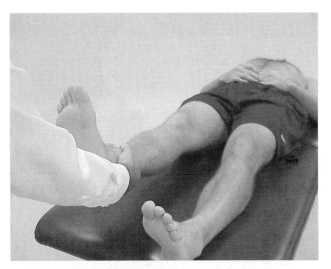

E X E R C I S E   3 3 - 5 5

Back-lying hip hike resisted.

8. The primary muscle groups that create low back pain in patients are the quadratus lumborum and the piriformis muscles.[18,32,35,36]

Travell and Simons have devoted two volumes to the causes and treatment of various myofascial pains.[35,36] They have done a very thorough job of describing the symptoms and signs of each area of the body, and they give very specific guidance on exercises and positioning in their treatment protocols.

REHABILITION TECHNIQUE

Myofascial trigger points may be treated using the following steps:

1. Position the patient comfortably but in a position that will lend itself to stretching the involved muscle group.
2. Caution the patient to use mild progressive stretches rather than sudden, sharp, hard stretches.
3. Hot pack the area for 10 minutes, and follow with an ultrasound-electrical stimulation treatment over the affected muscle.

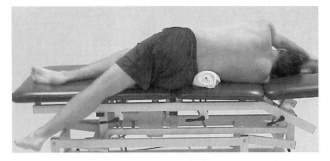

E X E R C I S E   3 3 - 5 6

Side-lying stretch over pillow roll.

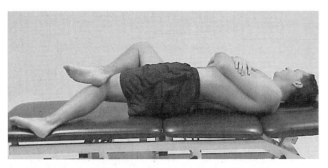

E X E R C I S E   3 3 - 5 7

Supine self-stretch legs crossed.

4. Use an ice cup, and use 2 or 3 slow strokes starting at the trigger point and moving in one direction toward the pain reference area and over the full length of the muscle.
5. Begin stretching well within the patient's comfort. A stretch should be maintained a minimum of 15 seconds. The stretch should be released until the patient is comfortable again. The next stretch repetition should then be progressively more intense if tolerated, and the position of the stretch should also be varied slightly. Repeat the stretch 4 to 6 times.
6. Hot pack the area, and have the patient go through some active stretches of the muscle.
7. Refer to Travell and Simons' manual for specific references on other muscle groups.[18,35,36]

Lumbar Facet Joint Sprains

PATHOMECHANICS AND INJURY MECHANISM

Sprains may occur in any of the ligaments in the lumbar spine, but the most common sprain involves lumbar facet joints. Facet joint sprain typically occurs when bending forward and twisting while lifting or moving some object. The patient will report a sudden acute episode that caused the problem, or they will give

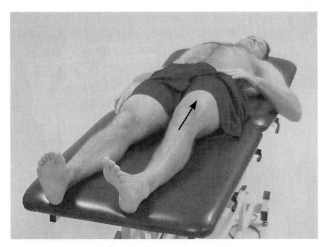

E X E R C I S E   3 3 - 5 8

Hip hike exercise with hand pressure.

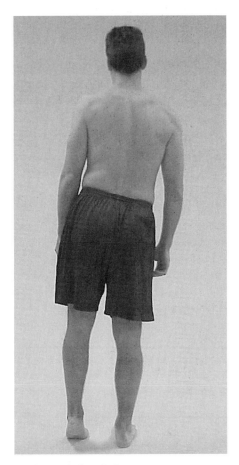

EXERCISE 33-59

Standing one leg up stretch.

a history of a chronic repetitive stress that caused the gradual onset of a pain that got progressively worse with continuing activity. The pain is local to the structure that has been injured, and the patient can clearly localize the area. The pain is described as a sore pain that gets sharper in response to certain movements or postures. The pain is located centrally or just lateral to the spinous process areas and is deep.

Local symptoms will occur in response to movements, and the patient will usually limit the movement in those ranges that are painful. When the vertebra is moved passively with a posteroanterior or rotational pressure through the spinous process, the pain may be provoked.

REHABILITATION PROGRESSION

The treatment should include the standard protection, ice, and compression as mentioned previously. Both pulsed ultrasound and electrical stimulation could also be used similarly to the treatment of muscle strains but localized to the specific joint area.

Joint mobilization using anteroposterior (see Exercise 33-30) and rotational glides (see Exercises 33-32 and 33-33) should help reduce pain and increase joint nutrition. The patient should be instructed in trunk stabilization exercises using

good postural control (see Exercises 33-39 to 33-43). Strengthening exercises for abdominals (see Exercises 33-12 to 33-14) and back extensors (see Exercises 33-6 to 33-9) should initially be limited to a pain-free range. Stretching in all ranges should start well within a comfort range and gradually increase until trunk movements reach normal ranges. Patients should be supported with a corset or range-limiting brace when they return to competitive activity, which should be used only temporarily until normal strength, muscle control, and pain-free range are achieved.[0,20,21,34,37] It is important to guard against the development of postural changes that may occur in response to pain.

Hypermobility Syndromes (Spondylolysis/Spondylolisthesis)

PATHOMECHANICS

Hypermobility of the low back may be attributed to spondylolysis or spondylolithesis. Spondylolysis refers to a degeneration of the vertebrae and, more commonly, a defect in the pars interarticularis of the articular processes of the vertebrae. It is often attributed to a congenital weakness with the defect occurring as a stress fracture. Spondylolysis may produce no symptoms unless a disk herniation occurs or there is sudden trauma such as hyperextension. Commonly, spondylolysis begins unilaterally. However, if it extends bilaterally, there may be some slipping of one vertebra on the one below it.

A spondylolisthesis is considered to be a complication of spondylolysis, often resulting in hypermobility of a vertebral segment.[11] Spondylolisthesis has the highest incidence with L5 slipping on S1.

INJURY MECHANISM

Movements that characteristically hyperextend the spine are most likely to cause this condition.

REHABILITATION CONCERNS

The patient usually has a relatively long history of feeling something "go" in the back. The patient complains of a low back pain described as a constant persistent ache across the back (belt type). This pain does not usually interfere with workout performance but is usually worse when fatigued or after sitting in a slumped posture for an extended time. The patient may also complain of a tired feeling in the low back. The patient describes the need to move frequently and get temporary relief of pain from self-manipulation. Patients often describe self-manipulative behavior more than 20 times a day. Their pain is relieved by rest, and they do not usually feel the pain during exercise. On physical examination, the patient usually will have full and painless trunk movements, but there will be a wiggle or hesitation at the midrange of forward bending. On backward bending, movement may appear to hinge at one spinal segment. When extremes of range are maintained for 15 to 30 seconds, the patient feels a lumbosacral ache. On return from forward bending, the patient will use thigh climbing to regain the neutral position. On palpation there may be tenderness localized to one spinal segment. Excessive movement may be noticed when applying posteroanterior pressure to the spinal segment.

REHABILITATION PROGRESSION

Patients with this problem will fall into the reinjury stage of back pain and may require extensive treatment to regain stability of the trunk. The patient's pain should be treated symptomatically. Initially, bracing and occasionally bed rest for 1 to 3 days will help to reduce pain. The major focus in rehabilitation should be directed toward exercises that control or stabilize the hypermobile segment (see Exercises 33-39 to 33-43). Progressive trunk-strengthening exercises, especially through the midrange, should be incorporated. Dynamic trunk-stabilization exercises, which concentrate on abdominal muscles, should also be used (see Exercises 33-12 to 33-14). The patient should avoid manipulation and self-manipulation as well as stretching and flexibility exercises. Corsets and braces are beneficial if the patient uses them only for support during higher-level activities and for short (1- to 2-hour) periods to help avoid fatigue (Exercise 33-60). [15,28] Hypermobility of a lumbar vertebra may make the patient more susceptible to lumbar muscle strains and ligament sprains. Thus it may be necessary for the patient to avoid vigorous activity. The use of a low back corset or brace may also make the patient more comfortable (Exercise 33-60).

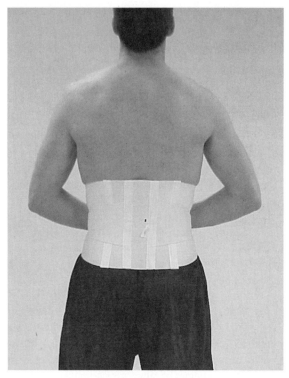

E X E R C I S E   3 3 - 6 0

A lower lumbar corset or brace.

Disk-Related Back Pain

PATHOMECHANICS

The lumbar disks are subject to constant abnormal stresses stemming from faulty body mechanics, trauma, or both, which over a period of time can cause degeneration, tears, and cracks in the annulus fibrosus.[6] The disk most often injured lies between the L4 and L5 vertebrae. The L5-S1 disk is the second most commonly affected.

INJURY MECHANISM

The mechanism of a disk injury is the same as for the lumbosacral sprain—forward bending and twisting that places abnormal strain on the lumbar region. The movement that produces herniation or bulging of the nucleus pulposus may be minimal, and associated pain may be significant. Besides injuring soft tissues, such a stress may herniate an already degenerated disk by causing the nucleus pulposus to protrude into or through the annulus fibrosis. As the disk progressively degenerates a prolapsed disk may develop in which the nucleus moves completely through the annulus. If the nucleus moves into the spinal canal and comes into contact with a nerve root, this is referred to as an extruded disk. This protrusion of the nucleus pulposus may place pressure on the cord of spinal nerves, thus causing radiating pains similar to those of sciatica as occurs in piriformis syndrome. If the material of the nucleus separates from the disk and begins to migrate, a sequestrated disk exists.

REHABILITATION CONCERNS

Patients will report a centrally located pain that radiates unilaterally or spreads across the back. They may describe a sudden or gradual onset that becomes particularly severe after they have rested and then tried to resume their activities. They may complain of tingling or numb feelings in a dermatomal pattern or sciatic radiation. Forward-bending and sitting postures increase their pain. Symptoms are usually worse in the morning on first arising and get better through the day. Coughing and sneezing may increase their pain.

On physical examination, the patient will have a hip shifted, forward-bent posture. On active movements, side-bending toward the hip shift is painful and limited. Side-bending away from the shift is more mobile and does not provoke the pain. Forward-bending is very limited and painful, and guarding is very apparent. On palpation there may be tenderness around the painful area. Posteroanterior pressure over the involved segment increases the pain. Passive straight-leg raising will increase the back or leg pain during the first 30 degrees of hip flexion. Bilateral knee-to-chest movement will increase the back pain. Neurologic testing (strength, sensory reflex) may be positive for differences between right and left.

REHABILITATION PROGRESSION

The patient should be treated with pain-reducing modalities (ice, electrical stimulation) initially. The therapist should then use the lateral shift correction and extension exercise (see Exercise 33-1). This should be followed by self-correction instruction and gentle strengthening and mobilizing exercises. Manual traction combined with passive backward bending or extension makes the patient more comfortable. The goal is to reduce the protrusion and restore normal posture. When pain and posture return to normal, abdominal and back extensor strengthening should be emphasized. This patient may recover easily from the first episode, but if repeated episodes occur, then the patient should also start on the reinjury stage of back rehabilitation.[7,10,12,14,17,27,30,33]

If the disk is extruded or sequestrated, about the only thing that can be done is to modulate pain with electrical stimulation. Flexion exercises and lying supine in a flexed position may help with comfort. The use of a low back corset or brace may also make the patient more comfortable (Fig. 33-19). Sometimes the symptoms will resolve with time. But if there are signs of nerve damage, surgery may be necessary.

Sacroiliac Joint Dysfunction

PATHOMECHANICS AND INJURY MECHANISM

A sprain of the sacroiliac joint may result from twisting with both feet on the ground, stumbling forward, falling backward, stepping too far down and landing heavily on one leg, or forward bending with the knees locked during lifting.[20] Athletic activities involving unilateral forceful movements, such as punting, hurdling, throwing, jumping, or trunk rotations with both feet fixed (swinging a club or bat), are the usual activities associated with the onset of pain. Any of these mechanisms can produce irritation and stretching of the sacrotuberous or sacrospinous ligaments. They may also cause either an anterior or posterior rotation of one side of the pelvis relative to the other. With rotation of the pelvis there is hypomobility. As healing occurs, the joint on the injured side may become hypermobile, allowing that joint to sublux in either an anteriorly or posteriorly rotated position.

REHABILITATION CONCERNS

On observation, the ASIS and/or PSIS may be asymmetrical when compared to the opposite side due to either anterior or posterior rotation of one side of the pelvis relative to the other. There may appear to be a measurable leg length difference.

The patient will relate a gradual onset of dull, achy back pain near or medial to the posterosuperior iliac spine (PSIS) with some associated muscle guarding. The pain may radiate into the buttocks and posterolateral thigh. The patient may describe a heaviness or dullness or deadness in the leg or referred pain to the groin, adductor, or hamstring on the same side. Doing a hip flexion activity with the affected leg may increase the pain. The pain may be more noticeable during the stance phase of walking.

On active movements in forward bending, there is a block to normal movement, and the PSIS on the affected side will move sooner than the normal side. Side-bending toward the painful side will increase the pain. Straight-leg raising will increase pain in the sacroiliac joint area after 45 degrees of motion. On palpation, there may be tenderness over the PSIS, medial to the PSIS, in the muscles of the buttocks, and anteriorly over the pubic symphysis. The back musculature will have increased tone on one side.

REHABILITATION PROGRESSION

To treat this problem, the therapist should mobilize the sacroiliac joint to correct the postural asymmetry (see Exercises 33-34 to 33-38). If the right side of the pelvis appears to be posteriorly rotated, it should be mobilized in an anterior direction. This should be followed by a contract–relax stretch of the hip, again aimed at correcting the postural asymmetry. Strengthening exercises should be used to help improve stability of a hypermobile joint. A bilateral hip lifting bridge exercise may be used to help stabilize the pelvis (Exercise 33-45). Corsets or belts may also help to stabilize the pelvis during activities (Exercise 33-60). Self-stretching to correct the postural asymmetry should also be taught to the patient.[4,5,11,16,40]

REHABILITATION TECHNIQUES FOR THE CERVICAL SPINE

Acute Facet Joint Lock

PATHOMECHANICS

Acute cervical joint lock is a very common condition, more frequently called wryneck or stiff neck. The patient usually complains of pain on one side of the neck following sudden backward bending, side-bending, and/or rotation of the neck. Pain can also occur after holding the head in an unusual position over a period of time as when awakening from sleep. This problem can also occasionally follow exposure to a cold draft of air. There is no report of other acute trauma that could have produced the pain. This usually occurs when a small piece of synovial membrane lining the joint capsule or a meniscoid body is impinged or trapped within a facet joint in the cervical vertebrae. During inspection, there is palpable point tenderness and marked muscle guarding. The patient will report that the neck is "locked." Side-bending and rotation are painful when moving in the direction opposite to the position in which there is locking. Other movements are relatively painless.[31]

REHABILITATION PROGRESSION

Various therapeutic modalities may be used to modulate pain in an attempt to break a pain–spasm–pain cycle. Joint mobilizations involving gentle traction (Exercise 33-61), rotation (Exercise 33-62), and lateral bending (Exercise 33-63)—first

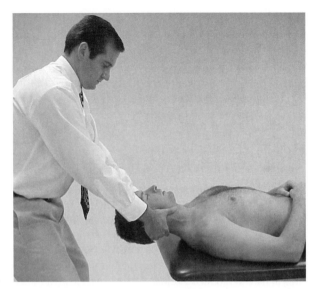

EXERCISE 33-61

Cervical traction

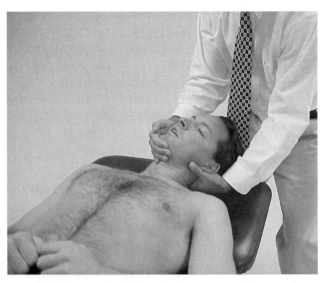

EXERCISE 33-63

Cervical vertebrae side bending may be used to treat pain or stiffness with resistance when side bending the neck.

Cervical Sprain

PATHOMECHANICS AND INJURY MECHANISM

A cervical sprain usually results from a moderate to severe trauma. Commonly, the head snaps suddenly, such as a case of "whiplash" occurring in an automobile accident. Frequently

in the pain-free direction and then in the direction of pain—can help reduce the guarding. Occasionally pain will be relieved almost immediately following mobilization. If not, it may be helpful to wear a soft cervical collar to provide for comfort (Exercise 33-64). This muscle guarding will generally last for 2 to 3 days as the patient progressively regains motion.

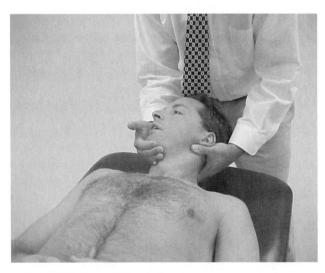

EXERCISE 33-62

Cervical vertebrae rotation oscillations are done with one hand supporting the weight of the head and the other rotating the head in the direction of the restriction. These oscillations treat pain or stiffness when there is some resistance in the same direction as the rotation.

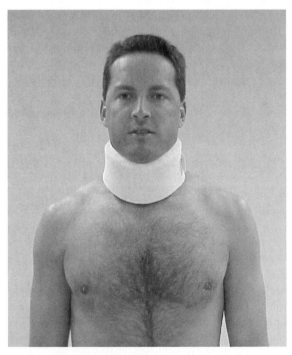

EXERCISE 33-64

The use of either a soft or hard collar can increase comfort.

muscle strains occur with ligament sprains. A sprain of the neck can produce tears in the major supporting tissue of the anterior or posterior longitudinal ligaments, the interspinous ligament, and the supraspinous ligament. There may be palpable tenderness over the transverse and spinous processes that serve as sites of attachment for the ligaments.

The sprain displays all the signs of the facet joint lock, but the movement restriction is much greater and can potentially involve more than one vertebral segment. The main difference between the two is that while acute joint lock can usually be dealt with in a very short period of time, a sprain will require a significantly longer period for rehabilitation. Pain may not be significant initially but always appears the day after the trauma. Pain stems from the inflammation of injured tissue and a protective muscle guarding that restricts motion.

REHABILITATION PROGRESSION

As soon as possible the patient should have a physician evaluation to rule out the possibility of fracture, dislocation, disk injury, or injury to the spinal cord or nerve root. A soft cervical collar may be applied to reduce muscle guarding (Exercise 33-64). Ice and electrical stimulation are used for 48 to 72 hours while the injury is in the acute stage of healing. In a patient with a severe injury, the physician may prescribe 2 to 3 days of bed rest, along with analgesics and anti-inflammatory medication. Range-of-motion exercises through a pain-free range should begin as soon as possible, including flexion (Exercise 33-65), extension (Exercise 33-66), rotation (Exercise 33-67), and side-bending (Exercise 33-68). It has been demonstrated that using

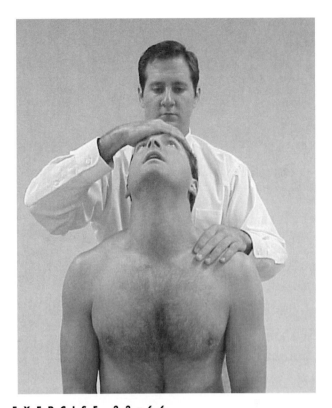

EXERCISE 33-66

Manually assisted extension stretching exercise.

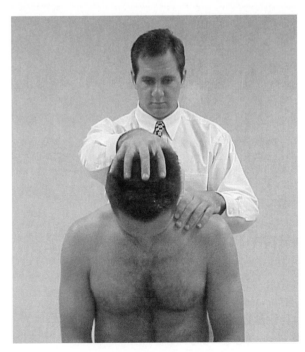

EXERCISE 33-65

Manually assisted flexion stretching exercise.

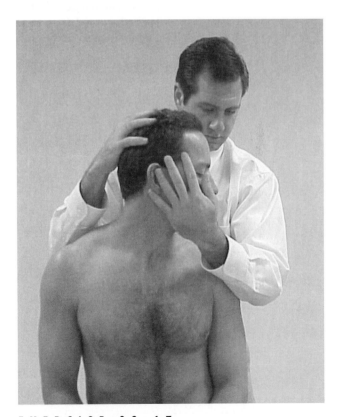

EXERCISE 33-67

Manually assisted rotation stretching exercise.

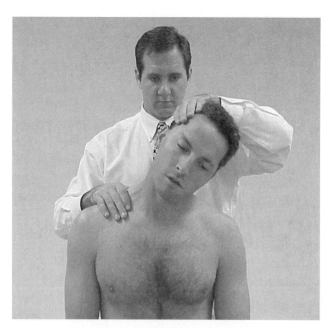

E X E R C I S E   3 3 - 6 8

Manually assisted side-bending stretching exercise.

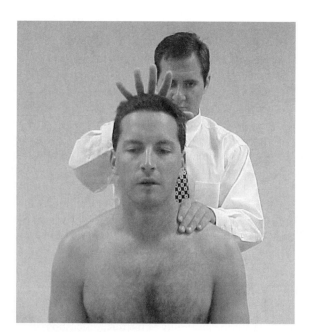

E X E R C I S E   3 3 - 7 0

Manually resisted extension strengthening exercise.

early ROM exercises, as opposed to long periods of immobility, tends to reduce the likelihood of neck hypomobility when the healing process is complete.[31] It is important to regain motion as soon as possible, but it is critical to understand that a sprain, particularly one that involes a complete ligament tear, causes

hypermobility. Thus strengthening exercises (Exercises 33-69 to 33-72), along with stabilization exercises (Exercises 33-73 and 33-74), should also be incorporated into the rehabilitation program. Mechanical traction may also be prescribed to relieve pain and muscle guarding (see Exercise 33-63).

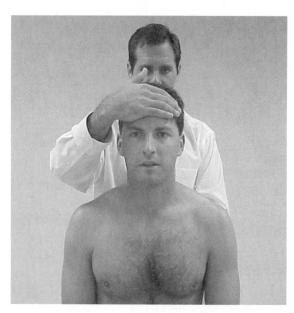

E X E R C I S E   3 3 - 6 9

Manually resisted flexion strengthening exercise.

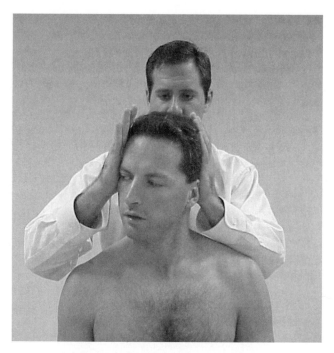

E X E R C I S E   3 3 - 7 1

Manually resisted rotation strengthening exercise.

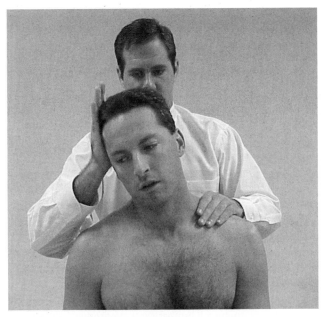

EXERCISE 33-72

Manually resisted side-bending strengthening exercise.

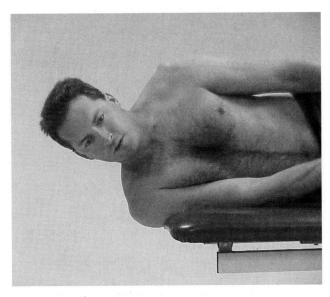

EXERCISE 33-73

Gravity assisted cervical stabilization exercise done on a treatment table with the head maintaining a static position. May be done sidelying (right and left), prone, supine.

EXERCISE 33-74

Cervical stabilization exercises done on a Swiss ball.

SUMMARY

- The low back pain that patients most often experience is an acute, painful experience of relatively short duration.
- Regardless of the diagnosis or the specificity of the diagnosis, a thorough evaluation of the patient's back pain is critical to good care.
- Back rehabilitation may be classified as a two-stage approach. Stage I (acute stage) treatment consists mainly of modality treatment and pain-relieving exercises. Stage II involves treating patients with a reinjury or exacerbation of a previous problem.
- The types of exercises that may be included in the initial pain management phase include lateral shift corrections, extension exercises, flexion exercises, mobilization exercises, and myofascial stretching exercises.
- It is suggested that the therapist use an eclectic approach to the selection of exercises, mixing the various protocols described according to the findings of the patient's evaluation.
- Specific goals and exercises included in stage II should address which structures to stretch, which structures to strengthen, incorporating dynamic stabilization into the patient's daily living and exercise routine, and which movements need a motor learning approach to control faulty mechanics.
- The rehabilitation program should be based on functional training, which may be divided into basic and advanced phases.
- Back pain can result from one or a combination of the following problems: muscle strain, piriformis muscle or quadratus lumborum myofascial pain or strain, myofascial trigger points, lumbar facet joint sprains, hypermobility syndromes, disk-related back problems, or sacroiliac joint dysfunction.
- Cervical pain can result from muscle strains, acute cervical joint lock, ligament sprains, and various other problems.

REFERENCES

1. Beattie P. The use of an eclectic approach for the treatment of low back pain: A case study. *Phys Ther* 72:923–928, 1992.

2. Binkley J, Finch E, Hall J, et al. Diagnostic classification of patients with low back pain: Report on a survey of physical therapy experts. *Phys Ther* 73:138–155, 1993.

3. Bittinger J. *Management of the Lumbar Pain Syndromes* Course Notes, Los Angeles, 1980.

4. Cibulka M. The treatment of the sacroiliac joint component to low back pain: A case report, *Phys Ther* 72:917–922, 1992.

5. Cibulka M, Delitto A, Koldehoff R. Changes in innominate tilt after manipulation of the sacroiliac joint in patients with low back pain: An experimental study. *Phys Ther* 68:1359–1370, 1988.

6. Cibulka M, Rose S, Delitto A, et al. Hamstring muscle strain treated by mobilizing the saroiliac joint. *Phys Ther* 66:1220–1223, 1986.

7. Crock H. Internal disk disruption: A challenge to disk-prolapse fifty years on. The presidential address, ISSLS. *Spine* 11:650–653, 1986.

8. DeRosa C, Porterfield J. A physical therapy model for the treatment of low back pain. *Phys Ther* 72:321–372, 1992.

9. Deyo R, Diehl A, Rosenthal M. How many days of bed rest for acute low back pain? A randomized clinical trial. *N Engl J Med* 315:1064–1070, 1986.

10. Donley P. Rehabilitation of low back pain in patients: The 1976 Schering symposium on low back problems. *Athl Train* 12(2):65–69, 1977.

11. Erhard R, Bowling R. The recognition and management of the pelvic component of low back and sciatic pain. *APTA* 2:4–13, 1979.

12. Farfan H. Muscular mechanism of the lumbar spine and the position of power and efficiency. *Orthop Clin North Am* 6:135–144, 1975.

13. Friberg O. Clinical symptoms and biomechanics of lumbar spine and hip joint in leg length inequality. *Spine* 8:643–650, 1983.

14. Frymoyer J. Back pain and sciatica: Medical progress. *N Engl J Med* 318:291–300, 1988.

15. Grieve G. Lumbar instability. Congress lecture *Physiotherapy* 68:2–9, 1982.

16. Grieve G. The sacro-iliac joint. *Physiotherapy* 62:384–400, 1976.

17. Jackson C, Brown M. Analysis of current approaches and a practical guide to prescription of exercise. *Clin Orthop Rel Res* 179:46–54, 1983.

18. Lewit K, Simons D. Myofascial pain: Relief by post-isometric relaxation. *Arch Phys Med Rehabil* 65:452–456, 1984.

19. Lindstrom I, Ohlund C, Eek C, et al. The effect of graded activity on patients with subacute low back pain: A randomized prospective clinical study with an operant-conditioning behavioral approach. *Phys Ther* 72:279–290, 1992.

20. Maigne R. Low back pain of thoracolumbar origin. *Arch Phys Med Rehabil* 61:391–395, 1980.

21. Maitland G. *Vertebral Manipulation*, 5th ed. London, Butterworth, 1990.

22. Mapa B. An Australian programme for management of low back problems. *Physiotherapy* 66:108–111, 1980.

23. McGraw M. *The Neuro-muscular Maturation of the Human Infant.* New York, Hafner, 1966.

24. McKenzie R. *The Lumbar Spine: Mechanical Diagnosis and Therapy.* Lower Hutt, New Zealand, Spinal Publications 1981.

25. McKenzie R. Manual correction of sciatic scoliosis. *NZ Med J* 76:194–199, 1972.

26. Porter R, Miller C. Back pain and trunk list. *Spine* 11:596–600, 1986.

27. Saal J. Dynamic muscular stabilization in the nonoperative treatment of lumbar pain syndromes. *Orthop Rev* 19:691–700, 1990.

28. Saal J. Rehabilitation of football players with lumbar spine injury. *Phys Sports Med* 16:61–68, 1988.

29. Saal J. Rehabilitation of football players with lumbar spine injury. *Phys Sports Med* 16:117–125, 1988.

30. Saal J, Saal J. Nonoperative treatment of herniated lumbar intervertebral disk with radiculopathy: An outcome study. *Spine* 14:431–437, 1989.

31. Saunders D. *Evaluation, Treatment, and Prevention of Musculoskeletal Disorders.* Bloomington, MN, Educational Opportunities, 1985.

32. Steiner C, Staubs C, Ganon M, et al. Piriformis syndrome: Pathogenesis, diagnosis, and treatment. *Am J Sports Med* 87:318–323, 1987.

33. Tenhula J, Rose S, Delitto A. Association between direction of lateral lumbar shift, movement tests, and side of symptoms in patients with low back pain syndrome. *Phys Ther* 70:480–486, 1990.

34. Threlkeld A. The effects of manual therapy on connective tissue. *Phys Ther* 72:893–902, 1992.

35. Travell J, Simons D. *Myofascial Pain and Dysfunction: The Lower Extremities.* Baltimore, MD, Williams & Wilkins, 1992.

36. Travell J, Simons D. *Myofascial Pain and Dysfunction: The Trigger Point Manual.* Baltimore, MD, Williams & Wilkins, 1992.

37. Twomey L. A rationale for treatment of back pain and joint pain by manual therapy. *Phys Ther* 72:885–892, 1992.

38. Waddell G. Clinical assessment of lumbar impairment. *Clin Orthop Rel Res* 221:110–120, 1987.

39. Waddell G. A new clinical model for the treatment of low-back pain. *Spine* 12:632–644, 1987.

40. Walker J. The sacroiliac joint: A critical review. *Phys Ther* 72:903–916, 1992.

PART 5

Special Considerations for Specific Patient Populations

CHAPTER 34

Rehabilitation Considerations With the Geriatric Patient

Cissy Voight

OBJECTIVES

After completing this chapter, the student therapist should be able to do the following:

- Describe the normal aging process in terms of successful aging.
- Discuss and describe the factors that contribute to disease, functional limitation, and disability.
- Understand the normal structure and function of bone, considering the normal and abnormal remodeling of bone during the process of fracture healing and the pathophysiologic process of osteoporosis.
- List and discuss the risk factors for the development of osteoporosis.
- Identify the usual mechanism of injury and treatment interventions for common fracture in the elderly.
- List and describe the indications for shoulder, hip, and knee arthroplasty.
- Describe the surgical and postsurgical considerations in the patient undergoing total joint arthroplasty of the shoulder, hip, and knee.
- Differentiate the principles of rehabilitation as they relate to the aging patient.

Rehabilitative care of older adults has evolved into a specialty area of practice for many clinicians. Geriatrics, or the care of the elderly, is based on the recognition that the aging process causes the body to respond differently to injury, disease, and medical care. The field of geriatrics continues to gain attention due to the rapid growth of this segment of the population and its predicted socioeconomic impact in the present century.

Traditionally, demographers have used age 65 to delineate one's reaching "old age." One of the reasons for this delineation is established social practice, such as retirement, Social Security, and Medicare. This segment of the population is growing steadily, both in absolute numbers and in proportion to the total population. A tremendous increase in the number of individuals reaching "old age" is projected during the next 40 to 50 years. In 1900, there were 3 million persons aged 65 years and above in the United States, representing 4 percent of the total population. In 1988, the number of persons age 65 years and older had grown to 31.6 million or 12.7 percent of the total population.[54] It is estimated that in 2020, 51 million individuals will be over the age of 65, representing 17.3

percent of the population. This dramatic growth is a result of the large cohorts born during the post-World War II "baby boom" that will be reaching old age, and the improved survivorship in all age cohorts, especially those regarded as the oldest-old at 100+ years. Since the mid-19th century, life expectancy in the United States has nearly doubled, from 40 years to almost 80 years, due in part to medical and scientific breakthroughs and improved health habits. Of this 65 and older category, it is estimated that 48 percent are actually over 75 years old. The number of elders aged 85 or older is predicted to triple in number by 2040.[9] As a result of this growth, the definition of "old age" is being redefined to better differentiate this large segment of the population (Table 34-1).

The purpose of this chapter is to provide an overview of the aging process in multiple systems and the impact of aging on the rehabilitation of acute and chronic musculoskeletal conditions common in the elderly. Orthopedic conditions commonly experienced by the older population will be addressed in regard to pathology, surgical intervention, and rehabilitation programs. Emphasis is placed on the importance of physical activity in

TABLE 34-1

Chronologic Age Descriptions

DESCRIPTION	AGE RANGE (YEARS)
Infant	0–2
Child	3–12
Adolescent	13–17
Young adult	18–24
Adult	25–44
Middle age	45–64
Young-old	65–74
Old	75–84
Old-old	85–99
Oldest-old	100+

preventing injury and minimizing functional decline. It is our goal to provide the physical therapist with knowledge that will facilitate development of effective rehabilitation interventions for this special population.

AGING DEFINED: IMPACT OF REHABILITATION

Although there is no perfect definition of the aging process, it can be loosely defined as the manifestations of biological events that occur over time. The term "aging" refers to a process or group of processes occurring in a living organism that, with the passage of time, leads to a loss of adaptability, impairment, functional limitation, and disability eventually leading to death. With increasing age comes an increased probability of experiencing a chronic debilitating condition and loss of functional capacity. Aging is often accompanied by a deterioration of general health. The incidence of chronic conditions has been shown to increase with advancing age, and this population is especially vulnerable to loss of function and independence following injury or illness. Elderly individuals often suffer from several diseases at the same time, such as cardiovascular disorders, arthritis, and diabetes with its various complications. These disease processes interact and their effects are additive.

Musculoskeletal impairments are among the most prevalent and symptomatic health problems of middle and old age.[9,31] By decreasing strength, restricting movement, and causing pain, musculoskeletal impairments prevent people who are middle-aged and older from making full use of their abilities for leisure or work, and from participating in the regular physical activity necessary to maintain optimum mobility and general health. For some individuals, declining mobility leads to loss of independence. Progress in medicine and surgery has made it possible for acutely or chronically ill elderly patients to survive for longer periods of time, but all too often the price of survival is a physical disability. The importance of rehabili-

tation programs that have the potential to restore function, prolong independence, and improve quality of life following injury or illness is readily apparent in this population. Rehabilitation professionals must be prepared to treat immediate acute conditions but also anticipate and manage the negative impact of pain, reduced activity, and immobilization on mobility and function in the aging adult. It is inevitable that future rehabilitation professionals will see an increase in the number of elderly individuals seeking services for the management of both acute and chronic conditions that can negatively impact active life expectancy or the number of years that an individual may expect to be independent in activities of daily living.[33] Older individuals fear nothing more than the prospect of losing their independence and having to rely on others for their daily care. Restoration of function and delay of functional decline and disability in order to help maintain independence must be of primary concern to those treating the elderly. Developing appropriate and cost-effective interventions with this purpose in mind is paramount.

FUNDAMENTALS FOR UNDERSTANDING THE AGING PROCESS

Biological Theories of Aging

Aging is a universal phenomenon that affects us all. Scientists have attempted to determine the underlying mechanisms responsible for the structural and functional changes that characterize advancing age. Genetic theories focus on the mechanisms for aging located in the nucleus of the cell. It is theorized that mutations and chromosomal anomalies accumulate with age, resulting in senescence. Based on the work of Leonard Hayflick, cells have a preprogrammed life span and genes control cell proliferation and cell death. Nongenetic theories focus on changes in function of control systems within the body—the immune system, neuroendocrine system, and central nervous system—and on the role of environment, lifestyle, exposure to toxins, and the cumulative effects of injury and illness. Whatever the cause, aging is most likely not a single biological process, but rather a wide variety of age-related changes that occur simultaneously in many different systems throughout the body. Together these changes impact the body's ability to adapt to everyday stresses and physical challenges, recover from physical insult, and continue to support vital function. Of immediate concern to the rehabilitation professional is an understanding of basic fundamental principles of the aging process and their impact on the ability of older adults to recover from injury or surgical intervention.

Aging Is Heterogeneous

Aging is a heterogeneous process and therefore differs greatly among individuals. The variability in health status and functional status is much greater in the older population as a whole than in the young. Older adults differ with regard to the degree that they experience functional limitations and disability associated with aging, disease, or injury. Many older adults retain high levels of activity and functional abilities well into advanced age. Conversely, some individuals demonstrate a physiologic age far exceeding their chronologic age because of chronic illnesses. Therefore, chronologic age should not be used to determine potential for recovery or the appropriateness of referral for rehabilitation. A comprehensive examination is necessary to determine individual impairments and functional limitations and will assist the therapist in determining the long-term prognosis for each patient and developing appropriate rehabilitation programs for minimizing disability.

Normal Versus Usual Aging

Normal aging is defined as "age-related changes that are the result of the passage of time and that are free of pathologic conditions."[7] Examples of normal age-related processes are farsightedness, hearing loss, decline in short-term memory, and menopause. The therapist must be able to recognize impairments associated with normal aging and consider the impact these changes will have on recovery and the ability of the individual to participate in or adhere to the prescribed rehabilitation program. Usual aging refers to the onset of age-related pathologic conditions such as osteoarthritis, osteoporosis, and coronary artery disease. Many of the age-dependent diseases previously thought to be a part of normal aging and inevitable are actually usual aging and may be positively impacted with early and effective interventions and patient education. The therapist treating an individual for an acute problem may provide invaluable education that could prevent or slow the progression of age-dependent conditions, especially those that are lifestyle dependent.

Successful aging represents efforts toward maximizing one's years of independence and compressing the onset of disease, disability, morbidity, and mortality.[21] Successful agers do not necessarily escape all disease or disability, but may delay the onset of age-related illness and decrease their overall morbidity. There is an emerging body of research supporting the importance of a healthy lifestyle, good nutrition, and exercise to successful aging.[3]

Comorbidity

Coexisting pathologic processes can exacerbate the effects of other conditions and result in greater functional limitations and disability. An older person's functional limitations may be a result of the sum of lost physiologic reserve in one or more systems. Rehabilitation programs must take into consideration the whole person with multiple system involvement and avoid interventions that may negatively impact one system while considered appropriate in the absence of comorbidity. Chronic conditions occur more frequently with age, accumulating as

TABLE 34-2

Chronic Conditions Often Experienced by Older Adults

Cardiovascular
  Heart disease
  Hypertension
Metabolic
  Diabetes
  Obesity
Pulmonary
  Asthma
  COPD
Neurologic
  Parkinson's disease
  Alzheimer's disease
Musculoskeletal
  Osteoarthritis
  Rheumatoid arthritis
Sensory
  Visual disorders
  Auditory disorders

people live longer. It is estimated that 80 percent of people 65 and older have one or more chronic diseases.[30] The most disabled patients are more likely to have a number of medical conditions that complicate assessment and treatment planning (Table 34-2).

Physiologic Reserve

The gradual decline of health and increased incidence of injury and diseases experienced by older individuals can be partially attributed to the gradual loss of physiologic reserves. Throughout youth and early adulthood, our bodies have reserve physiologic capacities and system redundancies that enable us to adapt to physical challenges and injury without loss in functional abilities. With aging, there is a loss in this reserve capacity and redundancy. Changes in muscle tissue, articular cartilage, intervertebral disks, tendons, ligaments, and joint capsules result in increased susceptibility to injury from repetitive use or trauma. Age-related alterations in bone dramatically increase the risk of fracture with age. The net result of these processes occurring over time is the loss of adaptability and development of impairment, functional limitation, and disability. This ensuing state of reduced physiologic reserve associated with increased susceptibility to functional limitations and disability has been defined as frailty.[20] Frailty is viewed as usual aging, and the opposite end of the spectrum from successful aging. A large percentage of loss in the musculoskeletal system and the cardiovascular system may be prevented with adherence to continued physical activity throughout the aging years.

T A B L E   3 4 - 3

Summary of the Physiologic Benefits of Physical Activity for Older Persons

- *Aerobic/cardiovascular endurance.* Substantial improvements in almost all aspects of cardiovascular functioning have been observed following appropriate physical training.
- *Muscle strength.* Individuals of all ages can benefit from muscle strengthening exercises. Resistance training can have a significant impact on the maintenance of independence in old age.
- *Flexibility.* Exercises that incorporate movement throughout the range of motion assist in the preservation and restoration of flexibility.
- *Balance/coordination.* Regular activity helps prevent and/or postpone the age-associated declines in balance and coordination that are risk factors for falls.
- *Velocity of movement.* Behavioral slowing is a characteristic of advancing age. Individuals who are regularly active can often postpone these age-related declines.

SOURCE: World Health Organization, 1997.

Hypokinetics

The deleterious effects of immobility are well documented. Due to the summative effects of aging on multiple systems, fatigue, reduction in sensory information, fear of falling, and effects of accumulated disease processes, many older adults experience a gradual reduction in activity level over time. This decreased activity, or hypokinetics, sets up a vicious cycle of disuse and loss of function. Loss of muscle mass, demineralization of bone, diminished cardiopulmonary function, and loss of neuromotor control have been directly related to lack of physical activity. Disuse exacerbates the aging process and negatively impacts physiologic reserve in the face of disease and injury. Participation in a regular exercise program has proven to be an effective intervention/modality to reduce or prevent functional declines associated with aging (Table 34-3). Regular exercise can also provide a number of psychological benefits related to preserved cognitive function, alleviation of depression symptoms, and behavior and an improved concept of personal control and self-efficacy.

AGE-RELATED CHANGES IN TISSUES AND SYSTEMS: OBSTACLES TO SUCCESSFUL REHABILITATION

Cardiovascular System

Age-related anatomic and physiologic changes of the heart and blood vessels result in reduced capacity for oxygen transport at rest and in response to situations imposing an increase in metabolic demand for oxygen. Maximal oxygen consumption (VO_2 max), an index of maximal cardiovascular function, decreases 5 to 15 percent per decade after the age of 25 years.[27] This decrease is a factor of a reduction in both cardiac output and maximal arteriovenous O_2 difference with advancing age. A reduction of maximum heart rate of 6 to 10 bpm per decade is responsibl for much of the age-associated decrease in maximal

cardiac output. At submaximal exercise heart rate responses, cardiac output, and stroke volume are lower in older adults at the same absolute work rates, while arteriovenous O_2 difference and blood pressures tend to be higher.[27]

Older adults elicit the same 10 to 30 percent increases in VO_2 max with prolonged endurance exercise training as young adults.[43] As with young adults, the magnitude of the increase in VO_2 max in older adults is also a function of training intensity, with light-intensity training eliciting minimal or no changes. While recent CDC/ACSM guidelines recommend light to moderate physical activities to optimize health and reduce the rate of age-related deterioration in numerous physiologic functions, moderate- or high-intensity exercise may be required to elicit adaptations in the cardiovascular system and in cardiovascular risk factors.[43] Older patients with cardiovascular disease appear to obtain the same beneficial cardiovascular adaptations with exercise training as younger patients. These changes include decreases in heart rate at rest and during submaximal exercise and decreases in other physiologic responses during submaximal exercise at the same absolute exercise intensity. Walking, swimming, and cycling are large-muscle rhythmic aerobic forms of exercise that reduce the risk of musculoskeletal injury in the older adult.

The patient admitted to a rehabilitation program may not have been physically active for some time, and the level of fitness may have declined considerably. In the rehabilitation setting, patients may be called upon to exert themselves well above their usual activity level and tolerance. Elderly patients, therefore, may become rapidly exhausted with moderate or even minimal exertion and develop signs of cardiovascular failure. Their participation in the rehabilitation program may quickly reach a limit. Therefore, elderly patients should have a physician's evaluation of their cardiovascular status before engaging in a rehabilitation program. In addition, the rehabilitation provider should carefully monitor cardiovascular responses and patient tolerance while the patient is exercising. The contraindications to exercise training for older adults are the same as for young adults; however, it is important to remember there is an increased prevalence of comorbidities in older adults that affect cardiovascular function, such as diabetes, hypertension, obesity, and left ventricular dysfunction. Careful assessment of risk factors and adherence to ACSM guidelines for the need for exercise testing prior to initiating an exercise program for older adults should be considered.[2]

Sensory Systems

SOMATOSENSATION

The somatosensory system is critical to balance and motor control because it provides information related to body contact and position. The somatosystem includes cutaneous receptors, which provide information about touch and vibration, and muscle and joint receptors, which provide information about position, limb movement, and body changes. Age-related somatosensory changes include reduced vibration sense, slowed nerve-conduction velocities, and a decrease in skin receptors and cutaneous awareness.[50] Age-related somatosensory changes are most often more pronounced in the lower extremities. Diminished or lost vibratory sensation in the lower extremities is present in 10 percent of individuals over 60 and in 50 percent of individuals over 75.[10] Proprioceptive organs in and around the joints have a diminished ability to detect small-amplitude joint movements, and position sense is decreased. Arthritic changes in the joints may result in additional loss of receptor function. Postural stability and overall balance performance may be impaired in persons with reductions in foot and ankle tactile/proprioceptive input.

VISION

Overall visual function deteriorates with age. Specific age-related impairments are reduced visual acuity, contrast sensitivity, and depth perception as well as impaired smooth pursuit (the ability to follow an object across the visual field while keeping the object in focus with the head not moving) and reduced ability to accommodate and adapt to darkness and changes in light. Common conditions affecting older adults are cataracts (clouding of the lens resulting in blurred vision), macular degeneration (deterioration of the retina and supportive structures causing loss of central vision), and glaucoma (increased intraocular pressure resulting in loss of peripheral vision). Reduction in visual function is a risk factor associated with increased incidence of postural instability and falls.

VESTIBULAR SYSTEM

The vestibular system experiences changes with advancing age. There is a reduction in sensory cells and primary neurons in the peripheral vestibular system, resulting in decreased sensitivity and reduced ability to stabilize vision during head movements. Blurred vision will affect postural stability during gait and possibly contribute to increased fall risk. Many older adults complain of dizziness, which may be a result of vestibular dysfunction. One of the most common causes of dizziness in older adults is benign paroxysmal positional vertigo, caused by free-floating calcium carbonate crystals forming a mass within the endolymph in the semicircular canals. The crystals overstimulate the hair cells in the semicircular canals, resulting in the perception of spinning during position changes and head movement. Clinicians trained in specialized techniques can treat this condition easily and effectively.

Any complaint of dizziness must be differentiated from postural hypotension (reduction in systolic blood pressure of 20 mmHg or more upon assuming standing from a supine position). Many older adults experience postural hypotension as an adverse side effect of common medications, following extended periods of inactivity or bed rest, and after major surgical procedures that may result in blood volume reduction.

FUNCTIONAL IMPLICATIONS OF SENSORY SYSTEM AGING

Functions of the nervous system slow down with age. This slowing is associated with fatigue, loss of memory, a decrease in motor skills, and changes in sensory perception. Due to the redundancy in physiologic systems, a significant loss of sensory system function may be tolerated with little or no observable deficits; however, significant decline in one or more sensory systems may result in the reduced ability to perceive changing environmental conditions and generate appropriate and timely balance strategies. Loss of balance, for example, is perceived more slowly and corrected less efficiently. In addition, the inability of an aging central nervous system to integrate the multiple sensory elements may be another factor that contributes to limitations in the postural control system. It is beyond the scope of this chapter to discuss the assessment and management of balance disorders in the elderly; however, any older adult with a history of falls, fractures resulting from falls, or significant sensory system impairment should undergo a risk assessment to determine the appropriateness of a comprehensive balance assessment and treatment program.

Musculoskeletal System

The biological and mechanical behaviors of all of the musculoskeletal soft tissues—including skeletal muscle, articular cartilage, intervertebral disks, tendons, ligaments, and joint capsules—are altered with age.

SKELETAL MUSCLE

Loss of skeletal muscle mass with age is well documented. Muscle size decreases an average of 30 to 40 percent over one's lifetime and affects the lower extremities more than the upper extremities.[22] This decrease in muscle mass is a direct result of a reduction in muscle fiber size and number with advancing age and is largely attributed to progressive inactivity and sedentary lifestyles.[22] Fiber loss appears to be more accelerated in type II muscle fibers, which decrease from an average of 60 percent in sedentary young men to below

30 percent after the age of 80.[37] Type II fibers have approximately twice the intrinsic strength per unit area, and twice the velocity of contraction, of type I fibers, and are used primarily in activities requiring more power such as sprinting or strength training and are not stimulated by normal activities of daily living (ADL).

STRENGTH CHANGES

With reduced muscle mass comes a reduction in muscle force production, strength, and aerobic fitness—frequently hallmarks of advancing age. Strength loss may begin slowly around the age of 50 and becomes more rapid with advancing age. Strength loss correlates with mass loss until advanced age, at which time fiber atrophy may not account fully for the observed strength loss, suggesting a possible neural influence. Loss of muscle strength with age is attributed to muscle fiber loss, muscle fiber atrophy, and denervated muscle fibers.[44]

STRENGTH TRAINING

Exercise intensity has been shown to be the most important variable for improving strength and function in the elderly.[11] High-intensity strength training (60 to 80 percent of one's 1-repetition max) has been shown to be safe and result in significant gains in muscle strength, size, and functional mobility even in the most frail elderly.[19] Improvements in lower-extremity strength positively impact mobility and independence with ADLs. Sedentary individuals should begin exercise programs initially at lower levels and progressively increase intensity as tolerance allows. Individuals with arthritic joint involvement may not tolerate large compressive forces across the joint and will require modifications in exercise position and intensity.

ARTICULAR CARTILAGE

Morphologic changes in articular cartilage with age are reduced number of chondrocytes, decreased rate of collagen and elastin synthesis, altered composition of fibril types, and reduced water content. Dehydrated cartilage may have a reduced ability to dissipate forces across the joint, leading to increased susceptibility to mechanical failure.[1] With aging and increased wear and tear, cartilage may break down, beginning with fibrillation and eventually leading to sclerosis of subchondral bone and continued cartilage degeneration. Some degree of mechanical breakdown seems to be part of the normal aging process, but severe destruction of cartilage and subchondral bone involvement leads to osteoarthritis, which is the most common form of joint disease in the United States. Osteoarthritis can lead to significant impairments in joint function and marked disability, leading to eventual joint replacement. Rehabilitation efforts should include reduction of pain, elimination of joint stress, maintenance of joint range of motion, maintenance of strength and endurance, and improvement in functional independence.

TENDON LIGAMENT AND JOINT CAPSULE

The most prevalent symptom of changes in periarticular connective tissue is loss of extensibility and reduction in joint motion. Changes in structure and function may occur as a result of normal aging and from disuse and inactivity. In addition, the tensile properties of some ligament–bone complexes show a decline in tensile stiffness and ultimate load to failure with increasing age.[57] Degenerative changes in dense fibrous tissues may result in spontaneous or low-energy-level ruptures of the rotator cuff of the shoulder, the long head of the biceps, and the posterior tibial tendon, patellar ligament, and Achilles tendon; they also may lead to sprains of joint capsules and ligaments, including those of the spine. Care should be taken with explosive, high-energy activities and loading of joints in the older individual, especially when initiating an exercise program in a previously sedentary person.

BONE

Bone mineral density is defined as bone mineral content relative to the area or volume of bone in the site of measurement and is expressed as g/cm^2, with $2\ g/cm^2$ considered a normal value. Strength of bone and ability to withstand compressive and tensile forces is related to bone mineral density. Bone mineral density reductions are known to occur with age and disuse, as are the strength properties of bone. Throughout life, women may lose as much as 35 to 40 percent of cortical bone and 50 to 60 percent of trabecular bone.[16] Men lose slightly less bone with age. Reduction of bone mineral density below $1\ g/cm^2$ is considered below the fracture threshold and increases the risk of osteoporotic-related fractures.

OSTEOPOROSIS

Osteoporosis is a generalized disease of bone in which there is a marked decrease in the amount of bone. The World Health Organization defines osteoporosis as a decrease in bone mineral density of more than 2.5 standard deviations below the mean as compared to young normals. Postmenopausal osteoporosis is caused by a decrease in estrogen and results in rapid bone loss 5 to 7 years following the onset of menopause. Women in this group have a high incidence of vertebral body fractures with subsequent postural changes, loss of body height, and often persistent pain and loss of function. Advancing age is among the risk factors for developing osteoporosis (Table 34-4). Age-related osteoporosis occurs equally in men and women ages 70 and greater and manifests mainly in hip and vertebral fractures. Fractures of the proximal humerus, proximal tibia, pelvis, and metatarsal bones are also common. It may be prudent to assume that even asymptomatic older adults may have a reduction in bone mineral density, as reduced bone mineral density of as much as 30 percent may be present before being evident on plain film x-ray. Exercise and mechanical stress to the bone, along with estrogen replacement and increased calcium consumption, have been well documented as preventative for the development and progression of osteoporosis.[36]

Osteoporosis Risk Factors

- Age (over 50 years)
- Genetic factors
  Sex (women > men)
  Race (white > black)
  Family history
  Body type (small frame > large frame)
- Postmenopause
- Nutritional factors
  Low body weight
  Low dietary intake of calcium
  High alcohol consumption
  Eating disorders
  High caffeine consumption
- Lifestyle factors
  Immobilization/inactivity
  Cigarette smoking
- Medical factors
  Early menopause
  Medication use: corticosteroids, antacids,
    anticoagulants
  Menstrual cycle disorders

Weight-bearing and strengthening exercises have been shown to maintain bone density and reduce the incidence of osteoporosis-related fractures.[36] A consistently sustained program of walking may be adequate for the lower extremities and spine, but upper-extremity exercises should also be given. For the older individual, safety and fall prevention during exercise are important concerns. The therapist should be creative in designing exercises that stress the skeletal system while ensuring safety of the patient.

Many patients who receive physical therapy have medical conditions that require long-term corticosteroid use. Corticosteroids assist in the management of inflammatory and autoimmune illnesses. Unfortunately, long-term corticosteroid use results in a significant decrease in bone density. Bone density for patients treated with corticosteroids for periods of 5 years is 20 to 40 percent less than density for nontreated control subjects.[46] Clinicians need to be aware of their patients' use of corticosteroids because exercise and activity protocols for these patients may need to be modified in order to prevent fractures from occurring.

SPECIAL CONSIDERATIONS

Polypharmacy

Older persons are more likely to have a number of medical problems and to be taking many medications. The excessive use of medication by elderly patients is known as polypharmacy.

Patients may take different medications prescribed by different physicians. It has been reported that 87 percent of older patients are taking at least one prescription medication and three over-the-counter drugs each day.[42] There is a linear relationship between the number of drugs taken and the increased potential for adverse drug reactions.[25] Approximately 19 percent of hospital admissions of older persons are attributable to drug reactions.[25] Increased sensitivity to drug effects can be due to changes in drug absorption with age, the number of drugs taken simultaneously, or failure of health care providers to take into account the proper way to prescribe and administer drugs to geriatric patients.

Although there are many potential adverse outcomes of polypharmacy, some are of particular interest here. The effects of drugs—particularly benzodiazepines, barbiturates, and antidepressants—are among the risk factors associated with falls. Even if the individual does not suffer a serious fall, the threat of a fall is often enough to cause one to limit activity, which results in deconditioning and functional decline. Delirium, a temporary change in attention and consciousness, may be mistaken for dementia (a permanent loss of intellectual abilities), when in fact it may be due to drug sensitivity. Confusion is especially common when drug reactions occur in someone with preexisting mild dementia. A person suffering from a mild adverse drug reaction that goes undetected for months may experience a gradual reduction in self-care skills and independence. Patients experiencing musculoskeletal complaints often are chronic users of nonsteroidal anti-inflammatory drugs, which can cause gastric bleeding. Narcotics may result in oversedation and loss of functional ability.

All medications taken by the elderly population should be regularly checked by their primary physician. The physician needs to know what drugs the patient is taking so that he or she can weed out duplications and generally be aware of and avoid adverse effects of drug interactions. A thorough history of the older adult seeking rehabilitation services should include a list of current medications. One should consider adverse reactions when evaluating acute changes in functional ability and mentation. Patients and families should be instructed to keep all medications in the original containers, never mix several drugs in one bottle, and throw away what is no longer in use.

Cognitive Impairment

A significant proportion of elderly persons will experience some form of cognitive dysfunction in their lifetime. The learning of new skills may be impaired, and this may be a major obstacle in the rehabilitation process. Early recognition and management can facilitate recovery from acute conditions and prevent adverse outcomes in both acute and chronic illnesses. The physical therapist should be cognizant of the characteristics of these disorders and facilitate referral to other health care providers where appropriate.

DELIRIUM

Acute cognitive dysfunction, or delirium, is often underdiagnosed or misdiagnosed. Older adults may experience delirium with acute medical illnesses, infections, or postoperatively. A variety of factors can increase the risk of delirium, including advanced age, cognitive impairment, sensory deprivation such as absence of glasses or hearing aid, unfamiliar surroundings, routine effects of medications, fractures, falls, low level of activity, and pain. Without adequate assessment, delirium may be attributed to advancing age or "senility." Failure to implement appropriate treatment promptly can lead to increased length of hospitalization, inappropriate placement in long-term care facilities, increased morbidity and mortality, an increased incidence of falls and incontinence, and perhaps inappropriate use of restraints and psychotropic medications. The presence of cognitive dysfunction may label a patient as inappropriate for rehabilitation services or incapable of achieving independence. With comprehensive assessment and aggressive intervention early in the development of acute confusion/delirium, most patients should be able to return to their previous level of cognitive function.

DEMENTIA

The distinctions between acute cognitive dysfunction (delirium) and chronic cognitive dysfunction (dementia) are at times difficult to discern, and patients may suffer from both simultaneously. Although the word "dementia" most often refers to progressive primary degenerative diseases of the cerebral cortex, including Alzheimer's disease, this general term also refers to a variety of cognitive deficits, including impaired memory and confusion, that can result from multiple causes. Dementia is not an inevitable consequence of age. Most people age without substantial loss of intellectual power. Nevertheless, dementia is considered to be age-related. About 11 percent of those over 65 in the United States show some degree of mental impairment.[23] The incidence of dementia is 2 percent higher per year for individuals over the age of 75.[23] Patients with dementia or suspected dementia should undergo a thorough neurologic and medical evaluation culminating in the implementation of an appropriate care plan that includes the patient's family and home and community-based services when possible.

For those patients with cognitive impairment receiving rehabilitation services, the following modifications may serve to improve patient participation and success: (1) providing consistency within the rehabilitation program and environment, (2) minimizing noise and distractions, (3) repetition of skills for enhanced learning, (4) incorporating familiar functional activities into treatment, and (5) modifying the pace of activities to the pace and abilities of the individual.

DEPRESSION

As many as one in five older persons living in the community report depressive signs and symptoms.[48] Patients with chronic medical conditions and those in hospitals and long-term care facilities experience a greater frequency of depressive symptoms and depressive illness. Many times the dominant theme in the predisposition of older persons to depression is loss. One of the most common and most serious losses is physical health. Other common losses are found in function, role, income, family, and friends. Disabling conditions are particularly likely to cause depression. The presentation of depression in the elderly is often loss of interest in or pleasure from usually pleasurable activities.[48] Other symptoms include weight loss, insomnia, fatigue, diminished ability to think or concentrate, and feelings of worthlessness or guilt. Dementia with depression is a common source of coexisting memory and depressive complaints, which can be difficult to differentiate from depression alone. Left untreated, depression can lead to the multiple consequences of immobility, deconditioning, failure to achieve restorative goals after a successful surgical procedure, and ultimately loss of independence. Elderly individuals and family members often attribute depressive symptoms to normal aging and fail to seek treatment. Identification and treatment of depression can usually result in successful treatment.

FRACTURES IN THE ELDERLY

Fractures are a common occurrence in older adults and are of both medical and socioeconomic importance. Approximately 250,000 individuals over the age of 65 experience a hip fracture in the United States each year.[53] Hip fractures alone have an associated mortality rate as high as 50 percent. Other common fracture sites include the proximal humerus, distal radius, and vertebrae. There are many reasons for the increased incidence of fractures in the elderly, but the two primary risk factors are osteoporosis and falls. Therefore, interventions for fractures in the elderly should also include measures to prevent osteoporosis and reduce the risk for falls. Once a fracture has occurred, the clinician must work toward the restoration of preinjury levels of function, mobility, and self-care.

Fracture Healing

Fracture healing is a very complex and highly ordered physiologic process. Unlike other tissues that heal by the formation of a fibrovascular scar, in fracture healing the original bone tissue is regenerated and the properties of the preexisting bone are restored. The first stage of fracture healing begins with the onset of a deforming force applied to the bone. At the moment of impact, the energy absorbed by the bone leads to mechanical and structural failure. A fracture may arise from forces of low magnitude that are cyclically repeated over a long period of time or from a force having sufficient magnitude to cause failure after a single application. The amount of energy that a bone can withstand without fracture is dependent upon several factors and is related to its crystal structure and collagen orientation, which reflect the viscoelastic properties of the bone.

Osteoporotic bone is not capable of withstanding as much force as young, healthy bone.

When there is an actual break in the continuity of the bone, there is a simultaneous disruption of the blood supply to the bone at the fracture site. Within a few hours after the fracture, the normal architecture of the bone marrow is lost and the blood vessels in the region adjacent to the fracture callus clot. The cellular complement of the bone marrow is reorganized. The result is a transformation of the endothelial cells to so-called polymorphic cells, which express an osteoblastic phenotype and begin to form new bone.

Fracture healing has often been subdivided into primary and secondary fracture healing. Primary healing, or primary cortical healing, involves a direct attempt by the cortex to reestablish itself when the continuity has been disrupted. If movement at the fracture site is eliminated and compression is applied during the fracture healing process (internal fixation), primary bone healing can occur. This process seems to occur only when there is anatomic restoration of the fracture fragments and when the stability of the fracture reduction is ensured by rigid internal fixation and a substantial decrease in interfragmentary strain. After stable fixation has been achieved, gaps will remain along the contact points. Healing within the gaps first occurs by the ingrowth of blood vessels, which begins soon after injury. Osteons bridge the fracture site and promote direct haversian remodeling. This process leads to new bone formation across the fracture site. Once healed, the fracture site continues to be protected from stress by the internal fixation device, and can develop osteopenia (subnormally mineralized bone).[28] For this reason, internal fixation devices are often removed once there is evidence of fracture union. The fracture site should be protected from excessive stresses for several months after removal of internal fixation devices. If a fracture is inherently stable, because of direct impaction of the bony ends or adjacent ligamentous and bony support, little additional effort is needed to maintain a minimal amount of interfragmentary motion and allow healing.[26] Cast or brace immobilization, or no immobilization, may be all that is needed for these nondisplaced or minimally displaced fractures. However, many fractures require additional internal or external support. Types of fracture fixation used include; compression plating or screws, external fixators, and intramedullary nails.

Secondary healing involves responses in the periosteum and external soft tissues. The response from the periosteum is a fundamental reaction to bone injury and is enhanced by motion and inhibited by rigid fixation. The fracture repair sequence follows at least four discrete stages of healing: inflammation, soft callus formation, hard callus formation, and eventual bone remodeling.

INFLAMMATION

An inflammatory response occurs immediately after a fracture has occurred. This response can last for up to 4 days.[28] As a result of the disruption of the vascular supply, a hematoma develops. The function of the hematoma formation is to serve as a source of signaling molecules with the capacity to initiate the cascades of cellular events necessary for fracture healing. Fibroblasts begin to form collagen, and granulation tissue replaces the hematoma.[15] A decrease in pain and swelling signals the end of the inflammatory stage.

SOFT CALLUS

Increased vascularity and osteoblastic activity signal the start of the soft-callus stage. By the middle of the second week after fracture healing is initiated, abundant cartilage overlies the fracture site, and this chondroid tissue initiates biochemical preparations to undergo calcification.[15] Both internal (endosteal) and external (subperiosteal) callus form.[28] Throughout this stage, these callus components are cartilaginous and are not visible on plain film radiographs. The external callus helps to stabilize the fracture and makes it possible to load the bone before healing is complete. This stage lasts 3 to 4 weeks and results in stability of the fracture site.

HARD CALLUS

As woven (fibrous) bone replaces the cartilaginous callus, the fracture is healed and able to withstand increased stress. Adult long bones require an average of 3 to 4 months to reach this stage; however, this period is variable and will be influenced by the available vascular supply and the physiologic health of the bone. Poorly vascularized or osteoporotic bone may take longer to reach clinical healing.

REMODELING

During the remodeling stage, the fibrous callus becomes lamellar (mature) bone. Osteoclastic activity gradually reduces the redundant callus and reforms the medullary canal.[28] The remodeling stage lasts from several months to years.[28]

Fractures of the Proximal Humerus

Fractures of the proximal humerus account for approximately 4 to 5 percent of all fractures.[6] Their incidence rises dramatically beyond the fifth decade and occurs more frequently among women than among men. Existing osteoporosis is a major risk factor for proximal humeral fractures in the senior population. The most common mechanism of injury is a fall on an outstretched hand from standing height or less. Fractures of the proximal humerus sustained in this manner are usually through the surgical neck and are nondisplaced or minimally displaced. When the mechanism involves a direct blow to the shoulder (as in a fall to the side without a protective response), the fracture pattern is usually much more complex.

CLASSIFICATION

About 85 percent of fractures at the proximal humerus are nondisplaced or minimally displaced.[13] The remaining 15 percent exhibit various fracture patterns. Neer developed the most commonly used classification system for these fractures

TABLE 34-5

Neer Classification of Proximal Humerus Fractures

CATEGORY	DESCRIPTION
1-Part	Nondisplaced or minimally displaced
2-Part	1 Part displaced >1 cm or angulated >45°
3-Part	2 Parts displaced and/or angulated from each other, and from the remaining part
4-Part	4 Parts displaced and/or angulated from each other
Fracture dislocation	Displacement of the humeral head from the joint space with fracture

(Table 34-5). The Neer system classifies fractures according to the number of parts or fracture fragments and the degree of angulation (or malalignment) of the parts. To be classified as displaced or angulated, the part must be displaced at least 1 cm or angulated at least 45 degrees.[14] The four important parts that may be displaced or angulated are the head (at the level of the surgical neck or anatomic neck), the greater and lesser tuberosities, and the shaft. When either of the tuberosities fracture, the pull of the attached muscles likely will cause displacement of the fracture's fragments. Fractures at the level of the anatomic neck frequently cause interruption of blood supply to the humeral head and may result in avascular osteonecrosis.

TREATMENT

Many methods of treatment of proximal humeral fractures have been proposed through the years. The disability that results from proximal humeral fracture is usually the result of lost range of motion and the development of a frozen shoulder. Shoulder range of motion can be lost by angular deformity of the proxi-

mal humerus, injury to the rotator cuff, or the development of arthrofibrosis secondary to prolonged immobilization.[14] The treatment goal for patients with a proximal humeral fracture is a united fracture with pain-free function. To achieve this goal, reasonable restoration of the normal anatomy and early rehabilitation are needed. Fortunately, the majority of proximal humeral fractures are nondisplaced or minimally displaced and can be satisfactorily treated with conservative measures. The arm is immobilized with a sling until pain and discomfort decrease. Active exercises for the elbow, wrist, and fingers should begin immediately to avoid stiffness and disability in these noninjured joints. Initial immobilization and early motion has been continually described as having a high degree of success because most proximal humeral fractures are minimally displaced. Because adhesive capsulitis is a frequent complication after fractures of the proximal humerus, early motion exercises should begin as soon as tolerated. Typically, active-assisted exercises can begin about 1 week after the injury. The patient should wear the sling during periods of activity (such as walking) or when sleeping until the soft callus has stabilized the fracture fragments (usually 3 to 4 weeks after injury). The patient may remove the sling while exercising or when inactive (such as resting in a chair). Attention should also be given to scapular stabilization exercises. The function of these muscles is important for normal scapulohumeral rhythm. As the fracture healing approaches a clinical union, strengthening exercise with external resistance should be added to the overall program (Table 34-6).

Displaced Fractures

Displaced fractures are difficult to treat by closed reduction. Even if closed reduction of the "two-part" and more severe fracture is successful, the rehabilitation program may need to be scaled back to avoid redisplacement. This becomes even more true if the pull of the muscle attachments displaced one of the

TABLE 34-6

Exercise Guidelines for Proximal Humeral Fracture

PROBLEM	EXERCISE	TIMELINE
Maintain or improve ROM	Assisted ROM (wand, wall climbs, pendulum)	End of inflammatory stage (usually 1 week)
	Passive overhead stretching (overhead pulley)	
Restore strength	Submaximal isometrics	No risk of fragment displacement, usually immediate
	Full active ROM against gravity	X-ray evidence of union, usually 6 weeks
	External resistance/isotonics	Ability to perform full active ROM against gravity, x-ray evidence of union, usually 6 weeks
Maximize function	Touch top of head, back of neck, low back	Assisted—evidence of callus
		Unassisted—x-ray evidence of union, usually 6 weeks

tuberosities. Fractures classified as two-part and above have a greater likelihood of operative reduction and internal fixation (ORIF) to achieve stable fixation.

For patients undergoing open reduction with internal fixation, the postoperative goals remain the same as with nondisplaced fractures: early return to function and avoiding the development of adhesive capsulitis. Because of the numerous types of fracture patterns and different surgical fixations, exercise guidelines must be individual and modified as needed. In some cases, the surgeon will be confident that the internal fixation is stable and the patient may progress through the exercise program more rapidly. In other cases, the rehabilitation program will be slowed down secondary to comminution, osteoporosis, or damage to the vascular supply. Each of these may compromise stability and/or delay healing.

Fractures of the Distal Radius

Fractures of the distal radius are one of the most common fractures encountered in orthopedics. These fractures constitute 15 percent of all fractures that result in emergency room visits.[18] The elderly have an increased number of distal radius fractures for two reasons. The first is related to the fragility of the bone secondary to postmenopausal osteoporosis. The second is related to the increased incidence of falls in the elderly as compared to younger individuals. As with proximal humeral fractures in older persons, the usual mechanism of injury is a fall on an outstretched arm.

CLASSIFICATION

No universally accepted classification of distal radius fractures has been developed to date. In order to be considered a distal radius fracture, the fracture must have occurred within 3 cm of the radiocarpal joint.[41] The Colles' fracture is the most common type of distal radius fracture and is by definition a dorsally angulated and displaced fracture of the radial metaphysis within 2 cm of the articular surface.[18] Comminution of the fracture is most common in the elderly. Because of the fracture fragment displacement, the majority of these fractures require some type of reduction to ensure anatomic alignment. Most Colles' fractures are managed by closed reduction and cast fixation. Open reduction with internal fixation, external fixators, or percutaneous pins and plaster may be used for severe cases with displacement. A Smith's fracture, conversely, is a volar angulated and displaced metaphyseal fracture that may be intraarticular, extraarticular, or part of a fracture dislocation.[18] This type of fracture usually occurs from a fall onto the dorsum of the hand. A Smith's fracture is often very unstable and may result in significant disability after it has healed. Carpal tunnel syndrome and RSD are potential complications of Smith's fracture.

TREATMENT

General principles for exercise and treatment are similar for both types of distal radial fracture. Nondisplaced fractures are treated nonoperatively. A short arm cast is usually applied and the fracture site immobilized for 3 to 4 weeks. If at that time there is radiographic evidence of healing and the fracture site is minimally tender, a removable splint is applied until the area is nontender. Overall, the most important rehabilitation consideration is early range of motion. Full active range-of-motion exercises for all nonimmobilized joints of the upper extremity should begin as soon as the fracture has been stabilized. This is most important for the glenohumeral joint in order to prevent the development of adhesive capsulitis. Although the cast should end at the proximal palmar crease to allow motion of the metacarpal phalangeal (MCP) joints, sometimes the cast nevertheless limits motion. Therefore, it is important to move the MCP joints as much as the cast will allow. The patient should also perform active exercises of the remaining thumb and finger joints. Strict compliance with active range-of-motion exercises several times a day will minimize loss of function during the immobilization period.

Typically, all immobilization is removed at about 6 weeks postinjury and range-of-motion and strengthening exercises for the immobilized joints are initiated at this time. Emphasis should be on restoring motion in wrist extension, forearm supination, thumb opposition, and finger MCP joint flexion. Restoring wrist extensor and grip strength exercises is very important to restore function of the hand and wrist.

With displaced fractures, surgical fixation is usually required. Types of surgical fixation include pins in plaster, percutaneous pinning, external fixation, and open reduction with internal fixation. Postreduction care will parallel that of nondisplaced fractures.

Fractures of the Proximal Femur

Fractures of the proximal femur are common problems for the older population and are one of the most potentially devastating injuries in the elderly. The incidence of hip fracture increases after the age of 50 and then doubles for each decade beyond 50 years of age.[34] More than 200,000 hip fractures occur in the United States each year, and the current mortality rate 1 year after hip fracture in elderly patients ranges from 12 to 36 percent.[3] Mortality is higher than for age-matched individuals without hip fractures, with the highest mortality rates occurring in institutionalized patients. After 1 year, mortality rates return to that for age- and sex-matched controls.[34]

Osteoporosis is a common predisposing factor for hip fractures. As many as 7 percent of hip fractures may occur spontaneously.[34] The most common mechanism for injury is a fall producing a direct blow over the greater trochanter. Following fracture, disability and functional dependence are common. Therefore, the overall goal of the treatment is to return the patient to the preinjury level of function.

CLASSIFICATION

The three common classifications of femoral neck fractures are those based on (1) anatomic location of the fracture, (2) direction of the fracture angle, and (3) displacement of the fracture fragments. With regard to anatomic location, surgeons divide fractures of the proximal femur into three groups. Femoral neck fractures are located from just below the articular surface to just superior to the intertrochanteric area. Intertrochanteric fractures are located between the greater and lesser trochanters. Subtrochanteric fractures occur in the proximal shaft below the level of the lesser trochanters. For patients over the age of 65, 95 percent of hip fractures are in the femoral neck or the intertrochanteric regions.[34]

TREATMENT

It is generally accepted that surgical management, followed by early mobilization, is the treatment of choice for hip fractures in the elderly. Historically, nonoperative management resulted in an excessive rate of medical morbidity and mortality as well as malunion and nonunion in displaced fractures. The overall goal of treatment for fracture of the proximal femur is to return the patient to the preinjury level of function as quickly and as safely as possible. Age, cognitive impairment, and coexisting morbidities may impact the level of independence the patient is able to achieve. The therapist should develop the postoperative care on an individual basis in consultation with the physician. Because of the high degree of variability in fracture patterns and postoperative fracture stability, ongoing communication is essential to developing a safe and effective rehabilitation program.

Physical therapy should begin on the first postoperative day. Patients who receive more than one physical therapy treatment session per day are more likely to regain functional independence and return home.[29] The treatment program should include range-of-motion and strengthening exercises, training in transfers and gait with an assistive device, and training in functional activities such as ADLs. The exercise program should increase in intensity and difficulty until the day of discharge. Some surgeons have recommended restricted weight bearing until the fracture has healed, whereas others have shown that unrestricted weight bearing can be started immediately without detrimental effects in the presence of stable internal fixation. Biomechanical data have shown that nonweight-bearing ambulation places significant stresses across the hip as a result of muscular contraction at the hip and knee.[34] Gait training with an assistive device should begin on the first postoperative day. Distance should be advanced and stair training introduced over the next couple of days. Ideally, the patient should be able to ambulate well enough to negotiate the indoor home environment by the time of discharge. Weight bearing as tolerated with a walker is appropriate for the majority of femoral neck and intertrochanteric fracture patients treated with ORIF or prosthetic replacement.

Cemented fixation of prosthetic replacements allow immediate full weight bearing, whereas biological growth fixation may delay full weight bearing for 6 to 12 weeks. Biological growth fixation is thought to have a lower fixation failure rate than cemented fixation and is preferable in younger, more active individuals. For older individuals who are at risk for greater morbidity and mortality after fracture, the early weight-bearing

status afforded by cemented fixation may be desirable. Because there is a greater likelihood of instability and healing complications with subtrochanteric fractures, patients with these types of fractures may require a longer period of protected weight bearing. The patient should advance to a cane and eventually eliminate the assistive devices when fracture healing and safety considerations permit.

During the first few weeks of fracture healing, emphasis should focus on active or active-assistive range-of-motion exercises with gravity eliminated, progressing to full active motion exercises against gravity as soon as allowed by adequate fracture healing. It is important that the patient begin the exercise program as tolerated on the first postoperative day. The exercise program should be designed to help prepare the patient for functional activities. Patients should perform the exercises in the supine, sitting, and standing positions. It is important for the patient to be able to move the operated limb through a full range of motion against gravity in order to perform simple ADLs, such as bed mobility and transfers. In most cases following ORIF, there is no restriction of the range-of-motion activities. In contrast, patients who undergo prosthetic replacement of the femoral head will likely be restricted in the amounts of hip flexion (less than 90 degrees), adduction (0 degrees), and internal rotation (0 degrees) allowed in the early postoperative period because of hip dislocation risk. Exercises should progress in intensity each day until the patient can move and control the limb independently. After some healing has occurred (3 to 4 weeks), external resistance may be added, provided the patient's strength is good enough to achieve full range of motion against gravity without assistance. Pain during resistance exercise may indicate that the exercise is too intensive and should be monitored by the therapist. Restoring hip-abductor and knee-extensor strength are critical for ambulatory function after hip fracture and should receive particular attention.

Fractures of the Spine

Compression fractures of the vertebrae are a common result of osteoporosis, leading to significant pain and functional limitation for seniors. Each year in the United States, an estimated 538,000 vertebral fractures occur in elderly patients with osteoporosis.[38] The rate of vertebral fractures rises sharply with advancing age. At age 70 years, for every 100 people, there are 20 vertebral fractures each year, and 90 percent of the population have vertebral body compression on plain film radiographs by age 75 years.[38]

Vertebral fractures in this group often result from relatively minor trauma. Osteoporotic compression fractures can be the result of a fall, but often occur spontaneously or in association with normal functional activities such as bending forward. There is a sudden onset of pain in the back and sometimes along the distribution of intercostal nerves. Because the fracture does not damage the posterior and middle columns of the vertebrae, there is no neurologic deficit. These fractures are sometimes called anterior wedge fractures because the anterior vertebral body collapses to form a triangular or trapezoidal shape. They are associated with an increase of kyphosis at the level of the fracture and a shortening in the height of the individual.

TREATMENT

The management of spinal fractures is guided by the same principal considerations that guide the management of spinal disorders in general: stability, deformity, and integrity of the neural elements.[38] Osteoporotic compression fractures take from 3 to 6 months to heal, but delayed union may result from interrupted vascular supply or from general poor health and old age.[40] The anterior wedge deformity most often persists, even if the bone heals. Initially there is severe pain associated with muscle spasm. The treatment program should be designed to provide symptomatic relief, restore mobility, and provide education in body mechanics to prevent further trauma and deformity. Modalities, massage, and bed rest may be applied to help patients control pain. Therapists should teach patients to avoid flexion postures and to log-roll onto their sides before sitting up. External supports such as corsets or braces help to maintain posture and relieve pain but many times are poorly tolerated by elderly individuals.

As soon as patients can tolerate movement (usually within 2 weeks), they should be taught how to arise and ambulate without flexing the spine. Patients should always keep the spine erect, avoiding flexion and rotation. Bending the knees should replace bending at the waist, and turning the whole body should replace twisting at the spine. Patients may use assistive devices for ambulation if needed, but this may encourage flexion postures. Safety and fall prevention are paramount and should determine progression to ambulation without an assistive device.

Sinaki and Mikkelsen advocate extension exercises to minimize the possibility of sustaining more compression fractures in the future. Flexion exercises greatly increased the frequency of additional compression fractures.[49] Extension exercises reverse kyphotic postures, unload the anterior vertebral bodies, and strengthen the erector spinae muscles.[49] The exercise program should be graded according to the stage of healing and the patient's symptoms. Initial exercises should consist of gentle elevation and retraction of the scapula while supine and sitting to reverse the kyphotic posture. Have the patient take a deep breath to elevate the ribcage while elevating and retracting the scapula. As symptoms allow, instruct the patient to raise the arms overhead in conjunction with scapular elevation and deep breathing. The patient should next gradually progress to the prone lying posture. When prone lying is tolerated and relatively asymptomatic (usually 4 to 6 weeks), erector spinae strengthening exercises should be added to the program. With the patient prone lying with the arms at the sides, have the patient raise the head and shoulders off the supporting surface without using the arms to push up. Intensity of exercise can be increased gradually by moving the arms from the sides to overhead. Eventually, the patient can advance to exercising on all fours by raising alternate arms and legs off of the supporting surface.

TOTAL JOINT ARTHROPLASTY

Hip, knee, and shoulder arthroplasty are increasingly common procedures. Replacement of damaged cartilage surfaces with artificial bearing materials has enabled surgeons to dramatically improve function and relieve pain in many patients.

Hip Arthroplasty

Sir John Charnley pioneered hip arthroplasty in the early 1960s. Since then, significant technologic advances in prosthetic design, materials, and technique have made hip arthroplasty a common and successful procedure. Hip arthroplasty that involves replacing only the femoral head component of the hip is a hemiarthroplasty. If both the femoral head and acetabular components are replaced, the procedure is a total hip arthroplasty. A hemiarthroplasty is usually performed for patients with an injury such as a femoral neck fracture, while a total hip arthroplasty is usually indicated for patients with disease involving both the femoral head and acetabulum.

INDICATIONS

Indications for hip arthroplasty include incapacitating pain, osteoarthritis, rheumatoid arthritis, osteonecrosis, fractures, failed previous reconstruction, and tumors. The surgical goals of total hip arthroplasty are alleviation of persistent pain and improvement in mobility, independence, and quality of life. Hemiarthroplasty, which can be converted later to a total hip arthroplasty (THA), is an alternative to THA, requiring that acetabular cartilage is intact and that joint pathology is limited to the femoral side of the hip joint.

OPERATIVE CONSIDERATIONS

Hip and knee arthroplasty procedures have the highest risk of mortality of all types of joint arthroplasty due to the increased incidence of postoperative thromboembolic events. Without anticoagulation therapy, high-risk orthopedic patients have a 40 to 70 percent chance of developing DVT. Nearly 20 percent will develop PE, with approximately 1 to 5 percent fatal. Several risk factors are identified for the development of DVT: age greater than 40 years, history of DVT or PE, malignant disease, major trauma, immobility, major surgical procedure, low cardiac output, varicose veins, obesity, oral contraceptives, invasive diagnostic procedures, and hemostatic disorders.

Signs and symptoms of DVT include peripheral edema in the involved area, skin discoloration, prominent superficial veins, Homan sign, leg pain, and tenderness. Signs and symptoms of PE include dyspnea, achypnea, and pleuritic chest pain. Prophylaxis in thromboembolic disease includes the use of antiembolic compression garments and the postoperative administration of various drug regimens of low-dose heparin and warfarin. Mobilization of the patient in the early postoperative period has been shown to reduce circulatory stasis and prevent complications.

An early complication after hip arthroplasty is dislocation. Dislocations reportedly occur in 1 to 9 percent of patients and most often in a posterior direction.[35] Initially, range-of-motion limitations are imposed to help prevent dislocation of the prosthesis following surgery (generally, dislocations may be caused by flexion, adduction, and internal rotation, as well as extension, adduction, and external rotation, depending upon the surgical approach used as well as the design of the prosthesis). There are conflicting opinions regarding the motion limitations used postoperatively. Some clinicians reinforce limitations in flexion, adduction, and internal rotation, while others allow full range of motion as long as no two motions are performed simultaneously. Ongoing communication with the referring orthopedic surgeon is warranted if there are questions regarding the postoperative motion restrictions.

Weight bearing after hip arthroplasty is another clinical variable. The weight-bearing status will be determined by the surgeon and is most often determined by the type of fixation of the prosthesis. If bone cement is used, a patient may be permitted to bear weight as tolerated postoperatively. If noncemented fixation was used, the patient may be restricted to some form of partial weight bearing for up to 6 to 8 weeks. Noncemented fixation relies on bone growth into the surface of the prosthesis, and weight bearing will be limited until the surgeon determines the bone density around the prosthetic components is sufficient to withstand weight-bearing stresses.

Preoperative patient education is a critical component for successful joint arthroplasty. A clear, concise description of the procedure helps many patients understand the need for postoperative therapy and clarifies the significance of the procedure. A preoperative discussion of weight-bearing status, postoperative dislocation precautions, exercises, ADL, and physical therapy interventions for pain and swelling can enhance postoperative recovery.

REHABILITATION

In the acute care setting, the primary goals for postoperative hip arthroplasty patients are independent mobility and restoration of motion and strength of the involved hip. Rehabilitation may be guided by an established clinical pathway, or criteria-based progression, which is established by the interdisciplinary team. Pathways should follow tissue-healing constraints, thereby allowing each patient to advance and progress through phases of rehabilitation at an individual rate of recovery. Desired outcomes include independence with bed mobility, chair and toilet transfers, dressing, ambulation, performance of a home exercise program, stair climbing, and incorporation of hip precautions. Mobility aids and adaptive equipment selection will depend on the needs of the individual patient. Elevated toilet seats are recommended to prevent excessive hip flexion and increase ease of rising to a standing position.

Patients with good family support systems and higher levels of independence may go directly home and continue their rehabilitation there or in the outpatient setting. Due to range-of-motion precautions and temporary deficits in strength and endurance, the home environment may require modifications such as bath benches, elevated toilet seats, and reaching devices. A home assessment by the therapist is often warranted. As part of the discharge plan, caregivers should receive instruction in patient handling and assistive techniques. Older patients who live alone and have multiple comorbidities may require admission to a rehabilitation facility prior to returning home.

Postoperative rehabilitation can be divided into three phases of recovery based on the healing constraints of the bone and soft tissue. Improvements in strength, weight-bearing status, reduced pain, bed mobility, transfers, and compliance with all total hip precautions guide the progression of the rehabilitation program. The initial phase is one of maximum protection and includes instruction in ankle pumps, quadriceps muscle sets, and active range-of-motion exercises avoiding excessive hip flexion, adduction, and medial rotation. The contralateral limb can be exercised with active range-of-motion, isometric, and resistance exercises. Weight-bearing status will depend upon the type of fixation used. The patient is progressed to the next phase of recovery when pain is reduced, there is compliance with all precautions and exercises, and the patient demonstrates independent bed mobility, transfers, and improved gait. The patient should demonstrate pain-free active motion against gravity within the range-of-motion restrictions prior to progressing to resistance exercises.

The moderate protection phase is generally characterized by an increase in functional resistance exercises, guided by healing constraints of bone and soft tissue and the method of fixation. A recumbent bicycle ergometer may be used to enhance reciprocal hip and knee motion. Closed-kinetic chain functional activities can begin between 2 and 4 weeks for a patient with a cemented prosthesis. A patient with an uncemented prosthesis requires an additional 2 to 3 weeks prior to the initiation of closed-chain exercises. Closed-chain exercises during this phase can include partial supported knee bends, weight shifting, treadmill walking, leg press, mini step-ups, and standing repeated hip and knee extension.

The minimal protection phase is initiated between 12 and 16 weeks after surgery. Prior to this phase, the patient must demonstrate the ability to perform all exercises in the moderate protection phase with increasing strength, motion, and confidence, reduced pain, and improved gait. The minimal protection phase classically emphasizes a normal gait without assistive devices, and instruction in balance, coordination, proprioception, and advanced closed-chain resistance functional activities that duplicate the patient's specific ADLs. When cleared by the surgeon, resumption of physical activities such as golf, swimming, doubles tennis, and biking are considered safe.

Knee Arthroplasty

INDICATIONS

Indications for total knee arthroplasty (TKA) include disabling knee pain with functional impairment, radiographic evidence of significant joint involvement, and failed conservative measures. Patient age is important to consider when planning knee arthroplasty. Young age is considered a relative contraindication due to the increased probability of revision. Male and female older patients have been found to benefit equally from knee arthroplasty; however, advanced age does influence overall outcome.[47] Patients over the age of 80 undergoing bilateral surgery are more prone to postoperative confusion and cardiopulmonary complications.[47]

REHABILITATION

Component design, fixation method, bone quality, and operative technique will all affect the rehabilitation process. In the immediate postoperative period, patients may require assistance in bed mobility, ADL transfers, and ambulation. Most often patients may begin ambulation with an assistive device (walker or crutches) as soon as postoperative day 1. Many surgeons use an identical routine, whether implants are cemented or noncemented, if initial fixation is sufficient to prevent loosening. If the bone is extremely osteoporotic, a delay in full weight bearing until the peri-implant bone plate develops may be indicated. The progression of weight bearing is based solely on the surgeon's discretion. It is important to monitor patients carefully when initiating ambulation because their cognition and vital signs may be altered by anesthesia and pain medications.

Restoration of range motion as quickly as possible in order to prevent adhesions and joint contracture is critical to successful outcome in total knee arthroplasty. Flexion of 90 degrees is required so the patient can negotiate stairs, and 105 degrees is required to arise easily from a low chair. Within 5 to 6 weeks following surgery, the patient should achieve full extension and 110 to 120 degrees of flexion. Continuous passive motion (CPM) has been frequently used in the postoperative period to gain range of motion. The literature reports conflicting results regarding long-term benefits with CPM. Knee arthroplasty patients using CPM gain greater knee flexion sooner than patients not using CPM; however, several studies point to no range-of-motion difference between CPM and non-CPM groups months or years after surgery.[55]

During the initial phase of rehabilitation, remedial exercises of quadriceps muscle sets, ankle pumps, gluteal muscle sets, active assisted straight-leg raises, and short-arc terminal knee extensions are initiated. Progressive active and active assistive range-of-motion exercises are used as regaining active knee flexion is a critical component during this phase of recovery. Supine hip and knee flexion, supine wall slides, and seated knee flexion will augment range of motion. Various modalities to control pain and swelling may be indicated. Once the patient achieves sufficient range of motion and strength, a gradual increase in strength training, aerobic fitness, range-of-motion exercises, and closed-chain functional activities should be undertaken. Balance and proprioception exercises should also be incorporated into the program. During this phase it is important to emphasize increased muscle contraction speeds. Im-

proved function following TKA dictates the need for progressive changes in muscle contraction speeds for improved balance, aerobic fitness, normal gait, and walking velocity. The minimum protection phase will focus on normal gait, advanced functional activities, and challenging proprioception and balance drills. All phases of recovery include a general conditioning program of flexibility, aerobic fitness (UBE, single-leg contralateral limb stationary-cycle ergometer), and strength training.

Complications following total knee arthroplasty are wound complications, deep vein thrombosis, peroneal nerve palsy, polyethylene wear, patellar fracture, supracondylar fracture, deep and superficial infection, and reduced range of motion. With time, prosthetic components may loosen. This may occur via microfractures in bone cement.

In cemented and noncemented arthroplasties, wear creates particular debris from the bearing surfaces that can produce an inflammatory response, contributing to bone resorption, which may result in prosthetic loosening. If loosening causes instability, the patient may be a candidate for revision arthroplasty. Revisions can be technically complex, and the result poor.[8]

Total Shoulder Arthroplasty

INDICATIONS

Indications for replacement of the humeral head (hemiarthroplasty) or total shoulder arthroplasty (replacement of the humeral head and the articulating surface of the glenoid) include displaced multipart fractures of the humeral head and painful and chronic shoulder conditions that are unresponsive to conservative measures such as medication and rehabilitation. Goals of shoulder replacement are alleviation of pain, restoration of normal anatomy, and restoration of function. In contrast to total hip and knee replacement surgery, where many of the procedures are performed on primarily older patients, hemiarthroplasty and total shoulder replacement may be performed on patients as young as in their 30s and 40s. The primary reason these procedures are available to younger patients is the fact that the components are nonweight-bearing, and thus there are fewer concerns surrounding component wear and loosening than there are in the lower-extremity procedures.

REHABILITATION

The ultimate functional outcome for those patients who have undergone total shoulder arthroplasty or hemiarthroplasty is significantly influenced by the postoperative care and rehabilitation provided by the rehabilitation team. Following surgery, older patients may remain hospitalized for a period of 2 to 5 days for pain control and due to possible disturbances in gait and balance following surgery. Patient education and performance of a carefully planned home rehabilitation program are critical. Rehabilitation is usually initiated on postoperative day 1 or 2 with passive range-of-motion and pendulum exercises and active wrist, finger, and elbow exercises. Active range of motion is discouraged. The preoperative condition of the rotator cuff is a significant factor following hemiarthroplasty or total shoulder arthroplasty. If a rotator cuff tear is repaired in addition to arthroplasty, postoperative immobilization may be as long as 6 to 8 weeks with the affected arm held in an abduction splint to allow for healing in the repaired cuff.

Postoperative rehabilitation is again divided into three phases. Phase 1 generally consists of passive or assisted exercise and the application of pain-relief modalities. In phase 1, the patient is taught self-assisted exercises and to avoid active use of the extremity above the elbow. Unless directed otherwise, passive stretching should be avoided. Exercises generally consist of active-assisted flexion to 90 degrees, internal rotation, and external rotation to 30 degrees. The program may include self-assisted exercise with a wand lying in supine for shoulder flexion and standing internal rotation behind the back movements.

Phase 2 begins 3 to 4 weeks postoperatively, when monitored isometric exercises are added to the program. The exercises may be done in the standing position with the elbow at 90 degrees, the arm held close to the side, and the opposite arm or a door frame used to stabilize the involved arm to guard against movement. At 6 weeks, repairs to the deltoid and rotator cuff musculature should be sufficiently healed to begin active exercises for these muscles.

During phase 2, the patient also may begin seated attempts at shoulder flexion with assistance by the therapist. It is in this phase that the therapist may begin gentle stretching of the shoulder musculature to increase the range of motion. Phase 2, which may take as long as 3 to 4 months from the date of the surgery, is considered complete when the patient can actively raise the arm in an unsupported manner and perform light overhead activities.

In phase 3, the patient is encouraged to begin an independent home exercise program. The patient may begin exercise consisting of light weightlifting, stretching, and mild sporting activities, with restrictions as outlined by the surgeon. Home exercise using elastic or rubber tubing is an excellent way of maintaining long-term range-of-motion gains, strength, and flexibility.

EXERCISE TRAINING GUIDELINES FOR OLDER ADULTS

Participation in a regular exercise program is an effective intervention/modality to reduce/prevent a number of functional declines associated with aging. Older individuals well into eighth and ninth decades of life respond to both endurance and strength training. Regular exercise and physical activity contribute to a more healthy, independent lifestyle and improved functional capacity and quality of life. Rehabilitation following injury or illness should include education regarding the benefits of physical activity and instruction for the implementation of and safe participation in a lifelong exercise program.

The American College of Sports Medicine has established guidelines for exercise testing and participation for older individuals. Prior to the initiation of any exercise program, it is recommended that all individuals undergo a physical examination and a diagnostic exercise workup. A proper warm-up routine is essential for all individuals engaged in an exercise program. The warm-up routine should involve some gentle stretching exercises that may last from 5 to 15 minutes. Some stretching activities and a cool-down period at the conclusion of the exercise program are also recommended. The intensity level is recommended to be 20 to 30 minutes a minimum of 3 times per week at light to moderate intensity levels to optimize health. Walking, running, swimming, and cycling are large-muscle rhythmic aerobic forms of exercise and minimize the risk of musculoskeletal injuries.

For resistance training, exercise should be performed with proper body mechanics and should include large-muscle groups. Attention should focus closely on the quality of movement rather than the quantity. Each exercise should be performed slowly and through a full range of motion if possible. Once muscle fatigue occurs, the movement pattern becomes poor, the smoothness of motion is reduced, and the range of motion is decreased, thereby reducing the training effect. Quick or ballistic movements should be avoided. It is best to use several sets of exercise (usually a minimum of 3) consisting of 7 to 10 repetitions. If the intent of the exercise program is to build muscular endurance and not muscle mass, the number of repetitions must be increased to 20 or more.

SUMMARY

- The field of geriatrics will continue to grow as the population ages. As life expectancy increases, rehabilitation of the physically disabled elderly will become an increasingly essential component of overall geriatric care.
- The aging process affects multiple systems in the body and has a direct impact on the rehabilitation of acute and chronic musculoskeletal conditions common in the elderly.
- Orthopedic conditions are commonly experienced by the older population. Fractures commonly occur and are often the result of osteoporosis and falls. When articular cartilage damage is severe or there is chronic joint pain, hip, knee, and shoulder arthroplasty are increasingly common procedures specifically designed to provide patients with dramatically improved lifestyle and function.
- Emphasis in the rehabilitation program should be placed upon the importance of physical activity in preventing injury and minimizing functional decline. Rehabilitation providers must be aware of the special needs that this population has in order to facilitate the development of effective rehabilitation interventions.

REFERENCES

1. Abyad A, Boyer JT. Arthritis and aging. *Curr Opin Rheumatol* 4:153–159, 1992.

2. American College of Sports Medicine. *Guidelines for Exercise Testing and Prescription,* 5th ed. Baltimore, Williams & Wilkins, 1995, pp. 1–373.

3. American College of Sports Medicine Position. The recommended quantity and quality of exercise for developing and maintaining cardiorespiratory and muscular fitness in healthy adults. *Med Sci Sport Exerc* 22:265–274, 1990.

4. Anderson LD, Meyer RN. Fractures of the shafts of the radius and ulna. In: Rockwood CA, Green DP, Bucholz RW, eds. *Fractures in Adults.* Philadelphia, Lippincott, 1991.

5. Barnes B, Donovan K. Functional outcomes after hip fracture. *Phys Ther* 67:1675–1679, 1987.

6. Bigliani LU, Craig EV, Butters KP. Fractures of the shoulder. In: Rockwood CA, Green DP, Bucholz RW, eds. *Fractures in Adults.* Philadelphia, Lippincott, 1991.

7. Bortz WM. On disease . . . aging . . . and disuse. *Exec Health* 20:1–6, 1983.

8. Bourne RB, Crawford HA. Principles of revision total knee arthroplasty. *Orthop Clin North Am* 29:331–337, 1998.

9. Brock DB, Guralnik JM, Brody JA. Demography and epidemiology of aging in the United States. In: Schneider EL, Rowe JW, eds. *Handbook of the Biology of Aging,* 3rd ed. San Diego, Academic Press, 1990.

10. Brocklehurst JC, Robertson D, James-Groom P. Clinical correlates of sway in old age: sensory modalities. *Age Ageing* 11:1–10, 1982.

11. Buchner DM. Understanding variability in studies of strength training in older adults: A meta-analytic perspective. *Top Geriatr Rehabil* 8:1–21, 1993.

12. Bugbee WD, Culpepper WJ, Engh CA. Long term clinical consequences of stress-shielding after total hip arthroplasty without cement. *J Bone Joint Surg Am* 79:1007–1012, 1997.

13. Connolly JF. Fractures of the upper end of the humerus. In: Connolly JF, ed. *Deplama's Management of Fractures and Dislocations: An Atlas,* 3rd ed. Philadelphia, Saunders, 1981, pp. 686–738.

14. Cornell CN, Schneider K. Proximal humerus. In: Koval KJ, Zuckerman JD, eds. *Fractures in the Elderly.* Philadelphia, Lippincott-Raven, 1998.

15. Day SM, Ostrum RF, Chao EY. Bone injury, regeneration, and repair. In: Buckwalter JA, Einhorn TA, Simm SR, eds. *Orthopedic Basic Science.* Chicago, AAOS, 2000.

16. Deal CL. Osteoporosis: Prevention, diagnosis, and management. *Am J Med* 102:35S–39S, 1997.

17. Delee JC. Fractures and dislocations of the hip. In: Rockwood CA, Green DP, Bucholz RW, eds. *Fractures in Adults.* Philadelphia, Lippincott, 1991.

18. Dinowitz MI, Koval KJ, Meadows. Distal radius. In: Koval KJ, Zuckerman JD, eds. *Fractures in the Elderly.* Philadelphia, Lippincott-Raven, 1998.

19. Fiatarone MA, Marks EC, Ryan ND, et al. High intensity strength training in nonagenarians: Effects on skeletal muscle. *JAMA* 263:3029–3034, 1990.

20. Fretwell MD. Acute hospital care for frail older patients. In: Hazzard WR, Andres R, Gierman EL, Blass JP, eds. *Principles of Geriatric Medicine and Gerontology,* 2nd ed. New York, McGraw-Hill, 1994.

21. Fries JF. The compression of morbidity: Miscellaneous comments about a theme. *Gerontologist* 24:354–359, 1984.

22. Gallagher D, Visser M, De Meersman RE, et al. Appendicular skeletal muscle mass: Effects of age, gender, and ethnicity. *J Appl Physiol* 83:229–239, 1997.

23. Goldman J, Coté L. Aging of the brain: Dementia of the Alzheimer's type. In: Kandel E, Schwartz JH, Jessell TM, eds. *Principles of Neural Science,* 3rd ed. Norwalk, CT, Appleton & Lange, 1991.

24. Greendale GA, Barrett-Conner E, Edelstein S, et al. Lifetime leisure exercise and osteoporosis: The Rancho Bernardo study. *Ann J Epidemiol* 141:951–959, 1995.

25. Grymonpre RE, Mitenko PA, Sitar DS, et al. Drug-associated hospital admissions in older medical patients. *J Am Geriatr Soc* 36:1092–1098, 1988.

26. Harkess JW, Ramsey WC. Principles of fractures and dislocations. In: Rockwood CA, Green DP, Bucholz RW, eds. *Fractures in Adults.* Philadelphia, Lippincott, 1991.

27. Heath G, Hagverg G, Ehsani A, et al. A physiological comparison of young and older endurance athletes. *J Appl Physiol* 51:634–640, 1981.

28. Heppenstall RB. Fracture healing. In: Heppenstall RB, ed. *Fracture Treatment and Healing.* Philadelphia, Saunders, 1980.

29. Hoenig H, Rubenstein LV, Sloane R, et al. What is the role of timing on the surgical and rehabilitative care of community dwelling older persons with acute hip fracture? *Arch Intern Med* 157:513–520, 1997.

30. Hoffman C, Rice D, Hai-Yen S. Persons with chronic conditions. *JAMA* 276:1473–1479, 1996.

31. Jette AM, Branch LG, Berlin J. Musculoskeletal impairments and physical disablement among the aged. *J Gerontol* 45:203–208, 1990.

32. Johnson H. Is aging physiological or pathological? In: Johnson H, ed. *Relations Between Normal Aging and Disease.* New York, Raven, 1985.

33. Katz S, et al. Active life expectancy. *N Engl J Med* 309:1218–1224, 1983.

34. Koval KJ, Zuckerman JD. Hip. In: Koval KJ, Zuckerman JD, eds. *Fractures in the Elderly.* Philadelphia, Lippincott-Raven, 1998.

35. Krotenberg RM, Stitik T, Johnston MV. Incidence of dislocation following hip arthroplasty for patients in the rehabilitation setting. *Am J Phys Med Rehabil* 74:444–447, 1995.

36. Lane JM. Osteoporosis: Medical prevention and treatment. *Spine* 22:32–37, 1997.

37. Larsson L, Sjodin B, Karlsson J. Histochemical and biochemical changes in human skeletal muscle with age in sedentary males, age 22–65 years. *Acta Physiol Scand* 103:31–39, 1978.

38. Main WK, Cammisa FP, O'Leary PF. The spine. In: Koval KJ, Zuckerman JD, eds. *Fractures in the Elderly*. Philadelphia, Lippincott-Raven, 1998.

39. Mauerhan DR, Campbell M, Miller JS, et al. Intraarticular morphine and/or bupivacaine in the management of pain after total knee arthroplasty. *J Arthroplasty* 12:546–552, 1997.

40. McKinnis LN. Thoracic spine, sternum, and ribs. In: McKinnis LN, ed. *Fundamentals of Orthopedic Radiology*. Philadelphia, Davis, 1997, pp. 135–176.

41. Melton LJ, Thamer M, Ran NF, et al. Fractures attributable to osteoporosis: Report from the National Osteoporosis Foundation. *J Bone Miner Res* 12:16–23, 1997.

42. Moellar JF, Mathiowetz NA. Prescribed medicines: A summary of use and expenditures for Medicare beneficiaries. Rockville, MD, U.S. Department of Health and Human Services, 1989, pub. no. PHC 89-3448.

43. Pate R, Pratt M, Blair N, et al. Physical activity and public health: A recommendation from the Centers for Disease Control and Prevention and the American College of Sports Medicine. *JAMA* 273:402–407, 1995.

44. Phillips SK, Bruce SA, Newton D, et al. The weakness of old age is not due to failure of muscle activation. *J Gerontol* 47:M45–M49, 1992.

45. Pope RO, Corcoran S, McCaul K, et al. Continuous passive motion in total knee arthroplasty. *Orthopedics* 13:291–295, 1990.

46. Reid IR. Glucocorticoid-induced osteoporosis: Assessment and treatment. *J Clin Densiometry* 1:65–73, 1998.

47. Ritter MA, Eizember L, Keating M, et al. The influence of age and gender on the outcome of total knee arthroplasty. *Todays OR Nurse* 17:12–15, 1995.

48. Robinson BE. Depression. *Arch Am Acad Orthop Surg* 2:33–37, 1998.

49. Sinaki M, Mikkelsen BA. Postmenopausal spinal osteoporosis: Flexion versus extension exercises. *Arch Phys Med Rehabil* 65:593–596, 1984.

50. Skinner HB, Barrack RL, Cook SD. Age-related declines in proprioception. *Clin Orthop* 184:208–211, 1988.

51. Stauffer ES, MacMillan M, Montessano PX. Fractures and dislocations of the spine. In: Rockwood CA, Green DP, Bucholz RW, eds. *Fractures in Adults*. Philadelphia, Lippincott, 1991.

52. Tankersley WS, Hungerford DS. Total knee arthroplasty in the very aged. *Clin Orthop* 316:45–49, 1995.

53. Tibbitts GM. Patients who fall: How to predict and prevent injuries. *Geriatrics* 51:24–31, 1996.

54. U.S. Bureau of the Census. Population Estimates by Age, Sex, Race, and Hispanic Origin: 1980–1988. Current Population Reports, series P-25, no. 1045. Washington, DC, U.S. Government Printing Office, 1990.

55. Ververeli PA, Sutton DC, Hearn SL, et al. Continuous possive motion after total knee arthroplasty. Analysis of cost and benefits. *Clin Orthop* 321:208–215, 1995.

56. Vince KG, Kelly MA, Beck J, et al. Continuous passive motion after total knee arthroplasty. *J Arthroplasty* 2:281–284, 1987.

57. Woo SL, Hollis JM, Adams DJ, et al. Tensile properties of the human femur–anterior cruciate ligament–tibia complex. The effects of specimen age and orientation. *Am J Sports Med* 19:217–225, 1991.

CHAPTER 35

Considerations with the Pediatric Patient

Steven R. Tippett

OBJECTIVES

After completing this chapter, the student therapist should be able to do the following:

- Describe common macrotraumatic and microtraumatic musculoskeletal injuries occurring in the skeletally immature patient.
- Describe selected congenital and acquired and musculoskeletal pathologies seen in active skeletally immature patients.
- Apply basic rehabilitation principles governing the care and prevention of macrotraumatic and microtraumatic musculoskeletal injuries in the skeletally immature patient.
- Differentiate between categories of growth plate fractures.
- Describe physiologic considerations unique to the active skeletally immature patient.
- Describe special psychological considerations for the skeletally immature athlete.
- Describe participation guidelines for the skeletally immature athlete.

Although the physical and psychological demands placed upon the young patient can be almost as rigorous as the demands placed upon an adult, young minds and bodies are often not suited to accept these demands. Growing musculoskeletal tissue is innately predisposed to specific injuries that vary greatly from the injuries sustained by their skeletally mature counterparts. This chapter briefly describes common macrotraumatic and microtraumatic injuries sustained by the young patient along with basic principles that govern the treatment of these injuries. Macrotraumatic injuries occur as a result of a single, supramaximal loading of bone, ligament, muscle, or tendon. Common youth macrotraumatic injuries that will be discussed include epiphyseal and avulsion fractures. Microtraumatic injuries, on the other hand, result from submaximal loading that occurs in a cyclic and repetitive fashion. Common microtraumatic injuries that occur in the immature musculoskeletal system that will be presented include osteochondroses and traction apophysites. Special concerns unique to the immature musculoskeletal system that do not fall neatly into the macrotraumatic or microtraumatic categories will also be presented in this chapter. Finally, physiologic and psychological issues unique to the youth patient will also be presented.

MACROTRAUMATIC MUSCULOSKELETAL INJURIES

Epiphyseal Fractures

Growing bone is the weak musculoskeletal link in the young athlete. Physical demands resulting in muscle strain or ligament sprain in the skeletally mature patient may result in epiphyseal plate injury in the young patient. The epiphyseal plate or growth plate is divided into zones differentiated from one another via structure and function. Beginning at the growth area of long bone and progressing in the direction of mature long bone, the four regions of the growth plate include the reserve zone, proliferative zone, hypertrophic zone, and bony metaphysis. The reserve zone produces and stores matrix; the proliferative zone also produces matrix and is the site for longitudinal bone cell growth. The hypertrophic zone is subdivided into the maturation zone, degenerative zone, and zone of provisional calcification. It is within the hypertrophic zone that matrix is prepared for calcification, and it is here that the matrix is ultimately calcified.[18]

It is difficult to predict the collective strength of the entire growth plate due to varying amounts and composition of matrix, along with varying cellular architecture and density.[18] Injury to the growth plate can occur when stress or tensile loads placed upon bone exceed mechanical strength of the growth plate–metaphysis complex. Two factors that impact epiphyseal plate injury are (1) the ability of the growth plate to resist failure and (2) the forces applied to bone or the stresses induced in the growth plate. Based upon results from animal studies, it has been determined that the weakest region of the growth plate is the hypertrophic zone. The hypertrophic zone is susceptible to injury because of the low volume of bone matrix and high amount of developing immature cells in this region.[18]

The majority of epiphyseal fractures are due to high-velocity injuries. Although growth plate fractures certainly result from youth sporting activities, a detailed description of all epiphyseal plate fractures is beyond the scope of this chapter. A brief description of the Salter–Harris classification of growth plate fractures along with some of the more common epiphyseal plate fractures in sports, however, is warranted.

The Salter–Harris classification of growth plate fracture consists of five types of fractures and is based upon the relationship of the fracture line to the growing cells of the epiphyseal plate as well as the mechanism of injury (Fig. 35-1). Type I fractures are due to shearing forces in which there is complete separation of the epiphysis without fracture through bone. Type I fractures are most commonly seen in the very young when the epiphyseal plate is relatively thick. Type II fractures are the most common type of growth plate fractures and result from shearing and bending forces. In the type II fracture, the line of separation traverses along the epiphyseal plate a variable distance and then makes its way through a segment of the bony metaphysis that results in a triangular-shaped metaphyseal fragment. Type II fractures usually occur in an older child who has a thin epiphyseal plate. Type III fractures usually result from shearing forces and result in intraarticular fractures from the joint surface to the deep zone of the growth plate and then along the growth plate to its periphery. Type IV fractures are intraarticular and also result from shearing forces. Type IV fractures extend from the joint surface through the epiphysis across the entire thickness of the growth plate and then through a segment of the bony metaphysis. Type V fractures are due to a crushing mechanism and are relatively uncommon.[34]

Salter–Harris type III fractures warrant special mention. These fractures are typically limited to the distal tibial epiphysis.[34] Injury to the proximal tibial epiphysis or distal femoral epiphysis may result from valgus loading of the knee, which is frequently encountered in contact and collision sports. The clinician can not rely solely on radiographic examination to confirm this type of injury. In a series of 6 high school athletes (5 playing football, 1 playing soccer), all injured by a valgus load, routine anterior–posterior and lateral x-rays did not demonstrate Salter–Harris type III fractures of the distal femoral epiphysis. Oblique x-rays with femoral rotation, cross-table lateral views demonstrating fat in the joint, or aspiration of a hemarthrosis with fat in the aspirate, will help confirm growth plate fracture with an intraarticular component.[46] A thorough ligamentous examination with careful palpation skills is required to help differentiate joint line opening from epiphyseal plate opening.

Other common epiphyseal fractures seen in children involve the medial epicondyle and the bones of the hand. The medial epicondyle epiphyseal fracture is the most common elbow fracture seen in the young patient. From a macrotraumatic standpoint, epiphyseal fracture of the medial epicondyle is frequently the childhood counterpart of elbow dislocation in the adult, and is typically caused by hyperextension and valgus loading.[1] Epiphyseal plate fractures of the medial epicondyle are typically Salter–Harris type I or II, although types III and IV injuries have also been reported. Medial epicondyle fractures typically result in the epicondyle being displaced inferiorly and possibly trapped in the elbow joint.[31] As the medial epicondyle serves as the attachment of the elbow and wrist flexors, avulsion fractures of the medial epicondyle also occur and will be discussed later in this chapter.

Epiphyseal fractures in children are more common in the hand than in other long bones of the upper extremity.[38] As a result, care must be taken by the parent, coach, or health care professional not to simply disregard finger injuries as simply a "jammed finger." Growth plate fractures in the hand usually involve the proximal and middle phalanges of the border digits. The most common epiphyseal plate fracture in the skeletally immature hand is a Salter–Harris type II at the base of the proximal phalanx of the little finger.[38]

The term "Little League shoulder" is used to describe an epiphyseal fracture of the proximal humeral epiphysis that typically occurs in the young baseball pitcher.[11] Although this injury can be macrotraumatic in nature (i.e., as a result of one specific throw), the condition is thought to be due to repetitive microtrauma. Fractures of the proximal humeral epiphysis are usually Salter–Harris type I or II. Radiographs demonstrate widening of the proximal humeral physis, and to a lesser degree may demonstrate lateral metaphyseal fragmentation, along with demineralization or sclerosis of the proximal humeral metaphysis. Avoiding all throwing until the patient is asymptomatic is vital in the treatment of this condition. Most patients are able to safely return to throwing with symptoms despite abnormal radiographs.[12]

Avulsion Fractures

As in the case with growing bone, much of the information regarding growing muscle is also based on animal studies. Although the physiology of the growth plate allows for bone growth, muscle does not inherently possess a specific structural site to allow for adaptation. It is clear that muscle adaptation does occur in order to accommodate for skeletal growth or as

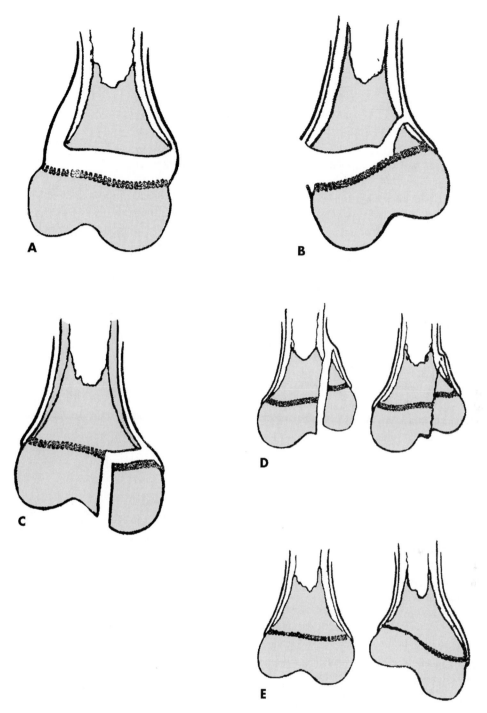

FIGURE 35-1

Growth plate fractures according to the Salter–Harris classification. **A,** Type I.
B, Type II. **C,** Type III. **D,** Type IV. **E,** Type V.

a response to therapeutic stretching exercise following periods of immobilization with muscle tissue in a shortened position. Based upon animal studies, it appears that a change in muscle length results from changes within the actual muscle belly itself and/or an increase in tendon length. In the skeletally immature animal model, change in muscle length occurs via changes in the length of both muscle and tendon. Research involving mature animals, on the other hand, indicates an increase in muscle length occurs primarily through elongation of the muscle belly.[14]

TABLE 35-1

Maturation of Bones of the Arm and Shoulder

BONE	MATURATION TIMETABLE
Clavicle, sternal epiphysis	Closure 18th–24th yr.
Acromion	Closure 18th–19th yr.
Coracoid	Closure 18th–21st yr.
Subcoracoid	Closure 18th–21st yr.
Scapula, vertebral margin and inferior angle	Closure 20th–21st yr.
Glenoid cavity	Closure 19th yr.
Humerus, head, center, and lesser tuberosities	Fuse together 4th–6th yr.; fuse to shaft 19th–21st yr. (males), 18th–20th yr. (females)
Humerus, capitulum, lateral epicondyle, and trochlea	Fuse together at puberty; fuse to shaft at 17th yr. in males, 14th yr. in females
Olecranon	Closure 15th–17th yr. in males, 14th–15th yr. in females
Radius, head	Closure 13th–17th yr. in males, 14th–15th yr. in females
Radial tuberosity	Closure 14th–18th yr.
Ulna, distal epiphysis	Closure 19th yr. in males, 17th yr. in females
Styloid of ulna	Closure 18th–20th yr.
Radius, distal epiphysis	Closure 19th yr. in males, 17th yr. in females
Styloid process, radius	Closure variable
Lunate	Appears 4th yr.
Navicular	Appears 6th yr.
Pisiform	Appears 12th yr.
Triquetrum	Appears 1st–2nd yr.
Hamate	Appears 6th mo.
Capitate	Appears 6th mo.
Trapezoid	Appears 4th yr.
Trapezium	Closure 5th yr.
Metacarpal I epiphysis	Closure 14th–21st yr.
Metacarpals II–IV, epiphysis	Closure 14th–21st yr.
Proximal phalanx I, epiphysis	Closure 14th–21st yr.
Distal phalanx I, epiphysis	Closure 14th–21st yr.

When changes in muscle length do not match the changes in long-bone growth, tensile loads placed within the muscle predispose the youngster to injury. Contractile unit injury from voluntary contraction or passive stretch can be exacerbated due to inadequate muscle length. Injuries can range from various degrees of muscle strain to situations where the bony attachment of the muscle fails prior to muscle damage. Common sites of avulsion fracture in the lower extremity include the anterior superior iliac spine, anterior inferior iliac spine, ischial tuberosity, and the base of the fifth metatarsal. As forces across the joints of the lower extremity due to running, jumping, and kicking exceed most forces across the upper extremity, avulsion fractures of the lower extremity outnumber avulsion fractures of the upper extremity. Stresses across the shoulder and elbow of

the young throwing athlete, however, are sufficient enough to result in avulsion of the medial humeral epicondyle and proximal humerus.

LOWER EXTREMITY

Anterior Superior Iliac Spine

Avulsion of the anterior superior iliac spine (ASIS) is caused by a contraction or stretch of the sartorius. The sartorius is the longest muscle in the body and crosses the anterior hip and proximal medial knee joints. The growth center at the ASIS appears between the ages of 13 and 15 years and fuses to the pelvis between the ages of 21 and 25 years (Table 35-1 and Fig. 35-2).[29] Excessive force from the pulling of the sartorius with the hip in

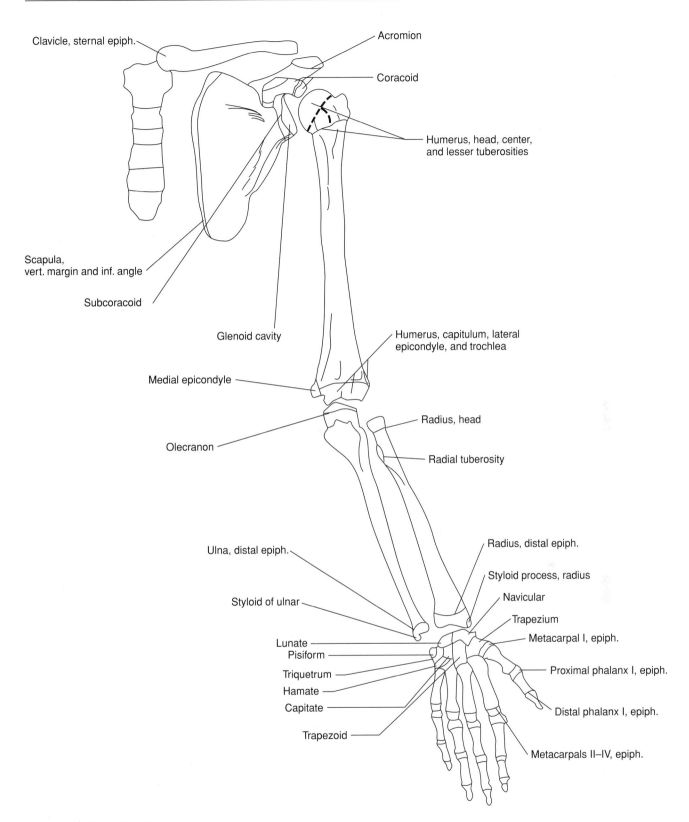

Clavicle, sternal epiph.

Acromion

Coracoid

Humerus, head, center, and lesser tuberosities

Scapula, vert. margin and inf. angle

Subcoracoid

Glenoid cavity

Humerus, capitulum, lateral epicondyle, and trochlea

Medial epicondyle

Radius, head

Olecranon

Radial tuberosity

Ulna, distal epiph.

Radius, distal epiph.

Styloid process, radius

Styloid of ulnar

Navicular

Trapezium

Lunate

Metacarpal I, epiph.

Pisiform

Triquetrum

Proximal phalanx I, epiph.

Hamate

Capitate

Distal phalanx I, epiph.

Trapezoid

Metacarpals II–IV, epiph.

FIGURE 35-2

A, Upper-extremity ossification and epiphyseal plate closure. **B,** Lower-extremity ossification and epiphyseal plate closure.

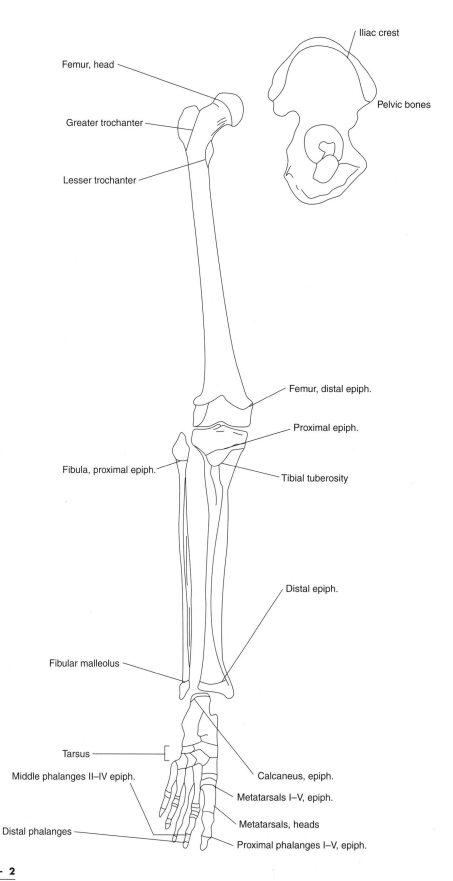

TABLE 35-2

Maturation of Bones of the Leg and Hip

BONE	MATURATION TIMETABLE
Pelvic bones	Fuse at puberty
Iliac crest	Closure 20th yr.
Femur, head	Closure 17th–18th yr. in males, 16th–17th yr. in females
Greater trochanter	Closure 16th–17th yr.
Lesser trochanter	Closure 16th–17th yr.
Femur, distal epiphysis	Closure 18th–19th yr. in males, 17th yr. in females
Proximal epiphysis	Closure 18th–19th yr. in males, 16th–17th yr. in females
Tibial tuberosity	Closure 19th yr.
Fibula, proximal epiphysis	Closure 18th–20th yr. in males, 16th–18th yr. in females
Fibular malleolus	Closure 17th–18th yr.
Distal epiphysis	Closure 17th–18th yr.
Calcaneus, epiphysis	Closure 12th–22nd yr.
Tarsus	Completion variable
Metatarsals I–V, epiphysis	Closure 18th yr. in males, 16th yr. in females
Metatarsals, heads	Closure 14th–21st yr.
Proximal phalanges I–V, epiphysis	Closure 18th yr.
Middle phalanges, II–IV, epiphysis	Closure 18th yr.
Distal phalanges	Closure 18th yr., beginning proximally

extension and knee in flexion may result in an avulsion of the ASIS. Positions of hip extension combined with knee flexion seen in the trail leg during sprinting and hurdling can predispose these athletes to ASIS avulsion fracture. When the growth center does avulse from the bony origin on the pelvis, displacement of the avulsed fragment is uncommon.[37]

Anterior Inferior Iliac Spine

Avulsion of the anterior-inferior iliac spine (AIIS) is caused by a stretch or contraction of the rectus femoris. The AIIS serves as the site of the direct (anterior, or straight) head of the rectus femoris. As in the case with ASIS avulsions, activities involving hyperextension of the hip combined with knee flexion can also result in AIIS avulsion. The growth center at the AIIS appears between the ages of 13 and 15 years and fuses at approximately 16 to 18 years.[29] Due to earlier ossification, avulsion fractures at the AIIS are less frequent than avulsion fractures involving the ASIS. Athletes involved in running, jumping, and kicking sports usually sustain AIIS avulsion fractures.[29] When avulsion occurs, displacement of the bony muscle origin is rare because the tensor fascia lata, inguinal ligament, and an intact reflected (posterior) head of the rectus femoris (which originates at the superior rim of the acetabulum) all serve to prevent significant AIIS displacement.[37]

With both ASIS and AIIS avulsion fractures, the youngster is typically able to remember a specific event and is usually unable to continue participation.[5] The patient demonstrates weakness of the involved muscle as evidenced by resisted hip flexion. In the avulsed ASIS, resisted hip flexion with the hip

in external rotation may be useful in the physical assessment. Point tenderness of the ASIS or AIIS is virtually always present. Swelling, if present, may be minimal, and there is minimal if any ecchymosis noted. Transfers from sit to supine are usually guarded and may require assistance from the patient's upper extremities or from the contralateral lower extremity. Assuming a prone position may be uncomfortable. Passive stretch into complete knee flexion may or may not produce pain. Passive stretch of the hip into extension with simultaneous knee flexion may increase symptoms. Gait is typically antalgic with increased trunk flexion during stance, decreased hip flexion during swing-through, and decreased hip extension during late stance.[44]

Peroneals

Inversion ankle sprains are sustained frequently by patients of all ages in a wide variety of sport and nonsport-related activities. As the patient inverts the ankle, stresses can be placed through the evertor muscle group, either by passive stretch and/or active contraction to pull the foot back into eversion. Excessive forces generated by the peroneus brevis may result in avulsion of its insertion at the base of the fifth metatarsal. Avulsion fracture of the base of the fifth metatarsal typically results in point tenderness along with weakness of resisted ankle eversion, especially when resisted at the athlete's available end-range inversion. Resisted eversion may or may not cause pain. Passive inversion of the ankle typically increases pain at the bony insertion. Swelling may be present, but occurs distal to the traditional location of swelling seen in ankle sprains. Ecchymosis, if present, typically does not arise until a few days following injury.[44]

Ischial Tuberosity

Avulsion of the hamstring origin at the ischial apophysis was first described in the middle 1850s and occurs with greater frequency than avulsions on the anterior aspect of the pelvis.[37] Growth centers in this region appear between the ages of 15 and 17 years and fuse to the ilia between the ages of 19 and 25 years.[29,37] Athletes with an avulsion fracture of the ischial tuberosity typically demonstrate discomfort with prolonged sitting. Assessment of hamstring length at 90 degrees of hip flexion will often show inadequate flexibility bilaterally, with more limitation on the involved side that is usually accompanied by pain. There may or may not be weakness with resisted knee flexion, but there is usually weakness noted with resisted or nonresisted prone active hip extension. There is typically minimal if any ecchymosis in the area, and swelling is usually not apparent.[44]

UPPER EXTREMITY

A medial epicondyle epiphyseal fracture is the most common elbow fracture seen in the young patient.[1] As discussed previously, this injury may occur as a result of a macrotraumatic hyperextension or valgus injury. The medial epicondyle serves as the attachment site of the forearm flexor/pronator group, and as such can also be a location for avulsion fracture. This type of injury is typically due to valgus loading during the acceleration phase of the throwing mechanism. Avulsion of the triceps attachment at the olecranon has also been reported. This condition has been seen to result in separated ossification centers that persist into adulthood with subsequent olecranon nonunion.[19]

TREATMENT PRINCIPLES

Conservative treatment of all avulsion fractures mimics that of a severe muscle strain. In fractures involving the lower extremity, assisted gait is a must until weight-bearing activities are pain free and without substitution. Compression of the area in the form of elastic wraps or neoprene sleeves may provide warmth and minimize discomfort experienced with activities of daily living and early rehabilitation efforts. Modalities to minimize pain and facilitate healing are indicated early in the treatment regimen. Once inflammation from the initial injury has subsided, gentle single-joint stretching exercises can begin. Two-joint stretching exercises should begin only after one-joint stretches are pain free. Submaximal single-joint strengthening exercises can begin when pain free. Strengthening efforts should be preceded by warm-up activities, and strengthening exercises should also be followed by stretching of the involved muscle. When isolated two-joint strengthening efforts are tolerated without difficulty, the young athlete can be allowed to return to a functional progression program.[44] Avulsion injuries of the upper extremity must be treated with rest until the youngster is asymptomatic. A gradual return to throwing sports through a supervised functional progression program is vital.

MICROTRAUMATIC INJURIES

Apophysitis

The apophysis of growing bone differs from the epiphysis of skeletally immature bone. The apophysis is an independent center of ossification that does not contribute to the longitudinal length of a long bone. An apophysis, however, does contribute to the structure and form of mature long bone by serving as a site of tendinous or ligamentous attachment. It is the role of the apophysis as the site for tendinous attachment that enters the picture of overuse injuries seen in the growing patient. At skeletal maturity, the apophysis fuses to its site of attachment to its respective long bone. Prior to skeletal maturity, however, traction placed upon an apophysis from an inflexible musculotendinous unit may result in apophyseal inflammation and delayed fusion to the long bone. Traction apophysitis commonly occurs at the tibial tubercle, calcaneus, and iliac crest.

LOWER EXTREMITY

Repetitive loading activities of the lower extremities in combination with muscle–tendon length insufficiency can yield traction forces through apophyseal centers that result in inflammation of the apophysis. Young patients involved in running, jumping, and kicking activities are inherently predisposed to large traction forces through apophyseal centers, especially during a growth spurt. These traction apophysites are typically self-limiting, but cases that do not respond to traditional conservative measures may require short-term immobilization to assist in eliminating pain and inflammation.

Calcaneal Apophysitis (Sever's disease)

Sever's disease is a traction apophysitis of the growth center of the calcaneus. Sever's disease typically affects youngsters 8 to 13 years of age, with the peak incidence occurring at 11 years in young females and at 12 years in young males.[24,28] Sever's disease frequently affects youngsters involved in outdoor fall sports following a dry summer that results in dry, hard ground. Soccer, football, and even band participants, especially early in the season, are commonly diagnosed with Sever's disease.[44] Young soccer players who routinely participate on artificial surfaces may also experience symptoms consistent with Sever's disease.[24] Spikes or other shoes lacking in adequate shock absorption and forefoot support, or shoes with broken-down heel counters, contribute to the incidence of Sever's disease.

Sever's disease is characterized by pain and point tenderness at the posterior calcaneus near the insertion of the Achilles tendon. Local signs of inflammation may be present in acute cases. Swelling at the calcaneal apophysis may also be present, but this is an exception rather than the rule. Patients with tight calves, internal tibial torsion, forefoot varus, a dorsally mobile first ray, weak dorsiflexors, and genu varus may be more susceptible to Sever's disease.

A

B

FIGURE 35-3

A, Front knee should be flexed for soleus stretching, back knee should be straight for gastrocnemius stretching, and heels should remain on the floor. **B,** Standing on a slantboard (see also Fig. 35-4) at the point of a discernable stretch for 10 minutes can be incorporated into a home stretching program.

Treatment of Sever's disease should focus on establishing normal flexibility of the gastrocnemius–soleus group (Figs. 35-3 and 35-4). Calf stretching should include exercises with the knee extended and the knee flexed. Just as importantly, stretching in a weight-bearing position should be performed with the correction of any rearfoot to lower leg or forefoot to rearfoot abnormality. Orthotic intervention may be a consideration in the treatment of Sever's disease and may range from temporary heel lifts or heel cups, to more sophisticated custom-fit orthotics to correct biomechanical abnormalities. Dorsiflexion strengthening exercises along with foot intrinsic strengthening may also help manage symptoms.[44]

Tibial Tubercle Apophysitis (Osgood–Schlatters Disease)

Initially described in 1903, Osgood–Schlatters disease (OSD) is commonly seen in active and nonactive youngsters alike.[22] Like all traction apophysites, the condition is usually self-limiting, but due to its prevalence and the ominous name, parents, and

young patients may mistakenly expect a poor prognosis. This is not to downplay the potential long-standing problems that can arise when the condition is not adequately diagnosed and treated.

Development of the tibial apophysis begins as a cartilaginous outgrowth. Secondary ossification centers appear with subsequent progression to an epiphyseal phase when the proximal tibial physis closes and the tibial apophysis fuses to the tibia.[16] Calcification of the apophysis begins distally at the average age of 9 years in females and at 11 years in males. Fusion of the apophysis to the tibia can take place via several ossification centers and occurs on average at 12 years in females and 13 years in males.[22] There is a normal transition from distal fibrocartilage to proximal fibrous tissue at the tibial apophysis. Fibrous tissue is more readily able to withstand the high tensile loads involved with athletic activities than is the weaker cartilage of the secondary ossification center. Microavulsions can occur through the area of bone and cartilage at the secondary ossification

SLANT BOARD DIAGRAM

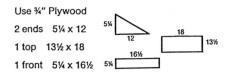

Use ¾" Plywood
2 ends   5¼ x 12
1 top   13½ x 18
1 front 5¼ x 16½

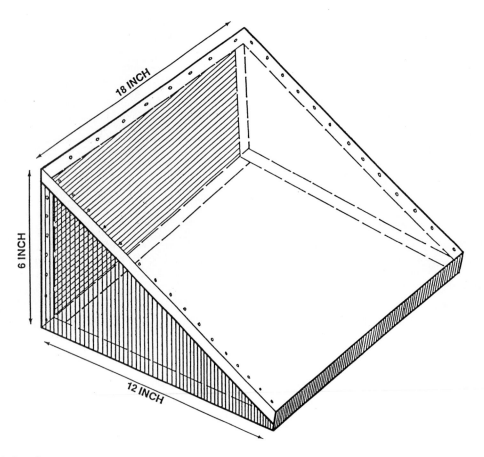

18 INCH

6 INCH

12 INCH

FIGURE 35-4

Directions for fabricating a slantboard to facilitate gastrocnemius–soleus stretching.

center, resulting in the potential for the development of separate ossicles, which can be a source of prolonged pain or reinjury.[22] Complications of OSD are few, but in addition to the formation of an accessory ossicle, patellar subluxation (secondary to patella alta), patella baja, nonunion of the tibial tubercle, and genu recurvatum have been reported.[20,23,50]

The diagnosis of OSD is not a clinical challenge. Symptoms are typically unilateral, although up to 25 percent of cases can be bilateral in nature.[16] There may or may not be a history of injury. Traditional literature reveals that OSD affects more young males than females; however, recent evidence suggests no significant difference between male and female involvement.[41] The youngster typically complains of aching around the tibial tubercle that is increased during or following jumping, climbing, or kneeling activities. The tibial tubercle may be reddened,

raised, or tender to palpation. Symptoms are usually confined to the tibial tubercle and are typically not present at the superior or inferior patellar poles or the patellar tendon; however, patellofemoral tenderness may be present.[39] Tenderness at the cartilaginous junction of the patella and patellar tendon at the inferior patellar pole is indicative of Sinding–Larsen–Johannson disease.[40] Findings on x-ray (especially if only performed unilaterally) are often misleading, as it is difficult to differentiate between abnormal fragmentation from normal centers of ossification. Radiographs, however, may reveal soft-tissue swelling. Some athletes with OSD also have patella alta, and some authors have noted a link between patients with OSD and Severs disease.[22]

Treatment of Osgood–Schlatter's disease should emphasize a judicious stretching program. Inadequate quadriceps flexibility is virtually always present. The shortened muscle group combined with the ballistic nature of quadriceps activity in jumping sports are at the heart of OSD. Overzealous stretching of the quadriceps, however, may increase the pull on the tibial tubercle and only serve to increase symptoms. Stretching of the quadriceps should begin prone, stressing an increase in quadriceps length at the knee joint only. A bolster under the hips may be required to place the muscle on slack at the hip joint. All stretching must be accompanied by a pull within the quadriceps muscle belly, not at the tibial tubercle. Two-joint stretching exercises should be instituted when adequate muscle length is established at the knee without an increase in tibial tubercle tenderness (Fig. 35-5). Quadriceps weakness is frequently not a major concern in this patient population; many of these youngsters have excellent quadriceps recruitment with no atrophy. Chronic cases, however, will result in quadriceps atrophy. Pain-free isometrics or low-load and high-repetition knee extension exercise may be incorporated if quadriceps atrophy is noted. Progressive resistive exercises of the quadriceps must be used judiciously, as they may only serve to increase pain at the tibial tubercle. As tight hamstrings require increased quadriceps force to overcome the tight posterior structures, hamstring exercises must be included in the comprehensive program to manage OSD (Figs. 35-6 and 35-7). If competing in a contact or collision sport, young athletes with OSD should be fit with a protective pad to minimize the risks of blunt trauma to the area. When the tibial tubercle area is inflamed, even when the athlete is not participating, protective padding should also be considered to minimize the incidence of inadvertent blunt trauma encountered in activities of daily living.[44]

Iliac Apophysitis

Iliac apophysitis is a condition typically seen in the older youngster involved in running sports. Active patients between the ages of 14 and 16 years are usually the prime candidates for iliac apophysitis.[13] The ossification center of the iliac crest appears anterolaterally and advances posteriorly until it reaches the posterior iliac spine. The average age of closure is 16 years in boys and 14 years in girls, but closure may be delayed up to 4 additional years.[28] The gluteus medius originates on the ilium just inferior to the iliac crest and is another muscle that may contribute to iliac apophysitis. The gluteus medius helps to maintain pelvic symmetry for single-leg stance activities during running and hopping. Inflammation of the iliac apophysis is thought to be due to a repetitive pull of the abdominal musculature at its insertion on the iliac crest.[37] During physical activities, the abdominal muscles serve as trunk stabilizers and accessory muscles of respiration. Although most commonly seen as an overuse apophysitis, incomplete avulsion fractures of the iliac apophysis have been reported from sudden contraction of the abdominals with a quick change in direction while running.

Patients who experience iliac apophysitis usually demonstrate exquisite point tenderness along the iliac crest, which is typically unilateral and located along the anterior one-half of the iliac crest. Seated or standing lateral trunk flexion away from the side of involvement is usually uncomfortable. Weakness or pain with resisted hip abduction, oblique abdominal muscular activity, and pain or compensation with hopping on the involved leg may also be present. A complete lower-extremity biomechanical examination may be indicated to determine structural or compensatory leg length inequality that may contribute to iliac apophysitis.

Treatment of iliac apophysitis should center on regaining normal flexibility of the iliotibial band, the abdominals, and gluteus medius. The patient at the outset of a flexibility program typically tolerates two-joint stretching of the iliotibial band with the knee extended (see Fig. 35-8 on page 710). The traditional Ober test position, along with variations, are efficient stretching activities, but are often accompanied by substitution of excessive hip flexion, trunk flexion, or rotation. Seated lateral flexion away from the side of involvement, progressed to standing lateral flexion, which is then progressed to standing lateral flexion with arms extended overhead, is a good stretching progression. Prone press-ups with rotation and lateral flexion may also be incorporated into the stretching program.[44]

Fifth Metatarsal Apophysitis (Iselin's Disease)

Of the many traction apophysites that affect the young patient, Iselin's disease is the most rarely encountered. The insertion of the peroneus brevis may be irritated by activities requiring fine foot control as in the case of dancers and gymnasts. Patients with abnormal relationships between the forefoot and rearfoot may be predisposed to Iselin's disease. A tight gastrocnemius–soleus complex or weak dorsiflexors may also contribute to apophysitis at the base of the fifth metatarsal.[28]

UPPER EXTREMITY

Because the stresses placed across an apophysis of the lower extremity usually exceed those placed across the upper extremity, most cases of apophysitis affect the legs of the growing patient. There are a few cases of upper-extremity apophysitis that do occur and warrant brief attention at this point. As previously noted, the elbow is subjected to large valgus forces during the acceleration phase of the throwing mechanism. In the skeletally mature patient, these valgus forces can result in medial elbow laxity. In the skeletally immature, these valgus forces may result in an apophysitis of the medial epicondyle.

Stretching and strengthening of the forearm and wrist musculature may be beneficial in minimizing the chances for upper-extremity overuse injuries in the growing patients. Abnormal throwing mechanics may contribute to youth upper-extremity overuse injury; however, the vast majority of injuries are due to training errors. The most frequently committed training error is the amount of pitching that a youngster is allowed to perform. In order to minimize the risk of overuse injury, the athlete must adhere to common-sense guidelines regarding the amount of pitching. Little League baseball and softball have established guidelines that govern the amount of pitching that a youngster can perform.[25]

A   **B**

FIGURE 35-5

Quadriceps stretching. **A,** Proper technique. **B,** Improper technique with excessive trunk flexion.

A   **B**

FIGURE 35-6

Long-sitting hamstring stretching. **A,** Proper technique. **B,** Improper technique with excessive thoracolumbar flexion.

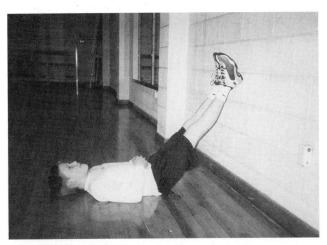

FIGURE 35-7

Wall stretch hamstring stretching. The youngster should maintain full knee extension and keep the buttocks on the floor. As hamstring flexibility improves, the youngster should ultimately be able to place the heels, backs of the knees, and buttocks against the wall.

While these guidelines are an important step in preventing upper-extremity overuse injury, they are only part of the story. Many youngsters participate in organized baseball programs that are not officially affiliated with Little League. These youngsters may not have guidelines to regulate how much an individual can pitch. These guidelines also do not apply to batting practice and often are not considered when youngsters pitch in tournament play. Finally, the number of innings may not be the best indicator to use, as an inning in baseball play by 9 to 12-year-olds ranges from 4 to 50 pitches per inning, and the number of pitches per pitching outing ranges from 4 to 100.[2]

SPINE

Most spine injuries involve the muscles, ligaments, and intervertebral disks. These injuries are usually self-limiting and rarely result in significant neurologic compromise.[43] Two conditions of the osseous structures of the spine, however, do involve the young patient: spondylolysis and spondylolisthesis. Spondylolysis is a bony defect in the pars interarticularis, a portion of the neural arch located between the superior and inferior articular facets. Physical forces encountered by youngsters involved in physical activities play a significant role in the development of spondylolysis. Activities that involve repetitive loading, especially with the lumbar spine in extension/hyperextension, such as ballet, gymnastics, diving, football, weight lifting, and wrestling, have been implicated in spondylolysis. Spondylolysis originates in children between the ages of 5 and 10 years of age and most frequently occurs at the fifth lumbar vertebra, with the fourth lumbar vertebra being involved second most frequently.[42] Many youngsters with sponylolysis remain asymptomatic for long periods of time and are not diagnosed until later in their skeletal development. X-rays from the lateral and oblique views are required in order to visualize the fracture in its entirety along the longitudinal plane. Positive x-ray findings include asymmetry of the neural arch, inferior apophyseal joint, and posterior elements with rotation of the spinous process away from a unilateral spondylolytic lesion. CT scan and bone scan with SPECT can aid in the radiologic diagnosis and staging of spondylolysis.[27] A common finding in patients with spondylolysis (symptomatic or asymptomatic) is hamstring spasm.[42] The etiology of this hamstring spasm is felt to be due to either a postural reflex to stabilize the L5-S1 segment or to nerve root irritation.[27,42]

Spondylolisthesis is a condition in which a vertebra slips anterior to the vertebra immediately below it. Spondylolisthesis most frequently takes place between the fifth lumbar and first sacral vertebrae, although the condition can occur at more than one spinal segment. The superior border of the inferior vertebra is divided into quarters, and the slip is described in terms of the width that the superior vertebra slips anteriorly in relation to the vertebra below it. A grade one spondylolisthesis is an anterior slip of 25 percent or less of the vertebral width, a grade two slip is up to 50 percent of the vertebral width, a grade three spondylolisthesis is a slip up to 75 percent of the vertebral width, and a grade four is a complete anterior slip. Spondylolisthesis is classified as degenerative, traumatic, pathologic, or isthmic. It is the isthmic classification that typically involves the young patient. In the isthmic category of spondylolisthesis, it is debatable whether a bilateral spondylolysis is a precursor for slippage and resultant instability of a spinal segment.

Treatment of spondylolysis and spondylolisthesis centers on healing of the bony defect and decreasing the patient's symptoms. Treatment depends upon the physician's personal preference and ranges from relative rest without a brace to 23 hours of bracing. When bracing is used, the brace is typically a rigid custom-fit lumbar spinal orthosis designed to keep the youngster out of extension. In addition to activity modification, hamstring stretching is an integral part of the treatment program.

SPECIAL CONSIDERATIONS

Musculoskeletal Considerations

Some conditions involving the young patient may actually be congenital in nature, but do not cause symptoms until the youngster becomes physically active in youth sports or physical education classes. Conditions such as these have unknown etiologies; some clearly have genetic predispositions, while others may be traced to excessive activity. Musculoskeletal conditions that will be discussed include tarsal coalition, Legg–Calvé–Perthes disease, slipped capital femoral epiphysis, osteochondroses, and patellofemoral pain syndrome.

A   **B**

FIGURE   35-8

A, Standing ITB stretching. The uninvolved leg is crossed over in front of the involved leg and the youngster dips the hips toward the wall. **B,** Side-lying ITB stretching. Lying on the involved side with feet, hips, and shoulders in a straight alignment, the athlete pushes up onto extended elbows.

TARSAL COALITION

Persistent ankle and foot pain in the young patient in conjunction with recurrent ankle sprains could possibly be due to an underlying tarsal coalition. A tarsal coalition is an abnormal fusion between tarsal bones in the rearfoot or midfoot due to a failure of bony segmentation. The most common tarsal coalitions occur between the calcaneus and navicular, the talus and the navicular, or the talus and calcaneus. Most tarsal coalitions present clinically in patients between the ages of 8 to 16 years, with anywhere from 50 to 60 percent of tarsal coalitions occurring bilaterally. There is familial predisposition in some cases of tarsal coalition.[24] As coalitions can be fibrous, cartilaginous, or osseous, X rays of the foot are many times interpreted as being unremarkable. Bone scan and CT scan may be of benefit in those cases where X rays fail to demonstrate pathologic findings. Stretching and strengthening of extrinsic and intrinsic ankle musculature may help to minimize motion and strength losses. A custom-made or off-the-shelf orthosis may also help to minimize symptoms.[36]

LEGG–CALVÉ–PERTHES DISEASE

Legg–Calvé–Perthes disease (LCPD) is an avascular necrosis of the femoral head thought to be due to an occlusion of the blood supply to the femoral head from excessive fluid pressure resulting from an inflammatory or traumatic synovial effusion of the hip joint. LCPD typically involves active youngsters between the ages of 3 and 11 years, and is found four times more frequently in young boys than young girls. LCPD is usually unilateral, although 15 percent of youngsters have bilateral involvement.[34] Youngsters diagnosed with LCPD may or may not be able to recall a history of trauma, but LCPD should be ruled out in any male athlete younger than 12 years of age with long-standing groin or knee pain worsened by a weight-bearing position. Young patients usually will present with a limp and a compensated or uncompensated gluteus medius gait. It should be noted that is not unusual for the youngster to have no complaints of hip pain. Pain, when present, is usually in the groin and is very frequently referred to the knee. In fact, LCPD can be misdiagnosed as patellofemoral pain.[45]

SLIPPED CAPITAL FEMORAL EPIPHYSIS

Slipped capital femoral epiphysis (SCFE), although rare, is a condition that may not manifest itself until a youngster becomes involved in sports activities. SCFE involves boys twice as often as girls and typically occurs between 10 and 15 years of age during a period of rapid growth.[37] A suspected causative factor is a potential hormonal imbalance; therefore SCFE should be suspected in youngsters who are tall and thin or short and obese who complain of long-standing thigh, groin, or knee pain. Progressive cases of SCFE may result in a varus deformity with concomitant external rotation.

There are also other conditions that may result in groin pain or pain around the pelvis that may be manifested after a macrotraumatic event. Musculoskeletal conditions include hernia, avulsion fracture of the lesser trochanter, iliopectineal bursitis/tendinitis (snapping hip), abdominal muscle strain, congenital dislocation of the hip, septic arthritis, and toxic synovitis. Nonmusculoskeletal differential diagnoses as a source of acute or persistent hip pain include leukemia and neuroblastoma.[48] Other potential causes of hip pain are bone tumor, appendicitis, pelvic inflammatory disease, hemophilia, arterial insufficiency, and sickle cell anemia.[15]

OSTEOCHONDROSES

Osteochondrosis and osteochondritis are two distinctly different pathologic entities. Osteochondrosis is typically a self-limiting disorder that involves a secondary epiphyseal center or pressure epiphysis at the end of a long bone or a primary epiphyseal center of a small bone.[34] Osteochondrosis involves degeneration or avascular necrosis with resultant regeneration or recalcification and typically does not demonstrate bony fragmentation.[6,34] Osteochondritis, on the other hand, is an inflammation of the subchondral bone and articular cartilage. Osteochondritis dissecans involves resultant fragmentation of articular cartilage within the joint. Many of the osteochondroses have their origins in chronic, repetitive trauma. The pathology and subsequent prognosis of osteochondrosis and osteochondritis of immature bone differ from that of mature bone.

Juvenile osteochondritis dissecans (JOCD) of the knee can be a devastating condition if not diagnosed and treated early. Although ischemia, genetic predisposition, and abnormal ossification are theoretical causes of JOCD,[17] growing evidence suggests that microtrauma to the immature knee over the course of months and years is the primary cause of JOCD.[7,9] The majority of JOCD lesions involve the medial femoral condyle, and most lesions occur on the weight-bearing surface. The site of JOCD pathology is subchondral bone, not articular cartilage.[9] Many lesions go undiagnosed or misdiagnosed. In a series of 192 patients, 80 percent of patients had symptoms for more than 15 months and 90 percent of patients had symptoms for greater than 8 months.[7] Symptoms center around an insidious onset of knee pain, with or without effusion, and knee pain that is increased with weight-bearing activities and typically reduced with rest. Youngsters with JOCD are usually involved in year-round physical activity, or participate in more than one sport with little if any rest between sporting seasons. Successful treatment is based upon accurate diagnosis, staging of the activity of the lesion, the ability of the lesion to heal, and subsequent nonoperative or operative intervention. Conservative treatment centers around minimizing weight-bearing and shear forces, activity modification, stretching of inflexible hamstrings and calves that serve to increase joint reaction forces, and appropriate quadriceps strengthening exercises initiated and progressed on an individual basis.

Another common site of osteochondrosis involves the elbow of a growing patient. Osteochondrosis of the capitellum of the elbow is called Panner's disease. Panner's disease is typically seen in young throwing athletes who complain of chronic dull aching in the elbow joint. Point tenderness at the lateral elbow is common, as is a subtle loss of elbow extension.[6] As the condition progresses the loss of extension can be more pronounced and can be accompanied by a loss of pronation and supination as well. Initially, rest and activity modification is important and should be followed by a range of motion and strengthening program along with a supervised functional progression program to return to throwing.

PATELLOFEMORAL PAIN

Patellofemoral pain is frequently encountered in many physical therapy clinics. Symptoms in youngsters are comparable to their adult counterparts. Dull peripatellar aching, pain with stairs or prolonged sitting, giving way of the knee, and pseudo-locking episodes in extension are classic signs of patellofemoral involvement. Treatment is symptomatic and should include pain-free quadriceps strengthening; hamstring, calf, and iliotibial band stretching; correction of biomechanical abnormalities; activity modification; bracing; and screening for signs of hyperelasticity that may indicate patellofemoral joint instability.

Physiologic Considerations

The youngster's cardiovascular response to exercise is related to the size of the youngster.[49] Children demonstrate a double sigmoid growth pattern from birth to adulthood. There is a rapid gain in growth in infancy and early childhood that slows down during middle childhood. The second rapid increase in growth occurs during adolescence. The peak height velocity is defined as the maximum rate of growth in stature and occurs in girls from 10.5 to 13 years but may start as early as 9 years or as late as 15 years. Peak height velocity of boys occurs from 12.5 to 15 years but may start as early as 10 years or as late as 16 years.[35]

As the youngster's heart is smaller than that of the mature adult, the capacity as a reservoir for blood is also smaller in the child's heart. Children, therefore, have a lower stroke volume at all levels of exercise.[49] The exercising youngster compensates for this lower stroke volume with an increased heart rate. As is seen in the adult, the youngster's systolic blood pressure rises during exercise, but the child's elevation in systolic blood pressure is less than that seen in the adult.[49] The red blood cell count for young boys and girls are similar with comparable abilities to carry oxygen to exercising organs. After menarche, however, females demonstrate lower blood volume and fewer red blood cells with a resultant decreased oxygen carrying capacity. Young girls, therefore, typically demonstrate a mean blood pressure lower than that seen in young boys.[35]

As the child's thoracic cavity is smaller than that of the mature adult, the child demonstrates a smaller vital capacity than the adult and also shows an elevated respiration rate as compared to the mature adult.[4,49] As the child matures, the ability to perform work (both aerobic and anaerobic) increases.[4,49] After menarche girls have a slightly lower oxygen uptake per kilogram of body weight, but are similar to boys per kilogram of lean body weight.[21] The maximum oxygen uptake is similar in young boys and girls until approximately 12 years of age. Males continue to demonstrate an increase until 16 to 18 years, with females failing to show significant gains after 12 to 14 years of age.[3,33] Young boys and girls have similar proportions of slow-twitch and fast-twitch muscle fiber. Strength differences between the genders are minimal when strength is expressed relative to fat-free weight.[47] Both young boys and young girls have been shown to be able to safely participate in strength-training programs.[8,26]

Independent of gender, the young athlete typically does not tolerate prolonged periods of heat exposure; therefore, care must be taken when the youngster participates in sports in a hot and humid environment. A child has a greater surface area-to-mass ratio than the typical adult, resulting in a greater transfer of heat into their young bodies. The child also has a higher production of metabolic heat per kilogram of body weight as compared to adult counterparts, which serves to further challenge the young thermoregulatory system.[4,49]

Psychological Considerations

To this point, the chapter has presented many physical and physiologic characteristics that constitute the unique challenges to evaluating and treating youth injuries. Before concluding this chapter, however, one other vital area must also be discussed, and that is the unique psychological demands placed upon young athletes, especially those involved in intense competition and training.

There are many benefits of physical activity in the youngster (Table 35-3).[10] There are many differences, however, between free-flowing play and organized sports. Organized sports, fortunately or unfortunately, carry the obligatory win or lose connotations of competition and also involve adults who coach and train the youngster as well as adults who interpret and enforce the rules that govern competition. The adverse effect of adult influences upon the young athlete is but one potential negative psychological aspect of youth sport participation.

Participation in organized sport can be taken to an extreme. Intensive participation can be described in terms of frequency and/or intensity. Examples of intensive participation include the ice skater or gymnast who trains daily for hours

T A B L E   3 5 - 3

Benefits of Physical Activity in Children

PHYSICAL
Increased maximal aerobic power and general stamina
Control of body mass and fat reduction
Increased muscle strength and endurance
Increased range of motion
Decreased blood lipid levels
Improved ventilatory efficiency
Increased oxygen consumption

PSYCHOLOGICAL
Feelings of competency and mastery
Personal self-esteem
Engaging in enjoyable behavior
Achieving desired goals
Gaining admiration of others
Safe training in risk-taking behavior
Satisfaction in achievement
Feeling of working toward a goal
Peer group interaction
Awareness of, and adherence to, rules
Personal role definition

and competes all year round for years on end. Other examples include the multisport athlete who trains and competes on a daily basis all year round. This intensive participation places significant physical demands on the body, demands that may result in serious overuse or stress–failure injury. Just as the young body grows to accept greater physical demands, so does the young mind. Intensive participation places many demands on the youngster, some of which may be unrealistic. As this relates to intense competition, research demonstrates that a child's cognitive ability to develop a mature understanding of the competition process does not occur until the age of 12. It is not until between the ages of 10 and 12 years of age that children develop the capacity to comprehend more than just one other viewpoint. Finally, after the age of 12 years the youngster can readily adopt a team perspective.[30] The negative psychological aspects of intense youth sport participation can be found in Table 35-4. Psychological issues may also enter the picture when rehabilitating youth sport participants involved in intense competition and training. Risk factors for psychological complications in the injured child include stress in the family, high-achieving siblings, over- or underinvolved parent(s), a paradoxical lack of leisure in athletic activity, self-esteem that is reliant on athletic prowess, and a narrow range of interests beyond athletics.[32]

This chapter has provided an overview of the unique physical and psychological issues that affect youth sport participants. The rehabilitation professional evaluating and treating the young athlete must be cognizant of these unique features.

TABLE 35-4

Potential Negative Aspects of Intensive Youth Sport Participation

- Children are not permitted to be children.
- Children are denied important social contacts and experiences.
- Children are victims of a disrupted family life.
- Children may experience impaired intellectual development.
- Children are exposed to excessive psychological/physiologic stress.
- Children may become so involved with sport that they become detached from society.
- Children may face a type of abandonment upon completion of their athletic career.

Evaluation and treatment principles must reflect the special circumstances that present in the youth athlete.

REFERENCES

1. Andrish JT. Upper extremity injuries in the skeletally immature athlete. In: Nicholas JA, Hershman EB, eds. *The Upper Extremity in Sports Medicine.* St. Louis, Mosby, 1990, p. 673.

2. Axe MJ, Snyder-Mackler L, Konin JG, Strube MJ. Development of a distance-based interval throwing program for Little League-aged athletes. *Am J Sports Med* 24:594, 1996.

3. Bar-Or O. The prepubescent female. In: Shangold M, Mirkin G, eds. *Women and Exercise,* 2nd ed. Philadelphia, Davis, 1994.

4. Bar-Or O. *Pediatric Sports Medicine for the Practitioner: From Physiologic Principles to Clinical Applications.* New York, Springer-Verlag, 1983.

5. Best TM. Muscle-tendon injuries in young athletes. *Clin Sports Med* 14:669, 1995.

6. Bianco AJ. Osteochondritis dissecans. In: Morrey BF, ed. *The Elbow and Its Disorders.* Philadelphia, Saunders, 1985, p. 254.

7. Cahill BR. Treatment of juvenile osteochondritis of the knee. *Sports Med Arthroscopy Rev* 2:65, 1994.

8. Cahill BR, moderator. Proceedings of the conference on strength training and the pubescent. Chicago, American Orthopaedic Society for Sports Medicine, 1988.

9. Cahill BR. Treatment of juvenile osteochondritis dissecans and osteochondritis dissecans of the knee. *Clin Sports Med* 4:367, 1985.

10. Cahill BR, Pearl AJ. *Intensive Participation in Children's Sports.* Champaign, IL, Human Kinetics, 1993.

11. Cahill BR, Tullos HS, Fain RH. Little League shoulder. *Sports Med* 2:150, 1974.

12. Carson WC, Gasser SI. Little Leaguer's shoulder: A report of 23 cases. *Am J Sports Med* 26:575, 1998.

13. Clancy WG. Running. In: Reider B, ed. *Sports Medicine: The School-Aged Athlete.* Philadelphia, Saunders, 1991, p. 632.

14. Garrett WE, Best TM. Anatomy, physiology, and mechanics of skeletal muscle. In: Simon SS, ed. *Orthopaedic Basic Science.* Rosemont, IL, American Academy of Orthopaedic Surgeons, 1994.

15. Goodman CG, Snyder TE. *Differential Diagnosis in Physical Therapy,* 2nd ed. Philadelphia, Saunders, 1995.

16. Graf BK, Fujisaki CK, Reider B. Disorders of the patellar tendon. In: Reider B, ed. *Sports Medicine: The School-Aged Athlete.* Philadelphia, Saunders, 1991, p. 355.

17. Graf BK, Lange RH. Osteochondritis dissecans. In: Reider B, ed. *Sports Medicine: The School-Aged Athlete.* Philadelphia, Saunders, 1991.

18. Iannotti JP, Goldstein S, Kuhn J, et al. Growth plate and bone development. In: Simon SS, ed. *Orthopaedic Basic Science.* Rosemont, IL, American Academy of Orthopaedic Surgeons, 1994.

19. Ireland ML, Andrews JR. Shoulder and elbow injuries in the young athlete. *Clin Sports Med* 7:473, 1988.

20. Jakob RP, Von Gumppenberg S, Engelhardt P. Does Osgood–Schlatter disease influence the position of the patella? *J Bone Joint Surg Br* 63:579, 1981.

21. Kemper HC. Exercise and training in childhood and adolescence. In: Torg JS, Welsh RP, Shephard RJ, eds. *Current Therapy in Sports Medicines* 2. Toronto, Decker, 1990.

22. Kujala UM, Kvist M, Heinonen O. Osgood–Schlatter's disease in adolescent athletes: Retrospective study of incidence and duration. *Am J Sports Med* 13:239, 1985.

23. Lancourt JE, Cristini JA. Patella alta and patella infera: Their etiological role in patellar dislocation, chondromalacia, and apophysitis of the tibial tubercle. *J Bone Joint Surg Am* 57:1112, 1975.

24. Larkin J, Brage M. Ankle, hindfoot, and midfoot injuries. In: Reider B, ed. *Sports Medicine: The School-Aged Athlete.* Philadelphia, Saunders, 1991, p. 365.

25. Little League Baseball, Inc. Williamsport, PA.

26. National Strength and Conditioning Association. Position paper on prepubescent strength training. *Natl Strength Train J* 7:27, 1985.

27. O'Leary PF, Boiardo RA. The diagnosis and treatment of injuries of the spine in athletes. In: Nicholas JA, Hershman EB, eds. *The Lower Extremity and Spine in Sports Medicine,* 3rd ed. St. Louis, Mosby, 1995, p. 1171.

28. Outerbridge AR, Micheli LJ. Overuse injuries in the young athlete. *Clin Sports Med* 14:503, 1995.

29. Paletta GA, Andrish JT. Injuries about the hip and pelvis in the young athlete. *Clin Sports Med* 14:59, 1995.

30. Passer MW. Determinants and consequences of children's competitive stress. In: Smoll FL, Magill RA, Ash MJ, eds. *Children in Sport,* 3rd ed. Champaign, IL, Human Kinetics, 1988.

31. Peterson HA. Physeal fractures. In: Morrey BF, ed. *The Elbow and Its Disorders.* Philadelphia, Saunders, 1985, p. 222.

32. Pillemer FG, Micheli LJ. Psychological considerations in youth sports. *Clin Sports Med* 7:679, 1988.

33. Roemmich JN, Rogol AD. Physiology of growth and development: Its relationship to performance in the young athlete. *Clin Sports Med* 14:483, 1995.

34. Salter RB. *Textbook of Disorders and Injuries of the Musculoskeletal System,* 2nd ed. Baltimore, Williams & Wilkins, 1983.

35. Sanborn CF, Jankowski CM. Physiological considerations for women in sport. *Clin Sports Med* 13:315, 1994.

36. Santopietro FJ. Foot and foot-related injuries in the young athlete. *Clin Sports Med* 7:563, 1988.

37. Sim FH, Rock MG, Scott SG. Pelvis and hip injuries in athletes: Anatomy and function. In: Nicholas JA, Hershman EB, eds. *The Lower Extremity and Spine in Sports Medicine,* 3rd ed. St. Louis, Mosby, 1995, p. 1025.

38. Simmons BP, Lovallo JL. Hand and wrist injuries in children. *Clin Sports Med* 7:495, 1988.

39. Smith AD, Tao SS. Knee injuries in young athletes. *Clin Sports Med* 14:650, 1995.

40. Stanitski CL. Anterior knee pain syndrome in the adolescent. *J Bone Joint Surg Am* 75:1407, 1993.

41. Stanitski CL. Combating overuse injuries: A focus on children and adolescents. *Phys Sports Med* 21:87, 1993.

42. Stinson JT. Spondylolysis and spondylolisthesis in the athlete. *Clin Sports Med* 12:517, 1993.

43. Tall RL, DeVault W. Spinal injury in sport: Epidemiologic considerations. *Clin Sports Med* 12:441, 1993.

44. Tippett SR. Lower extremity injuries in the young athlete. *Orthop Phys Ther Clin North Am* 6:471, 1997.

45. Tippett SR. Referred knee pain in a young athlete: A case study. *J Orthop Sports Phys Ther* 19:117, 1994.

46. Torg JS, Pavlov H, Morris VB. Salter–Harris type-III fracture of the medial femoral condyle occurring in the adolescent athlete. *J Bone Joint Surg Am* 63:586–591, 1981.

47. Van De Loo DA, Johnson MD. The young female athlete. *Clin Sports Med* 14:687, 1995.

48. Waters PM, Millis MB. Hip and pelvic injuries in the young athlete. *Clin Sports Med* 7:513, 1988.

49. Woodall WR, Weber MD. Exercise response and thermoregulation. *Orthop Phys Ther Clin North Am* 7:1, 1998.

50. Zimbler S, Merkow S. Genu recurvatum: A possible complication after Osgood–Schlatter disease. *J Bone Joint Surg Am* 66:1129, 1984.

CHAPTER 36

Considerations in Treating Amputees

Robert S. Gailey

OBJECTIVES

After completing this chapter, the student therapist should be able to do the following:

- Perform a postsurgical evaluation of the lower-limb amputee.
- Instruct the amputee on the care of the stump and prepare the limb for prosthetic fitting.
- Design a pre-prosthetic training plan for the care of the lower-limb amputee.
- Identify different designs of lower-limb prosthetics and discuss the functions of their principal components.
- Instruct the lower-limb amputee on the use of a prosthesis.
- Instruct the lower-limb amputee on the fundamentals of running.
- Identify different designs of upper-limb prosthetics and discuss the functions of their principal components.
- Design a prosthetic training plan for the care of the upper-limb amputee.

The prosthetist and the physical therapist, as members of the rehabilitation team, often develop a very close relationship when working together with lower-extremity amputees. The prosthetist is responsible for fabricating and modifying the specific socket design, and for providing prosthetic components that will best suit the lifestyle of a particular individual. The physical therapist's role is fourfold: First, the amputee must be properly evaluated to assess impairment, functional limitation, disability, or other health-related conditions in order to formulate an appropriate and focused rehabilitation program that will physically prepare the patient for prosthetic gait training. Second, the amputee must be educated about stump care, prior to being fitted with the prosthesis, in addition to learning how to use and care for the prosthesis. Third, the amputee must be reeducated in the biomechanics of gait while learning how to use a prosthesis. Once success is achieved with ambulation and the functional activities of that individual's daily routine, the amputee may look forward to resuming a productive life. Finally, the therapist should introduce the amputee to higher levels of activity beyond just learning to walk. The amputee may not be ready to participate in recreational activities immediately; however, providing the names of support groups and disabled recreational organizations can furnish the necessary information for the individual to seek involvement when ready.

EVALUATION OF THE AMPUTEE

Assessment of the amputee is extremely important and performed on a continual basis. The amputee acute assessment and progress form (Fig. 36-1) outlines the essential items for a complete evaluation. The following sections will briefly describe some of the procedures and findings specific to the amputee and to the formulation of an individual rehabilitation program.

Past Medical History

A complete medical history should be taken to provide the therapist with information that may be pertinent to the rehabilitation program.

Past Social History

Poor diet, the use of tobacco and alcohol, and lack of exercise often contribute to poor health, and possibly to the ill effects that led to amputation. Reinforcement of positive behaviors throughout rehabilitation can only help encourage patients to make better choices.

Amputee Acute Assessment and Progress Form

Admitting Diagnosis _____ **Admission Date** _____

Precautions _____

Surgical Procedure _____

Past Medical History _____

_____

Past Social History _____

_____

Fall History _____

_____

Current Medications _____

_____

Subjective Comments _____

_____

Mental Status

    Person/Place/Time _____

Observation/Inspection

    <u>Amputated Limb</u>

        Skin color _____

        Edema _____

        Temperature _____

        Pulses _____

    <u>Sound Limb</u>

        Skin color _____

        Edema _____

        Temperature _____

        Pulses _____

        Open lesions/ulcers _____

            Location _____

            Size/Description _____

Vital Signs

Date	_____	_____	_____	_____
Blood pressure	_____	_____	_____	_____
Heart rate	_____	_____	_____	_____

F I G U R E 3 6 - 1

Amputee acute assessment and progress form. (Reproduced, with permission, from *One Step Ahead: An Integrated Approach to Lower Extremity Prosthetics and Amputee Rehabilitation.* Course workbook. Miami, FL, Advanced Rehabilitation Therapy, 1996.)

Upper Extremity Screening

| | Strength | | ROM | |
	Right	Left	Right	Left
Shoulder				
Abduction	_____	_____	_____	_____
Adduction	_____	_____	_____	_____
Int. Rotation	_____	_____	_____	_____
Ext. Rotation	_____	_____	_____	_____
Elbow				
Flexion	_____	_____	_____	_____
Extension	_____	_____	_____	_____
Wrist				
Flexion	_____	_____	_____	_____
Extension	_____	_____	_____	_____
Grasp	_____	_____	_____	_____

Upper Extremity Screening

| | Strength | | ROM | |
	Right	Left	Right	Left
Hip				
Flexion	_____	_____	_____	_____
Extension	_____	_____	_____	_____
Abduction	_____	_____	_____	_____
Adduction	_____	_____	_____	_____
Int. Rotation	_____	_____	_____	_____
Ext. Rotation	_____	_____	_____	_____
Knee				
Flexion	_____	_____	_____	_____
Extension	_____	_____	_____	_____
Ankle				
Plantarflexion	_____	_____	_____	_____
Dorsiflexion	_____	_____	_____	_____

Sensation

| | Sharp/Dull | | Light Touch | | Proprioception | | Vibration | |
	Rt.	Lt.	Rt.	Lt.	Rt.	Lt.	Rt.	Lt.
L1	____	____	____	____	____	____	____	____
L2	____	____	____	____	____	____	____	____
L3	____	____	____	____	____	____	____	____
L4	____	____	____	____	____	____	____	____
L5	____	____	____	____	____	____	____	____
S1	____	____	____	____	____	____	____	____
S2	____	____	____	____	____	____	____	____

Deep Tendon Reflexes

	Right	Left			Right	Left
Triceps	____	____	Patella		____	____
Brachial	____	____	Achilles		____	____

Balance

	Unsteady	Steady with support	Steady Independent
Sitting eyes open	_____	_____	_____
Sitting eyes closed	_____	_____	_____
Sitting reach	_____	_____	_____
Sitting nudge	_____	_____	_____
Standing eyes open	_____	_____	_____
Standing eyes closed	_____	_____	_____
Standing reach	_____	_____	_____
Standing nudge	_____	_____	_____

FIGURE 36-1

(Continued). Reproduced, with permission, from *One Step Ahead: An Integrated Approach to Lower Extremity Prosthetics and Amputee Rehabilitation.* Course workbook. Miami, FL, Advanced Rehabilitation Therapy, 1996.

Bed Mobility and Transfers

	Assist × 2	Assist × 1	Standby	Independent
Bridging	_____	_____	_____	_____
Rolling	_____	_____	_____	_____
Supine to sit	_____	_____	_____	_____
Bed to Chair	_____	_____	_____	_____
Sit to Stand	_____	_____	_____	_____
Bed to Toilet	_____	_____	_____	_____

Ambulation

Assistive Device	WC ____	Walker ____	Crutches ____	Loft Strands ____	Cane ____
Date	____	____	____	____	____
Distance	____	____	____	____	____
Time	____	____	____	____	____

Compression Therapy

Wrap _____   Elastic Sleeve _____   Shrinker _____

Education

	Presented	Remembered
Positioning	_____	_____
Residual Limb Care	_____	_____
Skin Care	_____	_____
Sound Foot Care	_____	_____
Footwear	_____	_____
Home Exercise	_____	_____
Medication	_____	_____
Nutrition	_____	_____

Additional Identified Problems

1) _____
2) _____
3) _____
4) _____

Assessment

_____
_____
_____
_____
_____
_____
_____

Plan

Goals	Action
1) _____	_____
2) _____	_____
3) _____	_____
4) _____	_____
5) _____	_____
6) _____	_____

Clinician _____   Date _____

FIGURE 36-1

(Continued). Reproduced, with permission, from *One Step Ahead: An Integrated Approach to Lower Extremity Prosthetics and Amputee Rehabilitation.* Course workbook. Miami, FL, Advanced Rehabilitation Therapy, 1996.

Fall History

Assessment of falls is paramount, especially with elder amputees when determining their prosthetic candidacy. Preventing falls that could lead to additional health problems is important, especially as the amputee attempts to gain confidence in using a prosthesis.

Mental Status

The therapist should be concerned with assessing the patient's potential to perform activities such as donning and doffing the prosthesis, stump sock regulation, bed positioning, skin care, and safe ambulation.

Observation/Inspection

Inspection of the skin of both the intact limb and stump should include the following:

1. Skin color. Increased redness is indicative of infection, inflammation, or irritation. Blanching white suggests lack of circulation. Dark blackish color could indicate gangrene.
2. Edema. Swelling may relate to venous insufficiency, diet, or poor stump-wrapping technique.
3. Temperature. Increased warmth indicates infection or inflammation. Coolness demonstrates lack of circulation.
4. Pulses. Decreased pulses relate to poor circulation.
5. Lesions and ulcers. Any lesion or ulcer should be reported, treated, and monitored immediately.

Strength

Functional strength of the major muscle groups should be assessed through manual muscle testing of all extremities including the stump and the trunk. This will help determine the individual's potential skill level to perform activities such as transfers, wheelchair management, and ambulation, with and without the prosthesis.

Range of Motion

A functional assessment of gross upper extremity and sound lower limb motions should be made. A measurement of the stump's ROM should be recorded for future reference. Contractures are a complication that can greatly hinder the amputee's ability to ambulate efficiently using a prosthesis; thus, extra care should be taken to avoid this situation. The most common contracture for the transfemoral amputee is hip flexion, external rotation, and abduction; and for the transtibial amputee, the most frequently seen contracture is knee flexion.

Sensation

The evaluation of the amputee's sensation can provide insight into possible insensitivity of the stump and/or sound limb. This may affect proprioceptive feedback for balance and single-limb stance, which in turn can lead to gait difficulties. The patient must be made aware that decreased pain, temperature, and light touch sensation can increase the potential for injury and tissue breakdown to the intact foot or stump.

Balance/Coordination

The ability to maintain adequate sitting and standing balance demonstrates the amputee's control of center of gravity over the base of support. The ease of movement and refinement of motor skills relates to coordination. Both balance and coordination are required for weight shifting from one limb to another in sitting and standing and during dynamic activities such as walking.

Bed Mobility/Transfer

Bed mobility skills are essential for maintaining correct bed positioning and preventing contractures, and in avoiding excessive friction of the sheets against the suture line or frail skin of the insensitive foot. Adequate bed mobility is a splinter skill for higher-level skills, such as bed to wheelchair transfers; and if the patient is unable to perform these skills independently, assistance must be provided to prevent injury. More functional transfers such as toilet, shower, and car transfers must also be assessed before discharge, to more completely determine the individual's level of independence.

Ambulation With Assistive Devices Without a Prosthesis

The selection of an assistive device should meet with the amputee's level of skill, keeping in mind that, with time, the assistive device may change. For example, initially an individual may require a walker, but with proper training Lofstrand crutches may prove more beneficial as a long-term assistive device. The primary means of mobility for a large majority of amputees, either temporarily or permanently, will be a wheelchair. The energy conservation of the wheelchair over prosthetic ambulation is considerable for some levels of amputation, and therefore the use of a wheelchair should be positively introduced to those amputees, without implication of failure if used more for mobility than the prosthesis.

Stump Wrapping

Early wrapping of the stump can have a number of positive effects. It can decrease edema, increase circulation, assist in shaping, help counteract contractures, provide skin protection, reduce redundant tissue problems, reduce phantom limb pain/sensation, and desensitize local stump pain. Controversy does exist around the use of traditional Ace wrapping versus the use of stump shrinkers. Currently, many institutions prefer commercial shrinkers for their ease of donning. Advocates of Ace wrapping express that more control over the pressure gradient, and tissue shaping, is provided. Regardless of the individual preference, application must be performed correctly to prevent circulation constriction, poor stump shaping, and edema.

EDUCATION

The importance of educating the patient in self-care, management of the postsurgical stump, and preservation of the intact foot cannot be overstated. The following items are included in the evaluation process as a reminder that each topic must be presented to the client as early as feasible during rehabilitation.

Limb Management

POSITIONING

Prevention of decreased ROM and contractures is a major concern to all involved; therefore, proper limb positioning becomes important. The transfemoral amputee should place a pillow laterally along the stump to maintain neutral rotation with no abduction, when in a supine position. If the prone position is tolerable during the day or evening, then a pillow is placed under the stump to maintain hip extension. Transtibial amputees should avoid knee flexion for prolonged periods of time. A stump board will help maintain knee extension when using a wheelchair. All amputees must be made aware that continual sitting in a wheelchair without any effort to promote hip extension may lead to limited motion during prosthetic ambulation.

SKIN CARE

Every patient should be instructed to visually inspect the stump on a daily basis or after any strenuous activity. More frequent inspection of the stump should be routine in the initial months of prosthetic training. A hand mirror may be used to view the posterior stump and the plantar surface of the foot. Reddened areas should be monitored very closely as potential sites for abrasions. If a skin abrasion occurs, the patient must understand that in most cases the prosthesis should not be worn until healing occurs.

STUMP AND SOUND FOOT CARE

It is important that the amputee understands the care of the stump and sound limb. For example, the dysvascular patient's prosthetic gait training could be delayed 3 to 4 weeks if an abrasion should occur. The patient must be taught the difference between weight-bearing and pressure-sensitive areas when inspecting the skin. Preservation of the sound limb foot in many cases permits continued bipedal ambulation and delays further medical complications. One reason for this concern is that the sound limb routinely compensates for the amputee's inability to maintain equal weight distribution between limbs, resulting in altered gait mechanics. Two effects on the sound side limb raise concern: (1) the force being placed on the weight-bearing surfaces of the foot, and (2) the change in ground reaction forces (GRF) throughout the skeletal structures of the limb during

ambulation, with or without an assistive device. Increased forces placed on the intact limb can be of considerable concern during ambulation, because the foot often presents with neuropathic symptoms and is vulnerable to soft-tissue injury brought about by altered biomechanics.

Footwear

The need for appropriate footwear is extremely important, especially for the dysvascular amputee. Shoes should be made of soft leather or some other yielding lightweight material. A blucher-style closure for easier donning is suggested with an enlarged toe box, flat block heels, nonskid outer soles, and possibly a lateral toe flair for increased stability. Custom orthotic inserts are an excellent idea for every amputee to accommodate for the changes in weight-bearing forces and to maintain the arches of the foot. Shoes should be inspected daily for foreign objects inside the shoes, and for tacks or nails that may have penetrated the soles.

Home Exercise

Providing instruction for home exercise should be initiated from the time of discharge from the hospital. Typically, three types of exercises should be prescribed, with the selection of the exercises designed to prepare or augment prosthetic gait training. The three types are described next.

PREPROSTHETIC EXERCISE

Dynamic Stump Exercises

Eisert and Tester first described dynamic stump exercises in 1954.[3] Since then, these antigravity exercises have been the most favorable method of strengthening the stump. Dynamic stump exercises require little in the way of equipment. A towel roll and step stool is all that is required. These exercises offer additional benefits aside from strengthening, such as desensitization, bed mobility, and joint ROM. The exercises are relatively easy to learn and can be performed independently, permitting the therapist to spend patient contact time on other more advanced skills.

Incorporating isometric contractions at the peak of the isotonic movement will help to maximize strength increases. A period of a 10-second contraction followed by 10 seconds of relaxation for 10 repetitions gives the client an easy mnemonic to remember, the "rule of ten." The rationale behind a 10-second contraction is that a maximal isometric contraction can be maintained for 6 seconds; however, there is a 2-second rise time and a 2-second fall time. Thus, 2-second rise time plus 6-second maximal contraction plus 2-second fall = 10 seconds total time for each repetition.[2] Figure 36-2 demonstrates the basic dynamic strength-training program for transfemoral and transtibial amputees. Amputees who have access to isotonic and isokinetic strengthening equipment can take advantage of the

PROSTHETIC REHABILITATION PROGRAM EXERCISES

1. HIP EXTENSION   2. HIP ABDUCTION

3. HIP FLEXION   4. BACK EXTENSION   5. HIP ADDUCTION

9 a. KNEE FLEXION

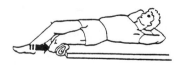

7. SIT-UPS

9 b. KNEE FLEXION

F. ANGULO

6. BRIDGING

8. KNEE EXTENSION

F I G U R E 3 6 - 2

Dynamic stump strengthening exercises. (Reproduced, with permission, from Advanced Rehabilitation Therapy, Inc., Miami, Florida.)

benefits derived from these forms of strengthening with few modifications in patient positioning on the weight machines.

General Activities and Cardiorespiratory Endurance Conditioning

Often, decreased general conditioning and endurance are contributory factors leading to difficulties in learning functional activities and prosthetic gait training. Regardless of age or present physical condition, a progressive general exercise prescription can be written for every patient, beginning immediately after surgery, going on through the preprosthetic period, and to be continued as part of the daily routine.

The list of possible general strengthening/endurance exercise activities is vast: cuff weights in bed, wheelchair propulsion for a predetermined distance, ambulation with assistive device prior to the prosthesis, lower- or upper-extremity ergometer, wheelchair aerobics, swimming, aquatic therapy, lower- and upper-body strengthening at the local fitness center, and any sport or recreational activity of interest. The amputee should select one or more of these activities and begin participation to tolerance, progressing to 1 hour or more a day.

Coordination and Balance Exercises

In preparation for ambulation without a prosthesis, all amputees must learn to compensate for the loss of weight of the amputated limb by balancing the center of mass (COM) over the sound limb. Preparing the amputee to control the COM can begin early as long sitting on a mat table and moving objects from one side of the body to the other. As the amputee progresses with trunk strength, raising the patient to high kneeling on a bolster will increase the difficulty of the exercise and improve motor patterning. Finally, single-limb balance must be learned initially to provide confidence during stand pivot transfers, ambulation with assistive devices, and eventually hopping, depending on the amputee's level of skill. After receiving the prosthesis, the same exercises may be continued standing, and the amputee should have greater success after progressing through this series of postures.

Exercises that can be performed with this postural progression include moving objects from side to side, progressing the weight of side-to-side objects (e.g., cups, 1-kg balls, to medicine balls), diagonal patterns with a stretch cord, and playing catch. Additionally, the surface that the amputee is sitting or standing on can be altered from a noncompliant to a compliant surface (Fig. 36-3).

LEVELS OF LOWER-EXTREMITY AMPUTATIONS AND PROSTHETIC COMPONENTS

Prosthetic components have advanced tremendously over the years, affording the amputee more comfortable and responsive prosthetic choices. Understanding the mechanical abilities and limitations of the prosthetic components for each level of amputation can be a terrific asset for the clinician, especially when assessing the amputee's gait and in instructing functional skills. Knowing the nomenclature and terms associated with the prosthesis can assist in gaining the patient's confidence and enable the therapist to communicate with the prosthetist and rehabilitation team more clearly and with a greater sense of comprehension about the amputee's rehabilitation program.

Partial Foot Amputations

PHALANGEAL (PARTIAL TOE)

The phalangeal amputation is the excision of any part of one or more toes. Typically, a prosthesis is not necessary unless the foot is at risk for deformity or further injury as a result of absent digits.

TRANSPHALANGEAL (TOE DISARTICULATION)

The disarticulation amputation is at the metatarsophalangeal joint of one or more toes. The prosthetic options vary depending on the number of digits involved. If one to three toes are involved, not including the first ray, a simple toe filler can be placed in the shoe, such as lamb's wool, sponge rubber, or foam filler. When the first digit or great toe is involved, a steel shank spring can be used in the sole of the shoe to assist with push-off, in addition to the toe filler, if needed. In the event that all toes have been removed, an insole with a metatarsal support is used to relieve weight from the metatarsal heads and a cavus support is provided for the high arch that often results from the lack of stretch to the plantar structures.

The following foot amputations identify the site of the surgical procedure (Fig. 36-4). Examples follow of prosthetic devices that could be employed to improve the amputee's overall functional ability.

METATARSAL RAY RESECTION (PARTIAL RAY RESECTION)

The resection of the third, fourth, and fifth metatarsals and digits.

TRANSMETATARSAL

Amputation through the midsection of all metatarsals.

TARSOMETATARSAL DISARTICULATION (LISFRANC OR MIDFOOT)

The disarticulation of all five metatarsals and the digits.

MIDTARSAL DISARTICULATION (CHOPART)

A disarticulation through the midtarsal joint leaving only the calcaneus and talus.

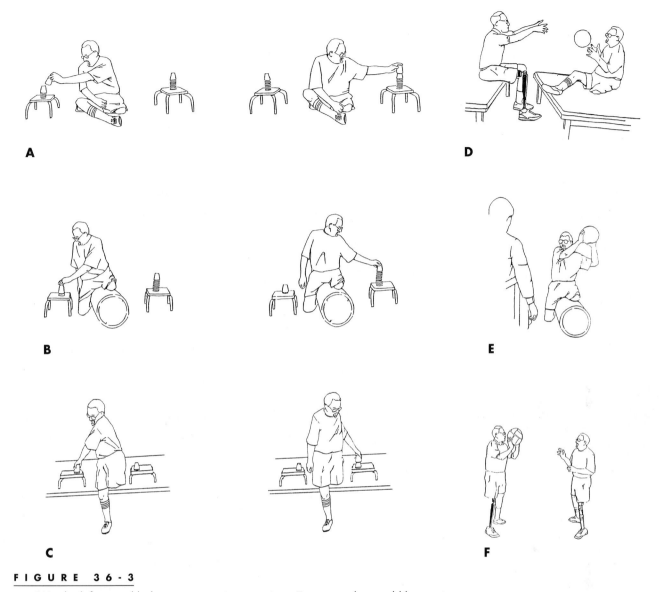

FIGURE 36-3

Weight-shifting and balance progression exercises. Two examples would be moving a cup from one side to the other. **A,** Sitting. **B,** Kneeling. **C,** Standing. Catching a ball. **D,** Sitting. **E,** Kneeling. **F,** Standing. (Reproduced, with permission, from Advanced Rehabilitation Therapy, Inc., Miami, Florida.)

PROSTHETIC DEVICES

Custom Molded Insole With Toe Filler

A simple foam filler with plastic insert for transverse arch of the foot and a heel counter for rear foot stability is widely accepted by many patients who do not experience foot or equinus deformity. To provide a smooth transition throughout the stance phase of gait, a rigid footplate is placed within the shoe or prosthesis, with a rocker bottom under the shoe.

Rigid Plate

To prevent the potential equinus deformity that can occur in the absence of the foot and the shortening of the gastrocnemius and soleus muscles, an ankle–foot orthosis-type appliance is coupled with a toe filler. A plate supports the residual foot and attaches to a shell that is formed around the calf, and the toe filler is fixed to the footplate.

Slipper-Type Elastomer Prosthesis

A more cosmetic approach is the slipper-type elastomer prosthesis (STEP), where semiflexible urethane elastomers are modeled to provide a foot-shaped prosthesis with a soft socket that conforms to the residual foot. The footplate and toe filler are incorporated into the STEP design.[1]

Syme Ankle Disarticulation

The Syme amputation is not a true disarticulation of the ankle, as the removal of the malleoli and distal tibial/fibular flares

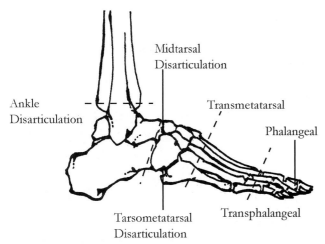

FIGURE 36-4

Surgical sites for partial foot amputations. (Reproduced, with permission, from Advanced Rehabilitation Therapy, Inc., Miami, Florida.)

occurs to create a smooth bony distal end with the attachment of the heel pad to the distal end of the tibia.

Veterans Administration Prosthetic Center (VAPC) Syme Prosthesis

A medial window or cutout at the distal end of the socket provides an opening for ease of donning for the bulbous end pad created by the anatomic heel pad. Velcro straps typically secure the removable doorpiece to the prosthesis. The device is usually fabricated with a prosthetic foot designed specifically for a Syme prosthesis (Fig. 36-5).

Elastic-Liner Syme Prosthesis (Miami Syme Prosthesis)

The inner liner is an expandable wall that permits the bulbous distal end of the stump to pass down and sit snugly within the

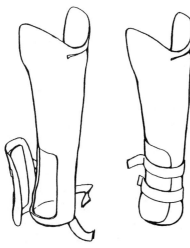

FIGURE 36-5

Veterans Administration Prosthetic Center (VAPC) Syme prosthesis. The medical window provides an opening for ease of donning. (Reproduced, with permission, from Advanced Rehabilitation Therapy, Inc., Miami, Florida.)

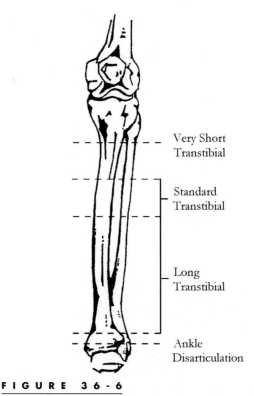

FIGURE 36-6

Surgical sites for transtibial amputations. (Reproduced with permission from Advanced Rehabilitation Therapy, Inc., Miami, Florida.)

socket as the flexible silastic elastomer walls envelop the limb for a total-contact fit, which prevents swelling. The absence of doors and windows on the socket's exterior provides a more cosmetic and stronger prosthesis. This prosthetic approach cannot be used with extremely bulbous or sensitive stumps.

Transtibial (Below Knee)

The most common surgery is the posterior flap procedure where approximately 40 percent of the tibia and fibula are retained, and the gastrocnemius and soleus muscles are wrapped around the distal end of the limb and sutured anteriorly (Fig. 36-6).

Knee Disarticulation

A number of surgical procedures exist for the knee disarticulation process, mostly describing the flap or how the muscles are secured. Today, most procedures require the shaping of the distal femur, squaring the condyles for an even weight-bearing surface.

Transfemoral (Above Knee)

Once again, many procedures exist for a transfemoral amputation; however, one procedure, the myocutaneous flap, attempts to maintain femoral adduction by performing a myodesis (surgical attachment of muscle to bone), suturing the adductor magnus to the lateral femur, and wrapping the quadriceps muscle over the adductor magnus and suturing it to the posterior femur.[4]

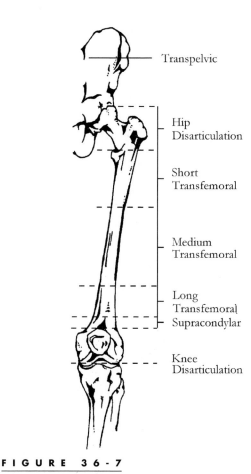

FIGURE 36-7

Surgical sites for femoral and pelvic amputations. (Reproduced, with permission, from Advanced Rehabilitation Therapy, Inc., Miami, Florida.)

Hip Disarticulation

Hip disarticulation is disarticulation of the femur and pelvis resulting in a myoplasty (surgical attachment of muscle to muscle) of the surrounding musculature (Fig. 36-7).

Prosthetic Devices

The selection of prosthetic components for the major amputations is very similar. Socket designs are fabricated, and the number of prosthetic joints are determined, according to the level of amputation; however, for the most part, the prosthetist can select from a wide variety of components to construct a prosthesis for each individual's needs. The components and socket designs are described generically in the next sections, with some isolated specific brand names discussed when necessary. There are literally hundreds of specific components, variations, and combinations of prosthetic design beyond what is presented here; however, the majority of components and socket designs are represented generically.

Foot–Ankle Assembly

The function of the foot–ankle assembly is threefold: (1) it provides a base of support during standing and in the stance phase of gait, (2) the heel provides shock attenuation at initial contact as the foot moves into plantarflexion, and (3) the forefoot is designed to stimulate metatarsophalangeal joint hyperextension during late stance. All foot motions occur passively, in response to the load applied by the amputee. Foot–ankle assemblies are divided into two general categories.

ARTICULATED FOOT–ANKLE ASSEMBLIES

Articulated foot–ankle assemblies provide motion at the level of the anatomic ankle in one or more planes.

Single-Axis Foot

The single-axis foot allows dorsiflexion (5 to 7 degrees) and plantarflexion (15 degrees), which are limited by rubber bumpers or spring systems. Single-axis feet offer adjustable plantar and dorsiflexion for greater ROM than nonarticulated foot–ankle designs, allowing foot-flat on low-grade ramps and terrain, but may not conform to steep ramps. No medial/lateral or rotary movements are permitted, and parts can be noisy as wear and fatigue occur over time.

Multiple-Axis Foot

In addition to sagittal motions, the lateral and rotary movements increase the foot–ankle assembly's ability to absorb the impact of uneven terrain, while reducing the torsional forces transmitted through the limb to the stump–socket interface. Although a large variety of excellent multiple-axis foot designs is commercially available, some can be bulky, maintenance and adjustments are frequent, and the additional components may increase the overall weight (Fig. 36-8).

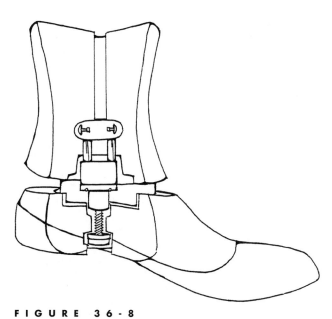

FIGURE 36-8

Multiple-axis foot. (Reproduced, with permission, from Advanced Rehabilitation Therapy, Inc., Miami, Florida.)

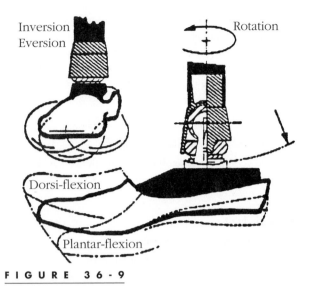

FIGURE   36-9

Endolite Multiflex ankle. (Reproduced, with permission, from Advanced Rehabilitation Therapy, Inc., Miami, Florida.)

Endolite Multiflex Ankle

The ball and snubber, or universal joint design, allows full ROM including inversion, eversion, and some rotation, in addition to plantar and dorsiflexion. The rotational component has the ability to absorb some of the torsional forces placed on the prosthesis. Thus, the foot is capable of adjusting to a wide variety of terrains. The keel is produced from a carbon-reinforced plastic (Fig. 36-9).

Tru-Step Foot

Designed to mimic the anatomic foot and ankle, the Tru-Step foot permits eight motions: plantarflexion, dorsiflexion, inversion, eversion, adduction, abduction, supination, and pronation. It features a three-point weight-transfer system and shock-absorbing heel to reduce ground reaction forces and provide stability. The three bumpers within the system can be changed by the prosthetist to provide the correct resistance for a smooth gait (Fig. 36-10).

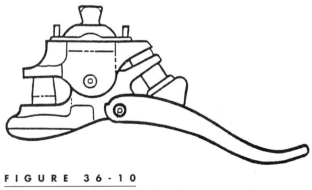

FIGURE   36-10

Tru-Step foot. (Reproduced, with permission, from Advanced Rehabilitation Therapy, Inc., Miami, Florida.)

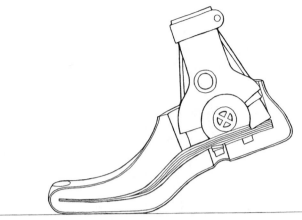

FIGURE   36-11

Total Concept foot. (Reproduced, with permission, from Advanced Rehabilitation Therapy, Inc., Miami, Florida.)

Total Concept Foot

The Total Concept foot functions as a dynamic response system with a single carbon fiber deflector plate, and the single-axis ankle has adjustable bumpers that control plantar and dorsiflexion. What makes the system unique is an innovative heel height adjustment at the ankle. A simple push of a release button allows for easy adjustment of up to 10 degrees of dorsiflexion for ascending, or 25 degrees of plantarflexion for descending ramps or hills. The plantarflexion adjustment is most commonly used for heel height adjustment, particularly for women who enjoy the option of wearing both flat and high-heel shoes (Fig. 36-11).

NONARTICULATED FOOT–ANKLE ASSEMBLIES

Nonarticulated foot–ankle assemblies have continuous external surfaces from the sole of the foot to the shank of the prosthesis. There is no articulated joint, and plantarflexion during early stance is achieved with the compression of a cushion heel or the deflection of a flexible heel.

Solid Ankle-Cushioned-Heel (SACH) Foot

As the most prescribed prosthetic foot worldwide, the molded heel cushion, made of a high-density foam rubber, forms the foot and ankle into one component. At heel strike, the rubber heel wedge compresses to stimulate plantarflexion. There are no moving parts, and thus no maintenance and no noise. The lightweight design offers good absorption of ground reaction forces, smooth transition of weight over the rubber forefoot, and resistance to toe extension during the late stance phase of gait. The limitations include limited adjustment of plantar/dorsiflexion, difficulty walking up inclines due to compression of the heel, limited motion for active people, and materials wear (Fig. 36-12).

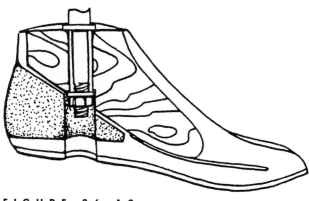

FIGURE 36-12

Solid ankle-cushioned-heel (SACH) foot. (Reproduced, with permission, from Advanced Rehabilitation Therapy, Inc., Miami, Florida.)

Stationary Attachment Flexible Endoskeletal II (SAFE II) Foot

Fashioned after the human foot, the SAFE II foot bolt block articulates with a rigid polyurethane elastomer keel section at a 45-degree angle in the sagittal plane to stimulate the human subtalar joint. Two bands made of Dacron polyester fiber further mimic the anatomic foot. The long plantar ligament band provides stability, while the plantar fascia band is designed to tighten, providing a semirigid lever for a smooth transition at toe-off. The flexible keel permits adaptation to various terrains, but it is not considered to be a dynamic response foot.

Seattle Foot

Designed for the more active individual, the Seattle foot was the first to provide dynamic keel or deflector plate capabilities. The keel is made of Delrin (acetal ploymer), a plastic that deflects during midstance to terminal stance, thus "storing energy," and that provides "spring" or "push-off" during toe-off. Two additional innovations made this foot very popular upon release in the early 1980s. The external foam covering is reinforced with Kevlar and has the appearance of an anatomic foot. The second is the cleft between the second and great toe, permitting the wearing of beach thongs. The Seattle Lite foot is one third lighter than the original foot because the bolt block has been decreased significantly. This permits use by the Symes amputee and adaptation to other ankle units. Currently, the Seattle Lite foot is becoming more popular than the original foot.

Carbon Copy II

Carbon Copy II is a solid ankle design with a heel polyurethane foam cushion. The keel is a unique dual-deflection plate structure made of a carbon composite, which provides two-stage resistance at terminal stance. In normal walking, the thin primary deflection plate provides gentle energy return, while the auxiliary deflection plate provides additional push-off during higher-cadence activities such as running. The Carbon Copy II

Light foot has recessed the bolt block and keel to permit the use of hybrid ankle systems, to fit Symes amputees, and to reduce the weight of the foot.

Flex Foot

The Modular III is a lightweight graphite composite foot designed with a keel consisting of two leaf springs, one arising from the heel and the other from the toe, both bound individually at the ankle. The Flex Foot uses the entire distance from the socket, not just the length of the keel, to "store energy" within the anterior deflector plate. As a result, the Flex Foot has been identified as the foot with the greatest energy return of the dynamic response feet. There is an optional "split toe," where from heel to toe, a split in the footplate enables the foot to function uniformly with the toe deflection on uneven terrain, including the capabilities of inversion and eversion. The Reflex Foot offers greater shock attenuation with the addition of a piston tube and carbon-fiber leaf spring designed to absorb ground reaction forces during ambulation. The Flex Foot design is also widely known as being popular with athletes. Although many variations of the foot are designed for amputees of all activity levels, the Sprint Flex is specifically designed for sprinting or long-distance running in a single direction (Fig. 36-13).

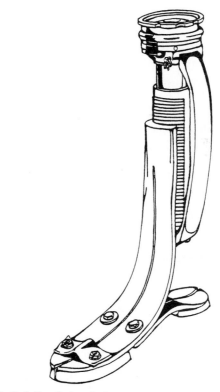

FIGURE 36-13

Flex Foot vertical shock pylon (VSP) or reflex foot. (Reproduced, with permission, from Advanced Rehabilitation Therapy, Inc., Miami, Florida.)

Shanks

The area between the knee and foot is commonly referred to as the shank. There are two basic structural designs of the shank that determine the general structural classification of a prosthesis:

1. The *exoskeletal design* (crustacean), where the exterior of the structure provides the required support for the weight of the body. Thermosetting plastic and wood are the common materials used to fabricate exoskeletal prostheses.
2. The *endoskeletal design* has an internal skeleton or pylon that supports the load with an outer covering, usually made of foam to give the shank a cosmetic shape. The *pylon* is a narrow vertical support typically made of metal or plastic tubing connecting the socket to the foot–ankle assembly. The endoskeletal design has become more popular over the years because it is typically lighter and allows the prosthetist to remove the cosmetic cover to make adjustments to the internal components.

Sockets

There are two general classifications of sockets: the hard socket, where there is direct contact between the socket's inner surface and stump, and the soft socket, which incorporates the use of a liner as a cushion between the socket and stump and in some cases provides suspension. Liners can be fabricated with pelite, silicone, or urethane. Stump socks do not constitute a soft socket and are normally used with all hard sockets.

Transtibial Amputee Socket Designs

PATELLAR TENDON-BEARING SOCKETS

The patellar tendon-bearing (PTB) socket is a total-contact design, which refers to the closed distal end creating a totally closed system around the skin, which offers a more intimate fit and avoids skin lesion problems that can occur when the soft tissues are not completely supported. The anterior wall is high enough to encompass the distal half of the patella, while the posterior wall rises slightly higher than the knee joint line. The posterior wall provides an anterior force to maintain the patella on the patellar bar (a small bulge in the socket), and it is also contoured with socket reliefs to prevent excessive pressure on the hamstrings. The medial and lateral walls are slightly higher than the anterior wall, adding stability, but for the most part, stability in the mediolateral plane is provided by the amputee's own knee. The patellar bar allows for weight to be borne on the patellar tendon; however, the weight bearing is also shared by the tibial flares. The PTB socket often requires cuff straps or other forms of suspension.

Two variations for the PTB are the PTB-supracondylar (PTB-SC) and the PTB-supracondylar/suprapatellar (PTB-SC/SP) socket. Both designs incorporate higher medial and lateral walls to encompass both femoral condyles to increase medial and lateral stability of the knee. The PTB-SC/SP raises the anterior wall to cover all of the patella, with the suprapatella area of the socket being contoured inward to create a "quadricep bar," resulting in additional suspension and resistance to recurvatum, in the case of very short stumps or unstable knees, respectively. The posterior wall remains unchanged in both socket variations (Fig. 36-14).

TRANSTIBIAL AMPUTEE SUCTION SOCKET DESIGNS

Because many of the suction sockets use the same proximal brim design, such as the PTB or PTB-SC, but use suction, a form of suspension, there is some gray area as to whether these sockets are a particular brim shape using a suction suspension or whether they constitute a separate category of socket design. Regardless of how they are categorized, they are very popular and warrant discussion.

Many sockets today are designed for a suction suspension, which means creating a vacuum between both a flexible roll-on sleeve and the skin, between the sleeve and the socket, or both, in order to hold the socket on the stump. The sleeves are made from silicon, urethane, or other composite gel materials, for the purpose of suspension, and in some cases act as soft liners to reduce pressure to bony prominences. All of the sleeves are rolled on over the stump, creating a sealed airless environment to keep the sleeve on the limb. The socket is connected to the sleeve by a pin and lock system or one-way valve system. Pin and lock systems use a small pin screwed into a hard cup at the end of the sleeve. When the sleeve-covered limb is placed completely into the socket, a locking mechanism at the distal socket receives the pin, locking the sleeve securely to the socket. A release pin is found on the exterior of the socket, or the sleeve can be removed. Suction sockets use a one-way valve system that permits the expulsion of air out of the socket but does not permit air to return back into the socket. So when the sleeve-covered stump is fully donned into the socket, and the air is evacuated, because the volume of the limb takes all the space, a vacuum is formed. To seal the top of the socket, an external suspension sleeve that covers the socket is rolled over the thigh, whereby an airtight suspension system is formed, and the prosthesis is suspended. Stump socks may be worn over the internal sleeves. The benefits of these suction systems include secure suspension, reduced pistoning, reduced friction, reduced perspiration, and the elimination of straps, cuffs, or sleeves. Some users have reported increased problems with swelling.

TRANSTIBIAL AMPUTEE SUSPENSION SYSTEMS

Methods for keeping the socket on the body for transtibial amputees are numerous, and there is no one method that works for all amputees. As a result, prosthetists have a wide variety of suspension techniques to meet the specific needs of each individual. Frequently more than one suspension system may be employed: a primary method that is chiefly responsible for suspending the socket, and a secondary system to provide an added sense of security, or improved suspension during higher-level activities.

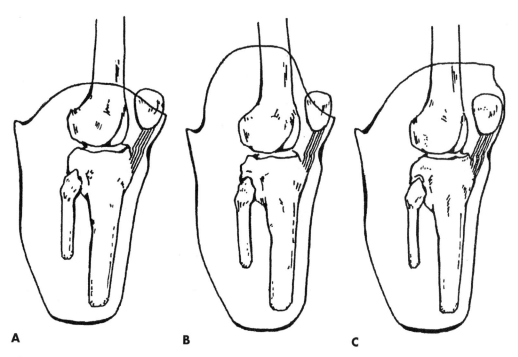

FIGURE 36-14

Comparison between the **A,** patella tendon-bearing (PTB) socket brim, **B,** patella tendon-bearing supracondylar (PTB-SC) socket brim, and **C,** patella tendon-bearing supracondylar/suprapatellar (PTB-SC/SP) socket brim. (Reproduced, with permission, from Advanced Rehabilitation Therapy, Inc., Miami, Florida.)

Common suspension methods include the supracondylar cuff, thigh corset or thigh lacer, inverted Y strap and waist belt, neoprene sleeve or latex sleeve, medial wedge, lateral wedge, suction, and removable medial brim.

Transfemoral Amputee Socket Designs

QUADRILATERAL SOCKET

The quadrilateral design is characterized by a series of reliefs or depressions in the socket designed to reduce pressure on relatively firm tissue, tendons, muscles, and bone and bulges, and prominent build-ups of materials intended to press on soft areas to provide load sharing. The socket allows for muscular contractions, reducing atrophy, and total contact is present between the socket and stump with a wider medial–lateral than anterior–posterior dimension. The basic concept of the quadrilateral socket is that the body sits on top of the socket and that all the soft tissue and bony prominences are accounted for with appropriate placement of the reliefs and bulges.

Some of the structural characteristics of the socket design consist of an ischial seat or a thickening on the medial part of posterior brim, where the majority of the weight-bearing area is intended via the ischial tuberosity. The medial brim is the same height as posterior brim or slightly lower, so the socket should not press on the pubic ramus. The anterior wall is 2.5 inches higher than the medial wall with the prominent Scarpa's bulge, maintaining the ischial tuberosity on the ischial seat by

providing counterpressure against the posterior wall. The lateral wall is higher than the anterior wall and set in 10 degrees of adduction (Fig. 36-15).

ISCHIAL CONTAINMENT SOCKET

Characterized by the encapsulation of the ischial tuberosity within the socket, and greater adduction of the femur, creating

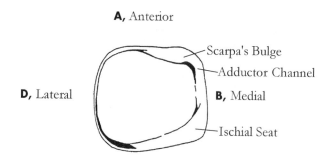

A, Anterior

Scarpa's Bulge
Adductor Channel
B, Medial
Ischial Seat

D, Lateral

C, Posterior

FIGURE 36-15

Quadrilateral socket design—a superior view. **A,** Anterior. **B,** Medial. **C,** Posterior. **D,** Lateral. (Reproduced, with permission, from Advanced Rehabilitation Therapy, Inc., Miami, Florida.)

a narrow medial–lateral dimension within the socket, the ischial containment (IC) socket design permits the pelvis and the socket to act as one for greater prosthetic control. Additionally, by adducting the femur, the muscles would theoretically be placed in an optimal length–tension position for better quality of muscular contraction. The contoured adducted trochanteric-controlled alignment (CAT-CAM) socket design is described as having a higher medial wall encapsulating the ischial ramus as well as the ischial tuberosity. However, because of the vast number of socket designs and names assigned to them, the generic description will be presented here.

The structural characteristics of the ischial containment socket create a high posterior wall where the ischial tuberosity is enclosed within the socket, and the gluteus maximus muscle is pocketed by the socket within a gluteal channel, applying a stretch to the hamstrings. The medial wall slants upward, encapsulating the ischial ramus with a counterpressure provided by the lateral wall. The anterior wall provides a counterpressure for the posterior wall. The lateral wall rises superiorly above the greater trochanter with femoral adduction (10 to 15 degrees) maintained by a force applied through the greater trochanter and the length of the shaft of the femur, with a counterforce applied at the ischial ramus. The weight should be distributed evenly throughout the lateral limb (Fig. 36-16).

The materials that sockets are currently constructed from enable prosthetists to design prostheses that have proximal brims that rise so high. The copolymer plastics such as polyethylene are very flexible, permitting greater sitting comfort and increased expandability of muscles as they contract.

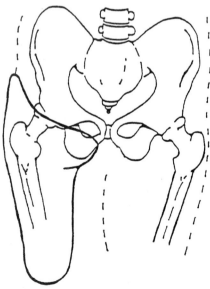

Ischial containment socket, anterior view. (Reproduced, with permission, from Advanced Rehabilitation Therapy, Inc., Miami, Florida.)

Transfemoral Amputee Suspension Systems

Suction is used with a well-shaped, fairly strong stump, and usually, for younger and active amputees who wear no stump socks and have the required ability to don and doff the prosthesis. The suspension systems described for the transtibial sockets apply for the transfemoral sockets. One form of suction, used only with transfemoral amputees, is a technique referred to as partial suction. In partial suction, stump socks are used but there is still a close fit. Because the suction is not complete, it does not fully suspend the prosthesis; therefore a secondary suspension system such as a Silesian bandage or a pelvic belt must be incorporated into the design. Suspension methods include the Silesian bandage, pelvic belt, neoprene belt, and internal suction sleeve.

Prosthetic Knee Units

Knee assembly provides stability during early stance through midstance, and controlled flexion and extension to allow the foot to clear the floor and advance the limb during swing. The speed of the lower leg as it extends should be dampened to control walking cadence and decrease terminal impact when the knee movement hits the extension stop. Additionally, flexion for sitting, kneeling, and related activities should not be restricted.

Because there are so many knee systems available today, it would be difficult to describe the various knee systems in detail. Understanding the three major mechanisms of knee units—the knee axis, swing phase control mechanism, and stance phase control mechanism—affords a good general understanding of prosthetic knees and how they function.

KNEE AXIS

There are two classifications of knee axes, single and polycentric. The single axis works like a hinge joint to maintain a single stationary axis point that either end may move around. This is the most common type of axis used in prosthetics. The polycentric axis is any knee unit with more than one axis. Traditionally, this type of knee axis was referred to as the four-bar linkage system, because there were usually four connecting rods or bars that created the knee joint mechanism. Today, this is no longer true because of some additional designs that are considered polycentric but do not use the four-bar system. The advantages to this knee axis design include an instantaneous center of rotation as the shank moves about the knee's axis. As a result, during sitting the shank moves under the distal end of the socket, preventing the prosthetic knee from protruding too far in front of the contralateral anatomic knee. During ambulation, as the shank moves posteriorly to the knee's center, greater toe clearance is permitted during swing.

SWING PHASE CONTROL MECHANISMS

Three general classifications of swing phase control mechanisms are available: mechanical constant friction, pneumatic or air control knee mechanism, and hydraulic or fluid control knee mechanisms. Extension-assist bias systems are designed to provide assistance with extension and do not constitute a category of swing phase control because these systems are used to aid with friction control knee systems.

Mechanical Constant Friction

The swing resistance is generated by a friction system that creates a drag on the prosthetic shank, or controls the speed of walking. The amount of resistance does not vary during the swing phase regardless of the angle of knee flexion or the cadence speed. The advantages of friction systems is that they are the simplest of knee units, typically lightweight, durable with few mechanical parts, and relatively low in cost. The main disadvantage is the inability to vary the speed of cadence.

Pneumatic Control Knee Mechanism

Pneumatic units are air-filled cylinders that provide cadence response using the spring action of a compressible medium, air. When the knee is flexed, the piston rod compresses the air, storing energy. As the knee moves into extension during late swing, the energy is returned, assisting with extension. To prevent an abnormal speed of return or terminal impact, a portion of the air is leaked off. The adjustment screw controls resistance. If the needle completely blocks the port at the top of the cylinder, no air is allowed to enter, and the knee is locked in extension. If the port is completely open, there is no resistance and the unit functions as a constant friction mechanism. A second adjustment screw can control extension in many manufacturers' designs. The key advantage to this system is the cadence-responsive function that is generally lighter weight than most hydraulic systems and is easier to maintain than many hydraulic units. The disadvantages when compared to friction units are the increased maintenance, increased weight, and higher cost.

Hydraulic Control Knee Mechanisms

The physical law that liquids are essentially incompressible is the fundamental principle behind hydraulic units. When the knee flexes, a piston rod is pushed into an oil-filled cylinder, forcing the oil through one or more chambers, thus regulating the speed of movement. The degree of resistance can be controlled by an adjustment screw, which varies the cross-sectional area of the chamber(s). If the amputee has a slow or weak gait, a greater cross-sectional area is created as the chambers open and in turn the resistance is lowered. With a faster walking speed, the cross-sectional area is decreased, the resistance increased, and speed of the limb accommodates accordingly. As the knee swings into extension, the piston rod returns to the top of the cylinder, collecting the oil as it passes each chamber.

The major advantages of hydraulic systems are the cadence-responsive function and the ability of most designs to withstand greater forces than pneumatic units. In general, the disadvantages are cost, weight, mechanical failure, and maintenance, which are overshadowed by the advantage of variable cadence without manual adjustment in those amputees who can walk at a variety of speeds.

Extension-Bias Assists

Although not really a knee design classification, the extension-bias assist units help advance the limb or extend the knee during swing. Two basic types are available, internal and external. With the internal unit, a spring provides assistance with extension once knee flexion is completed during ambulation. If the knee flexion is greater than 60 degrees, the knee will remain flexed as in sitting. With the external unit, an adjustable (or nonadjustable) elastic strap is attached to the socket anteriorly, descending to the anterior shank. As the knee is flexed, the strap is stretched. Once an extension force is initiated, the strap shortens. The strap, unless adjusted, will remain stretched during flexion as in sitting. The external types frequently provide a greater extension force than the internal type.

STANCE PHASE CONTROL MECHANISMS

Stance control can be established individually or in combination through five mechanisms: alignment, manual lock, friction brakes, fluid resistance, and polycentric linkage.

Alignment

All knee units require that the TKA (trochanter–knee–ankle) or weight line pass anterior to the axis creating an extension moment, and in turn, knee stability. There is one exception to this rule; the Total Knee requires that the weight line pass posteriorly to the knee axis. (The Total Knee is described in the subsequent "Polycentric Axis Knee Unit" section.)

Manual Locks

Designed to prevent any knee motion once engaged, manual locks are available with one of two basic lock systems: (1) manually operated, where a small lever or ring and cable system is accessible for the amputee to engage or disengage as needed; or (2) spring loaded, which engages automatically when the knee is extended.

Weight-Activated Friction Knee

With a weight-activated friction knee, the knee unit functions as a constant friction knee during swing phase; however, during weight bearing in the stance phase, a housing with a high coefficient of friction presses against the knee mechanism and prevents knee flexion. The "flexion stop," or brake mechanism, can be adjusted to the amputee's body weight. There are a variety of weight-activated friction or "safety" knees, all of which generally prevent flexion from the point of full extension to 25 degrees of flexion, decreasing the risk of buckling during initial contact to loading response.

Hydraulic Swing-N-Stance Control Units

The same hydraulic principles apply as described in the swing phase, but there is an additional advantage with stance control. As weight is applied when the knee is in full extension and up to 25 degrees of flexion, increased resistance is employed from the cylinder, as too rapid a fluid flow results in the immediate closing of valves that stop fluid flow, preventing the knee from buckling and allowing the amputee to regain balance.

Polycentric Axis Knee Unit

The polycentric knee system was historically considered only for knee disarticulation amputees; recently, however, greater acceptance for the general transfemoral amputee population has been observed. Prescription criteria for this knee system currently extend to (1) knee disarticulations, (2) short transfemoral amputees with less than 50 percent femur length, (3) amputees with weak hip extensors, and (4) amputees requiring greater stability.

One key advantage to the polycentric knee axis design in stance is that because there is no one center of rotation, a greater zone of stability exists. In other words, in a single-axis system, the weight line is either anterior, creating a stable knee, or posterior, resulting in an unstable knee. In the polycentric design, the area between the anterior and posterior bars is the zone of stability, or the area where the knee is neither too stable nor too unstable. The other key advantage for stability is the raised functional knee center, as the point where it takes the least amount of effort or force to control flexion and extension of the knee unit is moved proximally and posteriorly as a result of the four-bar linkage system. As a result, the easiest point for controlling the prosthetic knee within the socket is brought up to the level of the stump in very short limbs.

The Total Knee is also a polycentric knee, but does not have a four-bar linkage design and the weight-line characteristic varies from all other traditional knees. Because of its popularity, the Total Knee warrants description for the therapist who will work with this knee unit. This knee design offers a seven-axis system with a unique geometric locking and unlocking action. When the knee moves into extension during terminal swing, the knee is locked; as the body weight is shifted onto the prosthetic limb during loading response, the weight line moves posterior to the axis, flexing the knee to 15 degrees as the anatomic knee would flex. As the body weight moves over the prosthesis to terminal stance, the weight line moves anterior, releasing the locking mechanism and permitting free and easy knee flexion as the limb moves into swing phase. The cadence is controlled by a rack-and-pinion design where a piston drives the hydraulic fluid. Coupled with the dual flexion adjustment, the knee permits independent flexion control from 0 to 60 degrees and 60 to 160 degrees of knee flexion, reducing excessive heel rise and creating a smooth gait (Fig. 36-17).

Hip Disarticulation and Transpelvic Socket Designs

A hip disarticulation and transpelvic socket design are somewhat similar with the absence of bony structure making stability more difficult in the transpelvic socket. The essential concept of all the current socket designs is the encapsulation of the ischium and ascending ramus, and additionally, the soft tissues of the remaining musculature, extending to the gluteal fold, must be encased within the socket to create a pseudo-hydrostatic environment for the tissues and viscera. The socket extends around

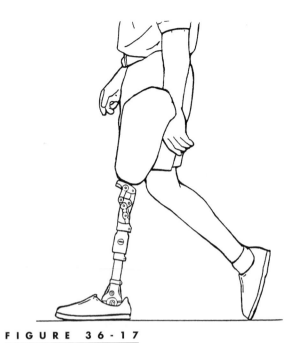

FIGURE 36-17

Total Knee polycentric knee design. (Reproduced, with permission, from Advanced Rehabilitation Therapy, Inc., Miami, Florida.)

both iliac crests, compressing the tissues snugly and providing a stable environment within the socket. The major difficulty is finding the balance between a well-fitting functional socket and patient comfort, both in standing and sitting. The flexible thermoplastics, silicones, and urethane materials have created a much more comfortable environment within the socket, while lighter-weight rigid material helps to maintain the much-needed external stability. As a result of the material advances, it appears that many more high-level amputees are using prostheses today than ever before.

Hip Joints

HIP FLEXION BIAS SYSTEM

A coil spring is compressed during midstance and released during preswing, thrusting the prosthetic thigh forward. The benefit to this design is the elimination of the excessive pelvic rocking required with traditional hip joint designs. The amputee has a much more natural gait, providing he or she fully loads the spring and rapidly transfers the weight to the sound limb, allowing the limb to thrust forward smoothly.

LITTIG HIP STRUT

A carbon composite strut in the shape of a band connects to the socket and the knee unit. As body weight is placed over the strut, it deflects or bends. As body weight is reduced during preswing and the limb moves into swing, the strut recoils or thrusts the prosthetic limb forward. The thickness and length of the hip strut vary according to the height and weight of the amputee. The need for excessive pelvic motion is eliminated as the amputee once again must confidently transfer body weight on and off the prosthesis as appropriate.

PROSTHETIC GAIT TRAINING

Orientation to Center of Gravity and Base of Support

Orientation of the center of mass (COM) over the base of support (BOS) in order to maintain balance requires that the amputee become familiar with these terms and aware of their relationship. The body's COM is located 2 inches anterior to the second sacral vertebra, and the average person stands with the feet 2 to 4 inches (5 to 10 cm) apart, both varying according to body height.[5,6] Various methods of proprioceptive and visual feedback may be employed to promote the amputee's ability to maximize the displacement of the COM over the BOS. The amputee must learn to displace the COM forward and backward, as well as from side to side (Fig. 36-18). These exercises

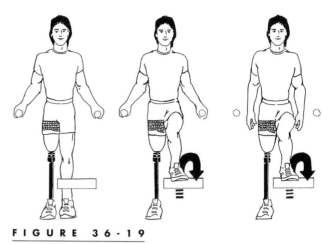

FIGURE 36-19

Stool-stepping exercise. (Reproduced, with permission, from Advanced Rehabilitation Therapy, Inc., Miami, Florida.)

vary little from traditional weight-shifting exercises, with the one exception that the concentration is placed on the movement of the COM over the BOS rather than weight bearing into the prosthesis. Increased weight bearing will be a direct result of improved COM displacement, and will establish a firm foundation for actual weight shifting during ambulation.

Single-Limb Standing

Single-limb balance over the prosthetic limb, while advancing the sound limb, should be practiced in a controlled manner so that, when called on to do so in a dynamic situation such as walking, this skill can be employed with relatively little difficulty. The stool-stepping exercise is an excellent method through which this skill may be learned. Have the amputee stand in the parallel bars with the sound limb in front of a 4- to 8-inch stool (or block), height depending on level of ability. Then ask the patient to step slowly onto the stool with the sound limb while using bilateral upper extremity support on the parallel bars. To further increase this weight-bearing skill, ask the patient to remove the sound side hand from the parallel bars, and eventually the other hand. Initially, the speed of the sound leg will increase when upper-extremity support is removed, but with practice, the speed will become slower and more controlled, promoting increased weight bearing on the prosthesis (Fig. 36-19).

The amputee's ability to control sound limb advancement is directly related to the ability to control prosthetic limb stance. The following are three contributing factors that may help the amputee achieve adequate balance over the prosthetic limb. The first is control of the musculature of the stump side to maintain balance over the prosthesis. Second, the client must learn to use the available sensation within the stump/socket interface, such as proprioception, in order to control the prosthesis. Third, the amputee must visualize the prosthetic foot and its relationship to the ground. New amputees will have difficulty understanding this concept at first, but will gain a greater appreciation as time goes on.

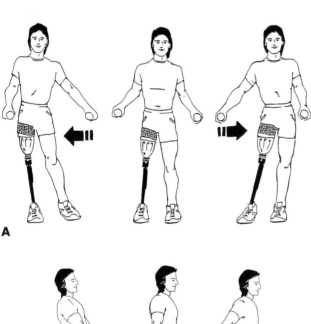

A

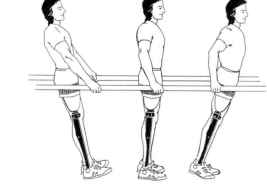

B

FIGURE 36-18

A, Lateral weight-shifting and balance orientation.
B, Sagittal weight-shifting and balance orientation. (Reproduced, with permission, from Advanced Rehabilitation Therapy, Inc., Miami, Florida.)

Gait Training Skills

SOUND AND PROSTHETIC LIMB TRAINING

Another component in adjusting to the amputation of a limb is the restoration of the gait biomechanics that were unique to a particular person prior to the amputation. That is to say, not everyone has the same gait pattern. Prosthetic developments in the last decade have provided limbs that replicate the mechanics of the human leg closely. Therefore, the goal of gait training should be the restoration of function to the remaining joints of the amputated limb. Prosthetic gait training should not alter the amputee's gait mechanics for the prosthesis; instead, the mechanics of the prosthesis should be designed around the amputee's individual gait.

PELVIC MOTIONS

The pelvis and the body's COM, as a unit, moves in four directions: (1) displaces vertically, (2) shifts laterally, (3) tilts horizontally, and (4) rotates transversely. Each of these motions can directly affect the amputee's gait, resulting in gait deviations or in a rise in energy expenditure during ambulation. If restoration of function to the remaining joints of the amputated limb is the goal of gait training, then the pelvic motions play a decisive role in determining the final outcome of an individual's gait pattern.

Normalization of trunk, pelvic, and extremity biomechanics can be taught to the amputee in a systematic way. First, independent movements of the various joint and muscle groups are developed. Second, the independent movements are incorporated into functional movement patterns of the gait cycle. Finally, all component movement patterns are integrated to produce a smooth normalized gait.

Resistive gait training techniques can be employed to restore the correct pelvic motion. The amputee places the prosthetic limb behind the sound limb while holding on to the P-bars with both hands. The therapist blocks the prosthetic foot to prevent forward movement of the prosthesis. Rhythmic initiation is employed, giving the amputee the feeling of rotating the pelvis forwardly as passive flexion of the prosthetic knee occurs. As the amputee becomes comfortable with the motion, he or she can begin to move the pelvis actively, eventually progressing to resistive movements when the therapist deems this appropriate (Fig. 36-20).

Once the amputee and therapist are satisfied with the pelvic motions, the swing phase of gait can be instructed. The amputee is now ready to step forward and backward with the prosthetic limb. Attention must be given to the pelvic motions: that the line of progression of the prosthesis remains constant without circumducting, and the heel contact occurs within boundaries of the BOS. As the amputee improves, release the sound side hand from the parallel bars and eventually both hands. There should be little if any loss of efficiency with the motion; but if there is, revert to the previous splinter skill.

Return to sound limb stepping with both hands on the P-bars. Observe that the mechanics are correct and that the

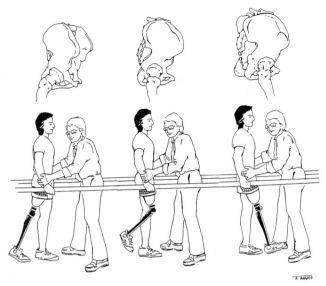

FIGURE   36-20

Resistive gait training techniques are proprioceptive neuromuscular facilitation techniques to assist and establish a normalized gait pattern. (Reproduced, with permission, from Advanced Rehabilitation Therapy, Inc., Miami, Florida.)

sound foot is not crossing midline as heel strike occurs. When ready, have the amputee remove the sound side hand from the P-bars. At this time, there may be an increase in the speed of the step, a decrease in step length, and/or lateral leaning of the trunk. This is a direct result of the inability to bear weight, or balance, over the prosthesis. Cue the amputee in remembering the skills learned while performing the stool-stepping exercise previously described.

When each of the skills described are developed to an acceptable level of competency, the amputee is ready to combine the individual skills and actually begin walking with the prosthesis. Initially, begin in the P-bars with the therapist and amputee facing each other, the therapist's hands on the amputee's anterior superior iliac spine (ASIS) and the amputee holding onto the P-bars. As the amputee ambulates within the P-bars, the therapist applies slight resistance through the hips, providing proprioceptive feedback for the pelvis and involved musculature of the lower extremity.

When both the therapist and the amputee are comfortable with the gait demonstrated in the P-bars, the same procedure as described is practiced out of the P-bars, with the amputee initially using the therapist's shoulders as support and progressing to both hands free when appropriate. The therapist may or may not continue to provide proprioceptive input to the pelvis.

Trunk rotation and arm swing are the final components needed to restore the complete biomechanics of gait. During human locomotion, the trunk and upper extremities rotate opposite to the pelvic girdle and lower extremities. Trunk rotation is necessary for balance, momentum, and symmetry of gait. Many amputees have decreased trunk rotation and arm swing,

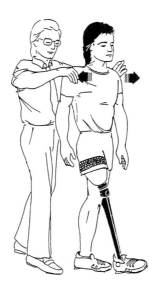

FIGURE 36-21

Passive trunk rotation will assist in restoring arm swing for improved balance, symmetry of gait, and momentum. (Reproduced, with permission, from Advanced Rehabilitation Therapy, Inc., Miami, Florida.)

especially on the prosthetic side. This may be the result of fear of displacing their COM too far forward or backward over the prosthesis (Fig. 36-21).

Instructing trunk rotation and arm swing is easily accomplished by using rhythmic initiation, or passively cueing the trunk as the amputee walks. The therapist stands behind the amputee with one hand on either shoulder. As the amputee walks, the therapist gently rotates the trunk. When the left leg steps forward, the right shoulder is rotated forward, and vice versa. Once the amputee feels comfortable with the motion, he or she can actively take over the motion.

Both amputees who will be independent ambulators and those who will require an assistive device can benefit to varying degrees from the above systematic rehabilitation program. Most patients can be progressed to the point of ambulating out of the P-bars. At that time, the amputee must practice ambulating with the chosen assistive device, maintaining pelvic rotation, adequate BOS, equal stance time, and equal stride length—all of which can have a direct influence on the energy cost of walking. Trunk rotation would be absent with amputees using a walker as an assistive device; however, those ambulating with crutches or a cane should be able to incorporate trunk rotation into their gait.

Advanced Gait Training Activities

STAIRS

Ascending and descending stairs is most safely and comfortably performed one step at a time (step-*by*-step). A few exceptional transfemoral amputees can descend stairs step-*over*-step, or by the "jackknifing" method, and even fewer, yet very strong amputees can ascend stairs step-*over*-step. Most transtibial

amputees have the option of either method, while hip disarticulation and hemipelvectomy amputees are limited to the step-*by*-step method.

CURBS

The methods described for stairs are identical for curbs. Depending on the level of skill, the amputee can step up or down curbs with either leg.

UNEVEN SURFACES

A good practice with gait training is to have the amputee ambulate over a variety of surfaces including concrete, grass, gravel, uneven terrain, and varied carpet heights. Initially, the new amputee will have difficulty in recognizing the different surfaces, secondary to the loss of proprioception. To promote an increased awareness, spending time on different surfaces and becoming visually aware of the changes help to initiate this learning process. Additionally, the amputee must realize that in some instances, it is important that he or she observe the terrain ahead to avoid any slippery surfaces or potholes that might result in a fall.

RAMPS AND HILLS

Ascending inclines presents a problem for all amputees because of the lack of dorsiflexion present within most prosthetic foot–ankle assemblies. For most amputees, descending inclines is even more difficult than ascending, primarily because of the lack of plantarflexion in the foot–ankle assembly. Transtibial amputees, and prosthetic wearers with knee joints, have the added dilemma of the weight line falling posterior to the knee joint, resulting in a flexion movement.

When ascending an incline, the body weight should be slightly more forward than normal to obtain maximal dorsiflexion with articulating foot–ankle assemblies, and to keep the knee in extension. Depending on the grade of the incline, pelvic rotation with additional acceleration may be required in order to achieve maximal knee flexion during swing.

Descent of an incline usually occurs at a more rapid pace than normal because of the lack of plantarflexion resulting in decreased stance time on the prosthetic limb. Amputees with prosthetic knees must exert a greater than normal force on the posterior wall of the socket to maintain knee extension.

Most amputees find it easier to ascend and descend inclines with short but equal strides. They prefer this method because it simulates a more normal appearance as opposed to the sidestepping or zigzag method.

When ascending and descending hills, the amputee will find side-stepping to be the most efficient means. The sound limb should lead, providing the power to lift the body to the next level, while the prosthetic limb remains slightly posterior to keep the weight line anterior to the knee and act as a firm base. During descents, the prosthetic limb leads but remains slightly posterior to the sound limb. The prosthetic knee remains in extension, again acting as a form of support so that the sound limb may lower the body.

BRAIDING

Braiding may be taught either in the P-bars or in an open area depending upon the person's ability. Simple braiding is one leg crossing in front of the other. As the amputee's skill improves, the crossing leg can alternate, first in front of and then behind the other leg. When ability improves, the speed of movement should increase. With increased speed, the arms will be required to assist with balance, and likewise, trunk rotation will increase, further emphasizing the need for independent movement between the trunk and pelvis.

FALLING

Falling, or lowering oneself to the floor, is an important skill to learn not only for safety reasons but also as a means to perform floor-level activities. During falling, the amputee must first discard any assistive device to avoid injury. He or she should land on the hands, with the elbows slightly flexed to dampen the force and decrease the possibility of injury. As the elbows flex, the amputee should roll to one side, further decreasing the impact of the fall.

Lowering the body to the floor in a controlled manner is initiated by squatting with the sound limb followed by gently leaning forward onto the slightly flexed upper extremities. From this position, the amputee has the choice of remaining in quadruped or assuming a sitting posture.

FLOOR TO STANDING

Many techniques exist for teaching the amputee how to rise from the floor to a standing position. The fundamental principle is to have the amputee use the assistive device for balance and the sound limb for power as the body begins to rise. Depending on the type of amputation and the level of skill, the amputee and therapist must work closely together to determine the most efficient and safe manner to successfully master this task.

RUNNING SKILLS

For most amputees, running is the single most commonly given reason for limiting participation in recreational activities—and yet it is the most wanted skill. Many amputees who do not have a strong desire to run for sport or leisure do have an interest in learning how to run for the simple peace of mind of knowing that they could move quickly to avoid a threatening situation. Rarely, if ever, is running taught in the rehabilitation setting. Running, as with all gait training and advanced skills, takes time and practice to master. If the amputee is exposed to the basic skills of running during rehabilitation, then the individual may make the decision to pursue running in the future.

The Syme and transtibial amputee does have the ability to achieve the same running biomechanics as able-bodied runners if emphasis is placed on the following:

1. At ground contact, the prosthetic limb hip should be flexed moving toward extension, the knee should be flexed, and the prosthetic foot dorsiflexed. The knee flexion not only permits greater shock absorption but in addition creates a backward force between the ground and the foot to provide additional forward momentum.

2. As the center of gravity is transferred over the prosthesis during the stance phase, the ipsilateral arm should be fully forward (shoulder flexed to 60 to 90 degrees), while at the same time the contralateral arm is backward (shoulder extended). Extreme arm movement can be difficult for the amputee concerned with maintaining balance.

3. The hip, during late midstance to toe-off, should be forcefully driving downward and backward through the prosthesis as the knee extends. If the prosthetic foot is "dynamic elastic response," the force produced by the hip extension should deflect the keel so that the prosthetic foot will provide additional push-off.

4. Forward swing and the float phase is a period when the hip should be rapidly flexing, elevating the thigh. The arms should again be opposing the advancing lower limb, with the ipsilateral arm backward and the contralateral arm forward.

5. During foot descent the hip should be flexed and beginning to extend as the knee is rapidly extending and reaching forward for a full stride.

Transfemoral and knee disarticulation amputees traditionally run with a period of double support on the sound limb during the running cycle, commonly referred to as the "hop-skip" running gait pattern. The typical running gait cycle begins with a long stride with the prosthetic leg, followed by a shorter stride with the sound leg. In order to give the prosthetic leg sufficient time to advance, the sound leg takes a small hop as the prosthetic limb clears the ground and moves forward to complete the stride. The speed that a transfemoral amputee runner may achieve will be hampered, because every time either foot makes contact with the ground, the foot's forces are traveling forward, and therefore the reaction force of the ground must be in a backward or opposite direction. The result is that each time the foot contacts the ground, forward momentum is decelerated. In other words, with every stride the amputee is slowing down when running with the "hop-skip" gait.

The ability to run "leg-over-leg" has been achieved by a number of transfemoral amputees who have developed this technique through training and working with knowledgeable coaches. The transfemoral amputee takes a full stride with the prosthetic leg, followed by a typically shorter stride with the sound leg. With training, equal stride length and stance time may be achieved. This running pattern is a more natural gait where the double support phase of the sound limb is eliminated, and both legs may maintain forward momentum. Initially, other problems that may occur include excessive vaulting off the sound limb to insure ground clearance of the prosthetic limb, decreased pelvic and trunk rotation, decreased and asymmetrical arm swing, and excessive trunk extension. Again with training, many of these deviations will decrease and possibly be eliminated.

INITIAL CONTACT   MID-STANCE   TAKE OFF   INITIAL SWING   MID-SWING   TERMINAL SWING

F. Aixulo

FIGURE 36-22

Transfemoral amputee running. (Reproduced, with permission, from Advanced Rehabilitation Therapy, Inc., Miami, Florida.)

The transfemoral amputee has an additional consideration when learning to run. To date, no knee system permits flexion during the prosthetic support phase, resulting in the stump having to absorb the ground reaction forces during initial ground contact. Other problems with present knee units that transfemoral amputees must contend with are maintaining cadence speed during swing. Hydraulic knee units offer the ability to adjust the hydraulic resistance during knee flexion and extension. During running, less resistance in extension permits faster knee extension, while increased resistance in flexion increases the amount of time until full knee flexion is achieved, allowing the same-side hip time to reach greater flexion, producing a more powerful stride. Seasoned runners often reduce both knee extension and flexion hydraulic resistance, permitting the prosthetic knee timing and mechanics to match the speed and ROM of the sound limb. As the runner's technique progresses and the level of competition elevates, it is important that the prosthesis be fine-tuned to match the athlete's abilities.

The "leg-over-leg" running style does permit the transfemoral amputee to run faster, for short distances, but at a greater metabolic cost. Although leg-over-leg is preferred, the hop-skip method is often more easily taught and less physically demanding on the amputee. If the sole purpose of instructing running is to permit the individual to move quickly in a safe manner, the hop-skip method is most frequently suggested (Fig. 36-22).

RECREATIONAL ACTIVITIES

By definition, recreation is any play or amusement used for the refreshment of the body or mind. That is to say, the term "recreational activities" need not exclusively mean athletics such as running or team sports. In fact, many people enjoy recreational activities such as gardening, shuffleboard, or playing cards as a means of socializing or relaxing. A comprehensive rehabilitation program should include educating the amputee on how to return to those activities that he or she finds pleasurable. For example, the therapist can teach the physical splinter skills such as weight shifting necessary to help the amputee participate in shuffleboard, or various methods of kneeling for gardening. In addition, there are many national and local recreational organizations and support groups, which provide clinics, coaching, or another amputee who can teach from experience how to perform various higher-level recreational skills. Providing the amputee with information on how to contact these groups is the first step to mainstreaming the patient back into a lifestyle complete with recreational skills as well as activities of daily living.

UPPER-LIMB PROSTHETIC REHABILITATION

Levels of Upper-Limb Amputation

The classification for upper limb amputees is based on the anatomic location of the amputation or surgical site (Fig. 36-23). When an amputation occurs to the digits of the hand, prosthetic fitting is most frequently for cosmetic rather than functional purposes. In some instances, custom-made prostheses are fabricated for functional purposes, especially when ROM or strength has been severely affected. The acceptance of upper-limb prosthetic devices varies depending on the age, activity level, and "gadget tolerance" of the amputee. Many amputees prefer to learn how to adapt with the sound arm and use the stump of the amputated side as an assist. Youngsters adapt very well without the use of a prosthesis, whereas adults who loose an upper extremity prefer to use a prosthesis for both aesthetic and functional reasons. This section will review the common components of an upper-limb prosthesis and outline the rehabilitation progression.

Terminal Devices

HOOKS

The most common terminal device (TD) used is the split-hook type. By allowing the amputee to open and close the hook, objects can be grasped between the "fingers" of the hook (each side of the metal hook is referred to as a finger). The fingers of the hook have the ability to carry, hold, or push objects (Fig. 36-24).

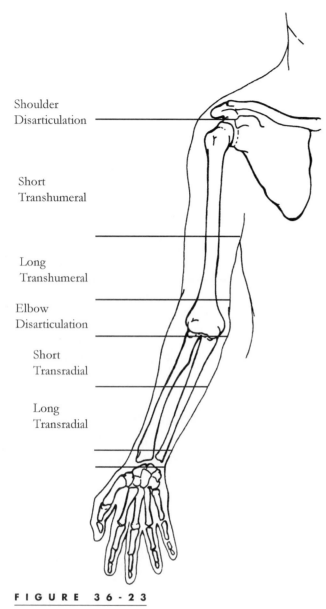

Shoulder
Disarticulation

Short
Transhumeral

Long
Transhumeral

Elbow
Disarticulation

Short
Transradial

Long
Transradial

FIGURE 36-23

Surgical sites for upper-limb amputations. (Reproduced, with permission, from Advanced Rehabilitation Therapy, Inc., Miami, Florida.)

Voluntary-Opening Hooks

The amputee exerts a force on the control cable of a voluntary-opening (VO) hook to open the fingers of the hook against the force of the rubber bands, which act as a spring to close the fingers and provide prehension, or pinch force. The force is approximately 1.5 pounds per rubber band. The standard hook is employed for general use and activities, while the farmer's hook is often prescribed for heavier work-related activities and for carrying loads.

Voluntary-Closing Hooks

The less commonly seen voluntary-closing (VC) hook permits the amputee more precise ability to close the device because the amputee powers the closing by use of cable control. Prehension

force ranges from 0.5 to 25 pounds. A self-locking mechanism automatically locks the hook in a grasp position. This TD is preferred for control of fine work without great exertion.

HANDS

More cosmetically appealing to some amputees, the prosthetic hand has become more popular over the years; however, it is not considered as functional as the hook. Many amputees use a hand on an interchangeable basis with a hook terminal device (Fig. 36-24).

Voluntary-Opening Hands

Operation of the VO hand is the same as the VO hook, except the fingers form the "three-jaw-chuck" pinch with the index and middle finger joining the thumb. The mechanics of the hand and fingers vary a little between the different manufacturers in that some hands offer multiple locking positions and different grips, and some vary the number of moveable fingers.

Passive or Cosmetic Hands

The passive hand has no functional mechanism and is intended purely for cosmetic effect. Many people will change to a cosmetic hand for formal dress or occasions where appearance exceeds the need for function.

WRIST UNITS

Wrist units are used for attaching the TD to the forearm and provide terminal device rotation (pronation/supination). Wrist units can be either constant-friction controlled or locking. TD rotation is performed passively by the sound hand or by pushing the TD against an object. Quick-change wrist units permit easy removal and replacement, offering the amputee a variety of terminal devices, depending on the activity.

Wrist flexion units are very practical adaptations permitting easier control for midline activities such as eating, grooming, and dressing. Bilateral upper-limb amputees find that one if not both wrist units must flex to perform everyday activities independently. There are two types of wrist flexion units, internal and external. The internal units combine a constant-friction wrist and a wrist-flexion unit that has locking settings of zero, 30, or 50 degrees of flexion. The external units are designed for manual positioning of the terminal device in either flexion or full extension.

TRANSRADIAL SOCKETS

Split Socket

Typically used with a very short transradial amputee (TRA), split sockets are used with step-up hinges because elbow flexion is often limited. The step-up gear ratio is 2:1, which permits 2 degrees of forearm shell movement for every degree of elbow flexion (Fig. 36-25).

Munster Socket

Often referred to as the self-suspending socket, the Munster socket was designed for short TRA. The extremely narrow

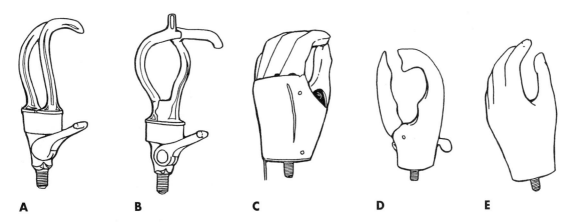

A   **B**   **C**   **D**   **E**

FIGURE 36-24

Terminal devices. *Hooks.* **A,** Standard voluntary opening (VO) hook. **B,** Farmer VO hook. **C,** Voluntary closing (VC) hook. *Hands.* **D,** Voluntary-opening (VO) hand. **E,** Passive or cosmetic hand. (Reproduced, with permission, from Advanced Rehabilitation Therapy, Inc., Miami, Florida.)

anterior–posterior dimension suspends the socket on the residual limb. The disadvantage of this socket is that the proximity of the anterior trim line frequently prevents full elbow flexion, and the forearm shell is often preflexed, limiting the appearance of full extension. When a manual terminal device is used, a harness is used to power the TD (figure-9). If a myoelectric control system is used, no other suspension device is necessary (Fig. 36-26).

Northwestern University Supracondylar Socket

Because of the ROM limitations associated with the Munster socket, the Northwestern University supracondylar design has become the most popular self-suspending socket design, where the medial and lateral walls of the socket narrow over the humeral epicondyles, suspending the prosthesis very adequately without any loss of ROM in the sagittal plane or the need to preflex the forearm shell (Fig. 36-27).

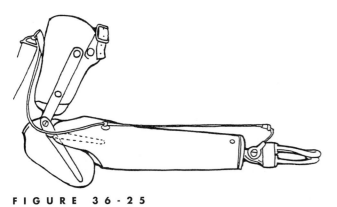

FIGURE 36-25

Split-socket design with triceps pad and a standard hook terminal device. (Reproduced, with permission, from Advanced Rehabilitation Therapy, Inc., Miami, Florida.)

HINGES

Transradial hinges connect the socket to a triceps cuff or pad on the posterior upper arm and assist with suspension and stability. Selection of the hinge type depends on the site of amputation and the residual function.

Flexible Elbow Hinges

Constructed of flexible materials such as Dacron webbing fabric, leather, or lightweight metals, flexible elbow hinges assist with suspension of the forearm shell and permit rotational motion of the forearm in long TRA and wrist disarticulations.

Rigid Elbow Hinges

Constructed of more rigid metals and composite plastics, rigid hinges are used for midforearm to short TRA with normal elbow ROM. Rigid hinges are also used with short TRA because little supination and pronation is available anatomically; also, a smaller stump requires greater stability in order to better control the prosthesis. The three major categories are (1) single-axis hinges, designed to provide rotational stability between the socket and forearm; (2) polycentric hinges, used with short TRA and designed to help increase elbow flexion by reducing the bunching of soft tissue in the cubital fossa; and (3) step-up hinges, used with the split socket and offering the 2:1 ratio of elbow motion to forearm movement.

TRANSRADIAL HARNESS AND CONTROLS

The function of the harness is to suspend the prosthesis from the shoulder so that the socket is held firmly in place on the stump. Movement of the scapulothoracic region, scapular abduction or protraction, and shoulder flexion increase pull on the control cable or create excursion, which in turn controls the terminal device or elbow joint as the amputee wishes. The harness is adjusted so the movements required by the shoulder or scapula are small and go relatively unnoticed.

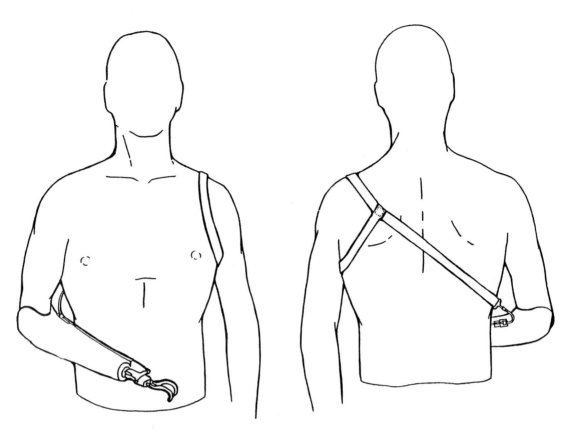

FIGURE 36-26

The Munster socket with figure-9 harness. (Reproduced, with permission, from Advanced Rehabilitation Therapy, Inc., Miami, Florida.)

Figure-Eight Harness

The figure-8 is the most commonly used harness. The axilla loop acts as a reaction point for the transmission of body forces to the terminal device. The anterior support strap and inverted-Y suspensor strap accept the major portion of the axial load (Fig. 36-28).

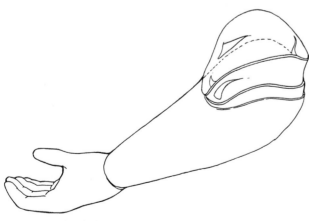

FIGURE 36-27

Northwestern University supracondylar socket. (Reproduced, with permission, from Advanced Rehabilitation Therapy, Inc., Miami, Florida.)

Chest-Strap Harness With Shoulder Saddle

Used when the amputee cannot tolerate an axilla loop, or if greater suspension is required for heavy lifting, the chest-strap harness is not appropriate for women as it has a tendency to rotate up on the chest when excessive forces are applied to the control cable (Fig. 36-29).

Figure-Nine Harness

Typically employed with a self-suspending prosthesis, the figure-9 harness consists of an axilla loop and a control attachment strap. The advantage over conventional harnesses is the greater freedom and comfort by eliminating the usual front support strap and triceps pad (Fig. 36-26).

ELBOW UNITS

External Elbow Units

External elbows are used with an elbow-disarticulation prosthesis with an outside-locking hinge system. For cosmetic and mechanical reasons it is not possible to use the standard internal elbow unit (Fig. 36-30).

Internal Elbow Units

Transhumeral amputees with at least 2 inches of the distal humerus removed have the space required to accommodate an inside-locking elbow unit. The elbow can be locked in 11

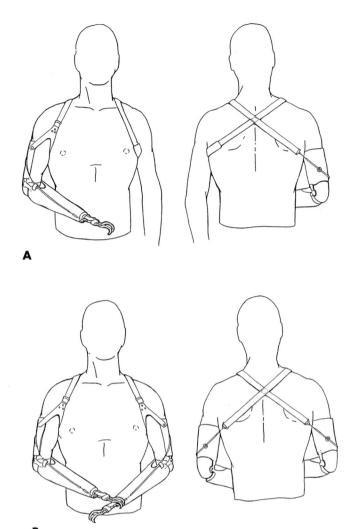

A

B

F I G U R E   3 6 - 2 8

Figure-8 harness used with **A,** a unilateral transradial
amputee, and **B,** a bilateral transradial amputee.
(Reproduced, with permission, from Advanced
Rehabilitation Therapy, Inc., Miami, Florida.)

different positions of flexion. Moreover, the friction turntable
offers the ability to manually rotate the prosthetic forearm, substituting for humeral internal and external rotation.

SHOULDER HARNESS AND CONTROL CABLES

Most shoulder systems are designed to meet the individual needs
of the user. A combination of chest, waist, and abdominal straps
is necessary for adequate stabilization of the prosthesis and control of the joints and terminal device. The harness and control
cables usually include a waistband with a strap connected to
the elbow-lock control cable. The most common control motions are shoulder-girdle flexion for elbow flexion and use of the
terminal device, with shoulder elevation for elbow locking and
unlocking.

   If the amputee cannot successfully operate the prosthesis
with the basic harness, three additions may be helpful: (1) an excursion amplifier will increase excursion with less force produced

by the body, (2) an axilla loop that operates as described previously, and (3) a shoulder sling with an axilla that provides a
wider area through which the extreme tip of the shoulder swings
when the scapulae are abducted, allowing greater excursion.

Prosthetic Training

COMPRESSION WRAPPING

Compression wrapping with elastic bandages or the use of elastic
shrinkers will reduce postoperative swelling. The amputee typically needs assistance wrapping, although the use of shrinkers
does provide a certain degree of independence with those individuals able to properly don the shrinkers. The reduction in
edema is necessary prior to casting for the prosthesis.

DESENSITIZATION

Upper-limb stumps are frequently highly sensitive postsurgically and must become tolerant to touch and pressure. A progression of contact with soft materials such as cotton or lamb's
wool, progressing to burlap-type materials, often assists with
the desensitization process. Rubbing, tapping, and performing
resistive exercises with the stump also assist in preparing the
limb for prosthetic fitting.

RANGE OF MOTION

Stretching and ROM exercises are extremely important postsurgically. Because an elbow or shoulder contracture can happen
relatively quickly, the amputee must be taught to perform a
simple independent stretching program daily to prevent loss of
ROM. It is also imperative that the scapulothoracic region be
stretched to ensure the mobility of the scapula so full excursion
may take place to control the prosthesis.

STRENGTH TRAINING

Selected strengthening exercises must be performed to increase
the strength of the residual musculature. Traditional isometric
exercises, progressing to isotonics with cuff weights, can be performed initially. As strength improves, simple adaptations with
traditional weight machines may be made for the amputee.
Some amputees find it comfortable to continue weight training
with the use of their prosthesis to maintain general fitness after
rehabilitation.

CHANGE OF HAND DOMINANCE

In many instances the amputated limb was the dominant hand.
Therefore, it becomes necessary to change hand dominance for
the majority of activities such as writing, eating, and grooming.
The prosthetic arm becomes the assistive limb. For adults this
can become a challenging and frustrating experience. The therapist must choose simple splinter skills to start and progress to
more complex skills as appropriate.

PROSTHETIC TRAINING

The amputee must learn how to don and doff the prosthesis independently and check the fit. Operation of the prosthesis can

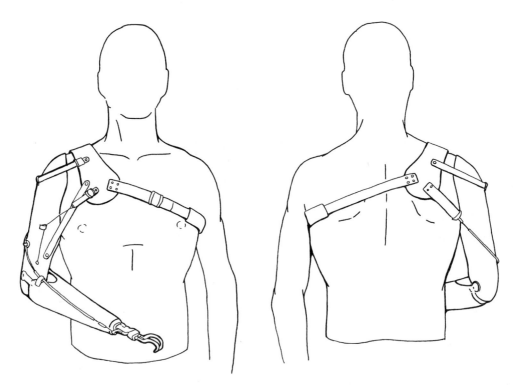

FIGURE   36-29

Chest-strap harness with shoulder saddle used with a transhumeral amputee.
(Reproduced, with permission, from Advanced Rehabilitation Therapy, Inc., Miami,
Florida.)

take some time and patience but can be mastered with practice and everyday use. Typically, gross movements are taught initially, and as control of the prosthesis improves, fine motor movements are introduced. Gross movements taught begin with dressing and light work activities such as light housework and cleaning. Learning hygiene and feeding skills require greater dexterity as both gross and fine motor skills are required. Skills such as tying shoes and fastening buttons can be very challenging. During the initial training period, the use of Velcro with

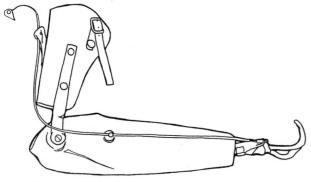

FIGURE   36-30

External elbow unit or outside-locking hinges used with an elbow-disarticulation prosthesis. (Reproduced, with permission, from Advanced Rehabilitation Therapy, Inc., Miami, Florida.)

some items can reduce the frustration level and permit the amputee to focus on other activities. As the skill level improves, and depending on the amputee's dedication to mastering prosthetic skills, even minute tasks can be performed by the accomplished prosthetic user. Returning the amputee to leisure and recreational activities enjoyed prior to the amputation is also paramount to a successful rehabilitation program. It is important that the amputee learn the correct terminology for the parts of the prosthesis and how to care for it by cleaning and simple maintenance of parts.

SUMMARY

- The physical therapist must work closely with the rehabilitation team to provide comprehensive care for the amputee.
- The therapist must carefully assess the amputee to ensure that rehabilitation goals for the amputee are designed to meet the patient's specific needs.
- Provide amputees with an individualized program that must be constructed according to the level of ability and skill of each patient.
- Understanding the function, fitting, and care of the prosthesis is important in the instruction of prosthetic use and will assist the amputee in obtaining the goal maximizing prosthetic control.

- Establishing long-term goals that will return the amputee to pre-amputation lifestyle is essential for a complete rehabilitation program. Recreational activities can assist the amputee in the process and restore the sense of being a productive member of society with the ability to live a life with choices.

The author would like to acknowledge Curtis Clark, PT, for his generous contributions to the material in this chapter.

REFERENCES

1. Condie D, Stills M. Prosthetic and orthotic management. In: Bowker JH, Michael JW, eds. *Atlas of Limb Prosthetics: Surgical, Prosthetic, and Rehabilitation Principles.* St. Louis, Mosby Year Book, 1992, p. 410.

2. Davis GJ. *A Compendium of Isokinetics in Clinical Usages and Rehabilitation Techniques,* 2nd ed. La Crosse, WI, S&S Publishing, 1985.

3. Eisert O, Tester OW. Dynamic exercises for lower extremity amputees. *Arch Phys Med Rehabil* 35:695–704, 1954.

4. Gottschalk F, Kourosh S, Stills M, et al. Does socket configuration influence the position of the femur in above-knee amputation? *J Prosthet Orthot* 2:94–102, 1989.

5. Murray MP. Gait as a total pattern of movement. *Am J Phys Med* 16:290–333, 1967.

6. Peizer E, Wright DW, Mason C. Human locomotion. *Bull Prosthet Res* 10:48–105, 1969.

Index